KEY TO WORLD MAP PAGES

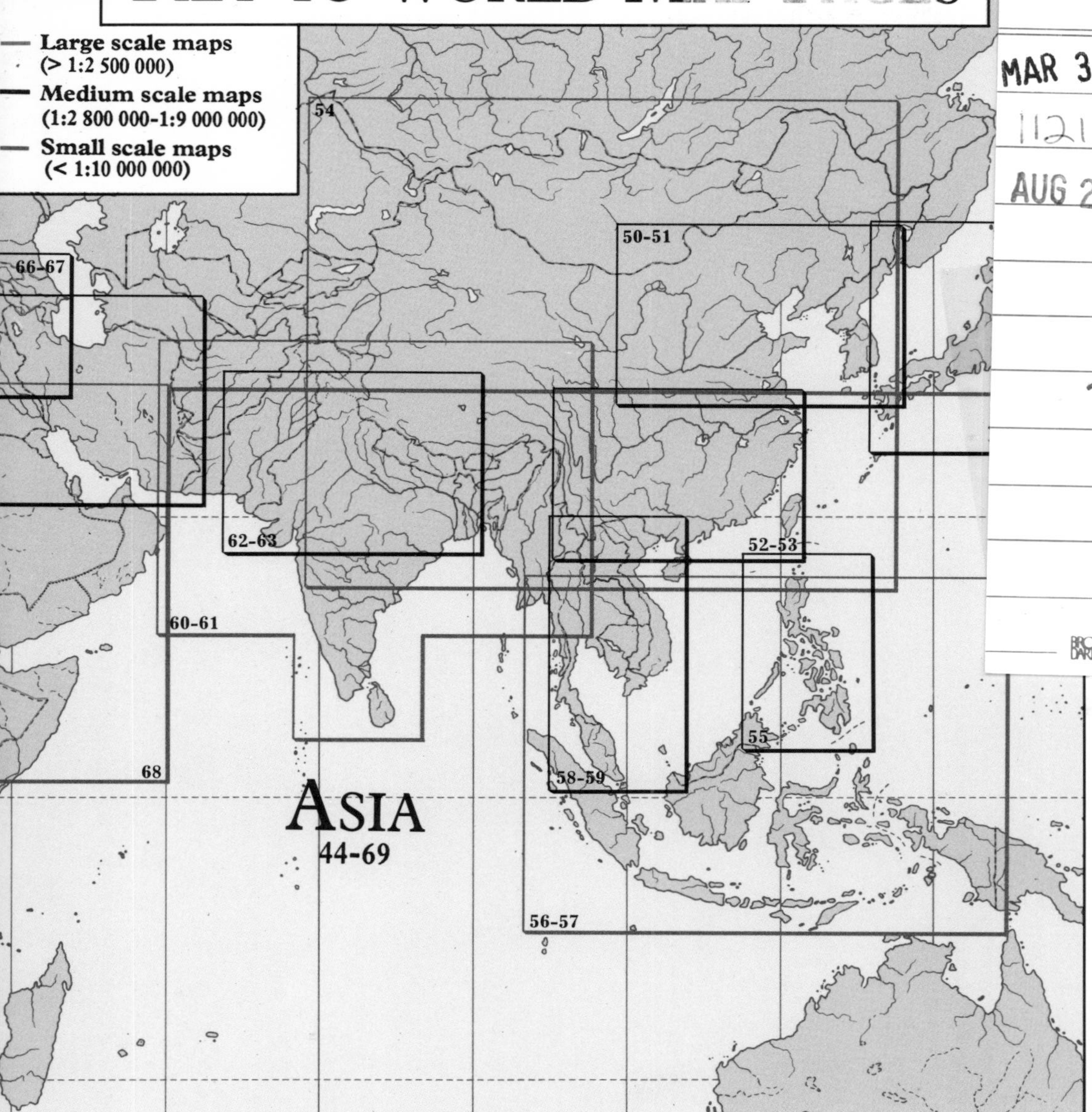

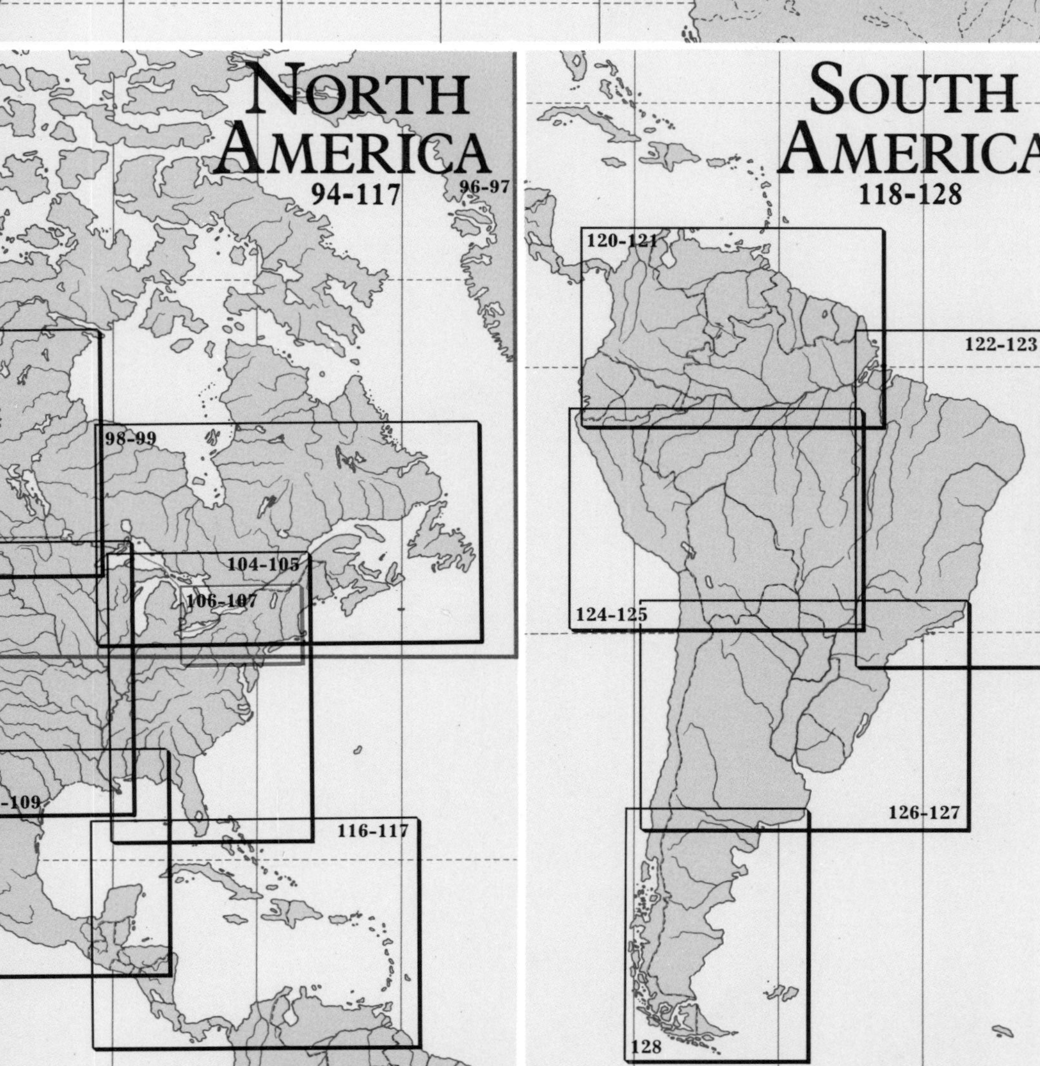

INDEX

Canada 96–101
Central African Republic 82
Chad 73
Chile 126, 128
China 50–54
Colombia 120
Congo 80
Costa Rica 116
Croatia 21
Cuba 116–117
Cyprus 37
Czech Republic 20–21

Denmark 11
Djibouti 68
Dominican Republic 117

Ecuador 120
Egypt 76
El Salvador 116
England 12–13
Equatorial Guinea 80
Eritrea 76–77
Estonia 40
Ethiopia 68, 77

Fiji 87
Finland 8–9
France 24–27
French Guiana 121

Gabon 80
Gambia 78
Georgia 43
Germany 18–19
Ghana 78–79
Greece 39
Greenland 4
Guatemala 116
Guinea 78
Guinea-Bissau 78
Guyana 121

Haiti 117
Honduras 116
Hong Kong 53
Hungary 21

Iceland 8
India 60–63
Indonesia 56–57
Iran 64–65
Iraq 64–65
Irish Republic 15
Israel 69
Italy 32–35
Ivory Coast 78

Jamaica 116
Japan 48–49
Jordan 69

Kazakstan 44
Kenya 82
Korea, North 51
Korea, South 51
Kuwait 64–65

Northern Ireland 15
Norway 8–9

Oman 68

Pakistan 62
Panama 116
Papua New Guinea 86
Paraguay 126–127
Peru 124
Philippines 55
Poland 20
Portugal 30–31
Puerto Rico 117

Qatar 65

Romania 38
Russia 40–45
Rwanda 82

Saudi Arabia 68
Scotland 14
Senegal 78
Sierra Leone 78
Singapore 59
Slovak Republic 20–21
Slovenia 33
Somali Republic 68
South Africa 84–85
Spain 28–31
Sri Lanka 60
Sudan 77
Surinam 121
Swaziland 85
Sweden 8–9
Switzerland 22–23
Syria 67

Taiwan 53
Tajikistan 44
Tanzania 82–83
Thailand 58–59
Togo 79
Trinidad and Tobago 117
Tunisia 75
Turkey 66–67
Turkmenistan 44

Uganda 82
Ukraine 41
United Arab Emirates 65
United Kingdom 12–15
USA 102–113
Uruguay 126–127
Uzbekistan 44

Venezuela 120–121
Vietnam 58–59

Wales 12–13

Yemen 68
Yugoslavia 38–39

Zaïre 80–81
Zambia 83
Zimbabwe 83

ATLAS OF CANADA AND THE WORLD

This edition published in 1996 by Key Porter Books Limited by arrangement with George Philip Limited, an imprint of Reed Books.

Canadian Cataloguing in Publication Data

Main entry under title:

Atlas of Canada and the world

ISBN 1-55013-816-2

1. Atlases, Canadian. 2. Canada – Maps.

G1021.A85 1996 912 C96-931075-7

Key Porter Books Limited
70 The Esplanade
Toronto, Ontario
Canada M5E 1R2

Cartography by Philip's

Printed and bound in China

96 97 98 99 6 5 4 3 2 1

ATLAS OF CANADA AND THE WORLD

KEY PORTER BOOKS

Contents

WORLD STATISTICS

Countries vi

CANADIAN MAPS

Map Symbols **1**

Canada
1:15 600 000
Canada: Political
1:35 600 000 **2–3**

Québec North and Labrador (Nfld)
1: 6 200 000 **4**

Newfoundland
1:2 200 000 **5**

Atlantic Provinces
1:2 200 000 **6–7**

Québec–South
1:2 200 000 **8–9**

Ontario–South
1:2 200 000 **10–11**

Central Ontario–Lake Superior
1:2 200 000 **12–13**

Manitoba and Saskatchewan–South
1:2 200 000 **14–15**

Alberta–South
1:2 200 000 **16–17**

British Columbia–South
1:2 200 000 **18–19**

Yukon and the Northwest Territories
1:8 900 000 **20–21**

Index to Canadian Maps **22–26**

WORLD MAPS

Map Symbols **1**

The World: Political
1:71 100 000 **2–3**

Arctic Ocean
1:31 100 000 **4**

Antarctica
1:31 100 000 **5**

EUROPE

Europe: Physical
1:17 800 000 **6**

Europe: Political
1:17 800 000 **7**

Scandinavia
1:4 400 000 **8–9**

Denmark and Southern Sweden
1:2 200 000 **10–11**

England and Wales
1:1 800 000 **12–13**

Scotland
1:1 800 000 **14**

Ireland
1:1 800 000 **15**

Netherlands, Belgium and Luxembourg
1:1 100 000 **16–17**

Germany
1:2 200 000 **18–19**

Middle Europe
1:3 100 000 **20–21**

Switzerland
1:900 000 **22–23**

Northern France
1:2 200 000 **24–25**

Southern France
1:2 200 000 **26–27**

Eastern Spain
1:2 200 000 **28–29**

Western Spain and Portugal
1:2 200 000 **30–31**

Northern Italy, Slovenia and Croatia
1:2 200 000 **32–33**

Southern Italy
1:2 200 000 **34–35**

Balearics, Canaries and Madeira
1:900 000 / 1:1 800 000 **36**

Malta, Crete, Corfu, Rhodes and Cyprus
1:900 000 / 1:1 200 000 **37**

The Balkans
1:3 100 000 **38–39**

Baltic States, Belarus and Ukraine
1:4 400 000 **40–41**

Volga Basin and the Caucasus
1:4 400 000 **42–43**

ASIA

Russia and Central Asia
1:17 800 000 **44–45**

Asia: Physical
1:44 400 000 **46**

Asia: Political
1:44 400 000 **47**

Japan
1:4 400 000 **48–49**

Northern China and Korea
1:5 300 000 **50–51**

Southern China
1:5 300 000 **52–53**

China
1:17 800 000 **54**

Philippines
1:6 700 000 **55**

Indonesia
1:11 100 000 **56–57**

Mainland South-east Asia
1:5 300 000 **58–59**

South Asia
1:8 900 000 **60–61**

The Indo-Gangetic Plain
1:5 300 000 **62–63**

The Middle East
1:6 200 000 **64–65**

Turkey and Transcaucasia
1:4 400 000 **66–67**

Arabia and the Horn of Africa
1:13 300 000 **68**

The Near East
1:2 200 000 **69**

AFRICA

Africa: Physical
1:37 300 000 **70**

Africa: Political
1:37 300 000 **71**

Northern Africa
1:13 300 000 **72–73**

North-west Africa
1:7 100 000 **74–75**

The Nile Valley
1:7 100 000
The Nile Delta
1:3 600 000 **76–77**

West Africa
1:7 100 000 **78–79**

Central and Southern Africa
1:13 300 000 **80–81**

East Africa
1:7 100 000 **82–83**

Southern Africa
1:7 100 000
Madagascar
1:7 100 000 **84–85**

AUSTRALIA AND OCEANIA

Australia and Oceania: Physical and Political
1:44 400 000 **86**

New Zealand
1:5 300 000 **87**

Western Australia
1:7 100 000 **88–89**

Eastern Australia
1:7 100 000 **90–91**

Pacific Ocean
1:48 000 000 **92–93**

NORTH AMERICA

North America: Physical
1:31 100 000 **94**

North America: Political
1:31 100 000 **95**

Canada
1:13 300 000
Alaska
1:26 700 000 **96–97**

Eastern Canada
1:6 200 000 **98–99**

Western Canada
1:6 200 000 **100–101**

United States
1:10 700 000
Hawaii
1:8 900 000 **102–103**

Eastern United States
1:5 300 000 **104–105**

Northeastern United States
1:2 200 000 **106–107**

Middle United States
1:5 300 000 **108–109**

Western United States
1:5 300 000 **110–111**

Central and Southern California and Washington
1:2 200 000 **112–113**

Mexico
1:7 100 000 **114–115**

Central America and the West Indies
1:7 100 000 **116–117**

SOUTH AMERICA

South America: Physical
1:31 100 000 **118**

South America: Political
1:31 100 000 **119**

South America–North-west
1:7 100 000 **120–121**

Eastern Brazil
1:7 100 000 **122–123**

South America–West
1:7 100 000 **124–125**

Central South America
1:7 100 000 **126–127**

Southern Chile and Argentina
1:7 100 000 **128**

INDEX TO WORLD MAPS **129–224**

World Statistics: Countries

This alphabetical list includes all the countries and territories of the world. If a territory is not completely independent, then the country it is associated with is named. The area figures give the total area of land, inland water and ice.

Units for areas and populations are thousands. The population figures are 1995 estimates. The annual income is the Gross National Product per capita in US dollars. The figures are the latest available, usually 1994.

Country/Territory	Area km² Thousands	Area miles² Thousands	Population Thousands	Capital	Annual Income US $
Afghanistan	652	252	19,509	Kabul	220
Albania	28.8	11.1	3,458	Tirana	340
Algeria	2,382	920	25,012	Algiers	1,650
American Samoa (US)	0.20	0.08	58	Pago Pago	2,600
Andorra	0.45	0.17	65	Andorra La Vella	14,000
Angola	1,247	481	10,020	Luanda	600
Anguilla (UK)	0.1	0.04	8	The Valley	6,800
Antigua & Barbuda	0.44	0.17	67	St John's	6,390
Argentina	2,767	1,068	34,663	Buenos Aires	7,290
Armenia	29.8	11.5	3,603	Yerevan	660
Aruba (Neths)	0.19	0.07	71	Oranjestad	17,500
Australia	7,687	2,968	18,107	Canberra	17,510
Austria	83.9	32.4	8,004	Vienna	23,120
Azerbaijan	86.6	33.4	7,559	Baku	730
Azores (Port.)	2.2	0.87	238	Ponta Delgada	–
Bahamas	13.9	5.4	277	Nassau	11,500
Bahrain	0.68	0.26	558	Manama	7,870
Bangladesh	144	56	118,342	Dhaka	220
Barbados	0.43	0.17	263	Bridgetown	6,240
Belarus	207.6	80.1	10,500	Minsk	2,930
Belgium	30.5	11.8	10,140	Brussels	21,210
Belize	23	8.9	216	Belmopan	2,440
Benin	113	43	5,381	Porto-Novo	420
Bermuda (UK)	0.05	0.02	64	Hamilton	27,000
Bhutan	47	18.1	1,639	Thimphu	170
Bolivia	1,099	424	7,900	La Paz/Sucre	770
Bosnia-Herzegovina	51	20	3,800	Sarajevo	2,500
Botswana	582	225	1,481	Gaborone	2,590
Brazil	8,512	3,286	161,416	Brasilia	3,020
Brunei	5.8	2.2	284	Bandar Seri Begawan	9,000
Bulgaria	111	43	8,771	Sofia	1,160
Burkina Faso	274	106	10,326	Ouagadougou	300
Burma (Myanmar)	677	261	46,580	Rangoon	950
Burundi	27.8	10.7	6,412	Bujumbura	180
Cambodia	181	70	10,452	Phnom Penh	600
Cameroon	475	184	13,232	Yaoundé	770
Canada	9,976	3,852	29,972	Ottawa	20,670
Canary Is. (Spain)	7.3	2.8	1,494	Las Palmas/Santa Cruz	–
Cape Verde Is.	4	1.6	386	Praia	870
Cayman Is. (UK)	0.26	0.10	31	George Town	20,000
Central African Republic	623	241	3,294	Bangui	390
Chad	1,284	496	6,314	Ndjaména	200
Chile	757	292	14,271	Santiago	3,070
China	9,597	3,705	1,226,944	Beijing	490
Colombia	1,139	440	34,948	Bogotá	1,400
Comoros	2.2	0.86	654	Moroni	520
Congo	342	132	2,593	Brazzaville	920
Cook Is. (NZ)	0.24	0.09	19	Avarua	900
Costa Rica	51.1	19.7	3,436	San José	2,160
Croatia	56.5	21.8	4,900	Zagreb	4,500
Cuba	111	43	11,050	Havana	1,250
Cyprus	9.3	3.6	742	Nicosia	10,380
Czech Republic	78.9	30.4	10,500	Prague	2,730
Denmark	43.1	16.6	5,229	Copenhagen	26,510
Djibouti	23.2	9	603	Djibouti	780
Dominica	0.75	0.29	89	Roseau	2,680
Dominican Republic	48.7	18.8	7,818	Santo Domingo	1,080
Ecuador	284	109	11,384	Quito	1,170
Egypt	1,001	387	64,100	Cairo	660
El Salvador	21	8.1	5,743	San Salvador	1,320
Equatorial Guinea	28.1	10.8	400	Malabo	360
Eritrea	94	36	3,850	Asmara	500
Estonia	44.7	17.3	1,531	Tallinn	3,040
Ethiopia	1,128	436	51,600	Addis Ababa	100
Faroe Is. (Den.)	1.4	0.54	47	Tórshavn	23,660
Fiji	18.3	7.1	773	Suva	2,140
Finland	338	131	5,125	Helsinki	18,970
France	552	213	58,286	Paris	22,360
French Guiana (Fr.)	90	34.7	154	Cayenne	5,000
French Polynesia (Fr.)	4	1.5	217	Papeete	7,000
Gabon	268	103	1,316	Libreville	4,050
Gambia, The	11.3	4.4	1,144	Banjul	360
Georgia	69.7	26.9	5,448	Tbilisi	560
Germany	357	138	82,000	Berlin/Bonn	23,560
Ghana	239	92	17,462	Accra	430
Gibraltar (UK)	0.007	0.003	28	Gibraltar Town	5,000
Greece	132	51	10,510	Athens	7,390
Greenland (Den.)	2,176	840	59	Godthåb (Nuuk)	9,000
Grenada	0.34	0.13	94	St George's	2,410
Guadeloupe (Fr.)	1.7	0.66	443	Basse-Terre	9,000
Guam (US)	0.55	0.21	155	Agana	6,000
Guatemala	109	42	10,624	Guatemala City	1,110
Guinea	246	95	6,702	Conakry	510
Guinea-Bissau	36.1	13.9	1,073	Bissau	220
Guyana	215	83	832	Georgetown	350
Haiti	27.8	10.7	7,180	Port-au-Prince	800
Honduras	112	43	5,940	Tegucigalpa	580
Hong Kong (UK)	1.1	0.40	6,000	–	17,860
Hungary	93	35.9	10,500	Budapest	3,330
Iceland	103	40	269	Reykjavik	23,620
India	3,288	1,269	942,989	New Delhi	290
Indonesia	1,905	735	198,644	Jakarta	730
Iran	1,648	636	68,885	Tehran	4,750
Iraq	438	169	20,184	Baghdad	2,000
Ireland	70.3	27.1	3,589	Dublin	12,580
Israel	27	10.3	5,696	Jerusalem	13,760
Italy	301	116	57,181	Rome	19,620
Ivory Coast	322	125	14,271	Yamoussoukro	630
Jamaica	11	4.2	2,700	Kingston	1,390
Japan	378	146	125,156	Tokyo	31,450
Jordan	89.2	34.4	5,547	Amman	1,190
Kazakstan	2,717	1,049	17,099	Alma-Ata	1,540
Kenya	580	224	28,240	Nairobi	270
Kiribati	0.72	0.28	80	Tarawa	710
Korea, North	121	47	23,931	Pyŏngyang	1,100
Korea, South	99	38.2	45,088	Seoul	7,670
Kuwait	17.8	6.9	1,668	Kuwait City	23,350
Kyrgyzstan	198.5	76.6	4,738	Bishkek	830
Laos	237	91	4,906	Vientiane	290
Latvia	65	25	2,558	Riga	2,030
Lebanon	10.4	4	2,971	Beirut	1,750
Lesotho	30.4	11.7	2,064	Maseru	660
Liberia	111	43	3,092	Monrovia	800
Libya	1,760	679	5,410	Tripoli	6,500
Liechtenstein	0.16	0.06	31	Vaduz	33,510
Lithuania	65.2	25.2	3,735	Vilnius	1,310
Luxembourg	2.6	1	408	Luxembourg	35,850
Macau (Port.)	0.02	0.006	490	Macau	7,500
Macedonia	25.7	9.9	2,173	Skopje	730
Madagascar	587	227	15,206	Antananarivo	240
Madeira (Port.)	0.81	0.31	253	Funchal	–
Malawi	118	46	9,800	Lilongwe	220
Malaysia	330	127	20,174	Kuala Lumpur	3,160
Maldives	0.30	0.12	254	Malé	820
Mali	1,240	479	10,700	Bamako	300
Malta	0.32	0.12	367	Valletta	6,800
Marshall Is.	0.18	0.07	55	Dalap-Uliga-Darrit	1,500
Martinique (Fr.)	1.1	0.42	384	Fort-de-France	3,500
Mauritania	1,025	396	2,268	Nouakchott	510
Mauritius	2.0	0.72	1,112	Port Louis	2,980
Mayotte (Fr.)	0.37	0.14	101	Mamoundzou	1,430
Mexico	1,958	756	93,342	Mexico City	3,750
Micronesia, Fed. States of	0.70	0.27	125	Palikir	1,560
Moldova	33.7	13	4,434	Chişinău	1,180
Monaco	0.002	0.0001	32	Monaco	16,000
Mongolia	1,567	605	2,408	Ulan Bator	400
Montserrat (UK)	0.10	0.04	11	Plymouth	4,500
Morocco	447	172	26,857	Rabat	1,030
Mozambique	802	309	17,800	Maputo	80
Namibia	825	318	1,610	Windhoek	1,660
Nauru	0.02	0.008	12	Yaren District	10,000
Nepal	141	54	21,953	Katmandu	160
Netherlands	41.5	16	15,495	Amsterdam/The Hague	20,710
Neths Antilles (Neths)	0.99	0.38	199	Willemstad	9,700
New Caledonia (Fr.)	19	7.3	181	Nouméa	6,000
New Zealand	269	104	3,567	Wellington	12,900
Nicaragua	130	50	4,544	Managua	360
Niger	1,267	489	9,149	Niamey	270
Nigeria	924	357	88,515	Abuja	310
Northern Mariana Is. (US)	0.48	0.18	47	Saipan	11,500
Norway	324	125	4,361	Oslo	26,340
Oman	212	82	2,252	Muscat	5,600
Pakistan	796	307	143,595	Islamabad	430
Palau	0.46	0.18	17	Koror	2,260
Panama	77.1	29.8	2,629	Panama City	2,580
Papua New Guinea	463	179	4,292	Port Moresby	1,120
Paraguay	407	157	4,979	Asunción	1,500
Peru	1,285	496	23,588	Lima	1,490
Philippines	300	116	67,167	Manila	830
Poland	313	121	38,587	Warsaw	2,270
Portugal	92.4	35.7	10,600	Lisbon	7,890
Puerto Rico (US)	9	3.5	3,689	San Juan	7,020
Qatar	11	4.2	594	Doha	15,140
Réunion (Fr.)	2.5	0.97	655	Saint-Denis	3,900
Romania	238	92	22,863	Bucharest	1,120
Russia	17,075	6,592	148,385	Moscow	2,350
Rwanda	26.3	10.2	7,899	Kigali	200
St Kitts & Nevis	0.36	0.14	45	Basseterre	4,470
St Lucia	0.62	0.24	147	Castries	3,040
St Vincent & Grenadines	0.39	0.15	111	Kingstown	1,730
San Marino	0.06	0.02	26	San Marino	20,000
São Tomé & Príncipe	0.96	0.37	133	São Tomé	330
Saudi Arabia	2,150	830	18,395	Riyadh	8,000
Senegal	197	76	8,308	Dakar	730
Seychelles	0.46	0.18	75	Victoria	6,370
Sierra Leone	71.7	27.7	4,467	Freetown	140
Singapore	0.62	0.24	2,990	Singapore	19,310
Slovak Republic	49	18.9	5,400	Bratislava	1,900
Slovenia	20.3	7.8	2,000	Ljubljana	6,310
Solomon Is.	28.9	11.2	378	Honiara	750
Somalia	638	246	9,180	Mogadishu	500
South Africa	1,220	471	44,000	C. Town/Pretoria/Bloemfontein	2,900
Spain	505	195	39,664	Madrid	13,650
Sri Lanka	65.6	25.3	18,359	Colombo	600
Sudan	2,506	967	29,980	Khartoum	750
Surinam	163	63	421	Paramaribo	1,210
Swaziland	17.4	6.7	849	Mbabane	1,050
Sweden	450	174	8,893	Stockholm	24,830
Switzerland	41.3	15.9	7,268	Bern	36,410
Syria	185	71	14,614	Damascus	5,700
Taiwan	36	13.9	21,100	Taipei	11,000
Tajikistan	143.1	55.2	6,102	Dushanbe	470
Tanzania	945	365	29,710	Dodoma	100
Thailand	513	198	58,432	Bangkok	2,040
Togo	56.8	21.9	4,140	Lomé	330
Tonga	0.75	0.29	107	Nuku'alofa	1,610
Trinidad & Tobago	5.1	2	1,295	Port of Spain	3,730
Tunisia	164	63	8,906	Tunis	1,780
Turkey	779	301	61,303	Ankara	2,120
Turkmenistan	488.1	188.5	4,100	Ashkhabad	1,400
Turks & Caicos Is. (UK)	0.43	0.17	15	Cockburn Town	5,000
Tuvalu	0.03	0.01	10	Fongafale	600
Uganda	236	91	21,466	Kampala	190
Ukraine	603.7	233.1	52,027	Kiev	1,910
United Arab Emirates	83.6	32.3	2,800	Abu Dhabi	22,470
United Kingdom	243.3	94	58,306	London	17,970
United States of America	9,373	3,619	263,563	Washington, DC	24,750
Uruguay	177	68	3,186	Montevideo	3,910
Uzbekistan	447.4	172.7	22,833	Tashkent	960
Vanuatu	12.2	4.7	167	Port-Vila	1,230
Venezuela	912	352	21,800	Caracas	2,840
Vietnam	332	127	74,580	Hanoi	170
Virgin Is. (UK)	0.15	0.06	20	Road Town	–
Virgin Is. (US)	0.34	0.13	105	Charlotte Amalie	12,000
Wallis & Futuna Is. (Fr.)	0.20	0.08	13	Mata-Utu	–
Western Sahara	266	103	220	El Aaiún	300
Western Samoa	2.8	1.1	169	Apia	980
Yemen	528	204	14,609	Sana	800
Yugoslavia	102.3	39.5	10,881	Belgrade	1,000
Zaïre	2,345	905	44,504	Kinshasa	500
Zambia	753	291	9,500	Lusaka	370
Zimbabwe	391	151	11,453	Harare	540

CANADIAN MAPS

SETTLEMENTS AND BOUNDARIES

Settlements in order of size :-

MONTRÉAL **Hamilton** **Moose Jaw** **Prince Rupert** **Gaspé** Banff Miquelon

International Boundaries

Internal Boundaries

Internal Boundaries (Undemarcated or Undefined)

These show the de facto situation where there are rival claims to territory.

National and Provincial Parks

COMMUNICATIONS

Freeways

Under construction

Trans-Canada Highway

Principal Roads

Other Roads

Trails and Seasonal Roads

Principal Railroads

Other Railroads

Under construction

Railroad Tunnels

Road Tunnels

Principal Canals

Passes

Airports

PHYSICAL FEATURES

Perennial Streams

8848 Spot Height in meters/metres

Seasonal Lakes, Salt Flats

Swamps, Marshes

8050 Sea Depths in meters/metres

Permanent Ice

1134 Height of Lake Surface Above Sea Level, in meters/metres

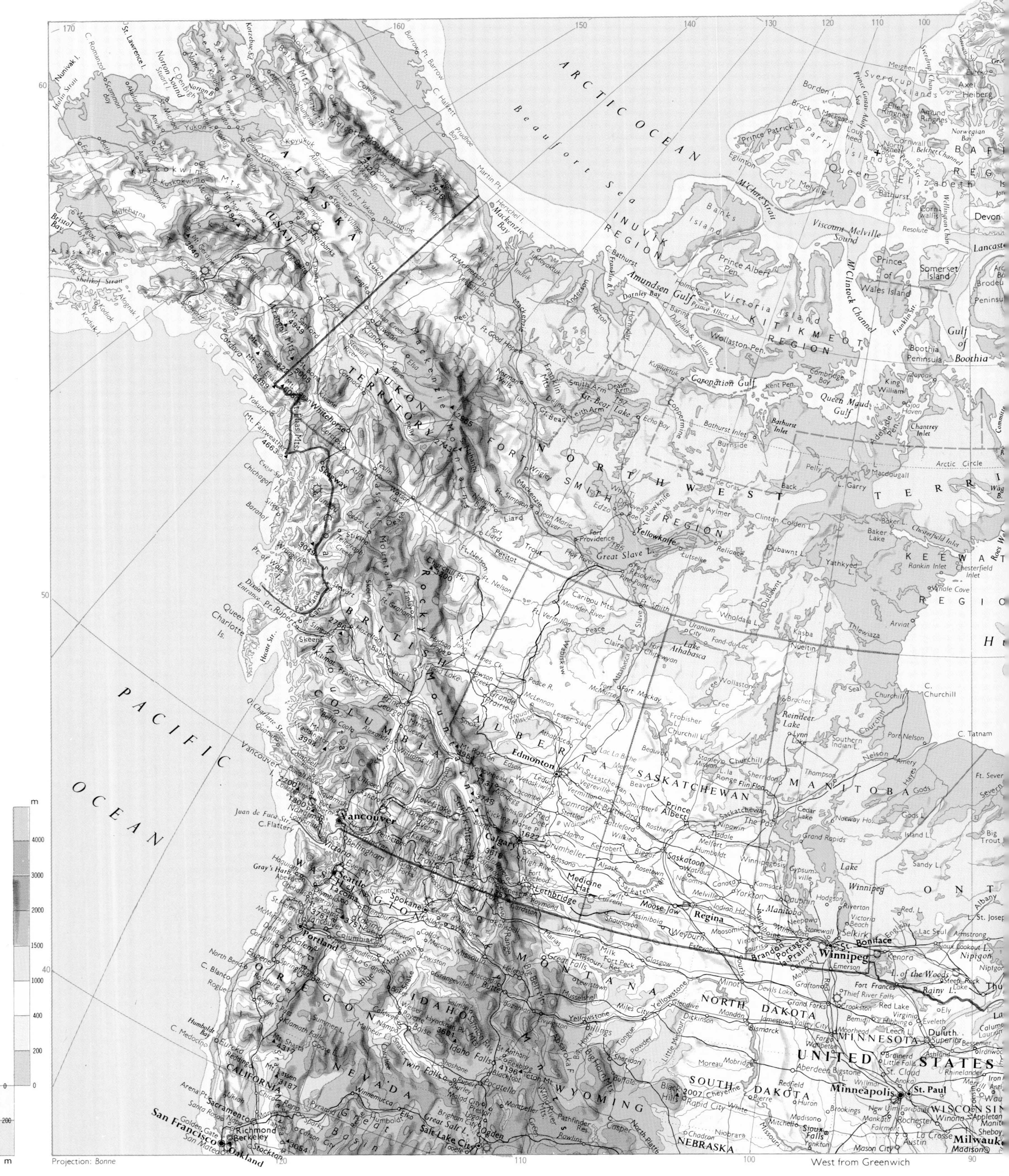
ARCTIC OCEAN
Beaufort Sea
PACIFIC OCEAN
ALASKA (U.S.A.)
YUKON TERRITORY
NORTHWEST TERRITORIES
INUVIK REGION
KITIKMEOT REGION
FORT SMITH REGION
KEEWATIN REGION
BRITISH COLUMBIA
ALBERTA
SASKATCHEWAN
MANITOBA
ONTARIO
WASHINGTON
OREGON
IDAHO
MONTANA
WYOMING
NEVADA
CALIFORNIA
NORTH DAKOTA
SOUTH DAKOTA
MINNESOTA
WISCONSIN
NEBRASKA
UNITED STATES
Rocky Mountains
Mackenzie Mountains
Coast Mountains
Great Basin
Victoria Island
Banks Island
Prince Patrick I.
Melville I.
Queen Elizabeth Islands
Sverdrup Islands
Axel Heiberg I.
Devon I.
Somerset Island
Prince of Wales Island
Boothia Peninsula
Gulf of Boothia
Amundsen Gulf
Coronation Gulf
Queen Maud Gulf
Viscount Melville Sound
M'Clure Strait
M'Clintock Channel
Great Bear Lake
Great Slave L.
Lake Athabasca
Reindeer Lake
L. Winnipeg
L. Manitoba
L. of the Woods
Queen Charlotte Is.
Vancouver I.
Juan de Fuca Str.
Kodiak I.
Bristol Bay
Arctic Circle
Whitehorse
Yellowknife
Edmonton
Calgary
Vancouver
Victoria
Regina
Saskatoon
Winnipeg
Prince Albert
Medicine Hat
Lethbridge
Moose Jaw
Brandon
Prince George
Prince Rupert
Kamloops
Dawson
Skagway
Fairbanks
Anchorage
Churchill
Seattle
Tacoma
Spokane
Portland
San Francisco
Oakland
Berkeley
Sacramento
Salt Lake City
Minneapolis
St. Paul
Duluth
Milwaukee
Projection: Bonne
West from Greenwich
170
160
150
140
130
120
110
100
90
60
50
40
m
4000
3000
2000
1500
1000
400
200
0
200

1 : 15 600 000

200 0 200 400 600 km
CANADA POLITICAL
1 : 35 600 000
National Capital
Provincial or Territorial Capital
Undemarcated boundary
District boundary
Western boundary of Nunavat from April 1999
ALASKA
GREENLAND
YUKON TERRITORY
Whitehorse
Inuvik Region
Kitikmeot Region
Baffin Region
NORTHWEST TERRITORIES
Fort Smith Region
Yellowknife
Keewatin Region
BRITISH COLUMBIA
Victoria
ALBERTA
Edmonton
SASKATCHEWAN
Regina
MANITOBA
Winnipeg
ONTARIO
Toronto
Ottawa
QUEBEC
Quebec
NEWFOUNDLAND
St John's
PRINCE EDWARD ISLAND
Charlottetown
NEW BRUNSWICK
Fredericton
NOVA SCOTIA
Halifax
UNITED STATES
West from Greenwich
GREENLAND
Qaanaaq (Thule)
Qimusseriarsuaq (Melville Bay)
Baffin Bay
Bylot I.
Pond Inlet
Cumberland Peninsula
Cumberland Sd.
Foxe Basin
Prince Charles I.
Nettilling L.
Amadjuak L.
Foxe Channel
Iqaluit
Frobisher Bay
Resolution I.
Hudson Strait
Southampton I.
Coats I.
Mansel I.
Akpatok I.
Ungava Bay
Hudson Bay
James Bay
Belcher Is.
Hebron
Nain
Hopedale
Labrador
Churchill Falls
Lac Bienville
La Grande
Labrador City
QUÉBEC
NEWFOUNDLAND
Gulf of St. Lawrence
St. Lawrence (St-Laurent)
I. d'Anticosti
Gaspé Pen.
PR. EDWARD I.
Cape Breton I.
Sydney
ST. PIERRE & MIQUELON (Fr.)
St. John's
Corner Brook
Gander
Bonavista
C. Race
NEW BRUNSWICK
Moncton
Saint John
NOVA SCOTIA
Halifax
Yarmouth
Sable I. (Nova Scotia)
ATLANTIC OCEAN
Chicoutimi
Québec
Trois-Rivières
MONTRÉAL
Hull
Ottawa
Kingston
Toronto
Hamilton
London
Windsor
DETROIT
Toledo
Cleveland
Erie
Buffalo
Rochester
Syracuse
Utica
Albany
NEW YORK
VERMONT
NEW HAMPSHIRE
MAINE
Boston
Providence
Worcester
Springfield
Hartford
Waterbury
Sherbrooke
Bangor
Portland
Sudbury
North Bay
Sault Ste. Marie
Timmins
Cochrane
Hearst
Lake Huron
Georgian Bay
Peterborough
Grand Rapids
Saginaw
COPYRIGHT, GEORGE PHILIP & SON, LTD.

QUÉBEC NORTH AND LABRADOR (NFLD)

1 : 6 200 000

Projection: Lambert's Equivalent Azimuthal

West from Greenwich

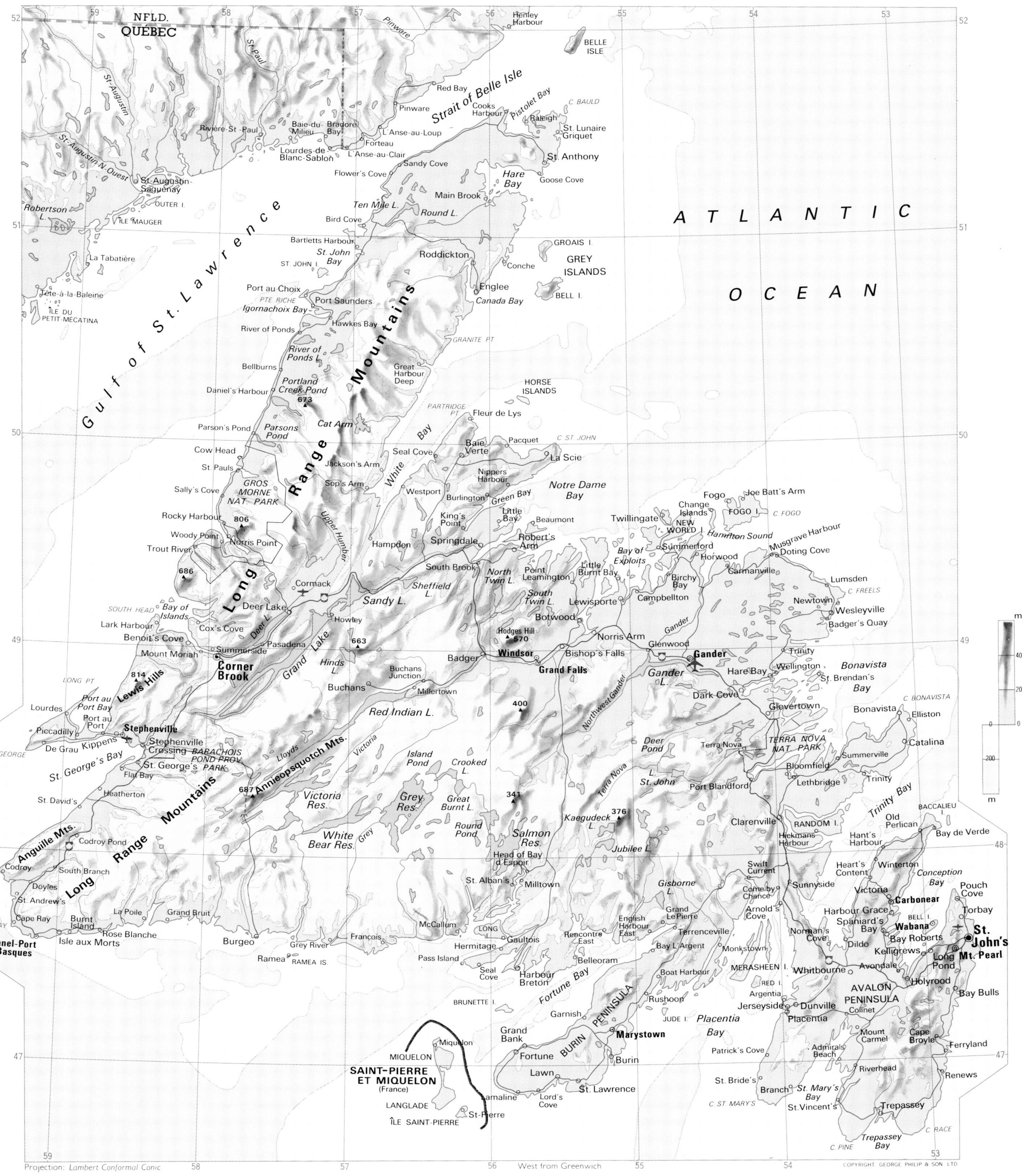
1 : 2 200 000
ATLANTIC OCEAN
Gulf of St. Lawrence
Strait of Belle Isle
Long Range Mountains
NFLD.
QUEBEC
Notre Dame Bay
White Bay
Bonavista Bay
Trinity Bay
Conception Bay
Placentia Bay
Fortune Bay
St. George's Bay
AVALON PENINSULA
BURIN PENINSULA
GROS MORNE NAT. PARK
TERRA NOVA NAT. PARK
Annieopsquotch Mts.
Lewis Hills
Anguille Mts.
Red Indian L.
Grand Lake
Gander L.
Sandy L.
Deer L.
Victoria Res.
Grey Res.
Salmon Res.
St. Anthony
Corner Brook
Stephenville
Gander
Grand Falls
Windsor
Carbonear
Wabana
St. John's
Mt. Pearl
Marystown
SAINT-PIERRE ET MIQUELON (France)
MIQUELON
LANGLADE
ÎLE SAINT-PIERRE
St-Pierre
BELLE ISLE
GREY ISLANDS
Projection: Lambert Conformal Conic
West from Greenwich
COPYRIGHT GEORGE PHILIP & SON LTD

QUÉBEC
NFLD.
QUEBEC
GULF OF ST. LAWRENCE
ÎLE D'ANTICOSTI
Détroit de Jacques-Cartier
Détroit d'Honguedo
St. Lawrence (Saint-Laurent)
Péninsule de Gaspé
MONTS CHIC-CHOCS
ÎLES DE MINGAN
Sept-Îles
Port-Cartier
Baie-Comeau
Matane
Gaspé
Percé
Labrador City
Wabush
Gagnon
Havre-St-Pierre
Natashquan
Kegaska
Musquaro
Harrington Harbour
Ste-Anne-des-Monts
Mont-Louis
Murdochville
Amqui
Causapscal
Chandler
New Richmond
Port-Menier
Baie-du-Renard
Rivière-au-Tonnerre
Longue-Pointe-de-Mingan
Mingan
Moisie
Magpie
Romaine
Natashquan-Est
Olomane
Petit-Mécatina
St-Augustin
Little Mecatina
Toulnustouc
Pentecôte
Godbout
Caopacho
Wacouno
PARC NATIONAL DE FORILLON
PARC PROV. DE LA GASPÉSIE
PARC PROV. DE MATANE
PARC PROV. DE PORT-DANIEL

1 : 2 200 000
10 0 10 20 30 40 50 60 70 80 90 100 km
NEW BRUNSWICK
NOVA SCOTIA
PRINCE EDWARD ISLAND
CAPE BRETON ISLAND
MAINE
ATLANTIC OCEAN
Bay of Fundy
Northumberland Strait
Chaleur Bay
Minas Basin
Minas Channel
ÎLES DE LA MADELEINE (QUÉBEC)
HALIFAX
Dartmouth
Saint John
Fredericton
Moncton
Charlottetown
Sydney
Truro
Yarmouth
Campbellton
Bathurst
Edmundston
Summerside
Antigonish
Newcastle
Chatham
Amherst
Kentville
Bridgewater
Glace Bay
MOUNT CARLETON PROV. PARK
CAPE BRETON HIGHLANDS NAT. PARK
PRINCE EDWARD ISLAND NAT. PARK
KOUCHIBOUGUAC NAT. PARK
FUNDY NAT. PARK
KEJIMKUJIK NAT. PARK
LOUISBOURG NAT. HISTORIC PARK
West from Greenwich
Projection: Bonne
COPYRIGHT GEORGE PHILIP & SON LTD.

L. Obamsca
L. Paul-Sauvé
L. Montreuil
L. Soscumica
L. Poncheville
L. Opataca
L. Lemieux
Brock
L. Sauvage
Little Abitibi
French
Harricana
L. Bouchier
Maicasagi
Abitibi
Kattawagami L.
L. Grasset
L. la Trêve
L. Opémisca
Island Falls
Matagami
L. au Goéland
Chibougamau
Chapais
L. Olga
Waswanipi
Pierre L.
Wawagosic
L. Waswanipi
Desmaraisville
L. Opawica
Little Abitibi L.
Kabika
L. Mistaouac
Bell
Turgeon
Miquelon
L. Surprise
Cochrane
Norembega
Bigniba
Normétal
Desméloizes
L. Turgeon
L. Quévillon
Lebel-sur-Quévillon
La Reine
Frederick House L.
Iroquois Falls
Lake Abitibi
Dupuy
La Sarre
L. Chicobi
Connaught
Val Gagné
Macamic
L. Obalski
Laflamme
Hoyle
KETTLE LAKES PROV PK
Timmins
Porcupine
South Porcupine
Matheson
Palmarolle
Taschereau
Rochebaucourt
L. Parent
Night Hawk L.
Holtyre
Villemontel
Amos
Landrienne
Champneuf
Obedjwan
L. Duparquet
Duparquet
PARC AIGUEBELLE
Mégiscane
Ramore
Barraute
Redstone
Watabeag L.
ESKER LAKES PROV. PARK
L. la Motte
Whitefish
Bourkes
L. Dasserat
L. Preissac
Belcourt
Senneterre
Kirkland Lake
Évain
Noranda
L. Faillon
Arntfield
Cadillac
L. Malartic
Swastika
Rouyn
Virginiatown
Paradis
Forsythe
Larder Lake
Larder L.
Malartic
Sullivan
Val-d'Or
L. Guéguen
Soucy
Clova
Oskélanéo
Matachewan
L. Opasatica
L. Lemoine
L. Matchi-Manitou
Rollet
L. Sabourin
Charlton
Englehart
Montreal
L. Roger
L. Villebon
L. Camachigama
Earlton
Rémigny
Réservoir Decelles
Gowganda
Elk Lake
Thornloe
Belle Vallée
Outaouais
Rapide-Sept
L. Granet
Capitachouane
L. Échouani
Notre-Dame-du-Nord
L. Simard
Grand Lac Victoria
Bazin
New Liskeard
Angliers
Makobe L.
Haileybury
Lake
Guigues
L. des Quinze
Laforce
Réservoir Dozois
L. des Augustines
Smoothwater L.
Cobalt
Laverlochère
Latulipe
Cawasachouane
Lorrainville
Belleterre
Réservoir Cabonga
Némiscachingue
Latchford
Ville-Marie
Béarn
Burwash L.
L. à la Truite
Rés. Mitchinamécus
Wanapitei
L. Ostaboningue
Fabre
PARC PROV DE LA VÉRENDRYE
L. Saseginaga
L. Ogascanane
Obabika L.
Timagami
Timiskaming
Lièvre
Bear Island
Lac Kipawa
L. aux Foins
Gatineau
L. de l'Écorce
L. Timagami
L. Wanapitei
L. Dumoine
Capreol
Marten River
Sturgeon
Kipawa
Val Caron
Hanmer
Témiscaming
Tee Lake
L. Sairs
Ste-Anne-du-Lac
Réservoir Baskatong
Azilda
Falconbridge
River Valley
L. Pin-Blanc
Sudbury
L. Beauchêne
L. du Fils
Ferme-Neuve
Copper Cliff
Coniston
Markstay
Field
Tomiko L.
L. Bleu
Warren
Verner
Sturgeon Falls
PARC PONTIAC
Montcerf
Mont-Laurier
Lac-des-Écorces
Cache Bay
Ottawa
Coulonge
L. des Îles
Val-Barrette
L. Nominingue
Burwash
Notre Dame du Lac
North Bay
Feronia
Mattawa
Dumoine
L. St-Patrice
Maniwaki
Nominingue
L'Annonciation
Lake Nipissing
Callander
Outaouais
Rutter
Noelville
Bonfield
Astorville
Deux-Rivières
Rapides des Joachims
Messine
Lac des Trente et un Milles
L. du Cerf
Labelle
French River
French
Powassan
Kiosk
Rolphton
Deep River
Bouchette
PARC PROV PAPINEAU-LABELLE
Mont-Tremblant
GRUNDY L. PROV PK
Port Loring
Commanda
Brent
Noire
Notre-Dame-du-Laus
L. Gagnon
La Conception
Key Harbour
Cedar L.
Trout Creek
Chalk River
Gracefield
St-Jovite
Britt
South River
Chapeau
Lac-Ste-Marie
Lac-Rémi
Byng Inlet
Drocourt
Sundridge
ALGONQUIN PROV. PARK
L. Lavieille
Waltham Sta.
Petawawa
L. du Poisson Blanc
Arundel
Big Trout L.
Pembroke
Fort-Coulonge
Venosta
Namur
Val-des-Bois
Chénéville
Pointe au Baril Sta.
Ardbeg
Magnetawan
Bernard L.
Opeongo L.
Alice
ÎLE DU GRAND CALUMET
Low
Poltimore
Ripon
Dunchurch
Burk's Falls
Bonnechère
Beachburg
Bryson
Campbell's Bay
Glen Almond
St-André-Avellin
Shawanaga
McKellar
Kearney
Algonquin Park
Round L.
Cobden
PARC DE LA GATINEAU
Papineauville
Montebello
Waubamik
Emsdale
Aylen L.
Golden Lake
Shawville
Buckingham
Thurso
Sprucedale
Killaloe Sta.
Eganville
L. des Chats
Bristol
Masson
Angers
Hawkesbury
Nobel
Parry Sound
Novar
Whitney
Madawaska
Barry's Bay
Golden L.
Douglas
Quyon
Pointe-Gatineau
Gatineau
Cumberland
Rockland
Vankleek Hill
Huntsville
Dwight
Bark L.
L. Clear
Renfrew
Braeside
Arnprior
Aylmer
Hull
OTTAWA
Bourget
Rosseau
Kawagama L.
Combermere
Kanata
Deschênes
Vars
Limoges
Glen Robertson
Georgian Bay
Rosseau L.
L. of Bays
Dorset
Lake St. Peter
Calabogie
Pakenham
Bells Corner
Alexandria
Joseph L.
Port Carling
Madawaska
White L.
Stittsville
Casselman
Maxville
MacTier
Baysville
Griffith
Almonte
Moose Creek
GEORGIAN BAY ISLANDS NATIONAL PARK
Muskoka L.
Bracebridge
Eagle Lake
Denbigh
Flower Sta.
Richmond
Manotick
Apple Hill
Bala
Haliburton
Osgoode
Avonmore
HOPE I.
Wilberforce
Bancroft
Mississippi L.
Carleton Place
Chesterville
Lancaster
Honey Harbour
Muskoka L.
Weslemkoon L.
Lavant Sta.
North Gower
Finch
Winchester
GRIFFITH I.
Gravenhurst
Minden
Plevna
Lanark
Kemptville
South Nation
Cornwall
CHRISTIAN I.
Goodreham
Elphin
Massena
O
N
T
A
R
I
O
Q
U
Projection: Bonne
81
80
79
78
77
76
75
50
49
48
47
46
45
m
1500
1000
400
200
0
200

1 : 2 200 000

10 0 10 20 30 40 50 60 70 80 90 100 km

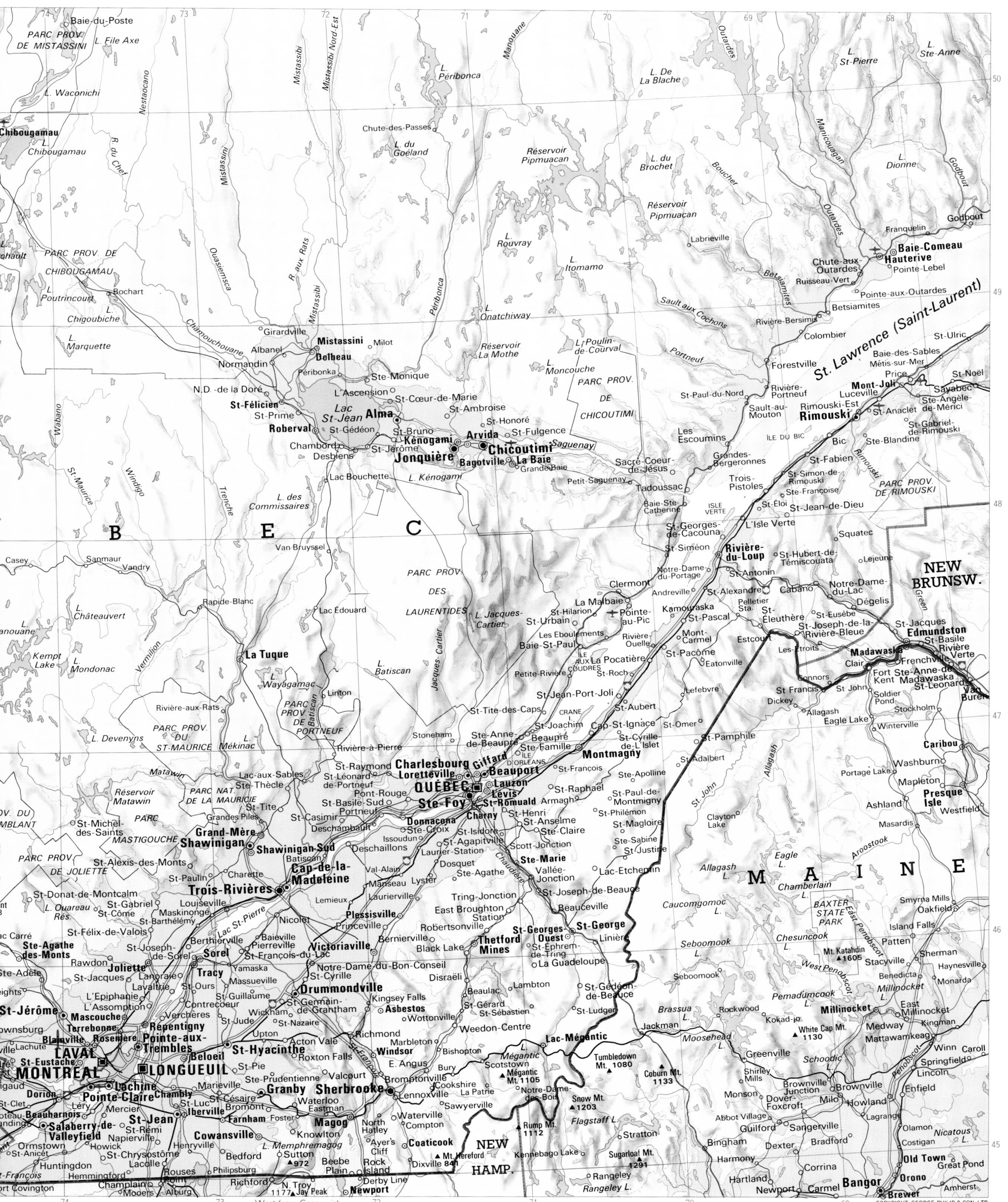

MICHIGAN

LAKE HURON

Georgian Bay

North Channel

LAKE ERIE

ONTARIO

OHIO

m
1500
1000
400
200
0
200
m

Projection: Bonne

Sault Sainte Marie
Whitefish Bay
Paradise
Newberry
Hulbert
Brimley
Echo Bay
Dafter
Strongs Corners
Rexton
Engadine
Naubinway
Brevort
Moran
Rudyard
Pickford
Hilton Beach
Thessalon
ST. JOSEPH I.
Trout Lake
Hessel
Goetzville
Drummond
De Tour
Cedarville
MACKINAC I.
BOIS BLANC I.
St. Ignace
Mackinaw City
Cheboygan
Levering
Pellston
Alanson
Burt L.
Indian River
Mullett L.
Hammond Bay
Rogers City
Onaway
Millersburg
Posen
Alpena
Vanderbilt
Gaylord
Atlanta
Hillman
Ossineke
Black River
Harrisville
Greenbush
Oscoda-Au Sable
East Tawas
Tawas City
Alabaster
Au Sable
Mio
Mikado
Glennie
Hubbard L.
Long Lake
Hale
West Branch
AU SABLE PT.
Rose City
Houghton L.
Lake City
Cadillac
Manton
Higgins L.
Roscommon
Grayling
Fairview
Curran
Lincoln
Harbor Springs
Charlevoix
Boyne City
East Jordan
Central Lake
Elk Rapids
Bellaire
Mancelona
Rapid City
Kalkaska
Walton
Manistee
Houghton Lake Heights
Marion
Harrison
Gladwin
Standish
Au Gres
CHARITY I.
Caseville
Bay Port
Pigeon
Elkton
Bad Axe
Harbor Beach
Port Hope
Kinde
Ruth
Palms
Deckerville
Sandusky
Port Sanilac
Croswell
Lexington
Saginaw Bay
Sebewaing
Unionville
Fairgrove
Caro
Cass City
Kingston
Peck
Brown City
Yale
Sand Beach
Mount Pleasant
Shepherd
Midland
Bay City
Carrollton
Zilwaukee
Saginaw
Bridgeport
Reese
Vassar
Millington
Birch Run
Montrose
Otter Lake
Columbiaville
Lapeer
Imlay City
Capac
Emmett
Port Huron
Sarnia
Marysville
Corunna
Wyoming
Petrolia
Watford
Strathroy
Flint
Grand Blanc
Swartz Creek
Durand
Davison
Flushing
Owosso
St. Johns
Ovid
Corunna
LANSING
East Lansing
Williamston
Howell
Pontiac
Birmingham
Royal Oak
Ferndale
Livonia
Dearborn
DETROIT
Ann Arbor
Ypsilanti
Wayne
Wyandotte
Trenton
Flat Rock
River Rouge
Ecorse
WINDSOR
Tecumseh
Essex
Amherstburg
Harrow
Kingsville
Leamington
Wheatley
POINT PELEE NAT. PARK
PELEE I.
Monroe
Dundee
Petersburg
Blissfield
Adrian
Morenci
Sylvania
Toledo
Rossford
Oregon
Maumee
Perrysburg
Bowling Green
Napoleon
Defiance

177

Elliot Lake
Sudbury
Onaping
Chelmsford
Azilda
Lively
Copper Cliff
Naughton
Whitefish
Espanola
Webbwood
Massey
Spanish
Blind River
Spragge
COCKBURN ISLAND
DRUMMOND ISLAND
Meldrum Bay
Gore Bay
Kagawong
Silver Water
WESTERN DUCK I.
GREAT DUCK I.
Providence Bay
South Baymouth
MANITOULIN ISLAND
Mindemoya
Manitowaning
Wikwemikong
Killarney
Little Current
KILLARNEY PROV. PARK
CLAPPERTON I.
Whitefish Falls
FITZWILLIAM I.
LONELY I.
Tobermory
COVE I.
BRUCE PENINSULA
Stokes Bay
Lion's Head
Wiarton
Hepworth
Southampton
Port Elgin
Shallow Lake
Owen Sound
Meaford
Thornbury
Collingwood
Kincardine
Tiverton
Paisley
Chesley
Markdale
Ripley
Lucknow
Walkerton
Hanover
Durham
Dundalk
Shelburne
Teeswater
Mildmay
Neustadt
Goderich
Blyth
Wingham
Harriston
Palmerston
Arthur
Clinton
Atwood
Listowel
Elmira
Fergus
Seaforth
Milverton
Linwood
Guelph
Mitchell
New Hamburg
Waterloo
KITCHENER
Cambridge
Exeter
Stratford
Woodstock
Brantford
Ingersoll
LONDON
Thamesford
Norwich
Tillsonburg
Aylmer
St. Thomas
Simcoe
Delhi
Port Stanley
Port Burwell
RONDEAU PROV. PARK
Chatham
Dresden
Wallaceburg
Thamesville
Ridgetown
Blenheim
Erieau
Comber

Parry Sound
Huntsville
North Bay
Lake Nipissing
Sturgeon Falls
GEORGIAN BAY ISLANDS NATIONAL PARK
Midland
Penetanguishene
Orillia
Barrie
Wasaga Beach
L. Simcoe
Orangeville
Brampton
Georgetown
Acton
Milton
Oakville
BURLINGTON
HAMILTON
Dundas
Grimsby
Stoney Creek
Beamsville
MISSISSAUGA
Niagara-on-the-Lake
Welland
Port Colborne
Dunnville

174

CLEVELAND
Lakewood
Euclid
Cleveland Heights
Parma
Elyria
Lorain
Avon Lake
Sandusky
ERIE
Ashtabula
Conneaut
Geneva
Painesville
Mentor
Willoughby

IND.

1 : 2 200 000

10 0 10 20 30 40 50 60 70 80 90 100 km

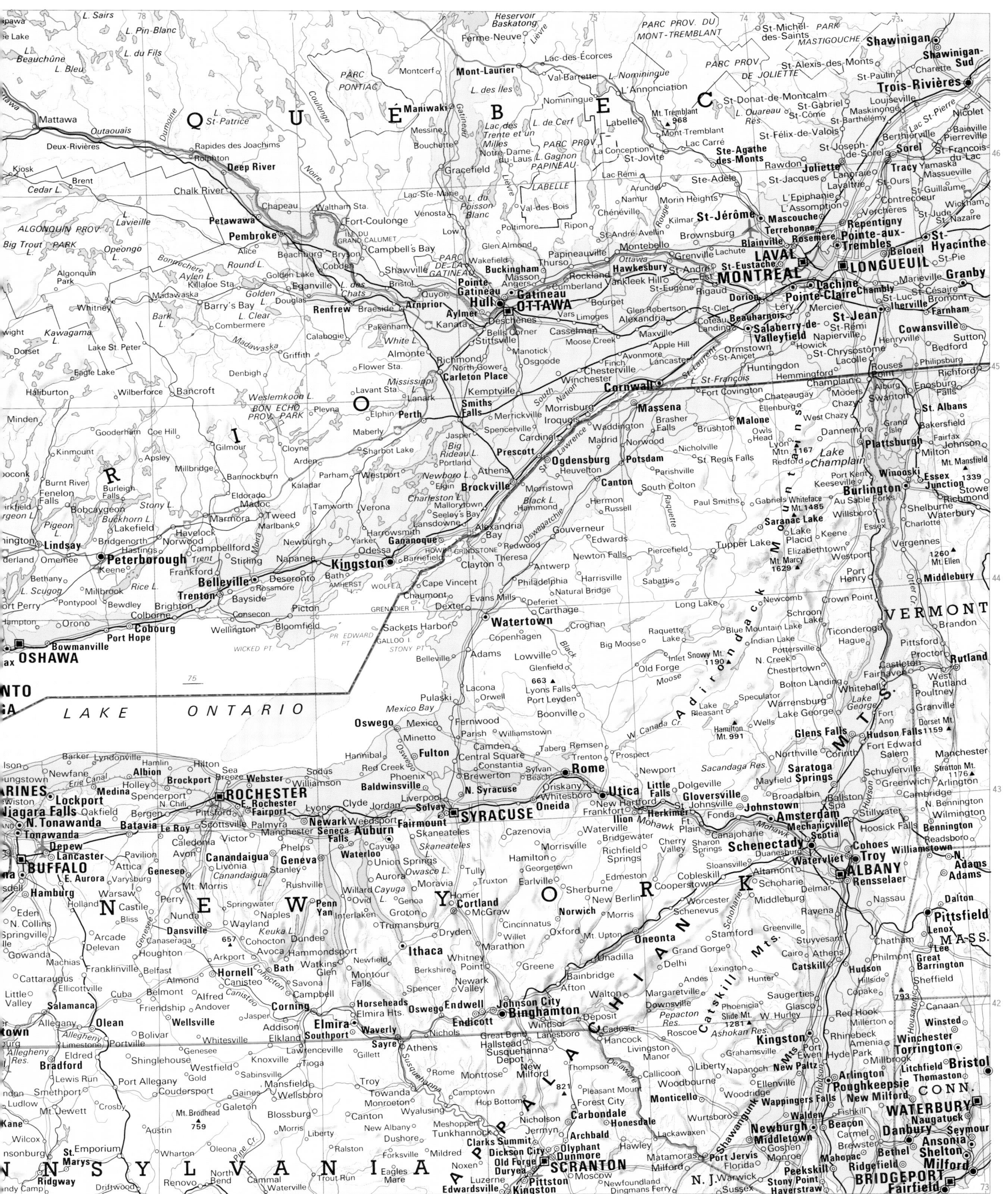

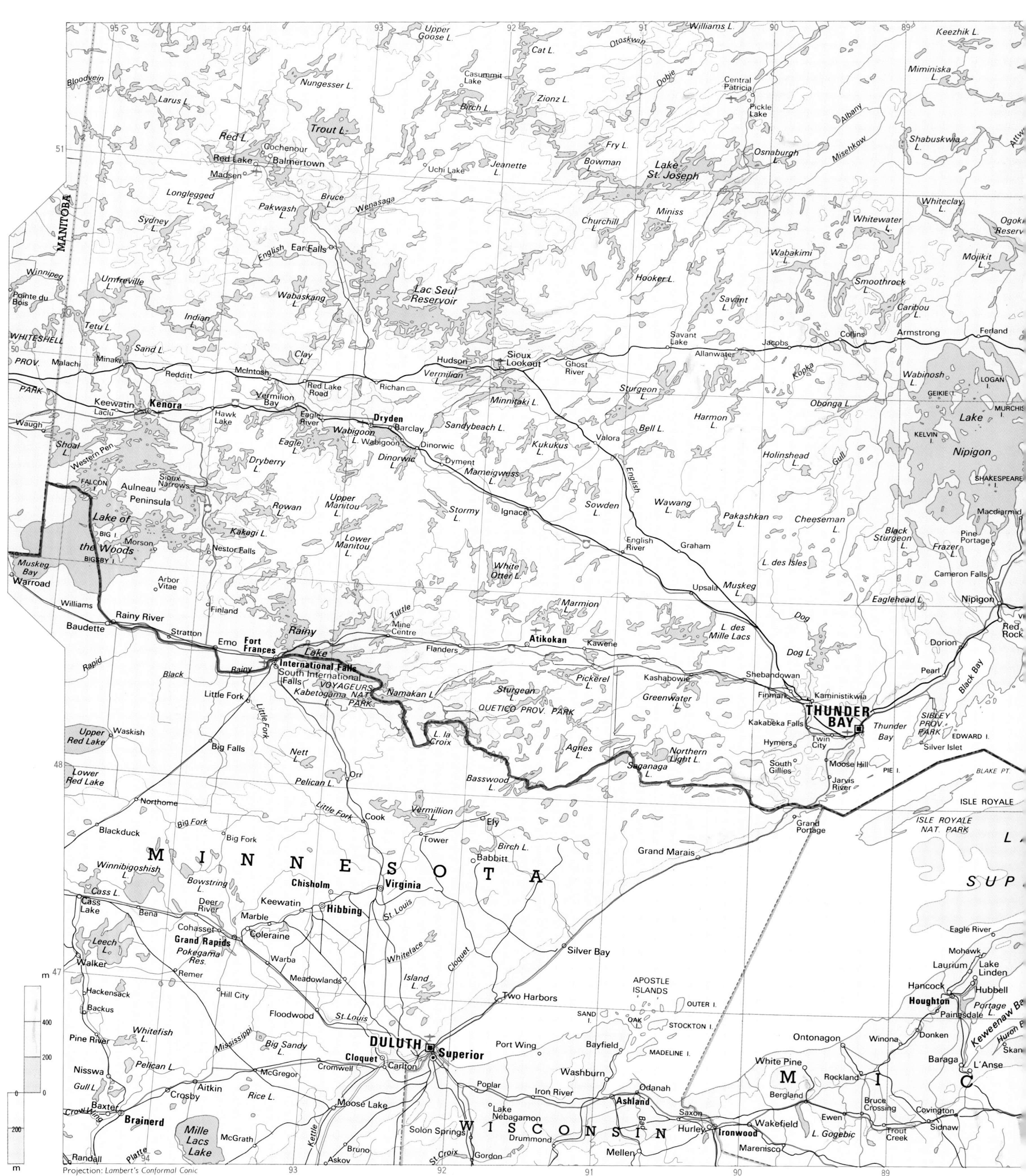
Projection: Lambert's Conformal Conic

1 : 2 200 000

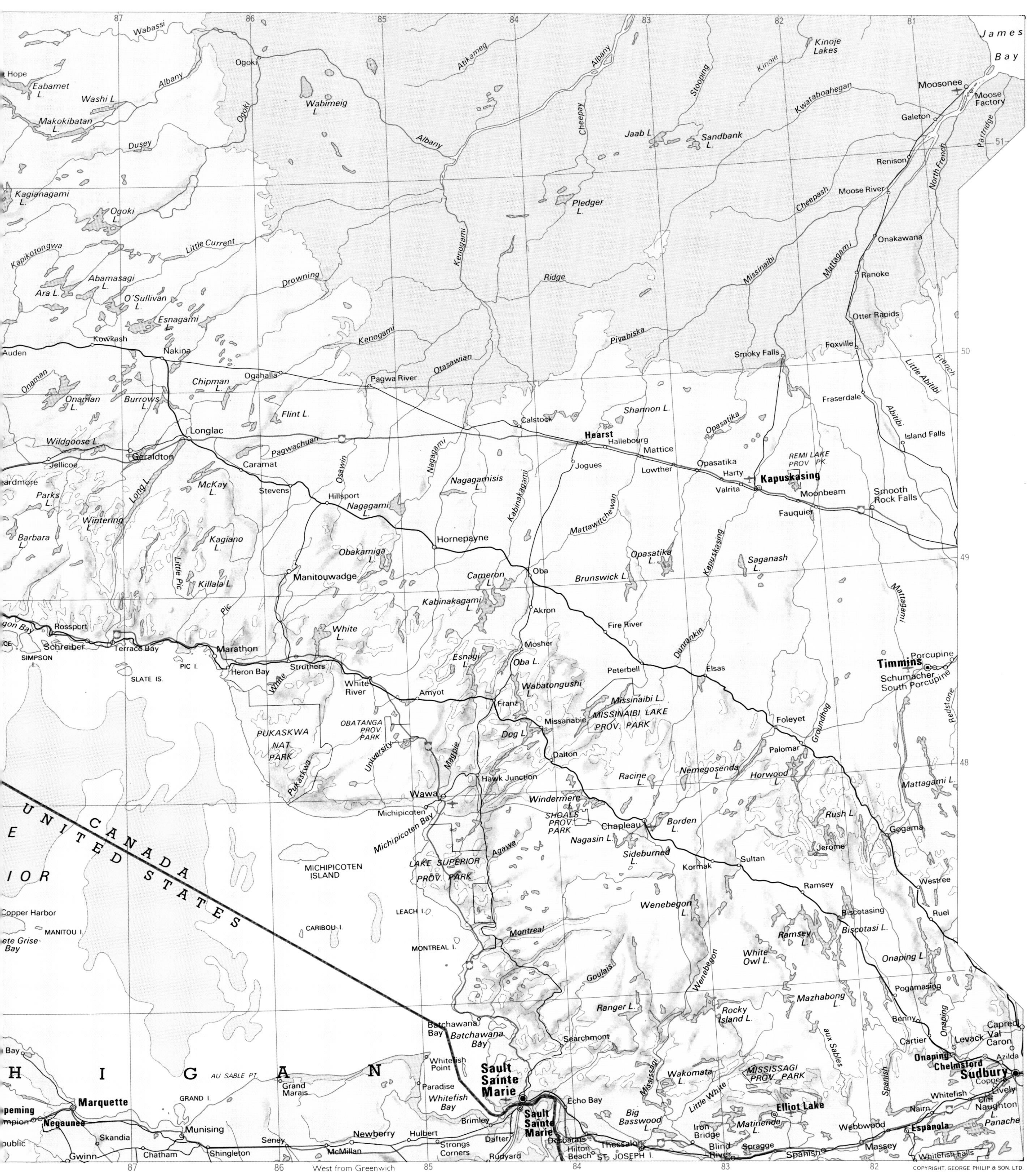
James Bay
Moosonee
Moose Factory
Kapuskasing
Hearst
Timmins
Sudbury
Sault Sainte Marie
Wawa
Chapleau
Marathon
Longlac
Geraldton
Hornepayne
Elliot Lake
Espanola
Marquette
CANADA
UNITED STATES
West from Greenwich

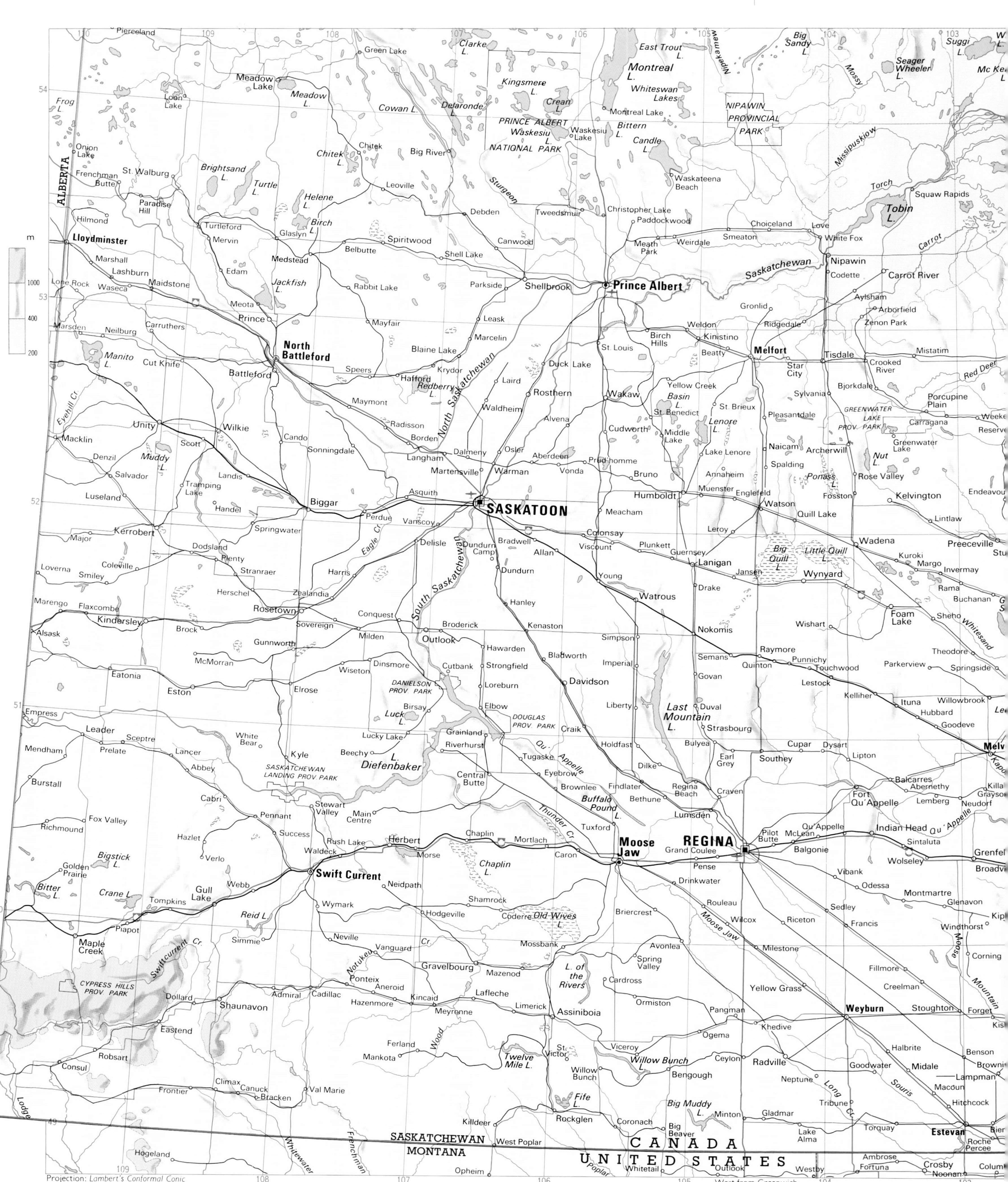
ALBERTA
Pierceland
Green Lake
Clarke L.
East Trout L.
Nipekamew
Big Sandy L.
Suggi L.
Seager Wheeler L.
Mossy
Mc Ke
Meadow Lake
Meadow L.
Loon Lake
Frog L.
Cowan L.
Delaronde L.
Kingsmere L.
Crean L.
Montreal L.
Whiteswan Lakes
Montreal Lake
NIPAWIN PROVINCIAL PARK
PRINCE ALBERT NATIONAL PARK
Waskesiu L.
Waskesiu Lake
Bittern L.
Candle L.
Missipuskiow
Onion Lake
Chitek L.
Chitek
Big River
Frenchman Butte
St. Walburg
Brightsand L.
Turtle L.
Sturgeon
Waskateena Beach
Torch
Squaw Rapids
Tobin L.
Paradise Hill
Helene L.
Leoville
Hilmond
Birch L.
Debden
Tweedsmuir
Christopher Lake
Paddockwood
Choiceland
Love
White Fox
Lloydminster
Turtleford
Glaslyn
Spiritwood
Canwood
Meath Park
Weirdale
Smeaton
Carrot
Mervin
Belbutte
Marshall
Lashburn
Medstead
Shell Lake
Saskatchewan
Nipawin
Codette
Carrot River
Edam
Jackfish L.
Lone Rock
Waseca
Maidstone
Rabbit Lake
Parkside
Shellbrook
Prince Albert
Meota
Aylsham
Arborfield
Prince
Gronlid
Zenon Park
Marsden
Neilburg
Carruthers
Mayfair
Leask
Weldon
Ridgedale
Kinistino
North Battleford
Marcelin
Birch Hills
Manito L.
Cut Knife
Blaine Lake
St. Louis
Beatty
Melfort
Tisdale
Crooked River
Mistatim
Battleford
Speers
Krydor
Hafford
Redberry L.
Laird
Duck Lake
Star City
Red Deer
Yellow Creek
Bjorkdale
Eyehill Cr.
Maymont
North Saskatchewan
Rosthern
Wakaw
Basin L.
Sylvania
Porcupine Plain
St. Brieux
St. Benedict
GREENWATER LAKE PROV. PARK
Weeke
Unity
Wilkie
Radisson
Waldheim
Alvena
Cudworth
Lenore L.
Pleasantdale
Carragana
Reserv
Macklin
Cando
Borden
Middle Lake
Greenwater Lake
Scott
Denzil
Muddy L.
Sonningdale
Langham
Dalmeny
Osler
Aberdeen
Prud'homme
Naicam
Archerwill
Nut L.
Lake Lenore
Spalding
Salvador
Landis
Martensville
Warman
Vonda
Bruno
Annaheim
Ponass L.
Rose Valley
Tramping Lake
Luseland
Asquith
Humboldt
Muenster
Englefeld
Fosston
Kelvington
Endeavou
Handel
Biggar
SASKATOON
Meacham
Watson
Quill Lake
Perdue
Lintlaw
Kerrobert
Springwater
Vanscoy
Colonsay
Leroy
Major
Dodsland
Delisle
Dundurn Camp
Bradwell
Viscount
Plunkett
Wadena
Preeceville
Plenty
Allan
Guernsey
Lanigan
Big Quill L.
Little Quill L.
Kuroki
Margo
Invermay
Loverna
Coleville
Smiley
Stranraer
Harris
Eagle Cr.
South Saskatchewan
Dundurn
Young
Jansen
Wynyard
Herschel
Zealandia
Watrous
Drake
Rama
Buchanan
Marengo
Flaxcombe
Rosetown
Hanley
Kindersley
Conquest
Foam Lake
Sheho
Alsask
Brock
Sovereign
Broderick
Kenaston
Wishart
Whitesand
Milden
Outlook
Nokomis
Gunnworth
Hawarden
Simpson
Raymore
Theodore
McMorran
Bladworth
Semans
Punnichy
Dinsmore
Cutbank
Strongfield
Imperial
Quinton
Touchwood
Parkerview
Springside
Eatonia
Wiseton
DANIELSON PROV. PARK
Loreburn
Davidson
Govan
Lestock
Eston
Elrose
Kelliher
Ituna
Willowbrook
Birsay
Elbow
Liberty
Last Mountain L.
Duval
Empress
Luck L.
DOUGLAS PROV. PARK
Hubbard
Goodeve
Leader
Sceptre
White Bear
Lucky Lake
Grainland
Craik
Strasbourg
Mendham
Prelate
Lancer
Kyle
Beechy
Riverhurst
Tugaske
Qu'Appelle
Holdfast
Bulyea
Cupar
Dysart
Lipton
Melv
Abbey
L. Diefenbaker
SASKATCHEWAN LANDING PROV. PARK
Eyebrow
Dilke
Earl Grey
Southey
Balcarres
Abernethy
Burstall
Central Butte
Brownlee
Findlater
Regina Beach
Craven
Fort Qu'Appelle
Lemberg
Neudorf
Cabri
Stewart Valley
Buffalo Pound L.
Bethune
Lumsden
Richmound
Fox Valley
Pennant
Main Centre
Thunder Cr.
Tuxford
Pilot Butte
McLean
Indian Head
Hazlet
Success
Rush Lake
Herbert
Chaplin
Mortlach
Moose Jaw
REGINA
Sintaluta
Bigstick L.
Verlo
Waldeck
Morse
Caron
Grand Coulee
Balgonie
Grenfel
Golden Prairie
Swift Current
Chaplin L.
Pense
Wolseley
Broadvi
Bitter L.
Crane L.
Gull Lake
Webb
Neidpath
Drinkwater
Vibank
Odessa
Tompkins
Wymark
Shamrock
Rouleau
Montmartre
Glenavon
Reid L.
Hodgeville
Coderre
Old Wives L.
Briercrest
Moose Jaw
Wilcox
Riceton
Sedley
Francis
Windthorst
Kip
Piapot
Simmie
Maple Creek
Swiftcurrent Cr.
Neville
Vanguard
Cr.
Mossbank
Avonlea
Milestone
Moose
Corning
Notukeu
Gravelbourg
Spring Valley
Fillmore
Mountain
CYPRESS HILLS PROV. PARK
Ponteix
Aneroid
Mazenod
L. of the Rivers
Cardross
Creelman
Admiral
Cadillac
Lafleche
Yellow Grass
Dollard
Kincaid
Hazenmore
Shaunavon
Meyronne
Limerick
Assiniboia
Ormiston
Weyburn
Stoughton
Forget
Kis
Eastend
Pangman
Khedive
Ogema
Wood
Ferland
Mankota
Robsart
Twelve Mile L.
St. Victor
Viceroy
Willow Bunch L.
Ceylon
Radville
Halbrite
Benson
Consul
Willow Bunch
Bengough
Goodwater
Midale
Browni
Lampman
Macoun
Climax
Canuck
Bracken
Val Marie
Frontier
Neptune
Long Cr.
Souris
Tribune
Hitchcock
Lodge
Fife L.
Big Muddy L.
Minton
Gladmar
Killdeer
Rockglen
Coronach
Big Beaver
Lake Alma
Torquay
Estevan
Bien
Frenchman
Whitewater
SASKATCHEWAN
MONTANA
West Poplar
CANADA
UNITED STATES
Roche Percee
Hogeland
Opheim
Poplar
Whitetail
Outlook
Westby
Ambrose
Fortuna
Crosby
Noonan
Colum
Projection: Lambert's Conformal Conic
West from Greenwich
m
1000
400
200
110
109
108
107
106
105
104
103
54
53
52
51
50
49

1 : 2 200 000

10 0 10 20 30 40 50 60 70 80 90 100 km

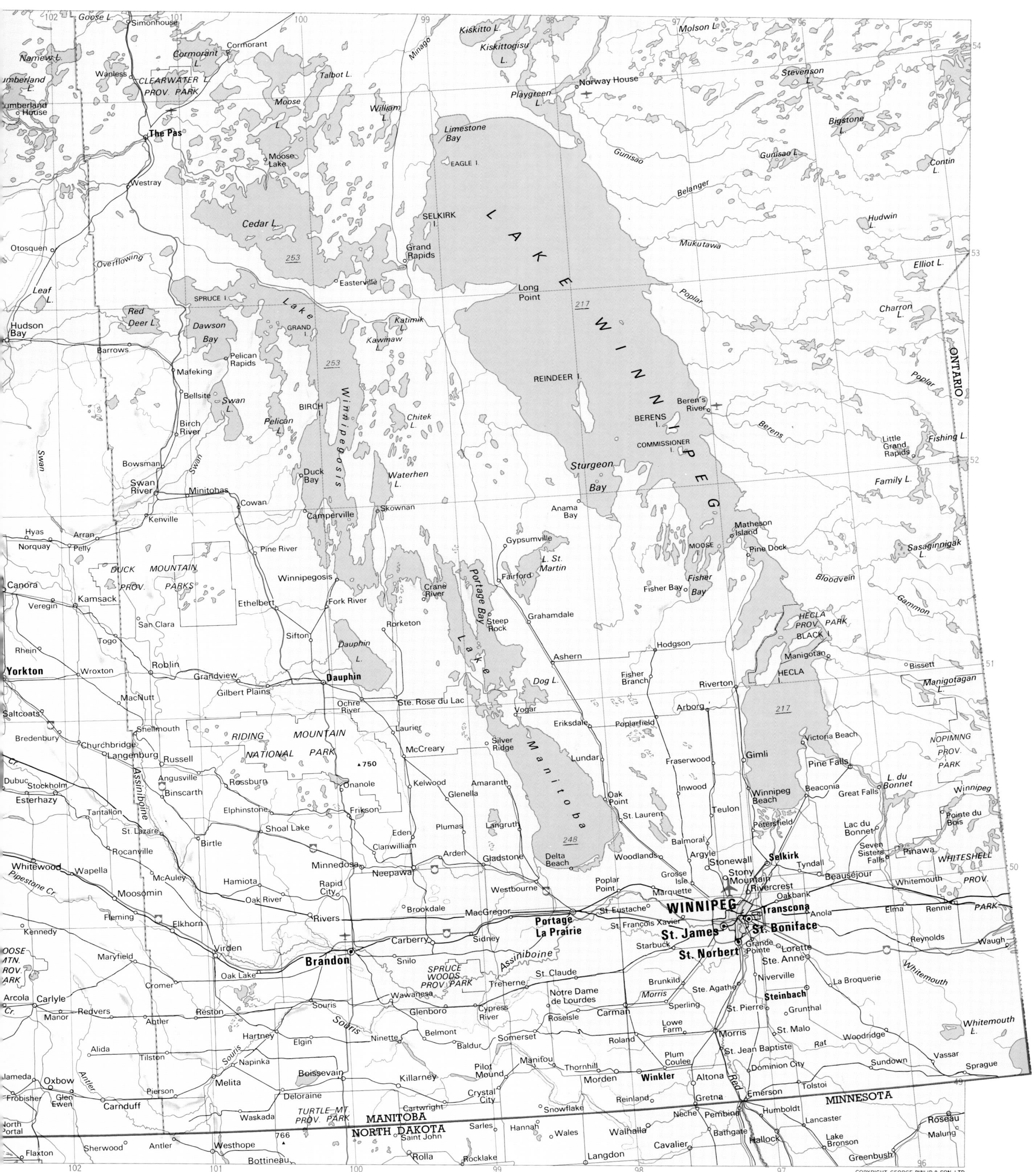

1 : 2 200 000

10 0 10 20 30 40 50 60 70 80 90 100 km

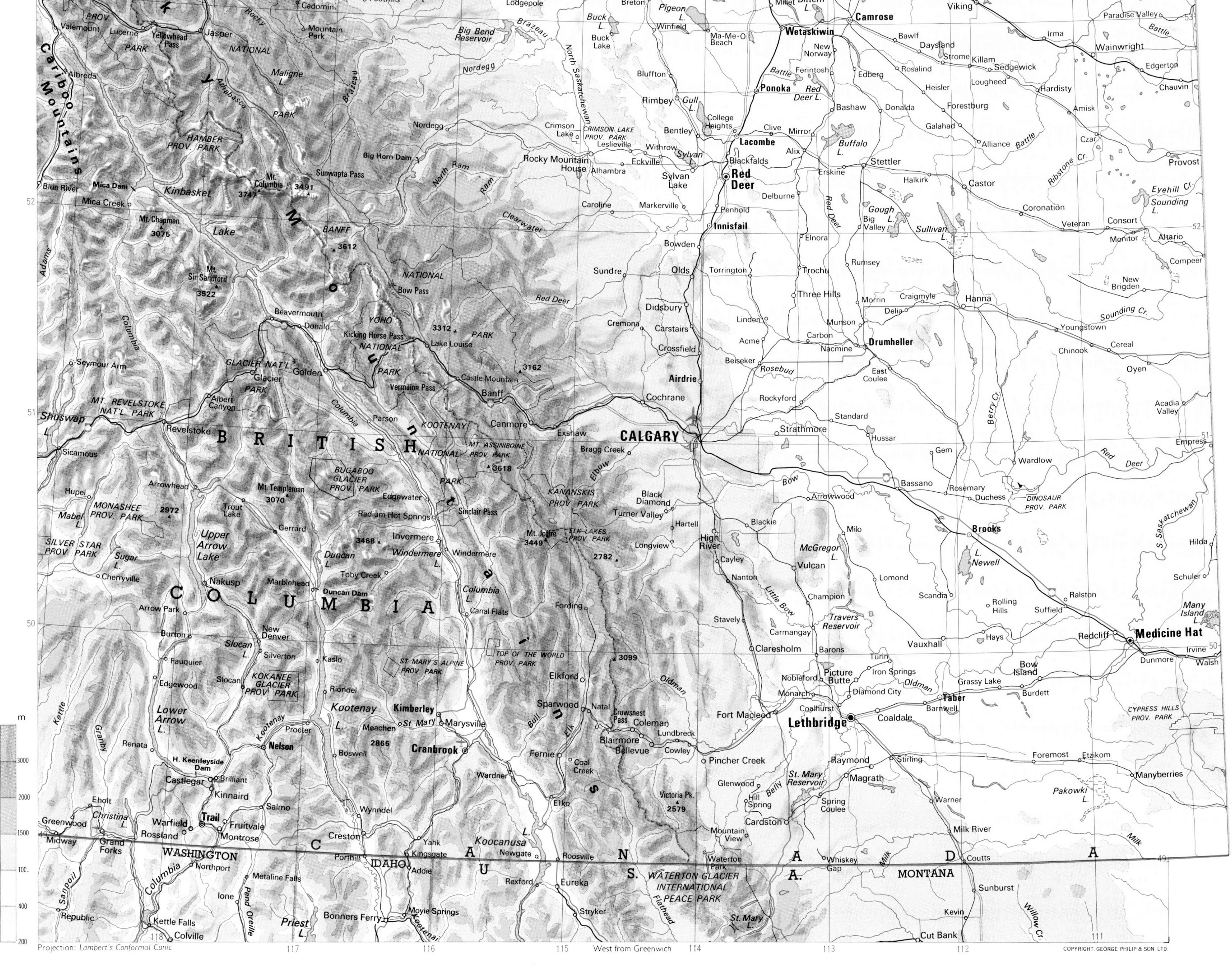
CALGARY
Medicine Hat
Lethbridge
Red Deer
Camrose
Wetaskiwin
Ponoka
Lacombe
Innisfail
Drumheller
Brooks
Airdrie
Banff
Canmore
Cochrane
Revelstoke
Golden
Nelson
Cranbrook
Kimberley
Trail
Castlegar
Nakusp
Jasper
Fernie
Sparwood
Taber
Fort Macleod
Pincher Creek
Cardston
BRITISH COLUMBIA
ROCKY MOUNTAINS
Cariboo Mountains
Kinbasket Lake
Upper Arrow Lake
Lower Arrow L.
Kootenay L.
Slocan L.
Koocanusa L.
BANFF NATIONAL PARK
YOHO NATIONAL PARK
KOOTENAY NATIONAL PARK
GLACIER NAT'L PARK
MT. REVELSTOKE NAT'L. PARK
WATERTON-GLACIER INTERNATIONAL PEACE PARK
CYPRESS HILLS PROV. PARK
DINOSAUR PROV. PARK
KANANSKIS PROV. PARK
U.S.A.
CANADA
MONTANA
IDAHO
WASHINGTON
North Saskatchewan
Red Deer
Bow
Oldman
Columbia
West from Greenwich
Projection: Lambert's Conformal Conic
COPYRIGHT GEORGE PHILIP & SON, LTD
m
3000
2000
1500
1000
400
200

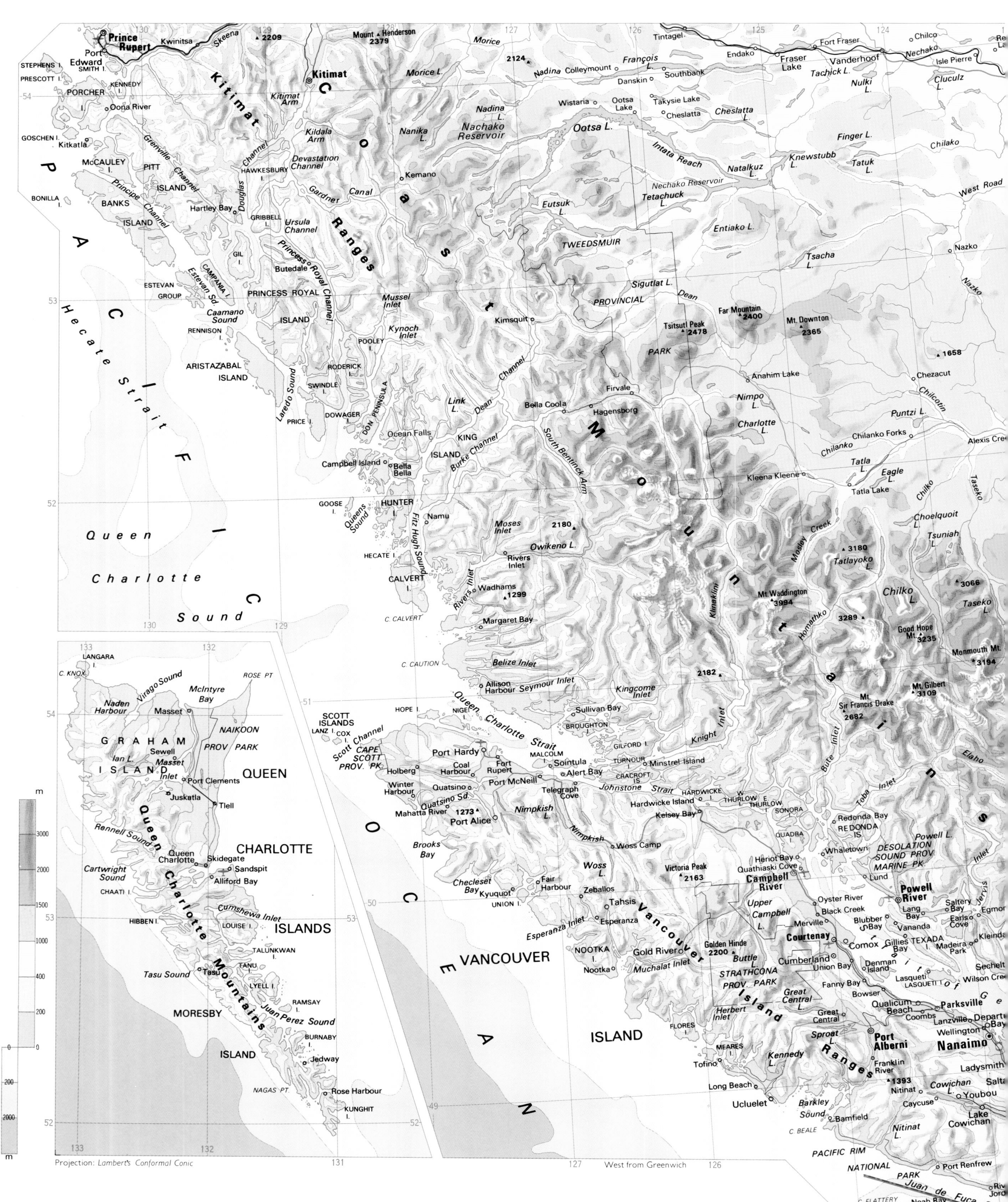
PACIFIC OCEAN
Queen Charlotte Sound
Hecate Strait
Coast Mountains
VANCOUVER ISLAND
Vancouver Island Ranges
Queen Charlotte Mountains
GRAHAM ISLAND
MORESBY ISLAND
QUEEN CHARLOTTE ISLANDS
Prince Rupert
Kitimat
Bella Coola
Port Hardy
Campbell River
Courtenay
Port Alberni
Nanaimo
Mt. Waddington 3994
Projection: Lambert's Conformal Conic
West from Greenwich

1 : 2 200 000

10 0 10 20 30 40 50 60 70 80 90 100 km

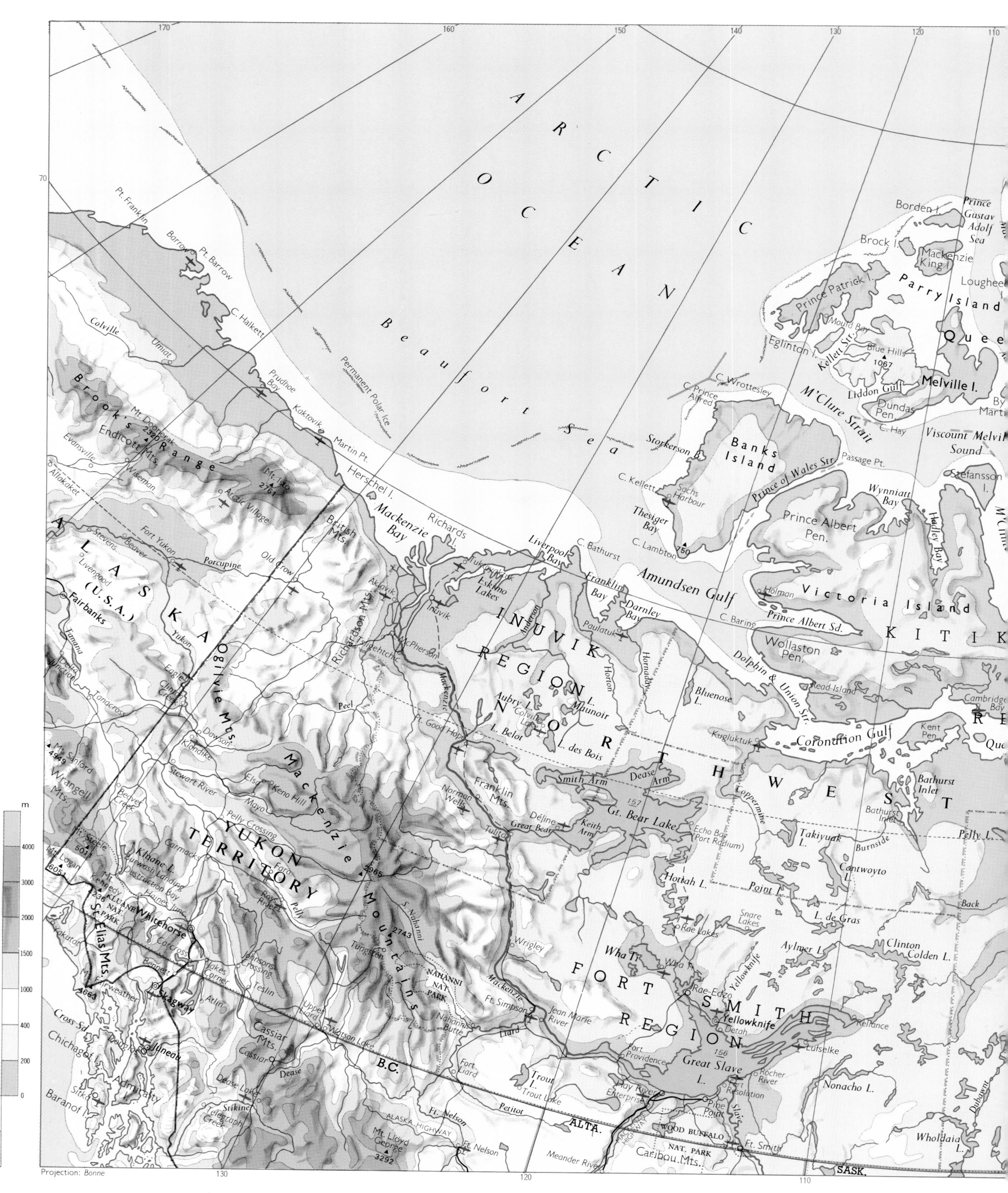
ARCTIC OCEAN
Beaufort Sea
Permanent Polar Ice
ALASKA (U.S.A.)
YUKON TERRITORY
NORTHWEST TERRITORIES
INUVIK REGION
FORT SMITH REGION
Brooks Range
Mackenzie Mountains
Ogilvie Mts.
Richardson Mts.
British Mts.
Franklin Mts.
St. Elias Mts.
Cassiar Mts.
Caribou Mts.
Banks Island
Victoria Island
Melville I.
Prince Patrick I.
Amundsen Gulf
Coronation Gulf
Gt. Bear Lake
Great Slave L.
Whitehorse
Yellowknife
Fairbanks
Dawson
Inuvik
Mackenzie Bay
Herschel I.
Fort Yukon
Old Crow
Aklavik
Tuktoyaktuk
Norman Wells
Ft. Simpson
Ft. Smith
Hay River
Juneau
Skagway
B.C.
ALTA.
SASK.
NAHANNI NAT. PARK
KLUANE NAT. PARK
WOOD BUFFALO NAT. PARK
ALASKA HIGHWAY
Projection: Bonne

1:8 900 000
100 0 100 200 300 400 km
GREENLAND
KALAALLIT NUNAAT
(DENMARK)
United States Range
Barbeau Pk. 2604
Victoria and Albert Mts.
Kennedy Chan.
Kane Basin
Smith Sound
C. Thomas Hubbard
Nansen Sd.
Greely Fd.
Eureka
Princess Margaret Range
2140
Axel Heiberg I.
Fosheim Pen.
Ellesmere Island
Sverdrup Is.
Raanes Pen.
Amund Ringnes I.
Ellef Ringnes I.
Norwegian Bay
Graham I.
Smith B.
Cornwall I.
Belcher Channel
Simmons Pen.
Glacier Str.
Coburg I.
Penny Str.
Lady Ann Str.
Jones Sound
Treuter Mts.
1887
Hyde Inlet
C. Cockburn
Devon I.
Bathurst I.
Cornwallis I.
Wellington Chan.
Resolute
C. Warrender
Qaanaaq (Thule)
Qimusseriarsuaq (Melville Bay)
Nuussuaq (Kraulshavn)
Upernavik
Kangersuatsiaq (Prøven)
Svartenhuk Peninsula
Uummannaq (Umanaq)
Ilulissat (Jakobshavn)
Qeqertarsuaq (Disko I.)
Qeqertarsuaq (Godhavn)
Sisimiut (Holsteinsborg)
Baffin Bay
Davis Strait
Lancaster Sound
Barrow Str.
Russell I.
C. Crauford
C. Liverpool
2134
Bylot I.
Pond Inlet
Nova Zembla I.
C. Jameson
C. Hunter
Nanisivik
Arctic Bay
Borden Peninsula
Eclipse Sd.
Bruce Mts.
Scott Inlet
Clyde River
C. Hewett
C. Raper
C. Henry Kater
Somerset I.
Prince Regent Inlet
Brodeur Peninsula
Admiralty Inlet
Barnes Icecap
Home B.
Kivitoo
Broughton Island
Padloping Island
Cape Dyer
Prince of Wales I.
Ft. Ross
C. Farrand
Franklin Str.
Bernier B.
Steensby Inlet
Baffin Island
AUYUITTUQ NAT. PARK
Penny Highland
2591
Cumberland Peninsula
Hoare B.
Boothia Peninsula
573
Gulf of Boothia
Gateshead I.
Fury & Hecla Str.
C. Englefield
Igloolik
Rowley I.
Baird Pen.
Foley I.
Hall Beach
Thom Bay
Taloyoak
Admiralty I.
King William I.
Gjoa Haven
Simpson Pen.
Pelly Bay
Committee B.
Melville Peninsula
Prince Charles I.
Air Force I.
Cumberland Sound
C. Mercy
Lemieux Islands
Nettilling L.
Foxe Basin
C. Dominion
Adelaide Pen.
Chantrey Inlet
Rae Isthmus
Repulse Bay
Amadjuak L.
Iqaluit
Hall Pen.
Frobisher Bay
Resolution I.
Arctic Circle
Vansittart I.
C. Dorchester
Foxe Pen.
Cape Dorset
Everett Mts.
Macdougall L.
Wager Bay
Wager B.
Torsill Mts.
Southampton I.
Foxe Channel
Salisbury I.
Hudson Strait
C. Chidley
Garry L.
Roes Welcome Sd.
Coral Harbour
Bell Pen.
Nottingham I.
Nottingham Island
Wolstenholme
Salluit
Digges Is.
C. Wolstenholme
Ivujivik
St. Louis Mts.
Kangiqsujuaq
Quaqtaq
C. Hopes Advance
Akpatok I.
Port Burwell
Baker Lake
Chesterfield Inlet
Fisher Strait
C. Low
Coats I.
Mansel I.
Kangirsuk
Ungava Bay
Arnaud (Payne)
KEEWATIN REGION
Dubawnt L.
Rankin Inlet
Whale Cove
Yathkyed L.
Kaminak L.
Padle
Tavani
Cape Smith
Povungnituk
Payne L.
Kuujjuaq
Koksoak
Hudson Bay
Arviat
Ottawa Is.
Portland Promontory
Feuilles (Leaf)
Mélèzes (Larch)
Nueltin L.
Thlewiaza
Kasba L.
Inukjuak
L. Minto
TERRITORIES
REGION
Macdougall
Chan.
100
90
80
70
60
50
40

INDEX TO CANADIAN MAPS

The first number in dark type after each name in the index refers to the number in the Canadian map section. These are followed by the geographical co-ordinates, in lighter type, which give the latitude and longitude of a particular place or feature.

The geographical co-ordinates which follow the name are sometimes only approximate but are close enough for the place or feature to be located. Rivers have been indexed to their mouth or confluence.

An open square □ signifies that the name is an administrative subdivision such as a province, county or district. An arrow → follows the name of a river.

A

Abbotsford .. **19** 49 5N 122 20W
Aberdeen ... **14** 52 20N 106 8W
Abitibi L. ... **8** 48 40N 79 40W
Acme **17** 51 33N 113 30W
Acton **10** 43 38N 80 3W
Acton Vale .. **9** 45 39N 72 34W
Adams L. ... **19** 51 10N 119 40W
Adelaide Pen. **21** 68 15N 97 30W
Adlavik Is. .. **4** 55 2N 57 45W
Agassiz **19** 49 14N 121 46W
Aguanish ... **4** 50 14N 62 2W
Aguanus → . **4** 50 13N 62 5W
Aiguebelle, Parc **8** 48 30N 78 45W
Aillik **4** 55 11N 59 18W
Ailsa Craig .. **10** 43 8N 81 33W
Ajax **11** 43 50N 79 1W
Akimiski I. .. **3** 52 50N 81 30W
Aklavik **20** 68 12N 135 0W
Akpatok I. ... **4** 60 25N 68 8W
Albanel **9** 48 53N 72 27W
Albanel, L. .. **4** 50 55N 73 12W
Albany → .. **3** 52 17N 81 31W
Albert Canyon **19** 51 8N 117 41W
Alberton **7** 46 50N 64 0W
Albreda **19** 52 35N 119 10W
Alert Bay ... **18** 50 30N 126 55W
Alexandria, *B.C.,* **19** 52 35N 122 27W
Alexandria, *Ont.,* **11** 45 19N 74 38W
Alexis → .. **4** 52 33N 56 8W
Alexis Creek . **18** 52 10N 123 20W
Algonquin Prov. Park . **11** 45 50N 78 30W
Alice **11** 45 47N 77 14W
Alida **15** 49 25N 101 55W
Alix **17** 52 24N 113 11W
Allan **14** 51 53N 106 4W
Allanwater .. **12** 50 14N 90 10W
Alliston **10** 44 9N 79 52W
Alluviaq, Fj. . **4** 59 27N 65 10W
Alma **9** 48 35N 71 40W
Almonte **8** 45 14N 76 12W
Alsask **14** 51 21N 109 59W
Alta Lake ... **19** 50 10N 123 0W
Alton **10** 43 54N 80 5W
Alvinston ... **10** 42 49N 81 52W
Amadjuak ... **21** 64 0N 72 39W
Amadjuak L. **21** 65 0N 71 8W
Amaranth ... **15** 50 36N 98 43W
Amherst **7** 45 48N 64 8W
Amherst I. .. **11** 44 8N 76 43W
Amherstburg **10** 42 6N 83 6W
Amos **8** 48 35N 78 5W
Amqui **6** 48 28N 67 27W
Amund Ringnes I. . **21** 78 20N 96 25W
Amundsen Gulf **20** 71 0N 124 0W
Anahim Lake **18** 52 28N 125 18W
Andreville .. **9** 47 41N 69 44W
Angers **8** 45 31N 75 29W
Angliers **8** 47 33N 79 14W
Angus **10** 44 19N 79 53W
Annapolis Royal **7** 44 44N 65 32W
Anticosti, I. d' **6** 49 30N 63 0W
Antigonish .. **7** 45 38N 61 58W
Antler → .. **15** 49 8N 101 0W
Apple Hill ... **11** 45 13N 74 46W
Apsley **11** 44 45N 78 6W
Arborfield ... **14** 53 6N 103 39W
Arborg **15** 50 54N 97 13W
Arcola **15** 49 40N 102 30W
Arctic Bay .. **21** 73 1N 85 7W
Arctic Red River = Tsiigehtchic **20** 67 15N 134 0W
Ardbeg **10** 45 38N 80 5W
Arden **11** 44 43N 76 56W
Argentia **5** 47 18N 53 58W
Aristazabal I. **18** 52 40N 129 10W
Arkona **10** 43 4N 81 50W
Armagh **9** 46 41N 70 32W
Armstrong, *B.C.,* **19** 50 25N 119 10W
Armstrong, *Ont.,* **12** 50 18N 89 4W
Arnaud → . **4** 59 59N 69 46W
Arnprior **11** 45 26N 76 21W
Arntfield **8** 48 12N 79 15W
Arrowhead .. **19** 50 40N 117 55W
Arthur **10** 43 50N 80 32W
Arundel **8** 45 58N 74 37W
Arviat **21** 61 10N 94 15W
Arvida **9** 48 25N 71 14W
Ashcroft **19** 50 40N 121 20W
Ashmont ... **16** 54 7N 111 35W
Ashuanipi, L. **4** 52 45N 66 15W
Asquith **14** 52 8N 107 13W
Assiniboia .. **14** 49 40N 105 59W
Assiniboine → **15** 49 53N 97 8W
Astorville ... **10** 46 11N 79 17W
Athabasca .. **16** 54 45N 113 20W
Athens **11** 44 38N 75 57W
Atherley **10** 44 37N 79 20W
Atholville ... **7** 47 59N 66 43W
Atikokan **12** 48 45N 91 37W
Atikonak L. .. **4** 52 40N 64 32W
Attawapiskat → **3** 52 57N 82 18W
Attikamagen L. **4** 55 0N 66 30W
Atwood **10** 43 40N 81 1W
Auden **13** 50 14N 87 53W
Augustines, L. des **8** 47 37N 75 56W
Ausable → . **10** 43 19N 81 46W
Avalon Pen. . **5** 47 30N 53 20W
Avola **19** 51 45N 119 19W
Avonlea **14** 50 0N 105 0W
Avonmore ... **8** 45 10N 74 58W
Axel Heiberg I. **21** 80 0N 90 0W
Ayer's Cliff .. **9** 45 10N 72 3W
Aylen L. **11** 45 37N 77 51W
Aylmer, *Ont.,* **10** 42 46N 80 59W
Aylmer, *Qué.,* **8** 45 24N 75 51W
Aylmer, L. .. **20** 64 0N 110 8W
Ayr **10** 43 17N 80 27W
Azilda **10** 46 33N 81 6W

B

Back → **20** 65 10N 104 0W
Badger **5** 49 0N 56 4W
Baffin I. **21** 68 0N 75 0W
Bagotville ... **9** 48 22N 70 54W
Baie Comeau **6** 49 12N 68 10W
Baie-du-Poste **4** 50 24N 73 56W
Baie-St-Paul . **9** 47 28N 70 32W
Baie-Ste-Catherine . **9** 48 6N 69 44W
Baie Trinité . **6** 49 25N 67 20W
Baie Verte .. **5** 49 55N 56 12W
Baieville **9** 46 8N 72 43W
Baker, L. **21** 64 0N 96 0W
Baker Lake .. **21** 64 20N 96 3W
Baker's Dozen Is. **4** 56 45N 78 45W
Bala **10** 45 1N 79 37W
Balcarres ... **14** 50 50N 103 35W
Bamfield **18** 48 45N 125 10W
Bancroft **11** 45 3N 77 51W
Banff **17** 51 10N 115 34W
Banff Nat. Park **17** 51 30N 116 15W
Banks I., *B.C.,* **18** 53 20N 130 0W
Banks I., *N.W.T.,* **20** 73 15N 121 30W
Bannockburn **11** 44 39N 77 33W
Baring, C. ... **20** 70 0N 117 30W
Bark L. **8** 45 27N 77 51W
Barkley Sound **18** 48 50N 125 10W
Barraute **8** 48 26N 77 38W
Barrhead ... **16** 54 10N 114 24W
Barrie **10** 44 24N 79 40W
Barriefield .. **11** 44 14N 76 28W
Barrière **19** 51 12N 120 7W
Barry's Bay . **11** 45 29N 77 41W
Baskatong, Rés. **8** 46 46N 75 50W
Bassano **17** 50 48N 112 20W
Bath **11** 44 11N 76 47W
Bathurst **7** 47 37N 65 43W
Bathurst, C. . **20** 70 34N 128 0W
Bathurst I. .. **21** 76 0N 100 30W
Bathurst Inlet **20** 66 50N 108 1W
Batiscan **9** 46 30N 72 15W
Batiscan → . **9** 46 16N 72 15W
Batiscan, L. . **9** 47 22N 71 55W
Battle → ... **14** 52 43N 108 15W
Battle Harbour **4** 52 16N 55 35W
Battleford ... **14** 52 45N 108 15W
Bay Bulls ... **5** 47 19N 52 50W
Bay de Verde **5** 48 5N 52 54W
Bayfield **10** 43 34N 81 42W
Bays, L. of .. **10** 45 15N 79 4W
Bayside **11** 44 7N 77 30W
Baysville **10** 45 9N 79 7W
Bazin → ... **8** 47 29N 75 22W
Beachburg .. **11** 45 44N 76 51W
Beachville ... **10** 43 5N 80 49W
Beaconia ... **15** 50 25N 96 31W
Beamsville ... **10** 43 12N 79 28W
Beardmore .. **13** 49 36N 87 57W
Béarn **8** 47 17N 79 20W
Beauceville .. **9** 46 13N 70 46W
Beauchûne, L. **8** 46 35N 78 55W
Beaufort Sea **2** 72 0N 140 0W
Beauharnois **9** 45 20N 73 52W
Beaulac **9** 45 50N 71 23W
Beauport ... **9** 46 52N 71 11W
Beaupré **9** 47 3N 70 54W
Beauséjour .. **15** 50 5N 96 35W
Beaverhill L. . **16** 53 27N 112 32W
Beaverlodge **16** 55 11N 119 29W
Beavermouth **19** 51 32N 117 23W
Beaverton .. **10** 44 26N 79 9W
Bedford **9** 45 7N 72 59W
Beebe Plain . **9** 45 1N 72 9W
Beechy **14** 50 53N 107 24W
Beeton **10** 44 5N 79 47W
Belcher Chan. **21** 77 15N 95 0W
Belcher Is. ... **4** 56 15N 78 45W
Belcourt **8** 48 24N 77 21W
Bell → **8** 49 48N 77 38W
Bell I. **5** 50 46N 55 35W
Bell Peninsula **21** 63 50N 82 0W
Bella Bella .. **18** 52 10N 128 10W
Bella Coola . **18** 52 25N 126 40W
Belle Isle ... **4** 51 57N 55 25W
Belle Isle, Str. of **4** 51 30N 56 30W
Belle River .. **10** 42 18N 82 43W
Belleoram ... **5** 47 31N 55 25W
Belleterre ... **8** 47 25N 78 41W
Belleville ... **11** 44 10N 77 23W
Bellevue **17** 49 35N 114 22W
Bellin = Kangirsuk . **4** 60 0N 70 0W
Bells Corners **11** 45 19N 75 50W
Belmont **10** 42 53N 81 5W
Beloeil **9** 45 34N 73 12W
Bengough ... **14** 49 25N 105 10W
Benny **10** 46 47N 81 38W
Berens → .. **15** 52 25N 97 2W
Berens I. **15** 52 18N 97 18W
Berens River **15** 52 25N 97 0W
Berland → . **16** 54 0N 116 50W
Bermen, L. .. **4** 53 35N 68 55W
Bernard L. .. **10** 45 45N 79 23W
Bernierville .. **9** 46 6N 71 34W
Berthierville . **9** 46 5N 73 10W
Bethany **11** 44 11N 78 34W
Betsiamites . **9** 48 56N 68 40W
Betsiamites → **9** 48 56N 68 38W
Bewdley **11** 44 5N 78 19W
Bic **9** 48 20N 68 41W
Bic, Île du ... **9** 48 24N 68 52W
Bienfait **14** 49 10N 102 50W
Bienville, L. . **4** 55 5N 72 40W
Big → **4** 54 50N 58 55W
Big B. **4** 55 43N 60 35W
Big Basswood L. **10** 46 25N 83 23W
Big Beaver .. **14** 49 10N 105 10W
Big Cr. → .. **19** 51 42N 122 41W
Big Quill L. .. **14** 51 55N 104 50W
Big Rideau L. **11** 44 40N 76 15W
Big River ... **14** 53 50N 107 0W
Big Trout L., *Ont.,* **11** 45 46N 78 37W
Big Trout L., *Ont.,* **2** 53 40N 90 0W
Biggar **14** 52 4N 108 0W
Bigniba → .. **8** 49 18N 77 20W
Bigstone L. .. **15** 53 42N 95 44W
Binscarth ... **15** 50 37N 101 17W
Birch Hills ... **14** 52 59N 105 25W
Birch I. **15** 52 26N 99 54W
Birch L. **12** 51 23N 92 18W
Birch River .. **15** 52 24N 101 6W
Birtle **15** 50 30N 101 5W
Biscostasing **13** 47 18N 82 9W
Bishop's Falls **5** 49 2N 55 30W
Bishopton ... **9** 45 35N 71 35W
Bissett **15** 51 2N 95 41W
Blache, L. de la **9** 50 5N 69 29W
Black → ... **10** 44 42N 79 19W
Black Diamond .. **17** 50 45N 114 14W
Black I. **15** 51 12N 96 30W
Black Lake .. **9** 46 1N 71 22W
Black Rock Pt. **4** 60 2N 64 10W
Blackie **17** 50 36N 113 37W
Blacks Harbour ... **7** 45 3N 66 49W
Blackville ... **7** 46 44N 65 50W
Blaine Lake . **14** 52 51N 106 52W
Blainville **9** 45 40N 73 52W
Blairmore ... **17** 49 40N 114 25W
Blenheim **10** 42 20N 82 0W
Bleu, L. **8** 46 35N 78 24W
Blind River .. **10** 46 10N 82 58W
Bloodvein → **15** 51 47N 96 43W
Bloomfield ... **11** 43 59N 77 14W
Blyth **10** 43 44N 81 26W
Bobcaygeon . **11** 44 33N 78 33W
Bochart **9** 49 10N 73 30W
Boissevain .. **15** 49 15N 100 5W
Bolton **10** 43 54N 79 45W
Bon Echo Prov. Park . **11** 45 0N 77 20W
Bonaventure **7** 48 5N 65 32W
Bonavista ... **5** 48 40N 53 5W
Bonavista, C. **5** 48 42N 53 5W
Bonfield **10** 46 14N 79 9W
Bonnechere → **11** 45 35N 77 50W
Bonnyville ... **16** 54 20N 110 45W
Boothia, Gulf of **21** 71 0N 90 0W
Borden **7** 46 18N 63 47W
Borden I. ... **20** 78 30N 111 30W
Boston Bar .. **19** 49 52N 121 30W
Boswell **19** 49 28N 116 45W
Bothwell **10** 42 38N 81 52W
Botwood **5** 49 6N 55 23W
Boucher → . **9** 49 10N 69 6W
Bouchette ... **8** 46 12N 75 57W
Bouchier, L. . **8** 50 6N 77 48W
Bourget **8** 45 26N 75 9W
Bow Island .. **17** 49 50N 111 23W
Bowmanville **11** 43 55N 78 41W
Bowron → .. **19** 54 3N 121 50W
Bowsman ... **15** 52 14N 101 12W
Boyd L. **4** 52 46N 76 42W
Bracebridge . **10** 45 2N 79 19W
Bradford **10** 44 7N 79 34W
Bradore Bay . **5** 51 27N 57 18W
Braeside **8** 45 28N 76 24W
Bralorne **19** 50 50N 122 50W
Brampton ... **10** 43 45N 79 45W
Brandon **15** 49 50N 99 57W
Brantford ... **10** 43 10N 80 15W
Bras d'Or, L. **7** 45 50N 60 50W
Brazeau → . **17** 52 55N 115 14W
Brechin **10** 44 32N 79 10W
Brent **11** 46 2N 78 29W
Breton **17** 53 7N 114 28W
Bridgenorth . **11** 44 23N 78 23W
Bridgeport .. **10** 43 29N 80 29W
Bridgetown .. **7** 44 55N 65 18W
Bridgewater . **7** 44 25N 64 31W
Brighton **11** 44 2N 77 44W
Brilliant **19** 49 19N 117 38W
Brion, I. **7** 47 46N 61 26W
Bristol **8** 45 32N 76 28W
Britt **10** 45 46N 80 34W
Broadback → **4** 51 21N 78 52W
Broadview .. **14** 50 22N 102 35W
Brochet, L. du **9** 49 40N 69 37W
Brock **14** 51 26N 108 43W
Brock → **8** 50 0N 75 5W
Brock I. **20** 77 52N 114 19W
Brockville ... **11** 44 35N 75 41W
Brodeur Pen. **21** 72 30N 88 10W
Bromont **9** 45 17N 72 39W
Bromptonville **9** 45 28N 71 57W
Brookmere .. **19** 49 52N 120 53W
Brooks **17** 50 35N 111 55W
Brooks B. ... **18** 50 15N 127 55W
Broughton Island **21** 67 33N 63 0W
Brownlee ... **14** 50 43N 106 1W
Brownsburg . **9** 45 41N 74 25W
Bruce Pen. .. **10** 45 0N 81 30W
Brûlé **16** 53 15N 117 58W
Bruno **14** 52 20N 105 30W
Brussels **10** 43 44N 81 15W
Bryson **8** 45 41N 76 37W
Buchanan ... **14** 51 40N 102 45W
Buchans **5** 48 50N 56 52W
Buckhorn L. . **11** 44 29N 78 23W
Buckingham . **8** 45 37N 75 24W
Buctouche .. **7** 46 30N 64 45W
Buffalo L. ... **17** 52 27N 112 54W
Burdett **17** 49 50N 111 32W
Burford **10** 43 7N 80 27W
Burgeo **5** 47 37N 57 38W
Burin **5** 47 1N 55 14W
Burk's Falls . **10** 45 37N 79 24W
Burleigh Falls **11** 44 33N 78 12W
Burlington ... **10** 43 18N 79 45W
Burnaby I. ... **18** 52 25N 131 19W
Burnside → . **20** 66 51N 108 4W
Burnt L. **4** 53 35N 64 4W
Burnt River .. **11** 44 41N 78 42W
Burstall **14** 50 39N 109 54W
Burton L. ... **4** 54 45N 78 20W
Burwash **10** 46 14N 80 51W
Bury **9** 45 28N 71 30W
Bute Inlet ... **18** 50 40N 124 53W
Button Is. ... **4** 60 38N 64 40W
Bylot I. **21** 73 13N 78 34W
Byng Inlet .. **10** 45 46N 80 33W

C

Caamano Sd. **18** 52 55N 129 25W
Cabano **9** 47 40N 68 56W
Cabonga, Réservoir .. **8** 47 20N 76 40W
Cabot Str. ... **3** 47 15N 59 40W
Cabri **14** 50 35N 108 25W
Cache Bay .. **10** 46 22N 80 0W
Cadillac **8** 48 14N 78 23W
Cadomin **17** 53 2N 117 20W
Cadotte → . **16** 56 43N 117 10W
Calabogie ... **11** 45 18N 76 43W
Caledonia ... **10** 43 7N 79 58W
Calgary **17** 51 0N 114 10W
Callander ... **10** 46 13N 79 22W
Calling Lake . **16** 55 15N 113 12W
Calstock **13** 49 47N 84 9W
Calvert I. **18** 51 30N 128 0W
Camachigama, L. **8** 47 50N 76 19W
Cambridge .. **10** 43 23N 80 15W
Cambridge Bay **20** 69 10N 105 0W
Cameron Falls **12** 49 8N 88 19W
Camp Borden **10** 44 18N 79 56W
Campbell River **18** 50 5N 125 20W
Campbellford **11** 44 18N 77 48W
Campbell's Bay **8** 45 44N 76 36W
Campbellton **7** 47 57N 66 43W
Camperville . **15** 51 59N 100 9W
Camrose ... **17** 53 0N 112 50W
Canada ■ ... **2** 60 0N 100 0W
Canadian Shield **3** 53 0N 75 0W
Canal Flats .. **17** 50 10N 115 48W
Candle L. ... **14** 53 50N 105 18W
Canim Lake . **19** 51 47N 120 54W
Canmore ... **17** 51 7N 115 18W
Cannington . **11** 44 20N 79 2W
Canora **15** 51 40N 102 30W
Canso **7** 45 20N 61 0W
Cap-aux-Meules ... **7** 47 23N 61 52W
Cap-Chat ... **6** 49 6N 66 40W
Cap-de-la-Madeleine **9** 46 22N 72 31W
Cap-St-Ignace **9** 47 2N 70 28W
Cape Breton Highlands Nat. Park .. **7** 46 50N 60 40W
Cape Breton I. **7** 46 0N 60 30W
Cape Dorset . **21** 64 14N 76 32W
Cape Dyer .. **21** 66 30N 61 22W
Cape Tormentine **7** 46 8N 63 47W
Capitachouane → **8** 47 40N 76 47W
Capreol **10** 46 43N 80 56W
Carberry **15** 49 50N 99 25W
Carbon **17** 51 30N 113 9W
Carbonear .. **5** 47 42N 53 13W
Carcross ... **20** 60 13N 134 45W
Cardinal **11** 44 47N 75 23W
Cardross ... **14** 49 50N 105 40W
Cardston ... **17** 49 15N 113 20W
Cariboo Mts. **19** 53 0N 121 0W
Caribou L. ... **13** 47 22N 85 49W
Caribou L. ... **12** 50 25N 89 5W
Carleton Place **11** 45 8N 76 9W
Carlyle **15** 49 40N 102 20W
Carmacks ... **20** 62 5N 136 16W
Carman **15** 49 30N 98 0W
Carmangay .. **17** 50 10N 113 10W
Carmanville . **5** 49 23N 54 19W
Carnduff ... **15** 49 10N 101 50W
Caron **14** 50 30N 105 50W
Carrot → .. **15** 53 50N 101 17W
Carrot River . **14** 53 17N 103 35W
Carruthers .. **14** 52 52N 109 16W
Cartier **10** 46 42N 81 33W
Cartwright ... **4** 53 41N 56 58W
Casey **9** 47 53N 74 11W
Caslan **16** 54 38N 112 31W
Casselman .. **8** 45 19N 75 5W
Castlegar ... **19** 49 20N 117 40W
Castor **17** 52 15N 111 50W
Castor → .. **4** 53 24N 78 58W
Casummit Lake **12** 51 29N 92 22W
Cat L. **12** 51 40N 91 50W
Catalina **5** 48 31N 53 4W
Causapscal .. **6** 48 19N 67 12W
Cawasachouane, L. **8** 47 27N 77 45W
Cayuga **10** 42 59N 79 50W
Cedar L., *Man.,* **15** 53 10N 100 0W
Cedar L., *Ont.,* **11** 46 2N 78 30W
Central Patricia ... **12** 51 30N 90 9W
Cerf, L. de .. **8** 46 16N 75 30W
Chakonipau, L. **4** 56 18N 68 30W
Chaleur B. .. **7** 47 55N 65 30W
Chalk River . **11** 46 1N 77 27W
Chambly **9** 45 27N 73 17W
Chambord ... **9** 48 25N 72 6W
Chamouchouane → **9** 48 37N 72 20W
Champdoré, L. **4** 55 55N 65 49W
Champneuf .. **8** 48 35N 77 30W
Chandler ... **6** 48 18N 64 46W
Channel-Port aux Basques .. **5** 47 30N 59 9W
Chantrey Inlet **21** 67 48N 96 20W
Chapais **8** 49 47N 74 51W
Chapeau **8** 45 54N 77 4W
Chapleau ... **13** 47 50N 83 24W
Chaplin **14** 50 28N 106 40W
Charette **9** 46 27N 72 56W
Charlesbourg **9** 46 51N 71 16W
Charleston L. **11** 44 32N 76 0W
Charlottetown **7** 46 14N 63 8W
Charlton I. .. **4** 52 0N 79 20W
Charny **9** 46 43N 71 15W
Châteauguay, L. **4** 56 26N 70 3W
Châteauvert, L. **9** 47 39N 73 56W
Chatham, *N.B.,* **7** 47 2N 65 28W
Chatham, *Ont.,* **10** 42 24N 82 11W
Chats, L. des **8** 45 30N 76 20W
Chatsworth . **10** 44 27N 80 54W
Chaudière → **9** 46 45N 71 17W
Chauvin **17** 52 45N 110 10W
Chavigny, L. . **4** 58 12N 75 8W
Checleset B. . **18** 50 5N 127 35W
Chedabucto B. **7** 45 25N 61 8W
Chef, R. du → **9** 49 21N 73 25W
Chemainus .. **19** 48 55N 123 42W
Chénéville .. **8** 45 53N 75 3W
Cheslatta L. . **18** 53 49N 125 20W
Chesley **10** 44 17N 81 5W
Chesterfield Inlet **21** 63 30N 90 45W
Chesterville . **8** 45 6N 75 14W
Chéticamp .. **7** 46 37N 60 59W
Chibougamau **9** 49 56N 74 24W
Chibougamau → **8** 49 42N 75 57W
Chibougamau, Parc Prov. de **9** 49 15N 73 45W
Chibougamau L. **9** 49 50N 74 20W
Chic-Chocs, Mts. **6** 48 55N 66 0W
Chicobi, L. .. **8** 48 53N 78 30W
Chicoutimi .. **9** 48 28N 71 5W
Chicoutimi, Parc Prov. de **9** 48 30N 70 20W
Chidley, C. .. **4** 60 23N 64 26W
Chiefs Pt. ... **10** 44 41N 81 18W
Chignecto B. **7** 45 30N 64 40W
Chigoubiche, L. **9** 49 7N 73 30W
Chilako → . **18** 53 53N 122 57W
Chilcotin → **19** 51 44N 122 23W
Chilko → .. **18** 52 0N 123 40W
Chilko, L. ... **18** 51 20N 124 10W
Chilliwack .. **19** 49 10N 121 54W
Chinook **17** 51 28N 110 59W
Chipman **7** 46 6N 65 53W
Chisasibi **4** 53 50N 79 0W
Chisholm ... **16** 54 55N 114 10W
Christian I. .. **8** 44 50N 80 12W
Christina → **16** 56 40N 111 3W
Chu Chua .. **19** 51 22N 120 10W
Churchill → . **4** 53 19N 60 10W
Churchill Falls **4** 53 36N 64 19W
Chute-aux-Outardes . **9** 49 7N 68 24W
Chute-des-Passes ... **9** 49 52N 71 16W
Clairambault, L. **4** 54 29N 69 0W
Claire **9** 47 15N 68 40W
Clapperton I. **10** 46 0N 82 14W
Clarenville .. **5** 48 10N 54 1W
Claresholm .. **17** 50 0N 113 33W
Clark, Pt. **10** 44 4N 81 45W
Clarke City .. **4** 50 12N 66 38W
Clarke L. **14** 54 24N 106 54W
Clark's Harbour .. **7** 43 25N 65 38W
Clear, L. **11** 45 26N 77 12W
Clearwater .. **19** 51 38N 120 2W
Clearwater →, *Alta.,* **16** 56 44N 111 23W
Clearwater →, *Alta.,* **17** 52 22N 114 57W
Clearwater Prov. Park . **15** 54 0N 101 0W
Clermont ... **9** 47 41N 70 14W
Climax **14** 49 10N 108 20W
Clinton, *B.C.,* **19** 51 6N 121 35W
Clinton, *Ont.,* **10** 43 37N 81 32W
Clinton Colden L. . **20** 63 58N 107 27W
Clinton Creek **20** 64 25N 140 37W
Clova **8** 48 7N 75 22W
Cloyne **11** 44 49N 77 11W
Clyde River . **21** 70 30N 68 30W
Coaldale **17** 49 45N 112 35W
Coast Mts. .. **18** 55 0N 129 20W
Coaticook ... **9** 45 10N 71 46W

Coats I. **21** 62 30N 83 0W
Cobalt **8** 47 25N 79 42W
Cobden ... **11** 45 38N 76 53W
Coboconk ... **11** 44 39N 78 48W
Cobourg ... **11** 43 58N 78 10W
Cochrane, *Alta.*, ... **17** 51 11N 114 30W
Cochrane, *Ont.*, ... **8** 49 0N 81 0W
Cockburn I. . **10** 45 55N 83 22W
Cod I. **4** 57 47N 61 47W
Coderre **14** 50 11N 106 31W
Coe Hill **11** 44 52N 77 50W
Colborne ... **11** 44 0N 77 53W
Coldwater ... **10** 44 42N 79 40W
Coleman **17** 49 40N 114 30W
Collingwood **10** 44 29N 80 13W
Collins **12** 50 17N 89 27W
Colombier .. **9** 48 52N 68 51W
Colonsay ... **14** 51 59N 105 52W
Columbia, Mt. **19** 52 8N 117 20W
Comber **10** 42 14N 82 33W
Combermere **11** 45 22N 77 37W
Commanda . **10** 45 57N 79 36W
Commissaires, L. des **9** 48 10N 72 16W
Committee B. **21** 68 30N 86 30W
Comox **18** 49 42N 124 55W
Compton ... **9** 45 14N 71 49W
Conche **5** 50 55N 55 58W
Congnarauya **4** 58 35N 68 1W
Coniston **10** 46 29N 80 51W
Conklin **16** 55 38N 111 5W
Connors **9** 47 10N 68 52W
Conquest ... **14** 51 32N 107 14W
Consecon ... **11** 44 0N 77 31W
Consort **17** 52 1N 110 46W
Consul **14** 49 20N 109 30W
Contrecoeur . **9** 45 51N 73 14W
Cookshire ... **9** 45 25N 71 38W
Copper Cliff . **10** 46 28N 81 4W
Coppermine = Kuglugtuk . **20** 67 50N 115 5W
Coppermine → **20** 67 49N 116 4W
Coral Harbour **21** 64 8N 83 10W
Cormorant .. **15** 54 14N 100 35W
Cormorant L. **15** 54 15N 100 50W
Corner Brook **5** 48 57N 57 58W
Cornwall **11** 45 2N 74 44W
Cornwall I. .. **21** 77 37N 94 38W
Cornwallis I. . **21** 75 8N 95 0W
Coronation .. **17** 52 5N 111 27W
Coronation Gulf **20** 68 25N 110 0W
Corunna **10** 42 53N 82 26W
Corvette, L. de la **4** 53 25N 74 3W
Coteau Landing .. **9** 45 15N 74 13W
Cottam **10** 42 8N 82 45W
Coudres, Ile aux **9** 47 24N 70 23W
Coulonge → **8** 45 52N 76 46W
Courtenay .. **18** 49 45N 125 0W
Courtland ... **10** 42 51N 80 38W
Courtright ... **10** 42 49N 82 28W
Coutts **17** 49 0N 111 57W
Couture, L. .. **4** 60 7N 75 20W
Cove I. **10** 45 17N 81 44W
Cowan **15** 52 5N 100 45W
Cowan L. ... **14** 54 0N 107 15W
Cowansville . **9** 45 14N 72 46W
Cox's Cove .. **5** 49 7N 58 5W
Cranbrook .. **17** 49 30N 115 46W
Crane I. **9** 47 4N 70 33W
Craven, L. ... **4** 54 20N 76 56W
Crean L. **14** 54 5N 106 9W
Crediton **10** 43 17N 81 33W
Creemore ... **10** 44 19N 80 6W
Creston **17** 49 10N 116 31W
Croix, L. La . **12** 48 20N 92 15W
Croker, C. ... **10** 44 58N 80 59W
Crossfield ... **17** 51 25N 114 0W
Crowsnest Pass **17** 49 40N 114 40W
Cumberland, *B.C.*, ... **18** 49 40N 125 0W
Cumberland, *Ont.*, ... **11** 45 29N 75 24W
Cumberland L. **15** 54 3N 102 18W
Cumberland Pen. **21** 67 0N 64 0W
Cumberland Sd. **21** 65 30N 66 0W
Cupar **14** 50 57N 104 10W
Cusson, Pte. . **4** 60 23N 77 46W
Czar **17** 52 27N 110 50W

D

Dalhousie ... **7** 48 5N 66 26W
Dalton **13** 48 11N 84 1W
Dana, L. **4** 50 53N 77 20W
Daniel's Harbour .. **5** 50 13N 57 35W
Dark Cove ... **5** 48 47N 54 13W
Darnley B. .. **20** 69 30N 123 30W
Dartmouth ... **7** 44 40N 63 30W
Dasserat, L. . **8** 48 16N 79 25W
Dauphin **15** 51 9N 100 5W
Dauphin L. .. **15** 51 20N 99 45W
Davidson ... **14** 51 16N 105 59W
Davis Inlet .. **4** 55 50N 60 59W
Dawson **20** 64 10N 139 30W
Daysland ... **17** 52 50N 112 20W
Dease Arm .. **20** 66 52N 119 37W
Debden **14** 53 30N 106 50W
Debolt **16** 55 12N 118 1W
Decelles, Rés. **8** 47 42N 78 8W
Déception, B. **4** 62 8N 74 41W
Deer Lake ... **5** 49 11N 57 27W
Dégelis **9** 47 30N 68 35W
Delhi **10** 42 51N 80 30W
Delia **17** 51 38N 112 23W
Déline **20** 65 10N 123 30W
Deloraine ... **15** 49 15N 100 29W
Denbigh **11** 45 8N 77 15W
Derwent **16** 53 41N 110 58W
Desbarats ... **10** 46 20N 83 56W
Desbiens ... **9** 48 25N 71 57W
Deschaillons **9** 46 32N 72 7W
Deschambault **9** 46 39N 71 56W
Deschênes .. **8** 45 23N 75 48W
Deseronto .. **11** 44 12N 77 3W
Desmaraisville **8** 49 32N 76 9W
Desméloizes **8** 48 57N 79 29W
Devenyns, L. **9** 47 5N 73 50W
Devon **16** 53 24N 113 44W
Devon I. **21** 75 10N 85 0W
Diana B. **4** 61 20N 70 0W
Didsbury ... **17** 51 35N 114 10W
Digby **7** 44 38N 65 50W
Digges Is. .. **4** 62 40N 77 50W
Disraëli **9** 45 54N 71 21W
Dixonville ... **16** 56 32N 117 40W
Dixville **9** 45 4N 71 46W
Dodsland ... **14** 51 50N 108 45W
Dog Creek .. **19** 51 35N 122 14W
Dog L., *Man.*, **15** 51 2N 98 31W
Dog L., *Ont.*, **12** 48 48N 89 30W
Dolbeau **9** 48 53N 72 18W
Dolphin and Union Str. . **20** 69 5N 114 45W
Donalda **17** 52 35N 112 34W
Donnaconna **9** 46 41N 71 41W
Dorchester, C. **21** 65 27N 77 27W
Dorion **9** 45 23N 74 3W
Dorset **8** 45 14N 78 54W
Dosquet **9** 46 28N 71 32W
Douglas **11** 45 31N 76 56W
Douglas Pt. . **10** 44 19N 81 37W
Douglastown **6** 48 46N 64 24W
Dozois, Rés. . **8** 47 30N 77 5W
Drayton **10** 43 46N 80 40W
Drayton Valley **16** 53 12N 114 58W
Dresden **10** 42 35N 82 11W
Drocourt **10** 45 46N 80 21W
Drumbo **10** 43 16N 80 35W
Drumheller .. **17** 51 25N 112 40W
Drummondville **9** 45 55N 72 25W
Dryden **12** 49 47N 92 50W
Du Gué → ... **4** 57 21N 70 45W
Dubawnt → **20** 64 33N 100 6W
Dubawnt, L. . **21** 63 4N 101 42W
Duck Lake ... **14** 52 50N 106 16W
Duck Mountain Prov. Park . **15** 51 45N 101 0W
Dufrost, Pte. . **4** 60 4N 77 39W
Dumoine → **8** 46 13N 77 51W
Dumoine L. . **8** 46 55N 77 55W
Duncan **19** 48 45N 123 40W
Duncan, L. .. **4** 53 29N 77 58W
Dunchurch .. **10** 45 39N 79 51W
Dundalk **10** 44 10N 80 24W
Dundas **10** 43 17N 79 59W
Dungannon .. **10** 43 51N 81 36W
Dunnville ... **10** 42 54N 79 36W
Dunster **19** 53 8N 119 50W
Duparquet .. **8** 48 30N 79 14W
Duparquet, L. **8** 48 28N 79 16W
Dupuy **8** 48 50N 79 21W
Durham **10** 44 10N 80 49W
Dutton **10** 42 39N 81 30W
Dwight **8** 45 20N 79 1W
Dyer, C. **21** 66 40N 61 0W
Dysart **14** 50 57N 104 2W

E

Eabamet, L. . **13** 51 30N 87 46W
Eagle → ... **4** 53 36N 57 26W
Eagle Lake .. **11** 45 8N 78 29W
Earl Grey ... **14** 50 57N 104 43W
East Angus .. **9** 45 30N 71 40W
East Broughton Station ... **9** 46 14N 71 5W
East Coulee . **17** 51 23N 112 27W
East Main = Eastmain **4** 52 10N 78 30W
East Pt. **7** 46 27N 61 58W
Eastend **14** 49 32N 108 50W
Easterville .. **15** 53 8N 99 49W
Eastmain **4** 52 10N 78 30W
Eastmain → **4** 52 27N 78 26W
Eastman **9** 45 18N 72 19W
Eatonia **14** 51 13N 109 25W
Eatonville ... **9** 47 20N 69 41W
Eau Claire, L. à l' **4** 56 10N 74 25W
Echo Bay, *N.W.T.*, ... **20** 66 5N 117 55W
Echo Bay, *Ont.*, ... **10** 46 29N 84 4W
Échouani, L. . **8** 47 46N 75 42W
Écorce, L. de l' **8** 47 5N 76 24W
Ecueils, Pte. aux **4** 59 47N 77 50W
Edam **14** 53 11N 108 46W
Edmonton .. **16** 53 30N 113 30W
Edmundston **7** 47 23N 68 20W
Edson **16** 53 35N 116 28W
Edward I. ... **12** 48 22N 88 37W
Eganville ... **11** 45 32N 77 5W
Eglington I. . **20** 75 48N 118 30W
Elbow **14** 51 7N 106 35W
Eldorado ... **11** 44 35N 77 31W
Elgin **11** 44 36N 76 13W
Elk Island Nat. Park **16** 53 35N 112 59W
Elk Lake **8** 47 40N 80 25W
Elk Point **16** 53 54N 110 55W
Elkhorn **15** 49 59N 101 14W
Elko **17** 49 20N 115 10W
Ellef Ringnes I. **21** 78 30N 102 2W
Ellesmere I. . **21** 79 30N 80 0W
Elliot Lake .. **10** 46 25N 82 35W
Ells → **16** 57 18N 111 40W
Elma **15** 49 52N 95 55W
Elmira **10** 43 36N 80 33W
Elmvale **10** 44 35N 79 52W
Elora **10** 43 41N 80 26W
Elphin **11** 44 55N 76 37W
Elrose **14** 51 12N 108 0W
Elsa **20** 63 55N 135 29W
Elsas **13** 48 32N 82 55W
Embro **10** 43 9N 80 54W
Emeril **4** 47 26N 75 47W
Emerson **15** 49 0N 97 10W
Empress **17** 50 57N 110 0W
Emsdale **8** 45 32N 79 19W
Endeavour .. **14** 52 10N 102 39W
Enderby **19** 50 35N 119 10W
Englee **5** 50 45N 56 5W
Englehart ... **8** 47 49N 79 52W
English → . **12** 50 35N 93 30W
English River **12** 49 14N 91 0W
Eric **4** 51 56N 65 45W
Erie, L. **10** 42 15N 81 0W
Erieau **10** 42 16N 81 57W
Eriksdale ... **15** 50 52N 98 7W
Erin **10** 43 45N 80 7W
Erlandson, L. **4** 57 3N 68 28W
Esker **4** 53 53N 66 25W
Eskimo Pt. = Arviat **21** 61 10N 94 15W
Espanola ... **10** 46 15N 81 46W
Essex **10** 42 10N 82 49W
Estcourt **9** 47 28N 69 14W
Esterhazy ... **15** 50 37N 102 5W
Estevan **14** 49 10N 102 59W
Estevan Group **18** 53 3N 129 38W
Eston **14** 51 8N 108 40W
Etamamu ... **4** 50 18N 59 59W
Ethelbert ... **15** 51 32N 100 25W
Eureka **21** 80 0N 85 56W
Eutsuk L. ... **18** 53 20N 126 45W
Evain **8** 48 14N 79 8W
Evans L. ... **4** 50 50N 77 0W
Exeter **10** 43 21N 81 29W

F

Fabre **8** 47 12N 79 22W
Faillon, L. ... **8** 48 21N 76 39W
Fairford **15** 51 37N 98 38W
Fairview **16** 56 5N 118 25W
Falconbridge **10** 46 35N 80 45W
Falher **16** 55 44N 117 15W
Family L. ... **15** 51 54N 95 27W
Fanny Bay .. **18** 49 37N 124 48W
Farnham **9** 45 17N 72 59W
Fatima **7** 47 24N 61 53W
Fenelon Falls **11** 44 32N 78 45W
Fergus **10** 43 43N 80 24W
Ferland **12** 50 19N 88 27W
Ferme-Neuve **8** 46 42N 75 27W
Fernie **17** 49 30N 115 5W
Feronia **10** 46 22N 79 19W
Ferryland ... **5** 47 2N 52 53W
Feuilles → . **4** 58 47N 70 4W
Feuilles, B. aux **4** 58 55N 69 20W
Field **10** 46 31N 80 1W
File Axe, L. .. **9** 50 18N 73 34W
Fillmore **14** 49 50N 103 25W
Fils, L. du ... **8** 46 37N 78 7W
Finch **8** 45 11N 75 7W
Fire River ... **13** 48 47N 83 21W
Firebag → . **16** 57 45N 111 21W
Firvale **18** 52 27N 126 13W
Fisher B. ... **15** 51 35N 97 13W
Fishing L. ... **15** 52 10N 95 24W
Fitzwilliam I. **10** 45 30N 81 45W
Flaherty I. ... **4** 56 15N 79 15W
Flesherton .. **10** 44 16N 80 33W
Flores I. **18** 49 20N 126 10W
Flower Station **8** 45 10N 76 41W
Flower's Cove **5** 51 14N 56 46W
Foam Lake .. **14** 51 40N 103 32W
Fogo **5** 49 43N 54 17W
Fogo I. **5** 49 40N 54 5W
Foins, L. aux **8** 47 5N 78 11W
Foleyet **13** 48 15N 82 25W
Foremost ... **17** 49 26N 111 34W
Forest **10** 43 6N 82 0W
Forestburg .. **17** 52 35N 112 1W
Forestville ... **9** 48 48N 69 2W
Forsythe **8** 48 14N 76 26W
Fort Albany . **2** 52 15N 81 35W
Fort Assiniboine **16** 54 20N 114 45W
Fort-Coulonge **8** 45 50N 76 45W
Fort Frances . **12** 48 36N 93 24W
Fort George = Chisasibi .. **4** 53 50N 79 0W
Fort Hope ... **13** 51 30N 88 0W
Fort Liard ... **20** 60 14N 123 30W
Fort Mackay . **16** 57 12N 111 41W
Fort McKenzie **4** 57 20N 69 0W
Fort Macleod **17** 49 45N 113 30W
Fort McMurray . **16** 56 44N 111 7W
Fort Norman = Tulita .. **20** 64 57N 125 30W
Fort Providence **20** 61 3N 117 40W
Fort Qu'Appelle **14** 50 45N 103 50W
Fort Resolution **20** 61 10N 113 40W
Fort Rupert = Waskaganish **4** 51 30N 78 40W
Fort Saskatchewan **16** 53 40N 113 15W
Fort Severn . **2** 56 0N 87 40W
Fort Simpson **20** 61 45N 121 15W
Forteau **4** 51 28N 56 58W
Fortune B. ... **5** 47 30N 55 22W
Foster **9** 45 17N 72 30W
Fourchu **7** 45 43N 60 17W
Fox Valley .. **14** 50 30N 109 25W
Foxe Basin .. **21** 66 0N 77 0W
Foxe Chan. .. **21** 65 0N 80 0W
Foxe Pen. ... **21** 65 0N 76 0W
François **5** 47 35N 56 45W
François L. .. **18** 54 0N 125 30W
Frankford ... **11** 44 12N 77 36W
Franklin B. .. **20** 69 45N 126 0W
Franklin Mts. **20** 65 0N 125 0W
Franklin Str. . **21** 72 0N 96 0W
Franz **13** 48 25N 84 30W
Fraser →, *B.C.*, ... **19** 49 7N 123 11W
Fraser →, *Nfld.*, ... **4** 56 39N 62 10W
Fraser Lake . **18** 54 0N 124 50W
Fraserdale .. **13** 49 55N 81 37W
Fredericton .. **7** 45 57N 66 40W
Fredericton Junc. **7** 45 41N 66 40W
Freels, C. **5** 49 15N 53 30W
Freeport **7** 44 15N 66 20W
French → .. **10** 46 2N 80 34W
French River **10** 46 2N 80 34W
Frenchman Butte **14** 53 35N 109 38W
Frobisher B. . **21** 62 30N 66 0W
Frobisher Bay = Iqaluit .. **21** 63 44N 68 31W
Fundy, B. of . **7** 45 0N 66 0W
Fury and Hecla Str. . **21** 69 56N 84 0W

G

Gagetown .. **7** 45 46N 66 10W
Gagnon **4** 51 50N 68 5W
Gagnon, L. .. **8** 46 7N 75 7W
Gammon → **15** 51 24N 95 44W
Gananoque . **11** 44 20N 76 10W
Gander **5** 48 58N 54 35W
Gander L. ... **5** 48 58N 54 35W
Gardner Canal **18** 53 27N 128 8W
Garibaldi Prov. Park . **19** 49 50N 122 40W
Garry, L. **21** 65 58N 100 18W
Garson L. ... **16** 56 19N 110 2W
Gaspé **6** 48 52N 64 30W
Gaspé, C. de **6** 48 48N 64 7W
Gaspé, Pén. de **6** 48 45N 65 40W
Gaspésie, Parc Prov. de la **6** 48 55N 65 50W
Gatineau ... **8** 45 29N 75 38W
Gatineau → **8** 45 27N 75 42W
Gatineau, Parc de la **8** 45 40N 76 0W
Gayot, L. **4** 55 43N 70 50W
George →, *Qué.*, ... **2** 58 49N 66 10W
George →, *Qué.*, ... **4** 58 49N 66 10W
George →, *Qué.*, ... **4** 49 21N 67 59W
George River = Kangiqsualujjuaq **4** 58 30N 65 59W
Georgetown, *Ont.*, ... **10** 43 40N 79 56W
Georgetown, *P.E.I.*, ... **7** 46 13N 62 24W
Georgia, Str. of **18** 49 25N 124 0W
Georgian B. . **10** 45 15N 81 0W
Georgina I. .. **10** 44 22N 79 17W
Geraldton ... **13** 49 44N 86 59W
Gerrard **19** 50 30N 117 17W
Gethsémani . **4** 50 13N 60 40W
Gibsons **19** 49 24N 123 32W
Giffard **9** 46 51N 71 12W
Gil I. **18** 53 12N 129 15W
Gilbert Plains **15** 51 9N 100 28W
Gilford I. **18** 50 40N 126 30W
Gilmour **11** 44 48N 77 37W
Girardville .. **9** 49 0N 72 32W
Gjoa Haven . **21** 68 38N 95 53W
Glace Bay .. **7** 46 11N 59 58W
Glacier Nat. Park **19** 51 15N 117 30W
Gladstone .. **15** 50 13N 98 57W
Glen Almond **8** 45 42N 75 29W
Glencoe **10** 42 45N 81 43W
Glenwood, *Alta.*, ... **17** 49 21N 113 31W
Glenwood, *Nfld.*, ... **5** 49 0N 54 58W
Godbout **6** 49 20N 67 38W
Goderich **10** 43 45N 81 41W
Goéland, L. au **8** 49 50N 76 48W
Gogama **13** 47 35N 81 43W
Golden **19** 51 20N 116 59W
Golden Hinde **18** 49 40N 125 44W
Golden Lake **8** 45 34N 77 21W
Golden Prairie **14** 50 13N 109 37W
Gooderham .. **11** 44 54N 78 21W
Goodeve **14** 51 4N 103 10W
Goose → .. **4** 53 20N 60 35W
Gordon L. ... **16** 56 30N 110 25W
Gore Bay ... **10** 45 57N 82 28W
Gouin, Rés. . **8** 48 35N 74 40W
Govan **14** 51 20N 105 0W
Gracefield ... **8** 46 6N 76 3W
Graham **12** 49 20N 90 30W
Graham I. ... **18** 53 40N 132 30W
Grahamdale . **15** 51 23N 98 30W
Granby **9** 45 25N 72 45W
Grand → ... **10** 42 51N 79 34W
Grand Bank . **5** 47 6N 55 48W
Grand Bend . **10** 43 19N 81 45W
Grand Calumet, Ile du **8** 45 44N 76 41W
Grand Falls .. **5** 48 56N 55 40W
Grand Forks . **19** 49 0N 118 30W
Grand L., *N.B.*, **7** 45 57N 66 7W
Grand L., *Nfld.*, ... **4** 53 40N 60 30W
Grand L., *Nfld.*, ... **5** 49 0N 57 30W
Grand Lac Victoria ... **8** 47 35N 77 35W
Grand Manan I. **7** 44 45N 66 52W
Grand Marais **12** 47 45N 90 25W
Grand-Mère . **9** 46 36N 72 40W
Grand Piles . **9** 46 40N 72 40W
Grand Rapids **15** 53 12N 99 19W
Grand View . **15** 51 10N 100 42W
Grande Baie . **9** 48 19N 70 52W
Grande Baleine, R. de la → .. **4** 55 16N 77 47W
Grande Cache **16** 53 53N 119 8W
Grande-Entrée **7** 47 30N 61 40W
Grande Prairie **16** 55 10N 118 50W
Grande-Rivière ... **6** 48 26N 64 30W
Grande-Vallée **6** 49 14N 65 8W
Grandes-Bergeronnes **9** 48 16N 69 35W
Granet, L. ... **8** 47 47N 77 31W
Gras, L. de .. **20** 64 30N 110 30W
Grasset, L. .. **8** 49 55N 78 10W
Gravelbourg **14** 49 50N 106 35W
Gravenhurst . **8** 44 52N 79 20W
Grayson **14** 50 45N 102 40W
Great Bear → .. **20** 65 0N 124 0W
Great Bear L. **20** 65 30N 120 0W
Great Central **18** 49 20N 125 10W
Great Duck I. **10** 45 40N 82 57W
Great Falls .. **15** 50 27N 96 1W
Great Harbour Deep **5** 50 25N 56 32W
Great Slave L. **20** 61 23N 115 38W
Greely Fd. .. **21** 80 30N 85 0W
Greenough Pt. **10** 44 58N 81 26W
Greenwater Lake Prov. Park **14** 52 32N 103 30W
Greenwood . **19** 49 10N 118 40W
Grenfell **14** 50 30N 102 56W
Grenville **8** 45 37N 74 36W
Grenville Chan. ... **18** 53 40N 129 46W
Grey Res. ... **5** 48 20N 56 30W
Gribbell I. ... **18** 53 23N 129 0W
Griffith **11** 45 15N 77 10W
Griffith I. **10** 44 50N 80 55W
Grimsby **10** 43 12N 79 34W
Grimshaw ... **16** 56 10N 117 40W
Grindstone I. **11** 44 43N 76 14W
Groais I. **5** 50 55N 55 35W
Groswater B. **4** 54 20N 57 40W
Grouard Mission ... **16** 55 33N 116 9W
Groundhog → **13** 48 45N 82 58W
Grundy Prov. Pk. **10** 45 58N 80 30W
Guéguen, L. . **8** 48 6N 77 13W
Guelph **10** 43 35N 80 20W
Guigues **8** 47 28N 79 26W
Guillaume-Delisle, L. .. **4** 56 15N 76 17W
Gull Lake ... **14** 50 10N 108 29W
Gunisao → **15** 53 56N 97 53W
Gunisao L. .. **15** 53 33N 96 15W
Gypsumville **15** 51 45N 98 40W

H

Hagersville .. **10** 42 58N 80 3W
Haileybury .. **8** 47 30N 79 38W
Haliburton .. **11** 45 3N 78 30W
Halifax **7** 44 38N 63 35W
Hall Beach .. **21** 68 46N 81 12W
Hamber Prov. Park **19** 52 20N 118 0W
Hamilton **10** 43 15N 79 50W
Hamiota **15** 50 11N 100 38W
Hampton ... **11** 43 58N 78 45W
Haney **19** 49 12N 122 40W
Hanmer **10** 46 39N 80 56W
Hanna **17** 51 40N 111 54W
Hanover **10** 44 9N 81 2W
Happy Valley-Goose Bay **4** 53 15N 60 20W
Harbour Breton **5** 47 29N 55 50W
Harbour Grace **5** 47 40N 53 22W
Hardisty **17** 52 40N 111 18W
Hare B. **5** 51 15N 55 45W
Harp L. **4** 55 5N 61 50W
Harricana → **8** 50 56N 79 32W
Harrington Harbour .. **4** 50 31N 59 30W
Harris Pt. ... **10** 43 6N 82 9W
Harrison, C. . **4** 54 55N 57 55W
Harrison L. .. **19** 49 33N 121 50W
Harriston ... **10** 43 57N 80 53W
Harrow **10** 42 2N 82 55W
Harrowsmith **11** 44 24N 76 40W
Hartland **7** 46 20N 67 32W
Hartley Bay . **18** 53 25N 129 15W
Hartney **15** 49 30N 100 35W
Hastings ... **11** 44 18N 77 57W
Hauterive ... **9** 49 10N 68 16W
Havelock, *N.B.*, ... **7** 46 2N 65 24W
Havelock, *Ont.*, ... **11** 44 26N 77 53W
Havre-Aubert **7** 47 12N 61 56W
Havre-St.-Pierre **4** 50 18N 63 33W
Hawarden .. **14** 51 25N 106 36W
Hawk Junction .. **13** 48 5N 84 38W
Hawkesbury I. **18** 53 37N 129 3W
Hay I. **10** 44 53N 80 58W
Hay Lakes .. **17** 53 12N 113 2W
Hay River ... **20** 60 51N 115 44W
Hays **17** 50 6N 111 48W
Hearst **13** 49 40N 83 41W
Heart's Content ... **5** 47 54N 53 27W
Heath Pt. ... **6** 49 8N 61 40W
Heath Steele **7** 47 17N 66 5W
Hebert **14** 50 30N 107 10W
Hebron **4** 58 5N 62 30W
Hebron Fd. .. **4** 58 9N 62 45W
Hecate Str. .. **18** 53 10N 130 30W
Hecla I. **15** 51 10N 96 43W
Hemmingford **9** 45 3N 73 35W
Henrietta Maria, C. .. **2** 55 9N 82 20W
Henryville ... **9** 45 8N 73 11W
Hensall **10** 43 26N 81 30W
Hepworth ... **10** 44 37N 81 9W
Hereford, Mt. **9** 45 5N 71 36W
Heron Bay .. **13** 48 40N 86 25W
Herschel, I. .. **20** 69 35N 139 5W
Hewett, C. .. **21** 70 16N 67 45W
High I. **4** 52 28N 55 40W
High Prairie . **16** 55 30N 116 30W
High River .. **17** 50 30N 113 50W
Hillmond ... **14** 53 26N 109 41W
Hillsport ... **13** 49 27N 85 34W
Hilton Beach **10** 46 15N 83 53W
Hines Creek . **16** 56 20N 118 40W
Hinton **16** 53 26N 117 34W
Hoare B. **21** 65 17N 62 30W
Hodgson **15** 51 13N 97 36W
Holden **16** 53 13N 112 11W
Holdfast **14** 50 58N 105 25W
Holman **20** 70 44N 117 44W
Holton **4** 54 31N 57 12W
Holyrood ... **5** 47 27N 53 8W
Home B. ... **21** 68 40N 67 10W
Honey Harbour .. **10** 44 52N 79 49W
Honguedo, Détroit d' .. **6** 49 15N 64 0W
Hope **19** 49 25N 121 25W
Hope I. **10** 44 55N 80 11W
Hopedale ... **4** 55 28N 60 13W
Hopes Advance, C. **4** 61 4N 69 34W
Hornaday → **20** 69 19N 123 48W
Hornepayne . **13** 49 14N 84 48W
Hornings Mills **10** 44 9N 80 12W
Horse Is. **5** 50 15N 55 50W
Horsefly L. .. **19** 52 25N 121 0W
Horton → .. **20** 69 56N 126 52W
Horwood, L. . **13** 48 5N 82 20W
Howe I. **11** 44 16N 76 17W
Howick **9** 45 11N 73 51W
Howley **5** 49 12N 57 2W
Hudson **12** 50 6N 92 9W
Hudson Bay, *N.W.T.*, ... **2** 60 0N 86 0W
Hudson Bay, *Sask.*, ... **15** 52 51N 102 23W
Hudson Str. . **2** 62 0N 70 0W
Hull **8** 45 25N 75 44W
Humboldt ... **14** 52 15N 105 9W
Hundred Mile House **19** 51 38N 121 18W
Hunter I. **18** 51 55N 128 0W
Huntingdon . **9** 45 6N 74 10W
Huntsville ... **10** 45 20N 79 14W
Huron, L. ... **10** 44 30N 82 40W
Hussar **17** 51 3N 112 41W
Hutte Sauvage, L. de la **4** 56 15N 64 45W

I

Iberville **9** 45 19N 73 17W
Iberville, Lac d' **4** 55 55N 73 15W
Iberville, Mt. d' **4** 58 50N 63 50W
Igloolik **21** 69 20N 81 49W
Ignace **12** 49 30N 91 40W
Iles, L. des .. **8** 46 20N 75 18W
Illukotat → . **4** 60 48N 78 11W
Imperial **14** 51 21N 105 28W
Indian Harbour .. **4** 54 27N 57 13W
Indian Head . **14** 50 30N 103 41W
Ingersoll **10** 43 4N 80 55W
Ingonish **7** 46 42N 60 18W
Innerkip **10** 43 13N 80 42W
Innetalling I. . **4** 56 0N 79 0W
Innisfail **17** 52 0N 113 57W
Inoucdjouac = Inukjuak .. **4** 58 25N 78 15W
Inukjuak .. **4** 58 25N 78 15W
Inuvik **20** 68 16N 133 40W
Invermere .. **17** 50 30N 116 2W
Inverness ... **7** 46 15N 61 19W
Iqaluit **21** 63 44N 68 31W
Irma **17** 52 55N 111 14W
Iron Bridge .. **10** 46 17N 83 14W
Iroquois **11** 44 51N 75 19W
Iroquois Falls **8** 48 46N 80 41W
Irvine **17** 49 57N 110 16W
Island Falls .. **8** 49 35N 81 20W
Islands, B. of **5** 49 11N 58 15W
Isle aux Morts **5** 47 35N 59 0W
Issoudun **9** 46 35N 71 38W
Itomamo, L. . **9** 49 11N 70 28W
Ituna **14** 51 10N 103 24W
Ivujivik **4** 62 24N 77 55W

J

Jacques-Cartier → **9** 46 40N 71 45W
Jacques Cartier, Dét. de **4** 50 0N 63 30W
Jacques-Cartier, L. . **9** 47 35N 71 13W

Jacques-Cartier, Mt. 6 48 57N 66 0W
James B. 3 51 30N 80 0W
Jarvis 10 42 53N 80 6W
Jasper, *Alta.*, 17 52 55N 118 5W
Jasper, *Ont.*, 11 44 50N 75 56W
Jasper Nat. Park 17 52 50N 118 8W
Jean Marie River 20 61 32N 120 38W
Jedway 18 52 17N 131 14W
Jellicoe 13 49 40N 87 30W
Joggins 7 45 42N 64 27W
Johnstone Str. 18 50 28N 126 0W
Joliette 9 46 3N 73 24W
Joliette, Parc Prov. de 9 46 30N 74 0W
Jonquière 9 48 27N 71 14W
Joseph, L., *Nfld.*, 4 52 45N 65 18W
Joseph, L., *Ont.*, 8 45 10N 79 44W
Joussard 16 55 22N 115 50W
Joy B. 4 61 30N 72 0W
Julian L. 4 54 25N 77 57W
Jupiter → 6 49 29N 63 37W

K

Kabinakagami L. 13 48 54N 84 25W
Kagawong L. 10 45 54N 82 15W
Kaipokok B. 4 54 54N 59 47W
Kakabeka Falls 12 48 24N 89 37W
Kakwa → 16 54 37N 118 28W
Kaladar 11 44 37N 77 5W
Kamloops 19 50 40N 120 20W
Kamouraska 9 47 34N 69 52W
Kamsack 15 51 34N 101 54W
Kanaaupscow 4 54 2N 76 30W
Kanaaupscow → 4 53 39N 77 9W
Kanairiktok → 4 55 2N 60 18W
Kanata 11 45 20N 75 59W
Kangiqsualujjuaq 4 58 30N 65 59W
Kangiqsujuaq 4 61 30N 72 0W
Kangirsuk 4 60 0N 70 0W
Kaniapiskau → 4 56 40N 69 30W
Kaniapiskau L. 4 54 10N 69 55W
Kapuskasing 13 49 25N 82 30W
Kapuskasing → 13 49 49N 82 0W
Kasba L. 2 60 20N 102 10W
Kashabowie 12 48 40N 90 26W
Kaslo 19 49 55N 116 55W
Kawagama L. 8 45 18N 78 45W
Kawene 12 48 45N 91 15W
Kearney 10 45 33N 79 13W
Kedgwick 7 47 40N 67 20W
Keene 11 44 15N 78 10W
Keewatin □ 21 63 20N 95 0W
Kegaska 4 50 9N 61 18W
Keglo, B. 4 58 40N 66 0W
Keith Arm 20 64 20N 122 15W
Kelowna 19 49 50N 119 25W
Kelsey Bay 18 50 25N 126 0W
Kelvington 14 52 10N 103 30W
Kemano 18 53 35N 128 0W
Kempt, L. 9 47 25N 74 22W
Kemptville 11 45 0N 75 38W
Kénogami 9 48 25N 71 15W
Kenogami → 13 51 6N 84 28W
Kénogami, L. 9 48 20N 71 23W
Kenora 12 49 47N 94 29W
Kensington 7 46 28N 63 34W
Kent Pen. 20 68 30N 107 0W
Kentville 7 45 6N 64 29W
Kerrobert 14 51 56N 109 8W
Keswick 10 44 15N 79 28W
Kettle Pt. 10 43 13N 82 1W
Key Harbour 10 45 50N 80 45W
Kicking Horse Pass 19 51 28N 116 16W
Kiglapait Mts. 4 57 6N 61 22W
Killaloe Sta. 8 45 33N 77 25W
Killam 17 52 47N 111 51W
Killarney 10 45 55N 81 30W
Killarney Prov. Park 10 46 2N 81 35W
Killdeer 14 49 6N 106 22W
Killinek I. 4 60 24N 64 37W
Kilmar 8 45 46N 74 37W
Kimberley 17 49 40N 115 59W
Kimmirut 21 62 50N 69 50W
Kimsquit 18 52 45N 126 57W
Kinbasket L. 19 52 0N 118 10W
Kincaid 14 49 40N 107 0W
Kincardine 10 44 10N 81 40W
Kindersley 14 51 30N 109 10W
King George Is. 4 57 20N 78 25W
King I. 18 52 10N 127 40W
King William I. 21 69 10N 97 25W
Kingsey Falls 9 45 51N 72 4W
Kingston 11 44 14N 76 30W
Kingsville 10 42 2N 82 45W
Kinistino 14 52 57N 105 2W
Kinmount 11 44 48N 78 45W
Kinnaird 19 49 17N 117 39W
Kinuso 16 55 20N 115 25W
Kiosk 11 46 6N 78 53W
Kipawa 8 46 47N 78 59W
Kipawa, L. 8 46 50N 79 0W
Kipawa, Parc de 8 47 0N 78 50W
Kipling 14 50 6N 102 38W
Kirkfield 11 44 34N 78 59W
Kirkland Lake 8 48 9N 80 2W
Kiskittogisu L. 15 54 13N 98 20W
Kitchener 10 43 27N 80 29W
Kitimat 18 54 3N 128 38W
Kittertoksoak, I. 4 58 50N 65 50W
Kleena Kleene 18 52 0N 124 59W
Klinaklini → 18 51 21N 125 40W
Klondike 20 64 0N 139 26W
Klotz, L. 4 60 32N 73 40W
Kluane L. 20 61 15N 138 40W
Knight Inlet 18 50 45N 125 40W
Knowlton 9 45 13N 72 31W
Knox, C. 18 54 11N 133 5W
Koartac = Quaqtaq 4 60 55N 69 40W
Kogaluk → 4 56 12N 61 44W
Kokanee Glacier Prov. Park 19 49 47N 117 10W
Koksoak → 4 58 30N 68 10W
Kootenay L. 19 49 45N 116 50W
Kootenay Nat. Park 17 51 0N 116 0W
Koroc → 4 58 50N 65 50W
Kovic, B. 4 61 35N 77 36W
Kowkash 13 50 20N 87 12W
Kugaluk, B. 4 59 10N 78 40W
Kuglugtuk 20 67 50N 115 5W
Kugong I. 4 56 18N 79 50W
Kunghit I. 18 52 6N 131 3W
Kuujjuaq 4 58 6N 68 15W
Kuujjuarapik 4 55 17N 77 45W
Kwataboahegan → 13 51 9N 80 50W
Kyuquot 18 50 3N 127 25W

L

La Conception 8 46 9N 74 42W
La Grande → 4 53 50N 79 0W
La Guadeloupe 9 45 57N 70 56W
La Malbaie 9 47 40N 70 10W
La Martre, L. = Wha Ti 20 63 0N 118 0W
La Mothe, Rés. 9 48 46N 71 9W
La Patrie 9 45 24N 71 15W
La Pocatière 9 47 22N 70 2W
La Reine 8 48 50N 79 30W
La Sarre 8 48 45N 79 15W
La Scie 5 49 57N 55 36W
La Tuque 9 47 30N 72 50W
Labrador, Coast of □ 4 53 20N 61 0W
Labrador City 4 52 57N 66 55W
Labrieville 9 49 18N 69 34W
Lac Allard 4 50 33N 63 24W
Lac-aux-Sables 9 46 51N 72 24W
Lac Bouchette 9 48 16N 72 11W
Lac Carré 9 46 7N 74 29W
Lac-des-Écorces 8 46 34N 75 22W
Lac Édouard 9 47 40N 72 16W
Lac-Etchemin 9 46 24N 70 30W
Lac La Biche 16 54 45N 111 58W
Lac-Mégantic 9 45 35N 70 53W
Lac-Rémi 8 46 1N 74 46W
Lac-Ste-Marie 8 45 57N 75 57W
Lac Seul, Res. 12 50 25N 92 30W
Lachine 9 45 30N 73 40W
Lachute 9 45 39N 74 21W
Lacolle 9 45 5N 73 22W
Lacombe 17 52 30N 113 44W
Ladysmith 18 49 0N 123 49W
Laflamme → 8 49 17N 77 9W
Lafleche 14 49 45N 106 40W
Laforce 8 47 32N 78 44W
Lake Harbour = Kimmirut 21 62 50N 69 50W
Lake Lenore 14 52 24N 104 59W
Lake Louise 17 51 30N 116 10W
Lake St. Peter 11 45 18N 78 2W
Lake Superior Prov. Park 13 47 45N 84 45W
Lakefield 11 44 25N 78 16W
Lambeth 10 42 54N 81 18W
Lambton 9 45 50N 71 5W
Lamèque 7 47 45N 64 38W
Lamont 16 53 46N 112 50W
Lampman 14 49 25N 102 50W
Lanark 8 45 1N 76 22W
Lancaster 8 45 10N 74 30W
Lancaster Sd. 21 74 13N 84 0W
Lancer 14 50 48N 108 53W
Landrienne 8 48 30N 77 50W
Lang Bay 18 49 45N 124 21W
Langara I. 18 54 14N 133 1W
Langenburg 15 50 51N 101 43W
Langlade 5 46 50N 56 20W
Lanigan 14 51 51N 105 2W
L'Annonciation 8 46 25N 74 55W
Lanoraie 9 45 58N 73 13W
Lansdowne 11 44 24N 76 1W
L'Anse au Loup 5 51 32N 56 50W
Larder Lake 8 48 5N 79 40W
Laredo Sd. 18 52 30N 128 53W
Lashburn 14 53 10N 109 40W
Last Mountain L. 14 51 5N 105 14W
Latchford 8 47 20N 79 50W
Latulipe 8 47 26N 79 2W
Laurentian Plateau 4 52 0N 70 0W
Laurentides, Parc Prov. des 9 47 45N 71 15W
Laurier-Station 9 46 32N 71 38W
Laurierville 9 46 18N 71 39W
Lauzon 9 46 48N 71 10W
Laval 9 45 35N 73 45W
Lavaltrie 9 45 53N 73 17W
Lavant Sta. 11 45 3N 76 42W
Laverlochère 8 47 26N 79 18W
Lavieille, L. 11 45 51N 78 14W
Leader 14 50 50N 109 30W
Leamington 10 42 3N 82 36W
Leask 14 53 5N 106 45W
Lebel-sur-Quévillon 8 49 3N 76 59W
Leduc 16 53 15N 113 30W
Lefebvre 9 47 12N 69 49W
Lefroy 10 44 16N 79 34W
Legal 16 53 55N 113 35W
Lejeune 9 47 46N 68 34W
Lemieux 9 46 18N 72 7W
Lemieux, L. 8 50 19N 74 38W
Lemoine, L. 8 48 0N 78 0W
Lennoxville 9 45 22N 71 51W
Lenore L. 14 52 30N 104 59W
Leoville 14 53 39N 107 33W
Lepellé → 4 59 58N 72 24W
L'Épiphanie 9 45 51N 73 29W
Leroy, L. 4 55 10N 67 15W
Léry 9 45 21N 73 48W
Les Éboulements 9 47 28N 70 21W
Les Escoumins 9 48 21N 69 24W
Les Étroits 9 47 24N 68 54W
Lesser Slave L. 16 55 30N 115 25W
Lestock 14 51 19N 103 59W
Lethbridge 17 49 45N 112 45W
Levack 10 46 38N 81 23W
Lévis 9 46 48N 71 9W
Lewisporte 5 49 15N 55 3W
Liard → 20 61 51N 121 18W
Lièvre → 8 45 31N 75 26W
Lillooet → 19 49 15N 121 57W
Limages 8 45 20N 75 16W
Limoges 11 45 20N 75 15W
Lincoln 10 43 10N 79 29W
Lindsay 11 44 22N 78 43W
Linière 9 46 4N 70 32W
Lintlaw 14 52 4N 103 14W
Linton 9 47 15N 72 16W
Linwood 10 43 35N 80 43W
Lion's Head 10 44 58N 81 15W
L'Isle Verte 9 48 1N 69 20W
Listowel 10 43 44N 80 58W
Little Cadotte → 16 56 41N 117 6W
Little Current 10 45 55N 82 0W
Little Current → 13 50 57N 84 36W
Little Grand Rapids 15 52 0N 95 29W
Little Smoky → 16 54 44N 117 11W
Little White → 10 46 23N 83 20W
Lively 10 46 26N 81 9W
Liverpool 7 44 5N 64 41W
Lloydminster 14 53 17N 110 0W
Lockeport 7 43 47N 65 4W
Lomond 17 50 24N 112 36W
London 10 42 59N 81 15W
Lonely I. 10 45 34N 81 28W
Long I. 4 54 50N 79 20W
Long L. 13 49 30N 86 50W
Long Point B. 10 42 40N 80 10W
Long Pt., *Nfld.*, 5 48 47N 58 46W
Long Pt., *Ont.*, 10 42 35N 80 2W
Long Range Mts. 5 49 30N 57 30W
Longlac 13 49 45N 86 25W
Longueuil 9 45 32N 73 30W
Longview 17 50 32N 114 10W
Loon → 16 57 8N 115 3W
Loon Lake 14 54 2N 109 10W
Loretteville 9 46 51N 71 21W
Lorrainville 8 47 21N 79 23W
Lougheed I. 20 77 26N 105 6W
Louis XIV, Pte. 4 54 37N 79 45W
Louisbourg 7 45 55N 60 0W
Louise I. 18 52 55N 131 50W
Louiseville 9 46 20N 72 56W
Loups Marins, Lacs des 4 56 30N 73 45W
Lourdes-du-Blanc-Sablon 4 51 24N 57 12W
Love 14 53 29N 104 10W
Low 8 45 50N 76 0W
Low L. 4 55 54N 67 5W
Lower Arrow L. 19 49 40N 118 5W
Lubicon L. 16 56 23N 115 56W
Lucan 10 43 11N 81 24W
Luceville 9 48 32N 68 22W
Lucknow 10 43 57N 81 31W
Lunenburg 7 44 22N 64 18W
Luseland 14 52 5N 109 24W
Lutselke 20 62 24N 110 44W
Lyal I. 10 44 57N 81 24W
Lyell I. 18 52 40N 131 35W
Lyster 9 46 22N 71 37W
Lytton 19 50 13N 121 31W

M

Mabel L. 19 50 35N 118 43W
Maberly 11 44 50N 76 32W
Macamic 8 48 45N 79 0W
McBride 19 53 20N 120 19W
McCauley I. 18 53 40N 130 15W
M'Clintock Chan. 21 72 0N 102 0W
M'Clure Str. 20 75 0N 119 0W
Macdougall L. 21 66 0N 98 27W
MacGregor 15 49 57N 98 48W
MacKay → 16 57 10N 111 38W
McKellar 10 45 30N 79 55W
Mackenzie → 20 69 10N 134 20W
Mackenzie Bay 20 69 0N 137 30W
Mackenzie King I. 20 77 45N 111 0W
Mackenzie Mts. 20 64 0N 130 0W
McLennan 16 55 42N 116 50W
McLure 19 51 2N 120 13W
McMorran 14 51 19N 108 42W
McMurray = Fort McMurray 16 56 44N 111 7W
MacNutt 15 51 5N 101 36W
MacTier 10 45 8N 79 47W
Madame I. 7 45 30N 60 58W
Madawaska 8 45 30N 78 0W
Madawaska → 11 45 27N 76 21W
Madeleine, Is. de la 7 47 30N 61 40W
Madoc 11 44 30N 77 28W
Mafeking 15 52 40N 101 10W
Magdalen Is. = Madeleine, Is. de la 7 47 30N 61 40W
Magnetawan 10 45 40N 79 39W
Magnetic Pole (North) = North Magnetic Pole 21 77 58N 102 8W
Magog 9 45 18N 72 9W
Magpie L. 6 51 0N 64 41W
Magrath 17 49 25N 112 50W
Maicasagi → 8 49 58N 76 33W
Maidstone 14 53 5N 109 20W
Main Centre 14 50 35N 107 21W
Major 14 51 52N 109 37W
Makkovik 4 55 10N 59 10W
Malartic 8 48 9N 78 9W
Malartic, L. 8 48 15N 78 5W
Mallorytown 11 44 29N 75 53W
Manicouagan → 9 49 30N 68 30W
Manicouagan, Rés. 4 51 5N 68 40W
Manigotagan 15 51 6N 96 18W
Manito L. 14 52 43N 109 43W
Manitoba □ 15 55 30N 97 0W
Manitoba, L. 15 51 0N 98 45W
Manitou 15 49 15N 98 32W
Manitou L., *Ont.*, 10 45 51N 82 0W
Manitou L., *Qué.*, 4 50 55N 65 17W
Manitoulin I. 10 45 40N 82 30W
Manitowaning 10 45 46N 81 49W
Maniwaki 8 46 23N 75 58W
Mankota 14 49 25N 107 5W
Manning 16 56 53N 117 39W
Manning Prov. Park 19 49 5N 120 45W
Manotick 11 45 13N 75 41W
Manouane, L., *Qué.*, 4 50 45N 70 45W
Manouane, L., *Qué.*, 9 47 33N 74 6W
Manseau 9 46 22N 72 0W
Mansel I. 4 62 0N 80 0W
Maple Creek 14 49 55N 109 29W
Marathon 13 48 44N 86 23W
Marbleton 9 45 37N 71 35W
Margaret Bay 18 51 20N 127 35W
Marguerite 19 52 30N 122 25W
Maricourt = Kangiqsujuaq 4 61 30N 72 0W
Marieville 9 45 26N 73 10W
Markdale 10 44 19N 80 39W
Markham 10 43 52N 79 16W
Markstay 10 46 29N 80 32W
Marlbank 11 44 26N 77 6W
Marmion L. 12 48 55N 91 20W
Marmora 11 44 28N 77 41W
Marquette, L. 9 48 54N 73 54W
Marten River 10 46 44N 79 49W
Maryfield 15 49 50N 101 35W
Mary's Harbour 4 52 18N 55 51W
Marystown 5 47 10N 55 10W
Marysville 17 49 35N 116 0W
Mascouche 9 45 45N 73 36W
Maskinongé 9 46 14N 73 1W
Masset 18 54 2N 132 10W
Massey 10 46 12N 82 5W
Masson 8 45 32N 75 25W
Massueville 9 45 55N 72 56W
Mastigouche, Parc 9 46 33N 73 41W
Matagami 4 49 45N 77 34W
Matagami, L. 4 49 50N 77 40W
Matane 6 48 50N 67 33W
Matapédia 7 48 0N 66 59W
Matawin → 9 46 54N 72 56W
Matawin, Rés. 9 46 46N 73 50W
Matchi-Manitou, L. 8 48 0N 77 4W
Matheson Island 15 51 45N 96 56W
Matinenda L. 10 46 22N 82 57W
Mattagami → 13 50 43N 81 29W
Mattice 13 49 40N 83 20W
Mauricie, Parc Nat. de la 9 46 45N 73 0W
Maxville 8 45 17N 74 51W
Mayerthorpe 16 53 57N 115 8W
Meadow Lake 14 54 10N 108 26W
Meaford 10 44 36N 80 35W
Meath Park 14 53 27N 105 22W
Medicine Hat 17 50 0N 110 45W
Medley 16 54 25N 110 16W
Medstead 14 53 19N 108 5W
Mégantic, L. 9 45 32N 70 53W
Mégantic, Mt. 9 45 28N 71 9W
Mégiscane → 8 48 29N 75 38W
Mégiscane, L. 8 48 35N 75 55W
Meighen I. 21 80 0N 99 30W
Mékinac, L. 9 47 3N 72 41W
Meldrum Bay 10 45 56N 83 6W
Mélèzes → 4 57 40N 69 29W
Melfort 14 52 50N 104 37W
Melita 15 49 15N 101 0W
Melville 14 50 55N 102 50W
Melville, L. 4 53 30N 60 0W
Melville I. 20 75 30N 112 0W
Melville Pen. 21 68 0N 84 0W
Memphrémagog, L. 9 45 8N 72 17W
Menihek 4 54 28N 56 36W
Menihek L. 4 54 0N 67 0W
Mercier 9 45 19N 73 45W
Mercy C. 21 65 0N 63 30W
Merrickville 11 44 55N 75 50W
Merritt 19 50 10N 120 45W
Merry I. 4 55 29N 77 31W
Mesgouez, L. 4 51 20N 75 0W
Messine 8 46 14N 76 2W
Michikamau L. 4 54 20N 63 10W
Michipicoten 13 47 55N 84 55W
Michipicoten I. 13 47 40N 85 40W
Midale 14 49 25N 103 20W
Middleton 7 44 57N 65 4W
Midland 10 44 45N 79 50W
Mikkwa → 16 58 25N 114 46W
Milden 14 51 29N 107 32W
Mildmay 10 44 3N 81 7W
Milestone 14 49 59N 104 31W
Milk River 17 49 10N 112 5W
Millbridge 11 44 41N 77 36W
Millbrook 11 44 10N 78 29W
Mille Lacs, L. des 12 48 45N 90 35W
Milne Inlet 3 72 30N 80 0W
Milo 17 50 34N 112 53W
Milot 9 48 54N 71 49W
Milton 10 43 31N 79 53W
Milverton 10 43 34N 80 55W
Minago → 15 54 33N 98 59W
Minaki 12 49 59N 94 40W
Minas Basin 7 45 20N 64 12W
Mindemoya 10 45 44N 82 10W
Minden 11 44 55N 78 43W
Mingan 4 50 20N 64 0W
Minipi, L. 6 52 25N 60 45W
Minnedosa 3 50 14N 99 50W
Minnitaki L. 12 49 57N 92 10W
Minto, L. 4 57 13N 75 0W
Minton 14 49 10N 104 35W
Miquelon 8 49 25N 76 27W
Miramichi B. 7 47 15N 65 0W
Mirror 17 52 30N 113 7W
Miscou I. 7 47 57N 64 31W
Missanabie 13 48 20N 84 6W
Missinaibi → 13 50 43N 81 29W
Missinaibi L. 13 48 23N 83 40W
Mission City 19 49 10N 122 15W
Missisicabi → 4 51 14N 79 31W
Mississagi → 10 46 15N 83 9W
Mississagi Prov. Park 10 46 30N 82 40W
Mississauga 10 43 32N 79 35W
Mississippi L. 8 45 5N 76 10W
Mistaouac, L. 8 49 25N 78 41W
Mistassibi → 9 48 53N 72 13W
Mistassibi Nord-Est → 9 49 31N 71 56W
Mistassini 9 48 53N 72 12W
Mistassini → 9 48 42N 72 20W
Mistassini, Parc Prov. de 9 50 20N 74 0W
Mistassini L. 4 51 0N 73 30W
Mistatim 14 52 52N 103 22W
Mitchell 10 43 28N 81 12W
Mitchinamécus, Rés. 8 47 19N 75 9W
Moira → 11 44 21N 77 24W
Moisie 4 50 12N 66 1W
Moisie → 6 50 14N 66 5W
Molson L. 15 54 22N 96 40W
Moncouche, L. 9 48 45N 70 42W
Moncton 7 46 7N 64 51W
Mondonac, L. 9 47 24N 73 58W
Monkton 10 43 35N 81 5W
Mont-Carmel 9 47 26N 69 52W
Mont-Joli 9 48 37N 68 10W
Mont-Laurier 8 46 35N 75 30W
Mont-Tremblant 8 46 13N 74 36W
Mont Tremblant Prov. Park 9 46 30N 74 30W
Montague 7 46 10N 62 39W
Montcerf 8 46 32N 76 3W
Montebello 8 45 40N 74 55W
Montmagny 9 46 58N 70 34W
Montmartre 14 50 14N 103 27W
Montréal 9 45 31N 73 34W
Montreal L. 14 54 20N 105 45W
Montreal Lake 14 54 3N 105 46W
Montreuil, L. 8 50 12N 77 40W
Monts, Pte. des 6 49 20N 67 12W
Moonbeam 13 49 20N 82 10W
Moose → 13 51 20N 80 25W
Moose Creek 11 45 15N 74 58W
Moose Factory 13 51 16N 80 32W
Moose I. 15 51 42N 97 10W
Moose Jaw 14 50 24N 105 30W
Moose Jaw → 14 50 34N 105 18W
Moose Lake 15 53 43N 100 20W
Moose Mountain Cr. → 14 49 13N 102 12W
Moose Mountain Prov. Park 15 49 48N 102 25W
Moose River 13 50 48N 81 17W
Moosomin 15 50 9N 101 40W
Moosonee 13 51 17N 80 39W
Morden 15 49 15N 98 10W
Moresby I. 18 52 30N 131 40W
Morice L. 18 53 50N 127 40W
Morin-Heights 9 45 54N 74 15W
Morinville 16 53 49N 113 41W
Morris 15 49 25N 97 22W
Morrisburg 11 44 55N 75 7W
Mosquito B. 4 61 10N 78 0W
Mossbank 14 49 56N 105 56W
Mossy → 14 54 5N 102 58W
Motte, L. la 8 48 20N 78 2W
Mouchalagane → 4 50 56N 68 41W
Mount Albert 10 44 8N 79 19W
Mount Brydges 10 42 54N 81 29W
Mount Forest 10 43 59N 80 43W
Mount Pearl 5 47 31N 52 47W
Mount Revelstoke Nat. Park 19 51 5N 118 30W
Mount Robson Prov. Park 19 53 0N 119 0W
Mountain Park 17 52 50N 117 15W
Mukutawa → 15 53 10N 97 24W
Mulgrave 7 45 38N 61 31W
Mundare 16 53 35N 112 20W
Murray Harbour 7 46 0N 62 28W
Murtle L. 19 52 8N 119 38W
Muskoka, L. 10 45 0N 79 25W
Musquaro, L. 4 50 38N 61 5W
Musquodoboit Harbour 7 44 50N 63 9W

N

Nabisipi → 4 50 14N 62 13W
Nachicapau, L. 4 56 40N 68 5W
Nachvak Fd. 4 59 3N 63 45W
Nagagami → 13 49 40N 84 40W
Nahanni Butte 20 61 2N 123 31W
Naicam 14 52 30N 104 30W
Nain 4 56 34N 61 40W
Nairn 10 46 20N 81 35W
Nakina 13 50 10N 86 40W
Nakusp 19 50 20N 117 45W
Namew L. 15 54 14N 101 56W
Namu 18 51 52N 127 50W
Namur 8 45 54N 74 56W
Nanaimo 18 49 10N 124 0W
Nansen Sd. 21 81 0N 91 0W
Nanton 17 50 21N 113 46W
Naococane L. 4 52 50N 70 45W
Napanee 11 44 15N 77 0W
Napartokh B. 4 58 1N 62 19W
Napierville 9 45 11N 73 25W
Napierville □ 9 45 10N 73 30W
Narraway → 16 55 44N 119 55W
Naskaupi → 4 53 47N 60 51W
Nastapoka → 4 56 55N 76 33W
Nastapoka, Is. 4 56 55N 76 50W
Natal 17 49 43N 114 51W
Natashquan 4 50 14N 61 46W
Natashquan → 4 50 7N 61 50W
Naughton 10 46 24N 81 12W
Nazko 18 53 1N 123 37W
Nazko → 18 53 7N 123 34W
Nechako → 19 53 30N 122 44W
Neepawa 15 50 15N 99 30W
Neidpath 14 50 12N 107 20W
Nelson 19 49 30N 117 20W
Némiscachingue, L. 8 47 25N 74 30W
Némiscau 4 51 18N 76 54W
Némiscau, L. 4 51 25N 76 40W
Neoskweskau 4 51 52N 74 17W
Néret L. 4 54 45N 70 44W
Nestaocano → 9 49 38N 73 28W
Nettilling L. 21 66 30N 71 0W
Neustadt 10 44 5N 81 0W
Neville 14 49 58N 107 39W
New Brunswick □ 7 46 50N 66 30W
New Denver 19 50 0N 117 25W
New Glasgow 7 45 35N 62 36W
New Hamburg 10 43 23N 80 42W
New Liskeard 8 47 31N 79 41W
New Waterford 7 46 13N 60 4W
New Westminster 19 49 13N 122 55W
Newboro L. 11 44 38N 76 20W
Newbrook 16 54 24N 112 57W
Newburgh 11 44 19N 76 52W
Newcastle 7 47 1N 65 38W
Newfoundland □ 3 53 0N 58 0W
Newmarket 10 44 3N 79 28W
Niagara Falls 10 43 7N 79 5W
Niagara-on-the-Lake 10 43 15N 79 4W
Nicola 19 50 12N 120 40W
Nicolet 9 46 17N 72 35W
Nioman 4 50 25N 66 5W
Nipawin 14 53 20N 104 0W
Nipawin Prov. Park 14 54 0N 104 37W
Nipigon 12 49 0N 88 17W
Nipigon, L. 12 49 50N 88 30W
Nipishish L. 4 54 12N 60 45W
Nipissing L. 10 46 20N 80 0W
Nipissis → 4 50 30N 66 5W
Nitchequon 4 53 10N 70 58W
Nith → 10 43 12N 80 23W
Nobel 10 45 25N 80 6W
Noelville 10 46 8N 80 26W
Noire → 8 45 54N 76 57W
Nokomis 14 51 35N 105 0W
Nominingue 8 46 24N 75 2W
Nominingue, L. 8 46 26N 74 59W
Nootka 18 49 38N 126 38W
Nootka I. 18 49 32N 126 42W
Noranda 8 48 20N 79 0W
Nordegg 17 52 29N 116 5W
Norembega 8 49 48N 80 43W
Norman Wells 20 65 17N 126 51W
Normandin 9 48 49N 72 31W

Normétal ... 8 49 0N 79 22W
Norquay 15 51 53N 102 5W
North → ... 4 57 30N 61 50W
North Aulatsivik I. 4 59 46N 64 5W
North Battleford . 14 52 50N 108 17W
North Bay .. 10 46 20N 79 30W
North Belcher Is. 4 56 50N 79 50W
North Bend . 19 49 50N 121 27W
North C. 7 47 2N 60 20W
North Channel 10 46 0N 83 0W
North Gower 11 45 8N 75 43W
North Hatley 9 45 17N 71 58W
North Magnetic Pole 21 77 58N 102 8W
North Portal . 15 49 0N 102 33W
North Pt. ... 7 47 5N 64 0W
North Saskatchewan → 14 53 15N 105 5W
North Sydney 7 46 12N 60 15W
North Thompson → 19 50 40N 120 20W
North Twin I. 4 53 20N 80 0W
North Vancouver 19 49 25N 123 3W
North Wabasca L. 16 56 0N 113 55W
North West River 4 53 30N 60 10W
North West Territories □ 20 67 0N 110 0W
Northern Light, L. .. 12 48 15N 90 39W
Northumberland Str. 7 46 20N 64 0W
Norway House 15 53 59N 97 50W
Norwegian B. 21 77 30N 90 0W
Norwich 10 42 59N 80 36W
Norwood 11 44 23N 77 59W
Notikewin → 16 57 2N 117 38W
Notre-Dame . 7 46 18N 64 46W
Notre Dame B. 5 49 45N 55 30W
Notre Dame de Koartac = Quaqtaq 4 60 55N 69 40W
Notre-Dame-de-la-Doré 9 48 43N 72 39W
Notre-Dame-des-Bois .. 9 45 24N 71 4W
Notre Dame d'Ivugivic = Ivujivik .. 4 62 24N 77 55W
Notre-Dame-du-Bon-Conseil ... 9 46 0N 72 21W
Notre Dame du Lac, Ont., ... 10 46 18N 80 11W
Notre-Dame-du-Lac, Qué., ... 9 47 36N 68 48W
Notre-Dame-du-Laus ... 8 46 5N 75 37W
Notre-Dame-du-Nord .. 8 47 36N 79 30W
Notre-Dame-du-Portage 9 47 46N 69 37W
Nottawasaga B. 10 44 35N 80 15W
Nottaway → 4 51 22N 78 55W
Nouveau Comptoir = Wemindji . 4 53 0N 78 49W
Nouveau-Québec ... 4 56 0N 71 0W
Nouvelle France, C. de 4 62 27N 73 42W
Nova Scotia □ 7 45 10N 63 0W
Novar 10 45 27N 79 15W
Nunaksaluk I. 4 55 49N 60 20W
Nutak 4 57 28N 61 59W
Nuvuk Is. ... 4 62 24N 78 3W

O

Oakville 10 43 27N 79 41W
Oba 13 49 4N 84 7W
Obalski, L. .. 8 48 43N 77 58W
Obamsca, L. . 8 50 24N 78 16W
Obed 16 53 30N 117 10W
Obedjwan .. 8 48 40N 74 56W
Ochre River . 15 51 4N 99 47W
Odessa 11 44 17N 76 43W
Ogahalla 13 50 6N 85 51W
Ogascanane, L. 8 47 5N 78 25W
Ogoki → ... 13 51 38N 85 57W
Ogoki L. ... 13 50 50N 87 10W
Ogoki Res. .. 12 50 45N 88 15W
Oil Springs . 10 42 47N 82 7W
Okak 4 57 33N 61 58W
Okak Is. 4 57 30N 61 30W
Okanagan L. 19 50 0N 119 30W
Old Wives L. 14 50 5N 106 0W
Oldman → . 17 49 57N 111 42W
Olds 17 51 50N 114 10W
Olga, L. 4 49 47N 77 15W
Oliver 19 49 13N 119 37W
Olomane → 4 50 14N 60 37W
Omemee ... 11 44 18N 78 33W
Onaping 10 46 37N 81 25W
Onaping → 10 46 37N 81 18W
Onaping L. 13 47 3N 81 30W
Onatchiway, L. 9 49 3N 71 5W
Ontario □ ... 3 48 0N 83 0W
Ontario, L. .. 11 43 20N 78 0W
Oona River .. 18 53 57N 130 16W
Ootsa L. 18 53 50N 126 2W
Opasatica, L. 8 48 5N 79 18W
Opasatika ... 13 49 30N 82 50W
Opataca, L. .. 8 50 22N 74 55W
Opawica, L. . 8 49 35N 75 55W
Opémisca, L. 4 49 56N 74 52W
Opeongo L. . 11 45 42N 78 23W
Opinaca → . 4 52 15N 78 2W
Opinaca L. .. 4 52 39N 76 20W
Opiscoteo, L. 4 53 10N 68 10W
Opiskotish, L. 4 53 10N 67 50W
Orangeville . 10 43 55N 80 5W
Orillia 10 44 40N 79 24W
Orléans, I. d' 9 46 54N 70 58W
Ormstown .. 9 45 8N 74 0W
Oromocto ... 7 45 54N 66 29W
Orono 11 43 59N 78 37W
Osgoode ... 11 45 8N 75 36W
Oshawa 11 43 50N 78 50W
Oskélanéo .. 8 48 5N 75 15W
Osoyoos 19 49 0N 119 30W
Ossokmanuan L. 4 53 25N 65 0W
Ostaboningue, L. 8 47 9N 78 53W
Otelnuk L. .. 4 56 9N 68 12W
Otish, Mts. .. 4 52 22N 70 30W
Otosquen ... 15 53 17N 102 1W
Ottawa = Outaouais → 9 45 27N 74 8W
Ottawa 11 45 27N 75 42W
Ottawa Is. .. 4 59 35N 80 10W
Otter Rapids 13 50 11N 81 39W
Otterville ... 10 42 55N 80 36W
Ouareau, Rés. du L. 9 46 17N 74 9W
Ouasiemsca → 9 49 0N 72 30W
Ouest, Pte. .. 6 49 52N 64 40W
Outaouais → 9 45 27N 74 8W
Outardes ... 9 50 20N 69 10W
Outardes → 9 49 24N 69 30W
Outer I. 4 51 10N 58 35W
Outlook 14 51 30N 107 0W
Owen Sound 10 44 35N 80 55W
Oyen 17 51 22N 110 28W

P

Packenham . 11 45 22N 76 25W
Paddockwood 14 53 30N 105 30W
Padloping Island 21 67 0N 62 50W
Pagwa River 13 50 2N 85 14W
Paint Hills = Wemindji .. 4 53 0N 78 49W
Paisley 10 44 18N 81 16W
Pakenham .. 8 45 18N 76 18W
Palmarolle .. 8 48 40N 79 12W
Palmerston . 10 43 50N 80 51W
Panache, L. 10 46 15N 81 20W
Pangnirtung . 21 66 8N 65 54W
Papineau-Labelle, Parc Prov. . 8 46 10N 75 15W
Papineauville 8 45 37N 75 1W
Paradis 8 48 15N 76 35W
Paradise → 4 53 27N 57 19W
Parent 8 47 55N 74 35W
Parent, L. ... 8 48 31N 77 1W
Parham 11 44 39N 76 43W
Paris 10 43 12N 80 25W
Parkerview .. 14 51 21N 103 18W
Parkhill 10 43 15N 81 38W
Parkside 14 53 10N 106 33W
Parksville ... 18 49 20N 124 21W
Parrsboro ... 7 45 30N 64 25W
Parry Is. 20 77 0N 110 0W
Parry Sound 10 45 20N 80 0W
Paspébiac ... 7 48 3N 65 17W
Paul I. 4 56 30N 61 20W
Paul-Sauvé, L. 8 50 15N 78 20W
Payne Bay = Kangirsuk . 4 60 0N 70 0W
Peace River . 16 56 15N 117 18W
Peel → 20 67 0N 135 0W
Peers 16 53 40N 116 0W
Pelee, Pt. ... 10 41 54N 82 31W
Pelee I. 10 41 47N 82 40W
Pélican, L. .. 4 59 47N 73 35W
Pelican L. ... 15 52 28N 100 20W
Pelican Rapids 15 52 45N 100 42W
Pelletier Sta. 9 47 33N 69 26W
Pelly → ... 20 62 47N 137 19W
Pelly Bay ... 21 68 38N 89 50W
Pelly L. 20 66 0N 102 0W
Pemberton .. 19 50 25N 122 50W
Pembroke .. 11 45 50N 77 7W
Penetanguishene 10 44 50N 79 55W
Pennant 14 50 32N 108 14W
Penny 19 53 51N 121 20W
Penny Str. .. 20 76 30N 97 0W
Pense 14 50 25N 104 59W
Penticton ... 19 49 30N 119 38W
Percé 6 48 31N 64 13W
Péribonca → 4 48 45N 72 5W
Péribonca, L. 9 50 1N 71 10W
Péribonka ... 9 48 46N 72 3W
Perth 11 44 55N 76 15W
Petawawa .. 11 45 54N 77 17W
Peterbell ... 13 48 36N 83 21W
Peterborough 11 44 20N 78 20W
Peters, L. ... 4 59 41N 70 53W
Petit-Cap ... 6 49 3N 64 30W
Petit Lac Manicouagan 6 51 25N 67 40W
Petit-Mécatina, I. du 4 50 30N 59 25W
Petitcodiac .. 7 45 57N 65 11W
Petite Baleine → 4 56 0N 76 45W
Petite-Rivière 9 47 20N 70 33W
Petite Saguenay . 9 48 15N 70 4W
Petitsikapau, L. 4 54 37N 66 25W
Petrolia 10 42 54N 82 9W
Philipsburg . 9 45 2N 73 5W
Piapot 14 49 59N 109 8W
Pickerel L. .. 12 48 40N 91 25W
Pickle Lake . 12 51 30N 90 12W
Picton 11 44 1N 77 9W
Pictou 7 45 41N 62 42W
Picture Butte 17 49 55N 112 45W
Pierreville ... 9 46 4N 72 49W
Pigeon L. ... 11 44 27N 78 30W
Pilot Mound . 15 49 15N 98 54W
Pin-Blanc, L. . 8 46 45N 78 8W
Pincher Creek 17 49 30N 113 57W
Pine, C. 5 46 37N 53 32W
Pine Falls ... 15 50 34N 96 11W
Pine Point .. 20 60 50N 114 28W
Pine River .. 15 51 45N 100 30W
Pins, Pte. aux 10 42 15N 81 51W
Pipestone Cr. → ... 15 49 38N 100 15W
Pipmuacan, Rés. 9 49 45N 70 30W
Pitt I. 18 53 30N 129 50W
Placentia ... 5 47 20N 54 0W
Placentia B. . 5 47 0N 54 40W
Plaster Rock . 7 46 53N 67 22W
Playgreen L. . 15 54 0N 98 15W
Plessisville .. 9 46 14N 71 47W
Pletipi L. 4 51 44N 70 6W
Plevna 11 44 58N 76 59W
Pogamasing . 13 46 55N 81 50W
Point Edward 10 43 0N 82 30W
Point Pelee Nat. Park .. 10 41 57N 82 31W
Pointe au Baril Sta. 10 45 35N 80 23W
Pointe-au-Pic 9 47 38N 70 9W
Pointe-aux-Outardes .. 9 49 3N 68 26W
Pointe-aux-Trembles . 9 45 40N 73 30W
Pointe-Claire 9 45 26N 73 50W
Pointe-Gatineau .. 11 45 28N 75 42W
Pointe-Lebel . 9 49 10N 68 12W
Poisson-Blanc, L. du 8 46 0N 75 45W
Poltimore ... 8 45 47N 75 43W
Ponass L. ... 14 52 16N 103 58W
Poncheville, L. 4 50 10N 76 55W
Pond Inlet .. 21 72 40N 77 0W
Ponds, I. of . 4 53 27N 55 52W
Ponoka 17 52 42N 113 40W
Pont-Rouge . 9 46 45N 71 42W
Ponteix 14 49 46N 107 29W
Pontiac, Parc 8 46 30N 76 30W
Pontypool ... 11 44 6N 78 38W
Pooley I. 18 52 45N 128 15W
Poplar → ... 15 53 0N 97 19W
Porcher I. ... 18 53 50N 130 30W
Porcupine ... 8 48 30N 81 11W
Port Alberni . 18 49 14N 124 50W
Port Alfred .. 9 48 18N 70 53W
Port Alice ... 18 50 20N 127 25W
Port au Port B. 5 48 40N 58 50W
Port Blandford 5 48 20N 54 10W
Port Burwell . 10 42 40N 80 48W
Port Carling . 10 45 7N 79 35W
Port-Cartier . 4 50 2N 66 50W
Port Clements 18 53 40N 132 10W
Port Colborne 10 42 50N 79 10W
Port Coquitlam . 19 49 15N 122 45W
Port Credit .. 10 43 33N 79 35W
Port Dover .. 10 42 47N 80 12W
Port Edward . 18 54 12N 130 10W
Port Elgin ... 10 44 25N 81 25W
Port Hardy .. 18 50 41N 127 30W
Port Harrison = Inukjuak 4 58 25N 78 15W
Port Hawkesbury 7 45 36N 61 22W
Port Hood ... 7 46 0N 61 32W
Port Hope ... 11 43 56N 78 20W
Port Loring .. 10 45 55N 80 0W
Port Mellon .. 19 49 32N 123 31W
Port-Menier . 6 49 51N 64 15W
Port Mouton 7 43 58N 64 50W
Port Nouveau-Québec = Kangiqsualujjuaq 4 58 30N 65 59W
Port Perry ... 11 44 6N 78 56W
Port Radium = Echo Bay 20 66 5N 117 55W
Port Renfrew 18 48 30N 124 20W
Port Rowan . 10 42 40N 80 30W
Port Saunders 5 50 40N 57 18W
Port Severn . 10 44 48N 79 43W
Port Stanley . 10 42 40N 81 10W
Portage La Prairie 15 49 58N 98 18W
Portland 11 44 42N 76 12W
Portland Prom. 4 58 40N 78 33W
Portneuf 9 46 43N 71 55W
Portneuf → . 9 48 38N 69 5W
Portneuf, Parc Prov. de 9 47 10N 72 25W
Poste-de-la-Baleine = Kuujjuarapik 4 55 17N 77 45W
Poulin-de-Courval, L. 9 48 52N 70 27W
Poutrincourt, L. 9 49 11N 74 7W
Povungnituk 4 60 2N 77 10W
Povungnituk → 4 60 3N 77 15W
Povungnituk, B. 4 60 0N 77 30W
Povungnituk, Mts. de 4 61 22N 75 5W
Powassan ... 10 46 5N 79 25W
Powell River 18 49 50N 124 35W
Preeceville .. 14 51 57N 102 40W
Preissac, L. .. 8 48 20N 78 20W
Prelate 14 50 51N 109 24W
Prescott 11 44 45N 75 30W
Price I. 18 52 23N 128 41W
Prince Albert 14 53 15N 105 50W
Prince Albert Nat. Park .. 14 54 0N 106 25W
Prince Albert Pen. 20 72 30N 116 0W
Prince Albert Sd. 20 70 25N 115 0W
Prince Charles I. 21 67 47N 76 12W
Prince Edward I. □ 7 46 20N 63 20W
Prince Edward Pt. 11 43 56N 76 52W
Prince George 19 53 55N 122 50W
Prince Gustav Adolf Sea . 20 78 30N 107 0W
Prince of Wales I. ... 21 73 0N 99 0W
Prince Patrick I. 20 77 0N 120 0W
Prince Rupert 18 54 20N 130 20W
Princess Royal I. 18 53 0N 128 40W
Princeton ... 19 49 27N 120 30W
Princeville .. 9 46 10N 71 53W
Principe Chan. 18 53 28N 130 0W
Providence Bay 10 45 41N 82 15W
Provost 17 52 25N 110 20W
Prud'homme 14 52 20N 105 54W

Q

Quaqtaq 4 60 55N 69 40W
Quatsino ... 18 50 30N 127 40W
Quatsino Sd. 18 50 25N 127 58W
Québec 9 46 52N 71 13W
Québec □ ... 3 48 0N 74 0W
Queen Charlotte .. 18 53 15N 132 2W
Queen Charlotte Is. 18 53 20N 132 10W
Queen Charlotte Str. 18 51 0N 128 0W
Queen Elizabeth Is. 21 76 0N 95 0W
Queen Maud G. 21 68 15N 102 30W
Quesnel 19 53 0N 122 30W
Quesnel → . 19 52 58N 122 29W
Quesnel L. .. 19 52 30N 121 20W
Quetico Prov. Park 12 48 30N 91 45W
Quévillon, L. 8 49 4N 76 57W
Quinze, L. des 8 47 35N 79 5W
Quyon 8 45 31N 76 14W

R

Rabbit Lake . 14 53 8N 107 46W
Race, C. 5 46 40N 53 5W
Radisson ... 14 52 30N 107 20W
Radium Hot Springs ... 17 50 35N 116 2W
Radville 14 49 30N 104 15W
Rae Isthmus . 21 66 40N 87 30W
Rainy L. 12 48 42N 93 10W
Rainy River . 12 48 43N 94 29W
Ramah 4 58 52N 63 15W
Ramah B. ... 4 58 52N 63 13W
Ramea 5 47 31N 57 23W
Ramore 8 48 30N 80 25W
Ramsey 13 47 25N 82 20W
Rankin Inlet . 21 62 30N 93 0W
Rapide-Blanc 9 47 48N 73 2W
Rapide-Sept . 8 47 46N 78 19W
Rapides des Joachims . 8 46 13N 77 43W
Rats, R. aux → ... 9 48 53N 72 14W
Rawdon 9 46 3N 73 40W
Ray, C. 5 47 33N 59 15W
Raymond ... 17 49 30N 112 35W
Raymore ... 14 51 25N 104 31W
Red → 15 49 0N 97 15W
Red Bay 4 51 44N 56 25W
Red Deer ... 17 52 20N 113 50W
Red Deer →, Alta., ... 17 50 58N 110 0W
Red Deer →, Man., ... 15 52 53N 101 1W
Red Deer L. . 15 52 55N 101 20W
Red Indian L. 5 48 35N 57 0W
Red Lake ... 12 51 3N 93 49W
Red Rock ... 12 48 55N 88 15W
Redcliff 17 50 10N 110 50W
Redvers 15 49 35N 101 40W
Redwater ... 16 53 55N 113 6W
Regina 14 50 27N 104 35W
Reindeer I. .. 15 52 30N 98 0W
Reliance ... 20 63 0N 109 20W
Rémigny 8 47 46N 79 12W
Renfrew 11 45 30N 76 40W
Rennell Sd. . 18 53 23N 132 35W
Repentigny . 9 45 44N 73 28W
Repulse Bay . 21 66 30N 86 30W
Reserve 14 52 28N 102 39W
Resolute ... 21 74 42N 94 54W
Resolution I. 21 61 30N 65 0W
Reston 15 49 33N 101 6W
Revelstoke . 19 51 0N 118 10W
Reynolds ... 15 49 40N 95 55W
Rhein 15 51 25N 102 15W
Rice L. 11 44 12N 78 10W
Rich, C. 10 44 43N 80 38W
Richibucto .. 7 46 42N 64 54W
Richmond, Ont., ... 11 45 11N 75 50W
Richmond, Qué., ... 9 45 40N 72 9W
Richmond Hill 10 43 52N 79 27W
Ridgedale ... 14 53 0N 104 10W
Ridgetown .. 10 42 26N 81 52W
Riding Mountain Nat. Park .. 15 50 50N 100 0W
Rigaud 9 45 29N 74 18W
Rigolet 4 54 10N 58 23W
Rimbey 17 52 35N 114 15W
Rimouski ... 9 48 27N 68 30W
Rimouski → 9 48 27N 68 32W
Rimouski, Parc Prov. de 9 48 0N 68 15W
Rimouski-Est 9 48 28N 68 31W
Ripley 10 44 4N 81 35W
Ripon 8 45 45N 75 10W
River Valley . 10 46 35N 80 11W
Riverhurst .. 14 50 55N 106 50W
Rivers 15 50 2N 100 14W
Rivers, L. of the 14 49 49N 105 44W
Rivers Inlet . 18 51 42N 127 15W
Riverton 15 51 1N 97 0W
Rivière-à-Pierre 9 46 59N 72 11W
Rivière-au-Renard ... 6 48 59N 64 23W
Rivière-aux-Rats 9 47 13N 72 53W
Rivière-Bersimis .. 9 48 56N 68 42W
Rivière-du-Loup 9 47 50N 69 30W
Rivière-Ouelle 9 47 26N 70 1W
Rivière-Pentecôte . 6 49 57N 67 1W
Rivière-Portneuf .. 9 48 38N 69 6W
Robertsonville 9 46 9N 71 13W
Roberval 9 48 32N 72 15W
Roblin 15 51 14N 101 21W
Robson, Mt. . 19 53 10N 119 10W
Rochebaucourt 8 48 41N 77 30W
Rochester ... 16 54 22N 113 27W
Rock Island .. 9 45 26N 73 54W
Rockglen ... 14 49 11N 105 57W
Rockland ... 8 45 33N 75 17W
Rockwood .. 10 43 37N 80 8W
Rocky Mountain House 17 52 22N 114 55W
Rockyford ... 17 51 14N 113 10W
Roddickton .. 5 50 51N 56 8W
Roderick I. .. 18 52 38N 128 22W
Rodney 10 42 34N 81 41W
Roes Welcome Sd. 21 65 0N 87 0W
Roger, L. 8 47 50N 78 59W
Roggan L. .. 4 54 8N 77 50W
Roggan River 4 54 25N 79 32W
Rohault, L. .. 9 49 23N 74 20W
Rollet 8 47 55N 79 15W
Romaine → . 4 50 18N 63 47W
Rondeau Prov. Park 10 42 19N 81 51W
Rorketon 15 51 24N 99 35W
Rose Blanche 5 47 38N 58 45W
Rose Harbour 18 52 15N 131 10W
Rose Pt. 18 54 11N 131 39W
Rose Valley . 14 52 19N 103 49W
Rosemary ... 17 50 46N 112 5W
Rosemère ... 9 45 38N 73 48W
Rosetown ... 14 51 35N 107 59W
Rossburn ... 15 50 40N 100 49W
Rosseau 10 45 16N 79 39W
Rosseau L. .. 10 45 10N 79 35W
Rossignol, L. 4 52 43N 73 40W
Rossignol Res. 7 44 12N 65 10W
Rossland ... 19 49 6N 117 50W
Rossmore ... 11 44 8N 77 23W
Rossport ... 13 48 50N 87 30W
Rosthern ... 14 52 40N 106 20W
Rothesay ... 7 45 23N 66 0W
Rouge → ... 8 45 17N 74 10W
Rouleau 14 50 10N 104 56W
Round L. ... 11 45 38N 77 30W
Rouvray, L. . 9 49 18N 70 49W
Rouyn 8 48 20N 79 0W
Roxton Falls . 9 45 34N 72 31W
Ruisseau-Vert 9 49 4N 68 28W
Rumsey 17 51 51N 112 48W
Rupert → ... 4 51 29N 78 45W
Rupert B. ... 4 51 35N 79 0W
Rupert House = Waskaganish 4 51 30N 78 40W
Rutter 10 46 6N 80 40W
Ryans B. 4 59 35N 64 3W

S

Sable, C. 7 43 29N 65 38W
Sable I. 3 44 0N 60 0W
Sables, R. aux → ... 10 46 13N 82 3W
Sabourin, L. . 8 47 58N 77 41W
Sacré-Coeur-de-Jésus .. 9 48 14N 69 48W
Saglek B. ... 4 58 30N 63 0W
Saglek Fd. .. 4 58 29N 63 15W
Saglouc = Salluit 4 62 14N 75 38W
Saguenay → 9 48 22N 71 0W
St-Adalbert . 9 46 51N 69 53W
St-Agapitville 9 46 34N 71 26W
St. Alban's .. 5 47 51N 55 50W
St. Albert ... 16 53 37N 113 32W
St-Alexandre 9 47 41N 69 38W
St-Alexis-des-Monts 9 46 28N 73 8W
St-Ambroise 9 48 33N 71 20W
St-Anaclet .. 9 48 29N 68 26W
St-André-Avellin ... 8 45 43N 75 3W
St-André-Est 9 45 34N 74 20W
St. Andrew's 5 47 45N 59 15W
St-Anicet ... 9 45 8N 74 22W
St. Ann B. .. 7 46 22N 60 25W
St-Anselme . 9 46 37N 70 58W
St. Anthony . 5 51 22N 55 35W
St-Antonin .. 9 47 46N 69 29W
St-Apolline .. 9 46 48N 70 12W
St. Arthur .. 7 47 33N 67 46W
St-Aubert ... 9 47 11N 70 13W
St-Augustin → 4 51 16N 58 40W
St-Augustin-Saguenay . 4 51 13N 58 38W
St-Barthélémy 9 46 11N 73 8W
St-Basile-Sud 9 46 45N 71 49W
St. Boniface . 15 49 53N 97 5W
St. Bride's ... 5 46 56N 54 10W
St-Bruno ... 9 48 28N 71 39W
St-Casimir .. 9 46 40N 72 8W
St. Catharines 10 43 10N 79 15W
St-Césaire .. 9 45 25N 73 0W
St-Chrysostôme 9 45 6N 73 46W
St. Clair, L. ... 10 42 30N 82 45W
St. Claude .. 15 49 40N 98 20W
St-Clet 9 45 21N 74 13W
St-Coeur de Marie 9 48 39N 71 43W
St-Côme 9 46 16N 73 47W
St-Cyrille-de-L'Islet 9 47 2N 70 17W
St. David's .. 5 48 12N 58 52W
St-Donat-de-Montcalm . 9 46 19N 74 13W
St. Elias Mts. 20 60 33N 139 28W
St-Éloi 9 48 2N 69 14W
St-Élouthère . 9 47 30N 69 15W
St-Éphrem-de-Tring 9 46 2N 70 59W
St. Eugène .. 8 45 30N 74 28W
St-Eusèbe ... 9 47 33N 68 55W
St-Eustache . 9 45 33N 73 54W
St-Fabien ... 9 48 18N 68 52W
St-Félicien .. 9 48 40N 72 25W
St-Félix-de-Valois 9 46 10N 73 26W
St-François .. 9 46 48N 70 49W
St-François → 9 46 7N 72 55W
St-François, L., Qué., .. 9 45 10N 74 22W
St-François, L., Qué., .. 9 45 10N 74 22W
St-François-du-Lac 9 46 5N 72 50W
St-Fulgence . 9 48 27N 70 54W
St-Gabriel-de-Brandon .. 9 46 17N 73 24W
St-Gabriel-de-Rimouski . 9 48 25N 68 10W
St-Gédéon ... 9 48 30N 71 46W
St-Gédéon-de-Beauce 9 45 45N 70 40W
St. George, N.B., ... 7 45 11N 66 50W
St. George, Ont., ... 10 43 15N 80 15W
St. George, C. 5 48 30N 59 16W
St. George's . 5 48 26N 58 31W
St-Georges .. 9 46 8N 70 40W
St. George's B. 5 48 24N 58 53W
St-Georges-de-Cacouna 9 47 55N 69 30W
St-Georges-Ouest 9 46 7N 70 40W
St-Gérard ... 9 45 46N 71 25W
St-Germain-de-Grantham . 9 45 50N 72 34W
St-Guillaume-d'Upton .. 9 45 53N 72 46W
St-Hilarion .. 9 47 34N 70 24W
St-Honoré .. 9 48 32N 71 5W
St-Hubert-de-Témiscouata 9 47 49N 69 9W
St-Hyacinthe 9 45 40N 72 58W
St. Ignace I. . 13 48 45N 88 0W
St-Isidore ... 9 45 20N 73 42W
St-Jacques .. 9 45 57N 73 34W
St-Jean 9 45 20N 73 20W
St-Jean → . 4 50 17N 64 20W
St-Jean, L. .. 9 48 40N 72 0W
St. Jean Baptiste .. 15 49 15N 97 20W
St-Jean-de-Dieu 9 48 0N 69 3W
St-Jean-Port-Joli 9 47 15N 70 13W
St-Jérôme, Qué., ... 9 48 26N 71 53W
St-Jérôme, Qué., ... 9 45 47N 74 0W
St-Joachim . 9 47 4N 70 50W
St. John 7 45 20N 66 8W
St. John, C. . 5 50 0N 55 32W
St. John's ... 5 47 35N 52 40W
St. Joseph, I. 10 46 12N 83 58W
St. Joseph, L. 12 51 10N 90 35W
St-Joseph-de-Beauce 9 46 18N 70 53W
St-Joseph-de-la-Rivière-Bleue 9 47 26N 69 3W
St-Joseph-de-Sorel 9 46 2N 73 7W
St-Jovite 8 46 8N 74 38W
St-Jude 9 45 46N 72 59W
St-Justine ... 9 46 24N 70 21W

St. Laurent .. 15 50 25N 97 58W
St. Lawrence 5 46 54N 55 23W
St. Lawrence → 3 49 30N 66 0W
St. Lawrence, Gulf of ... 3 48 25N 62 0W
St. Leonard 7 47 12N 67 58W
St-Léonard-de-Portneuf 9 46 53N 71 55W
St. Lewis → 4 52 26N 56 11W
St-Louis, Mts 4 46 13N 73 36W
St-Luc 9 45 22N 73 18W
St-Ludger ... 9 45 45N 70 42W
St. Lunaire-Griquet ... 5 51 31N 55 28W
St-Magloire . 9 46 35N 70 17W
St. Martin, L. 15 51 40N 98 30W
St. Martins .. 7 45 22N 65 34W
St. Marys ... 10 43 20N 81 10W
St. Mary's, C. 5 46 50N 54 12W
St. Marys Bay 7 44 25N 66 10W
St-Maurice → 9 46 21N 72 31W
St-Maurice, Parc Prov. du 9 47 5N 73 15W
St-Michel-des-Saints 9 46 41N 73 55W
St-Nazaire .. 9 45 44N 72 37W
St-Omer 9 47 3N 69 43W
St-Ours 9 45 53N 73 9W
St-Pacome .. 9 47 24N 69 58W
St-Pamphile . 9 46 58N 69 48W
St. Pascal ... 9 47 32N 69 48W
St-Patrice, L. 8 46 22N 77 20W
St. Paul 16 54 0N 111 17W
St-Paul → . 4 51 27N 57 42W
St-Paul-de-Montmigny 9 46 44N 70 22W
St-Paul-du-Nord 9 48 34N 69 14W
St. Paul I. ... 7 47 12N 60 9W
St-Paulin ... 9 46 25N 73 1W
St. Peters, N.S., ... 7 45 40N 60 53W
St. Peters, P.E.I., ... 7 46 25N 62 35W
St-Philemon . 9 46 41N 70 27W
St-Pie 9 45 30N 72 54W
St.-Pierre ... 5 46 46N 56 12W
St-Pierre, L., Qué., ... 9 50 8N 68 26W
St-Pierre, L., Qué., ... 9 46 12N 72 52W
St.-Pierre et Miquelon □ 5 46 55N 56 10W
St-Prime 9 48 35N 72 20W
St-Raphaël .. 9 46 48N 70 45W
St-Raymond . 9 46 54N 71 50W
St-Rémi 9 45 16N 73 37W
St-Roch 9 47 18N 70 12W
St-Romuald . 9 46 46N 71 20W
St-Sébastien 9 45 47N 70 58W
St-Siméon .. 9 47 51N 69 54W
St-Simon-de-Rimouski . 9 48 12N 69 3W
St. Stephen . 7 45 16N 67 17W
St. Thomas . 10 42 45N 81 10W
St-Tite 9 46 45N 72 34W
St-Tite-des-Caps 9 47 8N 70 47W
St-Urbain ... 9 47 33N 70 32W
Ste-Adèle ... 9 45 57N 74 7W
Ste-Agathe . 9 46 23N 71 25W
Ste-Agathe-des-Monts 9 46 3N 74 17W
Ste-Anne de Beaupré .. 9 47 2N 70 58W
Ste-Anne-des-Monts 6 49 8N 66 30W
Ste-Anne-du-Lac 8 46 48N 75 25W
Ste-Blandine 9 48 22N 68 28W
Ste-Claire ... 9 46 36N 70 51W
Ste-Croix ... 9 46 38N 71 44W
Ste-Famille .. 9 46 58N 70 58W
Ste-Foy 9 46 47N 71 17W
Ste-Françoise 9 48 6N 69 4W
Ste-Marguerite → 4 50 9N 66 36W
Ste-Marie de la Madeleine 9 46 26N 71 0W
Ste-Monique 9 48 44N 71 51W
Ste-Pudentienne 9 45 28N 72 40W
Ste. Rose du Lac 15 51 4N 99 30W
Ste-Sabine .. 9 45 15N 73 2W
Ste-Thècle .. 9 46 49N 72 31W
Sairs, L. 8 46 49N 78 26W
Sakami, L. .. 4 53 15N 77 0W
Salaberry-de-Valleyfield 9 45 15N 74 8W
Salluit 4 62 14N 75 38W
Salmo 19 49 10N 117 20W
Salmon Arm 19 50 40N 119 15W
Salmon Res. 5 48 5N 56 0W
Salvador 14 52 10N 109 32W
Sandspit 18 53 14N 131 49W
Sandwich B. 4 53 40N 57 15W
Sandy → .. 4 55 30N 68 21W
Sandy L. 2 53 2N 93 0W
Sangudo 16 53 50N 114 54W
Sanmaur 9 47 54N 73 47W
Sarnia 10 42 58N 82 23W
Saseginaga, L. 8 47 6N 78 35W
Saskatchewan → 15 53 37N 100 40W
Saskatoon .. 14 52 10N 106 38W
Saugeen → 10 44 30N 81 22W
Sault-au-Moulton .. 9 48 33N 69 15W
Sault aux Cochons → 9 48 44N 69 4W
Sault Ste. Marie 10 46 30N 84 20W
Sauvage, L. . 8 50 6N 74 30W
Savant L. ... 12 50 16N 90 44W
Savant Lake . 12 50 14N 90 40W
Sawyerville . 9 45 20N 71 34W
Sayabec 6 48 35N 67 41W
Scandia 17 50 20N 112 0W
Schefferville . 4 54 48N 66 50W
Schreiber 13 48 45N 87 20W
Schuler 17 50 20N 110 6W
Schumacher 13 48 30N 81 16W
Scotland 10 43 1N 80 22W
Scotstown ... 9 45 32N 71 17W
Scott Inlet .. 21 71 0N 71 0W
Scott Is. 18 50 48N 128 40W
Scott-Jonction 9 46 30N 71 4W
Scugog, L. .. 11 44 10N 78 55W
Seaforth 10 43 35N 81 25W
Seal Cove ... 5 49 57N 56 22W
Seal L. 4 54 20N 61 30W
Sebringville . 10 43 24N 81 4W
Sechelt 18 49 25N 123 42W
Sedgewick .. 17 52 48N 111 41W
Sedley 14 50 10N 104 0W
Seeley's Bay 11 44 29N 76 14W
Selkirk, Man., 15 50 10N 96 55W
Selkirk, Ont., 10 42 49N 79 56W
Selkirk I. 15 53 20N 99 6W
Senneterre . 8 48 25N 77 15W
Separation Point 4 53 37N 57 25W
Sept-Îles 4 50 13N 66 22W
Sérigny → . 4 56 47N 66 0W
Seven Islands B. 4 59 25N 63 45W
Severn → .. 2 56 2N 87 36W
Sexsmith ... 16 55 21N 118 47W
Shabogamo L. 4 53 15N 66 30W
Shallow Lake 10 44 36N 81 5W
Sharbot Lake 11 44 46N 76 41W
Shaunavon . 14 49 35N 108 25W
Shawanaga . 10 45 31N 80 17W
Shawinigan . 9 46 35N 72 50W
Shawinigan Sud 9 46 31N 72 45W
Shawville ... 8 45 36N 76 30W
Shediac 7 46 14N 64 32W
Sheet Harbour 7 44 56N 62 31W
Sheguiandah 10 45 54N 81 55W
Sheho 14 51 35N 103 13W
Shelburne, N.S., ... 7 43 47N 65 20W
Shelburne, Ont., ... 10 44 4N 80 15W
Sheldrake ... 4 50 20N 64 51W
Shell Lake .. 14 53 19N 107 2W
Shellbrook .. 14 53 13N 106 24W
Sherbrooke . 9 45 28N 71 57W
Shickshock Mts. = Chic-Chocs, Mts. 6 48 55N 66 0W
Shippegan .. 7 47 45N 64 45W
Shoal Lake .. 15 50 30N 100 35W
Shuswap L. . 19 50 55N 119 3W
Sicamous ... 19 50 49N 119 0W
Sidney 19 48 39N 123 24W
Sifton 15 51 21N 100 8W
Silver Water . 10 45 52N 82 52W
Simard, L. .. 8 47 40N 78 40W
Simcoe 10 42 50N 80 20W
Simcoe, L. .. 10 44 25N 79 20W
Simmie 14 49 56N 108 6W
Simonette → 16 55 9N 118 15W
Sioux Lookout 12 50 10N 91 50W
Skeena → .. 18 54 9N 130 5W
Skownan ... 15 51 58N 99 35W
Slate Is. 13 48 40N 87 0W
Slave Lake .. 16 55 17N 114 43W
Sleeper Is. .. 3 58 30N 81 0W
Slocan 19 49 48N 117 28W
Smeaton 14 53 30N 104 49W
Smiley 14 51 38N 109 29W
Smith 16 55 10N 114 0W
Smith Arm .. 20 66 15N 123 0W
Smith I. 4 54 13N 58 18W
Smiths Falls . 11 44 55N 76 0W
Smithville ... 10 43 6N 79 33W
Smoky → .. 16 56 10N 117 21W
Smoky Falls . 13 50 4N 82 10W
Smoky Lake . 16 54 10N 112 30W
Smooth Rock Falls 13 49 17N 81 37W
Snowdrift = Lutselke .. 20 62 24N 110 44W
Sombra 10 42 43N 82 29W
Somerset 15 49 25N 98 39W
Somerset I. . 21 73 30N 93 0W
Sop's Arm .. 5 49 46N 56 56W
Sorel 9 46 0N 73 10W
Soscumica, L. 4 50 15N 77 27W
Soucy 8 48 10N 75 30W
Souris 7 46 21N 62 15W
Souris → .. 15 49 40N 99 34W
South Aulatsivik I. 4 56 45N 61 30W
South Baymouth . 10 45 33N 82 1W
South Branch 5 47 55N 59 2W
South Brook 5 49 26N 56 5W
South Nahanni → 20 61 3N 123 21W
South Nation → 11 45 34N 75 6W
South Porcupine 8 48 30N 81 12W
South River 10 45 52N 79 23W
South Saskatchewan → 14 53 15N 105 5W
South Thompson → 19 50 40N 120 20W
South Twin I. 4 53 7N 79 52W
Southampton 10 44 30N 81 25W
Southampton I. 21 64 30N 84 0W
Spaniard's Bay 5 47 38N 53 20W
Spanish 10 46 12N 82 20W
Spanish → . 10 46 11N 82 19W
Speers 14 52 43N 107 34W
Spence Bay = Taloyoak .. 21 69 32N 93 32W
Spencerville . 11 44 51N 75 33W
Spences Bridge 19 50 25N 121 20W
Spirit River .. 16 55 45N 118 50W
Spiritwood .. 14 53 24N 107 33W
Spragge 10 46 15N 82 40W
Springdale .. 5 49 30N 56 6W
Springfield .. 10 42 50N 80 56W
Springhill ... 7 45 40N 64 4W
Springhouse 19 51 56N 122 7W
Springwater . 14 51 58N 108 23W
Sprucedale . 10 45 29N 79 28W
Spuzzum .. 19 49 37N 121 23W
Squamish .. 19 49 45N 123 10W
Square Islands 4 52 47N 55 47W
Squatec 9 47 53N 68 43W
Stanley 7 46 20N 66 44W
Star City 14 52 50N 104 20W
Stayner 10 44 25N 80 5W
Steep Rock .. 15 51 30N 98 48W
Steinbach ... 15 49 32N 96 40W
Stellarton ... 7 45 32N 62 30W
Stephens I. .. 18 54 10N 130 45W
Stephenville . 5 48 31N 58 35W
Stettler 17 52 19N 112 40W
Stevenson L. 15 53 55N 96 0W
Stewart River 20 63 19N 139 26W
Stewiacke ... 7 45 9N 63 22W
Stirling, Alta., 17 49 30N 112 30W
Stirling, Ont., 11 44 18N 77 33W
Stittsville ... 8 45 15N 75 55W
Stokes Bay .. 10 45 0N 81 28W
Stoneham ... 9 47 0N 71 22W
Stonewall ... 15 50 10N 97 19W
Stoney Creek 10 43 14N 79 45W
Stony L. 11 44 30N 78 5W
Stouffville ... 10 43 58N 79 15W
Stoughton ... 14 49 40N 103 0W
Strasbourg .. 14 51 4N 104 55W
Stratford ... 10 43 23N 81 0W
Strathcona Prov. Park . 18 49 38N 125 40W
Strathmore . 17 51 5N 113 18W
Strathnaver . 19 53 20N 122 33W
Strathroy ... 10 42 58N 81 38W
Streetsville .. 10 43 35N 79 42W
Stroud 10 44 19N 79 37W
Struthers ... 13 48 41N 85 51W
Sturgeon → . 10 46 35N 80 11W
Sturgeon B. . 15 52 0N 97 50W
Sturgeon Falls 10 46 25N 79 57W
Sturgeon L., Alta., ... 16 55 6N 117 32W
Sturgeon L., Ont., ... 11 44 28N 78 43W
Sturgeon L., Ont., ... 12 50 0N 90 45W
Success 14 50 28N 108 6W
Sud, Pte. ... 6 49 3N 62 14W
Sud-Ouest, Pte. du 6 49 23N 63 36W
Sudbury 10 46 30N 81 0W
Suffield 17 50 12N 111 10W
Sugluk = Salluit 4 62 14N 75 38W
Sullivan 8 48 7N 77 50W
Sullivan Bay 18 50 55N 126 50W
Sultan 13 47 36N 82 47W
Summerland 19 49 32N 119 41W
Summerside 7 46 24N 63 47W
Sunderland . 11 44 16N 79 4W
Sundre 17 51 49N 114 38W
Sundridge .. 10 45 45N 79 25W
Superior, L. . 13 47 0N 87 0W
Surprise, L. . 8 49 20N 74 55W
Sussex 7 45 45N 65 37W
Sutton, Ont., 10 44 18N 79 22W
Sutton, Qué., 9 45 6N 72 37W
Sverdrup Chan. 21 79 56N 96 25W
Sverdrup Is. . 21 79 0N 97 0W
Swan Hills .. 16 54 42N 115 24W
Swan L. 15 52 30N 100 40W
Swan River . 15 52 10N 101 16W
Swastika ... 8 48 7N 80 6W
Swift Current 14 50 20N 107 45W
Swiftcurrent → 14 50 38N 107 44W
Swindle, I. .. 18 52 30N 128 35W
Sydenham → 10 42 33N 82 25W
Sydney 7 46 7N 60 7W
Sydney Mines 7 46 18N 60 15W
Sylvan Lake . 17 52 20N 114 3W

T

Taber 17 49 47N 112 8W
Table B. 4 53 40N 56 25W
Tadoussac .. 9 48 11N 69 42W
Taloyoak ... 21 69 32N 93 32W
Tamworth ... 11 44 29N 77 0W
Tara 10 44 28N 81 9W
Taschereau . 8 48 40N 78 40W
Taseko → .. 18 52 8N 123 45W
Tassialuk, L. . 4 59 3N 74 0W
Tasu Sd. 18 52 47N 132 2W
Tavistock ... 10 43 19N 80 50W
Tecumseh ... 10 42 19N 82 54W
Tee Lake ... 8 46 40N 79 0W
Teeswater ... 10 43 59N 81 17W
Temiscamie → 4 50 59N 73 5W
Témiscaming 8 46 44N 79 5W
Témiscamingue, L. 8 47 10N 79 25W
Terrace Bay . 13 48 47N 87 5W
Terrebonne . 9 45 42N 73 38W
Terrenceville 5 47 40N 54 44W
Teslin 20 60 10N 132 43W
Tetachuck L. 18 53 18N 125 55W
Teulon 15 50 23N 97 16W
Texada I. 18 49 40N 124 25W
Thames → . 10 42 20N 82 25W
Thamesford . 10 43 4N 81 0W
Thamesville . 10 42 33N 81 59W
The Pas 15 53 45N 101 15W
Thedford 10 43 9N 81 51W
Thessalon ... 10 46 20N 83 30W
Thetford Mines 9 46 8N 71 18W
Thlewiaza → 21 60 29N 94 40W
Thompson → 19 50 15N 121 24W
Thornbury ... 10 44 34N 80 26W
Thorold 10 43 7N 79 12W
Three Hills .. 17 51 43N 113 15W
Thunder Bay 12 48 20N 89 15W
Thurso 8 45 36N 75 15W
Tignish 7 46 58N 64 2W
Tilbury 10 42 17N 82 23W
Tillsonburg . 10 42 53N 80 44W
Timagami L. 8 47 0N 80 10W
Timmins 8 48 28N 81 25W
Tisdale 14 52 50N 104 0W
Tiverton 10 44 16N 81 32W
Tlell 18 53 34N 131 56W
Tobermory .. 10 45 12N 81 40W
Tobin L. 14 53 35N 103 30W
Tofield 16 53 25N 112 40W
Tofino 18 49 11N 125 55W
Tomiko L. ... 10 46 32N 79 49W
Torbay 5 47 40N 52 42W
Torngat Mts. 4 59 0N 63 40W
Toronto 10 43 39N 79 20W
Torquay 14 49 9N 103 30W
Tottenham .. 10 44 1N 79 49W
Tracadie 7 47 30N 64 55W
Tracy 9 46 1N 73 9W
Trail 19 49 5N 117 40W
Transcona .. 15 49 55N 97 0W
Treherne ... 15 49 38N 98 42W
Tremblant, Mt. 8 46 16N 74 35W
Trenche → . 9 47 46N 72 53W
Trent → .. 11 44 6N 77 34W
Trente et un Milles, L. des 8 46 12N 75 49W
Trenton 11 44 10N 77 34W
Trepassey .. 5 46 43N 53 25W
Trêve, L. la .. 8 49 56N 75 30W
Tring-Jonction 9 46 16N 70 59W
Trinity 5 48 59N 53 55W
Trinity B. ... 5 48 20N 53 10W
Trochu 17 51 50N 113 13W
Trodely I. ... 4 52 15N 79 26W
Troilus, L. .. 4 50 50N 74 35W
Trois-Pistoles 9 48 5N 69 10W
Trois-Rivières 9 46 25N 72 34W
Trout Creek . 10 45 59N 79 22W
Trout L., N.W.T., ... 20 60 40N 121 14W
Trout L., Ont., 12 51 20N 93 15W
Trout River .. 5 49 29N 58 8W
Truite, L. à la 8 47 20N 78 20W
Truro 7 45 21N 63 14W
Tsiigehtchic . 20 67 15N 134 0W
Tudor, L. 4 55 50N 65 25W
Tukarak I. ... 4 56 15N 78 45W
Tuktoyaktuk . 20 69 27N 133 2W
Tulita 20 64 57N 125 30W
Tunulic → . 4 58 57N 66 50W
Tunungayualok I. 4 56 0N 61 0W
Turgeon → 8 50 0N 78 56W
Turgeon, L. . 8 49 2N 79 4W
Turin 17 49 58N 112 31W
Turner Valley 17 50 40N 114 17W
Turtle L. 14 53 36N 108 38W
Turtleford .. 14 53 23N 108 57W
Tweed 11 44 29N 77 19W
Tweedsmuir Prov. Park 18 53 0N 126 20W
Twillingate . 5 49 42N 54 45W
Two Hills ... 16 53 43N 111 52W

U

Uchi Lake ... 12 51 5N 92 35W
Ucluelet 18 48 57N 125 32W
Uivuk, C. 4 58 29N 62 34W
Ungava B. ... 4 59 30N 67 30W
Ungava Pen. 4 60 0N 74 0W
Unity 14 52 30N 109 5W
Upper Arrow L. 19 50 30N 117 50W
Upper Musquodoboit 7 45 10N 62 58W
Upton 9 45 39N 72 41W
Utikuma L. .. 16 55 50N 115 30W
Uxbridge ... 10 44 6N 79 7W

V

Val-Alain ... 9 46 24N 71 45W
Val-Barrette . 8 46 30N 75 21W
Val Caron ... 10 46 37N 81 1W
Val-des-Bois . 8 45 54N 75 35W
Val d'Or 8 48 7N 77 47W
Val Marie ... 14 49 15N 107 45W
Valcourt 9 45 29N 72 18W
Vallée-Jonction .. 9 46 22N 70 55W
Valleyview .. 16 55 5N 117 17W
Van Bruyssel 9 47 56N 72 9W
Van Buren .. 7 47 10N 67 55W
Vancouver .. 19 49 15N 123 10W
Vancouver I. 18 49 50N 126 0W
Vanderhoof . 18 54 0N 124 0W
Vandry 9 47 52N 73 34W
Vanguard ... 14 49 55N 107 20W
Vanier 11 45 27N 75 40W
Vankleek Hill 11 45 32N 74 40W
Vars 8 45 21N 75 21W
Vassar 15 49 10N 95 55W
Vauxhall 17 50 5N 112 9W
Vegreville ... 16 53 30N 112 5W
Venosta 8 45 52N 76 1W
Verchères ... 9 45 47N 73 21W
Vérendrye, Parc Prov. de la 8 47 20N 76 40W
Verlo 14 50 19N 108 35W
Vermeulle, L. 4 54 43N 69 24W
Vermilion ... 16 53 20N 110 50W
Vermilion →, Alta., ... 16 53 22N 110 51W
Vermilion →, Qué., ... 9 47 38N 72 56W
Vermilion Bay 12 49 51N 93 34W
Verner 10 46 25N 80 8W
Vernon 19 50 20N 119 15W
Verona 11 44 29N 76 42W
Verte, I. 9 48 2N 69 26W
Vibank 14 50 20N 103 56W
Victoria 19 48 30N 123 25W
Victoria, Grand L. .. 8 47 31N 77 30W
Victoria Beach 15 50 40N 96 35W
Victoria Harbour .. 10 44 45N 79 45W
Victoria I. .. 20 71 0N 111 0W
Victoria Res. 5 48 20N 57 27W
Victoriaville . 9 46 4N 71 56W
Vienna 10 42 41N 80 48W
Viking 17 53 7N 111 50W
Ville-Marie .. 8 47 20N 79 30W
Villebon, L. .. 8 47 58N 77 17W
Villemontel . 8 48 38N 78 22W
Vilna 16 54 7N 111 55W
Virago Sd. .. 18 54 0N 132 30W
Virden 15 49 50N 100 56W
Virginiatown 8 48 9N 79 36W
Viscount Melville Sd. 20 74 10N 108 0W
Voisey B. ... 4 56 15N 61 50W
Vulcan 17 50 25N 113 15W

W

Wabakimi L. . 12 50 38N 89 45W
Wabano → . 9 48 20N 74 3W
Wabasca ... 16 55 57N 113 56W
Wabigoon L. 12 49 44N 92 44W
Wabush 4 52 55N 66 52W
Waco 4 51 27N 65 37W
Waconichi, L. 9 50 8N 74 0W
Waddington, Mt. 18 51 23N 125 15W
Wadena 14 51 57N 103 47W
Wadhams ... 18 51 30N 127 30W
Wager B. ... 21 65 26N 88 40W
Wager Bay .. 21 65 56N 90 49W
Wainwright . 17 52 50N 110 50W
Wakaw 14 52 39N 105 44W
Wakefield ... 8 45 38N 75 56W
Wakeham Bay = Kangiqsujuaq 4 61 30N 72 0W
Wakomata L. 10 46 34N 83 22W
Wakuach L. . 4 55 34N 67 32W
Wales I. 4 62 0N 72 30W
Walker L. ... 4 50 20N 67 11W
Walkerton .. 10 44 10N 81 10W
Wallaceburg 10 42 34N 82 23W
Waltham Station ... 8 45 57N 76 57W
Wanapitei → 10 46 2N 80 51W
Wanapitei L. 10 46 45N 80 40W
Wanless 15 54 11N 101 21W
Wardlow ... 17 50 56N 111 31W
Warman 14 52 19N 106 30W
Warner 17 49 17N 112 12W
Warren 10 46 27N 80 18W
Wasaga Beach 10 44 31N 80 1W
Washago ... 10 44 45N 79 20W
Waskaganish 4 51 30N 78 40W
Waskesiu Lake 14 53 55N 106 5W
Waswanipi .. 4 49 40N 76 29W
Waswanipi → 4 49 40N 76 25W
Waswanipi, L. 8 49 35N 76 40W
Waterdown .. 10 43 20N 79 53W
Waterford ... 10 42 56N 80 17W
Waterhen L. . 15 52 10N 99 40W
Waterloo, Ont., ... 10 43 30N 80 32W
Waterloo, Qué., ... 9 45 22N 72 32W
Waterville ... 9 45 16N 71 54W
Watford 10 42 57N 81 53W
Watrous 14 51 40N 105 25W
Watson 14 52 10N 104 30W
Watson Lake 20 60 6N 128 49W
Waubamik .. 10 45 27N 80 1W
Waubaushene 10 44 45N 79 42W
Waugh 15 49 40N 95 11W
Wawa 13 47 59N 84 47W
Wawagosic → 8 49 58N 79 6W
Wawanesa .. 15 49 36N 99 40W
Wayagamac, L. 9 47 21N 72 39W
Webbwood .. 10 46 16N 81 52W
Wedgeport .. 7 43 44N 65 59W
Weedon-Centre 9 45 42N 71 27W
Welland 10 43 0N 79 15W
Wellington .. 11 43 57N 77 20W
Wellington Chan. 21 75 0N 93 0W
Wells Gray Prov. Park . 19 52 30N 120 15W
Wemindji ... 4 53 0N 78 49W
Weslemkoon L. 11 45 2N 77 25W
Wesleyville . 5 49 8N 53 36W
West Lorne . 10 42 36N 81 36W
West Magpie → 4 52 0N 65 0W
West Pt. = Ouest, Pte. 6 49 52N 64 40W
West Road → . 19 53 18N 122 53W
Western Duck I. 10 45 45N 83 0W
Westlock ... 16 54 9N 113 55W
Weston I. ... 4 52 33N 79 36W
Westport ... 11 44 40N 76 25W
Westray 15 53 36N 101 24W
Westree 13 47 26N 81 34W
Wetaskiwin . 17 52 55N 113 24W
Weyburn ... 14 49 40N 103 50W
Weymouth .. 7 44 30N 66 1W
Wha Ti 20 63 0N 118 0W
Whale → .. 4 58 15N 67 40W
Whale Cove . 21 62 11N 92 36W
Wheatley ... 10 42 6N 82 27W
Wheeler → . 4 57 2N 67 13W
Whiskey Gap 17 49 0N 113 3W
Whitby 11 43 52N 78 56W
White B. 5 50 0N 56 35W
White Bear Res. 5 48 10N 57 5W
White L. 8 45 18N 76 31W
White Otter L. 12 49 5N 91 55W
White River . 13 48 35N 85 20W
Whitecourt .. 16 54 10N 115 45W
Whitefish ... 10 46 23N 81 19W
Whitefish Falls 10 46 7N 81 44W
Whitegull, L. . 4 55 27N 64 17W
Whitehorse . 20 60 43N 135 3W
Whitemouth . 15 49 57N 95 58W
Whiteshell Prov. Park . 15 50 0N 95 40W
Whitewater L. 12 50 50N 89 10W
Whitewood .. 15 50 20N 102 20W
Whitney 8 45 31N 78 14W
Wholdaia L. . 20 60 43N 104 20W
Wiarton 10 44 40N 81 10W
Wicked Pt. .. 11 43 52N 77 15W
Wickham ... 9 45 45N 72 30W
Wikwemikong 10 45 48N 81 43W
Wilberforce . 8 45 2N 78 13W
Wilkie 14 52 27N 108 42W
Williams Lake 19 52 10N 122 10W
Willow Bunch 14 49 20N 105 35W
Winchester .. 11 45 6N 75 21W
Windfall 16 54 12N 116 13W
Windigo → 9 47 46N 73 19W
Windsor, N.S., 7 44 59N 64 5W
Windsor, Nfld., ... 5 48 57N 55 40W
Windsor, Ont., 10 42 18N 83 0W
Windsor, Qué., ... 9 45 34N 72 0W
Winefred L. . 16 55 30N 110 30W
Wingham ... 10 43 55N 81 20W
Winisk → .. 3 55 17N 85 5W
Winkler 15 49 10N 97 56W
Winnipeg ... 15 49 54N 97 9W
Winnipeg → 15 50 38N 96 19W
Winnipeg, L. 15 52 0N 97 0W
Winnipeg Beach 15 50 30N 96 58W
Winnipegosis 15 51 39N 99 55W
Winnipegosis L. 15 52 30N 100 0W
Winokapau, L. 4 53 15N 62 50W
Wolfe I. 11 44 7N 76 20W
Wollaston Pen. 20 69 30N 115 0W
Wolseley ... 14 50 25N 103 15W
Wolstenholme, C. 4 62 35N 77 30W
Woodbridge . 10 43 47N 79 36W
Woodpecker 19 53 30N 122 40W
Woodridge .. 15 49 20N 96 9W
Woods, L. ... 4 54 30N 65 13W
Woods, L. of the 12 49 15N 94 45W
Woodstock, N.B., ... 7 46 11N 67 37W
Woodstock, Ont., ... 10 43 10N 80 45W
Wottonville . 9 45 44N 71 48W
Wright 19 51 52N 121 40W
Wrigley 20 63 16N 123 37W
Wynyard 14 51 45N 104 10W
Wyoming ... 10 42 57N 82 7W

Y

Yahk 17 49 6N 116 10W
Yamaska ... 9 46 0N 72 55W
Yarker 11 44 23N 76 46W
Yarmouth ... 7 43 50N 66 7W
Yasinski, L. . 4 53 16N 77 35W
Yathkyed L. . 21 62 40N 98 0W
Yellowhead Pass 19 52 53N 118 25W
Yellowknife . 20 62 27N 114 29W
Yellowknife → 20 62 31N 114 19W
Yoho Nat. Park 19 51 25N 116 30W
Yorkton 15 51 11N 102 28W
Youbou 18 48 53N 124 13W
Young 14 51 47N 105 45W
Youngstown 17 51 35N 111 10W
Yukon Territory □ 20 63 0N 135 0W

Z

Zeballos 18 49 59N 126 50W
Zurich 10 43 26N 81 37W

WORLD MAPS

MAP SYMBOLS

SETTLEMENTS

PARIS Berne Livorno Brugge *Algeciras* *Fréjus* *Oberammergau* *Thira*

Settlement symbols and type styles vary according to the scale of each map and indicate the importance of towns on the map rather than specific population figures

∴ Ruins or Archæological Sites

Wells in Desert

ADMINISTRATION

International Boundaries

International Boundaries (Undefined or Disputed)

Internal Boundaries

National Parks

Country Names

NICARAGUA

Administrative Area Names

KENT

CALABRIA

International boundaries show the *de facto* situation where there are rival claims to territory

COMMUNICATIONS

Principal Roads

Other Roads

Trails and Seasonal Roads

Passes

Airfields

Principal Railways

Railways Under Construction

Other Railways

Railway Tunnels

Principal Canals

PHYSICAL FEATURES

Perennial Streams

Intermittent Streams

Perennial Lakes

Intermittent Lakes

Swamps and Marshes

Permanent Ice and Glaciers

8848 Elevations in metres

8050 Sea Depths in metres

1134 Height of Lake Surface Above Sea Level in metres

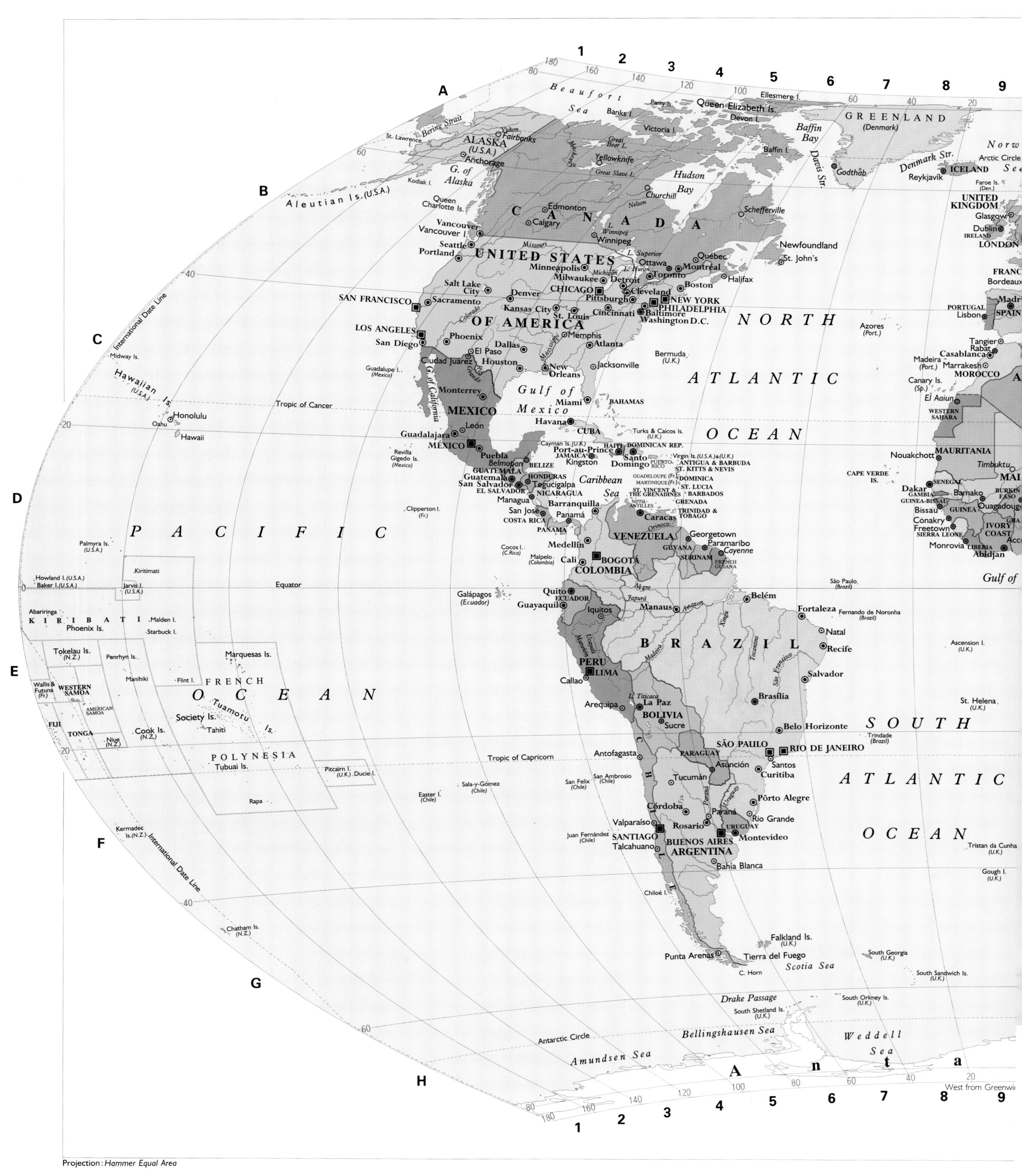

Projection: *Hammer Equal Area*

Hanoi ● Capital Cities

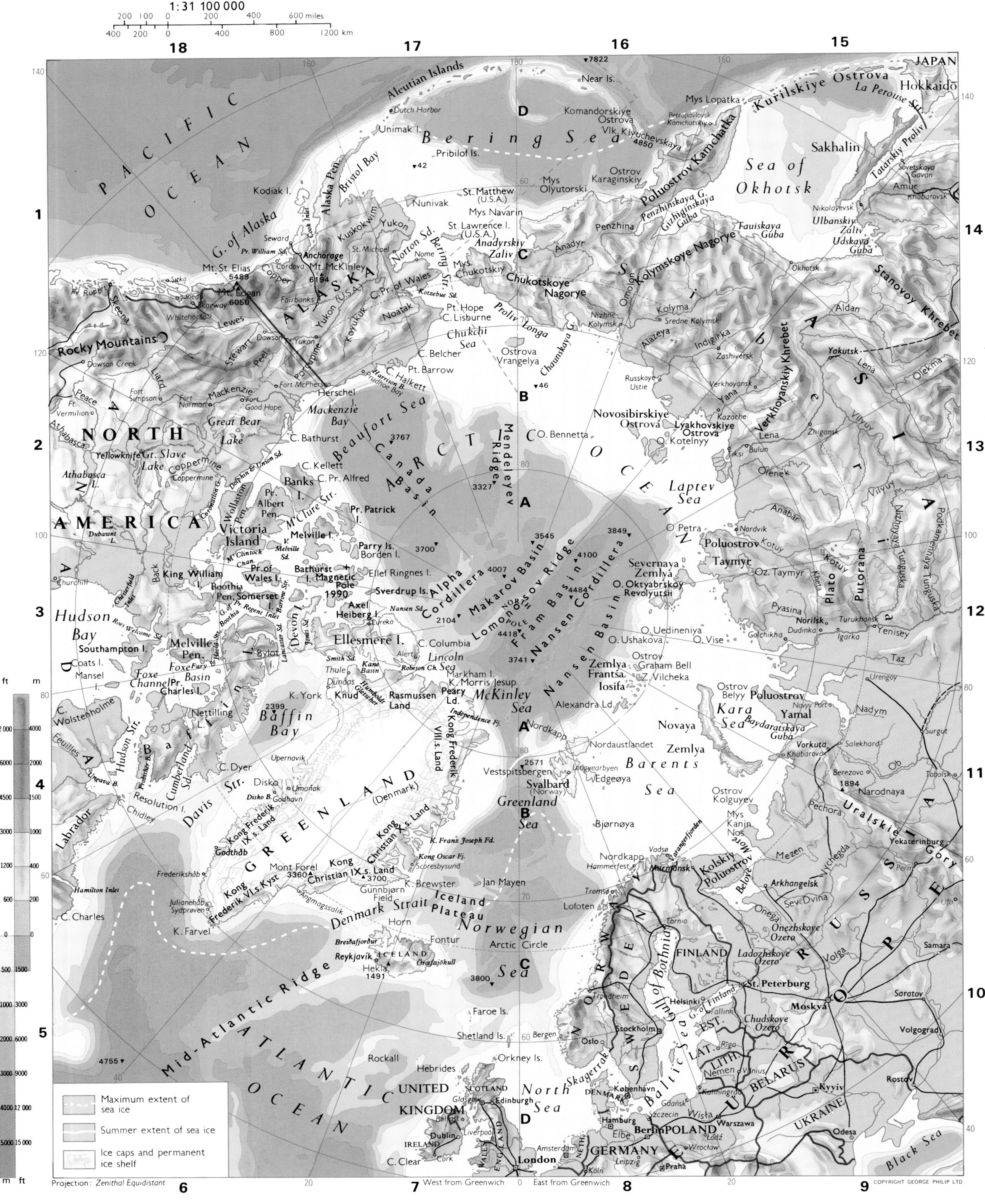
1:31 100 000
600 miles
1200 km
PACIFIC OCEAN
Aleutian Islands
Bering Sea
Sea of Okhotsk
Kurilskiye Ostrova
JAPAN
Hokkaido
La Perouse Str.
Sakhalin
Tatarskiy Proliv
Poluostrov Kamchatka
Mys Lopatka
Komandorskiye Ostrova
Vlk. Klyuchevskaya 4850
Near Is.
Dutch Harbor
Unimak I.
Pribilof Is.
Kodiak I.
Alaska Pen.
Bristol Bay
G. of Alaska
Nunivak
St. Matthew (U.S.A.)
Mys Navarin
Mys Olyutorski
Ostrov Karaginskiy
St Lawrence I. (U.S.A.)
Anadyrskiy Zaliv
Anadyr
Penzhina
Kuskokwim
Yukon
Norton Sd.
Bering Str.
Nome
Anchorage
Mt. McKinley 6194
Mt. St. Elias 5489
Mt. Logan 6050
ALASKA
Fairbanks
C. Pr. of Wales
Kotzebue Sd.
Chukotskoye Nagorye
Proliv Longa
Pt. Hope
C. Lisburne
Chukchi Sea
Ostrova Vrangelya
C. Belcher
Pt. Barrow
Rocky Mountains
Mackenzie
Great Bear Lake
Gt. Slave Lake
Yellowknife
Athabasca L.
NORTH AMERICA
Beaufort Sea
Canada Basin
Banks I.
Victoria Island
Melville I.
Pr. Patrick I.
Parry Is.
King William I.
Boothia Pen.
Somerset I.
Bathurst I.
Magnetic Pole 1990
Ellef Ringnes I.
Sverdrup Is.
Axel Heiberg I.
Devon I.
Ellesmere I.
Alpha Cordillera
Makarov Basin
Lomonosov Ridge
NORTH POLE
Fram Basin
Nansen Cordillera
Nansen Basin
Mendeleyev Ridge
ARCTIC OCEAN
Hudson Bay
Southampton I.
Melville Pen.
Foxe Basin
Foxe Channel
Baffin Bay
Baffin I.
Hudson Str.
Davis Str.
Labrador
C. Chidley
Resolution I.
GREENLAND (Denmark)
Godthåb
Frederikshåb
Julianehåb
K. Farvel
Denmark Strait
Iceland Plateau
Reykjavík
ICELAND
Hekla 1491
Jan Mayen
Norwegian Sea
Greenland Sea
Arctic Circle
Svalbard (Norway)
Vestspitsbergen
Nordaustlandet
Barents Sea
Zemlya Frantsa Iosifa
Novaya Zemlya
Kara Sea
Severnaya Zemlya
Laptev Sea
Novosibirskiye Ostrova
Poluostrov Taymyr
Poluostrov Yamal
Kolskiy Poluostrov
Murmansk
Arkhangelsk
Uralskie Gory
Yekaterinburg
SIBERIA
Lena
Yakutsk
Verkhoyanskiy Khrebet
Stanovoy Khrebet
Kolymskoye Nagorye
Yenisey
Ob
Norilsk
Vorkuta
Narodnaya 1894
Mid-Atlantic Ridge
ATLANTIC OCEAN
Faroe Is.
Shetland Is.
Orkney Is.
Rockall
Hebrides
UNITED KINGDOM
SCOTLAND
IRELAND
Edinburgh
Glasgow
Belfast
Dublin
Liverpool
London
North Sea
NORWAY
SWEDEN
FINLAND
Gulf of Bothnia
Baltic Sea
Oslo
Stockholm
Helsinki
St. Peterburg
Moskva
København
Hamburg
Berlin
POLAND
GERMANY
BELARUS
UKRAINE
RUSSIA
EUROPE
Volga
Kyyiv
Odesa
Black Sea
Maximum extent of sea ice
Summer extent of sea ice
Ice caps and permanent ice shelf
Projection: Zenithal Equidistant
West from Greenwich
East from Greenwich
COPYRIGHT GEORGE PHILIP LTD.

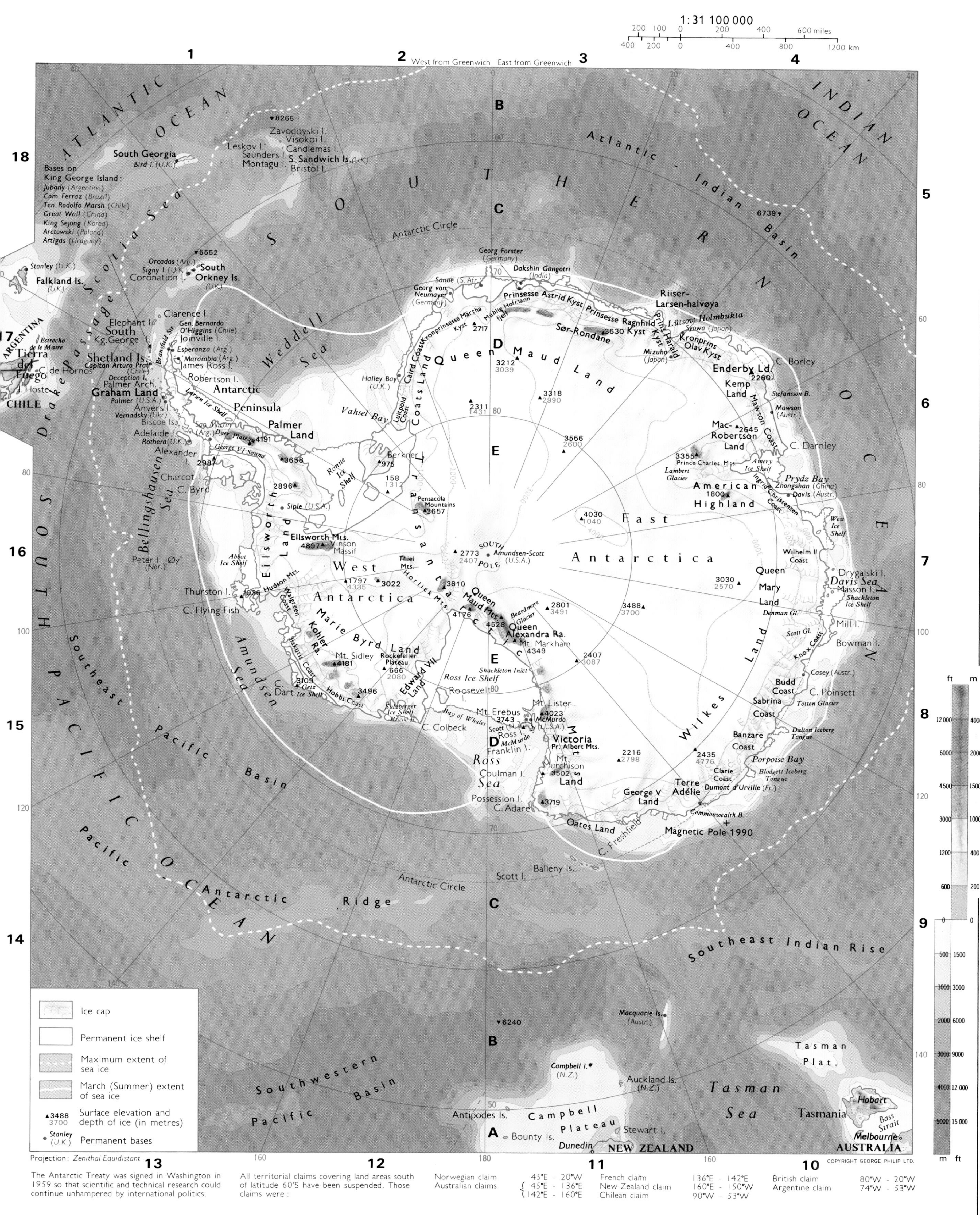

Projection: Zenithal Equidistant

The Antarctic Treaty was signed in Washington in 1959 so that scientific and technical research could continue unhampered by international politics.

All territorial claims covering land areas south of latitude 60°S have been suspended. Those claims were:

Norwegian claim	45°E - 20°W
Australian claims	45°E - 136°E; 142°E - 160°E
French claim	136°E - 142°E
New Zealand claim	160°E - 150°W
Chilean claim	90°W - 53°W
British claim	80°W - 20°W
Argentine claim	74°W - 53°W

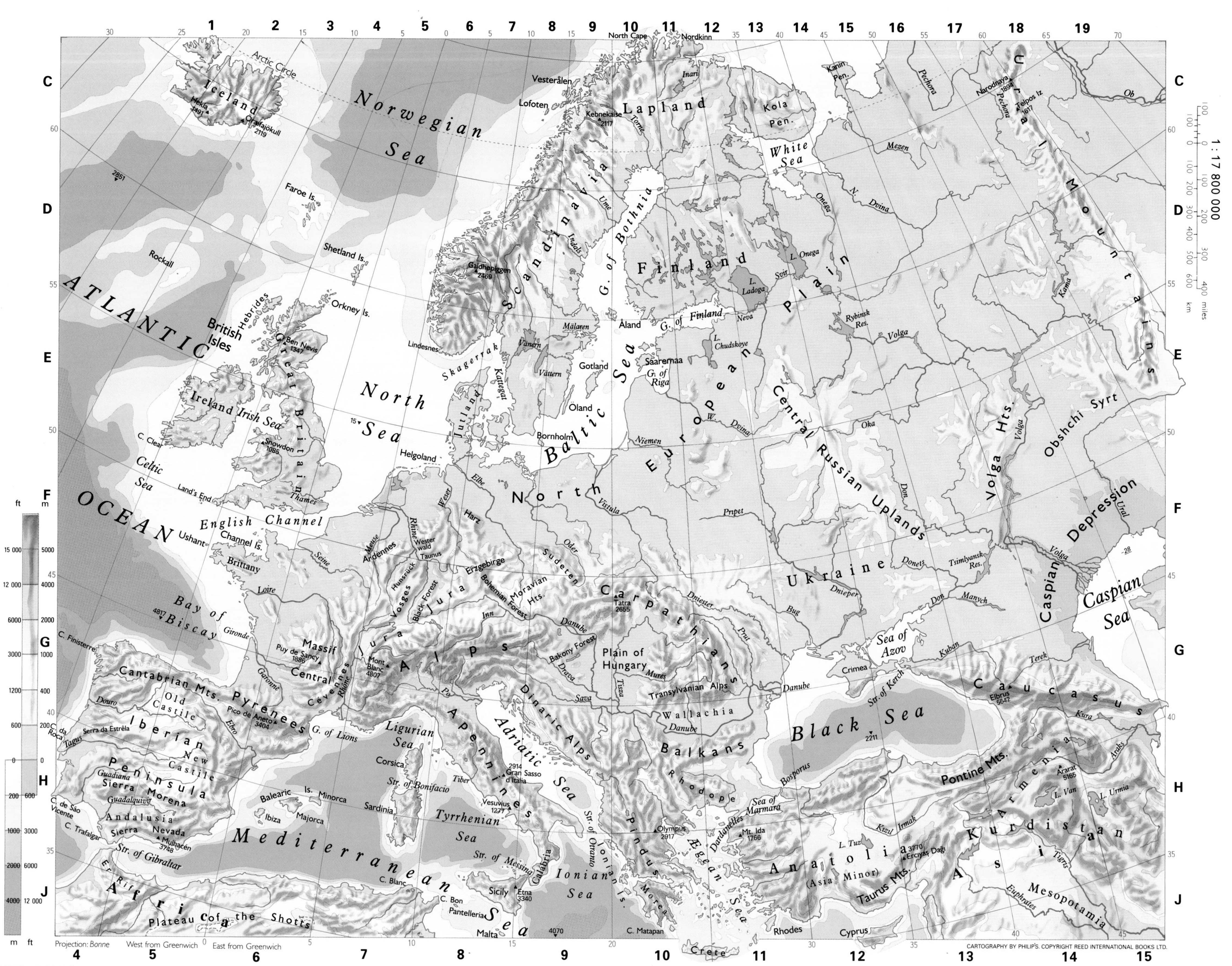
1 : 17 800 000
100 0 100 200 300 400 miles
100 0 100 200 300 400 500 600 km
Norwegian Sea
North Sea
ATLANTIC OCEAN
Iceland
Hekla 1491
Öraefajökull 2119
Arctic Circle
Faroe Is.
Shetland Is.
Orkney Is.
Rockall
Hebrides
British Isles
Great Britain
Ireland
Irish Sea
Ben Nevis 1347
Snowdon 1085
Thames
C. Clear
Celtic Sea
Land's End
English Channel
Channel Is.
Ushant
Brittany
Bay of Biscay
Loire
Seine
Gironde
Garonne
Massif Central
Puy de Sancy 1886
Cévennes
Rhône
G. of Lions
Pyrenees
Pico de Aneto 3404
Ebro
Cantabrian Mts.
Old Castile
New Castile
Iberian Peninsula
Sierra Morena
Sierra Nevada
Mulhacén 3478
Andalusia
Guadalquivir
Guadiana
Tagus
Douro
Serra da Estrêla
C. Finisterre
C. da Roca
C. de São Vicente
C. Trafalgar
Str. of Gibraltar
Er Rif
Africa
Plateau of the Shotts
Balearic Is.
Minorca
Majorca
Ibiza
Mediterranean Sea
Ligurian Sea
Corsica
Str. of Bonifacio
Sardinia
C. Blanc
C. Bon
Pantelleria
Malta
Sicily
Etna 3340
Str. of Messina
Tyrrhenian Sea
Vesuvius 1277
Tiber
Apennines
Gran Sasso d'Italia 2914
Adriatic Sea
Calabria
Ionian Sea
Ionian Is.
Str. of Otranto
Po
Alps
Mont Blanc 4807
Jura
Vosges
Black Forest
Hunsrück
Taunus
Westerwald
Ardennes
Meuse
Rhine
Weser
Elbe
Harz
Erzgebirge
Bohemian Forest
Moravian Hts.
Sudeten
Oder
Inn
Danube
Drava
Sava
Bakony Forest
Dinaric Alps
Plain of Hungary
Tisza
Mureș
Tatra 2655
Carpathians
Transylvanian Alps
Wallachia
Balkans
Rhodope
Olympus 2917
Pindus
Morea
C. Matapan
Ægean Sea
Crete
Dardanelles
Sea of Marmara
Mt. Ida 1766
Bosporus
Rhodes
Cyprus
Anatolia (Asia Minor)
Taurus Mts.
L. Tuz
Kizil Irmak
Erciyas Dağı
Pontine Mts.
Armenia
Kurdistan
Asia
Mesopotamia
Euphrates
Tigris
L. Van
L. Urmia
Ararat 5165
Araks
Kura
Caucasus
Elbrus 5642
Terek
Kuban
Black Sea
Crimea
Str. of Kerch
Sea of Azov
Don
Donets
Manych
Tsimlyansk Res.
Dnieper
Bug
Prut
Dniester
Pripet
Ukraine
Central Russian Uplands
Oka
Volga
Volga Hts.
Caspian Depression
Caspian Sea
Ural
Obshchi Syrt
Kama
Ural Mountains
Narodnaya 1894
Telpos Iz 1617
Pechora
Mezen
N. Dvina
Onega
Kanin Pen.
White Sea
Kola Pen.
L. Onega
Svir
L. Ladoga
Neva
L. Chudskoye
W. Dvina
Rybinsk Res.
Ob
North European Plain
Finland
G. of Finland
G. of Riga
Saaremaa
Åland
G. of Bothnia
Baltic Sea
Gotland
Öland
Bornholm
Niemen
Vistula
Mälaren
Vättern
Vänern
Kattegat
Skagerrak
Jutland
Helgoland
Lindesnes
Galdhøpiggen 2469
Scandinavia
Inari
Lapland
Torne
Ume
Indals
Kebnekaise 2117
North Cape
Nordkinn
Lofoten
Vesterålen
CARTOGRAPHY BY PHILIPS. COPYRIGHT REED INTERNATIONAL BOOKS LTD.
Projection: Bonne
West from Greenwich
East from Greenwich
ft m
15 000 5000
12 000 4000
6000 2000
3000 1000
1200 400
600 200
0 0
200 600
1000 3000
2000 6000
4000 12 000
m ft

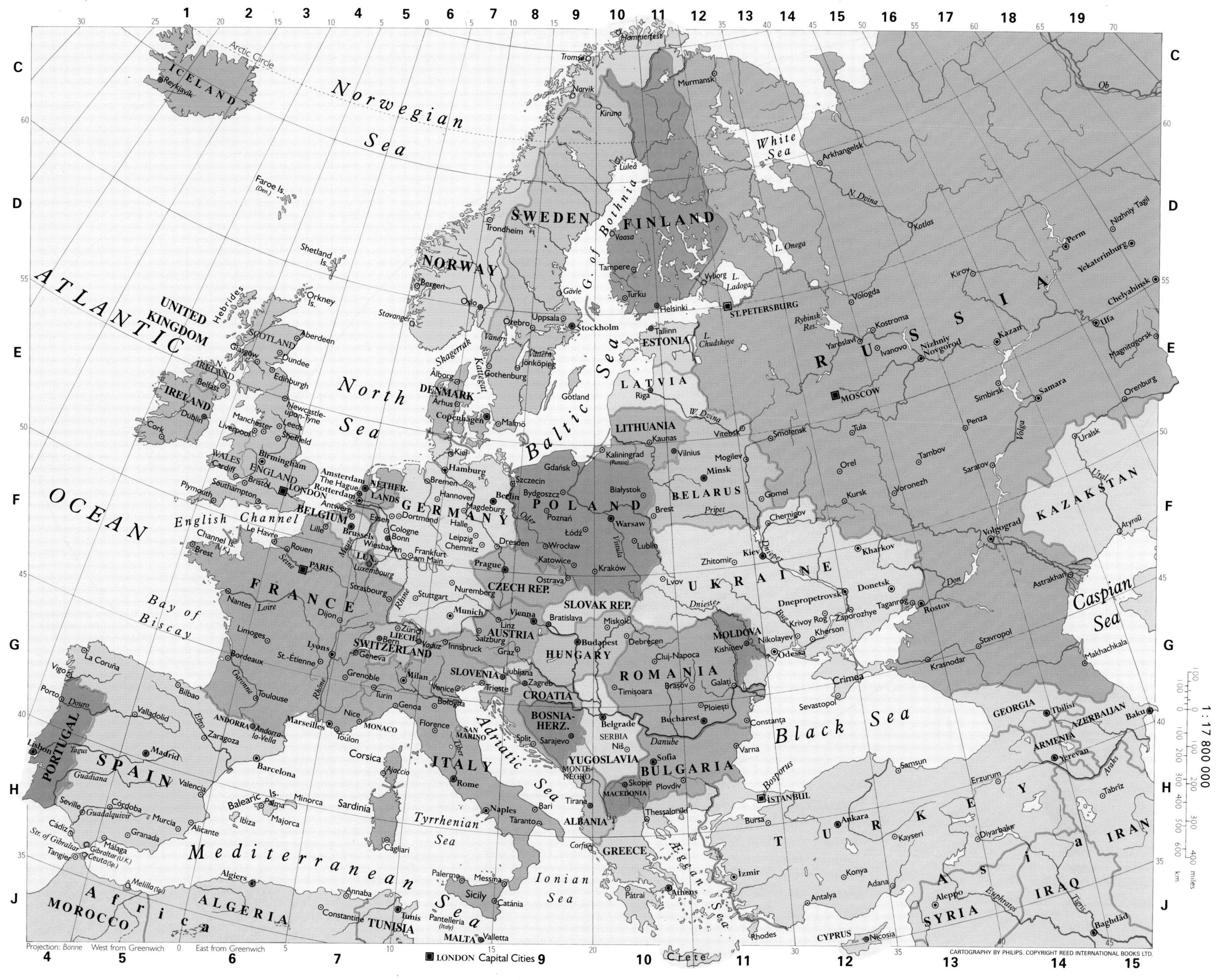

1 : 17 800 000
miles
km
Norwegian Sea
North Sea
Baltic Sea
White Sea
G. of Bothnia
ATLANTIC OCEAN
Bay of Biscay
English Channel
Mediterranean Sea
Tyrrhenian Sea
Adriatic Sea
Ionian Sea
Ægean Sea
Black Sea
Caspian Sea
ICELAND
UNITED KINGDOM
IRELAND
NORWAY
SWEDEN
FINLAND
DENMARK
ESTONIA
LATVIA
LITHUANIA
RUSSIA
BELARUS
UKRAINE
POLAND
GERMANY
NETHERLANDS
BELGIUM
LUX.
FRANCE
SWITZERLAND
LIECH.
AUSTRIA
CZECH REP.
SLOVAK REP.
HUNGARY
ROMANIA
MOLDOVA
SLOVENIA
CROATIA
BOSNIA-HERZ.
YUGOSLAVIA
MACEDONIA
ALBANIA
BULGARIA
GREECE
ITALY
SAN MARINO
MALTA
SPAIN
PORTUGAL
ANDORRA
MONACO
KAZAKSTAN
GEORGIA
ARMENIA
AZERBAIJAN
TURKEY
CYPRUS
SYRIA
IRAQ
IRAN
MOROCCO
ALGERIA
TUNISIA
Africa
LONDON
PARIS
MOSCOW
ST. PETERSBURG
ISTANBUL
LONDON Capital Cities
Projection: Bonne
West from Greenwich
East from Greenwich
CARTOGRAPHY BY PHILIPS. COPYRIGHT REED INTERNATIONAL BOOKS LTD.

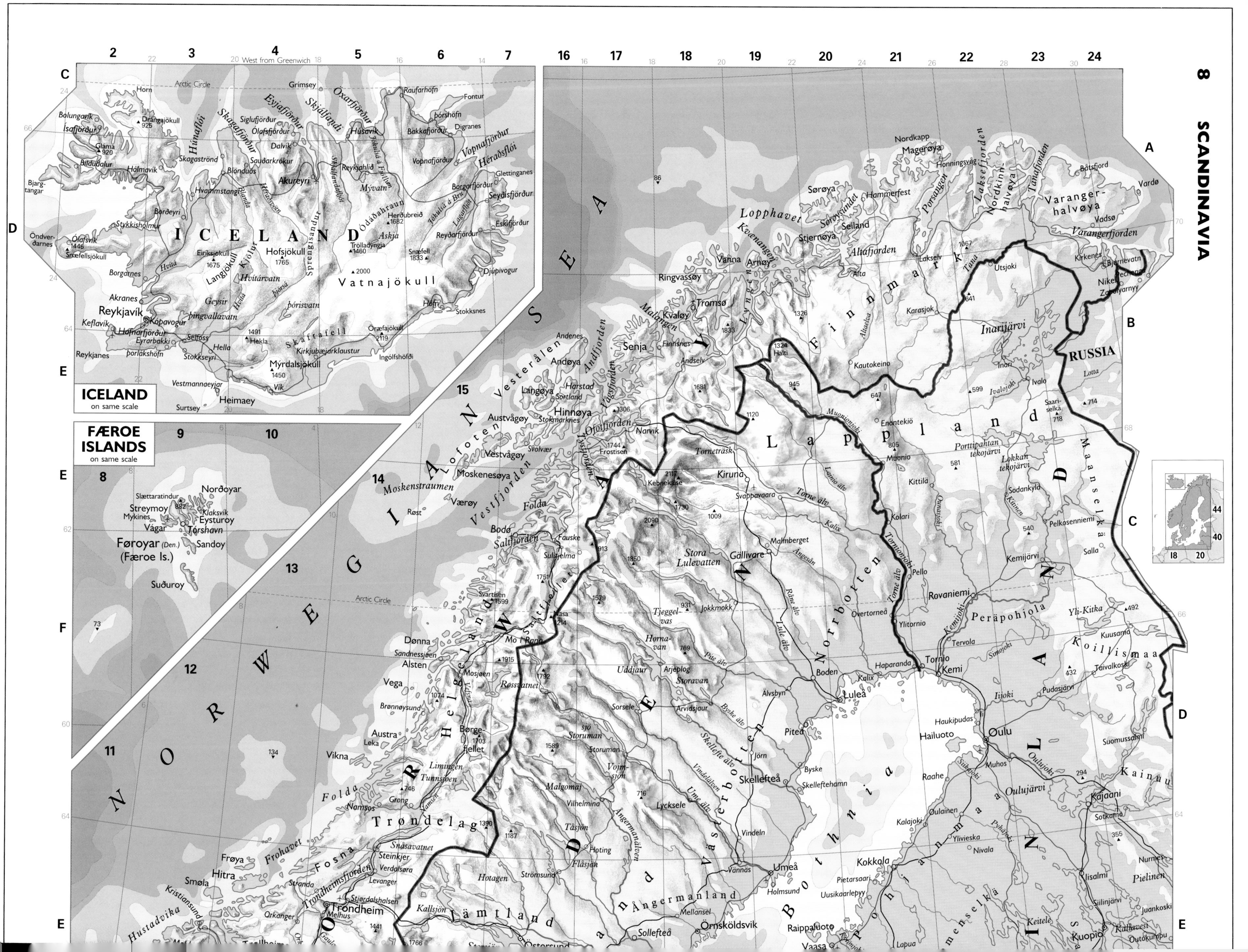
NORWEGIAN SEA
FINLAND
SWEDEN
NORWAY
RUSSIA
Lappland
Finnmark
Norrbotten
Västerbotten
Ångermanland
Jämtland
Trøndelag
Helgeland
Bothnia
Maanselkä
Kainuu
Koillismaa
Peräpohjola
Lofoten
Vesterålen
Vestfjorden
Lopphavet
Tromsø
Narvik
Kiruna
Gällivare
Luleå
Boden
Piteå
Skellefteå
Umeå
Örnsköldsvik
Haparanda
Tornio
Kemi
Rovaniemi
Oulu
Kajaani
Kokkola
Vaasa
Kuopio
Trondheim
Kristiansund
Namsos
Mo i Rana
Bodø
Hammerfest
Vadsø
Vardø
Kirkenes
Nordkapp
Magerøya
Varangerfjorden
Porsangen
Altafjorden
Inarijärvi
Oulujärvi
Stora Lulevatten
Arctic Circle
ICELAND on same scale
Reykjavík
Akureyri
Vatnajökull
Hofsjökull
Langjökull
Mýrdalsjökull
Heimaey
Surtsey
Vestmannaeyjar
Keflavík
Húsavík
Ísafjörður
Grímsey
FÆROE ISLANDS on same scale
Føroyar (Den.) (Færoe Is.)
Tórshavn
Streymoy
Eysturoy
Vágar
Sandoy
Suðuroy
Norðoyar
Klaksvík
West from Greenwich

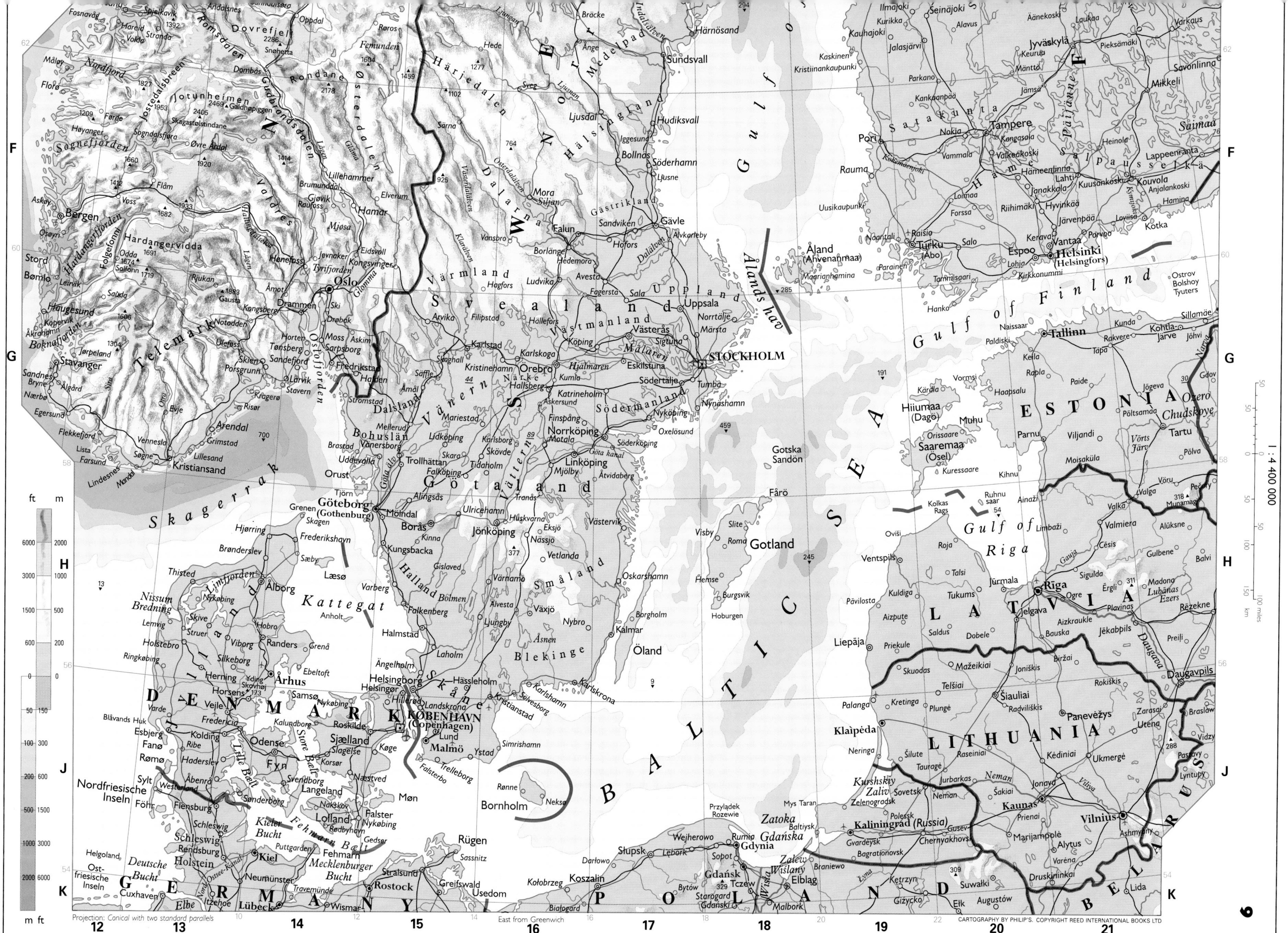

1 : 4 400 000

50 0 50 100 miles

50 0 50 100 150 km

ft m

6000 2000

3000 1000

1500 500

600 200

0 0

50 150

100 300

200 600

500 1500

1000 3000

2000 6000

m ft

NORWAY

SWEDEN

FINLAND

ESTONIA

LATVIA

LITHUANIA

BELARUS

POLAND

GERMANY

DENMARK

BALTIC SEA

Gulf of Bothnia

Gulf of Finland

Gulf of Riga

Ålands hav

Skagerrak

Kattegat

Svealand

Götaland

Västmanland

Södermanland

Uppland

Värmland

Dalarna

Härjedalen

Hälsingland

Medelpad

Gästrikland

Småland

Blekinge

Skåne

Halland

Bohuslän

Dalsland

Närke

Telemark

Jotunheimen

Hardangervidda

Østerdalen

Gudbrandsdalen

Valdres

Satakunta

Häme

Salpausselkä

Päijänne

Saimaa

Jylland

Sjælland

Fyn

Lolland

Falster

Møn

Bornholm

Gotland

Öland

Hiiumaa (Dago)

Saaremaa (Ösel)

Åland (Ahvenanmaa)

Vänern

Vättern

Mälaren

Hjälmaren

Ozero Chudskoye

Zatoka Gdańska

Kurshskiy Zaliv

Zalew Wiślany

STOCKHOLM

Oslo

Helsinki (Helsingfors)

Tallinn

Riga

Vilnius

KØBENHAVN (Copenhagen)

Göteborg (Gothenburg)

Malmö

Uppsala

Västerås

Örebro

Norrköping

Linköping

Jönköping

Gävle

Sundsvall

Bergen

Stavanger

Kristiansand

Drammen

Turku (Åbo)

Tampere

Pori

Espoo

Vantaa

Tartu

Pärnu

Liepāja

Ventspils

Daugavpils

Klaipėda

Kaunas

Šiauliai

Panevėžys

Kaliningrad (Russia)

Gdańsk

Gdynia

Elbląg

Koszalin

Słupsk

Rostock

Kiel

Lübeck

Flensburg

Århus

Ålborg

Odense

Esbjerg

Projection: Conical with two standard parallels

East from Greenwich

12 13 14 15 16 17 18 19 20 21

F G H J K

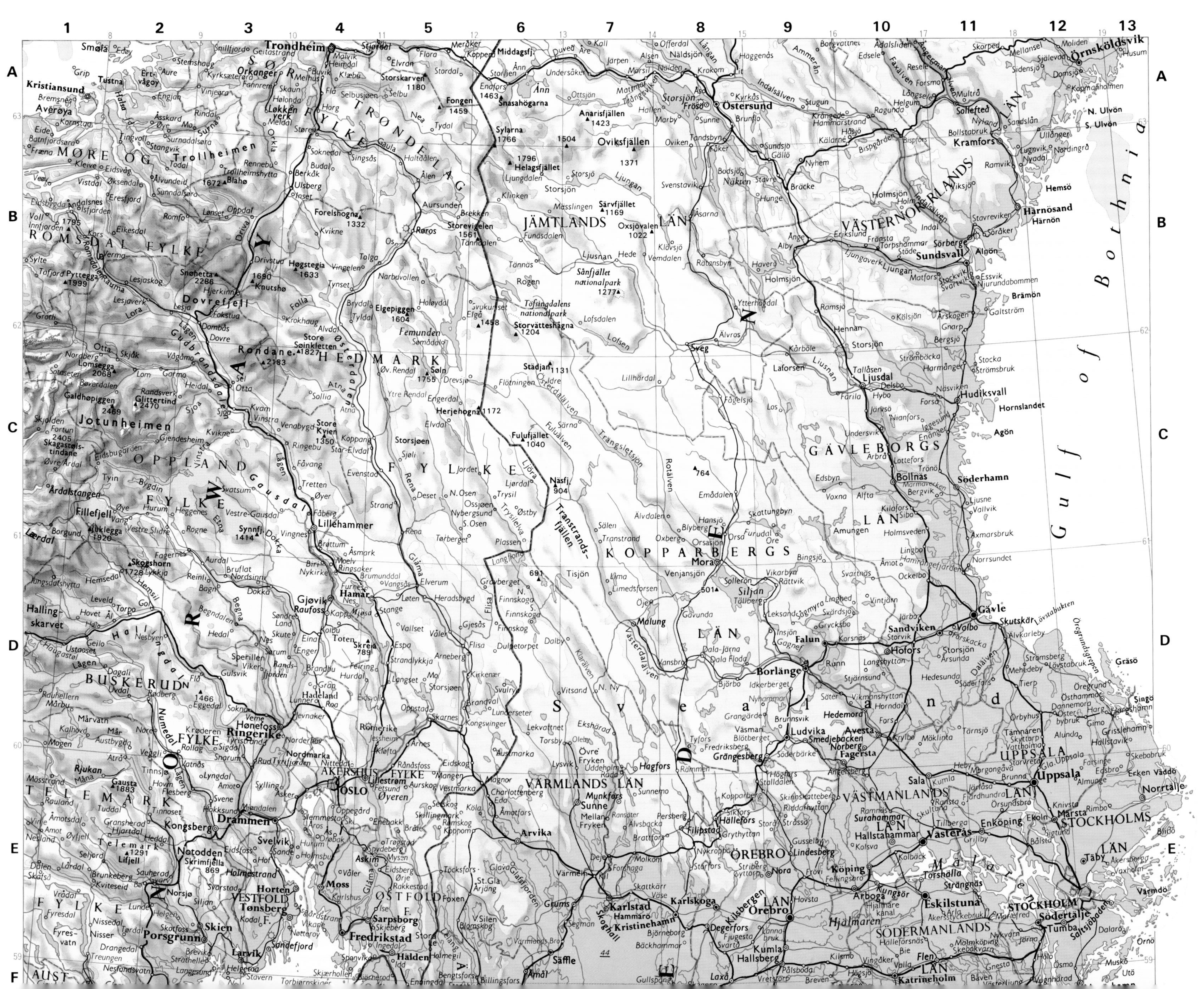
Gulf of Bothnia
Trondheim
Östersund
Sundsvall
Härnösand
Hudiksvall
Söderhamn
Gävle
Uppsala
STOCKHOLM
Västerås
Örebro
Karlstad
Falun
Borlänge
Mora
Lillehammer
Hamar
OSLO
Drammen
Hønefoss
Kongsberg
Skien
Porsgrunn
Larvik
Tønsberg
Moss
Fredrikstad
Sarpsborg
Halden
Kristiansund
JÄMTLANDS LÄN
GÄVLEBORGS LÄN
KOPPARBERGS LÄN
VÄRMLANDS LÄN
UPPSALA LÄN
STOCKHOLMS LÄN
SÖDERMANLANDS LÄN
VÄSTMANLANDS LÄN
ÖREBRO LÄN
VÄSTERNORRLANDS LÄN
SØR TRØNDELAG FYLKE
MØRE OG ROMSDAL FYLKE
HEDMARK FYLKE
OPPLAND FYLKE
BUSKERUD FYLKE
AKERSHUS FYLKE
ØSTFOLD FYLKE
VESTFOLD
TELEMARK FYLKE
Jotunheimen
Dovrefjell
Hjälmaren
Mälaren

1 : 2 200 000

10 0 10 20 30 40 50 miles

10 0 20 40 60 80 km

ft m

6000 2000

4500 1500

3000 1000

1200 400

600 200

0 0

200 600

m ft

Skagerrak

Norskerenna

Kattegat

BALTIC SEA

Jammerbugt

Ålborg Bugt

Kieler Bucht

Fehmarn Bælt

Femer Bælt

Store Bælt

Lille Bælt

Langelands Bælt

Hanöbukten

Kalmarsund

Bornholmsgattet

DENMARK

JYLLAND

SJÆLLAND

FYN

LOLLAND

FALSTER

Bornholm

Göteborg

Malmö

København (Copenhagen)

Helsingborg

Jönköping

Norrköping

Linköping

Kalmar

Karlskrona

Gotland

Öland

Visby

GERMANY

POLAND

Flensburg

Kiel

Rügen

Projection: Conical with two standard parallels

East from Greenwich

2 3 4 5 6 7 8 9 10 11

G H J K

NORTH SEA
IRISH SEA
SCOTLAND
Southern Uplands
Pennines
Cumbrian Mts.
Welsh Unitary Authorities
(from April 1996)
1. Neath Port Talbot
2. Rhondda Cynon Taff
3. Bridgend
4. Merthyr Tydfil
5. Caerphilly
6. Vale of Glamorgan
7. Cardiff
8. Blaenau Gwent
9. Torfaen
10. Newport
11. Monmouthshire
English Unitary Authorities
(from April 1996)
12. Hartlepool
13. Stockton-on-Tees
14. Middlesbrough
15. Redcar and Cleveland
16. Kingston upon Hull
17. York
18. South Gloucester
19. Bristol
20. North Somerset
21. Bath and N.E. Somerset

1 : 1 800 000
10 0 10 20 30 40 50 miles
10 0 10 20 30 40 50 60 70 80 km
ENGLISH CHANNEL
Bristol Channel
Channel Islands
SCILLY ISLES
On same Scale
Isles of Scilly
St. Mary's
Land's End
Penzance
St. Ives
Alderney
Guernsey
Sark
St. Peter Port
Jersey
St. Helier
C. de la Hague
Cherbourg
Barfleur
Quineville
Valognes
Carentan
Périers
Barneville
Isigny
Vierville
St. Lô
Bayeux
Arromanches
Caen
Trouville
Honfleur
Pont l'Évêque
Lisieux
Bernay
Le Havre
C. de la Hève
Etretat
C. d'Antifer
Fécamp
St. Valéry
Yvetot
Caudebec
Elbeuf
Louviers
Rouen
Dieppe
le Tréport
Seine
FRANCE
CORNWALL
DEVON
DORSET
SOMERSET
WILTS
HANTS
BERKS
OXFORD
BUCKS
BEDFORD
HERTFORD
ESSEX
SUFFOLK
KENT
SURREY
WEST SUSSEX
EAST SUSSEX
ISLE OF WIGHT
GLOUCESTER
WORCESTER
HEREFORD & WORCESTER
WARWICK
NORTHAMPTON
CAMBRIDGE
POWYS
CEREDIGION
CARMARTHENSHIRE
PEMBROKESHIRE
SHROPSHIRE
WEST MIDLANDS
Plymouth
Devonport
Exeter
Torquay (Torbay)
Paignton
Dartmouth
Dartmoor
Exmoor
Barnstaple
Bideford
Ilfracombe
Lynton
Minehead
Taunton
Bridgwater
Yeovil
Weymouth
Portland Bill
Poole
Bournemouth
Southampton
Portsmouth
Gosport
Winchester
Salisbury
Swindon
Bristol
Bath
Cardiff
Newport
Swansea
Port Talbot
Llanelli
Carmarthen
Pembroke
Milford Haven
Fishguard
Aberystwyth
Aberdovey
Hereford
Gloucester
Cheltenham
Worcester
Birmingham
Coventry
Oxford
Reading
Luton
Northampton
Bedford
Cambridge
Ipswich
Colchester
Chelmsford
Southend
Basildon
LONDON
Croydon
Brighton
Worthing
Eastbourne
Hastings
Folkestone
Dover
Deal
Ramsgate
Margate
Canterbury
Maidstone
Ashford
Gillingham
Chatham
Rochester
Guildford
Crawley
Horsham
Chichester
Bognor Regis
Selsey Bill
Newhaven
Beachy Hd.
Dungeness
New Romney
Felixstowe
Harwich
Clacton
Aldeburgh
Orford Ness
Southwold
Beccles
Lundy
Hartland Point
Lizard
Falmouth
Truro
St. Austell
Newquay
Padstow
Bude
Camborne
Redruth
St. Michael's Mount
Eddystone
Start Pt.
Lyme Regis
Sidmouth
Exmouth
Teignmouth
Weston-super-Mare
Mendip Hills
Quantock Hills
Salisbury Plain
Stonehenge
North Downs
South Downs
The Weald
Black Mts.
Brecon Beacons
Merthyr Tydfil
Rhondda
Pontypridd
St. Catherine's Point
St. Alban's Hd.
Needles
Swanage
I. of Purbeck
Portland I.
Projection: Conical with two standard parallels.
East from Greenwich
West from Greenwich
COPYRIGHT GEORGE PHILIP & SON, LTD.
ft
m
3000
1200
600
300
0
50
100
1000
400
200
100
0
150
300

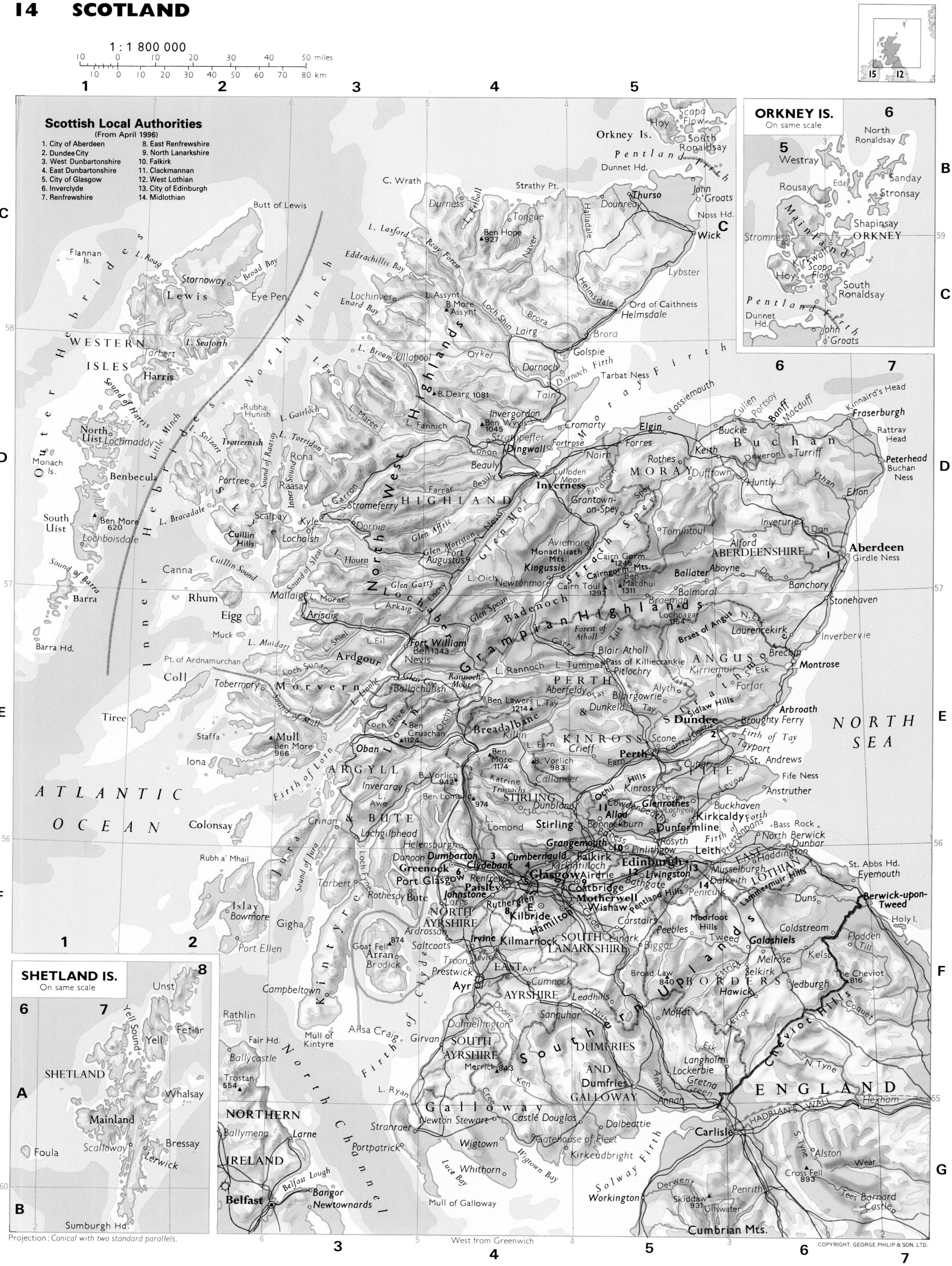
1 : 1 800 000
10 0 10 20 30 40 50 miles
10 0 10 20 30 40 50 60 70 80 km
Scottish Local Authorities
(From April 1996)
1. City of Aberdeen
2. Dundee City
3. West Dunbartonshire
4. East Dunbartonshire
5. City of Glasgow
6. Inverclyde
7. Renfrewshire
8. East Renfrewshire
9. North Lanarkshire
10. Falkirk
11. Clackmannan
12. West Lothian
13. City of Edinburgh
14. Midlothian
ORKNEY IS.
On same scale
North Ronaldsay
Westray
Sanday
Stronsay
Rousay
Eday
Shapinsay
ORKNEY
Mainland
Stromness
Kirkwall
Scapa Flow
Hoy
South Ronaldsay
Pentland Firth
Dunnet Hd.
John o'Groats
SHETLAND IS.
On same scale
Unst
Yell Sound
Yell
Fetlar
SHETLAND
Whalsay
Mainland
Foula
Scalloway
Bressay
Lerwick
Sumburgh Hd.
Butt of Lewis
Flannan Is.
L. Roag
Stornoway
Broad Bay
Lewis
Eye Pen.
WESTERN ISLES
Outer Hebrides
Tarbert
L. Seaforth
Harris
Sound of Harris
North Minch
Little Minch
North Uist
Lochmaddy
Monach Is.
Benbecula
South Uist
Ben More 620
Lochboisdale
Sound of Barra
Barra
Barra Hd.
Inner Hebrides
Rubha Hunish
Trotternish
Skye
Portree
Raasay
Rona
Cuillin Hills
Scalpay
Kyle of Lochalsh
Cuillin Sound
Canna
Rhum
Eigg
Muck
Coll
Tiree
Staffa
Mull
Ben More 966
Iona
Colonsay
Jura
Islay
Bowmore
Port Ellen
Gigha
Rubh a' Mhail
ATLANTIC OCEAN
C. Wrath
Durness
Ben Hope 927
Tongue
Strathy Pt.
Thurso
Dounreay
Orkney Is.
Pentland Firth
Dunnet Hd.
John o'Groats
Wick
Lybster
Helmsdale
Ord of Caithness
Brora
Golspie
Dornoch
Dornoch Firth
Tarbat Ness
Moray Firth
Lairg
Loch Shin
Lochinver
Ullapool
B. More Assynt
B. Dearg 1081
Invergordon
Ben Wyvis 1045
Cromarty
Dingwall
Inverness
Nairn
Forres
Elgin
Lossiemouth
Buckie
Banff
Macduff
Fraserburgh
Kinnaird's Head
Peterhead
Buchan
Rattray Head
Ellon
MORAY
HIGHLAND
North West Highlands
Glen Mor
Aviemore
Monadhliath Mts.
Kingussie
Cairn Gorm 1245
Cairngorm Mts.
Ben Macdhui 1311
Newtonmore
Fort Augustus
Kingussie
Inverurie
Aberdeen
Girdle Ness
ABERDEENSHIRE
Ballater
Aboyne
Banchory
Stonehaven
Braemar
Lochnagar 1154
Inverbervie
Laurencekirk
Grampian Highlands
Mallaig
Arisaig
Fort William
Ben Nevis 1343
Lochaber
Badenoch
Ardgour
Morvern
Tobermory
Glen Coe
Rannoch Moor
Pitlochry
Blair Atholl
ANGUS
Montrose
Brechin
Forfar
Arbroath
Dundee
Firth of Tay
St. Andrews
Fife Ness
Anstruther
PERTH & KINROSS
Perth
Crieff
Ben Lawers 1214
Breadalbane
Oban
Ben Cruachan 1124
Inveraray
ARGYLL & BUTE
Lochgilphead
Firth of Lorn
Ben Lomond 974
STIRLING
Stirling
Dunblane
Callander
Kinross
FIFE
Glenrothes
Kirkcaldy
Dunfermline
Alloa
Falkirk
Grangemouth
Linlithgow
Leith
Edinburgh
Livingston
Dalkeith
Penicuik
EAST LOTHIAN
Haddington
Dunbar
North Berwick
Bass Rock
St. Abbs Hd.
Eyemouth
Berwick-upon-Tweed
Glasgow
Paisley
Greenock
Dumbarton
Clydebank
Cumbernauld
Airdrie
Coatbridge
Motherwell
Hamilton
East Kilbride
Kilmarnock
NORTH AYRSHIRE
Ardrossan
Irvine
Arran
Goat Fell 874
Kintyre
Campbeltown
Mull of Kintyre
Ailsa Craig
Girvan
Ayr
EAST AYRSHIRE
SOUTH AYRSHIRE
SOUTH LANARKSHIRE
Lanark
Peebles
Galashiels
Melrose
Kelso
Coldstream
Jedburgh
Hawick
Selkirk
BORDERS
Southern Uplands
The Cheviot 816
Cheviot Hills
Moffat
Sanquhar
Dalmellington
Merrick 843
DUMFRIES AND GALLOWAY
Dumfries
Langholm
Lockerbie
Gretna Green
Annan
Galloway
Newton Stewart
Castle Douglas
Kirkcudbright
Wigtown
Whithorn
Luce Bay
Stranraer
Portpatrick
Mull of Galloway
Solway Firth
North Channel
NORTHERN IRELAND
Ballymena
Larne
Ballycastle
Belfast
Belfast Lough
Bangor
Newtownards
Rathlin
Fair Hd.
Trostan 554
ENGLAND
Hadrian's Wall
Hexham
Carlisle
Workington
Penrith
Skiddaw 931
Cumbrian Mts.
Cross Fell 893
Alston
Barnard Castle
Holy I.
NORTH SEA
West from Greenwich

Projection: *Conical with two standard parallels.*

COPYRIGHT, GEORGE PHILIP & SON, LTD.

1 : 1 800 000

10 0 10 20 30 40 50 miles
10 0 10 20 30 40 50 60 70 80 km
1 2 3 4 5 6
A B C D E
ATLANTIC OCEAN
IRISH SEA
North Channel
St. George's Channel
IRELAND
NORTHERN IRELAND
ULSTER
CONNACHT
LEINSTER
MUNSTER
DONEGAL
SLIGO
LEITRIM
MAYO
ROSCOMMON
GALWAY
LONGFORD
WESTMEATH
CAVAN
MONAGHAN
LOUTH
MEATH
DUBLIN
KILDARE
OFFALY
LAOIS
WICKLOW
CARLOW
KILKENNY
WEXFORD
TIPPERARY
CLARE
LIMERICK
KERRY
CORK
WATERFORD
Kintyre
Arran
Campbeltown
Rathlin I.
Mull of Kintyre
Ailsa Craig
Fair Hd.
Giant's Causeway
Portrush
Malin Hd.
Lough Swilly
Inishowen Pen.
Carndonagh
Moville
Buncrana
Tory I.
Horn Hd.
Sheep Haven
Bloody Foreland
Gweedore
Errigal 752
Derryveagh Mts.
Letterkenny
Aran I.
Gweebarra B.
Loughros More B.
Glenties
Bluestack 676
Finn
Lifford
Strabane
Rossan Pt.
Rathlin O Birne I.
Killybegs
Donegal
Donegal Bay
Bundoran
Ballyshannon
Coleraine
Limavady
Roe
Londonderry
Foyle
Sperrin Mts.
Sawel 683
Magherafelt
Mourne
Derg
Ballycastle
Ballymoney
Mts. of Antrim
554 Trostan
Bann
Main
Ballymena
Larne
I. Magee
Portpatrick
Stranraer
Carrickfergus
Antrim
Belfast L.
Bangor
Donaghadee
Newtownards
Belfast
Lisburn
Lagan
Strangford L.
Ards Pen.
Cookstown
Lough Neagh
Omagh
Irvinestown
Dungannon
Blackwater
Lurgan (Craigavon)
Portadown
Armagh
Banbridge
Downpatrick
Dundrum
Slieve Donard 852
Newcastle
Dundrum Bay
Mourne Mts.
Newry
St. Gullion 577
Warrenpoint
Castleblayney
Carlingford L.
Greenore
Dundalk
Dundalk Bay
Erne
Lower L. Erne
Enniskillen
Upper L. Erne
Clones
Monaghan
Sligo
Sligo B.
Collooney
L. Allen
Ox Mts.
Killala B.
Killala
Downpatrick Hd.
Broad Haven
Erris Hd.
Belmullet
Mullet Peninsula
Blacksod Bay
Ballina
Moy
L. Conn
Nephin 806
Achill Hd.
Achill I.
Achill
Castlebar
Clew Bay
Clare I.
Westport
Croagh Patrick 765
Mweelrea 819
Killary Harbour
L. Mask
Inishbofin
Claremorris
Castlerea
Robe
Ballinrobe
Tuam
Clifden
Twelve Pins
Connemara
L. Corrib
Slyne Hd.
Galway
Clare
Athenry
Ballinasloe
Kilkieran B.
Galway Bay
Inishmore
Aran Is.
Gort
Loughrea
Portumna
Slieve Aughty
Shannon
Suck
Arrow
Boyle
Leitrim
Carrick-on-Shannon
Belturbet
Annalee
Cootehill
Cavan
Carrickmacross
Kingscourt
Louth
Ardee
L. Gowna
Granard
L. Sheelin
Longford
Oldcastle
Ceanannas Mor (Kells)
An Uaimh (Navan)
Athboy
Trim
Boyne
Drogheda
Balbriggan
Lambay I.
Ireland's Eye
Howth Head
Swords
Dublin (Baile Atha Cliath)
Dublin Bay
Dun Laoghaire
Bray
Maynooth
Celbridge
Naas
Kippure 754
Poulaphouca Res.
Roscommon
L. Ree
Inny
Athlone
Mullingar
Edenderry
Clara
Tullamore
Daingean
Brosna
Droichead Nua
Kildare
Bog of Allen
Liffey
Birr
Portarlington
Mountmellick
Slieve Bloom
Port Laoise
Athy
Barrow
Wicklow
Wicklow Hd.
Rathdrum
Lugnaquilla 923
Wicklow Mts.
Mizen Hd.
Avoca
Arklow
Carlow
Tullow
Shillelagh
Gorey
Mune Bheag
Mt. Leinster 796
Slaney
Enniscorthy
Cahore Pt.
Nore
Kilkenny
Callan
Templemore
Thurles
Roscrea
L. Derg
Nenagh
Keeper 694
Ballina
Killaloe
Ardnacrusha
Rineanna
Ennistymon
Hags Hd.
Liscannor Bay
Mal Bay
Miltown Malbay
Ennis
Kilkee
Kilrush
Loop Hd.
R. Shannon
Foynes
Rathkeale
Limerick
Newcastle
Listowel
Feale
Kerry Hd.
Fenit
Tralee Bay
Brandon Bay
Brandon Mt. 953
Tralee
Sl. Mish
Maine
Dingle
Gt. Blasket I.
Dunmore Hd.
Dingle Bay
Laune
Killarney
Macgillycuddy's Reeks
Carrauntuohill 1040
Lakes of Killarney
Valencia Harbour
Valencia I.
Cahirciveen
Kenmare
Skellig Rocks
Ballinskelligs B.
Kenmare River
Caha Mts.
Glengarriff
Castletown Bearhaven
Bear I.
Bantry
Bantry Bay
Crow Hd.
Dunmanus Bay
Mizen Hd.
Fastnet Rock
Skull
Baltimore
Clear I.
C. Clear
Skibbereen
Clonakilty
Clonakilty Bay
Galley Hd.
Old Head of Kinsale
Kinsale
Bandon
Crosshaven
Cork Harbour
Cobh
Passage West
Midleton
Cork
Blarney
Lee
Macroom
Boggeragh Mts.
Mallow
Kanturk
Blackwater
Newmarket
Rath Luirc (Charleville)
Mitchelstown
Galtymore 920
Galty Mts.
Golden Vale
Tipperary
Cashel
Suir
Caher
Clonmel
Slievenamon 722
Carrick-on-Suir
Comeragh Mts.
Knockmealdown Mts.
Fermoy
Lismore
Dungarvan
Dungarvan Bay
Youghal
Youghal Harbour
Tramore
Waterford
Waterford Harbour
Hook Hd.
New Ross
Wexford
Wexford Harbour
Rosslare
Greenore Pt.
Tuscar Rock
Carnsore Pt.
Saltee Is.
St. David's Hd.
Projection: Conical with two standard parallels.
West from Greenwich
COPYRIGHT, GEORGE PHILIP & SON, LTD.
ft m
3000 1000
1200 400
600 200
300 100
0 0
100 300
200 600
m ft
Towns underlined in Northern Ireland give their names to the Districts in which they stand
The remaining Districts are:—
1 Fermanagh
2 Moyle
3 Newtownabbey
4 North Down
5 Castlereagh
6 Ards
7 Down
8 Newry & Mourne

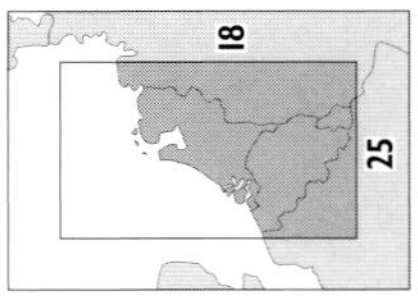
18
25

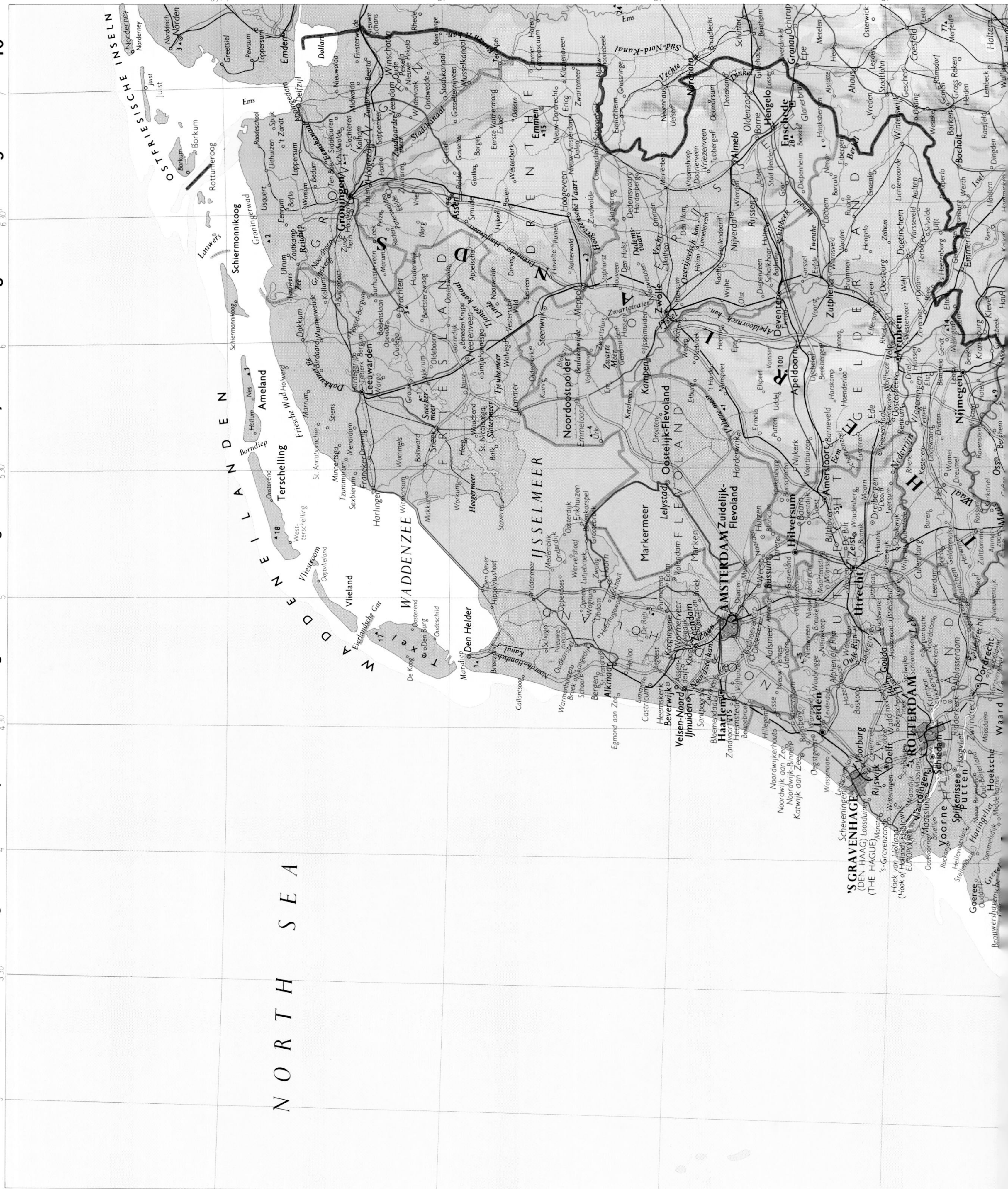
NORTH SEA
WADDENZEE
IJSSELMEER
WADDENEILANDEN
OSTFRIESISCHE INSELN
Markermeer
Noordoostpolder
Oostelijk-Flevoland
Zuidelijk-Flevoland
Schiermonnikoog
Ameland
Terschelling
Vlieland
Texel
Borkum
Juist
Norderney
Groningen
Leeuwarden
Assen
Emmen
Zwolle
Deventer
Apeldoorn
Hengelo
Enschede
Almelo
Arnhem
Nijmegen
Amersfoort
Utrecht
Hilversum
AMSTERDAM
Haarlem
Leiden
'S GRAVENHAGE
(DEN HAAG)
(THE HAGUE)
ROTTERDAM
Dordrecht
Den Helder
Alkmaar
Lelystad
Harlingen
Sneek
Drachten
Heerenveen
Hoogeveen
Meppel
Kampen
Zutphen
Emden
Delfzijl
Nordhorn
Gronau
Bocholt
Coesfeld
A
B
C
D
E
1
2
3
4
5
6
7
8
9
10

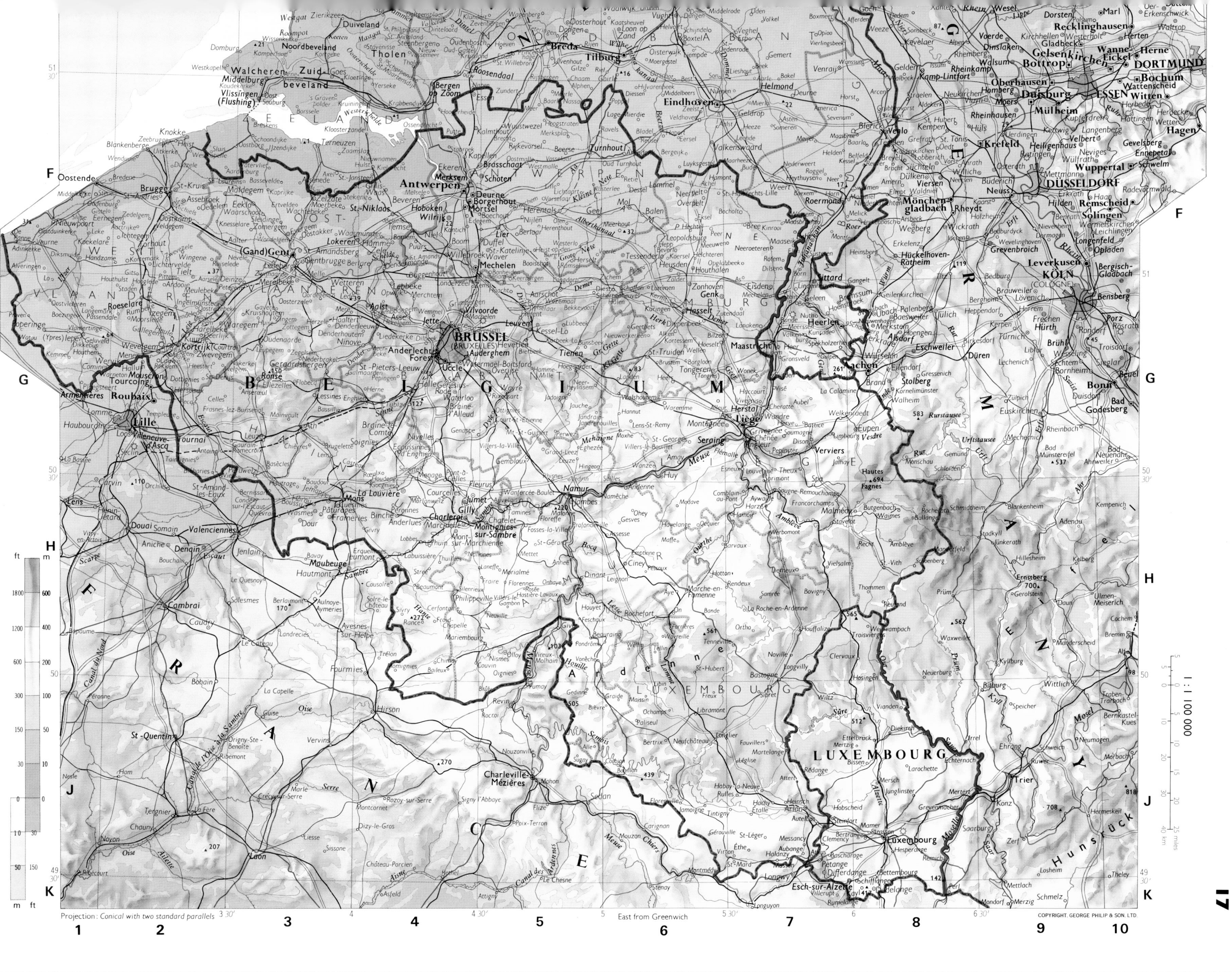
NEDERLAND
BELGIUM
LUXEMBOURG
GERMANY
FRANCE
BRUSSEL (BRUXELLES)
Antwerpen
(Gand) Gent
Brugge
Oostende
Lille
Roubaix
Tourcoing
Liège
Namur
Charleroi
Mons
Maastricht
Eindhoven
Tilburg
Breda
KÖLN (COLOGNE)
DÜSSELDORF
ESSEN
DORTMUND
Duisburg
Bonn
Aachen
Luxembourg
Esch-sur-Alzette
Charleville-Mézières
St-Quentin
Valenciennes
Cambrai
Laon
Trier
Middelburg
Vlissingen (Flushing)
Walcheren
Noordbeveland
Zuid-beveland
Ardenne
Hunsrück
Eifel
Meuse
Moselle
1 : 1 100 000
miles
km
East from Greenwich
Projection: Conical with two standard parallels
COPYRIGHT GEORGE PHILIP & SON, LTD.
ft
m

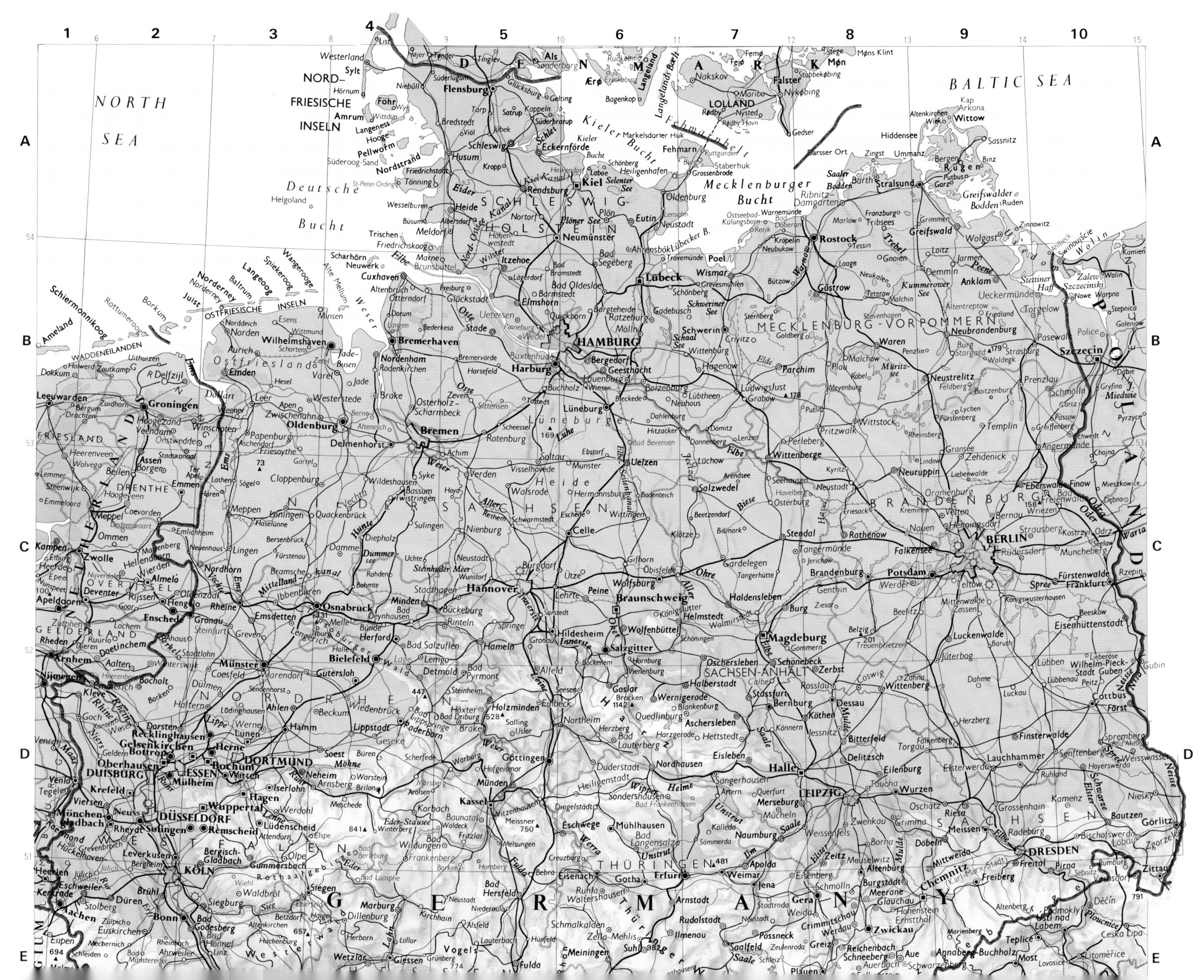
BALTIC SEA
NORTH SEA
NORD-FRIESISCHE INSELN
OSTFRIESISCHE INSELN
WADDENEILANDEN
Deutsche Bucht
Kieler Bucht
Mecklenburger Bucht
DENMARK
POLAND
GERMANY
NETHERLANDS
SCHLESWIG-HOLSTEIN
MECKLENBURG-VORPOMMERN
BRANDENBURG
NIEDERSACHSEN
SACHSEN-ANHALT
NORDRHEIN-WESTFALEN
THÜRINGEN
SACHSEN
Lüneburger Heide
BERLIN
HAMBURG
Bremen
Hannover
Kiel
Rostock
Lübeck
Magdeburg
Potsdam
DRESDEN
LEIPZIG
Halle
DORTMUND
ESSEN
DUISBURG
DÜSSELDORF
KÖLN
Bonn
Münster
Bielefeld
Osnabrück
Braunschweig
Kassel
Erfurt
Chemnitz
Szczecin
Groningen

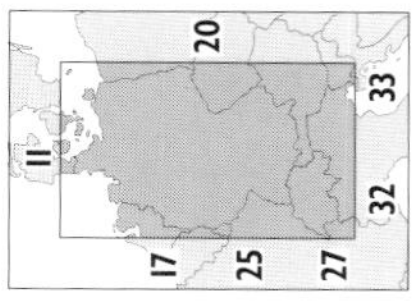

1 : 2 200 000

10 0 10 20 30 40 50 miles

10 0 10 20 30 40 50 60 70 80 km

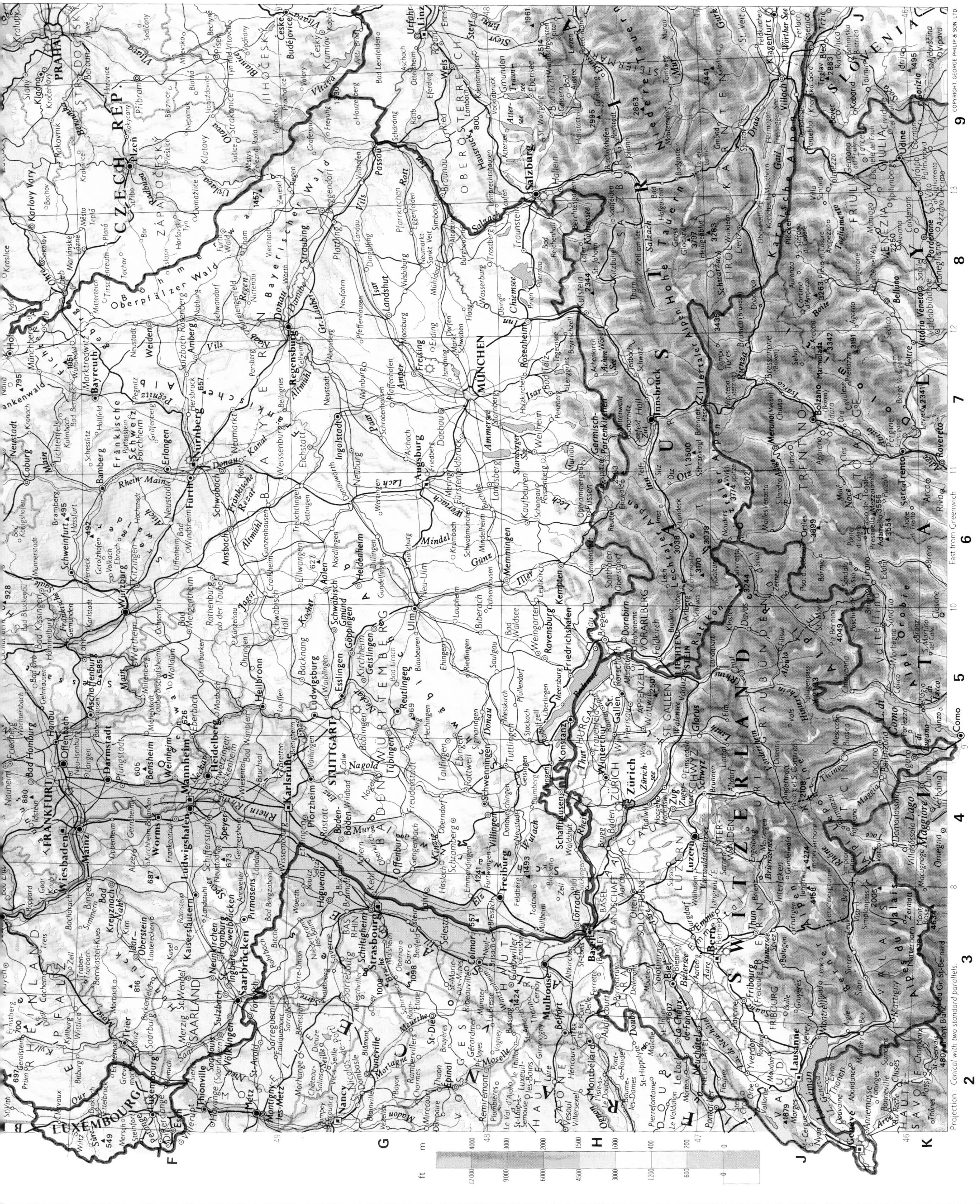

Projection: Conical with two standard parallels.

East from Greenwich

m	ft
4000	12000
3000	9000
2000	6000
1500	4500
1000	3000
400	1200
200	600
0	0

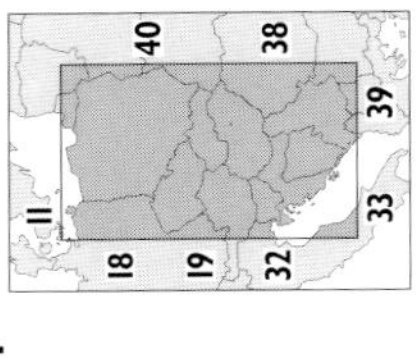
40
38
39
33
32
19
18
11

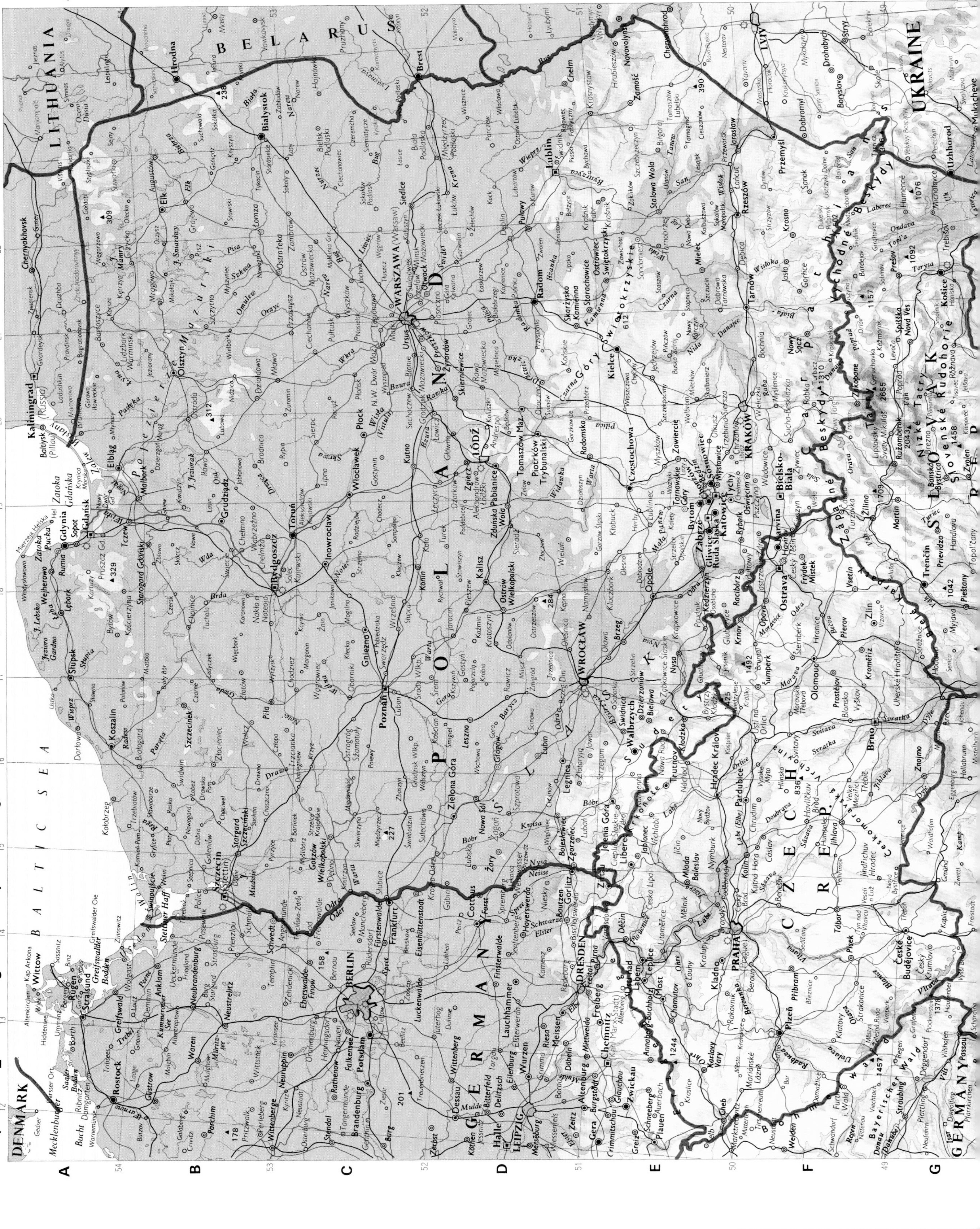
A
B
C
D
E
F
G
1
2
3
4
5
6
7
8
9
10
11
12
13
14
DENMARK
LITHUANIA
BELARUS
UKRAINE
POLAND
GERMANY
CZECH REP.
SLOVAKIA
BALTIC SEA
Kaliningrad (Russia)
WARSZAWA (Warsaw)
BERLIN
PRAHA (Prague)
Hrodna
Brest
Lviv
Gdańsk
Gdynia
Szczecin (Stettin)
Poznań
Wrocław
Łódź
Kraków
Katowice
Lublin
Białystok
Bydgoszcz
Toruń
Olsztyn
Rzeszów
Kielce
Częstochowa
Radom
Ostrava
Brno
Olomouc
Plzeň
Košice
Rostock
Stralsund
Dresden
Leipzig
Chemnitz
Potsdam
Frankfurt
Cottbus
Halle
Uzhhorod
Przemyśl
Vistula
Oder
Warta
Labe (Elbe)
Vltava
Morava
Wisła
Bug
Narew
Tatry

1 : 3 100 000
HUNGARY
ROMANIA
YUGOSLAVIA
CROATIA
SLOVENIA
BOSNIA-HERZEGOVINA
BULGARIA
MACEDONIA
ALBANIA
ITALY
MONTENEGRO
SERBIA
KOSOVO
VOJVODINA
ADRIATIC SEA
BUDAPEST
BEOGRAD
WIEN
Zagreb
Ljubljana
Sarajevo
SOFIYA
Bratislava
East from Greenwich
Projection: Conical with two standard parallels
---- Inter-entity boundaries as agreed at the 1995 Dayton Peace Agreement
m ft

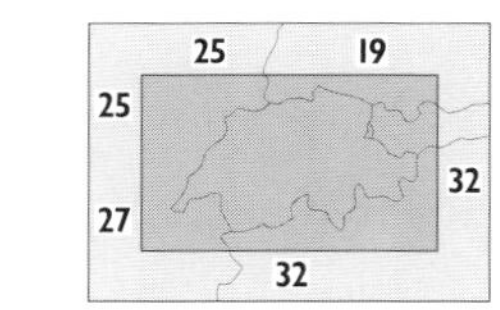

Projection: Conical with two standard parallels

1 : 900 000
5 0 5 10 15 20 miles
5 0 5 10 15 20 25 30 km
7
8
9
10
11
A
B
C
D
E
WÜRTTEMBERG
GERMANY
BAYERN
AUSTRIA
VORARLBERG
TIROL
LIECHTENSTEIN
THURGAU
ZÜRICH
SCHWYZ
ZUG
GLARUS
ST. GALLEN
APPENZELL
GRAUBÜNDEN
TICINO
ITALY
LOMBARDIA
TRENTINO
SCHAFFHAUSEN
Schaffhausen
Neuhausen a.Rh.
Singen
Radolfzell
Konstanz
Überlingen
Bodensee (L. Constance)
Friedrichshafen
Lindau
Bregenz
Ravensburg
Weingarten
Wangen i. A.
Kempten
Leutkirch
Marktoberdorf
Füssen
Schongau
Immenstadt i.A.
Sonthofen
Oberstdorf
Winterthur
Frauenfeld
Weinfelden
Romanshorn
Arbon
Rorschach
St. Gallen
Gossau
Wil
Herisau
Appenzell
Dornbirn
Lustenau
Hohenems
Götzis
Feldkirch
Bludenz
Vaduz
Buchs
Zürich
Uster
Wetzikon
Küsnacht
Thalwil
Horgen
Wädenswil
Rapperswil
Zug
Luzern
Schwyz
Einsiedeln
Glarus
Altdorf
Chur
Davos
Klosters
St. Moritz
Landeck
Imst
Bregenzer Wald
Lechtaler Alpen
Allgäuer Alpen
Rätikon
Silvretta-Gruppe
Glarner Alpen
Urner Alpen
Lepontine Alpen
Adula-Gruppe
Oberland
Unter Engadin
Ober Engadin
National-Park
Rätische Alpen
Alpi Orobie
Ötztaler Alpen
Vinschgau Val Venosta
Valtellina
Val Camonica
Val Seriana
Giudicarie
Bellinzona
Locarno
Lugano
Domodóssola
Lago Maggiore
Lago di Lugano
Lago di Como
Lago d'Iseo
Lago d'Idro
Lago di Garda
Chiavenna
Sóndrio
Tirano
Bórmio
Como
Lecco
Varese
Bergamo
Verbania
Gallarate
Mendrisio
Chiasso
Cantu
Seregno
Saronno
Riva del Garda
East from Greenwich
COPYRIGHT, GEORGE PHILIP & SON, LTD.

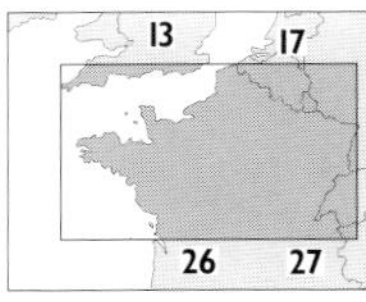

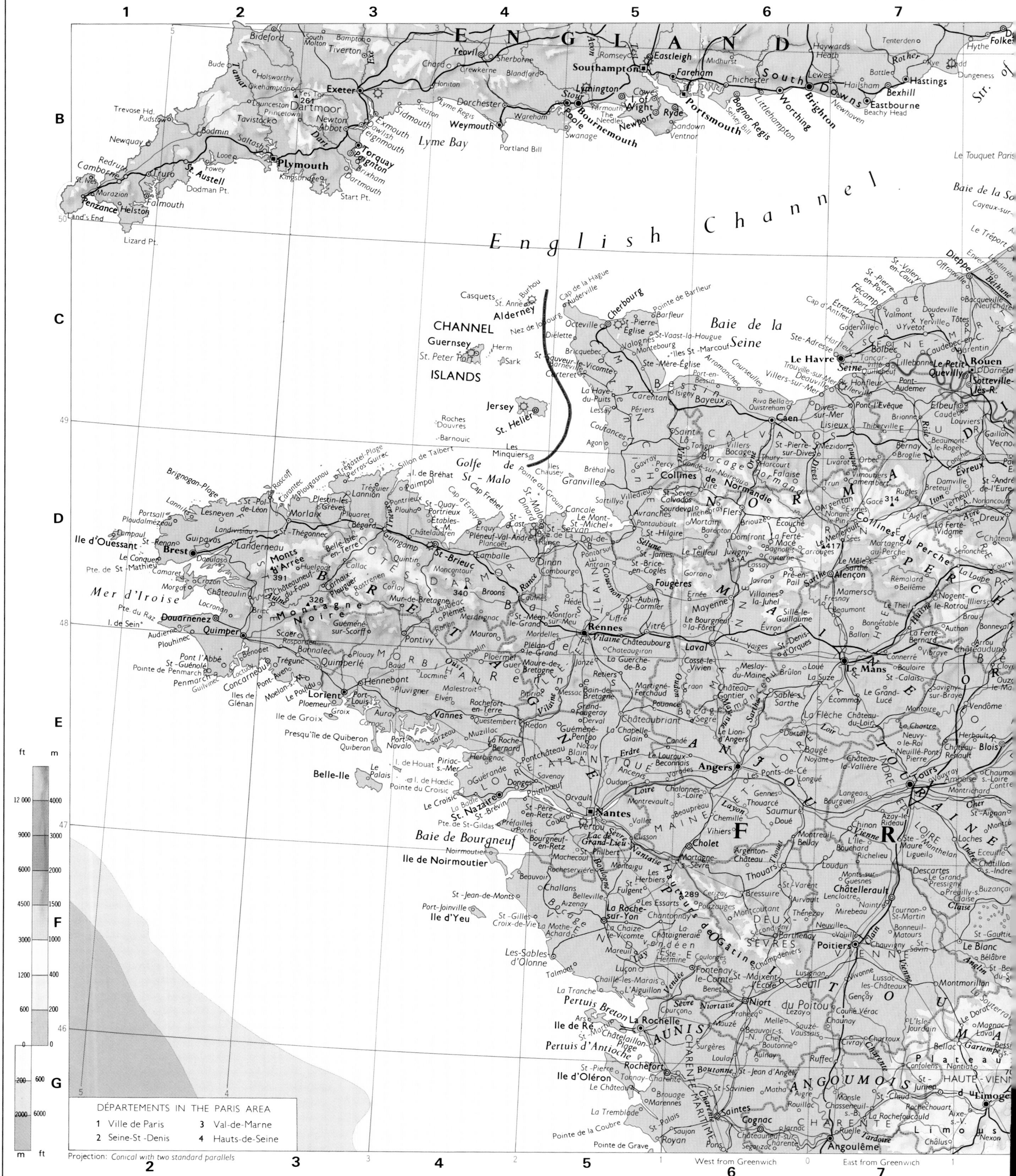

English Channel

CHANNEL ISLANDS

ENGLAND

NORMANDIE

BRETAGNE

ft	m
12 000	4000
9000	3000
6000	2000
4500	1500
3000	1000
1200	400
600	200
0	0
200	600
2000	6000
m	ft

DÉPARTEMENTS IN THE PARIS AREA

1	Ville de Paris	3	Val-de-Marne
2	Seine-St -Denis	4	Hauts-de-Seine

Projection: *Conical with two standard parallels*

West from Greenwich — East from Greenwich

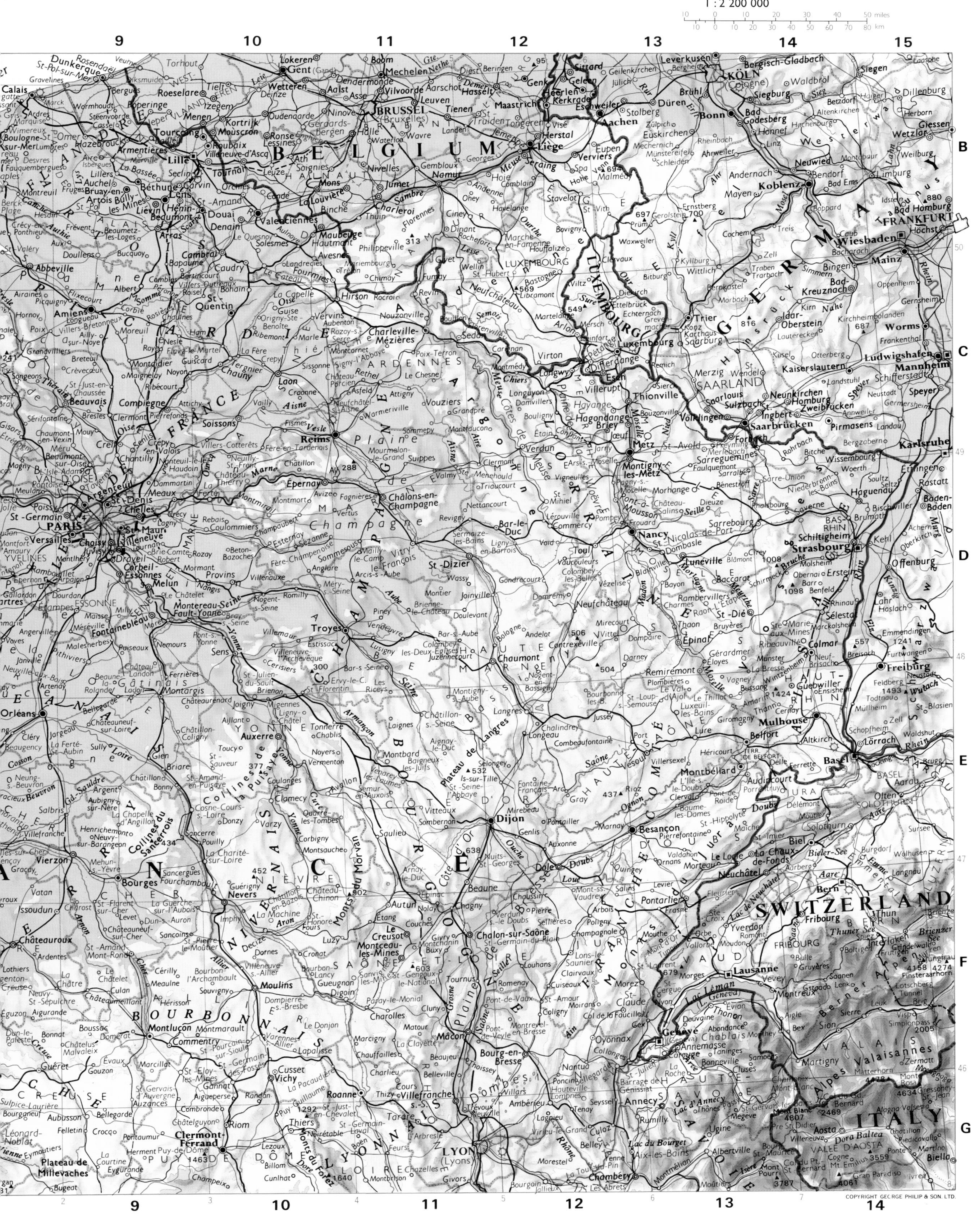
1 : 2 200 000
10 0 10 20 30 40 50 miles
10 0 10 20 30 40 50 60 70 80 km
9
10
11
12
13
14
15
B
C
D
E
F
G
BELGIUM
LUXEMBOURG
GERMANY
FRANCE
SWITZERLAND
ITALY
SAARLAND
Champagne
ARDENNES
LORRAINE
BOURGOGNE
VOSGES
JURA
BOURBONNAIS
NIVERNAIS
Calais
Dunkerque
Lille
Gent
BRUSSEL (Bruxelles)
Liège
Aachen
Köln
Bonn
Koblenz
Wiesbaden
Mainz
FRANKFURT
Amiens
Reims
PARIS
Versailles
Metz
Nancy
Strasbourg
Saarbrücken
Luxembourg
Troyes
Orléans
Dijon
Besançon
Basel
Bern
Lausanne
Genève
Annecy
Lyon (Lyons)
Clermont-Ferrand
Bourges
Nevers
Freiburg
Mulhouse
Colmar
Mâcon
Chambéry
Aosta
COPYRIGHT GEORGE PHILIP & SON, LTD.

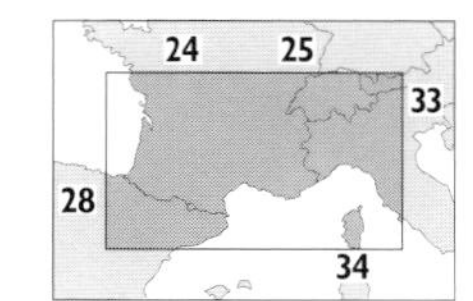

Projection: Conical with two standard parallels

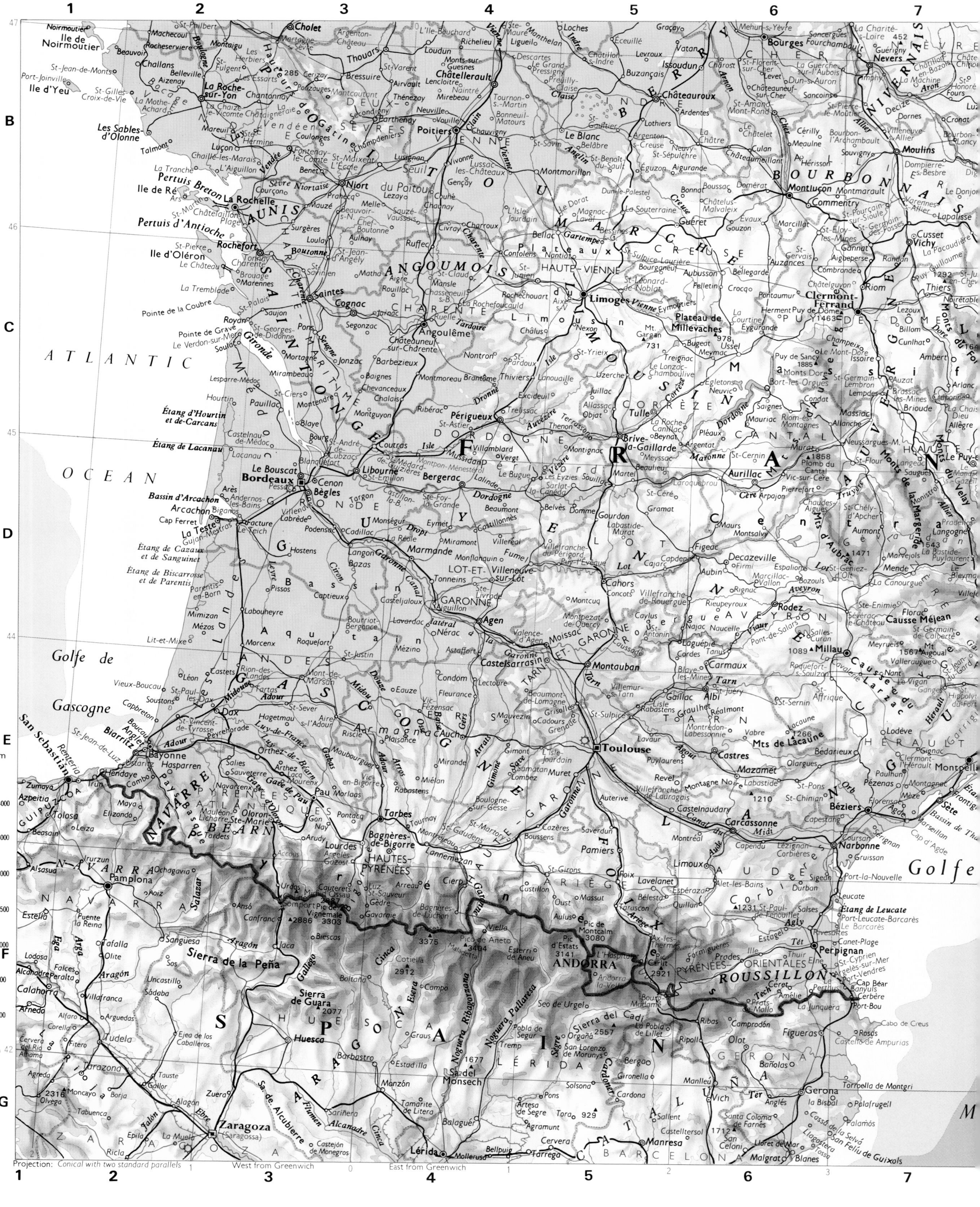

West from Greenwich

East from Greenwich

1 : 2 200 000
10 0 10 20 30 40 50 miles
10 0 10 20 30 40 50 60 70 80 km
8
9
10
11
12
13
14
B
C
D
E
F
G
SWITZERLAND
ITALY
LIGURIAN SEA
MEDITERRANEAN SEA
Golfo di Génova
CORSE (CORSICA)
HAUTE-CORSE
CORSE-DU-SUD
ALPES-DE-HAUTE-PROVENCE
ALPES-MARITIMES
VAUCLUSE
HAUTE-SAVOIE
SAVOIE
VALAIS
VAUD
FRIBOURG
JURA
DRÔME
LYON
MILANO
(Milan)
TORINO
(Turin)
GENOVA
(Genoa)
MARSEILLE
Genève
Lausanne
Grenoble
Avignon
Toulon
Nice
Cannes
MONACO
Monte-Carlo
San Remo
Bern
Luzern
Bastia
Ajaccio
Livorno
La Spezia
Parma
Bérgamo
Bréscia
Novara
Pavia
Alessándria
Asti
Savona
Aosta
Chambéry
Annecy
Valence
Arles
Nîmes
Aix-en-Provence
Montélimar
Mont Blanc
4807
ILES D'HYÈRES
Côte d'Azur
Elba
Capraia
Gorgona
COPYRIGHT, GEORGE PHILIP & SON, LTD.

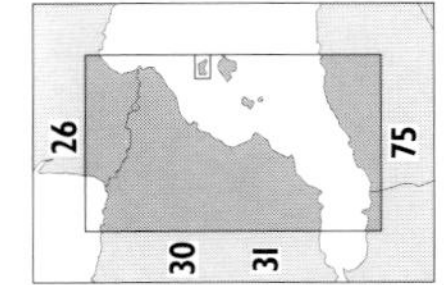
26
30
31
75

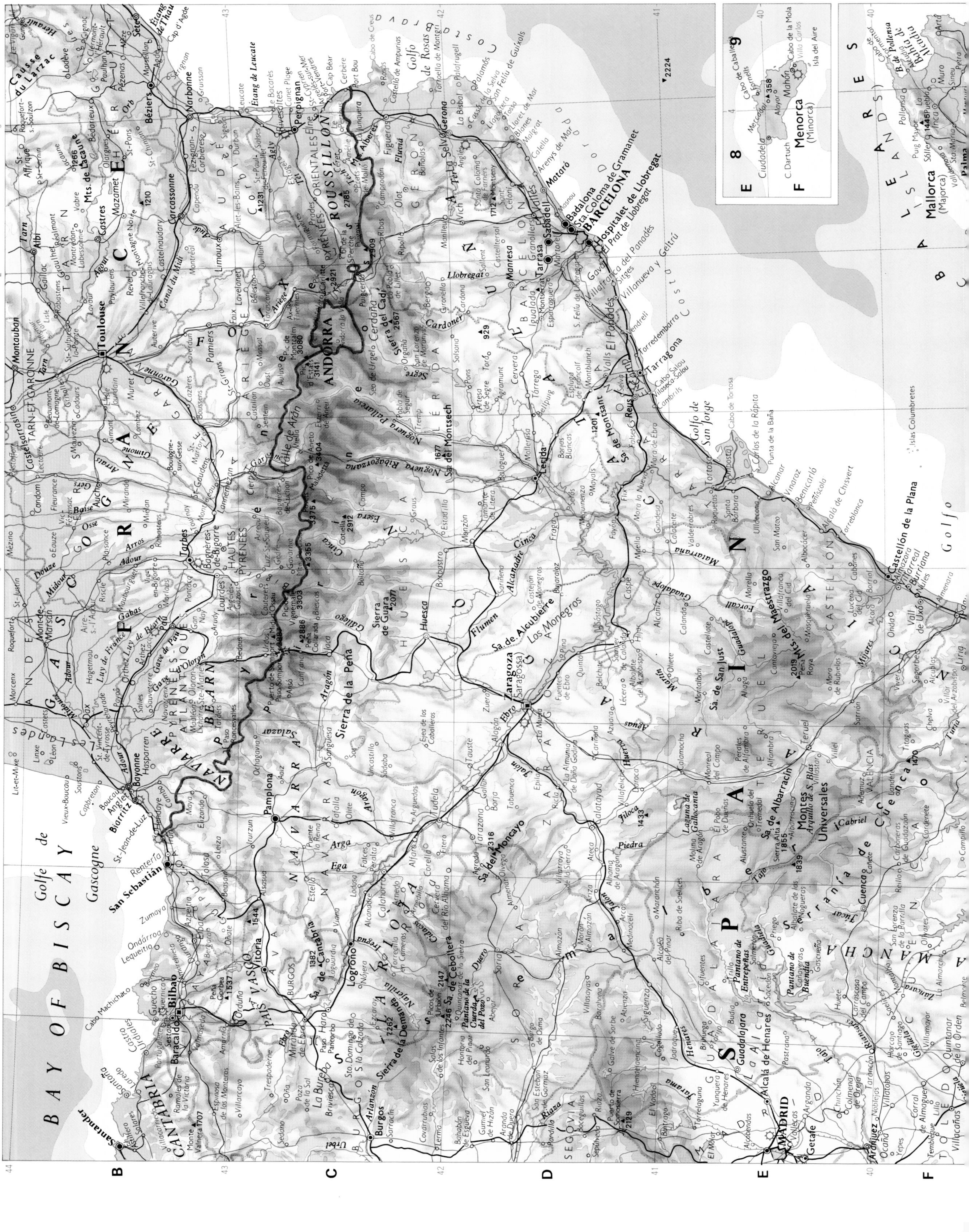

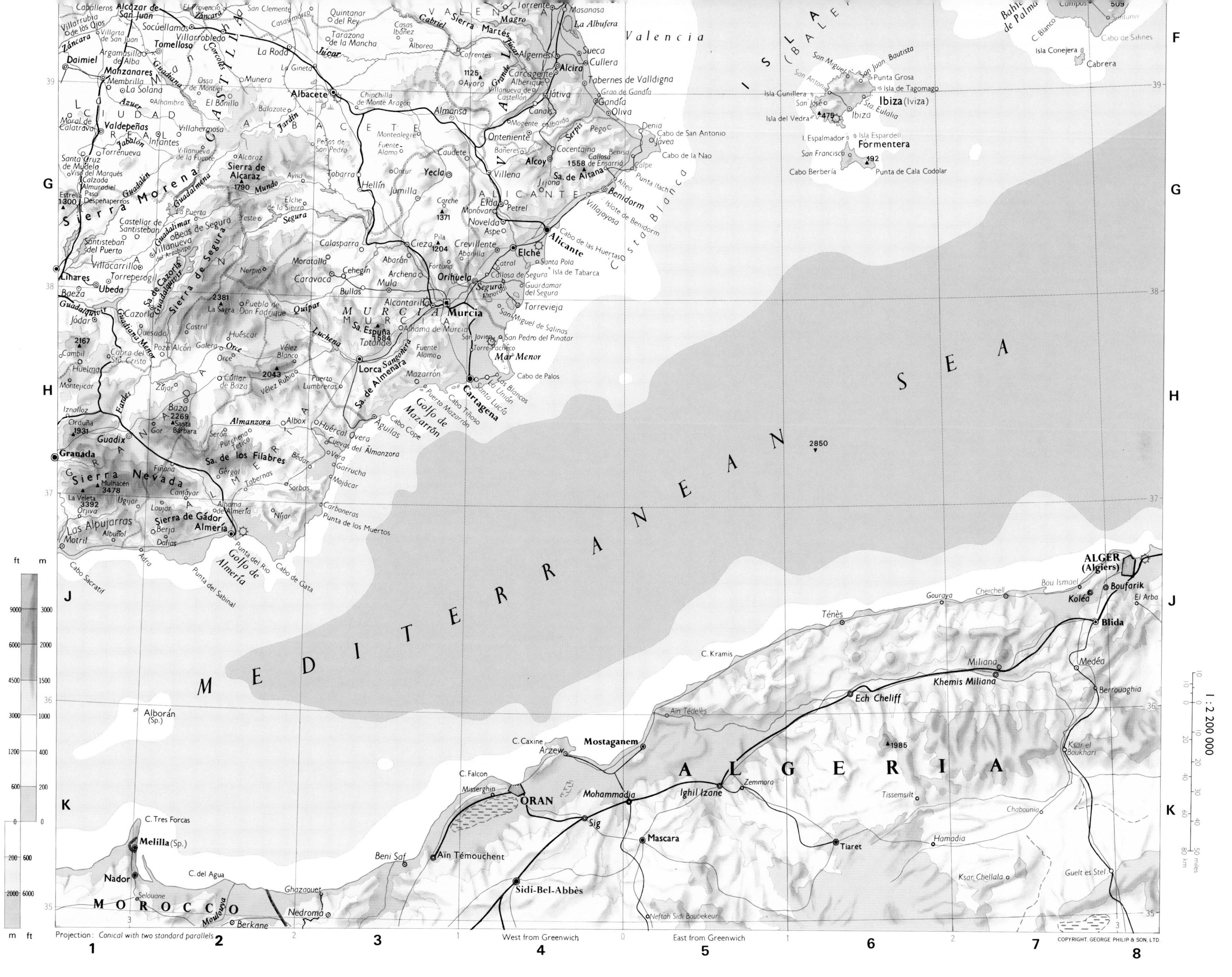

1 : 2 200 000
10 0 10 20 30 40 50 miles
10 0 20 40 60 80 km
F
G
H
J
K
1
2
3
4
5
6
7
8
MEDITERRANEAN SEA
ISLAS (BALEARES)
ALGERIA
MOROCCO
Valencia
Ibiza (Iviza)
Formentera
Cabrera
Isla Conejera
Bahía de Palma
Cabo de Salinas
Cabo de San Antonio
Cabo de la Nao
Costa Blanca
Alicante
Elche
Murcia
Cartagena
Cabo de Palos
Mar Menor
Golfo de Mazarrón
Lorca
Águilas
Almería
Golfo de Almería
Cabo de Gata
Granada
Sierra Nevada
Mulhacén 3478
Guadix
Linares
Úbeda
Baeza
Albacete
Hellín
Yecla
Jumilla
Almansa
Villena
Alcoy
Benidorm
Denia
Gandía
Sueca
Alcira
Játiva
Cullera
Torrevieja
Orihuela
Caravaca
Motril
Adra
Berja
Valdepeñas
Manzanares
Daimiel
Tomelloso
Sierra Morena
Sierra de Segura
Sierra de Alcaraz
Sa. de los Filabres
Sierra de Gádor
Las Alpujarras
Alborán (Sp.)
2850
ALGER (Algiers)
Blida
Boufarik
Koléa
Médéa
Miliana
Khemis Miliana
Cherchell
Ténès
Ech Cheliff
Tiaret
Mostaganem
Mascara
ORAN
Arzew
Sig
Sidi-Bel-Abbès
Aïn Témouchent
Nedroma
Ghazaouet
Beni Saf
C. Falcon
C. Kramis
Melilla (Sp.)
Nador
C. Tres Forcas
Berkane
West from Greenwich
East from Greenwich
Projection: Conical with two standard parallels
COPYRIGHT GEORGE PHILIP & SON, LTD.
ft m
9000 3000
6000 2000
4500 1500
3000 1000
1200 400
600 200
0 0

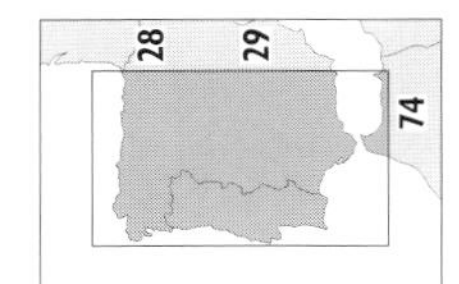
28
29
74

MEDITERRANEAN SEA
Golfo de Cádiz
Costa del Sol
Strait of Gibraltar
MOROCCO
Montes de Toledo
Sierra Morena
Sierra Nevada
Algarve
LISBOA (LISBON)
Sevilla
Córdoba
Granada
Málaga
Cádiz
Huelva
Almería
Jaén
Badajoz
Cáceres
Mérida
Ciudad Real
Gibraltar (Br.)
Ceuta (Sp.)
Melilla (Sp.)
Tanger (Tangier)
Tétouan
Larache
Faro
Évora
Setúbal
Algeciras
Jerez de la Frontera
Mulhacén 3478
Alborán (Sp.)
1 : 2 200 000
Projection: Conical with two standard parallels
West from Greenwich
COPYRIGHT. GEORGE PHILIP & SON, LTD.

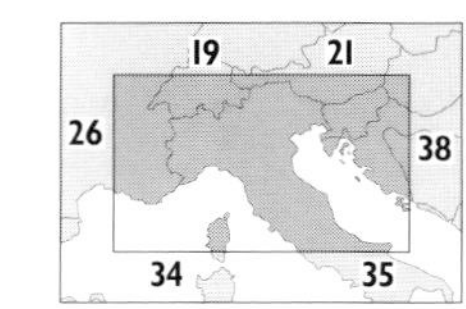

Projection: Conical with two standard parallels

East from Greenwich

---- Inter-entity boundaries as agreed at the 1995 Dayton Peace Agreement

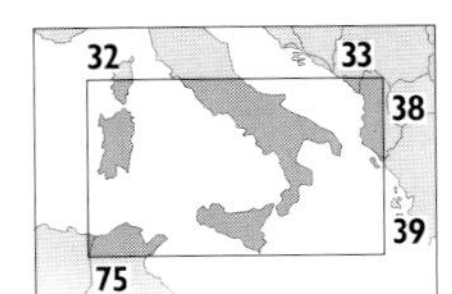

1 2 3 4 5 6

A B C D E F

Iles Sanguinaires
G. d'Ajaccio
C. di Muro
Petreto
Taravo
L'Incudine
2136
Zonza
Levie
Solenzara
Favone
CORSE
CORSICA
G. de Valinco
Propriano
Sartène
Porto-Vecchio
CORSE-DU-SUD
Iles Cerbicales
Bonifacio
I. de Cavallo
Bouches de Bonifacio
Santa Teresa Gallura
Maddalena
La Maddalena
Caprera
Asinara
Punta dello Scorno
Golfo dell' Asinara
Pto. Cervo
Arzachena
Costa Smeralda
Liscia
Coghinas
Àggius
Tempio Pausania
Calangianus
Golfo Aranci
G. di Òlbia
Tavolara
Òlbia
1362
M. Limbara
Porto Tòrres
Sorso
Sennori
Òsilo
Sàssari
C. dell'Argentiera
Òschiri
L. di Coghinas
Ozieri
Posada
Tanaunella
Fertilia
Ìttiri
Alghero
Villanova Monteleone
Pattada
Buddusò
Siniscola
C. Comino
1259
Bonorva
Tirso
Bitti
Orune
Bosa
Temo
Nùoro
Dorgali
Macomer
Oliena
Golfo di Orosei
SARDEGNA
Ghilarza
Cedrino
L. del Tirso
Fonni
C. Mannu
Sòrgono
Monti del Gennargentu
1834
Baunei
C. di Monte Santu
TYRRHENIAN
3719
Cabras
Oristano
SARDEGNA
Làconi
Arbatax
Lanusei
Golfo di Oristano
M. Arci
812
Arborea
Terralba
Nurri
Ìerzu
Campidano
Mannu
S. Gavino Monreale
Mandas
SARDINIA
Gùspini
Arbus
Sanluri
Flumendosa
C. Pècora
Gonnosfanàdiga
Senorbì
Fluminimaggiore
1236
M. Lìnas
Villacidro
Serramanna
S. Vito
Villaputzu
Muravera
Iglèsias
Cixerri
Dolianova
Pta. Serpeddi
1069
SEA
Portoscuso
Gonnesa
Siliqua
Assemini
Sestu
Sinnai
Selàrgius
C. Ferrato
Carloforte
Carbonia
1116
Cágliari
Quartu Sant'Elena
San Pietro
Sant'Antìoco
Santadi
Golfo di Cágliari
Serpentara
C. Carbonara
3589
Sant' Antìoco
Porto Botte
Pula
Teulada
G. di Pàlmas
C. Spartivento
Ustica
Iles de la Galite
C. Serrat
C. Blanc
Cani
Bizerte (Binzert)
Menzel-Bourguiba
Plane
Zembra
Golfe de Tunis
C. Bon
El Kala
Tabarka
Mateur
ALGERIA
Tébourba
TUNIS
Halq el Oued
Kelibia
Menzel-Temime
Bou Salem
Béja
Medjerda
Soliman
TUNISIA
Mellègue
Téboursouk
Nabeul
Zaghouan
Hammamet
Pantelleria
Pantelleria (It.)
836
1319
MEDITE
Vatican City
ROMA (Rome)
Tìvoli
Subiaco
Trasacco
Conca del Fùcino
Fregene
Tevere (Tiber)
Palestrina
Valmontone
Lido di Òstia (Lido di Roma)
Frascati
Anagni
Alatri
Vèroli
Sora
Pomèzia
Albano Laziale
Velletri
Cori
Ferentino
Ìsola del Liri
Arpino
Aprilia
Cisterna di Latina
Frosinone
Monte S. Giovanni
Latina
Sezze
Ceccano
Ceprano
Cassino
Ànzio
Nettuno
Priverno
Sonnino
Pontecorvo
Fondi
Liri
Pontina
1533
Sabàudia
Terracina
Fòrmia
Monte Circeo
541
Gaeta
Minturno
Garigliano
Golfo di Gaeta
Mondragone
Volturno
Zannone
Palmarola
Ìsole Ponziane
Ponza
283
Ventotene
Ìschia
788
C. San Vito
Castellammare del Golfo
G. di Castellammare
Terrasini
Favarotta
C. Gallo
PALERMO
Bagheria
1110
Levanzo
Trápani
Érice
Càrini
Monreale
Partinico
Misilmeri
Termini Imerese
Marèttimo
Ìsole Ègadi
Alcamo
S. Giuseppe Jato
Favignana
Paceco
Calatafimi
Marineo
Stagnone
Camporeale
Salemi
Corleone
1613
Belsito
Marsala
Gibellina
Partanna
Bisacquino
Prizzi
Lercara Friddi
Castelvetrano
Sambuca di Sicilia
Mazara del Vallo
Menfi
Bùrgio
Mussomeli
Campobello di Mazara
Belice
Sciacca
Caltabellotta
Ribera
Platani
San Cataldo
Racalmuto
Sicilian Channel
Cattòlica Eraclea
Raffadali
Aragona
Canicattì
Siculiana
Porto Empèdocle
Agrigento
Favara
Naro
Palma di Montechiaro
Campobello di Licata

ft m
9000 3000
6000 2000
4500 1500
3000 1000
1200 400
600 200
37
0 0
200 600
2000 6000
4000 12,000
m ft

Projection: Conical with two standard parallels

East from Greenwich

1 : 2 200 000

10 0 10 20 30 40 50 miles
10 0 20 40 60 80 km

7 8 9 10 11 12

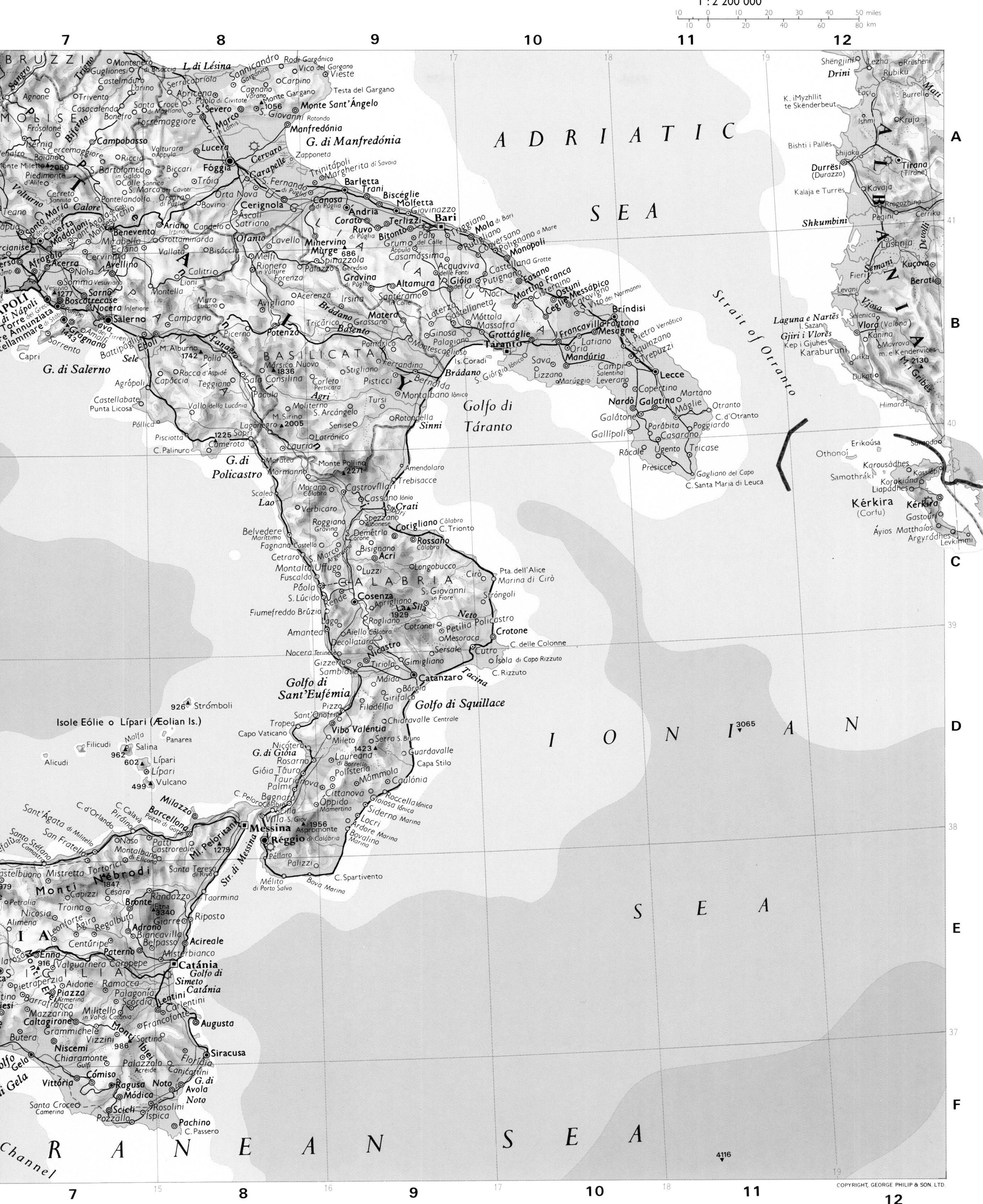

A B C D E F

7 8 9 10 11 12

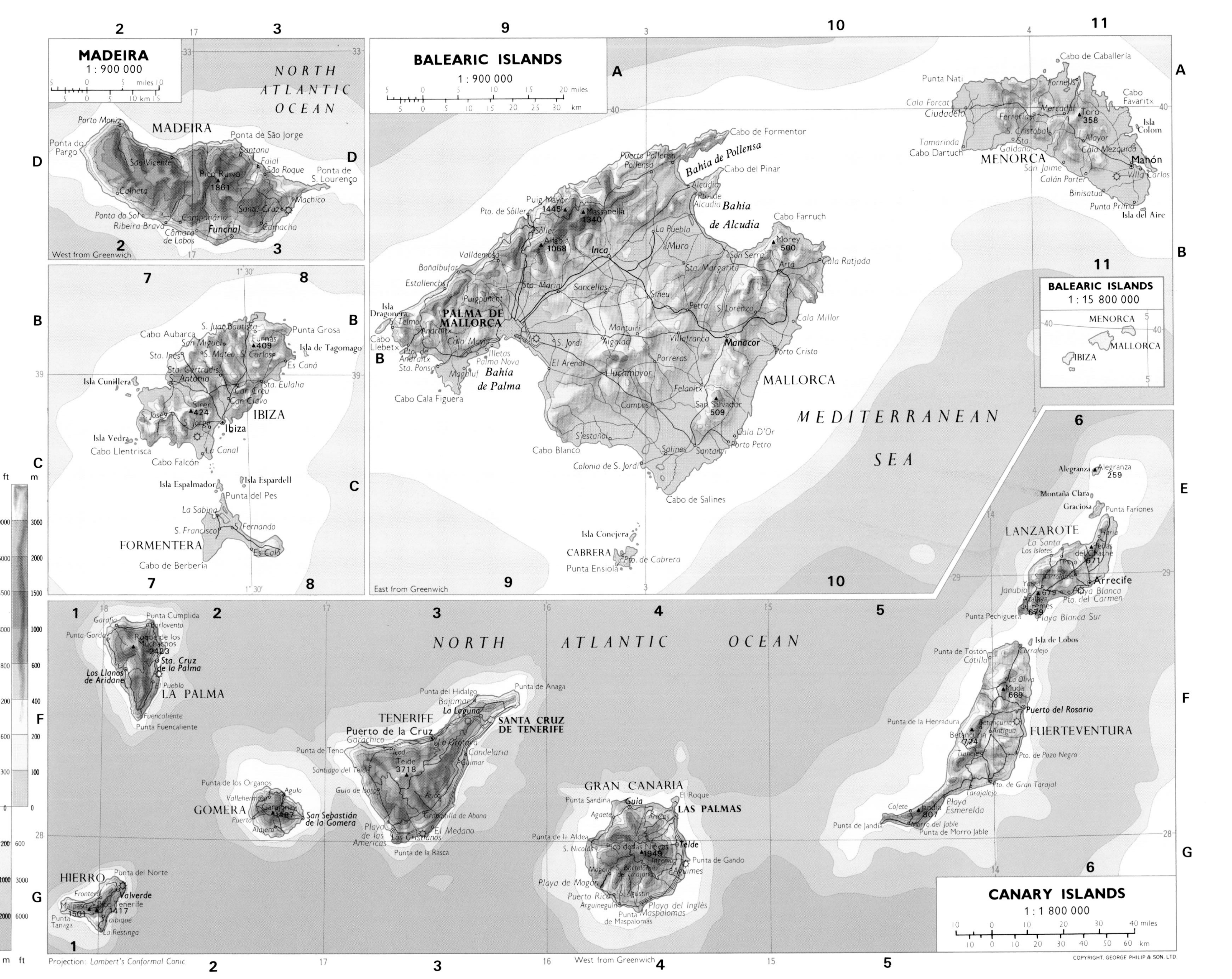

MADEIRA
1 : 900 000
NORTH ATLANTIC OCEAN
MADEIRA
Porto Moniz
Ponta do Pargo
São Vicente
Pico Ruivo
1861
Ponta de São Jorge
Santana
Faial
São Roque
Ponta de S. Lourenço
Machico
Santa Cruz
Camacha
Funchal
Câmara de Lobos
Ribeira Brava
Ponta do Sol
Calheta
West from Greenwich
BALEARIC ISLANDS
1 : 900 000
MALLORCA
MEDITERRANEAN SEA
PALMA DE MALLORCA
Cabo de Formentor
Bahia de Pollensa
Cabo del Pinar
Bahia de Alcudia
Cabo Farruch
Puerto Pollensa
Pollensa
Puig Mayor
1445
Massanella
1340
Alfabia
1068
Pto. de Sóller
Sóller
Valldemosa
Bañalbufar
Estallenchs
Isla Dragonera
Cabo Llebetx
Andraitx
Sta. Ponsa
Magaluf
Bahia de Palma
Cabo Cala Figuera
Inca
La Puebla
Muro
Alcudia
Sineu
Sancellas
Sta. Maria
Montuiri
Algaida
Llucmayor
Porreras
Villafranca
Manacor
Porto Cristo
Petra
S. Lorenzo
Sta. Margarita
San Serra
Arta
Morey
500
Cala Ratjada
Cala Millor
Felanitx
San Salvador
509
Cala D'Or
Porto Petro
Santanyi
Salines
Campos
S'estañol
Colonia de S. Jordi
Cabo Blanco
Cabo de Salines
El Arenal
S. Jordi
Isla Conejera
CABRERA
Pto. de Cabrera
Punta Ensiola
East from Greenwich
MENORCA
Cabo de Caballería
Punta Nati
Cala Forcat
Ciudadela
Tamarinda
Cabo Dartuch
Ferrerias
Mercadal
Toro
358
Fornells
Cabo Favaritx
Isla Colom
Alayor
Mahón
Villa Carlos
San Jaime
Calán Porter
Binisatua
Punta Prima
Isla del Aire
BALEARIC ISLANDS
1 : 15 800 000
MENORCA
MALLORCA
IBIZA
IBIZA
Ibiza
S. Juan Bautista
Punta Grosa
Isla de Tagomago
Cabo Aubarca
San Miguel
Sta. Inés
S. Mateo
S. Carlos
Furnas
409
Es Caná
Sta. Gertrudis
S. Antonio
Sta. Eulalia
Can Creu
Can Clavo
Isla Cunillera
S. José
Sirer
424
S. Jorge
Isla Vedra
Cabo Llentrisca
Cabo Falcón
La Canal
Isla Espalmador
Isla Espardell
Punta del Pes
La Sabina
S. Francisco
S. Fernando
Es Caló
FORMENTERA
Cabo de Berbería
NORTH ATLANTIC OCEAN
CANARY ISLANDS
1 : 1 800 000
LA PALMA
Punta Cumplida
Barlovento
Roque de los Muchachos
2423
Sta. Cruz de la Palma
Los Llanos de Aridane
El Pueblo
Fuencaliente
Punta Fuencaliente
Garafía
Punta Gorda
HIERRO
Punta del Norte
Valverde
Frontera
Malpaso
1501
1417
Punta Tanaga
La Restinga
GOMERA
San Sebastián de la Gomera
Punta de los Organos
Agulo
Vallehermoso
TENERIFE
Puerto de la Cruz
SANTA CRUZ DE TENERIFE
La Laguna
Punta de Anaga
Punta del Hidalgo
Bajamar
Punta de Teno
Garachico
La Orotava
Candelaria
Teide
3718
Santiago del Teide
Guía de Isora
Arico
El Médano
Playa de las Americas
Los Cristianos
Punta de la Rasca
GRAN CANARIA
LAS PALMAS
Guía
El Roque
Punta Sardina
Agaete
Arucas
Telde
Punta de Gando
Pico de las Nieves
1949
Punta de la Aldea
S. Nicolás
Playa de Mogán
Puerto Rico
Arguineguín
Playa del Inglés
Punta Maspalomas
LANZAROTE
Alegranza
259
Montaña Clara
Graciosa
Punta Fariones
La Santa
Los Islotes
Arrecife
Janubio
Playa Blanca
Pto. del Carmen
Punta Pechiguera
Playa Blanca Sur
FUERTEVENTURA
Isla de Lobos
Corralejo
Punta de Tostón
Cotillo
La Oliva
Muda
689
Puerto del Rosario
Punta de la Herradura
Betancuria
724
Antigua
Pto. de Pozo Negro
Pto. de Gran Tarajal
Tarajalejo
Playa Esmerelda
Cofete
Jandía
807
Morro del Jable
Punta de Morro Jable
Punta de Jandía
West from Greenwich
Projection: Lambert's Conformal Conic
COPYRIGHT GEORGE PHILIP & SON LTD.

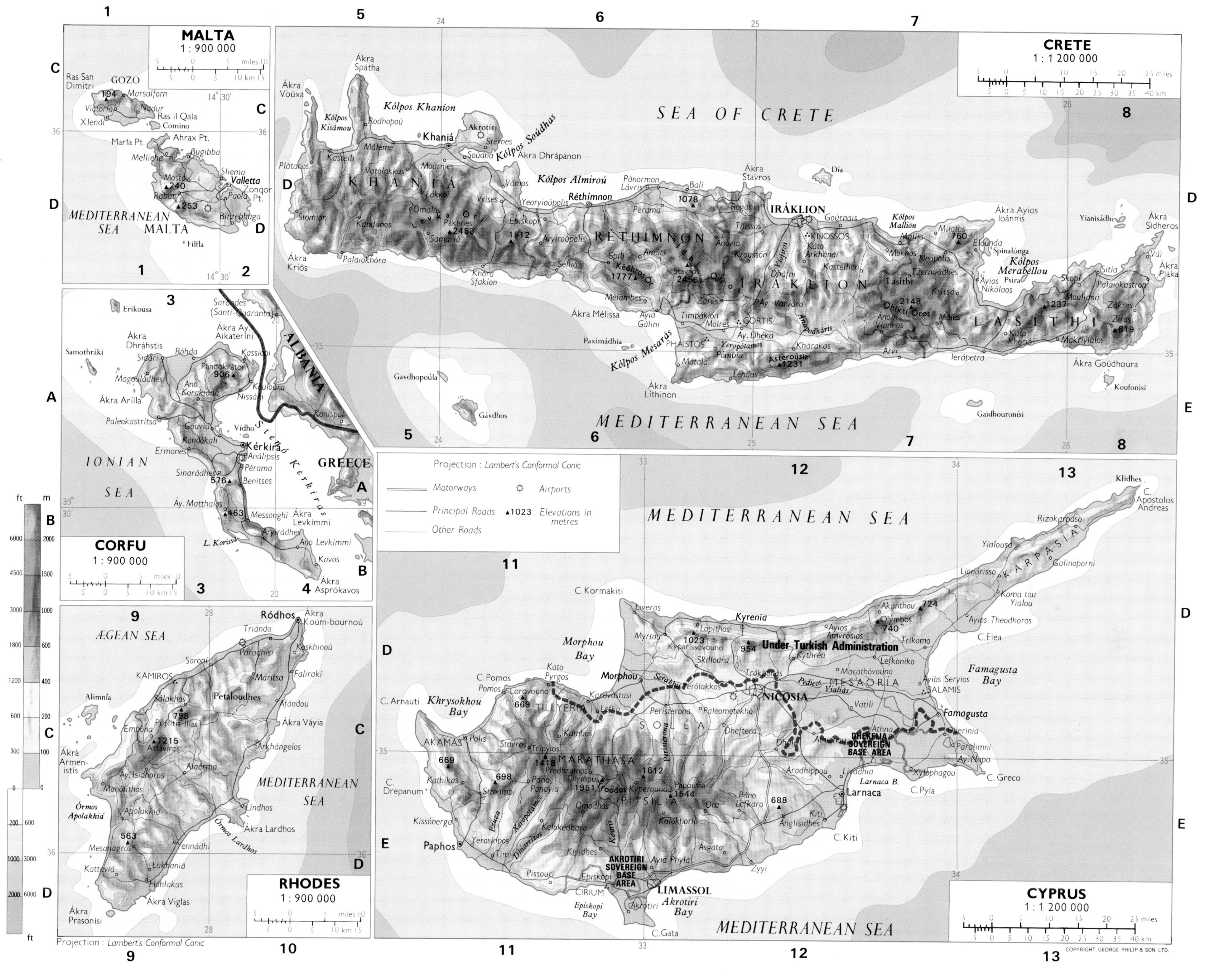

MALTA
1 : 900 000
GOZO
Comino
Valletta
MEDITERRANEAN SEA
MALTA
CRETE
1 : 1 200 000
SEA OF CRETE
Kólpos Khaníon
Khaniá
Kólpos Soúdhas
Kólpos Almiroú
Réthimnon
IRÁKLION
KNOSSOS
PHAISTOS
GORTIS
Kólpos Mesarás
Kólpos Merabéllou
Ierápetra
Sitía
Gávdhos
KHANIÁ
RÉTHIMNON
IRÁKLION
LASÍTHI
MEDITERRANEAN SEA
CORFU
1 : 900 000
ALBANIA
GREECE
Kérkira
Stenó Kerkíras
IONIAN SEA
Projection : Lambert's Conformal Conic
Motorways
Airports
Principal Roads
▲1023 Elevations in metres
Other Roads
MEDITERRANEAN SEA
CYPRUS
1 : 1 200 000
Under Turkish Administration
Kyrenia
NICOSIA
Famagusta
Famagusta Bay
Larnaca
Larnaca B.
LIMASSOL
Akrotiri Bay
Paphos
Morphou
Morphou Bay
Khrysokhou Bay
KARPASIA
MESAORIA
DHEKELIA SOVEREIGN BASE AREA
AKROTIRI SOVEREIGN BASE AREA
RHODES
1 : 900 000
Ródhos
ÆGEAN SEA
KAMIROS
Líndhos
MEDITERRANEAN SEA
Projection : Lambert's Conformal Conic
COPYRIGHT GEORGE PHILIP & SON LTD.

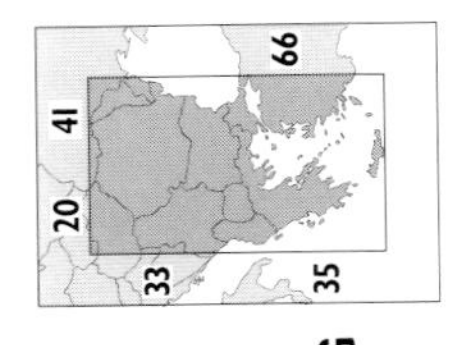

20
41
66
33
35

1 : 3 100 000
miles
km
TURKEY
MACEDONIA
AEGEAN SEA
IONIAN SEA
SEA OF CRETE
(Sea of Candia)
KIKLÁDHES
(CYCLADES)
DHODHEKÁNISOS
(DODECANESE)
Voríai Sporadhes
Marmara Denizi
Karadeniz Boğazı
(Bosporus)
Thrakikón Pélagos
İSTANBUL
Bursa
İZMİR
Edirne
Thessaloniki
(Salonica)
ATHÍNAI
Athens
Piraiévs
(Piræus)
Kórinthos
(Corinth)
Pátrai
Lárisa
Vólos
Tirana
(Tiranë)
Durrësi
(Durazzo)
Vlora (Valona)
Kérkira
(Corfu)
Kefallinía
(Cephalonia)
Zákinthos
(Zante)
Levkás
(Santa Maura)
Iráklion
Khaniá
Ródhos
(Rhodes)
Kárpathos
Kásos
Kos
Sámos
Ikaría
Khíos
(Chios)
Lesvos
(Lesbos)
Límnos
Thásos
Samothráki
Gökçeada
Çanakkale Boğazı
(Dardanelles)
Náxos
Páros
Thíra
Mílos
Ándros
Tínos
Kíthira
(Cerigo)
Pindus Mountains
Párnon Óros
Taïyetos Óros
Thermaïkós Kólpos
Saronikós Kólpos
Korinthiakós Kólpos
Argolikós Kólpos
Lakonikós Kólpos
Messiniakós Kólpos
Stenón Kásos
Stenón Karpáthos
East from Greenwich
Projection: Conical with two standard parallels
COPYRIGHT GEORGE PHILIP & SON, LTD
ft
m
9000
6000
4500
3000
1200
600
0
200
2000
3000
2000
1500
1000
400
200
0
600
6000

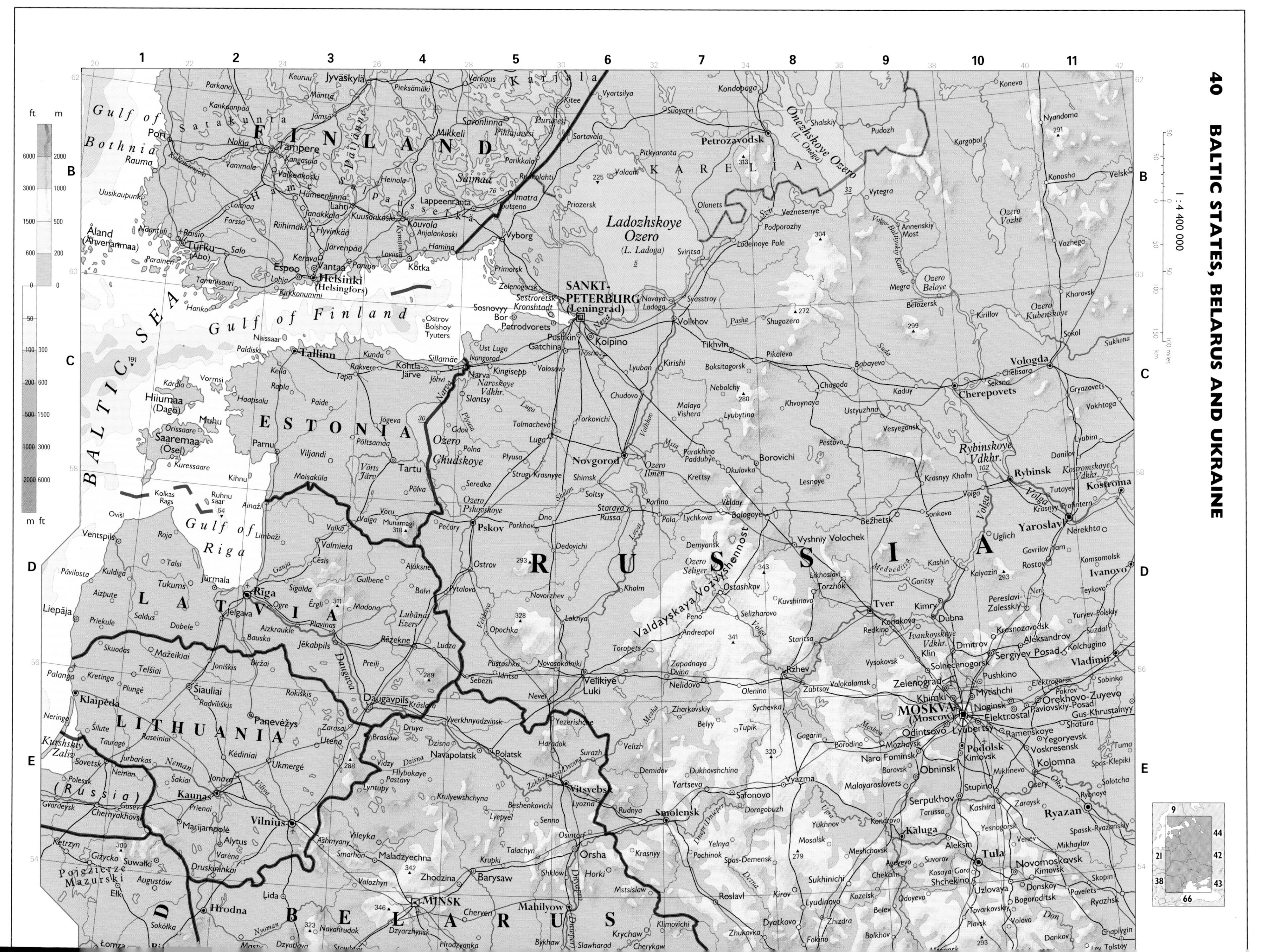
1 : 4 400 000
FINLAND
ESTONIA
LATVIA
LITHUANIA
BELARUS
RUSSIA
KARELIA
Gulf of Finland
Gulf of Riga
Gulf of Bothnia
BALTIC SEA
Ladozhskoye Ozero (L. Ladoga)
Onezhskoye Ozero (L. Onega)
Ozero Chudskoye
Valdayskaya Vozvyshennost
SANKT-PETERBURG (Leningrad)
MOSKVA (Moscow)
Helsinki (Helsingfors)
Tallinn
Riga
Vilnius
MINSK
Novgorod
Pskov
Tver
Smolensk
Yaroslavl
Vologda
Kaunas
Klaipėda
Daugavpils
Vitsyebsk
Hrodna
(Russia)
ft m
6000 2000
3000 1000
1500 500
600 200
0 0
50
100 300
200 600
500 1500
1000 3000
2000 6000
m ft

U K R A I N E
B L A C K S E A
Sea of Azov
Taganrogskiy Zaliv
Karkinitska Zatoka
Krymskyy Pivostriv
C R I M E A
M O L D O V A
R O M A N I A
B U L G A R I A
HUNGARY
SLOVAK REP.
KYYIV (Kiev)
KHARKIV (Kharkov)
DNIPROPETROVSK
DONETSK
ODESA
ROSTOV
BUCUREŞTI (Bucharest)
Zaporizhzhya
Kryvyy Rih
Mykolayiv
Kherson
Melitopol
Mariupol
Berdyansk
Luhansk
Kremenchuk
Poltava
Cherkasy
Kirovohrad
Bila Tserkva
Vinnytsya
Zhytomyr
Khmelnytskyy
Ternopil
Lviv (Lvov)
Lutsk
Rivne
Chernivtsi
Ivano-Frankivsk
Uzhhorod
Chernihiv
Homyel
Brest
Pinsk
Mazyr
Sumy
Kursk
Belgorod
Voronezh
Orel
Simferopol
Sevastopol
Kerch
Feodosiya
Yevpatoriya
Chişinău
Tiraspol
Iaşi
Galaţi
Brăila
Constanţa
Ploieşti
Braşov
Sibiu
Cluj-Napoca
Craiova
Lublin
Carpathians
Transilvania
Podilska Vysochyna
Pripet Marshes
Dnister
Dnipro
Desna
Prut
Siret
Donets
Dunărea (Danube)
East from Greenwich
Projection: Conical with two standard parallels
CARTOGRAPHY BY PHILIP'S. COPYRIGHT REED INTERNATIONAL BOOKS LTD
G H J K
6 7 8 9 10

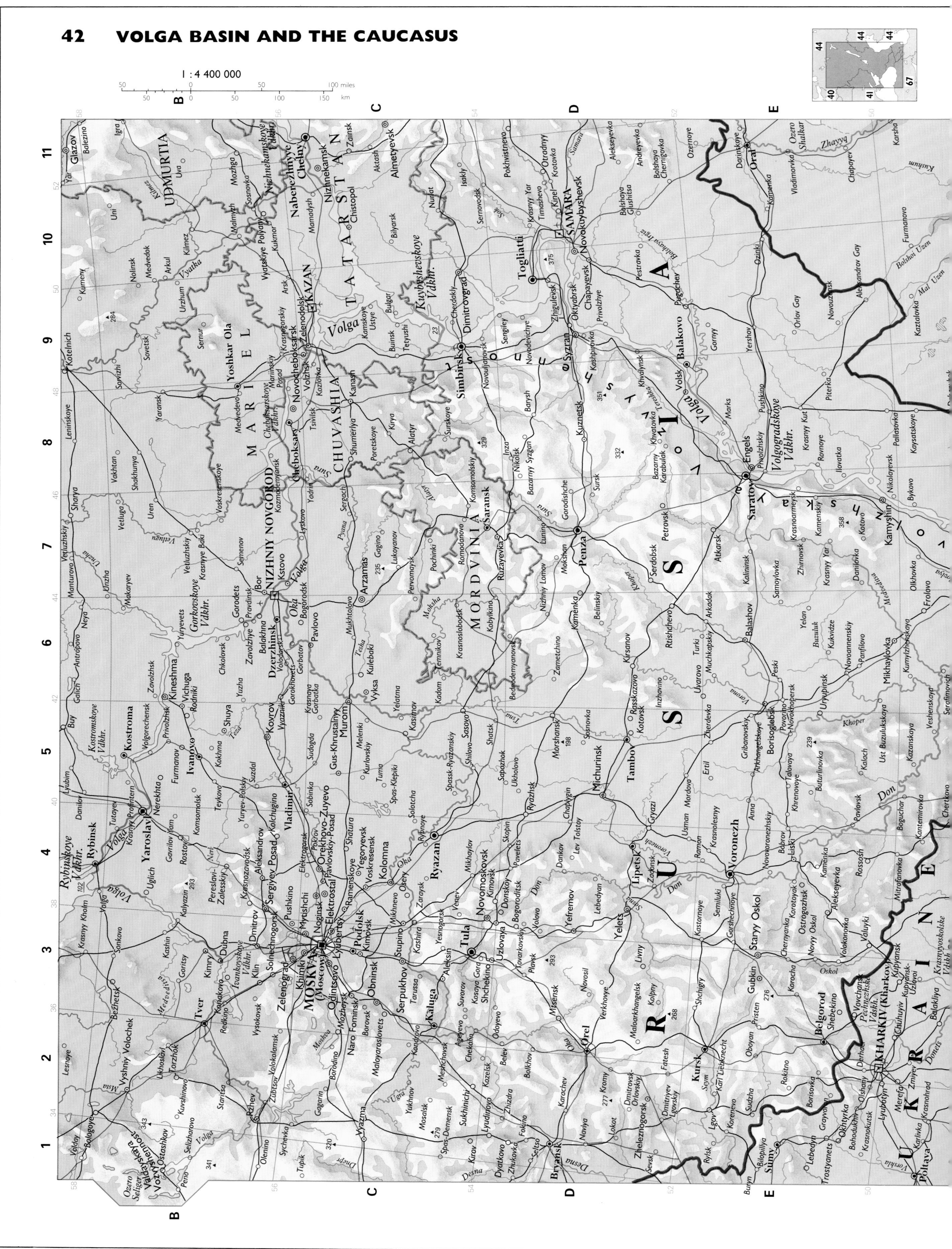
1 : 4 400 000
50 0 50 100 miles
50 0 50 100 150 km
RUSSIA
UKRAINE
UDMURTIA
TATARSTAN
MARI EL
CHUVASHIA
MORDVINIA
NIZHNIY NOVGOROD
MOSKVA (Moscow)
KAZAN
SAMARA
Saratov
Volgograd
Kharkiv (Kharkov)
Voronezh
Penza
Ryazan
Tula
Yaroslavl
Kostroma
Ivanovo
Vladimir
Tver
Kaluga
Orel
Kursk
Belgorod
Lipetsk
Tambov
Simbirsk
Togliatti
Engels
Syzran
Saransk
Cheboksary
Yoshkar Ola
Naberezhnyye Chelny
Volga

KAZAKSTAN
Rynsession Depression
Ryn Peski
CASPIAN SEA
BLACK SEA
Sea of Azov
Taganrogskiy Zaliv
KALMYKIA
Chernyye Zemli
Caspian
Yergeni Vozvyshennost
DAGESTAN
CHECHENIA
INGUSHETIA
NORTH OSSETIA
KABARDINO-BALKARIA
KARACHEY-CHERKESSIA
ADYGEA
ABKHAZIA
AJARIA
GEORGIA
South Ossetia
ARMENIA
AZERBAIJAN
TURKEY
CRIMEA
Caucasus Mountains
Samurskiy Khrebet
Kuzey Anadolu Dağları
Nagorno-Karabakh
Prikubanskaya Nizmennost
Tsimlyanskoye Vdkhr.
Veselovskoye Vdkhr.
Mingäçevir Su Anbarı
Sevana Lich
Kerchenskiy Proliv
Arabatskaya Strelka
Agrakhanskiy Poluostrov
Ostrova Tyuleni
VOLGOGRAD
ROSTOV
DONETSK
DNIPROPETROVSK
Zaporizhzhya
Astrakhan
Elista
Stavropol
Krasnodar
Makhachkala
Groznyy
Vladikavkaz
Nalchik
TBILISI
YEREVAN
BAKI
Sochi
Novorossiysk
Taganrog
Mariupol
Luhansk
Kutaisi
Batumi
Sokhumi
Trabzon
Samsun
Derbent
Sumqayıt
Gyumri
Gäncä
Kerch
Feodosiya
Melitopol
Berdyansk
Volzhskiy
Shakhty
Novocherkassk
Pyatigorsk
Kislovodsk
Cherkessk
Maykop
Armavir
Kropotkin
Tikhoretsk
Tuapse
Anapa
Yeysk
Budennovsk
Neftekumsk
Kizlyar
Rustavi
Poti
Elbrus 5642
Kazbek 5047
Projection: Conical with two standard parallels
East from Greenwich
CARTOGRAPHY BY PHILIP'S. COPYRIGHT REED INTERNATIONAL BOOKS LTD
ft
m
12000
9000
6000
3000
1500
600
0
4000
3000
2000
1000
500
200
0
50
100
200
500
1000
2000
150
300
600
1500
3000
6000
m
ft

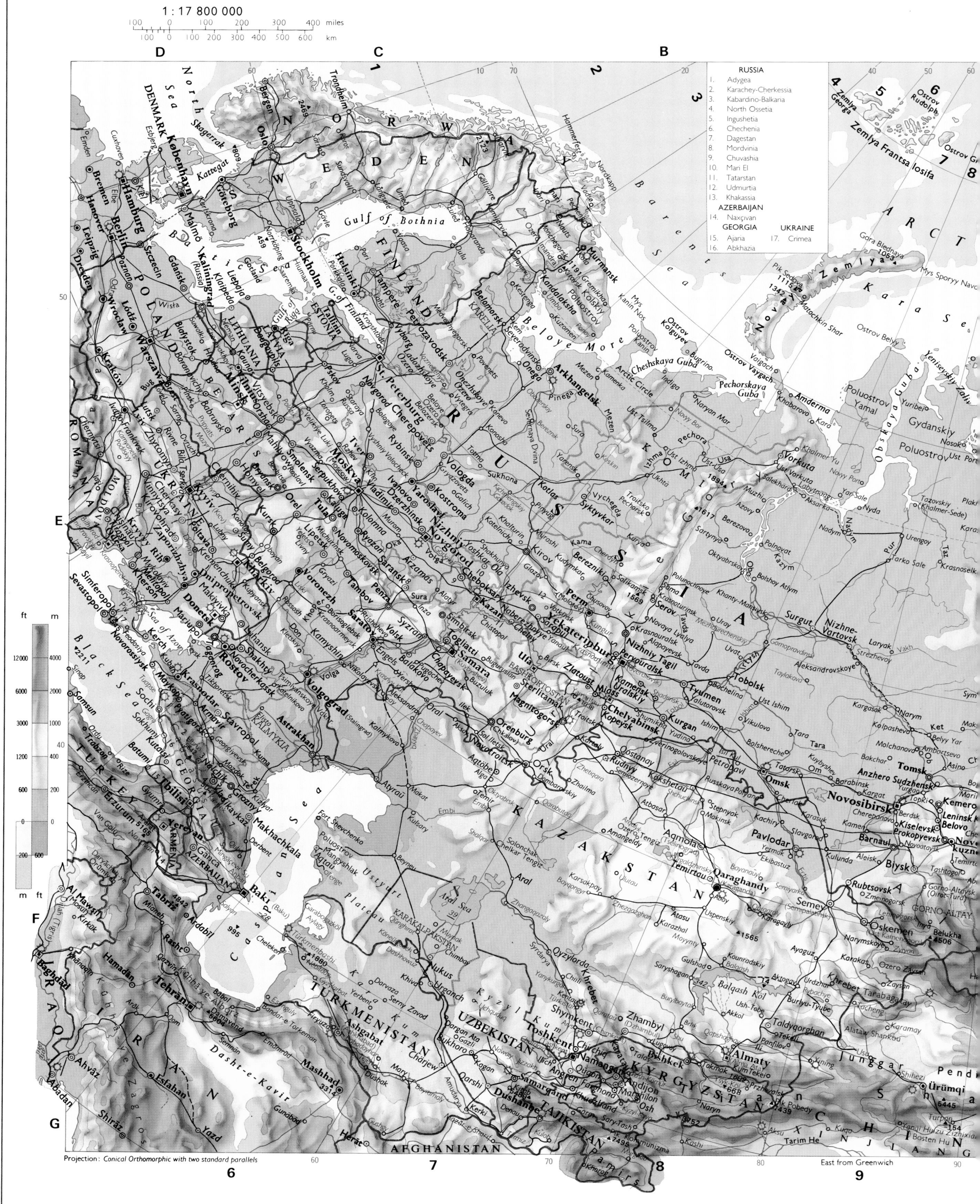
1 : 17 800 000
100 0 100 200 300 400 miles
100 0 100 200 300 400 500 600 km
RUSSIA
1. Adygea
2. Karachey-Cherkessia
3. Kabardino-Balkaria
4. North Ossetia
5. Ingushetia
6. Chechenia
7. Dagestan
8. Mordvinia
9. Chuvashia
10. Mari El
11. Tatarstan
12. Udmurtia
13. Khakassia
AZERBAIJAN
14. Naxçıvan
GEORGIA
15. Ajaria
16. Abkhazia
UKRAINE
17. Crimea
ft m
12000 4000
6000 2000
3000 1000
1200 400
600 200
0 0
200 600
m ft
Projection: Conical Orthomorphic with two standard parallels
East from Greenwich
RUSSIA
KAZAKSTAN
UZBEKISTAN
TURKMENISTAN
KYRGYZSTAN
TAJIKISTAN
AFGHANISTAN
IRAN
IRAQ
TURKEY
GEORGIA
ARMENIA
AZERBAIJAN
UKRAINE
BELARUS
MOLDOVA
ROMANIA
POLAND
LITHUANIA
LATVIA
ESTONIA
FINLAND
SWEDEN
NORWAY
DENMARK
Barents Sea
Kara Sea
Black Sea
Caspian Sea
Aral Sea
Baltic Sea
North Sea
Gulf of Bothnia
Beloye More
Zemlya Frantsa Iosifa
Novaya Zemlya
Moskva
St. Peterburg
Kyyiv
Minsk
Novosibirsk
Toshkent
Almaty
Tehran
Baku
Ashgabat
Bishkek
Dushanbe

A
B
C
D
E
F
10
11
12
13
14
Severnaya Zemlya
Ostrov Komsomolets
Ostrov Oktyabrskoy Revolyutsii
Ostrov Bolshevik
Proliv Vilkitskogo
Poluostrov Taymyr
Gory Byrranga
Laptev Sea
OCEAN
Novosibirskiye Ostrova
Ostrov Kotelnyy
Lyakhovskiye Ostrova
Proliv Dmitriya Lapteva
East Siberian Sea
Ostrov Vrangelya
Chukchi Sea
Mys Dezhneva (East C.)
St. Lawrence I. (U.S.A.)
Anadyrskiy Zaliv
Bering Sea
Chukotskoye Nagorye
Koryakskoye Nagorye
Kolymskoye Nagorye
Penzhinskaya Guba
Zaliv Shelikhova
Gizhiginskaya Guba
Poluostrov Kamchatka
Sredinnyy Khrebet
Petropavlovsk-Kamchatskiy
Komandorskiye Ostrova
Sea of Okhotsk
Kurilskiye Ostrova
Khrebet Cherskogo
Verkhoyanskiy Khrebet
Verkhoyansk
Tiksi
Norilsk
Arctic Circle
Yakutsk
Vilyuysk
Olekminsk
Srednekolymsk
Magadan
Okhotsk
Stanovoy Khrebet
Khrebet Dzhugdzur
Sakhalin
Ostrov Bolshoy Shantar
Sakhalinskiy Zaliv
Nikolayevsk-na-Amure
Komsomolsk
Khabarovsk
Sovetskaya Gavan
Yuzhno-Sakhalinsk
Khrebet Sikhote Alin
Blagoveshchensk
Kirensk
Bratsk
Krasnoyarsk
Kansk
Nizhneudinsk
Irkutsk
Angarsk
Usolye Sibirskoye
Cheremkhovo
Ulan Ude
Chita
Yablonovyy Khrebet
Vostochnyy Sayan
Tunguska
RUSSIA
Hovsgol Nuur
Uvs Nuur
Hangayn Nuruu
Hentiyn Nuruu
Ulaanbaatar (Ulan Bator)
MONGOLIA
GOBI
Edrengiyn Nuruu
Da Hinggan Ling
Hulun Nur
Qiqihar
Harbin
Jilin
Changchun
Shenyang
Fushun
Anshan
Dalian
Beijing
Hohhot
Baotou
Zhangjiakou
REPUBLIC
NORTH KOREA
Pyongyang
SOUTH KOREA
Sŏul (Seoul)
Inch'on
Taegu
Pusan
Vladivostok
Nakhodka
Ussuriysk
Sea of JAPAN
Japan
Hokkaido
Sapporo
Hakodate
Honshu
Niigata
Kanazawa
Boundaries of Republics

1 : 44 400 000

250 0 250 500 750 1000 miles

250 0 500 1000 1500 km

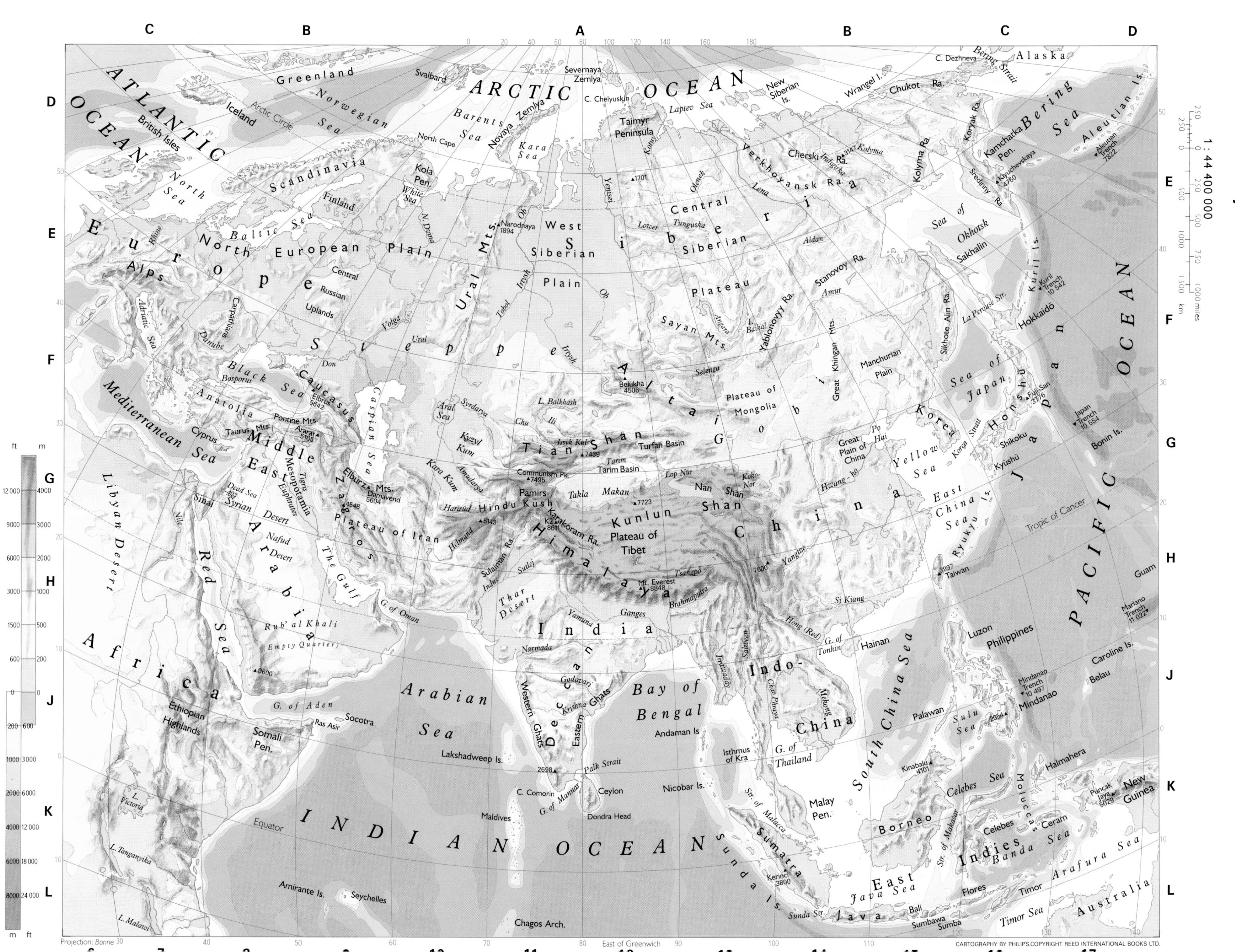

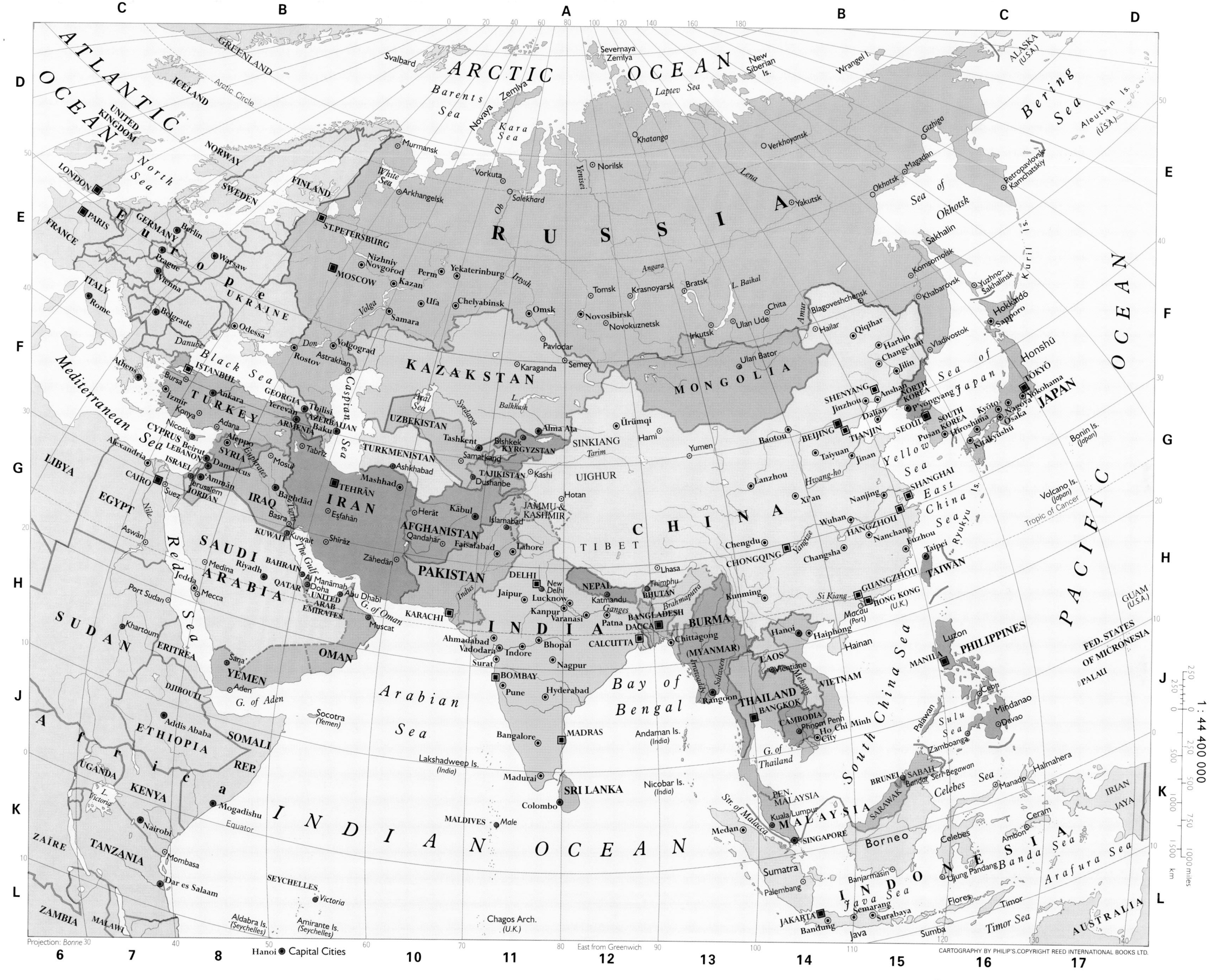
1 : 44 400 000
miles
km
ARCTIC OCEAN
PACIFIC OCEAN
INDIAN OCEAN
ATLANTIC OCEAN
RUSSIA
CHINA
MONGOLIA
KAZAKSTAN
INDIA
PAKISTAN
AFGHANISTAN
IRAN
IRAQ
SAUDI ARABIA
TURKEY
SYRIA
JORDAN
ISRAEL
LEBANON
CYPRUS
GEORGIA
ARMENIA
AZERBAIJAN
TURKMENISTAN
UZBEKISTAN
TAJIKISTAN
KYRGYZSTAN
NEPAL
BHUTAN
BANGLADESH
BURMA (MYANMAR)
THAILAND
LAOS
VIETNAM
CAMBODIA
MALAYSIA
SINGAPORE
BRUNEI
INDONESIA
PHILIPPINES
TAIWAN
JAPAN
NORTH KOREA
SOUTH KOREA
SRI LANKA
MALDIVES
OMAN
YEMEN
UNITED ARAB EMIRATES
QATAR
BAHRAIN
KUWAIT
EGYPT
SUDAN
ETHIOPIA
ERITREA
DJIBOUTI
SOMALI REP.
KENYA
UGANDA
TANZANIA
ZAÏRE
ZAMBIA
MALAWI
LIBYA
SEYCHELLES
UKRAINE
FINLAND
SWEDEN
NORWAY
ICELAND
GREENLAND
UNITED KINGDOM
FRANCE
GERMANY
ITALY
TIBET
UIGHUR
SINKIANG
JAMMU & KASHMIR
AUSTRALIA
Bering Sea
Sea of Okhotsk
Sea of Japan
Yellow Sea
East China Sea
South China Sea
Arabian Sea
Bay of Bengal
Caspian Sea
Black Sea
Mediterranean Sea
Red Sea
Barents Sea
Kara Sea
Laptev Sea
Java Sea
Banda Sea
Arafura Sea
Timor Sea
Celebes Sea
Sulu Sea
Tropic of Cancer
Equator
Arctic Circle
East from Greenwich
TOKYO
BEIJING
SEOUL
MOSCOW
ST. PETERSBURG
TEHRAN
DELHI
BOMBAY
CALCUTTA
MADRAS
KARACHI
BANGKOK
MANILA
JAKARTA
SHANGHAI
HONG KONG
ISTANBUL
CAIRO
Hanoi ● Capital Cities
Projection: Bonne 30
CARTOGRAPHY BY PHILIP'S.COPYRIGHT REED INTERNATIONAL BOOKS LTD.

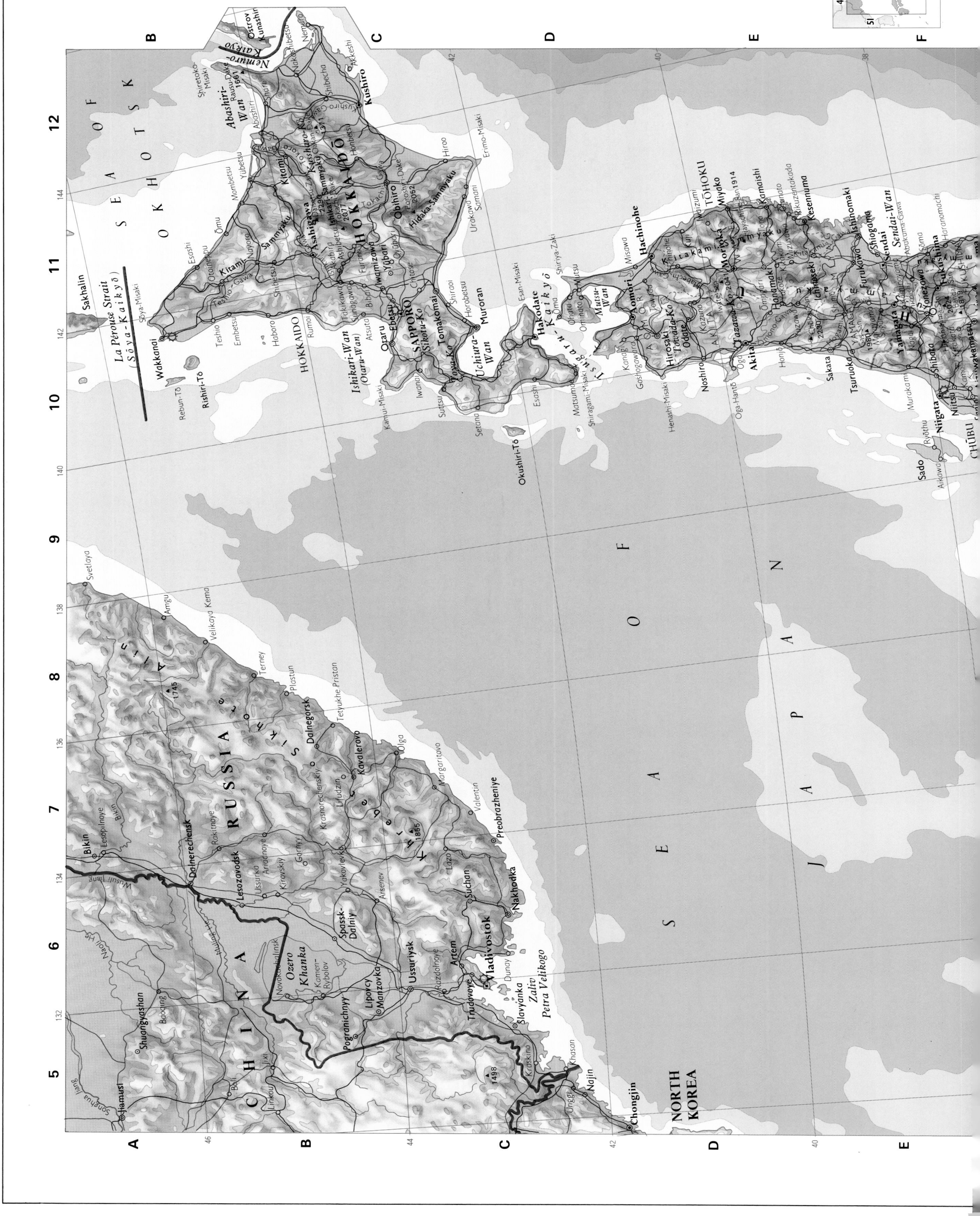

SEA OF OKHOTSK

SEA OF JAPAN

HOKKAIDŌ

La Pérouse Strait (Sōya-Kaikyō)

Nemuro-Kaikyō

Tsugaru-Kaikyō

Abashiri-Wan

Ishikari-Wan (Otaru-Wan)

Uchiura-Wan

Mutsu-Wan

Sendai-Wan

TŌHOKU

CHŪBU

RUSSIA

CHINA

NORTH KOREA

Sakhalin

Ostrov Kunashir

Rishiri-Tō

Rebun-Tō

Okushiri-Tō

Sado

Wakkanai

Kitami

Asahikawa

Abashiri

Kushiro

Obihiro

SAPPORO

Otaru

Tomakomai

Muroran

Hakodate

Aomori

Hachinohe

Hirosaki

Noshiro

Akita

Morioka

Miyako

Kamaishi

Sendai

Yamagata

Niigata

Sakata

Tsuruoka

Sikotu-Ko

Towada-Ko

Tazawa-Ko

Zaliv Petra Velikogo

Ozero Khanka

Vladivostok

Nakhodka

Ussuriysk

Artem

Spassk-Dalniy

Arsenev

Lesozavodsk

Dalnerechensk

Bikin

Dalnegorsk

Kavalerovo

Preobrazheniye

Olga

Terney

Plastun

Amgu

Svetlaya

Pogranichnyy

Slavyanka

Kraskino

Khasan

Najin

Chongjin

Jiamusi

Shuangyashan

Baoqing

Jixi

Linkou

Boli

Sikhote-Alin'

A B C D E F

5 6 7 8 9 10 11 12

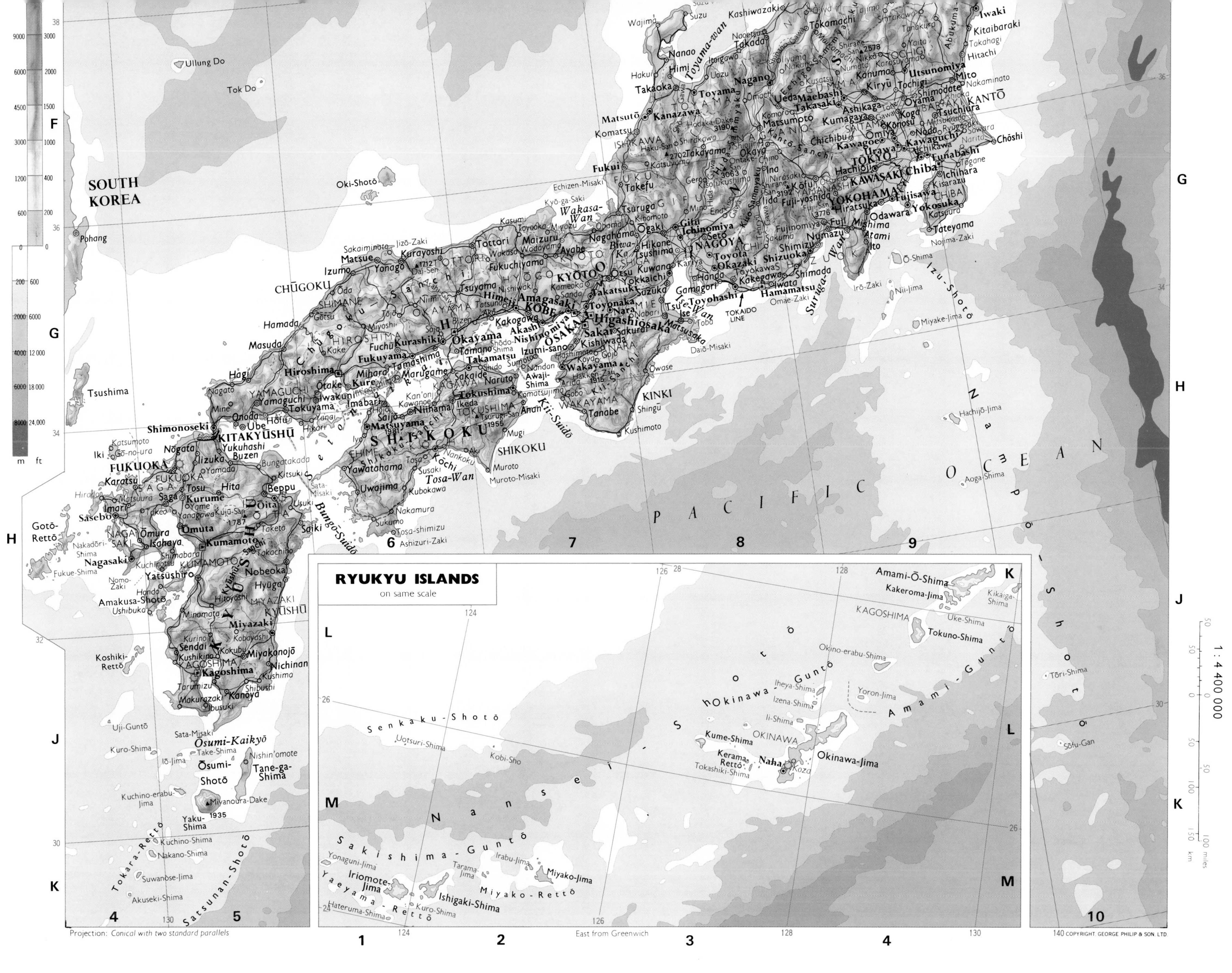
1 : 4 400 000
miles
km
SOUTH KOREA
Ullung Do
Tok Do
Pohang
Tsushima
Oki-Shotō
CHŪGOKU
SHIKOKU
KINKI
KANTŌ
KYŪSHŪ
P A C I F I C O C E A N
Kitakyūshū
Shimonoseki
Fukuoka
Nagasaki
Kumamoto
Kagoshima
Miyazaki
Hiroshima
Okayama
Matsuyama
Kōchi
Takamatsu
Tokushima
Kōbe
Ōsaka
Kyōto
Nagoya
Shizuoka
Yokohama
Kawasaki
Tōkyō
Chiba
Niigata
Kanazawa
Toyama
Nagano
Utsunomiya
Mito
Chōshi
Iwaki
Izu-Shotō
Hachijō-Jima
Tosa-Wan
Bungo-Suidō
Kii-Suidō
Ōsumi-Kaikyō
Tane-ga-Shima
Yaku-Shima
Tokara-Rettō
Satsunan-Shotō
Gotō-Rettō
Koshiki-Rettō
RYUKYU ISLANDS
on same scale
Amami-Ō-Shima
Tokuno-Shima
Okinawa-Jima
Naha
Miyako-Jima
Ishigaki-Shima
Iriomote-Jima
Senkaku-Shotō
Nansei-Shotō
Sakishima-Guntō
Projection: Conical with two standard parallels
East from Greenwich
COPYRIGHT GEORGE PHILIP & SON LTD

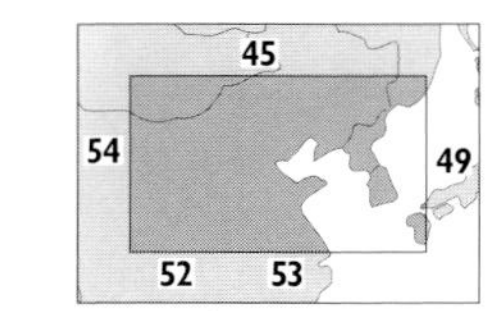

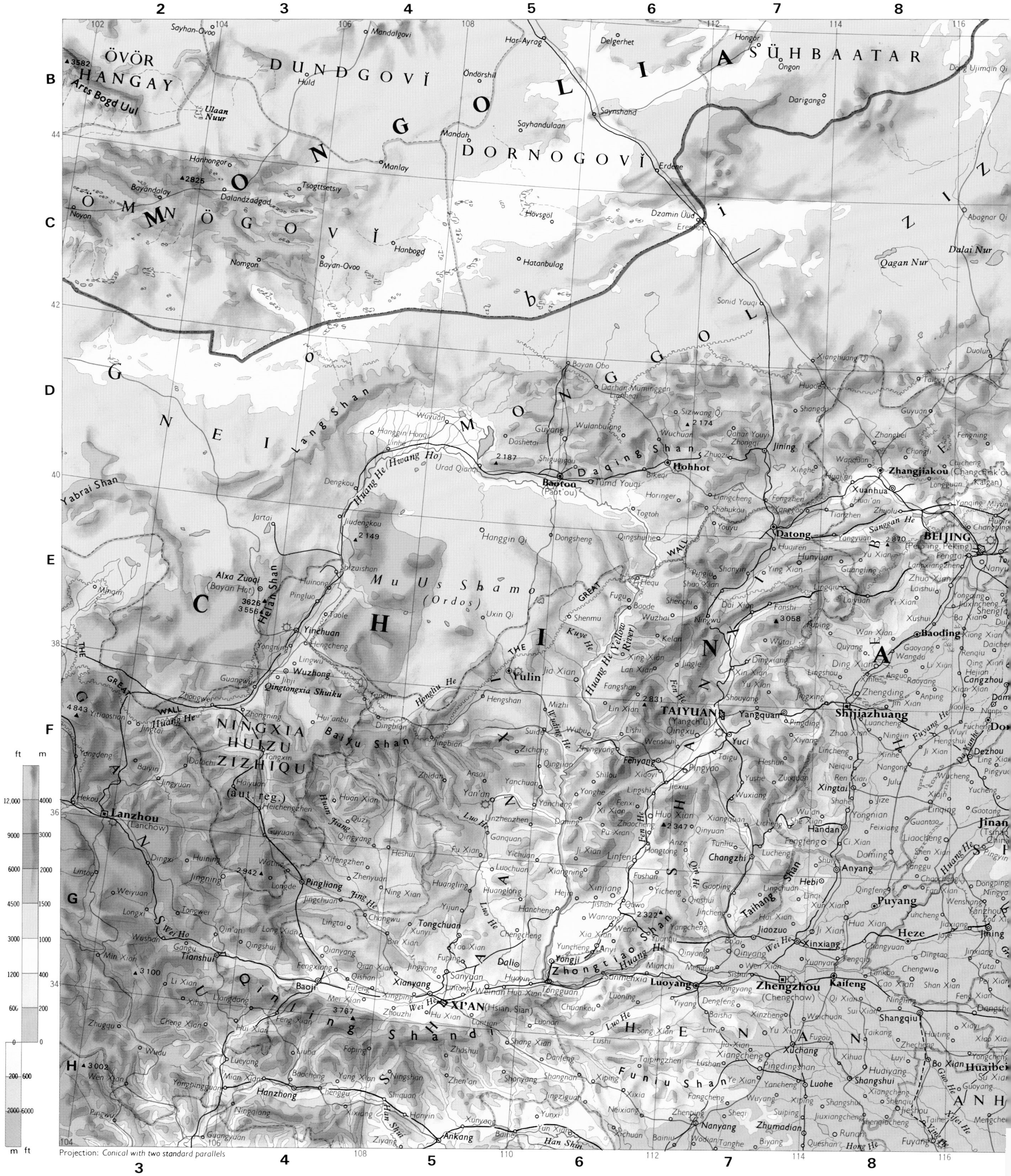

2 3 4 5 6 7 8

B C D E F G H

MONGOLIA
ÖVÖR HANGAY
DUNDGOVĬ
DORNOGOVĬ
SÜHBAATAR
ÖMNÖGOVĬ
Arts Bogd Uul
Sayhan-Ovoo
Mandalgovi
Har-Ayrag
Delgerhet
Hongor
Öngon
Dariganga
Huld
Öndörshil
Ulaan Nuur
Saynshand
Sayhandulaan
Mandah
Manlay
Hanhongor
Bayandalay
Dalandzadgad
Tsogttsetsiy
Noyon
Nomgon
Hanbogd
Bayan-Ovoo
Hövsgöl
Hatanbulag
Erdene
Dzamin Üüd
Erenhot
Abagnar Qi
Dalai Nur
Qagan Nur
Sonid Youqi
Xianghuang Qi
Duolun
Huade
Taibus Qi
Shangdu
Guyuan
Fengning
Zhangbei
Chongli
Zhangjiakou (Changchiak'ou; Kalgan)
Xuanhua
BEIJING (Peiping, Peking)
NEI MONGOL
GOBI
Lang Shan
Yabrai Shan
Bayan Obo
Darhan Muminggan Lianheqi
Siziwang Qi
Wuchuan
Qahar Youyi Zhongqi
Jining
Guyang
Wulanbulang
Wuyuan
Hanggin Houqi
Linhe
Dashetai
Shiguaigou
Daqing Shan
Hohhot
Urad Qianqi
Baotou (Pao-t'ou)
Tumd Youqi
Bikeqi
Huang He (Hwang Ho)
Dengkou
Horinger
Togtoh
Liangcheng
Fengzhen
Datong
Jartai
Jiudengkou
Hanggin Qi
Dongsheng
Qingshuihe
GREAT WALL
Youyu
Huairen
Hunyuan
Yangyuan
Yu Xian
Alxa Zuoqi (Bayan Hot)
Helan Shan
Shizuishan
Huinong
Pingluo
Mu Us Shamo (Ordos)
Uxin Qi
Taole
Yinchuan
Yongning
Hengcheng
Lingwu
Wuzhong
Qingtongxia Shuiku
Guangwu
Yulin
Jia Xian
Fugu
Hequ
Shenmu
Baode
Shenchi
Wuzhai
Ningwu
Kelan
Huang He (Yellow River)
Dai Xian
Fanshi
Wutai
Xinzhou
Ding Xiang
Baoding
Dingzhou
Quyang
NINGXIA HUIZU ZIZHIQU (aut. reg.)
Baixu Shan
Zhongwei
Zhongning
Tongxin
Haiyuan
Jingyuan
Jingbian
Hengshan
Suide
Mizhi
Zizhou
Wubu
Lishi
Fangshan
Lin Xian
TAIYUAN (Yangch'u)
Qingxu
Yuci
Yangquan
Shijiazhuang
Hekou
Lanzhou (Lanchow)
Baiyin
Jingyuan
Guyuan
Huan Xian
Qingyang
Ansai
Yan'an
Yanchang
Yanchuan
Fenyang
Wenshui
Pingyao
Xingtai
Handan
Changzhi
Linfen
Huo Xian
Anyang
Hebi
Dingxi
Huining
Jingning
Pingliang
Jing He
Huangling
Tongchuan
Yichuan
Hancheng
Jishan
Houma
Xinjiang
Yuncheng
Jiaozuo
Xinxiang
Puyang
Heze
Tianshui
Wei He
Baoji
Xianyang
XI'AN (Hsian, Sian)
Weinan
Huayin
Tongguan
Sanmenxia
Zhongtiao Shan
Luoyang
Zhengzhou (Chengchow)
Kaifeng
Shangqiu
Dali
Yongji
Qinling Shandi
Qin Ling
Min Xian
Li Xian
Zhouzhi
Hu Xian
Mei Xian
Feng Xian
Hui Xian
Shang Xian
Danfeng
Lushi
Luo He
Song Xian
HENAN
Yuzhou
Xuchang
Pingdingshan
Luohe
Shangshui
Zhoukou
Funiu Shan
Hanzhong
Ankang
Han Shui
Nanyang
Zhumadian
Xinyang
Bo Xian
Huaibei
Dezhou
Jinan
Cangzhou
Taihang Shan
Lueyang
Mian Xian
Yang Xian
Ningshan
Zhen'an
Shangnan
Xixia
Neixiang
Xichuan
Zhenping
Tanghe
Biyang
Xunyang
Baihe
Yun Xian
Guangyuan
Ningqiang
Zhugqu
Wudu
Wen Xian
SHAANXI
SHANXI
HEBEI
GANSU
CHINA

3626
3556
3582
2825
2187
2174
2149
2870
3058
2831
2347
2322
4843
2942
3100
3767
3002

102 104 106 108 110 112 114 116

44 42 40 38 36 34

ft m
12,000 4000
9000 3000
6000 2000
4500 1500
3000 1000
1200 400
600 200
0 0
200 600
2000 6000
m ft

Projection: Conical with two standard parallels

1 : 5 300 000
NORTH KOREA
SOUTH KOREA
SEA OF JAPAN
HUANG HAI (Yellow Sea)
Korea Bay
Bo Hai (Gulf of Chihli)
Liaodong Wan
Shandong Bandao
Liaodong Bandao
HARBIN
SHENYANG (Mukden)
DALIAN (Luda)
QINGDAO (Ch'ingtao)
P'YŎNGYANG
SŎUL (Seoul)
INCH'ŎN
PUSAN
TAEGU
Vladivostok
Changchun
Jilin
Tianjin
Cease Fire Line
Korea Strait
Tsushima-kaikyō
JAPAN
RUSSIA
Cheju-do
East from Greenwich
COPYRIGHT, GEORGE PHILIP & SON, LTD.

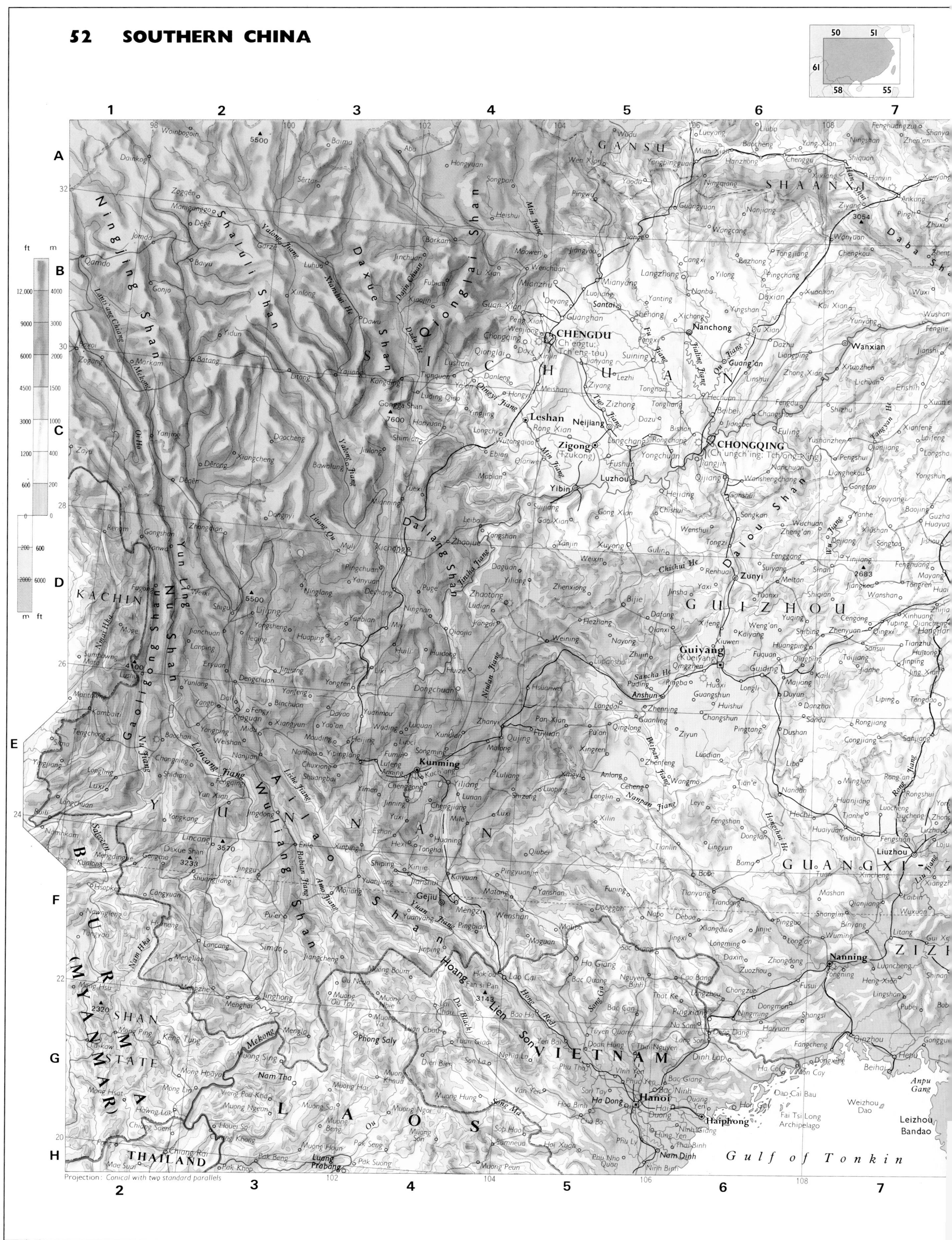

50
51
61
58
55
ft
m
12,000
4000
9000
3000
6000
2000
4500
1500
3000
1000
1200
400
600
200
0
200
600
2000
6000
GANSU
SHAANXI
SICHUAN
GUIZHOU
YUNNAN
GUANGXI
KACHIN
BURMA (MYANMAR)
SHAN STATE
LAOS
VIETNAM
THAILAND
CHENGDU
(Ch'engtu;
Tch'eng-tou)
CHONGQING
(Ch'ungch'ing; Tch'ong-King)
Guiyang
(Kueiyang)
Kunming
(K'unming)
Nanning
Hanoi
Haiphong
Leshan
Zigong
(Tzukong)
Neijiang
Yibin
Luzhou
Nanchong
Guang'an
Wanxian
Zunyi
Anshun
Liuzhou
Gejiu
Qamdo
Batang
Litang
Kangding
Xichang
Lijiang
Dali
Baoshan
Tengchong
Ruili
Lincang
Jinghong
Mengzi
Wenshan
Qujing
Zhaotong
Dukou
Lao Cai
Hoa Binh
Ha Dong
Nam Dinh
Phong Saly
Nam Tha
Luang Prabang
Chiang Rai
Mae Sai
Ningjing Shan
Shaluli Shan
Daxue Shan
Qionglai Shan
Daliang Shan
Dalou Shan
Daba Shan
Yun Ling
Nu Shan
Gaoligong Shan
Ailao Shan
Wuliang Shan
Hoang Lien Son
Min Jiang
Jialing Jiang
Yalong Jiang
Jinsha Jiang
Lancang Jiang
Nu Jiang
Mekong
Hong (Red)
Da (Black)
Song Ma
Wu Jiang
Beipan Jiang
Nanpan Jiang
Hongshui He
Gongga Shan
7600
5500
4100
3570
3233
3143
3054
2683
2320
Gulf of Tonkin
Leizhou Bandao
Weizhou Dao
Fai Tsi Long Archipelago
Anpu Gang
Projection: Conical with two standard parallels

1 : 5 300 000
50 0 50 100 miles
50 0 50 100 150 km
HENAN
HUBEI
ANHUI
JIANGSU
ZHEJIANG
JIANGXI
HUNAN
FUJIAN
GUANGDONG
TAIWAN
SHANGHAI
(Changhai)
NANJING
(Nanking; Nanching)
WUHAN
GUANGZHOU
HONG KONG (U.K.)
Kowloon
Macau (Macao) (Port.)
Hangzhou
(Hangchou; Hangchow)
Nanchang
Changsha
Fuzhou
Xiamen
(Hsiamen; Amoy)
Shantou
(Swatow)
Wenzhou
(Wenchow)
Ningbo
(Ningpo)
Hefei
Bengbu
Huainan
Nantong
Zhenjiang
(Chenchiang)
Changzhou
(Ch'angchou)
Wuxi
Suzhou
(Suchou)
Wuhu
Anqing
Jiujiang
Jingdezhen
Hengyang
Shaoyang
Zhuzhou
Xiangtan
Ganzhou
Shaoguan
Shenzhen
Foshan
Jiangmen
Zhanjiang
Wuzhou
Guilin
Zhangzhou
Quanzhou
Nanping
Sanming
Shaoxing
Jinhua
Linhai
Yichang
Shashi
Xiangfan
Nanyang
Macheng
Huangshi
Chao'an
T'AIPEI
Chilung
Hsinchu
T'aichung
Changhua
Chiai
T'ainan
Kaohsiung
P'ingtung
Hualien
T'aitung
Chang Jiang
Chongming Dao
Hangzhou Wan
Zhoushan Dao
Dabie Shan
Mufu Shan
Jiuling Shan
Wuyi Shan
Wugong Shan
Xuefeng Shan
Poyang Hu
Dongting Hu
Xi Jiang
Bei Jiang
Gan Jiang
Min Jiang
Xiang Jiang
Han Shui
Huai He
Formosa Strait
Luzon Strait
SOUTH CHINA SEA
Tropic of Cancer
Tungsha Tao
Matsu Tao
Chinmen Tao
Dangan Liedao
Hailing Dao
Shangchuan Dao
Xiachuan Dao
Donghai Dao
Naozhou Dao
Chungyang Shanmo
3931
3997
1834
1810
2120
1725
1629
2164
1703
A
B
C
D
E
F
G
H
8
9
10
11
12
13
14
East from Greenwich
COPYRIGHT. GEORGE PHILIP & SON. LTD.

1 : 17 800 000

100 0 100 200 300 400 miles

100 0 100 200 300 400 500 600 km

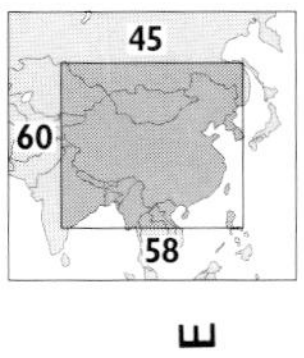

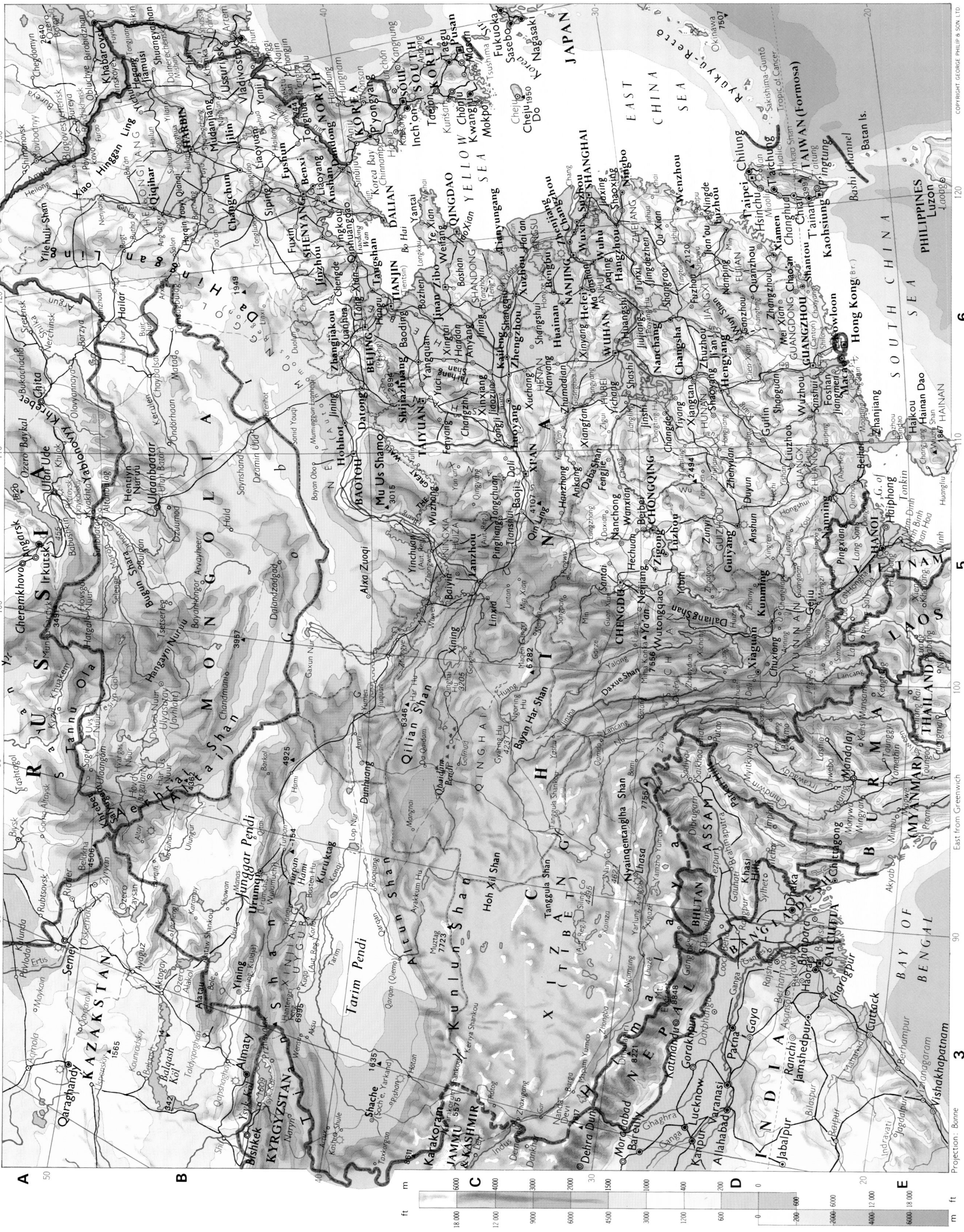

m	ft
6000	18 000
4000	12 000
3000	9000
2000	6000
1500	4500
1000	3000
400	1200
200	600
0	0
200	600
2000	6000
4000	12 000
6000	18 000

East from Greenwich

Projection : Bonne

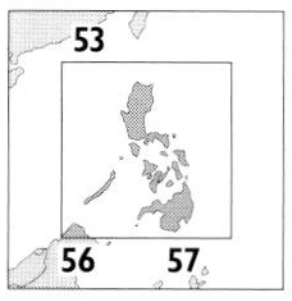

1 : 6 700 000

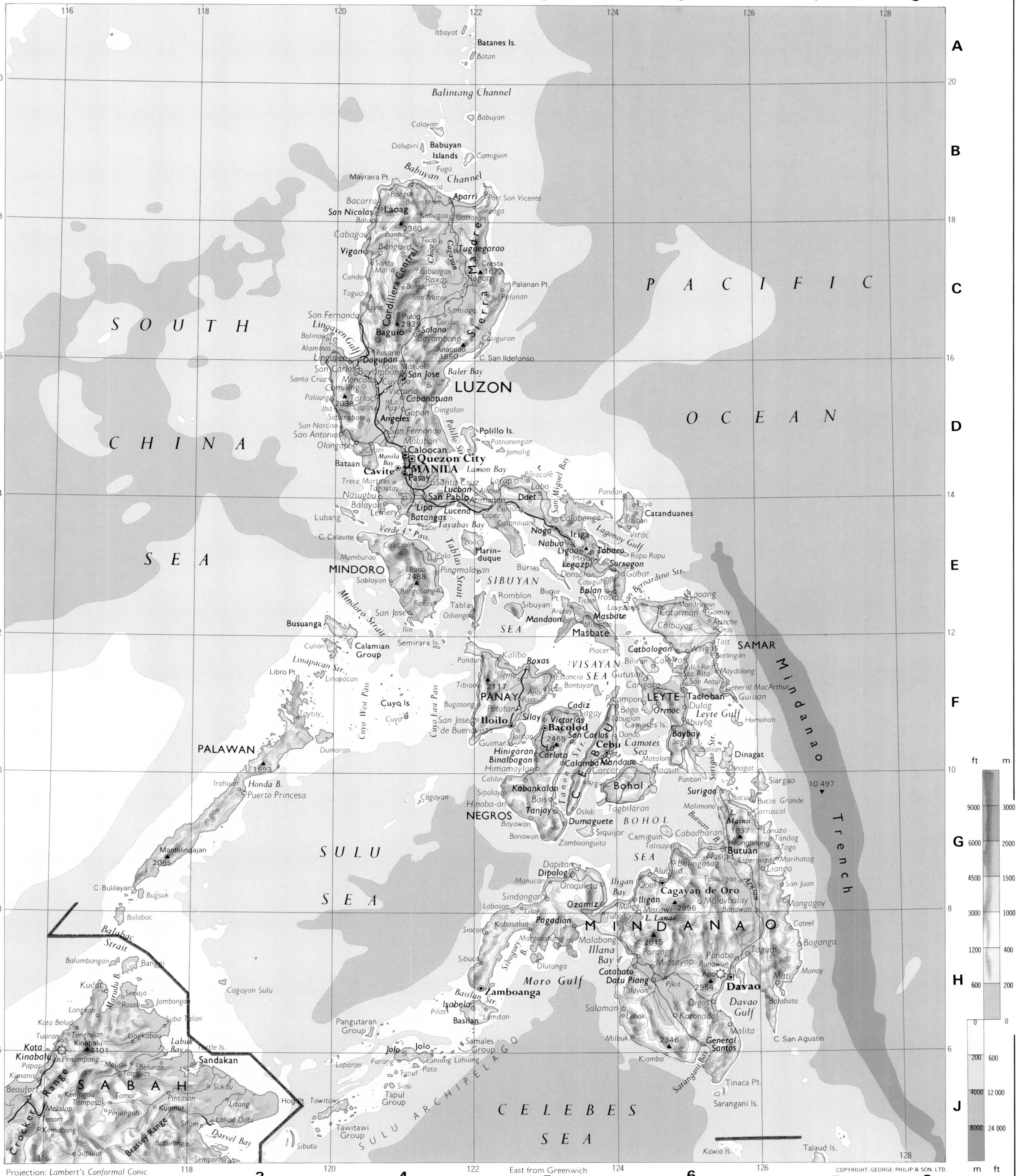

50 0 50 100 150 200 miles

50 0 50 100 150 200 250 300 km

PACIFIC OCEAN

SOUTH CHINA SEA

SULU SEA

CELEBES SEA

SIBUYAN SEA

VISAYAN SEA

BOHOL SEA

LUZON

MINDORO

PANAY

NEGROS

CEBU

LEYTE

SAMAR

MINDANAO

PALAWAN

SABAH

Batanes Is.

Balintang Channel

Babuyan Islands

Babuyan Channel

Cordillera Central

Sierra Madre

Lingayen Gulf

Baguio

Dagupan

Quezon City

MANILA

Cavite

Mindanao Trench

Mindoro Strait

Tablas Strait

Sulu Archipelago

Moro Gulf

Davao Gulf

Zamboanga

Cagayan de Oro

Davao

Iloilo

Bacolod

Cebu

Tacloban

Kota Kinabalu

Sandakan

Crocker Range

Projection: Lambert's Conformal Conic

East from Greenwich

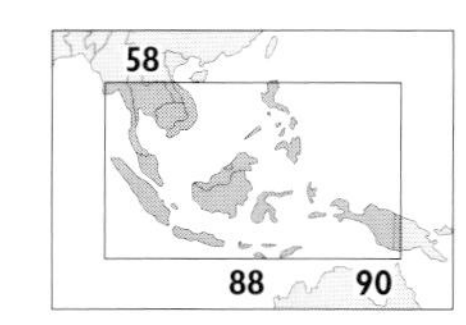

58
88
90

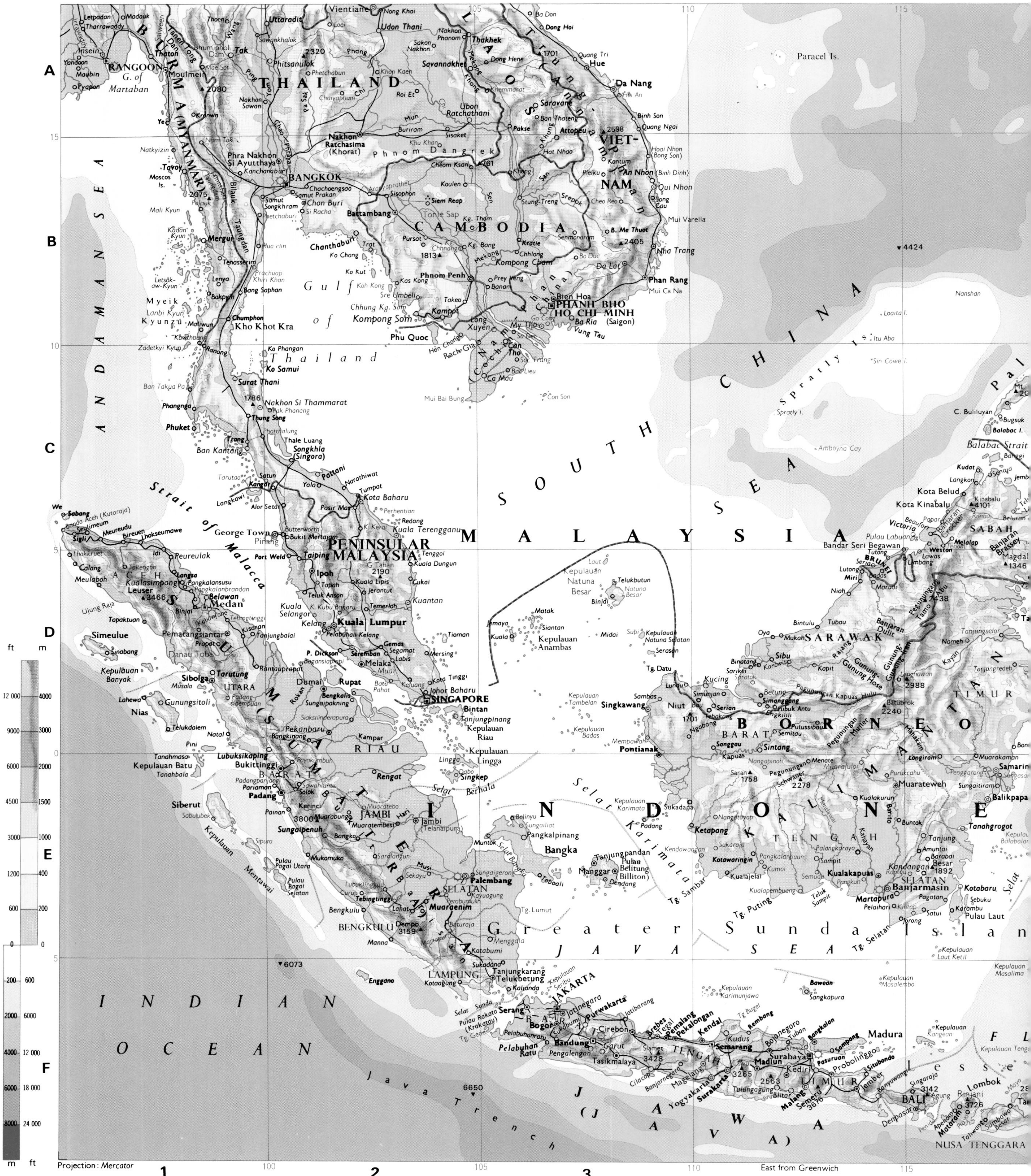

1
2
3
4
5
A
B
C
D
E
F
THAILAND
CAMBODIA
LAOS
VIET-NAM
BURMA (MYANMAR)
PENINSULAR MALAYSIA
MALAYSIA
SABAH
SARAWAK
BRUNEI
SINGAPORE
SUMATERA (SUMATRA)
BORNEO
KALIMANTAN
INDONESIA
JAWA (JAVA)
ANDAMAN SEA
Gulf of Thailand
SOUTH CHINA SEA
Strait of Malacca
INDIAN OCEAN
Java Trench
JAVA SEA
Greater Sunda Islands
Paracel Is.
Spratly Is.
G. of Martaban
Vientiane
Nong Khai
Udon Thani
Uttaradit
Tak
Phitsanulok
Nakhon Sawan
RANGOON
Moulmein
Thaton
Insein
Bassein
Pyapon
Ye
Tavoy
Mergui
Tenasserim
Phra Nakhon Si Ayutthaya
BANGKOK
Chon Buri
Nakhon Ratchasima (Khorat)
Ubon Ratchathani
Savannakhet
Thakhek
Dong Hoi
Hue
Quang Tri
Da Nang
Saravane
Pakse
Attopeu
Kontum
An Nhon
Qui Nhon
Pleiku
B. Me Thuot
Nha Trang
Da Lat
Phan Rang
Mui Varella
Mui Ca Na
Battambang
Siem Reap
Tonle Sap
Kratie
Kompong Cham
Phnom Penh
Chanthaburi
Kampot
Kompong Som
Phu Quoc
Bien Hoa
PHANH BHO HO CHI MINH (Saigon)
Vung Tau
My Tho
Can Tho
Rach Gia
Ca Mau
Mui Bai Bung
Con Son
Chumphon
Kho Khot Kra
Ranong
Ko Samui
Ko Phangan
Surat Thani
Nakhon Si Thammarat
Thung Song
Phuket
Trang
Ban Kantang
Songkhla (Singora)
Pattani
Yala
Narathiwat
Kota Baharu
Alor Setar
George Town
Pinang
Butterworth
Kuala Terengganu
Taiping
Ipoh
Port Weld
Kuantan
Kuala Lumpur
Kelang
Seremban
Melaka
Mersing
Johor Baharu
Tioman
Dumai
Rupat
Bintan
Tanjungpinang
Kepulauan Riau
Kepulauan Lingga
Singkep
Sabang
Banda Aceh (Kutaraja)
Sigli
Lhokseumawe
Langsa
Meulaboh
Belawan
Medan
Leuser 3466
Binjai
Pematangsiantar
Tanjungbalai
Simeulue
Sibolga
Nias
Gunungsitoli
Tarutung
Pekanbaru
RIAU
Padang
Bukittinggi
Siberut
Kepulauan Batu
Kepulauan Mentawai
Jambi
Sungaipenuh
Kerinci 3800
Rengat
Muntok
Bangka
Pangkalpinang
Palembang
Belitung (Billiton)
Tanjungpandan
Bengkulu
BENGKULU
Dempo 3159
Enggano
LAMPUNG
Tanjungkarang-Telukbetung
JAKARTA
Bogor
Bandung
Serang
Cirebon
Garut
Tasikmalaya
Semarang
Pekalongan
Yogyakarta
Surakarta
Madiun
Kediri
Surabaya
Madura
Malang
Semeru 3676
Jember
Banyuwangi
Probolinggo
BALI
Denpasar
Lombok
Rinjani 3726
Mataram
NUSA TENGGARA
Kepulauan Natuna Besar
Kepulauan Anambas
Natuna Selatan
Kuching
Sibu
Bintulu
Miri
Lutong
Labuan
Bandar Seri Begawan
Kota Kinabalu
Kinabalu 4101
Kudat
Sandakan
Pontianak
Singkawang
Ketapang
Sampit
Banjarmasin
Balikpapan
Samarinda
Muarateweh
Kotabaru
Pulau Laut
Selat Karimata
Selat Makasar
Balabac Strait
Projection: Mercator
East from Greenwich
100
105
110
115
ft
m
12 000
9000
6000
4500
3000
1200
600
4000
3000
2000
1500
1000
400
200
0
200
2000
4000
6000
8000
600
6000
12 000
18 000
24 000
6073
6650
4424

1 : 11 100 000
miles
km
JAVA AND MADURA
1 : 6 700 000
miles
km
Selat Sunda
JAKARTA
Bogor
Sukabumi
Bandung
Cirebon
Tegal
Pekalongan
Semarang
Kepulauan Karimunjawa
Bawean
TENGAH
TIMUR
Madura
Surabaya
Madiun
Kediri
Malang
Surakarta
Yogyakarta
Magelang
Salatiga
Probolinggo
Bali
Nusa Barung
LUZON
MANILA
Quezon City
Polillo Islands
Lamon Bay
Catanduanes
Mindoro
Marinduque
Sibuyan Sea
Masbate
Samar
Visayan Sea
Panay
Negros
Cebu
Leyte
Bohol
Mindanao
Dinagat
Siargao
Zamboanga
Davao
Cotabato
General Santos
Basilan
Sulu Arch.
SULU SEA
CELEBES SEA
PHILIPPINES
Mindanao Trench
PACIFIC OCEAN
FEDERATED STATES OF MICRONESIA
Yap Islands
Ulithi Atoll
PALAU
Babelthuap
Caroline Islands
Sorol Atoll
Ngulu Atoll
Sonsorol Islands
Pulo-Anna
Merir
Tobi
Helen Atoll
Kepulauan Talaud
Pulau Sangihe
Morotai
Halmahera
Ternate
Tidore
Kep. Bacan
Waigeo
Kepulauan Mapia
Kepulauan Asia
Equator
Manado
Gorontalo
Teluk Tomini
SULAWESI (CELEBES)
Kepulauan Banggai
Kepulauan Sula
Obi
MOLUCCA SEA
Misool
Jazirah Doberai
Manokwari
Sorong
Biak
Yapen
Supiori
Teluk Cenderawasih
IRIAN JAYA
Pegunungan Van Rees
Pegunungan Maoke
Pegunungan Sudirman
Pegunungan Jayawijaya
Puncak Jaya
Jayapura
Fakfak
Seram
Buru
Ambon
Ceram
Seram Sea
MALUKU
BANDA SEA
Buton
Muna
Kabaena
Kendari
Kepulauan Kai
Kepulauan Aru
Kepulauan Tanimbar
Yamdena
Trangan
Wetar
Flores
Flores Sea
Sumbawa
Sumba
Sawu Sea
Timor
Dili
Kupang
Roti
Alor
NUSA TENGGARA TIMUR
Ende
Bima
Kepulauan Leti
ARAFURA SEA
Pulau Yos Sudarso
Merauke
PAPUA NEW GUINEA
Teluk Flamingo
COPYRIGHT, GEORGE PHILIP & SON, LTD.

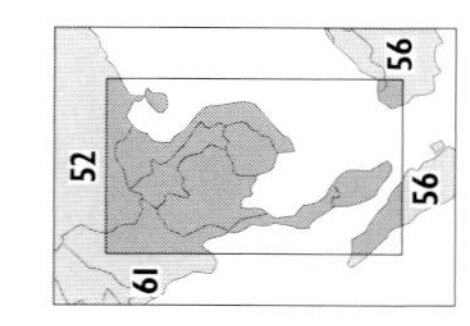
56
52
56
61

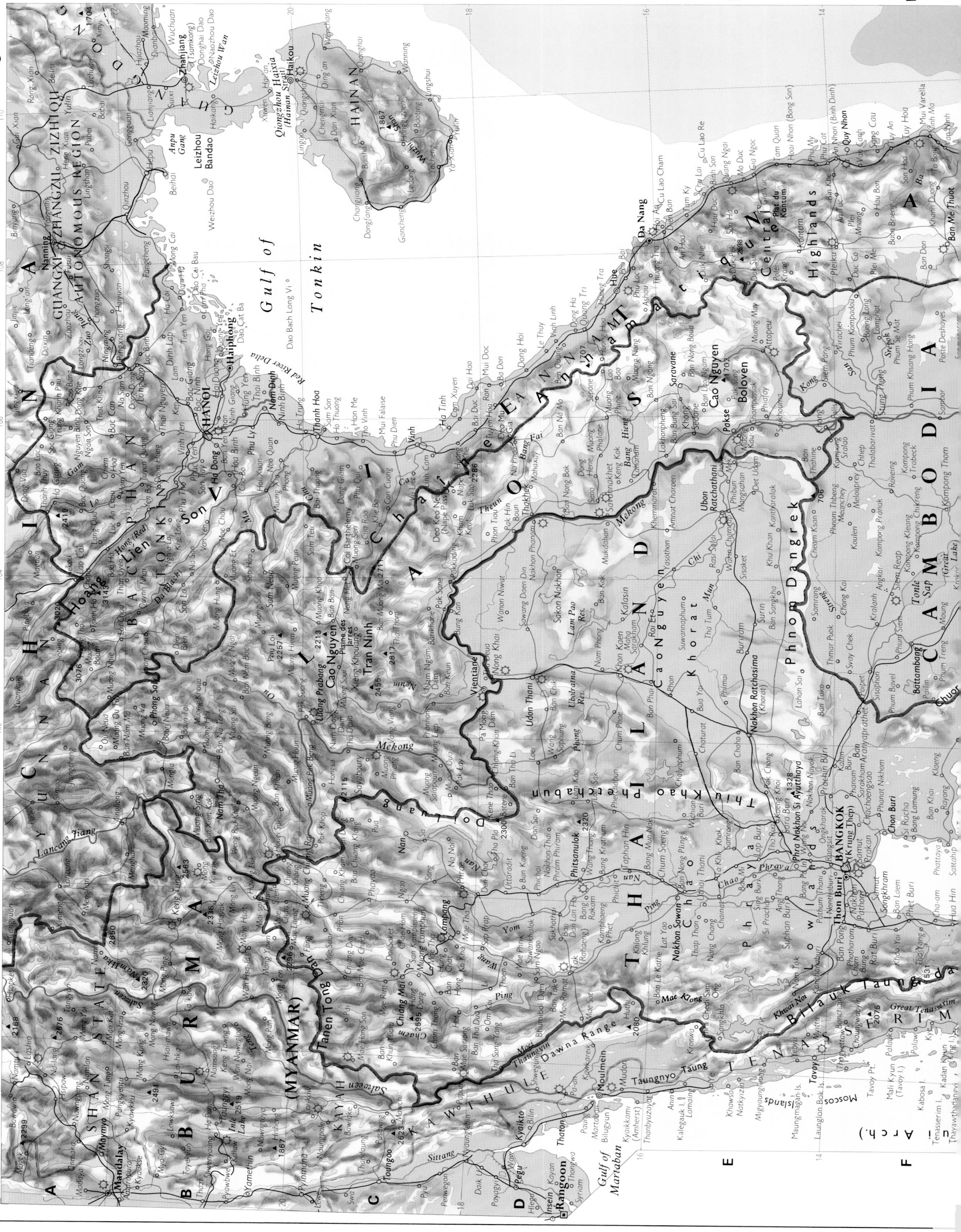

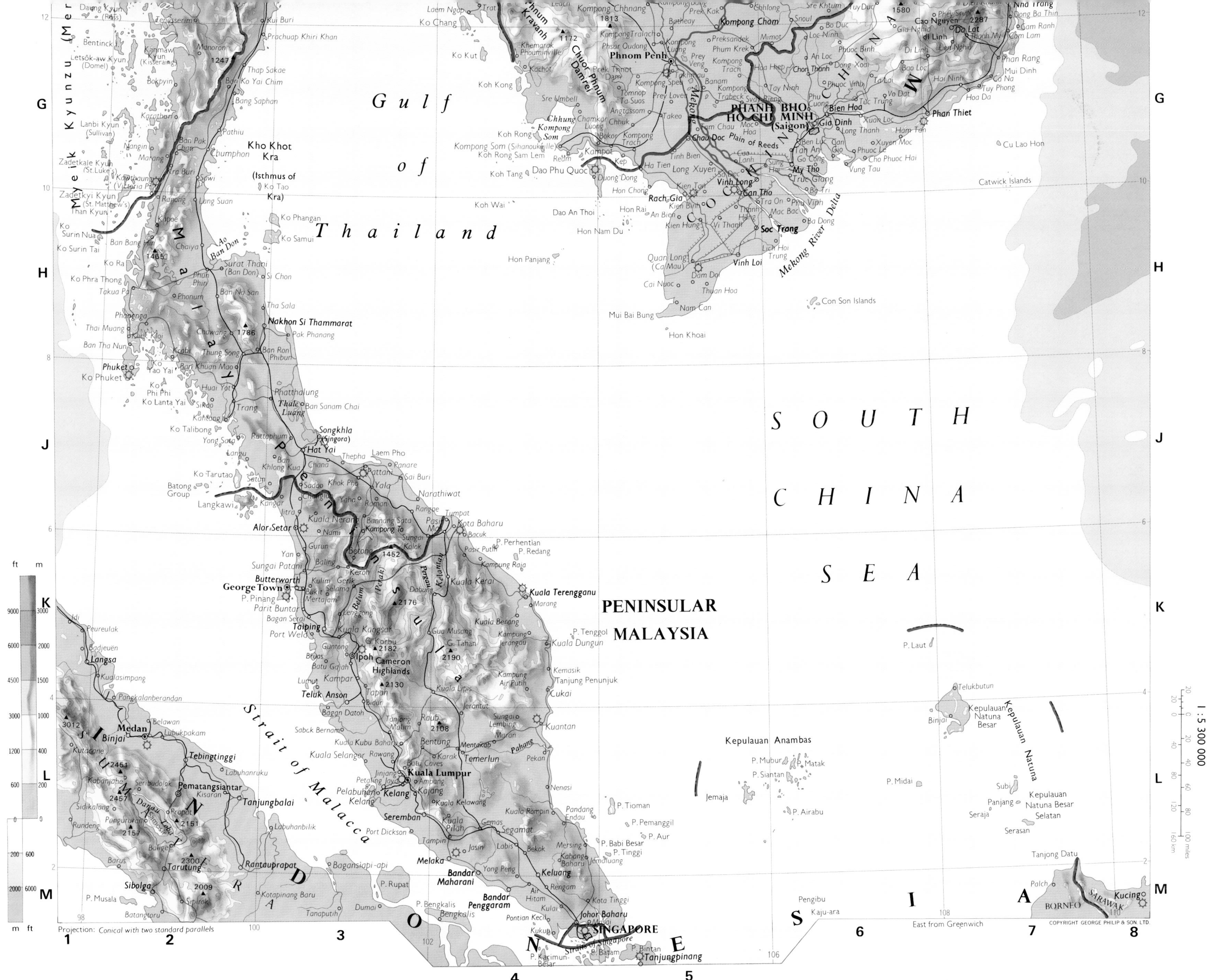

1 : 5 300 000
Gulf of Thailand
SOUTH CHINA SEA
PENINSULAR MALAYSIA
Strait of Malacca
INDONESIA
SUMATERA
Kho Khot Kra (Isthmus of Kra)
Phnom Penh
PHANH BHO HO CHI MINH (Saigon)
Mekong River Delta
Plain of Reeds
Kuala Lumpur
SINGAPORE
Johor Baharu
George Town
Butterworth
Ipoh
Cameron Highlands
Kuala Terengganu
Kota Baharu
Melaka
Seremban
Kuantan
Medan
Alor Setar
Hat Yai
Songkhla (Singora)
Nakhon Si Thammarat
Phuket
Langkawi
Kepulauan Anambas
Kepulauan Natuna
Kepulauan Natuna Besar
Kepulauan Natuna Selatan
Con Son Islands
Catwick Islands
Tanjungpinang
Kucing
SARAWAK
BORNEO
Phan Thiet
Soc Trang
Can Tho
Rach Gia
Dao Phu Quoc
East from Greenwich
Projection: Conical with two standard parallels
COPYRIGHT GEORGE PHILIP & SON LTD.

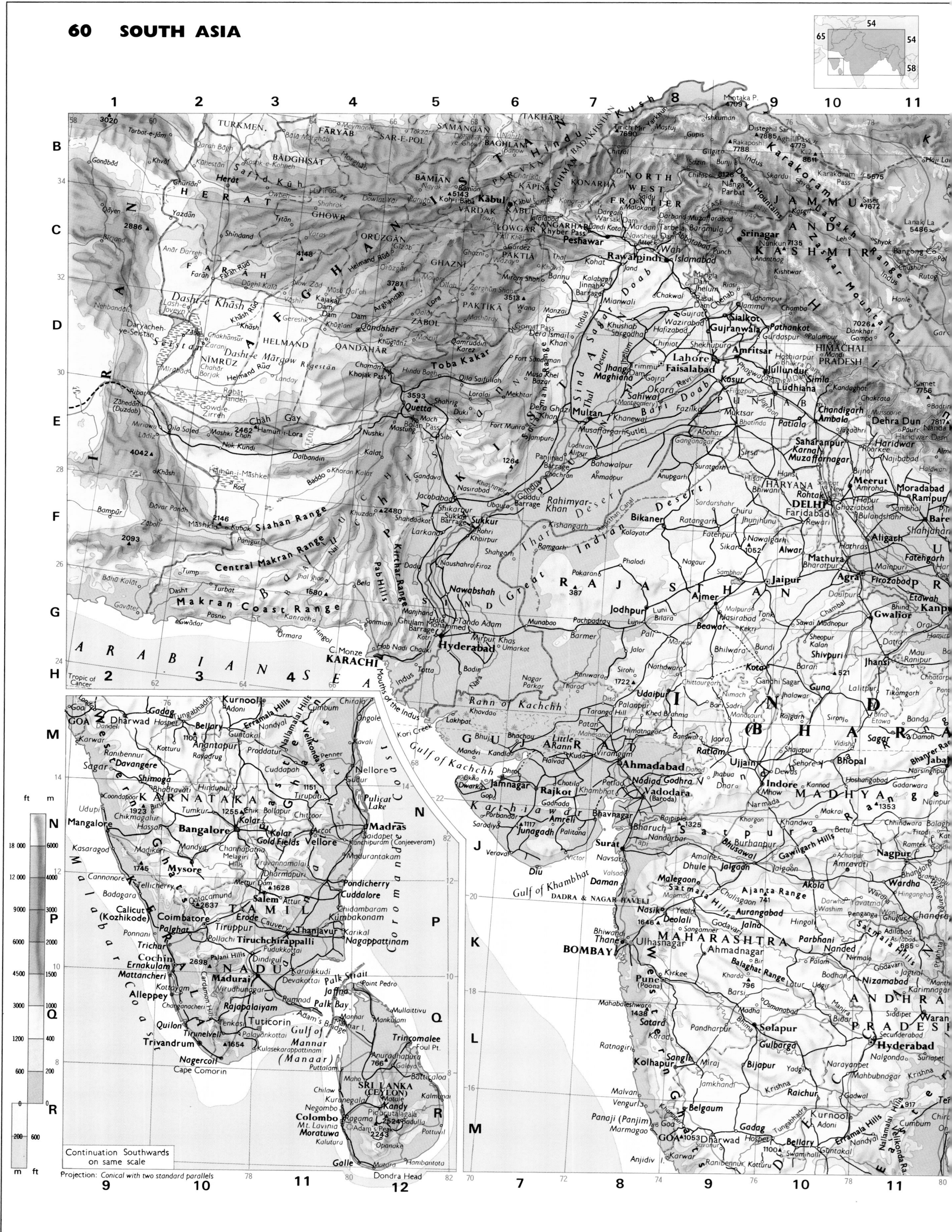

ARABIAN SEA
Tropic of Cancer
TURKMEN.
FĀRYĀB
SAR-E-POL
SAMANGĀN
BAGHLĀN
TAKHĀR
BĀDGHĪSĀT
HERĀT
Herāt
Safīd Kūh
BĀMIĀN
Kābul
KĀBUL
VARDAK
PARVĀN
KĀPĪSĀ
KONARHĀ
LOWGAR
NANGARHĀR
PAKTIĀ
GHOWR
ORŪZGĀN
GHAZNĪ
PAKTĪKĀ
ZĀBOL
QANDAHĀR
Qandahār
HELMAND
NĪMRŪZ
FARĀH
Dasht-e Khāsh
Dasht-e Māргow
Toba Kakar
Quetta
Khojak Pass
Bolan Pass
Nushki
Dalbandin
Siahan Range
Central Makran Range
Makran Coast Range
Pab Hills
Kirthar Range
KARACHI
C. Monze
Mouths of the Indus
Hyderabad
Sukkur
Nawabshah
Jacobabad
Larkana
Multan
Dera Ghazi Khan
Dera Ismail Khan
Bahawalpur
Rawalpindi
Islamabad
Peshawar
Khyber Pass
Kohat
Bannu
NORTH WEST FRONTIER
Hindu Kush
Tirich Mir 7690
Gilgit
Nanga Parbat 8126
Rakaposhi 7788
Karakoram Pass
Karakoram
JAMMU AND KASHMIR
Srinagar
Zaskar Mountains
Ladakh Range
Sialkot
Gujranwala
Lahore
Faisalabad
Amritsar
Jullundur
Ludhiana
Simla
HIMACHAL PRADESH
PUNJAB
Chandigarh
Ambala
Dehra Dun
Haridwar
Patiala
Saharanpur
Karnal
Muzaffarnagar
Meerut
Moradabad
Rampur
DELHI
Faridabad
Rohtak
HARYANA
Aligarh
Mathura
Agra
Firozabad
Etawah
Gwalior
Jhansi
Great Indian (Thar) Desert
Sind Sagar Doab
Thal Desert
Bari Doab
RAJASTHAN
Bikaner
Jaipur
Ajmer
Jodhpur
Alwar
Kota
Udaipur
Beawar
Bhilwara
Rann of Kachchh
Gulf of Kachchh
Kathiawar
Jamnagar
Rajkot
Junagadh
Bhavnagar
Porbandar
Veraval
Diu
Ahmadabad
Vadodara (Baroda)
Surat
Daman
Gulf of Khambhat
DADRA & NAGAR HAVELI
Bharuch
Ujjain
Indore
Bhopal
Ratlam
MADHYA PRADESH
Satpura Range
Narmada
Jalgaon
Dhule
Bhusawal
Akola
Amravati
Nagpur
Wardha
Gawilgarh Hills
Ajanta Range
Aurangabad
Nasik
BOMBAY
Thane
Ulhasnagar
MAHARASHTRA
Ahmadnagar
Pune (Poona)
Balaghat Range
Solapur
Satara
Kolhapur
Sangli
Gulbarga
Bijapur
Belgaum
Panaji (Panjim)
Marmagao
GOA
Dharwad
Hubli
Nanded
Parbhani
Latur
Nizamabad
ANDHRA PRADESH
Hyderabad
Secunderabad
Raichur
Kurnool
Bellary
Erramala Hills
Nallamalai Hills
Velikonda Range
INDIA (BHARAT)
Karwar
Davangere
Shimoga
KARNATAKA
Mangalore
Bangalore
Kolar Gold Fields
Mysore
Nellore
Madras
Pulicat Lake
Vellore
Kanchipuram (Conjeeveram)
Pondicherry
Cuddalore
Salem
Coimbatore
Erode
Tiruppur
Palghat
Calicut (Kozhikode)
Tellicherry
Cannanore
Ootacamund
TAMIL NADU
Tiruchchirappalli
Thanjavur
Nagappattinam
Kumbakonam
Dindigul
Madurai
Rajapalaiyam
Tuticorin
Tirunelveli
Nagercoil
Cape Comorin
Trivandrum
Quilon
Alleppey
Cochin
Ernakulam
Mattancheri
Trichur
KERALA
Malabar Coast
Coromandel Coast
Western Ghats
Eastern Ghats
Palk Strait
Palk Bay
Adam's Bridge
Gulf of Mannar
Jaffna
Trincomalee
Anuradhapura
SRI LANKA (CEYLON)
Kandy
Colombo
Mt. Lavinia
Moratuwa
Galle
Dondra Head
Adam's Peak
Pidurutalagala 2524
Batticaloa
Continuation Southwards on same scale
Projection: Conical with two standard parallels

1 : 8 900 000
100 50 0 50 100 150 200 miles
100 0 100 200 300 km
C H I N A
X I Z A N G
(T I B E T)
Q I N G H A I
S I C H U A N
Y U N N A N
Tanggula (Dangla) Shan
Bayan Har Shan
Xil Shan
Nyainqêntanglha Shan
Lhasa
Mt. Everest 8848
Kanchenjunga 8598
SIKKIM
BHUTAN
N E P A L
Katmandu
Siwalik Range
ASSAM
ARUNACHAL PRADESH
NAGALAND
MANIPUR
MIZORAM
TRIPURA
MEGHALAYA
WEST BENGAL
BIHAR
ORISSA
BANGLADESH
Dhaka
Chittagong
CALCUTTA
Haora
Patna
Varanasi
Lucknow
Ranchi
Jamshedpur
Cuttack
Bhubaneshwar
Vishakhapatnam
Kakinada (Cocanada)
Machilipatnam (Bandar)
Northern Circars
Shillong
Agartala
Mandalay
Rangoon
BURMA (MYANMAR)
CHIN
KACHIN
SHAN
KAYAH
THAILAND
Chiengmai
Tak (Raheng)
Tavoy
Moulmein
Arakan Yoma
Pegu Yoma
Arakan Coast
Ramree I.
Cheduba I.
Akyab
Gulf of Martaban
Mouths of the Ganga
Sundarbans
BAY OF BENGAL
INDIAN OCEAN
Preparis North Channel
Preparis South Channel
Pariparit Kyun (Burma)
Koko Kyunzu (Burma)
Tropic of Cancer
East from Greenwich

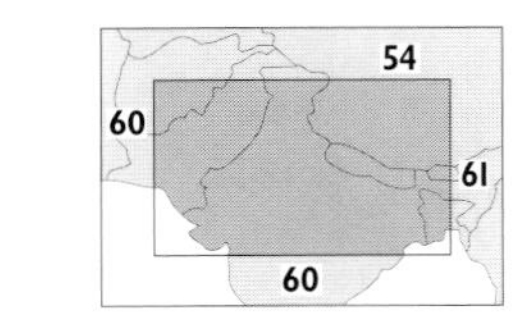

1 2 3 4 5 6 7

B C D E F G H J

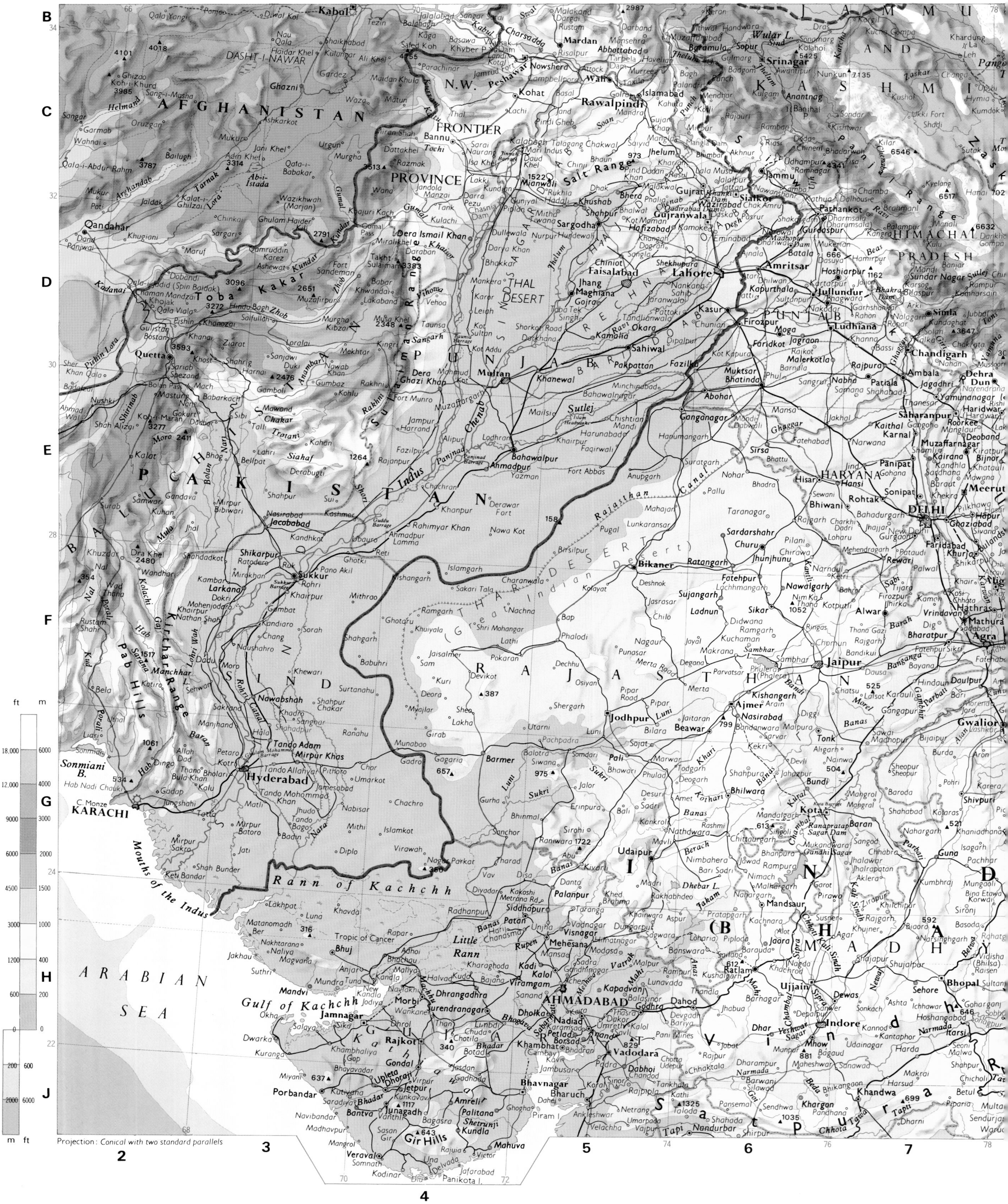

AFGHANISTAN
DASHT-I-NAWAR
N.W. FRONTIER PROVINCE
JAMMU AND KASHMIR
HIMACHAL PRADESH
PUNJAB
HARYANA
DELHI
PAKISTAN
BALUCHISTAN
PUNJAB
SIND
RAJASTHAN
THAR DESERT (Great Indian Desert)
THAL DESERT
SIND SAGAR DOAB
CHAJ DOAB
RECHNA DOAB
BARI DOAB
INDIA
MADHYA PRADESH
GUJARAT
Kathiawar
Vindhya Range
Satpura Range
Salt Range
Sulaiman Range
Kirthar Range
Pab Hills
Toba Kakar
Gir Hills
ARABIAN SEA
Gulf of Kachchh
Rann of Kachchh
Little Rann
Mouths of the Indus
Sonmiani B.
C. Monze
Tropic of Cancer

Kabul
Peshawar
Islamabad
Rawalpindi
Srinagar
Jammu
Lahore
Amritsar
Faisalabad
Multan
Quetta
Qandahar
Sukkur
Hyderabad
KARACHI
Jodhpur
Bikaner
Jaipur
Ajmer
DELHI
Agra
Gwalior
Chandigarh
Simla
Ludhiana
Jullundur
Udaipur
AHMADABAD
Vadodara
Rajkot
Jamnagar
Bhavnagar
Indore
Ujjain
Bhopal
Kota

Indus
Chenab
Jhelum
Ravi
Sutlej
Beas
Luni
Chambal
Narmada
Tapti
Mahi
Banas
Rajasthan Canal

ft m
18,000 6000
12,000 4000
9000 3000
6000 2000
4500 1500
3000 1000
1200 400
600 200
0 0
200 600
2000 6000
m ft

Projection: Conical with two standard parallels

2 3 4 5 6 7

1 : 5 300 000
50 0 50 100 150 miles
50 0 50 100 150 200 km
JAMMU AND KASHMIR
On same scale as Main Map
CHINA
Kunlun Shan
Karakoram Range
N.W. FRONTIER PROVINCE
PUNJAB
JAMMU AND KASHMIR
Zaskar Mountains
Ladakh Range
Deosai Mountains
HIMACHAL PRADESH
SODA PLAINS
Gilgit
Srinagar
Islamabad
Rawalpindi
Jammu
Sialkot
Leh
Anantnag
Abbottabad
Nanga Parbat 8126
Rakaposhi
Wular L.
Indus
Shyok
Nganglong Kangri
Gangdisê Shan
Mapam Yumco
Xizang (TIBET)
Yarlung Zangbo Jiang (Brahmaputra)
NEPAL
Mahabharat Lekh
Siwalik Range
Katmandu
Annapurna 8078
Mt. Everest 8848
Kanchenjunga
SIKKIM
Gangtok
Darjiling
BHUTAN
ASSAM
Garo Hills
UTTAR PRADESH
Moradabad
Bareilly
Shahjahanpur
Lucknow
KANPUR
Allahabad
Varanasi (Banaras, Benares)
Gorakhpur
Faizabad
Mirzapur
Jhansi
BIHAR
Patna
Gaya
Darbhanga
Munger
Bhagalpur
Ranchi
Jamshedpur
Rajmahal Hills
Kaimur Hills
MADHYA PRADESH
Jabalpur
Bilaspur
Maikala Range
Raigarh
Sambalpur
Hirakud Dam
Raurkela
WEST BENGAL
CALCUTTA
Haora
Kharagpur
Asansol
Durgapur
Bardhaman
Krishnanagar
BANGLADESH
DHAKA
Rajshahi
Jessore
Khulna
Barisal
Mymensingh
Sundarbans
Mouths of the Ganga
The Sandheads
Ganga
East from Greenwich
A B C D E F G H J
8 9 10 11 12 13

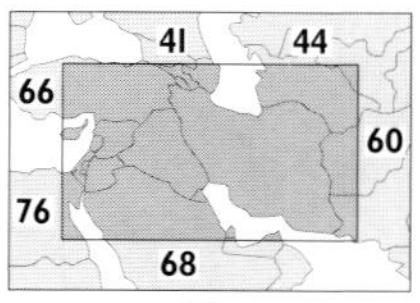

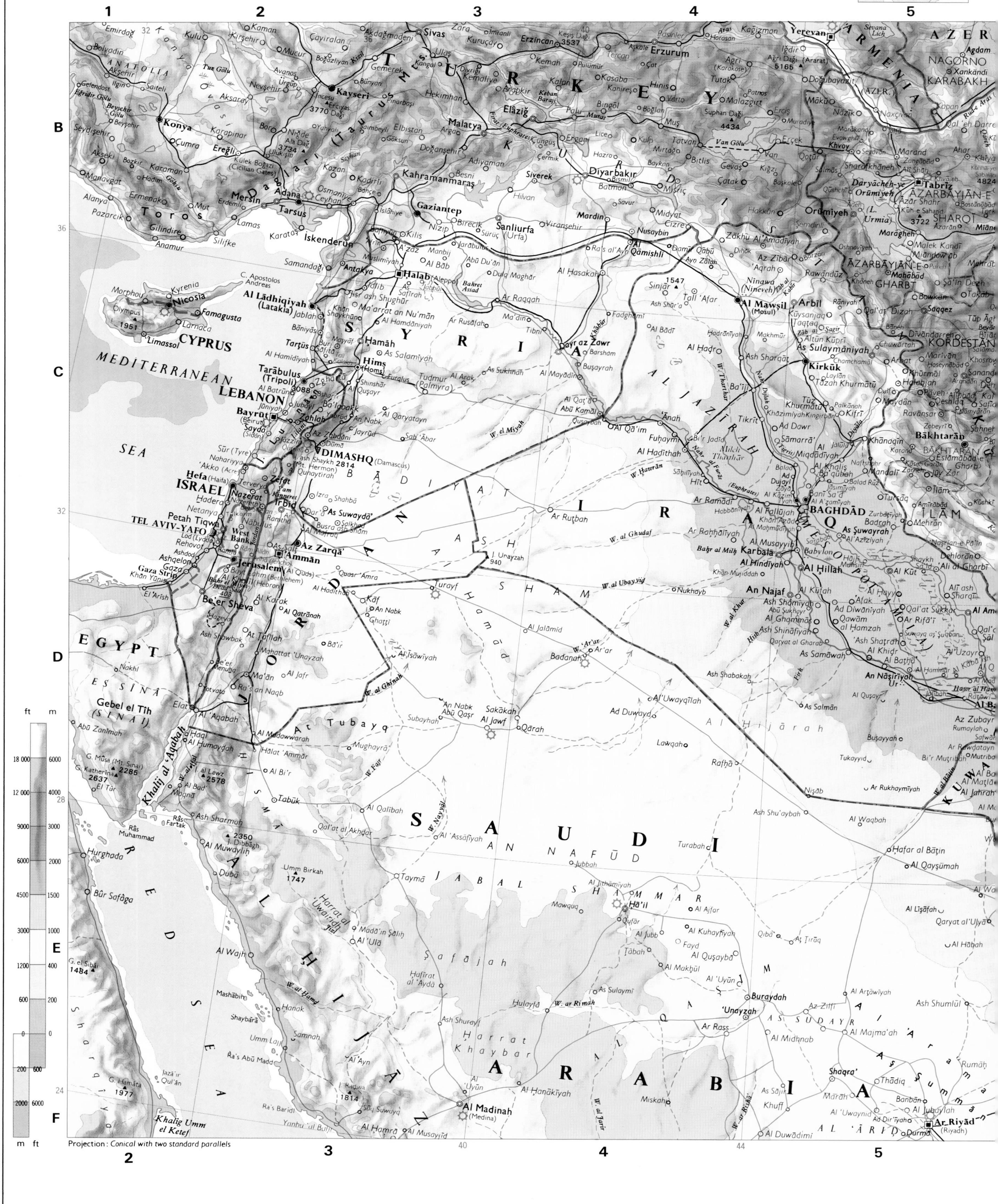

ft	m
18 000	6000
12 000	4000
9000	3000
6000	2000
4500	1500
3000	1000
1200	400
600	200
0	0
200	600
2000	6000
m	ft

1 **2** **3** **4** **5**

41 44
66 60
76
68

TURKEY

Emirdağ Kulu Kaman Kırşehir Akdağmadeni Sivas Zara İmranlı Erzincan 3537 Keşiş Dağı Aşkale Erzurum Pasinler Aras Kağızman Yerevan ARMENIA AZER

Bolvadin Kırşehir Çayıralan Kuruçay Tercan Kemah Pulumur Çat Ağrı (Karaköse) 5165 Ararat Iğdır Agdam NAGORNO KARABAKH Xankändi

Aksehir Ilgın Kaman Avanos Ürgüp Bünyan KAYSERİ Hekimhan Malatya Elazığ Palu Muradiye Nazik Maku Xankändi

ANATOLIA Nevşehir İncesu 3770 Dağı Pınarbaşı Malatya Elâzığ Çermik Muş Suphan Dağı 4434 Van Gölü Marand Ahar

Konya Niğde 3734 Fevzipaşa Gürün Darende Argaçan Bingöl Tatvan Van Gölü Khvoy AZER Naxçıvan

Ereğli Kulak Boğazı (Cilician Gates) Kozan Kahramanmaraş Besni Adıyaman Hazro Çermik Bitlis Gevaş Van Qotur Daryācheh-ye Orūmīyeh (L. Urmia) Tabrīz AZARBAYJAN-E SHARQI

Adana Osmaniye Bahçe Gaziantep Birecik Şanlıurfa (Urfa) Hilvan Siverek Batman Midyat Hakkâri Marāgheh 3722 Orūmīyeh Khoneh Qūshchī GHARBI

Mersin Tarsus İskenderun Kilis Nizip Suruç Viranşehir Mardin Nusaybin Cizre Zākhū Al 'Amādīyah Az Zibār Aqrah Rawāndūz Mahābād Sā'īn Dezh

CYPRUS

Morphou Kyrenia C. Apostolos Andreas Nicosia Famagusta Larnaca Limassol Olympus 1951

SYRIA

Al Lādhiqīyah (Latakia) Jablah İdlib Jisr ash Shughūr Ma'arrat an Nu'mān Al Bāb Manbij Ar Raqqah Ma'dīn Ash Shārā' Sinjār 1547 Tall 'Afar Al Mawṣil (Mosul) Arbīl Rānīyah Köysanjaq

Ḥamāh As Salamīyah Tibnī Ar Ruṣāfah Dayr az Zawr Barsham Al Ḥaḍr Ash Sharqāṭ Kirkūk

Ṭarṭūs Al Hamidiyah Bāniyās Maṣyaf Ḥimṣ (Homs) Tudmur (Palmyra) Abū Kamāl Āna Tikrīt Ad Dawr Sāmarrā

LEBANON

Ṭarābulus (Tripoli) Al Batrūn Jūniyah Bayrūt (Beirut) Ṣaydā (Sidon) Ṣūr (Tyre)

DIMASHQ (Damascus)

Ba'labakk An Nabk Al Qaryatayn Jayrūd W. el Miyāh Abū Kamāl Al Qā'im Al Hadīthah

ISRAEL

Hefa (Haifa) 'Akko (Acre) Nazerat Nahariyya Netanya Hadera Herzliyya PETAH TIQWA TEL AVIV-YAFO Lod (Lydda) Rehovot Ashdod Ashqelon Gaza Strip JERUSALEM (Al Quds) Be'er Sheva Ashqelon

WEST BANK

Nāblus Ramallāh Jericho Al Khalīl (Hebron) Bethlehem

JORDAN

'Ammān Az Zarqā' Irbid As Suwaydā' Al Karak Ma'ān At Ṭafīlah Ash Shawbak Al Qaṭrānah Qaṣr 'Amra

Turayf Al Ḥadīthah Kāf An Nabk Ghaṭṭī J. Unayzah 940 Ar Ruṭbah Ar Raḥḥālīyah

IRAQ

BAGHDAD Al Fallūjah Al Maḥmūdīyah Karbalā An Najaf Al Kūfah Al Ḥillah Al Kūt Al Musayyib As Samāwah An Nāṣirīyah Ur As Salmān Ash Shaṭrah Al Baṣrah

EGYPT

SINAI ESS SINĀ Gebel el Tih (SINAI) G. Mūsa (Mt. Sinai) 2285 G. Katherina 2637 El Ṭūr Nakhl Ras an Naqb Elat Al 'Aqabah

SAUDI ARABIA

Ḥaql Al Ḥumayḍah Al Bad' Maqnā Ṭābūk Al Qalībah Al Muwaylih Dubā Ḍibbah Al Wajh Ash Sharmah 2350 Al 'Ulā Madā'in Ṣāliḥ Taymā Jubbah AN NAFŪD

HISMĀ AL HIJĀZ Mashābīh Hanak Shaybārā Umm Lajj Ḥā'il Qafar Al Jubb Fayd Al Quṣayba Buraydah 'Unayzah

RED SEA Hurghada Bûr Safâga Ras Muhammad

Al Madīnah (Medina) Yanbu' al Baḥr Al Ḥamrā

Ḥā'il HARRAT KHAYBAR Miskah Al Ḥanākīyah An Nabhānīyah Ar Rass 'Unayzah Al Midhnab Shaqra' Thādiq Ar Riyāḍ (Riyadh)

AL 'ĀRIḌ

Al Duwādimī

Hafar al Bāṭin Al Qayṣūmah KUWAIT

MEDITERRANEAN SEA

BĀDIYAT ASH SHĀM Hamād

Al Ḥijārah

Ar'ar Ar'ar Badanah Rafḥā Niṣāb

Projection: *Conical with two standard parallels*

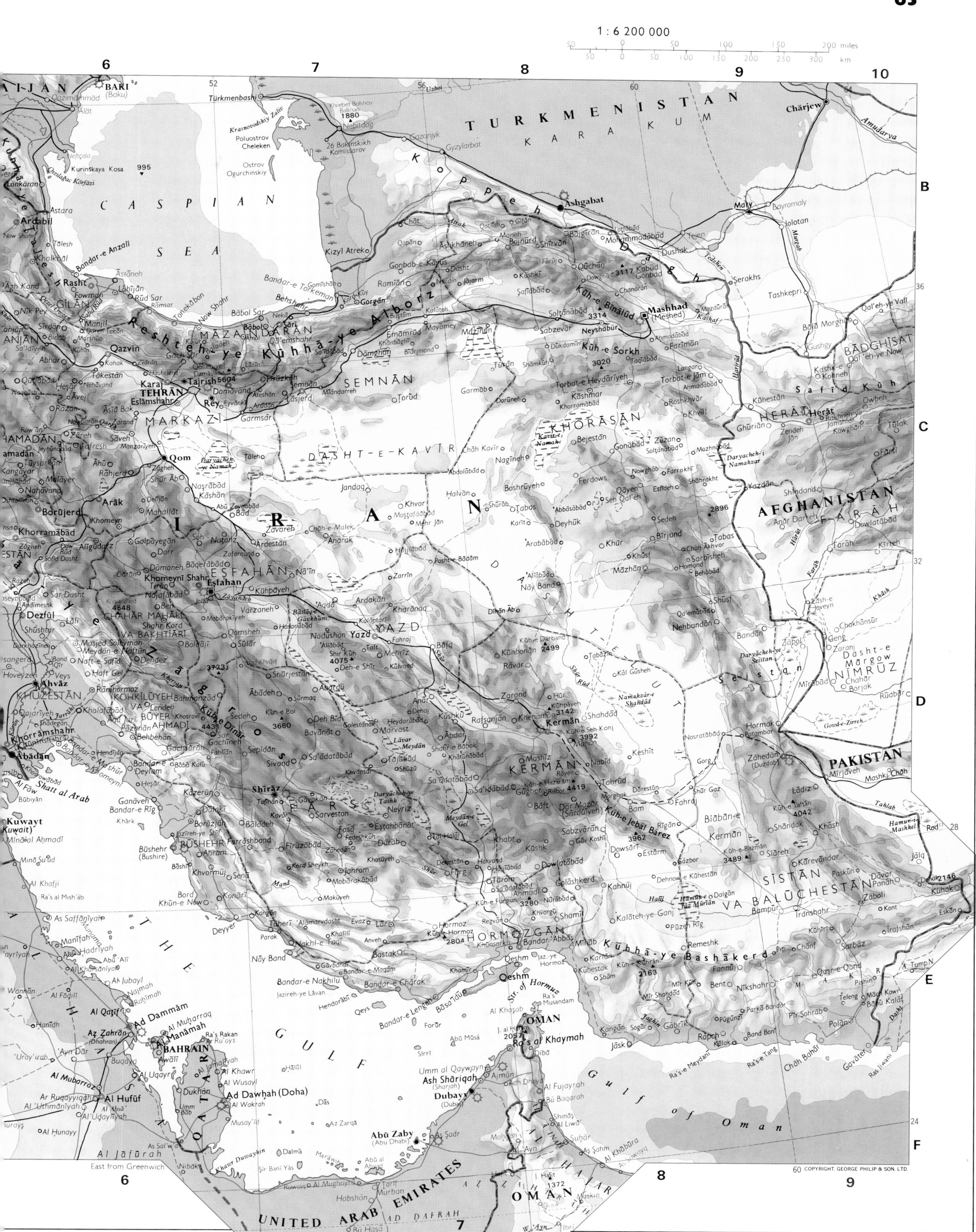

1 : 6 200 000
50 0 50 100 150 200 miles
50 0 50 100 150 200 250 300 km
6
7
8
9
10
B
C
D
E
F
TURKMENISTAN
KARAKUM
CASPIAN SEA
Kopet Dagh
Reshteh-ye Kūhhā-ye Alborz
IRAN
DASHT-E-KAVĪR
DASHT-E-LŪT
Zāgros
AFGHANISTAN
PAKISTAN
THE GULF
Gulf of Oman
Str. of Hormuz
OMAN
QATAR
BAHRAIN
UNITED ARAB EMIRATES
KHORĀSĀN
SEMNĀN
MARKAZĪ
ESFAHĀN
YAZD
KERMĀN
FĀRS
HORMOZGĀN
BUSHEHR
KHUZESTĀN
SĪSTĀN VA BALŪCHESTĀN
HERĀT
FARĀH
NĪMRŪZ
BĀDGHĪSĀT
Safīd Kūh
Kūhhā-ye Bashākerd
Kūh-e Bīnālūd
Kūh-e Sorkh
Kūh-e Dīnār
Kūh-e Jebāl Barez
BAKI (Baku)
Türkmenbashi
Ashgabat
Mashhad (Meshed)
Chārjew
Mary
Herāt
TEHRĀN
Qom
Esfahan
Yazd
Kermān
Shīrāz
Ahvāz
Ābādān
Khorramshahr
Bandar-e 'Abbās
Zāhedān (Duzdab)
Ad Dammām
Al Manāmah
Ad Dawḥah (Doha)
Abū Zaby (Abu Dhabi)
Dubayy (Dubai)
Ash Shāriqah (Sharjah)
Ra's al Khaymah
Al Hufūf
Kuwayt (Kuwait)
Shaṭṭ al Arab
Rasht
Qazvīn
Hamadān
Ardabīl
Arāk
Kāshān
Semnān
Gorgān
Sārī
Bābol
Neyshābūr
Sabzevār
Bīrjand
Zābol
Būshehr (Bushire)
Qeshm
Chāh Bahār
Jāsk
East from Greenwich
COPYRIGHT, GEORGE PHILIP & SON, LTD.

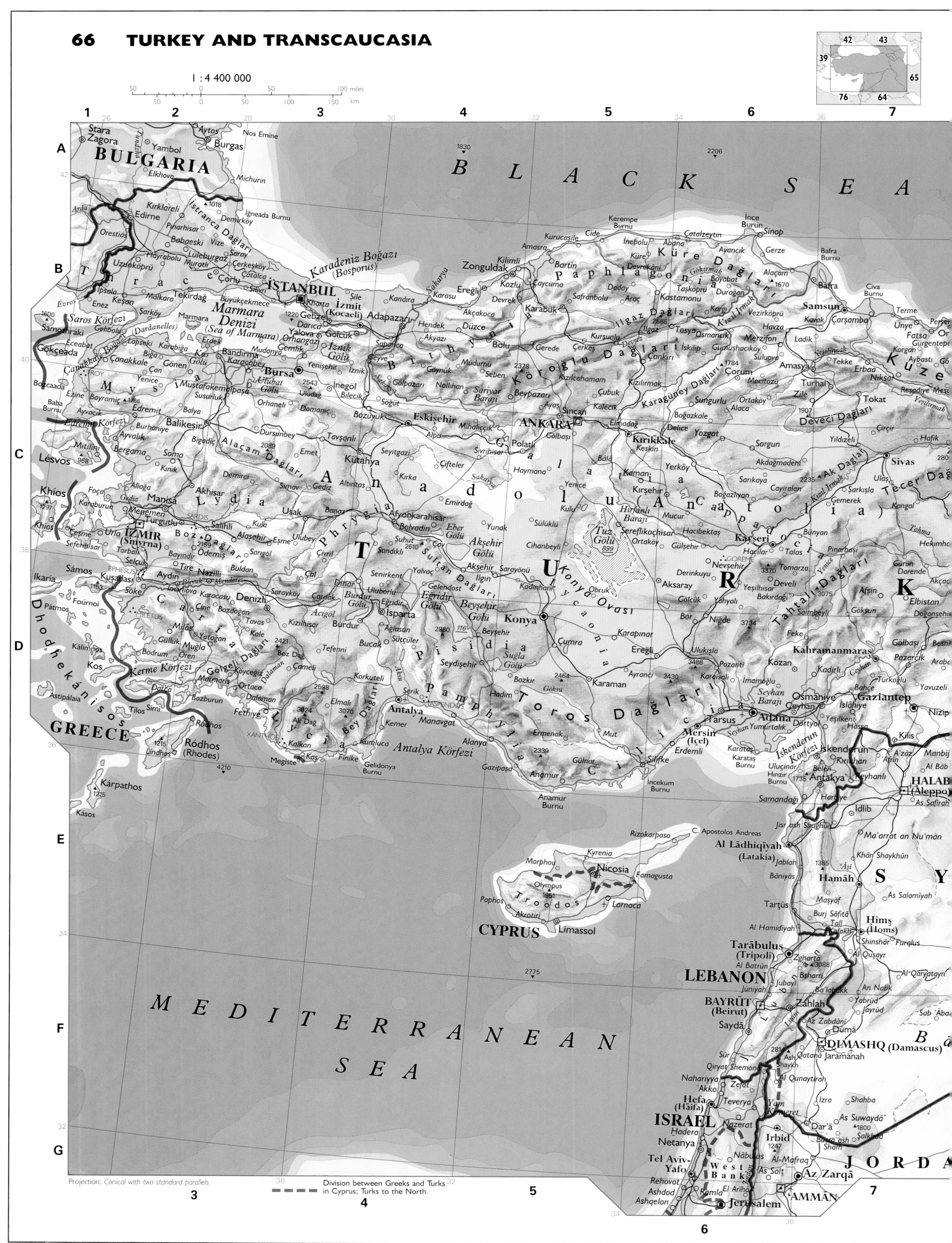
1 : 4 400 000
50 0 50 100 miles
50 0 50 100 150 km
BULGARIA
BLACK SEA
Stara Zagora
Yambol
Burgas
Aytos
Nos Emine
Elkhovo
Michurin
Edirne
Kırklareli
Orestiás
İğneada Burnu
Demirköy
Babaeski
Vize
Lüleburgaz
Uzunköprü
Hayrabolu
Muratlı
Saray
Çerkesköy
Çatalca
Çorlu
Silivri
Malkara
Tekirdağ
İpsala
Enez
Keşan
Évros
Saros Körfezi
Samothráki
Gökçeada
Gelibolu
Eceabat
(Dardanelles)
Lapseki
Çanakkale
Bozcaada
Biga
Karabiga
Erdek
Bandırma
Mudanya
Gemlik
Marmara
Marmara Denizi
(Sea of Marmara)
Büyükçekmece
İSTANBUL
Karadeniz Boğazı
(Bosporus)
Kartal
Gebze
Darıca
Yalova
Orhangazi
Gölcük
İzmit
(Kocaeli)
Şile
Kandıra
Adapazarı
Sakarya
Karasu
Akçakoca
Ereğli
Zonguldak
Kilimli
Kozlu
Devrek
Çaycuma
Bartın
Amasra
Karabük
Safranbolu
Kurucaşile
Cide
Kerempe Burnu
İnebolu
Abana
Küre
Devrekâni
Çatalzeytin
İnce Burun
Sinop
Gerze
Ayancık
Boyabat
Taşköprü
Durağan
Kastamonu
Küre Dağları
Paphlagonia
Bafra Burnu
Bafra
Alaçam
Samsun
Civa Burnu
Terme
Çarşamba
Ünye
Fatsa
Kavak
Vezirköprü
Havza
Ladik
Merzifon
Tosya
Osmancık
Kargı
Ilgaz Dağları
Ilgaz
Kurşunlu
Çerkeş
Gerede
Bolu
Düzce
Hendek
Akyazı
Sapanca
İznik Gölü
İznik
Geyve
Bithynia
Mudurnu
Göynük
Seben
Nallıhan
Gölpazarı
Köroğlu Dağları
Kızılcahamam
Beypazarı
Sarıyar Barajı
Çankırı
İskilip
Gümüşhacıköy
Suluova
Amasya
Çorum
Mecitözü
Tokat
Turhal
Zile
Niksar
Erbaa
Tekke
Yeşilırmak
Kızılırmak
Karagüney Dağları
Sungurlu
Ortaköy
Alaca
Boğazkale
Delice
Yozgat
Sorgun
Akdağmadeni
Sivas
Yıldızeli
Çamlıbel
Deveci Dağları
Hafik
Çubuk
Kalecik
Ayaş
Sincan
ANKARA
Gölbaşı
Elmadağ
Kırıkkale
Keskin
Polatlı
Sivrihisar
Mihalıççık
Eskişehir
Alpu
Bilecik
Söğüt
Bozüyük
İnegöl
Bursa
Yenişehir
Uludağ
Uluabat Gölü
Orhaneli
Mustafakemalpaşa
Karacabey
Susurluk
Gönen
Çan
Yenice
Bayramiç
Ezine
Baba Burnu
Ayvacık
Edremit Körfezi
Edremit
Burhaniye
Ayvalık
Balıkesir
Balya
Bigadiç
Dursunbey
Alaçam Dağları
Tavşanlı
Domaniç
Kütahya
Seyitgazi
Çifteler
Emet
Simav
Gediz
Demirci
Soma
Kınık
Bergama
Dikili
Mitilíni
Lésvos
Khíos
Foça
Aliağa
Menemen
Manisa
Akhisar
Lydia
Karaburun
Çeşme
Urla
İZMIR
(Smyrna)
Seferihisar
Torbalı
Selçuk
EPHESUS
Kuşadası
Sámos
Ikaria
Turgutlu
Salihli
Kula
Alaşehir
Eşme
Uşak
Ulubey
Banaz
Phrygia
Afyonkarahisar
Bolvadin
Eber Gölü
Emirdağ
Sandıklı
Şuhut
Çivril
Dinar
Bozdağ
Ödemiş
Bayındır
Tire
Nazilli
Aydın
Söke
Menderes
Denizli
Sarayköy
Çardak
Acıgöl
Burdur Gölü
Burdur
Isparta
Eğirdir Gölü
Eğirdir
Yalvaç
Akşehir Gölü
Akşehir
Sultan Dağları
Ilgın
Kadınhanı
Konya
Beyşehir Gölü
Beyşehir
Seydişehir
Suğla Gölü
Çumra
Karapınar
Ereğli
Konya Ovası
Lycaonia
Tuz Gölü
Cihanbeyli
Kulu
Yenice
Kırşehir
Kaman
Mucur
Hacıbektaş
Gülşehir
Nevşehir
GOREME
Kayseri
Cappadocia
Aksaray
Derinkuyu
Niğde
Bor
Ulukışla
Pozantı
Karaisalı
Kozan
Kahramanmaraş
Göksun
Elbistan
Afşin
Pınarbaşı
Sarız
Develi
Tomarza
Talas
Tahtalı Dağları
Ak Dağlar
Kangal
Gürün
Darende
Adana
Tarsus
Mersin
(İçel)
Erdemli
Silifke
Mut
Karaman
Ayrancı
Ermenek
Gülnar
Toros Dağları
Anamur
Anamur Burnu
Alanya
Gazipaşa
Manavgat
Serik
ASPENDOS
Antalya
Antalya Körfezi
Kemer
Kumluca
Finike
Gelidonya Burnu
Kaş
Kalkan
Megiste
Lycia
Elmalı
Fethiye
Dalaman
Köyceğiz
Marmaris
Datça
Ortaca
Kerme Körfezi
Bodrum
Milas
Muğla
Yatağan
Kale
Tavas
Çine
Bozdoğan
Karacasu
MILETUS
Gölgeli Dağları
Pisidia
Pamphylia
Cilicia
Caria
Kos
Kálimnos
Pátmos
Foúrnoi
Dhodhekánisos
Astipálaia
Tílos
Sími
Ródhos
Ródhos (Rhodes)
Líndhos
Kárpathos
Kásos
GREECE
Osmaniye
Ceyhan
Gaziantep
Nizip
İslâhiye
Kilis
Dörtyol
İskenderun
İskenderun Körfezi
Kırıkhan
Belen
Antakya
Reyhanlı
Samandağı
HALAB
(Aleppo)
Idlib
Ma'arrat an Nu'man
Karataş
Karataş Burnu
Yumurtalık
Seyhan Barajı
Al Lādhiqīyah
(Latakia)
Jablah
Bāniyās
Hamāh
Tartūs
Hims
(Homs)
SYRIA
Rizokarpaso
C. Apostolos Andreas
Kyrenia
Morphou
Nicosia
Famagusta
Olympus
Troodos
Paphos
Akrotiri
Larnaca
Limassol
CYPRUS
Tarābulus
(Tripoli)
LEBANON
BAYRŪT
(Beirut)
Saydā
Zahlah
DIMASHQ (Damascus)
Jaramānah
Sūr
Nahariyya
'Akko
Hefa
(Haifa)
Nazerat
Teverya
ISRAEL
Hadera
Netanya
Tel Aviv-Yafo
Rehovot
Ashdod
Ashqelon
West Bank
Jerusalem
Irbid
Dar'ā
As Suwaydā'
Al-Mafraq
Az Zarqā
AMMĀN
JORDAN
MEDITERRANEAN SEA
Projection: Conical with two standard parallels
Division between Greeks and Turks in Cyprus; Turks to the North.

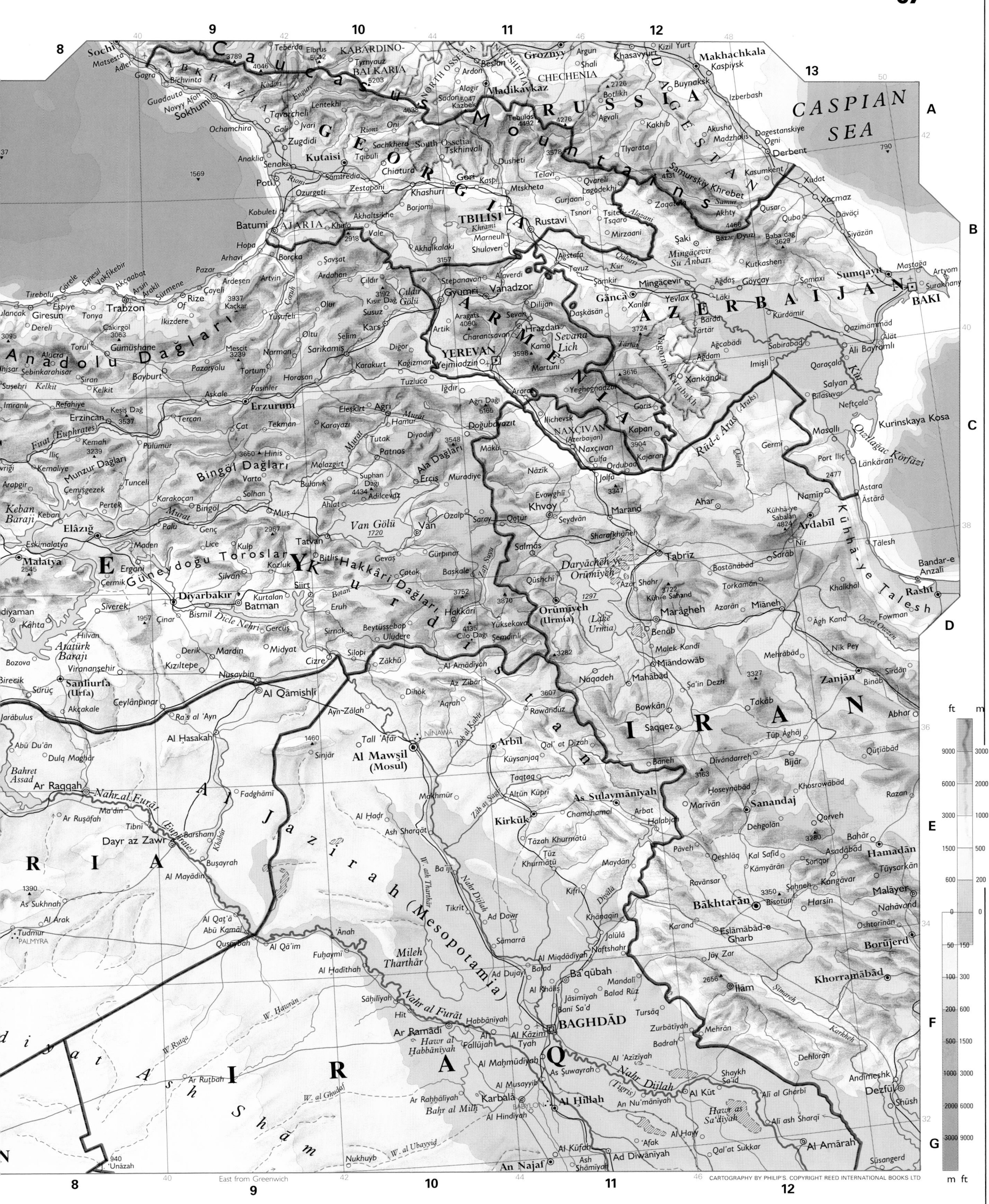

CASPIAN SEA
Caucasus Mountains
RUSSIA
GEORGIA
ARMENIA
AZERBAIJAN
TURKEY
IRAN
IRAQ
SYRIA
Kurdistan
Al Jazirah (Mesopotamia)
Bādiyat ash Shām
DAGESTAN
CHECHENIA
INGUSHETIA
NORTH OSSETIA
KABARDINO-BALKARIA
ABKHAZIA
AJARIA
South Ossetia
NAXÇIVAN (Azerbaijan)
Nagorno-Karabakh
Anadolu Dağları
Güneydoğu Toroslar
Hakkâri Dağları
Munzur Dağları
Bingöl Dağları
Ala Dağları
Kühhā-ye Ţālesh
Samurskiy Khrebet
TBILISI
YEREVAN
BAKI
BAGHDĀD
Sochi
Sokhumi
Batumi
Kutaisi
Rustavi
Gyumri
Vanadzor
Gäncä
Sumqayıt
Makhachkala
Derbent
Groznyy
Vladikavkaz
Trabzon
Rize
Giresun
Erzurum
Erzincan
Kars
Ağri
Van
Van Gölü
Muş
Bitlis
Elâzığ
Malatya
Diyarbakır
Batman
Siirt
Mardin
Şanlıurfa (Urfa)
Cizre
Tabrīz
Orūmīyeh (Urmia)
Daryācheh-ye Orūmīyeh (Lake Urmia)
Ardabīl
Rasht
Bandar-e Anzalī
Zanjān
Hamadān
Sanandaj
Bākhtarān
Khorramābād
Dezfūl
Borūjerd
Mahābād
Marāgheh
Khvoy
Ilām
Al Mawşil (Mosul)
Arbīl
Kirkūk
As Sulaymānīyah
Dahūk
Tikrīt
Sāmarrā
Ba'qūbah
Ar Ramādī
Al Fallūjah
Karbalā
Al Ḩillah
An Najaf
Al Kūt
Al 'Amārah
Ad Dīwānīyah
Ar Raqqah
Dayr az Zawr
Al Ḩasakah
Al Qāmishlī
Tudmur PALMYRA
Nahr al Furāt (Euphrates)
Nahr Dijlah (Tigris)
Rūd-e Aras (Araks)
Kur
Sevana Lich
Atatürk Barajı
Keban Barajı
Buḩayrat ath Tharthār
Hawr al Habbānīyah
Elbrus 5642
Kazbek 5047
Ağrı Dağı 5165
Aragats 4090
Süphan Dağı 4434
Sabalān 4824
East from Greenwich

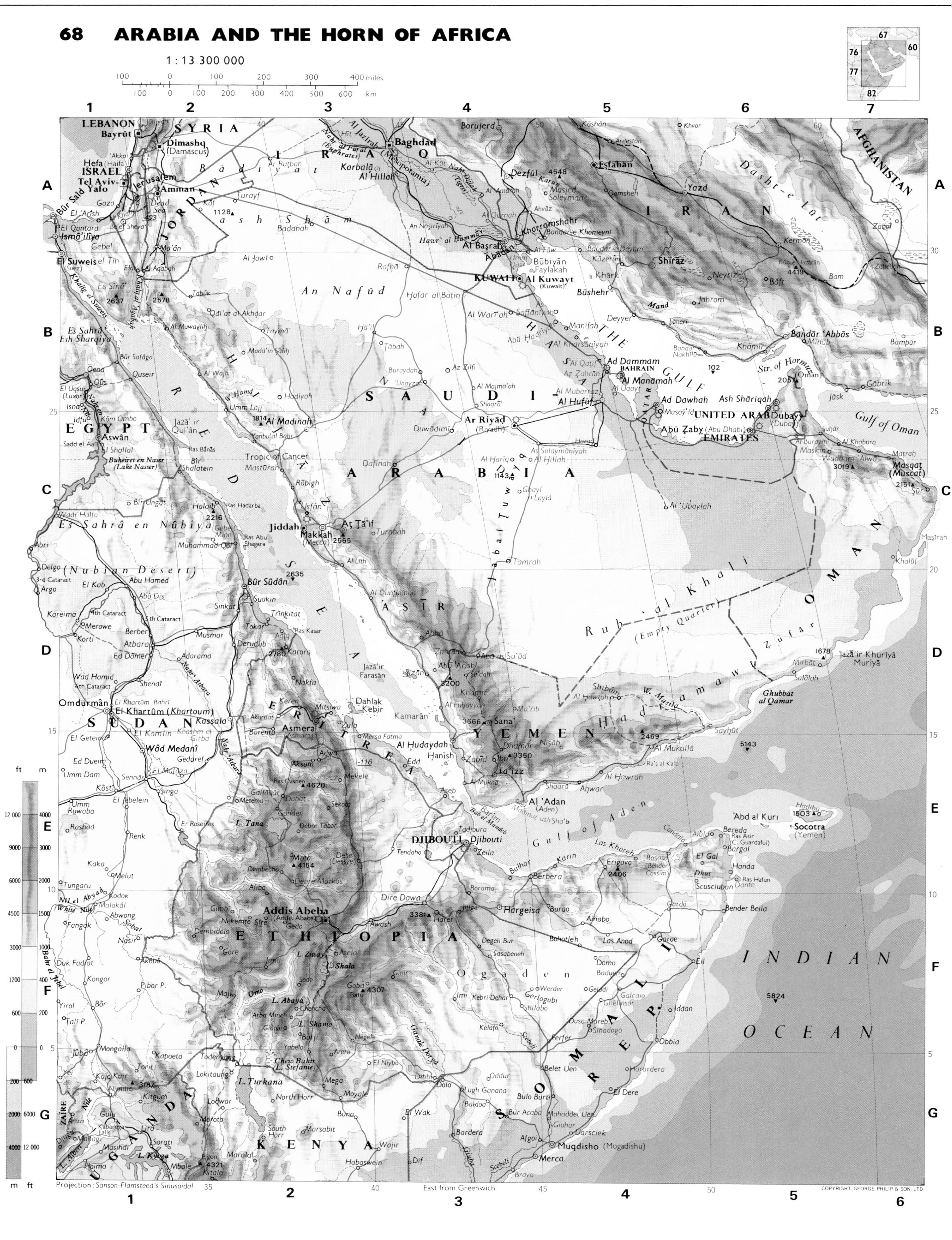
68 ARABIA AND THE HORN OF AFRICA
1 : 13 300 000
100 0 100 200 300 400 miles
100 0 100 200 300 400 500 600 km
67
76
60
77
82
LEBANON
SYRIA
ISRAEL
JORDAN
IRAQ
IRAN
AFGHANISTAN
KUWAIT
BAHRAIN
QATAR
UNITED ARAB EMIRATES
SAUDI ARABIA
OMAN
YEMEN
EGYPT
SUDAN
ERITREA
DJIBOUTI
ETHIOPIA
SOMALI REP.
KENYA
UGANDA
ZAIRE
RED SEA
THE GULF
Gulf of Oman
Gulf of Aden
INDIAN OCEAN
An Nafūd
Rub' al Khali (Empty Quarter)
Bādiyat ash Shām
Dasht-e Lūt
Es Sahrâ en Nûbîya
(Nubian Desert)
Ḥaḍramawt
Ogaden
Socotra (Yemen)
Tropic of Cancer
Projection: Sanson-Flamsteed's Sinusoidal
East from Greenwich
COPYRIGHT GEORGE PHILIP & SON LTD

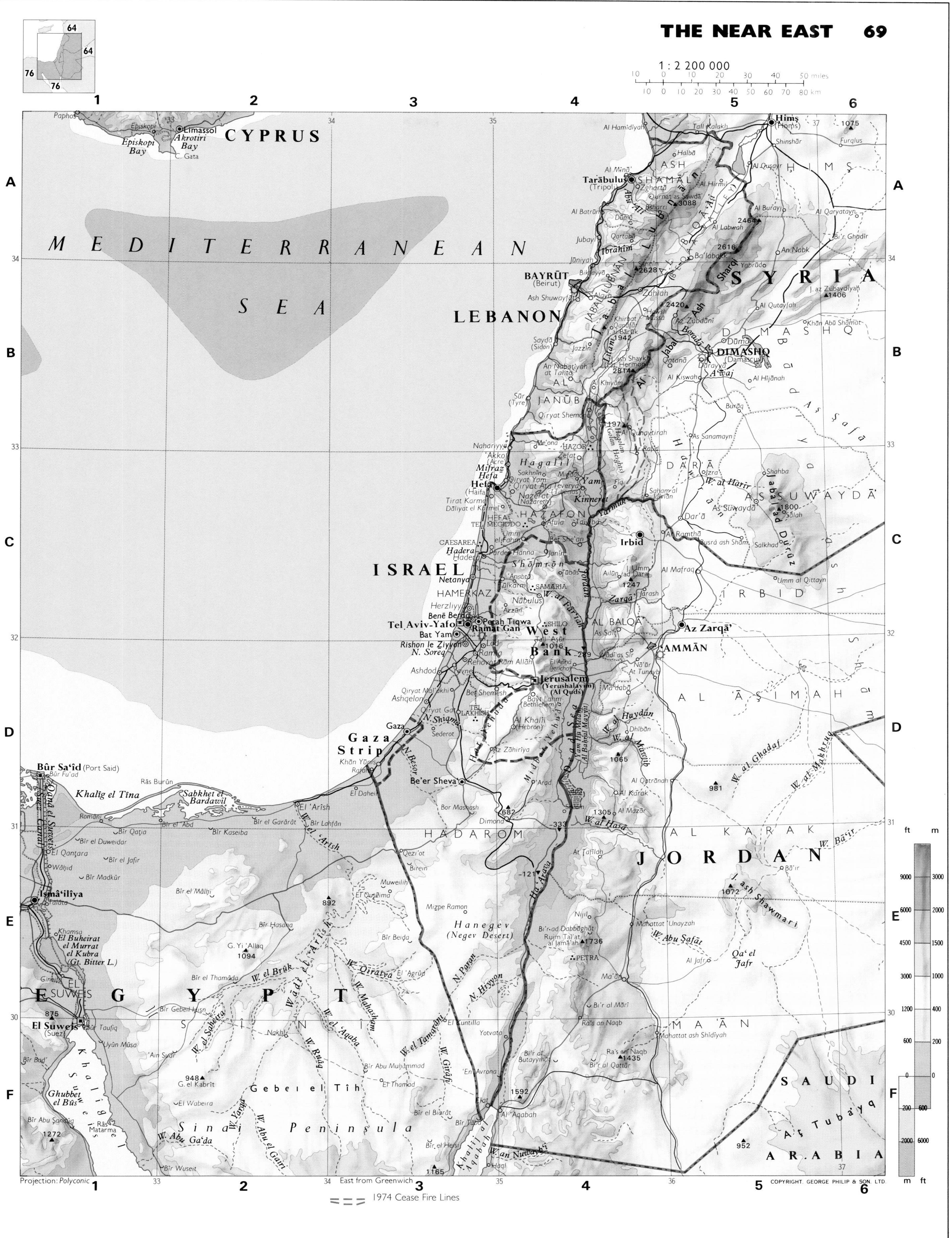
1 : 2 200 000
CYPRUS
MEDITERRANEAN SEA
LEBANON
SYRIA
ISRAEL
West Bank
Gaza Strip
JORDAN
EGYPT
SAUDI ARABIA
Sinai Peninsula
Jerusalem (Yerushalayim) (Al Quds)
AMMĀN
DIMASHQ (Damascus)
BAYRŪT (Beirut)
Tel Aviv-Yafo
Projection: Polyconic
East from Greenwich
1974 Cease Fire Lines
COPYRIGHT. GEORGE PHILIP & SON. LTD.

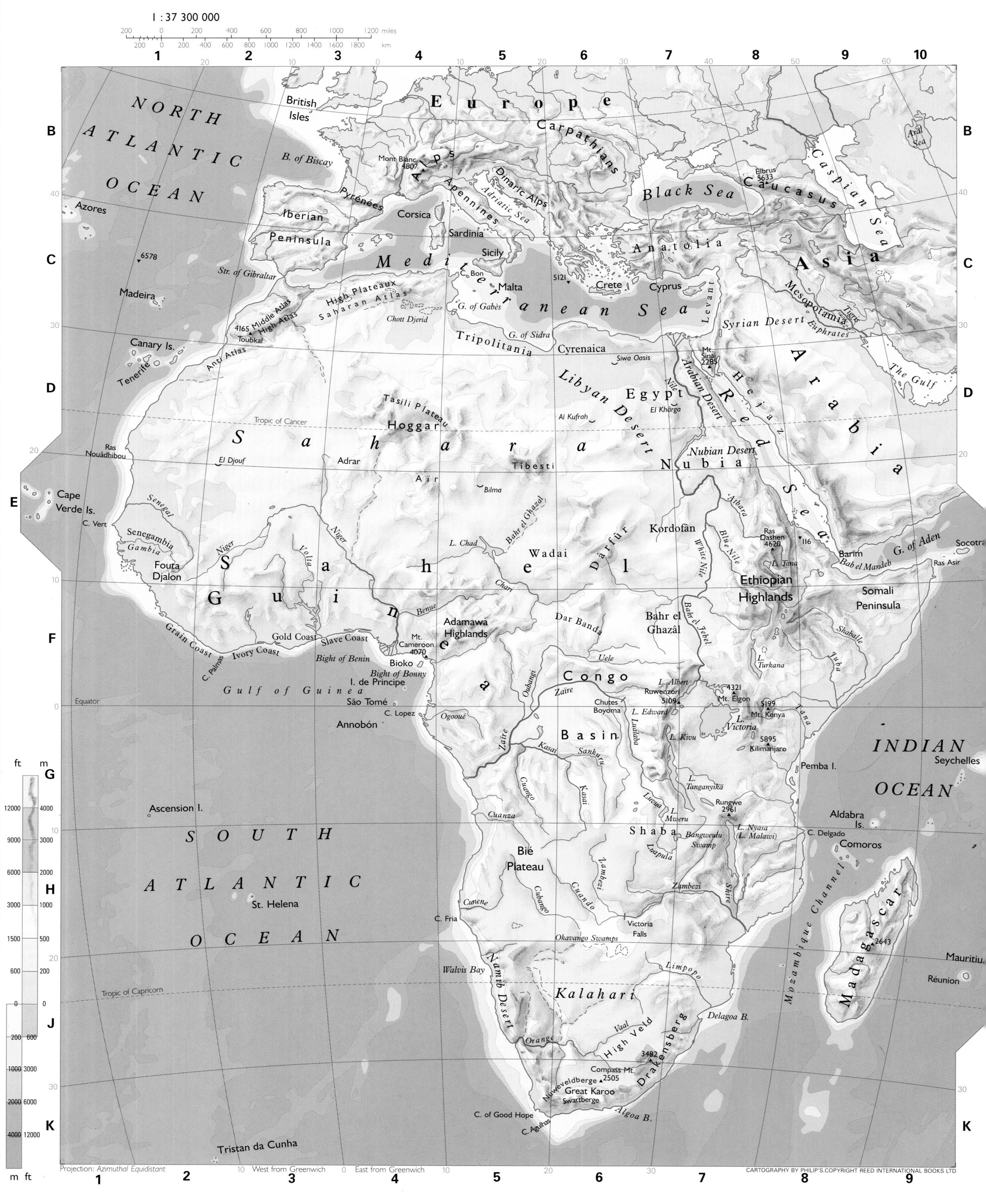
1 : 37 300 000
NORTH ATLANTIC OCEAN
Europe
British Isles
B. of Biscay
Carpathians
Mont Blanc 4807
Alps
Dinaric Alps
Apennines
Adriatic Sea
Black Sea
Elbrus 5633
Caucasus
Caspian Sea
Aral Sea
Azores
Pyrénées
Iberian Peninsula
Corsica
Sardinia
Sicily
Anatolia
Asia
6578
Str. of Gibraltar
Mediterranean Sea
C. Bon
Malta
5121
Crete
Cyprus
Levant
Mesopotamia
Tigris
Madeira
High Plateaux
Saharan Atlas
G. of Gabès
Chott Djerid
Syrian Desert
Euphrates
4165 Middle Atlas
High Atlas
Toubkal
G. of Sidra
Tripolitania
Cyrenaica
Siwa Oasis
Mt. Sinai 2285
Canary Is.
Anti Atlas
Tenerife
Libyan Desert
Arabian Desert
Hejaz
Arabia
The Gulf
Egypt
Nile
El Khârga
Red Sea
Tasili Plateau
Hoggar
Tropic of Cancer
Al Kufrah
Sahara
Ras Nouâdhibou
El Djouf
Adrar
Tibesti
Nubian Desert
Nubia
Aïr
Bilma
Cape Verde Is.
C. Vert
Senegal
Atbara
Senegambia
Gambia
Niger
Volta
Bahr el Ghazal
L. Chad
Kordofân
Ras Dashen 4620
116
Barim
G. of Aden
Socotra
Fouta Djalon
Sahel
Wadai
Dârfûr
White Nile
Blue Nile
L. Tana
Bab el Mandeb
Ras Asir
Ethiopian Highlands
Somali Peninsula
Guinea
Chari
Benue
Adamawa Highlands
Dar Banda
Bahr el Ghazâl
Bahr el Jebel
Shabelle
Grain Coast
Gold Coast
Slave Coast
Mt. Cameroon 4070
Ivory Coast
Bight of Benin
C. Palmas
Bioko
Bight of Bonny
Uele
L. Turkana
Juba
I. de Principe
Congo
L. Albert
Ruwenzori 5109
4321 Mt. Elgon
Gulf of Guinea
São Tomé
Zaïre
Oubangi
Chutes Boyoma
5199 Mt. Kenya
Equator
L. Edward
L. Victoria
Tana
C. Lopez
Ogooué
Annobón
Basin
Lualaba
L. Kivu
5895 Kilimanjaro
INDIAN OCEAN
Kasai
Sankuru
Seychelles
Pemba I.
Cuango
L. Tanganyika
Ascension I.
Rungwe 2961
Cuanza
Lucuta
L. Mweru
Aldabra Is.
SOUTH ATLANTIC OCEAN
Shaba
Bangweulu Swamp
L. Nyasa (L. Malawi)
C. Delgado
Comoros
Luapula
Bié Plateau
Zambezi
Mozambique Channel
Madagascar
St. Helena
Cunene
Cubango
Cuando
Shire
C. Fria
Victoria Falls
Okavango Swamps
2643
Walvis Bay
Namib Desert
Limpopo
Mauritius
Réunion
Tropic of Capricorn
Kalahari
Delagoa B.
Vaal
High Veld
Drakensberg
Orange
3482
Compass Mt. 2505
Nuweveldberge
Great Karoo
Swartberge
C. of Good Hope
C. Agulhas
Algoa B.
Tristan da Cunha
Projection: Azimuthal Equidistant
West from Greenwich
East from Greenwich
CARTOGRAPHY BY PHILIP'S.COPYRIGHT REED INTERNATIONAL BOOKS LTD

1 : 37 300 000
200 0 200 400 600 800 1000 1200 miles
200 0 200 400 600 800 1000 1200 1400 1600 1800 km
NORTH ATLANTIC OCEAN
Azores (Port.)
Madeira (Port.)
Canary Is. (Sp.)
B. of Biscay
UNITED KINGDOM
LONDON
NETH.
BELG.
PARIS
FRANCE
SWITZ.
GERMANY
POLAND
Warsaw
Prague
CZECH REP.
Vienna
AUSTRIA
SLOVAK REP.
HUNGARY
ROMANIA
CROATIA
BOS.-HERZ.
YUG.
BULGARIA
ALB.
MAC.
GREECE
Athens
Crete
ITALY
Rome
Corsica
Sardinia
Sicily
MALTA
Adriatic Sea
PORTUGAL
Lisbon
SPAIN
Madrid
RUSSIA
Kiev
UKRAINE
Odessa
Volgograd
KAZAKSTAN
Aral Sea
Caspian Sea
Black Sea
GEORGIA
ARM.
AZER.
Baku
TURKMEN.
TURKEY
Ankara
CYPRUS
Mosul
TEHRAN
Esfahan
IRAN
SYRIA
Aleppo
Damascus
LEB.
Tel Aviv-Jaffa
Jerusalem
ISRAEL
JORDAN
IRAQ
Baghdad
Tigris
Euphrates
Syrian Desert
Basra
KUWAIT
The Gulf
BAHRAIN
QATAR
SAUDI ARABIA
Riyadh
Medina
Jedda
Mecca
YEMEN
Socotra (Yemen)
G. of Aden
Ras Asir
Mediterranean Sea
Algiers
Annaba
Constantine
Tunis
TUNISIA
Sfax
Chott Djerid
Tripoli
Misrātah
Benghazi
Alexandria
Port Said
Suez
CAIRO
El Faiyûm
Asyût
Nile
EGYPT
Aswân
Red Sea
Rabat
Casablanca
Tetouan
Fès
MOROCCO
Marrakesh
ALGERIA
In Salah
LIBYA
Marzūq
Al Jawf
El Aaiún
WESTERN SAHARA
Dakhla
Fdérik
Tropic of Cancer
Sahara
Ras Nouâdhibou
MAURITANIA
Nouakchott
CAPE VERDE IS.
Praia
St-Louis
C. Vert
Dakar
SENEGAL
Senegal
GAMBIA
Banjul
GUINEA-BISSAU
Bissau
GUINEA
Conakry
Freetown
SIERRA LEONE
Monrovia
LIBERIA
Tombouctou
MALI
Bamako
Niger
NIGER
Agadès
Niamey
BURKINA FASO
Ouagadougou
Bobo-Dioulasso
IVORY COAST
Bouaké
Yamoussoukro
Abidjan
GHANA
Kumasi
Sekondi-Takoradi
Accra
TOGO
Lomé
BENIN
Porto Novo
NIGERIA
Kano
Maiduguri
Abuja
Ibadan
Lagos
Benue
Enugu
Port Harcourt
Bight of Benin
Gulf of Guinea
CHAD
L. Chad
Abéché
Ndjamena
Chari
SUDAN
El Fâsher
El Obeid
Wadi Halfa
Port Sudan
Atbara
Omdurmân
Khartoum
Wad Medani
White Nile
Blue Nile
Malakâl
Wau
Bahr el Jebel
ERITREA
Asmera
Mesewa
L. Tana
DJIBOUTI
Djibouti
Berbera
Addis Ababa
ETHIOPIA
Harer
Shabelle
SOMALI REP.
Mogadishu
Juba
Kismayu
CENTRAL AFRICAN REP.
Bangui
CAMEROON
Douala
Yaoundé
Malabo
EQUATORIAL GUINEA
SÃO TOMÉ & PRINCIPE
Annobón
Libreville
C. Lopez
GABON
CONGO
Oubangi
Equator
Pointe Noire
Brazzaville
Kinshasa
Matadi
CABINDA (Angola)
Zaïre
Mbandaka
ZAÏRE
Kisangani
Kasai
Kananga
L. Albert
L. Edward
Lualaba
L. Kivu
UGANDA
Kampala
Kisumu
L. Victoria
KENYA
Nairobi
L. Turkana
Tana
RWANDA
Kigali
BURUNDI
Bujumbura
TANZANIA
Dodoma
L. Tanganyika
Zanzibar
Dar es Salaam
Mombasa
INDIAN OCEAN
SEYCHELLES
Aldabra Is.
C. Delgado
COMOROS
Mayotte (Fr.)
Antsiranana
Mahajanga
Toamasina
Antananarivo
MADAGASCAR
Fianarantsoa
MAURITIUS
Réunion (Fr.)
Mozambique Channel
Ascension I. (U.K.)
SOUTH ATLANTIC OCEAN
St. Helena (U.K.)
Tristan da Cunha (U.K.)
Luanda
Cuango
Lobito
ANGOLA
Huambo
Namibe
Cunene
Cubango
C. Fria
L. Mweru
Likasi
Lubumbashi
Ndola
ZAMBIA
Lusaka
MALAWI
L. Malawi
Lilongwe
Blantyre
Zambezi
MOZAMBIQUE
Moçambique
Livingstone
Harare
ZIMBABWE
Bulawayo
Beira
NAMIBIA
Windhoek
BOTSWANA
Limpopo
Gaborone
Tropic of Capricorn
Pretoria
Johannesburg
Vaal
Mbabane
SWAZ.
Maputo
Kimberley
Orange
Maseru
LESOTHO
Durban
SOUTH AFRICA
Cape Town
C. of Good Hope
C. Agulhas
East London
Port Elizabeth
Projection: Azimuthal Equidistant
West from Greenwich
East from Greenwich
Dakar Capital Cities
CARTOGRAPHY BY PHILIP'S. COPYRIGHT REED INTERNATIONAL BOOKS LTD

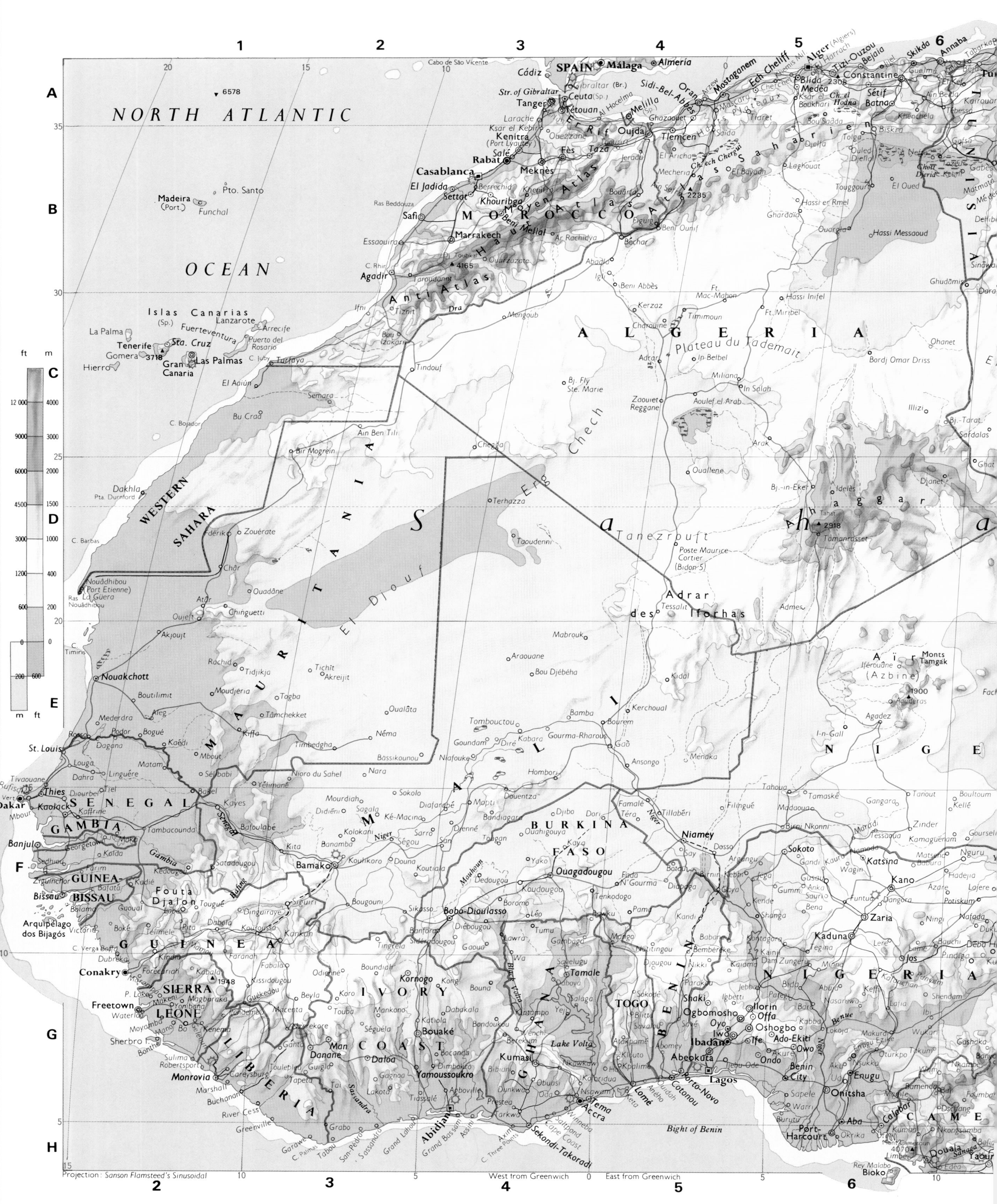
NORTH ATLANTIC
OCEAN
SPAIN
Málaga
Almería
Cádiz
Str. of Gibraltar
Gibraltar (Br.)
Tanger
Ceuta (Sp.)
Tétouan
Melilla (Sp.)
Oujda
Sidi-Bel-Abbès
Oran
Mostaganem
Ech Cheliff
Alger (Algiers)
Blida
Médéa
Tizi-Ouzou
Bejaia
Skikda
Annaba
Constantine
Sétif
Batna
Biskra
Tlemcen
Larache
Kenitra (Port Lyautey)
Salé
Rabat
Fès
Taza
Meknès
Casablanca
El Jadida
Settat
Khouribga
Safi
Essaouira
Marrakech
Beni Mellal
Ar Rachidiya
Béchar
Agadir
Tiznit
Tarfaya
Tindouf
Madeira (Port.)
Funchal
Pto. Santo
Islas Canarias (Sp.)
Lanzarote
Fuerteventura
Arrecife
Puerto del Rosario
La Palma
Tenerife
Sta. Cruz
Gomera
Hierro
Gran Canaria
Las Palmas
3718
6578
4165
2308
2235
2918
1948
1900
4070
M O R O C C O
Anti Atlas
Haut Atlas
Moyen Atlas
Er Rif
Atlas Saharien
Dra
Ghardaïa
Laghouat
Ouargla
Touggourt
El Oued
Hassi Messaoud
Hassi Inifel
Timimoun
Adrar
Reggane
In Salah
Plateau du Tademaït
A L G E R I A
Ahaggar
Tamanrasset
Djanet
Illizi
El Aaiún
Semara
Bu Craa
C. Bojador
Dakhla
WESTERN SAHARA
C. Barbas
Nouâdhibou (Port Etienne)
La Güera
Zouérate
Fdérik
Atar
Chinguetti
Ouadâne
Akjoujt
Nouakchott
Rosso
Kiffa
Néma
Tidjikja
M A U R I T A N I A
El Djouf
Taoudenni
Tanezrouft
Adrar des Iforhas
Kidal
Araouane
Tombouctou
Gao
Mopti
Ségou
Bamako
Kayes
M A L I
Niamey
Agadez
Aïr
N I G E R
St. Louis
Dakar
Thiès
Kaolack
S E N E G A L
GAMBIA
Banjul
GUINEA-BISSAU
Bissau
Arquipélago dos Bijagós
Fouta Djalon
G U I N E A
Conakry
Freetown
SIERRA LEONE
Monrovia
LIBERIA
IVORY COAST
Bouaké
Yamoussoukro
Abidjan
Ouagadougou
BURKINA FASO
Bobo-Dioulasso
GHANA
Tamale
Kumasi
Lake Volta
Accra
Tema
Sekondi-Takoradi
TOGO
Lomé
BENIN
Cotonou
Porto-Novo
Bight of Benin
Sokoto
Kano
Zaria
Kaduna
Jos
N I G E R I A
Ilorin
Ogbomosho
Oshogbo
Ibadan
Abeokuta
Lagos
Benin City
Onitsha
Enugu
Aba
Port-Harcourt
Calabar
Douala
Bioko
Projection: Sanson Flamsteed's Sinusoidal
West from Greenwich
East from Greenwich

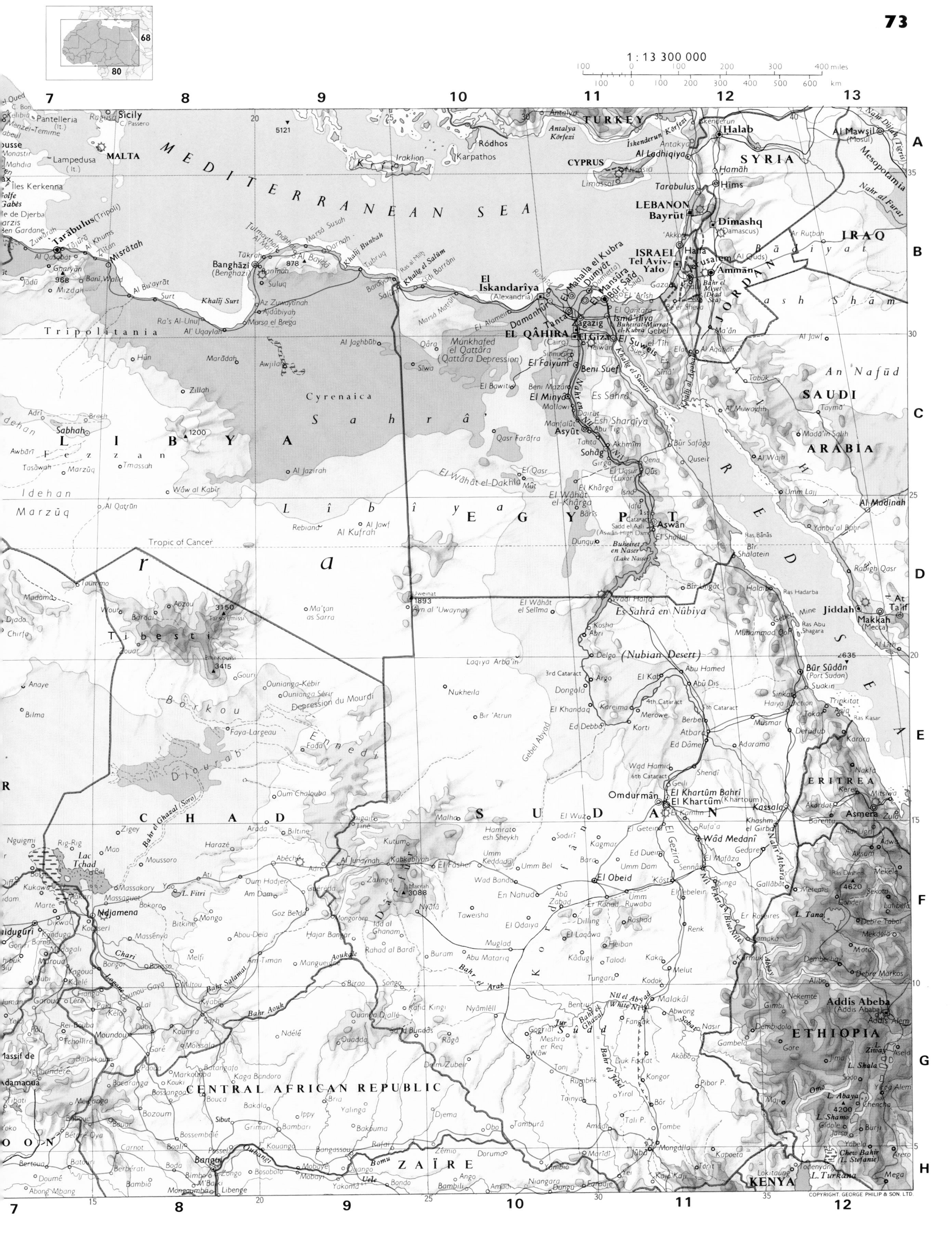
68
80
1 : 13 300 000
100 0 100 200 300 400 miles
100 0 100 200 300 400 500 600 km
7 8 9 10 11 12 13
A B C D E F G H
MEDITERRANEAN SEA
RED SEA
TURKEY
SYRIA
CYPRUS
LEBANON
ISRAEL
JORDAN
IRAQ
SAUDI ARABIA
LIBYA
EGYPT
SUDAN
CHAD
ERITREA
ETHIOPIA
CENTRAL AFRICAN REPUBLIC
ZAÏRE
KENYA
MALTA
Sicily
Pantelleria (It.)
Lampedusa (It.)
Îles Kerkenna
Golfe de Gabès
Île de Djerba
Tarābulus (Tripoli)
Misrātah
Al Khums
Gharyān
Mizdah
Tripolitania
Khalīj Surt
Surt
Banghāzī (Benghazi)
Ajdābiyah
Marsa el Brega
Tubruq
Khalīg el Salûm
Cyrenaica
Sahrâ' Lîbîya
Fezzan
Sabhah
Marzūq
Idehan Marzūq
Al Kufrah
Tropic of Cancer
Tibesti
Emi Koussi 3415
3150
Borkou
Ennedi
Djourab
Faya-Largeau
Depression du Mourdi
Ouanianga-Kébir
Bilma
Lac Tchad
Ndjamena
Abéché
Massenya
Chari
Moundou
Sarh
Bangui
Mongoumba
Ubangi
Bangassou
Rhodos
Karpathos
Iraklion
Kríti
Antalya Körfezi
İskenderun Körfezi
Halab
Al Lādhiqīyah
Hamāh
Hims
Tarabulus
Bayrūt
Dimashq (Damascus)
Haifa
Tel Aviv-Yafo
Jerusalem (Al Quds)
'Ammān
Bahr el Miyet (Dead Sea)
Bādiyat ash Shām
An Nafūd
Al Mawsil (Mosul)
Mesopotamia
Nahr al Furat
Nahr Dijlah (Tigris)
El Iskandarîya (Alexandria)
Damanhûr
Tanta
El Mahalla el Kubra
Dumyât
El Mansûra
Bûr Sa'îd (Port Said)
Zagazig
Ismâ'ilîya
EL QÂHIRA (Cairo)
El Gîza
El Suweis (Suez)
Khalîg el Suweis
Munkhafed el Qattâra (Qattara Depression)
Siwa
El Faiyûm
Beni Suef
El Minya
Nahr en Nîl
Asyût
Sohâg
Qena
El Uqsur (Luxor)
Aswân
Sadd el Aali (Aswan High Dam)
Buheiret en Naser (Lake Nasser)
El Wâhât el-Dakhla
El Wâhât el-Khârga
Es Sahrâ' Esh Sharqîya
Sînâ'
Jiddah
Makkah (Mecca)
Al Madînah
Bûr Sûdân (Port Sudan)
Suakin
Wadi Halfa
Es Sahrâ en Nûbiya
(Nubian Desert)
Dongola
Abu Hamed
Atbara
Omdurmân
El Khartûm (Khartoum)
El Khartûm Bahrî
Kassala
Wâd Medanî
El Obeid
Kordofân
Darfur
El Fasher
Nyala
3088
Malakâl
Bahr el Ghazal
Bahr el Jebel
Nîl el Abyad (White Nile)
Nîl el Azraq (Blue Nile)
Sobat
Jûba
Asmera
Mitsiwa
L. Tana
Addis Abeba
L. Turkana
L. Abaya
L. Shamo
Chew Bahir (L. Stefanie)
COPYRIGHT. GEORGE PHILIP & SON. LTD.

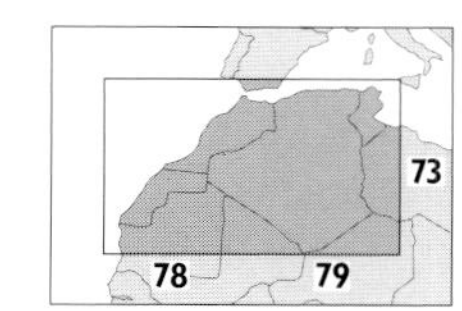

1 2 3

A B C D E

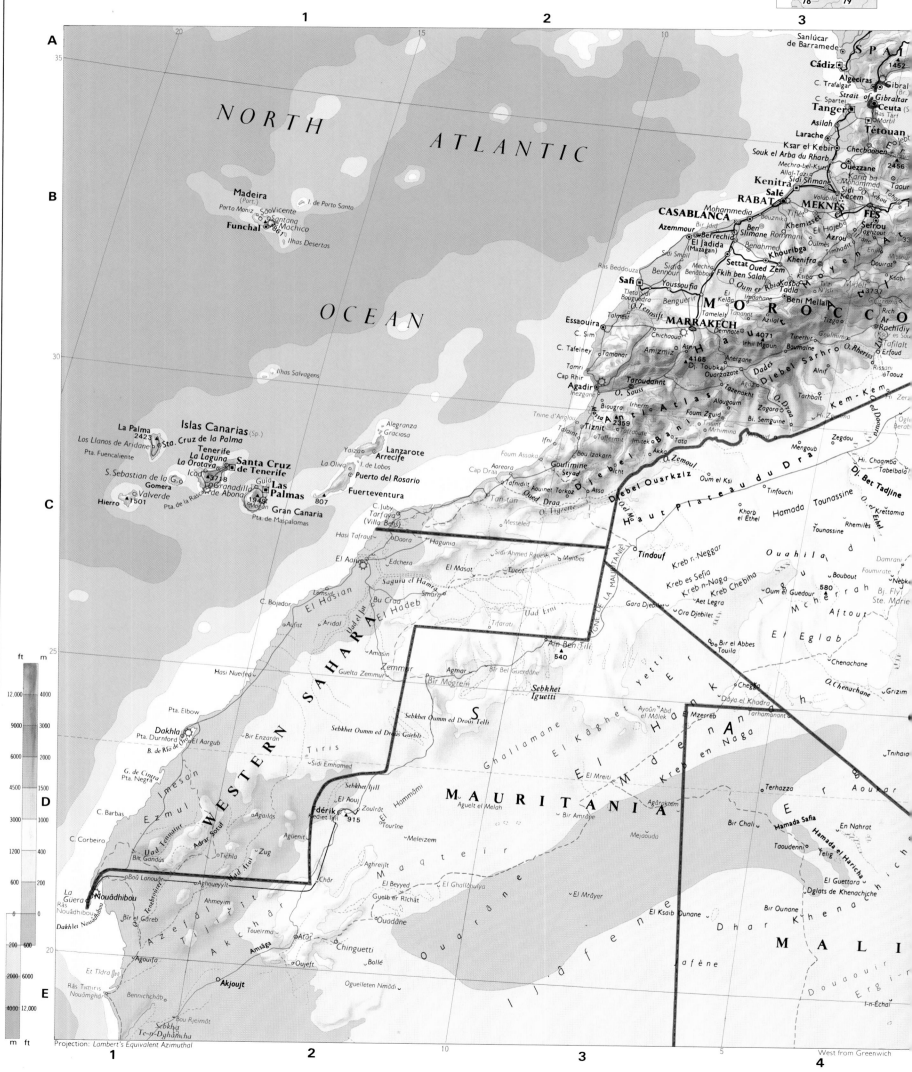

NORTH ATLANTIC OCEAN

Madeira (Port.)
Porto Moniz
São Vicente
Santana
Machico
Funchal
1861
I. de Porto Santo
Ilhas Desertas
Ilhas Salvagens

Islas Canarias (Sp.)
La Palma
2423
Sta. Cruz de la Palma
Los Llanos de Aridane
Pta. Fuencaliente
Tenerife
La Laguna
La Orotava
Santa Cruz de Tenerife
Icod
3718
S. Sebastian de la G.
Gomera
Granadilla de Abona
Valverde
Hierro
1501
Pta. de la Rasca
Guia
Las Palmas
1949
Mogán
Gran Canaria
Pta. de Maspalomas
Alegranza
Graciosa
Lanzarote
Arrecife
Yaiza
La Oliva
I. de Lobos
Puerto del Rosario
Fuerteventura
807

Sanlúcar de Barrameda
SPAIN
Cádiz
1452
Algeciras
Gibraltar (Br.)
C. Trafalgar
Strait of Gibraltar
C. Spartel
Tanger
Ceuta
Ras Tarf
Martil
Asilah
Tétouan
Larache
Ksar el Kebir
Chechaouen
Souk el Arba du Rharb
Mechra-bel-Ksiri
Allal-Tazi
Ouezzane
2456
Kenitra
Sidi Slimane
Karia ba Mohammed
Salé
RABAT
Sidi Kacem
MEKNÈS
FES
Volubilis
Taour
CASABLANCA
Mohammedia
Bouznika
Tiflet
Khemisset
Sefrou
Azemmour
Bir Jdid
Berrechid
Ben Slimane
Rommani
El Hajeb
Azrou
El Jadida (Mazagan)
Benahmed
Oulmès
Sidi Smaïl
Khouribga
Khenifra
Settat
Oued Zem
Sidi Bennour
Mechra Benâbbou
Fkih ben Salah
Ras Beddouza
Safi
Youssoufia
Oum er Rbia
Kasba Tadla
Tleta Sidi Bouguedra
Benguerir
El Kelâa
Beni Mellal
MOROCCO
Imdahane
Tamelelt
Tanannt
Azilal
3737
Essaouira
Talmest
O. Tensift
MARRAKECH
Demnate
Tizgà
Ar Rachidiya
C. Sim
Chichaoua
4071
Tinerhir
Goulmima
Tafilalt
Erfoud
C. Tafelney
Amizmiz
Asni
Imhil Mgoun
Boumalne
O. Rheris
Tamri
Tamanar
4165
Dj. Toubkal
Anergane
Ouarzazate
Dades
Djebel Sarhro
Alnif
Taouz
Cap Rhir
Agadir
Inezgane
Taroudannt
O. Souss
Tazenakht
Torhbalt
Biougra
Irherm
Alougoum
Zagora
O. Draa
Kem-Kem
Tnine d'Anglou
Massa
Anti Atlas
2359
Foum Zguid
Tiznit
Bi. Semguine
Talaint
Tafraoute
Tissint
Mrhimina
Ifni
Tafermit
Imitek
Tata
Mengoub
Zegdou
Foum Assaka
Bou Izakarn
Akka
O. Zemoul
Hi. Chagmba
Tabelbala
Aoreora
Goulimine
Seyad
Icht
Cap Draa
Tafnidilt
Aouinet Torkoz
Assa
Djebel Bani
Djebel Ouarkziz
Oum el Ksi
Dj. Bet Tadjine
Plateau du Dra
Tinfouchi
Tan-tan
Oued Draa
O. Tigzerte
Haut
Khorb el Ethel
Hamada
Tounassine
Krettamia
Rhemilès
Tounassine
Messeïed
C. Juby
Tarfaya (Villa Bens)
Hasi Tafraout
Daora
Hagunia
Tindouf
Kreb n-Neggar
Ouahila
Sidi Ahmed Rguibi
Mahbes
El Aaiún
Edchera
El Masat
Tucat
Kreb es Sefia
Kreb n-Naga
Kreb Chebiha
Boubout
580
Oum el Guedour
Meharrah
Bj. Flye Ste. Marie
Saguia el Hamra
Smara
Lemsid
El Hasian
C. Bojador
Bu Craa
El Hadeb
Ud Erni
Gara Djebilet
Aet Legra
Ora Djebilet
Aftout
Uad el Jat
Aridal
Tifarati
Bir el Abbes
Touila
El Eglab
Aufist
Aïn Ben Tili
540
Amasin
Chenachane
Hasi Nueifed
Zemmur
Agmar
Bir Bel Guerdâne
Guelta Zemmur
Bir Mogreïn
O. Chenachane
Grizim
Sebkhet Iguetti
Cheggâ
Daya el Khadra
Tarhamanant
Pta. Elbow
SAHARA
Yetti
Ayoûn Abd el Mâlek
Mzerreb
Sebkhet Oumm ed Drous Telli
Dakhla
Pta. Durnford
B. de Río de Oro
El Aargub
Bir Enzarán
Sebkhet Oumm ed Drous Guebli
Ghallamane
El Kâghet
El Hank
Kreb en Naga
Tiris
Sidi Emhamed
El Mreïti
El Mdena
Tnihaia
G. de Cintra
Pta. Negra
Imesan
Sebkhet Ijill
El Aouj
WESTERN
MAURITANIA
Terhazza
Aoukar
C. Barbas
Ezmul
Agaïlás
Fdérik
Kediet Ijill
Zouîrât
915
Hammâmi
Aguelt el Melah
Bir Amrâne
Agâraktem
Bir Chali
Hamada Safia
En Nahrat
Mejaouda
Tourine
Meleizem
C. Corbeiro
Uad Tenuaïvar
Adrar Sotuf
Agüenit
Taoudenni
Hamada el Haricha
Telig
Bir Gandús
Tichla
Zug
Uad Aïui
Aghreïjit
Maqteïr
El Guettara
Boû Lanouâr
Aghoueyyît
Châr
Dglats de Khenachiche
La Guera
Nouâdhibou
Râs Nouâdhibou
Dakhlet Nouâdhibou
Tmeïmichât
El Beyyed
El Ghallâouiya
Guelb er Richât
El Mrâyer
Ouarane
Bir Ounane
Ahmeyim
Tijirît
Bir el Gâreb
Azefâl
Ouadâne
El Ksaib Ounane
Khenachich
Akchâr
Toueirma
Atâr
Dhar
MALI
Agouïfa
Amsâga
Chinguetti
Ijâfene
Et Tidra
Oujeft
Bollé
Jafène
Douaouir
Râs Timiris
Nouâmghâr
Akjoujt
Oguileten Nmâdi
Erg Iguidi
Bennichchâb
Bou Rjeimât
I-n-Échaï
Sebkha Te-n-Dghâmcha

20 15 10 35 30 25 20 10 5

ft m
12,000 4000
9000 3000
6000 2000
4500 1500
3000 1000
1200 400
600 200
0 0
200 600
2000 6000
4000 12,000
m ft

Projection: Lambert's Equivalent Azimuthal

1 2 3 4

West from Greenwich

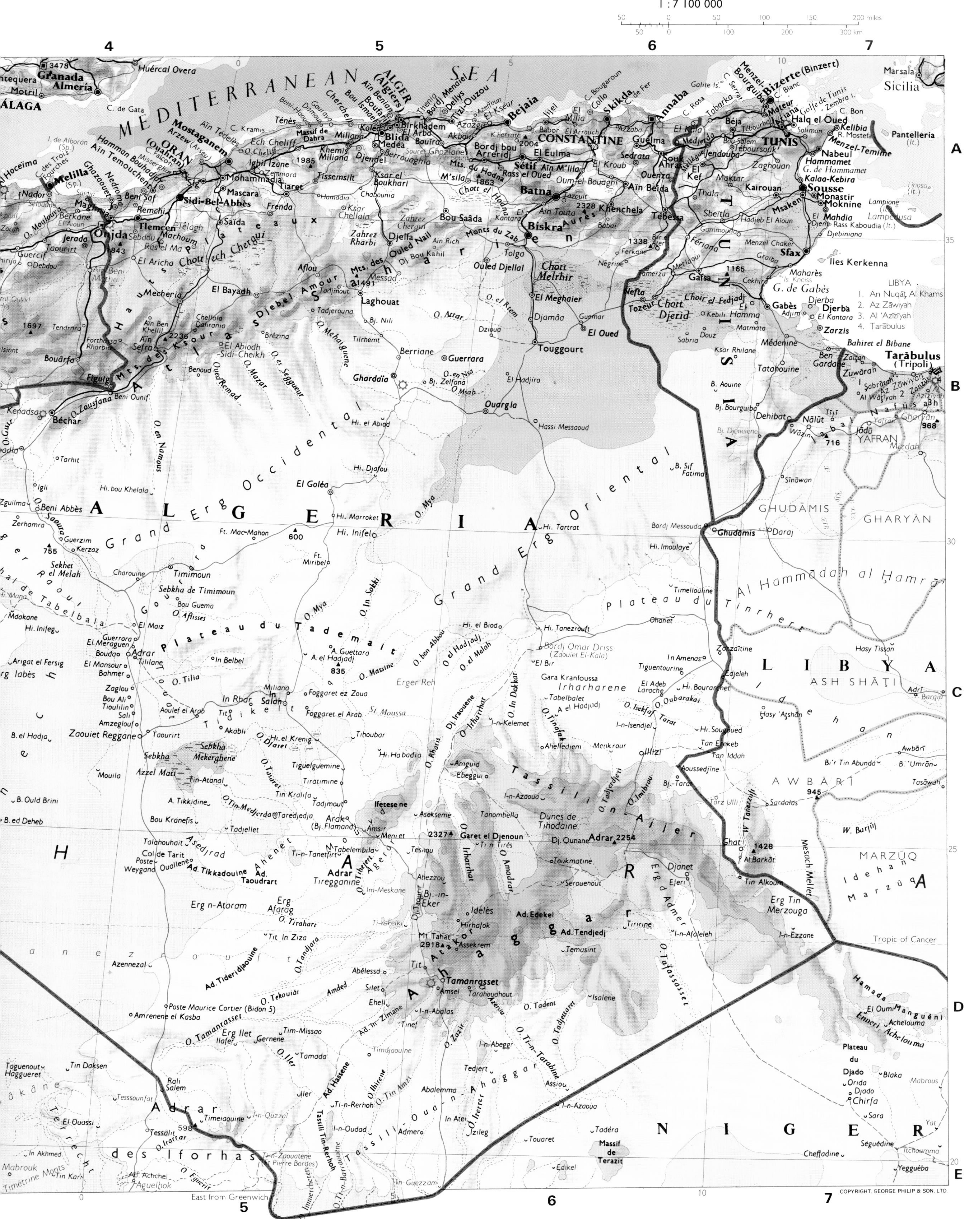

1 : 7 100 000
50 0 50 100 150 200 miles
50 0 100 200 300 km
4
5
6
7
MEDITERRANEAN SEA
ALGER (Algiers)
Granada
Almería
MÁLAGA
Huércal Overa
C. de Gata
Mostaganem
ORAN (Ouahran)
Arzew
Ténès
Cherchell
Blida
Médéa
Miliana
Boufarik
Bordj Menaïel
Tizi Ouzou
Dellys
Bejaia
Jijel
Skikda
Annaba
Collo
C. Bougaroun
C. de Fer
CONSTANTINE
Sétif
Bordj bou Arreridj
El Eulma
Batna
Biskra
M'sila
Khenchela
Tébessa
Guelma
Souk Ahras
Sidi-Bel-Abbès
Mascara
Tlemcen
Oujda
Melilla
Nador
Saïda
Tiaret
Frenda
Relizane
Chlef
Tissemsilt
Ksar el Boukhari
Djelfa
Bou Saâda
Laghouat
Aflou
El Bayadh
Mecheria
Aïn Sefra
Figuig
Béchar
Kenadsa
Ghardaïa
Guerrara
Berriane
Ouargla
Touggourt
El Oued
Hassi Messaoud
El Goléa
Timimoun
Adrar
Reggane
Zaouiet Reggane
In Salah
In Amenas
Illizi
Djanet
Tamanrasset
Assekrem
Mt. Tahat 2918
Bordj Omar Driss
Ghudāmis
Chott Melrhir
Chott Djerid
Chott ech Chergui
Grand Erg Occidental
Grand Erg Oriental
Erg Chech
Plateau du Tademaït
Plateau du Tinrhert
Tassili n Ajjer
Ahaggar
Tassili Oua-n-Ahaggar
Adrar des Iforhas
Tanezrouft
Tidikelt
Gourara
Mts. des Ksour
Djebel Amour
Monts du Zab
Monts des Ouled Nail
Aurès
Hauts Plateaux
Saharan Atlas
ALGERIA
TUNISIA
LIBYA
NIGER
Bizerte (Binzert)
TUNIS
Béja
Jendouba
El Kef
Kairouan
Sousse
Monastir
Moknine
Mahdia
Hammamet
Nabeul
Kelibia
Menzel-Temime
Sfax
Gafsa
Tozeur
Nefta
Gabès
Medenine
Tataouine
Ben Gardane
Djerba
Zarzis
Iles Kerkenna
G. de Gabès
Golfe de Tunis
G. de Hammamet
Pantelleria (It.)
Linosa (It.)
Lampione (It.)
Lampedusa
Sicilia
Marsala
Tarābulus (Tripoli)
Zuwārah
Şabrātah
Nālūt
Yafran
Mizdah
Al Ḩammādah al Ḩamrā'
Ghadāmis
Gharyān
Ash Shāţi
Awbārī
Idehan Awbārī
Idehan Marzūq
Marzūq
Ghat
Plateau du Djado
Djado
Chirfa
Séguédine
Yeggueba
Massif de Terazit
Ténéré du Tafassasset
Tropic of Cancer
LIBYA
1. An Nuqāţ Al Khams
2. Az Zāwiyah
3. Al 'Azīzīyah
4. Tarābulus
A
B
C
D
E
0
5
10
20
25
30
35
East from Greenwich
COPYRIGHT, GEORGE PHILIP & SON, LTD

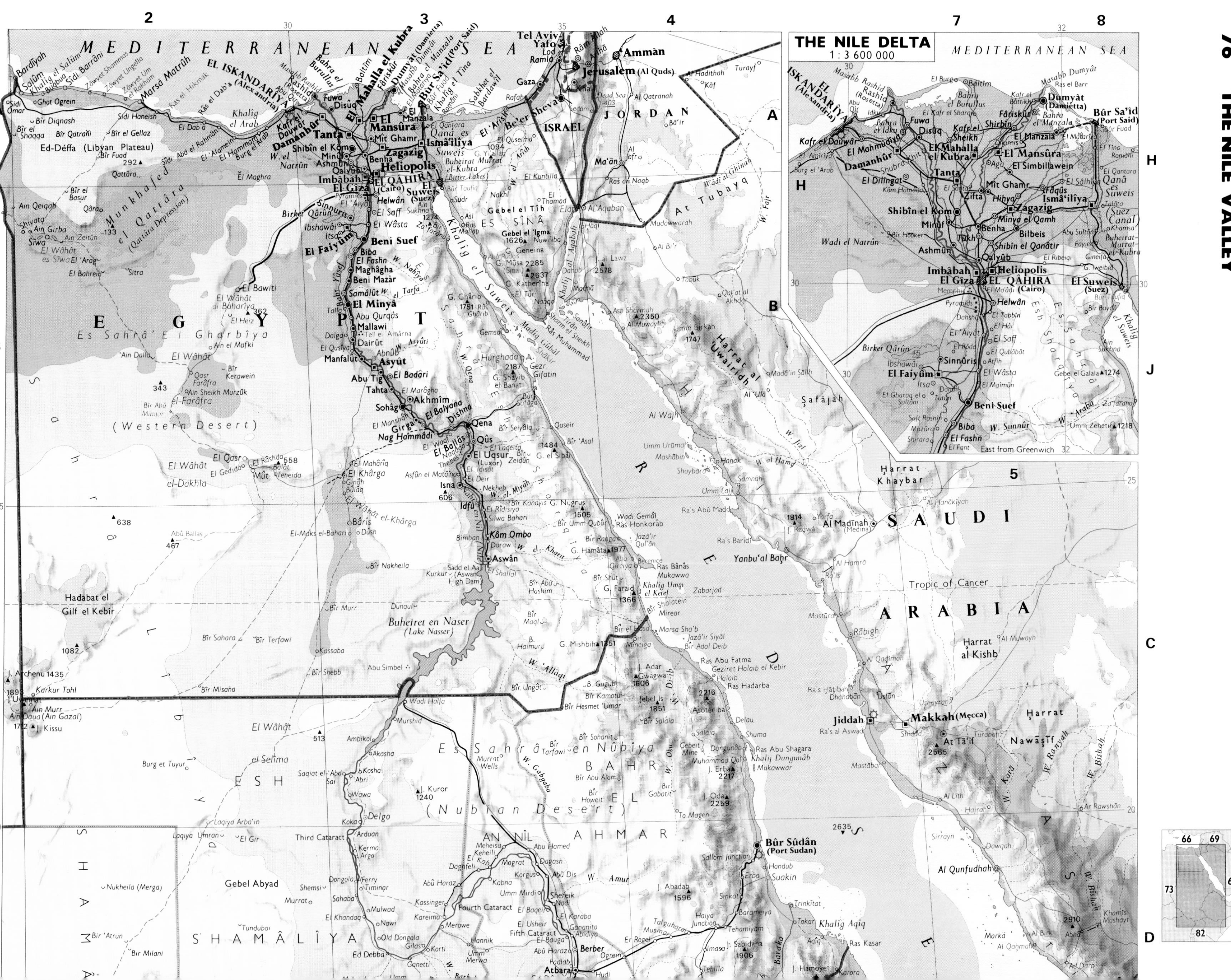

MEDITERRANEAN SEA
EL ISKANDARÎYA (Alexandria)
EL QÂHIRA (Cairo)
Bûr Sa'îd (Port Said)
Suweis (Suez)
E G Y P T
Es Sahrâ' El Gharbîya
(Western Desert)
Es Sahrâ' en Nûbîya
(Nubian Desert)
Buheiret en Naser (Lake Nasser)
Khalîg el Suweis
ES SÎNÂ
ISRAEL
JORDAN
Jerusalem (Al Quds)
'Ammân
Tel Aviv-Yafo
Gaza
S A U D I
A R A B I A
Tropic of Cancer
Al Madînah (Medina)
Makkah (Mecca)
Jiddah
Bûr Sûdân (Port Sudan)
Aswân
El Uqsur (Luxor)
Asyût
El Minya
Beni Suef
El Faiyûm
Qena
Wadi Halfa
Berber
Atbara
SHAMÂLÎYA
THE NILE DELTA
1 : 3 600 000
MEDITERRANEAN SEA
Dumyât (Damietta)
Tanta
El Mansûra
Zagazig
Ismâ'ilîya
Heliopolis
East from Greenwich

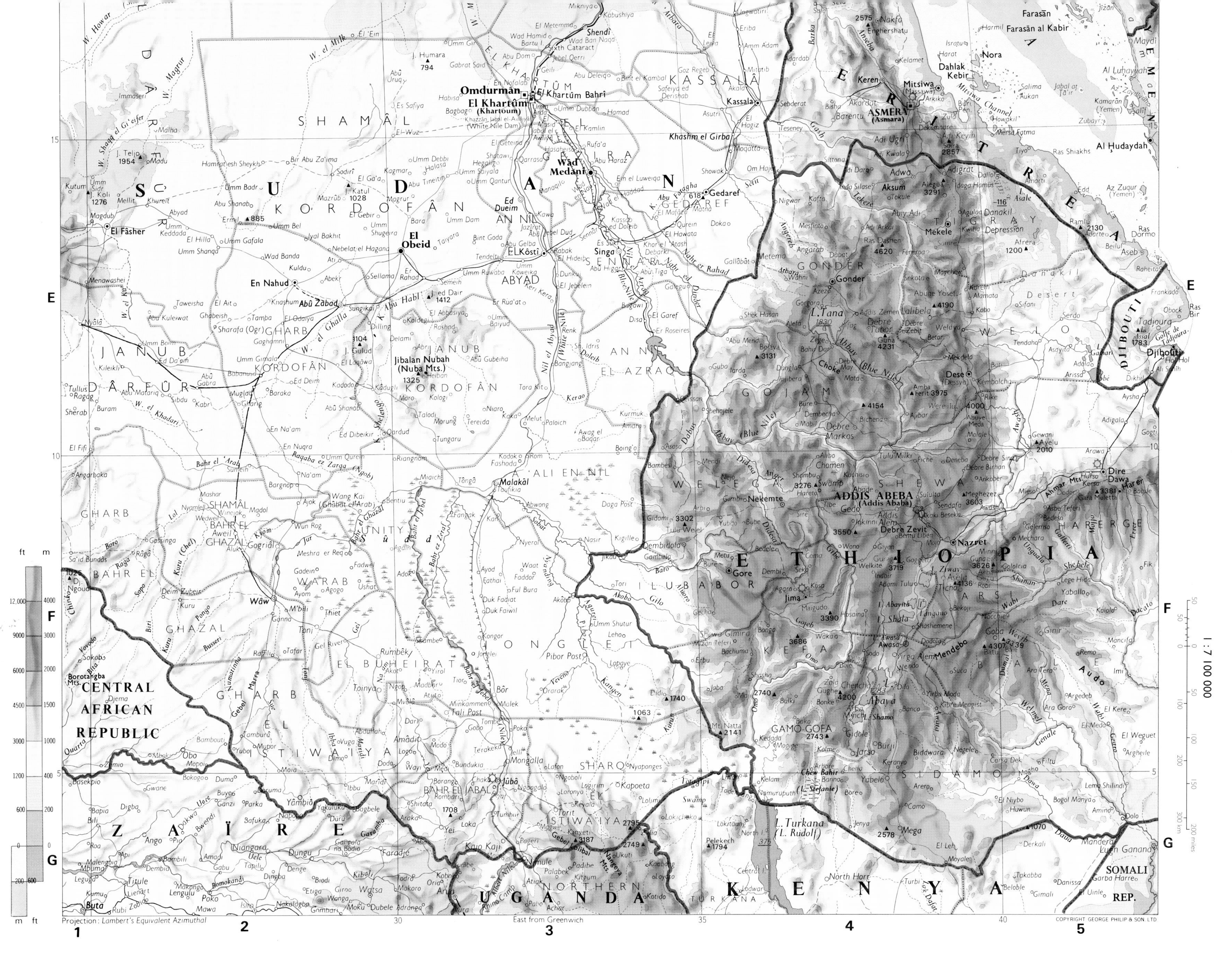
1 : 7 100 000
ETHIOPIA
ERITREA
DJIBOUTI
SUDAN
KENYA
UGANDA
ZAÏRE
CENTRAL AFRICAN REPUBLIC
SOMALI REP.
YEMEN
ADDIS ABEBA (Addis Ababa)
ASMERA (Asmara)
El Khartûm (Khartoum)
Omdurmân
El Khartûm Bahrî
Kassala
Gonder
Dese
Nazret
Dire Dawa
Harer
Gore
Jima
Malakâl
Wâw
Jûbâ
El Obeid
En Nahud
El Fâsher
Wad Medani
L. Tana
L. Turkana (L. Rudolf)
Projection: Lambert's Equivalent Azimuthal
East from Greenwich
COPYRIGHT GEORGE PHILIP & SON LTD

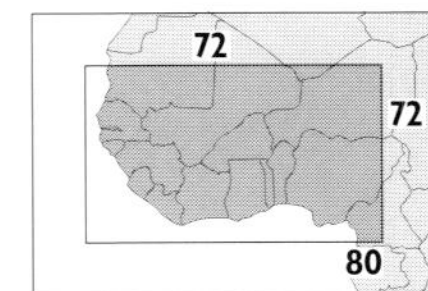

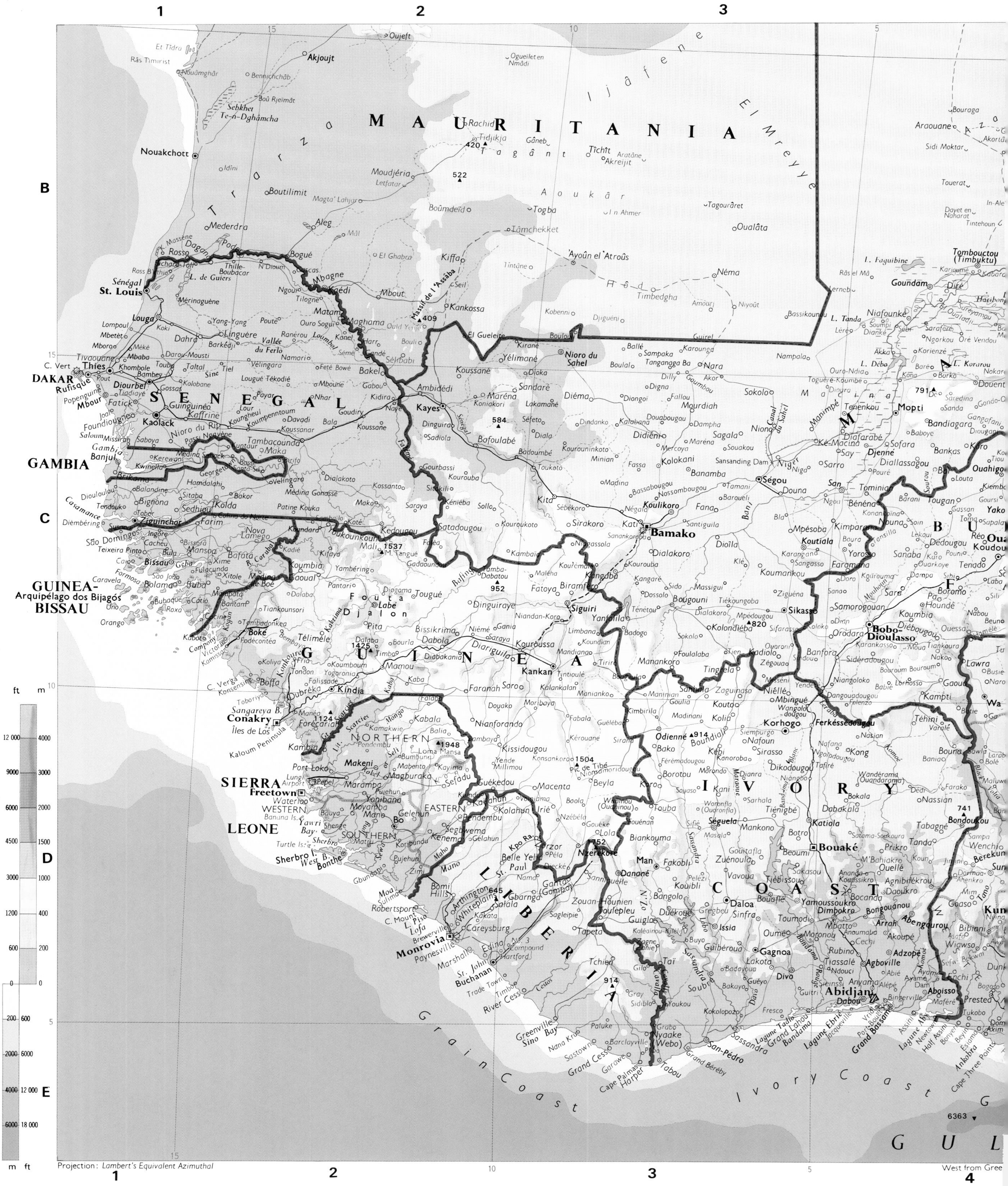

Projection: *Lambert's Equivalent Azimuthal*

West from Gree

1 : 7 100 000
50 0 50 100 150 200 miles
50 0 100 200 300 km
4
5
6
7
A
B
C
D
E
ALGERIA
NIGER
NIGERIA
BENIN
TOGO
GHANA
CHAD
CAMEROON
EQUATORIAL GUINEA
Adrar des Iforhas
Aïr
(Azbine)
Ténéré
Talak
Tahoua
Manga
Slave Coast
Bight of Benin
Niger Delta
GULF OF GUINEA
Bight of Bonny
Bioko (Fernando Poo)
Niamey
Agadez (Agadès)
Zinder
Maradi
Tahoua
Sokoto
Katsina
Kano
Zaria
Kaduna
Jos
Bauchi
Maiduguri
Ilorin
Ogbomosho
Oshogbo
IBADAN
Abeokuta
LAGOS
Porto-Novo
Cotonou
Lomé
ACCRA
Tema
Benin City
Enugu
Onitsha
Port-Harcourt
Calabar
DOUALA
Yaoundé
Malabo
Lac Tchad
N. E. NIGERIA
on same scale as general map
East from Greenwich
COPYRIGHT GEORGE PHILIP & SON, LTD

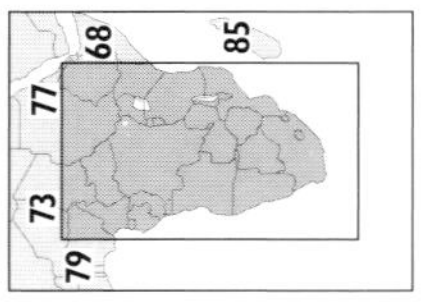
68
77
85
73
79

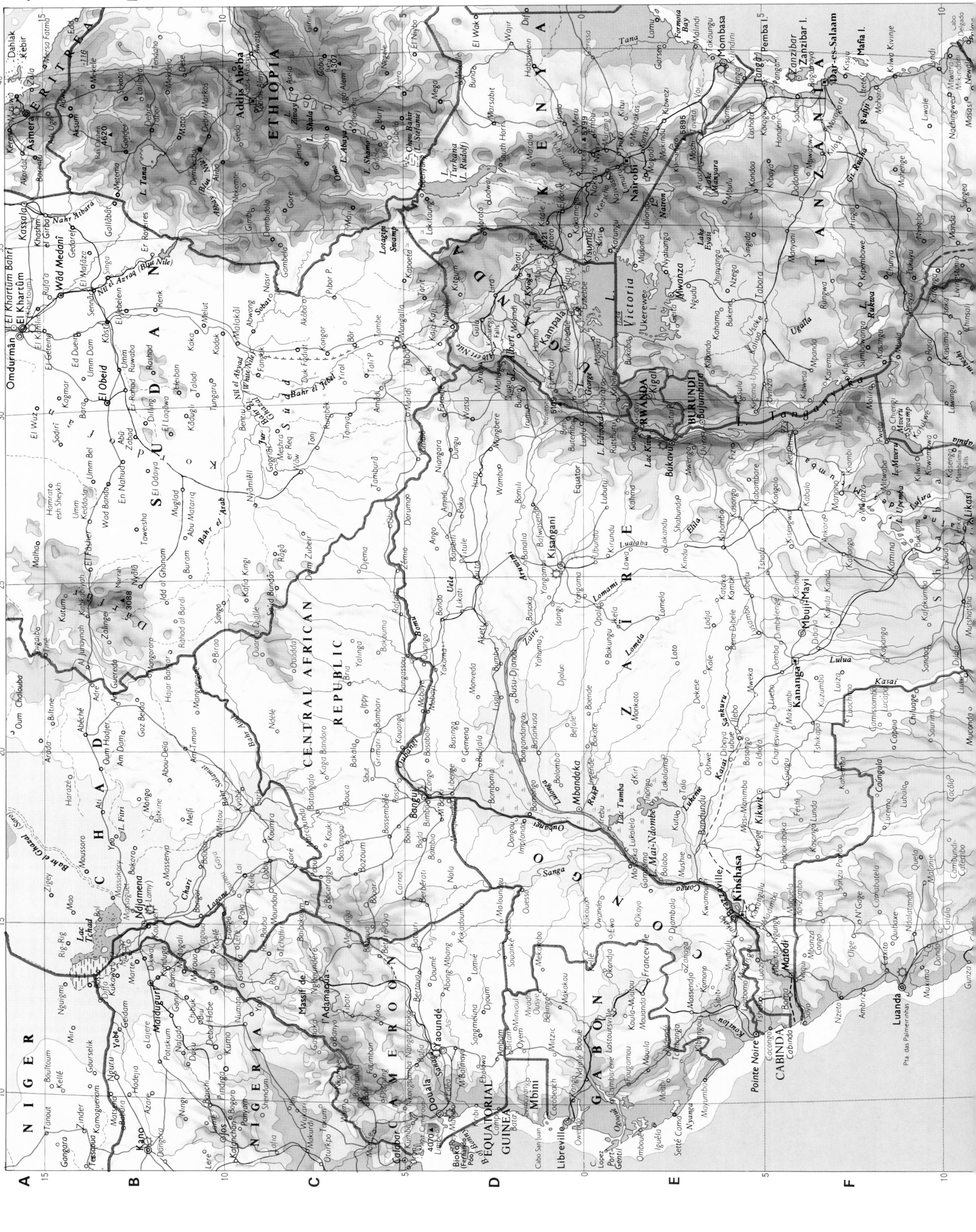
NIGER
NIGERIA
CHAD
SUDAN
ETHIOPIA
ERITREA
KENYA
UGANDA
RWANDA
BURUNDI
TANZANIA
CENTRAL AFRICAN REPUBLIC
CAMEROON
EQUATORIAL GUINEA
GABON
CONGO
ZAÏRE
CABINDA
Omdurman
El Khartûm
Asmera
Addis Abeba
Nairobi
Mombasa
Dar-es-Salaam
Kampala
Kigali
Bujumbura
Kisangani
Kinshasa
Brazzaville
Bangui
Ndjamena
Yaoundé
Douala
Libreville
Luanda
Pointe Noire
Kano
Mbuji-Mayi
Kananga
L. Victoria
L. Tana
L. Turkana (L. Rudolf)
Lac Tchad
L. Albert
Zanzibar
Mafia I.
Pemba I.
Bioko
Mbini

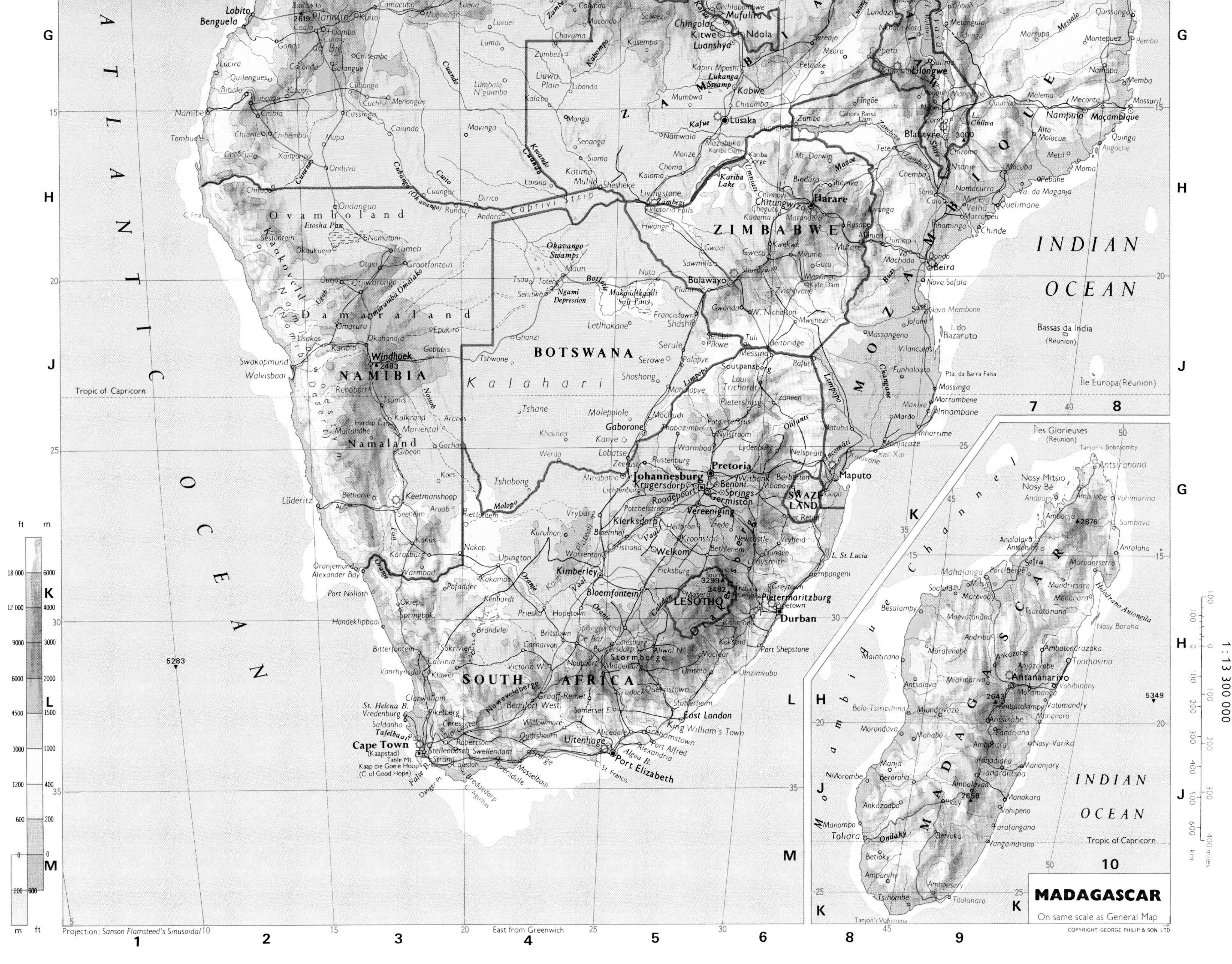

ATLANTIC OCEAN
INDIAN OCEAN
NAMIBIA
BOTSWANA
ZIMBABWE
ZAMBIA
MALAWI
MOZAMBIQUE
SOUTH AFRICA
LESOTHO
SWAZILAND
Kalahari
Ovamboland
Damaraland
Namaland
Namib Desert
Kaokoveld
Okavango Swamps
Ngami Depression
Makgadikgadi Salt Pans
Caprivi Strip
Windhoek
Gaborone
Harare
Lusaka
Lilongwe
Maputo
Pretoria
Johannesburg
Bloemfontein
Kimberley
Durban
Pietermaritzburg
East London
Port Elizabeth
Cape Town (Kaapstad)
Bulawayo
Beira
Blantyre
Ndola
Kitwe
Tropic of Capricorn
Projection: Sanson Flamsteed's Sinusoidal
East from Greenwich
Mozambique Channel
MADAGASCAR
On same scale as General Map
Antananarivo
Toamasina
Toliara
Fianarantsoa
Mahajanga
Antsiranana
Bassas da India (Réunion)
Île Europa (Réunion)
Îles Glorieuses (Réunion)
1 : 13 300 000
COPYRIGHT GEORGE PHILIP & SON LTD

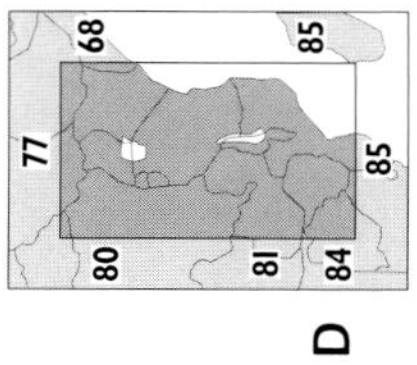

SOMALI REP.

ETHIOPIA

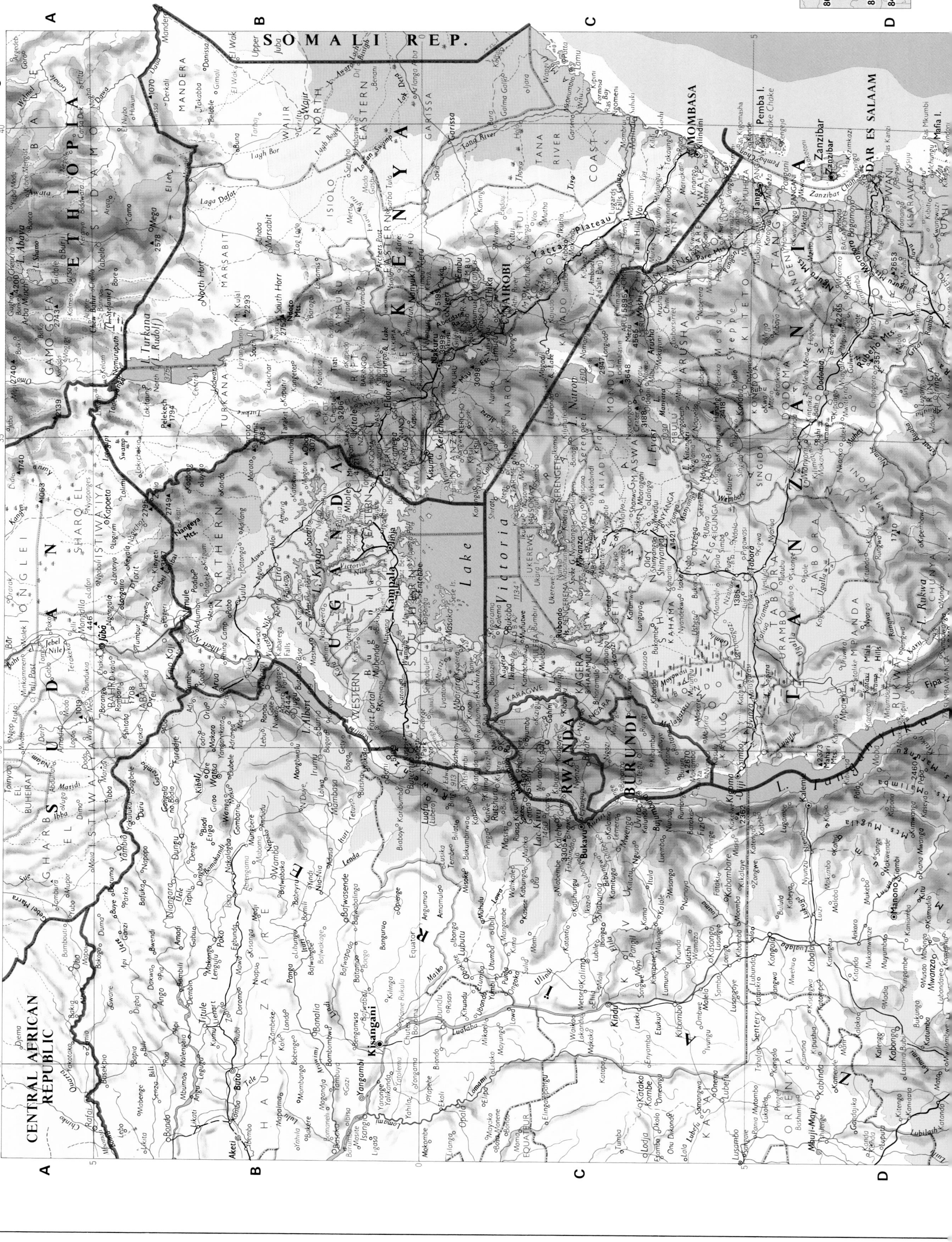

KENYA

UGANDA

RWANDA

BURUNDI

TANZANIA

SUDAN

CENTRAL AFRICAN REPUBLIC

ZAIRE

NAIROBI

MOMBASA

DAR ES SALAAM

Zanzibar

Pemba I.

Mafia I.

Kampala

Kisangani

Lake Victoria

L. Turkana (L. Rudolf)

L. Albert

L. Kyoga

L. Tanganyika

L. Rukwa

68 85 77 85 80 81 84

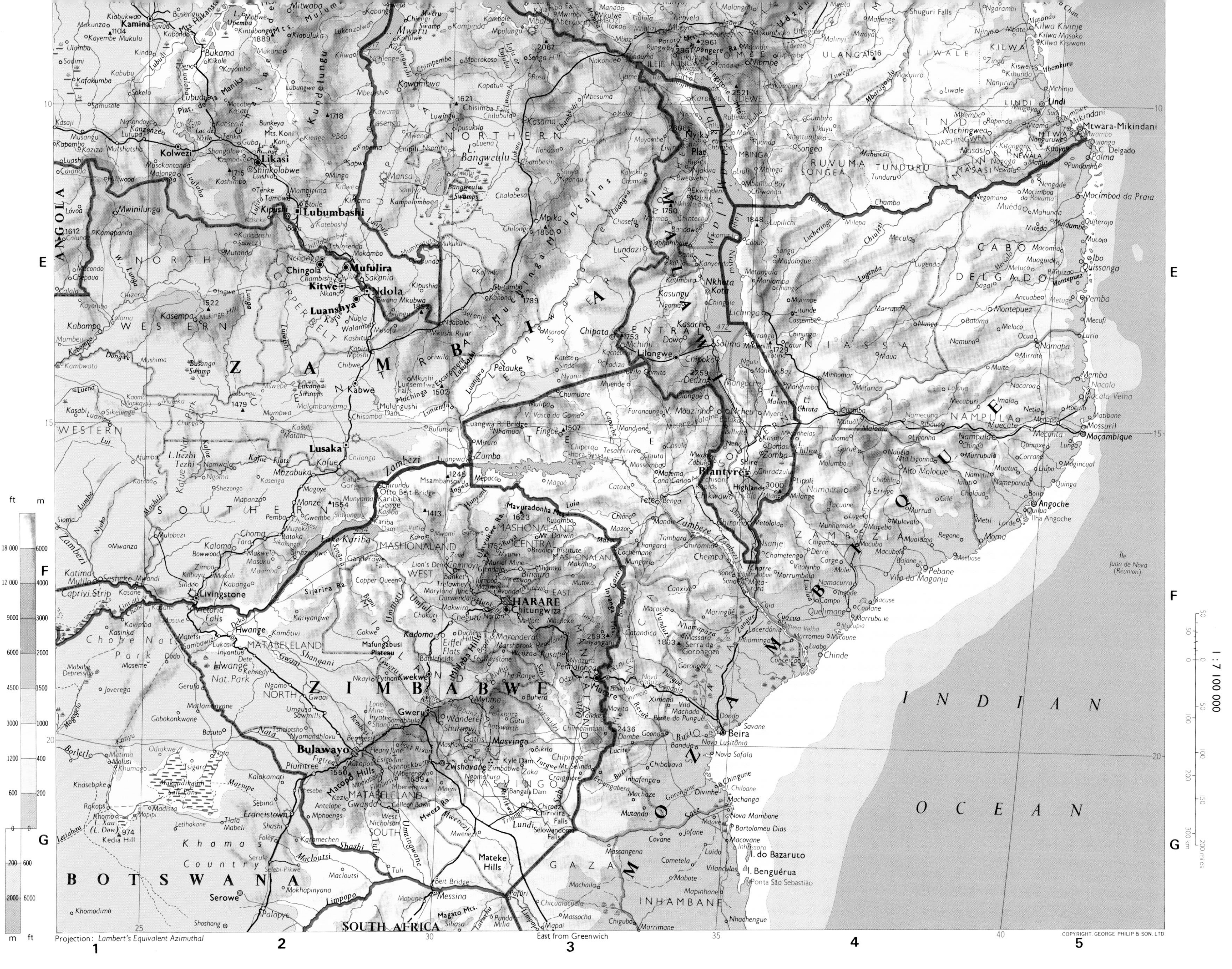
1 : 7 100 000
ANGOLA
ZAMBIA
MALAWI
MOZAMBIQUE
ZIMBABWE
BOTSWANA
SOUTH AFRICA
INDIAN OCEAN
Lusaka
HARARE
Lubumbashi
Likasi
Kolwezi
Kamina
Mufulira
Chingola
Kitwe
Ndola
Luanshya
Kabwe
Livingstone
Hwange
Bulawayo
Gweru
Kwekwe
Kadoma
Masvingo
Mutare
Chitungwiza
Lilongwe
Blantyre
Zomba
Chipata
Beira
Quelimane
Moçambique
Angoche
Nampula
Lindi
Mtwara-Mikindani
Songea
Serowe
Francistown
Messina
Tete
Zumbo
Lake Kariba
Zambezi
Limpopo
Lunga
Kafue
Luangwa
L. Bangweulu
Lago Niassa
Lake Malawi
NORTHERN
NORTH WESTERN
COPPERBELT
WESTERN
SOUTHERN
CENTRAL
EASTERN
MASHONALAND
MATABELELAND
MANICALAND
MIDLANDS
MASVINGO
CABO DELGADO
NIASSA
NAMPULA
ZAMBEZIA
TETE
MANICA
SOFALA
GAZA
INHAMBANE
RUVUMA
LINDI
MTWARA
Caprivi Strip
Chobe Nat. Park
Khama's Country
Matopo Hills
Mateke Hills
Muchinga Mountains
Inyanga Mts.
Projection: Lambert's Equivalent Azimuthal
East from Greenwich
COPYRIGHT. GEORGE PHILIP & SON. LTD.

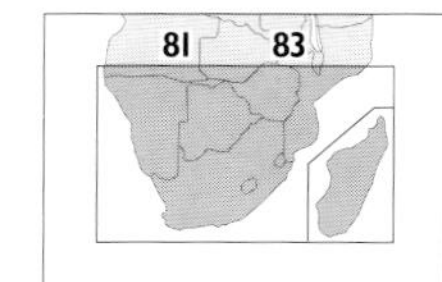

ANGOLA

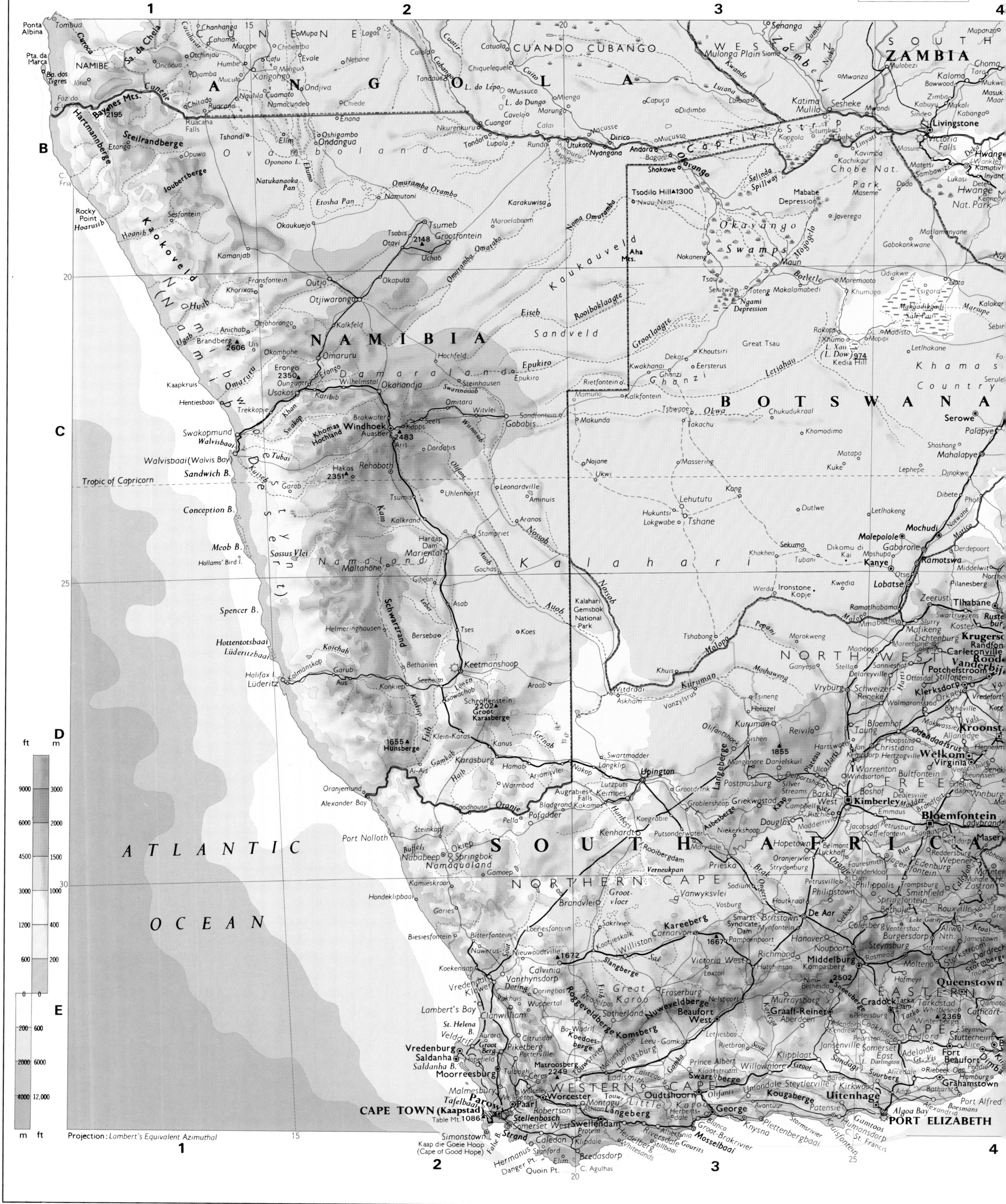

ZAMBIA

NAMIBIA

BOTSWANA

SOUTH AFRICA

ATLANTIC OCEAN

Tropic of Capricorn

ft	m
9000	3000
6000	2000
4500	1500
3000	1000
1200	400
600	200
0	0
200	600
2000	6000
4000	12,000
m	ft

Projection: *Lambert's Equivalent Azimuthal*

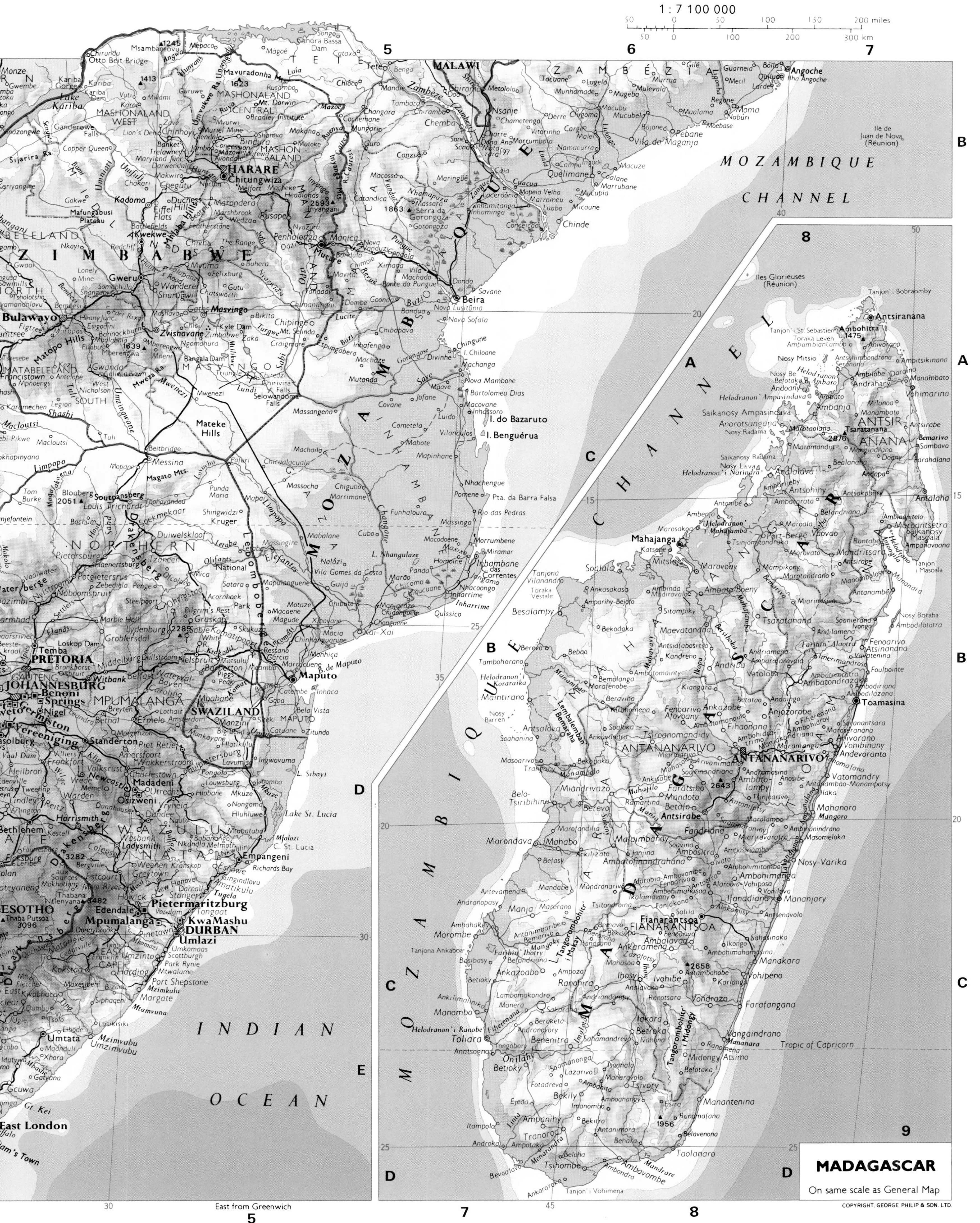

MADAGASCAR

On same scale as General Map

1 : 7 100 000

50 0 50 100 150 200 miles
50 0 100 200 300 km

MALAWI

ZIMBABWE

MOZAMBIQUE

MOZAMBIQUE

MOZAMBIQUE

CHANNEL

MOZAMBIQUE CHANNEL

CHANNEL

Beira

Bulawayo

HARARE
Chitungwiza

Kadoma

Gweru

Masvingo

Zvishavane

ZAMBÉZIA

Angoche

Quelimane

Ile de Juan de Nova (Réunion)

Iles Glorieuses (Réunion)

Antsiranana

Nosy Mitsio

Nosy Be

Mahajanga

ANTANANARIVO

Antsirabe

Toamasina

Fianarantsoa

Toliara

Tropic of Capricorn

I. do Bazaruto

I. Benguérua

Nova Sofala

Vilanculos

Inhambane

Maputo

SWAZILAND

PRETORIA

JOHANNESBURG

Vereeniging

DURBAN

Pietermaritzburg

KwaMashu

Umlazi

Empangeni

Richards Bay

Lake St. Lucia

Ladysmith

Harrismith

Bethlehem

LESOTHO

Umtata

East London

INDIAN

OCEAN

East from Greenwich

Tropic of Capricorn

Taolanaro

Tanjon'i Vohimena

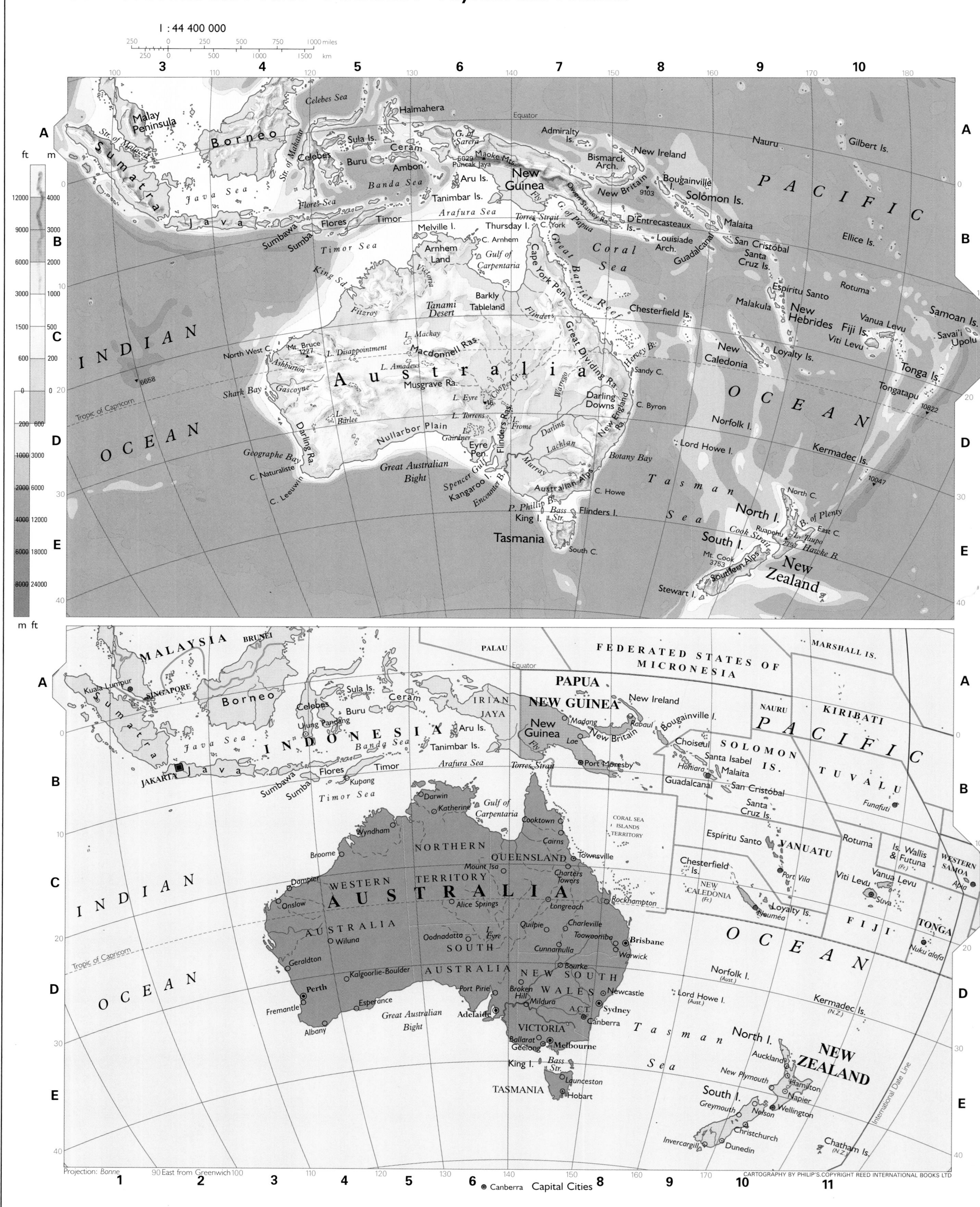

1 : 44 400 000
INDIAN OCEAN
PACIFIC OCEAN
Australia
Tasmania
New Guinea
New Zealand
Borneo
Sumatra
Java
Celebes
Coral Sea
Tasman Sea
Arafura Sea
Timor Sea
Great Australian Bight
Great Dividing Ra.
Great Barrier Reef
Nullarbor Plain
Macdonnell Ras.
Tanami Desert
Barkly Tableland
Gulf of Carpentaria
Cape York Pen.
North I.
South I.
Tropic of Capricorn
Equator
PAPUA NEW GUINEA
INDONESIA
MALAYSIA
BRUNEI
SINGAPORE
JAKARTA
FEDERATED STATES OF MICRONESIA
MARSHALL IS.
PALAU
NAURU
KIRIBATI
TUVALU
SOLOMON IS.
VANUATU
FIJI
TONGA
WESTERN SAMOA
NEW CALEDONIA (Fr.)
CORAL SEA ISLANDS TERRITORY
WESTERN AUSTRALIA
NORTHERN TERRITORY
QUEENSLAND
SOUTH AUSTRALIA
NEW SOUTH WALES
VICTORIA
TASMANIA
A.C.T.
Perth
Darwin
Brisbane
Sydney
Canberra
Melbourne
Adelaide
Hobart
Port Moresby
Wellington
Auckland
Christchurch
International Date Line
Projection: Bonne
East from Greenwich
Canberra Capital Cities
CARTOGRAPHY BY PHILIP'S.COPYRIGHT REED INTERNATIONAL BOOKS LTD

1: 5 300 000

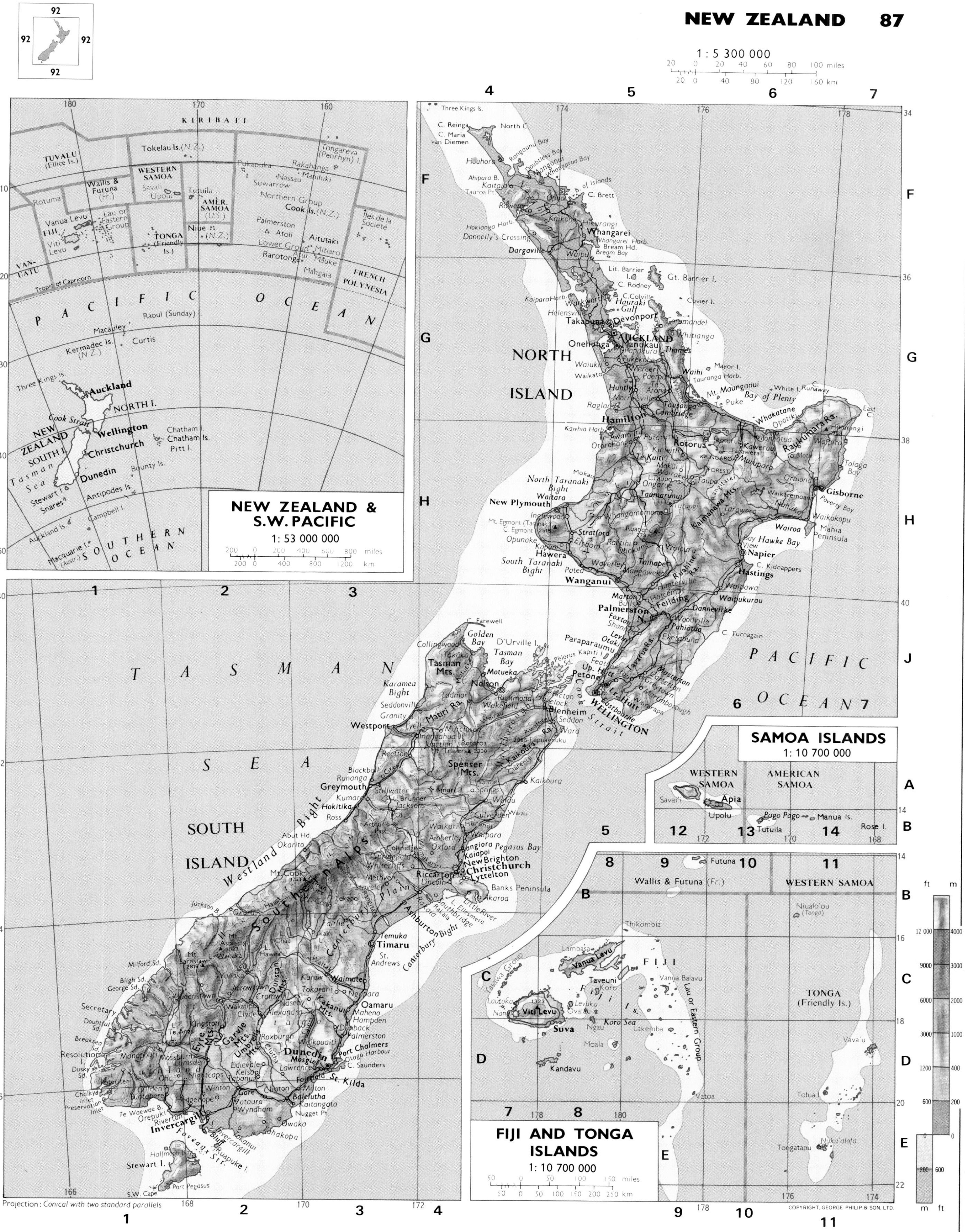
92
NEW ZEALAND & S.W. PACIFIC
1: 53 000 000
KIRIBATI
TUVALU (Ellice Is.)
Tokelau Is. (N.Z.)
WESTERN SAMOA
Savaii
Upolu
Tutuila
AMER. SAMOA (U.S.)
Wallis & Futuna (Fr.)
Rotuma
Vanua Levu
FIJI
Viti Levu
Lau or Eastern Group
TONGA (Friendly Is.)
Niue (N.Z.)
Tongareva (Penrhyn) I.
Pukapuka
Rakahanga
Manihiki
Nassau
Suwarrow
Northern Group
Cook Is. (N.Z.)
Palmerston Atoll
Aitutaki
Mitiaro
Lower Group
Atiu
Mauke
Rarotonga
Mangaia
Îles de la Société
FRENCH POLYNESIA
VANUATU
Tropic of Capricorn
PACIFIC OCEAN
Raoul (Sunday) I.
Macauley I.
Kermadec Is. (N.Z.)
Curtis
Three Kings Is.
Auckland
NORTH I.
Cook Strait
Wellington
NEW ZEALAND
SOUTH I.
Christchurch
Chatham I.
Chatham Is.
Pitt I.
Dunedin
Bounty Is.
Tasman Sea
Stewart I.
Snares
Antipodes Is.
Campbell I.
Auckland Is.
Macquarie I. (Austr.)
SOUTHERN OCEAN
NORTH ISLAND
SOUTH ISLAND
TASMAN SEA
PACIFIC OCEAN
Three Kings Is.
C. Reinga
North C.
C. Maria van Diemen
Houhora
Rangaunu Bay
Doubtless Bay
Mangonui
Whangaroa Bay
Ahipara B.
Kaitaia
Tauroa Pt.
B. of Islands
C. Brett
Opua
Rawene
Kaikohe
Hokianga Harb.
Donnelly's Crossing
Dargaville
Hikurangi
Whangarei
Whangarei Harb.
Bream Hd.
Bream Bay
Waipu
Lit. Barrier I.
C. Rodney
Gt. Barrier I.
Kaipara Harb.
Warkworth
C. Colville
Hauraki Gulf
Cuvier I.
Helensville
Takapuna
Devonport
Coromandel
AUCKLAND
Onehunga
Manukau
Papakura
Whitianga
Thames
Waiuku
Pukekohe
Mercer
Waikato
Paeroa
Waihi
Mayor I.
Tauranga Harb.
Huntly
Te Aroha
Mt. Maunganui
Te Puke
White I.
Runaway
Bay of Plenty
Raglan
Morrinsville
Tauranga
Cambridge
Hamilton
Whakatane
Opotiki
East C.
Kawhia Harb.
Te Awamutu
Otorohanga
Putaruru
Rotorua
Kawerau
Raukumara Ra.
Hikurangi
Te Kuiti
Tokoroa
Mokau
Murupara
Tolaga Bay
North Taranaki Bight
Taupo
Ormond
Waitara
Taumarunui
Gisborne
New Plymouth
Poverty Bay
Inglewood
Kaimanawa Mts.
Waikokopu
Mt. Egmont (Taranaki)
C. Egmont
Stratford
Wairoa
Mahia Peninsula
Opunake
Eltham
Raetihi
Ohakune
Hawke Bay
Hawera
Waiouru
Napier
Bay View
South Taranaki Bight
Taihape
C. Kidnappers
Patea
Waverley
Mangaweka
Hastings
Wanganui
Ruahine Ra.
Hunterville
Waipawa
Marton
Waipukurau
Feilding
Dannevirke
Palmerston N.
Foxton
Shannon
Woodville
Pahiatua
Levin
Otaki
Eketahuna
C. Turnagain
Paraparaumu
Kapiti I.
Tararua Ra.
Masterton
Featherston
Carterton
Martinborough
Petone
Up. Hutt
Lr. Hutt
WELLINGTON
Eastbourne
Cook Strait
C. Farewell
Golden Bay
Collingwood
D'Urville I.
Tasman Bay
Takaka
Tasman Mts.
Motueka
Pelorus Sd.
Karamea Bight
Nelson
Richmond
Wakefield
Picton
Havelock
Seddonville
Granity
Matiri Ra.
Blenheim
Seddon
Westport
Lyell
Murchison
Awatere
Ward
Inangahua Junction
Rotoroa
Kaikoura Ra.
Tapuaenuku
Reefton
Spenser Mts.
Blackball
Runanga
Greymouth
Kaikoura
Stillwater
L. Brunner
Kumara
Hokitika
Jacksons
Amuri
Hanmer Springs
Waiau
Ross
Culverden
Arthur's Pass
Waikari
Waipara
Abut Hd.
Okarito
Amberley
Oxford
Rangiora
Kaiapoi
Pegasus Bay
Westland Bight
New Brighton
Christchurch
Riccarton
Lyttelton
Lincoln
Mt. Cook
Southern Alps
Methven
Banks Peninsula
Akaroa
Ashburton
Rakaia
Southbridge
L. Ellesmere
Little River
Jackson B.
Tekapo
Canterbury Plains
Canterbury Bight
Fairlie
Pukaki
Temuka
Timaru
Mt. Aspiring
Ohau
Hawea
Wanaka
St. Andrews
Milford Sd.
Waimate
Bligh Sd.
George Sd.
Kurow
Arrowtown
Cromwell
Dunstan Mts.
Queenstown
Tokarahi
Kakanui Mts.
Ngapara
Oamaru
Secretary I.
Doubtful Sd.
Clyde
Alexandra
Maheno
Hampden
Te Anau
Kingston
Eyre Mts.
Garvie Mts.
Umbrella Mts.
Roxburgh
Dunback
Palmerston
Breaksea Sd.
Resolution I.
Dusky Sd.
Manapouri
Mossburn
Lumsden
Waikouaiti
Port Chalmers
Otago Harbour
Dunedin
Mosgiel
Lawrence
C. Saunders
Edievale
Kelso
Tapanui
Nightcaps
St. Kilda
Otautau
Ohai
Winton
Fairfield
Chalky Inlet
Preservation Inlet
Tuatapere
Hedgehope
Gore
Mataura
Wyndham
Clinton
Milton
Balclutha
Kaitangata
Nugget Pt.
Te Waewae B.
Orepuki
Riverton
Invercargill
Bluff
Owaka
Catlins
Waikawa
Foveaux Str.
Ruapuke I.
Halfmoon Bay
Stewart I.
Port Pegasus
S.W. Cape
SAMOA ISLANDS
1: 10 700 000
WESTERN SAMOA
AMERICAN SAMOA
Savai'i
Apia
Upolu
Pago Pago
Tutuila
Manua Is.
Rose I.
Futuna
Wallis & Futuna (Fr.)
WESTERN SAMOA
Niuafo'ou (Tonga)
Thikombia
Lambasa
Vanua Levu
FIJI
Taveuni
Koro
Vanua Balavu
Yasawa Group
Lautoka
Nandi
Viti Levu
Levuka
Ovalau
Fiji Is.
Lau or Eastern Group
Suva
Koro Sea
Ngau
Lakemba
Moala
Kandavu
Vatoa
TONGA (Friendly Is.)
Vava'u
Tofua
Tongatapu
Nuku'alofa
FIJI AND TONGA ISLANDS
1: 10 700 000
Projection: Conical with two standard parallels
COPYRIGHT, GEORGE PHILIP & SON, LTD.

A B C D
2 3 4 5
10 15 20 120 125 130

INDONESIA
TIMOR SEA
INDIAN OCEAN
NORTHERN TERRITORY
Timor
Sumba
Sumbawa
Lombok
Roti
Sawa
Semau
Melville I.
Bathurst I.
Darwin
Katherine
Van Diemen Gulf
Joseph Bonaparte Gulf
Bonaparte Archipelago
King Leopold Ranges
Durack Range
Great Sandy Desert
Tanami Desert
Gibson Desert
Hamersley Range
Macdonnell Ranges
Lake Mackay
Lake Disappointment
Port Hedland
Broome
Derby
Wyndham
Karratha
Roebourne
Newman
Onslow
Exmouth
Exmouth Gulf
Eighty Mile Beach
Rowley Shoals
Dampier Archipelago
Buccaneer Archipelago
King Sound
Fitzroy
Tropic of Capricorn

WESTERN AUSTRALIA
SOUTH AUSTRALIA
Great Victoria Desert
Nullarbor Plain
Hampton Tableland
Great Australian Bight
SOUTHERN OCEAN
PERTH
Fremantle
New Town
Kwinana
Rockingham
Mandurah
Bunbury
Busselton
Albany
Esperance
Norseman
Kalgoorlie-Boulder
Geraldton
Carnarvon
Shark Bay
Dirk Hartog I.
Houtman Abrolhos
Archipelago of the Recherche
Ayers Rock 868
Mt. Olga 1069
Musgrave Ranges
Mt. Woodroffe 1549
L. Carnegie
L. Wells
L. Moore
L. Barlee
L. Cowan
L. Dundas
Eucla Motel
1 : 7 100 000
Projection: Bonne
East from Greenwich
COPYRIGHT GEORGE PHILIP & SON, LTD.

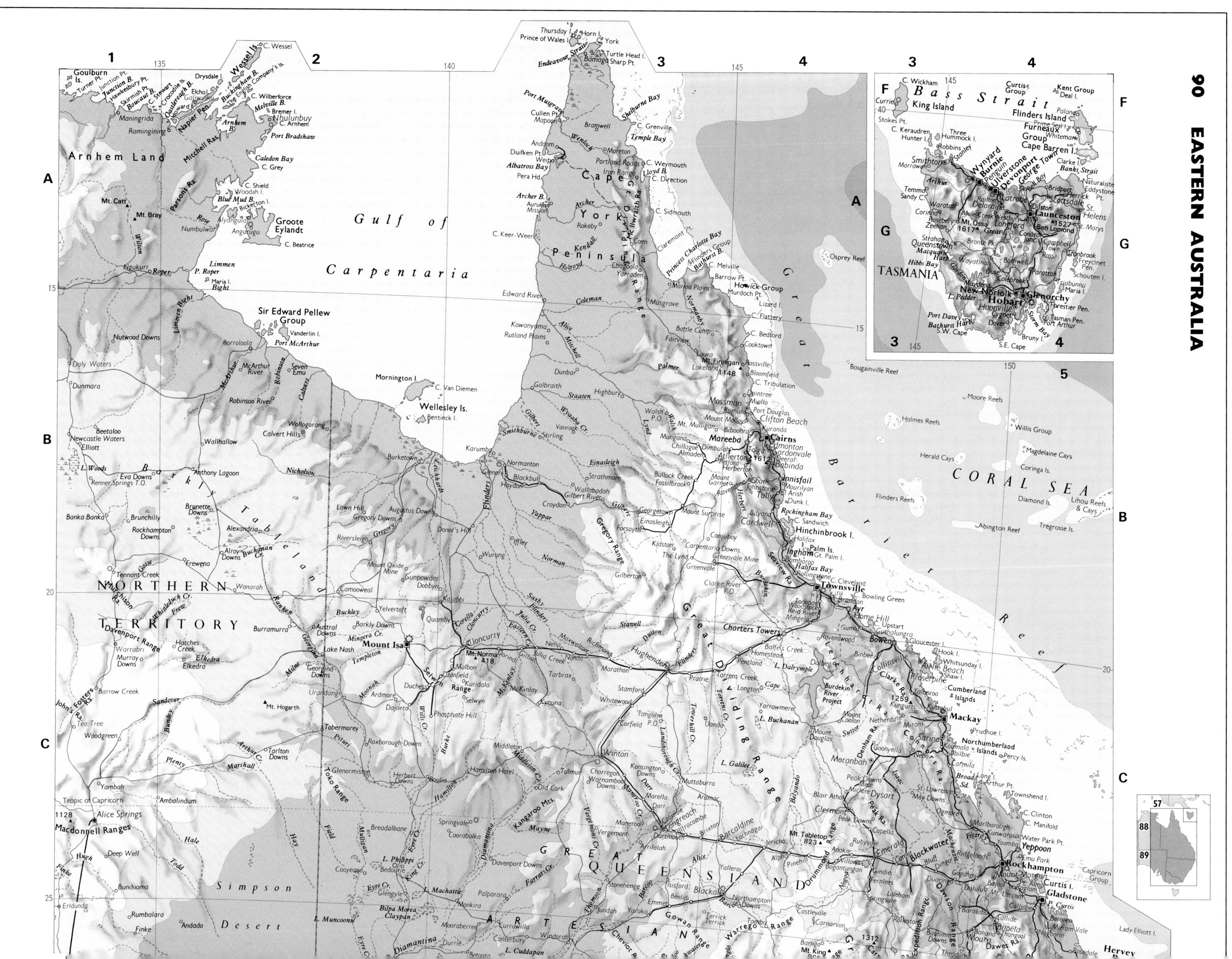
CORAL SEA
Great Barrier Reef
Gulf of Carpentaria
Great Dividing Range
Cape York Peninsula
QUEENSLAND
GREAT ARTESIAN BASIN
NORTHERN TERRITORY
Barkly Tableland
Arnhem Land
Simpson Desert
Bass Strait
TASMANIA
King Island
Flinders Island
Furneaux Group
Hobart
Launceston
Cairns
Townsville
Mackay
Rockhampton
Gladstone
Mount Isa
Charters Towers
Mareeba
Alice Springs
Macdonnell Ranges
Groote Eylandt
Wellesley Is.
Mornington I.
Sir Edward Pellew Group
Wessel Is.
Gregory Range
Selwyn Range
Toko Range
Dawson Range
Expedition Range
Gowan Range
Peak Ra.
Tropic of Capricorn
Curtis I.
Yeppoon
Bowen
Ayr
Ingham
Hinchinbrook I.
Cardwell
Innisfail
Atherton
Mossman
Cooktown
Normanton
Cloncurry
Hughenden
Winton
Longreach
Barcaldine
Blackall
Emerald
Clermont
Proserpine
Cumberland Islands
Northumberland Islands
Tennant Creek
Elliott
Borroloola

1 : 7 100 000
50 0 50 100 150 200 miles
50 0 100 200 300 km
SOUTH AUSTRALIA
NEW SOUTH WALES
VICTORIA
TASMAN SEA
Bass Strait
Spencer Gulf
Great Dividing Range
Flinders Ranges
Grey Range
Darling Downs
Barrier Range
Lake Eyre (North)
Lake Torrens
Lake Gairdner
Lake Frome
BRISBANE
SYDNEY
CANBERRA
MELBOURNE
ADELAIDE
Newcastle
Wollongong
Geelong
Ballarat
Bendigo
Broken Hill
Mildura
Wagga Wagga
Albury
Dubbo
Tamworth
Toowoomba
Maryborough
Charleville
Bourke
Port Augusta
Port Pirie
Whyalla
Port Lincoln
Mount Gambier
Kangaroo I.
King Island
Flinders Island
Furneaux Group
Cape Barren I.
Gold Coast
Coffs Harbour
Mt. Kosciusko 2230
East from Greenwich
Projection: Bonne
COPYRIGHT. GEORGE PHILIP & SON. LTD
m ft
1500 4500
1000 3000
400 1200
200 600
0 0
200 600
2000 6000
4000 12 000

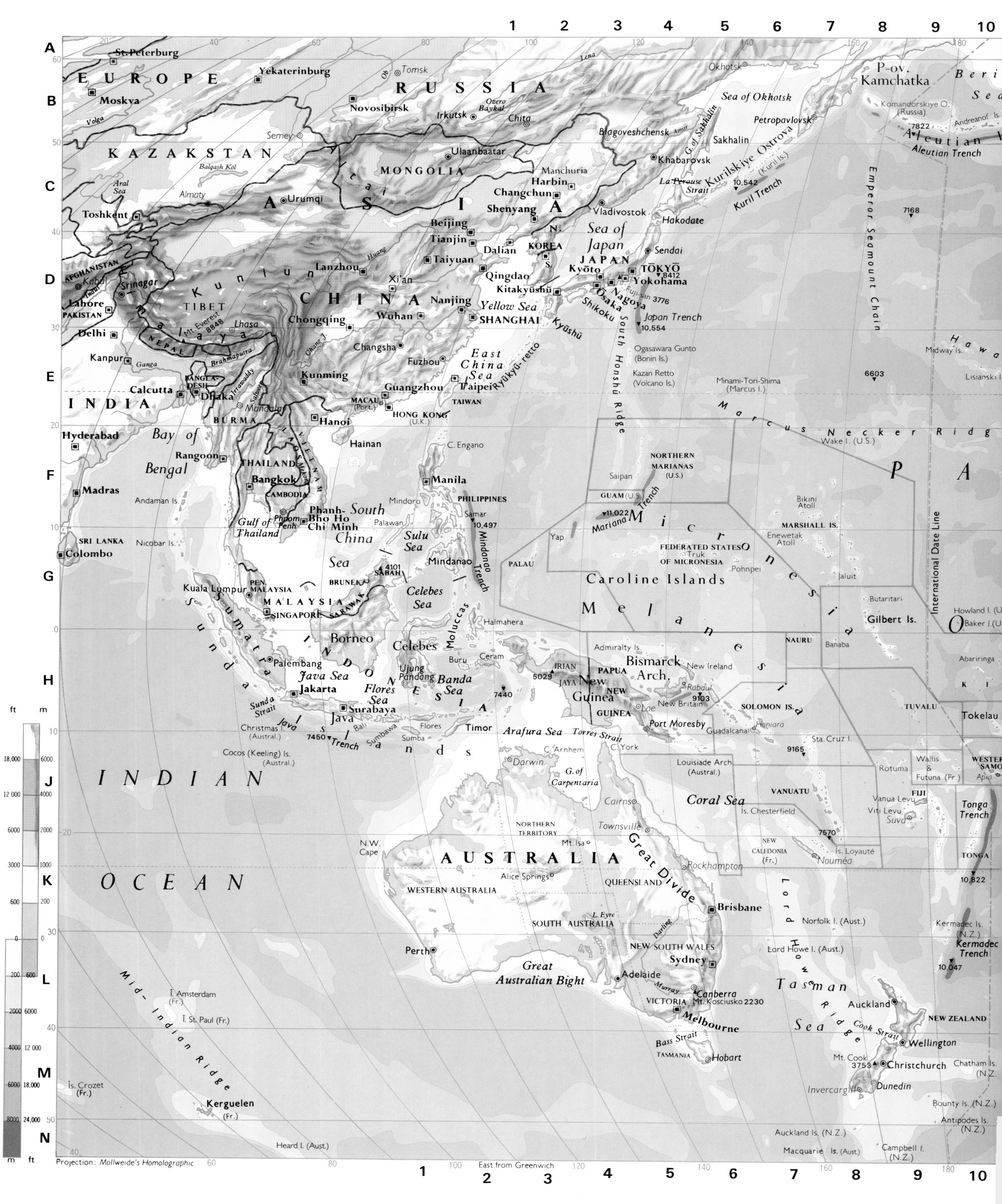
EUROPE
RUSSIA
KAZAKSTAN
MONGOLIA
ASIA
CHINA
TIBET
INDIA
JAPAN
St. Peterburg
Moskva
Yekaterinburg
Novosibirsk
Irkutsk
Tomsk
Chita
Okhotsk
Sea of Okhotsk
Petropavlovsk
P-ov. Kamchatka
Sakhalin
Khabarovsk
Blagoveshchensk
Ulaanbaatar
Semey
Almaty
Toshkent
Urumqi
Harbin
Changchun
Shenyang
Vladivostok
Hakodate
Beijing
Tianjin
Dalian
Taiyuan
Qingdao
Lanzhou
Xi'an
Nanjing
SHANGHAI
Wuhan
Chongqing
Changsha
Fuzhou
Kunming
Guangzhou
HONG KONG (U.K.)
MACAU (Port.)
Taipei
TAIWAN
Hanoi
Hainan
Sea of Japan
Yellow Sea
East China Sea
Kitakyushu
Kyoto
Osaka
Nagoya
TOKYO
Yokohama
Sendai
Fuji-san 3776
Japan Trench
10,554
Kuril Trench
10,542
Kurilskiye Ostrova
Emperor Seamount Chain
Aleutian Trench
7822
7168
6603
Ogasawara Gunto (Bonin Is.)
Kazan Retto (Volcano Is.)
Minami-Tori-Shima (Marcus I.)
Marcus Necker Ridge
Wake I. (U.S.)
Midway Is.
NORTHERN MARIANAS (U.S.)
Saipan
GUAM (U.S.)
Mariana Trench
11,022
Micronesia
FEDERATED STATES OF MICRONESIA
Caroline Islands
MARSHALL IS.
Bikini Atoll
Enewetak Atoll
Pohnpei
Jaluit
Butaritari
Gilbert Is.
International Date Line
Melanesia
NAURU
Banaba
Bismarck Arch.
New Ireland
Rabaul
New Britain
9103
PAPUA NEW GUINEA
IRIAN JAYA
5029
Port Moresby
SOLOMON IS.
Honiara
Guadalcanal
Sta. Cruz I.
9165
TUVALU
Tokelau
Wallis & Futuna (Fr.)
Rotuma
WESTERN SAMOA
FIJI
Vanua Levu
Viti Levu
Suva
Tonga Trench
TONGA
10,822
VANUATU
Coral Sea
Is. Chesterfield
NEW CALEDONIA (Fr.)
Nouméa
Is. Loyauté
7570
Louisiade Arch. (Austral.)
Kermadec Is. (N.Z.)
Kermadec Trench
10,047
Norfolk I. (Aust.)
Lord Howe I. (Aust.)
Lord Howe Ridge
Tasman Sea
Auckland
NEW ZEALAND
Wellington
Cook Strait
Christchurch
Mt. Cook 3753
Dunedin
Invercargill
Chatham Is. (N.Z.)
Bounty Is. (N.Z.)
Antipodes Is. (N.Z.)
Auckland Is. (N.Z.)
Macquarie Is. (Aust.)
Campbell I. (N.Z.)
AUSTRALIA
NORTHERN TERRITORY
WESTERN AUSTRALIA
QUEENSLAND
SOUTH AUSTRALIA
NEW SOUTH WALES
VICTORIA
TASMANIA
Darwin
C. Arnhem
C. York
G. of Carpentaria
Torres Strait
Arafura Sea
Cairns
Townsville
Mt. Isa
Rockhampton
Great Divide
Alice Springs
Brisbane
L. Eyre
Darling
Murray
Sydney
Canberra
Mt. Kosciusko 2230
Adelaide
Melbourne
Bass Strait
Hobart
Perth
N.W. Cape
Great Australian Bight
INDIAN OCEAN
Mid-Indian Ridge
Î. Amsterdam (Fr.)
Î. St. Paul (Fr.)
Îs. Crozet (Fr.)
Kerguelen (Fr.)
Heard I. (Aust.)
Cocos (Keeling) Is. (Austral.)
Christmas I. (Austral.)
Java Trench
7450
Sunda Strait
Sunda Islands
Java
Bali
Sumbawa
Sumba
Flores
Timor
Jakarta
Surabaya
Java Sea
Flores Sea
Banda Sea
7440
Ujung Pandang
Celebes
Borneo
INDONESIA
Sumatra
Palembang
Buru
Ceram
Moluccas
Halmahera
Celebes Sea
SINGAPORE
MALAYSIA
PEN. MALAYSIA
Kuala Lumpur
SARAWAK
SABAH
4101
BRUNEI
Sulu Sea
Mindanao
Mindanao Trench
10,497
Samar
PHILIPPINES
Manila
Mindoro
Palawan
C. Engano
PALAU
Yap
South China Sea
Phanh-Bho Ho Chi Minh
Phnom Penh
Gulf of Thailand
CAMBODIA
THAILAND
Bangkok
VIETNAM
LAOS
BURMA
Rangoon
Mandalay
Bay of Bengal
Andaman Is.
Nicobar Is.
SRI LANKA
Colombo
Madras
Hyderabad
Calcutta
BANGLADESH
Dhaka
Kanpur
Delhi
Lahore
PAKISTAN
AFGHANISTAN
Kabul
Srinagar
Kunlun
Himalaya
NEPAL
Mt. Everest 8848
Lhasa
Brahmaputra
Ganga
Irrawaddy
Salween
Mekong
Chang Jiang
Huang
Ob
Lena
Amur
Volga
Ozero Baykal
Aral Sea
Balqash Köl
Altai
G. of Sakhalin
La Pérouse Strait
Ryukyu-retto
Kyushu
Shikoku
South Honshu Ridge
KOREA
N.
S.
Manchuria
Komandorskiye O. (Russia)
Andreanof Is.
Aleutian Is.
Bering Sea
Hawaiian Is.
Lisianski I.
Howland I. (U.S.)
Baker I. (U.S.)
Abariringa
Apia
ft
m
18,000
12 000
6000
3000
600
0
200
2000
4000
6000
8000
6000
4000
2000
1000
200
600
12 000
18,000
24,000
Projection: Mollweide's Homolographic
East from Greenwich

1 : 48 000 000

GREENLAND
C. Farewell
Hudson Bay
Gulf of Alaska
Bristol Bay
Juneau
Prince of Wales I.
Prince Rupert
Kitimat
Queen Charlotte Is.
C A N A D A
Edmonton
L. Winnipeg
Labrador
N O R T H A M E R I C A
NORTH
Newfoundland
Rocky Mountains
Calgary
Regina
Winnipeg
Vancouver
Vancouver I.
Victoria
Seattle
St. Lawrence
Québec
Pr. Edward I.
Montréal
Ottawa
L. Superior
L. Huron
L. Michigan
L. Ontario
L. Erie
Toronto
Saint John
C. Sable
Boston
Portland
Minneapolis
Missouri
Boise
Snake
CHICAGO
Detroit
Buffalo
Pittsburgh
NEW YORK
Philadelphia
Baltimore
Washington
C. Mendocino
Salt Lake City
Colorado
Denver
Kansas City
St. Louis
Cincinnati
ATLANTIC
San Francisco
4418
UNITED STATES
Memphis
Appalachian Mts.
Oklahoma
Mississippi
C. Hatteras
6741
Los Angeles
San Diego
Atlanta
Dallas
Ciudad Juarez
Jacksonville
Bermuda (U.K.)
Houston
New Orleans
San Antonio
6225
I. Guadalupe (Mexico)
M E X I C O
Sierra Madre
Gulf of California
Gulf of Mexico
Miami
Florida Strait
OCEAN
Monterrey
BAHAMAS
Hawaiian Is. (U.S.)
Tropic of Cancer
La Habana
CUBA
Yucatan Channel
West Indies
Hispaniola
Oahu
Honolulu
Mérida
México
DOM. REP.
9200
4205
Hawaii
Is. Revilla Gigedo (Mexico)
Guadalajara
Puebla
5700
7680
JAMAICA
HAITI
Kingston
PUERTO RICO (U.S.)
Leeward Is.
Acapulco
BELIZE
I F I C
HONDURAS
Caribbean Sea
GUATEMALA
Guatemala
San Salvador
EL SALVADOR
NICARAGUA
Managua
BARBADOS
Windward Is.
TRINIDAD & TOBAGO
Barranquilla
Maracaibo
Caracas
Orinoco
CENTRAL AMERICA
Î. Clipperton (Fr.)
San José
COSTA RICA
Colón
Panama
PANAMA
Canal
VENEZUELA
Christmas Island Ridge
Palmyra Is. (U.S.)
I. del Coco (Costa Rica)
Medellín
Bogota
Teraina
Tabuaeran
Kiritimati
I. de Malpelo (Colombia)
Cali
COLOMBIA
E A N
Jarvis I. (U.S.)
Equator
Galápagos (Ecuador)
Quito
ECUADOR
Guayaquil
Amazonas
Manaus
Iquitos
Malden I.
Starbuck I.
C. Pariñas
BRAZIL
Îs. Marquises
East Pacific Ridge
Trujillo
SOUTH
Tongareva
Penrhyn Is.
Caroline I.
Manihiki
Vostok I.
Flint I.
6369
PERU
Lima
AMERICA
Suwarrow Is.
Cook Islands (N.Z.)
Îs. de la Société
Îs. Tuamotu
Tuamotu Ridge
Cuzco
L. Titicaca
Illampu & Ancohuma 6550
Arequipa
La Paz
BOLIVIA
Tahiti
Manuae
FRENCH POLYNESIA
6866
Peru-Chile Trench
Austral Seamount Chain
Iquique
Rarotonga
Pitcairn I. (U.K.)
Tropic of Capricorn
8050
Antofagasta
PARAGUAY
Îs. Tubuai (Îs. Australes)
Ducie I (U.K.)
Sala-y-Gomez (Chile)
San Félix (Chile)
Asunción
I. de Pascua (Easter I.) (Chile)
San Ambrosio (Chile)
Tucumán
Rapa
Pto. Alegre
Córdoba
6960
Arch. de Juan Fernández (Chile)
Valparaíso
Rosario
URUGUAY
Santiago
Buenos Aires
Montevideo
Pacific–Antarctic Ridge
Chile Rise
Concepción
ARGENTINA
Río de la Plata
Andes
SOUTH
ATLANTIC
OCEAN
Patagonia
6212
Falkland Is. (U.K.)
Punta Arenas
Str. of Magellan
Tierra del Fuego
South Georgia (U.K.)
C. Horn
West from Greenwich

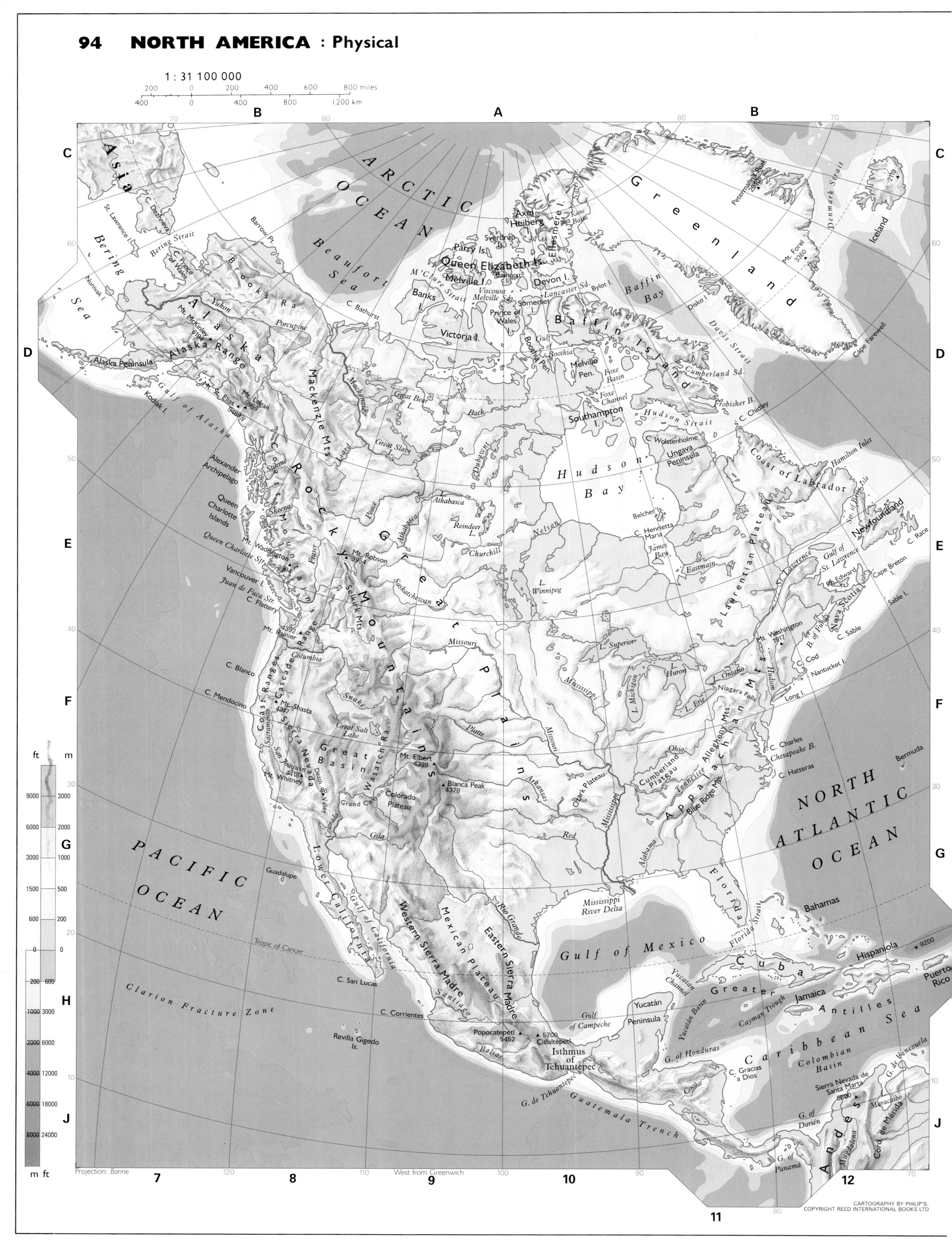
1 : 31 100 000
ARCTIC OCEAN
Beaufort Sea
Greenland
Baffin Bay
Baffin Island
Hudson Bay
Rocky Mountains
Great Plains
Alaska Range
Mackenzie Mts.
Coast Mountains
Cascade Range
Sierra Nevada
Great Basin
Colorado Plateau
Appalachian Mts.
Laurentian Plateau
Western Sierra Madre
Eastern Sierra Madre
Mexican Plateau
Gulf of Mexico
Caribbean Sea
Greater Antilles
NORTH ATLANTIC OCEAN
PACIFIC OCEAN
Gulf of Alaska
Bering Sea
Asia
Iceland
Newfoundland
Cuba
Hispaniola
Jamaica
Puerto Rico
Bahamas
Bermuda
Mt. McKinley 6194
Mt. Logan 5959
Mt. Elbert 4399
Mt. Whitney 4418
Popocatepetl 5452
Citlaltépetl 5700
Projection: Bonne
West from Greenwich

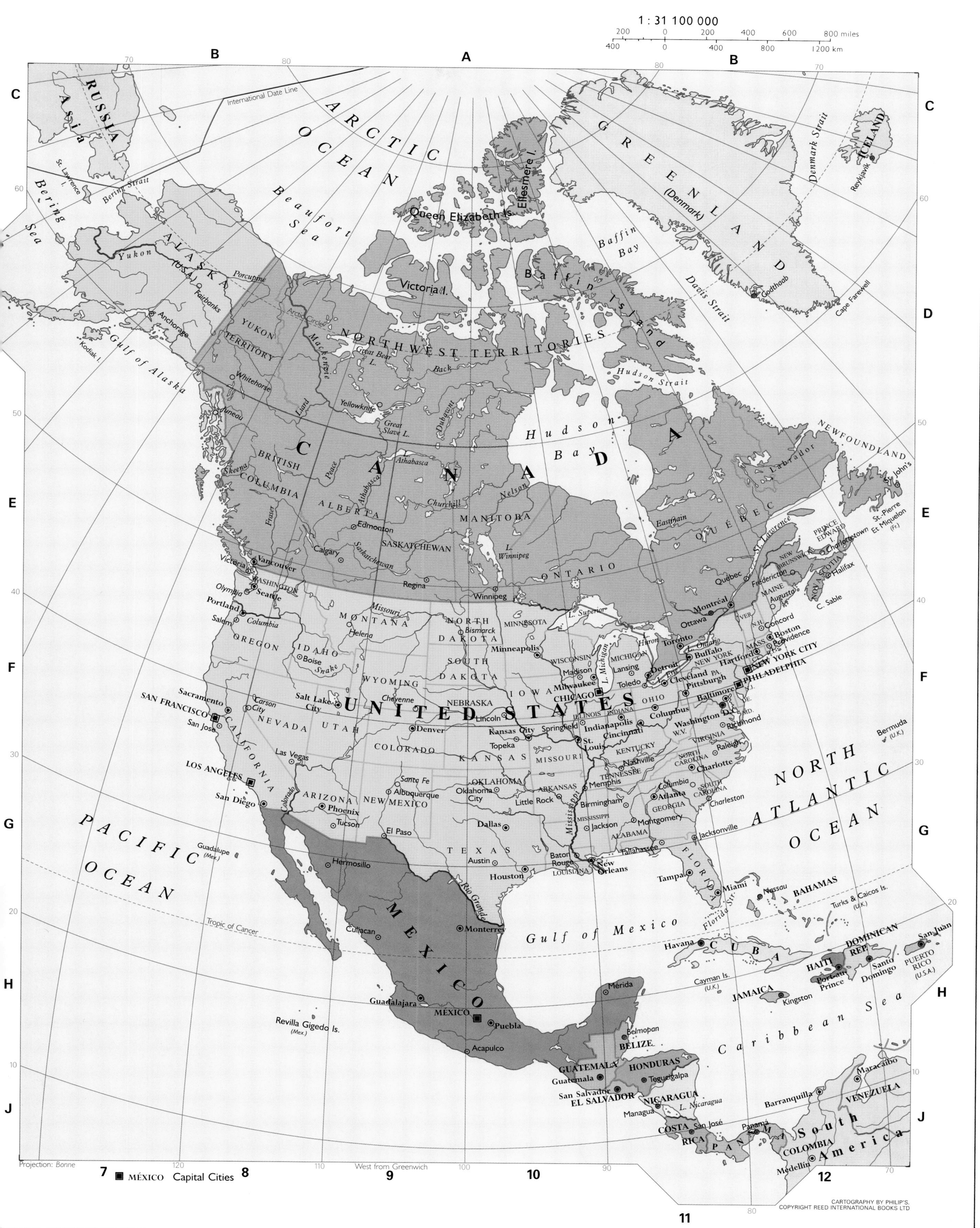
1 : 31 100 000
200 0 200 400 600 800 miles
400 0 400 800 1200 km
ARCTIC OCEAN
Beaufort Sea
Bering Sea
Bering Strait
St. Lawrence I.
RUSSIA
Asia
International Date Line
Queen Elizabeth Is.
Ellesmere I.
Victoria I.
Baffin Island
Baffin Bay
GREENLAND (Denmark)
Godthaab
Davis Strait
Cape Farewell
Denmark Strait
ICELAND
Reykjavik
ALASKA (U.S.A.)
Yukon
Porcupine
Fairbanks
Anchorage
Kodiak I.
Gulf of Alaska
Arctic Circle
YUKON TERRITORY
Whitehorse
Juneau
NORTHWEST TERRITORIES
Mackenzie
Great Bear L.
Back
Yellowknife
Great Slave L.
Liard
Dubawnt
Hudson Strait
Hudson Bay
CANADA
BRITISH COLUMBIA
Skeena
Peace
Athabasca
Fraser
ALBERTA
Edmonton
Calgary
SASKATCHEWAN
Saskatchewan
Churchill
Nelson
MANITOBA
L. Winnipeg
Regina
Winnipeg
ONTARIO
Eastmain
QUEBEC
Labrador
NEWFOUNDLAND
St John's
St.-Pierre Et Miquelon (Fr.)
PRINCE EDWARD I.
Charlottetown
NEW BRUNSWICK
NOVA SCOTIA
Halifax
Fredericton
C. Sable
St. Lawrence
Quebec
Montréal
Ottawa
L. Superior
Victoria
Vancouver
WASHINGTON
Olympia
Seattle
Portland
Salem
Columbia
OREGON
IDAHO
Boise
Snake
MONTANA
Helena
Missouri
NORTH DAKOTA
Bismarck
MINNESOTA
Minneapolis
SOUTH DAKOTA
WYOMING
Cheyenne
Salt Lake City
NEBRASKA
Lincoln
IOWA
WISCONSIN
Madison
Milwaukee
L. Michigan
MICHIGAN
Lansing
Huron
Detroit
Toledo
Erie
Cleveland
Toronto
L. Ontario
Buffalo
NEW YORK
Pittsburgh
MAINE
Augusta
Concord
Boston
Providence
Hartford
NEW YORK CITY
PHILADELPHIA
UNITED STATES
Sacramento
SAN FRANCISCO
San José
Carson City
NEVADA
UTAH
Denver
COLORADO
CALIFORNIA
Las Vegas
LOS ANGELES
San Diego
Colorado
ARIZONA
Phoenix
Tucson
NEW MEXICO
Santa Fe
Albuquerque
El Paso
KANSAS
Kansas City
Topeka
Springfield
ILLINOIS
INDIANA
Indianapolis
OHIO
Columbus
Cincinnati
St. Louis
MISSOURI
KENTUCKY
Nashville
TENNESSEE
Memphis
OKLAHOMA
Oklahoma City
ARKANSAS
Little Rock
Washington
Baltimore
Richmond
VIRGINIA
W.V.
Raleigh
NORTH CAROLINA
Charlotte
SOUTH CAROLINA
Columbia
Charleston
Atlanta
GEORGIA
Birmingham
Mississippi
MISSISSIPPI
Jackson
ALABAMA
Montgomery
Jacksonville
Tallahassee
FLORIDA
Tampa
Miami
Dallas
TEXAS
Austin
Houston
Baton Rouge
New Orleans
LOUISIANA
Rio Grande
Bermuda (U.K.)
NORTH ATLANTIC OCEAN
PACIFIC OCEAN
Guadalupe (Mex.)
Tropic of Cancer
Hermosillo
MEXICO
Culiacán
Monterrey
Gulf of Mexico
Florida Str.
Nassau
BAHAMAS
Turks & Caicos Is. (U.K.)
Havana
CUBA
HAITI
Port-au-Prince
DOMINICAN REP.
Santo Domingo
San Juan
PUERTO RICO (U.S.A.)
Cayman Is. (U.K.)
JAMAICA
Kingston
Caribbean Sea
Mérida
Guadalajara
MÉXICO
Puebla
Acapulco
Revilla Gigedo Is. (Mex.)
Belmopan
BELIZE
GUATEMALA
Guatemala
HONDURAS
Tegucigalpa
San Salvador
EL SALVADOR
NICARAGUA
Managua
L. Nicaragua
COSTA RICA
San José
Panamá
PANAMA
Barranquilla
Maracaibo
VENEZUELA
COLOMBIA
Medellín
South America
Projection: Bonne
West from Greenwich
■ MÉXICO Capital Cities
CARTOGRAPHY BY PHILIP'S.
COPYRIGHT REED INTERNATIONAL BOOKS LTD

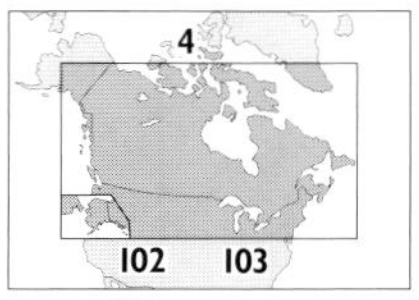
4
102
103

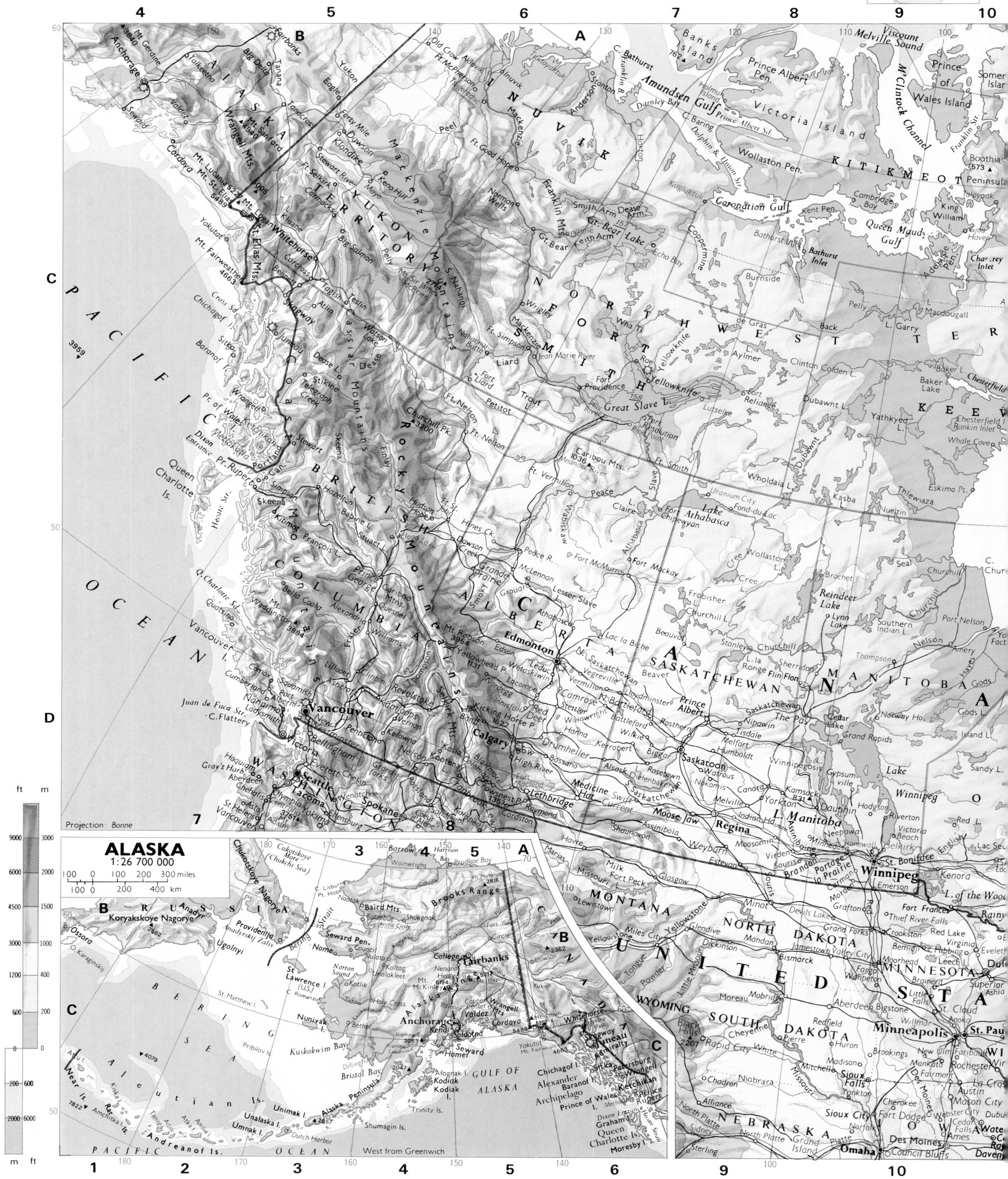
PACIFIC OCEAN
ALASKA
YUKON TERRITORY
NORTHWEST TERRITORIES
INUVIK
KITIKMEOT
KEEWATIN
BRITISH COLUMBIA
ALBERTA
SASKATCHEWAN
MANITOBA
WASHINGTON
MONTANA
NORTH DAKOTA
SOUTH DAKOTA
MINNESOTA
WYOMING
NEBRASKA
UNITED STATES
Mackenzie Mountains
Rocky Mountains
Coast Mountains
Cassiar Mountains
Selkirk Mts.
Columbia Mountains
Wrangell Mts.
Mt. Logan 5951
Mt. Lucania 5227
Mt. St. Elias 5489
Mt. Fairweather 4663
Mt. Robson 3954
Mt. Waddington 3994
Churchill Pk. 3200
Anchorage
Fairbanks
Whitehorse
Dawson
Skagway
Juneau
Sitka
Prince Rupert
Vancouver
Victoria
Seattle
Tacoma
Spokane
Kamloops
Prince George
Edmonton
Calgary
Lethbridge
Medicine Hat
Saskatoon
Regina
Moose Jaw
Prince Albert
Winnipeg
Minneapolis
Omaha
Yellowknife
Inuvik
Great Slave L.
Gt. Bear Lake
Lake Athabasca
Reindeer Lake
Lake Winnipeg
L. Manitoba
Victoria Island
Banks Island
Prince of Wales Island
Amundsen Gulf
Coronation Gulf
Queen Maud Gulf
M'Clintock Channel
Viscount Melville Sound
Queen Charlotte Is.
Vancouver I.
Juan de Fuca Str.
Projection: Bonne
ALASKA
1:26 700 000
100 0 100 200 300 miles
100 0 200 400 km
BERING SEA
GULF OF ALASKA
Aleutian Is.
Brooks Range
Seward Pen.
Alaska Peninsula
Kodiak I.
Nunivak I.
St. Lawrence I.
Mt. McKinley 6194
Kuskokwim Bay
Bristol Bay
RUSSIA
Koryakskoye Nagorye
West from Greenwich
ft m
9000 3000
6000 2000
4500 1500
3000 1000
1200 400
600 200
0 0
200 600
2000 6000
m ft

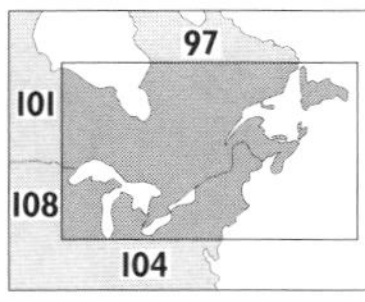

97
101
108
104

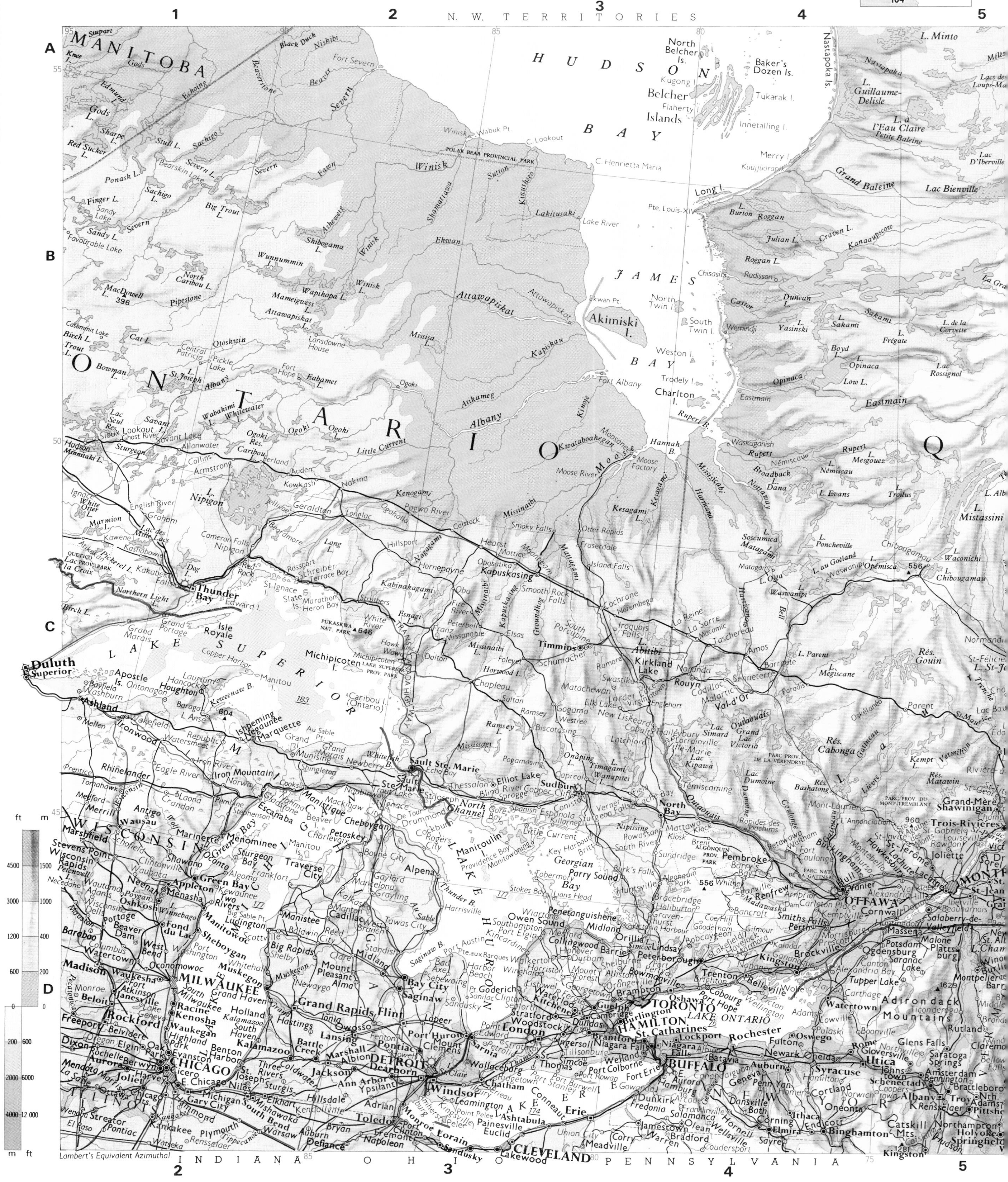

N. W. TERRITORIES

HUDSON BAY

JAMES BAY

MANITOBA

ONTARIO

QUEBEC

LAKE SUPERIOR

LAKE MICHIGAN

LAKE HURON

LAKE ONTARIO

LAKE ERIE

WISCONSIN

MICHIGAN

ILLINOIS

NEW YORK

INDIANA OHIO PENNSYLVANIA

ft m
4500 1500
3000 1000
1200 400
600 200
0 0
200 600
2000 6000
4000 12 000
m ft

Lambert's Equivalent Azimuthal

1 : 6 200 000
50 0 50 100 150 200 miles
50 0 50 100 150 200 250 300 km
6
7
8
9
A
B
C
D
NEWFOUNDLAND
COAST OF LABRADOR
LABRADOR
QUEBEC
NEW BRUNSWICK
NOVA SCOTIA
PRINCE EDWARD ISLAND
MAINE
NEWFOUNDLAND
GULF OF ST. LAWRENCE
ATLANTIC OCEAN
Cabot Strait
Str. of Belle Isle
Bay of Fundy
St. Lawrence
Northumberland Str.
Dét. de Jacques-Cartier
Dét. d'Honguedo
Î. d'Anticosti
Îs. de la Madeleine (Quebec)
Cape Breton Island
Sable I. (Nova Scotia)
SAINT PIERRE ET MIQUELON (Fr.)
Miquelon
Langlade
St. Pierre
Avalon Peninsula
Smallwood Res.
Churchill Falls
Happy Valley-Goose Bay
L. Melville
Mealy Mts.
Labrador City
Wabush
Res. Manicouagan
Kaniapiskau Lake
Nain
Hopedale
Cartwright
Battle Harbour
Belle I.
Sept-Îles
Port-Cartier
Havre-St-Pierre
Mingan
Natashquan
Mts. Chic-Chocs
Pén. de Gaspé
Gaspé
Percé
Chaleur Bay
Rimouski
Rivière-du-Loup
Chicoutimi
Jonquière
Alma
Dalhousie
Campbellton
Bathurst
Edmundston
Chatham
Newcastle
Moncton
Fredericton
Saint John
Charlottetown
Summerside
Amherst
Truro
New Glasgow
Halifax
Dartmouth
Yarmouth
Sydney
Glace Bay
North Sydney
New Waterford
Sydney Mines
Louisbourg
Corner Brook
Stephenville
Gander
Grand Falls
Botwood
Lewisporte
Clarenville
St. John's
Channel-Port aux Basques
Long Range Mts.
Notre Dame B.
Fogo I.
Bonavista
Trinity B.
Conception B.
Placentia B.
Fortune B.
St. Mary's B.
C. Race
Burin
Marystown
Grand Bank
Quebec
Lévis
Lauzon
Montmagny
Thetford Mines
Sherbrooke
Coaticook
Lac-Mégantic
Houlton
Presque Isle
Caribou
Millinocket
Bangor
Augusta
Waterville
Lewiston
Auburn
Portland
Biddeford
Saco
Rochester
Concord
Manchester
Nashua
Portsmouth
Haverhill
Lawrence
Lowell
Gloucester
Lynn
BOSTON
Brockton
Waltham
Rockland
Bath
Brunswick
Belfast
Calais
Eastport
Bar Harbor
Mt. Desert I.
West from Greenwich
70
65
60
55
50
45
COPYRIGHT, GEORGE PHILIP & SON, LTD.

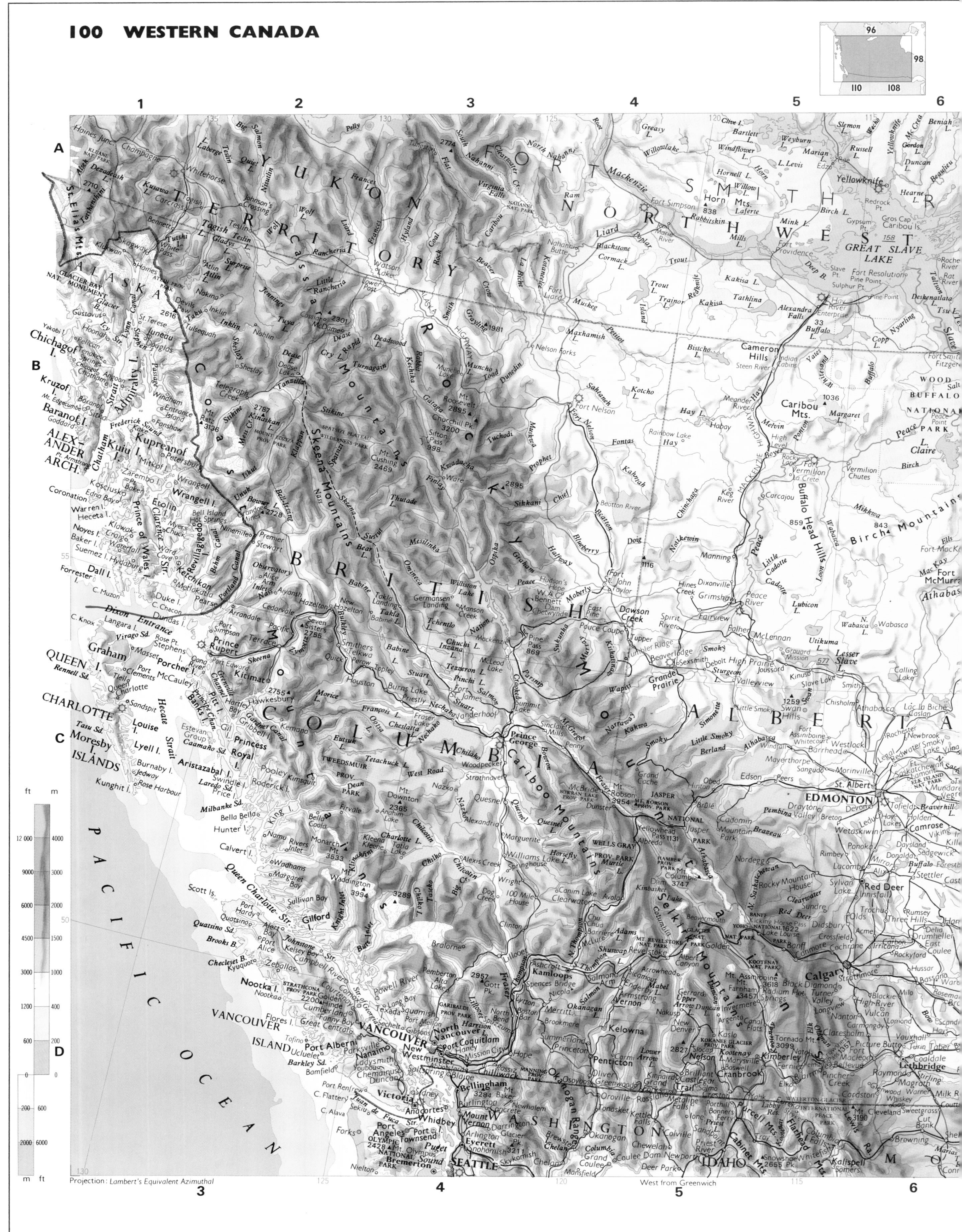
YUKON TERRITORY
NORTHWEST TERRITORIES
FORT SMITH
BRITISH COLUMBIA
ALBERTA
ALASKA
WASHINGTON
IDAHO
PACIFIC OCEAN
QUEEN CHARLOTTE ISLANDS
VANCOUVER ISLAND
ALEXANDER ARCH.
GREAT SLAVE LAKE
ROCKY MOUNTAINS
COAST MOUNTAINS
Skeena Mountains
Cariboo Mountains
Selkirk Mountains
Birch Mountains
Caribou Mts.
Horn Mts.
Cameron Hills
Buffalo Head Hills
WOOD BUFFALO NATIONAL PARK
JASPER NATIONAL PARK
TWEEDSMUIR PROV. PARK
WELLS GRAY PROV. PARK
Whitehorse
Yellowknife
Fort Simpson
Fort Nelson
Fort St. John
Dawson Creek
Grande Prairie
Peace River
Prince George
Prince Rupert
Kitimat
Terrace
Quesnel
Williams Lake
Kamloops
Kelowna
Penticton
Vernon
Nelson
Cranbrook
Trail
Revelstoke
Golden
Banff
Calgary
Red Deer
EDMONTON
St. Albert
Lethbridge
Camrose
Hinton
Edson
VANCOUVER
North Vancouver
New Westminster
Victoria
Nanaimo
Port Alberni
Bellingham
SEATTLE
Everett
Bremerton
Mt. Robson 3954
Dixon Entrance
Hecate Strait
Queen Charlotte Str.
Juan de Fuca Str.
Projection: Lambert's Equivalent Azimuthal
West from Greenwich

1 : 6 200 000
50 0 50 100 150 200 miles
50 0 50 100 150 200 250 300 km
7 8 9 10 11
A
B
C
D
KEEWATIN
REGION
HUDSON BAY
MANITOBA
SASKATCHEWAN
ONTARIO
NORTH DAKOTA
MINNESOTA
LAKE WINNIPEG
Lake Athabasca
Reindeer L.
Southern Indian L.
Wollaston L.
Cedar Lake
Lake Winnipegosis
Lake Manitoba
Lake of the Woods
Churchill
Flin Flon
The Pas
Prince Albert
North Battleford
Saskatoon
Regina
Moose Jaw
Swift Current
Medicine Hat
Yorkton
Brandon
WINNIPEG
Portage la Prairie
Kenora
Fort Frances
International Falls
Grand Forks
Minot
Devils Lake
Williston
Bemidji
Duluth
Virginia
Hibbing
Grand Rapids
7 8 9 10
110 105 100 95
COPYRIGHT GEORGE PHILIP & SON LTD

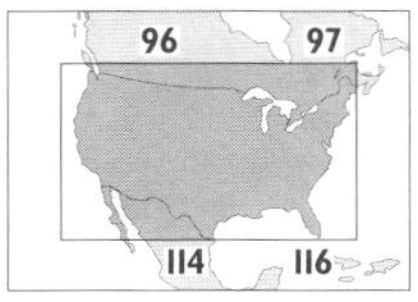

HAWAII

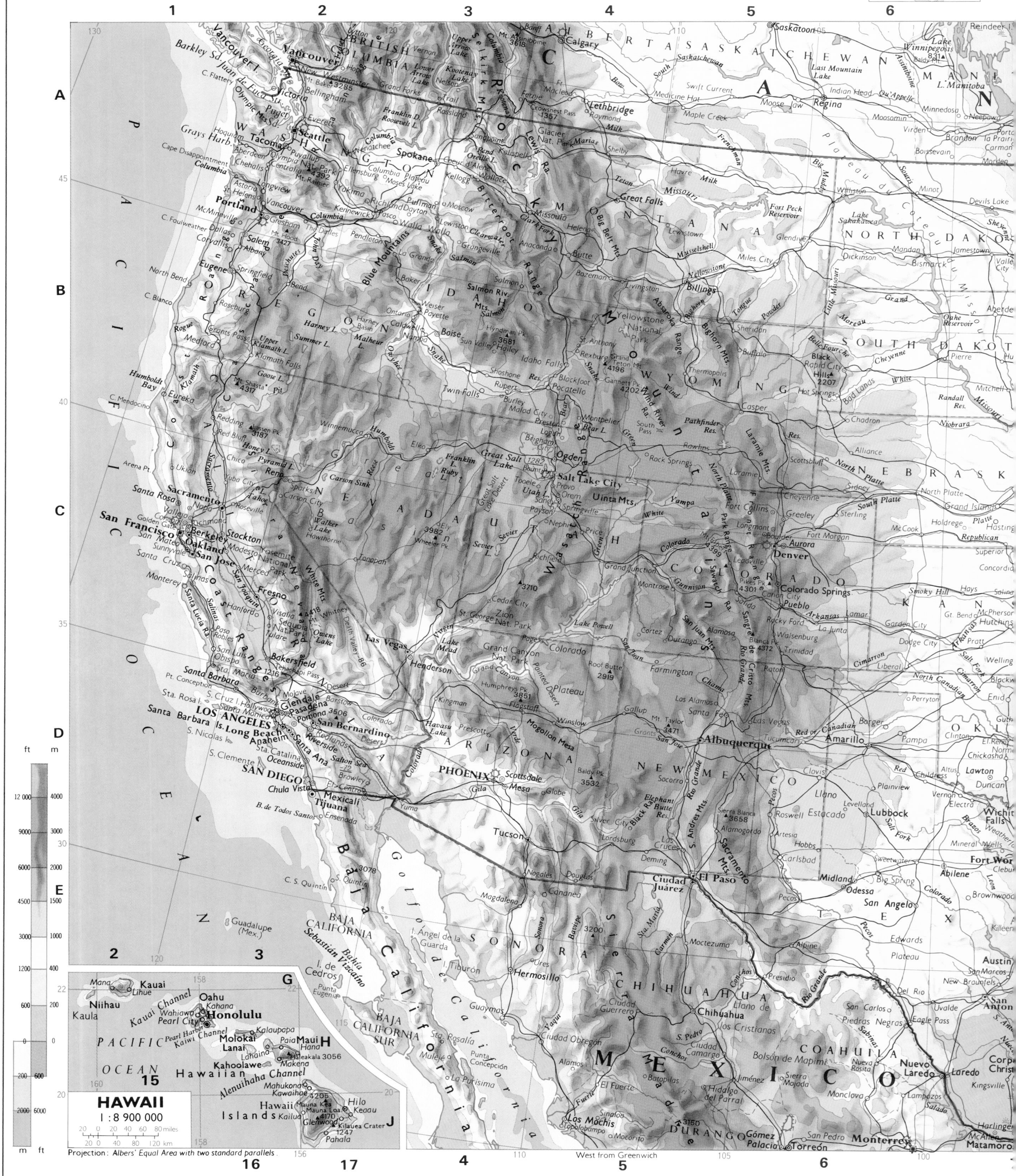

1 : 8 900 000

Projection: Albers' Equal Area with two standard parallels

West from Greenwich

ft	m
12 000	4000
9000	3000
6000	2000
4500	1500
3000	1000
1200	400
600	200
0	0
200	600
2000	6000
m	ft

96 97
114 116

1 2 3 4 5 6

A B C D E F

45

40

35

130 120 110 105 100

BRITISH COLUMBIA — **ALBERTA** — **SASKATCHEWAN** — **MANITOBA**

Saskatoon
Calgary
Lethbridge
Regina
Medicine Hat
Moose Jaw
Swift Current
Maple Creek

Vancouver I.
Vancouver
Victoria
New Westminster
Bellingham
C. Flattery

WASHINGTON
Seattle
Tacoma
Olympia
Spokane
Mt. Rainier 4392

OREGON
Portland
Salem
Eugene
Medford
Roseburg

MONTANA
Great Falls
Helena
Butte
Missoula
Billings
Miles City

IDAHO
Boise
Idaho Falls
Twin Falls
Pocatello

WYOMING
Yellowstone National Park
Casper
Cheyenne

NORTH DAKOTA
Bismarck
Dickinson
Jamestown

SOUTH DAKOTA
Pierre
Rapid City
Black Hills 2207

NEBRASKA
North Platte
Scottsbluff

NEVADA
Reno
Carson City
Las Vegas
Henderson

UTAH
Salt Lake City
Ogden
Provo
Great Salt Lake 1282

COLORADO
Denver
Colorado Springs
Pueblo
Pikes Pk. 4301

KANSAS
Dodge City
Garden City

CALIFORNIA
Sacramento
San Francisco
Oakland
Berkeley
San Jose
Stockton
Fresno
Bakersfield
LOS ANGELES
Long Beach
Pasadena
Glendale
Santa Ana
Anaheim
Riverside
San Bernardino
SAN DIEGO
Mt. Whitney 4418
Death Valley −86

ARIZONA
PHOENIX
Scottsdale
Mesa
Tucson
Yuma
Flagstaff
Grand Canyon National Park
Humphreys Pk. 3851

NEW MEXICO
Albuquerque
Santa Fe
Las Cruces
Roswell
Carlsbad

OKLAHOMA
Amarillo
Lubbock

TEXAS
El Paso
Midland
Odessa
San Angelo
Abilene
Austin
San Marcos
Fort Worth
Wichita Falls
Del Rio
Eagle Pass
Laredo

MEXICO
Tijuana
Mexicali
Ensenada
BAJA CALIFORNIA
BAJA CALIFORNIA SUR
SONORA
Hermosillo
Guaymas
Ciudad Obregón
Los Mochis
CHIHUAHUA
Ciudad Juárez
Chihuahua
COAHUILA
Nuevo Laredo
Monterrey
DURANGO
Gómez Palacio
Torreón

PACIFIC OCEAN

** HAWAII Inset**
Kauai
Lihue
Niihau
Oahu
Honolulu
Pearl Harbor
Wahiawa
Molokai
Lanai
Maui
Hana
Haleakala 3056
Kahoolawe

Hilo
Mauna Kea 4205
Mauna Loa 4170
Kilauea Crater 1247
Hawaiian Islands

1 : 10 700 000
50 0 50 100 150 200 250 300 miles
50 0 50 100 150 200 250 300 350 400 450 km
8
9
10
11
12
13
A
B
C
D
E
F
CANADA
ONTARIO
QUEBEC
Lake Winnipeg
Winnipeg
Lake of the Woods
Thunder Bay
Lake Superior
Lake Nipigon
Duluth
MINNESOTA
Minneapolis
St. Paul
WISCONSIN
Milwaukee
Lake Michigan
Lake Huron
Georgian Bay
Sudbury
Sault Ste. Marie
Ottawa
MONTREAL
Québec
NEW BRUNSWICK
MAINE
VERMONT
NEW HAMPSHIRE
Boston
TORONTO
Lake Ontario
Buffalo
NEW YORK
Lake Erie
DETROIT
Cleveland
CHICAGO
IOWA
Des Moines
Toledo
Pittsburgh
PENNSYLVANIA
PHILADELPHIA
Baltimore
Washington D.C.
NEW JERSEY
OHIO
Columbus
Cincinnati
Indianapolis
INDIANA
ILLINOIS
St. Louis
Kansas City
MISSOURI
WEST VIRGINIA
VIRGINIA
Richmond
Norfolk
KENTUCKY
Louisville
Nashville
TENNESSEE
Memphis
NORTH CAROLINA
SOUTH CAROLINA
Charlotte
Atlanta
GEORGIA
Birmingham
ALABAMA
MISSISSIPPI
ARKANSAS
Little Rock
OKLAHOMA
Oklahoma City
Tulsa
DALLAS
HOUSTON
LOUISIANA
New Orleans
Savannah
Jacksonville
FLORIDA
Tampa
Orlando
Miami
Key West
GULF OF MEXICO
ATLANTIC OCEAN
BAHAMAS
Nassau
Delta of the Mississippi
APPALACHIAN MTS.
COPYRIGHT. GEORGE PHILIP & SON. LTD

1 : 5 300 000
50 0 50 100 150 miles
50 0 50 100 150 200 km
TENNESSEE
NORTH CAROLINA
SOUTH CAROLINA
GEORGIA
ALABAMA
FLORIDA
MISSISSIPPI
MAINE
NEW HAMPSHIRE
CANADA
ATLANTIC OCEAN
GULF OF MEXICO
BAHAMAS
Nashville
Atlanta
Birmingham
Montgomery
Jacksonville
Savannah
Charleston
Columbia
Charlotte
Raleigh
Tampa
Orlando
Miami
Continuation Eastwards On same scale.
Projection: Alber's Equal Area with two standard parallels
West from Greenwich
COPYRIGHT GEORGE PHILIP & SON, LTD.

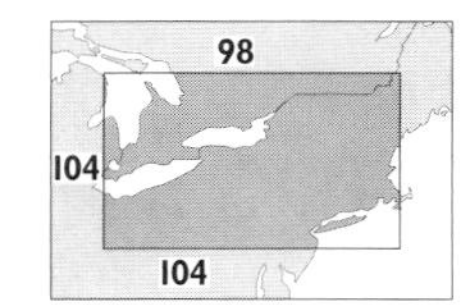

ft	m
6000	2000
4500	1500
3000	1000
1200	400
600	200
0	0
200	600
m	ft

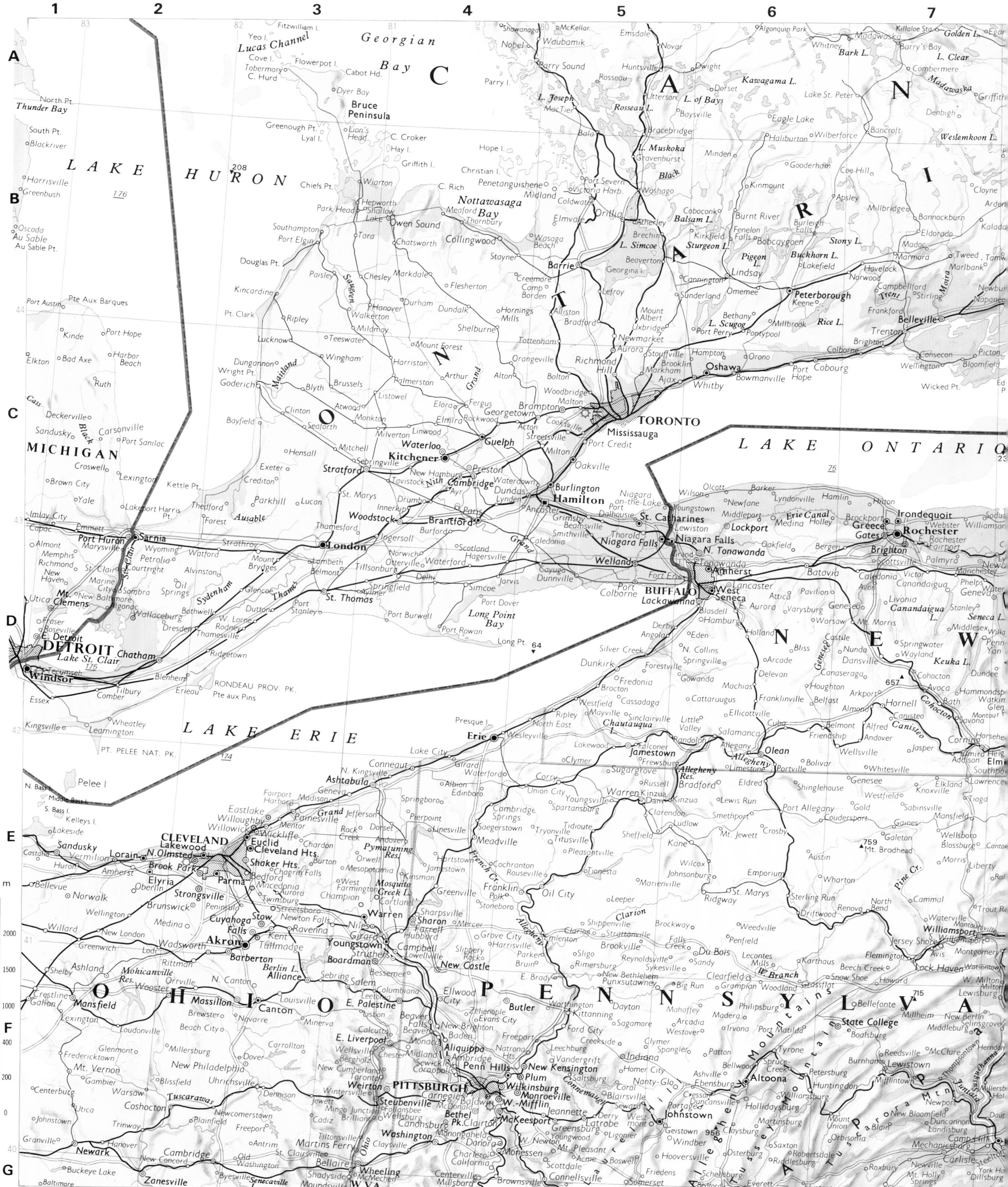

Projection: Bonne

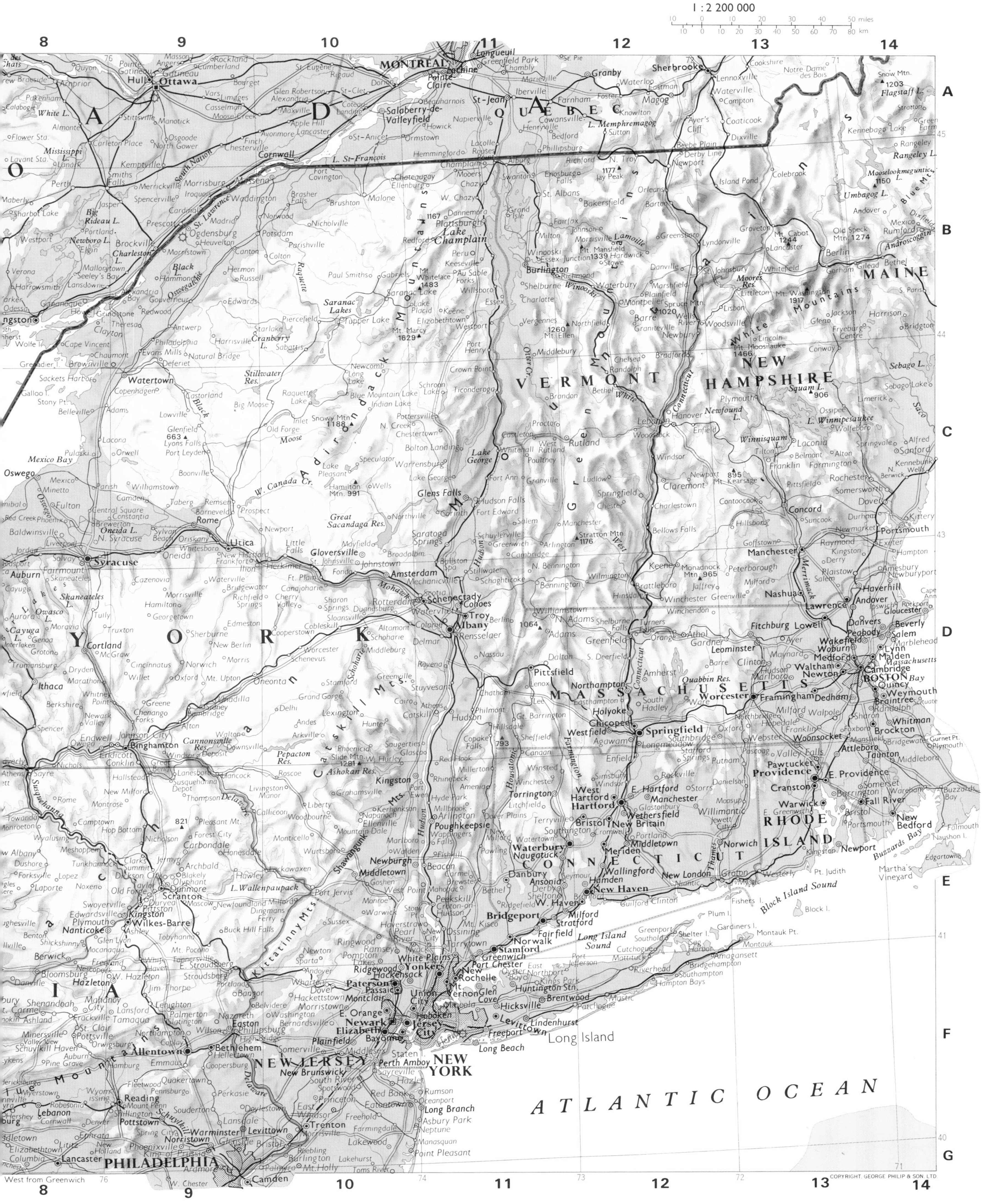
1 : 2 200 000
50 miles
80 km
MONTREAL
Ottawa
Sherbrooke
QUEBEC
MAINE
NEW HAMPSHIRE
VERMONT
MASSACHUSETTS
RHODE ISLAND
CONNECTICUT
NEW JERSEY
NEW YORK
YORK
Lake Champlain
Adirondack Mountains
Green Mountains
White Mountains
Catskill Mts.
Syracuse
Utica
Albany
Schenectady
Binghamton
Scranton
Wilkes-Barre
Allentown
Reading
PHILADELPHIA
Trenton
Newark
Jersey City
Burlington
Concord
Manchester
Worcester
BOSTON
Springfield
Hartford
New Haven
Bridgeport
Providence
Long Island
Long Island Sound
Block Island Sound
ATLANTIC OCEAN
West from Greenwich
COPYRIGHT. GEORGE PHILIP & SON, LTD

1 : 5 300 000

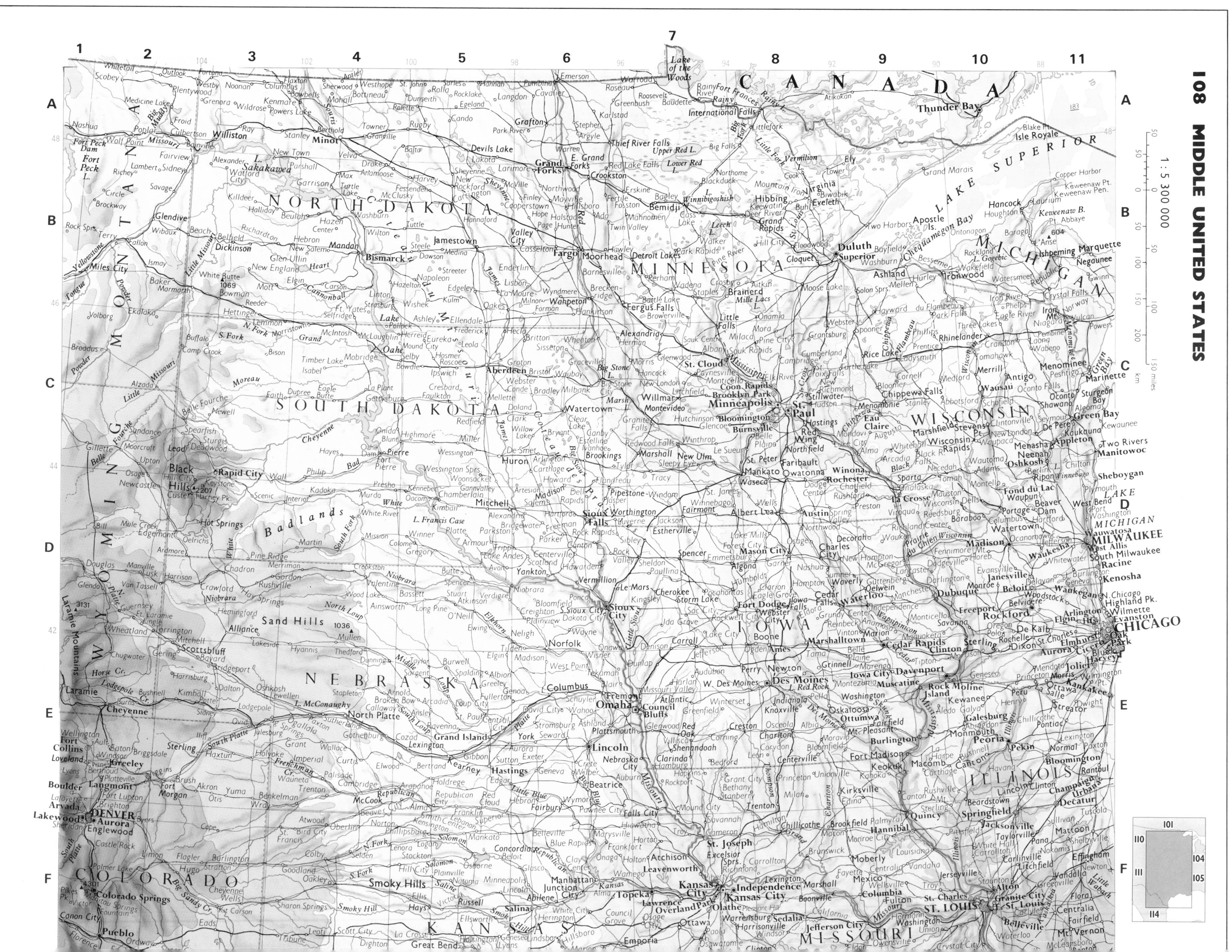
50 0 50 100 150 miles
50 0 50 100 150 200 km
CANADA
LAKE SUPERIOR
LAKE MICHIGAN
MICHIGAN
MINNESOTA
WISCONSIN
NORTH DAKOTA
SOUTH DAKOTA
IOWA
ILLINOIS
NEBRASKA
MISSOURI
KANSAS
COLORADO
WYOMING
MONTANA
CHICAGO
MILWAUKEE
ST. LOUIS
DENVER
Minneapolis
St. Paul
Des Moines
Omaha
Kansas City
Duluth
Thunder Bay
Black Hills
Sand Hills
Badlands
Laramie Mountains

OKLAHOMA
ARKANSAS
MISSISSIPPI
LOUISIANA
TEXAS
NEW MEXICO
TENNESSEE
MEXICO
COAHUILA
CHIHUAHUA
GULF OF MEXICO
Edwards Plateau
Llano Estacado
Sangre de Cristo Mts.
Ouachita Mts.
Boston Mts.
Balcones Escarpment
Stockton Plateau
DALLAS
HOUSTON
SAN ANTONIO
MEMPHIS
NEW ORLEANS
Oklahoma City
Little Rock
Jackson
Austin
Fort Worth
Shreveport
Corpus Christi
Tulsa
Wichita
Amarillo
Lubbock
Baton Rouge
El Paso
Continuation Southwards on same scale
Projection: Albers' Equal Area with two standard parallels
West from Greenwich
COPYRIGHT GEORGE PHILIP & SON, LTD

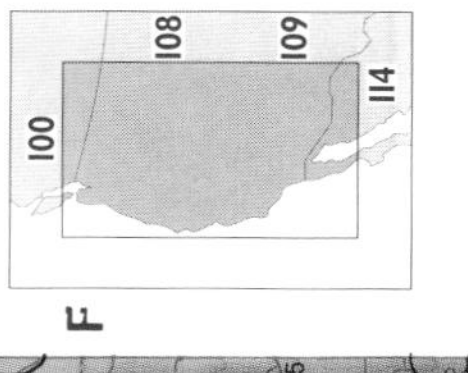

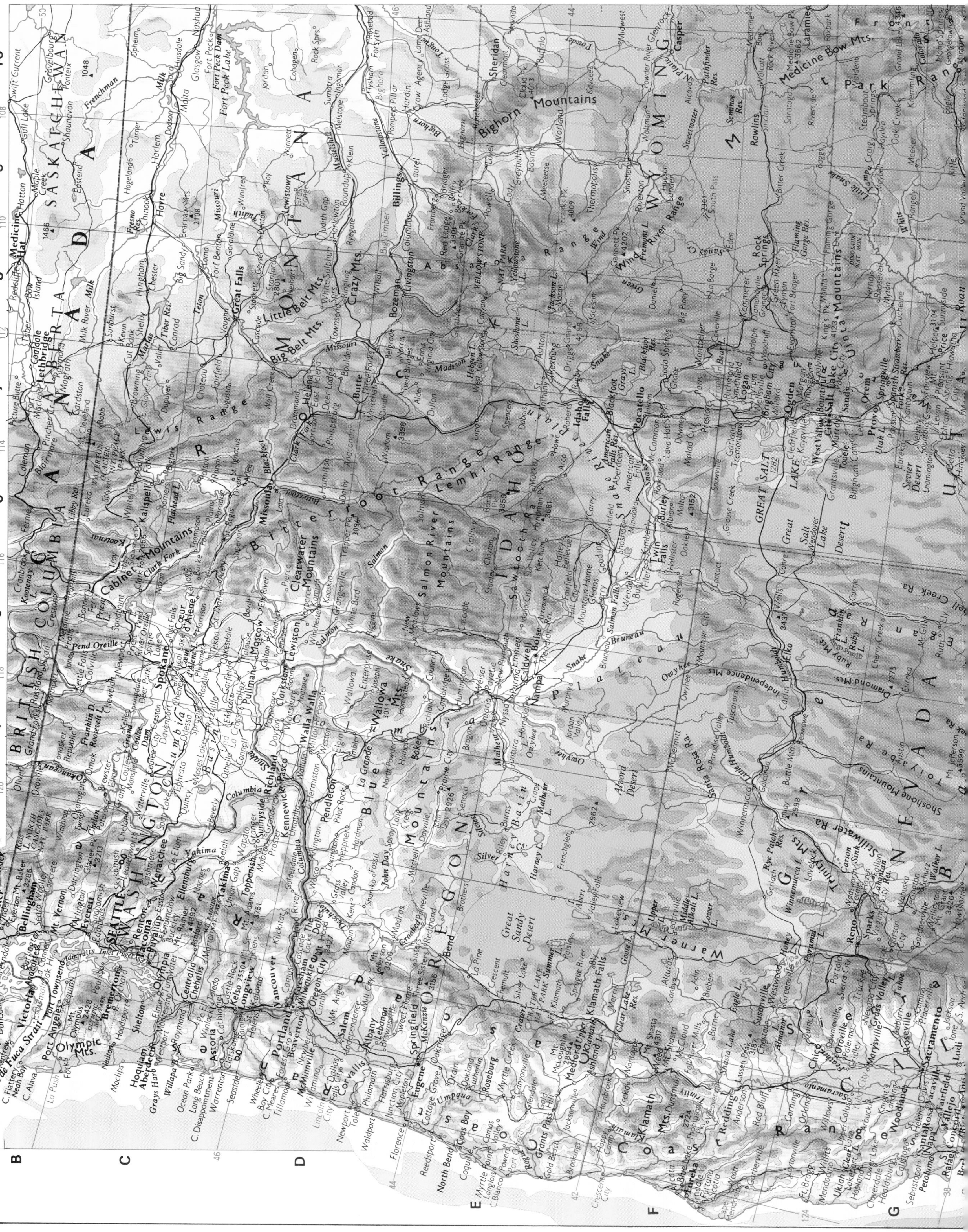

1 : 5 300 000

50 0 50 100 miles

50 0 50 100 150 km

COLORADO

NEW MEXICO

ARIZONA

CALIFORNIA

TEXAS

MEXICO

BAJA CALIFORNIA

SONORA

CHIHUAHUA

PACIFIC OCEAN

Golfo de California

Colorado Plateau

Sierra Nevada

West from Greenwich

Projection: Albers' Equal Area with two standard parallels

ft m

12 000 4000

9000 3000

6000 2000

4500 1500

3000 1000

1200 400

600 200

0 0

200 600

2000 6000

4000 12 000

m ft

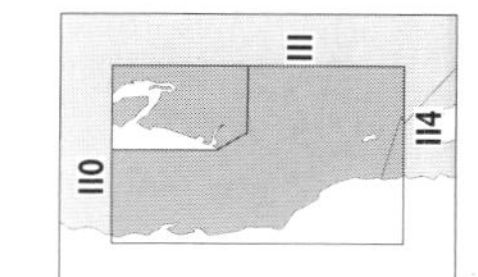

SEATTLE-PORTLAND REGION
On same scale

1 : 2 200 000

10 0 10 20 30 40 50 miles

10 0 20 40 60 80 km

NEVADA

CALIFORNIA

ARIZONA

MEXICO

PACIFIC OCEAN

Mojave Desert

Sonora Desert

LOS ANGELES

SAN DIEGO

SAN BERNARDINO

Tijuana

Mexicali

Las Vegas

Santa Barbara Channel

Gulf of Santa Catalina

Channel Islands

H J K L M

L M N P

8 9 10 11 12 13

West from Greenwich

Projection: Bonne

m 4000 3000 2000 1500 1000 400 200 0 200 2000 6000 m

ft 12 000 9000 6000 4500 3000 1200 600 0 600 6000 ft

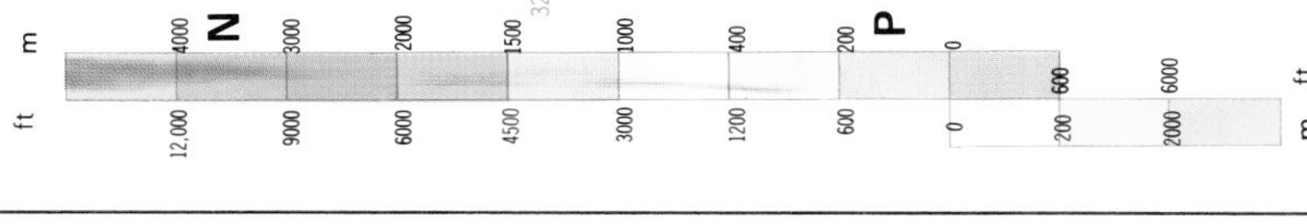

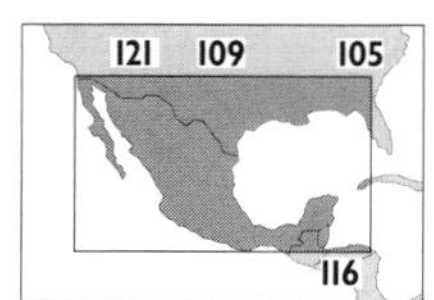

1 2 3 4

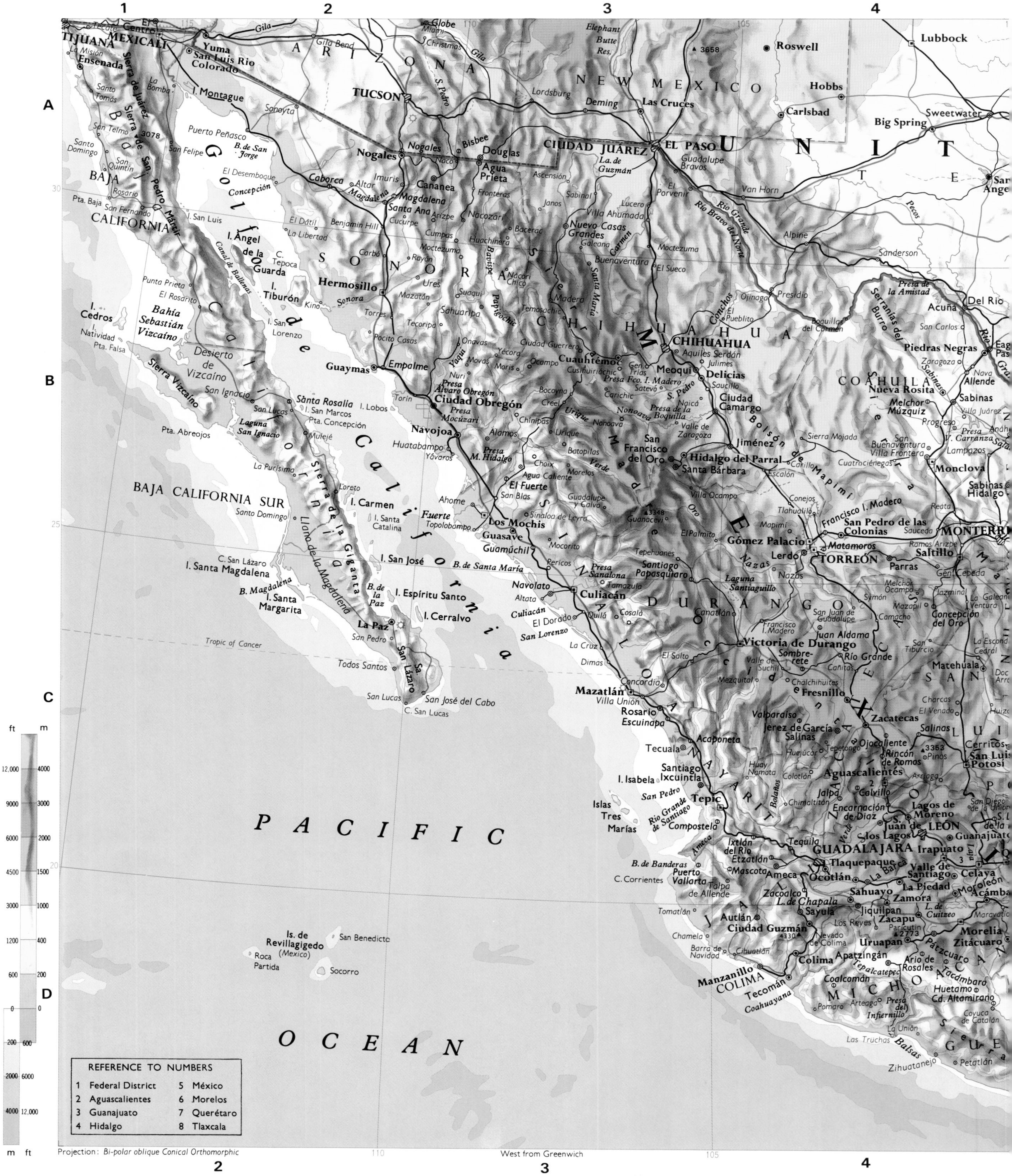

A

B

C

D

PACIFIC OCEAN

m	ft
4000	12,000
3000	9000
2000	6000
1500	4500
1000	3000
400	1200
200	600
0	0
200	600
2000	6000
4000	12,000

REFERENCE TO NUMBERS

1	Federal District	5	México
2	Aguascalientes	6	Morelos
3	Guanajuato	7	Querétaro
4	Hidalgo	8	Tlaxcala

Projection: *Bi-polar oblique Conical Orthomorphic*

West from Greenwich

2 3 4

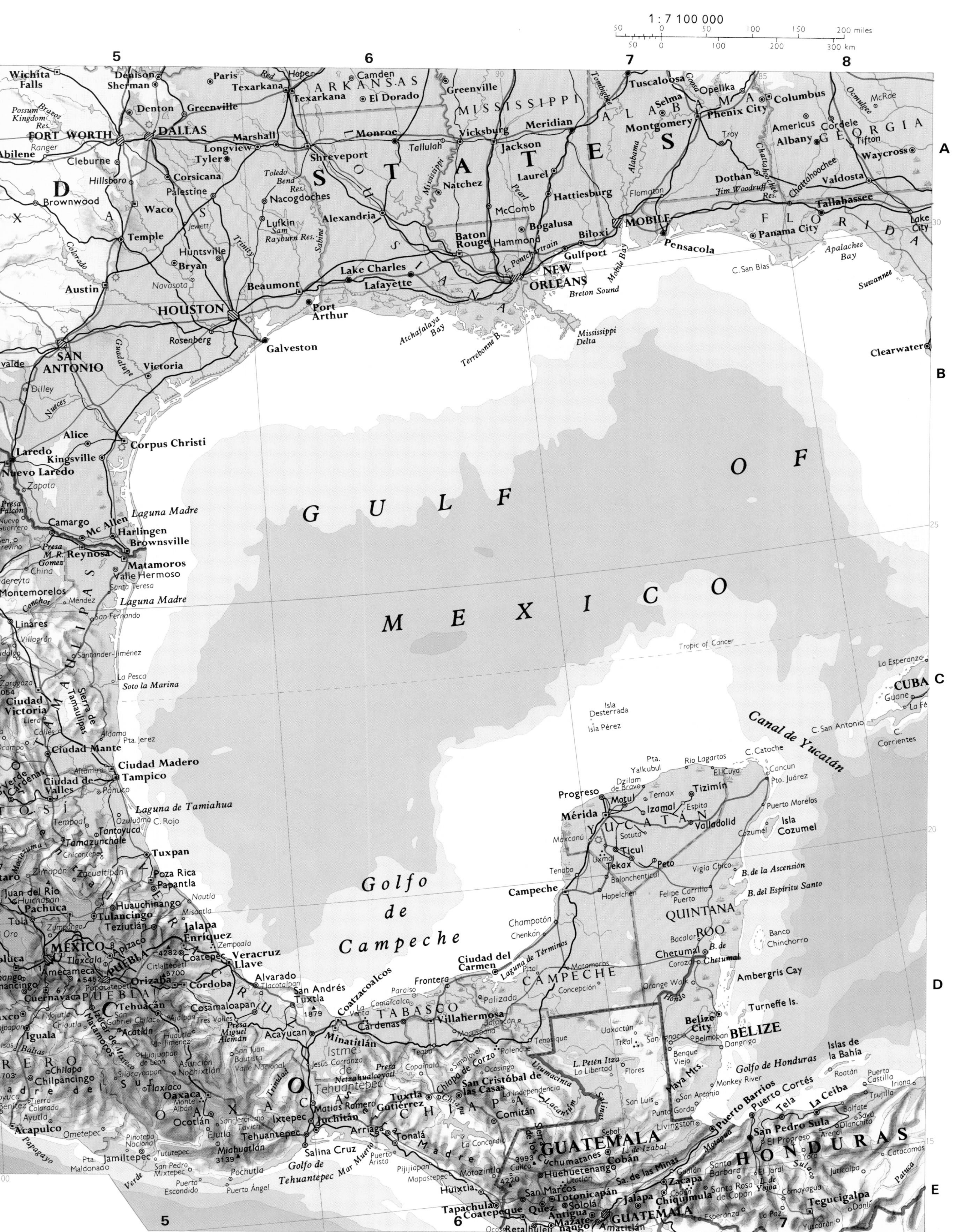
1 : 7 100 000
50 0 50 100 150 200 miles
50 0 100 200 300 km
5
6
7
8
A
B
C
D
E
GULF OF MEXICO
Golfo de Campeche
Canal de Yucatán
Golfo de Honduras
Golfo de Tehuantepec
Tropic of Cancer
UNITED STATES
TEXAS
ARKANSAS
LOUISIANA
MISSISSIPPI
ALABAMA
GEORGIA
FLORIDA
CUBA
YUCATÁN
QUINTANA ROO
CAMPECHE
TABASCO
CHIAPAS
OAXACA
VERACRUZ
PUEBLA
TAMAULIPAS
BELIZE
GUATEMALA
HONDURAS
Wichita Falls
Denison
Sherman
Paris
Texarkana
Hope
Camden
El Dorado
Greenville
Tuscaloosa
Opelika
Columbus
Denton
FORT WORTH
DALLAS
Marshall
Monroe
Vicksburg
Meridian
Selma
Montgomery
Phenix City
Americus
Cordele
Albany
Tifton
Abilene
Longview
Tyler
Shreveport
Tallulah
Jackson
Troy
Waycross
Cleburne
Corsicana
Palestine
Natchez
Laurel
Dothan
Valdosta
Hillsboro
Brownwood
Waco
Nacogdoches
Lufkin
Alexandria
McComb
Hattiesburg
Flomaton
Tallahassee
Lake City
Temple
Huntsville
Bryan
Baton Rouge
Hammond
Bogalusa
Biloxi
MOBILE
Pensacola
Panama City
Austin
Beaumont
Lake Charles
Lafayette
Gulfport
NEW ORLEANS
Apalachee Bay
HOUSTON
Port Arthur
Galveston
Breton Sound
Mississippi Delta
Atchafalaya Bay
Terrebonne B.
SAN ANTONIO
Victoria
Clearwater
Alice
Corpus Christi
Laredo
Kingsville
Nuevo Laredo
Camargo
Mc Allen
Harlingen
Brownsville
Reynosa
Laguna Madre
Matamoros
Valle Hermoso
Montemorelos
Linares
Ciudad Victoria
Sierra de Tamaulipas
Ciudad Mante
Ciudad Madero
Tampico
Ciudad de Valles
Laguna de Tamiahua
Tamazunchale
Tuxpan
Poza Rica
Papantla
Pachuca
Huauchinango
Tulancingo
Teziutlán
Jalapa Enríquez
MÉXICO
Tlaxcala
PUEBLA
Orizaba
Córdoba
Veracruz Llave
Alvarado
Cuernavaca
San Andrés Tuxtla
Coatzacoalcos
Tehuacán
Cosamaloapan
Acayucan
Minatitlán
Cárdenas
Villahermosa
Frontera
Ciudad del Carmen
Laguna de Términos
Champotón
Campeche
Iguala
Chilapa
Chilpancingo
Sierra Madre del Sur
Oaxaca
Ocotlán
Ixtepec
Juchitán
Tehuantepec
Salina Cruz
Acapulco
Ometepec
Jamiltepec
Miahuatlán
Pochutla
Puerto Ángel
Tuxtla Gutiérrez
San Cristóbal de las Casas
Comitán
Tonalá
Arriaga
Huixtla
Tapachula
Progreso
Mérida
Motul
Izamal
Tizimín
Valladolid
Ticul
Tekax
Peto
Isla Cozumel
Cancun
Pto. Juárez
C. Catoche
Isla Desterrada
Isla Pérez
Chetumal
B. de Chetumal
Ambergris Cay
Turneffe Is.
Belize City
Belmopan
Dangriga
Flores
L. Petén Itzá
Tikal
Puerto Barrios
Puerto Cortés
Tela
La Ceiba
San Pedro Sula
Islas de la Bahía
Cobán
Huehuetenango
Quezaltenango
Totonicapán
Sololá
Antigua
Jalapa
Chiquimula
Zacapa
GUATEMALA
Tegucigalpa
C. San Antonio
C. Corrientes
Guane
La Fé
C. San Blas
Suwannee
Mobile Bay
L. Pontchartrain

GULF OF MEXICO
U.S.A.
Fort Myers
West Palm Beach
Boca Raton
Fort Lauderdale
Hialeah
MIAMI
Key West
Florida Keys
Straits of Florida
L. Okeechobee
Everglades
Naples
C. Romano
C. Sable
Florida Bay
Dry Tortugas
Grand Bahama I.
Great Abaco I.
Northwest Providence Channel
Northeast Providence Channel
Bimini Is.
Berry Is.
Nassau
New Providence I.
Eleuthera I.
Andros Island
GREAT BAHAMA BANK
Santaren Channel
Cay Sal Bank
(Havana) LA HABANA
MARIANAO
Guanabacoa
Matanzas
Cárdenas
Colón
Sagua la Grande
Santa Clara
Caibarién
Pinar del Río
San Luis
Isla de la Juventud
Nueva Gerona
Archipiélago de los Canarreos
Cienfuegos
Trinidad
Sancti-Spíritus
Placetas
Morón
Ciego de Avila
Florida
Camagüey
Nuevitas
Victoria de las Tunas
Manzanillo
Bayamo
Palma Soriano
SANTIAGO DE CUBA
Sierra Maestra
CUBA
GREATER
CARIB
Canal Nicolás
Canal Viejo de Bahama
Golfo de Guacanayabo
Arch. de los Jardines de la Reina
C. Cruz
Cayman Islands (Br.)
Cayman Brac
Little Cayman
Georgetown
Grand Cayman
7680
Montego Bay
Falmouth
St. Ann's Bay
JAMAICA
KINGSTON
Spanish Town
May Pen
Mandeville
Black River
Savanna la Mar
South Negril Pt.
Lucea
Pedro Cays (Jamaica)
Swan Islands (U.S.A. & Honduras)
Bajo Nuevo (Colombia)
Canal de Yucatán
C. San Antonio
C. Corrientes
C. Catoche
Isla Desterrada
Isla Pérez
Progreso
Mérida
YUCATAN
Tizimín
Valladolid
Izamal
Ticul
Tekax
Peto
Campeche
Champotón
Ciudad del Carmen
Laguna de Términos
CAMPECHE
QUINTANA ROO
Felipe Carrillo Puerto
Isla Cozumel
Cancun
B. de la Ascensión
B. del Espíritu Santo
Banco Chinchorro
Chetumal
B. de Chetumal
Ambergris Cay
Turneffe Is.
BELIZE
Belize City
Belmopan
Dangriga
Maya Mts.
Punta Gorda
Golfo de Honduras
Islas de la Bahía
Roatán
L. Petén Itza
Flores
Comitán
GUATEMALA
Huehuetenango
Cobán
L. de Izabal
Livingston
Puerto Barrios
Puerto Cortés
Tela
La Ceiba
San Pedro Sula
HONDURAS
Tegucigalpa
Totonicapán
Quetzaltenango
Mazatenango
San Marcos
Sololá
Antigua
GUATEMALA
Escuintla
Jalapa
Zacapa
Chiquimula
Santa Ana
Ahuachapán
SAN SALVADOR
EL SALVADOR
Cojutepeque
Zacatecoluca
Usulután
San Miguel
Golfo de Fonseca
Choluteca
C. Camarón
Laguna Caratasca
C. Falso
C. Gracias á Dios
Mosquitia
Cayos Miskitos (Nicaragua)
Pta. Gorda
Puerto Cabezas
NICARAGUA
Estelí
Matagalpa
Chinandega
León
MANAGUA
Masaya
Granada
Diriamba
Boaco
Juigalpa
Lago de Nicaragua
Bluefields
Cord. de Yolaina
Bahía de San Juan del Norte
San Juan del Norte
I. de Providencia (Colombia)
Cayos Roncador (U.S.A. & Colombia)
I. de San Andrés (Colombia)
Cayos de Albuquerque (Colombia)
Islas del Maiz (Nicaragua, U.S.A.)
Golfo de Papagayo
COSTA RICA
Puntarenas
Alajuela
San José
Cartago
Limón
Pen. de Nicoya
Golfo de Nicoya
Bahía de Coronado
Pen. de Osa
Golfo Dulce
Puerto Armuelles
David
Colón
PANAMÁ
Archipiélago de San Blas
Golfo de Panamá
Arch. de las Perlas
Golfo de Chiriquí
Pen. de Azuero
Golfo del Darién
CARTAGENA
Monteria
Projection: Bi-polar oblique Conical Orthomorphic

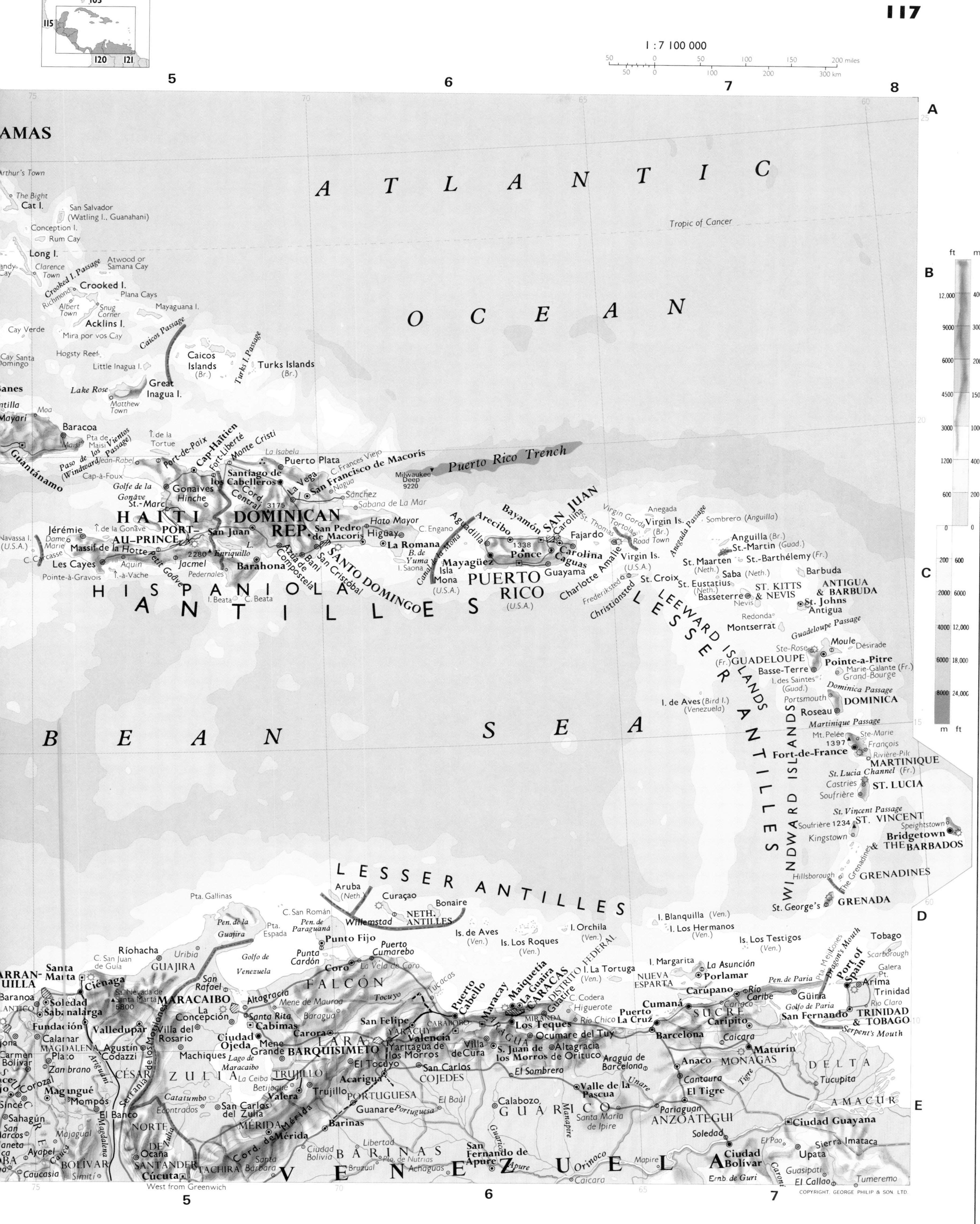
1 : 7 100 000
ATLANTIC OCEAN
CARIBBEAN SEA
Tropic of Cancer
Puerto Rico Trench
HAITI
DOMINICAN REP.
HISPANIOLA
ANTILLES
PUERTO RICO (U.S.A.)
LEEWARD ISLANDS
LESSER ANTILLES
WINDWARD ISLANDS
SAN JUAN
PORT-AU-PRINCE
SANTO DOMINGO
CARACAS
MARACAIBO
BARQUISIMETO
VENEZUELA
GUADELOUPE
DOMINICA
MARTINIQUE
ST. LUCIA
ST. VINCENT & THE GRENADINES
BARBADOS
GRENADA
TRINIDAD & TOBAGO
ANTIGUA & BARBUDA
ST. KITTS & NEVIS
NETH. ANTILLES
West from Greenwich
COPYRIGHT. GEORGE PHILIP & SON. LTD.

1:31 100 000
200 0 200 400 600 800 miles
400 0 400 800 1200 km
Tropic of Cancer
Turks & Caicos Is.
Yucatan Channel
Cuba
Greater Antilles
Gulf of Campeche
Yucatán Peninsula
Hispaniola
9200
Puerto Rico
NORTH ATLANTIC OCEAN
Jamaica
Isthmus of Tehuantepec
G. de Honduras
Lesser Antilles
Guadeloupe
Dominica
Martinique
St. Lucia
Barbados
St. Vincent
Grenada
Tobago
Trinidad
C. Gracias a Dios
Caribbean Sea
Guatemala Trench
Coco
L. Nicaragua
C. de la Aguja
5800
Sierra Nevada de Santa Marta
L. Maracaibo
I. Margarita
Panama Canal
G. of Darién
Orinoco
Llanos
Meta
Gulf of Panamá
Cordillera Occidental
Cordillera Central
Cordillera Oriental
Magdalena
Cord. de Mérida
Guiana Highlands
2810
Mt. Roraima
Sierra Pacaraima
Essequibo
Courantyne
Serra Tumucumaque
C. Orange
Guaviare
Branco
C. de San Francisco
Caquetá
Negro
Equator
Cotopaxi 6897
Chimborazo 6267
Japurá
Marajó I.
Amazon
Putumayo
Galapagos Is.
Napo
G. of Guayaquil
Marañón
Pta. Pariñas
Pta. Negra
Juruá
Ucayali
Selvas
Purus
Madeira
Tapajós
Xingu
Tocantins
Parnaíba
C. de São Roque
Aripuanã
Roosevelt
Teles Pires
Huascarán 6768
Plat. of Borborema
São Francisco
Araguaia
Chile Peru Trench
Madre de Dios
Arinos
Guaporé
Brazilian Highlands
Plateau of Mato Grosso
Chincha Alta
L. Titicaca
Nevada Ancohuma 6550
Mamoré
Bolivian Plateau
L. de Poopó
PACIFIC OCEAN
Abrolhos Bank
Gran Chaco
Paraguay
Paraná
Serra da Mantiqueira
2890
Pico da Bandeira
Pilcomayo
C. Frio
8050
Tropic of Capricorn
Atacama Desert
Andes
Cerro Ojos del Salado 6863
Iguaçu Falls
San Félix
San Ambrosio
Uruguay
Serra do Mar
Salado
Salinas Grandes
Entre Rios
L. Mar Chiquita
Sierra de Córdoba
Mt. Aconcagua 6960
L. dos Patos
Arch. de Juan Fernández
Pampas
Río de la Plata
SOUTH ATLANTIC OCEAN
Colorado
Bahía Blanca
Negro
Patagonia
G. San Matías
40
Valdés Peninsula
Chile Rise
Chiloé I.
Chubut
Argentine Basin
Chonos Archipelago
Mte. San Valentín 4058
Taitao Peninsula
Gulf of San Jorge
Gulf of Penas
6212
Wellington I.
Falkland Is.
West Falkland
East Falkland
Madre de Dios I.
Magellan's Str.
Santa Inés I.
Tierra del Fuego
Staten I.
South Georgia
Canal Cockburn
Canal Beagle
C. Horn
West from Greenwich
Projection: Lambert's Azimuthal Equal Area
CARTOGRAPHY BY PHILIP'S. COPYRIGHT REED INTERNATIONAL BOOKS LTD
ft m
12000 4000
9000 3000
6000 2000
3000 1000
1500 500
600 200
0 0
200 600
1000 3000
2000 6000
4000 12000
6000 18000
8000 24000
m ft

1 : 31 100 000
NORTH ATLANTIC OCEAN
PACIFIC OCEAN
SOUTH ATLANTIC OCEAN
Caribbean Sea
MEXICO
CUBA
Havana
BAHAMAS
Turks & Caicos Is. (U.K.)
HAITI
Port-au-Prince
DOMINICAN REP.
JAMAICA
Kingston
Virgin Is. (U.K.)
San Juan
PUERTO RICO (U.S.A.)
BELIZE
GUATEMALA
Guatemala
HONDURAS
Tegucigalpa
San Salvador
EL SALVADOR
NICARAGUA
Managua
COSTA RICA
San José
PANAMA
Panamá
COLOMBIA
Bogotá
VENEZUELA
Caracas
GUYANA
Georgetown
SURINAM
Paramaribo
FRENCH GUIANA
Cayenne
ECUADOR
Quito
Galapagos Is. (Ecuador)
PERU
LIMA
BOLIVIA
La Paz
BRAZIL
Brasília
PARAGUAY
Asunción
URUGUAY
Montevideo
ARGENTINA
BUENOS AIRES
CHILE
SANTIAGO
FALKLAND IS. (U.K.)
Stanley
South Georgia (U.K.)
Tierra del Fuego
C. Horn
Tropic of Cancer
Equator
Tropic of Capricorn
Projection: Lambert's Azimuthal Equal Area
LIMA Capital Cities
West from Greenwich
CARTOGRAPHY BY PHILIP'S. COPYRIGHT REED INTERNATIONAL BOOKS LTD

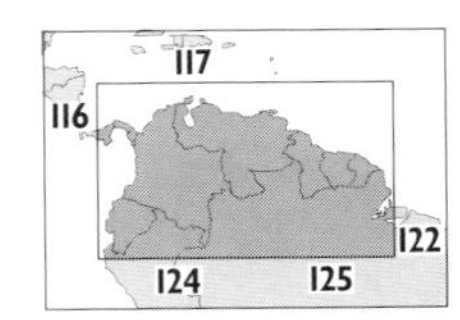

Projection: Lambert's Equivalent Azimuthal

1 : 7 100 000
50 0 50 100 150 200 miles
50 0 100 200 300 km
5
6
7
A
B
C
D
ATLANTIC OCEAN
GRENADA
St. George's
La Blanquilla (Ven.)
Los Hermanos (Ven.)
Is. Los Testigos (Ven.)
NUEVA ESPARTA
Margarita
I. La Tortuga (Ven.)
La Asunción
Porlamar
I. Coche
Carúpano
Pen. de Paria
Güiria
Tobago
Scarborough
Port of Spain
Arima
TRINIDAD AND TOBAGO
Trinidad
San Fernando
Galeota Point
Serpent's Mouth Boca de la Sierpe
Golfo de Paria
Pen. de Araya
Cumaná
Puerto La Cruz
Barcelona
SUCRE
Caripito
Maturín
Aragua de Barcelona
Anaco
Cantaura
MONAGAS
Zaraza
ANZOÁTEGUI
El Tigre
Pariaguán
Tucupita
DELTA AMACURO
Boca Grande
I. Corocoro
Orinoco
Ciudad Guayana
Pto. Ordaz
Soledad
Ciudad Bolívar
Upata
El Palmar
El Callao
Tumeremo
Embalse de Guri
El Dorado
Serranía Turagua
Angel Falls
2560
La Gran Sabana
Mt. Roraima 2772
Santa Elena
Sierra Pacaraima
Sa. Tepequem
Boa Vista
Serra do Apiaú
Serra do Mucajaí
Caracaraí
RORAIMA
Serra Tabatinga
Morawhanna
Mabaruma
BARIMA-WAINI
POMEROON-SUPERNAAM
ESSEQUIBO ISLANDS-WEST DEMERARA
Georgetown
DEMERARA-MAHAICA
MAHAICA-BERBICE
New Amsterdam
Port Mourant
CUYUNI-MAZARUNI
GUYANA
Bartica
Linden
(Mackenzie)
UPPER DEMERARA-BERBICE
Kaieteur Falls
POTARO-SIPARUNI
Pakaraima Mts.
Lethem
UPPER TAKUTU-UPPER ESSEQUIBO
EAST BERBICE-CORENTYNE
Kamoa Mts.
Serra Acaraí
734
Nieuw Nickerie
Paramaribo
CORONIE
Nieuw Amsterdam
Moengo
Albina
COMMEWIJNE
Brokopondo
SARAMACCA
Prof. Dr. Ir. W. J. Van Blommestein Meer
BROKOPONDO
SURINAM
NICKERIE
Wilhelmina Geb.
Julianatop 1280
MAROWIJNE
St. Laurent
Mana
I. du Diable
Iles du Salut
Kourou
Cayenne
FRENCH GUIANA
CAYENNE
INNINI
Saül
Maripasoula
Cabo Orange
Oiapoque
Serra Tumucumaque
690
AMAPÁ
Serra do Navio
Macapá
Ilha de Marajó
Almeirim
Prainha
Pôrto de Moz
Óbidos
Alenquer
Monte Alegre
Santarém
Parintins
MANAUS
BRAZIL
PARÁ
AMAZONAS
Amazonas
Altamira
Xingu
Tapajós
Madeira
Negro
Branco
Barcelos
Tefé
Coari
Itaituba
West from Greenwich
65
60
55
50
COPYRIGHT. GEORGE PHILIP & SON. LTD.

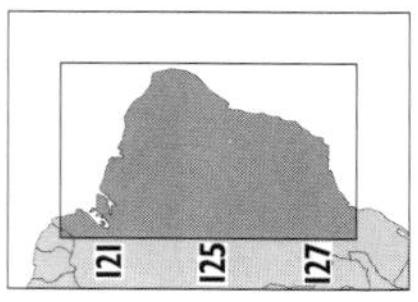

ATLANTIC OCEAN

AMAPÁ

PARÁ

MARANHÃO

CEARÁ

PIAUÍ

RIO GRANDE DO NORTE

PARAÍBA

PERNAMBUCO

ALAGOAS

TOCANTINS

BRAZIL

FORTALEZA (Ceará)

NATAL

João Pessoa (Paraíba)

RECIFE (Pernambuco)

MACEIÓ

BELÉM (Pará)

SÃO LUÍS

Teresina

Macapá

Ilha de Marajó

1 : 7 100 000
50 0 50 100 150 200 miles
50 0 100 200 300 km
ATLANTIC OCEAN
ESPÍRITO SANTO
Tropic of Capricorn
West from Greenwich
COPYRIGHT, GEORGE PHILIP & SON, LTD
Projection: Lambert's Equivalent Azimuthal
BAHIA
MINAS GERAIS
GOIÁS
SÃO PAULO
RIO DE JANEIRO
PARANÁ
DISTRITO FEDERAL
BRASÍLIA
SALVADOR (Bahia)
BELO HORIZONTE
RIO DE JANEIRO
NITERÓI
SÃO PAULO
SANTO ANDRÉ
SANTOS
CAMPINAS
CURITIBA
GOIÂNIA
Vitória
CAMPOS
Serra Geral de Goiás
Serra do Roncador
ft m
6000 2000
4500 1500
3000 1000
1200 400
600 200
0 0
200 600
2000 6000
4000 12,000
m ft

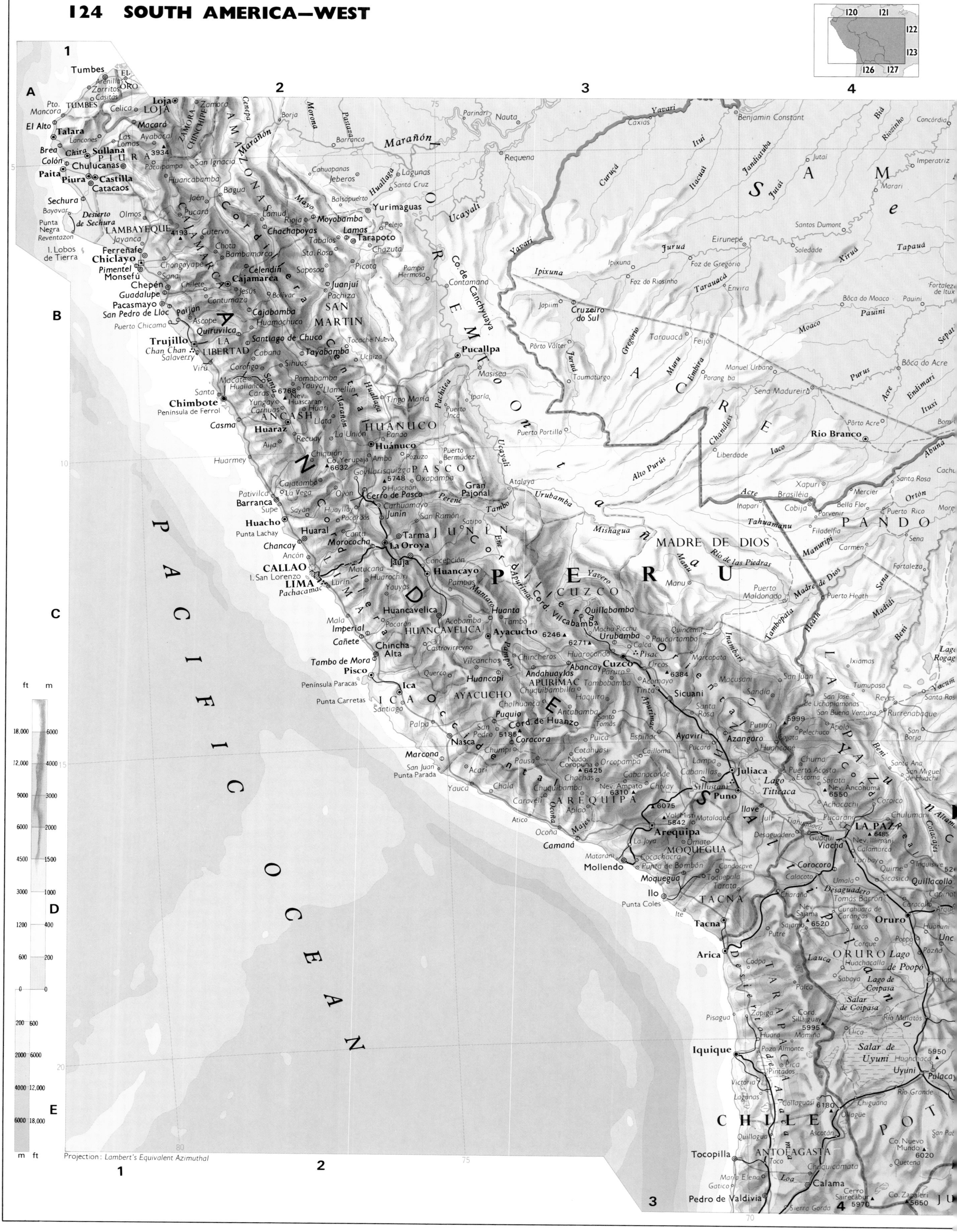
120
121
122
123
126
127
PACIFIC OCEAN
PERU
CHILE
A N D E S
Cordillera Central
Cordillera Occidental
Cordillera Oriental
A M A Z O N A S
L O R E T O
S A N M A R T I N
LA LIBERTAD
A N C A S H
H U Á N U C O
P A S C O
J U N Í N
L I M A
HUANCAVELICA
AYACUCHO
APURÍMAC
C U Z C O
MADRE DE DIOS
P U N O
A R E Q U I P A
MOQUEGUA
T A C N A
I C A
CAJAMARCA
LAMBAYEQUE
P I U R A
TUMBES
LOJA
ZAMORA CHINCHIPE
EL ORO
A C R E
P A N D O
A M A Z O N A S
ORURO
LA PAZ
TARAPACÁ
ANTOFAGASTA
POTOSÍ
Lago Titicaca
Lago de Poopó
Salar de Uyuni
Salar de Coipasa
Desierto de Sechura
Desierto de Atacama
Tumbes
Talara
Sullana
Paita
Piura
Castilla
Catacaos
Chulucanas
Sechura
Chiclayo
Ferreñafe
Pimentel
Monsefú
Chepén
Guadalupe
Pacasmayo
San Pedro de Lloc
Trujillo
Chan Chan
Salaverry
Chimbote
Casma
Huaraz
Huarmey
Barranca
Huacho
Huaral
Chancay
Ancón
CALLAO
LIMA
I. San Lorenzo
Pachacamac
Cañete
Chincha Alta
Pisco
Ica
Nasca
Marcona
Camaná
Mollendo
Ilo
Moquegua
Arequipa
Tacna
Arica
Iquique
Tocopilla
Calama
Pedro de Valdivia
Cajamarca
Chachapoyas
Moyobamba
Tarapoto
Yurimaguas
Pucallpa
Huánuco
Tingo María
Cerro de Pasco
Junín
Tarma
La Oroya
Jauja
Huancayo
Huancavelica
Ayacucho
Huanta
Andahuaylas
Abancay
Cuzco
Urubamba
Quillabamba
Machu Picchu
Sicuani
Juliaca
Puno
Azángaro
Ayaviri
Ilave
Puerto Maldonado
Rio Branco
Cruzeiro do Sul
Benjamin Constant
Requena
Nauta
Borja
Jaén
Bagua
Oruro
Uyuni
Viacha
Quillacollo
Marañón
Huallaga
Ucayali
Urubamba
Purus
Juruá
Yavari
Madre de Dios
Beni
Mamoré
Nev. Huascarán 6768
Co. Yerupajá 6632
Nev. Ampato 6310
Nudo Coropuna 6425
Vol. Misti 5842
Nev. Ancohuma 6550
Nev. Illimani 6485
Nev. Sajama 6520
Co. Nuevo Mundo 6020
ft
m
18,000
6000
12,000
4000
9000
3000
2000
4500
1500
3000
1000
1200
400
600
200
0
200
600
2000
6000
4000
12,000
6000
18,000
Projection: Lambert's Equivalent Azimuthal
1
2
3
4
A
B
C
D
E
5
10
15
20
75
80
70

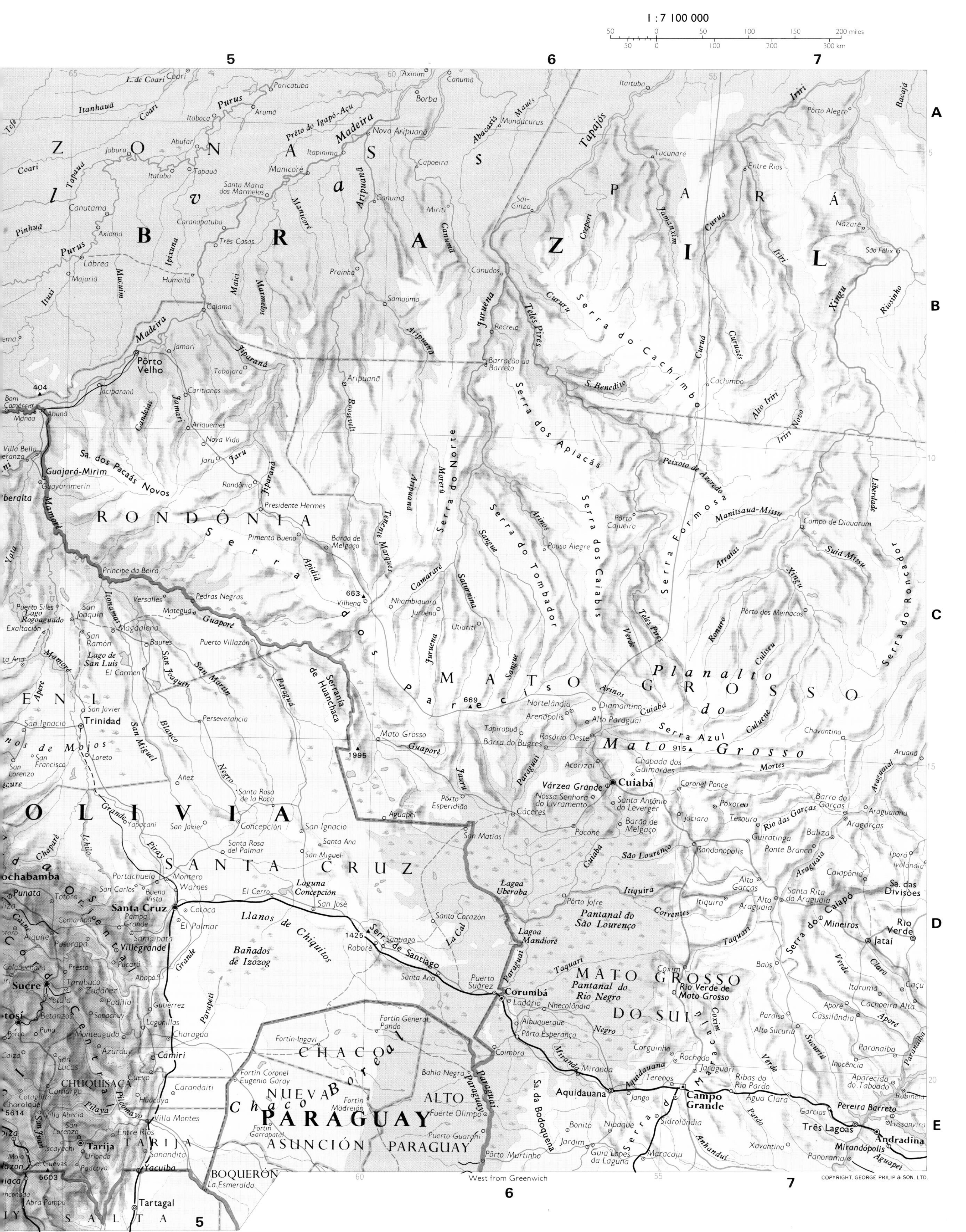
1 : 7 100 000
50 0 50 100 150 200 miles
50 0 100 200 300 km
5
6
7
A
B
C
D
E
BRAZIL
AMAZONAS
PARÁ
RONDÔNIA
MATO GROSSO
MATO GROSSO DO SUL
BOLIVIA
SANTA CRUZ
BENI
CHUQUISACA
TARIJA
SALTA
PARAGUAY
NUEVA ASUNCIÓN
ALTO PARAGUAY
BOQUERÓN
CHACO
Chaco Boreal
Planalto do Mato Grosso
Serra dos Parecis
Serra do Cachimbo
Serra dos Apiacás
Serra do Tombador
Serra dos Caiabis
Serra Formosa
Serra do Norte
Serra Azul
Serra do Roncador
Serra de Huanchaca
Serranía de Huanchaca
Serra de Santiago
Llanos de Chiquitos
Bañados de Izozog
Pantanal do São Lourenço
Pantanal do Rio Negro
Sa. dos Pacaás Novos
Sa. da Bodoquena
Serra de Maracaju
Serra do Caiapó
Sa. das Divisões
Madeira
Purus
Tapajós
Xingu
Iriri
Juruena
Teles Pires
Aripuanã
Guaporé
Mamoré
Paraguai
Araguaia
Pôrto Velho
Guajará-Mirim
Trinidad
Santa Cruz
Sucre
Tarija
Cuiabá
Várzea Grande
Corumbá
Campo Grande
Aquidauana
Camiri
Yacuiba
Tartagal
Humaitá
Manicoré
Borba
Novo Aripuanã
Vilhena
Cáceres
Rondonópolis
Jataí
Rio Verde
Três Lagoas
Andradina
Pereira Barreto
Coxim
Rio Verde de Mato Grosso
Diamantino
Rosário Oeste
Barra do Bugres
Pôrto Esperidião
Mato Grosso
Pimenta Bueno
Presidente Hermes
Ariquemes
Principe da Beira
Pedras Negras
Puerto Villazón
San Ignacio
Concepción
San José
Roboré
Puerto Suárez
Villamontes
Villa Montes
Lagoa Uberaba
Lagoa Mandioré
Laguna Concepción
Nossa Senhora do Livramento
Santo Antônio do Leverger
Barão de Melgaço
Chapada dos Guimarães
Cachimbo
Jacareacanga
Itaituba
Pôrto Alegre
São Félix
1995
1425
915
669
663
404
5614
5603
West from Greenwich
COPYRIGHT. GEORGE PHILIP & SON. LTD.

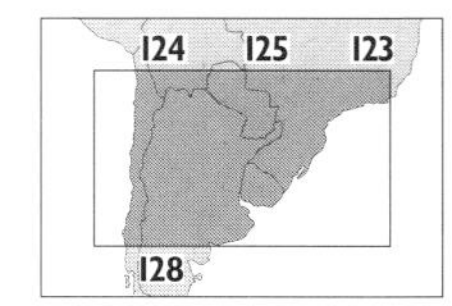

1 2 3 4

A B C D

PACIFIC OCEAN

BOLIVIA
PARAGUAY
ARGENTINA
CHILE
URUGUAY

ANDES
Gran Chaco

Iquique
TARAPACÁ
Salar de Uyuni
Uyuni
Pulacayo
POTOSÍ
Tupiza
Tarija
TARIJA
Villazón
La Quiaca
Tocopilla
Calama
Pedro de Valdivia
Mejillones
Antofagasta
ANTOFAGASTA
Salar de Atacama
San Pedro de Atacama
Desierto de Atacama
Cordillera Domeyko
JUJUY
S. Salvador de Jujuy
Salta
SALTA
Tartagal
Yacuiba
San Ramón de la Nueva Orán
Tabacal
Taltal
Chañaral
Copiapó
ATACAMA
CATAMARCA
Catamarca
TUCUMÁN
San Miguel de Tucumán
Santiago del Estero
SANTIAGO DEL ESTERO
Vallenar
La Serena
Coquimbo
COQUIMBO
Ovalle
La Rioja
LA RIOJA
Salinas Grandes
SAN JUAN
San Juan
Illapel
Córdoba
CÓRDOBA
Valparaíso
Viña del Mar
SANTIAGO
Los Andes
Aconcagua 6960
Mendoza
MENDOZA
San Luis
SAN LUIS
Rancagua
O'HIGGINS
San Rafael
Curicó
Talca
MAULE
Linares
Cauquenes
Chillán
Concepción
Talcahuano
Lota
BÍO-BÍO
Los Angeles
NEUQUÉN
LA PAMPA
Santa Rosa
General Acha
BUENOS AIRES
Bahía Blanca
Mar del Plata
Tandil
Olavarría
Azul
Necochea
Tres Arroyos
La Plata
BUENOS AIRES
Rosario
Santa Fe
SANTA FE
Paraná
ENTRE RÍOS
CORRIENTES
Corrientes
Resistencia
CHACO
FORMOSA
Formosa
ASUNCIÓN
Asunción
PRESIDENTE HAYES
BOQUERÓN
ALTO PARAGUAY
NUEVA ASUNCIÓN
Concepción
Paysandú
Salto
Concordia
Río Cuarto
Villa María
Venado Tuerto
Pergamino
Junín
San Nicolás de los Arroyos

Pilcomayo
Bermejo
Salado
Paraná
Uruguay
Colorado

ft m

18 000 6000
12 000 4000
9000 3000
6000 2000
4500 1500
3000 1000
1200 400
600 200
0 0
200 600
2000 6000
4000 12 000
6000 18 000

m ft

Projection: Lambert's Equivalent Azimuthal

70 65 60

1 2 3 4

1 : 7 100 000
200 miles
300 km
5
6
7
A
B
C
D
BELO HORIZONTE
Vitória
Vila Velha
Três Lagoas
Andradina
Araçatuba
S. José do Rio Prêto
Ribeirão Prêto
Campo Belo
São João del Rei
Juiz de Fora
CAMPOS
RIO DE JANEIRO
Petrópolis
DUQUE DE CAXIAS
SÃO GONÇALO
NITERÓI
Nova Iguaçu
Volta Redonda
Barra Mansa
Taubaté
S. J. dos Campos
Mogi das Cruzes
Jundiaí
CAMPINAS
Piracicaba
Sorocaba
SÃO PAULO
SANTO ANDRÉ
São Bernardo del Campo
São Vicente
SANTOS
Tropic of Capricorn
Bauru
Marília
Presidente Prudente
Londrina
Maringá
Apucarana
Umuarama
PARANÁ
BRAZIL
Ponta Grossa
Guarapuava
CURITIBA
Paranaguá
Foz do Iguaçu
Ciudad del Este
Joinvile
Blumenau
Itajaí
SANTA CATARINA
Florianópolis
Lajes
Passo Fundo
Santo Ângelo
Tubarão
Criciúma
Caxias do Sul
RIO GRANDE DO SUL
Santa Maria
Nôvo Hamburgo
São Leopoldo
PÔRTO ALEGRE
Pelotas
Lagoa dos Patos
Rio Grande
Bagé
Lagoa Mirim
Melo
Rocha
Maldonado
MONTEVIDEO
URUGUAY
ATLANTIC OCEAN
5304
West from Greenwich
COPYRIGHT GEORGE PHILIP & SON LTD

126 127
1 : 7 100 000
50 0 50 100 150 200 miles
50 0 100 200 300 km
LA PAMPA
BUENOS AIRES
NEUQUÉN
RÍO NEGRO
CHUBUT
SANTA CRUZ
ARAUCANIA
LOS LAGOS
ARGENTINA
CHILE
MAGALLANES
AISÉN
PATAGONIA
Cordillera de los Andes
TIERRA DEL FUEGO
SOUTH ATLANTIC OCEAN
PACIFIC OCEAN
FALKLAND ISLANDS
(ISLAS MALVINAS)
West Falkland
East Falkland
Stanley
Mt. Adam
Mt. Usborne
Jason Is.
Pebble I.
C. Dolphin
King George B.
Queen Charlotte B.
Weddell I.
C. Meredith
Falkland Sound
Port Darwin
Beauchêne I.
Golfo San Matías
Golfo San Jorge
Bahía Grande
Strait of Magellan
Estrecho de Magallanes
Isla Grande de Tierra del Fuego
Archipiélago de los Chonos
Isla de Chiloé
Golfo de Penas
Península de Taitao
Arch. Reina Adelaida
Bahía Blanca
Tres Arroyos
Necochea
Coronel Pringles
Coronel Dorrego
Balcarce
Juárez
Lobería
Quequén
Punta Alta
Neuquén
Cipolletti
Gral. Roca
Zapala
Choele Choel
Viedma
Carmen de Patagones
San Antonio Oeste
San Carlos de Bariloche
Temuco
Valdivia
Osorno
Puerto Montt
Puerto Varas
La Unión
Angol
Victoria
Traiguén
Lautaro
Pitrufquén
Mulchén
Ancud
Castro
Puerto Madryn
Rawson
Trelew
Esquel
Puerto Aisén
Coihaique
Comodoro Rivadavia
Caleta Olivia
Puerto Deseado
San Julián
Santa Cruz
Río Gallegos
Puerto Natales
Punta Arenas
Porvenir
Río Grande
Ushuaia
Península Valdés
Meseta de Somuncurá
Meseta de Montemayor
Altiplanicie Central
L. Nahuel Huapi
L. Buenos Aires
L. San Martín
L. Viedma
Lago Argentino
L. Musters
L. Colhué Huapi
L. Fagnano
Mt. San Valentín 4058
Mte. Fitzroy 3375
Mte. Darwin 2469
Mte. Tronador
Vol. Osorno 2660
I. de los Estados (Staten I.)
I. Navarino
I. Hoste
Is. Wollaston
Cabo de Hornos (Cape Horn)
Islas Diego Ramírez
Canal Beagle
Est. de Le Maire
Projection: Lambert's Equivalent Azimuthal
West from Greenwich
COPYRIGHT, GEORGE PHILIP & SON, LTD.

INDEX

The index contains the names of all the principal places and features shown on the World Maps. Each name is followed by an additional entry in italics giving the country or region within which it is located. The alphabetical order of names composed of two or more words is governed primarily by the first word and then by the second. This is an example of the rule:

Mīr Kūh, *Iran*	**65**	**E8**
Mīr Shahdād, *Iran*	**65**	**E8**
Miraj, *India*	**60**	**L9**
Miram Shah, *Pakistan*	**62**	**C4**
Miramar, *Mozam.*	**85**	**C6**

Physical features composed of a proper name (Erie) and a description (Lake) are positioned alphabetically by the proper name. The description is positioned after the proper name and is usually abbreviated:

Erie, L., *N. Amer.* **106** **D3**

Where a description forms part of a settlement or administrative name however, it is always written in full and put in its true alphabetic position:

Mount Morris, *U.S.A.* **106** **D7**

Names beginning with M' and Mc are indexed as if they were spelt Mac. Names beginning St. are alphabetised under Saint, but Sankt, Sint, Sant', Santa and San are all spelt in full and are alphabetised accordingly. If the same place name occurs two or more times in the index and all are in the same country, each is followed by the name of the administrative subdivision in which it is located. The names are placed in the alphabetical order of the subdivisions. For example:

Jackson, *Ky., U.S.A.*	**104**	**G4**
Jackson, *Mich., U.S.A.*	**104**	**D3**
Jackson, *Minn., U.S.A.*	**108**	**D7**

The number in bold type which follows each name in the index refers to the number of the map page where that feature or place will be found. This is usually the largest scale at which the place or feature appears. The letter and figure which are in bold type immediately after the page number give the grid square on the map page, within which the feature is situated. The letter represents the latitude and the figure the longitude.

In some cases the feature itself may fall within the specified square, while the name is outside. This is usually the case only with features which are larger than a grid square. Rivers are indexed to their mouths or confluences, and carry the symbol → after their names. A solid square ■ follows the name of a country while, an open square □ refers to a first order administrative area.

ABBREVIATIONS USED IN THE INDEX

A.C.T. — Australian Capital Territory
Afghan. — Afghanistan
Ala. — Alabama
Alta. — Alberta
Amer. — America(n)
Arch. — Archipelago
Ariz. — Arizona
Ark. — Arkansas
Atl. Oc. — Atlantic Ocean
B. — Baie, Bahía, Bay, Bucht, Bugt
B.C. — British Columbia
Bangla. — Bangladesh
Barr. — Barrage
Bos.-H. — Bosnia-Herzegovina
C. — Cabo, Cap, Cape, Coast
C.A.R. — Central African Republic
C. Prov. — Cape Province
Calif. — California
Cent. — Central
Chan. — Channel
Colo. — Colorado
Conn. — Connecticut
Cord. — Cordillera
Cr. — Creek
Czech. — Czech Republic
D.C. — District of Columbia
Del. — Delaware
Dep. — Dependency
Des. — Desert
Dist. — District
Dj. — Djebel
Domin. — Dominica
Dom. Rep. — Dominican Republic
E. — East
El Salv. — El Salvador
Eq. Guin. — Equatorial Guinea
Fla. — Florida
Falk. Is. — Falkland Is.
G. — Golfe, Golfo, Gulf, Guba, Gebel
Ga. — Georgia
Gt. — Great, Greater
Guinea-Biss. — Guinea-Bissau
H.K. — Hong Kong
H.P. — Himachal Pradesh
Hants. — Hampshire
Harb. — Harbor, Harbour
Hd. — Head
Hts. — Heights
I.(s). — Île, Ilha, Insel, Isla, Island, Isle
Ill. — Illinois
Ind. — Indiana
Ind. Oc. — Indian Ocean
Ivory C. — Ivory Coast
J. — Jabal, Jebel, Jazira
Junc. — Junction
K. — Kap, Kapp
Kans. — Kansas
Kep. — Kepulauan
Ky. — Kentucky
L. — Lac, Lacul, Lago, Lagoa, Lake, Limni, Loch, Lough
La. — Louisiana
Liech. — Liechtenstein
Lux. — Luxembourg
Mad. P. — Madhya Pradesh
Madag. — Madagascar
Man. — Manitoba
Mass. — Massachusetts
Md. — Maryland
Me. — Maine
Medit. S. — Mediterranean Sea
Mich. — Michigan
Minn. — Minnesota
Miss. — Mississippi
Mo. — Missouri
Mont. — Montana
Moza. — Mozambique
Mt.(e). — Mont, Monte, Monti, Montaña, Mountain
N. — Nord, Norte, North, Northern, Nouveau
N.B. — New Brunswick
N.C. — North Carolina
N. Cal. — New Caledonia
N. Dak. — North Dakota
N.H. — New Hampshire
N.I. — North Island
N.J. — New Jersey
N. Mex. — New Mexico
N.S. — Nova Scotia
N.S.W. — New South Wales
N.W.T. — North West Territory
N.Y. — New York
N.Z. — New Zealand
Nebr. — Nebraska
Neths. — Netherlands
Nev. — Nevada
Nfld. — Newfoundland
Nic. — Nicaragua
O. — Oued, Ouadi
Occ. — Occidentale
Okla. — Oklahoma
Ont. — Ontario
Or. — Orientale
Oreg. — Oregon
Os. — Ostrov
Oz. — Ozero
P. — Pass, Passo, Pasul, Pulau
P.E.I. — Prince Edward Island
Pa. — Pennsylvania
Pac. Oc. — Pacific Ocean
Papua N.G. — Papua New Guinea
Pass. — Passage
Pen. — Peninsula, Péninsule
Phil. — Philippines
Pk. — Park, Peak
Plat. — Plateau
P-ov. — Poluostrov
Prov. — Province, Provincial
Pt. — Point
Pta. — Ponta, Punta
Pte. — Pointe
Qué. — Québec
Queens. — Queensland
R. — Rio, River
R.I. — Rhode Island
Ra.(s). — Range(s)
Raj. — Rajasthan
Reg. — Region
Rep. — Republic
Res. — Reserve, Reservoir
S. — San, South, Sea
Si. Arabia — Saudi Arabia
S.C. — South Carolina
S. Dak. — South Dakota
S.I. — South Island
S. Leone — Sierra Leone
Sa. — Serra, Sierra
Sask. — Saskatchewan
Scot. — Scotland
Sd. — Sound
Sev. — Severnaya
Sib. — Siberia
Sprs. — Springs
St. — Saint, Sankt, Sint
Sta. — Santa, Station
Ste. — Sainte
Sto. — Santo
Str. — Strait, Stretto
Switz. — Switzerland
Tas. — Tasmania
Tenn. — Tennessee
Tex. — Texas
Tg. — Tanjung
Trin. & Tob. — Trinidad & Tobago
U.A.E. — United Arab Emirates
U.K. — United Kingdom
U.S.A. — United States of America
Ut. P. — Uttar Pradesh
Va. — Virginia
Vdkhr. — Vodokhranilishche
Vf. — Vîrful
Vic. — Victoria
Vol. — Volcano
Vt. — Vermont
W. — Wadi, West
W. Va. — West Virginia
Wash. — Washington
Wis. — Wisconsin
Wlkp. — Wielkopolski
Wyo. — Wyoming
Yorks. — Yorkshire
Yug. — Yugoslavia

A

A Coruña = La Coruña, *Spain* 30 B2
Aachen, *Germany* 18 E2
Aadorf, *Switz.* 23 B7
Aalborg = Ålborg, *Denmark* 11 G3
Aalen, *Germany* 19 G6
A'âli en Nîl □, *Sudan* 77 F3
Aalsmeer, *Neths.* 16 D5
Aalst, *Belgium* 17 G4
Aalst, *Neths.* 17 F6
Aalten, *Neths.* 16 E9
Aalter, *Belgium* 17 F2
Äänekoski, *Finland* 9 E21
Aarau, *Switz.* 22 B6
Aarberg, *Switz.* 22 B4
Aardenburg, *Belgium* 17 F2
Aare →, *Switz.* 22 A6
Aargau □, *Switz.* 22 B6
Aarhus = Århus, *Denmark* 11 H4
Aarle, *Neths.* 17 E7
Aarschot, *Belgium* 17 G5
Aarsele, *Belgium* 17 G2
Aartrijke, *Belgium* 17 F2
Aarwangen, *Switz.* 22 B5
Aba, *China* 52 A3
Aba, *Nigeria* 79 D6
Aba, *Zaïre* 82 B3
Âbâ, Jazîrat, *Sudan* 77 E3
Abacaxis →, *Brazil* 121 D6
Ābādān, *Iran* 65 D6
Abade, *Ethiopia* 77 F4
Ābādeh, *Iran* 65 D7
Abadin, *Spain* 30 B3
Abadla, *Algeria* 75 B4
Abaeté, *Brazil* 123 E2
Abaeté →, *Brazil* 123 E2
Abaetetuba, *Brazil* 122 B2
Abagnar Qi, *China* 50 C9
Abai, *Paraguay* 127 B4
Abak, *Nigeria* 79 E6
Abakaliki, *Nigeria* 79 D6
Abakan, *Russia* 45 D10
Abalemma, *Niger* 79 B6
Abana, *Turkey* 66 B6
Abancay, *Peru* 124 C3
Abanilla, *Spain* 29 G3
Abano Terme, *Italy* 33 C8
Abapó, *Bolivia* 125 D5
Abarán, *Spain* 29 G3
Abariringa, *Kiribati* 92 H10
Abarqū, *Iran* 65 D7
Abashiri, *Japan* 48 B12
Abashiri-Wan, *Japan* 48 B12
Abaújszántó, *Hungary* 21 G11
Abay, *Kazakstan* 44 E8
Abaya, L., *Ethiopia* 77 F4
Abaza, *Russia* 44 D10
Abbadia San Salvatore, *Italy* 33 F8
'Abbāsābād, *Iran* 65 C8
Abbay = Nîl el Azraq →, *Sudan* 77 D3
Abbaye, Pt., *U.S.A.* 104 B1
Abbé, L., *Ethiopia* 77 E5
Abbeville, *France* 25 B8
Abbeville, *La., U.S.A.* 109 K8
Abbeville, *S.C., U.S.A.* 105 H4
Abbiategrasso, *Italy* 32 C5
Abbieglassie, *Australia* 91 D4
Abbot Ice Shelf, *Antarctica* 5 D16
Abbotsford, *Canada* 100 D4
Abbotsford, *U.S.A.* 108 C9
Abbottabad, *Pakistan* 62 B5
Abcoude, *Neths.* 16 D5
Abd al Kūrī, *Ind. Oc.* 68 E5
Ābdar, *Iran* 65 D7
'Abdolābād, *Iran* 65 C8
Abéché, *Chad* 73 F9
Abejar, *Spain* 28 D2
Abekr, *Sudan* 77 E2
Abêlessa, *Algeria* 75 D5
Abengourou, *Ivory C.* 78 D4
Åbenrå, *Denmark* 11 J3
Abensberg, *Germany* 19 G7
Abeokuta, *Nigeria* 79 D5
Aber, *Uganda* 82 B3
Aberaeron, *U.K.* 13 E3
Aberayron = Aberaeron, *U.K.* 13 E3
Aberconwy & Colwyn □, *U.K.* 12 D4
Abercorn = Mbala, *Zambia* 83 D3
Abercorn, *Australia* 91 D5
Aberdare, *U.K.* 13 F4
Aberdare Ra., *Kenya* 82 C4
Aberdeen, *Australia* 91 E5
Aberdeen, *Canada* 101 C7
Aberdeen, *S. Africa* 84 E3
Aberdeen, *U.K.* 14 D6
Aberdeen, *Ala., U.S.A.* 105 J1
Aberdeen, *Idaho, U.S.A.* 110 E7
Aberdeen, *S. Dak., U.S.A.* 108 C5
Aberdeen, *Wash., U.S.A.* 112 D3
Aberdeenshire □, *U.K.* 14 D6
Aberdovey = Aberdyfi, *U.K.* 13 E3
Aberdyfi, *U.K.* 13 E3
Aberfeldy, *U.K.* 14 E5
Abergaria-a-Velha, *Portugal* 30 E2
Abergavenny, *U.K.* 13 F4
Abernathy, *U.S.A.* 109 J4
Abert, L., *U.S.A.* 110 E3
Aberystwyth, *U.K.* 13 E3
Abha, *Si. Arabia* 76 D5
Abhar, *Iran* 67 D13
Abhayapuri, *India* 63 F14
Abia □, *Nigeria* 79 D6
Abidiya, *Sudan* 76 D3
Abidjan, *Ivory C.* 78 D4
Abilene, *Kans., U.S.A.* 108 F6
Abilene, *Tex., U.S.A.* 109 J5
Abingdon, *U.K.* 13 F6
Abingdon, *Ill., U.S.A.* 108 E9
Abingdon, *Va., U.S.A.* 105 G5
Abington Reef, *Australia* 90 B4
Abitau →, *Canada* 101 B7
Abitau L., *Canada* 101 A7
Abitibi L., *Canada* 98 C4
Abiy Adi, *Ethiopia* 77 E4
Abkhaz Republic □ = Abkhazia □, *Georgia* 43 J5
Abkhazia □, *Georgia* 43 J5
Abkit, *Russia* 45 C16
Abminga, *Australia* 91 D1
Abnûb, *Egypt* 76 B3
Åbo = Turku, *Finland* 9 F20
Abocho, *Nigeria* 79 D6
Abohar, *India* 62 D6
Aboisso, *Ivory C.* 78 D4
Abomey, *Benin* 79 D5
Abondance, *France* 27 B10
Abong-Mbang, *Cameroon* 80 D2
Abonnema, *Nigeria* 79 E6
Abony, *Hungary* 21 H10
Aboso, *Ghana* 78 D4
Abou-Deïa, *Chad* 73 F8
Aboyne, *U.K.* 14 D6
Abra Pampa, *Argentina* 126 A2
Abrantes, *Portugal* 31 F2
Abraveses, *Portugal* 30 E3
Abreojos, Pta., *Mexico* 114 B2
Abreschviller, *France* 25 D14
Abri, *Esh Shamâliya, Sudan* 76 C3
Abri, *Janub Kordofân, Sudan* 77 E3
Abrolhos, Banka, *Brazil* 123 E4
Abruzzi □, *Italy* 33 F10
Absaroka Range, *U.S.A.* 110 D9
Abū al Khaṣīb, *Iraq* 65 D6
Abū 'Alī, *Si. Arabia* 65 E6
Abū 'Alī →, *Lebanon* 69 A4
Abu 'Arīsh, *Si. Arabia* 68 D3
Abû Ballas, *Egypt* 76 C2
Abu Deleiq, *Sudan* 77 D3
Abu Dhabi = Abū Ẓāby, *U.A.E.* 65 E7
Abû Dis, *Sudan* 76 D3
Abû Dom, *Sudan* 77 D3
Abū Du'ān, *Syria* 67 D8
Abu el Gairi, W. →, *Egypt* 69 F2
Abû Gabra, *Sudan* 77 E2
Abu Ga'da, W. →, *Egypt* 69 F1
Abû Gubeiha, *Sudan* 77 E3
Abu Habl, Khawr →, *Sudan* 77 E3
Abū Ḥadrīyah, *Si. Arabia* 65 E6
Abu Hamed, *Sudan* 76 D3
Abu Haraz, *An Nîl el Azraq, Sudan* 77 E3
Abû Haraz, *Esh Shamâliya, Sudan* 76 D3
Abû Higar, *Sudan* 77 E3
Abū Kamāl, *Syria* 67 E9
Abū Madd, Ra's, *Si. Arabia* 64 E3
Abu Matariq, *Sudan* 77 E2
Abu Qir, *Egypt* 76 H7
Abu Qireiya, *Egypt* 76 C4
Abu Qurqâs, *Egypt* 76 J7
Abu Ṣafāt, W. →, *Jordan* 69 E5
Abû Simbel, *Egypt* 76 C3
Abū Şukhayr, *Iraq* 67 G11
Abu Tig, *Egypt* 76 B3
Abu Tiga, *Sudan* 77 E3
Abû Zabad, *Sudan* 77 E2
Abū Ẓāby, *U.A.E.* 65 E7
Abū Zeydābād, *Iran* 65 C6
Abufari, *Brazil* 125 B5
Abuja, *Nigeria* 79 D6
Abukuma-Gawa →, *Japan* 48 E10
Abukuma-Sammyaku, *Japan* 48 F10
Abunã, *Brazil* 125 B4
Abunã →, *Brazil* 125 B4
Aburo, *Zaïre* 82 B3
Abut Hd., *N.Z.* 87 K3
Abwong, *Sudan* 77 F3
Åby, *Sweden* 11 F10
Aby, Lagune, *Ivory C.* 78 D4
Acacías, *Colombia* 120 C3
Acajutla, *El Salv.* 116 D2
Açailândia, *Brazil* 122 C2
Acámbaro, *Mexico* 114 C4
Acaponeta, *Mexico* 114 C3
Acapulco, *Mexico* 115 D5
Acarai, Serra, *Brazil* 121 C6
Acaraú, *Brazil* 122 B3
Acari, *Brazil* 122 C4
Acarí, *Peru* 124 D3
Acarigua, *Venezuela* 120 B4
Acatlán, *Mexico* 115 D5
Acayucan, *Mexico* 115 D6
Accéglio, *Italy* 32 D3
Accomac, *U.S.A.* 104 G8
Accous, *France* 26 E3
Accra, *Ghana* 79 D4
Accrington, *U.K.* 12 D5
Acebal, *Argentina* 126 C3
Aceh □, *Indonesia* 56 D1
Acerenza, *Italy* 35 B8
Acerra, *Italy* 35 B7
Aceuchal, *Spain* 31 G4
Achacachi, *Bolivia* 124 D4
Achaguas, *Venezuela* 120 B4
Achalpur, *India* 60 J10
Achao, *Chile* 128 B2
Achel, *Belgium* 17 F6
Acheng, *China* 51 B14
Achenkirch, *Austria* 19 H7
Achensee, *Austria* 19 H7
Acher, *India* 62 H5
Achern, *Germany* 19 G4
Achill, *Ireland* 15 C2
Achill Hd., *Ireland* 15 C1
Achill I., *Ireland* 15 C1
Achill Sd., *Ireland* 15 C2
Achim, *Germany* 18 B5
Achinsk, *Russia* 45 D10
Achol, *Sudan* 77 F3
Acıgöl, *Turkey* 66 D3
Acireale, *Italy* 35 E8
Ackerman, *U.S.A.* 109 J10
Acklins I., *Bahamas* 117 B5
Acme, *Canada* 100 C6
Acobamba, *Peru* 124 C3
Acomayo, *Peru* 124 C3
Aconcagua, Cerro, *Argentina* 126 C2
Aconquija, Mt., *Argentina* 126 B2
Acopiara, *Brazil* 122 C4
Açores, Is. dos = Azores, *Atl. Oc.* 70 C1
Acorizal, *Brazil* 125 D6
Acquapendente, *Italy* 33 F8
Acquasanta Terme, *Italy* 33 F10
Acquaviva delle Fonti, *Italy* 35 B9
Acqui Terme, *Italy* 32 D5
Acraman, L., *Australia* 91 E2
Acre = 'Akko, *Israel* 69 C4
Acre □, *Brazil* 124 B3
Acre →, *Brazil* 124 B4
Acri, *Italy* 35 C9
Acs, *Hungary* 21 H8
Acton, *Canada* 106 C4
Açu, *Brazil* 122 C4
Ad Dammām, *Si. Arabia* 65 E6
Ad Dawhah, *Qatar* 65 E6
Ad Dawr, *Iraq* 67 E10
Ad Dir'īyah, *Si. Arabia* 64 E5
Ad Dīwānīyah, *Iraq* 67 F11
Ad Dujayl, *Iraq* 67 F11
Ad Durūz, J., *Jordan* 69 C5
Ada, *Ghana* 79 D5
Ada, *Serbia, Yug.* 21 K10
Ada, *Minn., U.S.A.* 108 B6
Ada, *Okla., U.S.A.* 109 H6
Adaja →, *Spain* 30 D6
Ådalsliden, *Sweden* 10 A10
Adam, Mt., *Falk. Is.* 128 D4
Adamantina, *Brazil* 123 F1
Adamaoua, Massif de l', *Cameroon* 79 D7
Adamawa □, *Nigeria* 79 D7
Adamawa Highlands = Adamaoua, Massif de l', *Cameroon* 79 D7
Adamello, Mte., *Italy* 32 B7
Adami Tulu, *Ethiopia* 77 F4
Adaminaby, *Australia* 91 F4
Adams, *Mass., U.S.A.* 107 D11
Adams, *N.Y., U.S.A.* 107 C8
Adams, *Wis., U.S.A.* 108 D10
Adam's Bridge, *Sri Lanka* 60 Q11
Adams L., *Canada* 100 C5
Adams Mt., *U.S.A.* 112 D5
Adam's Peak, *Sri Lanka* 60 R12
Adamuz, *Spain* 31 G6
Adana, *Turkey* 66 D6
Adanero, *Spain* 30 E6
Adapazarı, *Turkey* 66 B4
Adarama, *Sudan* 77 D3
Adare, C., *Antarctica* 5 D11
Adaut, *Indonesia* 57 F8
Adavale, *Australia* 91 D3
Adda →, *Italy* 32 C6
Addis Ababa = Addis Abeba, *Ethiopia* 77 F4
Addis Abeba, *Ethiopia* 77 F4
Addis Alem, *Ethiopia* 77 F4
Addison, *U.S.A.* 106 D7
Addo, *S. Africa* 84 E4
Adebour, *Niger* 79 C7
Ādeh, *Iran* 64 B5
Adel, *U.S.A.* 105 K4
Adelaide, *Australia* 91 E2
Adelaide, *Bahamas* 116 A4
Adelaide, *S. Africa* 84 E4
Adelaide I., *Antarctica* 5 C17
Adelaide Pen., *Canada* 96 B10
Adelaide River, *Australia* 88 B5
Adelanto, *U.S.A.* 113 L9
Adelboden, *Switz.* 22 D5
Adele I., *Australia* 88 C3
Adélie, Terre, *Antarctica* 5 C10
Adélie Land = Adélie, Terre, *Antarctica* 5 C10
Ademuz, *Spain* 28 E3
Aden = Al 'Adan, *Yemen* 68 E4
Aden, G. of, *Asia* 68 E4
Adendorp, *S. Africa* 84 E3
Adh Dhayd, *U.A.E.* 65 E7
Adhoi, *India* 62 H4
Adi, *Indonesia* 57 E8
Adi Daro, *Ethiopia* 77 E4
Adi Keyih, *Eritrea* 77 E4
Adi Kwala, *Eritrea* 77 E4
Adi Ugri, *Eritrea* 77 E4
Adieu, C., *Australia* 89 F5
Adieu Pt., *Australia* 88 C3
Adigala, *Ethiopia* 77 E5
Adige →, *Italy* 33 C9
Adigrat, *Ethiopia* 77 E4
Adilabad, *India* 60 K11
Adilcevaz, *Turkey* 67 C10
Adin, *U.S.A.* 110 F3
Adin Khel, *Afghan.* 60 C6
Adinkerke, *Belgium* 17 F1
Adirondack Mts., *U.S.A.* 107 C10
Adıyaman, *Turkey* 67 D8
Adjim, *Tunisia* 75 B7
Adjohon, *Benin* 79 D5
Adjud, *Romania* 38 C10
Adjumani, *Uganda* 82 B3
Adlavik Is., *Canada* 99 B8
Adler, *Russia* 43 J4
Adliswil, *Switz.* 23 B7
Admer, *Algeria* 75 D6
Admer, Erg d', *Algeria* 75 D6
Admiralty G., *Australia* 88 B4
Admiralty I., *U.S.A.* 96 C6
Admiralty Inlet, *U.S.A.* 110 C2
Admiralty Is., *Papua N. G.* 92 H6
Ado, *Nigeria* 79 D5
Ado-Ekiti, *Nigeria* 79 D6
Adok, *Sudan* 77 F3
Adola, *Ethiopia* 77 E5
Adonara, *Indonesia* 57 F6
Adoni, *India* 60 M10
Adony, *Hungary* 21 H8
Adour →, *France* 26 E2
Adra, *India* 63 H12
Adra, *Spain* 29 J1
Adrano, *Italy* 35 E7
Adrar, *Algeria* 75 C4
Adré, *Chad* 73 F9
Adrī, *Libya* 75 C7
Ádria, *Italy* 33 C9
Adrian, *Mich., U.S.A.* 104 E3
Adrian, *Tex., U.S.A.* 109 H3
Adriatic Sea, *Medit. S.* 6 G9
Adua, *Indonesia* 57 E7
Adula, *Switz.* 23 D8
Adwa, *Ethiopia* 77 E4
Adygea □, *Russia* 43 H5
Adzhar Republic □ = Ajaria □, *Georgia* 43 K6
Adzopé, *Ivory C.* 78 D4
Ægean Sea, *Medit. S.* 39 L8
Aerhtai Shan, *Mongolia* 54 B4
Ærø, *Denmark* 11 K4
Ærøskøbing, *Denmark* 11 K4
Aesch, *Switz.* 22 B5
'Afak, *Iraq* 67 F11
Afándou, *Greece* 37 C10
Afarag, Erg, *Algeria* 75 D5
Affreville = Khemis Miliana, *Algeria* 75 A5
Afghanistan ■, *Asia* 60 C4
Afgoi, *Somali Rep.* 68 G3
Afikpo, *Nigeria* 79 D6
Aflou, *Algeria* 75 B5
Afogados da Ingàzeira, *Brazil* 122 C4
Afognak I., *U.S.A.* 96 C4
Afragola, *Italy* 35 B7
Afrera, *Ethiopia* 77 E5
'Afrīn, *Syria* 66 D7
Afşin, *Turkey* 66 C7
Afton, *U.S.A.* 107 D9
Aftout, *Algeria* 74 C4
Afuá, *Brazil* 121 D7
Afula, *Israel* 69 C4
Afyonkarahisar, *Turkey* 66 C4
Aga, *Egypt* 76 H7
Agadès = Agadez, *Niger* 79 B6
Agadez, *Niger* 79 B6
Agadir, *Morocco* 74 B3
Agaete, *Canary Is.* 36 F4
Agailás, *Mauritania* 74 D2
Agapa, *Russia* 45 B9
Agar, *India* 62 H7
Agaro, *Ethiopia* 77 F4
Agartala, *India* 61 H17
Agassiz, *Canada* 100 D4
Agats, *Indonesia* 57 F9
Agbélouvé, *Togo* 79 D5
Agboville, *Ivory C.* 78 D4
Ağcabädi, *Azerbaijan* 43 K8
Ağdam, *Azerbaijan* 43 L8
Ağdaş, *Azerbaijan* 43 K8
Agde, *France* 26 E7
Agde, C. d', *France* 26 E7
Agdz, *Morocco* 74 B3
Agdzhabedi = Ağcabädi, *Azerbaijan* 43 K8
Agen, *France* 26 D4
Agersø, *Denmark* 11 J5
Ageyevo, *Russia* 42 C3
Agger, *Denmark* 11 H2
Ággius, *Italy* 34 B2
Āgh Kand, *Iran* 67 D13
Aghoueyyît, *Mauritania* 74 D1
Aginskoye, *Russia* 45 D12
Agira, *Italy* 35 E7
Ağlasun, *Turkey* 66 D4
Agly →, *France* 26 F7
Agnibilékrou, *Ivory C.* 78 D4
Agnita, *Romania* 38 D7
Agnone, *Italy* 35 A7
Agofie, *Ghana* 79 D5
Agogna →, *Italy* 32 C5
Agogo, *Sudan* 77 F2
Agon, *France* 24 C5
Agön, *Sweden* 10 C11
Ágordo, *Italy* 33 B9
Agout →, *France* 26 E5
Agra, *India* 62 F7
Agrakhanskiuy Poluostrov, *Russia* 43 J8
Agramunt, *Spain* 28 D6
Agreda, *Spain* 28 D3
Ağri, *Turkey* 67 C10
Agri →, *Italy* 35 B9
Ağrı Dağı, *Turkey* 67 C11
Agrigento, *Italy* 34 E6
Agrinion, *Greece* 39 L4
Agrópoli, *Italy* 35 B7
Ağstafa, *Azerbaijan* 43 K7
Água Branca, *Brazil* 122 C3
Agua Caliente, *Baja Calif., Mexico* 113 N10
Agua Caliente, *Sinaloa, Mexico* 114 B3
Agua Caliente Springs, *U.S.A.* 113 N10
Água Clara, *Brazil* 125 E7
Agua Hechicero, *Mexico* 113 N10
Agua Preta →, *Brazil* 121 D5
Agua Prieta, *Mexico* 114 A3
Aguachica, *Colombia* 120 B3
Aguada Cecilio, *Argentina* 128 B3
Aguadas, *Colombia* 120 B2
Aguadilla, *Puerto Rico* 117 C6
Aguadulce, *Panama* 116 E3
Aguanga, *U.S.A.* 113 M10
Aguanish, *Canada* 99 B7
Aguanus →, *Canada* 99 B7
Aguapeí, *Brazil* 125 D6
Aguapeí →, *Brazil* 123 F1
Aguapey →, *Argentina* 126 B4
Aguaray Guazú →, *Paraguay* 126 A4
Aguarico →, *Ecuador* 120 D2
Aguas →, *Spain* 28 D4
Aguas Blancas, *Chile* 126 A2
Aguas Calientes, Sierra de, *Argentina* 126 B2
Águas Formosas, *Brazil* 123 E3
Aguascalientes, *Mexico* 114 C4
Aguascalientes □, *Mexico* 114 C4
Agudo, *Spain* 31 G6
Águeda, *Portugal* 30 E2
Agueda →, *Spain* 30 D4
Aguié, *Niger* 79 C6
Aguilafuente, *Spain* 30 D6
Aguilar, *Spain* 31 H6
Aguilar de Campóo, *Spain* 30 C6
Aguilares, *Argentina* 126 B2
Aguilas, *Spain* 29 H3
Agüimes, *Canary Is.* 36 G4
Aguja, C. de la, *Colombia* 120 A3
Agulaa, *Ethiopia* 77 E4
Agulhas, C., *S. Africa* 84 E3
Agulo, *Canary Is.* 36 F2
Agung, *Indonesia* 56 F5
Agur, *Uganda* 82 B3
Agusan →, *Phil.* 55 G6
Agustín Codazzi, *Colombia* 120 A3
Agvali, *Russia* 43 J8
Aha Mts., *Botswana* 84 B3
Ahaggar, *Algeria* 75 D6
Ahamansu, *Ghana* 79 D5
Ahar, *Iran* 67 C12
Ahaus, *Germany* 18 C3
Ahelledjem, *Algeria* 75 C6
Ahipara B., *N.Z.* 87 F4
Ahiri, *India* 60 K12
Ahlat, *Turkey* 67 C10
Ahlen, *Germany* 18 D3
Ahmad Wal, *Pakistan* 62 E1
Ahmadabad, *India* 62 H5
Aḥmadābād, *Khorāsān, Iran* 65 C9
Aḥmadābād, *Khorāsān, Iran* 65 C8
Aḥmadī, *Iran* 65 E8
Ahmadnagar, *India* 60 K9
Ahmadpur, *Pakistan* 62 E4
Ahmar, *Ethiopia* 77 F5
Ahmedabad = Ahmadabad, *India* 62 H5
Ahmednagar = Ahmadnagar, *India* 60 K9
Ahoada, *Nigeria* 79 D6
Ahome, *Mexico* 114 B3
Ahr →, *Germany* 18 E3
Ahram, *Iran* 65 D6
Ahrax Pt., *Malta* 37 D1
Ahrensbök, *Germany* 18 A6
Ahrweiler, *Germany* 18 E3
Āhū, *Iran* 65 C6
Ahuachapán, *El Salv.* 116 D2
Ahvāz, *Iran* 65 D6
Ahvenanmaa = Åland, *Finland* 9 F19
Aḥwar, *Yemen* 68 E4
Ahzar, *Mali* 79 B5
Aiari →, *Brazil* 120 C4
Aichach, *Germany* 19 G7
Aichi □, *Japan* 49 G8
Aidone, *Italy* 35 E7
Aiello Cálabro, *Italy* 35 C9
Aigle, *Switz.* 22 D3
Aignay-le-Duc, *France* 25 E11
Aigoual, Mt., *France* 26 D7
Aigre, *France* 26 C4
Aigua, *Uruguay* 127 C5
Aigueperse, *France* 26 B7
Aigues →, *France* 27 D8
Aigues-Mortes, *France* 27 E8
Aigues-Mortes, G. d', *France* 27 E8

Aiguilles, *France* 27 D10
Aiguillon, *France* 26 D4
Aigurande, *France* 26 B5
Aihui, *China* 54 A7
Aija, *Peru* 124 B2
Aikawa, *Japan* 48 E9
Aiken, *U.S.A.* 105 J5
Ailao Shan, *China* 52 F3
Aillant-sur-Tholon, *France* 25 E10
Aillik, *Canada* 99 A8
Ailly-sur-Noye, *France* 25 C9
Ailsa Craig, *U.K.* 14 F3
'Ailūn, *Jordan* 69 C4
Aim, *Russia* 45 D14
Aimere, *Indonesia* 57 F6
Aimogasta, *Argentina* 126 B2
Aimorés, *Brazil* 123 E3
Ain □, *France* 27 B9
Ain →, *France* 27 C9
Aïn Beïda, *Algeria* 75 A6
Aïn Ben Khellil, *Algeria* 75 B4
Aïn Ben Tili, *Mauritania* 74 C3
Aïn Beni Mathar, *Morocco* 75 B4
Aïn Benian, *Algeria* 75 A5
Ain Dalla, *Egypt* 76 B2
Ain el Mafki, *Egypt* 76 B2
Ain Girba, *Egypt* 76 B2
Aïn M'lila, *Algeria* 75 A6
Ain Qeiqab, *Egypt* 76 B1
Aïn-Sefra, *Algeria* 75 B4
Ain Sheikh Murzûk, *Egypt* 76 B2
'Ain Sudr, *Egypt* 69 F2
Ain Sukhna, *Egypt* 76 J8
Aïn Tédelès, *Algeria* 75 A5
Aïn-Témouchent, *Algeria* 75 A4
Aïn Touta, *Algeria* 75 A6
Ain Zeitûn, *Egypt* 76 B2
Aïn Zorah, *Morocco* 75 B4
Ainabo, *Somali Rep.* 68 F4
Ainaži, *Latvia* 9 H21
Aínos Óros, *Greece* 39 L3
Ainsworth, *U.S.A.* 108 D5
Aipe, *Colombia* 120 C2
Aiquile, *Bolivia* 125 D4
Aïr, *Niger* 79 B6
Air Hitam, *Malaysia* 59 M4
Airaines, *France* 25 C8
Airão, *Brazil* 121 D5
Airdrie, *U.K.* 14 F5
Aire →, *France* 25 C11
Aire →, *U.K.* 12 D7
Aire, I. del, *Spain* 36 B11
Aire-sur-la-Lys, *France* 25 B9
Aire-sur-l'Adour, *France* 26 E3
Airlie Beach, *Australia* 90 C4
Airolo, *Switz.* 23 C7
Airvault, *France* 24 F6
Aisch →, *Germany* 19 F7
Aisen □, *Chile* 128 C2
Aisne □, *France* 25 C10
Aisne →, *France* 25 C9
Aitana, Sierra de, *Spain* 29 G4
Aitkin, *U.S.A.* 108 B8
Aitolikón, *Greece* 39 L4
Aiuaba, *Brazil* 122 C3
Aiud, *Romania* 38 C6
Aix-en-Provence, *France* 27 E9
Aix-la-Chapelle = Aachen, *Germany* 18 E2
Aix-les-Bains, *France* 27 C9
Aixe-sur-Vienne, *France* 26 C5
Aiyansh, *Canada* 100 B3
Aíyina, *Greece* 39 M6
Aiyínion, *Greece* 39 J5
Aiyion, *Greece* 39 L5
Aizawl, *India* 61 H18
Aizenay, *France* 24 F5
Aizkraukle, *Latvia* 9 H21
Aizpute, *Latvia* 9 H19
Aizuwakamatsu, *Japan* 48 F9
Ajaccio, *France* 27 G12
Ajaccio, G. d', *France* 27 G12
Ajaju →, *Colombia* 120 C3
Ajalpan, *Mexico* 115 D5
Ajanta Ra., *India* 60 J9
Ajari Rep. = Ajaria □, *Georgia* 43 K6
Ajaria □, *Georgia* 43 K6
Ajax, *Canada* 106 C5
Ajdâbiyah, *Libya* 73 B9
Ajdovščina, *Slovenia* 33 C10
Ajibar, *Ethiopia* 77 E4
Ajka, *Hungary* 21 H7
'Ajmān, *U.A.E.* 65 E7
Ajmer, *India* 62 F6
Ajo, *U.S.A.* 111 K7
Ajoie, *Switz.* 22 B4
Ajok, *Sudan* 77 F2
Ajuy, *Phil.* 55 F5
Ak Dağ, *Turkey* 66 D3
Ak Dağlař, *Turkey* 66 C7
Akaba, *Togo* 79 D5
Akabira, *Japan* 48 C11
Akabli, *Algeria* 75 C5
Akaki Beseka, *Ethiopia* 77 F4
Akala, *Sudan* 77 D4
Akamas □, *Cyprus* 37 D11
Akanthou, *Cyprus* 37 D12
Akaroa, *N.Z.* 87 K4
Akasha, *Sudan* 76 C3
Akashi, *Japan* 49 G7
Akbou, *Algeria* 75 A5
Akçaabat, *Turkey* 67 B8
Akçadağ, *Turkey* 66 C7
Akçakale, *Turkey* 67 D8
Akçakoca, *Turkey* 66 B4
Akchâr, *Mauritania* 74 D2
Akdağmadeni, *Turkey* 66 C6
Akelamo, *Indonesia* 57 D7
Akershus fylke □, *Norway* 10 E5
Aketi, *Zaïre* 80 D4
Akhalkalaki, *Georgia* 43 K6
Akhaltsikhe, *Georgia* 43 K6
Akharnaí, *Greece* 39 L6
Akhelóös →, *Greece* 39 L4
Akhendria, *Greece* 39 Q8
Akhéron →, *Greece* 39 K3
Akhisar, *Turkey* 66 C2
Akhladhókambos, *Greece* 39 M5
Akhmîm, *Egypt* 76 B3
Akhnur, *India* 63 C6
Akhtuba →, *Russia* 43 G8
Akhtubinsk, *Russia* 43 F8
Akhty, *Russia* 43 K8
Akhtyrka = Okhtyrka, *Ukraine* 41 G8
Aki, *Japan* 49 H6
Akimiski I., *Canada* 98 B3
Akimovka, *Ukraine* 41 J8
Akita, *Japan* 48 E10
Akita □, *Japan* 48 E10
Akjoujt, *Mauritania* 78 B2
Akka, *Morocco* 74 C3
Akkeshi, *Japan* 48 C12
'Akko, *Israel* 69 C4
Akkol, *Kazakstan* 44 E8
Akkrum, *Neths.* 16 B7
Aklampa, *Benin* 79 D5
Aklavik, *Canada* 96 B6
Akmolinsk = Aqmola, *Kazakstan* 44 D8
Akmonte, *Spain* 31 H4
Aknoul, *Morocco* 75 B4
Akō, *Japan* 49 G7
Ako, *Nigeria* 79 C7
Akobo →, *Ethiopia* 77 F3
Akola, *India* 60 J10
Akonolinga, *Cameroon* 79 E7
Akordat, *Eritrea* 77 D4
Akosombo Dam, *Ghana* 79 D5
Akot, *Sudan* 77 F3
Akpatok I., *Canada* 97 B13
Åkrahamn, *Norway* 9 G11
Akranes, *Iceland* 8 D2
Akreïjit, *Mauritania* 78 B3
Akrítas Venétiko, Ákra, *Greece* 39 N4
Akron, *Colo., U.S.A.* 108 E3
Akron, *Ohio, U.S.A.* 106 E3
Akrotiri, *Cyprus* 66 E5
Akrotíri, Ákra, *Greece* 39 J8
Akrotiri Bay, *Cyprus* 37 E12
Aksai Chin, *India* 63 B8
Aksaray, *Turkey* 66 C6
Aksarka, *Russia* 44 C7
Aksay, *Kazakstan* 44 D6
Akşehir, *Turkey* 66 C4
Akşehir Gölü, *Turkey* 66 C4
Aksenovo Zilovskoye, *Russia* 45 D12
Akstafa = Ağstafa, *Azerbaijan* 43 K7
Aksu, *China* 54 B3
Aksu →, *Turkey* 66 D4
Aksum, *Ethiopia* 77 E4
Aktash, *Russia* 42 C11
Aktogay, *Kazakstan* 44 E8
Aktsyabrski, *Belarus* 41 F5
Aktyubinsk = Aqtöbe, *Kazakstan* 44 D6
Aku, *Nigeria* 79 D6
Akure, *Nigeria* 79 D6
Akureyri, *Iceland* 8 D4
Akuseki-Shima, *Japan* 49 K4
Akusha, *Russia* 43 J8
Akwa-Ibom □, *Nigeria* 79 E6
Akyab = Sittwe, *Burma* 61 J18
Akyazı, *Turkey* 66 B4
Al 'Adan, *Yemen* 68 E4
Al Aḩsā, *Si. Arabia* 65 E6
Al Ajfar, *Si. Arabia* 64 E4
Al Amādīyah, *Iraq* 67 D10
Al Amārah, *Iraq* 67 G12
Al 'Aqabah, *Jordan* 69 F4
Al Arak, *Syria* 67 E8
Al 'Aramah, *Si. Arabia* 64 E5
Al Arṭāwīyah, *Si. Arabia* 64 E5
Al 'Āṣimah □, *Jordan* 69 D5
Al' Assāfīyah, *Si. Arabia* 64 D3
Al 'Ayn, *Oman* 65 E7
Al 'Ayn, *Si. Arabia* 64 E3
Al A'ẓamīyah, *Iraq* 64 C5
Al 'Azīzīyah, *Iraq* 67 F11
Al 'Azīzīyah, *Libya* 75 B7
Al Bāb, *Syria* 66 D7
Al Bad', *Si. Arabia* 64 D2
Al Bādī, *Iraq* 64 C4
Al Baḩrah, *Kuwait* 64 D5
Al Balqā' □, *Jordan* 69 C4
Al Barkāt, *Libya* 75 D7
Al Bārūk, J., *Lebanon* 69 B4
Al Başrah, *Iraq* 64 D5
Al Baṭḩā, *Iraq* 64 D5
Al Batrūn, *Lebanon* 69 A4
Al Bayḑā, *Libya* 73 B9
Al Biqā □, *Lebanon* 69 A5
Al Bi'r, *Si. Arabia* 64 D3
Al Bu'ayrāt al Ḩasūn, *Libya* 73 B8
Al Burayj, *Syria* 69 A5
Al Fallūjah, *Iraq* 67 F10
Al Fāw, *Iraq* 65 D6
Al Fujayrah, *U.A.E.* 65 E8
Al Ghadaf, W. →, *Jordan* 69 D5
Al Ghammās, *Iraq* 64 D5
Al Ḩābah, *Si. Arabia* 64 E5
Al Ḩadīthah, *Iraq* 67 E10
Al Ḩadīthah, *Si. Arabia* 64 D3
Al Ḩaḑr, *Iraq* 67 E10
Al Ḩājānah, *Syria* 69 B5
Al Ḩāmad, *Si. Arabia* 64 D3
Al Hamdānīyah, *Syria* 64 C3
Al Ḩamidīyah, *Syria* 69 A4
Al Ḩammādah al Ḩamrā', *Libya* 75 C7
Al Ḩammār, *Iraq* 64 D5
Al Ḩarīr, W. →, *Syria* 69 C4
Al Ḩasā, W. →, *Jordan* 69 D4
Al Ḩasakah, *Syria* 67 D9
Al Ḩawrah, *Yemen* 68 E4
Al Ḩaydān, W. →, *Jordan* 69 D4
Al Ḩayy, *Iraq* 67 F12
Al Ḩijāz, *Si. Arabia* 68 B2
Al Ḩillah, *Iraq* 67 F11
Al Ḩillah, *Si. Arabia* 68 C4
Al Hindīyah, *Iraq* 67 F11
Al Hirmil, *Lebanon* 69 A5
Al Hoceïma, *Morocco* 74 A4
Al Ḩudaydah, *Yemen* 68 E3
Al Hufūf, *Si. Arabia* 65 E6
Al Ḩumayḑah, *Si. Arabia* 64 D2
Al Ḩunayy, *Si. Arabia* 65 E6
Al Īsāwīyah, *Si. Arabia* 64 D3
Al Ittihad = Madīnat ash Sha'b, *Yemen* 68 E3
Al Jafr, *Jordan* 69 E5
Al Jaghbūb, *Libya* 73 C9
Al Jahrah, *Kuwait* 64 D5
Al Jalāmīd, *Si. Arabia* 64 D3
Al Jamalīyah, *Qatar* 65 E6
Al Janūb □, *Lebanon* 69 B4
Al Jawf, *Libya* 73 D9
Al Jawf, *Si. Arabia* 64 D3
Al Jazirah, *Iraq* 67 E10
Al Jazirah, *Libya* 73 C9
Al Jithāmīyah, *Si. Arabia* 64 E4
Al Jubayl, *Si. Arabia* 65 E6
Al Jubaylah, *Si. Arabia* 64 E5
Al Jubb, *Si. Arabia* 64 E4
Al Junaynah, *Sudan* 73 F9
Al Kabā'ish, *Iraq* 64 D5
Al Karak, *Jordan* 69 D4
Al Karak □, *Jordan* 69 E5
Al Kāẓim Tyah, *Iraq* 67 F11
Al Khalīl, *West Bank* 69 D4
Al Khāliş, *Iraq* 67 F11
Al Khawr, *Qatar* 65 E6
Al Khiḑr, *Iraq* 64 D5
Al Khiyām, *Lebanon* 69 B4
Al Kiswah, *Syria* 69 B5
Al Kūfah, *Iraq* 67 F11
Al Kufrah, *Libya* 73 D9
Al Kuhayfīyah, *Si. Arabia* 64 E4
Al Kūt, *Iraq* 67 F11
Al Kuwayt, *Kuwait* 64 D5
Al Labwah, *Lebanon* 69 A5
Al Lādhiqīyah, *Syria* 66 E6
Al Līth, *Si. Arabia* 76 C5
Al Liwā', *Oman* 65 E8
Al Luḩayyah, *Yemen* 68 D3
Al Madīnah, *Iraq* 64 D5
Al Madīnah, *Si. Arabia* 64 E3
Al-Mafraq, *Jordan* 69 C5
Al Maḩmūdīyah, *Iraq* 67 F11
Al Majma'ah, *Si. Arabia* 64 E5
Al Makhruq, W. →, *Jordan* 69 D6
Al Makḩūl, *Si. Arabia* 64 E4
Al Manāmah, *Bahrain* 65 E6
Al Maqwa', *Kuwait* 64 D5
Al Marj, *Libya* 73 B9
Al Maţlā, *Kuwait* 64 D5
Al Mawjib, W. →, *Jordan* 69 D4
Al Mawşil, *Iraq* 67 D10
Al Mayādin, *Syria* 67 E9
Al Mazār, *Jordan* 69 D4
Al Midhnab, *Si. Arabia* 64 E5
Al Minā', *Lebanon* 69 A4
Al Miqdādīyah, *Iraq* 67 E11
Al Mubarraz, *Si. Arabia* 65 E6
Al Mughayrā', *U.A.E.* 65 E7
Al Muḩarraq, *Bahrain* 65 E6
Al Mukallā, *Yemen* 68 E4
Al Mukhā, *Yemen* 68 E3
Al Musayjīd, *Si. Arabia* 64 E3
Al Musayyib, *Iraq* 67 F11
Al Muwayliḩ, *Si. Arabia* 64 E2
Al Owuho = Otukpa, *Nigeria* 79 D6
Al Qā'im, *Iraq* 67 E9
Al Qalībah, *Si. Arabia* 64 D3
Al Qāmishlī, *Syria* 67 D9
Al Qaryatayn, *Syria* 69 A6
Al Qaşabát, *Libya* 73 B7
Al Qaţ'ā, *Syria* 67 E9
Al Qaţīf, *Si. Arabia* 65 E6
Al Qatrānah, *Jordan* 69 D5
Al Qaţrūn, *Libya* 73 D8
Al Qayşūmah, *Si. Arabia* 64 D5
Al Quds = Jerusalem, *Israel* 69 D4
Al Qunaytirah, *Syria* 69 C4
Al Qunfudhah, *Si. Arabia* 76 D5
Al Qurnah, *Iraq* 64 D5
Al Quşayr, *Iraq* 64 D5
Al Quşayr, *Syria* 69 A5
Al Qutayfah, *Syria* 69 B5
Al' Uḑaylīyah, *Si. Arabia* 65 E6
Al 'Ulā, *Si. Arabia* 64 E3
Al Uqaylah ash Sharqīgah, *Libya* 73 B8
Al Uqayr, *Si. Arabia* 65 E6
Al 'Uwaynid, *Si. Arabia* 64 E5
Al 'Uwayqīlah, *Si. Arabia* 64 D4
Al 'Uyūn, *Si. Arabia* 64 E4
Al 'Uyūn, *Si. Arabia* 64 E3
Al Wajh, *Si. Arabia* 64 E3
Al Wakrah, *Qatar* 65 E6
Al Wannān, *Si. Arabia* 65 E6
Al Waqbah, *Si. Arabia* 64 D5
Al Wari'āh, *Si. Arabia* 64 E5
Al Wātīyah, *Libya* 75 B7
Al Wusayl, *Qatar* 65 E6
Ala, *Italy* 32 C8
Ala Dağları, *Turkey* 67 C10
Alabama □, *U.S.A.* 105 J2
Alabama →, *U.S.A.* 105 K2
Alaca, *Turkey* 66 B6
Alaçam, *Turkey* 66 B6
Alaçam Dağları, *Turkey* 66 C3
Alaejos, *Spain* 30 D5
Alaérma, *Greece* 37 C9
Alagir, *Russia* 43 J7
Alagna Valsésia, *Italy* 32 C4
Alagoa Grande, *Brazil* 122 C4
Alagoas □, *Brazil* 122 C4
Alagoinhas, *Brazil* 123 D4
Alagón, *Spain* 28 D3
Alagón →, *Spain* 31 F4
Alajero, *Canary Is.* 36 F2
Alajuela, *Costa Rica* 116 D3
Alakamisy, *Madag.* 85 C8
Alalapura, *Surinam* 121 C6
Alalaú →, *Brazil* 121 D5
Alameda, *Spain* 31 H6
Alameda, *Calif., U.S.A.* 112 H4
Alameda, *N. Mex., U.S.A.* 111 J10
Alaminos, *Phil.* 55 C3
Alamo, *U.S.A.* 113 J11
Alamo Crossing, *U.S.A.* 113 L13
Alamogordo, *U.S.A.* 111 K11
Alamos, *Mexico* 114 B3
Alamosa, *U.S.A.* 111 H11
Åland, *Finland* 9 F19
Alandroal, *Portugal* 31 G3
Ålands hav, *Sweden* 9 F18
Alandur, *India* 60 N12
Alange, Presa de, *Spain* 31 G4
Alania = North Ossetia □, *Russia* 43 J7
Alanis, *Spain* 31 G5
Alanya, *Turkey* 66 D5
Alaotra, Farihin', *Madag.* 85 B8
Alapayevsk, *Russia* 44 D7
Alar del Rey, *Spain* 30 C6
Alaraz, *Spain* 30 E5
Alaşehir, *Turkey* 66 C3
Alaska □, *U.S.A.* 96 B5
Alaska, G. of, *Pac. Oc.* 96 C5
Alaska Highway, *Canada* 100 B3
Alaska Peninsula, *U.S.A.* 96 C4
Alaska Range, *U.S.A.* 96 B4
Alássio, *Italy* 32 D5
Älät, *Azerbaijan* 43 L9
Alataw Shankou, *China* 54 B3
Alatri, *Italy* 34 A6
Alatyr, *Russia* 42 C8
Alatyr →, *Russia* 42 C8
Alausi, *Ecuador* 120 D2
Álava □, *Spain* 28 C2
Alava, C., *U.S.A.* 110 B1
Alaverdi, *Armenia* 43 K7
Alavus, *Finland* 9 E20
Alawoona, *Australia* 91 E3
'Alayh, *Lebanon* 69 B4
Alayor, *Spain* 36 B11
Alazani →, *Azerbaijan* 43 K8
Alba, *Italy* 32 D5
Alba de Tormes, *Spain* 30 E5
Alba-Iulia, *Romania* 38 C6
Albac, *Romania* 38 C6
Albacete, *Spain* 29 G3
Albacete □, *Spain* 29 G3
Albacutya, L., *Australia* 91 F3
Ålbæk, *Denmark* 11 G4
Ålbæk Bugt, *Denmark* 11 G4
Albaida, *Spain* 29 G4
Albalate de las Nogueras, *Spain* 28 E2
Albalate del Arzobispo, *Spain* 28 D4
Albania ■, *Europe* 39 J3
Albano Laziale, *Italy* 34 A5
Albany, *Australia* 89 G2
Albany, *Ga., U.S.A.* 105 K3
Albany, *Minn., U.S.A.* 108 C7
Albany, *N.Y., U.S.A.* 107 D11
Albany, *Oreg., U.S.A.* 110 D2
Albany, *Tex., U.S.A.* 109 J5
Albany →, *Canada* 98 B3
Albardón, *Argentina* 126 C2
Albarracín, *Spain* 28 E3
Albarracín, Sierra de, *Spain* 28 E3
Albatross B., *Australia* 90 A3
Albegna →, *Italy* 33 F8
Albemarle, *U.S.A.* 105 H5
Albemarle Sd., *U.S.A.* 105 H7
Albenga, *Italy* 32 D5
Alberche →, *Spain* 30 F6
Alberdi, *Paraguay* 126 B4
Alberes, Mts., *Spain* 28 C7
Alberique, *Spain* 29 F4
Albersdorf, *Germany* 18 A5
Albert, *France* 25 B9
Albert, L., *Australia* 91 F2
Albert Canyon, *Canada* 100 C5
Albert Edward Ra., *Australia* 88 C4
Albert L., *Africa* 82 B3
Albert Lea, *U.S.A.* 108 D8
Albert Nile →, *Uganda* 82 B3
Albert Town, *Bahamas* 117 B5
Alberta □, *Canada* 100 C6
Alberti, *Argentina* 126 D3
Albertinia, *S. Africa* 84 E3
Albertkanaal →, *Belgium* 17 F4
Alberton, *Canada* 99 C7
Albertville = Kalemie, *Zaïre* 82 D2
Albertville, *France* 27 C10
Albi, *France* 26 E6
Albia, *U.S.A.* 108 E8
Albina, *Surinam* 121 B7
Albina, Ponta, *Angola* 84 B1
Albino, *Italy* 32 C6
Albion, *Idaho, U.S.A.* 110 E7
Albion, *Mich., U.S.A.* 104 D3
Albion, *Nebr., U.S.A.* 108 E5
Albion, *Pa., U.S.A.* 106 E4
Alblasserdam, *Neths.* 16 E5
Albocácer, *Spain* 28 E5
Alborán, *Medit. S.* 31 K7
Alborea, *Spain* 29 F3
Ålborg, *Denmark* 11 G3
Ålborg Bugt, *Denmark* 11 H4
Alborz, Reshteh-ye Kūhhā-ye, *Iran* 65 C7
Albox, *Spain* 29 H2
Albreda, *Canada* 100 C5
Albufeira, *Portugal* 31 H2
Albula →, *Switz.* 23 C8
Albuñol, *Spain* 29 J1
Albuquerque, *Brazil* 125 D6
Albuquerque, *U.S.A.* 111 J10
Albuquerque, Cayos de, *Caribbean* 116 D3
Alburg, *U.S.A.* 107 B11
Alburno, Mte., *Italy* 35 B8
Alburquerque, *Spain* 31 F4
Albury, *Australia* 91 F4
Alby, *Sweden* 10 B9
Alcácer do Sal, *Portugal* 31 G2
Alcaçovas, *Portugal* 31 G2
Alcalá de Chisvert, *Spain* 28 E5
Alcalá de Guadaira, *Spain* 31 H5
Alcalá de Henares, *Spain* 28 E1
Alcalá de los Gazules, *Spain* 31 J5
Alcalá la Real, *Spain* 31 H7
Alcamo, *Italy* 34 E5
Alcanadre, *Spain* 28 C2
Alcanadre →, *Spain* 28 D4
Alcanar, *Spain* 28 E5
Alcanede, *Portugal* 31 F2
Alcanena, *Portugal* 31 F2
Alcañices, *Spain* 30 D4
Alcañiz, *Spain* 28 D4
Alcântara, *Brazil* 122 B3
Alcántara, *Spain* 31 F4
Alcantara L., *Canada* 101 A7
Alcantarilla, *Spain* 29 H3
Alcaracejos, *Spain* 31 G6
Alcaraz, *Spain* 29 G2
Alcaraz, Sierra de, *Spain* 29 G2
Alcaudete, *Spain* 31 H6
Alcázar de San Juan, *Spain* 29 F1
Alchevsk, *Ukraine* 41 H10
Alcira, *Spain* 29 F4
Alcoa, *U.S.A.* 105 H4
Alcobaça, *Portugal* 31 F2
Alcobendas, *Spain* 28 E1
Alcolea del Pinar, *Spain* 28 D2
Alcora, *Spain* 28 E4
Alcorcón, *Spain* 30 E7
Alcoutim, *Portugal* 31 H3
Alcova, *U.S.A.* 110 E10
Alcoy, *Spain* 29 G4
Alcubierre, Sierra de, *Spain* 28 D4
Alcublas, *Spain* 28 F4
Alcudia, *Spain* 36 B10
Alcudia, B. de, *Spain* 36 B10
Alcudia, Sierra de la, *Spain* 31 G6
Aldabra Is., *Seychelles* 70 G8
Aldama, *Mexico* 115 C5
Aldan, *Russia* 45 D13
Aldan →, *Russia* 45 C13
Aldea, Pta. de la, *Canary Is.* 36 G4
Aldeburgh, *U.K.* 13 E9
Aldeia Nova, *Portugal* 31 H3
Alder, *U.S.A.* 110 D7
Alder Pk., *U.S.A.* 112 K5
Alderney, *U.K.* 13 H5
Aldershot, *U.K.* 13 F7
Aledo, *U.S.A.* 108 E9
Alefa, *Ethiopia* 77 E4
Aleg, *Mauritania* 78 B2
Alegranza, *Canary Is.* 36 E6
Alegranza, I., *Canary Is.* 36 E6
Alegre, *Brazil* 123 F3
Alegrete, *Brazil* 127 B4
Aleisk, *Russia* 44 D9
Aleksandriya = Oleksandriya, *Ukraine* 41 H7
Aleksandriya = Oleksandriya, *Ukraine* 41 G4
Aleksandriyskaya, *Russia* 43 J8
Aleksandrov, *Russia* 42 B4
Aleksandrov Gay, *Russia* 42 E9
Aleksandrovac, *Serbia, Yug.* 21 L11
Aleksandrovka = Oleksandrovka, *Ukraine* 41 H7
Aleksandrovo, *Bulgaria* 38 F7
Aleksandrovsk-Sakhalinskiy, *Russia* 45 D15
Aleksandrovskiy Zavod, *Russia* 45 D12
Aleksandrovskoye, *Russia* 44 C8

Aleksandrów Kujawski, *Poland* 20 C8
Aleksandrów Łódzki, *Poland* 20 D9
Alekseyevka, *Russia* 42 D10
Alekseyevka, *Russia* 42 E4
Aleksin, *Russia* 42 C3
Aleksinac, *Serbia, Yug.* 21 M11
Além Paraíba, *Brazil* 123 F3
Alemania, *Argentina* 126 B2
Alemania, *Chile* 126 B2
Ålen, *Norway* 10 B5
Alençon, *France* 24 D7
Alenuihaha Channel, *U.S.A.* 102 H17
Aleppo = Ḥalab, *Syria* 66 D7
Aléria, *France* 27 F13
Alert Bay, *Canada* 100 C3
Alès, *France* 27 D8
Aleşd, *Romania* 38 B5
Alessándria, *Italy* 32 D5
Ålestrup, *Denmark* 11 H3
Ålesund, *Norway* 9 E12
Alet-les-Bains, *France* 26 F6
Aletschhorn, *Switz.* 22 D6
Aleutian Is., *Pac. Oc.* 96 C2
Aleutian Trench, *Pac. Oc.* 92 B10
Alexander, *U.S.A.* 108 B3
Alexander, Mt., *Australia* 89 E3
Alexander Arch., *U.S.A.* 100 B2
Alexander Bay, *S. Africa* 84 D2
Alexander City, *U.S.A.* 105 J3
Alexander I., *Antarctica* 5 C17
Alexandra, *Australia* 91 F4
Alexandra, *N.Z.* 87 L2
Alexandra Falls, *Canada* 100 A5
Alexandria = El Iskandarîya, *Egypt* 76 H6
Alexandria, *Australia* 90 B2
Alexandria, *B.C., Canada* 100 C4
Alexandria, *Ont., Canada* 98 C5
Alexandria, *Romania* 38 F8
Alexandria, *S. Africa* 84 E4
Alexandria, *Ind., U.S.A.* 104 E3
Alexandria, *La., U.S.A.* 109 K8
Alexandria, *Minn., U.S.A.* 108 C7
Alexandria, *S. Dak., U.S.A.* 108 D6
Alexandria, *Va., U.S.A.* 104 F7
Alexandria Bay, *U.S.A.* 107 B9
Alexandrina, L., *Australia* 91 F2
Alexandroúpolis, *Greece* 39 J8
Alexis →, *Canada* 99 B8
Alexis Creek, *Canada* 100 C4
Alfabia, *Spain* 36 B9
Alfambra, *Spain* 28 E3
Alfândega da Fé, *Portugal* 30 D4
Alfaro, *Spain* 28 C3
Alfeld, *Germany* 18 D5
Alfenas, *Brazil* 127 A6
Alfiós →, *Greece* 39 M4
Alfonsine, *Italy* 33 D9
Alford, *U.K.* 14 D6
Alfred, *Maine, U.S.A.* 107 C14
Alfred, *N.Y., U.S.A.* 106 D7
Alfreton, *U.K.* 12 D6
Alga, *Kazakstan* 44 E6
Algaida, *Spain* 36 B9
Algar, *Spain* 31 J5
Algård, *Norway* 9 G11
Algarinejo, *Spain* 31 H6
Algarve, *Portugal* 31 J2
Algeciras, *Spain* 31 J5
Algemesí, *Spain* 29 F4
Alger, *Algeria* 75 A5
Algeria ■, *Africa* 75 C5
Alghero, *Italy* 34 B1
Algiers = Alger, *Algeria* 75 A5
Algoa B., *S. Africa* 84 E4
Algodonales, *Spain* 31 J5
Algodor →, *Spain* 30 F7
Algoma, *U.S.A.* 104 C2
Algona, *U.S.A.* 108 D7
Algonac, *U.S.A.* 106 D2
Alhama de Almería, *Spain* 29 J2
Alhama de Aragón, *Spain* 28 D3
Alhama de Granada, *Spain* 31 J7
Alhama de Murcia, *Spain* 29 H3
Alhambra, *Spain* 29 G1
Alhambra, *U.S.A.* 102 D3
Alhaurín el Grande, *Spain* 31 J6
Alhucemas = Al Hoceïma, *Morocco* 74 A4
'Alī al Gharbī, *Iraq* 67 F12
Alī ash Sharqī, *Iraq* 67 F12
Äli Bayramlı, *Azerbaijan* 43 L9
'Alī Khēl, *Afghan.* 62 C3
Ali Sahîh, *Djibouti* 77 E5
Alī Shāh, *Iran* 64 B5
Ália, *Italy* 34 E6
'Alīābād, *Khorāsān, Iran* 65 C8
'Alīābād, *Kordestān, Iran* 64 C5
'Alīābād, *Yazd, Iran* 65 D7
Aliaga, *Spain* 28 E4
Aliağa, *Turkey* 66 C2
Aliákmon →, *Greece* 39 J5
Alibo, *Ethiopia* 77 F4
Alibunar, *Serbia, Yug.* 21 K10
Alicante, *Spain* 29 G4
Alicante □, *Spain* 29 G4
Alice, *S. Africa* 84 E4
Alice, *U.S.A.* 109 M5
Alice →, *Queens., Australia* 90 C3
Alice →, *Queens., Australia* 90 B3
Alice, Punta dell', *Italy* 35 C10
Alice Arm, *Canada* 100 B3
Alice Downs, *Australia* 88 C4
Alice Springs, *Australia* 90 C1
Alicedale, *S. Africa* 84 E4
Aliceville, *U.S.A.* 105 J1
Alick Cr. →, *Australia* 90 C3
Alicudi, I., *Italy* 35 D7
Alida, *Canada* 101 D8
Aligarh, *Raj., India* 62 G7
Aligarh, *Ut. P., India* 62 F8
Alīgūdarz, *Iran* 65 C6
Alijó, *Portugal* 30 D3
Alimena, *Italy* 35 E7
Alimnía, *Greece* 37 C9
Alingsås, *Sweden* 11 G6
Alipur, *Pakistan* 62 E4
Alipur Duar, *India* 61 F16
Aliquippa, *U.S.A.* 106 F4
Aliste →, *Spain* 30 D5
Alitus = Alytus, *Lithuania* 9 J21
Alivérion, *Greece* 39 L7
Aliwal North, *S. Africa* 84 E4
Alix, *Canada* 100 C6
Aljezur, *Portugal* 31 H2
Aljustrel, *Portugal* 31 H2
Alkamari, *Niger* 79 C7
Alken, *Belgium* 17 G6
Alkmaar, *Neths.* 16 C5
All American Canal, *U.S.A.* 111 K6
Allada, *Benin* 79 D5
Allah Dad, *Pakistan* 62 G2
Allahabad, *India* 63 G9
Allakh-Yun, *Russia* 45 C14
Allal Tazi, *Morocco* 74 B3
Allan, *Canada* 101 C7
Allanche, *France* 26 C6
Allanmyo, *Burma* 61 K19
Allanridge, *S. Africa* 84 D4
Allanwater, *Canada* 98 B1
Allaqi, Wadi →, *Egypt* 76 C3
Allariz, *Spain* 30 C3
Allassac, *France* 26 C5
Alle, *Belgium* 17 J5
Allegan, *U.S.A.* 104 D3
Allegany, *U.S.A.* 106 D6
Allegheny →, *U.S.A.* 106 F5
Allegheny Mts., *U.S.A.* 94 F11
Allegheny Plateau, *U.S.A.* 104 G6
Allegheny Reservoir, *U.S.A.* 106 E6
Allègre, *France* 26 C7
Allen, *Argentina* 128 A3
Allen, Bog of, *Ireland* 15 C4
Allen, L., *Ireland* 15 B3
Allende, *Mexico* 114 B4
Allentown, *U.S.A.* 107 F9
Alleppey, *India* 60 Q10
Aller →, *Germany* 18 C5
Alleur, *Belgium* 17 G7
Allevard, *France* 27 C10
Alliance, *Surinam* 121 B7
Alliance, *Nebr., U.S.A.* 108 D3
Alliance, *Ohio, U.S.A.* 106 F3
Allier □, *France* 26 B6
Allier →, *France* 25 F10
Allingåbro, *Denmark* 11 H4
Alliston, *Canada* 98 D4
Alloa, *U.K.* 14 E5
Allora, *Australia* 91 D5
Allos, *France* 27 D10
Alluitsup Paa = Sydprøven, *Greenland* 4 C5
Alma, *Canada* 99 C5
Alma, *Ga., U.S.A.* 105 K4
Alma, *Kans., U.S.A.* 108 F6
Alma, *Mich., U.S.A.* 104 D3
Alma, *Nebr., U.S.A.* 108 E5
Alma, *Wis., U.S.A.* 108 C9
Alma Ata = Almaty, *Kazakstan* 44 E8
Almada, *Portugal* 31 G1
Almaden, *Australia* 90 B3
Almadén, *Spain* 31 G6
Almagro, *Spain* 31 G7
Almanor, L., *U.S.A.* 110 F3
Almansa, *Spain* 29 G3
Almanza, *Spain* 30 C5
Almanzor, Pico del Moro, *Spain* 30 E5
Almanzora →, *Spain* 29 H3
Almas, *Brazil* 123 D2
Almaty, *Kazakstan* 44 E8
Almazán, *Spain* 28 D2
Almazora, *Spain* 28 F4
Almeirim, *Brazil* 121 D7
Almeirim, *Portugal* 31 F2
Almelo, *Neths.* 16 D9
Almenar, *Spain* 28 D2
Almenara, *Brazil* 123 E3
Almenara, *Spain* 28 F4
Almenara, Sierra de, *Spain* 29 H3
Almendralejo, *Spain* 31 G4
Almería, *Spain* 29 J2
Almería □, *Spain* 29 H2
Almería, G. de, *Spain* 29 J2
Almetyevsk, *Russia* 42 C11
Almirante, *Panama* 116 E3
Almirante Montt, G., *Chile* 128 D2
Almirós, *Greece* 39 K5
Almiroú, Kólpos, *Greece* 37 D6
Almodôvar, *Portugal* 31 H2
Almodóvar del Campo, *Spain* 31 G6
Almogia, *Spain* 31 J6
Almonaster la Real, *Spain* 31 H4
Almont, *U.S.A.* 106 D1
Almonte, *Canada* 107 A8
Almonte →, *Spain* 31 F4
Almora, *India* 63 E8
Almoradí, *Spain* 29 G4
Almorox, *Spain* 30 E6
Almoustarat, *Mali* 79 B5
Almuñécar, *Spain* 31 J7
Alnif, *Morocco* 74 B3
Alnwick, *U.K.* 12 B6
Aloi, *Uganda* 82 B3
Alon, *Burma* 61 H19
Alor, *Indonesia* 57 F6
Alor Setar, *Malaysia* 59 J3
Alora, *Spain* 31 J6
Alosno, *Spain* 31 H3
Alougoum, *Morocco* 74 B3
Aloysius, Mt., *Australia* 89 E4
Alpaugh, *U.S.A.* 112 K7
Alpedrinha, *Portugal* 30 E3
Alpena, *U.S.A.* 104 C4
Alpercatas →, *Brazil* 122 C3
Alpes-de-Haute-Provence □, *France* 27 D10
Alpes-Maritimes □, *France* 27 E11
Alpha, *Australia* 90 C4
Alphen, *Neths.* 17 F5
Alphen aan den Rijn, *Neths.* 16 D5
Alpiarça, *Portugal* 31 F2
Alpine, *Ariz., U.S.A.* 111 K9
Alpine, *Calif., U.S.A.* 113 N10
Alpine, *Tex., U.S.A.* 109 K3
Alpnach, *Switz.* 23 C6
Alps, *Europe* 6 F7
Alpu, *Turkey* 66 C4
Alrø, *Denmark* 11 J4
Alroy Downs, *Australia* 90 B2
Alsace, *France* 25 D14
Alsask, *Canada* 101 C7
Alsásua, *Spain* 28 C2
Alsdorf, *Germany* 18 E2
Alsen, *Sweden* 10 A7
Alsfeld, *Germany* 18 E5
Alsten, *Norway* 8 D15
Alta, *Norway* 8 B20
Alta, Sierra, *Spain* 28 E3
Alta Gracia, *Argentina* 126 C3
Alta Lake, *Canada* 100 C4
Alta Sierra, *U.S.A.* 113 K8
Altaelva →, *Norway* 8 B20
Altafjorden, *Norway* 8 A20
Altagracia, *Venezuela* 120 A3
Altagracia de Orituco, *Venezuela* 120 B4
Altai = Aerhtai Shan, *Mongolia* 54 B4
Altamachi →, *Bolivia* 124 D4
Altamaha →, *U.S.A.* 105 K5
Altamira, *Brazil* 121 D7
Altamira, *Chile* 126 B2
Altamira, *Colombia* 120 C2
Altamira, *Mexico* 115 C5
Altamira, Cuevas de, *Spain* 30 B6
Altamont, *U.S.A.* 107 D10
Altamura, *Italy* 35 B9
Altanbulag, *Mongolia* 54 A5
Altar, *Mexico* 114 A2
Altata, *Mexico* 114 C3
Altavista, *U.S.A.* 104 G6
Altay, *China* 54 B3
Altdorf, *Switz.* 23 C7
Alte Mellum, *Germany* 18 B4
Altea, *Spain* 29 G4
Altenberg, *Germany* 18 E9
Altenbruch, *Germany* 18 B4
Altenburg, *Germany* 18 E8
Altenkirchen, *Mecklenburg-Vorpommern, Germany* 18 A9
Altenkirchen, *Rhld-Pfz., Germany* 18 E3
Altentreptow, *Germany* 18 B9
Alter do Chão, *Portugal* 31 F3
Altıntaş, *Turkey* 66 C4
Altiplano, *Bolivia* 124 D4
Altkirch, *France* 25 E14
Altmühl →, *Germany* 19 G7
Alto Adige = Trentino-Alto Adige □, *Italy* 32 B8
Alto Araguaia, *Brazil* 125 D7
Alto Cuchumatanes = Cuchumatanes, Sierra de los, *Guatemala* 116 C1
Alto del Inca, *Chile* 126 A2
Alto Garças, *Brazil* 125 D7
Alto Iriri →, *Brazil* 125 B7
Alto Ligonha, *Mozam.* 83 F4
Alto Molocue, *Mozam.* 83 F4
Alto Paraguai, *Brazil* 125 C6
Alto Paraguay □, *Paraguay* 126 A4
Alto Paraná □, *Paraguay* 127 B5
Alto Parnaíba, *Brazil* 122 C2
Alto Purús →, *Peru* 124 B3
Alto Río Senguerr, *Argentina* 128 C2
Alto Santo, *Brazil* 122 C4
Alto Sucuriú, *Brazil* 125 D7
Alto Turi, *Brazil* 122 B2
Alton, *Canada* 106 C4
Alton, *U.S.A.* 108 F9
Alton Downs, *Australia* 91 D2
Altoona, *U.S.A.* 106 F6
Altopáscio, *Italy* 32 E7
Altos, *Brazil* 122 C3
Altötting, *Germany* 19 G8
Altstätten, *Switz.* 23 B9
Altūn Kūprī, *Iraq* 67 E11
Altun Shan, *China* 54 C3
Alturas, *U.S.A.* 110 F3
Altus, *U.S.A.* 109 H5
Alubijid, *Phil.* 55 G6
Alucra, *Turkey* 67 B8
Alūksne, *Latvia* 9 H22
Alùla, *Somali Rep.* 68 E5
Alunite, *U.S.A.* 113 K12
Alupka, *Ukraine* 41 K8
Alushta, *Ukraine* 41 K8
Alusi, *Indonesia* 57 F8
Alustante, *Spain* 28 E3
Al'Uzayr, *Iraq* 64 D5
Alva, *U.S.A.* 109 G5
Alvaiázere, *Portugal* 30 F2
Älvängen, *Sweden* 11 G6
Alvarado, *Mexico* 115 D5
Alvarado, *U.S.A.* 109 J6
Alvarães, *Brazil* 121 D5
Alvaro Obregón, Presa, *Mexico* 114 B3
Alvdal, *Norway* 10 B4
Alvear, *Argentina* 126 B4
Alverca, *Portugal* 31 G1
Alveringen, *Belgium* 17 F1
Alvesta, *Sweden* 9 H16
Alvie, *Australia* 91 F3
Alvin, *U.S.A.* 109 L7
Alvinston, *Canada* 106 D3
Alvito, *Portugal* 31 G3
Älvkarleby, *Sweden* 9 F17
Älvros, *Sweden* 10 B8
Älvsborgs län □, *Sweden* 11 F6
Älvsbyn, *Sweden* 8 D19
Älvsered, *Sweden* 11 G6
Alwar, *India* 62 F7
Alxa Zuoqi, *China* 50 E3
Alyaskitovyy, *Russia* 45 C15
Alyata = Älät, *Azerbaijan* 43 L9
Alyth, *U.K.* 14 E5
Alytus, *Lithuania* 9 J21
Alzada, *U.S.A.* 108 C2
Alzano Lombardo, *Italy* 32 C6
Alzette →, *Lux.* 17 J8
Alzey, *Germany* 19 F4
Am Dam, *Chad* 73 F9
Am-Timan, *Chad* 73 F9
Amacuro □, *Venezuela* 121 B5
Amadeus, L., *Australia* 89 D5
Amâdi, *Sudan* 77 F3
Amadi, *Zaïre* 82 B2
Amadjuak, *Canada* 97 B12
Amadjuak L., *Canada* 97 B12
Amadora, *Portugal* 31 G1
Amagasaki, *Japan* 49 G7
Amager, *Denmark* 11 J6
Amakusa-Shotō, *Japan* 49 H5
Åmål, *Sweden* 9 G15
Amalfi, *Colombia* 120 B2
Amalfi, *Italy* 35 B7
Amaliás, *Greece* 39 M4
Amalner, *India* 60 J9
Amambaí, *Brazil* 127 A4
Amambaí →, *Brazil* 127 A5
Amambay □, *Paraguay* 127 A4
Amambay, Cordillera de, *S. Amer.* 127 A4
Amami-Guntō, *Japan* 49 L4
Amami-Ō-Shima, *Japan* 49 L4
Amana →, *Venezuela* 121 B5
Amaná, L., *Brazil* 121 D5
Amanda Park, *U.S.A.* 112 C3
Amándola, *Italy* 33 F10
Amangeldy, *Kazakstan* 44 D7
Amantea, *Italy* 35 C9
Amapá, *Brazil* 121 C7
Amapá □, *Brazil* 121 C7
Amapari, *Brazil* 121 C7
Amara, *Sudan* 77 E3
Amarante, *Brazil* 122 C3
Amarante, *Portugal* 30 D2
Amarante do Maranhão, *Brazil* 122 C2
Amaranth, *Canada* 101 C9
Amareleja, *Portugal* 31 G3
Amargosa, *Brazil* 123 D4
Amargosa →, *U.S.A.* 113 J10
Amargosa Range, *U.S.A.* 113 J10
Amári, *Greece* 37 D6
Amarillo, *U.S.A.* 109 H4
Amaro, Mte., *Italy* 33 F11
Amaro Leite, *Brazil* 123 D2
Amarpur, *India* 63 G12
Amasra, *Turkey* 66 B5
Amassama, *Nigeria* 79 D6
Amasya, *Turkey* 66 B6
Amataurá, *Brazil* 120 D4
Amatikulu, *S. Africa* 85 D5
Amatitlán, *Guatemala* 116 D1
Amatrice, *Italy* 33 F10
Amay, *Belgium* 17 G6
Amazon = Amazonas →, *S. Amer.* 121 D7
Amazonas □, *Brazil* 125 B5
Amazonas □, *Peru* 124 B2
Amazonas □, *Venezuela* 120 C4
Amazonas →, *S. Amer.* 121 D7
Ambahakily, *Madag.* 85 C7
Ambala, *India* 62 D7
Ambalavao, *Madag.* 85 C8
Ambalindum, *Australia* 90 C2
Ambam, *Cameroon* 80 D2
Ambanja, *Madag.* 85 A8
Ambarchik, *Russia* 45 C17
Ambarijeby, *Madag.* 85 A8
Ambaro, Helodranon', *Madag.* 85 A8
Ambartsevo, *Russia* 44 D9
Ambato, *Ecuador* 120 D2
Ambato, Sierra de, *Argentina* 126 B2
Ambato Boeny, *Madag.* 85 B8
Ambatofinandrahana, *Madag.* 85 C8
Ambatolampy, *Madag.* 85 B8
Ambatondrazaka, *Madag.* 85 B8
Ambatosoratra, *Madag.* 85 B8
Ambenja, *Madag.* 85 B8
Amberg, *Germany* 19 F7
Ambergris Cay, *Belize* 115 D7
Ambérieu-en-Bugey, *France* 27 C9
Amberley, *N.Z.* 87 K4
Ambert, *France* 26 C7
Ambidédi, *Mali* 78 C2
Ambikapur, *India* 63 H10
Ambikol, *Sudan* 76 C3
Ambilobé, *Madag.* 85 A8
Ambinanindrano, *Madag.* 85 C8
Ambjörnarp, *Sweden* 11 G7
Ambleside, *U.K.* 12 C5
Amblève, *Belgium* 17 H8
Amblève →, *Belgium* 17 H7
Ambo, *Ethiopia* 77 E4
Ambo, *Peru* 124 C2
Ambodifototra, *Madag.* 85 B8
Ambodilazana, *Madag.* 85 B8
Ambohimahasoa, *Madag.* 85 C8
Ambohimanga, *Madag.* 85 C8
Ambohitra, *Madag.* 85 A8
Amboise, *France* 24 E8
Ambon, *Indonesia* 57 E7
Amboseli L., *Kenya* 82 C4
Ambositra, *Madag.* 85 C8
Ambovombé, *Madag.* 85 D8
Amboy, *U.S.A.* 113 L11
Amboyna Cay, *S. China Sea* 56 C4
Ambridge, *U.S.A.* 106 F4
Ambriz, *Angola* 80 F2
Amby, *Australia* 91 D4
Amchitka I., *U.S.A.* 96 C1
Amderma, *Russia* 44 C7
Ameca, *Mexico* 114 C4
Ameca →, *Mexico* 114 C3
Amecameca, *Mexico* 115 D5
Ameland, *Neths.* 16 B7
Amélia, *Italy* 33 F9
Amélie-les-Bains-Palalda, *France* 26 F6
Amen, *Russia* 45 C18
Amendolara, *Italy* 35 C9
America, *Neths.* 17 F7
American Falls, *U.S.A.* 110 E7
American Falls Reservoir, *U.S.A.* 110 E7
American Highland, *Antarctica* 5 D6
American Samoa ■, *Pac. Oc.* 87 B13
Americana, *Brazil* 127 A6
Americus, *U.S.A.* 105 J3
Amersfoort, *Neths.* 16 D6
Amersfoort, *S. Africa* 85 D4
Amery, *Australia* 89 F2
Amery, *Canada* 101 B10
Amery Ice Shelf, *Antarctica* 5 C6
Ames, *U.S.A.* 108 E8
Amesbury, *U.S.A.* 107 D14
Amfíklia, *Greece* 39 L5
Amfilokhía, *Greece* 39 L4
Amga, *Russia* 45 C14
Amga →, *Russia* 45 C14
Amgu, *Russia* 45 E14
Amgun →, *Russia* 45 D14
Amherst, *Burma* 61 L20
Amherst, *Canada* 99 C7
Amherst, *Mass., U.S.A.* 107 D12
Amherst, *N.Y., U.S.A.* 106 D6
Amherst, *Ohio, U.S.A.* 106 E2
Amherst, *Tex., U.S.A.* 109 H3
Amherst I., *Canada* 107 B8
Amherstburg, *Canada* 98 D3
Amiata, Mte., *Italy* 33 F8
Amiens, *France* 25 C9
Amindaion, *Greece* 39 J4
Amīrābād, *Iran* 64 C5
Amirante Is., *Seychelles* 46 K9
Amisk L., *Canada* 101 C8
Amistad, Presa de la, *Mexico* 114 B4
Amite, *U.S.A.* 109 K9
Amizmiz, *Morocco* 74 B3
Åmli, *Norway* 11 F2
Amlwch, *U.K.* 12 D3
Amm Adam, *Sudan* 77 D4
'Ammān, *Jordan* 69 D4
Ammanford, *U.K.* 13 F3
Ammassalik = Angmagssalik, *Greenland* 4 C6
Ammerån, *Sweden* 10 A10
Ammerån →, *Sweden* 10 A10
Ammersee, *Germany* 19 G7
Ammerzoden, *Neths.* 16 E6
Amnat Charoen, *Thailand* 58 E5
Amo Jiang →, *China* 52 F3
Āmol, *Iran* 65 B7
Amorebieta, *Spain* 28 B2
Amorgós, *Greece* 39 N8
Amory, *U.S.A.* 105 J1
Amos, *Canada* 98 C4
Åmot, *Buskerud, Norway* 10 E3
Åmot, *Telemark, Norway* 10 E2
Åmotsdal, *Norway* 10 E2
Amour, Djebel, *Algeria* 75 B5
Amoy = Xiamen, *China* 53 E12
Ampang, *Malaysia* 59 L3
Ampanihy, *Madag.* 85 C7

Ampasindava, Helodranon', *Madag.* 85 A8
Ampasindava, Saikanosy, *Madag.* 85 A8
Ampato, Nevado, *Peru* 124 D3
Ampenan, *Indonesia* 56 F5
Amper, *Nigeria* 79 D6
Amper →, *Germany* 19 G7
Ampezzo, *Italy* 33 B9
Amposta, *Spain* 28 E5
Ampotaka, *Madag.* 85 D7
Ampoza, *Madag.* 85 C7
Amqui, *Canada* 99 C6
Amravati, *India* 60 J10
Amreli, *India* 62 J4
Amrenene el Kasba, *Algeria* 75 D5
Amriswil, *Switz.* 23 A8
Amritsar, *India* 62 D6
Amroha, *India* 63 E8
Amrum, *Germany* 18 A4
Amsel, *Algeria* 75 D6
Amsterdam, *Neths.* 16 D5
Amsterdam, *U.S.A.* 107 D10
Amsterdam, I., *Ind. Oc.* 3 F13
Amstetten, *Austria* 21 G4
Amudarya →, *Uzbekistan* 44 E6
Amundsen Gulf, *Canada* 96 A7
Amundsen Sea, *Antarctica* 5 D15
Amuntai, *Indonesia* 56 E5
Amur →, *Russia* 45 D15
Amurang, *Indonesia* 57 D6
Amuri Pass, *N.Z.* 87 K4
Amurrio, *Spain* 28 B1
Amursk, *Russia* 45 D14
Amurzet, *Russia* 45 E14
Amusco, *Spain* 30 C6
Amvrakikós Kólpos, *Greece* 39 L4
Amvrosiyivka, *Ukraine* 41 J10
Amyderya = Amudarya →, *Uzbekistan* 44 E6
Amzeglouf, *Algeria* 75 C5
An Bien, *Vietnam* 59 H5
An Hoa, *Vietnam* 58 E7
An Khe, *Vietnam* 58 F7
An Nabatīyah at Tahta, *Lebanon* 69 B4
An Nabk, *Si. Arabia* 64 D3
An Nabk, *Syria* 69 A5
An Nabk Abū Qaṣr, *Si. Arabia* 64 D3
An Nafūd, *Si. Arabia* 64 D4
An Najaf, *Iraq* 67 G11
An Nāṣirīyah, *Iraq* 64 D5
An Nhon, *Vietnam* 58 F7
An Nîl □, *Sudan* 76 D3
An Nîl el Abyad □, *Sudan* 77 E3
An Nîl el Azraq □, *Sudan* 77 E3
An Nu'ayrīyah, *Si. Arabia* 65 E6
An Nu'mānīyah, *Iraq* 67 F11
An Nuwayb'ī, W. →, *Si. Arabia* 69 F3
An Thoi, Dao, *Vietnam* 59 H4
An Uaimh, *Ireland* 15 C5
Anabar →, *Russia* 45 B12
'Anabtā, *West Bank* 69 C4
Anaco, *Venezuela* 121 B5
Anaconda, *U.S.A.* 110 C7
Anacortes, *U.S.A.* 112 B4
Anacuao, Mt., *Phil.* 55 C4
Anadarko, *U.S.A.* 109 H5
Anadia, *Brazil* 122 C4
Anadia, *Portugal* 30 E2
Anadolu, *Turkey* 66 C5
Anadyr, *Russia* 45 C18
Anadyr →, *Russia* 45 C18
Anadyrskiy Zaliv, *Russia* 45 C19
Anáfi, *Greece* 39 N8
Anafópoulo, *Greece* 39 N8
Anaga, Pta. de, *Canary Is.* 36 F3
Anagni, *Italy* 34 A6
'Ānah, *Iraq* 67 E10
Anaheim, *U.S.A.* 113 M9
Anahim Lake, *Canada* 100 C3
Anáhuac, *Mexico* 114 B4
Anajás, *Brazil* 122 B2
Anajatuba, *Brazil* 122 B3
Anakapalle, *India* 61 L13
Anakie, *Australia* 90 C4
Anaklia, *Georgia* 43 J5
Analalava, *Madag.* 85 A8
Análipsis, *Greece* 37 A3
Anamã, *Brazil* 121 D5
Anambar →, *Pakistan* 62 D3
Anambas, Kepulauan, *Indonesia* 56 D3
Anambas Is. = Anambas, Kepulauan, *Indonesia* 56 D3
Anambra □, *Nigeria* 79 D6
Anamoose, *U.S.A.* 108 B4
Anamosa, *U.S.A.* 108 D9
Anamur, *Turkey* 66 D5
Anamur Burnu, *Turkey* 66 D5
Anan, *Japan* 49 H7
Anand, *India* 62 H5
Anantnag, *India* 63 C6
Ananyiv, *Ukraine* 41 J5
Anapa, *Russia* 43 H3
Anapodháris →, *Greece* 37 E7
Anápolis, *Brazil* 123 E2
Anapu →, *Brazil* 121 D7
Anār, *Iran* 65 D7
Anārak, *Iran* 65 C7
Anatolia = Anadolu, *Turkey* 66 C5
Anatone, *U.S.A.* 110 C5
Anatsogno, *Madag.* 85 C7
Añatuya, *Argentina* 126 B3
Anauá →, *Brazil* 121 C5
Anaunethad L., *Canada* 101 A8
Anavilhanas, Arquipélago das, *Brazil* 121 D5
Anaye, *Niger* 73 E7
Anbyŏn, *N. Korea* 51 E14
Ancash □, *Peru* 124 B2
Ancenis, *France* 24 E5
Ancho, Canal, *Chile* 128 D2
Anchor Bay, *U.S.A.* 112 G3
Anchorage, *U.S.A.* 96 B5
Anci, *China* 50 E9
Ancohuma, Nevada, *Bolivia* 124 D4
Ancón, *Peru* 124 C2
Ancona, *Italy* 33 E10
Ancud, *Chile* 128 B2
Ancud, G. de, *Chile* 128 B2
Andacollo, *Argentina* 126 D1
Andacollo, *Chile* 126 C1
Andado, *Australia* 90 D2
Andahuaylas, *Peru* 124 C3
Andalgalá, *Argentina* 126 B2
Åndalsnes, *Norway* 10 B1
Andalucía □, *Spain* 31 H6
Andalusia, *U.S.A.* 105 K2
Andalusia □ = Andalucía □, *Spain* 31 H6
Andaman Is., *Ind. Oc.* 46 H13
Andaman Sea, *Ind. Oc.* 56 B1
Andara, *Namibia* 84 B3
Andaraí, *Brazil* 123 D3
Andeer, *Switz.* 23 C8
Andelfingen, *Switz.* 23 A7
Andelot, *France* 25 D12
Andenes, *Norway* 8 B17
Andenne, *Belgium* 17 H6
Andéranboukane, *Mali* 79 B5
Anderlecht, *Belgium* 17 G4
Anderlues, *Belgium* 17 H4
Andermatt, *Switz.* 23 C7
Andernach, *Germany* 18 E3
Andernos-les-Bains, *France* 26 D2
Anderslöv, *Sweden* 11 J7
Anderson, *Calif., U.S.A.* 110 F2
Anderson, *Ind., U.S.A.* 104 E3
Anderson, *Mo., U.S.A.* 109 G7
Anderson, *S.C., U.S.A.* 105 H4
Anderson →, *Canada* 96 B7
Andes = Andes, Cord. de los, *S. Amer.* 124 C3
Andes, *S. Amer.* 124 C2
Andes, Cord. de los, *S. Amer.* 124 C3
Andfjorden, *Norway* 8 B17
Andhra Pradesh □, *India* 60 L11
Andijon, *Uzbekistan* 44 E8
Andikíthira, *Greece* 39 P6
Andīmeshk, *Iran* 67 F13
Andímilos, *Greece* 39 N7
Andípaxoi, *Greece* 39 K3
Andizhan = Andijon, *Uzbekistan* 44 E8
Andoany, *Madag.* 85 A8
Andoas, *Peru* 120 D2
Andong, *S. Korea* 51 F15
Andongwei, *China* 51 G10
Andorra ■, *Europe* 28 C6
Andorra La Vella, *Andorra* 28 C6
Andover, *U.K.* 13 F6
Andover, *Mass., U.S.A.* 107 D13
Andover, *N.Y., U.S.A.* 106 D7
Andover, *Ohio, U.S.A.* 106 E4
Andøya, *Norway* 8 B16
Andradina, *Brazil* 123 F1
Andrahary, Mt., *Madag.* 85 A8
Andraitx, *Spain* 36 B9
Andramasina, *Madag.* 85 B8
Andranopasy, *Madag.* 85 C7
Andreanof Is., *U.S.A.* 96 C2
Andreapol, *Russia* 40 D7
Andrespol, *Poland* 20 D9
Andrewilla, *Australia* 91 D2
Andrews, *S.C., U.S.A.* 105 J6
Andrews, *Tex., U.S.A.* 109 J3
Andreyevka, *Russia* 42 D10
Ándria, *Italy* 35 A9
Andriba, *Madag.* 85 B8
Andrijevica, *Montenegro, Yug.* 21 N9
Andrítsaina, *Greece* 39 M4
Androka, *Madag.* 85 C7
Andropov = Rybinsk, *Russia* 42 A4
Ándros, *Greece* 39 M7
Andros I., *Bahamas* 116 B4
Andros Town, *Bahamas* 116 B4
Andselv, *Norway* 8 B18
Andújar, *Spain* 31 G6
Andulo, *Angola* 80 G3
Anegada, B., *Argentina* 128 B4
Anegada I., *Virgin Is.* 117 C7
Anegada Passage, *W. Indies* 117 C7
Aného, *Togo* 79 D5
Añelo, *Argentina* 128 A3
Anergane, *Morocco* 74 B3
Aneto, Pico de, *Spain* 28 C5
Añez, *Bolivia* 125 D5
Anfu, *China* 53 D10
Ang Thong, *Thailand* 58 E3
Angamos, Punta, *Chile* 126 A1
Ang'angxi, *China* 54 B7
Angara →, *Russia* 45 D10
Angarab, *Ethiopia* 77 E4
Angarsk, *Russia* 45 D11
Angas Downs, *Australia* 89 E5
Angas Hills, *Australia* 88 D4
Angaston, *Australia* 91 E2
Ånge, *Sweden* 10 B9
Ángel, Salto = Angel Falls, *Venezuela* 121 B5
Ángel de la Guarda, I., *Mexico* 114 B2
Angel Falls, *Venezuela* 121 B5
Angeles, *Phil.* 55 D4
Ängelholm, *Sweden* 11 H6
Angellala, *Australia* 91 D4
Angels Camp, *U.S.A.* 111 G3
Anger →, *Ethiopia* 77 F4
Angereb →, *Ethiopia* 77 E4
Ångermanälven →, *Sweden* 10 B12
Ångermanland, *Sweden* 8 E18
Angermünde, *Germany* 18 B10
Angers, *Canada* 107 A9
Angers, *France* 24 E6
Angerville, *France* 25 D8
Ångesån →, *Sweden* 8 C20
Anghiari, *Italy* 33 E9
Angical, *Brazil* 123 D3
Angikuni L., *Canada* 101 A9
Angkor, *Cambodia* 58 F4
Anglés, *Spain* 28 D7
Anglesey, *U.K.* 12 D3
Anglesey □, *U.K.* 12 D3
Anglet, *France* 26 E2
Angleton, *U.S.A.* 109 L7
Angleur, *Belgium* 17 G7
Anglin →, *France* 26 B4
Anglisidhes, *Cyprus* 37 E12
Anglure, *France* 25 D10
Angmagssalik, *Greenland* 4 C6
Ango, *Zaïre* 82 B2
Angoche, *Mozam.* 83 F4
Angoche, I., *Mozam.* 83 F4
Angol, *Chile* 126 D1
Angola, *Ind., U.S.A.* 104 E3
Angola, *N.Y., U.S.A.* 106 D5
Angola ■, *Africa* 81 G3
Angoon, *U.S.A.* 100 B2
Angoulême, *France* 26 C4
Angoumois, *France* 26 C4
Angra dos Reis, *Brazil* 127 A7
Angren, *Uzbekistan* 44 E8
Angtassom, *Cambodia* 59 G5
Angu, *Zaïre* 82 B1
Anguang, *China* 51 B12
Anguilla ■, *W. Indies* 117 C7
Anguo, *China* 50 E8
Angurugu, *Australia* 90 A2
Angus □, *U.K.* 14 E6
Angus, Braes of, *U.K.* 14 E5
Anhanduí →, *Brazil* 127 A5
Anhée, *Belgium* 17 H5
Anholt, *Denmark* 11 H5
Anhua, *China* 53 C8
Anhui □, *China* 53 B11
Anhwei □ = Anhui □, *China* 53 B11
Anichab, *Namibia* 84 C1
Anicuns, *Brazil* 123 E2
Ánidhros, *Greece* 39 N8
Anie, *Togo* 79 D5
Animas, *U.S.A.* 111 L9
Änimskog, *Sweden* 11 F6
Anina, *Romania* 38 D4
Anivorano, *Madag.* 85 B8
Anjalankoski, *Finland* 9 F22
Anjar, *India* 62 H4
Anjidiv I., *India* 60 M9
Anjou, *France* 24 E6
Anjozorobe, *Madag.* 85 B8
Anju, *N. Korea* 51 E13
Anka, *Nigeria* 79 C6
Ankaboa, Tanjona, *Madag.* 85 C7
Ankang, *China* 50 H5
Ankara, *Turkey* 66 C5
Ankaramena, *Madag.* 85 C8
Ankazoabo, *Madag.* 85 C7
Ankazobe, *Madag.* 85 B8
Ankisabe, *Madag.* 85 B8
Anklam, *Germany* 18 B9
Ankober, *Ethiopia* 77 F4
Ankoro, *Zaïre* 82 D2
Anlong, *China* 52 E5
Anlu, *China* 53 B9
Anmyŏn-do, *S. Korea* 51 F14
Ånn, *Sweden* 10 A6
Ann, C., *U.S.A.* 107 D14
Ann Arbor, *U.S.A.* 104 D4
Anna, *Russia* 42 E5
Anna, *U.S.A.* 109 G10
Anna Plains, *Australia* 88 C3
Anna Regina, *Guyana* 121 B6
Annaba, *Algeria* 75 A6
Annaberg-Buchholz, *Germany* 18 E8
Annalee →, *Ireland* 15 B4
Annam = Trung-Phan, *Vietnam* 58 E7
Annamitique, Chaîne, *Asia* 58 D6
Annan, *U.K.* 14 G5
Annan →, *U.K.* 14 G5
Annapolis, *U.S.A.* 104 F7
Annapolis Royal, *Canada* 99 D6
Annapurna, *Nepal* 63 E10
Annean, L., *Australia* 89 E2
Anneberg, *Sweden* 11 G6
Annecy, *France* 27 C10
Annecy, L. d', *France* 27 C10
Annemasse, *France* 27 B10
Annenskiy Most, *Russia* 40 B9
Anning, *China* 52 E4
Anningie, *Australia* 88 D5
Anniston, *U.S.A.* 105 J3
Annobón, *Atl. Oc.* 70 G4
Annonay, *France* 27 C8
Annot, *France* 27 E10
Annotto Bay, *Jamaica* 116 C4
Annuello, *Australia* 91 E3
Annville, *U.S.A.* 107 F8
Annweiler, *Germany* 19 F3
Áno Viánnos, *Greece* 37 D7
Anoka, *U.S.A.* 103 A8
Anorotsangana, *Madag.* 85 A8
Anóyia, *Greece* 37 D6
Anping, *Hebei, China* 50 E8
Anping, *Liaoning, China* 51 D12
Anpu Gang, *China* 52 G7
Anqing, *China* 53 B11
Anqiu, *China* 51 F10
Anren, *China* 53 D9
Ans, *Belgium* 17 G7
Ansai, *China* 50 F5
Ansbach, *Germany* 19 F6
Anseba →, *Eritrea* 77 D4
Anserma, *Colombia* 120 B2
Anseroeul, *Belgium* 17 G3
Anshan, *China* 51 D12
Anshun, *China* 52 D5
Ansião, *Portugal* 30 F2
Ansirabe, *Madag.* 85 B8
Ansley, *U.S.A.* 108 E5
Ansó, *Spain* 28 C4
Anson, *U.S.A.* 109 J5
Anson B., *Australia* 88 B5
Ansongo, *Mali* 79 B5
Ansonia, *U.S.A.* 107 E11
Anstruther, *U.K.* 14 E6
Ansudu, *Indonesia* 57 E9
Antabamba, *Peru* 124 C3
Antakya, *Turkey* 66 D7
Antalaha, *Madag.* 85 A9
Antalya, *Turkey* 66 D4
Antalya Körfezi, *Turkey* 66 D4
Antananarivo, *Madag.* 85 B8
Antananarivo □, *Madag.* 85 B8
Antanimbaribe, *Madag.* 85 C7
Antarctic Pen., *Antarctica* 5 C18
Antarctica 5 E3
Antelope, *Zimbabwe* 83 G2
Antenor Navarro, *Brazil* 122 C4
Antequera, *Paraguay* 126 A4
Antequera, *Spain* 31 H6
Antero, Mt., *U.S.A.* 111 G10
Anthony, *Kans., U.S.A.* 109 G5
Anthony, *N. Mex., U.S.A.* 111 K10
Anthony Lagoon, *Australia* 90 B2
Anti Atlas, *Morocco* 74 C2
Anti-Lebanon = Ash Sharqi, Al Jabal, *Lebanon* 69 B5
Antibes, *France* 27 E11
Antibes, C. d', *France* 27 E11
Anticosti, I. d', *Canada* 99 C7
Antifer, C. d', *France* 24 C7
Antigo, *U.S.A.* 108 C10
Antigonish, *Canada* 99 C7
Antigua, *Canary Is.* 36 F5
Antigua, *Guatemala* 116 D1
Antigua, *W. Indies* 117 C7
Antigua & Barbuda ■, *W. Indies* 117 C7
Antilla, *Cuba* 116 B4
Antimony, *U.S.A.* 111 G8
Antioch, *U.S.A.* 112 G5
Antioche, Pertuis d', *France* 26 B2
Antioquia, *Colombia* 120 B2
Antioquia □, *Colombia* 120 B2
Antipodes Is., *Pac. Oc.* 92 M9
Antler, *U.S.A.* 108 A4
Antler →, *Canada* 101 D8
Antlers, *U.S.A.* 109 H7
Antofagasta, *Chile* 126 A1
Antofagasta □, *Chile* 126 A2
Antofagasta de la Sierra, *Argentina* 126 B2
Antofalla, *Argentina* 126 B2
Antofalla, Salar de, *Argentina* 126 B2
Antoing, *Belgium* 17 G2
Anton, *U.S.A.* 109 J3
Anton Chico, *U.S.A.* 111 J11
Antongila, Helodrano, *Madag.* 85 B8
Antonibé, *Madag.* 85 B8
Antonibé, Presqu'île d', *Madag.* 85 A8
Antonina, *Brazil* 127 B6
Antonito, *U.S.A.* 111 H10
Antrain, *France* 24 D5
Antrim, *U.K.* 15 B5
Antrim □, *U.K.* 15 B5
Antrim, Mts. of, *U.K.* 15 B5
Antrim Plateau, *Australia* 88 C4
Antrodoco, *Italy* 33 F10
Antropovo, *Russia* 42 A6
Antsalova, *Madag.* 85 B7
Antsiranana, *Madag.* 85 A8
Antsohihy, *Madag.* 85 A8
Antsohimbondrona Seranana, *Madag.* 85 A8
Antu, *China* 51 C15
Antwerp = Antwerpen, *Belgium* 17 F4
Antwerp, *U.S.A.* 107 B9
Antwerpen, *Belgium* 17 F4
Antwerpen □, *Belgium* 17 F5
Anupgarh, *India* 62 E5
Anuradhapura, *Sri Lanka* 60 Q12
Anveh, *Iran* 65 E7
Anvers = Antwerpen, *Belgium* 17 F4
Anvers I., *Antarctica* 5 C17
Anxi, *Fujian, China* 53 E12
Anxi, *Gansu, China* 54 B4
Anxiang, *China* 53 C9
Anxious B., *Australia* 91 E1
Anyama, *Ivory C.* 78 D4
Anyang, *China* 50 F8
Anyi, *Jiangxi, China* 53 C10
Anyi, *Shanxi, China* 50 G6
Anyuan, *China* 53 E10
Anza, *U.S.A.* 113 M10
Anze, *China* 50 F7
Anzhero-Sudzhensk, *Russia* 44 D9
Ánzio, *Italy* 34 A5
Anzoátegui □, *Venezuela* 121 B5
Aoga-Shima, *Japan* 49 H9
Aoiz, *Spain* 28 C3
Aomori, *Japan* 48 D10
Aomori □, *Japan* 48 D10
Aonla, *India* 63 E8
Aosta, *Italy* 32 C4
Aoudéras, *Niger* 79 B6
Aouinet Torkoz, *Morocco* 74 C3
Aoukar, *Mali* 74 D4
Aouker, *Mauritania* 78 B3
Aoulef el Arab, *Algeria* 75 C5
Apa →, *S. Amer.* 126 A4
Apache, *U.S.A.* 109 H5
Apalachee B., *U.S.A.* 105 L3
Apalachicola, *U.S.A.* 105 L3
Apalachicola →, *U.S.A.* 105 L3
Apapa, *Nigeria* 79 D5
Apaporis →, *Colombia* 120 D4
Aparecida do Taboado, *Brazil* 123 F1
Aparri, *Phil.* 55 B4
Aparurén, *Venezuela* 121 B5
Apateu, *Romania* 38 C4
Apatin, *Serbia, Yug.* 21 K8
Apatzingán, *Mexico* 114 D4
Apeldoorn, *Neths.* 16 D7
Apeldoornsch Kanal →, *Neths.* 16 D8
Apen, *Germany* 18 B3
Apennines = Appennini, *Italy* 32 D7
Apere →, *Bolivia* 125 C4
Apia, *W. Samoa* 87 A13
Apiacás, Serra dos, *Brazil* 125 B6
Apiaú →, *Brazil* 121 C5
Apiaú, Serra do, *Brazil* 121 C5
Apidiá →, *Brazil* 125 C5
Apinajé, *Brazil* 123 D2
Apizaco, *Mexico* 115 D5
Aplao, *Peru* 124 D3
Apo, Mt., *Phil.* 57 C7
Apodi, *Brazil* 122 C4
Apolakkiá, *Greece* 37 C9
Apolakkiá, Órmos, *Greece* 37 C9
Apolda, *Germany* 18 D7
Apollonia = Marsá Susah, *Libya* 73 B9
Apollonia, *Greece* 39 N7
Apolo, *Bolivia* 124 C4
Apónguao →, *Venezuela* 121 C5
Aporé, *Brazil* 125 D7
Aporé →, *Brazil* 123 E1
Aporema, *Brazil* 122 A1
Apostle Is., *U.S.A.* 108 B9
Apóstoles, *Argentina* 127 B4
Apostolos Andreas, C., *Cyprus* 66 E6
Apostolovo, *Ukraine* 41 J7
Apoteri, *Guyana* 121 C6
Appalachian Mts., *U.S.A.* 104 G6
Appelscha, *Neths.* 16 C8
Appennini, *Italy* 32 D7
Appennino Ligure, *Italy* 32 D5
Appenzell, *Switz.* 23 B8
Appenzell-Ausser Rhoden □, *Switz.* 23 B8
Appenzell-Inner Rhoden □, *Switz.* 23 B8
Appiano, *Italy* 33 B8
Appingedam, *Neths.* 16 B9
Apple Hill, *Canada* 107 A10
Apple Valley, *U.S.A.* 113 L9
Appleby-in-Westmorland, *U.K.* 12 C5
Appleton, *U.S.A.* 104 C1
Approuague, *Fr. Guiana* 121 C7
Approuague →, *Fr. Guiana* 121 C7
Apricena, *Italy* 35 A8
Aprigliano, *Italy* 35 C9
Aprília, *Italy* 34 A5
Apsheronsk, *Russia* 43 H4
Apt, *France* 27 E9
Apuane, Alpi, *Italy* 32 D7
Apuaú, *Brazil* 121 D5
Apucarana, *Brazil* 127 A5
Apulia = Púglia □, *Italy* 35 B9
Apure □, *Venezuela* 120 B4
Apure →, *Venezuela* 120 B4
Apurímac □, *Peru* 124 C3
Apurimac →, *Peru* 124 C3
Apuseni, Munţii, *Romania* 38 C5
Aqabah = Al 'Aqabah, *Jordan* 69 F4
'Aqabah, Khalīj al, *Red Sea* 64 D2
'Aqdā, *Iran* 65 C7
Aqîq, *Sudan* 76 D4
Aqîq, Khalîg, *Sudan* 76 D4
Aqmola, *Kazakstan* 44 D8
Aqrah, *Iraq* 67 D10
Aqtöbe, *Kazakstan* 44 D6

Aquidauana, *Brazil* 125 E6
Aquidauana →, *Brazil* 125 D6
Aquiles Serdán, *Mexico* 114 B3
Aquin, *Haiti* 117 C5
Ar Rachidiya, *Morocco* 74 B4
Ar Rafid, *Syria* 69 C4
Ar Raḩḩālīyah, *Iraq* 67 F10
Ar Ramādī, *Iraq* 67 F10
Ar Ramthā, *Jordan* 69 C5
Ar Raqqah, *Syria* 67 E8
Ar Rass, *Si. Arabia* 64 E4
Ar Rifā'ī, *Iraq* 64 D5
Ar Riyāḑ, *Si. Arabia* 64 E5
Ar Ru'ays, *Qatar* 65 E6
Ar Rukhaymīyah, *Iraq* 64 D5
Ar Ruqayyidah, *Si. Arabia* 65 E6
Ar Ruşāfah, *Syria* 67 E8
Ar Ruţbah, *Iraq* 67 F9
Ara, *India* 63 G11
'Arab, Bahr el →, *Sudan* 77 F2
Arab, Khalîg el, *Egypt* 76 H6
'Arabābād, *Iran* 65 C8
Araban, *Turkey* 66 D7
Arabatskaya Strelka, *Ukraine* 41 K8
Arabba, *Italy* 33 B8
Arabelo, *Venezuela* 121 C5
Arabia, *Asia* 68 C4
Arabian Desert = Es Sahrâ' Esh Sharqîya, *Egypt* 76 B3
Arabian Gulf = Gulf, The, *Asia* 65 E6
Arabian Sea, *Ind. Oc.* 47 H10
Araç, *Turkey* 66 B5
Aracaju, *Brazil* 122 D4
Aracataca, *Colombia* 120 A3
Aracati, *Brazil* 122 B4
Araçatuba, *Brazil* 127 A5
Aracena, *Spain* 31 H4
Aracena, Sierra de, *Spain* 31 H4
Araçuaí, *Brazil* 123 E3
Araçuaí →, *Brazil* 123 E3
'Arad, *Israel* 69 D4
Arad, *Romania* 38 C4
Arada, *Chad* 73 F9
Aradhippou, *Cyprus* 37 E12
Arafura Sea, *E. Indies* 57 F8
Aragarças, *Brazil* 125 D7
Aragats, *Armenia* 43 K7
Aragón □, *Spain* 28 D4
Aragón →, *Spain* 28 C3
Aragona, *Italy* 34 E6
Aragua □, *Venezuela* 120 B4
Aragua de Barcelona, *Venezuela* 121 B5
Araguacema, *Brazil* 122 C2
Araguaçu, *Brazil* 123 D2
Araguaia →, *Brazil* 122 C2
Araguaiana, *Brazil* 125 D7
Araguaína, *Brazil* 122 C2
Araguari, *Brazil* 123 E2
Araguari →, *Brazil* 121 C8
Araguatins, *Brazil* 122 C2
Araioses, *Brazil* 122 B3
Arak, *Algeria* 75 C5
Arāk, *Iran* 65 C6
Arakan Coast, *Burma* 61 K19
Arakan Yoma, *Burma* 61 K19
Arakli, *Turkey* 67 B8
Araks = Aras, Rūd-e →, *Azerbaijan* 43 K9
Aral, *Kazakstan* 44 E7
Aral Sea, *Asia* 44 E7
Aral Tengizi = Aral Sea, *Asia* 44 E7
Aralsk = Aral, *Kazakstan* 44 E7
Aralskoye More = Aral Sea, *Asia* 44 E7
Aralsor, Ozero, *Kazakstan* 43 F9
Aramac, *Australia* 90 C4
Arambag, *India* 63 H12
Aran I., *Ireland* 15 B3
Aran Is., *Ireland* 15 C2
Aranda de Duero, *Spain* 28 D1
Arandān, *Iran* 64 C5
Aranjuez, *Spain* 30 E7
Aranos, *Namibia* 84 C2
Aransas Pass, *U.S.A.* 109 M6
Aranzazu, *Colombia* 120 B2
Araouane, *Mali* 78 B4
Arapahoe, *U.S.A.* 108 E5
Arapari, *Brazil* 122 C2
Arapey Grande →, *Uruguay* 126 C4
Arapgir, *Turkey* 67 C8
Arapiraca, *Brazil* 122 C4
Arapongas, *Brazil* 127 A5
Ar'ar, *Si. Arabia* 64 D4
Araracuara, *Colombia* 120 D3
Araranguá, *Brazil* 127 B6
Araraquara, *Brazil* 123 F2
Ararás, Serra das, *Brazil* 127 B5
Ararat, *Armenia* 67 C11
Ararat, *Australia* 91 F3
Ararat, Mt. = Ağrı Dağı, *Turkey* 67 C11
Arari, *Brazil* 122 B3
Araria, *India* 63 F12
Araripe, Chapada do, *Brazil* 122 C3
Araripina, *Brazil* 122 C3
Araruama, L. de, *Brazil* 123 F3
Araruna, *Brazil* 122 C4
Aras, Rūd-e →, *Azerbaijan* 43 K9
Araticu, *Brazil* 122 B2
Arauca, *Colombia* 120 B3
Arauca □, *Colombia* 120 B3
Arauca →, *Venezuela* 120 B4
Arauco, *Chile* 126 D1
Arauco □, *Chile* 126 D1
Araújos, *Brazil* 123 E2
Arauquita, *Colombia* 120 B3
Araure, *Venezuela* 120 B4
Arawa, *Ethiopia* 77 F5
Araxá, *Brazil* 123 E2
Araya, Pen. de, *Venezuela* 121 A5
Arba Minch, *Ethiopia* 77 F4
Arbat, *Iraq* 67 E11
Arbatax, *Italy* 34 C2
Arbedo, *Switz.* 23 D8
Arbīl, *Iraq* 67 D11
Arbois, *France* 25 F12
Arboletes, *Colombia* 120 B2
Arbon, *Switz.* 23 A8
Arbore, *Ethiopia* 77 F4
Arboréa, *Italy* 34 C1
Arborfield, *Canada* 101 C8
Arborg, *Canada* 101 C9
Arbrå, *Sweden* 10 C10
Arbroath, *U.K.* 14 E6
Arbuckle, *U.S.A.* 112 F4
Arbus, *Italy* 34 C1
Arc, *France* 25 E12
Arc →, *France* 27 C10
Arcachon, *France* 26 D2
Arcachon, Bassin d', *France* 26 D2
Arcade, *U.S.A.* 106 D6
Arcadia, *Fla., U.S.A.* 105 M5
Arcadia, *La., U.S.A.* 109 J8
Arcadia, *Nebr., U.S.A.* 108 E5
Arcadia, *Pa., U.S.A.* 106 F6
Arcadia, *Wis., U.S.A.* 108 C9
Arcata, *U.S.A.* 110 F1
Arcévia, *Italy* 33 E9
Archangel = Arkhangelsk, *Russia* 44 C5
Archar, *Bulgaria* 38 F5
Archbald, *U.S.A.* 107 E9
Archena, *Spain* 29 G3
Archer →, *Australia* 90 A3
Archer B., *Australia* 90 A3
Archers Post, *Kenya* 82 B4
Archidona, *Spain* 31 H6
Arci, Mte., *Italy* 34 C1
Arcidosso, *Italy* 33 F8
Arcila = Asilah, *Morocco* 74 A3
Arcis-sur-Aube, *France* 25 D11
Arckaringa, *Australia* 91 D1
Arckaringa Cr. →, *Australia* 91 D2
Arco, *Italy* 32 C7
Arco, *U.S.A.* 110 E7
Arcola, *Canada* 101 D8
Arcos, *Spain* 28 D2
Arcos de la Frontera, *Spain* 31 J5
Arcos de Valdevez, *Portugal* 30 D2
Arcot, *India* 60 N11
Arcoverde, *Brazil* 122 C4
Arctic Bay, *Canada* 97 A11
Arctic Ocean, *Arctic* 4 B18
Arctic Red River, *Canada* 96 B6
Arda →, *Bulgaria* 39 H9
Arda →, *Italy* 32 D6
Ardabīl, *Iran* 67 C13
Ardahan, *Turkey* 67 B10
Ardakān = Sepīdān, *Iran* 65 D7
Ardales, *Spain* 31 J6
Årdalstangen, *Norway* 10 C1
Ardea, *Greece* 39 J5
Ardèche □, *France* 27 D8
Ardèche →, *France* 27 D8
Ardee, *Ireland* 15 C5
Arden, *Canada* 106 B8
Arden, *Denmark* 11 H3
Arden, *Calif., U.S.A.* 112 G5
Arden, *Nev., U.S.A.* 113 J11
Ardenne, *Belgium* 25 C12
Ardennes = Ardenne, *Belgium* 25 C12
Ardennes □, *France* 25 C11
Ardentes, *France* 25 F8
Ardeşen, *Turkey* 67 B9
Ardestān, *Iran* 65 C7
Ardgour, *U.K.* 14 E3
Árdhas →, *Greece* 39 H9
Ardila →, *Portugal* 31 G3
Ardlethan, *Australia* 91 E4
Ardmore, *Australia* 90 C2
Ardmore, *Okla., U.S.A.* 109 H6
Ardmore, *Pa., U.S.A.* 107 G9
Ardmore, *S. Dak., U.S.A.* 108 D3
Ardnacrusha, *Ireland* 15 D3
Ardnamurchan, Pt. of, *U.K.* 14 E2
Ardon, *Russia* 43 J7
Ardooie, *Belgium* 17 G2
Ardore, *Italy* 35 D9
Ardres, *France* 25 B8
Ardrossan, *Australia* 91 E2
Ardrossan, *U.K.* 14 F4
Ards □, *U.K.* 15 B6
Ards Pen., *U.K.* 15 B6
Ardud, *Romania* 38 B5
Åre, *Sweden* 10 A7
Arecibo, *Puerto Rico* 117 C6
Areia Branca, *Brazil* 122 B4
Arena, Pt., *U.S.A.* 112 G3
Arenales, Cerro, *Chile* 128 C2
Arenápolis, *Brazil* 125 C6
Arenas, *Spain* 30 B6
Arenas de San Pedro, *Spain* 30 E5
Arendal, *Norway* 11 F2
Arendonk, *Belgium* 17 F6
Arendsee, *Germany* 18 C7
Arenillas, *Ecuador* 120 D1
Arenys de Mar, *Spain* 28 D7
Arenzano, *Italy* 32 D5
Areópolis, *Greece* 39 N5
Arequipa, *Peru* 124 D3
Arequipa □, *Peru* 124 D3
Arere, *Brazil* 121 D7
Arero, *Ethiopia* 77 G4
Arès, *France* 26 D2
Arévalo, *Spain* 30 D6
Arezzo, *Italy* 33 E8
Arga →, *Spain* 28 C3
Argalastí, *Greece* 39 K6
Argamakmur, *Indonesia* 56 E2
Argamasilla de Alba, *Spain* 29 F1
Arganda, *Spain* 28 E1
Arganil, *Portugal* 30 E2
Argelès-Gazost, *France* 26 F3
Argelès-sur-Mer, *France* 26 F7
Argens →, *France* 27 E10
Argent-sur-Sauldre, *France* 25 E9
Argenta, *Italy* 33 D8
Argentan, *France* 24 D6
Argentário, Mte., *Italy* 33 F8
Argentat, *France* 26 C5
Argentera, *Italy* 32 D3
Argentera, Monte del, *Italy* 32 D4
Argenteuil, *France* 25 D9
Argentia, *Canada* 99 C9
Argentiera, C. dell', *Italy* 34 B1
Argentière, Aiguilles d', *Switz.* 22 E4
Argentina ■, *S. Amer.* 128 B3
Argentina Is., *Antarctica* 5 C17
Argentino, L., *Argentina* 128 D2
Argenton-Château, *France* 24 F6
Argenton-sur-Creuse, *France* 26 B5
Argeş →, *Romania* 38 E9
Arghandab →, *Afghan.* 62 D1
Argo, *Sudan* 76 D3
Argolikós Kólpos, *Greece* 39 M5
Argonne, *France* 25 C12
Árgos, *Greece* 39 M5
Argostólion, *Greece* 39 L3
Arguedas, *Spain* 28 C3
Arguello, Pt., *U.S.A.* 113 L6
Arguineguín, *Canary Is.* 36 G4
Argun, *Russia* 43 J7
Argun →, *Russia* 45 D13
Argungu, *Nigeria* 79 C5
Argus Pk., *U.S.A.* 113 K9
Argyle, *U.S.A.* 108 A6
Argyle, L., *Australia* 88 C4
Argyll & Bute □, *U.K.* 14 E3
Arhavi, *Turkey* 67 B9
Århus, *Denmark* 11 H4
Århus Amtskommune □, *Denmark* 11 H4
Ariadnoye, *Russia* 48 B7
Ariamsvlei, *Namibia* 84 D2
Ariana, *Tunisia* 75 A7
Ariano Irpino, *Italy* 35 A8
Ariano nel Polèsine, *Italy* 33 D9
Ariari →, *Colombia* 120 C3
Aribinda, *Burkina Faso* 79 C4
Arica, *Chile* 124 D3
Arica, *Colombia* 120 D3
Arico, *Canary Is.* 36 F3
Arid, C., *Australia* 89 F3
Arida, *Japan* 49 G7
Ariège □, *France* 26 F5
Ariège →, *France* 26 E5
Arieş →, *Romania* 38 C6
Arīḩā, *Syria* 64 C3
Arílla, Ákra, *Greece* 37 A3
Arima, *Trin. & Tob.* 117 D7
Arinos →, *Brazil* 125 C6
Ario de Rosales, *Mexico* 114 D4
Aripuanã, *Brazil* 125 B5
Aripuanã →, *Brazil* 125 B5
Ariquemes, *Brazil* 125 B5
Arisaig, *U.K.* 14 E3
Arîsh, W. el →, *Egypt* 76 H8
Arismendi, *Venezuela* 120 B4
Arissa, *Ethiopia* 77 E5
Aristazabal I., *Canada* 100 C3
Arivaca, *U.S.A.* 111 L8
Arivonimamo, *Madag.* 85 B8
Ariza, *Spain* 28 D2
Arizaro, Salar de, *Argentina* 126 A2
Arizona, *Argentina* 126 D2
Arizona □, *U.S.A.* 111 J8
Arizpe, *Mexico* 114 A2
Arjeplog, *Sweden* 8 D18
Arjona, *Colombia* 120 A2
Arjona, *Spain* 31 H6
Arjuno, *Indonesia* 57 G15
Arka, *Russia* 45 C15
Arkadak, *Russia* 42 E6
Arkadelphia, *U.S.A.* 109 H8
Arkaig, L., *U.K.* 14 E3
Arkalyk = Arqalyk, *Kazakstan* 44 D7
Arkansas □, *U.S.A.* 109 H8
Arkansas →, *U.S.A.* 109 J9
Arkansas City, *U.S.A.* 109 G6
Arkathos →, *Greece* 39 K4
Arkhángelos, *Greece* 37 C10
Arkhangelsk, *Russia* 44 C5
Arkhangelskoye, *Russia* 42 E5
Arkiko, *Eritrea* 77 D4
Arklow, *Ireland* 15 D5
Arkona, Kap, *Germany* 18 A9
Arkösund, *Sweden* 11 F10
Arkticheskiy, Mys, *Russia* 45 A10
Arkul, *Russia* 42 B10
Arlanc, *France* 26 C7
Arlanza →, *Spain* 30 C6
Arlanzón →, *Spain* 30 C6
Arlberg P., *Austria* 19 H6
Arlee, *U.S.A.* 110 C6
Arles, *France* 27 E8
Arlesheim, *Switz.* 22 B5
Arlington, *S. Africa* 85 D4
Arlington, *Oreg., U.S.A.* 110 D3
Arlington, *S. Dak., U.S.A.* 108 C6
Arlington, *Va., U.S.A.* 104 F7
Arlington, *Wash., U.S.A.* 112 B4
Arlington Heights, *U.S.A.* 104 D2
Arlon, *Belgium* 17 J7
Arlöv, *Sweden* 11 J7
Arly, *Burkina Faso* 79 C5
Armagh, *U.K.* 15 B5
Armagh □, *U.K.* 15 B5
Armagnac, *France* 26 E4
Armançon →, *France* 25 E10
Armavir, *Russia* 43 H5
Armenia, *Colombia* 120 C2
Armenia ■, *Asia* 43 K7
Armenistís, Ákra, *Greece* 37 C9
Armentières, *France* 25 B9
Armidale, *Australia* 91 E5
Armour, *U.S.A.* 108 D5
Armstrong, *B.C., Canada* 100 C5
Armstrong, *Ont., Canada* 98 B2
Armstrong, *U.S.A.* 109 M6
Armstrong →, *Australia* 88 C5
Arnarfjörður, *Iceland* 8 D2
Arnaud →, *Canada* 97 B12
Arnauti, C., *Cyprus* 37 D11
Arnay-le-Duc, *France* 25 E11
Arnedillo, *Spain* 28 C2
Arnedo, *Spain* 28 C2
Arnemuiden, *Neths.* 17 F3
Årnes, *Norway* 10 D5
Arnett, *U.S.A.* 109 G5
Arnhem, *Neths.* 16 E7
Arnhem, C., *Australia* 90 A2
Arnhem B., *Australia* 90 A2
Arnhem Land, *Australia* 90 A1
Arno →, *Italy* 32 E7
Arno Bay, *Australia* 91 E2
Arnold, *Calif., U.S.A.* 112 G6
Arnold, *Nebr., U.S.A.* 108 E4
Arnoldstein, *Austria* 21 J3
Arnon →, *France* 25 E9
Arnot, *Canada* 101 B9
Arnøy, *Norway* 8 A19
Arnprior, *Canada* 98 C4
Arnsberg, *Germany* 18 D4
Arnstadt, *Germany* 18 E6
Aro →, *Venezuela* 121 B5
Aroab, *Namibia* 84 D2
Aroche, *Spain* 31 H4
Aroeiras, *Brazil* 122 C4
Arolla, *Switz.* 22 D4
Arolsen, *Germany* 18 D5
Aron →, *France* 26 B7
Arona, *Italy* 32 C5
Aroroy, *Phil.* 55 E5
Arosa, *Switz.* 23 C9
Arosa, Ria de, *Spain* 30 C2
Arpajon, *France* 25 D9
Arpajon-sur-Cère, *France* 26 D6
Arpino, *Italy* 34 A6
Arqalyk, *Kazakstan* 44 D7
Arque, *Bolivia* 124 D4
Arrabury, *Australia* 91 D3
Arrah = Ara, *India* 63 G11
Arraias, *Brazil* 123 D2
Arraias →, *Mato Grosso, Brazil* 125 C7
Arraias →, *Pará, Brazil* 122 C2
Arraiolos, *Portugal* 31 G3
Arran, *U.K.* 14 F3
Arrandale, *Canada* 100 C3
Arras, *France* 25 B9
Arrats →, *France* 26 D4
Arreau, *France* 26 F4
Arrecife, *Canary Is.* 36 F6
Arrecifes, *Argentina* 126 C3
Arrée, Mts. d', *France* 24 D3
Arriaga, *Chiapas, Mexico* 115 D6
Arriaga, *San Luis Potosí, Mexico* 114 C4
Arrilalah P.O., *Australia* 90 C3
Arrino, *Australia* 89 E2
Arrojado →, *Brazil* 123 D3
Arromanches-les-Bains, *France* 24 C6
Arronches, *Portugal* 31 F3
Arros →, *France* 26 E3
Arrou, *France* 24 D8
Arrow, L., *Ireland* 15 B3
Arrow Rock Res., *U.S.A.* 110 E6
Arrowhead, *Canada* 100 C5
Arrowhead, L., *U.S.A.* 113 L9
Arrowtown, *N.Z.* 87 L2
Arroyo de la Luz, *Spain* 31 F4
Arroyo Grande, *U.S.A.* 113 K6
Ārs, *Denmark* 11 H3
Ars, *Iran* 64 B5
Ars-en-Ré, *France* 26 B2
Ars-sur-Moselle, *France* 25 C13
Arsenault L., *Canada* 101 B7
Arsenev, *Russia* 48 B6
Arsi □, *Ethiopia* 77 F4
Arsiero, *Italy* 33 C8
Arsin, *Turkey* 67 B8
Arsk, *Russia* 42 B9
Árta, *Greece* 39 K4
Artá, *Spain* 36 B10
Arteaga, *Mexico* 114 D4
Arteche, *Phil.* 55 E6
Arteijo, *Spain* 30 B2
Artem = Artyom, *Azerbaijan* 43 K10
Artem, *Russia* 48 C6
Artemovsk, *Russia* 45 D10
Artemovsk, *Ukraine* 41 H9
Artemovskiy, *Russia* 43 G5
Artenay, *France* 25 D8
Artern, *Germany* 18 D7
Artesa de Segre, *Spain* 28 D6
Artesia = Mosomane, *Botswana* 84 C4
Artesia, *U.S.A.* 109 J2
Artesia Wells, *U.S.A.* 109 L5
Artesian, *U.S.A.* 108 C6
Arth, *Switz.* 23 B7
Arthez-de-Béarn, *France* 26 E3
Arthington, *Liberia* 78 D2
Arthur →, *Australia* 90 G3
Arthur Cr. →, *Australia* 90 C2
Arthur Pt., *Australia* 90 C5
Arthur's Pass, *N.Z.* 87 K3
Arthur's Town, *Bahamas* 117 B4
Artigas, *Uruguay* 126 C4
Artik, *Armenia* 43 K6
Artillery L., *Canada* 101 A7
Artois, *France* 25 B9
Artsyz, *Ukraine* 41 J5
Artvin, *Turkey* 67 B9
Artyom, *Azerbaijan* 43 K10
Aru, Kepulauan, *Indonesia* 57 F8
Aru Is. = Aru, Kepulauan, *Indonesia* 57 F8
Aru Meru □, *Tanzania* 82 C4
Arua, *Uganda* 82 B3
Aruanã, *Brazil* 123 D1
Aruba ■, *W. Indies* 117 D6
Arucas, *Canary Is.* 36 F4
Arudy, *France* 26 E3
Arumã, *Brazil* 121 D5
Arumpo, *Australia* 91 E3
Arun →, *Nepal* 63 F12
Arunachal Pradesh □, *India* 61 E19
Arusha, *Tanzania* 82 C4
Arusha □, *Tanzania* 82 C4
Arusha Chini, *Tanzania* 82 C4
Aruwimi →, *Zaïre* 82 B1
Arvada, *U.S.A.* 110 D10
Arvayheer, *Mongolia* 54 B5
Arve →, *France* 27 B10
Árvi, *Greece* 37 E7
Arvida, *Canada* 99 C5
Arvidsjaur, *Sweden* 8 D18
Arvika, *Sweden* 9 G15
Arvin, *U.S.A.* 113 K8
Arxan, *China* 54 B6
Aryirádhes, *Greece* 37 B3
Aryiroúpolis, *Greece* 37 D6
Arys, *Kazakstan* 44 E7
Arzachena, *Italy* 34 A2
Arzamas, *Russia* 42 C6
Arzew, *Algeria* 75 A4
Arzgir, *Russia* 43 H7
Arzignano, *Italy* 33 C8
As, *Belgium* 17 F7
Aş Şadr, *U.A.E.* 65 E7
Aş Şafā, *Syria* 69 B6
'As Saffānīyah, *Si. Arabia* 65 D6
As Safīrah, *Syria* 66 D7
Aş Şahm, *Oman* 65 E8
As Sājir, *Si. Arabia* 64 E5
As Salamīyah, *Syria* 66 E7
As Salţ, *Jordan* 69 C4
As Sal'w'a, *Qatar* 65 E6
As Samāwah, *Iraq* 64 D5
As Sanamayn, *Syria* 69 B5
As Sukhnah, *Syria* 67 E8
As Sulaymānīyah, *Iraq* 67 E11
As Sulaymī, *Si. Arabia* 64 E4
As Summān, *Si. Arabia* 64 E5
As Suwaydā', *Syria* 69 C5
As Suwaydā' □, *Syria* 69 C5
As Şuwayrah, *Iraq* 67 F11
Asab, *Namibia* 84 D2
Asaba, *Nigeria* 79 D6
Asadābād, *Iran* 67 E13
Asafo, *Ghana* 78 D4
Asahi-Gawa →, *Japan* 49 G6
Asahigawa, *Japan* 48 C11
Asale, L., *Ethiopia* 77 E5
Asamankese, *Ghana* 79 D4
Asansol, *India* 63 H12
Åsarna, *Sweden* 10 B8
Asbe Teferi, *Ethiopia* 77 F5
Asbesberge, *S. Africa* 84 D3
Asbestos, *Canada* 99 C5
Asbury Park, *U.S.A.* 107 F10
Ascensión, *Mexico* 114 A3
Ascensión, B. de la, *Mexico* 115 D7
Ascension I., *Atl. Oc.* 70 G2
Aschaffenburg, *Germany* 19 F5
Aschendorf, *Germany* 18 B3
Aschersleben, *Germany* 18 D7
Asciano, *Italy* 33 E8
Áscoli Piceno, *Italy* 33 F10
Áscoli Satriano, *Italy* 35 A8
Ascona, *Switz.* 23 D7
Ascope, *Peru* 124 B2
Ascotán, *Chile* 126 A2
Aseb, *Eritrea* 68 E3
Asedjrad, *Algeria* 75 D5
Asela, *Ethiopia* 77 F4
Asenovgrad, *Bulgaria* 39 G7

Asfeld, France 25 C11
Asfûn el Matâ'na, Egypt 76 B3
Åsgårdstrand, Norway 10 E4
Asgata, Cyprus 37 E12
Ash Fork, U.S.A. 111 J7
Ash Grove, U.S.A. 109 G8
Ash Shām, Bādiyat, Asia 46 F7
Ash Shamāl □, Lebanon 69 A5
Ash Shāmīyah, Iraq 67 G11
Ash Shāriqah, U.A.E. 65 E7
Ash Sharmah, Si. Arabia 64 D2
Ash Sharqāt, Iraq 67 E10
Ash Sharqi, Al Jabal, Lebanon 69 B5
Ash Shaṭrah, Iraq 64 D5
Ash Shawbak, Jordan 64 D2
Ash Shawmari, J., Jordan 69 E5
Ash Shaykh, J., Lebanon 69 B4
Ash Shināfīyah, Iraq 64 D5
Ash Shu'aybah, Si. Arabia 64 E5
Ash Shumlūl, Si. Arabia 64 E5
Ash Shūr'a, Iraq 64 C4
Ash Shurayf, Si. Arabia 64 E3
Ash Shuwayfāt, Lebanon 69 B4
Ashanti □, Ghana 79 D4
Ashau, Vietnam 58 D6
Ashburn, U.S.A. 105 K4
Ashburton, N.Z. 87 K3
Ashburton →, Australia 88 D1
Ashburton Downs, Australia 88 D2
Ashby de la Zouch, U.K. 12 E6
Ashcroft, Canada 100 C4
Ashdod, Israel 69 D3
Asheboro, U.S.A. 105 H6
Asherton, U.S.A. 109 L5
Asheville, U.S.A. 105 H4
Asheweig →, Canada 98 B2
Ashford, Australia 91 D5
Ashford, U.K. 13 F8
Ashford, U.S.A. 110 C2
Ashgabat, Turkmenistan 44 F6
Ashibetsu, Japan 48 C11
Ashikaga, Japan 49 F9
Ashizuri-Zaki, Japan 49 H6
Ashkarkot, Afghan. 62 C2
Ashkhabad = Ashgabat, Turkmenistan 44 F6
Ashland, Kans., U.S.A. 109 G5
Ashland, Ky., U.S.A. 104 F4
Ashland, Maine, U.S.A. 99 C6
Ashland, Mont., U.S.A. 110 D10
Ashland, Nebr., U.S.A. 108 E6
Ashland, Ohio, U.S.A. 106 F2
Ashland, Oreg., U.S.A. 110 E2
Ashland, Pa., U.S.A. 107 F8
Ashland, Va., U.S.A. 104 G7
Ashland, Wis., U.S.A. 108 B9
Ashley, N. Dak., U.S.A. 108 B5
Ashley, Pa., U.S.A. 107 E9
Ashmont, Canada 100 C6
Ashmore Reef, Australia 88 B3
Ashmûn, Egypt 76 H7
Ashmyany, Belarus 9 J21
Ashqelon, Israel 69 D3
Ashtabula, U.S.A. 106 E4
Ashton, S. Africa 84 E3
Ashton, U.S.A. 110 D8
Ashton under Lyne, U.K. 12 D5
Ashuanipi, L., Canada 99 B6
'Āṣī →, Asia 66 D6
Asia, Kepulauan, Indonesia 57 D8
Āsīā Bak, Iran 65 C6
Asiago, Italy 33 C8
Asidonhoppo, Surinam 121 C6
Asifabad, India 60 K11
Asike, Indonesia 57 F10
Asilah, Morocco 74 A3
Asinara, Italy 34 A1
Asinara, G. dell', Italy 34 B1
Asino, Russia 44 D9
Asipovichy, Belarus 40 F5
'Asīr □, Si. Arabia 68 D3
Asir, Ras, Somali Rep. 68 E5
Aşkale, Turkey 67 C9
Asker, Norway 10 E4
Askersund, Sweden 11 F8
Askham, S. Africa 84 D3
Askim, Norway 10 E5
Askja, Iceland 8 D5
Askøy, Norway 9 F11
Asl, Egypt 76 J8
Asmara = Asmera, Eritrea 77 D4
Asmera, Eritrea 77 D4
Asnæs, Denmark 11 J5
Åsnen, Sweden 9 H16
Asni, Morocco 74 B3
Ásola, Italy 32 C7
Asoteriba, Jebel, Sudan 76 C4
Asotin, U.S.A. 110 C5
Aspe, Spain 29 G4
Aspen, U.S.A. 111 G10
Aspendos, Turkey 66 D4
Aspermont, U.S.A. 109 J4
Aspiring, Mt., N.Z. 87 L2
Aspres-sur-Buëch, France 27 D9
Asprókavos, Ákra, Greece 37 B4
Aspromonte, Italy 35 D8
Aspur, India 62 H6
Asquith, Canada 101 C7
Assa, Morocco 74 C3
Assâba, Mauritania 78 B2
Assad, Bahret, Syria 67 D8
Assam □, India 61 F18
Assamakka, Niger 79 B6
Asse, Belgium 17 H4
Assebroek, Belgium 17 F2
Assekrem, Algeria 75 D6
Assémini, Italy 34 C2
Assen, Neths. 16 C9
Assendelft, Neths. 16 D5
Assenede, Belgium 17 F3
Assens, Århus, Denmark 11 H4
Assens, Fyn, Denmark 11 J3
Assesse, Belgium 17 H6
Assini, Ivory C. 78 D4
Assiniboia, Canada 101 D7
Assiniboine →, Canada 101 D9
Assis, Brazil 127 A5
Assisi, Italy 33 E9
Assynt, L., U.K. 14 C3
Astaffort, France 26 D4
Astara, Azerbaijan 67 C13
Āstārā, Iran 67 C13
Asten, Neths. 17 F7
Asteroúsia, Greece 37 E7
Asti, Italy 32 D5
Astipálaia, Greece 39 N9
Astorga, Spain 30 C4
Astoria, U.S.A. 112 D3
Åstorp, Sweden 11 H6
Astrakhan, Russia 43 G9
Astudillo, Spain 30 C6
Asturias □, Spain 30 B5
Asunción, Paraguay 126 B4
Asunción Nochixtlán, Mexico 115 D5
Asutri, Sudan 77 D4
Aswa →, Uganda 82 B3
Aswad, Ras al, Si. Arabia 76 C4
Aswân, Egypt 76 C3
Aswân High Dam = Sadd el Aali, Egypt 76 C3
Asyût, Egypt 76 B3
Asyûti, Wadi →, Egypt 76 B3
Aszód, Hungary 21 H9
At Ṭafīlah, Jordan 69 E4
At Tā'if, Si. Arabia 68 C3
Aṭ Ṭirāq, Si. Arabia 64 E5
Atacama □, Chile 126 B2
Atacama, Desierto de, Chile 126 A2
Atacama, Salar de, Chile 126 A2
Ataco, Colombia 120 C2
Atakor, Algeria 75 D6
Atakpamé, Togo 79 D5
Atalándi, Greece 39 L5
Atalaya, Peru 124 C3
Atalaya de Femes, Canary Is. 36 F6
Ataléia, Brazil 123 E3
Atami, Japan 49 G9
Atapupu, Indonesia 57 F6
Atâr, Mauritania 74 D2
Ataram, Erg n-, Algeria 75 D5
Atarfe, Spain 31 H7
Atascadero, U.S.A. 111 J3
Atasu, Kazakstan 44 E8
Atatürk Barajı, Turkey 67 D8
Atauro, Indonesia 57 F7
Atbara, Sudan 76 D3
'Atbara →, Sudan 76 D3
Atbasar, Kazakstan 44 D7
Atchafalaya B., U.S.A. 109 L9
Atchison, U.S.A. 108 F7
Atebubu, Ghana 79 D4
Ateca, Spain 28 D3
Aterno →, Italy 33 F10
Atesine, Alpi, Italy 32 B8
Atessa, Italy 33 F11
Ath, Belgium 17 G3
Athabasca, Canada 100 C6
Athabasca →, Canada 101 B6
Athabasca, L., Canada 101 B7
Athboy, Ireland 15 C5
Athenry, Ireland 15 C3
Athens = Athínai, Greece 39 M6
Athens, Ala., U.S.A. 105 H2
Athens, Ga., U.S.A. 105 J4
Athens, N.Y., U.S.A. 107 D11
Athens, Ohio, U.S.A. 104 F4
Athens, Pa., U.S.A. 107 E8
Athens, Tenn., U.S.A. 105 H3
Athens, Tex., U.S.A. 109 J7
Atherley, Canada 106 B5
Atherton, Australia 90 B4
Athiéme, Benin 79 D5
Athienou, Cyprus 37 D12
Athínai, Greece 39 M6
Athlone, Ireland 15 C4
Athna, Cyprus 37 D12
Atholl, Forest of, U.K. 14 E5
Atholville, Canada 99 C6
Áthos, Greece 39 J7
Athus, Belgium 17 J7
Athy, Ireland 15 D5
Ati, Chad 73 F8
Ati, Sudan 77 E2
Atiak, Uganda 82 B3
Atico, Peru 124 D3
Atienza, Spain 28 D2
Atikokan, Canada 98 C1
Atikonak L., Canada 99 B7
Atimonan, Phil. 55 E4
Atka, Russia 45 C16
Atkarsk, Russia 42 E7
Atkinson, U.S.A. 108 D5
Atlanta, Ga., U.S.A. 105 J3
Atlanta, Tex., U.S.A. 109 J7
Atlantic, U.S.A. 108 E7
Atlantic City, U.S.A. 104 F8
Atlantic Ocean 2 E9
Atlántico □, Colombia 120 A2
Atlas Mts. = Haut Atlas, Morocco 74 B3
Atlin, Canada 100 B2
Atlin, L., Canada 100 B2
Atmore, U.S.A. 105 K2
Atoka, U.S.A. 109 H6
Atókos, Greece 39 L3
Atolia, U.S.A. 113 K9
Atouguia, Portugal 31 F1
Atoyac →, Mexico 115 D5
Atrak = Atrek →, Turkmenistan 65 B8
Ätran, Sweden 11 G6
Atrato →, Colombia 120 B2
Atrauli, India 62 E8
Atrek →, Turkmenistan 65 B8
Atri, Italy 33 F10
Atsbi, Ethiopia 77 E4
Atsoum, Mts., Cameroon 79 D7
Atsuta, Japan 48 C10
Attalla, U.S.A. 105 H2
Attáviros, Greece 37 C9
Attawapiskat, Canada 98 B3
Attawapiskat →, Canada 98 B3
Attawapiskat, L., Canada 98 B2
Attendorn, Germany 18 D3
Attert, Belgium 17 J7
Attica, U.S.A. 104 E2
Attichy, France 25 C10
Attigny, France 25 C11
Attikamagen L., Canada 99 A6
Attleboro, U.S.A. 107 E13
Attock, Pakistan 62 C5
Attopeu, Laos 58 E6
Attur, India 60 P11
Atuel →, Argentina 126 D2
Åtvidaberg, Sweden 11 F10
Atwater, U.S.A. 111 H3
Atwood, Canada 106 C3
Atwood, U.S.A. 108 F4
Atyraū, Kazakstan 44 E6
Au Sable →, U.S.A. 104 C4
Au Sable Pt., U.S.A. 98 C2
Aubagne, France 27 E9
Aubange, Belgium 17 J7
Aubarca, C., Spain 36 B7
Aube □, France 25 D11
Aube →, France 25 D10
Aubel, Belgium 17 G7
Aubenas, France 27 D8
Aubenton, France 25 C11
Auberry, U.S.A. 112 H7
Aubigny-sur-Nère, France 25 E9
Aubin, France 26 D6
Aubrac, Mts. d', France 26 D7
Auburn, Ala., U.S.A. 105 J3
Auburn, Calif., U.S.A. 112 G5
Auburn, Ind., U.S.A. 104 E3
Auburn, N.Y., U.S.A. 107 D8
Auburn, Nebr., U.S.A. 108 E7
Auburn, Wash., U.S.A. 112 C4
Auburn Ra., Australia 91 D5
Auburndale, U.S.A. 105 L5
Aubusson, France 26 C6
Auch, France 26 E4
Auchel, France 25 B9
Auchi, Nigeria 79 D6
Auckland, N.Z. 87 G5
Auckland Is., Pac. Oc. 92 N8
Aude □, France 26 E6
Aude →, France 26 E7
Auden, Canada 98 B2
Auderghem, Belgium 17 G4
Auderville, France 24 C5
Audierne, France 24 D2
Audincourt, France 25 E13
Audo, Ethiopia 77 F5
Audubon, U.S.A. 108 E7
Aue, Germany 18 E8
Auer = Ora, Italy 33 B8
Auerbach, Germany 18 E8
Aueti Paraná →, Brazil 120 D4
Aufist, W. Sahara 74 C2
Augathella, Australia 91 D4
Augrabies Falls, S. Africa 84 D3
Augsburg, Germany 19 G6
Augusta, Italy 35 E8
Augusta, Ark., U.S.A. 109 H9
Augusta, Ga., U.S.A. 105 J5
Augusta, Kans., U.S.A. 109 G6
Augusta, Maine, U.S.A. 99 D6
Augusta, Mont., U.S.A. 110 C7
Augusta, Wis., U.S.A. 108 C9
Augustenborg, Denmark 11 K3
Augustów, Poland 20 B12
Augustus, Mt., Australia 88 D2
Augustus Downs, Australia 90 B2
Augustus I., Australia 88 C3
Aukan, Eritrea 77 D5
Aukum, U.S.A. 112 G6
Auld, L., Australia 88 D3
Aulla, Italy 32 D6
Aulnay, France 26 B3
Aulne →, France 24 D2
Aulnoye-Aymeries, France 25 B10
Ault, France 24 B8
Ault, U.S.A. 108 E2
Aulus-les-Bains, France 26 F5
Aumale, France 25 C8
Aumont-Aubrac, France 26 D7
Auna, Nigeria 79 C5
Aunis, France 26 B3
Auponhia, Indonesia 57 E7
Aups, France 27 E10
Aur, P., Malaysia 59 L5
Auraiya, India 63 F8
Aurangabad, Bihar, India 63 G11
Aurangabad, Maharashtra, India 60 K9
Auray, France 24 E4
Aurès, Algeria 75 A6
Aurich, Germany 18 B3
Aurilândia, Brazil 123 E1
Aurillac, France 26 D6
Auronzo di Cadore, Italy 33 B9
Aurora, Canada 106 C5
Aurora, S. Africa 84 E2
Aurora, Colo., U.S.A. 108 F2
Aurora, Ill., U.S.A. 104 E1
Aurora, Mo., U.S.A. 109 G8
Aurora, Nebr., U.S.A. 108 E6
Aurora, Ohio, U.S.A. 106 E3
Aursmoen, Norway 10 E5
Aurukun Mission, Australia 90 A3
Aus, Namibia 84 D2
Auschwitz = Oświęcim, Poland 20 E9
Austin, Minn., U.S.A. 108 D8
Austin, Nev., U.S.A. 110 G5
Austin, Pa., U.S.A. 106 E6
Austin, Tex., U.S.A. 109 K6
Austin, L., Australia 89 E2
Austra, Norway 8 D14
Austral Downs, Australia 90 C2
Austral Is. = Tubuai Is., Pac. Oc. 93 K12
Austral Seamount Chain, Pac. Oc. 93 K13
Australia ■, Oceania 92 K5
Australian Alps, Australia 91 F4
Australian Capital Territory □, Australia 91 F4
Austria ■, Europe 21 H4
Austvågøy, Norway 8 B16
Autazes, Brazil 121 D6
Autelbas, Belgium 17 J7
Auterive, France 26 E5
Authie →, France 25 B8
Authon-du-Perche, France 24 D7
Autlán, Mexico 114 D4
Autun, France 25 F11
Auvelais, Belgium 17 H5
Auvergne, Australia 88 C5
Auvergne, France 26 C7
Auvergne, Mts. d', France 26 C6
Auvézère →, France 26 C4
Auxerre, France 25 E10
Auxi-le-Château, France 25 B9
Auxonne, France 25 E12
Auzances, France 26 B6
Auzat-sur-Allier, France 26 C7
Avallon, France 25 E10
Avalon, U.S.A. 113 M8
Avalon Pen., Canada 99 C9
Avaré, Brazil 127 A6
Ávas, Greece 39 J8
Avawatz Mts., U.S.A. 113 K10
Aveiro, Brazil 121 D6
Aveiro, Portugal 30 E2
Aveiro □, Portugal 30 E2
Āvej, Iran 65 C6
Avelgem, Belgium 17 G2
Avellaneda, Argentina 126 C4
Avellino, Italy 35 B7
Avenal, U.S.A. 112 K6
Avenches, Switz. 22 C4
Averøya, Norway 10 A1
Aversa, Italy 35 B7
Avery, U.S.A. 110 C6
Aves, I. de, W. Indies 117 C7
Aves, Is. de, Venezuela 117 D6
Avesnes-sur-Helpe, France 25 B10
Avesta, Sweden 9 F17
Aveyron □, France 26 D6
Aveyron →, France 26 D5
Avezzano, Italy 33 F10
Aviá Terai, Argentina 126 B3
Aviano, Italy 33 B9
Avigliana, Italy 32 C4
Avigliano, Italy 35 B8
Avignon, France 27 E8
Ávila, Spain 30 E6
Ávila □, Spain 30 E6
Ávila, Sierra de, Spain 30 E5
Avila Beach, U.S.A. 113 K6
Avilés, Spain 30 B5
Avísio →, Italy 33 B8
Aviz, Portugal 31 F3
Avize, France 25 D11
Avoca, Ireland 15 D5
Avoca, U.S.A. 106 D7
Avoca →, Australia 91 F3
Avola, Canada 100 C5
Avola, Italy 35 F8
Avon, N.Y., U.S.A. 106 D7
Avon, S. Dak., U.S.A. 108 D5
Avon →, Australia 89 F2
Avon →, Bristol, U.K. 13 F5
Avon →, Dorset, U.K. 13 G6
Avon →, Warks., U.K. 13 F5
Avondale, Zimbabwe 83 F3
Avonlea, Canada 101 D7
Avonmore, Canada 107 A10
Avonmouth, U.K. 13 F5
Avranches, France 24 D5
Avre →, France 24 D8
Awag el Baqar, Sudan 77 E3
A'waj →, Syria 69 B5
Awaji-Shima, Japan 49 G7
'Awālī, Bahrain 65 E6
Awantipur, India 63 C6
Awasa, L., Ethiopia 77 F4
Awash, Ethiopia 68 F3
Awash →, Ethiopia 77 E5
Awaso, Ghana 78 D4
Awatere →, N.Z. 87 J5
Awbārī, Libya 75 C7
Awbārī □, Libya 75 C7
Awe, L., U.K. 14 E3
Aweil, Sudan 77 F2
Awgu, Nigeria 79 D6
Awjilah, Libya 73 C9
Ax-les-Thermes, France 26 F5
Axel, Neths. 17 F3
Axel Heiberg I., Canada 4 B3
Axim, Ghana 78 E4
Axinim, Brazil 121 D6
Axintele, Romania 38 E9
Axioma, Brazil 125 B5
Axiós →, Greece 39 J5
Axminster, U.K. 13 G4
Axvall, Sweden 11 F7
Aÿ, France 25 C11
Ayabaca, Peru 124 A2
Ayabe, Japan 49 G7
Ayacucho, Argentina 126 D4
Ayacucho, Peru 124 C3
Ayaguz, Kazakstan 44 E9
Ayamonte, Spain 31 H3
Ayan, Russia 45 D14
Ayancık, Turkey 66 B6
Ayapel, Colombia 120 B2
Ayas, Turkey 66 B5
Ayaviri, Peru 124 C3
Aybastı, Turkey 66 B7
Aydın, Turkey 66 D2
Aye, Belgium 17 H6
Ayenngré, Togo 79 D5
Ayer's Cliff, Canada 107 A12
Ayers Rock, Australia 89 E5
Ayiá, Greece 39 K5
Ayia Aikateríni, Ákra, Greece 37 A3
Ayia Dhéka, Greece 37 D6
Ayia Gálini, Greece 37 D6
Ayía Marína, Greece 39 M9
Ayia Napa, Cyprus 37 E13
Ayía Paraskeví, Greece 39 K9
Ayia Phyla, Cyprus 37 E12
Ayía Rouméli, Greece 39 P6
Ayia Varvára, Greece 37 D7
Áyios Amvrósios, Cyprus 37 D12
Áyios Andréas, Greece 39 M5
Áyios Evstrátios, Greece 39 K7
Áyios Ioánnis, Ákra, Greece 37 D7
Áyios Isídhoros, Greece 37 C9
Áyios Kiríkos, Greece 39 M9
Áyios Matthaíos, Greece 37 B3
Áyios Mírono, Greece 39 P8
Áyios Nikólaos, Greece 37 D7
Áyios Seryios, Cyprus 37 D12
Ayios Theodhoros, Cyprus 37 D13
Aykathonisi, Greece 39 M9
Aylesbury, U.K. 13 F7
Aylmer, Canada 106 D4
Aylmer, L., Canada 96 B8
Ayn Zālah, Iraq 67 D10
Ayna, Spain 29 G2
Ayolas, Paraguay 126 B4
Ayom, Sudan 77 F2
Ayon, Ostrov, Russia 45 C17
Ayora, Spain 29 F3
Ayr, Australia 90 B4
Ayr, U.K. 14 F4
Ayr →, U.K. 14 F4
Ayrancı, Turkey 66 D5
Ayre, Pt. of, U.K. 12 C3
Aysha, Ethiopia 77 E5
Aytos, Bulgaria 38 G10
Ayu, Kepulauan, Indonesia 57 D8
Ayutla, Guatemala 116 D1
Ayutla, Mexico 115 D5
Ayvacık, Turkey 66 C2
Ayvalık, Turkey 66 C2
Aywaille, Belgium 17 H7
Az Zabdānī, Syria 69 B5
Aẓ Ẓāhirīyah, West Bank 69 D3
Aẓ Ẓahrān, Si. Arabia 65 E6
Az Zarqā, Jordan 69 C5
Az Zāwiyah, Libya 75 B7
Az Zībār, Iraq 67 D11
Az-Zilfī, Si. Arabia 64 E5
Az Zubayr, Iraq 64 D5
Az Zuwaytīnah, Libya 73 B9
Azambuja, Portugal 31 F2
Azamgarh, India 63 F10
Azangaro, Peru 124 C3
Azaouak, Vallée de l', Mali 79 B5
Āzār Shahr, Iran 67 D11
Azarān, Iran 67 D12
Azärbayjan = Azerbaijan ■, Asia 43 K9
Āzarbāyjān-e Gharbī □, Iran 64 B5
Āzarbāyjān-e Sharqī □, Iran 64 B5
Azare, Nigeria 79 C7
Azay-le-Rideau, France 24 E7
A'zāz, Syria 66 D7
Azazga, Algeria 75 A5
Azbine = Aïr, Niger 79 B6
Azefal, Mauritania 74 D2
Azeffoun, Algeria 75 A5
Azemmour, Morocco 74 B3
Azerbaijan ■, Asia 43 K9
Azerbaijchan = Azerbaijan ■, Asia 43 K9
Azezo, Ethiopia 77 E4
Azimganj, India 63 G13
Aznalcóllar, Spain 31 H4
Azogues, Ecuador 120 D2
Azores, Atl. Oc. 70 C1
Azov, Russia 43 G4
Azov, Sea of, Europe 43 H3
Azovskoye More = Azov, Sea of, Europe 43 H3

Azovy, *Russia* 44 C7
Azpeitia, *Spain* 28 B2
Azrou, *Morocco* 74 B3
Aztec, *U.S.A.* 111 H10
Azúa, *Dom. Rep.* 117 C5
Azuaga, *Spain* 31 G5
Azuara, *Spain* 28 D4
Azuay □, *Ecuador* 120 D2
Azuer →, *Spain* 31 F7
Azuero, Pen. de, *Panama* 116 E3
Azul, *Argentina* 126 D4
Azul, Serra, *Brazil* 125 C7
Azurduy, *Bolivia* 125 D5
Azusa, *U.S.A.* 113 L9
Azzaba, *Algeria* 75 A6
Azzano Décimo, *Italy* 33 C9
'Azzūn, *West Bank* 69 C4

B

Ba Don, *Vietnam* 58 D6
Ba Dong, *Vietnam* 59 H6
Ba Ngoi = Cam Lam, *Vietnam* 59 G7
Ba Ria, *Vietnam* 59 G6
Ba Tri, *Vietnam* 59 G6
Ba Xian, *China* 50 E9
Baa, *Indonesia* 57 F6
Baamonde, *Spain* 30 B3
Baar, *Switz.* 23 B7
Baarle Nassau, *Belgium* 17 F5
Baarlo, *Neths.* 17 F8
Baarn, *Neths.* 16 D6
Bab el Mandeb, *Red Sea* 68 E3
Baba Burnu, *Turkey* 66 C2
Baba dag, *Azerbaijan* 43 K9
Bābā Kalū, *Iran* 65 D6
Babaçulândia, *Brazil* 122 C2
Babadag, *Romania* 38 E11
Babadayhan, *Turkmenistan* 44 F7
Babaeski, *Turkey* 66 B2
Babahoyo, *Ecuador* 120 D2
Babakin, *Australia* 89 F2
Babana, *Nigeria* 79 C5
Babar, *Algeria* 75 A6
Babar, *Indonesia* 57 F7
Babar, *Pakistan* 62 D3
Babarkach, *Pakistan* 62 E2
Babayevo, *Russia* 40 C8
Babb, *U.S.A.* 110 B7
Babenhausen, *Germany* 19 F4
Babi Besar, P., *Malaysia* 59 L4
Babian Jiang →, *China* 52 F3
Babile, *Ethiopia* 77 F5
Babinda, *Australia* 90 B4
Babine, *Canada* 100 B3
Babine →, *Canada* 100 B3
Babine L., *Canada* 100 C3
Babo, *Indonesia* 57 E8
Bābol, *Iran* 65 B7
Bābol Sar, *Iran* 65 B7
Baboua, *C.A.R.* 80 C2
Babruysk, *Belarus* 41 F5
Babura, *Nigeria* 79 C6
Babusar Pass, *Pakistan* 63 B5
Babušnica, *Serbia, Yug.* 21 M12
Babuyan Chan., *Phil.* 55 B4
Babuyan Is., *Phil.* 55 B4
Babylon, *Iraq* 67 F11
Bac Can, *Vietnam* 58 A5
Bac Giang, *Vietnam* 58 B6
Bac Ninh, *Vietnam* 58 B6
Bac Phan, *Vietnam* 58 B5
Bac Quang, *Vietnam* 58 A5
Bacabal, *Brazil* 122 B3
Bacajá →, *Brazil* 121 D7
Bacalar, *Mexico* 115 D7
Bacan, Kepulauan, *Indonesia* 57 E7
Bacan, Pulau, *Indonesia* 57 E7
Bacarra, *Phil.* 55 B4
Bacău, *Romania* 38 C9
Baccarat, *France* 25 D13
Bacerac, *Mexico* 114 A3
Băceşti, *Romania* 38 C10
Bach Long Vi, Dao, *Vietnam* 58 B6
Bachaquero, *Venezuela* 120 B3
Bacharach, *Germany* 19 E3
Bachelina, *Russia* 44 D7
Bachuma, *Ethiopia* 77 F4
Bačina, *Serbia, Yug.* 21 M11
Back →, *Canada* 96 B9
Bačka Palanka, *Serbia, Yug.* 21 K9
Bačka Topola, *Serbia, Yug.* 21 K9
Bäckefors, *Sweden* 11 F6
Backnang, *Germany* 19 G5
Backstairs Passage, *Australia* 91 F2
Baco, Mt., *Phil.* 55 E4
Bacolod, *Phil.* 55 F5
Bacqueville-en-Caux, *France* 24 C8
Bácsalmás, *Hungary* 21 J9
Bacuag, *Phil.* 55 G6
Bacuk, *Malaysia* 59 J4
Bād, *Iran* 65 C7
Bad →, *U.S.A.* 108 C4
Bad Axe, *U.S.A.* 106 C2
Bad Bergzabern, *Germany* 19 F4
Bad Berleburg, *Germany* 18 D4
Bad Bevensen, *Germany* 18 B6
Bad Bramstedt, *Germany* 18 B5
Bad Brückenau, *Germany* 19 E5
Bad Doberan, *Germany* 18 A7
Bad Driburg, *Germany* 18 D5
Bad Ems, *Germany* 19 E3
Bad Frankenhausen, *Germany* 18 D7
Bad Freienwalde, *Germany* 18 C10
Bad Godesberg, *Germany* 18 E3
Bad Hersfeld, *Germany* 18 E5
Bad Hofgastein, *Austria* 21 H3
Bad Homburg, *Germany* 19 E4
Bad Honnef, *Germany* 18 E3
Bad Ischl, *Austria* 21 H3
Bad Kissingen, *Germany* 19 E6
Bad Königshofen, *Germany* 19 E6
Bad Kreuznach, *Germany* 19 F3
Bad Laasphe, *Germany* 18 E4
Bad Lands, *U.S.A.* 108 D3
Bad Langensalza, *Germany* 18 D6
Bad Lauterberg, *Germany* 18 D6
Bad Lippspringe, *Germany* 18 D4
Bad Mergentheim, *Germany* 19 F5
Bad Münstereifel, *Germany* 18 E2
Bad Muskau, *Germany* 18 D10
Bad Nauheim, *Germany* 19 E4
Bad Oeynhausen, *Germany* 18 C4
Bad Oldesloe, *Germany* 18 B6
Bad Orb, *Germany* 19 E5
Bad Pyrmont, *Germany* 18 D5
Bad Ragaz, *Switz.* 23 B9
Bad Reichenhall, *Germany* 19 H8
Bad Säckingen, *Germany* 19 H3
Bad Salzuflen, *Germany* 18 C4
Bad Segeberg, *Germany* 18 B6
Bad Tölz, *Germany* 19 H7
Bad Urach, *Germany* 19 G5
Bad Waldsee, *Germany* 19 H5
Bad Wildungen, *Germany* 18 D5
Bad Wimpfen, *Germany* 19 F5
Bad Windsheim, *Germany* 19 F6
Badagara, *India* 60 P9
Badagri, *Nigeria* 79 D5
Badajós, L., *Brazil* 121 D5
Badajoz, *Spain* 31 G4
Badajoz □, *Spain* 31 G4
Badalona, *Spain* 28 D7
Badalzai, *Afghan.* 62 E1
Badampahar, *India* 61 H15
Badanah, *Si. Arabia* 64 D4
Badarinath, *India* 63 D8
Badas, *Brunei* 56 D4
Badas, Kepulauan, *Indonesia* 56 D3
Baddo →, *Pakistan* 60 F4
Bade, *Indonesia* 57 F9
Baden, *Austria* 21 G6
Baden, *Switz.* 23 B6
Baden-Baden, *Germany* 19 G4
Baden-Württemberg □, *Germany* 19 G5
Badenoch, *U.K.* 14 E4
Badger, *Canada* 99 C8
Badger, *U.S.A.* 112 J7
Bādghīsāt □, *Afghan.* 60 B3
Badgom, *India* 63 B6
Badhoevedorp, *Neths.* 16 D5
Badia Polésine, *Italy* 33 C8
Badin, *Pakistan* 62 G3
Badogo, *Mali* 78 C3
Badong, *China* 53 B8
Badrah, *Iraq* 67 F11
Baduen, *Somali Rep.* 68 F4
Badulla, *Sri Lanka* 60 R12
Baena, *Spain* 31 H6
Baexem, *Neths.* 17 F7
Baeza, *Ecuador* 120 D2
Baeza, *Spain* 29 H1
Bafang, *Cameroon* 79 D7
Bafatá, *Guinea-Biss.* 78 C2
Baffin B., *Canada* 4 B4
Baffin I., *Canada* 97 B12
Bafia, *Cameroon* 79 E7
Bafilo, *Togo* 79 D5
Bafing →, *Mali* 78 C2
Bafliyūn, *Syria* 64 B3
Baflo, *Neths.* 16 B9
Bafoulabé, *Mali* 78 C2
Bafoussam, *Cameroon* 79 D7
Bāfq, *Iran* 65 D7
Bafra, *Turkey* 66 B6
Bafra Burnu, *Turkey* 66 B7
Bāft, *Iran* 65 D8
Bafut, *Cameroon* 79 D7
Bafwasende, *Zaïre* 82 B2
Bagamoyo, *Tanzania* 82 D4
Bagamoyo □, *Tanzania* 82 D4
Bagan Datoh, *Malaysia* 59 L3
Bagan Serai, *Malaysia* 59 K3
Baganga, *Phil.* 55 H7
Bagani, *Namibia* 84 B3
Bagansiapiapi, *Indonesia* 56 D2
Bagasra, *India* 62 J4
Bagawi, *Sudan* 77 E3
Bagdad, *U.S.A.* 113 L11
Bagdarin, *Russia* 45 D12
Bagé, *Brazil* 127 C5
Bagenalstown = Muine Bheag, *Ireland* 15 D5
Baggs, *U.S.A.* 110 F10
Bagh, *Pakistan* 63 C5
Baghdād, *Iraq* 67 F11
Bagheria, *Italy* 34 D6
Baghlān, *Afghan.* 60 A6
Bagley, *U.S.A.* 108 B7
Bagnacavallo, *Italy* 33 D8
Bagnara Cálabra, *Italy* 35 D8
Bagnères-de-Bigorre, *France* 26 E4
Bagnères-de-Luchon, *France* 26 F4
Bagni di Lucca, *Italy* 32 D7
Bagno di Romagna, *Italy* 33 E8
Bagnoles-de-l'Orne, *France* 24 D6
Bagnoli di Sopra, *Italy* 33 C8
Bagnolo Mella, *Italy* 32 C7
Bagnols-sur-Cèze, *France* 27 D8
Bagnorégio, *Italy* 33 F9
Bagolino, *Italy* 32 C7
Bagotville, *Canada* 99 C5
Bagrationovsk, *Russia* 9 J19
Bagua, *Peru* 124 B2
Baguio, *Phil.* 55 C4
Bahabón de Esgueva, *Spain* 28 D1
Bahadurgarh, *India* 62 E7
Bahama, Canal Viejo de, *W. Indies* 116 B4
Bahamas ■, *N. Amer.* 117 B5
Bahār, *Iran* 67 E13
Baharampur, *India* 63 G13
Baharîya, El Wâhât al, *Egypt* 76 J6
Bahau, *Malaysia* 59 L4
Bahawalnagar, *Pakistan* 62 D5
Bahawalpur, *Pakistan* 62 E4
Bahçe, *Turkey* 66 D7
Baheri, *India* 63 E8
Bahi, *Tanzania* 82 D4
Bahi Swamp, *Tanzania* 82 D4
Bahía = Salvador, *Brazil* 123 D4
Bahía □, *Brazil* 123 D3
Bahía, Is. de la, *Honduras* 116 C2
Bahía Blanca, *Argentina* 126 D3
Bahía de Caráquez, *Ecuador* 120 D1
Bahía Honda, *Cuba* 116 B3
Bahía Laura, *Argentina* 128 C3
Bahía Negra, *Paraguay* 125 E6
Bahir Dar, *Ethiopia* 77 E4
Bahmanzād, *Iran* 65 D6
Bahmer, *Algeria* 75 C4
Bahönye, *Hungary* 21 J7
Bahr Aouk →, *C.A.R.* 80 C3
Bahr el Ahmar □, *Sudan* 76 C3
Bahr el Ghazâl □, *Sudan* 77 F2
Bahr Salamat →, *Chad* 73 G8
Bahr Yûsef →, *Egypt* 76 J7
Bahra el Burullus, *Egypt* 76 H7
Bahraich, *India* 63 F9
Bahrain ■, *Asia* 65 E6
Bahror, *India* 62 F7
Bāhū Kalāt, *Iran* 65 E9
Bai, *Mali* 78 C4
Bai Bung, Mui, *Vietnam* 59 H5
Bai Duc, *Vietnam* 58 C5
Bai Thuong, *Vietnam* 58 C5
Baia Mare, *Romania* 38 B6
Baia-Sprie, *Romania* 38 B6
Baião, *Brazil* 122 B2
Baïbokoum, *Chad* 73 G8
Baicheng, *China* 51 B12
Baidoa, *Somali Rep.* 68 G3
Baie Comeau, *Canada* 99 C6
Baie-St-Paul, *Canada* 99 C5
Baie Trinité, *Canada* 99 C6
Baie Verte, *Canada* 99 C8
Baignes-Ste.-Radegonde, *France* 26 C3
Baigneux-les-Juifs, *France* 25 E11
Baihe, *China* 50 H6
Ba'ījī, *Iraq* 67 E10
Baikal, L. = Baykal, Oz., *Russia* 45 D11
Baile Atha Cliath = Dublin, *Ireland* 15 C5
Bailei, *Ethiopia* 77 F5
Bailén, *Spain* 31 G7
Băileşti, *Romania* 38 E6
Baileux, *Belgium* 17 H4
Bailique, Ilha, *Brazil* 122 A2
Bailleul, *France* 25 B9
Bailundo, *Angola* 81 G3
Baima, *China* 52 A3
Bain-de-Bretagne, *France* 24 E5
Bainbridge, *Ga., U.S.A.* 105 K3
Bainbridge, *N.Y., U.S.A.* 107 D9
Baing, *Indonesia* 57 F6
Bainiu, *China* 50 H7
Bainville, *U.S.A.* 108 A2
Bā'ir, *Jordan* 69 E5
Baird, *U.S.A.* 109 J5
Baird Mts., *U.S.A.* 96 B3
Bairin Youqi, *China* 51 C10
Bairin Zuoqi, *China* 51 C10
Bairnsdale, *Australia* 91 F4
Bais, *Phil.* 55 G5
Baisha, *China* 50 G7
Baïsole →, *France* 26 E4
Baissa, *Nigeria* 79 D7
Baitadi, *Nepal* 63 E9
Baixa Grande, *Brazil* 123 D3
Baiyin, *China* 50 F3
Baiyü, *China* 52 B2
Baiyu Shan, *China* 50 F4
Baiyuda, *Sudan* 76 D3
Baj Baj, *India* 63 H13
Baja, *Hungary* 21 J8
Baja, Pta., *Mexico* 114 B1
Baja California, *Mexico* 114 A1
Baja California □, *Mexico* 114 B2
Baja California Sur □, *Mexico* 114 B2
Bajamar, *Canary Is.* 36 F3
Bajana, *India* 62 H4
Bājgīrān, *Iran* 65 B8
Bajimba, Mt., *Australia* 91 D5
Bajo Nuevo, *Caribbean* 116 C4
Bajoga, *Nigeria* 79 C7
Bajool, *Australia* 90 C5
Bakala, *C.A.R.* 73 G9
Bakar, *Croatia* 33 C11
Bakchar, *Russia* 44 D9
Bakel, *Neths.* 17 E7
Bakel, *Senegal* 78 C2
Baker, *Calif., U.S.A.* 113 K10
Baker, *Mont., U.S.A.* 108 B2
Baker, *Oreg., U.S.A.* 110 D5
Baker, Canal, *Chile* 128 C2
Baker, L., *Canada* 96 B10
Baker I., *Pac. Oc.* 92 G10
Baker L., *Australia* 89 E4
Baker Lake, *Canada* 96 B10
Baker Mt., *U.S.A.* 110 B3
Bakers Creek, *Australia* 90 C4
Baker's Dozen Is., *Canada* 98 A4
Bakersfield, *Calif., U.S.A.* 113 K7
Bakersfield, *Vt., U.S.A.* 107 B12
Bakhchysaray, *Ukraine* 41 K7
Bakhmach, *Ukraine* 41 G7
Bākhtarān, *Iran* 67 E12
Bākhtarān □, *Iran* 64 C5
Bakı, *Azerbaijan* 43 K9
Bakırdaği, *Turkey* 66 C6
Bakırköy, *Turkey* 39 H11
Bakkafjörður, *Iceland* 8 C6
Bakony →, *Hungary* 21 H7
Bakony Forest = Bakony Hegyseg, *Hungary* 21 H7
Bakony Hegyseg, *Hungary* 21 H7
Bakori, *Nigeria* 79 C6
Bakouma, *C.A.R.* 73 G9
Baksan, *Russia* 43 J6
Baku = Bakı, *Azerbaijan* 43 K9
Bakutis Coast, *Antarctica* 5 D15
Baky = Bakı, *Azerbaijan* 43 K9
Bala, *Canada* 106 A5
Bâlâ, *Turkey* 66 C5
Bala, L., *U.K.* 12 E4
Balabac I., *Phil.* 55 H2
Balabac Str., *E. Indies* 56 C5
Balabagh, *Afghan.* 62 B4
Ba'labakk, *Lebanon* 69 A5
Balabalangan, Kepulauan, *Indonesia* 56 E5
Bălăciţa, *Romania* 38 E6
Balad, *Iraq* 67 F11
Balad Rūz, *Iraq* 67 F11
Bālādeh, *Fārs, Iran* 65 D6
Bālādeh, *Māzandaran, Iran* 65 B6
Balaghat, *India* 60 J12
Balaghat Ra., *India* 60 K10
Balaguer, *Spain* 28 D5
Balakhna, *Russia* 42 B6
Balaklava, *Australia* 91 E2
Balaklava, *Ukraine* 41 K7
Balakliya, *Ukraine* 41 H9
Balakovo, *Russia* 42 D8
Balancán, *Mexico* 115 D6
Balashov, *Russia* 42 E6
Balasinor, *India* 62 H5
Balasore = Baleshwar, *India* 61 J15
Balassagyarmat, *Hungary* 21 G9
Balât, *Egypt* 76 B2
Balaton, *Hungary* 21 J7
Balayan, *Phil.* 55 E4
Balazote, *Spain* 29 G2
Balbina, Represa de, *Brazil* 121 D6
Balboa, *Panama* 116 E4
Balbriggan, *Ireland* 15 C5
Balcarce, *Argentina* 126 D4
Balcarres, *Canada* 101 C8
Balchik, *Bulgaria* 38 F11
Balclutha, *N.Z.* 87 M2
Bald Hd., *Australia* 89 G2
Bald I., *Australia* 89 F2
Bald Knob, *U.S.A.* 109 H9
Baldock L., *Canada* 101 B9
Baldwin, *Fla., U.S.A.* 105 K4
Baldwin, *Mich., U.S.A.* 104 D3
Baldwinsville, *U.S.A.* 107 C8
Baldy Peak, *U.S.A.* 111 K9
Bale, *Croatia* 33 C10
Bale □, *Ethiopia* 77 F5
Baleares □, *Spain* 28 F7
Baleares, Is., *Spain* 36 B10
Balearic Is. = Baleares, Is., *Spain* 36 B10
Baleia, Pta. da, *Brazil* 123 E4
Balen, *Belgium* 17 F6
Baler, *Phil.* 55 D4
Baler Bay, *Phil.* 55 D4
Balerna, *Switz.* 23 E8
Baleshwar, *India* 61 J15
Balezino, *Russia* 42 B11
Balfate, *Honduras* 116 C2
Balfe's Creek, *Australia* 90 C4
Bali, *Cameroon* 79 D6
Balí, *Greece* 37 D6
Bali, *Indonesia* 56 F5
Bali □, *Indonesia* 56 F5
Bali, Selat, *Indonesia* 57 H16
Baligród, *Poland* 20 F12
Balıkeşir, *Turkey* 66 C2
Balikpapan, *Indonesia* 56 E5
Balimbing, *Phil.* 57 C5
Baling, *Malaysia* 59 K3
Balintang Channel, *Phil.* 55 B4
Balipara, *India* 61 F18
Baliza, *Brazil* 125 D7
Balk, *Neths.* 16 C7
Balkan Mts. = Stara Planina, *Bulgaria* 38 F6
Balkhash = Balqash, *Kazakstan* 44 E8
Balkhash, Ozero = Balqash Köl, *Kazakstan* 44 E8
Balla, *Bangla.* 61 G17
Ballachulish, *U.K.* 14 E3
Balladonia, *Australia* 89 F3
Ballarat, *Australia* 91 F3
Ballard, L., *Australia* 89 E3
Ballater, *U.K.* 14 D5
Ballenas, Canal de, *Mexico* 114 B2
Balleny Is., *Antarctica* 5 C11
Ballesteros, *Phil.* 55 B4
Ballia, *India* 63 G11
Ballidu, *Australia* 89 F2
Ballina, *Australia* 91 D5
Ballina, *Mayo, Ireland* 15 B2
Ballina, *Tipp., Ireland* 15 D3
Ballinasloe, *Ireland* 15 C3
Ballinger, *U.S.A.* 109 K5
Ballinrobe, *Ireland* 15 C2
Ballinskelligs B., *Ireland* 15 E1
Ballon, *France* 24 D7
Ballycastle, *U.K.* 15 A5
Ballymena, *U.K.* 15 B5
Ballymena □, *U.K.* 15 B5
Ballymoney, *U.K.* 15 A5
Ballymoney □, *U.K.* 15 A5
Ballyshannon, *Ireland* 15 B3
Balmaceda, *Chile* 128 C2
Balmazújváros, *Hungary* 21 H11
Balmhorn, *Switz.* 22 D5
Balmoral, *Australia* 91 F3
Balmoral, *U.K.* 14 D5
Balmorhea, *U.S.A.* 109 K3
Balonne →, *Australia* 91 D4
Balqash, *Kazakstan* 44 E8
Balqash Köl, *Kazakstan* 44 E8
Balrampur, *India* 63 F10
Balranald, *Australia* 91 E3
Balş, *Romania* 38 E7
Balsapuerto, *Peru* 124 B2
Balsas, *Mexico* 115 D5
Balsas →, *Maranhão, Brazil* 122 C3
Balsas →, *Tocantins, Brazil* 122 C2
Balsas →, *Mexico* 114 D4
Bålsta, *Sweden* 10 E11
Balsthal, *Switz.* 22 B5
Balston Spa, *U.S.A.* 107 D11
Balta, *Romania* 38 E5
Balta, *Ukraine* 41 H5
Balta, *U.S.A.* 108 A4
Baltanás, *Spain* 30 D6
Bălţi, *Moldova* 41 J4
Baltic Sea, *Europe* 9 H18
Baltîm, *Egypt* 76 H7
Baltimore, *Ireland* 15 E2
Baltimore, *U.S.A.* 104 F7
Baltit, *Pakistan* 63 A6
Baltiysk, *Russia* 9 J18
Baltrum, *Germany* 18 B3
Baluchistan □, *Pakistan* 60 F4
Balurghat, *India* 63 G13
Balvi, *Latvia* 9 H22
Balya, *Turkey* 66 C2
Balygychan, *Russia* 45 C16
Balzar, *Ecuador* 120 D2
Bam, *Iran* 65 D8
Bama, *China* 52 E6
Bama, *Nigeria* 79 C7
Bamako, *Mali* 78 C3
Bamba, *Mali* 79 B4
Bambamarca, *Peru* 124 B2
Bambari, *C.A.R.* 73 G9
Bambaroo, *Australia* 90 B4
Bamberg, *Germany* 19 F6
Bamberg, *U.S.A.* 105 J5
Bambesi, *Ethiopia* 77 F3
Bambey, *Senegal* 78 C1
Bambili, *Zaïre* 82 B2
Bambuí, *Brazil* 123 F2
Bamenda, *Cameroon* 79 D7
Bamfield, *Canada* 100 D3
Bāmīān □, *Afghan.* 60 B5
Bamiancheng, *China* 51 C13
Bamkin, *Cameroon* 79 D7
Bampūr, *Iran* 65 E9
Ban Aranyaprathet, *Thailand* 58 F4
Ban Ban, *Laos* 58 C4
Ban Bang Hin, *Thailand* 59 H2
Ban Chiang Klang, *Thailand* 58 C3
Ban Chik, *Laos* 58 D4
Ban Choho, *Thailand* 58 E4
Ban Dan Lan Hoi, *Thailand* 58 D2
Ban Don = Surat Thani, *Thailand* 59 H2
Ban Don, *Vietnam* 58 F6
Ban Don, Ao, *Thailand* 59 H2
Ban Dong, *Thailand* 58 C3
Ban Hong, *Thailand* 58 C2
Ban Kaeng, *Thailand* 58 D3
Ban Keun, *Laos* 58 C4
Ban Khai, *Thailand* 58 F3
Ban Kheun, *Laos* 58 B3
Ban Khlong Kua, *Thailand* 59 J3
Ban Khuan Mao, *Thailand* 59 J2
Ban Khun Yuam, *Thailand* 58 C1
Ban Ko Yai Chim, *Thailand* 59 G2
Ban Kok, *Thailand* 58 D4
Ban Laem, *Thailand* 58 F2
Ban Lao Ngam, *Laos* 58 E6
Ban Le Kathe, *Thailand* 58 E2
Ban Mae Chedi, *Thailand* 58 C2
Ban Mae Laeng, *Thailand* 58 B2

Ban Mae Sariang, *Thailand* 58 C1
Ban Mê Thuôt = Buon Me Thuot, *Vietnam* 58 F7
Ban Mi, *Thailand* 58 E3
Ban Muong Mo, *Laos* 58 C4
Ban Na Mo, *Laos* 58 D5
Ban Na San, *Thailand* 59 H2
Ban Na Tong, *Laos* 58 B3
Ban Nam Bac, *Laos* 58 B4
Ban Nam Ma, *Laos* 58 A3
Ban Ngang, *Laos* 58 E6
Ban Nong Bok, *Laos* 58 D5
Ban Nong Boua, *Laos* 58 E6
Ban Nong Pling, *Thailand* 58 E3
Ban Pak Chan, *Thailand* 59 G2
Ban Phai, *Thailand* 58 D4
Ban Pong, *Thailand* 58 F2
Ban Ron Phibun, *Thailand* 59 H2
Ban Sanam Chai, *Thailand* 59 J3
Ban Sangkha, *Thailand* 58 E4
Ban Tak, *Thailand* 58 D2
Ban Tako, *Thailand* 58 E4
Ban Tha Dua, *Thailand* 58 D2
Ban Tha Li, *Thailand* 58 D3
Ban Tha Nun, *Thailand* 59 H2
Ban Thahine, *Laos* 58 E5
Ban Xien Kok, *Laos* 58 B3
Ban Yen Nhan, *Vietnam* 58 B6
Baña, Punta de la, *Spain* 28 E5
Banaba, *Kiribati* 92 H8
Bañalbufar, *Spain* 36 B9
Banalia, *Zaïre* 82 B2
Banam, *Cambodia* 59 G5
Banamba, *Mali* 78 C3
Banana, *Australia* 90 C5
Bananal, I. do, *Brazil* 123 D1
Banaras = Varanasi, *India* 63 G10
Banas →, *Gujarat, India* 62 H4
Banas →, *Mad. P., India* 63 G9
Bânâs, Ras, *Egypt* 76 C4
Banaz, *Turkey* 66 C3
Banbān, *Si. Arabia* 64 E5
Banbridge, *U.K.* 15 B5
Banbridge □, *U.K.* 15 B5
Banbury, *U.K.* 13 E6
Banchory, *U.K.* 14 D6
Bancroft, *Canada* 98 C4
Band Bonī, *Iran* 65 E8
Band Qīr, *Iran* 65 D6
Banda, *India* 63 G9
Banda, Kepulauan, *Indonesia* 57 E7
Banda Aceh, *Indonesia* 56 C1
Banda Banda, Mt., *Australia* 91 E5
Banda Elat, *Indonesia* 57 F8
Banda Is. = Banda, Kepulauan, *Indonesia* 57 E7
Banda Sea, *Indonesia* 57 F7
Bandai-San, *Japan* 48 F10
Bandama →, *Ivory C.* 78 D3
Bandān, *Iran* 65 D9
Bandanaira, *Indonesia* 57 E7
Bandanwara, *India* 62 F6
Bandar = Machilipatnam, *India* 61 L12
Bandār 'Abbās, *Iran* 65 E8
Bandar-e Anzalī, *Iran* 67 D13
Bandar-e Bushehr = Būshehr, *Iran* 65 D6
Bandar-e Chārak, *Iran* 65 E7
Bandar-e Deylam, *Iran* 65 D6
Bandar-e Khomeynı, *Iran* 65 D6
Bandar-e Lengeh, *Iran* 65 E7
Bandar-e Maqām, *Iran* 65 E7
Bandar-e Ma'shur, *Iran* 65 D6
Bandar-e Nakhīlū, *Iran* 65 E7
Bandar-e Rīg, *Iran* 65 D6
Bandar-e Torkeman, *Iran* 65 B7
Bandar Maharani = Muar, *Malaysia* 59 L4
Bandar Penggaram = Batu Pahat, *Malaysia* 59 M4
Bandar Seri Begawan, *Brunei* 56 C4
Bandawe, *Malawi* 83 E3
Bande, *Belgium* 17 H6
Bande, *Spain* 30 C3
Bandeira, Pico da, *Brazil* 123 F3
Bandeirante, *Brazil* 123 D1
Bandera, *Argentina* 126 B3
Bandera, *U.S.A.* 109 L5
Banderas, B. de, *Mexico* 114 C3
Bandiagara, *Mali* 78 C4
Bandırma, *Turkey* 66 B3
Bandon, *Ireland* 15 E3
Bandon →, *Ireland* 15 E3
Bandula, *Mozam.* 83 F3
Bandundu, *Zaïre* 80 E3
Bandung, *Indonesia* 57 G12
Bandya, *Australia* 89 E3
Bāneh, *Iran* 67 E11
Bañeres, *Spain* 29 G4
Banes, *Cuba* 117 B4
Banff, *Canada* 100 C5
Banff, *U.K.* 14 D6
Banff Nat. Park, *Canada* 100 C5
Banfora, *Burkina Faso* 78 C4
Bang Fai →, *Laos* 58 D5
Bang Hieng →, *Laos* 58 D5
Bang Krathum, *Thailand* 58 D3
Bang Lamung, *Thailand* 58 F3
Bang Mun Nak, *Thailand* 58 D3
Bang Pa In, *Thailand* 58 E3
Bang Rakam, *Thailand* 58 D3
Bang Saphan, *Thailand* 59 G2
Bangala Dam, *Zimbabwe* 83 G3
Bangalore, *India* 60 N10
Bangante, *Cameroon* 79 D7
Bangaon, *India* 63 H13
Bangassou, *C.A.R.* 80 D4
Banggai, Kepulauan, *Indonesia* 57 E6
Banggi, P., *Malaysia* 56 C5
Banghāzī, *Libya* 73 B9
Bangil, *Indonesia* 57 G15
Bangjang, *Sudan* 77 E3
Bangka, P., *Sulawesi, Indonesia* 57 D7
Bangka, P., *Sumatera, Indonesia* 56 E3
Bangka, Selat, *Indonesia* 56 E3
Bangkalan, *Indonesia* 57 G15
Bangkinang, *Indonesia* 56 D2
Bangko, *Indonesia* 56 E2
Bangkok, *Thailand* 58 F3
Bangladesh ■, *Asia* 61 H17
Bangolo, *Ivory C.* 78 D3
Bangong Co, *India* 63 B8
Bangor, *Down, U.K.* 15 B6
Bangor, *Gwynedd, U.K.* 12 D3
Bangor, *Maine, U.S.A.* 99 D6
Bangor, *Pa., U.S.A.* 107 F9
Bangued, *Phil.* 55 C4
Bangui, *C.A.R.* 80 D3
Bangui, *Phil.* 55 B4
Banguru, *Zaïre* 82 B2
Bangweulu, L., *Zambia* 83 E3
Bangweulu Swamp, *Zambia* 83 E3
Bani, *Dom. Rep.* 117 C5
Bani →, *Mali* 78 C4
Bani, Djebel, *Morocco* 74 C3
Bani Bangou, *Niger* 79 B5
Banī Sa'd, *Iraq* 67 F11
Banī Walīd, *Libya* 73 B7
Bania, *Ivory C.* 78 D4
Banihal Pass, *India* 63 C6
Banīnah, *Libya* 73 B9
Bāniyās, *Syria* 66 E6
Banja Luka, *Bos.-H.* 21 L7
Banjar, *Indonesia* 57 G13
Banjarmasin, *Indonesia* 56 E4
Banjarnegara, *Indonesia* 57 G13
Banjul, *Gambia* 78 C1
Banka Banka, *Australia* 90 B1
Banket, *Zimbabwe* 83 F3
Bankilaré, *Niger* 79 C5
Bankipore, *India* 63 G11
Banks I., *B.C., Canada* 100 C3
Banks I., *N.W.T., Canada* 96 A7
Banks Pen., *N.Z.* 87 K4
Banks Str., *Australia* 90 G4
Bankura, *India* 63 H12
Bann →, *Arm., U.K.* 15 B5
Bann →, *L'derry., U.K.* 15 A5
Banna, *Phil.* 55 C4
Bannalec, *France* 24 E3
Bannang Sata, *Thailand* 59 J3
Banning, *U.S.A.* 113 M10
Banningville = Bandundu, *Zaïre* 80 E3
Bannockburn, *Canada* 106 B7
Bannockburn, *U.K.* 14 E5
Bannockburn, *Zimbabwe* 83 G2
Bannu, *Pakistan* 60 C7
Bañolas, *Spain* 28 C7
Banon, *France* 27 D9
Baños de la Encina, *Spain* 31 G7
Baños de Molgas, *Spain* 30 C3
Banská Bystrica, *Slovak Rep.* 20 G9
Banská Štiavnica, *Slovak Rep.* 21 G8
Banswara, *India* 62 H6
Bantayan, *Phil.* 55 F5
Banten, *Indonesia* 57 G12
Bantry, *Ireland* 15 E2
Bantry B., *Ireland* 15 E2
Bantul, *Indonesia* 57 G14
Bantva, *India* 62 J4
Banu, *Afghan.* 60 B6
Banyak, Kepulauan, *Indonesia* 56 D1
Banyo, *Cameroon* 79 D7
Banyuls-sur-Mer, *France* 26 F7
Banyumas, *Indonesia* 57 G13
Banyuwangi, *Indonesia* 57 H16
Banzare Coast, *Antarctica* 5 C9
Banzyville = Mobayi, *Zaïre* 80 D4
Bao Ha, *Vietnam* 58 A5
Bao Lac, *Vietnam* 58 A5
Bao Loc, *Vietnam* 59 G6
Bao'an = Shenzhen, *China* 53 F10
Baocheng, *China* 50 H4
Baode, *China* 50 E6
Baodi, *China* 51 E9
Baoding, *China* 50 E8
Baoji, *China* 50 G4
Baojing, *China* 52 C7
Baokang, *China* 53 B8
Baoshan, *Shanghai, China* 53 B13
Baoshan, *Yunnan, China* 52 E2
Baotou, *China* 50 D6
Baoying, *China* 51 H10
Bap, *India* 62 F5
Bapatla, *India* 61 M12
Bapaume, *France* 25 B9
Bāqerābād, *Iran* 65 C6
Ba'qūbah, *Iraq* 67 F11
Baquedano, *Chile* 126 A2
Bar, *Montenegro, Yug.* 21 N9
Bar, *Ukraine* 41 H4
Bar Bigha, *India* 63 G11
Bar Harbor, *U.S.A.* 99 D6
Bar-le-Duc, *France* 25 D12
Bar-sur-Aube, *France* 25 D11
Bar-sur-Seine, *France* 25 D11
Barabai, *Indonesia* 56 E5
Barabinsk, *Russia* 44 D8
Baraboo, *U.S.A.* 108 D10
Baracaldo, *Spain* 28 B2
Baracoa, *Cuba* 117 B5
Baradero, *Argentina* 126 C4
Baraga, *U.S.A.* 108 B10
Barahona, *Dom. Rep.* 117 C5
Barahona, *Spain* 28 D2
Barail Range, *India* 61 G18
Baraka →, *Sudan* 76 D4
Barakhola, *India* 61 G18
Barakot, *India* 63 J11
Barakpur, *India* 63 H13
Barakula, *Australia* 91 D5
Baralaba, *Australia* 90 C4
Baralzon L., *Canada* 101 B9
Barameiya, *Sudan* 76 D4
Baramula, *India* 63 B6
Baran, *India* 62 G7
Baranavichy, *Belarus* 41 F4
Baranoa, *Colombia* 120 A3
Baranof I., *U.S.A.* 100 B1
Barão de Cocais, *Brazil* 123 E3
Barão de Grajaú, *Brazil* 122 C3
Barão de Melgaço, *Mato Grosso, Brazil* 125 D6
Barão de Melgaço, *Rondônia, Brazil* 125 C5
Baraolt, *Romania* 38 C8
Barapasi, *Indonesia* 57 E9
Barasat, *India* 63 H13
Barat Daya, Kepulauan, *Indonesia* 57 F7
Barataria B., *U.S.A.* 109 L10
Baraut, *India* 62 E7
Baraya, *Colombia* 120 C2
Barbacena, *Brazil* 123 F3
Barbacoas, *Colombia* 120 C2
Barbacoas, *Venezuela* 120 B4
Barbados ■, *W. Indies* 117 D8
Barbalha, *Brazil* 122 C4
Barban, *Croatia* 33 C11
Barbastro, *Spain* 28 C5
Barbate, *Spain* 31 J5
Barberino di Mugello, *Italy* 33 D8
Barberton, *S. Africa* 85 D5
Barberton, *U.S.A.* 106 E3
Barbezieux, *France* 26 C3
Barbosa, *Colombia* 120 B3
Barbourville, *U.S.A.* 105 G4
Barbuda, *W. Indies* 117 C7
Barcaldine, *Australia* 90 C4
Barcarrota, *Spain* 31 G4
Barcellona Pozzo di Gotto, *Italy* 35 D8
Barcelona, *Spain* 28 D7
Barcelona, *Venezuela* 121 A5
Barcelona □, *Spain* 28 D7
Barcelonette, *France* 27 D10
Barcelos, *Brazil* 121 D5
Barcoo →, *Australia* 90 D3
Barcs, *Hungary* 21 K7
Bärdä, *Azerbaijan* 43 K8
Barda del Medio, *Argentina* 128 A3
Bardai, *Chad* 73 D8
Bardas Blancas, *Argentina* 126 D2
Barddhaman, *India* 63 H12
Bardejov, *Slovak Rep.* 20 F11
Bardera, *Somali Rep.* 68 G3
Bardi, *Italy* 32 D6
Bardīyah, *Libya* 73 B9
Bardolino, *Italy* 32 C7
Bardsey I., *U.K.* 12 E3
Bardstown, *U.S.A.* 104 G3
Bareilly, *India* 63 E8
Barentin, *France* 24 C7
Barenton, *France* 24 D6
Barents Sea, *Arctic* 4 B9
Barentu, *Eritrea* 77 D4
Barfleur, *France* 24 C5
Barfleur, Pte. de, *France* 24 C5
Barga, *China* 54 C3
Barga, *Italy* 32 D7
Bargal, *Somali Rep.* 68 E5
Bargara, *Australia* 90 C5
Barge, *Italy* 32 D4
Bargnop, *Sudan* 77 F2
Bargteheide, *Germany* 18 B6
Barguzin, *Russia* 45 D11
Barh, *India* 63 G11
Barhaj, *India* 63 F10
Barhi, *India* 63 G11
Bari, *India* 62 F7
Bari, *Italy* 35 A9
Bari Doab, *Pakistan* 62 D5
Bariadi □, *Tanzania* 82 C3
Barīm, *Yemen* 68 E3
Barima →, *Guyana* 121 B5
Barinas, *Venezuela* 120 B3
Barinas □, *Venezuela* 120 B4
Baring, C., *Canada* 96 B8
Baringo, *Kenya* 82 B4
Baringo □, *Kenya* 82 B4
Baringo, L., *Kenya* 82 B4
Barinitas, *Venezuela* 120 B3
Bariri, *Brazil* 123 F2
Bârîs, *Egypt* 76 C3
Barisal, *Bangla.* 61 H17
Barisan, Bukit, *Indonesia* 56 E2
Barito →, *Indonesia* 56 E4
Barjac, *France* 27 D8
Barjols, *France* 27 E10
Barjūj, Wadi →, *Libya* 75 C7
Bark L., *Canada* 106 A7
Barka = Baraka →, *Sudan* 76 D4
Barkam, *China* 52 B4
Barker, *U.S.A.* 106 C6
Barkley Sound, *Canada* 100 D3
Barkly Downs, *Australia* 90 C2
Barkly East, *S. Africa* 84 E4
Barkly Tableland, *Australia* 90 B2
Barkly West, *S. Africa* 84 D3
Barkol, Wadi →, *Sudan* 76 D3
Barksdale, *U.S.A.* 109 L4
Barlee, L., *Australia* 89 E2
Barlee, Mt., *Australia* 89 D4
Barletta, *Italy* 35 A9
Barlinek, *Poland* 20 C5
Barlovento, *Canary Is.* 36 F2
Barlow L., *Canada* 101 A8
Barmedman, *Australia* 91 E4
Barmer, *India* 62 G4
Barmera, *Australia* 91 E3
Barmouth, *U.K.* 12 E3
Barmstedt, *Germany* 18 B5
Barnagar, *India* 62 H6
Barnard Castle, *U.K.* 12 C6
Barnato, *Australia* 91 E3
Barnaul, *Russia* 44 D9
Barnesville, *U.S.A.* 105 J3
Barnet, *U.K.* 13 F7
Barneveld, *Neths.* 16 D7
Barneveld, *U.S.A.* 107 C9
Barneville-Cartevert, *France* 24 C5
Barngo, *Australia* 90 D4
Barnhart, *U.S.A.* 109 K4
Barnsley, *U.K.* 12 D6
Barnstaple, *U.K.* 13 F3
Barnsville, *U.S.A.* 108 B6
Baro, *Nigeria* 79 D6
Baro →, *Ethiopia* 77 F3
Baroda = Vadodara, *India* 62 H5
Baroda, *India* 62 G7
Baroe, *S. Africa* 84 E3
Baron Ra., *Australia* 88 D4
Barpeta, *India* 61 F17
Barques, Pt. Aux, *U.S.A.* 104 C4
Barquinha, *Portugal* 31 F2
Barquísimeto, *Venezuela* 120 A4
Barr, *France* 25 D14
Barra, *Brazil* 122 D3
Barra, *U.K.* 14 E1
Barra, Sd. of, *U.K.* 14 D1
Barra da Estiva, *Brazil* 123 D3
Barra de Navidad, *Mexico* 114 D4
Barra do Corda, *Brazil* 122 C2
Barra do Mendes, *Brazil* 123 D3
Barra do Piraí, *Brazil* 123 F3
Barra Falsa, Pta. da, *Mozam.* 85 C6
Barra Hd., *U.K.* 14 E1
Barra Mansa, *Brazil* 123 F3
Barraba, *Australia* 91 E5
Barracão do Barreto, *Brazil* 125 B6
Barrackpur = Barakpur, *India* 63 H13
Barrafranca, *Italy* 35 E7
Barraigh = Barra, *U.K.* 14 E1
Barranca, *Lima, Peru* 124 C2
Barranca, *Loreto, Peru* 120 D2
Barrancabermeja, *Colombia* 120 B3
Barrancas, *Colombia* 120 A3
Barrancas, *Venezuela* 121 B5
Barrancos, *Portugal* 31 G4
Barranqueras, *Argentina* 126 B4
Barranquilla, *Colombia* 120 A3
Barras, *Brazil* 122 B3
Barras, *Colombia* 120 D3
Barraute, *Canada* 98 C4
Barre, *Mass., U.S.A.* 107 D12
Barre, *Vt., U.S.A.* 107 B12
Barre do Bugres, *Brazil* 125 C6
Barreal, *Argentina* 126 C2
Barreiras, *Brazil* 123 D3
Barreirinha, *Brazil* 121 D6
Barreirinhas, *Brazil* 122 B3
Barreiro, *Portugal* 31 G1
Barreiros, *Brazil* 122 C4
Barrême, *France* 27 E10
Barren, Nosy, *Madag.* 85 B7
Barretos, *Brazil* 123 F2
Barrhead, *Canada* 100 C6
Barrie, *Canada* 98 D4
Barrier Ra., *Australia* 91 E3
Barrière, *Canada* 100 C4
Barrington, *U.S.A.* 107 E13
Barrington L., *Canada* 101 B8
Barrington Tops, *Australia* 91 E5
Barringun, *Australia* 91 D4
Barro do Garças, *Brazil* 125 D7
Barrow, *U.S.A.* 96 A4
Barrow →, *Ireland* 15 D4
Barrow Creek, *Australia* 90 C1
Barrow I., *Australia* 88 D2
Barrow-in-Furness, *U.K.* 12 C4
Barrow Pt., *Australia* 90 A3
Barrow Pt., *U.S.A.* 94 B4
Barrow Ra., *Australia* 89 E4
Barrow Str., *Canada* 4 B3
Barruecopardo, *Spain* 30 D4
Barruelo, *Spain* 30 C6
Barry, *U.K.* 13 F4
Barry's Bay, *Canada* 98 C4
Barsalogho, *Burkina Faso* 79 C4
Barsat, *Pakistan* 63 A5
Barsham, *Syria* 67 E9
Barsi, *India* 60 K9
Barsø, *Denmark* 11 J3
Barsoi, *India* 61 G15
Barstow, *Calif., U.S.A.* 113 L9
Barstow, *Tex., U.S.A.* 109 K3
Barth, *Germany* 18 A8
Barthélemy, Col, *Vietnam* 58 C5
Bartica, *Guyana* 121 B6
Bartin, *Turkey* 66 B5
Bartlesville, *U.S.A.* 109 G7
Bartlett, *Calif., U.S.A.* 112 J8
Bartlett, *Tex., U.S.A.* 109 K6
Bartlett, L., *Canada* 100 A5
Bartolomeu Dias, *Mozam.* 83 G4
Barton, *Australia* 89 F5
Barton upon Humber, *U.K.* 12 D7
Bartoszyce, *Poland* 20 A10
Bartow, *U.S.A.* 105 M5
Barú, I. de, *Colombia* 120 A2
Barú, Volcan, *Panama* 116 E3
Barumba, *Zaïre* 82 B1
Baruth, *Germany* 18 C9
Barvaux, *Belgium* 17 H6
Barvinkove, *Ukraine* 41 H9
Barwani, *India* 62 H6
Barysaw, *Belarus* 40 E5
Barysh, *Russia* 42 D8
Barzān, *Iraq* 64 B5
Bas-Rhin □, *France* 25 D14
Bašaid, *Serbia, Yug.* 21 K10
Bāsa'idū, *Iran* 65 E7
Basal, *Pakistan* 62 C5
Basankusa, *Zaïre* 80 D3
Basarabeasca, *Moldova* 41 J5
Basawa, *Afghan.* 62 B4
Bascharage, *Lux.* 17 J7
Bascuñán, C., *Chile* 126 B1
Basècles, *Belgium* 17 G3
Basel, *Switz.* 22 A5
Basel-Stadt □, *Switz.* 22 A5
Baselland □, *Switz.* 22 B5
Basento →, *Italy* 35 B9
Bāshī, *Iran* 65 D6
Bashi Channel, *Phil.* 54 D7
Bashkir Republic = Bashkortostan □, *Russia* 44 D6
Bashkortostan □, *Russia* 44 D6
Basilan, *Phil.* 55 H5
Basilan Str., *Phil.* 55 H5
Basildon, *U.K.* 13 F8
Basilicata □, *Italy* 35 B9
Basim = Washim, *India* 60 J10
Basin, *U.S.A.* 110 D9
Basingstoke, *U.K.* 13 F6
Baška, *Croatia* 33 D11
Başkale, *Turkey* 67 C10
Baskatong, Rés., *Canada* 98 C4
Basle = Basel, *Switz.* 22 A5
Basoda, *India* 62 H7
Basodino, *Switz.* 23 D6
Basoka, *Zaïre* 82 B1
Basongo, *Zaïre* 80 E4
Basque, Pays, *France* 26 E2
Basque Provinces = País Vasco □, *Spain* 28 C2
Basra = Al Başrah, *Iraq* 64 D5
Bass Rock, *U.K.* 14 E6
Bass Str., *Australia* 90 F4
Bassano, *Canada* 100 C6
Bassano del Grappa, *Italy* 33 C8
Bassar, *Togo* 79 D5
Bassas da India, *Ind. Oc.* 81 J7
Basse Santa-Su, *Gambia* 78 C2
Basse-Terre, *Guadeloupe* 117 C7
Bassecourt, *Switz.* 22 B4
Bassein, *Burma* 61 L19
Basseterre, *St. Kitts & Nevis* 117 C7
Bassett, *Nebr., U.S.A.* 108 D5
Bassett, *Va., U.S.A.* 105 G6
Bassevelde, *Belgium* 17 F3
Bassi, *India* 62 D7
Bassigny, *France* 25 E12
Bassikounou, *Mauritania* 78 B3
Bassilly, *Belgium* 17 G3
Bassum, *Germany* 18 C4
Båstad, *Sweden* 11 H6
Bastak, *Iran* 65 E7
Baştām, *Iran* 65 B7
Bastar, *India* 61 K12
Bastelica, *France* 27 F13
Basti, *India* 63 F10
Bastia, *France* 27 F13
Bastia Umbra, *Italy* 33 E9
Bastogne, *Belgium* 17 H7
Bastrop, *U.S.A.* 109 K6
Bat Yam, *Israel* 69 C3
Bata, *Eq. Guin.* 80 D1
Bata, *Romania* 38 C5
Bataan, *Phil.* 55 D4
Batabanó, *Cuba* 116 B3
Batabanó, G. de, *Cuba* 116 B3
Batac, *Phil.* 55 B4
Batagoy, *Russia* 45 C14
Batak, *Bulgaria* 39 H7
Batalha, *Portugal* 31 F2
Batama, *Zaïre* 82 B2
Batamay, *Russia* 45 C13
Batan I., *Phil.* 55 A4
Batanes Is., *Phil.* 55 A4
Batang, *China* 52 B2
Batang, *Indonesia* 57 G13
Batangafo, *C.A.R.* 73 G8
Batangas, *Phil.* 55 E4
Batanta, *Indonesia* 57 E8
Batatais, *Brazil* 127 A6
Batavia, *U.S.A.* 106 D6
Bataysk, *Russia* 43 G4
Batchelor, *Australia* 88 B5
Bateman's B., *Australia* 91 F5
Batemans Bay, *Australia* 91 F5
Bates Ra., *Australia* 89 E3
Batesburg, *U.S.A.* 105 J5
Batesville, *Ark., U.S.A.* 109 H9
Batesville, *Miss., U.S.A.* 109 H10

Batesville, *Tex., U.S.A.* 109 L5
Bath, *U.K.* 13 F5
Bath, *Maine, U.S.A.* 99 D6
Bath, *N.Y., U.S.A.* 106 D7
Bath & North East Somerset □, *U.K.* 13 F5
Batheay, *Cambodia* 59 G5
Bathgate, *U.K.* 14 F5
Bathmen, *Neths.* 16 D8
Bathurst = Banjul, *Gambia* 78 C1
Bathurst, *Australia* 91 E4
Bathurst, *Canada* 99 C6
Bathurst, *S. Africa* 84 E4
Bathurst, C., *Canada* 96 A7
Bathurst B., *Australia* 90 A3
Bathurst Harb., *Australia* 90 G4
Bathurst I., *Australia* 88 B5
Bathurst I., *Canada* 4 B2
Bathurst Inlet, *Canada* 96 B9
Batie, *Burkina Faso* 78 D4
Batlow, *Australia* 91 F4
Batman, *Turkey* 67 D9
Batna, *Algeria* 75 A6
Batobato, *Phil.* 55 H7
Batoka, *Zambia* 83 F2
Baton Rouge, *U.S.A.* 109 K9
Batong, Ko, *Thailand* 59 J2
Batopilas, *Mexico* 114 B3
Batouri, *Cameroon* 80 D2
Båtsfjord, *Norway* 8 A23
Battambang, *Cambodia* 58 F4
Batticaloa, *Sri Lanka* 60 R12
Battice, *Belgium* 17 G7
Battipáglia, *Italy* 35 B7
Battle, *U.K.* 13 G8
Battle →, *Canada* 101 C7
Battle Camp, *Australia* 90 B3
Battle Creek, *U.S.A.* 104 D3
Battle Ground, *U.S.A.* 112 E4
Battle Harbour, *Canada* 99 B8
Battle Lake, *U.S.A.* 108 B7
Battle Mountain, *U.S.A.* 110 F5
Battlefields, *Zimbabwe* 83 F2
Battleford, *Canada* 101 C7
Battonya, *Hungary* 21 J11
Batu, *Ethiopia* 68 F2
Batu, Kepulauan, *Indonesia* 56 E1
Batu Caves, *Malaysia* 59 L3
Batu Gajah, *Malaysia* 59 K3
Batu Is. = Batu, Kepulauan, *Indonesia* 56 E1
Batu Pahat, *Malaysia* 59 M4
Batuata, *Indonesia* 57 F6
Batumi, *Georgia* 43 K5
Baturaja, *Indonesia* 56 E2
Baturité, *Brazil* 122 B4
Bau, *Malaysia* 56 D4
Baubau, *Indonesia* 57 F6
Bauchi, *Nigeria* 79 C6
Bauchi □, *Nigeria* 79 C6
Baud, *France* 24 E3
Baudette, *U.S.A.* 108 A7
Baudour, *Belgium* 17 H3
Bauer, C., *Australia* 91 E1
Baugé, *France* 24 E6
Bauhinia Downs, *Australia* 90 C4
Baukau, *Indonesia* 57 F7
Bauma, *Switz.* 23 B7
Baume-les-Dames, *France* 25 E13
Baunatal, *Germany* 18 D5
Baunei, *Italy* 34 B2
Baures, *Bolivia* 125 C5
Bauru, *Brazil* 127 A6
Baús, *Brazil* 125 D7
Bauska, *Latvia* 9 H21
Bautino, *Kazakstan* 43 H10
Bautzen, *Germany* 18 D10
Bavānāt, *Iran* 65 D7
Bavaria = Bayern □, *Germany* 19 F7
Båven, *Sweden* 10 F10
Bavi Sadri, *India* 62 G6
Bavispe →, *Mexico* 114 B3
Bawdwin, *Burma* 61 H20
Bawean, *Indonesia* 56 F4
Bawku, *Ghana* 79 C4
Bawlake, *Burma* 61 K20
Bawolung, *China* 52 C3
Baxley, *U.S.A.* 105 K4
Baxoi, *China* 52 B1
Baxter Springs, *U.S.A.* 109 G7
Bay, L. de, *Phil.* 57 B6
Bay Bulls, *Canada* 99 C9
Bay City, *Mich., U.S.A.* 104 D4
Bay City, *Oreg., U.S.A.* 110 D2
Bay City, *Tex., U.S.A.* 109 L7
Bay de Verde, *Canada* 99 C9
Bay Minette, *U.S.A.* 105 K2
Bay St. Louis, *U.S.A.* 109 K10
Bay Springs, *U.S.A.* 109 K10
Bay View, *N.Z.* 87 H6
Baya, *Zaïre* 83 E2
Bayamo, *Cuba* 116 B4
Bayamón, *Puerto Rico* 117 C6
Bayan Har Shan, *China* 54 C4
Bayan Hot = Alxa Zuoqi, *China* 50 E3
Bayan Obo, *China* 50 D5
Bayan-Ovoo, *Mongolia* 50 C4
Bayana, *India* 62 F7
Bayanaûyl, *Kazakstan* 44 D8
Bayandalay, *Mongolia* 50 C2
Bayanhongor, *Mongolia* 54 B5
Bayard, *U.S.A.* 108 E3
Bayawan, *Phil.* 55 G5
Baybay, *Phil.* 55 F6
Bayburt, *Turkey* 67 B9
Bayerischer Wald, *Germany* 19 F8
Bayern □, *Germany* 19 F7
Bayeux, *France* 24 C6
Bayfield, *Canada* 106 C3
Bayfield, *U.S.A.* 108 B9
Bayındır, *Turkey* 66 C2
Baykal, Oz., *Russia* 45 D11
Baykit, *Russia* 45 C10
Baykonur = Bayqongyr, *Kazakstan* 44 E7
Baynes Mts., *Namibia* 84 B1
Bayombong, *Phil.* 55 C4
Bayon, *France* 25 D13
Bayona, *Spain* 30 C2
Bayonne, *France* 26 E2
Bayonne, *U.S.A.* 107 F10
Bayovar, *Peru* 124 B1
Bayqongyr, *Kazakstan* 44 E7
Bayram-Ali = Bayramaly, *Turkmenistan* 44 F7
Bayramaly, *Turkmenistan* 44 F7
Bayramiç, *Turkey* 66 C2
Bayreuth, *Germany* 19 F7
Bayrischzell, *Germany* 19 H8
Bayrūt, *Lebanon* 69 B4
Bayt Lahm, *West Bank* 69 D4
Baytown, *U.S.A.* 109 L7
Bayzo, *Niger* 79 C5
Baza, *Spain* 29 H2
Bazar Dyuzi, *Russia* 43 K8
Bazardüzü = Bazar Dyuzi, *Russia* 43 K8
Bazarny Karabulak, *Russia* 42 D8
Bazarnyy Syzgan, *Russia* 42 D8
Bazaruto, I. do, *Mozam.* 85 C6
Bazas, *France* 26 D3
Bazhong, *China* 52 B6
Bazmān, Kūh-e, *Iran* 65 D9
Beach, *U.S.A.* 108 B3
Beach City, *U.S.A.* 106 F3
Beachport, *Australia* 91 F2
Beachy Hd., *U.K.* 13 G8
Beacon, *Australia* 89 F2
Beacon, *U.S.A.* 107 E11
Beaconia, *Canada* 101 C9
Beagle, Canal, *S. Amer.* 128 E3
Beagle Bay, *Australia* 88 C3
Bealanana, *Madag.* 85 A8
Beamsville, *Canada* 106 C5
Bear →, *U.S.A.* 112 G5
Béar, C., *France* 26 F7
Bear I., *Ireland* 15 E2
Bear L., *B.C., Canada* 100 B3
Bear L., *Man., Canada* 101 B9
Bear L., *U.S.A.* 110 E8
Bearcreek, *U.S.A.* 110 D9
Beardmore, *Canada* 98 C2
Beardmore Glacier, *Antarctica* 5 E11
Beardstown, *U.S.A.* 108 F9
Béarn, *France* 26 E3
Bearpaw Mts., *U.S.A.* 110 B9
Bearskin Lake, *Canada* 98 B1
Beas de Segura, *Spain* 29 G2
Beasain, *Spain* 28 B2
Beata, C., *Dom. Rep.* 117 C5
Beata, I., *Dom. Rep.* 117 C5
Beatrice, *U.S.A.* 108 E6
Beatrice, *Zimbabwe* 83 F3
Beatrice, C., *Australia* 90 A2
Beatton →, *Canada* 100 B4
Beatton River, *Canada* 100 B4
Beatty, *U.S.A.* 111 H5
Beaucaire, *France* 27 E8
Beauce, Plaine de la, *France* 25 D8
Beauceville, *Canada* 99 C5
Beauchêne, I., *Falk. Is.* 128 D5
Beaudesert, *Australia* 91 D5
Beaufort, *Malaysia* 56 C5
Beaufort, *N.C., U.S.A.* 105 H7
Beaufort, *S.C., U.S.A.* 105 J5
Beaufort Sea, *Arctic* 4 B1
Beaufort West, *S. Africa* 84 E3
Beaugency, *France* 25 E8
Beauharnois, *Canada* 98 C5
Beaujeu, *France* 27 B8
Beaulieu →, *Canada* 100 A6
Beaulieu-sur-Dordogne, *France* 26 D5
Beaulieu-sur-Mer, *France* 27 E11
Beauly, *U.K.* 14 D4
Beauly →, *U.K.* 14 D4
Beaumaris, *U.K.* 12 D3
Beaumetz-lès-Loges, *France* 25 B9
Beaumont, *Belgium* 17 H4
Beaumont, *France* 26 D4
Beaumont, *U.S.A.* 109 K7
Beaumont-de-Lomagne, *France* 26 E4
Beaumont-le-Roger, *France* 24 C7
Beaumont-sur-Oise, *France* 25 C9
Beaumont-sur-Sarthe, *France* 24 D7
Beaune, *France* 25 E11
Beaune-la-Rolande, *France* 25 D9
Beaupréau, *France* 24 E6
Beauraing, *Belgium* 17 H5
Beauséjour, *Canada* 101 C9
Beauvais, *France* 25 C9
Beauval, *Canada* 101 B7
Beauvoir-sur-Mer, *France* 24 F4
Beauvoir-sur-Niort, *France* 26 B3
Beaver, *Alaska, U.S.A.* 96 B5
Beaver, *Okla., U.S.A.* 109 G4
Beaver, *Pa., U.S.A.* 106 F4
Beaver, *Utah, U.S.A.* 111 G7
Beaver →, *B.C., Canada* 100 B4
Beaver →, *Ont., Canada* 98 A2
Beaver →, *Sask., Canada* 101 B7
Beaver City, *U.S.A.* 108 E5
Beaver Dam, *U.S.A.* 108 D10
Beaver Falls, *U.S.A.* 106 F4
Beaver Hill L., *Canada* 101 C10
Beaver I., *U.S.A.* 104 C3
Beaverhill L., *Alta., Canada* 100 C6
Beaverhill L., *N.W.T., Canada* 101 A8
Beaverlodge, *Canada* 100 B5
Beavermouth, *Canada* 100 C5
Beaverstone →, *Canada* 98 B2
Beaverton, *Canada* 106 B5
Beaverton, *U.S.A.* 112 E4
Beawar, *India* 62 F6
Bebedouro, *Brazil* 127 A6
Beboa, *Madag.* 85 B7
Bebra, *Germany* 18 E5
Beccles, *U.K.* 13 E9
Bečej, *Serbia, Yug.* 21 K10
Becerreá, *Spain* 30 C3
Béchar, *Algeria* 75 B4
Beckley, *U.S.A.* 104 G5
Beckum, *Germany* 18 D4
Bečva →, *Czech.* 20 F7
Bédar, *Spain* 29 H3
Bédarieux, *France* 26 E7
Bédarrides, *France* 27 D8
Beddouza, Ras, *Morocco* 74 B3
Bedele, *Ethiopia* 77 F4
Bederkesa, *Germany* 18 B4
Bedeso, *Ethiopia* 77 F5
Bedford, *Canada* 98 C5
Bedford, *S. Africa* 84 E4
Bedford, *U.K.* 13 E7
Bedford, *Ind., U.S.A.* 104 F2
Bedford, *Iowa, U.S.A.* 108 E7
Bedford, *Ohio, U.S.A.* 106 E3
Bedford, *Pa., U.S.A.* 106 F6
Bedford, *Va., U.S.A.* 104 G6
Bedford, C., *Australia* 90 B4
Bedford Downs, *Australia* 88 C4
Bedfordshire □, *U.K.* 13 E7
Będków, *Poland* 20 D9
Bednja →, *Croatia* 33 B13
Bednodemyanovsk, *Russia* 42 D6
Bedónia, *Italy* 32 D6
Bedourie, *Australia* 90 C2
Bedretto, *Switz.* 23 C7
Bedum, *Neths.* 16 B9
Będzin, *Poland* 20 E9
Beech Grove, *U.S.A.* 104 F2
Beechy, *Canada* 101 C7
Beek, *Gelderland, Neths.* 16 E8
Beek, *Limburg, Neths.* 17 G7
Beek, *Noord-Brabant, Neths.* 17 E7
Beekbergen, *Neths.* 16 D7
Beelitz, *Germany* 18 C8
Beenleigh, *Australia* 91 D5
Be'er Menuha, *Israel* 64 D2
Be'er Sheva, *Israel* 69 D3
Beersheba = Be'er Sheva, *Israel* 69 D3
Beerta, *Neths.* 16 B10
Beerze →, *Neths.* 16 E6
Beesd, *Neths.* 16 E6
Beeskow, *Germany* 18 C10
Beeston, *U.K.* 12 E6
Beetaloo, *Australia* 90 B1
Beetsterzwaag, *Neths.* 16 B8
Beetzendorf, *Germany* 18 C7
Beeville, *U.S.A.* 109 L6
Befale, *Zaïre* 80 D4
Befandriana, *Madag.* 85 C7
Befotaka, *Madag.* 85 C8
Bega, *Australia* 91 F4
Bega, Canalul, *Romania* 38 D3
Bégard, *France* 24 D3
Bègles, *France* 26 D3
Begna →, *Norway* 10 D4
Begonte, *Spain* 30 B3
Begusarai, *India* 63 G12
Behābād, *Iran* 65 C8
Behara, *Madag.* 85 C8
Behbehān, *Iran* 65 D6
Behshahr, *Iran* 65 B7
Bei Jiang →, *China* 53 F9
Bei'an, *China* 54 B7
Beibei, *China* 52 C6
Beihai, *China* 52 G7
Beijing, *China* 50 E9
Beijing □, *China* 50 E9
Beilen, *Neths.* 16 C8
Beiliu, *China* 53 F8
Beilngries, *Germany* 19 F7
Beilpajah, *Australia* 91 E3
Beilul, *Eritrea* 77 E5
Beinn na Faoghla = Benbecula, *U.K.* 14 D1
Beipiao, *China* 51 D11
Beira, *Mozam.* 83 F3
Beirut = Bayrūt, *Lebanon* 69 B4
Beitaolaizhao, *China* 51 B13
Beitbridge, *Zimbabwe* 83 G3
Beiuş, *Romania* 38 C5
Beizhen, *Liaoning, China* 51 D11
Beizhen, *Shandong, China* 51 F10
Beizhengzhen, *China* 51 B12
Beja, *Portugal* 31 G3
Béja, *Tunisia* 75 A6
Beja □, *Portugal* 31 H3
Bejaia, *Algeria* 75 A6
Béjar, *Spain* 30 E5
Bejestān, *Iran* 65 C8
Bekaa Valley = Al Biqā □, *Lebanon* 69 A5
Bekasi, *Indonesia* 57 G12
Békés, *Hungary* 21 J11
Békéscsaba, *Hungary* 21 J11
Bekily, *Madag.* 85 C8
Bekkevoort, *Belgium* 17 G5
Bekoji, *Ethiopia* 77 F4
Bekok, *Malaysia* 59 L4
Bekwai, *Ghana* 79 D4
Bela, *India* 63 G9
Bela, *Pakistan* 62 F2
Bela Crkva, *Serbia, Yug.* 21 L11
Bela Palanka, *Serbia, Yug.* 21 M12
Bela Vista, *Brazil* 126 A4
Bela Vista, *Mozam.* 85 D5
Bélâbre, *France* 26 B5
Belalcázar, *Spain* 31 G5
Belarus ■, *Europe* 40 F4
Belau = Palau ■, *Pac. Oc.* 46 J17
Belavenona, *Madag.* 85 C8
Belawan, *Indonesia* 56 D1
Belaya, *Ethiopia* 77 E4
Belaya Glina, *Russia* 43 G5
Belaya Kalitva, *Russia* 43 F5
Belaya Tserkov = Bila Tserkva, *Ukraine* 41 H6
Belcher Is., *Canada* 97 C12
Belchite, *Spain* 28 D4
Belden, *U.S.A.* 112 E5
Belém, *Brazil* 122 B2
Belém de São Francisco, *Brazil* 122 C4
Belén, *Argentina* 126 B2
Belén, *Colombia* 120 C2
Belén, *Paraguay* 126 A4
Belen, *U.S.A.* 111 J10
Beleni, *Turkey* 66 D7
Bélesta, *France* 26 F5
Belet Uen, *Somali Rep.* 68 G4
Belev, *Russia* 42 D3
Belfair, *U.S.A.* 112 C4
Belfast, *S. Africa* 85 D5
Belfast, *U.K.* 15 B6
Belfast, *Maine, U.S.A.* 99 D6
Belfast, *N.Y., U.S.A.* 106 D6
Belfast □, *U.K.* 15 B6
Belfast L., *U.K.* 15 B6
Belfeld, *Neths.* 17 F8
Belfield, *U.S.A.* 108 B3
Belfort, *France* 25 E13
Belfort, Territoire de □, *France* 25 E13
Belfry, *U.S.A.* 110 D9
Belgaum, *India* 60 M9
Belgioioso, *Italy* 32 C6
Belgium ■, *Europe* 17 G5
Belgorod, *Russia* 42 E3
Belgorod-Dnestrovskiy = Bilhorod-Dnistrovskyy, *Ukraine* 41 J6
Belgrade = Beograd, *Serbia, Yug.* 21 L10
Belgrade, *U.S.A.* 110 D8
Belhaven, *U.S.A.* 105 H7
Beli Drim →, *Europe* 21 N10
Beli Manastir, *Croatia* 21 K8
Belice →, *Italy* 34 E5
Belin-Béliet, *France* 26 D3
Belinga, *Gabon* 80 D2
Belinskiy, *Russia* 42 D6
Belinyu, *Indonesia* 56 E3
Beliton Is. = Belitung, *Indonesia* 56 E3
Belitung, *Indonesia* 56 E3
Beliu, *Romania* 38 C5
Belize ■, *Cent. Amer.* 115 D7
Belize City, *Belize* 115 D7
Beljanica, *Serbia, Yug.* 21 L11
Belkovskiy, Ostrov, *Russia* 45 B14
Bell →, *Canada* 98 C4
Bell Bay, *Australia* 90 G4
Bell I., *Canada* 99 B8
Bell-Irving →, *Canada* 100 B3
Bell Peninsula, *Canada* 97 B11
Bell Ville, *Argentina* 126 C3
Bella Bella, *Canada* 100 C3
Bella Coola, *Canada* 100 C3
Bella Flor, *Bolivia* 124 C4
Bella Unión, *Uruguay* 126 C4
Bella Vista, *Corrientes, Argentina* 126 B4
Bella Vista, *Tucuman, Argentina* 126 B2
Bellac, *France* 26 B5
Bellágio, *Italy* 32 C6
Bellaire, *U.S.A.* 106 F4
Bellary, *India* 60 M10
Bellata, *Australia* 91 D4
Belle Fourche, *U.S.A.* 108 C3
Belle Fourche →, *U.S.A.* 108 C3
Belle Glade, *U.S.A.* 105 M5
Belle-Ile, *France* 24 E3
Belle Isle, *Canada* 99 B8
Belle Isle, Str. of, *Canada* 99 B8
Belle-Isle-en-Terre, *France* 24 D3
Belle Plaine, *Iowa, U.S.A.* 108 E8
Belle Plaine, *Minn., U.S.A.* 108 C8
Belle Yella, *Liberia* 78 D3
Belledonne, Chaîne de, *France* 27 C10
Belledune, *Canada* 99 C6
Bellefontaine, *U.S.A.* 104 E4
Bellefonte, *U.S.A.* 106 F7
Bellegarde, *France* 25 E9
Bellegarde-en-Marche, *France* 26 C6
Bellegarde-sur-Valserine, *France* 27 B9
Bellême, *France* 24 D7
Belleoram, *Canada* 99 C8
Belleville, *Canada* 98 D4
Belleville, *France* 27 B8
Belleville, *Ill., U.S.A.* 108 F10
Belleville, *Kans., U.S.A.* 108 F6
Belleville, *N.Y., U.S.A.* 107 C8
Belleville-sur-Vie, *France* 24 F5
Bellevue, *Canada* 100 D6
Bellevue, *Idaho, U.S.A.* 110 E6
Bellevue, *Ohio, U.S.A.* 106 E2
Bellevue, *Wash., U.S.A.* 112 C4
Belley, *France* 27 C9
Bellin = Kangirsuk, *Canada* 97 B13
Bellingen, *Australia* 91 E5
Bellingham, *U.S.A.* 112 B4
Bellingshausen Sea, *Antarctica* 5 C17
Bellinzona, *Switz.* 23 D8
Bello, *Colombia* 120 B2
Bellows Falls, *U.S.A.* 107 C12
Bellpat, *Pakistan* 62 E3
Bellpuig, *Spain* 28 D6
Belluno, *Italy* 33 B9
Bellville, *U.S.A.* 109 L6
Bellwood, *U.S.A.* 106 F6
Bélmez, *Spain* 31 G5
Belmont, *Australia* 91 E5
Belmont, *Canada* 106 D3
Belmont, *S. Africa* 84 D3
Belmont, *U.S.A.* 106 D6
Belmonte, *Brazil* 123 E4
Belmonte, *Portugal* 30 E3
Belmonte, *Spain* 28 F2
Belmopan, *Belize* 115 D7
Belmullet, *Ireland* 15 B2
Belo Horizonte, *Brazil* 123 E3
Belo Jardim, *Brazil* 122 C4
Belo-sur-Mer, *Madag.* 85 C7
Belo-Tsiribihina, *Madag.* 85 B7
Belogorsk = Bilohirsk, *Ukraine* 41 K8
Belogorsk, *Russia* 45 D13
Belogradchik, *Bulgaria* 38 F5
Beloha, *Madag.* 85 D8
Beloit, *Kans., U.S.A.* 108 F5
Beloit, *Wis., U.S.A.* 108 D10
Belokorovichi, *Ukraine* 41 G5
Belomorsk, *Russia* 44 C4
Belonia, *India* 61 H17
Belopolye = Bilopillya, *Ukraine* 41 G8
Belorechensk, *Russia* 43 H4
Belorussia ■ = Belarus ■, *Europe* 40 F4
Belovo, *Russia* 44 D9
Belovodsk, *Ukraine* 41 H10
Beloye, Ozero, *Russia* 40 B9
Beloye More, *Russia* 44 C4
Belozersk, *Russia* 40 B9
Belpasso, *Italy* 35 E7
Belsele, *Belgium* 17 F4
Belsito, *Italy* 34 E6
Beltana, *Australia* 91 E2
Belterra, *Brazil* 121 D7
Beltinci, *Slovenia* 33 B13
Belton, *S.C., U.S.A.* 105 H4
Belton, *Tex., U.S.A.* 109 K6
Belton Res., *U.S.A.* 109 K6
Beltsy = Bălţi, *Moldova* 41 J4
Belturbet, *Ireland* 15 B4
Belukha, *Russia* 44 E9
Beluran, *Malaysia* 56 C5
Belvedere Marittimo, *Italy* 35 C8
Belvès, *France* 26 D5
Belvidere, *Ill., U.S.A.* 108 D10
Belvidere, *N.J., U.S.A.* 107 F9
Belvis de la Jara, *Spain* 31 F6
Belyando →, *Australia* 90 C4
Belyy, *Russia* 40 E7
Belyy, Ostrov, *Russia* 44 B8
Belyy Yar, *Russia* 44 D9
Belzig, *Germany* 18 C8
Belzoni, *U.S.A.* 109 J9
Bemaraha, Lembalemban' i, *Madag.* 85 B7
Bemarivo, *Madag.* 85 C7
Bemarivo →, *Madag.* 85 B8
Bemavo, *Madag.* 85 C8
Bembéréke, *Benin* 79 C5
Bembesi, *Zimbabwe* 83 F2
Bembesi →, *Zimbabwe* 83 F2
Bembézar →, *Spain* 31 H5
Bemidji, *U.S.A.* 108 B7
Bemmel, *Neths.* 16 E7
Ben, *Iran* 65 C6
Ben Cruachan, *U.K.* 14 E3
Ben Dearg, *U.K.* 14 D4
Ben Gardane, *Tunisia* 75 B7
Ben Hope, *U.K.* 14 C4
Ben Lawers, *U.K.* 14 E4
Ben Lomond, *N.S.W., Australia* 91 E5
Ben Lomond, *Tas., Australia* 90 G4
Ben Lomond, *U.K.* 14 E4
Ben Luc, *Vietnam* 59 G6
Ben Macdhui, *U.K.* 14 D5
Ben Mhor, *U.K.* 14 D1
Ben More, *Arg. & Bute, U.K.* 14 E2
Ben More, *Stirl., U.K.* 14 E4
Ben More Assynt, *U.K.* 14 C4
Ben Nevis, *U.K.* 14 E4
Ben Quang, *Vietnam* 58 D6

Ben Slimane, *Morocco* 74 B3
Ben Tre, *Vietnam* 59 G6
Ben Vorlich, *U.K.* 14 E4
Ben Wyvis, *U.K.* 14 D4
Bena, *Nigeria* 79 C6
Bena Dibele, *Zaïre* 80 E4
Benāb, *Iran* 67 D12
Benagalbón, *Spain* 31 J6
Benagerie, *Australia* 91 E3
Benahmed, *Morocco* 74 B3
Benalla, *Australia* 91 F4
Benambra, Mt., *Australia* 91 F4
Benamejí, *Spain* 31 H6
Benares = Varanasi, *India* 63 G10
Bénat, C., *France* 27 E10
Benavente, *Portugal* 31 G2
Benavente, *Spain* 30 C5
Benavides, *Spain* 30 C5
Benavides, *U.S.A.* 109 M5
Benbecula, *U.K.* 14 D1
Benbonyathe, *Australia* 91 E2
Bencubbin, *Australia* 89 F2
Bend, *U.S.A.* 110 D3
Bender Beila, *Somali Rep.* 68 F5
Bendering, *Australia* 89 F2
Bendery = Tighina, *Moldova* 41 J5
Bendigo, *Australia* 91 F3
Bendorf, *Germany* 18 E3
Benē Beraq, *Israel* 69 C3
Beneden Knijpe, *Neths.* 16 C7
Beneditinos, *Brazil* 122 C3
Benedito Leite, *Brazil* 122 C3
Bénéna, *Mali* 78 C4
Benenitra, *Madag.* 85 C8
Benešŏv, *Czech.* 20 F4
Bénestroff, *France* 25 D13
Benet, *France* 26 B3
Benevento, *Italy* 35 A7
Benfeld, *France* 25 D14
Benga, *Mozam.* 83 F3
Bengal, Bay of, *Ind. Oc.* 61 K16
Bengbu, *China* 51 H9
Benghazi = Banghāzī, *Libya* 73 B9
Bengkalis, *Indonesia* 56 D2
Bengkulu, *Indonesia* 56 E2
Bengkulu □, *Indonesia* 56 E2
Bengough, *Canada* 101 D7
Benguela, *Angola* 81 G2
Benguerir, *Morocco* 74 B3
Benguérua, I., *Mozam.* 85 C6
Benha, *Egypt* 76 H7
Beni, *Zaïre* 82 B2
Beni □, *Bolivia* 125 C4
Beni →, *Bolivia* 125 C4
Beni Abbès, *Algeria* 75 B4
Beni-Haoua, *Algeria* 75 A5
Beni Mazâr, *Egypt* 76 J7
Beni Mellal, *Morocco* 74 B3
Beni Ounif, *Algeria* 75 B4
Beni Saf, *Algeria* 75 A4
Beni Suef, *Egypt* 76 J7
Beniah L., *Canada* 100 A6
Benicarló, *Spain* 28 E5
Benicia, *U.S.A.* 112 G4
Benidorm, *Spain* 29 G4
Benidorm, Islote de, *Spain* 29 G4
Benin ■, *Africa* 79 D5
Benin, Bight of, *W. Afr.* 79 D5
Benin City, *Nigeria* 79 D6
Benisa, *Spain* 29 G5
Benitses, *Greece* 37 A3
Benjamin Aceval, *Paraguay* 126 A4
Benjamin Constant, *Brazil* 120 D3
Benjamin Hill, *Mexico* 114 A2
Benkelman, *U.S.A.* 108 E4
Benkovac, *Croatia* 33 D12
Benlidi, *Australia* 90 C3
Bennebroek, *Neths.* 16 D5
Bennekom, *Neths.* 16 D7
Bennett, *Canada* 100 B2
Bennett, L., *Australia* 88 D5
Bennett, Ostrov, *Russia* 45 B15
Bennettsville, *U.S.A.* 105 H6
Bennington, *U.S.A.* 107 D11
Bénodet, *France* 24 E2
Benoni, *S. Africa* 85 D4
Benoud, *Algeria* 75 B5
Benque Viejo, *Belize* 115 D7
Bensheim, *Germany* 19 F4
Benson, *U.S.A.* 111 L8
Bent, *Iran* 65 E8
Benteng, *Indonesia* 57 F6
Bentinck I., *Australia* 90 B2
Bentiu, *Sudan* 77 F2
Bento Gonçalves, *Brazil* 127 B5
Benton, *Ark., U.S.A.* 109 H8
Benton, *Calif., U.S.A.* 112 H8
Benton, *Ill., U.S.A.* 108 F10
Benton Harbor, *U.S.A.* 104 D2
Bentu Liben, *Ethiopia* 77 F4
Bentung, *Malaysia* 59 L3
Benue □, *Nigeria* 79 D6
Benue →, *Nigeria* 79 D6
Benxi, *China* 51 D12
Benzdorp, *Surinam* 121 C7
Beo, *Indonesia* 57 D7
Beograd, *Serbia, Yug.* 21 L10
Beowawe, *U.S.A.* 110 F5
Bepan Jiang →, *China* 52 E6
Beppu, *Japan* 49 H5
Beqaa Valley = Al Biqā □, *Lebanon* 69 A5
Berati, *Albania* 39 J2
Berau, Teluk, *Indonesia* 57 E8
Berber, *Sudan* 76 D3
Berbera, *Somali Rep.* 68 E4
Berbérati, *C.A.R.* 80 D3
Berberia, C. del, *Spain* 36 C7
Berbice →, *Guyana* 121 B6
Berceto, *Italy* 32 D7
Berchtesgaden, *Germany* 19 H8
Berck-Plage, *France* 25 B8
Berdichev = Berdychiv, *Ukraine* 41 H5
Berdsk, *Russia* 44 D9
Berdyansk, *Ukraine* 41 J9
Berdychiv, *Ukraine* 41 H5
Berea, *U.S.A.* 104 G3
Berebere, *Indonesia* 57 D7
Bereda, *Somali Rep.* 68 E5
Berehove, *Ukraine* 41 H2
Berekum, *Ghana* 78 D4
Berenice, *Egypt* 76 C4
Berens →, *Canada* 101 C9
Berens I., *Canada* 101 C9
Berens River, *Canada* 101 C9
Berestechko, *Ukraine* 41 G3
Bereşti, *Romania* 38 C10
Beretău →, *Romania* 38 B4
Berettyo →, *Hungary* 21 J11
Berettyóújfalu, *Hungary* 21 H11
Berevo, *Mahajanga, Madag.* 85 B7
Berevo, *Toliara, Madag.* 85 B7
Bereza, *Belarus* 41 F3
Berezhany, *Ukraine* 41 H3
Berezina = Byarezina →, *Belarus* 41 F6
Berezivka, *Ukraine* 41 J6
Berezna, *Ukraine* 41 G6
Berezniki, *Russia* 44 D6
Berezovo, *Russia* 44 C7
Berga, *Spain* 28 C6
Bergama, *Turkey* 66 C2
Bergambacht, *Neths.* 16 E5
Bérgamo, *Italy* 32 C6
Bergantiños, *Spain* 30 B2
Bergara, *Spain* 28 B2
Bergedorf, *Germany* 18 B6
Bergeijk, *Neths.* 17 F6
Bergen, *Germany* 18 A9
Bergen, *Neths.* 16 C5
Bergen, *Norway* 9 F11
Bergen, *U.S.A.* 106 C7
Bergen-op-Zoom, *Neths.* 17 F4
Bergerac, *France* 26 D4
Bergheim, *Germany* 18 E2
Berghem, *Neths.* 16 E7
Bergisch Gladbach, *Germany* 18 E3
Bergschenhoek, *Neths.* 16 E5
Bergsjö, *Sweden* 10 C11
Bergues, *France* 25 B9
Bergum, *Neths.* 16 B7
Bergville, *S. Africa* 85 D4
Berhala, Selat, *Indonesia* 56 E2
Berhampore = Baharampur, *India* 63 G13
Berhampur, *India* 61 K14
Berheci →, *Romania* 38 C10
Bering Sea, *Pac. Oc.* 96 C1
Bering Strait, *U.S.A.* 96 B3
Beringen, *Belgium* 17 F6
Beringen, *Switz.* 23 A7
Beringovskiy, *Russia* 45 C18
Berisso, *Argentina* 126 C4
Berja, *Spain* 29 J2
Berkane, *Morocco* 75 B4
Berkel →, *Neths.* 16 D8
Berkeley, *U.K.* 13 F5
Berkeley, *U.S.A.* 112 H4
Berkeley Springs, *U.S.A.* 104 F6
Berkhout, *Neths.* 16 C5
Berkner I., *Antarctica* 5 D18
Berkovitsa, *Bulgaria* 38 F6
Berkshire □, *U.K.* 13 F6
Berlaar, *Belgium* 17 F5
Berland →, *Canada* 100 C5
Berlanga, *Spain* 31 G5
Berlare, *Belgium* 17 F4
Berlenga, I., *Portugal* 31 F1
Berlin, *Germany* 18 C9
Berlin, *Md., U.S.A.* 104 F8
Berlin, *N.H., U.S.A.* 107 B13
Berlin, *Wis., U.S.A.* 104 D1
Bermeja, Sierra, *Spain* 31 J5
Bermejo →, *Formosa, Argentina* 126 B4
Bermejo →, *San Juan, Argentina* 126 C2
Bermeo, *Spain* 28 B2
Bermillo de Sayago, *Spain* 30 D4
Bermuda ■, *Atl. Oc.* 94 F13
Bern, *Switz.* 22 C4
Bern □, *Switz.* 22 C5
Bernado, *U.S.A.* 111 J10
Bernalda, *Italy* 35 B9
Bernalillo, *U.S.A.* 111 J10
Bernardo de Irigoyen, *Argentina* 127 B5
Bernardo O'Higgins □, *Chile* 126 C1
Bernasconi, *Argentina* 126 D3
Bernau, *Bayern, Germany* 19 H8
Bernau, *Brandenburg, Germany* 18 C9
Bernay, *France* 24 C7
Bernburg, *Germany* 18 D7
Berne = Bern, *Switz.* 22 C4
Berne = Bern □, *Switz.* 22 C5
Berner Alpen, *Switz.* 22 D5
Bernese Oberland = Oberland, *Switz.* 22 C5
Bernier I., *Australia* 89 D1
Bernina, Piz, *Switz.* 23 D9
Bernissart, *Belgium* 17 H3
Bernkastel-Kues, *Germany* 19 F3
Beroroha, *Madag.* 85 C8
Béroubouay, *Benin* 79 C5
Beroun, *Czech.* 20 F4
Berounka →, *Czech.* 20 F4
Berovo, *Macedonia* 39 H5
Berrahal, *Algeria* 75 A6
Berre, Étang de, *France* 27 E9
Berrechid, *Morocco* 74 B3
Berri, *Australia* 91 E3
Berriane, *Algeria* 75 B5
Berrouaghia, *Algeria* 75 A5
Berry, *Australia* 91 E5
Berry, *France* 25 F8
Berry Is., *Bahamas* 116 A4
Berryessa L., *U.S.A.* 112 G4
Berryville, *U.S.A.* 109 G8
Bersenbrück, *Germany* 18 C3
Bershad, *Ukraine* 41 H5
Berthold, *U.S.A.* 108 A4
Berthoud, *U.S.A.* 108 E2
Bertincourt, *France* 25 B9
Bertoua, *Cameroon* 80 D2
Bertrand, *U.S.A.* 108 E5
Bertrange, *Lux.* 17 J8
Bertrix, *Belgium* 17 J6
Beruri, *Brazil* 121 D5
Berwick, *U.S.A.* 107 E8
Berwick-upon-Tweed, *U.K.* 12 B5
Berwyn Mts., *U.K.* 12 E4
Beryslav, *Ukraine* 41 J7
Berzasca, *Romania* 38 E4
Besal, *Pakistan* 63 B5
Besalampy, *Madag.* 85 B7
Besançon, *France* 25 E13
Besar, *Indonesia* 56 E5
Beshenkovichi, *Belarus* 40 E5
Beslan, *Russia* 43 J7
Besnard L., *Canada* 101 B7
Besni, *Turkey* 66 D7
Besor, N. →, *Egypt* 69 D3
Bessarabiya, *Moldova* 41 J5
Bessarabka = Basarabeasca, *Moldova* 41 J5
Bessèges, *France* 27 D8
Bessemer, *Ala., U.S.A.* 105 J2
Bessemer, *Mich., U.S.A.* 108 B9
Bessin, *France* 24 C5
Bessines-sur-Gartempe, *France* 26 B5
Best, *Neths.* 17 E6
Bet She'an, *Israel* 69 C4
Bet Shemesh, *Israel* 69 D3
Bet Tadjine, Djebel, *Algeria* 74 C4
Betafo, *Madag.* 85 B8
Betancuria, *Canary Is.* 36 F5
Betanzos, *Bolivia* 125 D4
Betanzos, *Spain* 30 B2
Bétaré Oya, *Cameroon* 80 C2
Bétera, *Spain* 28 F4
Bethal, *S. Africa* 85 D4
Bethanien, *Namibia* 84 D2
Bethany, *U.S.A.* 108 E7
Bethel, *Alaska, U.S.A.* 96 B3
Bethel, *Vt., U.S.A.* 107 C12
Bethel Park, *U.S.A.* 106 F4
Bethlehem = Bayt Lahm, *West Bank* 69 D4
Bethlehem, *S. Africa* 85 D4
Bethlehem, *U.S.A.* 107 F9
Bethulie, *S. Africa* 84 E4
Béthune, *France* 25 B9
Béthune →, *France* 24 C8
Bethungra, *Australia* 91 E4
Betijoque, *Venezuela* 120 B3
Betim, *Brazil* 123 E3
Betioky, *Madag.* 85 C7
Beton-Bazoches, *France* 25 D10
Betong, *Thailand* 59 K3
Betoota, *Australia* 90 D3
Betroka, *Madag.* 85 C8
Betsiamites, *Canada* 99 C6
Betsiamites →, *Canada* 99 C6
Betsiboka →, *Madag.* 85 B8
Bettembourg, *Lux.* 17 J8
Bettiah, *India* 63 F11
Bèttola, *Italy* 32 D6
Betul, *India* 60 J10
Betung, *Malaysia* 56 D4
Betzdorf, *Germany* 18 E3
Beuca, *Romania* 38 E7
Beuil, *France* 27 D10
Beulah, *U.S.A.* 108 B4
Beuvron →, *France* 24 E8
Beveren, *Belgium* 17 F4
Beverley, *Australia* 89 F2
Beverley, *U.K.* 12 D7
Beverlo, *Belgium* 17 F6
Beverly, *Mass., U.S.A.* 107 D14
Beverly, *Wash., U.S.A.* 110 C4
Beverly Hills, *U.S.A.* 113 L8
Beverwijk, *Neths.* 16 D5
Bex, *Switz.* 22 D4
Bey Dağları, *Turkey* 66 D4
Beya, *Russia* 45 D10
Beyānlū, *Iran* 64 C5
Beyin, *Ghana* 78 D4
Beyla, *Guinea* 78 D3
Beynat, *France* 26 C5
Beyneu, *Kazakstan* 44 E6
Beypazarı, *Turkey* 66 B4
Beyşehir, *Turkey* 66 D4
Beyşehir Gölü, *Turkey* 66 D4
Beytüşşebap, *Turkey* 67 D10
Bezhetsk, *Russia* 42 B3
Bezhitsa, *Russia* 44 D4
Béziers, *France* 26 E7
Bezwada = Vijayawada, *India* 61 L12
Bhachau, *India* 60 H7
Bhadarwah, *India* 63 C6
Bhadrakh, *India* 61 J15
Bhadravati, *India* 60 N9
Bhagalpur, *India* 63 G12
Bhakkar, *Pakistan* 62 D4
Bhakra Dam, *India* 62 D7
Bhamo, *Burma* 61 G20
Bhandara, *India* 60 J11
Bhanrer Ra., *India* 62 H8
Bharat = India ■, *Asia* 60 K11
Bharatpur, *India* 62 F7
Bhatinda, *India* 62 D6
Bhatpara, *India* 63 H13
Bhaun, *Pakistan* 62 C5
Bhaunagar = Bhavnagar, *India* 62 J5
Bhavnagar, *India* 62 J5
Bhawanipatna, *India* 61 K12
Bhera, *Pakistan* 62 C5
Bhilsa = Vidisha, *India* 62 H7
Bhilwara, *India* 62 G6
Bhima →, *India* 60 L10
Bhimavaram, *India* 61 L12
Bhimbar, *Pakistan* 63 C6
Bhind, *India* 63 F8
Bhiwandi, *India* 60 K8
Bhiwani, *India* 62 E7
Bhola, *Bangla.* 61 H17
Bhopal, *India* 62 H7
Bhubaneshwar, *India* 61 J14
Bhuj, *India* 62 H3
Bhumiphol Dam = Phumiphon, Khuan, *Thailand* 58 D2
Bhusaval, *India* 60 J9
Bhutan ■, *Asia* 61 F17
Biá →, *Brazil* 120 D4
Biafra, B. of = Bonny, Bight of, *Africa* 79 E6
Biak, *Indonesia* 57 E9
Biała →, *Poland* 20 E10
Biała Podlaska, *Poland* 20 C13
Białogard, *Poland* 20 A5
Białystok, *Poland* 20 B13
Biancavilla, *Italy* 35 E7
Bīārjmand, *Iran* 65 B7
Biaro, *Indonesia* 57 D7
Biarritz, *France* 26 E2
Biasca, *Switz.* 23 D7
Biba, *Egypt* 76 J7
Bibai, *Japan* 48 C10
Bibala, *Angola* 81 G2
Bibane, Bahiret el, *Tunisia* 75 B7
Bibbiena, *Italy* 33 E8
Bibby I., *Canada* 101 A10
Biberach, *Germany* 19 G5
Biberist, *Switz.* 22 B5
Bibey →, *Spain* 30 C3
Bibiani, *Ghana* 78 D4
Biboohra, *Australia* 90 B4
Bibungwa, *Zaïre* 82 C2
Bic, *Canada* 99 C6
Bicaz, *Romania* 38 C9
Biccari, *Italy* 35 A8
Bichena, *Ethiopia* 77 E4
Bichvinta, *Georgia* 43 J5
Bickerton I., *Australia* 90 A2
Bicknell, *Ind., U.S.A.* 104 F2
Bicknell, *Utah, U.S.A.* 111 G8
Bida, *Nigeria* 79 D6
Bidar, *India* 60 L10
Biddeford, *U.S.A.* 99 D5
Biddwara, *Ethiopia* 77 F4
Bideford, *U.K.* 13 F3
Bidon 5 = Poste Maurice Cortier, *Algeria* 75 D5
Bidor, *Malaysia* 59 K3
Bié, Planalto de, *Angola* 81 G3
Bieber, *U.S.A.* 110 F3
Biel, *Switz.* 22 B4
Bielawa, *Poland* 20 E6
Bielé Karpaty, *Europe* 20 F7
Bielefeld, *Germany* 18 C4
Bielersee, *Switz.* 22 B4
Biella, *Italy* 32 C5
Bielsk Podlaski, *Poland* 20 C13
Bielsko-Biała, *Poland* 20 F9
Bien Hoa, *Vietnam* 59 G6
Bienfait, *Canada* 101 D8
Bienne = Biel, *Switz.* 22 B4
Bienvenida, *Spain* 31 G4
Bienvenue, *Fr. Guiana* 121 C7
Bienville, L., *Canada* 98 A5
Biescas, *Spain* 28 C4
Biese →, *Germany* 18 C7
Biesiesfontein, *S. Africa* 84 E2
Bietigheim, *Germany* 19 G5
Bievre, *Belgium* 17 J6
Biferno →, *Italy* 35 A8
Big →, *Canada* 99 B8
Big B., *Canada* 99 A7
Big Bear City, *U.S.A.* 113 L10
Big Bear Lake, *U.S.A.* 113 L10
Big Beaver, *Canada* 101 D7
Big Belt Mts., *U.S.A.* 110 C8
Big Bend, *Swaziland* 85 D5
Big Bend National Park, *U.S.A.* 109 L3
Big Black →, *U.S.A.* 109 J9
Big Blue →, *U.S.A.* 108 F6
Big Cr. →, *Canada* 100 C4
Big Creek, *U.S.A.* 112 H7
Big Cypress Swamp, *U.S.A.* 105 M5
Big Falls, *U.S.A.* 108 A8
Big Fork →, *U.S.A.* 108 A8
Big Horn Mts. = Bighorn Mts., *U.S.A.* 110 D10
Big Lake, *U.S.A.* 109 K4
Big Moose, *U.S.A.* 107 C10
Big Muddy Cr. →, *U.S.A.* 108 A2
Big Pine, *U.S.A.* 111 H4
Big Piney, *U.S.A.* 110 E8
Big Quill L., *Canada* 101 C8
Big Rapids, *U.S.A.* 104 D3
Big River, *Canada* 101 C7
Big Run, *U.S.A.* 106 F6
Big Sable Pt., *U.S.A.* 104 C2
Big Sand L., *Canada* 101 B9
Big Sandy, *U.S.A.* 110 B8
Big Sandy Cr. →, *U.S.A.* 108 F3
Big Sioux →, *U.S.A.* 108 D6
Big Spring, *U.S.A.* 109 J4
Big Springs, *U.S.A.* 108 E3
Big Stone City, *U.S.A.* 108 C6
Big Stone Gap, *U.S.A.* 105 G4
Big Stone L., *U.S.A.* 108 C6
Big Sur, *U.S.A.* 112 J5
Big Timber, *U.S.A.* 110 D9
Big Trout L., *Canada* 98 B1
Biğa, *Turkey* 66 B2
Bigadiç, *Turkey* 66 C3
Biganos, *France* 26 D3
Bigfork, *U.S.A.* 110 B6
Biggar, *Canada* 101 C7
Biggar, *U.K.* 14 F5
Bigge I., *Australia* 88 B4
Biggenden, *Australia* 91 D5
Biggs, *U.S.A.* 112 F5
Bighorn, *U.S.A.* 110 C10
Bighorn →, *U.S.A.* 110 C10
Bighorn Mts., *U.S.A.* 110 D10
Bignona, *Senegal* 78 C1
Bigorre, *France* 26 E4
Bigstone L., *Canada* 101 C9
Biguglia, Étang de, *France* 27 F13
Bigwa, *Tanzania* 82 D4
Bihać, *Bos.-H.* 33 D12
Bihar, *India* 63 G11
Bihar □, *India* 63 G11
Biharamulo, *Tanzania* 82 C3
Biharamulo □, *Tanzania* 82 C3
Bihor, Munţii, *Romania* 38 C5
Bijagós, Arquipélago dos, *Guinea-Biss.* 78 C1
Bijaipur, *India* 62 F7
Bijapur, *Karnataka, India* 60 L9
Bijapur, *Mad. P., India* 61 K12
Bījār, *Iran* 67 E12
Bijeljina, *Bos.-H.* 21 L9
Bijelo Polje, *Montenegro, Yug.* 21 M9
Bijie, *China* 52 D5
Bijnor, *India* 62 E8
Bikaner, *India* 62 E5
Bikapur, *India* 63 F10
Bikeqi, *China* 50 D6
Bikfayyā, *Lebanon* 69 B4
Bikin, *Russia* 45 E14
Bikin →, *Russia* 48 A7
Bikini Atoll, *Pac. Oc.* 92 F8
Bikoué, *Cameroon* 79 E7
Bila Tserkva, *Ukraine* 41 H6
Bilara, *India* 62 F5
Bilaspur, *Mad. P., India* 63 H10
Bilaspur, *Punjab, India* 62 D7
Biläsuvar, *Azerbaijan* 67 C13
Bilauk Taungdan, *Thailand* 58 F2
Bilbao, *Spain* 28 B2
Bilbeis, *Egypt* 76 H7
Bilbo = Bilbao, *Spain* 28 B2
Bilbor, *Romania* 38 B8
Bíldudalur, *Iceland* 8 D2
Bileća, *Bos.-H.* 21 N8
Bilecik, *Turkey* 66 B4
Biłgoraj, *Poland* 20 E12
Bilhorod-Dnistrovskyy, *Ukraine* 41 J6
Bilibino, *Russia* 45 C17
Bilibiza, *Mozam.* 83 E5
Bilir, *Russia* 45 C14
Biliran I., *Phil.* 55 F6
Bill, *U.S.A.* 108 D2
Billabalong, *Australia* 89 E2
Billiluna, *Australia* 88 C4
Billingham, *U.K.* 12 C6
Billings, *U.S.A.* 110 D9
Billiton Is. = Belitung, *Indonesia* 56 E3
Billom, *France* 26 C7
Bilma, *Niger* 73 E7
Bilo Gora, *Croatia* 21 K7
Biloela, *Australia* 90 C5
Bilohirsk, *Ukraine* 41 K8
Biloku, *Guyana* 121 C6
Bilopillya, *Ukraine* 41 G8
Biloxi, *U.S.A.* 109 K10
Bilpa Morea Claypan, *Australia* 90 D2
Bilthoven, *Neths.* 16 D6
Biltine, *Chad* 73 F9
Bilyana, *Australia* 90 B4
Bilyarsk, *Russia* 42 C10
Bilzen, *Belgium* 17 G7
Bima, *Indonesia* 57 F5
Bimban, *Egypt* 76 C3
Bimbila, *Ghana* 79 D5
Bimbo, *C.A.R.* 80 D3
Bimini Is., *Bahamas* 116 A4

Bin Xian, *Heilongjiang, China* 51 B14
Bin Xian, *Shaanxi, China* 50 G5
Bina-Etawah, *India* 62 G8
Bināb, *Iran* 67 D13
Binalbagan, *Phil.* 55 F5
Binalong, *Australia* 91 E4
Bīnālūd, Kūh-e, *Iran* 65 B8
Binatang, *Malaysia* 56 D4
Binbee, *Australia* 90 C4
Binche, *Belgium* 17 H4
Binchuan, *China* 52 E3
Binda, *Australia* 91 D4
Bindle, *Australia* 91 D4
Bindura, *Zimbabwe* 83 F3
Bingara, *N.S.W., Australia* 91 D5
Bingara, *Queens., Australia* 91 D3
Bingen, *Germany* 19 F3
Bingerville, *Ivory C.* 78 D4
Bingham, *U.S.A.* 99 C6
Bingham Canyon, *U.S.A.* 110 F7
Binghamton, *U.S.A.* 107 D9
Bingöl, *Turkey* 67 C9
Bingöl Dağları, *Turkey* 67 C9
Binh Dinh = An Nhon, *Vietnam* 58 F7
Binh Khe, *Vietnam* 58 F7
Binh Son, *Vietnam* 58 E7
Binhai, *China* 51 G10
Binisatua, *Spain* 36 B11
Binjai, *Indonesia* 56 D1
Binnaway, *Australia* 91 E4
Binongko, *Indonesia* 57 F6
Binscarth, *Canada* 101 C8
Bintan, *Indonesia* 56 D2
Bintulu, *Malaysia* 56 D4
Bintuni, *Indonesia* 57 E8
Binyang, *China* 52 F7
Binz, *Germany* 18 A9
Binzert = Bizerte, *Tunisia* 75 A6
Bío Bío □, *Chile* 126 D1
Biograd, *Croatia* 33 E12
Bioko, *Eq. Guin.* 79 E6
Biougra, *Morocco* 74 B3
Bir, *India* 60 K9
Bir, Ras, *Djibouti* 77 E5
Bîr Abu Hashim, *Egypt* 76 C3
Bîr Abu M'nqar, *Egypt* 76 B2
Bîr Abu Muḥammad, *Egypt* 69 F3
Bi'r ad Dabbāghāt, *Jordan* 69 E4
Bir Adal Deib, *Sudan* 76 C4
Bi'r al Butayyihāt, *Jordan* 69 F4
Bi'r al Mārī, *Jordan* 69 E4
Bi'r al Qattār, *Jordan* 69 F4
Bir Aouine, *Tunisia* 75 B6
Bîr 'Asal, *Egypt* 76 B3
Bir Autrun, *Sudan* 76 D2
Bîr Beiḍa, *Egypt* 69 E3
Bîr Diqnash, *Egypt* 76 A2
Bir el Abbes, *Algeria* 74 C3
Bîr el 'Abd, *Egypt* 69 D2
Bir el Ater, *Algeria* 75 B6
Bîr el Basur, *Egypt* 76 B2
Bîr el Biarât, *Egypt* 69 F3
Bîr el Duweidar, *Egypt* 69 E1
Bîr el Garârât, *Egypt* 69 D2
Bîr el Gellaz, *Egypt* 76 A2
Bîr el Heisi, *Egypt* 69 F3
Bîr el Jafir, *Egypt* 69 E1
Bîr el Mâlḥi, *Egypt* 69 E2
Bîr el Shaqqa, *Egypt* 76 A2
Bîr el Thamâda, *Egypt* 69 E2
Bîr Fuad, *Egypt* 76 A2
Bîr Gebeil Ḥiṣn, *Egypt* 69 E2
Bi'r Ghadīr, *Syria* 69 A6
Bîr Haimur, *Egypt* 76 C3
Bîr Ḥasana, *Egypt* 69 E2
Bi'r Jadīd, *Iraq* 64 C4
Bir Jdid, *Morocco* 74 B3
Bîr Kanayis, *Egypt* 76 C3
Bîr Kaseiba, *Egypt* 69 E2
Bîr Kerawein, *Egypt* 76 B2
Bîr Lahfân, *Egypt* 69 D2
Bir Lahrache, *Algeria* 75 B6
Bîr Madkûr, *Egypt* 69 E1
Bîr Maql, *Egypt* 76 C3
Bîr Misaha, *Egypt* 76 C2
Bir Mogrein, *Mauritania* 74 C2
Bîr Murr, *Egypt* 76 C3
Bi'r Muṭribah, *Kuwait* 64 D5
Bîr Nakheila, *Egypt* 76 C3
Bîr Qaṭia, *Egypt* 69 E1
Bîr Qatrani, *Egypt* 76 A2
Bîr Ranga, *Egypt* 76 C4
Bîr Sahara, *Egypt* 76 C2
Bîr Seiyâla, *Egypt* 76 B3
Bir Semguine, *Morocco* 74 B3
Bîr Shalatein, *Egypt* 76 C4
Bîr Shebb, *Egypt* 76 C2
Bîr Shût, *Egypt* 76 C4
Bîr Terfawi, *Egypt* 76 C2
Bîr Umm Qubûr, *Egypt* 76 C3
Bîr Ungât, *Egypt* 76 C3
Bîr Za'farâna, *Egypt* 76 J8
Bîr Zeidûn, *Egypt* 76 B3
Bira, *Indonesia* 57 E8
Bîra, *Romania* 38 B10
Biramféro, *Guinea* 78 C3
Birao, *C.A.R.* 73 F9
Birawa, *Zaïre* 82 C2
Bîrca, *Romania* 38 F6
Birch Hills, *Canada* 101 C7
Birch I., *Canada* 101 C9
Birch L., *N.W.T., Canada* 100 A5
Birch L., *Ont., Canada* 98 B1
Birch L., *U.S.A.* 98 C1
Birch Mts., *Canada* 100 B6
Birch River, *Canada* 101 C8
Birchip, *Australia* 91 F3
Bird, *Canada* 101 B10
Bird City, *U.S.A.* 108 F4
Bird I. = Aves, I. de, *W. Indies* 117 C7
Birdaard, *Neths.* 16 B7
Birdlip, *U.K.* 13 F5
Birdsville, *Australia* 90 D2
Birdum, *Australia* 88 C5
Birecik, *Turkey* 67 D8
Birein, *Israel* 69 E3
Bireuen, *Indonesia* 56 C1
Birifo, *Gambia* 78 C2
Birigui, *Brazil* 127 A5
Birkenfeld, *Germany* 19 F3
Birkenhead, *U.K.* 12 D4
Birket Qârûn, *Egypt* 76 J7
Birkhadem, *Algeria* 75 A5
Bîrlad, *Romania* 38 C10
Birmingham, *U.K.* 13 E6
Birmingham, *U.S.A.* 105 J2
Birmitrapur, *India* 61 H14
Birni Ngaouré, *Niger* 79 C5
Birni Nkonni, *Niger* 79 C6
Birnin Gwari, *Nigeria* 79 C6
Birnin Kebbi, *Nigeria* 79 C5
Birnin Kudu, *Nigeria* 79 C6
Birobidzhan, *Russia* 45 E14
Birr, *Ireland* 15 C4
Birrie →, *Australia* 91 D4
Birs →, *Switz.* 22 B5
Birsilpur, *India* 62 E5
Birsk, *Russia* 44 D6
Birtin, *Romania* 38 C5
Birtle, *Canada* 101 C8
Birur, *India* 60 N9
Biryuchiy, *Ukraine* 41 J8
Biržai, *Lithuania* 9 H21
Bîrzava, *Romania* 38 C4
Birzebugga, *Malta* 37 D2
Bisa, *Indonesia* 57 E7
Bisáccia, *Italy* 35 A8
Bisacquino, *Italy* 34 E6
Bisalpur, *India* 63 E8
Bisbee, *U.S.A.* 111 L9
Biscarrosse et de Parentis, Étang de, *France* 26 D2
Biscay, B. of, *Atl. Oc.* 6 F5
Biscayne B., *U.S.A.* 105 N5
Biscéglie, *Italy* 35 A9
Bischofshofen, *Austria* 21 H3
Bischofswerda, *Germany* 18 D10
Bischofszell, *Switz.* 23 B8
Bischwiller, *France* 25 D14
Biscoe Bay, *Antarctica* 5 D13
Biscoe Is., *Antarctica* 5 C17
Biscostasing, *Canada* 98 C3
Biscucuy, *Venezuela* 120 B4
Biševo, *Croatia* 33 F13
Bisha, *Eritrea* 77 D4
Bishah, W. →, *Si. Arabia* 76 C5
Bishan, *China* 52 C6
Bishkek, *Kyrgyzstan* 44 E8
Bishnupur, *India* 63 H12
Bisho, *S. Africa* 85 E4
Bishop, *Calif., U.S.A.* 111 H4
Bishop, *Tex., U.S.A.* 109 M6
Bishop Auckland, *U.K.* 12 C6
Bishop's Falls, *Canada* 99 C8
Bishop's Stortford, *U.K.* 13 F8
Bisignano, *Italy* 35 C9
Bisina, L., *Uganda* 82 B3
Biskra, *Algeria* 75 B6
Bislig, *Phil.* 57 C7
Bismarck, *U.S.A.* 108 B4
Bismarck Arch., *Papua N. G.* 92 H6
Bismark, *Germany* 18 C7
Bismil, *Turkey* 67 D9
Biso, *Uganda* 82 B3
Bison, *U.S.A.* 108 C3
Bīsotūn, *Iran* 67 E12
Bispgården, *Sweden* 10 A10
Bissagos = Bijagós, Arquipélago dos, *Guinea-Biss.* 78 C1
Bissau, *Guinea-Biss.* 78 C1
Bissett, *Canada* 101 C9
Bissikrima, *Guinea* 78 C2
Bistcho L., *Canada* 100 B5
Bistreṭu, *Romania* 38 F6
Bistrica = Ilirska-Bistrica, *Slovenia* 33 C11
Bistriṭa, *Romania* 38 B7
Bistriṭa →, *Romania* 38 C9
Bistriṭei, Munṭii, *Romania* 38 B8
Biswan, *India* 63 F9
Bitam, *Gabon* 80 D2
Bitburg, *Germany* 19 F2
Bitche, *France* 25 C14
Bithynia, *Turkey* 66 B4
Bitkine, *Chad* 73 F8
Bitlis, *Turkey* 67 C10
Bitola, *Macedonia* 39 H4
Bitolj = Bitola, *Macedonia* 39 H4
Bitonto, *Italy* 35 A9
Bitter Creek, *U.S.A.* 110 F9
Bitter L. = Buheirat-Murrat-el-Kubra, *Egypt* 76 H8
Bitterfeld, *Germany* 18 D8
Bitterfontein, *S. Africa* 84 E2
Bitterroot →, *U.S.A.* 110 C6
Bitterroot Range, *U.S.A.* 110 D6
Bitterwater, *U.S.A.* 112 J6
Bitti, *Italy* 34 B2
Bittou, *Burkina Faso* 79 C4
Biu, *Nigeria* 79 C7
Bivolari, *Romania* 38 B10
Biwa-Ko, *Japan* 49 G8
Biwabik, *U.S.A.* 108 B8
Bixad, *Romania* 38 B6
Biyang, *China* 50 H7
Biysk, *Russia* 44 D9
Bizana, *S. Africa* 85 E4
Bizen, *Japan* 49 G7
Bizerte, *Tunisia* 75 A6
Bjargtangar, *Iceland* 8 D1
Bjelasica, *Montenegro, Yug.* 21 N9
Bjelovar, *Croatia* 21 K6
Bjerringbro, *Denmark* 11 H3
Bjervamoen, *Norway* 10 E3
Bjørnevatn, *Norway* 8 B23
Bjørnøya, *Arctic* 4 B8
Bjuv, *Sweden* 11 H6
Blace, *Serbia, Yug.* 21 M11
Black = Da →, *Vietnam* 58 B5
Black →, *Canada* 106 B5
Black →, *Ark., U.S.A.* 109 H9
Black →, *N.Y., U.S.A.* 107 C8
Black →, *Wis., U.S.A.* 108 D9
Black Diamond, *Canada* 100 C6
Black Forest = Schwarzwald, *Germany* 19 H4
Black Hills, *U.S.A.* 108 C3
Black I., *Canada* 101 C9
Black L., *Canada* 101 B7
Black L., *U.S.A.* 104 C3
Black Mesa, *U.S.A.* 109 G3
Black Mt. = Mynydd Du, *U.K.* 13 F4
Black Mts., *U.K.* 13 F4
Black Range, *U.S.A.* 111 K10
Black River, *Jamaica* 116 C4
Black River Falls, *U.S.A.* 108 C9
Black Sea, *Eurasia* 6 G12
Black Volta →, *Africa* 78 D4
Black Warrior →, *U.S.A.* 105 J2
Blackall, *Australia* 90 C4
Blackball, *N.Z.* 87 K3
Blackbull, *Australia* 90 B3
Blackburn, *U.K.* 12 D5
Blackduck, *U.S.A.* 108 B7
Blackfoot, *U.S.A.* 110 E7
Blackfoot →, *U.S.A.* 110 C7
Blackfoot River Reservoir, *U.S.A.* 110 E8
Blackie, *Canada* 100 C6
Blackpool, *U.K.* 12 D4
Blackriver, *U.S.A.* 106 B1
Blacks Harbour, *Canada* 99 C6
Blacksburg, *U.S.A.* 104 G5
Blacksod B., *Ireland* 15 B2
Blackstone, *U.S.A.* 104 G6
Blackstone →, *Canada* 100 A4
Blackstone Ra., *Australia* 89 E4
Blackville, *Canada* 99 C6
Blackwater, *Australia* 90 C4
Blackwater →, *Ireland* 15 E4
Blackwater →, *U.K.* 15 B5
Blackwater Cr. →, *Australia* 91 D3
Blackwell, *U.S.A.* 109 G6
Blackwells Corner, *U.S.A.* 113 K7
Bladel, *Neths.* 17 F6
Blaenau Ffestiniog, *U.K.* 12 E4
Blaenau Gwent □, *U.K.* 13 F4
Blagodarnoye = Blagodarnyy, *Russia* 43 H6
Blagodarnyy, *Russia* 43 H6
Blagoevgrad, *Bulgaria* 39 G6
Blagoveshchensk, *Russia* 45 D13
Blain, *France* 24 E5
Blaine, *U.S.A.* 112 B4
Blaine Lake, *Canada* 101 C7
Blainville-sur-l'Eau, *France* 25 D13
Blair, *U.S.A.* 108 E6
Blair Athol, *Australia* 90 C4
Blair Atholl, *U.K.* 14 E5
Blairgowrie, *U.K.* 14 E5
Blairmore, *Canada* 100 D6
Blairsden, *U.S.A.* 112 F6
Blairsville, *U.S.A.* 106 F5
Blaj, *Romania* 38 C6
Blake Pt., *U.S.A.* 108 A10
Blakely, *U.S.A.* 105 K3
Blâmont, *France* 25 D13
Blanc, C., *Tunisia* 75 A6
Blanc, Mont, *Alps* 27 C10
Blanca, B., *Argentina* 128 A4
Blanca Peak, *U.S.A.* 111 H11
Blanchard, *U.S.A.* 109 H6
Blanche, C., *Australia* 91 E1
Blanche, L., *S. Austral., Australia* 91 D2
Blanche, L., *W. Austral., Australia* 88 D3
Blanco, *S. Africa* 84 E3
Blanco, *U.S.A.* 109 K5
Blanco →, *Argentina* 126 C2
Blanco, C., *Costa Rica* 116 E2
Blanco, C., *Spain* 36 B9
Blanco, C., *U.S.A.* 110 E1
Blanda →, *Iceland* 8 D3
Blandford Forum, *U.K.* 13 G5
Blanding, *U.S.A.* 111 H9
Blanes, *Spain* 28 D7
Blangy-sur-Bresle, *France* 25 C8
Blanice →, *Czech.* 20 F4
Blankenberge, *Belgium* 17 F2
Blankenburg, *Germany* 18 D6
Blanquefort, *France* 26 D3
Blanquillo, *Uruguay* 127 C4
Blansko, *Czech.* 20 F6
Blantyre, *Malawi* 83 F4
Blaricum, *Neths.* 16 D6
Blarney, *Ireland* 15 E3
Blato, *Croatia* 33 F13
Blatten, *Switz.* 22 D5
Blaubeuren, *Germany* 19 G5
Blåvands Huk, *Denmark* 9 J13
Blaydon, *U.K.* 12 C6
Blaye, *France* 26 C3
Blaye-les-Mines, *France* 26 D6
Blayney, *Australia* 91 E4
Blaze, Pt., *Australia* 88 B5
Bleckede, *Germany* 18 B6
Bled, *Slovenia* 33 B11
Blednaya, Gora, *Russia* 44 B7
Bléharis, *Belgium* 17 G2
Blejeşti, *Romania* 38 E8
Blekinge, *Sweden* 9 H16
Blenheim, *Canada* 106 D2
Blenheim, *N.Z.* 87 J4
Bléone →, *France* 27 D10
Blerick, *Neths.* 17 F8
Bletchley, *U.K.* 13 F7
Blida, *Algeria* 75 A5
Blidet Amor, *Algeria* 75 B6
Blidö, *Sweden* 10 E12
Bligh Sound, *N.Z.* 87 L1
Blind River, *Canada* 98 C3
Blinnenhorn, *Switz.* 23 D6
Blitar, *Indonesia* 57 H15
Blitta, *Togo* 79 D5
Block I., *U.S.A.* 107 E13
Block Island Sd., *U.S.A.* 107 E13
Blodgett Iceberg Tongue, *Antarctica* 5 C9
Bloemendaal, *Neths.* 16 D5
Bloemfontein, *S. Africa* 84 D4
Bloemhof, *S. Africa* 84 D4
Blois, *France* 24 E8
Blokziji, *Neths.* 16 C7
Blönduós, *Iceland* 8 D3
Bloodvein →, *Canada* 101 C9
Bloody Foreland, *Ireland* 15 A3
Bloomer, *U.S.A.* 108 C9
Bloomfield, *Australia* 90 B4
Bloomfield, *Canada* 106 C7
Bloomfield, *Iowa, U.S.A.* 108 E8
Bloomfield, *N. Mex., U.S.A.* 111 H10
Bloomfield, *Nebr., U.S.A.* 108 D6
Bloomington, *Ill., U.S.A.* 108 E10
Bloomington, *Ind., U.S.A.* 104 F2
Bloomington, *Minn., U.S.A.* 108 C8
Bloomsburg, *U.S.A.* 107 F8
Blora, *Indonesia* 57 G14
Blossburg, *U.S.A.* 106 E7
Blouberg, *S. Africa* 85 C4
Blountstown, *U.S.A.* 105 K3
Bludenz, *Austria* 19 H5
Blue Island, *U.S.A.* 104 E2
Blue Lake, *U.S.A.* 110 F2
Blue Mesa Reservoir, *U.S.A.* 111 G10
Blue Mts., *Oreg., U.S.A.* 110 D4
Blue Mts., *Pa., U.S.A.* 107 F8
Blue Mud B., *Australia* 90 A2
Blue Nile = Nîl el Azraq →, *Sudan* 77 D3
Blue Rapids, *U.S.A.* 108 F6
Blue Ridge Mts., *U.S.A.* 105 G5
Blue Stack Mts., *Ireland* 15 B3
Blueberry →, *Canada* 100 B4
Bluefield, *U.S.A.* 104 G5
Bluefields, *Nic.* 116 D3
Bluff, *Australia* 90 C4
Bluff, *N.Z.* 87 M2
Bluff, *U.S.A.* 111 H9
Bluff Knoll, *Australia* 89 F2
Bluff Pt., *Australia* 89 E1
Bluffton, *U.S.A.* 104 E3
Blumenau, *Brazil* 127 B6
Blümlisalphorn, *Switz.* 22 D5
Blunt, *U.S.A.* 108 C4
Bly, *U.S.A.* 110 E3
Blyth, *Canada* 106 C3
Blyth, *U.K.* 12 B6
Blythe, *U.S.A.* 113 M12
Blythe Bridge, *U.K.* 12 E5
Bø, *Norway* 10 E3
Bo, *S. Leone* 78 D2
Bo Duc, *Vietnam* 59 G6
Bo Hai, *China* 51 E10
Bo Xian, *China* 50 H8
Boa Esperança, *Brazil* 121 C5
Boa Esperança, Reprêsa, *Brazil* 122 C3
Boa Nova, *Brazil* 123 D3
Boa Viagem, *Brazil* 122 C4
Boa Vista, *Brazil* 121 C5
Boac, *Phil.* 55 E4
Boaco, *Nic.* 116 D2
Bo'ai, *China* 50 G7
Boal, *Spain* 30 B4
Boardman, *U.S.A.* 106 E4
Boatman, *Australia* 91 D4
Bobadah, *Australia* 91 E4
Bobai, *China* 52 F7
Bobbili, *India* 61 K13
Bòbbio, *Italy* 32 D6
Bobcaygeon, *Canada* 98 D4
Böblingen, *Germany* 19 G5
Bobo-Dioulasso, *Burkina Faso* 78 C4
Boboc, *Romania* 38 D9
Bobonaza →, *Ecuador* 120 D2
Bobov Dol, *Bulgaria* 38 G5
Bóbr →, *Poland* 20 C5
Bobraomby, Tanjon' i, *Madag.* 85 A8
Bobrinets, *Ukraine* 41 H7
Bobrov, *Russia* 42 E5
Bobrovitsa, *Ukraine* 41 G6
Bobruysk = Babruysk, *Belarus* 41 F5
Bobures, *Venezuela* 120 B3
Boca de Drago, *Venezuela* 121 A5
Bôca do Acre, *Brazil* 124 B4
Bôca do Jari, *Brazil* 121 D7
Bôca do Moaco, *Brazil* 124 B4
Boca Grande, *Venezuela* 121 B5
Boca Raton, *U.S.A.* 105 M5
Bocaiúva, *Brazil* 123 E3
Bocanda, *Ivory C.* 78 D4
Bocaranga, *C.A.R.* 73 G8
Bocas del Toro, *Panama* 116 E3
Boceguillas, *Spain* 28 D1
Bochnia, *Poland* 20 F10
Bocholt, *Belgium* 17 F7
Bocholt, *Germany* 18 D2
Bochum, *Germany* 18 D3
Bockenem, *Germany* 18 C6
Bocognano, *France* 27 F13
Boconó, *Venezuela* 120 B3
Boconó →, *Venezuela* 120 B4
Bocoyna, *Mexico* 114 B3
Bocq →, *Belgium* 17 H5
Boda, *C.A.R.* 80 D3
Bodaybo, *Russia* 45 D12
Boddington, *Australia* 89 F2
Bodega Bay, *U.S.A.* 112 G3
Bodegraven, *Neths.* 16 D5
Boden, *Sweden* 8 D19
Bodensee, *Europe* 23 A8
Bodenteich, *Germany* 18 C6
Bodhan, *India* 60 K10
Bodinga, *Nigeria* 79 C6
Bodio, *Switz.* 23 D7
Bodmin, *U.K.* 13 G3
Bodmin Moor, *U.K.* 13 G3
Bodø, *Norway* 8 C16
Bodoquena, Serra da, *Brazil* 125 E6
Bodrog →, *Hungary* 21 G11
Bodrum, *Turkey* 66 D2
Boechout, *Belgium* 17 F5
Boekelo, *Neths.* 16 D9
Boelenslaan, *Neths.* 16 B8
Boën, *France* 27 C8
Boende, *Zaïre* 80 E4
Boerne, *U.S.A.* 109 L5
Boertange, *Neths.* 16 B10
Boezinge, *Belgium* 17 G1
Boffa, *Guinea* 78 C2
Bogalusa, *U.S.A.* 109 K10
Bogan Gate, *Australia* 91 E4
Bogantungan, *Australia* 90 C4
Bogata, *U.S.A.* 109 J7
Bogatić, *Serbia, Yug.* 21 L9
Boğazkale, *Turkey* 66 B6
Boğazlıyan, *Turkey* 66 C6
Bogense, *Denmark* 11 J4
Boggabilla, *Australia* 91 D5
Boggabri, *Australia* 91 E5
Boggeragh Mts., *Ireland* 15 D3
Bognor Regis, *U.K.* 13 G7
Bogø, *Denmark* 11 K6
Bogo, *Phil.* 55 F6
Bogodukhov = Bohodukhiv, *Ukraine* 41 G8
Bogong, Mt., *Australia* 91 F4
Bogor, *Indonesia* 57 G12
Bogoroditsk, *Russia* 42 D4
Bogorodsk, *Russia* 42 B6
Bogorodskoye, *Russia* 45 D15
Bogoso, *Ghana* 78 D4
Bogotá, *Colombia* 120 C3
Bogotol, *Russia* 44 D9
Bogra, *Bangla.* 61 G16
Boguchany, *Russia* 45 D10
Boguchar, *Russia* 42 F5
Bogué, *Mauritania* 78 B2
Boguslav, *Ukraine* 41 H6
Bohain-en-Vermandois, *France* 25 C10
Bohemia Downs, *Australia* 88 C4
Bohemian Forest = Böhmerwald, *Germany* 19 F8
Bohena Cr. →, *Australia* 91 E4
Bohinjska Bistrica, *Slovenia* 33 B11
Böhmerwald, *Germany* 19 F8
Bohmte, *Germany* 18 C4
Bohodukhiv, *Ukraine* 41 G8
Bohol, *Phil.* 55 G6
Bohol Sea, *Phil.* 57 C6
Bohotleh, *Somali Rep.* 68 F4
Bohuslän, *Sweden* 9 G14
Boi, *Nigeria* 79 D6
Boi, Pta. de, *Brazil* 127 A6
Boiaçu, *Brazil* 121 D5
Boiano, *Italy* 35 A7
Boileau, C., *Australia* 88 C3
Boipeba, I. de, *Brazil* 123 D4
Bois →, *Brazil* 123 E1
Boischot, *Belgium* 17 F5
Boise, *U.S.A.* 110 E5
Boise City, *U.S.A.* 109 G3
Boissevain, *Canada* 101 D8
Boite →, *Italy* 33 B9
Boitzenburg, *Germany* 18 B9
Boizenburg, *Germany* 18 B6
Bojador C., *W. Sahara* 74 C2
Bojnūrd, *Iran* 65 B8
Bojonegoro, *Indonesia* 57 G14
Boju, *Nigeria* 79 D6

Boka Kotorska, *Montenegro, Yug.* 21 N8
Bokala, *Ivory C.* 78 D4
Boké, *Guinea* 78 C2
Bokhara →, *Australia* 91 D4
Bokkos, *Nigeria* 79 D6
Boknafjorden, *Norway* 9 G11
Bokoro, *Chad* 73 F8
Bokote, *Zaïre* 80 E4
Boksitogorsk, *Russia* 40 C7
Bokungu, *Zaïre* 80 E4
Bol, *Chad* 73 F7
Bol, *Croatia* 33 E13
Bolama, *Guinea-Biss.* 78 C1
Bolan Pass, *Pakistan* 60 E5
Bolaños →, *Mexico* 114 C4
Bolbec, *France* 24 C7
Boldājī, *Iran* 65 D6
Boldeşti, *Romania* 38 D9
Bole, *China* 54 B3
Bole, *Ethiopia* 77 F4
Bolekhiv, *Ukraine* 41 H2
Bolekhov = Bolekhiv, *Ukraine* 41 H2
Bolesławiec, *Poland* 20 D5
Bolgatanga, *Ghana* 79 C4
Bolgrad = Bolhrad, *Ukraine* 41 K5
Bolhrad, *Ukraine* 41 K5
Boli, *Sudan* 77 F2
Bolinao, *Phil.* 55 C3
Bolinao C., *Phil.* 57 A5
Bolívar, *Argentina* 126 D3
Bolívar, *Antioquía, Colombia* 120 B2
Bolívar, *Cauca, Colombia* 120 C2
Bolívar, *Peru* 124 B2
Bolivar, *Mo., U.S.A.* 109 G8
Bolivar, *Tenn., U.S.A.* 109 H10
Bolívar □, *Colombia* 120 B3
Bolívar □, *Ecuador* 120 D2
Bolívar □, *Venezuela* 121 B5
Bolivia ■, *S. Amer.* 125 D5
Bolivian Plateau, *S. Amer.* 118 E4
Bolkhov, *Russia* 42 D3
Bollène, *France* 27 D8
Bollnäs, *Sweden* 10 C10
Bollon, *Australia* 91 D4
Bollstabruk, *Sweden* 10 A11
Bollullos, *Spain* 31 H4
Bolmen, *Sweden* 9 H15
Bolobo, *Zaïre* 80 E3
Bologna, *Italy* 33 D8
Bologne, *France* 25 D12
Bologoye, *Russia* 42 B2
Bolomba, *Zaïre* 80 D3
Bolonchenticul, *Mexico* 115 D7
Bolong, *Phil.* 57 C6
Boloven, Cao Nguyen, *Laos* 58 E6
Bolpur, *India* 63 H12
Bolsena, *Italy* 33 F8
Bolsena, L. di, *Italy* 33 F8
Bolshaya Chernigovka, *Russia* 42 D10
Bolshaya Glushitsa, *Russia* 42 D10
Bolshaya Martynovka, *Russia* 43 G5
Bolshaya Vradiyevka, *Ukraine* 41 J6
Bolshereche, *Russia* 44 D8
Bolshevik, Ostrov, *Russia* 45 B11
Bolshoi Kavkas = Caucasus Mountains, *Eurasia* 43 J7
Bolshoy Anyuy →, *Russia* 45 C17
Bolshoy Atlym, *Russia* 44 C7
Bolshoy Begichev, Ostrov, *Russia* 45 B12
Bolshoy Lyakhovskiy, Ostrov, *Russia* 45 B15
Bolshoy Tokmak = Tokmak, *Ukraine* 41 J8
Bolshoy Tyuters, Ostrov, *Russia* 9 G22
Bolsward, *Neths.* 16 B7
Boltaña, *Spain* 28 C5
Boltigen, *Switz.* 22 C4
Bolton, *Canada* 106 C5
Bolton, *U.K.* 12 D5
Bolu, *Turkey* 66 B4
Bolungavík, *Iceland* 8 C2
Boluo, *China* 53 F10
Bolvadin, *Turkey* 66 C4
Bolzano, *Italy* 33 B8
Bom Comércio, *Brazil* 125 B4
Bom Conselho, *Brazil* 122 C4
Bom Despacho, *Brazil* 123 E2
Bom Jesus, *Brazil* 122 C3
Bom Jesus da Gurguéia, Serra, *Brazil* 122 C3
Bom Jesus da Lapa, *Brazil* 123 D3
Boma, *Zaïre* 80 F2
Bomaderry, *Australia* 91 E5
Bombala, *Australia* 91 F4
Bombarral, *Portugal* 31 F1
Bombay, *India* 60 K8
Bomboma, *Zaïre* 80 D3
Bombombwa, *Zaïre* 82 B2
Bomi Hills, *Liberia* 78 D2
Bomili, *Zaïre* 82 B2
Bømlo, *Norway* 9 G11
Bommel, *Neths.* 16 E4
Bomokandi →, *Zaïre* 82 B2
Bomongo, *Zaïre* 80 D3
Bomu →, *C.A.R.* 80 D4
Bon, C., *Tunisia* 75 A7
Bon Sar Pa, *Vietnam* 58 F6
Bonaduz, *Switz.* 23 C8
Bonaire, *Neth. Ant.* 117 D6
Bonang, *Australia* 91 F4
Bonanza, *Nic.* 116 D3
Bonaparte Arch., *Australia* 88 B3
Boñar, *Spain* 30 C5
Bonaventure, *Canada* 99 C6
Bonavista, *Canada* 99 C9
Bonavista, C., *Canada* 99 C9
Bonawan, *Phil.* 55 G5
Bondeno, *Italy* 33 D8
Bondo, *Zaïre* 82 B1
Bondoukou, *Ivory C.* 78 D4
Bondowoso, *Indonesia* 57 G15
Bone, Teluk, *Indonesia* 57 E6
Bonefro, *Italy* 35 A7
Bonerate, *Indonesia* 57 F6
Bonerate, Kepulauan, *Indonesia* 57 F6
Bo'ness, *U.K.* 14 E5
Bonete, Cerro, *Argentina* 126 B2
Bong Son = Hoai Nhon, *Vietnam* 58 E7
Bongabong, *Phil.* 55 E4
Bongandanga, *Zaïre* 80 D4
Bongor, *Chad* 73 F8
Bongouanou, *Ivory C.* 78 D4
Bonham, *U.S.A.* 109 J6
Bonheiden, *Belgium* 17 F5
Bonifacio, *France* 27 G13
Bonifacio, Bouches de, *Medit. S.* 34 A2
Bonin Is. = Ogasawara Gunto, *Pac. Oc.* 46 G18
Bonke, *Ethiopia* 77 F4
Bonn, *Germany* 18 E3
Bonnat, *France* 26 B5
Bonne Terre, *U.S.A.* 109 G9
Bonners Ferry, *U.S.A.* 110 B5
Bonnétable, *France* 24 D7
Bonneuil-Matours, *France* 24 F7
Bonneval, *France* 24 D8
Bonneville, *France* 27 B10
Bonney, L., *Australia* 91 F3
Bonnie Downs, *Australia* 90 C3
Bonnie Rock, *Australia* 89 F2
Bonny, *Nigeria* 79 E6
Bonny →, *Nigeria* 79 E6
Bonny, Bight of, *Africa* 79 E6
Bonny-sur-Loire, *France* 25 E9
Bonnyville, *Canada* 101 C6
Bonoi, *Indonesia* 57 E9
Bonorva, *Italy* 34 B1
Bonsall, *U.S.A.* 113 M9
Bontang, *Indonesia* 56 D5
Bonthain, *Indonesia* 57 F5
Bonthe, *S. Leone* 78 D2
Bontoc, *Phil.* 55 C4
Bonyeri, *Ghana* 78 D4
Bonython Ra., *Australia* 88 D4
Bookabie, *Australia* 89 F5
Booker, *U.S.A.* 109 G4
Boolaboolka L., *Australia* 91 E3
Booligal, *Australia* 91 E3
Boom, *Belgium* 17 F4
Boonah, *Australia* 91 D5
Boone, *Iowa, U.S.A.* 108 D8
Boone, *N.C., U.S.A.* 105 G5
Booneville, *Ark., U.S.A.* 109 H8
Booneville, *Miss., U.S.A.* 105 H1
Boonville, *Calif., U.S.A.* 112 F3
Boonville, *Ind., U.S.A.* 104 F2
Boonville, *Mo., U.S.A.* 108 F8
Boonville, *N.Y., U.S.A.* 107 C9
Boorindal, *Australia* 91 E4
Boorowa, *Australia* 91 E4
Boothia, Gulf of, *Canada* 97 A11
Boothia Pen., *Canada* 96 A10
Bootle, *U.K.* 12 D4
Booué, *Gabon* 80 E2
Boppard, *Germany* 19 E3
Boquerón □, *Paraguay* 125 E5
Boquete, *Panama* 116 E3
Boquilla, Presa de la, *Mexico* 114 B3
Boquillas del Carmen, *Mexico* 114 B4
Bor, *Czech.* 20 F2
Bor, *Russia* 42 B7
Bor, *Serbia, Yug.* 21 L12
Bôr, *Sudan* 77 F3
Bor, *Turkey* 66 D6
Bor Mashash, *Israel* 69 D3
Boradā →, *Syria* 69 B5
Borah Peak, *U.S.A.* 110 D7
Borama, *Somali Rep.* 68 F3
Borang, *Sudan* 77 G3
Borås, *Sweden* 11 G6
Borāzjān, *Iran* 65 D6
Borba, *Brazil* 121 D6
Borba, *Portugal* 31 G3
Borborema, Planalto da, *Brazil* 122 C4
Borçka, *Turkey* 67 B9
Borculo, *Neths.* 16 D9
Bord Khūn-e Now, *Iran* 65 D6
Borda, C., *Australia* 91 F2
Bordeaux, *France* 26 D3
Borden, *Australia* 89 F2
Borden, *Canada* 99 C7
Borden I., *Canada* 4 B2
Borders □, *U.K.* 14 F6
Bordertown, *Australia* 91 F3
Borðeyri, *Iceland* 8 D3
Bordighera, *Italy* 32 E4
Bordj bou Arreridj, *Algeria* 75 A5
Bordj Bourguiba, *Tunisia* 75 B7
Bordj Fly Ste. Marie, *Algeria* 74 C4
Bordj-in-Eker, *Algeria* 75 D6
Bordj Menaiel, *Algeria* 75 A5
Bordj Messouda, *Algeria* 75 B6
Bordj Nili, *Algeria* 75 B5
Bordj Omar Driss, *Algeria* 75 C6
Bordj Sif Fatima, *Algeria* 75 B6
Bordj-Tarat, *Algeria* 75 C6
Bordj Zelfana, *Algeria* 75 B5
Borensberg, *Sweden* 11 F9
Borgå = Porvoo, *Finland* 9 F21
Borgarfjörður, *Iceland* 8 D7
Borgarnes, *Iceland* 8 D3
Børgefjellet, *Norway* 8 D15
Borger, *Neths.* 16 C9
Borger, *U.S.A.* 109 H4
Borgerhout, *Belgium* 17 F4
Borghamn, *Sweden* 11 F8
Borgholm, *Sweden* 9 H17
Bórgia, *Italy* 35 D9
Borgloon, *Belgium* 17 G6
Borgo San Dalmazzo, *Italy* 32 D4
Borgo San Lorenzo, *Italy* 33 E8
Borgo Valsugano, *Italy* 33 B8
Borgomanero, *Italy* 32 C5
Borgonovo Val Tidone, *Italy* 32 C6
Borgorose, *Italy* 33 F10
Borgosésia, *Italy* 32 C5
Borgvattnet, *Sweden* 10 A9
Borikhane, *Laos* 58 C4
Borisoglebsk, *Russia* 42 E6
Borisov = Barysaw, *Belarus* 40 E5
Borisovka, *Russia* 42 E3
Borja, *Peru* 120 D2
Borja, *Spain* 28 D3
Borjas Blancas, *Spain* 28 D5
Borjomi, *Georgia* 43 K6
Borken, *Germany* 18 D2
Borkou, *Chad* 73 E8
Borkum, *Germany* 18 B2
Borlänge, *Sweden* 9 F16
Borley, C., *Antarctica* 5 C5
Bormida →, *Italy* 32 D5
Bórmio, *Italy* 32 B7
Born, *Neths.* 17 F7
Borna, *Germany* 18 D8
Borndiep, *Neths.* 16 B7
Borne, *Neths.* 16 D9
Bornem, *Belgium* 17 F4
Borneo, *E. Indies* 56 D5
Bornholm, *Denmark* 9 J16
Borno □, *Nigeria* 79 C7
Bornos, *Spain* 31 J5
Bornu Yassa, *Nigeria* 79 C7
Borobudur, *Indonesia* 57 G14
Borodino, *Russia* 42 C2
Borogontsy, *Russia* 45 C14
Boromo, *Burkina Faso* 78 C4
Boron, *U.S.A.* 113 L9
Borongan, *Phil.* 55 F6
Bororen, *Australia* 90 C5
Borotangba Mts., *C.A.R.* 77 F1
Borovan, *Bulgaria* 38 F6
Borovichi, *Russia* 40 C7
Borovsk, *Russia* 42 C3
Borrego Springs, *U.S.A.* 113 M10
Borriol, *Spain* 28 E4
Borroloola, *Australia* 90 B2
Borşa, *Romania* 38 B7
Borssele, *Neths.* 17 F3
Bort-les-Orgues, *France* 26 C6
Borth, *U.K.* 13 E3
Borūjerd, *Iran* 67 F13
Boryslav, *Ukraine* 41 H2
Boryspil, *Ukraine* 41 G6
Borzhomi = Borjomi, *Georgia* 43 K6
Borzna, *Ukraine* 41 G7
Borzya, *Russia* 45 D12
Bosa, *Italy* 34 B1
Bosanska Dubica, *Bos.-H.* 33 C13
Bosanska Gradiška, *Bos.-H.* 21 K7
Bosanska Kostajnica, *Bos.-H.* 33 C13
Bosanska Krupa, *Bos.-H.* 33 D13
Bosanski Novi, *Bos.-H.* 33 C13
Bosanski Šamac, *Bos.-H.* 21 K8
Bosansko Grahovo, *Bos.-H.* 33 D13
Bosansko Petrovac, *Bos.-H.* 33 D13
Bosaso, *Somali Rep.* 68 E4
Boscastle, *U.K.* 13 G3
Boscotrecase, *Italy* 35 B7
Bose, *China* 52 F6
Boshan, *China* 51 F9
Boshof, *S. Africa* 84 D4
Boshrūyeh, *Iran* 65 C8
Bosilegrad, *Serbia, Yug.* 21 N12
Boskoop, *Neths.* 16 D5
Bosna →, *Bos.-H.* 21 K8
Bosna i Hercegovina = Bosnia-Herzegovina ■, *Europe* 21 L7
Bosnia-Herzegovina ■, *Europe* 21 L7
Bosnik, *Indonesia* 57 E9
Bosobolo, *Zaïre* 80 D3
Bosporus = Karadeniz Boğazı, *Turkey* 66 B3
Bossangoa, *C.A.R.* 73 G8
Bossembélé, *C.A.R.* 73 G8
Bossier City, *U.S.A.* 109 J8
Bosso, *Niger* 79 C7
Bostānābād, *Iran* 67 D12
Bosten Hu, *China* 54 B3
Boston, *U.K.* 12 E7
Boston, *U.S.A.* 107 D13
Boston Bar, *Canada* 100 D4
Bosut →, *Croatia* 21 K8
Boswell, *Canada* 100 D5
Boswell, *Okla., U.S.A.* 109 H7
Boswell, *Pa., U.S.A.* 106 F5
Botad, *India* 62 H4
Botan →, *Turkey* 67 D10
Botany B., *Australia* 91 E5
Botene, *Laos* 58 D3
Botevgrad, *Bulgaria* 38 G6
Bothaville, *S. Africa* 84 D4
Bothnia, G. of, *Europe* 8 E19
Bothwell, *Australia* 90 G4
Bothwell, *Canada* 106 D3
Boticas, *Portugal* 30 D3
Botletle →, *Botswana* 84 C3
Botlikh, *Russia* 43 J8
Botoşani, *Romania* 38 B9
Botro, *Ivory C.* 78 D3
Botswana ■, *Africa* 84 C3
Bottineau, *U.S.A.* 108 A4
Bottrop, *Germany* 17 E9
Botucatu, *Brazil* 127 A6
Botwood, *Canada* 99 C8
Bou Alam, *Algeria* 75 B5
Bou Ali, *Algeria* 75 C4
Bou Djébéha, *Mali* 78 B4
Bou Guema, *Algeria* 75 C5
Bou Ismael, *Algeria* 75 A5
Bou Izakarn, *Morocco* 74 C3
Boû Lanouâr, *Mauritania* 74 D1
Bou Saâda, *Algeria* 75 A5
Bou Salem, *Tunisia* 75 A6
Bouaké, *Ivory C.* 78 D3
Bouar, *C.A.R.* 80 C3
Bouârfa, *Morocco* 75 B4
Bouca, *C.A.R.* 73 G8
Boucau, *France* 26 E2
Boucaut B., *Australia* 90 A1
Bouches-du-Rhône □, *France* 27 E9
Bouda, *Algeria* 75 C4
Boudenib, *Morocco* 74 B4
Boudry, *Switz.* 22 C3
Boufarik, *Algeria* 75 A5
Bougainville, C., *Australia* 88 B4
Bougainville Reef, *Australia* 90 B4
Bougaroun, C., *Algeria* 75 A6
Bougie = Bejaia, *Algeria* 75 A6
Bougouni, *Mali* 78 C3
Bouillon, *Belgium* 17 J6
Bouïra, *Algeria* 75 A5
Boulder, *Colo., U.S.A.* 108 E2
Boulder, *Mont., U.S.A.* 110 C7
Boulder City, *U.S.A.* 113 K12
Boulder Creek, *U.S.A.* 112 H4
Boulder Dam = Hoover Dam, *U.S.A.* 113 K12
Bouli, *Mauritania* 78 B2
Boulia, *Australia* 90 C2
Bouligny, *France* 25 C12
Boulogne →, *France* 24 E5
Boulogne-sur-Gesse, *France* 26 E4
Boulogne-sur-Mer, *France* 25 B8
Bouloire, *France* 24 E7
Boulsa, *Burkina Faso* 79 C4
Boultoum, *Niger* 79 C7
Boumalne, *Morocco* 74 B3
Boun Neua, *Laos* 58 B3
Boun Tai, *Laos* 58 B3
Bouna, *Ivory C.* 78 D4
Boundary Peak, *U.S.A.* 112 H8
Boundiali, *Ivory C.* 78 D3
Bountiful, *U.S.A.* 110 F8
Bounty Is., *Pac. Oc.* 92 M9
Bourbon-Lancy, *France* 26 B7
Bourbon-l'Archambault, *France* 26 B7
Bourbonnais, *France* 26 B7
Bourbonne-les-Bains, *France* 25 E12
Bourem, *Mali* 79 B4
Bourg, *France* 26 C3
Bourg-Argental, *France* 27 C8
Bourg-de-Péage, *France* 27 C9
Bourg-en-Bresse, *France* 27 B9
Bourg-St.-Andéol, *France* 27 D8
Bourg-St.-Maurice, *France* 27 C10
Bourg-St.-Pierre, *Switz.* 22 E4
Bourganeuf, *France* 26 C5
Bourges, *France* 25 E9
Bourget, *Canada* 107 A9
Bourget, L. du, *France* 27 C9
Bourgneuf, B. de, *France* 24 E4
Bourgneuf-en-Retz, *France* 24 E5
Bourgogne, *France* 25 F11
Bourgoin-Jallieu, *France* 27 C9
Bourgueil, *France* 24 E7
Bourke, *Australia* 91 E4
Bournemouth, *U.K.* 13 G6
Bourriot-Bergonce, *France* 26 D3
Bouse, *U.S.A.* 113 M13
Boussac, *France* 26 B6
Boussens, *France* 26 E4
Bousso, *Chad* 73 F8
Boussu, *Belgium* 17 H3
Boutilimit, *Mauritania* 78 B2
Boutonne →, *France* 26 C3
Bouvet I. = Bouvetøya, *Antarctica* 3 G10
Bouvetøya, *Antarctica* 3 G10
Bouznika, *Morocco* 74 B3
Bouzonville, *France* 25 C13
Bova Marina, *Italy* 35 E8
Bovalino Marina, *Italy* 35 D9
Bovec, *Slovenia* 33 B10
Bovenkarspel, *Neths.* 16 C6
Bovigny, *Belgium* 17 H7
Bovill, *U.S.A.* 110 C5
Bovino, *Italy* 35 A8
Bow Island, *Canada* 100 D6
Bowbells, *U.S.A.* 108 A3
Bowdle, *U.S.A.* 108 C5
Bowelling, *Australia* 89 F2
Bowen, *Australia* 90 C4
Bowen Mts., *Australia* 91 F4
Bowie, *Ariz., U.S.A.* 111 K9
Bowie, *Tex., U.S.A.* 109 J6
Bowkān, *Iran* 67 D12
Bowland, Forest of, *U.K.* 12 D5
Bowling Green, *Ky., U.S.A.* 104 G2
Bowling Green, *Ohio, U.S.A.* 104 E4
Bowling Green, C., *Australia* 90 B4
Bowman, *U.S.A.* 108 B3
Bowman I., *Antarctica* 5 C8
Bowmans, *Australia* 91 E2
Bowmanville, *Canada* 98 D4
Bowmore, *U.K.* 14 F2
Bowral, *Australia* 91 E5
Bowraville, *Australia* 91 E5
Bowron →, *Canada* 100 C4
Bowser L., *Canada* 100 B3
Bowsman, *Canada* 101 C8
Bowwood, *Zambia* 83 F2
Boxholm, *Sweden* 11 F9
Boxmeer, *Neths.* 17 E7
Boxtel, *Neths.* 17 E6
Boyabat, *Turkey* 66 B6
Boyaca = Casanare □, *Colombia* 120 B3
Boyce, *U.S.A.* 109 K8
Boyer →, *Canada* 100 B5
Boyle, *Ireland* 15 C3
Boyne →, *Ireland* 15 C5
Boyne City, *U.S.A.* 104 C3
Boynton Beach, *U.S.A.* 105 M5
Boyoma, Chutes, *Zaïre* 82 B2
Boyup Brook, *Australia* 89 F2
Boz Dağ, *Turkey* 66 D3
Boz Dağları, *Turkey* 66 C3
Bozburun, *Turkey* 66 D3
Bozcaada, *Turkey* 66 C2
Bozdoğan, *Turkey* 66 D3
Bozeman, *U.S.A.* 110 D8
Bozen = Bolzano, *Italy* 33 B8
Bozkır, *Turkey* 66 D5
Bozouls, *France* 26 D6
Bozoum, *C.A.R.* 73 G8
Bozova, *Turkey* 67 D8
Bozovici, *Romania* 38 E5
Bozüyük, *Turkey* 66 C4
Bra, *Italy* 32 D4
Brabant □, *Belgium* 17 G5
Brabant L., *Canada* 101 B8
Brabrand, *Denmark* 11 H4
Brač, *Croatia* 33 E13
Bracadale, L., *U.K.* 14 D2
Bracciano, *Italy* 33 F9
Bracciano, L. di, *Italy* 33 F9
Bracebridge, *Canada* 98 C4
Brach, *Libya* 73 C7
Bracieux, *France* 25 E8
Bräcke, *Sweden* 10 B9
Brackettville, *U.S.A.* 109 L4
Bracki Kanal, *Croatia* 33 E13
Brad, *Romania* 38 C5
Brádano →, *Italy* 35 B9
Bradenton, *U.S.A.* 105 M4
Bradford, *Canada* 106 B5
Bradford, *U.K.* 12 D6
Bradford, *Pa., U.S.A.* 106 E6
Bradford, *Vt., U.S.A.* 107 C12
Brădiceni, *Romania* 38 D6
Bradley, *Ark., U.S.A.* 109 J8
Bradley, *Calif., U.S.A.* 112 K6
Bradley, *S. Dak., U.S.A.* 108 C6
Bradley Institute, *Zimbabwe* 83 F3
Bradore Bay, *Canada* 99 B8
Bradshaw, *Australia* 88 C5
Brady, *U.S.A.* 109 K5
Brædstrup, *Denmark* 11 J3
Braemar, *Australia* 91 E2
Braeside, *Canada* 107 A8
Braga, *Portugal* 30 D2
Braga □, *Portugal* 30 D2
Bragado, *Argentina* 126 D3
Bragança, *Brazil* 122 B2
Bragança, *Portugal* 30 D4
Bragança □, *Portugal* 30 D4
Bragança Paulista, *Brazil* 127 A6
Brahmanbaria, *Bangla.* 61 H17
Brahmani →, *India* 61 J15
Brahmaputra →, *India* 63 G13
Braich-y-pwll, *U.K.* 12 E3
Braidwood, *Australia* 91 F4
Brăila, *Romania* 38 D10
Braine-l'Alleud, *Belgium* 17 G4
Braine-le-Comte, *Belgium* 17 G4
Brainerd, *U.S.A.* 108 B7
Braintree, *U.K.* 13 F8
Braintree, *U.S.A.* 107 D14
Brak →, *S. Africa* 84 D3
Brake, *Germany* 18 B4
Brakel, *Germany* 18 D5

Brakel, *Neths.* 16 E6
Brakwater, *Namibia* 84 C2
Brålanda, *Sweden* 11 F6
Bralorne, *Canada* 100 C4
Bramberg, *Germany* 19 E6
Bramming, *Denmark* 11 J2
Brämön, *Sweden* 10 B11
Brampton, *Canada* 98 D4
Bramsche, *Germany* 18 C3
Bramwell, *Australia* 90 A3
Branco →, *Brazil* 121 D5
Branco, C., *Brazil* 122 C5
Brande, *Denmark* 11 J3
Brandenburg = Neubrandenburg, *Germany* 18 B9
Brandenburg, *Germany* 18 C8
Brandenburg □, *Germany* 18 C9
Brandfort, *S. Africa* 84 D4
Brandon, *Canada* 101 D9
Brandon, *U.S.A.* 107 C11
Brandon B., *Ireland* 15 D1
Brandon Mt., *Ireland* 15 D1
Brandsen, *Argentina* 126 D4
Brandval, *Norway* 10 D6
Brandvlei, *S. Africa* 84 E3
Brandýs, *Czech.* 20 E4
Branford, *U.S.A.* 107 E12
Braniewo, *Poland* 20 A9
Bransfield Str., *Antarctica* 5 C18
Branson, *Colo., U.S.A.* 109 G3
Branson, *Mo., U.S.A.* 109 G8
Brantford, *Canada* 98 D3
Brantôme, *France* 26 C4
Branxholme, *Australia* 91 F3
Branzi, *Italy* 32 B6
Bras d'Or, L., *Canada* 99 C7
Brasil, Planalto, *Brazil* 118 E6
Brasiléia, *Brazil* 124 C4
Brasília, *Brazil* 123 E2
Brasília Legal, *Brazil* 121 D6
Braslaw, *Belarus* 9 J22
Braslovce, *Slovenia* 33 B12
Brașov, *Romania* 38 D8
Brass, *Nigeria* 79 E6
Brass →, *Nigeria* 79 E6
Brassac-les-Mines, *France* 26 C7
Brasschaat, *Belgium* 17 F4
Brassey, Banjaran, *Malaysia* 56 D5
Brassey Ra., *Australia* 89 E3
Brasstown Bald, *U.S.A.* 105 H4
Brastad, *Sweden* 9 G14
Bratislava, *Slovak Rep.* 21 G7
Bratsk, *Russia* 45 D11
Brattleboro, *U.S.A.* 107 D12
Braunau, *Austria* 21 G3
Braunschweig, *Germany* 18 C6
Braunton, *U.K.* 13 F3
Brava, *Somali Rep.* 68 G3
Bråviken, *Sweden* 10 F10
Bravo del Norte →, *Mexico* 114 B5
Bravo del Norte, R. → = Grande, Rio →, *U.S.A.* 109 N6
Brawley, *U.S.A.* 113 N11
Bray, *Ireland* 15 C5
Bray, Mt., *Australia* 90 A1
Bray, Pays de, *France* 25 C8
Bray-sur-Seine, *France* 25 D10
Brazeau →, *Canada* 100 C5
Brazil, *U.S.A.* 104 F2
Brazil ■, *S. Amer.* 123 D2
Brazilian Highlands = Brasil, Planalto, *Brazil* 118 E6
Brazo Sur →, *S. Amer.* 126 B4
Brazos →, *U.S.A.* 109 L7
Brazzaville, *Congo* 80 E3
Brčko, *Bos.-H.* 21 L8
Brea, *Peru* 124 A1
Breadalbane, *Australia* 90 C2
Breadalbane, *U.K.* 14 E4
Breaden, L., *Australia* 89 E4
Breaksea Sd., *N.Z.* 87 L1
Bream B., *N.Z.* 87 F5
Bream Hd., *N.Z.* 87 F5
Breas, *Chile* 126 B1
Brebes, *Indonesia* 57 G13
Brechin, *Canada* 106 B5
Brechin, *U.K.* 14 E6
Brecht, *Belgium* 17 F5
Breckenridge, *Colo., U.S.A.* 110 G10
Breckenridge, *Minn., U.S.A.* 108 B6
Breckenridge, *Tex., U.S.A.* 109 J5
Breckland, *U.K.* 13 E8
Brecknock, Pen., *Chile* 128 D2
Břeclav, *Czech.* 20 G6
Brecon, *U.K.* 13 F4
Brecon Beacons, *U.K.* 13 F4
Breda, *Neths.* 17 E5
Bredasdorp, *S. Africa* 84 E3
Bredbo, *Australia* 91 F4
Bredene, *Belgium* 17 F1
Bredstedt, *Germany* 18 A4
Bree, *Belgium* 17 F7
Breezand, *Neths.* 16 C5
Bregalnica →, *Macedonia* 39 H5
Bregenz, *Austria* 19 H5
Bréhal, *France* 24 D5
Bréhat, I. de, *France* 24 D4
Breiðafjörður, *Iceland* 8 D2
Breil-sur-Roya, *France* 27 E11
Breisach, *Germany* 19 G3
Brejinho de Nazaré, *Brazil* 122 D2
Brejo, *Brazil* 122 B3
Bremen, *Germany* 18 B4
Bremen □, *Germany* 18 B4
Bremer I., *Australia* 90 A2
Bremerhaven, *Germany* 18 B4
Bremerton, *U.S.A.* 112 C4
Bremervörde, *Germany* 18 B5
Bremsnes, *Norway* 10 A1
Brenes, *Spain* 31 H5
Brenham, *U.S.A.* 109 K6
Brenner P., *Austria* 19 H7
Breno, *Italy* 32 C7
Brent, *Canada* 98 C4
Brent, *U.K.* 13 F7
Brenta →, *Italy* 33 C9
Brentwood, *U.K.* 13 F8
Brentwood, *U.S.A.* 107 F11
Bréscia, *Italy* 32 C7
Breskens, *Neths.* 17 F3
Breslau = Wrocław, *Poland* 20 D7
Bresle →, *France* 24 B8
Bresles, *France* 25 C9
Bressanone, *Italy* 33 B8
Bressay, *U.K.* 14 A7
Bresse, *France* 25 F12
Bressuire, *France* 24 F6
Brest, *Belarus* 41 F2
Brest, *France* 24 D2
Brest-Litovsk = Brest, *Belarus* 41 F2
Bretagne, *France* 24 D4
Bretçu, *Romania* 38 C9
Breteuil, *Eure, France* 24 D7
Breteuil, *Oise, France* 25 C9
Breton, *Canada* 100 C6
Breton, Pertuis, *France* 26 B2
Breton Sd., *U.S.A.* 109 L10
Brett, C., *N.Z.* 87 F5
Bretten, *Germany* 19 F4
Breukelen, *Neths.* 16 D6
Brevard, *U.S.A.* 105 H4
Breves, *Brazil* 122 B1
Brevik, *Norway* 10 E3
Brewarrina, *Australia* 91 D4
Brewer, *U.S.A.* 99 D6
Brewer, Mt., *U.S.A.* 112 J8
Brewster, *N.Y., U.S.A.* 107 E11
Brewster, *Wash., U.S.A.* 110 B4
Brewster, Kap, *Greenland* 4 B6
Brewton, *U.S.A.* 105 K2
Breyten, *S. Africa* 85 D4
Brezhnev = Naberezhnyye Chelny, *Russia* 42 C11
Brežice, *Slovenia* 33 C12
Brézina, *Algeria* 75 B5
Březnice, *Czech.* 20 F3
Breznik, *Bulgaria* 38 G5
Brezno, *Slovak Rep.* 20 G9
Bria, *C.A.R.* 73 G9
Briançon, *France* 27 D10
Briare, *France* 25 E9
Bribie I., *Australia* 91 D5
Bricquebec, *France* 24 C5
Bridgehampton, *U.S.A.* 107 F12
Bridgend, *U.K.* 13 F4
Bridgend □, *U.K.* 13 F4
Bridgeport, *Calif., U.S.A.* 111 G4
Bridgeport, *Conn., U.S.A.* 107 E11
Bridgeport, *Nebr., U.S.A.* 108 E3
Bridgeport, *Tex., U.S.A.* 109 J6
Bridger, *U.S.A.* 110 D9
Bridgeton, *U.S.A.* 104 F8
Bridgetown, *Australia* 89 F2
Bridgetown, *Barbados* 117 D8
Bridgetown, *Canada* 99 D6
Bridgewater, *Canada* 99 D7
Bridgewater, *Mass., U.S.A.* 107 E14
Bridgewater, *S. Dak., U.S.A.* 108 D6
Bridgewater, C., *Australia* 91 F3
Bridgnorth, *U.K.* 13 E5
Bridgton, *U.S.A.* 107 B14
Bridgwater, *U.K.* 13 F4
Bridlington, *U.K.* 12 C7
Bridport, *Australia* 90 G4
Bridport, *U.K.* 13 G5
Brie, Plaine de la, *France* 25 D10
Brie-Comte-Robert, *France* 25 D9
Briec, *France* 24 D2
Brielle, *Neths.* 16 E4
Brienne-le-Château, *France* 25 D11
Brienon-sur-Armançon, *France* 25 E10
Brienz, *Switz.* 22 C6
Brienzersee, *Switz.* 22 C5
Brig, *Switz.* 22 D5
Brigg, *U.K.* 12 D7
Briggsdale, *U.S.A.* 108 E2
Brigham City, *U.S.A.* 110 F7
Bright, *Australia* 91 F4
Brighton, *Australia* 91 F2
Brighton, *Canada* 98 D4
Brighton, *U.K.* 13 G7
Brighton, *U.S.A.* 108 F2
Brignogan-Plage, *France* 24 D2
Brignoles, *France* 27 E10
Brihuega, *Spain* 28 E2
Brikama, *Gambia* 78 C1
Brilliant, *Canada* 100 D5
Brilliant, *U.S.A.* 106 F4
Brilon, *Germany* 18 D4
Bríndisi, *Italy* 35 B10
Brinje, *Croatia* 33 D12
Brinkley, *U.S.A.* 109 H9
Brinkworth, *Australia* 91 E2
Brinnon, *U.S.A.* 112 C4
Brion, I., *Canada* 99 C7
Brionne, *France* 24 C7
Brionski, *Croatia* 33 D10
Brioude, *France* 26 C7
Briouze, *France* 24 D6
Brisbane, *Australia* 91 D5
Brisbane →, *Australia* 91 D5
Brisighella, *Italy* 33 D8
Bristol, *U.K.* 13 F5
Bristol, *Conn., U.S.A.* 107 E12
Bristol, *Pa., U.S.A.* 107 F10
Bristol, *R.I., U.S.A.* 107 E13
Bristol, *S. Dak., U.S.A.* 108 C6
Bristol, *Tenn., U.S.A.* 105 G4
Bristol □, *U.K.* 13 F5
Bristol B., *U.S.A.* 96 C4
Bristol Channel, *U.K.* 13 F3
Bristol I., *Antarctica* 5 B1
Bristol L., *U.S.A.* 111 J5
Bristow, *U.S.A.* 109 H6
British Columbia □, *Canada* 100 C3
British Isles, *Europe* 6 E5
Brits, *S. Africa* 85 D4
Britstown, *S. Africa* 84 E3
Britt, *Canada* 98 C3
Brittany = Bretagne, *France* 24 D4
Britton, *U.S.A.* 108 C6
Brive-la-Gaillarde, *France* 26 C5
Briviesca, *Spain* 28 C1
Brixen = Bressanone, *Italy* 33 B8
Brixton, *Australia* 90 C3
Brlik, *Kazakstan* 44 E8
Brno, *Czech.* 20 F6
Bro, *Sweden* 10 E11
Broad →, *U.S.A.* 105 J5
Broad Arrow, *Australia* 89 F3
Broad B., *U.K.* 14 C2
Broad Haven, *Ireland* 15 B2
Broad Law, *U.K.* 14 F5
Broad Sd., *Australia* 90 C4
Broadhurst Ra., *Australia* 88 D3
Broads, The, *U.K.* 12 E9
Broadus, *U.S.A.* 108 C2
Broadview, *Canada* 101 C8
Broager, *Denmark* 11 K3
Broaryd, *Sweden* 11 G7
Brochet, *Canada* 101 B8
Brochet, L., *Canada* 101 B8
Brock, *Canada* 101 C7
Brocken, *Germany* 18 D6
Brockport, *U.S.A.* 106 C7
Brockton, *U.S.A.* 107 D13
Brockville, *Canada* 98 D4
Brockway, *Mont., U.S.A.* 108 B2
Brockway, *Pa., U.S.A.* 106 E6
Brocton, *U.S.A.* 106 D5
Brod, *Macedonia* 39 H4
Brodarevo, *Serbia, Yug.* 21 M9
Brodeur Pen., *Canada* 97 A11
Brodick, *U.K.* 14 F3
Brodnica, *Poland* 20 B9
Brody, *Ukraine* 41 G3
Broechem, *Belgium* 17 F5
Broek, *Neths.* 16 D6
Broek op Langedijk, *Neths.* 16 C5
Brogan, *U.S.A.* 110 D5
Broglie, *France* 24 C7
Broken Arrow, *U.S.A.* 109 G7
Broken Bow, *Nebr., U.S.A.* 108 E5
Broken Bow, *Okla., U.S.A.* 109 H7
Broken Hill = Kabwe, *Zambia* 83 E2
Broken Hill, *Australia* 91 E3
Brokind, *Sweden* 11 F9
Brokopondo, *Surinam* 121 B7
Brokopondo □, *Surinam* 121 C6
Bromfield, *U.K.* 13 E5
Bromley, *U.K.* 13 F8
Brønderslev, *Denmark* 11 G3
Brong-Ahafo □, *Ghana* 78 D4
Bronkhorstspruit, *S. Africa* 85 D4
Brønnøysund, *Norway* 8 D15
Bronte, *Italy* 35 E7
Bronte, *U.S.A.* 109 K4
Bronte Park, *Australia* 90 G4
Brook Park, *U.S.A.* 106 E4
Brookfield, *U.S.A.* 108 F8
Brookhaven, *U.S.A.* 109 K9
Brookings, *Oreg., U.S.A.* 110 E1
Brookings, *S. Dak., U.S.A.* 108 C6
Brooklin, *Canada* 106 C6
Brooklyn Park, *U.S.A.* 108 C8
Brookmere, *Canada* 100 D4
Brooks, *Canada* 100 C6
Brooks B., *Canada* 100 C3
Brooks L., *Canada* 101 A7
Brooks Ra., *U.S.A.* 96 B5
Brooksville, *U.S.A.* 105 L4
Brookville, *U.S.A.* 104 F3
Brooloo, *Australia* 91 D5
Broom, L., *U.K.* 14 D3
Broome, *Australia* 88 C3
Broomehill, *Australia* 89 F2
Brooms, *France* 24 D4
Brora, *U.K.* 14 C5
Brora →, *U.K.* 14 C5
Brosna →, *Ireland* 15 C4
Broșteni, *Romania* 38 B8
Brotas de Macaúbas, *Brazil* 123 D3
Brothers, *U.S.A.* 110 E3
Brøttum, *Norway* 10 C4
Brou, *France* 24 D8
Brouage, Ramparts de, *France* 26 C2
Brough, *U.K.* 12 C5
Broughton Island, *Canada* 97 B13
Broughty Ferry, *U.K.* 14 E6
Brouwershaven, *Neths.* 16 E3
Brouwershavensche Gat, *Neths.* 16 E3
Brovary, *Ukraine* 41 G6
Brovst, *Denmark* 11 G3
Browerville, *U.S.A.* 108 B7
Brown, Pt., *Australia* 91 E1
Brown Willy, *U.K.* 13 G3
Brownfield, *U.S.A.* 109 J3
Browning, *U.S.A.* 110 B7
Brownlee, *Canada* 101 C7
Brownsville, *Oreg., U.S.A.* 110 D2
Brownsville, *Tenn., U.S.A.* 109 H10
Brownsville, *Tex., U.S.A.* 109 N6
Brownsweg, *Surinam* 121 B6
Brownwood, *U.S.A.* 109 K5
Brownwood, L., *U.S.A.* 109 K5
Browse I., *Australia* 88 B3
Broye →, *Switz.* 22 C3
Brozas, *Spain* 31 F4
Bruas, *Malaysia* 59 K3
Bruay-en-Artois, *France* 25 B9
Bruce, Mt., *Australia* 88 D2
Bruce Pen., *Canada* 106 A3
Bruce Rock, *Australia* 89 F2
Bruche →, *France* 25 D14
Bruchsal, *Germany* 19 F4
Bruck an der Leitha, *Austria* 21 G6
Bruck an der Mur, *Austria* 21 H5
Brue →, *U.K.* 13 F5
Brugelette, *Belgium* 17 G3
Bruges = Brugge, *Belgium* 17 F2
Brugg, *Switz.* 22 B6
Brugge, *Belgium* 17 F2
Brühl, *Germany* 18 E2
Bruinisse, *Neths.* 17 E4
Brûlé, *Canada* 100 C5
Brûlon, *France* 24 E6
Brûly, *Belgium* 17 J5
Brumado, *Brazil* 123 D3
Brumado →, *Brazil* 123 D3
Brumath, *France* 25 D14
Brummen, *Neths.* 16 D8
Brumunddal, *Norway* 10 D4
Brunchilly, *Australia* 90 B1
Brundidge, *U.S.A.* 105 K3
Bruneau, *U.S.A.* 110 E6
Bruneau →, *U.S.A.* 110 E6
Bruneck = Brunico, *Italy* 33 B8
Brunei = Bandar Seri Begawan, *Brunei* 56 C4
Brunei ■, *Asia* 56 D4
Brunette Downs, *Australia* 90 B2
Brunflo, *Sweden* 10 A8
Brunico, *Italy* 33 B8
Brünig, P., *Switz.* 22 C6
Brunkeberg, *Norway* 10 E2
Brunna, *Sweden* 10 E11
Brunnen, *Switz.* 23 C7
Brunner, L., *N.Z.* 87 K3
Bruno, *Canada* 101 C7
Brunsbüttel, *Germany* 18 B5
Brunssum, *Neths.* 17 G7
Brunswick = Braunschweig, *Germany* 18 C6
Brunswick, *Ga., U.S.A.* 105 K5
Brunswick, *Maine, U.S.A.* 99 D6
Brunswick, *Md., U.S.A.* 104 F7
Brunswick, *Mo., U.S.A.* 108 F8
Brunswick, *Ohio, U.S.A.* 106 E3
Brunswick, Pen. de, *Chile* 128 D2
Brunswick B., *Australia* 88 C3
Brunswick Junction, *Australia* 89 F2
Bruntál, *Czech.* 20 F7
Bruny I., *Australia* 90 G4
Brus Laguna, *Honduras* 116 C3
Brusartsi, *Bulgaria* 38 F6
Brush, *U.S.A.* 108 E3
Brushton, *U.S.A.* 107 B10
Brusio, *Switz.* 23 D10
Brusque, *Brazil* 127 B6
Brussel, *Belgium* 17 G4
Brussels = Brussel, *Belgium* 17 G4
Brussels, *Canada* 106 C3
Brustem, *Belgium* 17 G6
Bruthen, *Australia* 91 F4
Bruxelles = Brussel, *Belgium* 17 G4
Bruyères, *France* 25 D13
Bryan, *Ohio, U.S.A.* 104 E3
Bryan, *Tex., U.S.A.* 109 K6
Bryan, Mt., *Australia* 91 E2
Bryanka, *Ukraine* 41 H10
Bryansk, *Russia* 42 D2
Bryansk, *Russia* 43 H8
Bryanskoye = Bryansk, *Russia* 43 H8
Bryant, *U.S.A.* 108 C6
Bryne, *Norway* 9 G11
Bryson City, *U.S.A.* 105 H4
Bryukhovetskaya, *Russia* 43 H4
Brza Palanka, *Serbia, Yug.* 21 L12
Brzava →, *Serbia, Yug.* 21 K10
Brzeg, *Poland* 20 E7
Brzeg Din, *Poland* 20 D6
Bsharri, *Lebanon* 69 A5
Bū Baqarah, *U.A.E.* 65 E8
Bu Craa, *W. Sahara* 74 C2
Bū Ḩasā, *U.A.E.* 65 F7
Bua Yai, *Thailand* 58 E4
Buapinang, *Indonesia* 57 E6
Buayan, *Phil.* 57 C7
Buba, *Guinea-Biss.* 78 C2
Bubanza, *Burundi* 82 C2
Būbiyān, *Kuwait* 65 D6
Bucak, *Turkey* 66 D4
Bucaramanga, *Colombia* 120 B3
Bucas Grande I., *Phil.* 55 G6
Buccaneer Arch., *Australia* 88 C3
Bucchiánico, *Italy* 33 F11
Bucecea, *Romania* 38 B9
Buchach, *Ukraine* 41 H3
Buchan, *U.K.* 14 D6
Buchan Ness, *U.K.* 14 D7
Buchanan, *Canada* 101 C8
Buchanan, *Liberia* 78 D2
Buchanan, L., *Queens., Australia* 90 C4
Buchanan, L., *W. Austral., Australia* 89 E3
Buchanan, L., *U.S.A.* 109 K5
Buchanan Cr. →, *Australia* 90 B2
Buchans, *Canada* 99 C8
Bucharest = București, *Romania* 38 E9
Buchholz, *Germany* 18 B5
Buchloe, *Germany* 19 G6
Buchon, Pt., *U.S.A.* 112 K6
Buchs, *Switz.* 23 B8
Bückeburg, *Germany* 18 C5
Buckeye, *U.S.A.* 111 K7
Buckhannon, *U.S.A.* 104 F5
Buckhaven, *U.K.* 14 E5
Buckie, *U.K.* 14 D6
Buckingham, *Canada* 98 C4
Buckingham, *U.K.* 13 F7
Buckingham B., *Australia* 90 A2
Buckinghamshire □, *U.K.* 13 F7
Buckle Hd., *Australia* 88 B4
Buckleboo, *Australia* 91 E2
Buckley, *U.S.A.* 110 C2
Buckley →, *Australia* 90 C2
Bucklin, *U.S.A.* 109 G5
Bucks L., *U.S.A.* 112 F5
Bucquoy, *France* 25 B9
Buctouche, *Canada* 99 C7
București, *Romania* 38 E9
Bucyrus, *U.S.A.* 104 E4
Budafok, *Hungary* 21 H9
Budalin, *Burma* 61 H19
Budapest, *Hungary* 21 H9
Budaun, *India* 63 E8
Budd Coast, *Antarctica* 5 C8
Buddusò, *Italy* 34 B2
Bude, *U.K.* 13 G3
Budel, *Neths.* 17 F7
Budennovsk, *Russia* 43 H7
Budești, *Romania* 38 E9
Budge Budge = Baj Baj, *India* 63 H13
Budgewoi, *Australia* 91 E5
Budia, *Spain* 28 E2
Budjala, *Zaïre* 80 D3
Búdrio, *Italy* 33 D8
Buea, *Cameroon* 79 E6
Buellton, *U.S.A.* 113 L6
Buena Park, *U.S.A.* 113 M9
Buena Vista, *Bolivia* 125 D5
Buena Vista, *Colo., U.S.A.* 111 G10
Buena Vista, *Va., U.S.A.* 104 G6
Buena Vista L., *U.S.A.* 113 K7
Buenaventura, *Colombia* 120 C2
Buenaventura, *Mexico* 114 B3
Buenaventura, B. de, *Colombia* 120 C2
Buendía, Pantano de, *Spain* 28 E2
Buenópolis, *Brazil* 123 E3
Buenos Aires, *Argentina* 126 C4
Buenos Aires, *Colombia* 120 C3
Buenos Aires, *Costa Rica* 116 E3
Buenos Aires □, *Argentina* 126 D4
Buenos Aires, L., *Chile* 128 C2
Buesaco, *Colombia* 120 C2
Buffalo, *Mo., U.S.A.* 109 G8
Buffalo, *N.Y., U.S.A.* 106 D6
Buffalo, *Okla., U.S.A.* 109 G5
Buffalo, *S. Dak., U.S.A.* 108 C3
Buffalo, *Wyo., U.S.A.* 110 D10
Buffalo →, *Canada* 100 A5
Buffalo Head Hills, *Canada* 100 B5
Buffalo L., *Canada* 100 C6
Buffalo Narrows, *Canada* 101 B7
Buffels →, *S. Africa* 84 D2
Buford, *U.S.A.* 105 H4
Bug → = Buh →, *Ukraine* 41 J6
Bug →, *Poland* 20 C11
Buga, *Colombia* 120 C2
Buganda, *Uganda* 82 C3
Buganga, *Uganda* 82 C3
Bugasong, *Phil.* 55 F5
Bugeat, *France* 26 C5
Bugel, Tanjung, *Indonesia* 56 F4
Buggenhout, *Belgium* 17 F4
Bugibba, *Malta* 37 D1
Bugsuk, *Phil.* 55 G2
Buguma, *Nigeria* 79 E6
Bugun Shara, *Mongolia* 54 B5
Buguruslan, *Russia* 44 D6
Buh →, *Ukraine* 41 J6
Buhăești, *Romania* 38 C10
Buheirat-Murrat-el-Kubra, *Egypt* 76 H8
Buhl, *Idaho, U.S.A.* 110 E6
Buhl, *Minn., U.S.A.* 108 B8
Buick, *U.S.A.* 109 G9
Builth Wells, *U.K.* 13 E4
Buinsk, *Russia* 42 C9
Buíque, *Brazil* 122 C4

Buir Nur, *Mongolia* 54 B6
Buis-les-Baronnies, *France* 27 D9
Buitenpost, *Neths.* 16 B8
Buitrago, *Spain* 30 E7
Bujalance, *Spain* 31 H6
Buján, *Spain* 30 C2
Bujaraloz, *Spain* 28 D4
Buje, *Croatia* 33 C10
Bujumbura, *Burundi* 82 C2
Bukachacha, *Russia* 45 D12
Bukama, *Zaïre* 83 D2
Bukavu, *Zaïre* 82 C2
Bukene, *Tanzania* 82 C3
Bukhara = Bukhoro, *Uzbekistan* 44 F7
Bukhoro, *Uzbekistan* 44 F7
Bukima, *Tanzania* 82 C3
Bukit Mertajam, *Malaysia* 59 K3
Bukittinggi, *Indonesia* 56 E2
Bukoba, *Tanzania* 82 C3
Bukoba □, *Tanzania* 82 C3
Bukuru, *Nigeria* 79 D6
Bukuya, *Uganda* 82 B3
Bula, *Guinea-Biss.* 78 C1
Bula, *Indonesia* 57 E8
Bülach, *Switz.* 23 A7
Bulahdelah, *Australia* 91 E5
Bulan, *Phil.* 55 E5
Bulancak, *Turkey* 67 B8
Bulandshahr, *India* 62 E7
Bulanık, *Turkey* 67 C10
Bûlâq, *Egypt* 76 B3
Bulawayo, *Zimbabwe* 83 G2
Buldan, *Turkey* 66 C3
Bulgan, *Mongolia* 54 B5
Bulgar, *Russia* 42 C9
Bulgaria ■, *Europe* 38 G8
Bulgroo, *Australia* 91 D3
Bulgunnia, *Australia* 91 E1
Bulhar, *Somali Rep.* 68 E3
Buli, Teluk, *Indonesia* 57 D7
Buliluyan, C., *Phil.* 55 G2
Bulki, *Ethiopia* 77 F4
Bulkley →, *Canada* 100 B3
Bull Shoals L., *U.S.A.* 109 G8
Bullange, *Belgium* 17 H8
Bullaque →, *Spain* 31 G6
Bullara, *Australia* 88 D1
Bullaring, *Australia* 89 F2
Bullas, *Spain* 29 G3
Bulle, *Switz.* 22 C4
Bulli, *Australia* 91 E5
Bullock Creek, *Australia* 90 B3
Bulloo →, *Australia* 91 D3
Bulloo Downs, *Queens., Australia* 91 D3
Bulloo Downs, *W. Austral., Australia* 88 D2
Bulloo L., *Australia* 91 D3
Bulls, *N.Z.* 87 J5
Bully-les-Mines, *France* 25 B9
Bulnes, *Chile* 126 D1
Bulo Burti, *Somali Rep.* 68 G4
Bulsar = Valsad, *India* 60 J8
Bultfontein, *S. Africa* 84 D4
Bulukumba, *Indonesia* 57 F6
Bulun, *Russia* 45 B13
Bulus, *Russia* 45 C13
Bumba, *Zaïre* 80 D4
Bumbiri I., *Tanzania* 82 C3
Bumhpa Bum, *Burma* 61 F20
Bumi →, *Zimbabwe* 83 F2
Buna, *Kenya* 82 B4
Bunawan, *Agusan del S., Phil.* 55 G6
Bunawan, *Davao del S., Phil.* 55 H6
Bunazi, *Tanzania* 82 C3
Bunbah, Khalīj, *Libya* 73 B9
Bunbury, *Australia* 89 F2
Buncrana, *Ireland* 15 A4
Bundaberg, *Australia* 91 C5
Bünde, *Germany* 18 C4
Bundey →, *Australia* 90 C2
Bundi, *India* 62 G6
Bundooma, *Australia* 90 C1
Bundoran, *Ireland* 15 B3
Bundukia, *Sudan* 77 F3
Bung Kan, *Thailand* 58 C4
Bungatakada, *Japan* 49 H5
Bungil Cr. →, *Australia* 90 D4
Bungo-Suidō, *Japan* 49 H6
Bungoma, *Kenya* 82 B3
Bungu, *Tanzania* 82 D4
Bunia, *Zaïre* 82 B3
Bunji, *Pakistan* 63 B6
Bunkie, *U.S.A.* 109 K8
Bunnell, *U.S.A.* 105 L5
Bunnik, *Neths.* 16 D6
Buñol, *Spain* 29 F4
Bunsbeek, *Belgium* 17 G5
Bunschoten, *Neths.* 16 D6
Buntok, *Indonesia* 56 E4
Bununu, *Nigeria* 79 D6
Bununu Dass, *Nigeria* 79 C6
Bünyan, *Turkey* 66 C6
Bunyu, *Indonesia* 56 D5
Bunza, *Nigeria* 79 C5
Buol, *Indonesia* 57 D6
Buon Brieng, *Vietnam* 58 F7
Buon Me Thuot, *Vietnam* 58 F7
Buong Long, *Cambodia* 58 F6
Buorkhaya, Mys, *Russia* 45 B14
Buqayq, *Si. Arabia* 65 E6
Buqbua, *Egypt* 76 A2
Bur Acaba, *Somali Rep.* 68 G3
Bûr Fuad, *Egypt* 76 H8
Bûr Safâga, *Egypt* 76 B3
Bûr Sa'îd, *Egypt* 76 H8
Bûr Sûdân, *Sudan* 76 D4
Bûr Taufiq, *Egypt* 76 J8
Bura, *Kenya* 82 C4
Burao, *Somali Rep.* 68 F4
Burâq, *Syria* 69 B5
Buras, *U.S.A.* 109 L10
Buraydah, *Si. Arabia* 64 E5
Burbank, *U.S.A.* 113 L8
Burcher, *Australia* 91 E4
Burdekin →, *Australia* 90 B4
Burdett, *Canada* 100 D6
Burdur, *Turkey* 66 D4
Burdur Gölü, *Turkey* 66 D4
Burdwan = Barddhaman, *India* 63 H12
Bure, *Ethiopia* 77 E4
Bure →, *U.K.* 12 E9
Büren, *Germany* 18 D4
Buren, *Neths.* 16 E6
Bureya →, *Russia* 45 E13
Burford, *Canada* 106 C4
Burg, *Germany* 18 C7
Burg auf Fehmarn, *Germany* 18 A7
Burg el Arab, *Egypt* 76 H6
Burg et Tuyur, *Sudan* 76 C2
Burg Stargard, *Germany* 18 B9
Burgas, *Bulgaria* 38 G10
Burgdorf, *Germany* 18 C5
Burgdorf, *Switz.* 22 B5
Burgeo, *Canada* 99 C8
Burgersdorp, *S. Africa* 84 E4
Burges, Mt., *Australia* 89 F3
Burghausen, *Germany* 19 G8
Búrgio, *Italy* 34 E6
Bürglen, *Switz.* 23 C7
Burglengenfeld, *Germany* 19 F8
Burgo de Osma, *Spain* 28 D1
Burgohondo, *Spain* 30 E6
Burgos, *Spain* 28 C1
Burgos □, *Spain* 28 C1
Burgstädt, *Germany* 18 E8
Burgsvik, *Sweden* 9 H18
Burguillos del Cerro, *Spain* 31 G4
Burgundy = Bourgogne, *France* 25 F11
Burhaniye, *Turkey* 66 C2
Burhanpur, *India* 60 J10
Burhou, *U.K.* 24 C4
Buri Pen., *Eritrea* 77 D4
Burias, *Phil.* 55 E5
Burica, Pta., *Costa Rica* 116 E3
Burigi, L., *Tanzania* 82 C3
Burin, *Canada* 99 C8
Buriram, *Thailand* 58 E4
Buriti Alegre, *Brazil* 123 E2
Buriti Bravo, *Brazil* 122 C3
Buriti dos Lopes, *Brazil* 122 B3
Burj Sāfitā, *Syria* 66 E7
Burji, *Ethiopia* 77 F4
Burkburnett, *U.S.A.* 109 H5
Burke, *U.S.A.* 110 C6
Burke →, *Australia* 90 C2
Burketown, *Australia* 90 B2
Burkina Faso ■, *Africa* 78 C4
Burk's Falls, *Canada* 98 C4
Burley, *U.S.A.* 110 E7
Burlingame, *U.S.A.* 112 H4
Burlington, *Canada* 106 C5
Burlington, *Colo., U.S.A.* 108 F3
Burlington, *Iowa, U.S.A.* 108 E9
Burlington, *Kans., U.S.A.* 108 F7
Burlington, *N.C., U.S.A.* 105 G6
Burlington, *N.J., U.S.A.* 107 F10
Burlington, *Vt., U.S.A.* 107 B11
Burlington, *Wash., U.S.A.* 112 B4
Burlington, *Wis., U.S.A.* 104 D1
Burlyu-Tyube, *Kazakstan* 44 E8
Burma ■, *Asia* 61 J20
Burnaby I., *Canada* 100 C2
Burnet, *U.S.A.* 109 K5
Burney, *U.S.A.* 110 F3
Burngup, *Australia* 89 F2
Burnham, *U.S.A.* 106 F7
Burnie, *Australia* 90 G4
Burnley, *U.K.* 12 D5
Burns, *Oreg., U.S.A.* 110 E4
Burns, *Wyo., U.S.A.* 108 E2
Burns Lake, *Canada* 100 C3
Burnside →, *Canada* 96 B9
Burnside, L., *Australia* 89 E3
Burnsville, *U.S.A.* 108 C8
Burnt River, *Canada* 106 B6
Burntwood →, *Canada* 101 B9
Burntwood L., *Canada* 101 B8
Burqān, *Kuwait* 64 D5
Burqin, *China* 54 B3
Burra, *Australia* 91 E2
Burramurra, *Australia* 90 C2
Burreli, *Albania* 39 H3
Burren Junction, *Australia* 91 E4
Burrendong Dam, *Australia* 91 E4
Burriana, *Spain* 28 F4
Burrinjuck Res., *Australia* 91 F4
Burro, Serranías del, *Mexico* 114 B4
Burruyacú, *Argentina* 126 B3
Burry Port, *U.K.* 13 F3
Bursa, *Turkey* 66 B3
Burseryd, *Sweden* 11 G7
Burstall, *Canada* 101 C7
Burton L., *Canada* 98 B4
Burton upon Trent, *U.K.* 12 E6
Burtundy, *Australia* 91 E3
Buru, *Indonesia* 57 E7
Burullus, Bahra el, *Egypt* 76 H7
Burûn, Râs, *Egypt* 69 D2
Burundi ■, *Africa* 82 C3
Bururi, *Burundi* 82 C2
Burutu, *Nigeria* 79 D6
Burwell, *U.S.A.* 108 E5
Bury, *U.K.* 12 D5
Bury St. Edmunds, *U.K.* 13 E8
Buryatia □, *Russia* 45 D11
Buryn, *Ukraine* 41 G7
Busalla, *Italy* 32 D5
Busango Swamp, *Zambia* 83 E2
Buşayrah, *Syria* 67 E9
Buşayyah, *Iraq* 64 D5
Busca, *Italy* 32 D4
Būshehr, *Iran* 65 D6
Būshehr □, *Iran* 65 D6
Bushell, *Canada* 101 B7
Bushenyi, *Uganda* 82 C3
Bushire = Būshehr, *Iran* 65 D6
Bushnell, *Ill., U.S.A.* 108 E9
Bushnell, *Nebr., U.S.A.* 108 E3
Busia □, *Kenya* 82 B3
Busie, *Ghana* 78 C4
Businga, *Zaïre* 80 D4
Buskerud fylke □, *Norway* 10 D3
Busko Zdrój, *Poland* 20 E10
Busovača, *Bos.-H.* 21 L7
Busra ash Shām, *Syria* 69 C5
Bussang, *France* 25 E13
Busselton, *Australia* 89 F2
Busseto, *Italy* 32 D7
Bussigny, *Switz.* 22 C3
Bussum, *Neths.* 16 D6
Bustamante, B., *Argentina* 128 C3
Busto, C., *Spain* 30 B4
Busto Arsízio, *Italy* 32 C5
Busu-Djanoa, *Zaïre* 80 D4
Busuanga, *Phil.* 55 E3
Büsum, *Germany* 18 A4
Buta, *Zaïre* 82 B1
Butare, *Rwanda* 82 C2
Butaritari, *Kiribati* 92 G9
Bute, *U.K.* 14 F3
Bute Inlet, *Canada* 100 C4
Butemba, *Uganda* 82 B3
Butembo, *Zaïre* 82 B2
Butera, *Italy* 35 E7
Bütgenbach, *Belgium* 17 H8
Butha Qi, *China* 54 B7
Butiaba, *Uganda* 82 B3
Butler, *Mo., U.S.A.* 108 F7
Butler, *Pa., U.S.A.* 106 F5
Buton, *Indonesia* 57 E6
Bütschwil, *Switz.* 23 B8
Butte, *Mont., U.S.A.* 110 C7
Butte, *Nebr., U.S.A.* 108 D5
Butte Creek →, *U.S.A.* 112 F5
Butterworth = Gcuwa, *S. Africa* 85 E4
Butterworth, *Malaysia* 59 K3
Buttfield, Mt., *Australia* 89 D4
Button B., *Canada* 101 B10
Buttonwillow, *U.S.A.* 113 K7
Butty Hd., *Australia* 89 F3
Butuan, *Phil.* 55 G6
Butuku-Luba, *Eq. Guin.* 79 E6
Butung = Buton, *Indonesia* 57 E6
Buturlinovka, *Russia* 42 E5
Butzbach, *Germany* 18 E4
Bützow, *Germany* 18 B7
Buxar, *India* 63 G10
Buxton, *Guyana* 121 B6
Buxton, *U.K.* 12 D6
Buxy, *France* 25 F11
Buy, *Russia* 42 A5
Buynaksk, *Russia* 43 J8
Büyük Menderes →, *Turkey* 66 D2
Büyükçekmece, *Turkey* 66 B3
Buzançais, *France* 24 F8
Buzău, *Romania* 38 D9
Buzău →, *Romania* 38 D10
Buzău, Pasul, *Romania* 38 D9
Buzen, *Japan* 49 H5
Buzet, *Croatia* 33 C10
Buzi →, *Mozam.* 83 F3
Buziaş, *Romania* 38 D4
Buzuluk, *Russia* 44 D6
Buzuluk →, *Russia* 42 E6
Buzzards Bay, *U.S.A.* 107 E14
Bwana Mkubwe, *Zaïre* 83 E2
Byala, *Bulgaria* 38 F8
Byala Slatina, *Bulgaria* 38 F6
Byarezina →, *Belarus* 41 F6
Bychawa, *Poland* 20 D12
Bydgoszcz, *Poland* 20 B8
Byelarus = Belarus ■, *Europe* 40 F4
Byelorussia = Belarus ■, *Europe* 40 F4
Byers, *U.S.A.* 108 F2
Byesville, *U.S.A.* 106 G3
Byhalia, *U.S.A.* 109 H10
Bykhaw, *Belarus* 40 F6
Bykhov = Bykhaw, *Belarus* 40 F6
Bykovo, *Russia* 42 F7
Bylas, *U.S.A.* 111 K8
Bylderup-Bov, *Denmark* 11 K3
Bylot I., *Canada* 97 A12
Byrd, C., *Antarctica* 5 C17
Byro, *Australia* 89 E2
Byrock, *Australia* 91 E4
Byron Bay, *Australia* 91 D5
Byrranga, Gory, *Russia* 45 B11
Byrranga Mts. = Byrranga, Gory, *Russia* 45 B11
Byrum, *Denmark* 11 G5
Byske, *Sweden* 8 D19
Byske älv →, *Sweden* 8 D19
Bystrzyca Kłodzka, *Poland* 20 E6
Bytom, *Poland* 20 E8
Bytów, *Poland* 20 A7
Byumba, *Rwanda* 82 C3

C

Ca →, *Vietnam* 58 C5
Ca Mau = Quan Long, *Vietnam* 59 H5
Ca Mau, Mui = Bai Bung, Mui, *Vietnam* 59 H5
Ca Na, *Vietnam* 59 G7
Caacupé, *Paraguay* 126 B4
Caála, *Angola* 81 G3
Caamano Sd., *Canada* 100 C3
Caapiranga, *Brazil* 121 D5
Caazapá, *Paraguay* 126 B4
Caazapá □, *Paraguay* 127 B4
Cabadbaran, *Phil.* 55 G6
Cabalian, *Phil.* 55 F6
Caballeria, C. de, *Spain* 36 A11
Cabana, *Peru* 124 B2
Cabanaconde, *Peru* 124 D3
Cabañaquinta, *Spain* 30 B5
Cabanatuan, *Phil.* 55 D4
Cabanes, *Spain* 28 E5
Cabanillas, *Peru* 124 D3
Cabano, *Canada* 99 C6
Čabar, *Croatia* 33 C11
Cabazon, *U.S.A.* 113 M10
Cabedelo, *Brazil* 122 C5
Cabeza del Buey, *Spain* 31 G5
Cabildo, *Chile* 126 C1
Cabimas, *Venezuela* 120 A3
Cabinda, *Angola* 80 F2
Cabinda □, *Angola* 80 F2
Cabinet Mts., *U.S.A.* 110 C6
Cabo Blanco, *Argentina* 128 C3
Cabo Frio, *Brazil* 123 F3
Cabo Pantoja, *Peru* 120 D2
Cabo Raso, *Argentina* 128 B3
Cabonga, Réservoir, *Canada* 98 C4
Cabool, *U.S.A.* 109 G8
Caboolture, *Australia* 91 D5
Cabora Bassa Dam = Cahora Bassa Dam, *Mozam.* 83 F3
Caborca, *Mexico* 114 A2
Cabot, Mt., *U.S.A.* 107 B13
Cabot Str., *Canada* 99 C8
Cabra, *Spain* 31 H6
Cabra del Santo Cristo, *Spain* 29 H1
Cábras, *Italy* 34 C1
Cabrera, *Spain* 36 B9
Cabrera, Sierra, *Spain* 30 C4
Cabri, *Canada* 101 C7
Cabriel →, *Spain* 29 F3
Cabruta, *Venezuela* 120 B4
Cabugao, *Phil.* 55 C4
Cabuyaro, *Colombia* 120 C3
Cacabelos, *Spain* 30 C4
Čačak, *Serbia, Yug.* 21 M10
Cacao, *Fr. Guiana* 121 C7
Cáceres, *Brazil* 125 D6
Cáceres, *Colombia* 120 B2
Cáceres, *Spain* 31 F4
Cáceres □, *Spain* 31 F4
Cache Bay, *Canada* 98 C4
Cache Cr. →, *U.S.A.* 112 G5
Cachepo, *Portugal* 31 H3
Cachéu, *Guinea-Biss.* 78 C1
Cachi, *Argentina* 126 B2
Cachimbo, *Brazil* 125 B7
Cachimbo, Serra do, *Brazil* 125 B6
Cachoeira, *Brazil* 123 D4
Cachoeira Alta, *Brazil* 123 E1
Cachoeira de Itapemirim, *Brazil* 123 F3
Cachoeira do Sul, *Brazil* 127 C5
Cachoeiro do Arari, *Brazil* 122 B2
Cachopo, *Portugal* 31 H3
Cachuela Esperanza, *Bolivia* 125 C4
Cacólo, *Angola* 80 G3
Caconda, *Angola* 81 G3
Cacongo, *Angola* 80 F2
Caçu, *Brazil* 123 E1
Caculé, *Brazil* 123 D3
Cadarache, *France* 27 E9
Čadca, *Slovak Rep.* 20 F8
Caddo, *U.S.A.* 109 H6
Cadell Cr. →, *Australia* 90 C3
Cadenazzo, *Switz.* 23 D7
Cader Idris, *U.K.* 12 E4
Cadí, Sierra del, *Spain* 28 C6
Cadibarrawirracanna, L., *Australia* 91 D2
Cadillac, *Canada* 98 C4
Cadillac, *France* 26 D3
Cadillac, *U.S.A.* 104 C3
Cadiz, *Phil.* 55 F5
Cádiz, *Spain* 31 J4
Cadiz, *U.S.A.* 106 F4
Cádiz □, *Spain* 31 J5
Cádiz, G. de, *Spain* 31 J4
Cadney Park, *Australia* 91 D1
Cadomin, *Canada* 100 C5
Cadotte →, *Canada* 100 B5
Cadours, *France* 26 E5
Cadoux, *Australia* 89 F2
Caen, *France* 24 C6
Caernarfon, *U.K.* 12 D3
Caernarfon B., *U.K.* 12 D3
Caernarvon = Caernarfon, *U.K.* 12 D3
Caerphilly, *U.K.* 13 F4
Caerphilly □, *U.K.* 13 F4
Caesarea, *Israel* 69 C3
Caeté, *Brazil* 123 E3
Caetité, *Brazil* 123 D3
Cafayate, *Argentina* 126 B2
Cafifi, *Colombia* 120 B3
Cafu, *Angola* 84 B2
Cagayan →, *Phil.* 55 B4
Cagayan de Oro, *Phil.* 55 G6
Cagayan Is., *Phil.* 55 G4
Cagayan Sulu I., *Phil.* 55 H3
Cagli, *Italy* 33 E9
Cágliari, *Italy* 34 C2
Cágliari, G. di, *Italy* 34 C2
Cagnano Varano, *Italy* 35 A8
Cagnes-sur-Mer, *France* 27 E11
Caguán →, *Colombia* 120 D3
Caguas, *Puerto Rico* 117 C6
Caha Mts., *Ireland* 15 E2
Cahama, *Angola* 84 B1
Caher, *Ireland* 15 D4
Caherciveen, *Ireland* 15 E1
Cahora Bassa Dam, *Mozam.* 83 F3
Cahore Pt., *Ireland* 15 D5
Cahors, *France* 26 D5
Cahuapanas, *Peru* 124 B2
Cahuinari →, *Colombia* 120 D3
Cahul, *Moldova* 41 K5
Cai Bau, Dao, *Vietnam* 58 B6
Cai Nuoc, *Vietnam* 59 H5
Caia, *Mozam.* 83 F4
Caiabis, Serra dos, *Brazil* 125 C6
Caianda, *Angola* 83 E1
Caiapó, Serra do, *Brazil* 125 D7
Caiapônia, *Brazil* 125 D7
Caibarién, *Cuba* 116 B4
Caibiran, *Phil.* 55 F6
Caicara, *Bolívar, Venezuela* 120 B4
Caicara, *Monagas, Venezuela* 121 B5
Caicó, *Brazil* 122 C4
Caicos Is., *W. Indies* 117 B5
Caicos Passage, *W. Indies* 117 B5
Cailloma, *Peru* 124 D3
Caine →, *Bolivia* 125 D4
Caird Coast, *Antarctica* 5 D1
Cairn Gorm, *U.K.* 14 D5
Cairn Toul, *U.K.* 14 D5
Cairngorm Mts., *U.K.* 14 D5
Cairns, *Australia* 90 B4
Cairo = El Qâhira, *Egypt* 76 H7
Cairo, *Ga., U.S.A.* 105 K3
Cairo, *Ill., U.S.A.* 109 G10
Cairo Montenotte, *Italy* 32 D5
Caithness, Ord of, *U.K.* 14 C5
Caiundo, *Angola* 81 H3
Caiza, *Bolivia* 125 E4
Cajabamba, *Peru* 124 B2
Cajamarca, *Peru* 124 B2
Cajamarca □, *Peru* 124 B2
Cajapió, *Brazil* 122 B3
Cajarc, *France* 26 D5
Cajatambo, *Peru* 124 C2
Cajàzeiras, *Brazil* 122 C4
Čajetina, *Serbia, Yug.* 21 M9
Çakirgol, *Turkey* 67 B8
Čakovec, *Croatia* 33 B13
Çal, *Turkey* 66 C3
Cala, *Spain* 31 H4
Cala →, *Spain* 31 H4
Cala Cadolar, Punta de, *Spain* 29 G6
Cala d'Or, *Spain* 36 B10
Cala Figuera, C., *Spain* 36 B9
Cala Forcat, *Spain* 36 A10
Cala Mayor, *Spain* 36 B9
Cala Mezquida, *Spain* 36 B11
Cala Millor, *Spain* 36 B10
Cala Ratjada, *Spain* 36 B10
Calabanga, *Phil.* 55 E5
Calabar, *Nigeria* 79 E6
Calabozo, *Venezuela* 120 B4
Calábria □, *Italy* 35 C9
Calaburras, Pta. de, *Spain* 31 J6
Calaceite, *Spain* 28 D5
Calacota, *Bolivia* 124 D4
Calafate, *Argentina* 128 D2
Calahorra, *Spain* 28 C3
Calais, *France* 25 B8
Calais, *U.S.A.* 99 C6
Calais, Pas de, *France* 25 B8
Calalaste, Cord. de, *Argentina* 126 B2
Calama, *Brazil* 125 B5
Calama, *Chile* 126 A2
Calamar, *Bolívar, Colombia* 120 A3
Calamar, *Vaupés, Colombia* 120 C3
Calamarca, *Bolivia* 124 D4
Calamba, *Phil.* 55 F5
Calamian Group, *Phil.* 55 F3
Calamocha, *Spain* 28 E3
Calán Porter, *Spain* 36 B11
Calañas, *Spain* 31 H4
Calanda, *Spain* 28 E4
Calang, *Indonesia* 56 D1
Calangiánus, *Italy* 34 B2
Calapan, *Phil.* 55 E4
Călărași, *Romania* 38 E10
Calasparra, *Spain* 29 G3

Calatafimi, *Italy* 34 E5
Calatayud, *Spain* 28 D3
Calato = Kálathos, *Greece* 39 N11
Calauag, *Phil.* 55 E5
Calavà, C., *Italy* 35 D7
Calavite, C., *Phil.* 55 E4
Calayan, *Phil.* 55 B4
Calbayog, *Phil.* 55 E6
Calbe, *Germany* 18 D7
Calca, *Peru* 124 C3
Calcasieu L., *U.S.A.* 109 L8
Calci, *Italy* 32 E7
Calcutta, *India* 63 H13
Caldaro, *Italy* 33 B8
Caldas □, *Colombia* 120 B2
Caldas da Rainha, *Portugal* 31 F1
Caldas de Reyes, *Spain* 30 C2
Caldas Novas, *Brazil* 123 E2
Calder →, *U.K.* 12 D6
Caldera, *Chile* 126 B1
Caldwell, *Idaho, U.S.A.* 110 E5
Caldwell, *Kans., U.S.A.* 109 G6
Caldwell, *Tex., U.S.A.* 109 K6
Caledon, *S. Africa* 84 E2
Caledon →, *S. Africa* 84 E4
Caledon B., *Australia* 90 A2
Caledonia, *Canada* 106 C5
Caledonia, *U.S.A.* 106 D7
Calella, *Spain* 28 D7
Calemba, *Angola* 84 B2
Calenzana, *France* 27 F12
Caleta Olivia, *Argentina* 128 C3
Calexico, *U.S.A.* 113 N11
Calf of Man, *U.K.* 12 C3
Calgary, *Canada* 100 C6
Calheta, *Madeira* 36 D2
Calhoun, *U.S.A.* 105 H3
Cali, *Colombia* 120 C2
Calicut, *India* 60 P9
Caliente, *U.S.A.* 111 H6
California, *Mo., U.S.A.* 108 F8
California, *Pa., U.S.A.* 106 F5
California □, *U.S.A.* 111 H4
California, Baja, *Mexico* 114 A1
California, Baja, T.N. □ = Baja California □, *Mexico* 114 B2
California, Baja, T.S. □ = Baja California Sur □, *Mexico* 114 B2
California, G. de, *Mexico* 114 B2
California City, *U.S.A.* 113 K9
California Hot Springs, *U.S.A.* 113 K8
Călimănești, *Romania* 38 D7
Călimani, Munții, *Romania* 38 B8
Călinești, *Romania* 38 D7
Calingasta, *Argentina* 126 C2
Calipatria, *U.S.A.* 113 M11
Calistoga, *U.S.A.* 112 G4
Calitri, *Italy* 35 B8
Calitzdorp, *S. Africa* 84 E3
Callabonna, L., *Australia* 91 D3
Callac, *France* 24 D3
Callan, *Ireland* 15 D4
Callander, *U.K.* 14 E4
Callantsoog, *Neths.* 16 C5
Callao, *Peru* 124 C2
Callaway, *U.S.A.* 108 E5
Calles, *Mexico* 115 C5
Callide, *Australia* 90 C5
Calling Lake, *Canada* 100 B6
Calliope, *Australia* 90 C5
Callosa de Ensarriá, *Spain* 29 G4
Callosa de Segura, *Spain* 29 G4
Calola, *Angola* 84 B2
Calolbon, *Phil.* 55 E6
Caloocan, *Phil.* 55 D4
Calore →, *Italy* 35 A7
Caloundra, *Australia* 91 D5
Calpe, *Spain* 29 G5
Calpella, *U.S.A.* 112 F3
Calpine, *U.S.A.* 112 F6
Calstock, *Canada* 98 C3
Caltabellotta, *Italy* 34 E6
Caltagirone, *Italy* 35 E7
Caltanissetta, *Italy* 35 E7
Calulo, *Angola* 80 G2
Calumet, *U.S.A.* 104 B1
Calunda, *Angola* 81 G4
Caluso, *Italy* 32 C4
Calvados □, *France* 24 C6
Calvert, *U.S.A.* 109 K6
Calvert →, *Australia* 90 B2
Calvert Hills, *Australia* 90 B2
Calvert I., *Canada* 100 C3
Calvert Ra., *Australia* 88 D3
Calvi, *France* 27 F12
Calvillo, *Mexico* 114 C4
Calvinia, *S. Africa* 84 E2
Calw, *Germany* 19 G4
Calwa, *U.S.A.* 112 J7
Calzada Almuradiel, *Spain* 29 G1
Calzada de Calatrava, *Spain* 31 G7
Cam →, *U.K.* 13 E8
Cam Lam, *Vietnam* 59 G7
Cam Pha, *Vietnam* 58 B6
Cam Ranh, *Vietnam* 59 G7
Cam Xuyen, *Vietnam* 58 C6
Camabatela, *Angola* 80 F3
Camacã, *Brazil* 123 E4
Camaçari, *Brazil* 123 D4
Camacha, *Madeira* 36 D3
Camacho, *Mexico* 114 C4
Camacupa, *Angola* 81 G3
Camaguán, *Venezuela* 120 B4
Camagüey, *Cuba* 116 B4
Camaiore, *Italy* 32 E7
Camamu, *Brazil* 123 D4
Camaná, *Peru* 124 D3
Camanche Reservoir, *U.S.A.* 112 G6
Camaquã →, *Brazil* 127 C5
Câmara de Lobos, *Madeira* 36 D3
Camararé →, *Brazil* 125 C6
Camarat, C., *France* 27 E10
Camaret, *France* 24 D2
Camargo, *Bolivia* 125 E4
Camargue, *France* 27 E8
Camarillo, *U.S.A.* 113 L7
Camariñas, *Spain* 30 B1
Camarón, C., *Honduras* 116 C2
Camarones, *Argentina* 128 B3
Camarones, B., *Argentina* 128 B3
Camas, *U.S.A.* 112 E4
Camas Valley, *U.S.A.* 110 E2
Cambados, *Spain* 30 C2
Cambará, *Brazil* 127 A5
Cambay = Khambhat, *India* 62 H5
Cambay, G. of = Khambat, G. of, *India* 62 J5
Cambil, *Spain* 29 H1
Cambo-les-Bains, *France* 26 E2
Cambodia ■, *Asia* 58 F5
Camborne, *U.K.* 13 G2
Cambrai, *France* 25 B10
Cambria, *U.S.A.* 111 J3
Cambrian Mts., *U.K.* 13 E4
Cambridge, *Canada* 98 D3
Cambridge, *Jamaica* 116 C4
Cambridge, *N.Z.* 87 G5
Cambridge, *U.K.* 13 E8
Cambridge, *Idaho, U.S.A.* 110 D5
Cambridge, *Mass., U.S.A.* 107 D13
Cambridge, *Md., U.S.A.* 104 F7
Cambridge, *Minn., U.S.A.* 108 C8
Cambridge, *N.Y., U.S.A.* 107 C11
Cambridge, *Nebr., U.S.A.* 108 E4
Cambridge, *Ohio, U.S.A.* 106 F3
Cambridge Bay, *Canada* 96 B9
Cambridge G., *Australia* 88 B4
Cambridge Springs, *U.S.A.* 106 E4
Cambridgeshire □, *U.K.* 13 E8
Cambrils, *Spain* 28 D6
Cambuci, *Brazil* 123 F3
Cambundi-Catembo, *Angola* 80 G3
Camden, *Ala., U.S.A.* 105 K2
Camden, *Ark., U.S.A.* 109 J8
Camden, *Maine, U.S.A.* 99 D6
Camden, *N.J., U.S.A.* 107 G9
Camden, *S.C., U.S.A.* 105 H5
Camden Sd., *Australia* 88 C3
Camdenton, *U.S.A.* 109 F8
Çameli, *Turkey* 66 D3
Camembert, *France* 24 D7
Cámeri, *Italy* 32 C5
Camerino, *Italy* 33 E10
Cameron, *Ariz., U.S.A.* 111 J8
Cameron, *La., U.S.A.* 109 L8
Cameron, *Mo., U.S.A.* 108 F7
Cameron, *Tex., U.S.A.* 109 K6
Cameron Falls, *Canada* 98 C2
Cameron Highlands, *Malaysia* 59 K3
Cameron Hills, *Canada* 100 B5
Cameroon ■, *Africa* 73 G7
Camerota, *Italy* 35 B8
Cameroun →, *Cameroon* 79 E6
Cameroun, Mt., *Cameroon* 79 E6
Cametá, *Brazil* 122 B2
Camiguin □, *Phil.* 55 G6
Camiguin I., *Phil.* 55 B4
Camiling, *Phil.* 55 D4
Caminha, *Portugal* 30 D2
Camino, *U.S.A.* 112 G6
Camira Creek, *Australia* 91 D5
Camiranga, *Brazil* 122 B2
Camiri, *Bolivia* 125 E5
Camissombo, *Angola* 80 F4
Cammal, *U.S.A.* 106 E7
Camocim, *Brazil* 122 B3
Camogli, *Italy* 32 D6
Camooweal, *Australia* 90 B2
Camopi, *Fr. Guiana* 121 C7
Camopi →, *Fr. Guiana* 121 C7
Camotes Is., *Phil.* 55 F6
Camotes Sea, *Phil.* 55 F6
Camp Crook, *U.S.A.* 108 C3
Camp Nelson, *U.S.A.* 113 J8
Camp Wood, *U.S.A.* 109 L4
Campagna, *Italy* 35 B8
Campana, *Argentina* 126 C4
Campana, I., *Chile* 128 C1
Campanário, *Madeira* 36 D2
Campanario, *Spain* 31 G5
Campània □, *Italy* 35 B7
Campbell, *S. Africa* 84 D3
Campbell, *Calif., U.S.A.* 112 H5
Campbell, *Ohio, U.S.A.* 106 E4
Campbell I., *Pac. Oc.* 92 N8
Campbell L., *Canada* 101 A7
Campbell River, *Canada* 100 C3
Campbell Town, *Australia* 90 G4
Campbellford, *Canada* 106 B7
Campbellpur, *Pakistan* 62 C5
Campbellsville, *U.S.A.* 104 G3
Campbellton, *Canada* 99 C6
Campbelltown, *Australia* 91 E5
Campbeltown, *U.K.* 14 F3
Campeche, *Mexico* 115 D6
Campeche □, *Mexico* 115 D6
Campeche, B. de, *Mexico* 115 D6
Camperdown, *Australia* 91 F3
Camperville, *Canada* 101 C8
Campi Salentina, *Italy* 35 B11
Campidano, *Italy* 34 C1
Campíglia Maríttima, *Italy* 32 E7
Campillo de Altobuey, *Spain* 28 F3
Campillo de Llerena, *Spain* 31 G5
Campillos, *Spain* 31 H6
Campina Grande, *Brazil* 122 C4
Campina Verde, *Brazil* 123 E2
Campinas, *Brazil* 127 A6
Campine, *Belgium* 17 F6
Campli, *Italy* 33 F10
Campo, *Cameroon* 80 D1
Campo, *Spain* 28 C5
Campo Belo, *Brazil* 123 F2
Campo de Criptana, *Spain* 29 F1
Campo de Diauarum, *Brazil* 125 C7
Campo de Gibraltar, *Spain* 31 J5
Campo Flórido, *Brazil* 123 E2
Campo Formoso, *Brazil* 122 D3
Campo Grande, *Brazil* 125 E7
Campo Maíor, *Brazil* 122 B3
Campo Maior, *Portugal* 31 G3
Campo Mourão, *Brazil* 127 A5
Campo Tencia, *Switz.* 23 D7
Campo Túres, *Italy* 33 B8
Campoalegre, *Colombia* 120 C2
Campobasso, *Italy* 35 A7
Campobello di Licata, *Italy* 34 E6
Campobello di Mazara, *Italy* 34 E5
Campofelice di Roccella, *Italy* 34 E6
Camporeale, *Italy* 34 E6
Campos, *Brazil* 123 F3
Campos Altos, *Brazil* 123 E2
Campos Belos, *Brazil* 123 D2
Campos del Puerto, *Spain* 36 B10
Campos Novos, *Brazil* 127 B5
Campos Sales, *Brazil* 122 C3
Camprodón, *Spain* 28 C7
Camptonville, *U.S.A.* 112 F5
Campuya →, *Peru* 120 D3
Camrose, *Canada* 100 C6
Camsell Portage, *Canada* 101 B7
Çan, *Turkey* 66 B2
Can Clavo, *Spain* 36 C7
Can Creu, *Spain* 36 C7
Can Gio, *Vietnam* 59 G6
Can Tho, *Vietnam* 59 G5
Canaan, *U.S.A.* 107 D11
Canada ■, *N. Amer.* 96 C10
Cañada de Gómez, *Argentina* 126 C3
Canadian, *U.S.A.* 109 H4
Canadian →, *U.S.A.* 109 H7
Canadian Shield, *Canada* 97 C10
Çanakkale, *Turkey* 66 B2
Çanakkale Boğazı, *Turkey* 66 B2
Canal Flats, *Canada* 100 C5
Canalejas, *Argentina* 126 D2
Canals, *Argentina* 126 C3
Canals, *Spain* 29 G4
Canandaigua, *U.S.A.* 106 D7
Cananea, *Mexico* 114 A2
Cañar, *Ecuador* 120 D2
Cañar □, *Ecuador* 120 D2
Canarias, Is., *Atl. Oc.* 36 F4
Canarreos, Arch. de los, *Cuba* 116 B3
Canary Is. = Canarias, Is., *Atl. Oc.* 36 F4
Canastra, Serra da, *Brazil* 123 F2
Canatlán, *Mexico* 114 C4
Canaveral, C., *U.S.A.* 105 L5
Cañaveras, *Spain* 28 E2
Canavieiras, *Brazil* 123 E4
Canbelego, *Australia* 91 E4
Canberra, *Australia* 91 F4
Canby, *Calif., U.S.A.* 110 F3
Canby, *Minn., U.S.A.* 108 C6
Canby, *Oreg., U.S.A.* 112 E4
Cancale, *France* 24 D5
Canche →, *France* 25 B8
Canchyuaya, Cordillera de, *Peru* 124 B3
Cancún, *Mexico* 115 C7
Candala, *Somali Rep.* 68 E4
Candarave, *Peru* 124 D3
Candas, *Spain* 30 B5
Candé, *France* 24 E5
Candeias →, *Brazil* 125 B5
Candela, *Italy* 35 A8
Candelaria, *Argentina* 127 B4
Candelaria, *Canary Is.* 36 F3
Candelaria, Pta. de la, *Spain* 30 B2
Candeleda, *Spain* 30 E5
Candelo, *Australia* 91 F4
Candia = Iráklion, *Greece* 37 D7
Candia, Sea of = Crete, Sea of, *Greece* 39 N8
Cândido de Abreu, *Brazil* 123 F1
Cândido Mendes, *Brazil* 122 B2
Candle L., *Canada* 101 C7
Candlemas I., *Antarctica* 5 B1
Cando, *U.S.A.* 108 A5
Candon, *Phil.* 55 C4
Canea = Khaniá, *Greece* 37 D6
Canela, *Brazil* 122 D2
Canelli, *Italy* 32 D5
Canelones, *Uruguay* 127 C4
Canet-Plage, *France* 26 F7
Cañete, *Chile* 126 D1
Cañete, *Peru* 124 C2
Cañete, *Spain* 28 E3
Cañete de las Torres, *Spain* 31 H6
Canfranc, *Spain* 28 C4
Cangas, *Spain* 30 C2
Cangas de Narcea, *Spain* 30 B4
Cangas de Onís, *Spain* 30 B5
Canguaretama, *Brazil* 122 C4
Canguçu, *Brazil* 127 C5
Cangxi, *China* 52 B5
Cangyuan, *China* 52 F2
Cangzhou, *China* 50 E9
Canicattì, *Italy* 34 E6
Canicattini Bagni, *Italy* 35 E8
Canim Lake, *Canada* 100 C4
Canindé, *Brazil* 122 B4
Canindé →, *Brazil* 122 C3
Canindeyu □, *Paraguay* 127 A4
Canipaan, *Phil.* 56 C5
Canisteo, *U.S.A.* 106 D7
Canisteo →, *U.S.A.* 106 D7
Cañitas, *Mexico* 114 C4
Cañizal, *Spain* 30 D5
Canjáyar, *Spain* 29 H2
Çankırı, *Turkey* 66 B5
Cankuzo, *Burundi* 82 C3
Canmore, *Canada* 100 C5
Cann River, *Australia* 91 F4
Canna, *U.K.* 14 D2
Cannanore, *India* 60 P9
Cannes, *France* 27 E11
Canning Town = Port Canning, *India* 63 H13
Cannington, *Canada* 106 B5
Cannock, *U.K.* 12 E5
Cannon Ball →, *U.S.A.* 108 B4
Cannondale Mt., *Australia* 90 D4
Caño Colorado, *Colombia* 120 C4
Canoas, *Brazil* 127 B5
Canoe L., *Canada* 101 B7
Canon City, *U.S.A.* 108 F2
Canora, *Canada* 101 C8
Canosa di Púglia, *Italy* 35 A9
Canowindra, *Australia* 91 E4
Canso, *Canada* 99 C7
Canta, *Peru* 124 C2
Cantabria □, *Spain* 30 B6
Cantabria, Sierra de, *Spain* 28 C2
Cantabrian Mts. = Cantábrica, Cordillera, *Spain* 30 C5
Cantábrica, Cordillera, *Spain* 30 C5
Cantal □, *France* 26 C6
Cantal, Plomb du, *France* 26 C6
Cantanhede, *Portugal* 30 E2
Cantaura, *Venezuela* 121 B5
Cantavieja, *Spain* 28 E4
Canterbury, *Australia* 90 D3
Canterbury, *U.K.* 13 F9
Canterbury □, *N.Z.* 87 K3
Canterbury Bight, *N.Z.* 87 L3
Canterbury Plains, *N.Z.* 87 K3
Cantil, *U.S.A.* 113 K9
Cantillana, *Spain* 31 H5
Canto do Buriti, *Brazil* 122 C3
Canton = Guangzhou, *China* 53 F9
Canton, *Ga., U.S.A.* 105 H3
Canton, *Ill., U.S.A.* 108 E9
Canton, *Miss., U.S.A.* 109 J9
Canton, *Mo., U.S.A.* 108 E9
Canton, *N.Y., U.S.A.* 107 B9
Canton, *Ohio, U.S.A.* 106 F3
Canton, *Okla., U.S.A.* 109 G5
Canton, *S. Dak., U.S.A.* 108 D6
Canton L., *U.S.A.* 109 G5
Cantù, *Italy* 32 C6
Canudos, *Brazil* 125 B6
Canumã, *Amazonas, Brazil* 121 D6
Canumã, *Amazonas, Brazil* 125 B5
Canumã →, *Brazil* 125 A6
Canutama, *Brazil* 125 B5
Canutillo, *U.S.A.* 111 L10
Canyon, *Tex., U.S.A.* 109 H4
Canyon, *Wyo., U.S.A.* 110 D8
Canyonlands National Park, *U.S.A.* 111 G9
Canyonville, *U.S.A.* 110 E2
Canzo, *Italy* 32 C6
Cao Bang, *Vietnam* 58 A6
Cao He →, *China* 51 D13
Cao Lanh, *Vietnam* 59 G5
Cao Xian, *China* 50 G8
Cáorle, *Italy* 33 C9
Cap-aux-Meules, *Canada* 99 C7
Cap-Chat, *Canada* 99 C6
Cap-de-la-Madeleine, *Canada* 98 C5
Cap-Haïtien, *Haiti* 117 C5
Cap St-Jacques = Vung Tau, *Vietnam* 59 G6
Capa, *Vietnam* 58 A4
Capa Stilo, *Italy* 35 D9
Capáccio, *Italy* 35 B8
Capaia, *Angola* 80 F4
Capanaparo →, *Venezuela* 120 B4
Capanema, *Brazil* 122 B2
Caparo →, *Barinas, Venezuela* 120 B3
Caparo →, *Bolívar, Venezuela* 121 B5
Capatárida, *Venezuela* 120 A3
Capbreton, *France* 26 E2
Capdenac, *France* 26 D6
Cape →, *Australia* 90 C4
Cape Barren I., *Australia* 90 G4
Cape Breton Highlands Nat. Park, *Canada* 99 C7
Cape Breton I., *Canada* 99 C7
Cape Charles, *U.S.A.* 104 G8
Cape Coast, *Ghana* 79 D4
Cape Coral, *U.S.A.* 105 M5
Cape Dorset, *Canada* 97 B12
Cape Dyer, *Canada* 97 B13
Cape Fear →, *U.S.A.* 105 H6
Cape Girardeau, *U.S.A.* 109 G10
Cape Jervis, *Australia* 91 F2
Cape May, *U.S.A.* 104 F8
Cape May Point, *U.S.A.* 103 C12
Cape Palmas, *Liberia* 78 E3
Cape Tormentine, *Canada* 99 C7
Cape Town, *S. Africa* 84 E2
Cape Verde Is. ■, *Atl. Oc.* 70 E1
Cape Vincent, *U.S.A.* 107 B8
Cape York Peninsula, *Australia* 90 A3
Capela, *Brazil* 122 D4
Capela de Campo, *Brazil* 122 B3
Capelinha, *Brazil* 123 E3
Capella, *Australia* 90 C4
Capendu, *France* 26 E6
Capestang, *France* 26 E7
Capim, *Brazil* 122 B2
Capim →, *Brazil* 122 B2
Capinópolis, *Brazil* 123 E2
Capinota, *Bolivia* 124 D4
Capitan, *U.S.A.* 111 K11
Capitán Aracena, I., *Chile* 128 D2
Capitán Pastene, *Chile* 128 A2
Capitola, *U.S.A.* 112 J5
Capivara, Serra da, *Brazil* 123 D3
Capizzi, *Italy* 35 E7
Čapljina, *Bos.-H.* 21 M7
Capoche →, *Mozam.* 83 F3
Capoeira, *Brazil* 125 B6
Cappadocia, *Turkey* 66 C6
Capraia, *Italy* 32 E6
Caprarola, *Italy* 33 F9
Capreol, *Canada* 98 C3
Caprera, *Italy* 34 A2
Capri, *Italy* 35 B7
Capricorn Group, *Australia* 90 C5
Capricorn Ra., *Australia* 88 D2
Caprino Veronese, *Italy* 32 C7
Caprivi Strip, *Namibia* 84 B3
Captainganj, *India* 63 F10
Captain's Flat, *Australia* 91 F4
Captieux, *France* 26 D3
Cápua, *Italy* 35 A7
Caquetá □, *Colombia* 120 C3
Caquetá →, *Colombia* 120 D4
Carabobo, *Venezuela* 120 A4
Carabobo □, *Venezuela* 120 A4
Caracal, *Romania* 38 E7
Caracaraí, *Brazil* 121 C5
Caracas, *Venezuela* 120 A4
Caracol, *Brazil* 122 C3
Caracollo, *Bolivia* 124 D4
Caradoc, *Australia* 91 E3
Caráglio, *Italy* 32 D4
Carahue, *Chile* 128 A2
Caraí, *Brazil* 123 E3
Carajás, Serra dos, *Brazil* 122 C1
Caranapatuba, *Brazil* 125 B5
Carandaiti, *Bolivia* 125 E5
Carangola, *Brazil* 123 F3
Carani, *Australia* 89 F2
Caransebeş, *Romania* 38 D5
Carantec, *France* 24 D3
Caraparaná →, *Colombia* 120 D3
Carapelle →, *Italy* 35 A8
Caras, *Peru* 124 B2
Caratasca, L., *Honduras* 116 C3
Caratinga, *Brazil* 123 E3
Caraúbas, *Brazil* 122 C4
Caravaca, *Spain* 29 G3
Caravággio, *Italy* 32 C6
Caravelas, *Brazil* 123 E4
Caraveli, *Peru* 124 D3
Caràzinho, *Brazil* 127 B5
Carballino, *Spain* 30 C2
Carballo, *Spain* 30 B2
Carberry, *Canada* 101 D9
Carbia, *Spain* 30 C2
Carbó, *Mexico* 114 B2
Carbon, *Canada* 100 C6
Carbonara, C., *Italy* 34 C2
Carbondale, *Colo., U.S.A.* 110 G10
Carbondale, *Ill., U.S.A.* 109 G10
Carbondale, *Pa., U.S.A.* 107 E9
Carbonear, *Canada* 99 C9
Carboneras, *Spain* 29 J3
Carboneras de Guadazaón, *Spain* 28 F3
Carbonia, *Italy* 34 C1
Carcabuey, *Spain* 31 H6
Carcagente, *Spain* 29 F4
Carcajou, *Canada* 100 B5
Carcar, *Phil.* 55 F5
Carcasse, C., *Haiti* 117 C5
Carcassonne, *France* 26 E6
Carche, *Spain* 29 G3
Carchi □, *Ecuador* 120 C2
Carcross, *Canada* 96 B6
Cardabia, *Australia* 88 D1
Çardak, *Turkey* 66 D3
Cardamon Hills, *India* 60 Q10
Cárdenas, *Cuba* 116 B3
Cárdenas, *San Luis Potosí, Mexico* 115 C5
Cárdenas, *Tabasco, Mexico* 115 D6
Cardenete, *Spain* 28 F3
Cardiel, L., *Argentina* 128 C2
Cardiff, *U.K.* 13 F4
Cardiff □, *U.K.* 13 F4
Cardiff-by-the-Sea, *U.S.A.* 113 M9
Cardigan, *U.K.* 13 E3

Cardigan B., *U.K.* 13 E3
Cardinal, *Canada* 107 B9
Cardón, Punta, *Venezuela* 120 A3
Cardona, *Spain* 28 D6
Cardona, *Uruguay* 126 C4
Cardoner →, *Spain* 28 D6
Cardross, *Canada* 101 D7
Cardston, *Canada* 100 D6
Cardwell, *Australia* 90 B4
Careen L., *Canada* 101 B7
Carei, *Romania* 38 B5
Careiro, *Brazil* 121 D6
Careme, *Indonesia* 57 G13
Carentan, *France* 24 C5
Carey, *Idaho, U.S.A.* 110 E7
Carey, *Ohio, U.S.A.* 104 E4
Carey, L., *Australia* 89 E3
Carey L., *Canada* 101 A8
Careysburg, *Liberia* 78 D2
Cargèse, *France* 27 F12
Carhaix-Plouguer, *France* 24 D3
Carhuamayo, *Peru* 124 C2
Carhuas, *Peru* 124 B2
Carhué, *Argentina* 126 D3
Caria, *Turkey* 66 D3
Cariacica, *Brazil* 123 F3
Caribbean Sea, *W. Indies* 117 C5
Cariboo Mts., *Canada* 100 C4
Caribou, *U.S.A.* 99 C6
Caribou →, *Man., Canada* 101 B10
Caribou →, *N.W.T., Canada* 100 A3
Caribou I., *Canada* 98 C2
Caribou Is., *Canada* 100 A6
Caribou L., *Man., Canada* 101 B9
Caribou L., *Ont., Canada* 98 B2
Caribou Mts., *Canada* 100 B5
Carichic, *Mexico* 114 B3
Carigara, *Phil.* 55 F6
Carignan, *France* 25 C12
Carignano, *Italy* 32 D4
Carillo, *Mexico* 114 B4
Carinda, *Australia* 91 E4
Cariñena, *Spain* 28 D3
Carinhanha, *Brazil* 123 D3
Carinhanha →, *Brazil* 123 D3
Carini, *Italy* 34 D6
Carinola, *Italy* 34 A6
Caripito, *Venezuela* 121 A5
Caritianas, *Brazil* 125 B5
Carlbrod = Dimitrovgrad, *Serbia, Yug.* 21 M12
Carlentini, *Italy* 35 E8
Carleton Place, *Canada* 98 C4
Carletonville, *S. Africa* 84 D4
Carlin, *U.S.A.* 110 F5
Carlingford L., *U.K.* 15 B5
Carlinville, *U.S.A.* 108 F10
Carlisle, *U.K.* 12 C5
Carlisle, *U.S.A.* 106 F7
Carlit, Pic, *France* 26 F5
Carloforte, *Italy* 34 C1
Carlos Casares, *Argentina* 126 D3
Carlos Chagas, *Brazil* 123 E3
Carlos Tejedor, *Argentina* 126 D3
Carlow, *Ireland* 15 D5
Carlow □, *Ireland* 15 D5
Carlsbad, *Calif., U.S.A.* 113 M9
Carlsbad, *N. Mex., U.S.A.* 109 J2
Carlyle, *Canada* 101 D8
Carlyle, *U.S.A.* 108 F10
Carmacks, *Canada* 96 B6
Carmagnola, *Italy* 32 D4
Carman, *Canada* 101 D9
Carmangay, *Canada* 100 C6
Carmanville, *Canada* 99 C9
Carmarthen, *U.K.* 13 F3
Carmarthen B., *U.K.* 13 F3
Carmarthenshire □, *U.K.* 13 F3
Carmaux, *France* 26 D6
Carmel, *U.S.A.* 107 E11
Carmel-by-the-Sea, *U.S.A.* 111 H3
Carmel Valley, *U.S.A.* 112 J5
Carmelo, *Uruguay* 126 C4
Carmen, *Bolivia* 124 C4
Carmen, *Colombia* 120 B2
Carmen, *Paraguay* 127 B4
Carmen →, *Mexico* 114 A3
Carmen, I., *Mexico* 114 B2
Carmen de Patagones, *Argentina* 128 B4
Cármenes, *Spain* 30 C5
Carmensa, *Argentina* 126 D2
Carmi, *U.S.A.* 104 F1
Carmichael, *U.S.A.* 112 G5
Carmila, *Australia* 90 C4
Carmona, *Spain* 31 H5
Carnac, *France* 24 E3
Carnarvon, *Queens., Australia* 90 C4
Carnarvon, *W. Austral., Australia* 89 D1
Carnarvon, *S. Africa* 84 E3
Carnarvon Ra., *Queens., Australia* 90 D4
Carnarvon Ra., *W. Austral., Australia* 89 E3
Carnation, *U.S.A.* 112 C5
Carnaxide, *Portugal* 31 G1
Carndonagh, *Ireland* 15 A4
Carnduff, *Canada* 101 D8
Carnegie, *U.S.A.* 106 F4
Carnegie, L., *Australia* 89 E3
Carnic Alps = Karnische Alpen, *Europe* 21 J3
Carniche Alpi = Karnische Alpen, *Europe* 21 J3
Carnot, *C.A.R.* 80 D3
Carnot, C., *Australia* 91 E2
Carnot B., *Australia* 88 C3
Carnsore Pt., *Ireland* 15 D5
Caro, *U.S.A.* 104 D4
Carol City, *U.S.A.* 105 N5
Carolina, *Brazil* 122 C2
Carolina, *Puerto Rico* 117 C6
Carolina, *S. Africa* 85 D5
Caroline I., *Kiribati* 93 H12
Caroline Is., *Pac. Oc.* 46 J17
Caron, *Canada* 101 C7
Caroni →, *Venezuela* 121 B5
Caroníe = Nébrodi, Monti, *Italy* 35 E7
Caroona, *Australia* 91 E5
Carora, *Venezuela* 120 A3
Carovigno, *Italy* 35 B10
Carpathians, *Europe* 20 F11
Carpaţii Meridionali, *Romania* 38 D8
Carpenédolo, *Italy* 32 C7
Carpentaria, G. of, *Australia* 90 A2
Carpentaria Downs, *Australia* 90 B3
Carpentras, *France* 27 D9
Carpi, *Italy* 32 D7
Carpina, *Brazil* 122 C4
Carpino, *Italy* 35 A8
Carpinteria, *U.S.A.* 113 L7
Carpio, *Spain* 30 D5
Carpolac = Morea, *Australia* 91 F3
Carr Boyd Ra., *Australia* 88 C4
Carrabelle, *U.S.A.* 105 L3
Carranya, *Australia* 88 C4
Carrara, *Italy* 32 D7
Carrascal, *Phil.* 55 G6
Carrascosa del Campo, *Spain* 28 E2
Carrauntoohill, *Ireland* 15 E2
Carretas, Punta, *Peru* 124 C2
Carrick-on-Shannon, *Ireland* 15 C3
Carrick-on-Suir, *Ireland* 15 D4
Carrickfergus, *U.K.* 15 B6
Carrickfergus □, *U.K.* 15 B6
Carrickmacross, *Ireland* 15 C5
Carrieton, *Australia* 91 E2
Carrington, *U.S.A.* 108 B5
Carrión →, *Spain* 30 D6
Carrión de los Condes, *Spain* 30 C6
Carrizal Bajo, *Chile* 126 B1
Carrizalillo, *Chile* 126 B1
Carrizo Cr. →, *U.S.A.* 109 G3
Carrizo Springs, *U.S.A.* 109 L5
Carrizozo, *U.S.A.* 111 K11
Carroll, *U.S.A.* 108 D7
Carrollton, *Ga., U.S.A.* 105 J3
Carrollton, *Ill., U.S.A.* 108 F9
Carrollton, *Ky., U.S.A.* 104 F3
Carrollton, *Mo., U.S.A.* 108 F8
Carrollton, *Ohio, U.S.A.* 106 F3
Carron →, *U.K.* 14 D3
Carron, L., *U.K.* 14 D3
Carrot →, *Canada* 101 C8
Carrot River, *Canada* 101 C8
Carrouges, *France* 24 D6
Carruthers, *Canada* 101 C7
Çarşamba, *Turkey* 66 B7
Carse of Gowrie, *U.K.* 14 E5
Carsóli, *Italy* 33 F10
Carson, *Calif., U.S.A.* 113 M8
Carson, *N. Dak., U.S.A.* 108 B4
Carson →, *U.S.A.* 112 F8
Carson City, *U.S.A.* 112 F7
Carson Sink, *U.S.A.* 110 G4
Carstairs, *U.K.* 14 F5
Cartagena, *Colombia* 120 A2
Cartagena, *Spain* 29 H4
Cartago, *Colombia* 120 C2
Cartago, *Costa Rica* 116 E3
Cartaxo, *Portugal* 31 F2
Cartaya, *Spain* 31 H3
Carteret, *France* 24 C5
Cartersville, *U.S.A.* 105 H3
Carterton, *N.Z.* 87 J5
Carthage, *Ark., U.S.A.* 109 H8
Carthage, *Ill., U.S.A.* 108 E9
Carthage, *Mo., U.S.A.* 109 G7
Carthage, *S. Dak., U.S.A.* 108 C6
Carthage, *Tex., U.S.A.* 109 J7
Cartier I., *Australia* 88 B3
Cartwright, *Canada* 99 B8
Caruaru, *Brazil* 122 C4
Carúpano, *Venezuela* 121 A5
Carutapera, *Brazil* 122 B2
Caruthersville, *U.S.A.* 109 G10
Carvalho, *Brazil* 121 D7
Carvin, *France* 25 B9
Carvoeiro, *Brazil* 121 D5
Carvoeiro, C., *Portugal* 31 F1
Cary, *U.S.A.* 105 H6
Casa Branca, *Brazil* 123 F2
Casa Branca, *Portugal* 31 G2
Casa Grande, *U.S.A.* 111 K8
Casablanca, *Chile* 126 C1
Casablanca, *Morocco* 74 B3
Casacalenda, *Italy* 35 A7
Casal di Principe, *Italy* 35 B7
Casalbordino, *Italy* 33 F11
Casale Monferrato, *Italy* 32 C5
Casalmaggiore, *Italy* 32 D7
Casalpusterlengo, *Italy* 32 C6
Casamance →, *Senegal* 78 C1
Casamássima, *Italy* 35 B9
Casanare □, *Colombia* 120 B3
Casanare →, *Colombia* 120 B4
Casarano, *Italy* 35 B11
Casares, *Spain* 31 J5
Casas Grandes, *Mexico* 114 A3
Casas Ibañez, *Spain* 29 F3
Casasimarro, *Spain* 29 F2
Casatejada, *Spain* 30 F5
Casavieja, *Spain* 30 E6
Cascade, *Idaho, U.S.A.* 110 D5
Cascade, *Mont., U.S.A.* 110 C8
Cascade Locks, *U.S.A.* 112 E5
Cascade Ra., *U.S.A.* 112 D5
Cascade Range, *U.S.A.* 94 E7
Cascais, *Portugal* 31 G1
Cascavel, *Brazil* 127 A5
Cáscina, *Italy* 32 E7
Caselle Torinese, *Italy* 32 C4
Caserta, *Italy* 35 A7
Cashel, *Ireland* 15 D4
Cashmere, *U.S.A.* 110 C3
Cashmere Downs, *Australia* 89 E2
Casibare →, *Colombia* 120 C3
Casiguran, *Phil.* 55 C5
Casilda, *Argentina* 126 C3
Casino, *Australia* 91 D5
Casiquiare →, *Venezuela* 120 C4
Casitas, *Peru* 124 A1
Caslan, *Canada* 100 C6
Čáslav, *Czech.* 20 F5
Casma, *Peru* 124 B2
Casmalia, *U.S.A.* 113 L6
Casola Valsenio, *Italy* 33 D8
Cásoli, *Italy* 33 F11
Caspe, *Spain* 28 D4
Casper, *U.S.A.* 110 E10
Caspian Depression, *Eurasia* 43 G9
Caspian Sea, *Eurasia* 44 E6
Casquets, *U.K.* 24 C4
Cass City, *U.S.A.* 104 D4
Cass Lake, *U.S.A.* 108 B7
Cassá de la Selva, *Spain* 28 D7
Cassano Iónio, *Italy* 35 C9
Cassel, *France* 25 B9
Casselman, *Canada* 107 A9
Casselton, *U.S.A.* 108 B6
Cassiar, *Canada* 100 B3
Cassiar Mts., *Canada* 100 B2
Cassilândia, *Brazil* 125 D7
Cassinga, *Angola* 81 H3
Cassino, *Italy* 34 A6
Cassis, *France* 27 E9
Cassville, *U.S.A.* 109 G8
Cástagneto Carducci, *Italy* 32 E7
Castaic, *U.S.A.* 113 L8
Castanhal, *Brazil* 122 B2
Casteau, *Belgium* 17 G4
Castéggio, *Italy* 32 C6
Castejón de Monegros, *Spain* 28 D4
Castel di Sangro, *Italy* 33 G11
Castel San Giovanni, *Italy* 32 C6
Castel San Pietro Terme, *Italy* 33 D8
Castelbuono, *Italy* 35 E7
Casteldelfino, *Italy* 32 D4
Castelfiorentino, *Italy* 32 E7
Castelfranco Emília, *Italy* 32 D8
Castelfranco Véneto, *Italy* 33 C8
Casteljaloux, *France* 26 D4
Castellabate, *Italy* 35 B7
Castellammare, G. di, *Italy* 34 D5
Castellammare del Golfo, *Italy* 34 D5
Castellammare di Stábia, *Italy* 35 B7
Castellamonte, *Italy* 32 C4
Castellana Grotte, *Italy* 35 B10
Castellane, *France* 27 E10
Castellaneta, *Italy* 35 B9
Castellar de Santisteban, *Spain* 29 G1
Castelleone, *Italy* 32 C6
Castelli, *Argentina* 126 D4
Castelló de Ampurias, *Spain* 28 C8
Castellón □, *Spain* 28 E4
Castellón de la Plana, *Spain* 28 F4
Castellote, *Spain* 28 E4
Castelltersol, *Spain* 28 D7
Castelmáuro, *Italy* 35 A7
Castelnau-de-Médoc, *France* 26 C3
Castelnaudary, *France* 26 E5
Castelnovo ne' Monti, *Italy* 32 D7
Castelnuovo di Val di Cécina, *Italy* 32 E7
Castelo, *Brazil* 123 F3
Castelo Branco, *Portugal* 30 F3
Castelo Branco □, *Portugal* 30 F3
Castelo de Paiva, *Portugal* 30 D2
Castelo de Vide, *Portugal* 31 F3
Castelo do Piauí, *Brazil* 122 C3
Castelsarrasin, *France* 26 D5
Casteltérmini, *Italy* 34 E6
Castelvetrano, *Italy* 34 E5
Casterton, *Australia* 91 F3
Castets, *France* 26 E2
Castiglione del Lago, *Italy* 33 E9
Castiglione della Pescáia, *Italy* 32 F7
Castiglione delle Stiviere, *Italy* 32 C7
Castiglione Fiorentino, *Italy* 33 E8
Castilblanco, *Spain* 31 F5
Castilla, *Peru* 124 B1
Castilla, Playa de, *Spain* 31 H4
Castilla La Mancha □, *Spain* 31 F7
Castilla y Leon □, *Spain* 30 D6
Castillon, Barr. de, *France* 27 E10
Castillon-en-Couserans, *France* 26 F5
Castillon-la-Bataille, *France* 26 D3
Castillonès, *France* 26 D4
Castillos, *Uruguay* 127 C5
Castle Dale, *U.S.A.* 110 G8
Castle Douglas, *U.K.* 14 G5
Castle Rock, *Colo., U.S.A.* 108 F2
Castle Rock, *Wash., U.S.A.* 112 D4
Castlebar, *Ireland* 15 C2
Castleblaney, *Ireland* 15 B5
Castlegar, *Canada* 100 D5
Castlemaine, *Australia* 91 F3
Castlerea, *Ireland* 15 C3
Castlereagh □, *U.K.* 15 B6
Castlereagh →, *Australia* 91 E4
Castlereagh B., *Australia* 90 A2
Castletown, *U.K.* 12 C3
Castletown Bearhaven, *Ireland* 15 E2
Castlevale, *Australia* 90 C4
Castor, *Canada* 100 C6
Castres, *France* 26 E6
Castricum, *Neths.* 16 C5
Castries, *St. Lucia* 117 D7
Castril, *Spain* 29 H2
Castro, *Brazil* 127 A5
Castro, *Chile* 128 B2
Castro Alves, *Brazil* 123 D4
Castro del Río, *Spain* 31 H6
Castro Marim, *Portugal* 31 H3
Castro Urdiales, *Spain* 28 B1
Castro Verde, *Portugal* 31 H2
Castrojeriz, *Spain* 30 C6
Castropol, *Spain* 30 B3
Castroreale, *Italy* 35 D8
Castrovíllari, *Italy* 35 C9
Castroville, *Calif., U.S.A.* 112 J5
Castroville, *Tex., U.S.A.* 109 L5
Castrovirreyna, *Peru* 124 C2
Castuera, *Spain* 31 G5
Casummit Lake, *Canada* 98 B1
Çat, *Turkey* 67 C9
Cat Ba, Dao, *Vietnam* 58 B6
Cat I., *Bahamas* 117 B4
Cat I., *U.S.A.* 109 K10
Cat L., *Canada* 98 B1
Catacamas, *Honduras* 116 D2
Catacáos, *Peru* 124 B1
Cataguases, *Brazil* 123 F3
Catahoula L., *U.S.A.* 109 K8
Çatak, *Turkey* 67 C10
Catalão, *Brazil* 123 E2
Çatalca, *Turkey* 66 B3
Catalina, *Canada* 99 C9
Catalonia = Cataluña □, *Spain* 28 D6
Cataluña □, *Spain* 28 D6
Çatalzeytin, *Turkey* 66 B6
Catamarca, *Argentina* 126 B2
Catamarca □, *Argentina* 126 B2
Catanauan, *Phil.* 55 E5
Catanduanes, *Phil.* 55 E6
Catanduva, *Brazil* 127 A6
Catánia, *Italy* 35 E8
Catánia, G. di, *Italy* 35 E8
Catanzaro, *Italy* 35 D9
Catarman, *Phil.* 55 E6
Catbalogan, *Phil.* 55 F6
Cateel, *Phil.* 55 H7
Catende, *Brazil* 122 C4
Cathcart, *S. Africa* 84 E4
Cathlamet, *U.S.A.* 112 D3
Catio, *Guinea-Biss.* 78 C1
Catismiña, *Venezuela* 121 C5
Catita, *Brazil* 122 C3
Catlettsburg, *U.S.A.* 104 F4
Catoche, C., *Mexico* 115 C7
Catolé do Rocha, *Brazil* 122 C4
Catral, *Spain* 29 G4
Catria, Mt., *Italy* 33 E9
Catrimani, *Brazil* 121 C5
Catrimani →, *Brazil* 121 C5
Catskill, *U.S.A.* 107 D11
Catskill Mts., *U.S.A.* 107 D10
Catt, Mt., *Australia* 90 A1
Cattaraugus, *U.S.A.* 106 D6
Cattólica, *Italy* 33 E9
Cattólica Eraclea, *Italy* 34 E6
Catu, *Brazil* 123 D4
Catuala, *Angola* 84 B2
Catur, *Mozam.* 83 E4
Catwick Is., *Vietnam* 59 G7
Cauca □, *Colombia* 120 C2
Cauca →, *Colombia* 120 B3
Caucaia, *Brazil* 122 B4
Caucasia, *Colombia* 120 B2
Caucasus Mountains, *Eurasia* 43 J7
Caudebec-en-Caux, *France* 24 C7
Caudebec-lès-Elbeuf, *France* 24 C8
Caudete, *Spain* 29 G3
Caudry, *France* 25 B10
Caulnes, *France* 24 D4
Caulónia, *Italy* 35 D9
Caúngula, *Angola* 80 F3
Cauquenes, *Chile* 126 D1
Caura →, *Venezuela* 121 B5
Caurés →, *Brazil* 121 D5
Cauresi →, *Mozam.* 83 F3
Causapscal, *Canada* 99 C6
Caussade, *France* 26 D5
Causse-Méjean, *France* 26 D7
Cauterets, *France* 26 F3
Cautín □, *Chile* 128 A2
Cauvery →, *India* 60 P11
Caux, Pays de, *France* 24 C7
Cava dei Tirreni, *Italy* 35 B7
Cávado →, *Portugal* 30 D2
Cavaillon, *France* 27 E9
Cavalaire-sur-Mer, *France* 27 E10
Cavalcante, *Brazil* 123 D2
Cavalese, *Italy* 33 B8
Cavalier, *U.S.A.* 108 A6
Cavalla = Cavally →, *Africa* 78 E3
Cavallo, I. de, *France* 27 G13
Cavally →, *Africa* 78 E3
Cavan, *Ireland* 15 C4
Cavan □, *Ireland* 15 C4
Cavárzere, *Italy* 33 C9
Cave City, *U.S.A.* 104 G3
Cavenagh Ra., *Australia* 89 E4
Cavendish, *Australia* 91 F3
Caviana, I., *Brazil* 121 C7
Cavite, *Phil.* 55 D4
Cavour, *Italy* 32 D4
Cavtat, *Croatia* 21 N8
Cawndilla L., *Australia* 91 E3
Cawnpore = Kanpur, *India* 63 F9
Caxias, *Brazil* 122 B3
Caxias do Sul, *Brazil* 127 B5
Caxito, *Angola* 80 F2
Çay, *Turkey* 66 C4
Cay Sal Bank, *Bahamas* 116 B3
Cayambe, *Napo, Ecuador* 120 C2
Cayambe, *Quito, Ecuador* 120 C2
Çaycuma, *Turkey* 66 B5
Çayeli, *Turkey* 67 B9
Cayenne, *Fr. Guiana* 121 B7
Cayenne □, *Fr. Guiana* 121 C7
Cayeux-sur-Mer, *France* 25 B8
Cayiralan, *Turkey* 66 C6
Caylus, *France* 26 D5
Cayman Brac, *Cayman Is.* 116 C4
Cayman Is. ■, *W. Indies* 116 C3
Cayo Romano, *Cuba* 117 B4
Cayuga, *Canada* 106 D5
Cayuga, *U.S.A.* 107 D8
Cayuga L., *U.S.A.* 107 D8
Cazalla de la Sierra, *Spain* 31 H5
Căzăneşti, *Romania* 38 E10
Cazaux et de Sanguinet, Étang de, *France* 26 D2
Cazères, *France* 26 E5
Cazin, *Bos.-H.* 33 D12
Čazma, *Croatia* 33 C13
Čazma →, *Croatia* 33 C13
Cazombo, *Angola* 81 G4
Cazorla, *Spain* 29 H1
Cazorla, *Venezuela* 120 B4
Cazorla, Sierra de, *Spain* 29 G2
Cea →, *Spain* 30 C5
Ceadâr-Lunga, *Moldova* 41 J5
Ceanannus Mor, *Ireland* 15 C5
Ceará = Fortaleza, *Brazil* 122 B4
Ceará □, *Brazil* 122 C4
Ceará Mirim, *Brazil* 122 C4
Cebaco, I. de, *Panama* 116 E3
Cebollar, *Argentina* 126 B2
Cebollera, Sierra de, *Spain* 28 D2
Cebreros, *Spain* 30 E6
Cebu, *Phil.* 55 F5
Ceccano, *Italy* 34 A6
Cechi, *Ivory C.* 78 D4
Čechy, *Czech.* 19 F9
Cecil Plains, *Australia* 91 D5
Cécina, *Italy* 32 E7
Cécina →, *Italy* 32 E7
Ceclavin, *Spain* 30 F4
Cedar →, *U.S.A.* 108 E9
Cedar City, *U.S.A.* 111 H7
Cedar Creek Reservoir, *U.S.A.* 109 J6
Cedar Falls, *Iowa, U.S.A.* 108 D8
Cedar Falls, *Wash., U.S.A.* 112 C5
Cedar Key, *U.S.A.* 105 L4
Cedar L., *Canada* 101 C8
Cedar Rapids, *U.S.A.* 108 E9
Cedartown, *U.S.A.* 105 H3
Cedarvale, *Canada* 100 B3
Cedarville, *S. Africa* 85 E4
Cedarville, *U.S.A.* 110 F3
Cedeira, *Spain* 30 B2
Cedral, *Mexico* 114 C4
Cedrino →, *Italy* 34 B2
Cedro, *Brazil* 122 C4
Cedros, I. de, *Mexico* 114 B1
Ceduna, *Australia* 91 E1
Cefalù, *Italy* 35 D7
Cega →, *Spain* 30 D6
Cegléd, *Hungary* 21 H9
Céglie Messápico, *Italy* 35 B10
Cehegín, *Spain* 29 G3
Ceheng, *China* 52 E5
Cehu-Silvaniei, *Romania* 38 B6
Ceira →, *Portugal* 30 E2
Cekhira, *Tunisia* 75 B7
Celano, *Italy* 33 F10
Celanova, *Spain* 30 C3
Celaya, *Mexico* 114 C4
Celbridge, *Ireland* 15 C5
Celebes = Sulawesi □, *Indonesia* 57 E6
Celebes Sea, *Indonesia* 57 D6
Čelendín, *Peru* 124 B2
Čelić, *Bos.-H.* 21 L8
Celica, *Ecuador* 120 D2
Celina, *U.S.A.* 104 E3
Celje, *Slovenia* 33 B12

Celle, Germany 18 C6
Celles, Belgium 17 G2
Celorico da Beira, Portugal 30 E3
Cement, U.S.A. 109 H5
Çemişgezek, Turkey 67 C8
Cenepa →, Peru 120 D2
Cengong, China 52 D7
Ceno →, Italy 32 D7
Cenon, France 26 D3
Centallo, Italy 32 D4
Centenário do Sul, Brazil 123 F1
Center, N. Dak., U.S.A. 108 B4
Center, Tex., U.S.A. 109 K7
Centerfield, U.S.A. 111 G8
Centerville, Calif., U.S.A. 112 J7
Centerville, Iowa, U.S.A. 108 E8
Centerville, Pa., U.S.A. 106 F5
Centerville, S. Dak., U.S.A. 108 D6
Centerville, Tenn., U.S.A. 105 H2
Centerville, Tex., U.S.A. 109 K7
Cento, Italy 33 D8
Central, Brazil 122 D3
Central, U.S.A. 111 K9
Central □, Kenya 82 C4
Central □, Malawi 83 E3
Central □, Zambia 83 E2
Central, Cordillera, Bolivia 125 D5
Central, Cordillera, Colombia 120 C2
Central, Cordillera, Costa Rica 116 D3
Central, Cordillera, Dom. Rep. 117 C5
Central, Cordillera, Peru 124 B2
Central, Cordillera, Phil. 55 C4
Central, Sistema, Spain 30 E5
Central African Rep. ■, Africa 73 G9
Central City, Ky., U.S.A. 104 G2
Central City, Nebr., U.S.A. 108 E5
Central I., Kenya 82 B4
Central Makran Range, Pakistan 60 F4
Central Patricia, Canada 98 B1
Central Russian Uplands, Europe 6 E13
Central Siberian Plateau, Russia 46 C14
Centralia, Ill., U.S.A. 108 F10
Centralia, Mo., U.S.A. 108 F8
Centralia, Wash., U.S.A. 112 D4
Centreville, Ala., U.S.A. 105 J2
Centreville, Miss., U.S.A. 109 K9
Centúripe, Italy 35 E7
Cephalonia = Kefallinía, Greece 39 L3
Ceprano, Italy 34 A6
Cepu, Indonesia 57 G14
Ceram = Seram, Indonesia 57 E7
Ceram Sea = Seram Sea, Indonesia 57 E7
Cerbère, France 26 F7
Cerbicales, Is., France 27 G13
Cercal, Portugal 31 H2
Cercemaggiore, Italy 35 A7
Cerdaña, Spain 28 C6
Cerdedo, Spain 30 C2
Cère →, France 26 D5
Cerea, Italy 33 C8
Ceres, Argentina 126 B3
Ceres, Brazil 123 E2
Ceres, Italy 32 C4
Ceres, S. Africa 84 E2
Ceres, U.S.A. 112 H6
Céret, France 26 F6
Cereté, Colombia 120 B2
Cerfontaine, Belgium 17 H4
Ceridigion □, U.K. 13 E3
Cerignola, Italy 35 A8
Cerigo = Kíthira, Greece 39 N7
Cérilly, France 26 B6
Cerisiers, France 25 D10
Cerizay, France 24 F6
Çerkeş, Turkey 66 B5
Çerkeşköy, Turkey 66 B2
Cerknica, Slovenia 33 C11
Çermik, Turkey 67 C8
Cerna →, Romania 38 E7
Cernavodă, Romania 38 E11
Cernay, France 25 E14
Cernik, Croatia 21 K7
Cerralvo, I., Mexico 114 C3
Cerreto Sannita, Italy 35 A7
Cerritos, Mexico 114 C4
Cerro Sombrero, Chile 128 D3
Certaldo, Italy 32 E8
Cervaro →, Italy 35 A8
Cervera, Spain 28 D6
Cervera de Pisuerga, Spain 30 C6
Cervera del Río Alhama, Spain 28 C3
Cérvia, Italy 33 D9
Cervignano del Friuli, Italy 33 C10
Cervinara, Italy 35 A7
Cervione, France 27 F13
Cervo, Spain 30 B3
César □, Colombia 120 B3
Cesaro, Italy 35 E7
Cesena, Italy 33 D9
Cesenático, Italy 33 D9
Cēsis, Latvia 9 H21
Česká Lípa, Czech. 20 E4
Česká Republika = Czech Rep. ■, Europe 20 F4
České Budějovice, Czech. 20 G4
Ceskomoravská Vrchovina, Czech. 20 F5
Český Brod, Czech. 20 E4
Český Krumlov, Czech. 20 G4
Český Těšin, Czech. 20 F8
Çeşme, Turkey 66 C2
Cessnock, Australia 91 E5
Cestos →, Liberia 78 D3
Cétin Grad, Croatia 33 C12
Cetina →, Croatia 33 E13
Cetraro, Italy 35 C8
Ceuta, N. Afr. 74 A3
Ceva, Italy 32 D5
Cévennes, France 26 D7
Ceyhan, Turkey 66 D6
Ceyhan →, Turkey 66 D6
Ceylânpınar, Turkey 67 D9
Ceylon = Sri Lanka ■, Asia 60 R12
Cèze →, France 27 D8
Cha-am, Thailand 58 F2
Chaam, Neths. 17 E5
Chabeuil, France 27 D9
Chablais, France 27 B10
Chablis, France 25 E10
Chabounia, Algeria 75 A5
Chacabuco, Argentina 126 C3
Chachapoyas, Peru 124 B2
Chachasp, Peru 124 D3
Chachoengsao, Thailand 58 F3
Chachran, Pakistan 60 E7
Chachro, Pakistan 62 G4
Chaco □, Argentina 126 B3
Chaco □, Paraguay 126 B3
Chad ■, Africa 73 E8
Chad, L. = Tchad, L., Chad 73 F7
Chadan, Russia 45 D10
Chadileuvú →, Argentina 126 D2
Chadiza, Zambia 83 E3
Chadron, U.S.A. 108 D3
Chadyr-Lunga = Ceadâr-Lunga, Moldova 41 J5
Chae Hom, Thailand 58 C2
Chaem →, Thailand 58 C2
Chaeryŏng, N. Korea 51 E13
Chagai Hills, Afghan. 60 E3
Chagda, Russia 45 D14
Chagny, France 25 F11
Chagoda, Russia 40 C8
Chagos Arch., Ind. Oc. 47 K11
Chāh Ākhvor, Iran 65 C8
Chāh Bahār, Iran 65 E9
Chāh-e-Malek, Iran 65 D8
Chāh Kavīr, Iran 65 D7
Chahar Burjak, Afghan. 60 D3
Chaibasa, India 61 H14
Chaillé-les-Marais, France 26 B2
Chainat, Thailand 58 E3
Chaitén, Chile 128 B2
Chaiya, Thailand 59 H2
Chaj Doab, Pakistan 62 C5
Chajari, Argentina 126 C4
Chake Chake, Tanzania 82 D4
Chakhānsūr, Afghan. 60 D3
Chakonipau, L., Canada 99 A6
Chakradharpur, India 63 H11
Chakwal, Pakistan 62 C5
Chala, Peru 124 D3
Chalais, France 26 C4
Chalchihuites, Mexico 114 C4
Chalcis = Khalkís, Greece 39 L6
Chaleur B., Canada 99 C6
Chalfant, U.S.A. 112 H8
Chalhuanca, Peru 124 C3
Chalindrey, France 25 E12
Chaling, China 53 D9
Chalisgaon, India 60 J9
Chalky Inlet, N.Z. 87 M1
Challans, France 24 F5
Challapata, Bolivia 124 D4
Challis, U.S.A. 110 D6
Chalna, India 63 H13
Chalon-sur-Saône, France 25 F11
Chalonnes-sur-Loire, France 24 E6
Châlons-en-Champagne, France 25 D11
Châlus, France 26 C4
Chalyaphum, Thailand 58 E4
Cham, Germany 19 F8
Cham, Switz. 23 B6
Cham, Cu Lao, Vietnam 58 E7
Chama, U.S.A. 111 H10
Chaman, Pakistan 60 D5
Chamba, India 62 C7
Chamba, Tanzania 83 E4
Chambal →, India 63 F8
Chamberlain, U.S.A. 108 D5
Chamberlain →, Australia 88 C4
Chambers, U.S.A. 111 J9
Chambersburg, U.S.A. 104 F7
Chambéry, France 27 C9
Chambly, Canada 107 A11
Chambord, Canada 99 C5
Chamchamal, Iraq 67 E11
Chamela, Mexico 114 D3
Chamical, Argentina 126 C2
Chamkar Luong, Cambodia 59 G4
Chamonix-Mont Blanc, France 27 C10
Champa, India 63 H10
Champagne, Canada 100 A1
Champagne, France 25 D11
Champagne, Plaine de, France 25 D11
Champagnole, France 25 F12
Champaign, U.S.A. 104 E1
Champassak, Laos 58 E5
Champaubert, France 25 D10
Champdeniers, France 26 B3
Champeix, France 26 C7
Champlain, Canada 104 B9
Champlain, U.S.A. 107 B11
Champlain, L., U.S.A. 107 B11
Champotón, Mexico 115 D6
Chamusca, Portugal 31 F2
Chan Chan, Peru 124 B2
Chana, Thailand 59 J3
Chañaral, Chile 126 B1
Chanārān, Iran 65 B8
Chanasma, India 62 H5
Chancay, Peru 124 C2
Chancy, Switz. 22 D1
Chandannagar, India 63 H13
Chandausi, India 63 E8
Chandeleur Is., U.S.A. 109 L10
Chandeleur Sd., U.S.A. 109 L10
Chandigarh, India 62 D7
Chandler, Australia 91 D1
Chandler, Canada 99 C7
Chandler, Ariz., U.S.A. 111 K8
Chandler, Okla., U.S.A. 109 H6
Chandless →, Brazil 124 B4
Chandmani, Mongolia 54 B4
Chandpur, Bangla. 61 H17
Chandpur, India 62 E8
Chandrapur, India 60 K11
Chānf, Iran 65 E9
Chang, Pakistan 62 F3
Chang, Ko, Thailand 59 F4
Ch'ang Chiang = Chang Jiang →, China 53 B13
Chang Jiang →, China 53 B13
Changa, India 63 C7
Changanacheri, India 60 Q10
Changane →, Mozam. 85 C5
Changbai, China 51 D15
Changbai Shan, China 51 C15
Changchiak'ou = Zhangjiakou, China 50 D8
Ch'angchou = Changzhou, China 53 B12
Changchun, China 51 C13
Changchunling, China 51 B13
Changde, China 53 C8
Changdo-ri, N. Korea 51 E14
Changfeng, China 53 A11
Changhai = Shanghai, China 53 B13
Changhua, China 53 B12
Changhua, Taiwan 53 E13
Changhŭng, S. Korea 51 G14
Changhŭngni, N. Korea 51 D15
Changjiang, China 54 E5
Changjin, N. Korea 51 D14
Changjin-chŏsuji, N. Korea 51 D14
Changle, China 53 E12
Changli, China 51 E10
Changling, China 51 B12
Changlun, Malaysia 59 J3
Changning, Hunan, China 53 D9
Changning, Yunnan, China 52 E2
Changping, China 50 D9
Changsha, China 53 C9
Changshan, China 53 C12
Changshou, China 52 C6
Changshu, China 53 B13
Changshun, China 52 D6
Changtai, China 53 E11
Changting, China 53 E11
Changwu, China 50 G4
Changxing, China 53 B12
Changyang, China 53 B8
Changyi, China 51 F10
Changyŏn, N. Korea 51 E13
Changyuan, China 50 G8
Changzhi, China 50 F7
Changzhou, China 53 B12
Chanhanga, Angola 84 B1
Chanlar = Xanlar, Azerbaijan 43 K8
Channapatna, India 60 N10
Channel Is., U.K. 13 H5
Channel Is., U.S.A. 113 M7
Channel-Port aux Basques, Canada 99 C8
Channing, Mich., U.S.A. 104 B1
Channing, Tex., U.S.A. 109 H3
Chantada, Spain 30 C3
Chanthaburi, Thailand 58 F4
Chantilly, France 25 C9
Chantonnay, France 24 F5
Chantrey Inlet, Canada 96 B10
Chanute, U.S.A. 109 G7
Chanza →, Spain 31 H3
Chao Hu, China 53 B11
Chao Phraya →, Thailand 58 F3
Chao Phraya Lowlands, Thailand 58 E3
Chao Xian, China 53 B11
Chao'an, China 53 F11
Chaocheng, China 50 F8
Chaoyang, Guangdong, China 53 F11
Chaoyang, Liaoning, China 51 D11
Chapada dos Guimarães, Brazil 125 D6
Chapala, Mozam. 83 F4
Chapala, L. de, Mexico 114 C4
Chaparé →, Bolivia 125 D5
Chaparral, Colombia 120 C2
Chapayev, Kazakstan 42 E10
Chapayevsk, Russia 42 D9
Chapecó, Brazil 127 B5
Chapel Hill, U.S.A. 105 H6
Chapleau, Canada 98 C3
Chaplin, Canada 101 C7
Chaplino, Ukraine 41 H9
Chaplygin, Russia 42 D5
Chapra = Chhapra, India 63 G11
Châr, Mauritania 74 D2
Chara, Russia 45 D12
Charadai, Argentina 126 B4
Charagua, Bolivia 125 D5
Charalá, Colombia 120 B3
Charambirá, Punta, Colombia 120 C2
Charaña, Bolivia 124 D4
Charantsavan, Armenia 43 K7
Charapita, Colombia 120 D3
Charata, Argentina 126 B3
Charcas, Mexico 114 C4
Charcoal L., Canada 101 B8
Chard, U.K. 13 G5
Chardara, Kazakstan 44 E7
Chardon, U.S.A. 106 E3
Chardzhou = Chärjew, Turkmenistan 44 F7
Charente □, France 26 C4
Charente →, France 26 C2
Charente-Maritime □, France 26 C3
Chari →, Chad 73 F7
Chārīkār, Afghan. 60 B6
Chariton →, U.S.A. 108 F8
Charity, Guyana 121 B6
Chärjew, Turkmenistan 44 F7
Charkhari, India 63 G8
Charkhi Dadri, India 62 E7
Charleroi, Belgium 17 H4
Charleroi, U.S.A. 106 F5
Charles, C., U.S.A. 104 G8
Charles City, U.S.A. 108 D8
Charles L., Canada 101 B6
Charles Town, U.S.A. 104 F7
Charleston, Ill., U.S.A. 104 F1
Charleston, Miss., U.S.A. 109 H9
Charleston, Mo., U.S.A. 109 G10
Charleston, S.C., U.S.A. 105 J6
Charleston, W. Va., U.S.A. 104 F5
Charleston Peak, U.S.A. 113 J11
Charlestown, S. Africa 85 D4
Charlestown, U.S.A. 104 F3
Charlesville, Zaïre 80 F4
Charleville = Rath Luirc, Ireland 15 D3
Charleville, Australia 91 D4
Charleville-Mézières, France 25 C11
Charlevoix, U.S.A. 104 C3
Charlieu, France 27 B8
Charlotte, Mich., U.S.A. 104 D3
Charlotte, N.C., U.S.A. 105 H5
Charlotte Amalie, Virgin Is. 117 C7
Charlotte Harbor, U.S.A. 105 M4
Charlottesville, U.S.A. 104 F6
Charlottetown, Canada 99 C7
Charlton, Australia 91 F3
Charlton, U.S.A. 108 E8
Charlton I., Canada 98 B4
Charmes, France 25 D13
Charny, Canada 99 C5
Charolles, France 27 B8
Chârost, France 25 F9
Charouine, Algeria 75 C4
Charre, Mozam. 83 F4
Charroux, France 26 B4
Charsadda, Pakistan 62 B4
Charters Towers, Australia 90 C4
Chartres, France 24 D8
Chascomús, Argentina 126 D4
Chasefu, Zambia 83 E3
Chasovnya-Uchurskaya, Russia 45 D14
Chasseneuil-sur-Bonnieure, France 26 C4
Chāt, Iran 65 B7
Chatal Balkan = Udvoy Balkan, Bulgaria 38 G9
Château-Arnoux, France 27 D10
Château-Chinon, France 25 E10
Château d'Oex, Switz. 22 D4
Château-du-Loir, France 24 E7
Château-Gontier, France 24 E6
Château-la-Vallière, France 24 E7
Château-Landon, France 25 D9
Château-Porcien, France 25 C11
Château-Renault, France 24 E7
Château-Salins, France 25 D13
Château-Thierry, France 25 C10
Châteaubourg, France 24 D5
Châteaubriant, France 24 E5
Châteaudun, France 24 D8
Châteaugiron, France 24 D5
Châteaulin, France 24 D2
Châteaumeillant, France 26 B6
Châteauneuf-du-Faou, France 24 D3
Châteauneuf-en-Thymerais, France 24 D8
Châteauneuf-sur-Charente, France 26 C3
Châteauneuf-sur-Cher, France 25 F9
Châteauneuf-sur-Loire, France 25 E9
Châteaurenard, Bouches-du-Rhône, France 27 E8
Châteaurenard, Loiret, France 25 E9
Châteauroux, France 25 F8
Châtel-St.-Denis, Switz. 22 C3
Châtelaillon-Plage, France 26 B2
Châtelaudren, France 24 D4
Chatelet, Belgium 17 H5
Châtelguyon, France 26 C7
Châtellerault, France 24 F7
Châtelus-Malvaleix, France 26 B6
Chatfield, U.S.A. 108 D9
Chatham, N.B., Canada 99 C6
Chatham, Ont., Canada 98 D3
Chatham, U.K. 13 F8
Chatham, La., U.S.A. 109 J8
Chatham, N.Y., U.S.A. 107 D11
Chatham, I., Chile 128 D2
Chatham Is., Pac. Oc. 92 M10
Chatham Str., U.S.A. 100 B2
Châtillon, Italy 32 C4
Châtillon-Coligny, France 25 E9
Châtillon-en-Bazois, France 25 E10
Châtillon-en-Diois, France 27 D9
Châtillon-sur-Indre, France 24 F8
Châtillon-sur-Loire, France 25 E9
Châtillon-sur-Marne, France 25 C10
Châtillon-sur-Seine, France 25 E11
Chatmohar, Bangla. 63 G13
Chatra, India 63 G11
Chatrapur, India 61 K14
Chats, L. des, Canada 107 A8
Chatsworth, Canada 106 B4
Chatsworth, Zimbabwe 83 F3
Chattahoochee →, U.S.A. 105 K3
Chattanooga, U.S.A. 105 H3
Chaturat, Thailand 58 E3
Chau Doc, Vietnam 59 G5
Chaudanne, Barr. de, France 27 E10
Chaudes-Aigues, France 26 D7
Chauffailles, France 27 B8
Chauk, Burma 61 J19
Chaukan La, Burma 61 F20
Chaulnes, France 25 C9
Chaumont, France 25 D12
Chaumont, U.S.A. 107 B8
Chaumont-en-Vexin, France 25 C8
Chaumont-sur-Loire, France 24 E8
Chaunay, France 26 B4
Chauny, France 25 C10
Chausey, Is., France 24 D5
Chaussin, France 25 F12
Chautauqua L., U.S.A. 106 D5
Chauvigny, France 24 F7
Chauvin, Canada 101 C6
Chavantina, Brazil 125 C7
Chaves, Brazil 122 B2
Chaves, Portugal 30 D3
Chavuma, Zambia 81 G4
Chawang, Thailand 59 H2
Chazelles-sur-Lyon, France 27 C8
Chazuta, Peru 124 B2
Chazy, U.S.A. 107 B11
Cheb, Czech. 20 E2
Cheboksarskoye Vdkhr., Russia 42 B8
Cheboksary, Russia 42 B8
Cheboygan, U.S.A. 104 C3
Chebsara, Russia 40 C10
Chech, Erg, Africa 74 D4
Chechaouen, Morocco 74 A3
Chechen, Ostrov, Russia 43 H8
Chechenia □, Russia 43 J7
Checheno-Ingush Republic = Chechenia □, Russia 43 J7
Chechnya = Chechenia □, Russia 43 J7
Chechon, S. Korea 51 F15
Chęciny, Poland 20 E10
Checleset B., Canada 100 C3
Checotah, U.S.A. 109 H7
Chedabucto B., Canada 99 C7
Cheduba I., Burma 61 K18
Cheepie, Australia 91 D4
Chef-Boutonne, France 26 B3
Chegdomyn, Russia 45 D14
Chegga, Mauritania 74 C3
Chegutu, Zimbabwe 83 F3
Chehalis, U.S.A. 112 D4
Cheiron, Mt., France 27 E10
Cheju Do, S. Korea 51 H14
Chekalin, Russia 42 C3
Chekiang = Zhejiang □, China 53 C13
Chel = Kuru, Bahr el →, Sudan 77 F2
Chela, Sa. da, Angola 84 B1
Chelan, U.S.A. 110 C4
Chelan, L., U.S.A. 110 C3
Cheleken, Turkmenistan 44 F6
Chelforó, Argentina 128 A3
Chéliff, O. →, Algeria 75 A5
Chelkar = Shalqar, Kazakstan 44 E6
Chelkar Tengiz, Solonchak, Kazakstan 44 E7
Chellala Dahrania, Algeria 75 B5
Chelles, France 25 D9
Chełm, Poland 20 D13
Chełmek, Poland 20 E9
Chełmno, Poland 20 B8
Chelmsford, U.K. 13 F8
Chełmża, Poland 20 B8
Chelsea, Okla., U.S.A. 109 G7
Chelsea, Vt., U.S.A. 107 C12
Cheltenham, U.K. 13 F5
Chelva, Spain 28 F4
Chelyabinsk, Russia 44 D7
Chelyuskin, C., Russia 46 B14

Chemainus, *Canada* 100 D4
Chembar = Belinskiy, *Russia* 42 D6
Chemillé, *France* 24 E6
Chemnitz, *Germany* 18 E8
Chemult, *U.S.A.* 110 E3
Chen, Gora, *Russia* 45 C15
Chen Xian, *China* 53 E9
Chenab →, *Pakistan* 62 D4
Chenachane, O. →, *Algeria* 74 C4
Chenango Forks, *U.S.A.* 107 D9
Chencha, *Ethiopia* 77 F4
Chenchiang = Zhenjiang, *China* 53 A12
Chênée, *Belgium* 17 G7
Cheney, *U.S.A.* 110 C5
Cheng Xian, *China* 50 H3
Chengbu, *China* 53 D8
Chengcheng, *China* 50 G5
Chengchou = Zhengzhou, *China* 50 G7
Chengde, *China* 51 D9
Chengdong Hu, *China* 53 A11
Chengdu, *China* 52 B5
Chenggong, *China* 52 E4
Chenggu, *China* 50 H4
Chengjiang, *China* 52 E4
Chengkou, *China* 52 B7
Ch'engtu = Chengdu, *China* 52 B5
Chengwu, *China* 50 G8
Chengxi Hu, *China* 53 A11
Chengyang, *China* 51 F11
Chenjiagang, *China* 51 G10
Chenkán, *Mexico* 115 D6
Chenxi, *China* 53 C8
Cheo Reo, *Vietnam* 58 F7
Cheom Ksan, *Cambodia* 58 E5
Chepelare, *Bulgaria* 39 H7
Chepén, *Peru* 124 B2
Chepes, *Argentina* 126 C2
Chepo, *Panama* 116 E4
Cheptulil, Mt., *Kenya* 82 B4
Chequamegon B., *U.S.A.* 108 B9
Cher □, *France* 25 E9
Cher →, *France* 24 E7
Cherasco, *Italy* 32 D4
Cheratte, *Belgium* 17 G7
Cheraw, *U.S.A.* 105 H6
Cherbourg, *France* 24 C5
Cherchell, *Algeria* 75 A5
Cherdakly, *Russia* 42 C9
Cherdyn, *Russia* 44 C6
Cheremkhovo, *Russia* 45 D11
Cherepanovo, *Russia* 44 D9
Cherepovets, *Russia* 40 C9
Chergui, Chott ech, *Algeria* 75 B5
Cherikov = Cherykaw, *Belarus* 40 F6
Cherkasy, *Ukraine* 41 H7
Cherkessk, *Russia* 43 H6
Cherlak, *Russia* 44 D8
Chernaya, *Russia* 45 B9
Cherni, *Bulgaria* 38 G6
Chernigov = Chernihiv, *Ukraine* 41 G6
Chernihiv, *Ukraine* 41 G6
Chernivtsi, *Ukraine* 41 H3
Chernobyl = Chornobyl, *Ukraine* 41 G6
Chernogorsk, *Russia* 45 D10
Chernomorskoye = Chornomorske, *Ukraine* 41 K7
Chernovtsy = Chernivtsi, *Ukraine* 41 H3
Chernyakhovsk, *Russia* 9 J19
Chernyanka, *Russia* 42 E3
Chernyshovskiy, *Russia* 45 C12
Chernyye Zemli, *Russia* 43 H8
Cherokee, *Iowa, U.S.A.* 108 D7
Cherokee, *Okla., U.S.A.* 109 G5
Cherokees, Lake O' The, *U.S.A.* 109 G7
Cherquenco, *Chile* 128 A2
Cherrapunji, *India* 61 G17
Cherry Creek, *U.S.A.* 110 G6
Cherry Valley, *U.S.A.* 113 M10
Cherryvale, *U.S.A.* 109 G7
Cherskiy, *Russia* 45 C17
Cherskogo Khrebet, *Russia* 45 C15
Chertkovo, *Russia* 42 F5
Cherven, *Belarus* 40 F5
Cherven-Bryag, *Bulgaria* 38 F7
Chervonohrad, *Ukraine* 41 G3
Cherwell →, *U.K.* 13 F6
Cherykaw, *Belarus* 40 F6
Chesapeake, *U.S.A.* 104 G7
Chesapeake B., *U.S.A.* 104 F7
Cheshire □, *U.K.* 12 D5
Cheshskaya Guba, *Russia* 44 C5
Cheslatta L., *Canada* 100 C3
Chesley, *Canada* 106 B3
Cheste, *Spain* 29 F4
Chester, *U.K.* 12 D5
Chester, *Calif., U.S.A.* 110 F3
Chester, *Ill., U.S.A.* 109 G10
Chester, *Mont., U.S.A.* 110 B8
Chester, *Pa., U.S.A.* 104 F8
Chester, *S.C., U.S.A.* 105 H5
Chesterfield, *U.K.* 12 D6
Chesterfield, Is., *N. Cal.* 92 J7
Chesterfield Inlet, *Canada* 96 B10
Chesterton Ra., *Australia* 91 D4
Chesterville, *Canada* 107 A9
Chesuncook L., *U.S.A.* 99 C6
Chéticamp, *Canada* 99 C7
Chetumal, B. de, *Mexico* 115 D7
Chetwynd, *Canada* 100 B4
Chevanceaux, *France* 26 C3
Cheviot, The, *U.K.* 12 B5
Cheviot Hills, *U.K.* 12 B5
Cheviot Ra., *Australia* 90 D3
Chew Bahir, *Ethiopia* 77 G4
Chewelah, *U.S.A.* 110 B5
Cheyenne, *Okla., U.S.A.* 109 H5
Cheyenne, *Wyo., U.S.A.* 108 E2
Cheyenne →, *U.S.A.* 108 C4
Cheyenne Wells, *U.S.A.* 108 F3
Cheyne B., *Australia* 89 F2
Chhabra, *India* 62 G7
Chhapra, *India* 63 G11
Chhata, *India* 62 F7
Chhatarpur, *India* 63 G8
Chhep, *Cambodia* 58 F5
Chhindwara, *India* 63 H8
Chhlong, *Cambodia* 59 F5
Chhuk, *Cambodia* 59 G5
Chi →, *Thailand* 58 E5
Chiai, *Taiwan* 53 F13
Chiali, *Taiwan* 53 F13
Chiamis, *Indonesia* 57 G13
Chiamussu = Jiamusi, *China* 54 B8
Chiang Dao, *Thailand* 58 C2
Chiang Kham, *Thailand* 58 C3
Chiang Khan, *Thailand* 58 D3
Chiang Khong, *Thailand* 58 B3
Chiang Mai, *Thailand* 58 C2
Chiang Saen, *Thailand* 58 B3
Chiange, *Angola* 81 H2
Chiapa →, *Mexico* 115 D6
Chiapa de Corzo, *Mexico* 115 D6
Chiapas □, *Mexico* 115 D6
Chiaramonte Gulfi, *Italy* 35 E7
Chiaravalle, *Italy* 33 E10
Chiaravalle Centrale, *Italy* 35 D9
Chiari, *Italy* 32 C6
Chiasso, *Switz.* 23 E8
Chiatura, *Georgia* 43 J6
Chiautla, *Mexico* 115 D5
Chiávari, *Italy* 32 D6
Chiavenna, *Italy* 32 B6
Chiba, *Japan* 49 G10
Chibabava, *Mozam.* 85 C5
Chibatu, *Indonesia* 57 G12
Chibemba, *Cunene, Angola* 81 H2
Chibemba, *Huila, Angola* 84 B2
Chibia, *Angola* 81 H2
Chibougamau, *Canada* 98 C5
Chibougamau L., *Canada* 98 C5
Chibuk, *Nigeria* 79 C7
Chic-Chocs, Mts., *Canada* 99 C6
Chicacole = Srikakulam, *India* 61 K13
Chicago, *U.S.A.* 104 E2
Chicago Heights, *U.S.A.* 104 E2
Chichagof I., *U.S.A.* 100 B1
Chichaoua, *Morocco* 74 B3
Chicheng, *China* 50 D8
Chichester, *U.K.* 13 G7
Chichibu, *Japan* 49 F9
Ch'ich'ihaerh = Qiqihar, *China* 45 E13
Chickasha, *U.S.A.* 109 H5
Chiclana de la Frontera, *Spain* 31 J4
Chiclayo, *Peru* 124 B2
Chico, *U.S.A.* 112 F5
Chico →, *Chubut, Argentina* 128 B3
Chico →, *Santa Cruz, Argentina* 128 C3
Chicomo, *Mozam.* 85 C5
Chicontepec, *Mexico* 115 C5
Chicopee, *U.S.A.* 107 D12
Chicoutimi, *Canada* 99 C5
Chicualacuala, *Mozam.* 85 C5
Chidambaram, *India* 60 P11
Chidenguele, *Mozam.* 85 C5
Chidley, C., *Canada* 97 B13
Chiede, *Angola* 84 B2
Chiefs Pt., *Canada* 106 B3
Chiem Hoa, *Vietnam* 58 A5
Chiemsee, *Germany* 19 H8
Chiengi, *Zambia* 83 D2
Chiengmai = Chiang Mai, *Thailand* 58 C2
Chienti →, *Italy* 33 E10
Chieri, *Italy* 32 D4
Chiers →, *France* 25 C11
Chiese →, *Italy* 32 C7
Chieti, *Italy* 33 F11
Chièvres, *Belgium* 17 G3
Chifeng, *China* 51 C10
Chigirin, *Ukraine* 41 H7
Chignecto B., *Canada* 99 C7
Chigorodó, *Colombia* 120 B2
Chiguana, *Bolivia* 126 A2
Chiha-ri, *N. Korea* 51 E14
Chihli, G. of = Bo Hai, *China* 51 E10
Chihli, G. of = Po Hai, *China* 46 F15
Chihuahua, *Mexico* 114 B3
Chihuahua □, *Mexico* 114 B3
Chiili, *Kazakstan* 44 E7
Chik Bollapur, *India* 60 N10
Chikmagalur, *India* 60 N9
Chikwawa, *Malawi* 83 F3
Chilac, *Mexico* 115 D5
Chilako →, *Canada* 100 C4
Chilam Chavki, *Pakistan* 63 B6
Chilanga, *Zambia* 83 F2
Chilapa, *Mexico* 115 D5
Chilas, *Pakistan* 63 B6
Chilaw, *Sri Lanka* 60 R11
Chilcotin →, *Canada* 100 C4
Childers, *Australia* 91 D5
Childress, *U.S.A.* 109 H4
Chile ■, *S. Amer.* 128 B2
Chile Chico, *Chile* 128 C2
Chile Rise, *Pac. Oc.* 93 L18
Chilecito, *Argentina* 126 B2
Chilete, *Peru* 124 B2
Chilia, Braţul →, *Romania* 38 D12
Chililabombwe, *Zambia* 83 E2
Chilin = Jilin, *China* 51 C14
Chilka L., *India* 61 K14
Chilko →, *Canada* 100 C4
Chilko, L., *Canada* 100 C4
Chillagoe, *Australia* 90 B3
Chillán, *Chile* 126 D1
Chillicothe, *Ill., U.S.A.* 108 E10
Chillicothe, *Mo., U.S.A.* 108 F8
Chillicothe, *Ohio, U.S.A.* 104 F4
Chilliwack, *Canada* 100 D4
Chilo, *India* 62 F5
Chiloane, I., *Mozam.* 85 C5
Chiloé □, *Chile* 128 B2
Chiloé, I. de, *Chile* 128 B2
Chilpancingo, *Mexico* 115 D5
Chiltern Hills, *U.K.* 13 F7
Chilton, *U.S.A.* 104 C1
Chiluage, *Angola* 80 F4
Chilubi, *Zambia* 83 E2
Chilubula, *Zambia* 83 E3
Chilumba, *Malawi* 83 E3
Chilung, *Taiwan* 53 E13
Chilwa, L., *Malawi* 83 F4
Chimaltitán, *Mexico* 114 C4
Chimán, *Panama* 116 E4
Chimay, *Belgium* 17 H4
Chimbay, *Uzbekistan* 44 E6
Chimborazo, *Ecuador* 120 D2
Chimborazo □, *Ecuador* 120 D2
Chimbote, *Peru* 124 B2
Chimkent = Shymkent, *Kazakstan* 44 E7
Chimoio, *Mozam.* 83 F3
Chimpembe, *Zambia* 83 D2
Chin □, *Burma* 61 J18
Chin Ling Shan = Qinling Shandi, *China* 50 H5
China, *Mexico* 115 B5
China ■, *Asia* 50 E3
China Lake, *U.S.A.* 113 K9
Chinacota, *Colombia* 120 B3
Chinan = Jinan, *China* 50 F9
Chinandega, *Nic.* 116 D2
Chinati Peak, *U.S.A.* 109 K2
Chincha Alta, *Peru* 124 C2
Chinchilla, *Australia* 91 D5
Chinchilla de Monte Aragón, *Spain* 29 G3
Chinchón, *Spain* 28 E1
Chinchorro, Banco, *Mexico* 115 D7
Chinchou = Jinzhou, *China* 51 D11
Chincoteague, *U.S.A.* 104 G8
Chinde, *Mozam.* 83 F4
Chindo, *S. Korea* 51 G14
Chindwin →, *Burma* 61 J19
Chineni, *India* 63 C6
Chinga, *Mozam.* 83 F4
Chingola, *Zambia* 83 E2
Chingole, *Malawi* 83 E3
Ch'ingtao = Qingdao, *China* 51 F11
Chinguetti, *Mauritania* 74 D2
Chingune, *Mozam.* 85 C5
Chinhae, *S. Korea* 51 G15
Chinhanguanine, *Mozam.* 85 D5
Chinhoyi, *Zimbabwe* 83 F3
Chiniot, *Pakistan* 62 D5
Chínipas, *Mexico* 114 B3
Chinju, *S. Korea* 51 G15
Chinle, *U.S.A.* 111 H9
Chinmen, *Taiwan* 53 E13
Chinmen Tao, *Taiwan* 53 E13
Chinnampo, *N. Korea* 51 E13
Chino, *Japan* 49 G9
Chino, *U.S.A.* 113 L9
Chino Valley, *U.S.A.* 111 J7
Chinon, *France* 24 E7
Chinook, *Canada* 101 C6
Chinook, *U.S.A.* 110 B9
Chinsali, *Zambia* 83 E3
Chióggia, *Italy* 33 C9
Chíos = Khíos, *Greece* 39 L9
Chipata, *Zambia* 83 E3
Chipewyan L., *Canada* 101 B9
Chipinge, *Zimbabwe* 83 G3
Chipiona, *Spain* 31 J4
Chipley, *U.S.A.* 105 K3
Chipman, *Canada* 99 C6
Chipoka, *Malawi* 83 E3
Chippenham, *U.K.* 13 F5
Chippewa →, *U.S.A.* 108 C8
Chippewa Falls, *U.S.A.* 108 C9
Chiquián, *Peru* 124 C2
Chiquimula, *Guatemala* 116 D2
Chiquinquira, *Colombia* 120 B3
Chiquitos, Llanos de, *Bolivia* 125 D5
Chir →, *Russia* 43 F6
Chirala, *India* 60 M12
Chiramba, *Mozam.* 83 F3
Chirawa, *India* 62 E6
Chirchiq, *Uzbekistan* 44 E7
Chirgua →, *Venezuela* 120 B4
Chiricahua Peak, *U.S.A.* 111 L9
Chiriquí, G. de, *Panama* 116 E3
Chiriquí, L. de, *Panama* 116 E3
Chirivira Falls, *Zimbabwe* 83 G3
Chirmiri, *India* 61 H13
Chiromo, *Malawi* 81 H7
Chirpan, *Bulgaria* 38 G8
Chirripó Grande, Cerro, *Costa Rica* 116 E3
Chisamba, *Zambia* 83 E2
Chisapani Garhi, *Nepal* 61 F14
Chisasibi, *Canada* 98 B4
Ch'ishan, *Taiwan* 53 F13
Chisholm, *Canada* 100 C6
Chishtian Mandi, *Pakistan* 62 E5
Chishui, *China* 52 C5
Chishui He →, *China* 52 C5
Chisimaio, *Somali Rep.* 71 G8
Chisimba Falls, *Zambia* 83 E3
Chişinău, *Moldova* 41 J5
Chisone →, *Italy* 32 D4
Chisos Mts., *U.S.A.* 109 L3
Chistopol, *Russia* 42 C10
Chita, *Colombia* 120 B3
Chita, *Russia* 45 D12
Chitado, *Angola* 81 H2
Chitembo, *Angola* 81 G3
Chitipa, *Malawi* 83 D3
Chitose, *Japan* 48 C10
Chitral, *Pakistan* 60 B7
Chitré, *Panama* 116 E3
Chittagong, *Bangla.* 61 H17
Chittagong □, *Bangla.* 61 G17
Chittaurgarh, *India* 62 G6
Chittoor, *India* 60 N11
Chitungwiza, *Zimbabwe* 83 F3
Chiusa, *Italy* 33 B8
Chiusi, *Italy* 33 E8
Chiva, *Spain* 29 F4
Chivacoa, *Venezuela* 120 A4
Chivasso, *Italy* 32 C4
Chivay, *Peru* 124 D3
Chivhu, *Zimbabwe* 83 F3
Chivilcoy, *Argentina* 126 C4
Chiwanda, *Tanzania* 83 E3
Chixi, *China* 53 G9
Chizera, *Zambia* 83 E1
Chkalov = Orenburg, *Russia* 44 D6
Chkolovsk, *Russia* 42 B6
Chloride, *U.S.A.* 113 K12
Cho Bo, *Vietnam* 58 B5
Cho-do, *N. Korea* 51 E13
Cho Phuoc Hai, *Vietnam* 59 G6
Choba, *Kenya* 82 B4
Chobe National Park, *Botswana* 84 B3
Chochiwŏn, *S. Korea* 51 F14
Chociwel, *Poland* 20 B5
Chocó □, *Colombia* 120 B2
Chocontá, *Colombia* 120 B3
Choctawhatchee B., *U.S.A.* 103 D9
Chodecz, *Poland* 20 C9
Chodziez, *Poland* 20 C6
Choele Choel, *Argentina* 128 A3
Choisy-le-Roi, *France* 25 D9
Choix, *Mexico* 114 B3
Chojnice, *Poland* 20 B7
Chojnów, *Poland* 20 D5
Chŏkai-San, *Japan* 48 E10
Choke, *Ethiopia* 77 E4
Chokurdakh, *Russia* 45 B15
Cholame, *U.S.A.* 112 K6
Cholet, *France* 24 E6
Choluteca, *Honduras* 116 D2
Choluteca →, *Honduras* 116 D2
Chom Bung, *Thailand* 58 F2
Chom Thong, *Thailand* 58 C2
Choma, *Zambia* 83 F2
Chomen Swamp, *Ethiopia* 77 F4
Chomun, *India* 62 F6
Chomutov, *Czech.* 20 E3
Chon Buri, *Thailand* 58 F3
Chon Thanh, *Vietnam* 59 G6
Chonan, *S. Korea* 51 F14
Chone, *Ecuador* 120 D2
Chong Kai, *Cambodia* 58 F4
Chong Mek, *Thailand* 58 E5
Chong'an, *China* 53 D12
Chongde, *China* 53 B13
Chŏngdo, *S. Korea* 51 G15
Chŏngha, *S. Korea* 51 F15
Chŏngjin, *N. Korea* 51 D15
Chŏngju, *N. Korea* 51 E13
Chŏngju, *S. Korea* 51 F14
Chongli, *China* 50 D8
Chongming, *China* 53 B13
Chongming Dao, *China* 53 B13
Chongoyape, *Peru* 124 B2
Chongqing, *Sichuan, China* 52 C6
Chongqing, *Sichuan, China* 52 B4
Chongren, *China* 53 D11
Chŏngŭp, *S. Korea* 51 G14
Chongzuo, *China* 52 F6
Chŏnju, *S. Korea* 51 G14
Chonos, Arch. de los, *Chile* 128 C2
Chop, *Ukraine* 41 H2
Chopim →, *Brazil* 127 B5
Chorbat La, *India* 63 B7
Chorley, *U.K.* 12 D5
Chornobyl, *Ukraine* 41 G6
Chornomorske, *Ukraine* 41 K7
Chorolque, Cerro, *Bolivia* 126 A2
Chorregon, *Australia* 90 C3
Chortkiv, *Ukraine* 41 H3
Chŏrwŏn, *S. Korea* 51 E14
Chorzów, *Poland* 20 E8
Chos-Malal, *Argentina* 126 D1
Chosan, *N. Korea* 51 D13
Choszczno, *Poland* 20 B5
Chota, *Peru* 124 B2
Choteau, *U.S.A.* 110 C7
Chotila, *India* 62 H4
Chowchilla, *U.S.A.* 111 H3
Choybalsan, *Mongolia* 54 B6
Christchurch, *N.Z.* 87 K4
Christchurch, *U.K.* 13 G6
Christian I., *Canada* 106 B4
Christiana, *S. Africa* 84 D4
Christiansfeld, *Denmark* 11 J3
Christiansted, *Virgin Is.* 117 C7
Christie B., *Canada* 101 A6
Christina →, *Canada* 101 B6
Christmas Cr. →, *Australia* 88 C4
Christmas Creek, *Australia* 88 C4
Christmas I. = Kiritimati, *Kiribati* 93 G12
Christmas I., *Ind. Oc.* 92 J2
Christopher L., *Australia* 89 D4
Chrudim, *Czech.* 20 F5
Chrzanów, *Poland* 20 E9
Chtimba, *Malawi* 83 E3
Chu = Shu, *Kazakstan* 44 E8
Chu → = Shu →, *Kazakstan* 46 E10
Chu →, *Vietnam* 58 C5
Chu Chua, *Canada* 100 C4
Chu Lai, *Vietnam* 58 E7
Chu Xian, *China* 53 A12
Ch'uanchou = Quanzhou, *China* 53 E12
Chuankou, *China* 50 G6
Chūbu □, *Japan* 49 F8
Chubut □, *Argentina* 128 B3
Chubut →, *Argentina* 128 B3
Chuchi L., *Canada* 100 B4
Chudovo, *Russia* 40 C6
Chudskoye, Oz., *Russia* 9 G22
Chūgoku □, *Japan* 49 G6
Chūgoku-Sanchi, *Japan* 49 G6
Chuguyev = Chuhuyiv, *Ukraine* 41 H9
Chugwater, *U.S.A.* 108 E2
Chuhuyiv, *Ukraine* 41 H9
Chukchi Sea, *Russia* 45 C19
Chukotskoye Nagorye, *Russia* 45 C18
Chula Vista, *U.S.A.* 113 N9
Chulman, *Russia* 45 D13
Chulucanas, *Peru* 124 B1
Chulumani, *Bolivia* 124 D4
Chulym →, *Russia* 44 D9
Chum Phae, *Thailand* 58 D4
Chum Saeng, *Thailand* 58 E3
Chuma, *Bolivia* 124 D4
Chumar, *India* 63 C8
Chumbicha, *Argentina* 126 B2
Chumerna, *Bulgaria* 38 G8
Chumikan, *Russia* 45 D14
Chumphon, *Thailand* 59 G2
Chumpi, *Peru* 124 D3
Chumuare, *Mozam.* 83 E3
Chumunjin, *S. Korea* 51 F15
Chuna →, *Russia* 45 D10
Chun'an, *China* 53 C12
Chunchŏn, *S. Korea* 51 F14
Chunchura, *India* 63 H13
Chunga, *Zambia* 83 F2
Chunggang-ŭp, *N. Korea* 51 D14
Chunghwa, *N. Korea* 51 E13
Chungju, *S. Korea* 51 F14
Chungking = Chongqing, *China* 52 C6
Chungli, *Taiwan* 53 E13
Chungmu, *S. Korea* 51 G15
Chungt'iaoshan = Zhongtiao Shan, *China* 50 G6
Chungyang Shanmo, *Taiwan* 53 F13
Chunian, *Pakistan* 62 D6
Chunya, *Tanzania* 83 D3
Chunya □, *Tanzania* 82 D3
Chunyang, *China* 51 C15
Chuquibamba, *Peru* 124 D3
Chuquibambilla, *Peru* 124 C3
Chuquicamata, *Chile* 126 A2
Chuquisaca □, *Bolivia* 125 E5
Chur, *Switz.* 23 C9
Churachandpur, *India* 61 G18
Churchill, *Canada* 101 B10
Churchill →, *Man., Canada* 101 B10
Churchill →, *Nfld., Canada* 99 B7
Churchill, C., *Canada* 101 B10
Churchill Falls, *Canada* 99 B7
Churchill L., *Canada* 101 B7
Churchill Pk., *Canada* 100 B3
Churfisten, *Switz.* 23 B8
Churu, *India* 62 E6
Churún Merú = Angel Falls, *Venezuela* 121 B5
Churwalden, *Switz.* 23 C9
Chushal, *India* 63 C8
Chusovoy, *Russia* 44 D6
Chuuronjang, *N. Korea* 51 D15
Chuvash Republic □ = Chuvashia □, *Russia* 42 C8
Chuvashia □, *Russia* 42 C8
Chuwārtah, *Iraq* 64 C5
Chuxiong, *China* 52 E3
Ci Xian, *China* 50 F8
Ciacova, *Romania* 38 D4
Cianjur, *Indonesia* 57 G12
Cibadok, *Indonesia* 57 G12
Cibatu, *Indonesia* 57 G12
Cibola, *U.S.A.* 113 M12
Cicero, *U.S.A.* 104 E2
Cícero Dantas, *Brazil* 122 D4
Cidacos →, *Spain* 28 C3

Cide, Turkey 66 B5
Ciechanów, Poland 20 C10
Ciego de Avila, Cuba 116 B4
Ciénaga, Colombia 120 A3
Ciénaga de Oro, Colombia 120 B2
Cienfuegos, Cuba 116 B3
Cieplice Śląskie Zdrój, Poland 20 E5
Cierp, France 26 F4
Cíes, Is., Spain 30 C2
Cieszyn, Poland 20 F8
Cieza, Spain 29 G3
Çifteler, Turkey 66 C4
Cifuentes, Spain 28 E2
Cihanbeyli, Turkey 66 C5
Cihuatlán, Mexico 114 D4
Cijara, Pantano de, Spain 31 F6
Cijulang, Indonesia 57 G13
Cikajang, Indonesia 57 G12
Cikampek, Indonesia 57 G12
Cilacap, Indonesia 57 G13
Çıldır, Turkey 67 B10
Çıldır Gölü, Turkey 67 B10
Cili, China 53 C8
Cilicia, Turkey 66 D5
Cill Chainnigh = Kilkenny, Ireland 15 D4
Cilo Dağı, Turkey 67 D10
Cima, U.S.A. 113 K11
Cimahi, Indonesia 57 G12
Cimarron, Kans., U.S.A. 109 G4
Cimarron, N. Mex., U.S.A. 109 G2
Cimarron →, U.S.A. 109 G6
Cimişlia, Moldova 41 J5
Cimone, Mte., Italy 32 D7
Cîmpina, Romania 38 D8
Cîmpulung, Argeş, Romania 38 D8
Cîmpulung, Suceava, Romania 38 B8
Çinar, Turkey 67 D9
Cinca →, Spain 28 D5
Cincinnati, U.S.A. 104 F3
Cîndeşti, Romania 38 D9
Çine, Turkey 66 D3
Ciney, Belgium 17 H6
Cíngoli, Italy 33 E10
Cinigiano, Italy 33 F8
Cinto, Mte., France 27 F12
Ciorani, Romania 38 E9
Čiovo, Croatia 33 E13
Cipó, Brazil 122 D4
Circeo, Mte., Italy 34 A6
Çirçir, Turkey 66 C7
Circle, Alaska, U.S.A. 96 B5
Circle, Mont., U.S.A. 108 B2
Circleville, Ohio, U.S.A. 104 F4
Circleville, Utah, U.S.A. 111 G7
Cirebon, Indonesia 57 G13
Cirencester, U.K. 13 F6
Cirey-sur-Vezouze, France 25 D13
Ciriè, Italy 32 C4
Cirium, Cyprus 37 E11
Cirò, Italy 35 C10
Ciron →, France 26 D3
Cisco, U.S.A. 109 J5
Cislău, Romania 38 D9
Cisneros, Colombia 120 B2
Cisterna di Latina, Italy 34 A5
Cisternino, Italy 35 B10
Citaré →, Brazil 121 C7
Citeli-Ckaro = Tsiteli-Tsqaro, Georgia 43 K8
Citlaltépetl, Mexico 115 D5
Citrus Heights, U.S.A. 112 G5
Citrusdal, S. Africa 84 E2
Città della Pieve, Italy 33 F9
Città di Castello, Italy 33 E9
Città Sant' Angelo, Italy 33 F11
Cittadella, Italy 33 C8
Cittaducale, Italy 33 F9
Cittanova, Italy 35 D9
City of Aberdeen □, U.K. 14 D6
City of Edinburgh □, U.K. 14 F5
City of Glasgow □, U.K. 14 F4
Ciucaş, Romania 38 D8
Ciudad Altamirano, Mexico 114 D4
Ciudad Bolívar, Venezuela 121 B5
Ciudad Camargo, Mexico 114 B3
Ciudad Chetumal, Mexico 115 D7
Ciudad de Valles, Mexico 115 C5
Ciudad del Carmen, Mexico 115 D6
Ciudad del Este, Paraguay 127 B5
Ciudad Delicias = Delicias, Mexico 114 B3
Ciudad Guayana, Venezuela 121 B5
Ciudad Guerrero, Mexico 114 B3
Ciudad Guzmán, Mexico 114 D4
Ciudad Juárez, Mexico 114 A3
Ciudad Madero, Mexico 115 C5
Ciudad Mante, Mexico 115 C5
Ciudad Obregón, Mexico 114 B3
Ciudad Ojeda, Venezuela 120 A3
Ciudad Real, Spain 31 G7
Ciudad Real □, Spain 31 G7
Ciudad Rodrigo, Spain 30 E4
Ciudad Trujillo = Santo Domingo, Dom. Rep. 117 C6
Ciudad Victoria, Mexico 115 C5
Ciudadela, Spain 36 B10
Ciulniţa, Romania 38 E10
Civa Burnu, Turkey 66 B7
Cividale del Friuli, Italy 33 B10
Cívita Castellana, Italy 33 F9
Civitanova Marche, Italy 33 E10
Civitavécchia, Italy 33 F8
Civitella del Tronto, Italy 33 F10
Civray, France 26 B4
Çivril, Turkey 66 C3
Cixerri →, Italy 34 C1
Cizre, Turkey 67 D10
Clackmannan □, U.K. 14 E5
Clacton-on-Sea, U.K. 13 F9
Clain →, France 24 F7
Claire, L., Canada 100 B6
Clairemont, U.S.A. 109 J4
Clairton, U.S.A. 106 F5
Clairvaux-les-Lacs, France 27 B9
Clallam Bay, U.S.A. 112 B2
Clamecy, France 25 E10
Clanton, U.S.A. 105 J2
Clanwilliam, S. Africa 84 E2
Clara, Ireland 15 C4
Clara →, Australia 90 B3
Claraville, U.S.A. 113 K8
Clare, Australia 91 E2
Clare, U.S.A. 104 D3
Clare □, Ireland 15 D3
Clare →, Ireland 15 C2
Clare I., Ireland 15 C2
Claremont, Calif., U.S.A. 113 L9
Claremont, N.H., U.S.A. 107 C12
Claremont Pt., Australia 90 A3
Claremore, U.S.A. 109 G7
Claremorris, Ireland 15 C3
Clarence →, Australia 91 D5
Clarence →, N.Z. 87 K4
Clarence, I., Chile 128 D2
Clarence I., Antarctica 5 C18
Clarence Str., Australia 88 B5
Clarence Str., U.S.A. 100 B2
Clarence Town, Bahamas 117 B5
Clarendon, Ark., U.S.A. 109 H9
Clarendon, Tex., U.S.A. 109 H4
Clarenville, Canada 99 C9
Claresholm, Canada 100 C6
Clarie Coast, Antarctica 5 C9
Clarinda, U.S.A. 108 E7
Clarion, Iowa, U.S.A. 108 D8
Clarion, Pa., U.S.A. 106 E5
Clarion →, U.S.A. 106 E5
Clark, U.S.A. 108 C6
Clark, Pt., Canada 106 B3
Clark Fork, U.S.A. 110 B5
Clark Fork →, U.S.A. 110 B5
Clark Hill Res., U.S.A. 105 J4
Clarkdale, U.S.A. 111 J7
Clarke City, Canada 99 B6
Clarke I., Australia 90 G4
Clarke L., Canada 101 C7
Clarke Ra., Australia 90 C4
Clark's Fork →, U.S.A. 110 D9
Clark's Harbour, Canada 99 D6
Clarks Summit, U.S.A. 107 E9
Clarksburg, U.S.A. 104 F5
Clarksdale, U.S.A. 109 H9
Clarkston, U.S.A. 110 C5
Clarksville, Ark., U.S.A. 109 H8
Clarksville, Tenn., U.S.A. 105 G2
Clarksville, Tex., U.S.A. 109 J7
Claro →, Brazil 123 E1
Clatskanie, U.S.A. 112 D3
Claude, U.S.A. 109 H4
Claveria, Phil. 55 B4
Clay, U.S.A. 112 G5
Clay Center, U.S.A. 108 F6
Claypool, U.S.A. 111 K8
Claysville, U.S.A. 106 F4
Clayton, Idaho, U.S.A. 110 D6
Clayton, N. Mex., U.S.A. 109 G3
Cle Elum, U.S.A. 110 C3
Clear, C., Ireland 15 E2
Clear I., Ireland 15 E2
Clear L., U.S.A. 112 F4
Clear Lake, S. Dak., U.S.A. 108 C6
Clear Lake, Wash., U.S.A. 110 B2
Clear Lake Reservoir, U.S.A. 110 F3
Clearfield, Pa., U.S.A. 104 E6
Clearfield, Utah, U.S.A. 110 F7
Clearlake Highlands, U.S.A. 112 G4
Clearmont, U.S.A. 110 D10
Clearwater, Canada 100 C4
Clearwater, U.S.A. 105 M4
Clearwater →, Alta., Canada 100 C6
Clearwater →, Alta., Canada 101 B6
Clearwater Cr. →, Canada 100 A3
Clearwater Mts., U.S.A. 110 C6
Clearwater Prov. Park, Canada 101 C8
Cleburne, U.S.A. 109 J6
Cleethorpes, U.K. 12 D7
Cleeve Hill, U.K. 13 F6
Clelles, France 27 D9
Clemency, Lux. 17 J7
Clerke Reef, Australia 88 C2
Clermont, Australia 90 C4
Clermont, France 25 C9
Clermont-en-Argonne, France 25 C12
Clermont-Ferrand, France 26 C7
Clermont-l'Hérault, France 26 E7
Clerval, France 25 E13
Clervaux, Lux. 17 H8
Cléry-St.-André, France 25 E8
Cles, Italy 32 B8
Cleveland, Australia 91 D5
Cleveland, Miss., U.S.A. 109 J9
Cleveland, Ohio, U.S.A. 106 E3
Cleveland, Okla., U.S.A. 109 G6
Cleveland, Tenn., U.S.A. 105 H3
Cleveland, Tex., U.S.A. 109 K7
Cleveland, C., Australia 90 B4
Cleveland Heights, U.S.A. 106 E3
Clevelândia, Brazil 127 B5
Clevelândia do Norte, Brazil 121 C7
Clew B., Ireland 15 C2
Clewiston, U.S.A. 105 M5
Clifden, Ireland 15 C1
Clifden, N.Z. 87 M1
Cliffdell, U.S.A. 112 D5
Clifton, Australia 91 D5
Clifton, Ariz., U.S.A. 111 K9
Clifton, Tex., U.S.A. 109 K6
Clifton Beach, Australia 90 B4
Clifton Forge, U.S.A. 104 G6
Clifton Hills, Australia 91 D2
Climax, Canada 101 D7
Clinch →, U.S.A. 105 H3
Clingmans Dome, U.S.A. 105 H4
Clint, U.S.A. 111 L10
Clinton, B.C., Canada 100 C4
Clinton, Ont., Canada 98 D3
Clinton, N.Z. 87 M2
Clinton, Ark., U.S.A. 109 H8
Clinton, Ill., U.S.A. 108 E10
Clinton, Ind., U.S.A. 104 F2
Clinton, Iowa, U.S.A. 108 E9
Clinton, Mass., U.S.A. 107 D13
Clinton, Mo., U.S.A. 108 F8
Clinton, N.C., U.S.A. 105 H6
Clinton, Okla., U.S.A. 109 H5
Clinton, S.C., U.S.A. 105 H5
Clinton, Tenn., U.S.A. 105 G3
Clinton, Wash., U.S.A. 112 C4
Clinton C., Australia 90 C5
Clinton Colden L., Canada 96 B9
Clintonville, U.S.A. 108 C10
Clipperton, I., Pac. Oc. 93 F17
Clisson, France 24 E5
Clive L., Canada 100 A5
Cliza, Bolivia 125 D4
Cloates, Pt., Australia 88 D1
Clocolan, S. Africa 85 D4
Clodomira, Argentina 126 B3
Clonakilty, Ireland 15 E3
Clonakilty B., Ireland 15 E3
Cloncurry, Australia 90 C3
Cloncurry →, Australia 90 B3
Clones, Ireland 15 B4
Clonmel, Ireland 15 D4
Cloppenburg, Germany 18 C4
Cloquet, U.S.A. 108 B8
Clorinda, Argentina 126 B4
Cloud Peak, U.S.A. 110 D10
Cloudcroft, U.S.A. 111 K11
Cloverdale, U.S.A. 112 G4
Clovis, Calif., U.S.A. 111 H4
Clovis, N. Mex., U.S.A. 109 H3
Cloyes-sur-le-Loir, France 24 E8
Cluj-Napoca, Romania 38 C6
Clunes, Australia 91 F3
Cluny, France 27 B8
Cluses, France 27 B10
Clusone, Italy 32 C6
Clutha →, N.Z. 87 M2
Clwyd →, U.K. 12 D4
Clyde, N.Z. 87 L2
Clyde, U.S.A. 106 C8
Clyde →, U.K. 14 F4
Clyde, Firth of, U.K. 14 F4
Clyde River, Canada 97 A13
Clydebank, U.K. 14 F4
Clymer, U.S.A. 106 D5
Côa →, Portugal 30 D3
Coachella, U.S.A. 113 M10
Coachella Canal, U.S.A. 113 N12
Coahoma, U.S.A. 109 J4
Coahuayana →, Mexico 114 D4
Coahuayutla, Mexico 114 D4
Coahuila □, Mexico 114 B4
Coal →, Canada 100 B3
Coalane, Mozam. 83 F4
Coalcomán, Mexico 114 D4
Coaldale, Canada 100 D6
Coalgate, U.S.A. 109 H6
Coalinga, U.S.A. 111 H3
Coalville, U.K. 12 E6
Coalville, U.S.A. 110 F8
Coaraci, Brazil 123 D4
Coari, Brazil 121 D5
Coari →, Brazil 121 D5
Coari, L. de, Brazil 121 D5
Coast □, Kenya 82 C4
Coast Mts., Canada 100 C3
Coast Ranges, U.S.A. 112 G4
Coatbridge, U.K. 14 F4
Coatepec, Mexico 115 D5
Coatepeque, Guatemala 116 D1
Coatesville, U.S.A. 104 F8
Coaticook, Canada 99 C5
Coats I., Canada 97 B11
Coats Land, Antarctica 5 D1
Coatzacoalcos, Mexico 115 D6
Cobalt, Canada 98 C4
Cobán, Guatemala 116 C1
Cobar, Australia 91 E4
Cóbh, Ireland 15 E3
Cobham, Australia 91 E3
Cobija, Bolivia 124 C4
Cobleskill, U.S.A. 107 D10
Coboconk, Canada 106 B6
Cobourg, Canada 98 D4
Cobourg Pen., Australia 88 B5
Cobram, Australia 91 F4
Cobre, U.S.A. 110 F6
Cóbué, Mozam. 83 E3
Coburg, Germany 19 E6
Coca, Spain 30 D6
Coca →, Ecuador 120 D2
Cocachacra, Peru 124 D3
Cocal, Brazil 122 B3
Cocanada = Kakinada, India 61 L13
Cocentaina, Spain 29 G4
Cochabamba, Bolivia 125 D4
Coche, I., Venezuela 121 A5
Cochem, Germany 19 E3
Cochemane, Mozam. 83 F3
Cochin, India 60 Q10
Cochin China = Nam-Phan, Vietnam 59 G6
Cochise, U.S.A. 111 K9
Cochran, U.S.A. 105 J4
Cochrane, Alta., Canada 100 C6
Cochrane, Ont., Canada 98 C3
Cochrane →, Canada 101 B8
Cochrane, L., Chile 128 C2
Cockburn, Australia 91 E3
Cockburn, Canal, Chile 128 D2
Cockburn I., Canada 98 C3
Cockburn Ra., Australia 88 C4
Cocklebiddy Motel, Australia 89 F4
Coco →, Cent. Amer. 116 D3
Coco, Pta., Colombia 120 C2
Cocoa, U.S.A. 105 L5
Cocobeach, Gabon 80 D1
Côcos, Brazil 123 D3
Côcos →, Brazil 123 D3
Cocos, I. del, Pac. Oc. 93 G19
Cocos Is., Ind. Oc. 92 J1
Cod, C., U.S.A. 103 B13
Codajás, Brazil 121 D5
Codera, C., Venezuela 120 A4
Coderre, Canada 101 C7
Codigoro, Italy 33 D9
Codó, Brazil 122 B3
Codogno, Italy 32 C6
Codpa, Chile 124 D4
Codroipo, Italy 33 C10
Cody, U.S.A. 110 D9
Coe Hill, Canada 98 D4
Coelemu, Chile 126 D1
Coelho Neto, Brazil 122 B3
Coen, Australia 90 A3
Coeroeni →, Surinam 121 C6
Coesfeld, Germany 18 D3
Cœur d'Alene, U.S.A. 110 C5
Cœur d'Alene L., U.S.A. 110 C5
Coevorden, Neths. 16 C9
Cofete, Canary Is. 36 F5
Coffeyville, U.S.A. 109 G7
Coffin B., Australia 91 E2
Coffin Bay Peninsula, Australia 91 E2
Coffs Harbour, Australia 91 E5
Cofrentes, Spain 29 F3
Cogealac, Romania 38 E11
Coghinas →, Italy 34 B1
Coghinas, L. di, Italy 34 B2
Cognac, France 26 C3
Cogne, Italy 32 C4
Cogolludo, Spain 28 E1
Cohagen, U.S.A. 110 C10
Cohoes, U.S.A. 107 D11
Cohuna, Australia 91 F3
Coiba, I., Panama 116 E3
Coig →, Argentina 128 D3
Coihaique, Chile 128 C2
Coimbatore, India 60 P10
Coimbra, Brazil 125 D6
Coimbra, Portugal 30 E2
Coimbra □, Portugal 30 E2
Coín, Spain 31 J6
Coipasa, L. de, Bolivia 124 D4
Coipasa, Salar de, Bolivia 124 D4
Cojata, Peru 124 D4
Cojedes □, Venezuela 120 B4
Cojedes →, Venezuela 120 B4
Cojimies, Ecuador 120 C1
Cojocna, Romania 38 C6
Cojutepequé, El Salv. 116 D2
Cokeville, U.S.A. 110 E8
Colac, Australia 91 F3
Colares, Portugal 31 G1
Colatina, Brazil 123 E3
Colbeck, C., Antarctica 5 D13
Colbinabbin, Australia 91 F3
Colborne, Canada 106 B7
Colby, U.S.A. 108 F4
Colchagua □, Chile 126 C1
Colchester, U.K. 13 F8
Coldstream, U.K. 14 F6
Coldwater, Canada 106 B5
Coldwater, U.S.A. 109 G5
Colebrook, Australia 90 G4
Colebrook, U.S.A. 107 B13
Coleman, Canada 100 D6
Coleman, U.S.A. 109 K5
Coleman →, Australia 90 B3
Colenso, S. Africa 85 D4
Coleraine, Australia 91 F3
Coleraine, U.K. 15 A5
Coleraine □, U.K. 15 A5
Coleridge, L., N.Z. 87 K3
Colesberg, S. Africa 84 E4
Coleville, U.S.A. 112 G7
Colfax, Calif., U.S.A. 112 F6
Colfax, La., U.S.A. 109 K8
Colfax, Wash., U.S.A. 110 C5
Colhué Huapi, L., Argentina 128 C3
Cólico, Italy 32 B6
Coligny, France 27 B9
Coligny, S. Africa 85 D4
Colima, Mexico 114 D4
Colima □, Mexico 114 D4
Colima, Nevado de, Mexico 114 D4
Colina, Chile 126 C1
Colina do Norte, Guinea-Biss. 78 C2
Colinas, Goiás, Brazil 123 D2
Colinas, Maranhão, Brazil 122 C3
Coll, U.K. 14 E2
Collaguasi, Chile 126 A2
Collarada, Peña, Spain 28 C4
Collarenebri, Australia 91 D4
Collbran, U.S.A. 111 G10
Colle di Val d'Elsa, Italy 33 E8
Colle Salvetti, Italy 32 E7
Colle Sannita, Italy 35 A7
Collécchio, Italy 32 D7
Colleen Bawn, Zimbabwe 83 G2
College Park, U.S.A. 105 J3
College Station, U.S.A. 109 K6
Collette, Canada 99 C6
Collie, Australia 89 F2
Collier B., Australia 88 C3
Collier Ra., Australia 88 D2
Colline Metallifere, Italy 32 E7
Collingwood, Canada 98 D3
Collingwood, N.Z. 87 J4
Collins, Canada 98 B2
Collinsville, Australia 90 C4
Collipulli, Chile 126 D1
Collo, Algeria 75 A6
Collonges, France 27 B9
Collooney, Ireland 15 B3
Colmar, France 25 D14
Colmars, France 27 D10
Colmenar, Spain 31 J6
Colmenar de Oreja, Spain 28 E1
Colmenar Viejo, Spain 30 E7
Colne, U.K. 12 D5
Colo →, Australia 91 E5
Cologna Véneta, Italy 33 C8
Cologne = Köln, Germany 18 E2
Colom, I., Spain 36 B11
Coloma, U.S.A. 112 G6
Colomb-Béchar = Béchar, Algeria 75 B4
Colombey-les-Belles, France 25 D12
Colombey-les-Deux-Églises, France 25 D11
Colômbia, Brazil 123 F2
Colombia ■, S. Amer. 120 C3
Colombian Basin, S. Amer. 94 H12
Colombier, Switz. 22 C3
Colombo, Sri Lanka 60 R11
Colome, U.S.A. 108 D5
Colón, Argentina 126 C4
Colón, Cuba 116 B3
Colón, Panama 116 E4
Colón, Peru 124 A1
Colona, Australia 89 F5
Colonella, Italy 33 F10
Colonia, Uruguay 126 C4
Colonia de San Jordi, Spain 36 B9
Colonia Dora, Argentina 126 B3
Colonial Heights, U.S.A. 104 G7
Colonne, C. delle, Italy 35 C10
Colonsay, Canada 101 C7
Colonsay, U.K. 14 E2
Colorado □, U.S.A. 111 G10
Colorado →, Argentina 128 A4
Colorado →, N. Amer. 111 L6
Colorado →, U.S.A. 109 L7
Colorado City, U.S.A. 109 J4
Colorado Desert, U.S.A. 102 D3
Colorado Plateau, U.S.A. 111 H8
Colorado River Aqueduct, U.S.A. 113 L12
Colorado Springs, U.S.A. 108 F2
Colorno, Italy 32 D7
Colotlán, Mexico 114 C4
Colquechaca, Bolivia 125 D4
Colton, N.Y., U.S.A. 107 B10
Colton, Wash., U.S.A. 110 C5
Columbia, La., U.S.A. 109 J8
Columbia, Miss., U.S.A. 109 K10
Columbia, Mo., U.S.A. 108 F8
Columbia, Pa., U.S.A. 107 F8
Columbia, S.C., U.S.A. 105 H5
Columbia, Tenn., U.S.A. 105 H2
Columbia →, U.S.A. 110 C1
Columbia, C., Canada 4 A4
Columbia, District of □, U.S.A. 104 F7
Columbia, Mt., Canada 100 C5
Columbia Basin, U.S.A. 110 C4
Columbia Falls, U.S.A. 110 B6
Columbia Heights, U.S.A. 108 C8
Columbiana, U.S.A. 106 F4
Columbretes, Is., Spain 28 F5
Columbus, Ga., U.S.A. 105 J3
Columbus, Ind., U.S.A. 104 F3
Columbus, Kans., U.S.A. 109 G7
Columbus, Miss., U.S.A. 105 J1
Columbus, Mont., U.S.A. 110 D9
Columbus, N. Dak., U.S.A. 108 A3
Columbus, N. Mex., U.S.A. 111 L10
Columbus, Nebr., U.S.A. 108 E6
Columbus, Ohio, U.S.A. 104 F4
Columbus, Tex., U.S.A. 109 L6
Columbus, Wis., U.S.A. 108 D10
Colunga, Spain 30 B5
Colusa, U.S.A. 112 F4
Colville, U.S.A. 110 B5
Colville →, U.S.A. 96 A4
Colville, C., N.Z. 87 G5

Colwyn Bay, *U.K.* 12 D4
Coma, *Ethiopia* 77 F4
Comácchio, *Italy* 33 D9
Comalcalco, *Mexico* 115 D6
Comallo, *Argentina* 128 B2
Comanche, *Okla., U.S.A.* 109 H6
Comanche, *Tex., U.S.A.* 109 K5
Comandante Luis Piedrabuena, *Argentina* 128 C3
Comănești, *Romania* 38 C9
Comarapa, *Bolivia* 125 D5
Comayagua, *Honduras* 116 D2
Combahee →, *U.S.A.* 105 J5
Combeaufontaine, *France* 25 E12
Comber, *Canada* 106 D2
Comblain-au-Pont, *Belgium* 17 H7
Combles, *France* 25 B9
Combourg, *France* 24 D5
Combronde, *France* 26 C7
Comeragh Mts., *Ireland* 15 D4
Comet, *Australia* 90 C4
Comilla, *Bangla.* 61 H17
Comines, *Belgium* 17 G1
Comino, *Malta* 37 C1
Comino, C., *Italy* 34 B2
Cómiso, *Italy* 35 F7
Comitán, *Mexico* 115 D6
Commentry, *France* 26 B6
Commerce, *Ga., U.S.A.* 105 H4
Commerce, *Tex., U.S.A.* 109 J7
Commercy, *France* 25 D12
Commewijne □, *Surinam* 121 B7
Committee B., *Canada* 97 B11
Commonwealth B., *Antarctica* 5 C10
Commoron Cr. →, *Australia* 91 D5
Communism Pk. = Kommunizma, Pik, *Tajikistan* 44 F8
Como, *Italy* 32 C6
Como, L. di, *Italy* 32 B6
Comodoro Rivadavia, *Argentina* 128 C3
Comorin, C., *India* 60 Q10
Comoro Is. = Comoros ■, *Ind. Oc.* 70 H8
Comoros ■, *Ind. Oc.* 70 H8
Comox, *Canada* 100 D4
Compiègne, *France* 25 C9
Comporta, *Portugal* 31 G2
Compostela, *Mexico* 114 C4
Comprida, I., *Brazil* 127 A6
Compton, *U.S.A.* 113 M8
Compton Downs, *Australia* 91 E4
Comrat, *Moldova* 41 J5
Con Cuong, *Vietnam* 58 C5
Con Son, *Vietnam* 59 H6
Cona Niyeu, *Argentina* 128 B3
Conakry, *Guinea* 78 D2
Conara Junction, *Australia* 90 G4
Concarneau, *France* 24 E3
Conceição, *Brazil* 122 C4
Conceição, *Mozam.* 83 F4
Conceição da Barra, *Brazil* 123 E4
Conceição do Araguaia, *Brazil* 122 C2
Conceição do Canindé, *Brazil* 122 C3
Concepción, *Argentina* 126 B2
Concepción, *Bolivia* 125 D5
Concepción, *Chile* 126 D1
Concepción, *Mexico* 115 D6
Concepción, *Paraguay* 126 A4
Concepción, *Peru* 124 C2
Concepción □, *Chile* 126 D1
Concepción →, *Mexico* 114 A2
Concepción, Est. de, *Chile* 128 D2
Concepción, L., *Bolivia* 125 D5
Concepción, Punta, *Mexico* 114 B2
Concepción del Oro, *Mexico* 114 C4
Concepción del Uruguay, *Argentina* 126 C4
Conception, Pt., *U.S.A.* 113 L6
Conception B., *Namibia* 84 C1
Conception I., *Bahamas* 117 B4
Concession, *Zimbabwe* 83 F3
Conchas Dam, *U.S.A.* 109 H2
Conche, *Canada* 99 B8
Conches-en-Ouche, *France* 24 D7
Concho, *U.S.A.* 111 J9
Concho →, *U.S.A.* 109 K5
Conchos →, *Chihuahua, Mexico* 114 B4
Conchos →, *Tamaulipas, Mexico* 115 B5
Concord, *Calif., U.S.A.* 112 H4
Concord, *N.C., U.S.A.* 105 H5
Concord, *N.H., U.S.A.* 107 C13
Concordia, *Argentina* 126 C4
Concórdia, *Brazil* 120 D4
Concordia, *Mexico* 114 C3
Concordia, *U.S.A.* 108 F6
Concots, *France* 26 D5
Concrete, *U.S.A.* 110 B3
Condamine, *Australia* 91 D5
Condat, *France* 26 C6
Conde, *Brazil* 123 D4
Conde, *U.S.A.* 108 C5
Condé-sur-l'Escaut, *France* 25 B10
Condé-sur-Noireau, *France* 24 D6
Condeúba, *Brazil* 123 D3
Condobolin, *Australia* 91 E4
Condom, *France* 26 E4
Condon, *U.S.A.* 110 D3
Condove, *Italy* 32 C4
Conegliano, *Italy* 33 C9
Conejera, I., *Spain* 36 B9
Conejos, *Mexico* 114 B4
Conflans-en-Jarnisy, *France* 25 C12
Confolens, *France* 26 B4
Confuso →, *Paraguay* 126 B4
Congjiang, *China* 52 E7
Congleton, *U.K.* 12 D5
Congo = Zaïre →, *Africa* 80 F2
Congo, *Brazil* 122 C4
Congo (Kinshasa) = Zaïre ■, *Africa* 80 E4
Congo ■, *Africa* 80 E3
Congo Basin, *Africa* 70 G6
Congonhas, *Brazil* 123 F3
Congress, *U.S.A.* 111 J7
Conil, *Spain* 31 J4
Coniston, *Canada* 98 C3
Conjeeveram = Kanchipuram, *India* 60 N11
Conjuboy, *Australia* 90 B3
Conklin, *Canada* 101 B6
Conlea, *Australia* 91 E3
Conn, L., *Ireland* 15 B2
Connacht □, *Ireland* 15 C3
Conneaut, *U.S.A.* 106 E4
Connecticut □, *U.S.A.* 107 E12
Connecticut →, *U.S.A.* 107 E12
Connell, *U.S.A.* 110 C4
Connellsville, *U.S.A.* 106 F5
Connemara, *Ireland* 15 C2
Connemaugh →, *U.S.A.* 106 F5
Connerré, *France* 24 D7
Connersville, *U.S.A.* 104 F3
Connors Ra., *Australia* 90 C4
Conoble, *Australia* 91 E3
Cononaco →, *Ecuador* 120 D2
Cononbridge, *U.K.* 14 D4
Conquest, *Canada* 101 C7
Conrad, *U.S.A.* 110 B8
Conran, C., *Australia* 91 F4
Conroe, *U.S.A.* 109 K7
Conselheiro Lafaiete, *Brazil* 123 F3
Conselheiro Pena, *Brazil* 123 E3
Consort, *Canada* 101 C6
Constance = Konstanz, *Germany* 19 H5
Constance, L. = Bodensee, *Europe* 23 A8
Constanța, *Romania* 38 E11
Constantina, *Spain* 31 H5
Constantine, *Algeria* 75 A6
Constitución, *Chile* 126 D1
Constitución, *Uruguay* 126 C4
Consuegra, *Spain* 31 F7
Consul, *Canada* 101 D7
Contact, *U.S.A.* 110 F6
Contai, *India* 63 J12
Contamana, *Peru* 124 B3
Contarina, *Italy* 33 C9
Contas →, *Brazil* 123 D4
Contes, *France* 27 E11
Conthey, *Switz.* 22 D4
Contoocook, *U.S.A.* 107 C13
Contra Costa, *Mozam.* 85 D5
Contres, *France* 24 E8
Contrexéville, *France* 25 D12
Contumaza, *Peru* 124 B2
Convención, *Colombia* 120 B3
Conversano, *Italy* 35 B10
Conway = Conwy, *U.K.* 12 D4
Conway = Conwy →, *U.K.* 12 D4
Conway, *Ark., U.S.A.* 109 H8
Conway, *N.H., U.S.A.* 107 C13
Conway, *S.C., U.S.A.* 105 J6
Conway, L., *Australia* 91 D2
Conwy, *U.K.* 12 D4
Conwy →, *U.K.* 12 D4
Coober Pedy, *Australia* 91 D1
Cooch Behar = Koch Bihar, *India* 61 F16
Coodardy, *Australia* 89 E2
Cook, *Australia* 89 F5
Cook, *U.S.A.* 108 B8
Cook, B., *Chile* 128 E2
Cook, Mt., *N.Z.* 87 K3
Cook Inlet, *U.S.A.* 96 C4
Cook Is., *Pac. Oc.* 93 J11
Cook Strait, *N.Z.* 87 J5
Cookeville, *U.S.A.* 105 G3
Cookhouse, *S. Africa* 84 E4
Cookshire, *Canada* 107 A13
Cookstown, *U.K.* 15 B5
Cookstown □, *U.K.* 15 B5
Cooksville, *Canada* 106 C5
Cooktown, *Australia* 90 B4
Coolabah, *Australia* 91 E4
Cooladdi, *Australia* 91 D4
Coolah, *Australia* 91 E4
Coolamon, *Australia* 91 E4
Coolangatta, *Australia* 91 D5
Coolgardie, *Australia* 89 F3
Coolibah, *Australia* 88 C5
Coolidge, *U.S.A.* 111 K8
Coolidge Dam, *U.S.A.* 111 K8
Cooma, *Australia* 91 F4
Coon Rapids, *U.S.A.* 108 C8
Coonabarabran, *Australia* 91 E4
Coonamble, *Australia* 91 E4
Coonana, *Australia* 89 F3
Coondapoor, *India* 60 N9
Coongie, *Australia* 91 D3
Coongoola, *Australia* 91 D4
Cooninie, L., *Australia* 91 D2
Cooper, *U.S.A.* 109 J7
Cooper →, *U.S.A.* 105 J6
Cooper Cr. →, *Australia* 91 D2
Cooperstown, *N. Dak., U.S.A.* 108 B5
Cooperstown, *N.Y., U.S.A.* 107 D10
Coorabie, *Australia* 89 F5
Coorabulka, *Australia* 90 C3
Coorow, *Australia* 89 E2
Cooroy, *Australia* 91 D5
Coos Bay, *U.S.A.* 110 E1
Cootamundra, *Australia* 91 E4
Cootehill, *Ireland* 15 B4
Cooyar, *Australia* 91 D5
Cooyeana, *Australia* 90 C2
Copahue Paso, *Argentina* 126 D1
Copainalá, *Mexico* 115 D6
Copán, *Honduras* 116 D2
Copatana, *Brazil* 120 D4
Cope, *U.S.A.* 108 F3
Cope, C., *Spain* 29 H3
Copenhagen = København, *Denmark* 11 J6
Copertino, *Italy* 35 B11
Copiapó, *Chile* 126 B1
Copiapó →, *Chile* 126 B1
Copley, *Australia* 91 E2
Copp L., *Canada* 100 A6
Copparo, *Italy* 33 D8
Coppename →, *Surinam* 121 B6
Copper Center, *U.S.A.* 96 B5
Copper Cliff, *Canada* 98 C3
Copper Harbor, *U.S.A.* 104 B2
Copper Queen, *Zimbabwe* 83 F2
Copperbelt □, *Zambia* 83 E2
Coppermine = Kuglugtuk, *Canada* 96 B8
Coppermine →, *Canada* 96 B8
Copperopolis, *U.S.A.* 112 H6
Coquet →, *U.K.* 12 B6
Coquilhatville = Mbandaka, *Zaïre* 80 D3
Coquille, *U.S.A.* 110 E1
Coquimbo, *Chile* 126 B1
Coquimbo □, *Chile* 126 C1
Corabia, *Romania* 38 F7
Coração de Jesus, *Brazil* 123 E3
Coracora, *Peru* 124 D3
Coradi, Is., *Italy* 35 B10
Coral Gables, *U.S.A.* 105 N5
Coral Harbour, *Canada* 97 B11
Coral Sea, *Pac. Oc.* 92 J7
Coral Springs, *U.S.A.* 105 M5
Corantijn →, *Surinam* 121 B6
Coraopolis, *U.S.A.* 106 F4
Corato, *Italy* 35 A9
Corbeil-Essonnes, *France* 25 D9
Corbie, *France* 25 C9
Corbières, *France* 26 F6
Corbigny, *France* 25 E10
Corbin, *U.S.A.* 104 G3
Corbion, *Belgium* 17 J6
Corbones →, *Spain* 31 H5
Corby, *U.K.* 13 E7
Corby Glen, *U.K.* 13 E7
Corcaigh = Cork, *Ireland* 15 E3
Corcoles →, *Spain* 29 F1
Corcoran, *U.S.A.* 111 H4
Corcubión, *Spain* 30 C1
Cordele, *U.S.A.* 105 K4
Cordell, *U.S.A.* 109 H5
Cordenons, *Italy* 33 C9
Cordes, *France* 26 D5
Cordisburgo, *Brazil* 123 E3
Córdoba, *Argentina* 126 C3
Córdoba, *Mexico* 115 D5
Córdoba, *Spain* 31 H6
Córdoba □, *Argentina* 126 C3
Córdoba □, *Colombia* 120 B2
Córdoba □, *Spain* 31 G6
Córdoba, Sierra de, *Argentina* 126 C3
Cordon, *Phil.* 55 C4
Cordova, *Ala., U.S.A.* 105 J2
Cordova, *Alaska, U.S.A.* 96 B5
Corella, *Spain* 28 C3
Corella →, *Australia* 90 B3
Coremas, *Brazil* 122 C4
Corentyne →, *Guyana* 121 B6
Corfield, *Australia* 90 C3
Corfu = Kérkira, *Greece* 37 A3
Corfu, Str of, *Greece* 37 A4
Corgo, *Spain* 30 C3
Corguinho, *Brazil* 125 D7
Cori, *Italy* 34 A5
Coria, *Spain* 30 F4
Corigliano Cálabro, *Italy* 35 C9
Coringa Is., *Australia* 90 B4
Corinna, *Australia* 90 G4
Corinth = Kórinthos, *Greece* 39 M5
Corinth, *Miss., U.S.A.* 105 H1
Corinth, *N.Y., U.S.A.* 107 C11
Corinth, G. of = Korinthiakós Kólpos, *Greece* 39 L5
Corinth Canal, *Greece* 39 M6
Corinto, *Brazil* 123 E3
Corinto, *Nic.* 116 D2
Cork, *Ireland* 15 E3
Cork □, *Ireland* 15 E3
Cork Harbour, *Ireland* 15 E3
Corlay, *France* 24 D3
Corleone, *Italy* 34 E6
Corleto Perticara, *Italy* 35 B9
Çorlu, *Turkey* 66 B2
Cormack L., *Canada* 100 A4
Cormòns, *Italy* 33 C10
Cormorant, *Canada* 101 C8
Cormorant L., *Canada* 101 C8
Corn Is. = Maiz, Is. del, *Nic.* 116 D3
Cornélio Procópio, *Brazil* 127 A5
Cornell, *U.S.A.* 108 C9
Corner Brook, *Canada* 99 C8
Cornești, *Moldova* 41 J5
Corníglio, *Italy* 32 D7
Corning, *Ark., U.S.A.* 109 G9
Corning, *Calif., U.S.A.* 110 G2
Corning, *Iowa, U.S.A.* 108 E7
Corning, *N.Y., U.S.A.* 106 D7
Corno, Monte, *Italy* 33 F10
Cornwall, *Canada* 98 C5
Cornwall □, *U.K.* 13 G3
Corny Pt., *Australia* 91 E2
Coro, *Venezuela* 120 A4
Coroaci, *Brazil* 123 E3
Coroatá, *Brazil* 122 B3
Corocoro, *Bolivia* 124 D4
Corocoro, I., *Venezuela* 121 B5
Coroico, *Bolivia* 124 D4
Coromandel, *Brazil* 123 E2
Coromandel, *N.Z.* 87 G5
Coromandel Coast, *India* 60 N12
Corona, *Australia* 91 E3
Corona, *Calif., U.S.A.* 113 M9
Corona, *N. Mex., U.S.A.* 111 J11
Coronado, *U.S.A.* 113 N9
Coronado, B. de, *Costa Rica* 116 E3
Coronados, G. de los, *Chile* 128 B2
Coronados, Is. los, *U.S.A.* 113 N9
Coronation, *Canada* 100 C6
Coronation Gulf, *Canada* 96 B8
Coronation I., *Antarctica* 5 C18
Coronation I., *U.S.A.* 100 B2
Coronation Is., *Australia* 88 B3
Coronda, *Argentina* 126 C3
Coronel, *Chile* 126 D1
Coronel Bogado, *Paraguay* 126 B4
Coronel Dorrego, *Argentina* 126 D3
Coronel Fabriciano, *Brazil* 123 E3
Coronel Murta, *Brazil* 123 E3
Coronel Oviedo, *Paraguay* 126 B4
Coronel Ponce, *Brazil* 125 D6
Coronel Pringles, *Argentina* 126 D3
Coronel Suárez, *Argentina* 126 D3
Coronel Vidal, *Argentina* 126 D4
Corongo, *Peru* 124 B2
Coronie □, *Surinam* 121 B6
Coropuna, Nevado, *Peru* 124 D3
Çorovoda, *Albania* 39 J3
Corowa, *Australia* 91 F4
Corozal, *Belize* 115 D7
Corozal, *Colombia* 120 B2
Corps, *France* 27 D9
Corpus, *Argentina* 127 B4
Corpus Christi, *U.S.A.* 109 M6
Corpus Christi, L., *U.S.A.* 109 L6
Corque, *Bolivia* 124 D4
Corral, *Chile* 128 A2
Corral de Almaguer, *Spain* 28 F1
Corralejo, *Canary Is.* 36 F6
Corréggio, *Italy* 32 D7
Corrente, *Brazil* 122 D2
Corrente →, *Brazil* 123 D3
Correntes →, *Brazil* 125 D6
Correntes, C. das, *Mozam.* 85 C6
Correntina, *Brazil* 123 D3
Corrèze □, *France* 26 C5
Corrèze →, *France* 26 C5
Corrib, L., *Ireland* 15 C2
Corrientes, *Argentina* 126 B4
Corrientes □, *Argentina* 126 B4
Corrientes →, *Argentina* 126 C4
Corrientes →, *Peru* 120 D3
Corrientes, C., *Colombia* 120 B2
Corrientes, C., *Cuba* 116 B3
Corrientes, C., *Mexico* 114 C3
Corrigan, *U.S.A.* 109 K7
Corrigin, *Australia* 89 F2
Corry, *U.S.A.* 106 E5
Corse, *France* 27 F13
Corse, C., *France* 27 E13
Corse-du-Sud □, *France* 27 G13
Corsica = Corse, *France* 27 F13
Corsicana, *U.S.A.* 109 J6
Corte, *France* 27 F13
Corte do Pinto, *Portugal* 31 H3
Cortegana, *Spain* 31 H4
Cortez, *U.S.A.* 111 H9
Cortina d'Ampezzo, *Italy* 33 B9
Cortland, *U.S.A.* 107 D8
Cortona, *Italy* 33 E8
Coruche, *Portugal* 31 G2
Çoruh →, *Turkey* 43 K5
Çorum, *Turkey* 66 B6
Corumbá, *Brazil* 125 D6
Corumbá →, *Brazil* 123 E2
Corumbá de Goiás, *Brazil* 123 E2
Corumbaíba, *Brazil* 123 E2
Corunna = La Coruña, *Spain* 30 B2
Corvallis, *U.S.A.* 110 D2
Corvette, L. de la, *Canada* 98 B5
Corydon, *U.S.A.* 108 E8
Cosalá, *Mexico* 114 C3
Cosamaloapan, *Mexico* 115 D5
Cosenza, *Italy* 35 C9
Coshocton, *U.S.A.* 106 F3
Cosmo Newberry, *Australia* 89 E3
Cosne-sur-Loire, *France* 25 E9
Coso Junction, *U.S.A.* 113 J9
Coso Pk., *U.S.A.* 113 J9
Cospeito, *Spain* 30 B3
Cosquín, *Argentina* 126 C3
Cossato, *Italy* 32 C5
Cossé-le-Vivien, *France* 24 E6
Cosson →, *France* 24 E8
Costa Blanca, *Spain* 29 G4
Costa Brava, *Spain* 28 D8
Costa del Sol, *Spain* 31 J6
Costa Dorada, *Spain* 28 E6
Costa Mesa, *U.S.A.* 113 M9
Costa Rica ■, *Cent. Amer.* 116 D3
Costa Smeralda, *Italy* 34 A2
Costigliole d'Asti, *Italy* 32 D5
Costilla, *U.S.A.* 111 H11
Cosumnes →, *U.S.A.* 112 G5
Coswig, *Germany* 18 D8
Cotabato, *Phil.* 55 H6
Cotacajes →, *Bolivia* 124 D4
Cotagaita, *Bolivia* 126 A2
Cotahuasi, *Peru* 124 D3
Côte d'Azur, *France* 27 E11
Côte-d'Ivoire ■ = Ivory Coast ■, *Africa* 78 D3
Côte d'Or, *France* 25 E11
Côte-d'Or □, *France* 25 E11
Coteau des Prairies, *U.S.A.* 108 C6
Coteau du Missouri, *U.S.A.* 108 B4
Coteau Landing, *Canada* 107 A10
Cotegipe, *Brazil* 123 D3
Cotentin, *France* 24 C5
Côtes-d'Armor □, *France* 24 D4
Côtes de Meuse, *France* 25 C12
Côtes-du-Nord = Côtes-d'Armor □, *France* 24 D4
Cotiella, *Spain* 28 C5
Cotillo, *Canary Is.* 36 F5
Cotina →, *Bos.-H.* 21 M8
Cotoca, *Bolivia* 125 D5
Cotonou, *Benin* 79 D5
Cotopaxi, *Ecuador* 120 D2
Cotopaxi □, *Ecuador* 120 D2
Cotronei, *Italy* 35 C9
Cotswold Hills, *U.K.* 13 F5
Cottage Grove, *U.S.A.* 110 E2
Cottbus, *Germany* 18 D10
Cottingham, *U.K.* 12 C5
Cottonwood, *U.S.A.* 111 J7
Cotulla, *U.S.A.* 109 L5
Coubre, Pte. de la, *France* 26 C2
Couches, *France* 25 F11
Couço, *Portugal* 31 G2
Coudersport, *U.S.A.* 106 E6
Couedic, C. du, *Australia* 91 F2
Couëron, *France* 24 E5
Couesnon →, *France* 24 D5
Couhé, *France* 26 B4
Coulanges-sur-Yonne, *France* 25 E10
Coulee City, *U.S.A.* 110 C4
Coulman I., *Antarctica* 5 D11
Coulommiers, *France* 25 D10
Coulon →, *France* 27 E9
Coulonge →, *Canada* 98 C4
Coulonges-sur-l'Autize, *France* 26 B3
Coulterville, *U.S.A.* 112 H6
Council, *Alaska, U.S.A.* 96 B3
Council, *Idaho, U.S.A.* 110 D5
Council Bluffs, *U.S.A.* 108 E7
Council Grove, *U.S.A.* 108 F6
Coupeville, *U.S.A.* 112 B4
Courantyne →, *S. Amer.* 121 B6
Courcelles, *Belgium* 17 H4
Courçon, *France* 26 B3
Couronne, C., *France* 27 E9
Cours-la-Ville, *France* 27 B8
Coursan, *France* 26 E7
Courseulles-sur-Mer, *France* 24 C6
Court-St.-Etienne, *Belgium* 17 G5
Courtenay, *Canada* 100 D3
Courtland, *U.S.A.* 112 G5
Courtrai = Kortrijk, *Belgium* 17 G2
Courtright, *Canada* 106 D2
Courville-sur-Eure, *France* 24 D8
Coushatta, *U.S.A.* 109 J8
Coutances, *France* 24 C5
Couterne, *France* 24 D6
Coutras, *France* 26 C3
Coutts, *Canada* 100 D6
Couvet, *Switz.* 22 C3
Couvin, *Belgium* 17 H4
Covarrubias, *Spain* 28 C1
Coveñas, *Colombia* 120 B2
Coventry, *U.K.* 13 E6
Coventry L., *Canada* 101 A7
Covilhã, *Portugal* 30 E3
Covington, *Ga., U.S.A.* 105 J4
Covington, *Ky., U.S.A.* 104 F3
Covington, *Okla., U.S.A.* 109 G6
Covington, *Tenn., U.S.A.* 109 H10
Cowal, L., *Australia* 91 E4
Cowan, *Canada* 101 C8
Cowan, L., *Australia* 89 F3
Cowan L., *Canada* 101 C7
Cowangie, *Australia* 91 F3
Cowansville, *Canada* 107 A12
Cowarie, *Australia* 91 D2
Cowcowing Lakes, *Australia* 89 F2
Cowdenbeath, *U.K.* 14 E5
Cowell, *Australia* 91 E2
Cowes, *U.K.* 13 G6
Cowlitz →, *U.S.A.* 112 D4
Cowra, *Australia* 91 E4
Coxilha Grande, *Brazil* 127 B5
Coxim, *Brazil* 125 D7
Coxim →, *Brazil* 125 D7
Cox's Bazar, *Bangla.* 61 J17
Cox's Cove, *Canada* 99 C8

Coyame, *Mexico* 114 B3
Coyote Wells, *U.S.A.* 113 N11
Coyuca de Benítez, *Mexico* 115 D4
Coyuca de Catalan, *Mexico* 114 D4
Cozad, *U.S.A.* 108 E5
Cozumel, *Mexico* 115 C7
Cozumel, I. de, *Mexico* 115 C7
Craboon, *Australia* 91 E4
Cracow = Kraków, *Poland* 20 E9
Cracow, *Australia* 91 D5
Cradock, *S. Africa* 84 E4
Craig, *Alaska, U.S.A.* 100 B2
Craig, *Colo., U.S.A.* 110 F10
Craigavon, *U.K.* 15 B5
Craigmore, *Zimbabwe* 83 G3
Crailsheim, *Germany* 19 F6
Craiova, *Romania* 38 E6
Cramsie, *Australia* 90 C3
Cranberry Portage, *Canada* 101 C8
Cranbrook, *Tas., Australia* 90 G4
Cranbrook, *W. Austral., Australia* 89 F2
Cranbrook, *Canada* 100 D5
Crandon, *U.S.A.* 108 C10
Crane, *Oreg., U.S.A.* 110 E4
Crane, *Tex., U.S.A.* 109 K3
Cranston, *U.S.A.* 107 E13
Craon, *France* 24 E6
Craonne, *France* 25 C10
Craponne-sur-Arzon, *France* 26 C7
Crasna, *Romania* 38 C10
Crater L., *U.S.A.* 110 E2
Crateús, *Brazil* 122 C3
Crati →, *Italy* 35 C9
Crato, *Brazil* 122 C4
Crato, *Portugal* 31 F3
Cravo Norte, *Colombia* 120 B3
Cravo Norte →, *Colombia* 120 B3
Crawford, *U.S.A.* 108 D3
Crawfordsville, *U.S.A.* 104 E2
Crawley, *U.K.* 13 F7
Crazy Mts., *U.S.A.* 110 C8
Crean L., *Canada* 101 C7
Crécy-en-Brie, *France* 25 D9
Crécy-en-Ponthieu, *France* 25 B8
Crediton, *Canada* 106 C3
Credo, *Australia* 89 F3
Cree →, *Canada* 101 B7
Cree →, *U.K.* 14 G4
Cree L., *Canada* 101 B7
Creede, *U.S.A.* 111 H10
Creel, *Mexico* 114 B3
Creighton, *U.S.A.* 108 D6
Creil, *France* 25 C9
Crema, *Italy* 32 C6
Cremona, *Italy* 32 C7
Crepori →, *Brazil* 125 B6
Crépy, *France* 25 C10
Crépy-en-Valois, *France* 25 C9
Cres, *Croatia* 33 D11
Cresbard, *U.S.A.* 108 C5
Crescent, *Okla., U.S.A.* 109 H6
Crescent, *Oreg., U.S.A.* 110 E3
Crescent City, *U.S.A.* 110 F1
Crescentino, *Italy* 32 C5
Crespino, *Italy* 33 D8
Crespo, *Argentina* 126 C3
Cressy, *Australia* 91 F3
Crest, *France* 27 D9
Cresta, Mt., *Phil.* 55 C5
Crested Butte, *U.S.A.* 111 G10
Crestline, *Calif., U.S.A.* 113 L9
Crestline, *Ohio, U.S.A.* 106 F2
Creston, *Canada* 100 D5
Creston, *Calif., U.S.A.* 112 K6
Creston, *Iowa, U.S.A.* 108 E7
Creston, *Wash., U.S.A.* 110 C4
Crestview, *Calif., U.S.A.* 112 H8
Crestview, *Fla., U.S.A.* 105 K2
Crete = Kríti, *Greece* 37 D7
Crete, *U.S.A.* 108 E6
Crete, Sea of, *Greece* 39 N8
Creus, C. de, *Spain* 28 C8
Creuse □, *France* 26 B6
Creuse →, *France* 26 B4
Creuzburg, *Germany* 18 D6
Crevalcore, *Italy* 33 D8
Crèvecœur-le-Grand, *France* 25 C9
Crevillente, *Spain* 29 G4
Crewe, *U.K.* 12 D5
Criciúma, *Brazil* 127 B6
Crieff, *U.K.* 14 E5
Crikvenica, *Croatia* 33 C11
Crimea □, *Ukraine* 41 K8
Crimean Pen. = Krymskyy Pivostriv, *Ukraine* 41 K8
Crimmitschau, *Germany* 18 E8
Cristalândia, *Brazil* 122 D2
Cristino Castro, *Brazil* 122 C3
Crişul Alb →, *Romania* 38 C4
Crişul Negru →, *Romania* 38 C4
Crişul Repede →, *Romania* 38 C3
Crivitz, *Germany* 18 B7
Crixás, *Brazil* 123 D2
Crna Gora = Montenegro □, *Yugoslavia* 21 N9
Crni Drim →, *Macedonia* 39 H3
Črnomelj, *Slovenia* 33 C12
Croagh Patrick, *Ireland* 15 C2
Croatia ■, *Europe* 33 C13
Crocker, Banjaran, *Malaysia* 56 C5
Crockett, *U.S.A.* 109 K7
Crocodile = Krokodil →, *Mozam.* 85 D5
Crocodile Is., *Australia* 90 A1
Crocq, *France* 26 C6
Croisette, C., *France* 27 E9
Croisic, Pte. du, *France* 24 E4
Croix, L. La, *Canada* 98 C1
Croker, C., *Australia* 88 B5
Croker I., *Australia* 88 B5
Cromarty, *Canada* 101 B10
Cromarty, *U.K.* 14 D4
Cromer, *U.K.* 12 E9
Cromwell, *N.Z.* 87 L2
Cronat, *France* 25 F10
Cronulla, *Australia* 91 E5
Crooked →, *Canada* 100 C4
Crooked →, *U.S.A.* 110 D3
Crooked I., *Bahamas* 117 B5
Crooked Island Passage, *Bahamas* 117 B5
Crookston, *Minn., U.S.A.* 108 B6
Crookston, *Nebr., U.S.A.* 108 D4
Crooksville, *U.S.A.* 104 F4
Crookwell, *Australia* 91 E4
Crosby, *Minn., U.S.A.* 108 B8
Crosby, *N. Dak., U.S.A.* 101 D8
Crosby, *Pa., U.S.A.* 106 E6
Crosbyton, *U.S.A.* 109 J4
Cross →, *Nigeria* 79 E6
Cross City, *U.S.A.* 105 L4
Cross Fell, *U.K.* 12 C5
Cross L., *Canada* 101 C9
Cross Plains, *U.S.A.* 109 J5
Cross River □, *Nigeria* 79 D6
Cross Sound, *U.S.A.* 96 C6
Crossett, *U.S.A.* 109 J9
Crossfield, *Canada* 100 C6
Crosshaven, *Ireland* 15 E3
Croton-on-Hudson, *U.S.A.* 107 E11
Crotone, *Italy* 35 C10
Crow →, *Canada* 100 B4
Crow Agency, *U.S.A.* 110 D10
Crow Hd., *Ireland* 15 E1
Crowell, *U.S.A.* 109 J5
Crowley, *U.S.A.* 109 K8
Crowley, L., *U.S.A.* 112 H8
Crown Point, *U.S.A.* 104 E2
Crows Landing, *U.S.A.* 112 H5
Crows Nest, *Australia* 91 D5
Crowsnest Pass, *Canada* 100 D6
Croydon, *Australia* 90 B3
Croydon, *U.K.* 13 F7
Crozet Is., *Ind. Oc.* 3 G12
Crozon, *France* 24 D2
Cruz, C., *Cuba* 116 C4
Cruz Alta, *Brazil* 127 B5
Cruz das Almas, *Brazil* 123 D4
Cruz de Malta, *Brazil* 122 C3
Cruz del Eje, *Argentina* 126 C3
Cruzeiro, *Brazil* 123 F2
Cruzeiro do Oeste, *Brazil* 127 A5
Cruzeiro do Sul, *Brazil* 124 B3
Cry L., *Canada* 100 B3
Crystal Bay, *U.S.A.* 112 F7
Crystal Brook, *Australia* 91 E2
Crystal City, *Mo., U.S.A.* 108 F9
Crystal City, *Tex., U.S.A.* 109 L5
Crystal Falls, *U.S.A.* 104 B1
Crystal River, *U.S.A.* 105 L4
Crystal Springs, *U.S.A.* 109 K9
Csongrád, *Hungary* 21 J10
Csorna, *Hungary* 21 H7
Csurgo, *Hungary* 21 J7
Cu Lao Hon, *Vietnam* 59 G7
Cua Rao, *Vietnam* 58 C5
Cuácua →, *Mozam.* 83 F4
Cuamato, *Angola* 84 B2
Cuamba, *Mozam.* 83 E4
Cuando →, *Angola* 81 H4
Cuando Cubango □, *Angola* 84 B3
Cuangar, *Angola* 84 B2
Cuanza →, *Angola* 70 G5
Cuarto →, *Argentina* 126 C3
Cuatrociénegas, *Mexico* 114 B4
Cuauhtémoc, *Mexico* 114 B3
Cuba, *Portugal* 31 G3
Cuba, *N. Mex., U.S.A.* 111 J10
Cuba, *N.Y., U.S.A.* 106 D6
Cuba ■, *W. Indies* 116 B4
Cuballing, *Australia* 89 F2
Cubango →, *Africa* 84 B3
Çubuk, *Turkey* 66 B5
Cuchi, *Angola* 81 G3
Cuchillo-Có, *Argentina* 128 A4
Cuchivero →, *Venezuela* 120 B4
Cuchumatanes, Sierra de los, *Guatemala* 116 C1
Cucuí, *Brazil* 120 C4
Cucurpe, *Mexico* 114 A2
Cucurrupí, *Colombia* 120 C2
Cúcuta, *Colombia* 120 B3
Cudalbi, *Romania* 38 D10
Cuddalore, *India* 60 P11
Cuddapah, *India* 60 M11
Cuddapan, L., *Australia* 90 D3
Cudgewa, *Australia* 91 F4
Cudillero, *Spain* 30 B4
Cue, *Australia* 89 E2
Cuéllar, *Spain* 30 D6
Cuenca, *Ecuador* 120 D2
Cuenca, *Spain* 28 E2
Cuenca □, *Spain* 28 F2
Cuenca, Serranía de, *Spain* 28 F3
Cuerdo del Pozo, Pantano de la, *Spain* 28 D2
Cuernavaca, *Mexico* 115 D5
Cuero, *U.S.A.* 109 L6
Cuers, *France* 27 E10
Cuervo, *U.S.A.* 109 H2
Cuesmes, *Belgium* 17 H3
Cuevas, Cerro, *Bolivia* 125 E4
Cuevas del Almanzora, *Spain* 29 H3
Cuevo, *Bolivia* 125 E5
Cuiabá, *Brazil* 125 D6
Cuiabá →, *Brazil* 125 D6
Cuilco, *Guatemala* 116 C1
Cuillin Hills, *U.K.* 14 D2
Cuillin Sd., *U.K.* 14 D2
Cuima, *Angola* 81 G3
Cuiseaux, *France* 27 B9
Cuité, *Brazil* 122 C4
Cuito →, *Angola* 84 B3
Cuitzeo, L. de, *Mexico* 114 D4
Cuiuni →, *Brazil* 121 D5
Cukai, *Malaysia* 59 K4
Culan, *France* 26 B6
Culbertson, *U.S.A.* 108 A2
Culcairn, *Australia* 91 F4
Culebra, Sierra de la, *Spain* 30 D4
Culemborg, *Neths.* 16 E6
Culfa, *Azerbaijan* 67 C11
Culgoa →, *Australia* 91 D4
Culiacán, *Mexico* 114 C3
Culiacán →, *Mexico* 114 C3
Culion, *Phil.* 55 F4
Culiseu →, *Brazil* 125 C7
Cúllar de Baza, *Spain* 29 H2
Cullarin Ra., *Australia* 91 E4
Cullen, *U.K.* 14 D6
Cullen Pt., *Australia* 90 A3
Cullera, *Spain* 29 F4
Cullman, *U.S.A.* 105 H2
Culloden, *U.K.* 14 D4
Culoz, *France* 27 C9
Culpeper, *U.S.A.* 104 F7
Culuene →, *Brazil* 125 C7
Culver, Pt., *Australia* 89 F3
Culverden, *N.Z.* 87 K4
Cumaná, *Venezuela* 121 A5
Cumare, *Colombia* 120 C3
Cumari, *Brazil* 123 E2
Cumberland, *Canada* 100 D3
Cumberland, *Md., U.S.A.* 104 F6
Cumberland, *Wis., U.S.A.* 108 C8
Cumberland →, *U.S.A.* 105 G2
Cumberland I., *U.S.A.* 105 K5
Cumberland Is., *Australia* 90 C4
Cumberland L., *Canada* 101 C8
Cumberland Pen., *Canada* 97 B13
Cumberland Plateau, *U.S.A.* 105 H3
Cumberland Sd., *Canada* 97 B13
Cumborah, *Australia* 91 D4
Cumbres Mayores, *Spain* 31 G4
Cumbria □, *U.K.* 12 C5
Cumbrian Mts., *U.K.* 12 C4
Cumbum, *India* 60 M11
Cuminá →, *Brazil* 121 D6
Cuminapanema →, *Brazil* 121 D7
Cummings Mt., *U.S.A.* 113 K8
Cummins, *Australia* 91 E2
Cumnock, *Australia* 91 E4
Cumnock, *U.K.* 14 F4
Cumpas, *Mexico* 114 A3
Cumplida, Pta., *Canary Is.* 36 F2
Çumra, *Turkey* 66 D5
Cuncumén, *Chile* 126 C1
Cundeelee, *Australia* 89 F3
Cunderdin, *Australia* 89 F2
Cundinamarca □, *Colombia* 120 C3
Cunene →, *Angola* 84 B1
Cúneo, *Italy* 32 D4
Cunillera, I., *Spain* 36 C7
Cunlhat, *France* 26 C7
Cunnamulla, *Australia* 91 D4
Cuorgnè, *Italy* 32 C4
Cupar, *Canada* 101 C8
Cupar, *U.K.* 14 E5
Cupica, G. de, *Colombia* 120 B2
Ćuprija, *Serbia, Yug.* 21 M11
Curaçá, *Brazil* 122 C4
Curaçao, *Neth. Ant.* 117 D6
Curacautín, *Chile* 128 A2
Curahuara de Carangas, *Bolivia* 124 D4
Curanilahue, *Chile* 126 D1
Curaray →, *Peru* 120 D3
Curatabaca, *Venezuela* 121 B5
Cure →, *France* 25 E10
Curepto, *Chile* 126 D1
Curiapo, *Venezuela* 121 B5
Curicó, *Chile* 126 C1
Curicó □, *Chile* 126 C1
Curicuriari →, *Brazil* 120 D4
Curimatá, *Brazil* 122 D3
Curiplaya, *Colombia* 120 C3
Curitiba, *Brazil* 127 B6
Currabubula, *Australia* 91 E5
Currais Novos, *Brazil* 122 C4
Curralinho, *Brazil* 122 B2
Currant, *U.S.A.* 110 G6
Curraweena, *Australia* 91 E4
Currawilla, *Australia* 90 D3
Current →, *U.S.A.* 109 G9
Currie, *Australia* 90 F3
Currie, *U.S.A.* 110 F6
Currituck Sd., *U.S.A.* 105 G8
Curtea de Argeş, *Romania* 38 D7
Curtis, *Spain* 30 B2
Curtis, *U.S.A.* 108 E4
Curtis Group, *Australia* 90 F4
Curtis I., *Australia* 90 C5
Curuá →, *Pará, Brazil* 121 D7
Curuá →, *Pará, Brazil* 125 B7
Curuá, I., *Brazil* 122 A1
Curuaés →, *Brazil* 125 B7
Curuápanema →, *Brazil* 121 D6
Curuçá, *Brazil* 122 B2
Curuguaty, *Paraguay* 127 A4
Curup, *Indonesia* 56 E2
Curupira, Serra, *S. Amer.* 121 C5
Cururu →, *Brazil* 125 B6
Cururupu, *Brazil* 122 B3
Curuzú Cuatiá, *Argentina* 126 B4
Curvelo, *Brazil* 123 E3
Cushing, *U.S.A.* 109 H6
Cushing, Mt., *Canada* 100 B3
Cusihuiráchic, *Mexico* 114 B3
Cusna, Mte., *Italy* 32 D7
Cusset, *France* 26 B7
Custer, *U.S.A.* 108 D3
Cut Bank, *U.S.A.* 110 B7
Cutervo, *Peru* 124 B2
Cuthbert, *U.S.A.* 105 K3
Cutler, *U.S.A.* 112 J7
Cutral-Có, *Argentina* 128 A3
Cutro, *Italy* 35 C9
Cuttaburra →, *Australia* 91 D3
Cuttack, *India* 61 J14
Cuvier, C., *Australia* 89 D1
Cuvier I., *N.Z.* 87 G5
Cuxhaven, *Germany* 18 B4
Cuyabeno, *Ecuador* 120 D2
Cuyahoga Falls, *U.S.A.* 106 E3
Cuyapo, *Phil.* 55 D4
Cuyo, *Phil.* 55 F4
Cuyo East Pass, *Phil.* 55 F4
Cuyo West Pass, *Phil.* 55 F4
Cuyuni →, *Guyana* 121 B6
Cuzco, *Bolivia* 124 E4
Cuzco, *Peru* 124 C3
Cuzco □, *Peru* 124 C3
Cwmbran, *U.K.* 13 F4
Cyangugu, *Rwanda* 82 C2
Cyclades = Kikládhes, *Greece* 39 M7
Cygnet, *Australia* 90 G4
Cynthiana, *U.S.A.* 104 F3
Cypress Hills, *Canada* 101 D7
Cyprus ■, *Asia* 66 E5
Cyrenaica, *Libya* 73 C9
Cyrene = Shaḩḩāt, *Libya* 73 B9
Czar, *Canada* 101 C6
Czarne, *Poland* 20 B6
Czech Rep. ■, *Europe* 20 F4
Czersk, *Poland* 20 B7
Częstochowa, *Poland* 20 E9

D

Da →, *Vietnam* 58 B5
Da Hinggan Ling, *China* 54 B7
Da Lat, *Vietnam* 59 G7
Da Nang, *Vietnam* 58 D7
Da Qaidam, *China* 54 C4
Da Yunhe →, *China* 51 G11
Da'an, *China* 51 B13
Daarlerveen, *Neths.* 16 D9
Dab'a, Râs el, *Egypt* 76 H6
Daba Shan, *China* 52 B7
Dabai, *Nigeria* 79 C6
Dabajuro, *Venezuela* 120 A3
Dabakala, *Ivory C.* 78 D4
Dabeiba, *Colombia* 120 B2
Dabhoi, *India* 62 H5
Dąbie, *Poland* 20 B4
Dabie Shan, *China* 53 B10
Dabo, *Indonesia* 56 E2
Dabola, *Guinea* 78 C2
Dabou, *Ivory C.* 78 D4
Daboya, *Ghana* 79 D4
Dabrowa Tarnówska, *Poland* 20 E10
Dabu, *China* 53 E11
Dabung, *Malaysia* 59 K4
Dabus →, *Ethiopia* 77 E4
Dacato →, *Ethiopia* 77 F5
Dacca = Dhaka, *Bangla.* 63 H14
Dacca = Dhaka □, *Bangla.* 63 G14
Dachau, *Germany* 19 G7
Dadanawa, *Guyana* 121 C6
Daday, *Turkey* 66 B5
Dade City, *U.S.A.* 105 L4
Dades, Oued →, *Morocco* 74 B3
Dadiya, *Nigeria* 79 D7
Dadra and Nagar Haveli □, *India* 60 J8
Dadri = Charkhi Dadri, *India* 62 E7
Dadu, *Pakistan* 62 F2
Dadu He →, *China* 52 C4
Dăeni, *Romania* 38 E11
Daet, *Phil.* 55 D5
Dafang, *China* 52 D5
Dagana, *Senegal* 78 B1
Dagash, *Sudan* 76 D3
Dagestan □, *Russia* 43 J8
Dagestanskiye Ogni, *Russia* 43 J9
Daggett, *U.S.A.* 113 L10
Daghestan Republic = Dagestan □, *Russia* 43 J8
Daghfeli, *Sudan* 76 D3
Dağlıq Qarabağ = Nagorno-Karabakh, *Azerbaijan* 67 C12
Dagö = Hiiumaa, *Estonia* 9 G20
Dagu, *China* 51 E9
Daguan, *China* 52 D4
Dagupan, *Phil.* 55 C4
Dahab, *Egypt* 76 B3
Dahlak Kebir, *Eritrea* 68 D3
Dahlenburg, *Germany* 18 B6
Dahlonega, *U.S.A.* 105 H4
Dahme, *Germany* 18 D9
Dahod, *India* 62 H6
Dahomey = Benin ■, *Africa* 79 D5
Dahong Shan, *China* 53 B9
Dahra, *Senegal* 78 B1
Dahra, Massif de, *Algeria* 75 A5
Dai Hao, *Vietnam* 58 C6
Dai-Sen, *Japan* 49 G6
Dai Shan, *China* 53 B14
Dai Xian, *China* 50 E7
Daicheng, *China* 50 E9
Daimiel, *Spain* 29 F1
Daingean, *Ireland* 15 C4
Dainkog, *China* 52 A1
Daintree, *Australia* 90 B4
Daiō-Misaki, *Japan* 49 G8
Dairût, *Egypt* 76 B3
Daisetsu-Zan, *Japan* 48 C11
Dajarra, *Australia* 90 C2
Dajin Chuan →, *China* 52 B3
Dak Dam, *Cambodia* 58 F6
Dak Nhe, *Vietnam* 58 E6
Dak Pek, *Vietnam* 58 E6
Dak Song, *Vietnam* 59 F6
Dak Sui, *Vietnam* 58 E6
Dakar, *Senegal* 78 C1
Dakhla, *W. Sahara* 74 D1
Dakhla, El Wâhât el-, *Egypt* 76 B2
Dakingari, *Nigeria* 79 C5
Dakor, *India* 62 H5
Dakoro, *Niger* 79 C6
Dakota City, *U.S.A.* 108 D6
Đakovica, *Serbia, Yug.* 21 N10
Đakovo, *Croatia* 21 K8
Dalaba, *Guinea* 78 C2
Dalachi, *China* 50 F3
Dalai Nur, *China* 50 C9
Dālakī, *Iran* 65 D6
Dalälven, *Sweden* 9 F17
Dalaman, *Turkey* 66 D3
Dalaman →, *Turkey* 66 D3
Dalandzadgad, *Mongolia* 50 C3
Dalarna, *Sweden* 9 F16
Dālbandīn, *Pakistan* 60 E4
Dalbeattie, *U.K.* 14 G5
Dalbosjön, *Sweden* 11 F6
Dalby, *Australia* 91 D5
Dalby, *Sweden* 11 J7
Dalen, *Neths.* 16 C9
Dalen, *Norway* 10 E2
Dalfsen, *Neths.* 16 C8
Dalga, *Egypt* 76 B3
Dalgān, *Iran* 65 E8
Dalhart, *U.S.A.* 109 G3
Dalhousie, *Canada* 99 C6
Dalhousie, *India* 62 C6
Dali, *Shaanxi, China* 50 G5
Dali, *Yunnan, China* 52 E3
Dalian, *China* 51 E11
Daliang Shan, *China* 52 D4
Dalias, *Spain* 29 J2
Daling He →, *China* 51 D11
Dāliyat el Karmel, *Israel* 69 C4
Dalkeith, *U.K.* 14 F5
Dall I., *U.S.A.* 100 C2
Dallarnil, *Australia* 91 D5
Dallas, *Oreg., U.S.A.* 110 D2
Dallas, *Tex., U.S.A.* 109 J6
Dallol, *Ethiopia* 77 E5
Dalmacija, *Croatia* 21 M7
Dalmatia = Dalmacija, *Croatia* 21 M7
Dalmellington, *U.K.* 14 F4
Dalnegorsk, *Russia* 45 E14
Dalnerechensk, *Russia* 45 E14
Daloa, *Ivory C.* 78 D3
Dalou Shan, *China* 52 C6
Dalsjöfors, *Sweden* 11 G7
Dalskog, *Sweden* 11 F6
Dalsland, *Sweden* 9 G14
Daltenganj, *India* 63 G11
Dalton, *Canada* 98 C3
Dalton, *Ga., U.S.A.* 105 H3
Dalton, *Mass., U.S.A.* 107 D11
Dalton, *Nebr., U.S.A.* 108 E3
Dalton Iceberg Tongue, *Antarctica* 5 C9
Dalupiri I., *Phil.* 55 B4
Dalvík, *Iceland* 8 D4
Daly →, *Australia* 88 B5
Daly City, *U.S.A.* 112 H4
Daly L., *Canada* 101 B7
Daly Waters, *Australia* 90 B1
Dam Doi, *Vietnam* 59 H5
Dam Ha, *Vietnam* 58 B6
Daman, *India* 60 J8
Dāmaneh, *Iran* 65 C6
Damanhûr, *Egypt* 76 H7
Damanzhuang, *China* 50 E9
Damar, *Indonesia* 57 F7
Damaraland, *Namibia* 84 C2
Damascus = Dimashq, *Syria* 69 B5
Damaturu, *Nigeria* 79 C7
Damāvand, *Iran* 65 C7
Damāvand, Qolleh-ye, *Iran* 65 C7
Damba, *Angola* 80 F3
Dame Marie, *Haiti* 117 C5
Dāmghān, *Iran* 65 B7
Dămienesti, *Romania* 38 C10
Damietta = Dumyât, *Egypt* 76 H7
Daming, *China* 50 F8

Damīr Qābū, Syria 64 B4
Dammam = Ad Dammām, Si. Arabia 65 E6
Dammarie, France 24 D8
Dammartin-en-Goële, France 25 C9
Dammastock, Switz. 23 C6
Damme, Germany 18 C4
Damodar →, India 63 H12
Damoh, India 63 H8
Damous, Algeria 75 A5
Dampier, Australia 88 D2
Dampier, Selat, Indonesia 57 E8
Dampier Arch., Australia 88 D2
Damrei, Chuor Phnum, Cambodia 59 G4
Damville, France 24 D8
Damvillers, France 25 C12
Dan-Gulbi, Nigeria 79 C6
Dana, Indonesia 57 F6
Dana, L., Canada 98 B4
Dana, Mt., U.S.A. 112 H7
Danakil Depression, Ethiopia 77 E5
Danao, Phil. 55 F6
Danbury, U.S.A. 107 E11
Danby L., U.S.A. 111 J6
Dand, Afghan. 62 D1
Dandaragan, Australia 89 F2
Dandeldhura, Nepal 63 E9
Dandeli, India 60 M9
Dandenong, Australia 91 F4
Dandong, China 51 D13
Danfeng, China 50 H6
Danforth, U.S.A. 99 C6
Dangan Liedao, China 53 F10
Danger Is. = Pukapuka, Cook Is. 93 J11
Danger Pt., S. Africa 84 E2
Dangla, Ethiopia 77 E4
Dangora, Nigeria 79 C6
Dangrek, Phnom, Thailand 58 E5
Dangriga, Belize 115 D7
Dangshan, China 50 G9
Dangtu, China 53 B12
Dangyang, China 53 B8
Daniel, U.S.A. 110 E8
Daniel's Harbour, Canada 99 B8
Danielskuil, S. Africa 84 D3
Danielson, U.S.A. 107 E13
Danilov, Russia 42 A5
Danilovka, Russia 42 E7
Daning, China 50 F6
Danissa, Kenya 82 B5
Danja, Nigeria 79 C6
Dankalwa, Nigeria 79 C7
Dankama, Nigeria 79 C6
Dankhar Gompa, India 60 C11
Dankov, Russia 42 D4
Danleng, China 52 B4
Danlí, Honduras 116 D2
Dannemora, U.S.A. 107 B11
Dannenberg, Germany 18 B7
Dannevirke, N.Z. 87 J6
Dannhauser, S. Africa 85 D5
Dansville, U.S.A. 106 D7
Dantan, India 63 J12
Dante, Somali Rep. 68 E5
Danube = Dunărea →, Europe 41 K5
Danube →, Europe 6 F11
Danvers, U.S.A. 107 D14
Danville, Ill., U.S.A. 104 E2
Danville, Ky., U.S.A. 104 G3
Danville, Va., U.S.A. 105 G6
Danyang, China 53 B12
Danzhai, China 52 D6
Danzig = Gdańsk, Poland 20 A8
Dao, Phil. 57 B6
Dão →, Portugal 30 E2
Dao Xian, China 53 E8
Daocheng, China 52 C3
Daora, W. Sahara 74 C2
Daoud = Aïn Beïda, Algeria 75 A6
Daoulas, France 24 D2
Dapaong, Togo 79 C5
Dapitan, Phil. 55 G5
Daqing Shan, China 50 D6
Daqu Shan, China 53 B14
Dar Banda, Africa 70 F6
Dar el Beida = Casablanca, Morocco 74 B3
Dar es Salaam, Tanzania 82 D4
Dar Mazār, Iran 65 D8
Dar'ā, Syria 69 C5
Dar'ā □, Syria 69 C5
Dārāb, Iran 65 D7
Daraj, Libya 75 B7
Dārān, Iran 65 C6
Daravica, Serbia, Yug. 21 N10
Daraw, Egypt 76 C3
Dārayyā, Syria 69 B5
Darazo, Nigeria 79 C7
Darband, Pakistan 62 B5
Darband, Kūh-e, Iran 65 D8
Darbhanga, India 63 F11
Darby, U.S.A. 110 C6
Dardanelle, Ark., U.S.A. 109 H8
Dardanelle, Calif., U.S.A. 112 G7
Dardanelles = Çanakkale Boğazı, Turkey 66 B2
Darende, Turkey 66 C7
Dārestān, Iran 65 D8
Darfo, Italy 32 C7
Dârfûr, Sudan 73 F9
Dargai, Pakistan 62 B4
Dargan Ata, Uzbekistan 44 E7
Dargaville, N.Z. 87 F4
Darhan Muminggan Lianheqi, China 50 D6
Dari, Sudan 77 F3
Darıca, Turkey 66 B3
Darién, G. del, Colombia 120 B2
Darién, Serranía del, Colombia 120 B2
Dariganga, Mongolia 50 B7
Darinskoye, Kazakstan 42 E10
Darjeeling = Darjiling, India 63 F13
Darjiling, India 63 F13
Dark Cove, Canada 99 C9
Darkan, Australia 89 F2
Darkhazīneh, Iran 65 D6
Darkot Pass, Pakistan 63 A5
Darling →, Australia 91 E3
Darling Downs, Australia 91 D5
Darling Ra., Australia 89 F2
Darlington, U.K. 12 C6
Darlington, S.C., U.S.A. 105 H6
Darlington, Wis., U.S.A. 108 D9
Darlington, L., S. Africa 84 E4
Darlot, L., Australia 89 E3
Darłowo, Poland 20 A6
Darmstadt, Germany 19 F4
Darnah, Libya 73 B9
Darnall, S. Africa 85 D5
Darnétal, France 24 C8
Darney, France 25 D13
Darnley, C., Antarctica 5 C6
Darnley B., Canada 96 B7
Daroca, Spain 28 D3
Darr, Australia 90 C3
Darr →, Australia 90 C3
Darrington, U.S.A. 110 B3
Darsser Ort, Germany 18 A8
Dart →, U.K. 13 G4
Dart, C., Antarctica 5 D14
Dartmoor, U.K. 13 G4
Dartmouth, Australia 90 C3
Dartmouth, Canada 99 D7
Dartmouth, U.K. 13 G4
Dartmouth, L., Australia 91 D4
Dartuch, C., Spain 36 B10
Darvaza, Turkmenistan 44 E6
Darvel, Teluk, Malaysia 57 D5
Darwha, India 60 J10
Darwin, Australia 88 B5
Darwin, U.S.A. 113 J9
Darwin, Mt., Chile 128 D3
Darwin River, Australia 88 B5
Daryoi Amu = Amudarya →, Uzbekistan 44 E6
Dās, U.A.E. 65 E7
Dashetai, China 50 D5
Dashhowuz, Turkmenistan 44 E6
Dashkesan = Daşkäsän, Azerbaijan 43 K7
Dasht, Iran 65 B8
Dasht →, Pakistan 60 G2
Dasht-e Mārgow, Afghan. 60 D3
Dasht-i-Nawar, Afghan. 62 C3
Daska, Pakistan 62 C6
Daşkäsän, Azerbaijan 43 K7
Dassa-Zoume, Benin 79 D5
Datça, Turkey 66 D2
Datia, India 63 G8
Datian, China 53 E11
Datong, Anhui, China 53 B11
Datong, Shanxi, China 50 D7
Datu, Tanjung, Indonesia 56 D3
Datu Piang, Phil. 55 H6
Daugava →, Latvia 9 H21
Daugavpils, Latvia 9 J22
Daule, Ecuador 120 D2
Daule →, Ecuador 120 D2
Daulpur, India 62 F7
Daun, Germany 19 E2
Dauphin, Canada 101 C8
Dauphin I., U.S.A. 105 K1
Dauphin L., Canada 101 C9
Dauphiné, France 27 C9
Daura, Borno, Nigeria 79 C7
Daura, Kaduna, Nigeria 79 C6
Dausa, India 62 F7
Däväçi, Azerbaijan 43 K9
Davangere, India 60 M9
Davao, Phil. 55 H6
Davao, G. of, Phil. 55 H6
Dāvar Panāh, Iran 65 E9
Davenport, Calif., U.S.A. 112 H4
Davenport, Iowa, U.S.A. 108 E9
Davenport, Wash., U.S.A. 110 C4
Davenport Downs, Australia 90 C3
Davenport Ra., Australia 90 C1
David, Panama 116 E3
David City, U.S.A. 108 E6
David Gorodok = Davyd Haradok, Belarus 41 F4
Davidson, Canada 101 C7
Davis, U.S.A. 112 G5
Davis Dam, U.S.A. 113 K12
Davis Inlet, Canada 99 A7
Davis Mts., U.S.A. 109 K2
Davis Sea, Antarctica 5 C7
Davis Str., N. Amer. 97 B14
Davos, Switz. 23 C9
Davy L., Canada 101 B7
Davyd Haradok, Belarus 41 F4
Dawa →, Ethiopia 77 G5
Dawaki, Bauchi, Nigeria 79 D6
Dawaki, Kano, Nigeria 79 C6
Dawes Ra., Australia 90 C5
Dawson, Canada 96 B6
Dawson, Ga., U.S.A. 105 K3
Dawson, N. Dak., U.S.A. 108 B5
Dawson, I., Chile 128 D2
Dawson Creek, Canada 100 B4
Dawson Inlet, Canada 101 A10
Dawson Ra., Australia 90 C4
Dawu, China 52 B3
Dax, France 26 E2
Daxian, China 52 B6
Daxin, China 52 F6
Daxindian, China 51 F11
Daxinggou, China 51 C15
Daxue Shan, Sichuan, China 52 B3
Daxue Shan, Yunnan, China 52 F2
Dayao, China 52 E3
Daye, China 53 B10
Dayi, China 52 B4
Daylesford, Australia 91 F3
Dayong, China 53 C8
Dayr az Zawr, Syria 67 E9
Daysland, Canada 100 C6
Dayton, Nev., U.S.A. 112 F7
Dayton, Ohio, U.S.A. 104 F3
Dayton, Pa., U.S.A. 106 F5
Dayton, Tenn., U.S.A. 105 H3
Dayton, Wash., U.S.A. 110 C4
Daytona Beach, U.S.A. 105 L5
Dayu, China 53 E10
Dayville, U.S.A. 110 D4
Dazhu, China 52 B6
Dazu, China 52 C5
De Aar, S. Africa 84 E3
De Bilt, Neths. 16 D6
De Funiak Springs, U.S.A. 105 K2
De Grey, Australia 88 D2
De Grey →, Australia 88 D2
De Kalb, U.S.A. 108 E10
De Koog, Neths. 16 B5
De Land, U.S.A. 105 L5
De Leon, U.S.A. 109 J5
De Panne, Belgium 17 F1
De Pere, U.S.A. 104 C1
De Queen, U.S.A. 109 H7
De Quincy, U.S.A. 109 K8
De Ridder, U.S.A. 109 K8
De Rijp, Neths. 16 C5
De Smet, U.S.A. 108 C6
De Soto, U.S.A. 108 F9
De Tour Village, U.S.A. 104 C4
De Witt, U.S.A. 109 H9
Dead Sea, Asia 69 D4
Deadwood, U.S.A. 108 C3
Deadwood L., Canada 100 B3
Deakin, Australia 89 F4
Deal, U.K. 13 F9
Deal I., Australia 90 F4
Dealesville, S. Africa 84 D4
De'an, China 53 C10
Dean, Forest of, U.K. 13 F5
Deán Funes, Argentina 126 C3
Dearborn, U.S.A. 98 D3
Dease →, Canada 100 B3
Dease L., Canada 100 B2
Dease Lake, Canada 100 B2
Death Valley, U.S.A. 113 J10
Death Valley Junction, U.S.A. 113 J10
Death Valley National Monument, U.S.A. 113 J10
Deauville, France 24 C7
Deba Habe, Nigeria 79 C7
Debaltsevo, Ukraine 41 H10
Debao, China 52 F6
Debar, Macedonia 39 H3
Debden, Canada 101 C7
Debdou, Morocco 75 B4
Dębica, Poland 20 E11
Dęblin, Poland 20 D11
Débo, L., Mali 78 B4
Debolt, Canada 100 B5
Deborah East, L., Australia 89 F2
Deborah West, L., Australia 89 F2
Debre Birhan, Ethiopia 77 F4
Debre Markos, Ethiopia 77 E4
Debre May, Ethiopia 77 E4
Debre Sina, Ethiopia 77 F4
Debre Tabor, Ethiopia 77 E4
Debre Zebit, Ethiopia 77 E4
Debrecen, Hungary 21 H11
Dečani, Serbia, Yug. 21 N10
Decatur, Ala., U.S.A. 105 H2
Decatur, Ga., U.S.A. 105 J3
Decatur, Ill., U.S.A. 108 F10
Decatur, Ind., U.S.A. 104 E3
Decatur, Tex., U.S.A. 109 J6
Decazeville, France 26 D6
Deccan, India 60 M10
Deception L., Canada 101 B8
Dechang, China 52 D4
Děčín, Czech. 20 E4
Decize, France 25 F10
Deckerville, U.S.A. 106 C2
Decollatura, Italy 35 C9
Decorah, U.S.A. 108 D9
Dedéagach = Alexandroúpolis, Greece 39 J8
Dedemsvaart, Neths. 16 C8
Dedham, U.S.A. 107 D13
Dédougou, Burkina Faso 78 C4
Dedovichi, Russia 40 D5
Dedza, Malawi 83 E3
Dee →, C. of Aberd., U.K. 14 D6
Dee →, Wales, U.K. 12 D4
Deep B., Canada 100 A5
Deep Well, Australia 90 C1
Deepwater, Australia 91 D5
Deer →, Canada 101 B10
Deer Lake, Nfld., Canada 99 C8
Deer Lake, Ont., Canada 101 C10
Deer Lodge, U.S.A. 110 C7
Deer Park, U.S.A. 110 C5
Deer River, U.S.A. 108 B8
Deeral, Australia 90 B4
Deerdepoort, S. Africa 84 C4
Deerlijk, Belgium 17 G2
Deferiet, U.S.A. 107 B9
Defiance, U.S.A. 104 E3
Dêgê, China 52 B2
Degebe →, Portugal 31 G3
Degeh Bur, Ethiopia 68 F3
Degema, Nigeria 79 E6
Degersheim, Switz. 23 B8
Deggendorf, Germany 19 G8
Deh Bīd, Iran 65 D7
Deh-e Shīr, Iran 65 D7
Dehaj, Iran 65 D7
Dehdez, Iran 65 D6
Dehestān, Iran 65 D7
Dehgolān, Iran 67 E12
Dehi Titan, Afghan. 60 C3
Dehibat, Tunisia 75 B7
Dehlorān, Iran 67 F12
Dehnow-e Kūhestān, Iran 65 E8
Dehra Dun, India 62 D8
Dehri, India 63 G11
Dehua, China 53 E12
Dehui, China 51 B13
Deinze, Belgium 17 G3
Dej, Romania 38 B6
Dejiang, China 52 C7
Dekemhare, Eritrea 77 D4
Dekese, Zaïre 80 E4
Del Mar, U.S.A. 113 N9
Del Norte, U.S.A. 111 H10
Del Rio, U.S.A. 109 L4
Delai, Sudan 76 D4
Delano, U.S.A. 113 K7
Delareyville, S. Africa 84 D4
Delavan, U.S.A. 108 D10
Delaware, U.S.A. 104 E4
Delaware □, U.S.A. 104 F8
Delaware →, U.S.A. 104 F8
Delaware B., U.S.A. 103 C12
Delegate, Australia 91 F4
Delémont, Switz. 22 B4
Delft, Neths. 16 D4
Delfzijl, Neths. 16 B9
Delgado, C., Mozam. 83 E5
Delgerhet, Mongolia 50 B6
Delgo, Sudan 76 C3
Delhi, Canada 106 D4
Delhi, India 62 E7
Delhi, U.S.A. 107 D10
Delia, Canada 100 C6
Delice, Turkey 66 C6
Delicias, Mexico 114 B3
Delījān, Iran 65 C6
Déline, Canada 96 B7
Delitzsch, Germany 18 D8
Dell City, U.S.A. 111 L11
Dell Rapids, U.S.A. 108 D6
Delle, France 25 E14
Dellys, Algeria 75 A5
Delmar, U.S.A. 107 D11
Delmenhorst, Germany 18 B4
Delmiro Gouveia, Brazil 122 C4
Delnice, Croatia 33 C11
Delong, Ostrova, Russia 45 B15
Deloraine, Australia 90 G4
Deloraine, Canada 101 D8
Delphi, U.S.A. 104 E2
Delphos, U.S.A. 104 E3
Delportshoop, S. Africa 84 D3
Delray Beach, U.S.A. 105 M5
Delsbo, Sweden 10 C10
Delta, Colo., U.S.A. 111 G9
Delta, Utah, U.S.A. 110 G7
Delta □, Nigeria 79 D6
Delta Amacuro □, Venezuela 121 B5
Delungra, Australia 91 D5
Delvinákion, Greece 39 K3
Delvinë, Albania 39 K3
Demanda, Sierra de la, Spain 28 C1
Demavand = Damāvand, Iran 65 C7
Demba, Zaïre 80 F4
Dembecha, Ethiopia 77 E4
Dembi, Ethiopia 77 F4
Dembia, Zaïre 82 B2
Dembidolo, Ethiopia 77 F3
Demer →, Belgium 17 G5
Demidov, Russia 40 E6
Deming, N. Mex., U.S.A. 111 K10
Deming, Wash., U.S.A. 112 B4
Demini →, Brazil 121 D5
Demirci, Turkey 66 C3
Demirköy, Turkey 66 B2
Demmin, Germany 18 B9
Demnate, Morocco 74 B3
Demonte, Italy 32 D4
Demopolis, U.S.A. 105 J2
Dempo, Indonesia 56 E2
Demyansk, Russia 40 D7
Den Burg, Neths. 16 B5
Den Chai, Thailand 58 D3
Den Dungen, Neths. 17 E6
Den Haag = 's-Gravenhage, Neths. 16 D4
Den Ham, Neths. 16 D8
Den Helder, Neths. 16 C5
Den Hulst, Neths. 16 C8
Den Oever, Neths. 16 C6
Denain, France 25 B10
Denair, U.S.A. 112 H6
Denau, Uzbekistan 44 F7
Denbigh, U.K. 12 D4
Denbighshire □, U.K. 12 D4
Dendang, Indonesia 56 E3
Dender →, Belgium 17 F4
Denderhoutem, Belgium 17 G4
Denderleeuw, Belgium 17 G4
Dendermonde, Belgium 17 F4
Deneba, Ethiopia 77 F4
Denekamp, Neths. 16 D10
Deng Xian, China 53 A9
Dengchuan, China 52 E3
Denge, Nigeria 79 C6
Dengfeng, China 50 G7
Dengi, Nigeria 79 D6
Dengkou, China 50 D4
Denham, Australia 89 E1
Denham Ra., Australia 90 C4
Denham Sd., Australia 89 E1
Denia, Spain 29 G5
Denial B., Australia 91 E1
Deniliquin, Australia 91 F3
Denison, Iowa, U.S.A. 108 D7
Denison, Tex., U.S.A. 109 J6
Denison Plains, Australia 88 C4
Denizli, Turkey 66 D3
Denman Glacier, Antarctica 5 C7
Denmark, Australia 89 F2
Denmark ■, Europe 11 J3
Denmark Str., Atl. Oc. 4 C6
Dennison, U.S.A. 106 F3
Denpasar, Indonesia 56 F5
Denton, Mont., U.S.A. 110 C9
Denton, Tex., U.S.A. 109 J6
D'Entrecasteaux, Pt., Australia 89 F2
Dents du Midi, Switz. 22 D3
Denu, Ghana 79 D5
Denver, U.S.A. 108 F2
Denver City, U.S.A. 109 J3
Deoband, India 62 E7
Deoghar, India 63 G12
Deolali, India 60 K8
Deoli = Devli, India 62 G6
Deoria, India 63 F10
Deosai Mts., Pakistan 63 B6
Deping, China 51 F9
Deposit, U.S.A. 107 D9
Depot Springs, Australia 89 E3
Deputatskiy, Russia 45 C14
Dêqên, China 52 C2
Deqing, China 53 F8
Dera Ghazi Khan, Pakistan 62 D4
Dera Ismail Khan, Pakistan 62 D4
Derbent, Russia 43 J9
Derby, Australia 88 C3
Derby, U.K. 12 E6
Derby, Conn., U.S.A. 107 E11
Derby, N.Y., U.S.A. 106 D6
Derbyshire □, U.K. 12 E6
Dereli, Turkey 67 B8
Derg →, U.K. 15 B4
Derg, L., Ireland 15 D3
Dergachi = Derhaci, Ukraine 41 G9
Dergaon, India 61 F19
Derhaci, Ukraine 41 G9
Derik, Turkey 67 D9
Derinkuyu, Turkey 66 C6
Dernieres, Isles, U.S.A. 109 L9
Dêrong, China 52 C2
Derry = Londonderry, U.K. 15 B4
Derryveagh Mts., Ireland 15 B3
Derudub, Sudan 76 D4
Derval, France 24 E5
Dervéni, Greece 39 L5
Derwent, Canada 101 C6
Derwent →, Derby, U.K. 12 E6
Derwent →, N. Yorks., U.K. 12 D7
Derwent Water, U.K. 12 C4
Des Moines, Iowa, U.S.A. 108 E8
Des Moines, N. Mex., U.S.A. 109 G3
Des Moines →, U.S.A. 108 E9
Desaguadero →, Argentina 126 C2
Desaguadero →, Bolivia 124 D4
Descanso, Pta., Mexico 113 N9
Descartes, France 26 B4
Deschaillons, Canada 99 C5
Descharme →, Canada 101 B7
Deschutes →, U.S.A. 110 D3
Dese, Ethiopia 68 E2
Deseado, C., Chile 128 D2
Desenzano del Garda, Italy 32 C7
Desert Center, U.S.A. 113 M11
Desert Hot Springs, U.S.A. 113 M10
Désirade, I., Guadeloupe 117 C7
Deskenatlata L., Canada 100 A6
Desna →, Ukraine 41 G6
Desnătui →, Romania 38 E6
Desolación, I., Chile 128 D2
Despeñaperros, Paso, Spain 29 G1
Despotovac, Serbia, Yug. 21 L11
Dessau, Germany 18 D8
Dessel, Belgium 17 F6
Dessye = Dese, Ethiopia 68 E2
D'Estrees B., Australia 91 F2
Desuri, India 62 G5
Desvres, France 25 B8
Det Udom, Thailand 58 E5
Dete, Zimbabwe 83 F2
Detinja →, Serbia, Yug. 21 M9

Detmold, *Germany* 18 D4
Detour, Pt., *U.S.A.* 104 C2
Detroit, *Mich., U.S.A.* 98 D3
Detroit, *Tex., U.S.A.* 109 J7
Detroit Lakes, *U.S.A.* 108 B7
Deurne, *Belgium* 17 F4
Deurne, *Neths.* 17 F7
Deutsche Bucht, *Germany* 18 A4
Deutschlandsberg, *Austria* 21 J5
Deux-Sèvres □, *France* 24 F6
Deva, *Romania* 38 D5
Devakottai, *India* 60 Q11
Devaprayag, *India* 63 D8
Dévaványa, *Hungary* 21 H10
Deveci Dağları, *Turkey* 66 B7
Develi, *Turkey* 66 C6
Deventer, *Neths.* 16 D8
Deveron →, *U.K.* 14 D6
Devgadh Bariya, *India* 62 H5
Devils Den, *U.S.A.* 112 K7
Devils Lake, *U.S.A.* 108 A5
Devils Paw, *Canada* 100 B2
Devizes, *U.K.* 13 F6
Devli, *India* 62 G6
Devnya, *Bulgaria* 38 F10
Devolii →, *Albania* 39 J3
Devon, *Canada* 100 C6
Devon □, *U.K.* 13 G4
Devon I., *Canada* 4 B3
Devonport, *Australia* 90 G4
Devonport, *N.Z.* 87 G5
Devonport, *U.K.* 13 G3
Devrek, *Turkey* 66 B4
Devrekâni, *Turkey* 66 B5
Devrez →, *Turkey* 66 B6
Dewas, *India* 62 H7
Dewetsdorp, *S. Africa* 84 D4
Dewsbury, *U.K.* 12 D6
Dexing, *China* 53 C11
Dexter, *Mo., U.S.A.* 109 G9
Dexter, *N. Mex., U.S.A.* 109 J2
Dey-Dey, L., *Australia* 89 E5
Deyang, *China* 52 B5
Deyhūk, *Iran* 65 C8
Deyyer, *Iran* 65 E6
Dezadeash L., *Canada* 100 A1
Dezfūl, *Iran* 67 F13
Dezhneva, Mys, *Russia* 45 C19
Dezhou, *China* 50 F9
Dháfni, *Greece* 37 D7
Dhahaban, *Si. Arabia* 76 C4
Dhahiriya = Az̧ Z̧āhirīyah, *West Bank* 69 D3
Dhahran = Az̧ Z̧ahrān, *Si. Arabia* 65 E6
Dhaka, *Bangla.* 63 H14
Dhaka □, *Bangla.* 63 G14
Dhali, *Cyprus* 37 D12
Dhamar, *Yemen* 68 E3
Dhamási, *Greece* 39 K5
Dhampur, *India* 63 E8
Dhamtari, *India* 61 J12
Dhanbad, *India* 63 H12
Dhangarhi, *Nepal* 61 E12
Dhankuta, *Nepal* 63 F12
Dhar, *India* 62 H6
Dharampur, *India* 62 H6
Dharamsala = Dharmsala, *India* 62 C7
Dharmapuri, *India* 60 N11
Dharmsala, *India* 62 C7
Dharwad, *India* 60 M9
Dhaulagiri, *Nepal* 63 E10
Dhebar, L., *India* 62 G6
Dheftera, *Cyprus* 37 D12
Dhenkanal, *India* 61 J14
Dhenoúsa, *Greece* 39 M8
Dherinia, *Cyprus* 37 D12
Dheskáti, *Greece* 39 K4
Dhespotikó, *Greece* 39 N7
Dhestina, *Greece* 39 L5
Dhiarrizos →, *Cyprus* 37 E11
Dhībān, *Jordan* 69 D4
Dhíkti Óros, *Greece* 37 D7
Dhimitsána, *Greece* 39 M5
Dhírfis, *Greece* 39 L6
Dhodhekánisos, *Greece* 39 N10
Dholiana, *Greece* 39 K3
Dholka, *India* 62 H5
Dhoraji, *India* 62 J4
Dhoxáton, *Greece* 39 H7
Dhráhstis, Ákra, *Greece* 37 A3
Dhrangadhra, *India* 62 H4
Dhrápanon, Ákra, *Greece* 37 D6
Dhrol, *India* 62 H4
Dhuburi, *India* 61 F16
Dhule, *India* 60 J9
Dhut →, *Somali Rep.* 68 E5
Di Linh, *Vietnam* 59 G7
Di Linh, Cao Nguyen, *Vietnam* 59 G7
Día, *Greece* 37 D7
Diablo, Mt., *U.S.A.* 112 H5
Diablo Range, *U.S.A.* 112 J5
Diafarabé, *Mali* 78 C4
Diala, *Mali* 78 C3
Dialakoro, *Mali* 78 C3
Diallassagou, *Mali* 78 C4
Diamante, *Argentina* 126 C3
Diamante →, *Argentina* 126 C2
Diamantina, *Brazil* 123 E3
Diamantina →, *Australia* 91 D2
Diamantino, *Brazil* 125 C6
Diamond Bar, *U.S.A.* 113 L9
Diamond Harbour, *India* 63 H13
Diamond Is., *Australia* 90 B5
Diamond Mts., *U.S.A.* 110 G6
Diamond Springs, *U.S.A.* 112 G6
Diamondville, *U.S.A.* 110 F8
Dianbai, *China* 53 G8
Diancheng, *China* 53 G8
Diano Marina, *Italy* 32 E5
Dianópolis, *Brazil* 123 D2
Dianra, *Ivory C.* 78 D3
Diapaga, *Burkina Faso* 79 C5
Diapangou, *Burkina Faso* 79 C5
Diariguila, *Guinea* 78 C2
Dībā, *Oman* 65 E8
Dibaya, *Zaïre* 80 F4
Dibaya-Lubue, *Zaïre* 80 E3
Dibbi, *Ethiopia* 68 G3
Dibete, *Botswana* 84 C4
Dibrugarh, *India* 61 F19
Dickinson, *U.S.A.* 108 B3
Dickson, *Russia* 44 B9
Dickson, *U.S.A.* 105 G2
Dickson City, *U.S.A.* 107 E9
Dicle Nehri →, *Turkey* 67 D9
Dicomano, *Italy* 33 E8
Didam, *Neths.* 16 E8
Didesa, W. →, *Ethiopia* 77 E4
Didiéni, *Mali* 78 C3
Didsbury, *Canada* 100 C6
Didwana, *India* 62 F6
Die, *France* 27 D9
Diébougou, *Burkina Faso* 78 C4
Diefenbaker L., *Canada* 101 C7
Diego Garcia, *Ind. Oc.* 3 E13
Diekirch, *Lux.* 17 J8
Diélette, *France* 24 C5
Diéma, *Mali* 78 C3
Diémbéring, *Senegal* 78 C1
Diemen, *Neths.* 16 D5
Dien Ban, *Vietnam* 58 E7
Dien Bien, *Vietnam* 58 B4
Dien Khanh, *Vietnam* 59 F7
Diepenbeek, *Belgium* 17 G6
Diepenheim, *Neths.* 16 D9
Diepenveen, *Neths.* 16 D8
Diepholz, *Germany* 18 C4
Diepoldsau, *Switz.* 23 B9
Dieppe, *France* 24 C8
Dieren, *Neths.* 16 D8
Dierks, *U.S.A.* 109 H7
Diessen, *Neths.* 17 F6
Diessenhofen, *Switz.* 23 A7
Diest, *Belgium* 17 G6
Dietikon, *Switz.* 23 B6
Dieulefit, *France* 27 D9
Dieuze, *France* 25 D13
Diever, *Neths.* 16 C8
Differdange, *Lux.* 17 J7
Dig, *India* 62 F7
Digba, *Zaïre* 82 B2
Digby, *Canada* 99 D6
Digges, *Canada* 101 B10
Digges Is., *Canada* 97 B12
Dighinala, *Bangla.* 61 H18
Dighton, *U.S.A.* 108 F4
Digne-les-Bains, *France* 27 D10
Digoin, *France* 26 B7
Digor, *Turkey* 67 B10
Digos, *Phil.* 55 H6
Digranes, *Iceland* 8 C6
Digul →, *Indonesia* 57 F9
Dihang →, *India* 61 F19
Dīhōk, *Iraq* 67 D10
Dijlah, Nahr →, *Asia* 64 D5
Dijle →, *Belgium* 17 G5
Dijon, *France* 25 E12
Dikala, *Sudan* 77 G3
Dikimdya, *Russia* 45 D13
Dikkil, *Djibouti* 77 E5
Dikomu di Kai, *Botswana* 84 C3
Diksmuide, *Belgium* 17 F1
Dikson = Dickson, *Russia* 44 B9
Dikwa, *Nigeria* 79 C7
Dila, *Ethiopia* 77 F4
Dilbeek, *Belgium* 17 G4
Dili, *Indonesia* 57 F7
Dilijan, *Armenia* 43 K7
Dilizhan = Dilijan, *Armenia* 43 K7
Dillenburg, *Germany* 18 E4
Dilley, *U.S.A.* 109 L5
Dilling, *Sudan* 77 E2
Dillingen, *Germany* 19 G6
Dillingham, *U.S.A.* 96 C4
Dillon, *Canada* 101 B7
Dillon, *Mont., U.S.A.* 110 D7
Dillon, *S.C., U.S.A.* 105 H6
Dillon →, *Canada* 101 B7
Dilolo, *Zaïre* 80 G4
Dilsen, *Belgium* 17 F7
Dilston, *Australia* 90 G4
Dimas, *Mexico* 114 C3
Dimashq, *Syria* 69 B5
Dimashq □, *Syria* 69 B5
Dimbaza, *S. Africa* 85 E4
Dimbokro, *Ivory C.* 78 D4
Dimboola, *Australia* 91 F3
Dîmbovița →, *Romania* 38 E9
Dîmbovnic →, *Romania* 38 E8
Dimbulah, *Australia* 90 B4
Dimitrovgrad, *Bulgaria* 39 G8
Dimitrovgrad, *Russia* 42 C9
Dimitrovgrad, *Serbia, Yug.* 21 M12
Dimitrovo = Pernik, *Bulgaria* 38 G6
Dimmitt, *U.S.A.* 109 H3
Dimo, *Sudan* 77 F2
Dimona, *Israel* 69 D4
Dimovo, *Bulgaria* 38 F5
Dinagat, *Phil.* 55 F6
Dinajpur, *Bangla.* 61 G16
Dinan, *France* 24 D4
Dīnān Āb, *Iran* 65 C8
Dinant, *Belgium* 17 H5
Dinapur, *India* 63 G11
Dinar, *Turkey* 66 C4
Dīnār, Kūh-e, *Iran* 65 D6
Dinara Planina, *Croatia* 33 E13
Dinard, *France* 24 D4
Dinaric Alps = Dinara Planina, *Croatia* 33 E13
Dinder, Nahr ed →, *Sudan* 77 E3
Dindigul, *India* 60 P11
Ding Xian, *China* 50 E8
Dingalan, *Phil.* 55 D4
Dingbian, *China* 50 F4
Dingelstädt, *Germany* 18 D6
Dinghai, *China* 53 B14
Dingle, *Ireland* 15 D1
Dingle B., *Ireland* 15 D1
Dingmans Ferry, *U.S.A.* 107 E10
Dingnan, *China* 53 E10
Dingo, *Australia* 90 C4
Dingolfing, *Germany* 19 G8
Dingtao, *China* 50 G8
Dinguiraye, *Guinea* 78 C2
Dingwall, *U.K.* 14 D4
Dingxi, *China* 50 G3
Dingxiang, *China* 50 E7
Dingyuan, *China* 53 A11
Dinh, Mui, *Vietnam* 59 G7
Dinh Lap, *Vietnam* 58 B6
Dinkel →, *Neths.* 16 D9
Dinokwe, *Botswana* 84 C4
Dinosaur National Monument, *U.S.A.* 110 F9
Dinslaken, *Germany* 17 E9
Dintel →, *Neths.* 17 E4
Dinteloord, *Neths.* 17 E4
Dinuba, *U.S.A.* 111 H4
Dinxperlo, *Neths.* 16 E9
Diósgyör, *Hungary* 21 G10
Diourbel, *Senegal* 78 C1
Diplo, *Pakistan* 62 G3
Dipolog, *Phil.* 55 G5
Dipşa, *Romania* 38 C7
Dir, *Pakistan* 60 B7
Diré, *Mali* 78 B4
Dire Dawa, *Ethiopia* 68 F3
Diriamba, *Nic.* 116 D2
Dirico, *Angola* 81 H4
Dirk Hartog I., *Australia* 89 E1
Dirranbandi, *Australia* 91 D4
Disa, *India* 62 G5
Disa, *Sudan* 77 E3
Disappointment, C., *U.S.A.* 110 C1
Disappointment, L., *Australia* 88 D3
Disaster B., *Australia* 91 F4
Discovery B., *Australia* 91 F3
Disentis, *Switz.* 23 C7
Dishna, *Egypt* 76 B3
Disina, *Nigeria* 79 C6
Disko, *Greenland* 4 C5
Disko Bugt, *Greenland* 4 C5
Disna = Dzisna →, *Belarus* 40 E5
Dison, *Belgium* 17 G7
Disteghil Sar, *Pakistan* 63 A6
Distrito Federal □, *Brazil* 123 E2
Distrito Federal □, *Venezuela* 120 A4
Disûq, *Egypt* 76 H7
Diu, *India* 62 J4
Dīvāndarreh, *Iran* 67 E12
Dives →, *France* 24 C6
Dives-sur-Mer, *France* 24 C6
Divichi = Däväçi, *Azerbaijan* 43 K9
Divide, *U.S.A.* 110 D7
Dividing Ra., *Australia* 89 E2
Divinópolis, *Brazil* 123 F3
Divisões, Serra dos, *Brazil* 123 E1
Divnoye, *Russia* 43 H6
Divo, *Ivory C.* 78 D3
Divriği, *Turkey* 67 C8
Dīwāl Kol, *Afghan.* 62 B2
Dixie Mt., *U.S.A.* 112 F6
Dixon, *Calif., U.S.A.* 112 G5
Dixon, *Ill., U.S.A.* 108 E10
Dixon, *Mont., U.S.A.* 110 C6
Dixon, *N. Mex., U.S.A.* 111 H11
Dixon Entrance, *U.S.A.* 100 C2
Dixonville, *Canada* 100 B5
Diyadin, *Turkey* 67 C10
Diyālā →, *Iraq* 67 F11
Diyarbakır, *Turkey* 67 D9
Djado, *Niger* 73 D7
Djakarta = Jakarta, *Indonesia* 57 G12
Djamâa, *Algeria* 75 B6
Djamba, *Angola* 84 B1
Djambala, *Congo* 80 E2
Djanet, *Algeria* 75 D6
Djawa = Jawa, *Indonesia* 57 G14
Djebiniana, *Tunisia* 75 A7
Djelfa, *Algeria* 75 B5
Djema, *C.A.R.* 82 A2
Djendel, *Algeria* 75 A5
Djeneïene, *Tunisia* 75 B7
Djenné, *Mali* 78 C4
Djenoun, Garet el, *Algeria* 75 C6
Djerba, *Tunisia* 75 B7
Djerba, I. de, *Tunisia* 73 B7
Djerid, Chott, *Tunisia* 75 B6
Djibo, *Burkina Faso* 79 C4
Djibouti, *Djibouti* 68 E3
Djibouti ■, *Africa* 68 E3
Djolu, *Zaïre* 80 D4
Djougou, *Benin* 79 D5
Djoum, *Cameroon* 80 D2
Djourab, *Chad* 73 E8
Djugu, *Zaïre* 82 B3
Djúpivogur, *Iceland* 8 D6
Djursholm, *Sweden* 10 E12
Djursland, *Denmark* 11 H4
Dmitriya Lapteva, Proliv, *Russia* 45 B15
Dmitriyev Lgovskiy, *Russia* 42 D2
Dmitrov, *Russia* 42 B3
Dmitrovsk-Orlovskiy, *Russia* 42 D2
Dnepr → = Dnipro →, *Ukraine* 41 J7
Dneprodzerzhinsk = Dniprodzerzhynsk, *Ukraine* 41 H8
Dneprodzerzhinskoye Vdkhr. = Dniprodzerzhynske Vdskh., *Ukraine* 41 H8
Dnepropetrovsk = Dnipropetrovsk, *Ukraine* 41 H8
Dneprorudnoye = Dniprorudne, *Ukraine* 41 J8
Dnestr → = Dnister →, *Europe* 41 J6
Dnestrovski = Belgorod, *Russia* 42 E3
Dnieper = Dnipro →, *Ukraine* 41 J7
Dniester = Dnister →, *Europe* 41 J6
Dnipro →, *Ukraine* 41 J7
Dniprodzerzhynsk, *Ukraine* 41 H8
Dniprodzerzhynske Vdskh., *Ukraine* 41 H8
Dnipropetrovsk, *Ukraine* 41 H8
Dniprorudne, *Ukraine* 41 J8
Dnister →, *Europe* 41 J6
Dnistrovskyy Lyman, *Ukraine* 41 J6
Dno, *Russia* 40 D5
Dnyapro = Dnipro →, *Ukraine* 41 J7
Doan Hung, *Vietnam* 58 B5
Doba, *Chad* 73 G8
Dobbiaco, *Italy* 33 B9
Dobbyn, *Australia* 90 B3
Dobele, *Latvia* 9 H20
Döbeln, *Germany* 18 D9
Doberai, Jazirah, *Indonesia* 57 E8
Dobiegniew, *Poland* 20 C5
Doblas, *Argentina* 126 D3
Dobo, *Indonesia* 57 F8
Doboj, *Bos.-H.* 21 L8
Dobra, *Dîmbovita, Romania* 38 E8
Dobra, *Hunedoara, Romania* 38 D5
Dobreta-Turnu-Severin, *Romania* 38 E5
Dobrich, *Bulgaria* 38 F10
Dobrinishta, *Bulgaria* 39 H6
Dobrodzień, *Poland* 20 E8
Dobropole, *Ukraine* 41 H9
Dobruja, *Romania* 38 E11
Dobrush, *Belarus* 41 F6
Dobtong, *Sudan* 77 F3
Doc, Mui, *Vietnam* 58 D6
Doce →, *Brazil* 123 E4
Doda, *India* 63 C6
Dodecanese = Dhodhekánisos, *Greece* 39 N10
Dodewaard, *Neths.* 16 E7
Dodge Center, *U.S.A.* 108 C8
Dodge City, *U.S.A.* 109 G5
Dodge L., *Canada* 101 B7
Dodgeville, *U.S.A.* 108 D9
Dodo, *Sudan* 77 F2
Dodola, *Ethiopia* 77 F4
Dodoma, *Tanzania* 82 D4
Dodoma □, *Tanzania* 82 D4
Dodsland, *Canada* 101 C7
Dodson, *U.S.A.* 110 B9
Doesburg, *Neths.* 16 D8
Doetinchem, *Neths.* 16 E8
Dog Creek, *Canada* 100 C4
Dog L., *Man., Canada* 101 C9
Dog L., *Ont., Canada* 98 C2
Doğanşehir, *Turkey* 66 C7
Dogi, *Afghan.* 60 C3
Dogliani, *Italy* 32 D4
Dogondoutchi, *Niger* 79 C5
Dogran, *Pakistan* 62 D5
Doğubayazıt, *Turkey* 67 C11
Doguéraoua, *Niger* 79 C6
Doha = Ad Dawhah, *Qatar* 65 E6
Dohazari, *Bangla.* 61 H18
Doi, *Indonesia* 57 D7
Doi Luang, *Thailand* 58 C3
Doi Saket, *Thailand* 58 C2
Doig →, *Canada* 100 B4
Dois Irmãos, Sa., *Brazil* 122 C3
Dokka →, *Norway* 10 D4
Dokkum, *Neths.* 16 B7
Dokkumer Ee →, *Neths.* 16 B7
Dokri, *Pakistan* 62 F3
Dokuchayevsk, *Ukraine* 41 J9
Dol-de-Bretagne, *France* 24 D5
Doland, *U.S.A.* 108 C5
Dolbeau, *Canada* 99 C5
Dole, *France* 25 E12
Doleib, Wadi →, *Sudan* 77 E3
Dolgellau, *U.K.* 12 E4
Dolgelley = Dolgellau, *U.K.* 12 E4
Dolianova, *Italy* 34 C2
Dolinskaya = Dolynska, *Ukraine* 41 H7
Dollart, *Neths.* 16 B10
Dolna Banya, *Bulgaria* 38 G6
Dolni Dŭbnik, *Bulgaria* 38 F7
Dolo, *Ethiopia* 77 G5
Dolo, *Italy* 33 C9
Dolomites = Dolomiti, *Italy* 33 B8
Dolomiti, *Italy* 33 B8
Dolores, *Argentina* 126 D4
Dolores, *Uruguay* 126 C4
Dolores, *U.S.A.* 111 H9
Dolores →, *U.S.A.* 111 G9
Dolphin, C., *Falk. Is.* 128 D5
Dolphin and Union Str., *Canada* 96 B8
Dolynska, *Ukraine* 41 H7
Dolzhanskaya, *Russia* 43 G3
Dom, *Switz.* 22 D5
Dom Joaquim, *Brazil* 123 E3
Dom Pedrito, *Brazil* 127 C5
Dom Pedro, *Brazil* 122 B3
Doma, *Nigeria* 79 D6
Domaniç, *Turkey* 66 C3
Domasi, *Malawi* 83 F4
Domat Ems, *Switz.* 23 C8
Domazlice, *Czech.* 20 F2
Dombarovskiy, *Russia* 44 D6
Dombås, *Norway* 9 E13
Dombasle-sur-Meurthe, *France* 25 D13
Dombes, *France* 27 B8
Dombóvár, *Hungary* 21 J8
Domburg, *Neths.* 17 E3
Domérat, *France* 26 B6
Domeyko, *Chile* 126 B1
Domeyko, Cordillera, *Chile* 126 A2
Domfront, *France* 24 D6
Dominador, *Chile* 126 A2
Dominica ■, *W. Indies* 117 C7
Dominica Passage, *W. Indies* 117 C7
Dominican Rep. ■, *W. Indies* 117 C5
Dömitz, *Germany* 18 B7
Domme, *France* 26 D5
Dommel →, *Neths.* 17 E6
Domo, *Ethiopia* 68 F4
Domodóssola, *Italy* 32 B5
Dompaire, *France* 25 D13
Dompierre-sur-Besbre, *France* 26 B7
Dompim, *Ghana* 78 D4
Domrémy-la-Pucelle, *France* 25 D12
Domsjö, *Sweden* 10 A12
Domville, Mt., *Australia* 91 D5
Domvraína, *Greece* 39 L5
Domžale, *Slovenia* 33 B11
Don →, *Russia* 43 G4
Don →, *C. of Aberd., U.K.* 14 D6
Don →, *S. Yorks., U.K.* 12 D7
Don, C., *Australia* 88 B5
Don Benito, *Spain* 31 G5
Don Duong, *Vietnam* 59 G7
Don Martín, Presa de, *Mexico* 114 B4
Dona Ana = Nhamaabué, *Mozam.* 83 F4
Donaghadee, *U.K.* 15 B6
Donald, *Australia* 91 F3
Donalda, *Canada* 100 C6
Donaldsonville, *U.S.A.* 109 K9
Donalsonville, *U.S.A.* 105 K3
Donau = Dunărea →, *Europe* 41 K5
Donau →, *Austria* 21 G7
Donaueschingen, *Germany* 19 H4
Donauwörth, *Germany* 19 G6
Doncaster, *U.K.* 12 D6
Dondo, *Angola* 80 F2
Dondo, *Mozam.* 83 F3
Dondo, Teluk, *Indonesia* 57 D6
Dondra Head, *Sri Lanka* 60 S12
Donegal, *Ireland* 15 B3
Donegal □, *Ireland* 15 B4
Donegal B., *Ireland* 15 B3
Donets →, *Russia* 43 G5
Donetsk, *Ukraine* 41 J9
Dong Ba Thin, *Vietnam* 59 F7
Dong Dang, *Vietnam* 58 B6
Dong Giam, *Vietnam* 58 C5
Dong Ha, *Vietnam* 58 D6
Dong Hene, *Laos* 58 D5
Dong Hoi, *Vietnam* 58 D6
Dong Jiang →, *China* 53 F10
Dong Khe, *Vietnam* 58 A6
Dong Ujimqin Qi, *China* 50 B9
Dong Van, *Vietnam* 58 A5
Dong Xoai, *Vietnam* 59 G6
Donga, *Nigeria* 79 D7
Dong'an, *China* 53 D8
Dongara, *Australia* 89 E1
Dongbei, *China* 51 D13
Dongchuan, *China* 52 D4
Dongen, *Neths.* 17 E5
Donges, *France* 24 E4
Dongfang, *China* 58 C7
Dongfeng, *China* 51 C13
Donggala, *Indonesia* 57 E5
Donggan, *China* 52 F5
Donggou, *China* 51 E13
Dongguan, *China* 53 F9
Dongguang, *China* 50 F9
Donghai Dao, *China* 53 G8

Dongjingcheng, China 51 B15
Donglan, China 52 E6
Dongliu, China 53 B11
Dongmen, China 52 F6
Dongning, China 51 B16
Dongnyi, China 52 C3
Dongola, Sudan 76 D3
Dongou, Congo 80 D3
Dongping, China 50 G9
Dongshan, China 53 F11
Dongsheng, China 50 E6
Dongtai, China 51 H11
Dongting Hu, China 53 C9
Dongxiang, China 53 C11
Dongxing, China 52 G7
Dongyang, China 53 C13
Dongzhi, China 53 B11
Donington, C., Australia 91 E2
Doniphan, U.S.A. 109 G9
Donja Stubica, Croatia 33 C13
Donji Dušnik, Serbia, Yug. 21 M12
Donji Miholjac, Croatia 21 K8
Donji Milanovac, Serbia, Yug. 21 L12
Donji Vakuf, Bos.-H. 21 L7
Dønna, Norway 8 C15
Donna, U.S.A. 109 M5
Donnaconna, Canada 99 C5
Donnelly's Crossing, N.Z. 87 F4
Donnybrook, Australia 89 F2
Donnybrook, S. Africa 85 D4
Donora, U.S.A. 106 F5
Donor's Hill, Australia 90 B3
Donostia = San Sebastián, Spain 28 B3
Donskoy, Russia 42 D4
Donsol, Phil. 55 E5
Donya Lendava, Slovenia 33 B13
Donzère, France 27 D8
Donzère-Mondragon, Barr. de, France 27 D8
Donzy, France 25 E10
Doon →, U.K. 14 F4
Doorn, Neths. 16 D6
Dora, L., Australia 88 D3
Dora Báltea →, Italy 32 C5
Dora Ripária →, Italy 32 C4
Doran L., Canada 101 A7
Dorchester, U.K. 13 G5
Dorchester, C., Canada 97 B12
Dordogne □, France 26 C4
Dordogne →, France 26 C3
Dordrecht, Neths. 16 E5
Dordrecht, S. Africa 84 E4
Dore →, France 26 C7
Dore, Mts., France 26 C6
Doré L., Canada 101 C7
Doré Lake, Canada 101 C7
Dores do Indaiá, Brazil 123 E2
Dorfen, Germany 19 G8
Dorgali, Italy 34 B2
Dori, Burkina Faso 79 C4
Doring →, S. Africa 84 E2
Doringbos, S. Africa 84 E2
Dorion, Canada 98 C5
Dormaa-Ahenkro, Ghana 78 D4
Dormo, Ras, Eritrea 77 E5
Dornach, Switz. 22 B5
Dornberg, Slovenia 33 C10
Dornbirn, Austria 19 H5
Dornes, France 25 F10
Dornoch, U.K. 14 D4
Dornoch Firth, U.K. 14 D4
Dornogovĭ □, Mongolia 50 B6
Doro, Mali 79 B4
Dorogobuzh, Russia 40 E7
Dorohoi, Romania 38 B9
Döröö Nuur, Mongolia 54 B4
Dorr, Iran 65 C6
Dorre I., Australia 89 E1
Dorrigo, Australia 91 E5
Dorris, U.S.A. 110 F3
Dorset, Canada 106 A6
Dorset, U.S.A. 106 E4
Dorset □, U.K. 13 G5
Dorsten, Germany 18 D2
Dortmund, Germany 18 D3
Dörtyol, Turkey 66 D7
Dorum, Germany 18 B4
Doruma, Zaïre 82 B2
Dorūneh, Iran 65 C8
Dos Bahías, C., Argentina 128 B3
Dos Hermanas, Spain 31 H5
Dos Palos, U.S.A. 112 J6
Dosso, Niger 79 C5
Dothan, U.S.A. 105 K3
Dottignies, Belgium 17 G2
Doty, U.S.A. 112 D3
Douai, France 25 B10
Douala, Cameroon 79 E6
Douarnenez, France 24 D2
Double Island Pt., Australia 91 D5
Doubrava →, Czech. 20 F5
Doubs □, France 25 E13
Doubs →, France 25 F12
Doubtful Sd., N.Z. 87 L1
Doubtless B., N.Z. 87 F4
Doudeville, France 24 C7
Doué-la-Fontaine, France 24 E6
Douentza, Mali 78 C4
Douglas, S. Africa 84 D3
Douglas, U.K. 12 C3
Douglas, Alaska, U.S.A. 100 B2
Douglas, Ariz., U.S.A. 111 L9
Douglas, Ga., U.S.A. 105 K4
Douglas, Wyo., U.S.A. 108 D2
Douglastown, Canada 99 C7
Douglasville, U.S.A. 105 J3
Douirat, Morocco 74 B4
Doukáton, Ákra, Greece 39 L3
Doulevant-le-Château, France 25 D11
Doullens, France 25 B9
Doumé, Cameroon 80 D2
Douna, Mali 78 C3
Dounreay, U.K. 14 C5
Dour, Belgium 17 H3
Dourada, Serra, Brazil 123 D2
Dourados, Brazil 127 A5
Dourados →, Brazil 127 A5
Dourdan, France 25 D9
Douro →, Europe 30 D2
Douvaine, France 27 B10
Douz, Tunisia 75 B6
Douze →, France 26 E3
Dove →, U.K. 12 E6
Dove Creek, U.S.A. 111 H9
Dover, Australia 90 G4
Dover, U.K. 13 F9
Dover, Del., U.S.A. 104 F8
Dover, N.H., U.S.A. 107 C14
Dover, N.J., U.S.A. 107 F10
Dover, Ohio, U.S.A. 106 F3
Dover, Pt., Australia 89 F4
Dover, Str. of, Europe 24 B8
Dover-Foxcroft, U.S.A. 99 C6
Dover Plains, U.S.A. 107 E11
Dovey = Dyfi →, U.K. 13 E4
Dovrefjell, Norway 10 B3
Dow Rūd, Iran 65 C6
Dowa, Malawi 83 E3
Dowagiac, U.S.A. 104 E2
Dowgha'i, Iran 65 B8
Dowlatābād, Iran 65 D8
Down □, U.K. 15 B6
Downey, Calif., U.S.A. 113 M8
Downey, Idaho, U.S.A. 110 E7
Downham Market, U.K. 13 E8
Downieville, U.S.A. 112 F6
Downpatrick, U.K. 15 B6
Downpatrick Hd., Ireland 15 B2
Dowsārī, Iran 65 D8
Doyle, U.S.A. 112 E6
Doylestown, U.S.A. 107 F9
Draa, C., Morocco 74 C2
Draa, Oued →, Morocco 74 C2
Drac →, France 27 C9
Drachten, Neths. 16 B8
Drăgănești, Romania 38 E7
Drăgănești-Viașca, Romania 38 E8
Dragaš, Serbia, Yug. 21 N10
Drăgășani, Romania 38 E7
Dragichyn, Belarus 41 F3
Dragonera, I., Spain 36 B9
Draguignan, France 27 E10
Drain, U.S.A. 110 E2
Drake, Australia 91 D5
Drake, U.S.A. 108 B4
Drake Passage, S. Ocean 5 B17
Drakensberg, S. Africa 85 E4
Dráma, Greece 39 H7
Drammen, Norway 10 E4
Drangajökull, Iceland 8 C2
Drangedal, Norway 10 E3
Dranov, Ostrov, Romania 38 E12
Dras, India 63 B6
Drau = Drava →, Croatia 21 K8
Drava →, Croatia 21 K8
Draveil, France 25 D9
Dravograd, Slovenia 33 B12
Drawa →, Poland 20 C5
Drawno, Poland 20 B5
Drayton Valley, Canada 100 C6
Dreibergen, Neths. 16 D6
Drenthe □, Neths. 16 C9
Drentsche Hoofdvaart, Neths. 16 C8
Drepanum, C., Cyprus 37 E11
Dresden, Canada 106 D2
Dresden, Germany 18 D9
Dreux, France 24 D8
Driel, Neths. 16 E7
Driffield, U.K. 12 C7
Driftwood, U.S.A. 106 E6
Driggs, U.S.A. 110 E8
Drin i zi →, Albania 39 H3
Drina →, Bos.-H. 21 L9
Drincea →, Romania 38 E5
Drini →, Albania 38 G3
Drinjača →, Bos.-H. 21 L9
Drissa = Vyerkhnyadzvinsk, Belarus 40 E4
Drivstua, Norway 10 B3
Drniš, Croatia 33 E13
Drøbak, Norway 10 E4
Drochia, Moldova 41 H4
Drogheda, Ireland 15 C5
Drogichin = Dragichyn, Belarus 41 F3
Drogobych = Drohobych, Ukraine 41 H2
Drohobych, Ukraine 41 H2
Droichead Atha = Drogheda, Ireland 15 C5
Droichead Nua, Ireland 15 C5
Droitwich, U.K. 13 E5
Drôme □, France 27 D9
Drôme →, France 27 D8
Dromedary, C., Australia 91 F5
Dronero, Italy 32 D4
Dronfield, Australia 90 C3
Dronne →, France 26 C3
Dronninglund, Denmark 11 G4
Dronrijp, Neths. 16 B7
Dropt →, France 26 D3
Drumbo, Canada 106 C4
Drumheller, Canada 100 C6
Drummond, U.S.A. 110 C7
Drummond I., U.S.A. 98 C3
Drummond Pt., Australia 91 E2
Drummond Ra., Australia 90 C4
Drummondville, Canada 98 C5
Drumright, U.S.A. 109 H6
Drunen, Neths. 17 E6
Druskininkai, Lithuania 9 J20
Drut →, Belarus 41 F6
Druten, Neths. 16 E7
Druya, Belarus 40 E4
Druzhina, Russia 45 C15
Drvar, Bos.-H. 33 D13
Drvenik, Croatia 33 E13
Dry Tortugas, U.S.A. 116 B3
Dryanovo, Bulgaria 38 G8
Dryden, Canada 101 D10
Dryden, U.S.A. 109 K3
Drygalski I., Antarctica 5 C7
Drysdale →, Australia 88 B4
Drysdale I., Australia 90 A2
Dschang, Cameroon 79 D7
Du Bois, U.S.A. 106 E6
Du Quoin, U.S.A. 108 G10
Duanesburg, U.S.A. 107 D10
Duaringa, Australia 90 C4
Ḍubā, Si. Arabia 64 E2
Dubai = Dubayy, U.A.E. 65 E7
Dubăsari, Moldova 41 J5
Dubăsari Vdkhr., Moldova 41 J5
Dubawnt →, Canada 101 A8
Dubawnt, L., Canada 101 A8
Dubayy, U.A.E. 65 E7
Dubbeldam, Neths. 16 E5
Dubbo, Australia 91 E4
Dubele, Zaïre 82 B2
Dübendorf, Switz. 23 B7
Dubica, Croatia 33 C13
Dublin, Ireland 15 C5
Dublin, Ga., U.S.A. 105 J4
Dublin, Tex., U.S.A. 109 J5
Dublin □, Ireland 15 C5
Dublin B., Ireland 15 C5
Dubna, Russia 42 B3
Dubno, Ukraine 41 G3
Dubois, U.S.A. 110 D7
Dubossary = Dubăsari, Moldova 41 J5
Dubossary Vdkhr. = Dubăsari Vdkhr., Moldova 41 J5
Dubovka, Russia 43 F7
Dubovskoye, Russia 43 G6
Dubrajpur, India 63 H12
Dubréka, Guinea 78 D2
Dubrovitsa = Dubrovytsya, Ukraine 41 G4
Dubrovnik, Croatia 21 N8
Dubrovskoye, Russia 45 D12
Dubrovytsya, Ukraine 41 G4
Dubuque, U.S.A. 108 D9
Duchang, China 53 C11
Duchesne, U.S.A. 110 F8
Duchess, Australia 90 C2
Ducie I., Pac. Oc. 93 K15
Duck Cr. →, Australia 88 D2
Duck Lake, Canada 101 C7
Duck Mountain Prov. Park, Canada 101 C8
Duckwall, Mt., U.S.A. 112 H6
Düdelange, Lux. 17 K8
Duderstadt, Germany 18 D6
Dudhi, India 61 G13
Düdingen, Switz. 22 C4
Dudinka, Russia 45 C9
Dudley, U.K. 13 E5
Dueñas, Spain 30 D6
Dueré, Brazil 123 D2
Duero = Douro →, Europe 30 D2
Duffel, Belgium 17 F5
Dufftown, U.K. 14 D5
Dufourspitz, Switz. 22 E5
Dugi Otok, Croatia 33 E12
Dugo Selo, Croatia 33 C13
Duifken Pt., Australia 90 A3
Duisburg, Germany 18 D2
Duitama, Colombia 120 B3
Duiveland, Neths. 17 E4
Duiwelskloof, S. Africa 85 C5
Dūkdamīn, Iran 65 C8
Duke I., U.S.A. 100 C2
Dukhān, Qatar 65 E6
Dukhovshchina, Russia 40 E7
Duki, Pakistan 60 D6
Duku, Bauchi, Nigeria 79 C7
Duku, Sokoto, Nigeria 79 C5
Dulag, Phil. 55 F6
Dulce →, Argentina 126 C3
Dulce, G., Costa Rica 116 E3
Dulf, Iraq 64 C5
Dŭlgopol, Bulgaria 38 F10
Dulit, Banjaran, Malaysia 56 D4
Duliu, China 50 E9
Dullewala, Pakistan 62 D4
Dülmen, Germany 18 D3
Dulovo, Bulgaria 38 F10
Dulq Maghār, Syria 67 D8
Dululu, Australia 90 C5
Duluth, U.S.A. 108 B8
Dum Dum, India 63 H13
Dum Duma, India 61 F19
Dum Hadjer, Chad 73 F8
Dūmā, Lebanon 69 A4
Dūmā, Syria 69 B5
Dumaguete, Phil. 55 G5
Dumai, Indonesia 56 D2
Dumaran, Phil. 55 F3
Dumas, Ark., U.S.A. 109 J9
Dumas, Tex., U.S.A. 109 H4
Dumbarton, U.K. 14 F4
Dumbleyung, Australia 89 F2
Dumfries, U.K. 14 F5
Dumfries & Galloway □, U.K. 14 F5
Dumka, India 63 G12
Dümmer See, Germany 18 C4
Dumoine →, Canada 98 C4
Dumoine L., Canada 98 C4
Dumraon, India 63 G11
Dumyât, Egypt 76 H7
Dumyât, Masabb, Egypt 76 H7
Dún Dealgan = Dundalk, Ireland 15 B5
Dun Laoghaire, Ireland 15 C5
Dun-le-Palestel, France 26 B5
Dun-sur-Auron, France 25 F9
Duna = Dunărea →, Europe 41 K5
Duna →, Hungary 21 K8
Dunaföldvár, Hungary 21 J8
Dunaj = Dunărea →, Europe 41 K5
Dunaj →, Slovak Rep. 21 H8
Dunajec →, Poland 20 E10
Dunajska Streda, Slovak Rep. 21 H7
Dunapatai, Hungary 21 J9
Dunărea →, Europe 41 K5
Dunaújváros, Hungary 21 J8
Dunav = Dunărea →, Europe 41 K5
Dunav →, Serbia, Yug. 21 L11
Dunay, Russia 48 C6
Dunback, N.Z. 87 L3
Dunbar, Australia 90 B3
Dunbar, U.K. 14 E6
Dunblane, U.K. 14 E5
Duncan, Canada 100 D4
Duncan, Ariz., U.S.A. 111 K9
Duncan, Okla., U.S.A. 109 H6
Duncan, L., Canada 98 B4
Duncan L., Canada 100 A6
Duncan Town, Bahamas 116 B4
Duncannon, U.S.A. 106 F7
Dundalk, Canada 106 B4
Dundalk, Ireland 15 B5
Dundalk Bay, Ireland 15 C5
Dundas, Canada 98 D4
Dundas, L., Australia 89 F3
Dundas I., Canada 100 C2
Dundas Str., Australia 88 B5
Dundee, S. Africa 85 D5
Dundee, U.K. 14 E6
Dundee City □, U.K. 14 E6
Dundgovĭ □, Mongolia 50 B4
Dundoo, Australia 91 D3
Dundrum, U.K. 15 B6
Dundrum B., U.K. 15 B6
Dundwara, India 63 F8
Dunedin, N.Z. 87 L3
Dunedin, U.S.A. 105 L4
Dunedin →, Canada 100 B4
Dunfermline, U.K. 14 E5
Dungannon, Canada 106 C3
Dungannon, U.K. 15 B5
Dungannon □, U.K. 15 B5
Dungarpur, India 62 H5
Dungarvan, Ireland 15 D4
Dungarvan Harbour, Ireland 15 D4
Dungeness, U.K. 13 G8
Dungo, L. do, Angola 84 B2
Dungog, Australia 91 E5
Dungu, Zaïre 82 B2
Dungunâb, Sudan 76 C4
Dungunâb, Khalij, Sudan 76 C4
Dunhua, China 51 C15
Dunhuang, China 54 B4
Dunières, France 27 C8
Dunk I., Australia 90 B4
Dunkeld, U.K. 14 E5
Dunkerque, France 25 A9
Dunkery Beacon, U.K. 13 F4
Dunkirk = Dunkerque, France 25 A9
Dunkirk, U.S.A. 106 D5
Dunkuj, Sudan 77 E3
Dunkwa, Central, Ghana 78 D4
Dunkwa, Central, Ghana 79 D4
Dunlap, U.S.A. 108 E7
Dúnleary = Dun Laoghaire, Ireland 15 C5
Dunmanus B., Ireland 15 E2
Dunmara, Australia 90 B1
Dunmore, U.S.A. 107 E9
Dunmore Hd., Ireland 15 D1
Dunmore Town, Bahamas 116 A4
Dunn, U.S.A. 105 H6
Dunnellon, U.S.A. 105 L4
Dunnet Hd., U.K. 14 C5
Dunning, U.S.A. 108 E4
Dunnville, Canada 106 D5
Dunolly, Australia 91 F3
Dunoon, U.K. 14 F4
Dunqul, Egypt 76 C3
Duns, U.K. 14 F6
Dunseith, U.S.A. 108 A4
Dunsmuir, U.S.A. 110 F2
Dunstable, U.K. 13 F7
Dunstan Mts., N.Z. 87 L2
Dunster, Canada 100 C5
Dunvegan L., Canada 101 A7
Duolun, China 50 C9
Duong Dong, Vietnam 59 G4
Dupree, U.S.A. 108 C4
Dupuyer, U.S.A. 110 B7
Duque de Caxias, Brazil 123 F3
Duque de York, I., Chile 128 D1
Durack →, Australia 88 C4
Durack Ra., Australia 88 C4
Durağan, Turkey 66 B6
Durance →, France 27 E8
Durand, U.S.A. 104 D4
Durango = Victoria de Durango, Mexico 114 C4
Durango, Spain 28 B2
Durango, U.S.A. 111 H10
Durango □, Mexico 114 C4
Duranillin, Australia 89 F2
Durant, U.S.A. 109 J6
Duratón →, Spain 30 D6
Durazno, Uruguay 126 C4
Durazzo = Durrësi, Albania 39 H2
Durban, France 26 F6
Durban, S. Africa 85 D5
Dúrcal, Spain 31 J7
Düren, Germany 18 E2
Durg, India 61 J12
Durgapur, India 63 H12
Durham, Canada 98 D3
Durham, U.K. 12 C6
Durham, Calif., U.S.A. 112 F5
Durham, N.C., U.S.A. 105 G6
Durham □, U.K. 12 C6
Durham Downs, Australia 91 D4
Durmitor, Montenegro, Yug. 21 M9
Durness, U.K. 14 C4
Durrësi, Albania 39 H2
Durrie, Australia 90 D3
Dursunbey, Turkey 66 C3
Durtal, France 24 E6
Duru, Zaïre 82 B2
D'Urville, Tanjung, Indonesia 57 E9
D'Urville I., N.Z. 87 J4
Duryea, U.S.A. 107 E9
Dusa Mareb, Somali Rep. 68 F4
Dûsh, Egypt 76 C3
Dushak, Turkmenistan 44 F7
Dushan, China 52 E6
Dushanbe, Tajikistan 44 F7
Dusheti, Georgia 43 J7
Dusky Sd., N.Z. 87 L1
Dussejour, C., Australia 88 B4
Düsseldorf, Germany 18 D2
Dussen, Neths. 16 E5
Dutch Harbor, U.S.A. 96 C3
Dutlwe, Botswana 84 C3
Dutsan Wai, Nigeria 79 C6
Dutton, Canada 106 D3
Dutton →, Australia 90 C3
Duved, Sweden 10 A6
Duvno, Bos.-H. 21 M7
Duyun, China 52 D6
Düzce, Turkey 66 B4
Duzdab = Zāhedān, Iran 65 D9
Dvina, Severnaya →, Russia 44 C5
Dvinsk = Daugavpils, Latvia 9 J22
Dvor, Croatia 33 C13
Dwarka, India 62 H3
Dwellingup, Australia 89 F2
Dwight, Canada 106 A5
Dwight, U.S.A. 104 E1
Dyatkovo, Russia 42 D2
Dyatlovo = Dzyatlava, Belarus 40 F3
Dyer, C., Canada 97 B13
Dyer Plateau, Antarctica 5 D17
Dyersburg, U.S.A. 109 G10
Dyfi →, U.K. 13 E4
Dyje →, Czech. 20 G6
Dyle →, Belgium 17 G5
Dymer, Ukraine 41 G6
Dynevor Downs, Australia 91 D3
Dynów, Poland 20 F12
Dysart, Canada 101 C8
Dzamin Üüd, Mongolia 50 C6
Dzerzhinsk, Russia 42 B6
Dzhalinda, Russia 45 D13
Dzhambul = Zhambyl, Kazakstan 44 E8
Dzhankoy, Ukraine 41 K8
Dzhanybek, Kazakstan 42 F8
Dzhardzhan, Russia 45 C13
Dzharylhach, Ostriv, Ukraine 41 J7
Dzhetygara = Zhetiqara, Kazakstan 44 D7
Dzhezkazgan = Zhezqazghan, Kazakstan 44 E7
Dzhizak = Jizzakh, Uzbekistan 44 E7
Dzhugdzur, Khrebet, Russia 45 D14
Dzhvari = Jvari, Georgia 43 J6
Działdowa, Poland 20 B10
Działoszyn, Poland 20 D8
Dzierzgoń, Poland 20 B9
Dzierzoniów, Poland 20 E6
Dzilam de Bravo, Mexico 115 C7
Dzioua, Algeria 75 B6
Dzisna, Belarus 40 E5
Dzisna →, Belarus 40 E5

Dzungaria = Junggar Pendi, China 54 B3
Dzungarian Gate = Alataw Shankou, China 54 B3
Dzuumod, Mongolia 54 B5
Dzyarzhynsk, Belarus 40 F4
Dzyatlava, Belarus 40 F3

E

Eabamet, L., Canada 98 B2
Eads, U.S.A. 108 F3
Eagle, U.S.A. 110 G10
Eagle →, Canada 99 B8
Eagle Butte, U.S.A. 108 C4
Eagle Grove, U.S.A. 108 D8
Eagle L., Calif., U.S.A. 110 F3
Eagle L., Maine, U.S.A. 99 C6
Eagle Lake, U.S.A. 109 L6
Eagle Mountain, U.S.A. 113 M11
Eagle Nest, U.S.A. 111 H11
Eagle Pass, U.S.A. 109 L4
Eagle Pk., U.S.A. 112 G7
Eagle Pt., Australia 88 C3
Eagle River, U.S.A. 108 C10
Ealing, U.K. 13 F7
Earaheedy, Australia 89 E3
Earl Grey, Canada 101 C8
Earle, U.S.A. 109 H9
Earlimart, U.S.A. 113 K7
Earn →, U.K. 14 E5
Earn, L., U.K. 14 E4
Earnslaw, Mt., N.Z. 87 L2
Earth, U.S.A. 109 H3
Easley, U.S.A. 105 H4
East Angus, Canada 99 C5
East Aurora, U.S.A. 106 D6
East Ayrshire □, U.K. 14 F4
East B., U.S.A. 109 L10
East Bengal, Bangla. 61 G17
East Beskids = Vychodné Beskydy, Europe 41 H2
East Brady, U.S.A. 106 F5
East C., N.Z. 87 G7
East Chicago, U.S.A. 104 E2
East China Sea, Asia 54 C7
East Coulee, Canada 100 C6
East Dunbartonshire □, U.K. 14 F4
East Falkland, Falk. Is. 128 D5
East Grand Forks, U.S.A. 108 B6
East Greenwich, U.S.A. 107 E13
East Hartford, U.S.A. 107 E12
East Helena, U.S.A. 110 C8
East Indies, Asia 57 E6
East Jordan, U.S.A. 104 C3
East Lansing, U.S.A. 104 D3
East Liverpool, U.S.A. 106 F4
East London, S. Africa 85 E4
East Lothian □, U.K. 14 F6
East Main = Eastmain, Canada 98 B4
East Orange, U.S.A. 107 F10
East Pacific Ridge, Pac. Oc. 93 J17
East Palestine, U.S.A. 106 F4
East Pine, Canada 100 B4
East Point, U.S.A. 105 J3
East Providence, U.S.A. 107 E13
East Pt., Canada 99 C7
East Renfrewshire □, U.K. 14 F4
East Retford = Retford, U.K. 12 D7
East Riding □, U.K. 12 D7
East St. Louis, U.S.A. 108 F9
East Schelde → = Oosterschelde, Neths. 17 E4
East Siberian Sea, Russia 45 B17
East Stroudsburg, U.S.A. 107 E9
East Sussex □, U.K. 13 G8
East Tawas, U.S.A. 104 C4
East Toorale, Australia 91 E4
East Walker →, U.S.A. 112 G7
Eastbourne, N.Z. 87 J5
Eastbourne, U.K. 13 G8
Eastend, Canada 101 D7
Easter Islands = Pascua, I. de, Pac. Oc. 93 K17
Eastern □, Kenya 82 B4
Eastern □, Uganda 82 B3
Eastern Cape □, S. Africa 84 E4
Eastern Cr. →, Australia 90 C3
Eastern Ghats, India 60 N11
Eastern Group = Lau Group, Fiji 87 C9
Eastern Group, Australia 89 F3
Eastern Province □, S. Leone 78 D2
Eastern Transvaal = Mpumalanga □, S. Africa 85 B5
Easterville, Canada 101 C9
Easthampton, U.S.A. 107 D12
Eastland, U.S.A. 109 J5
Eastleigh, U.K. 13 G6
Eastmain, Canada 98 B4
Eastmain →, Canada 98 B4
Eastman, Canada 107 A12
Eastman, U.S.A. 105 J4
Easton, Md., U.S.A. 104 F7
Easton, Pa., U.S.A. 107 F9
Easton, Wash., U.S.A. 112 C5
Eastport, U.S.A. 99 D6
Eastsound, U.S.A. 112 B4
Eaton, U.S.A. 108 E2
Eatonia, Canada 101 C7
Eatonton, U.S.A. 105 J4
Eatontown, U.S.A. 107 F10
Eatonville, U.S.A. 112 D4
Eau Claire, Fr. Guiana 121 C7
Eau Claire, U.S.A. 108 C9
Eauze, France 26 E4
Ebagoola, Australia 90 A3
Eban, Nigeria 79 D5
Ebbw Vale, U.K. 13 F4
Ebeggui, Algeria 75 C6
Ebeltoft, Denmark 9 H14
Ebensburg, U.S.A. 106 F6
Ebensee, Austria 21 H3
Eber Gölü, Turkey 66 C4
Eberbach, Germany 19 F4
Eberswalde-Finow, Germany 18 C9
Ebetsu, Japan 48 C10
Ebian, China 52 C4
Ebikon, Switz. 23 B6
Ebingen, Germany 19 G5
Ebnat-Kappel, Switz. 23 B8
Eboli, Italy 35 B8
Ebolowa, Cameroon 79 E7
Ebrach, Germany 19 F6
Ébrié, Lagune, Ivory C. 78 D4
Ebro →, Spain 28 E5
Ebro, Pantano del, Spain 30 B7
Ebstorf, Germany 18 B6
Ecaussines-d' Enghien, Belgium 17 G4
Eceabat, Turkey 66 B2
Ech Cheliff, Algeria 75 A5
Echallens, Switz. 22 C3
Echeng, China 53 B10
Echigo-Sammyaku, Japan 49 F9
Echizen-Misaki, Japan 49 G7
Echmiadzin = Yejmiadzin, Armenia 43 K7
Echo Bay, N.W.T., Canada 96 B8
Echo Bay, Ont., Canada 98 C3
Echoing →, Canada 101 B10
Echt, Neths. 17 F7
Echternach, Lux. 17 J8
Echuca, Australia 91 F3
Ecija, Spain 31 H5
Eckernförde, Germany 18 A5
Eclipse Is., Australia 88 B4
Écommoy, France 24 E7
Ecoporanga, Brazil 123 E3
Écos, France 25 C8
Écouché, France 24 D6
Ecuador ■, S. Amer. 120 D2
Écueillé, France 24 E8
Ed, Sweden 11 F5
Ed Dabbura, Sudan 76 D3
Ed Dâmer, Sudan 76 D3
Ed Debba, Sudan 76 D3
Ed-Déffa, Egypt 76 A2
Ed Deim, Sudan 77 E2
Ed Dueim, Sudan 77 E3
Edah, Australia 89 E2
Edam, Canada 101 C7
Edam, Neths. 16 C6
Eday, U.K. 14 B6
Edd, Eritrea 68 E3
Eddrachillis B., U.K. 14 C3
Eddystone, U.K. 13 G3
Eddystone Pt., Australia 90 G4
Ede, Neths. 16 D7
Ede, Nigeria 79 D5
Édea, Cameroon 79 E7
Edegem, Belgium 17 F4
Edehon L., Canada 101 A9
Edekel, Adrar, Algeria 75 D6
Eden, Australia 91 F4
Eden, N.C., U.S.A. 105 G6
Eden, N.Y., U.S.A. 106 D6
Eden, Tex., U.S.A. 109 K5
Eden, Wyo., U.S.A. 110 E9
Eden →, U.K. 12 C4
Eden L., Canada 101 B8
Edenburg, S. Africa 84 D4
Edendale, S. Africa 85 D5
Edenderry, Ireland 15 C4
Edenton, U.S.A. 105 G7
Edenville, S. Africa 85 D4
Eder →, Germany 18 D5
Eder-Stausee, Germany 18 D4
Edgar, U.S.A. 108 E5
Edgartown, U.S.A. 107 E14
Edge Hill, U.K. 13 E6
Edgefield, U.S.A. 105 J5
Edgeley, U.S.A. 108 B5
Edgemont, U.S.A. 108 D3
Edgeøya, Svalbard 4 B9
Édhessa, Greece 39 J5
Edievale, N.Z. 87 L2
Edina, Liberia 78 D2
Edina, U.S.A. 108 E8
Edinburg, U.S.A. 109 M5
Edinburgh, U.K. 14 F5
Ediniţa, Moldova 41 H4
Edirne, Turkey 66 B2
Edison, U.S.A. 112 B4
Edithburgh, Australia 91 F2
Edjeleh, Algeria 75 C6
Edjudina, Australia 89 E3
Edmeston, U.S.A. 107 D9
Edmond, U.S.A. 109 H6
Edmonds, U.S.A. 112 C4
Edmonton, Australia 90 B4
Edmonton, Canada 100 C6
Edmund L., Canada 101 C10
Edmundston, Canada 99 C6
Edna, U.S.A. 109 L6
Edna Bay, U.S.A. 100 B2
Edo □, Nigeria 79 D6
Edolo, Italy 32 B7
Edremit, Turkey 66 C2
Edremit Körfezi, Turkey 66 C2
Edsbyn, Sweden 10 C9
Edsele, Sweden 10 A10
Edson, Canada 100 C5
Eduardo Castex, Argentina 126 D3
Edward →, Australia 91 F3
Edward, L., Africa 82 C2
Edward I., Canada 98 C2
Edward River, Australia 90 A3
Edward VII Land, Antarctica 5 E13
Edwards, U.S.A. 113 L9
Edwards Plateau, U.S.A. 109 K4
Edwardsville, U.S.A. 107 E9
Edzo, Canada 100 A5
Eefde, Neths. 16 D8
Eeklo, Belgium 17 F3
Eelde, Neths. 16 B9
Eem →, Neths. 16 D6
Eems →, Neths. 16 B9
Eems Kanaal, Neths. 16 B9
Eenrum, Neths. 16 B8
Eernegem, Belgium 17 F2
Eerste Valthermond, Neths. 16 C9
Eferi, Algeria 75 D6
Effingham, U.S.A. 104 F1
Effretikon, Switz. 23 B7
Eforie Sud, Romania 38 E11
Ega →, Spain 28 C3
Égadi, Ísole, Italy 34 E5
Eganville, Canada 98 C4
Egeland, U.S.A. 108 A5
Egenolf L., Canada 101 B9
Eger = Cheb, Czech. 20 E2
Eger, Hungary 21 H10
Eger →, Hungary 21 H10
Egersund, Norway 9 G12
Egg L., Canada 101 B7
Eggenburg, Austria 20 G5
Eggenfelden, Germany 19 G8
Eggiwil, Switz. 22 C5
Éghezée, Belgium 17 G5
Eginbah, Australia 88 D2
Égletons, France 26 C6
Eglisau, Switz. 23 A7
Egmond-aan-Zee, Neths. 16 C5
Egmont, C., N.Z. 87 H4
Egmont, Mt., N.Z. 87 H5
Eğridir, Turkey 66 D4
Eğridir Gölü, Turkey 66 D4
Egtved, Denmark 11 J3
Éguas →, Brazil 123 D3
Egume, Nigeria 79 D6
Éguzon, France 26 B5
Egvekinot, Russia 45 C19
Egypt ■, Africa 76 J7
Eha Amufu, Nigeria 79 D6
Ehime □, Japan 49 H6
Ehingen, Germany 19 G5
Ehrenberg, U.S.A. 113 M12
Ehrwald, Austria 19 H6
Eibar, Spain 28 B2
Eibergen, Neths. 16 D9
Eichstätt, Germany 19 G7
Eider →, Germany 18 A4
Eidsvold, Australia 91 D5
Eidsvoll, Norway 9 F14
Eifel, Germany 19 E2
Eiffel Flats, Zimbabwe 83 F3
Eigg, U.K. 14 E2
Eighty Mile Beach, Australia 88 C3
Eil, Somali Rep. 68 F4
Eil, L., U.K. 14 E3
Eildon, L., Australia 91 F4
Eileen L., Canada 101 A7
Eilenburg, Germany 18 D8
Ein el Luweiqa, Sudan 77 E3
Einasleigh, Australia 90 B3
Einasleigh →, Australia 90 B3
Einbeck, Germany 18 D5
Eindhoven, Neths. 17 F6
Einsiedeln, Switz. 23 B7
Eire = Ireland ■, Europe 15 D4
Eiríksjökull, Iceland 8 D3
Eirlandsche Gat, Neths. 16 B5
Eirunepé, Brazil 124 B4
Eisden, Belgium 17 G7
Eisenach, Germany 18 E6
Eisenberg, Germany 18 E7
Eisenerz, Austria 21 H4
Eisenhüttenstadt, Germany 18 C10
Eisenstadt, Austria 21 H6
Eiserfeld, Germany 18 E3
Eisfeld, Germany 18 E6
Eisleben, Germany 18 D7
Eivissa = Ibiza, Spain 36 C7
Ejby, Denmark 11 J3
Eje, Sierra del, Spain 30 C4
Ejea de los Caballeros, Spain 28 C3
Ejutla, Mexico 115 D5
Ekalaka, U.S.A. 108 C2
Ekeren, Belgium 17 F4
Eket, Nigeria 79 E6
Eketahuna, N.Z. 87 J5
Ekhínos, Greece 39 H8
Ekibastuz, Kazakstan 44 D8
Ekimchan, Russia 45 D14
Ekoli, Zaïre 82 C1
Eksel, Belgium 17 F6
Eksjö, Sweden 9 H16
Ekwan →, Canada 98 B3
Ekwan Pt., Canada 98 B3
El Aaiún, W. Sahara 74 C2
El Aargub, Mauritania 74 D1
El Abiodh-Sidi-Cheikh, Algeria 75 B5
El 'Agrûd, Egypt 69 E3
El Aïoun, Morocco 75 B4
El 'Aiyat, Egypt 76 J7
El Alamein, Egypt 76 H6
El Alto, Peru 124 A1
El 'Aqaba, W. →, Egypt 69 E2
El 'Arag, Egypt 76 B2
El Arahal, Spain 31 H5
El Arenal, Spain 36 B9
El Aricha, Algeria 75 B4
El Arīhā, West Bank 69 D4
El Arish, Australia 90 B4
El 'Arîsh, Egypt 69 D2
El 'Arîsh, W. →, Egypt 69 D2
El Arrouch, Algeria 75 A6
El Asnam = Ech Cheliff, Algeria 75 A5
El Astillero, Spain 30 B7
El Badâri, Egypt 76 B3
El Bahrein, Egypt 76 B2
El Ballâs, Egypt 76 B3
El Balyana, Egypt 76 B3
El Banco, Colombia 120 B3
El Baqeir, Sudan 76 D3
El Barco de Ávila, Spain 30 E5
El Barco de Valdeorras, Spain 30 C4
El Bauga, Sudan 76 D3
El Baúl, Venezuela 120 B4
El Bawiti, Egypt 76 J6
El Bayadh, Algeria 75 B5
El Bierzo, Spain 30 C4
El Bluff, Nic. 116 D3
El Bolsón, Argentina 128 B2
El Bonillo, Spain 29 G2
El Brûk, W. →, Egypt 69 E2
El Buheirat □, Sudan 77 F2
El Caín, Argentina 128 B3
El Cajon, U.S.A. 113 N10
El Callao, Venezuela 121 B5
El Camp, Spain 28 D6
El Campo, U.S.A. 109 L6
El Carmen, Bolivia 125 C5
El Carmen, Venezuela 120 C4
El Castillo, Spain 31 H4
El Centro, U.S.A. 113 N11
El Cerro, Bolivia 125 D5
El Cerro, Spain 31 H4
El Cocuy, Colombia 120 B3
El Compadre, Mexico 113 N10
El Corcovado, Argentina 128 B2
El Coronil, Spain 31 H5
El Cuy, Argentina 128 A3
El Cuyo, Mexico 115 C7
El Dab'a, Egypt 76 H6
El Daheir, Egypt 69 D3
El Deir, Egypt 76 B3
El Dere, Somali Rep. 68 G4
El Descanso, Mexico 113 N10
El Desemboque, Mexico 114 A2
El Dilingat, Egypt 76 H7
El Diviso, Colombia 120 C2
El Djem, Tunisia 75 A7
El Djouf, Mauritania 72 E3
El Dorado, Ark., U.S.A. 109 J8
El Dorado, Kans., U.S.A. 109 G6
El Dorado, Venezuela 121 B5
El Eglab, Algeria 74 C4
El Escorial, Spain 30 E6
El Eulma, Algeria 75 A6
El Faiyûm, Egypt 76 J7
El Fâsher, Sudan 77 E2
El Fashn, Egypt 76 J7
El Ferrol, Spain 30 B2
El Fifi, Sudan 77 E1
El Fuerte, Mexico 114 B3
El Gal, Somali Rep. 68 E5
El Gebir, Sudan 77 E2
El Gedida, Egypt 76 B2
El Geneina = Al Junaynah, Sudan 73 F9
El Geteina, Sudan 77 E3
El Gezira □, Sudan 77 E3
El Giza, Egypt 76 H7
El Goléa, Algeria 75 B5
El Hadeb, W. Sahara 74 C2
El Hadjira, Algeria 75 B6
El Hagiz, Sudan 77 D4
El Hajeb, Morocco 74 B3
El Hammam, Egypt 76 H6
El Hammâmi, Mauritania 74 D2
El Hank, Mauritania 74 D3
El Hasian, W. Sahara 74 C2
El Hawata, Sudan 77 E3
El Heiz, Egypt 76 B2
El 'Idisât, Egypt 76 B3
El Iskandarîya, Egypt 76 H6
El Jadida, Morocco 74 B3
El Jebelein, Sudan 77 E3
El Kab, Sudan 76 D3
El Kabrît, G., Egypt 69 F2
El Kala, Algeria 75 A6
El Kalâa, Morocco 74 B3
El Kamlin, Sudan 77 D3
El Kantara, Algeria 75 A6
El Kantara, Tunisia 75 B7
El Karaba, Sudan 76 D3
El Kef, Tunisia 75 A6
El Khandaq, Sudan 76 D3
El Khârga, Egypt 76 B3
El Khartûm, Sudan 77 D3
El Khartûm □, Sudan 77 D3
El Khartûm Bahrî, Sudan 77 D3
El Khroub, Algeria 75 A6
El Kseur, Algeria 75 A5
El Ksiba, Morocco 74 B3
El Kuntilla, Egypt 69 E3
El Laqâwa, Sudan 77 E2
El Laqeita, Egypt 76 B3
El Leiya, Sudan 77 D4
El Mafâza, Sudan 77 E3
El Mahalla el Kubra, Egypt 76 H7
El Mahârîq, Egypt 76 B3
El Mahmûdîya, Egypt 76 H7
El Maitén, Argentina 128 B2
El Maiz, Algeria 75 C4
El-Maks el-Bahari, Egypt 76 C3
El Manshâh, Egypt 76 B3
El Mansour, Algeria 75 C4
El Mansûra, Egypt 76 H7
El Mantico, Venezuela 121 B5
El Manzala, Egypt 76 H7
El Marâgha, Egypt 76 B3
El Masid, Sudan 77 D3
El Matariya, Egypt 76 H8
El Medano, Canary Is. 36 F3
El Meghaier, Algeria 75 B6
El Meraguen, Algeria 75 C4
El Metemma, Sudan 77 D3
El Miamo, Venezuela 121 B5
El Milagro, Argentina 126 C2
El Milia, Algeria 75 A6
El Minyâ, Egypt 76 J7
El Molar, Spain 28 E1
El Monte, U.S.A. 113 L8
El Mreyye, Mauritania 78 B3
El Obeid, Sudan 77 E3
El Odaiya, Sudan 77 E2
El Oro, Mexico 115 D4
El Oro □, Ecuador 120 D2
El Oued, Algeria 75 B6
El Palmar, Bolivia 125 D5
El Palmar, Venezuela 121 B5
El Palmito, Presa, Mexico 114 B3
El Panadés, Spain 28 D6
El Pardo, Spain 30 E7
El Paso, U.S.A. 111 L10
El Paso Robles, U.S.A. 112 K6
El Pedernoso, Spain 29 F2
El Pedroso, Spain 31 H5
El Pobo de Dueñas, Spain 28 E3
El Portal, U.S.A. 111 H4
El Porvenir, Mexico 114 A3
El Prat de Llobregat, Spain 28 D7
El Progreso, Honduras 116 C2
El Provencío, Spain 29 F2
El Pueblito, Mexico 114 B3
El Pueblo, Canary Is. 36 F2
El Puerto de Santa María, Spain 31 J4
El Qâhira, Egypt 76 H7
El Qantara, Egypt 69 E1
El Qasr, Egypt 76 B2
El Quseima, Egypt 69 E3
El Qusîya, Egypt 76 B3
El Râshda, Egypt 76 B2
El Reno, U.S.A. 109 H6
El Ribero, Spain 30 C2
El Rîdisiya, Egypt 76 C3
El Rio, U.S.A. 113 L7
El Ronquillo, Spain 31 H4
El Roque, Pta., Canary Is. 36 F4
El Rosarito, Mexico 114 B2
El Rubio, Spain 31 H5
El Saff, Egypt 76 J7
El Saheira, W. →, Egypt 69 E2
El Salto, Mexico 114 C3
El Salvador ■, Cent. Amer. 116 D2
El Sancejo, Spain 31 H5
El Sauce, Nic. 116 D2
El Shallal, Egypt 76 C3
El Simbillawein, Egypt 76 H7
El Sombrero, Venezuela 120 B4
El Suweis, Egypt 76 J8
El Tamarâni, W. →, Egypt 69 E3
El Thamad, Egypt 69 F3
El Tigre, Venezuela 121 B5
El Tîh, G., Egypt 69 F2
El Tîna, Khalîg, Egypt 69 D1
El Tocuyo, Venezuela 120 B4
El Tofo, Chile 126 B1
El Tránsito, Chile 126 B1
El Tûr, Egypt 76 J8
El Turbio, Argentina 128 D2
El Uqsur, Egypt 76 B3
El Vado, Spain 28 D1
El Vallés, Spain 28 D7
El Venado, Mexico 114 C4
El Vigía, Venezuela 120 B3
El Wabeira, Egypt 69 F2
El Wak, Kenya 82 B5
El Waqf, Egypt 76 B3
El Wâsta, Egypt 76 J7
El Weguet, Ethiopia 77 F5
El Wuz, Sudan 77 D3
Elafónisos, Greece 39 N5
Élassa, Greece 39 P9
Elassón, Greece 39 K5
Elat, Israel 69 F3
Elâzığ, Turkey 67 C8
Elba, Italy 32 F7
Elba, U.S.A. 105 K2
Elbasani, Albania 39 H3
Elbe, U.S.A. 112 D4
Elbe →, Europe 18 B4
Elbe-Seiten Kanal, Germany 18 C6
Elbert, Mt., U.S.A. 111 G10
Elberta, U.S.A. 104 C2
Elberton, U.S.A. 105 H4
Elbeuf, France 24 C8
Elbing = Elbląg, Poland 20 A9
Elbistan, Turkey 66 C7
Elbląg, Poland 20 A9

Elbow, *Canada* 101 C7
Elbrus, *Asia* 43 J6
Elburg, *Neths.* 16 D7
Elburz Mts. = Alborz, Reshteh-ye Kūhhā-ye, *Iran* 65 C7
Elche, *Spain* 29 G4
Elche de la Sierra, *Spain* 29 G2
Elcho I., *Australia* 90 A2
Elda, *Spain* 29 G4
Eldon, *Mo., U.S.A.* 108 F8
Eldon, *Wash., U.S.A.* 112 C3
Eldora, *U.S.A.* 108 D8
Eldorado, *Argentina* 127 B5
Eldorado, *Canada* 101 B7
Eldorado, *Mexico* 114 C3
Eldorado, *Ill., U.S.A.* 104 G1
Eldorado, *Tex., U.S.A.* 109 K4
Eldorado Springs, *U.S.A.* 109 G8
Eldoret, *Kenya* 82 B4
Eldred, *U.S.A.* 106 E6
Elea, C., *Cyprus* 37 D13
Electra, *U.S.A.* 109 H5
Elefantes →, *Mozam.* 85 C5
Elefantes, G., *Chile* 128 C2
Elektrogorsk, *Russia* 42 C4
Elektrostal, *Russia* 42 C4
Elele, *Nigeria* 79 D6
Elephant Butte Reservoir, *U.S.A.* 111 K10
Elephant I., *Antarctica* 5 C18
Elesbão Veloso, *Brazil* 122 C3
Eleşkirt, *Turkey* 67 C10
Eleuthera, *Bahamas* 116 A4
Elgepiggen, *Norway* 10 B5
Elgeyo-Marakwet □, *Kenya* 82 B4
Elgg, *Switz.* 23 B7
Elgin, *N.B., Canada* 99 C6
Elgin, *Ont., Canada* 107 B8
Elgin, *U.K.* 14 D5
Elgin, *Ill., U.S.A.* 104 D1
Elgin, *N. Dak., U.S.A.* 108 B4
Elgin, *Nebr., U.S.A.* 108 E5
Elgin, *Nev., U.S.A.* 111 H6
Elgin, *Oreg., U.S.A.* 110 D5
Elgin, *Tex., U.S.A.* 109 K6
Elgon, Mt., *Africa* 82 B3
Eliase, *Indonesia* 57 F8
Elida, *U.S.A.* 109 J3
Elikón, *Greece* 39 L5
Elim, *S. Africa* 84 E2
Elisabethville = Lubumbashi, *Zaïre* 83 E2
Eliseu Martins, *Brazil* 122 C3
Elista, *Russia* 43 G7
Elizabeth, *Australia* 91 E2
Elizabeth, *U.S.A.* 107 F10
Elizabeth City, *U.S.A.* 105 G7
Elizabethton, *U.S.A.* 105 G4
Elizabethtown, *Ky., U.S.A.* 104 G3
Elizabethtown, *N.Y., U.S.A.* 107 B11
Elizabethtown, *Pa., U.S.A.* 107 F8
Elizondo, *Spain* 28 B3
Ełk, *Poland* 20 B12
Elk City, *U.S.A.* 109 H5
Elk Creek, *U.S.A.* 112 F4
Elk Grove, *U.S.A.* 112 G5
Elk Island Nat. Park, *Canada* 100 C6
Elk Lake, *Canada* 98 C3
Elk Point, *Canada* 101 C6
Elk River, *Idaho, U.S.A.* 110 C5
Elk River, *Minn., U.S.A.* 108 C8
Elkedra, *Australia* 90 C2
Elkedra →, *Australia* 90 C2
Elkhart, *Ind., U.S.A.* 104 E3
Elkhart, *Kans., U.S.A.* 109 G4
Elkhorn, *Canada* 101 D8
Elkhorn →, *U.S.A.* 108 E6
Elkhovo, *Bulgaria* 38 G9
Elkin, *U.S.A.* 105 G5
Elkins, *U.S.A.* 104 F6
Elko, *Canada* 100 D5
Elko, *U.S.A.* 110 F6
Ell, L., *Australia* 89 E4
Ellecom, *Neths.* 16 D8
Ellef Ringnes I., *Canada* 4 B2
Ellendale, *Australia* 88 C3
Ellendale, *U.S.A.* 108 B5
Ellensburg, *U.S.A.* 110 C3
Ellenville, *U.S.A.* 107 E10
Ellery, Mt., *Australia* 91 F4
Ellesmere, L., *N.Z.* 87 M4
Ellesmere I., *Canada* 4 B4
Ellesmere Port, *U.K.* 12 D5
Ellezelles, *Belgium* 17 G3
Ellice Is. = Tuvalu ■, *Pac. Oc.* 92 H9
Ellinwood, *U.S.A.* 108 F5
Elliot, *Australia* 90 B1
Elliot, *S. Africa* 85 E4
Elliot Lake, *Canada* 98 C3
Elliotdale = Xhora, *S. Africa* 85 E4
Ellis, *U.S.A.* 108 F5
Elliston, *Australia* 91 E1
Ellisville, *U.S.A.* 109 K10
Ellon, *U.K.* 14 D6
Ellore = Eluru, *India* 61 L12
Ells →, *Canada* 100 B6
Ellsworth, *U.S.A.* 108 F5
Ellsworth Land, *Antarctica* 5 D16
Ellsworth Mts., *Antarctica* 5 D16
Ellwangen, *Germany* 19 G6
Ellwood City, *U.S.A.* 106 F4
Elm, *Switz.* 23 C8
Elma, *Canada* 101 D9
Elma, *U.S.A.* 112 D3
Elmadağ, *Turkey* 66 C5
Elmalı, *Turkey* 66 D3
Elmhurst, *U.S.A.* 104 E2
Elmina, *Ghana* 79 D4
Elmira, *Canada* 106 C4
Elmira, *U.S.A.* 106 D8
Elmore, *Australia* 91 F3
Elmore, *U.S.A.* 113 M11
Elmshorn, *Germany* 18 B5
Elmvale, *Canada* 106 B5
Elne, *France* 26 F6
Elora, *Canada* 106 C4
Elorza, *Venezuela* 120 B4
Eloúnda, *Greece* 37 D7
Eloy, *U.S.A.* 111 K8
Éloyes, *France* 25 D13
Elrose, *Canada* 101 C7
Elsas, *Canada* 98 C3
Elsie, *U.S.A.* 112 E3
Elsinore = Helsingør, *Denmark* 11 H6
Elsinore, *U.S.A.* 111 G7
Elspe, *Germany* 18 D4
Elspeet, *Neths.* 16 D7
Elst, *Neths.* 16 E7
Elster →, *Germany* 18 D7
Elsterwerda, *Germany* 18 D9
Elten, *Neths.* 16 E8
Eltham, *N.Z.* 87 H5
Elton, *Russia* 43 F8
Elton, Ozero, *Russia* 43 F8
Eluru, *India* 61 L12
Elvas, *Portugal* 31 G3
Elven, *France* 24 E4
Elverum, *Norway* 10 D5
Elvire →, *Australia* 88 C4
Elvo →, *Italy* 32 C5
Elvran, *Norway* 10 A5
Elwood, *Ind., U.S.A.* 104 E3
Elwood, *Nebr., U.S.A.* 108 E5
Elx = Elche, *Spain* 29 G4
Ely, *U.K.* 13 E8
Ely, *Minn., U.S.A.* 108 B9
Ely, *Nev., U.S.A.* 110 G6
Elyria, *U.S.A.* 106 E2
Elz →, *Germany* 19 G3
Emāmrūd, *Iran* 65 B7
Emba = Embi, *Kazakstan* 44 E6
Emba → = Embi →, *Kazakstan* 44 E6
Embarcación, *Argentina* 126 A3
Embarras Portage, *Canada* 101 B6
Embetsu, *Japan* 48 B10
Embi, *Kazakstan* 44 E6
Embi →, *Kazakstan* 44 E6
Embira →, *Brazil* 124 B3
Embóna, *Greece* 37 C9
Embrach, *Switz.* 23 A7
Embrun, *France* 27 D10
Embu, *Kenya* 82 C4
Embu □, *Kenya* 82 C4
Emden, *Germany* 18 B3
Emerald, *Australia* 90 C4
Emerson, *Canada* 101 D9
Emery, *U.S.A.* 111 G8
Emet, *Turkey* 66 C3
Emi Koussi, *Chad* 73 E8
Emília-Romagna □, *Italy* 32 D7
Emílius, Mte., *Italy* 32 C4
Eminabad, *Pakistan* 62 C6
Emirdağ, *Turkey* 66 C4
Emlenton, *U.S.A.* 106 E5
Emlichheim, *Germany* 18 C2
Emme →, *Switz.* 22 B5
Emmeloord, *Neths.* 16 C7
Emmen, *Neths.* 16 C9
Emmendingen, *Germany* 19 G3
Emmental, *Switz.* 22 C4
Emmer-Compascuum, *Neths.* 16 C10
Emmerich, *Germany* 18 D2
Emmet, *Australia* 90 C3
Emmetsburg, *U.S.A.* 108 D7
Emmett, *U.S.A.* 110 E5
Empalme, *Mexico* 114 B2
Empangeni, *S. Africa* 85 D5
Empedrado, *Argentina* 126 B4
Emperor Seamount Chain, *Pac. Oc.* 92 D9
Empoli, *Italy* 32 E7
Emporia, *Kans., U.S.A.* 108 F6
Emporia, *Va., U.S.A.* 105 G7
Emporium, *U.S.A.* 106 E6
Empress, *Canada* 101 C6
Emptinne, *Belgium* 17 H6
Empty Quarter = Rub' al Khali, *Si. Arabia* 68 D4
Ems →, *Germany* 18 B3
Emsdale, *Canada* 106 A5
Emsdetten, *Germany* 18 C3
Emu, *China* 51 C15
Emu Park, *Australia* 90 C5
'En 'Avrona, *Israel* 69 F3
En Nahud, *Sudan* 77 E2
Ena, *Japan* 49 G8
Enafors, *Sweden* 10 A6
Enambú, *Colombia* 120 C3
Enana, *Namibia* 84 B2
Enånger, *Sweden* 10 C11
Enaratoli, *Indonesia* 57 E9
Enard B., *U.K.* 14 C3
Enare = Inarijärvi, *Finland* 8 B22
Encantadas, Serra, *Brazil* 127 C5
Encanto, C., *Phil.* 57 A6
Encarnación, *Paraguay* 127 B4
Encarnación de Diaz, *Mexico* 114 C4
Enchi, *Ghana* 78 D4
Encinal, *U.S.A.* 109 L5
Encinitas, *U.S.A.* 113 M9
Encino, *U.S.A.* 111 J11
Encontrados, *Venezuela* 120 B3
Encounter B., *Australia* 91 F2
Encruzilhada, *Brazil* 123 E3
Ende, *Indonesia* 57 F6
Endeavour, *Canada* 101 C8
Endeavour Str., *Australia* 90 A3
Endelave, *Denmark* 11 J4
Enderbury I., *Kiribati* 92 H10
Enderby, *Canada* 100 C5
Enderby I., *Australia* 88 D2
Enderby Land, *Antarctica* 5 C5
Enderlin, *U.S.A.* 108 B6
Endicott, *N.Y., U.S.A.* 107 D8
Endicott, *Wash., U.S.A.* 110 C5
Endimari →, *Brazil* 124 B4
Endyalgout I., *Australia* 88 B5
Ene →, *Peru* 124 C3
Enewetak Atoll, *Pac. Oc.* 92 F8
Enez, *Turkey* 66 B2
Enfield, *U.K.* 13 F7
Engadin, *Switz.* 19 J6
Engaño, C., *Dom. Rep.* 117 C6
Engaño, C., *Phil.* 57 A6
Engcobo, *S. Africa* 85 E4
Engelberg, *Switz.* 23 C6
Engels, *Russia* 42 E8
Engemann L., *Canada* 101 B7
Enger, *Norway* 10 D4
Enggano, *Indonesia* 56 F2
Enghien, *Belgium* 17 G4
Engil, *Morocco* 74 B4
Engkilili, *Malaysia* 56 D4
England, *U.S.A.* 109 H9
England □, *U.K.* 7 E5
Englee, *Canada* 99 B8
Englehart, *Canada* 98 C4
Engler L., *Canada* 101 B7
Englewood, *Colo., U.S.A.* 108 F2
Englewood, *Kans., U.S.A.* 109 G5
English →, *Canada* 101 C10
English Bazar = Ingraj Bazar, *India* 63 G13
English Channel, *Europe* 13 G6
English River, *Canada* 98 C1
Enguri →, *Georgia* 43 J5
Enid, *U.S.A.* 109 G6
Enipévs →, *Greece* 39 K5
Enkhuizen, *Neths.* 16 C6
Enköping, *Sweden* 10 E11
Enle, *China* 52 E3
Enna, *Italy* 35 E7
Ennadai, *Canada* 101 A8
Ennadai L., *Canada* 101 A8
Ennedi, *Chad* 73 E9
Enngonia, *Australia* 91 D4
Ennis, *Ireland* 15 D3
Ennis, *Mont., U.S.A.* 110 D8
Ennis, *Tex., U.S.A.* 109 J6
Enniscorthy, *Ireland* 15 D5
Enniskillen, *U.K.* 15 B4
Ennistimon, *Ireland* 15 D2
Enns →, *Austria* 21 G4
Enontekiö, *Finland* 8 B20
Enping, *China* 53 F9
Enriquillo, L., *Dom. Rep.* 117 C5
Ens, *Neths.* 16 C7
Enschede, *Neths.* 16 D9
Ensenada, *Argentina* 126 C4
Ensenada, *Mexico* 114 A1
Enshi, *China* 52 B7
Ensiola, Pta., *Spain* 36 B9
Ensisheim, *France* 25 E14
Entebbe, *Uganda* 82 B3
Enter, *Neths.* 16 D9
Enterprise, *Canada* 100 A5
Enterprise, *Oreg., U.S.A.* 110 D5
Enterprise, *Utah, U.S.A.* 111 H7
Entlebuch, *Switz.* 22 C6
Entre Ríos, *Bolivia* 126 A3
Entre Rios, *Bahia, Brazil* 123 D4
Entre Rios, *Pará, Brazil* 125 B7
Entre Ríos □, *Argentina* 126 C4
Entrepeñas, Pantano de, *Spain* 28 E2
Enugu, *Nigeria* 79 D6
Enugu □, *Nigeria* 79 D6
Enugu Ezike, *Nigeria* 79 D6
Enumclaw, *U.S.A.* 112 C5
Envermeu, *France* 24 C8
Envigado, *Colombia* 120 B2
Envira, *Brazil* 124 B3
Enz →, *Germany* 19 F5
Enza →, *Italy* 32 D7
Eólie, Ís., *Italy* 35 D7
Epanomí, *Greece* 39 J5
Epe, *Neths.* 16 D7
Epe, *Nigeria* 79 D5
Épernay, *France* 25 C10
Épernon, *France* 25 D8
Ephesus, *Turkey* 66 D2
Ephraim, *U.S.A.* 110 G8
Ephrata, *U.S.A.* 110 C4
Epila, *Spain* 28 D3
Épinac-les-Mines, *France* 25 F11
Épinal, *France* 25 D13
Epira, *Guyana* 121 B6
Episkopi, *Cyprus* 37 E11
Episkopí, *Greece* 37 D6
Episkopi Bay, *Cyprus* 37 E11
Eppan = Appiano, *Italy* 33 B8
Epping, *U.K.* 13 F8
Epukiro, *Namibia* 84 C2
Equatorial Guinea ■, *Africa* 80 D1
Equeipa, *Venezuela* 121 B5
Er Rahad, *Sudan* 77 E3
Er Rif, *Morocco* 75 A4
Er Roseires, *Sudan* 77 E3
Erāwadī Myit = Irrawaddy →, *Burma* 61 M19
Erba, *Italy* 32 C6
Erba, *Sudan* 76 D4
Erbaa, *Turkey* 66 B7
Erbil = Arbīl, *Iraq* 67 D11
Erçis, *Turkey* 67 C10
Erdao Jiang →, *China* 51 C14
Erdek, *Turkey* 66 B2
Erdemli, *Turkey* 66 D6
Erdene, *Mongolia* 50 B6
Erding, *Germany* 19 G7
Erdre →, *France* 24 E5
Erebato →, *Venezuela* 121 B5
Erebus, Mt., *Antarctica* 5 D11
Erechim, *Brazil* 127 B5
Ereğli, *Konya, Turkey* 66 D6
Ereğli, *Zonguldak, Turkey* 66 B4
Erei, Monti, *Italy* 35 E7
Erembodegem, *Belgium* 17 G4
Erenhot, *China* 50 C7
Eresma →, *Spain* 30 D6
Erewadi Myitwanya, *Burma* 61 M19
Erfenisdam, *S. Africa* 84 D4
Erfoud, *Morocco* 74 B4
Erft →, *Germany* 18 D2
Erfurt, *Germany* 18 E7
Ergani, *Turkey* 67 C8
Ergeni Vozvyshennost, *Russia* 43 G7
Ērgli, *Latvia* 9 H21
Erhlin, *Taiwan* 53 F13
Eria →, *Spain* 30 C5
Eriba, *Sudan* 77 D4
Eriboll, L., *U.K.* 14 C4
Erica, *Neths.* 16 C9
Érice, *Italy* 34 D5
Erie, *U.S.A.* 106 D4
Erie, L., *N. Amer.* 106 D3
Erie Canal, *U.S.A.* 106 C6
Erieau, *Canada* 106 D3
Erigavo, *Somali Rep.* 68 E4
Erikoúsa, *Greece* 37 A3
Eriksdale, *Canada* 101 C9
Erikslund, *Sweden* 10 B9
Erímanthos, *Greece* 39 M4
Erimo-misaki, *Japan* 48 D11
Eriswil, *Switz.* 22 B5
Erithraí, *Greece* 39 L6
Eritrea ■, *Africa* 77 E4
Erjas →, *Portugal* 31 F3
Erlangen, *Germany* 19 F7
Erldunda, *Australia* 90 D1
Ermelo, *Neths.* 16 D7
Ermelo, *S. Africa* 85 D4
Ermenak, *Turkey* 66 D5
Ermióni, *Greece* 39 M6
Ermones, *Greece* 37 A3
Ermoúpolis = Síros, *Greece* 39 M7
Ernakulam = Cochin, *India* 60 Q10
Erne →, *Ireland* 15 B3
Erne, Lower L., *U.K.* 15 B4
Erne, Upper L., *U.K.* 15 B4
Ernée, *France* 24 D6
Ernest Giles Ra., *Australia* 89 E3
Ernstberg, *Germany* 19 E2
Erode, *India* 60 P10
Eromanga, *Australia* 91 D3
Erongo, *Namibia* 84 C2
Erp, *Neths.* 17 E7
Erquelinnes, *Belgium* 17 H4
Erquy, *France* 24 D4
Erquy, C. d', *France* 24 D4
Err, Piz d', *Switz.* 23 C9
Errabiddy, *Australia* 89 E2
Erramala Hills, *India* 60 M11
Errer →, *Ethiopia* 77 F5
Errigal, *Ireland* 15 A3
Erris Hd., *Ireland* 15 B1
Erseka, *Albania* 39 J3
Erskine, *U.S.A.* 108 B7
Erstein, *France* 25 D14
Erstfeld, *Switz.* 23 C7
Ertil, *Russia* 42 E5
Ertis → = Irtysh →, *Russia* 44 C7
Ertvelde, *Belgium* 17 F3
Eruh, *Turkey* 67 D10
Eruwa, *Nigeria* 79 D5
Ervy-le-Châtel, *France* 25 D10
Erwin, *U.S.A.* 105 G4
Eryuan, *China* 52 D2
Erzgebirge, *Germany* 18 E9
Erzin, *Russia* 45 D10
Erzincan, *Turkey* 67 C8
Erzurum, *Turkey* 67 C9
Es Caló, *Spain* 36 C8
Es Caná, *Spain* 36 B8
Es Sahrâ' Esh Sharqîya, *Egypt* 76 B3
Es Sînâ', *Egypt* 76 J8
Es Sûkî, *Sudan* 77 E3
Esambo, *Zaïre* 82 C1
Esan-Misaki, *Japan* 48 D10
Esashi, *Hokkaidō, Japan* 48 B11
Esashi, *Hokkaidō, Japan* 48 D10
Esbjerg, *Denmark* 11 J2
Escada, *Brazil* 122 C4
Escalante, *U.S.A.* 111 H8
Escalante →, *U.S.A.* 111 H8
Escalón, *Mexico* 114 B4
Escalona, *Spain* 30 E6
Escambia →, *U.S.A.* 105 K2
Escanaba, *U.S.A.* 104 C2
Escaut →, *Belgium* 17 F3
Esch-sur-Alzette, *Lux.* 17 J7
Eschede, *Germany* 18 C6
Escholzmatt, *Switz.* 22 C5
Eschwege, *Germany* 18 D6
Eschweiler, *Germany* 18 E2
Escoma, *Bolivia* 124 D4
Escondido, *U.S.A.* 113 M9
Escuinapa, *Mexico* 114 C3
Escuintla, *Guatemala* 116 D1
Eséka, *Cameroon* 79 E7
Esenguly, *Turkmenistan* 44 F6
Esens, *Germany* 18 B3
Esera →, *Spain* 28 C5
Eşfahān, *Iran* 65 C6
Esfīdeh, *Iran* 65 C8
Esgueva →, *Spain* 30 D6
Esh Sham = Dimashq, *Syria* 69 B5
Esh Shamâlîya □, *Sudan* 76 D2
Eshan, *China* 52 E4
Eshowe, *S. Africa* 85 D5
Esiama, *Ghana* 78 E4
Esil → = Ishim →, *Russia* 44 D8
Esino →, *Italy* 33 E10
Esk →, *Cumb., U.K.* 14 G5
Esk →, *N. Yorks., U.K.* 12 C7
Eskifjörður, *Iceland* 8 D7
Eskilstuna, *Sweden* 10 E10
Eskimalatya, *Turkey* 67 C8
Eskimo Pt., *Canada* 101 A10
Eskişehir, *Turkey* 66 C4
Esla →, *Spain* 30 D4
Esla, Pantano del, *Spain* 30 D4
Eslāmābād-e Gharb, *Iran* 67 E12
Eslöv, *Sweden* 11 J7
Eşme, *Turkey* 66 C3
Esmeralda, I., *Chile* 128 C1
Esmeraldas, *Ecuador* 120 C2
Esmeraldas □, *Ecuador* 120 C2
Esmeraldas →, *Ecuador* 120 C2
Esneux, *Belgium* 17 G7
Espada, Pta., *Colombia* 120 A3
Espalion, *France* 26 D6
Espalmador, I., *Spain* 36 C7
Espanola, *Canada* 98 C3
Espardell, I. del, *Spain* 36 C7
Esparraguera, *Spain* 28 D6
Esparta, *Costa Rica* 116 E3
Espejo, *Spain* 31 H6
Esperança, *Brazil* 122 C4
Esperance, *Australia* 89 F3
Esperance B., *Australia* 89 F3
Esperantinópolis, *Brazil* 122 B3
Esperanza, *Santa Cruz, Argentina* 128 D2
Esperanza, *Santa Fe, Argentina* 126 C3
Esperanza, *Phil.* 55 G6
Espéraza, *France* 26 F6
Espichel, C., *Portugal* 31 G1
Espiel, *Spain* 31 G5
Espigão, Serra do, *Brazil* 127 B5
Espinal, *Colombia* 120 C3
Espinar, *Peru* 124 C3
Espinazo, Sierra del = Espinhaço, Serra do, *Brazil* 123 E3
Espinhaço, Serra do, *Brazil* 123 E3
Espinho, *Portugal* 30 D2
Espinilho, Serra do, *Brazil* 127 B5
Espino, *Venezuela* 120 B4
Espinosa de los Monteros, *Spain* 30 B7
Espírito Santo □, *Brazil* 123 F3
Espíritu Santo, B. del, *Mexico* 115 D7
Espíritu Santo, I., *Mexico* 114 C2
Espita, *Mexico* 115 C7
Espiye, *Turkey* 67 B8
Esplanada, *Brazil* 123 D4
Espluga de Francolí, *Spain* 28 D6
Espoo, *Finland* 9 F21
Espuña, Sierra, *Spain* 29 H3
Espungabera, *Mozam.* 85 C5
Esquel, *Argentina* 128 B2
Esquina, *Argentina* 126 B4
Essaouira, *Morocco* 74 B3
Essebie, *Zaïre* 82 B3
Essen, *Belgium* 17 F4
Essen, *Germany* 18 D2
Essendon, Mt., *Australia* 89 E3
Essequibo →, *Guyana* 121 B6
Essex, *Canada* 106 D2
Essex, *Calif., U.S.A.* 113 L11
Essex, *N.Y., U.S.A.* 107 B11
Essex □, *U.K.* 13 F8
Esslingen, *Germany* 19 G5
Essonne □, *France* 25 D9
Essvik, *Sweden* 10 B11
Estaca, Pta. del, *Spain* 30 B3
Estadilla, *Spain* 28 C5
Estados, I. de Los, *Argentina* 128 D4
Estagel, *France* 26 F6
Eşţahbānāt, *Iran* 65 D7
Estallenchs, *Spain* 36 B9
Estância, *Brazil* 122 D4
Estancia, *U.S.A.* 111 J10
Estārm, *Iran* 65 D8
Estarreja, *Portugal* 30 E2
Estats, Pic d', *Spain* 28 C6
Estavayer-le-Lac, *Switz.* 22 C3
Estcourt, *S. Africa* 85 D4
Este, *Italy* 33 C8
Esteban, *Spain* 36 B4
Estelí, *Nic.* 116 D2
Estella, *Spain* 28 C2

Estelline, S. Dak., U.S.A. 108 C6
Estelline, Tex., U.S.A. 109 H4
Estena →, Spain 31 F6
Estepa, Spain 31 H6
Estepona, Spain 31 J5
Esterhazy, Canada 101 C8
Esternay, France 25 D10
Esterri de Aneu, Spain 28 C6
Estevan, Canada 101 D8
Estevan Group, Canada 100 C3
Estherville, U.S.A. 108 D7
Estissac, France 25 D10
Eston, Canada 101 C7
Estonia ■, Europe 9 G21
Estoril, Portugal 31 G1
Estouk, Mali 79 B5
Estrêla, Serra da, Portugal 30 E3
Estrella, Spain 29 G1
Estremoz, Portugal 31 G3
Estrondo, Serra do, Brazil 122 C2
Esztergom, Hungary 21 H8
Et Tîdra, Mauritania 78 B1
Étables-sur-Mer, France 24 D4
Etadunna, Australia 91 D2
Etah, India 63 F8
Étain, France 25 C12
Etalle, Belgium 17 J7
Etamamu, Canada 99 B8
Étampes, France 25 D9
Étang-sur-Arroux, France 27 B8
Etanga, Namibia 84 B1
Étaples, France 25 B8
Etawah, India 63 F8
Etawah →, U.S.A. 105 H3
Etawney L., Canada 101 B9
Ete, Nigeria 79 D6
Éthe, Belgium 17 J7
Ethel, U.S.A. 112 D4
Ethel, Oued el →, Algeria 74 C4
Ethel Creek, Australia 88 D3
Ethelbert, Canada 101 C8
Ethiopia ■, Africa 68 F3
Ethiopian Highlands, Ethiopia 46 J7
Etive, L., U.K. 14 E3
Etna, Italy 35 E8
Etoile, Zaïre 83 E2
Etolin I., U.S.A. 100 B2
Etosha Pan, Namibia 84 B2
Etowah, U.S.A. 105 H3
Étrépagny, France 25 C8
Étretat, France 24 C7
Ettelbruck, Lux. 17 J8
Etten, Neths. 17 E5
Ettlingen, Germany 19 G4
Ettrick Water →, U.K. 14 F6
Etuku, Zaïre 82 C2
Etzatlán, Mexico 114 C4
Eu, France 24 B8
Euboea = Évvoia, Greece 39 L7
Eucla Motel, Australia 89 F4
Euclid, U.S.A. 106 E3
Euclides da Cunha, Brazil 122 D4
Eucumbene, L., Australia 91 F4
Eudora, U.S.A. 109 J9
Eufaula, Ala., U.S.A. 105 K3
Eufaula, Okla., U.S.A. 109 H7
Eufaula L., U.S.A. 109 H7
Eugene, U.S.A. 110 E2
Eugowra, Australia 91 E4
Eulo, Australia 91 D4
Eunice, La., U.S.A. 109 K8
Eunice, N. Mex., U.S.A. 109 J3
Eupen, Belgium 17 G8
Euphrates = Furāt, Nahr al →, Asia 64 D5
Eure □, France 24 C8
Eure →, France 24 C8
Eure-et-Loir □, France 24 D8
Eureka, Canada 4 B3
Eureka, Calif., U.S.A. 110 F1
Eureka, Kans., U.S.A. 109 G6
Eureka, Mont., U.S.A. 110 B6
Eureka, Nev., U.S.A. 110 G5
Eureka, S. Dak., U.S.A. 108 C5
Eureka, Utah, U.S.A. 110 G7
Eureka, Mt., Australia 89 E3
Euroa, Australia 91 F4
Europa, I., Ind. Oc. 81 J8
Europa, Picos de, Spain 30 B6
Europa, Pta. de, Gib. 31 J5
Europa Pt. = Europa, Pta. de, Gib. 31 J5
Europoort, Neths. 16 E4
Euskirchen, Germany 18 E2
Eustis, U.S.A. 105 L5
Eutin, Germany 18 A6
Eutsuk L., Canada 100 C3
Eva, Brazil 121 D6
Eva Downs, Australia 90 B1
Evale, Angola 84 B2
Evans, U.S.A. 108 E2
Evans Head, Australia 91 D5
Evans L., Canada 98 B4
Evans Mills, U.S.A. 107 B9
Evanston, Ill., U.S.A. 104 D2
Evanston, Wyo., U.S.A. 110 F8
Evansville, Ind., U.S.A. 104 F2
Evansville, Wis., U.S.A. 108 D10
Évaux-les-Bains, France 26 B6
Evaz, Iran 65 E7
Eveleth, U.S.A. 108 B8
Evensk, Russia 45 C16
Evenstad, Norway 10 C5
Everard, L., Australia 91 E1
Everard Park, Australia 89 E5
Everard Ras., Australia 89 E5
Evere, Belgium 17 G4
Everest, Mt., Nepal 63 E12
Everett, Pa., U.S.A. 106 F6
Everett, Wash., U.S.A. 112 C4
Evergem, Belgium 17 F3
Everglades, The, U.S.A. 105 N5
Everglades City, U.S.A. 105 N5
Everglades National Park, U.S.A. 105 N5
Evergreen, U.S.A. 105 K2
Everson, U.S.A. 110 B2
Evesham, U.K. 13 E6
Évian-les-Bains, France 27 B10
Evinayong, Eq. Guin. 80 D2
Évinos →, Greece 39 L4
Évisa, France 27 F12
Evje, Norway 9 G12
Évora, Portugal 31 G3
Évora □, Portugal 31 G3
Evowghlī, Iran 67 C11
Évreux, France 24 C8
Évron, France 24 D6
Évros →, Bulgaria 66 B2
Evrótas →, Greece 39 N5
Évvoia, Greece 39 L7
Évvoia □, Greece 39 L6
Ewe, L., U.K. 14 D3
Ewing, U.S.A. 108 D5
Ewo, Congo 80 E2
Exaltación, Bolivia 125 C4
Excelsior Springs, U.S.A. 108 F7
Excideuil, France 26 C5
Exe →, U.K. 13 G4
Exeter, Canada 106 C3
Exeter, U.K. 13 G4
Exeter, Calif., U.S.A. 111 H4
Exeter, N.H., U.S.A. 107 D14
Exeter, Nebr., U.S.A. 108 E6
Exloo, Neths. 16 C9
Exmes, France 24 D7
Exmoor, U.K. 13 F4
Exmouth, Australia 88 D1
Exmouth, U.K. 13 G4
Exmouth G., Australia 88 D1
Expedition Ra., Australia 90 C4
Extremadura □, Spain 31 F4
Exuma Sound, Bahamas 116 B4
Eyasi, L., Tanzania 82 C4
Eyeberry L., Canada 101 A8
Eyemouth, U.K. 14 F6
Eygurande, France 26 C6
Eyjafjörður, Iceland 8 C4
Eymet, France 26 D4
Eymoutiers, France 26 C5
Eynesil, Turkey 67 B8
Eyre, Australia 89 F4
Eyre (North), L., Australia 91 D2
Eyre (South), L., Australia 91 D2
Eyre Cr. →, Australia 91 D2
Eyre Mts., N.Z. 87 L2
Eyre Pen., Australia 91 E2
Eysturoy, Færoe Is. 8 E9
Eyvānkī, Iran 65 C6
Ez Zeidab, Sudan 76 D3
Ezcaray, Spain 28 C2
Ezine, Turkey 66 C2
Ezmul, Mauritania 74 D1
Ezouza →, Cyprus 37 E11

F

F.Y.R.O.M. = Macedonia ■, Europe 39 H4
Fabens, U.S.A. 111 L10
Fåborg, Denmark 11 J4
Fabriano, Italy 33 E9
Făcăeni, Romania 38 E10
Facatativá, Colombia 120 C3
Fachi, Niger 72 E7
Facture, France 26 D3
Fada, Chad 73 E9
Fada-n-Gourma, Burkina Faso 79 C5
Faddeyevskiy, Ostrov, Russia 45 B15
Fadghāmī, Syria 67 E9
Fadlab, Sudan 76 D3
Faenza, Italy 33 D8
Færoe Is. = Føroyar, Atl. Oc. 8 F9
Fafa, Mali 79 B5
Fafe, Portugal 30 D2
Fagam, Nigeria 79 C7
Făgăras, Romania 38 D7
Făgăras, Munţii, Romania 38 D7
Fågelsjö, Sweden 10 C8
Fagersta, Sweden 9 F16
Făget, Romania 38 D5
Fagnano, L., Argentina 128 D3
Fagnano Castello, Italy 35 C9
Fagnières, France 25 D11
Fahlīān, Iran 65 D6
Fahraj, Kermān, Iran 65 D8
Fahraj, Yazd, Iran 65 D7
Faial, Madeira 36 D3
Faido, Switz. 23 D7
Fair Hd., U.K. 15 A5
Fair Oaks, U.S.A. 112 G5
Fairbank, U.S.A. 111 L8
Fairbanks, U.S.A. 96 B5
Fairbury, U.S.A. 108 E6
Fairfax, U.S.A. 109 G6
Fairfield, Ala., U.S.A. 105 J2
Fairfield, Calif., U.S.A. 112 G4
Fairfield, Conn., U.S.A. 107 E11
Fairfield, Idaho, U.S.A. 110 E6
Fairfield, Ill., U.S.A. 104 F1
Fairfield, Iowa, U.S.A. 108 E9
Fairfield, Mont., U.S.A. 110 C8
Fairfield, Tex., U.S.A. 109 K7
Fairford, Canada 101 C9
Fairhope, U.S.A. 105 K2
Fairlie, N.Z. 87 L3
Fairmead, U.S.A. 112 H6
Fairmont, Minn., U.S.A. 108 D7
Fairmont, W. Va., U.S.A. 104 F5
Fairmount, U.S.A. 113 L8
Fairplay, U.S.A. 111 G11
Fairport, U.S.A. 106 C7
Fairport Harbor, U.S.A. 106 E3
Fairview, Australia 90 B3
Fairview, Canada 100 B5
Fairview, Mont., U.S.A. 108 B2
Fairview, Okla., U.S.A. 109 G5
Fairview, Utah, U.S.A. 110 G8
Fairweather, Mt., U.S.A. 96 C6
Faisalabad, Pakistan 62 D5
Faith, U.S.A. 108 C3
Faizabad, India 63 F10
Fajardo, Puerto Rico 117 C6
Fakfak, Indonesia 57 E8
Fakobli, Ivory C. 78 D3
Fakse, Denmark 11 J6
Fakse Bugt, Denmark 11 J6
Fakse Ladeplads, Denmark 11 J6
Faku, China 51 C12
Falaise, France 24 D6
Falaise, Mui, Vietnam 58 C5
Falam, Burma 61 H18
Falces, Spain 28 C3
Fălciu, Romania 38 C11
Falcón □, Venezuela 120 A4
Falcon, C., Algeria 75 A4
Falcón, C., Spain 36 C7
Falcon Dam, U.S.A. 109 M5
Falconara Marittima, Italy 33 E10
Falconer, U.S.A. 106 D5
Faléa, Mali 78 C2
Faleshty = Fălești, Moldova 41 J4
Fălești, Moldova 41 J4
Falfurrias, U.S.A. 109 M5
Falher, Canada 100 B5
Falirakí, Greece 37 C10
Falkenberg, Germany 18 D9
Falkenberg, Sweden 11 H6
Falkensee, Germany 18 C9
Falkenstein, Germany 18 E8
Falkirk, U.K. 14 F5
Falkirk □, U.K. 14 F5
Falkland, East, I., Falk. Is. 128 D5
Falkland, West, I., Falk. Is. 128 D4
Falkland Is. □, Atl. Oc. 128 D5
Falkland Sd., Falk. Is. 128 D5
Falköping, Sweden 11 F7
Fall River, U.S.A. 107 E13
Fall River Mills, U.S.A. 110 F3
Fallbrook, U.S.A. 111 K5
Fallbrook, Calif., U.S.A. 113 M9
Fallon, Mont., U.S.A. 108 B2
Fallon, Nev., U.S.A. 110 G4
Falls City, Nebr., U.S.A. 108 E7
Falls City, Oreg., U.S.A. 110 D2
Falls Creek, U.S.A. 106 E6
Falmouth, Jamaica 116 C4
Falmouth, U.K. 13 G2
Falmouth, U.S.A. 104 F3
False B., S. Africa 84 E2
Falset, Spain 28 D5
Falso, C., Honduras 116 C3
Falster, Denmark 11 K5
Falsterbo, Sweden 11 J6
Fălticeni, Romania 38 B9
Falun, Sweden 9 F16
Famagusta, Cyprus 66 E5
Famagusta Bay, Cyprus 37 D13
Famatina, Sierra de, Argentina 126 B2
Family L., Canada 101 C9
Famoso, U.S.A. 113 K7
Fan Xian, China 50 G8
Fana, Mali 78 C3
Fandriana, Madag. 85 C8
Fang, Thailand 58 C2
Fang Xian, China 53 A8
Fangchang, China 53 B12
Fangcheng, Guangxi Zhuangzu, China 52 G7
Fangcheng, Henan, China 50 H7
Fangliao, Taiwan 53 F13
Fangshan, China 50 E6
Fangzi, China 51 F10
Fani i Madh →, Albania 39 H3
Fanjiatun, China 51 C13
Fannich, L., U.K. 14 D4
Fannūj, Iran 65 E8
Fanny Bay, Canada 100 D4
Fanø, Denmark 11 J2
Fano, Italy 33 E10
Fanshaw, U.S.A. 100 B2
Fanshi, China 50 E7
Fao = Al Fāw, Iraq 65 D6
Faqirwali, Pakistan 62 E5
Fara in Sabina, Italy 33 F9
Faradje, Zaïre 82 B2
Farafangana, Madag. 85 C8
Farâfra, El Wâhât el-, Egypt 76 B2
Farāh, Afghan. 60 C3
Farāh □, Afghan. 60 C3
Farahalana, Madag. 85 A9
Faraid, Gebel, Egypt 76 C4
Faramana, Burkina Faso 78 C4
Faranah, Guinea 78 C2
Farasān, Jazā'ir, Si. Arabia 68 D3
Farasan Is. = Farasān, Jazā'ir, Si. Arabia 68 D3
Faratsiho, Madag. 85 B8
Fardes →, Spain 29 H1
Fareham, U.K. 13 G6
Farewell, C., N.Z. 87 J4
Farewell C. = Farvel, Kap, Greenland 4 D5
Farghona, Uzbekistan 44 E8
Fargo, U.S.A. 108 B6
Fār'iah, W. al →, West Bank 69 C4
Faribault, U.S.A. 108 C8
Faridkot, India 62 D6
Faridpur, Bangla. 63 H13
Färila, Sweden 10 C9
Farim, Guinea-Biss. 78 C1
Farīmān, Iran 65 C8
Farina, Australia 91 E2
Farinha →, Brazil 122 C2
Fariones, Pta., Canary Is. 36 E6
Fâriskûr, Egypt 76 H7
Farmerville, U.S.A. 109 J8
Farmington, Calif., U.S.A. 112 H6
Farmington, N.H., U.S.A. 107 C13
Farmington, N. Mex., U.S.A. 111 H9
Farmington, Utah, U.S.A. 110 F8
Farmington →, U.S.A. 107 E12
Farmville, U.S.A. 104 G6
Farnborough, U.K. 13 F7
Farne Is., U.K. 12 B6
Farnham, Canada 107 A12
Faro, Brazil 121 D6
Faro, Portugal 31 H3
Fårö, Sweden 9 H18
Faro □, Portugal 31 H2
Farquhar, C., Australia 89 D1
Farrars Cr. →, Australia 90 D3
Farrāshband, Iran 65 D7
Farrell, U.S.A. 106 E4
Farrell Flat, Australia 91 E2
Farrokhī, Iran 65 C8
Farruch, C., Spain 36 B10
Farrukhabad-cum-Fatehgarh, India 63 F8
Fārs □, Iran 65 D7
Fársala, Greece 39 K5
Farsø, Denmark 11 H3
Farsund, Norway 9 G12
Fartak, Râs, Si. Arabia 64 D2
Fartura, Serra da, Brazil 127 B5
Faru, Nigeria 79 C6
Fārūj, Iran 65 B8
Farum, Denmark 11 J6
Farvel, Kap, Greenland 4 D5
Farwell, U.S.A. 109 H3
Fasā, Iran 65 D7
Fasano, Italy 35 B10
Fashoda, Sudan 77 F3
Fastiv, Ukraine 41 G5
Fastnet Rock, Ireland 15 E2
Fastov = Fastiv, Ukraine 41 G5
Fatagar, Tanjung, Indonesia 57 E8
Fatehgarh, India 63 F8
Fatehpur, Raj., India 62 F6
Fatehpur, Ut. P., India 63 G9
Fatesh, Russia 42 D2
Fatick, Senegal 78 C1
Fatima, Canada 99 C7
Fátima, Portugal 31 F2
Fatoya, Guinea 78 C3
Fatsa, Turkey 66 B7
Faucille, Col de la, France 27 B10
Faulkton, U.S.A. 108 C5
Faulquemont, France 25 C13
Fauquembergues, France 25 B9
Faure I., Australia 89 E1
Făurei, Romania 38 D10
Fauresmith, S. Africa 84 D4
Fauske, Norway 8 C16
Fauvillers, Belgium 17 J7
Favara, Italy 34 E6
Favaritx, C., Spain 36 A11
Favignana, Italy 34 E5
Favignana, I., Italy 34 E5
Favourable Lake, Canada 98 B1
Fawn →, Canada 98 A2
Fawnskin, U.S.A. 113 L10
Faxaflói, Iceland 8 D2
Faya-Largeau, Chad 73 E8
Fayd, Si. Arabia 64 E4
Fayence, France 27 E10
Fayette, Ala., U.S.A. 105 J2
Fayette, Mo., U.S.A. 108 F8
Fayetteville, Ark., U.S.A. 109 G7
Fayetteville, N.C., U.S.A. 105 H6
Fayetteville, Tenn., U.S.A. 105 H2
Fayón, Spain 28 D5
Fazenda Nova, Brazil 123 E1
Fazilka, India 62 D6
Fazilpur, Pakistan 62 E4
Fdérik, Mauritania 74 D2
Feale →, Ireland 15 D2
Fear, C., U.S.A. 105 J7
Feather →, U.S.A. 110 G3
Feather Falls, U.S.A. 112 F5
Featherston, N.Z. 87 J5
Featherstone, Zimbabwe 83 F3
Fécamp, France 24 C7
Fedala = Mohammedia, Morocco 74 B3
Federación, Argentina 126 C4
Fedeshkūh, Iran 65 D7
Fedjadj, Chott el, Tunisia 75 B6
Fehmarn, Germany 18 A7
Fehmarn Bælt, Europe 9 J14
Fei Xian, China 51 G9
Feijó, Brazil 124 B3
Feilding, N.Z. 87 J5
Feira de Santana, Brazil 123 D4
Feixiang, China 50 F8
Fejø, Denmark 11 K5
Feke, Turkey 66 D6
Felanitx, Spain 36 B10
Feldberg, Baden-W., Germany 19 H3
Feldberg, Mecklenburg-Vorpommern, Germany 18 B9
Feldkirch, Austria 19 H5
Felipe Carrillo Puerto, Mexico 115 D7
Felixlândia, Brazil 123 E3
Felixstowe, U.K. 13 F9
Felletin, France 26 C6
Felton, U.K. 12 B6
Felton, U.S.A. 112 H4
Feltre, Italy 33 B8
Femø, Denmark 11 K5
Femunden, Norway 10 B5
Fen He →, China 50 G6
Fenelon Falls, Canada 106 B6
Feneroa, Ethiopia 77 E4
Feng Xian, Jiangsu, China 50 G9
Feng Xian, Shaanxi, China 50 H4
Fengári, Greece 39 J8
Fengcheng, Jiangxi, China 53 C10
Fengcheng, Liaoning, China 51 D13
Fengdu, China 52 C6
Fengfeng, China 50 F8
Fenggang, China 52 D6
Fenghua, China 53 C13
Fenghuang, China 52 D7
Fenghuangzui, China 52 A7
Fengjie, China 52 B7
Fengkai, China 53 F8
Fengle, China 53 B9
Fengning, China 50 D9
Fengqing, China 52 E2
Fengqiu, China 50 G8
Fengrun, China 51 E10
Fengshan, Guangxi Zhuangzu, China 52 E7
Fengshan, Guangxi Zhuangzu, China 52 E6
Fengtai, Anhui, China 53 A11
Fengtai, Beijing, China 50 E9
Fengxian, China 53 B13
Fengxiang, China 50 G4
Fengxin, China 53 C10
Fengyang, China 51 H9
Fengyi, China 52 E3
Fengzhen, China 50 D7
Fenit, Ireland 15 D2
Fennimore, U.S.A. 108 D9
Feno, C. de, France 27 G12
Fenoarivo Afovoany, Madag. 85 B8
Fenoarivo Atsinanana, Madag. 85 B8
Fens, The, U.K. 12 E8
Fenton, U.S.A. 104 D4
Fenxi, China 50 F6
Fenyang, China 50 F6
Fenyi, China 53 D10
Feodosiya, Ukraine 41 K8
Fer, C. de, Algeria 75 A6
Ferdows, Iran 65 C8
Fère-Champenoise, France 25 D10
Fère-en-Tardenois, France 25 C10
Ferentino, Italy 34 A6
Ferfer, Somali Rep. 68 F4
Fergana = Farghona, Uzbekistan 44 E8
Fergus, Canada 98 D3
Fergus Falls, U.S.A. 108 B6
Fériana, Tunisia 75 B6
Feričanci, Croatia 21 K8
Ferkane, Algeria 75 B6
Ferkéssédougou, Ivory C. 78 D3
Ferlach, Austria 21 J4
Ferland, Canada 98 B2
Ferlo, Vallée du, Senegal 78 B2
Fermanagh □, U.K. 15 B4
Fermo, Italy 33 E10
Fermoselle, Spain 30 D4
Fermoy, Ireland 15 D3
Fernán Nuñéz, Spain 31 H6
Fernández, Argentina 126 B3
Fernandina Beach, U.S.A. 105 K5
Fernando de Noronha, Brazil 122 B5
Fernando Póo = Bioko, Eq. Guin. 79 E6
Fernandópolis, Brazil 123 F1
Ferndale, Calif., U.S.A. 110 F1
Ferndale, Wash., U.S.A. 112 B4
Fernie, Canada 100 D5
Fernlees, Australia 90 C4
Fernley, U.S.A. 110 G4
Ferozepore = Firozpur, India 62 D6
Férrai, Greece 39 J9
Ferrandina, Italy 35 B9
Ferrara, Italy 33 D8
Ferrato, C., Italy 34 C2
Ferreira do Alentejo, Portugal 31 G2
Ferreñafe, Peru 124 B2
Ferrerías, Spain 36 B11

Ferret, C., France 26 D2
Ferrette, France 25 E14
Ferriday, U.S.A. 109 K9
Ferrières, France 25 D9
Ferriete, Italy 32 D6
Ferrol = El Ferrol, Spain 30 B2
Ferrol, Pen. de, Peru 124 B2
Ferron, U.S.A. 111 G8
Ferros, Brazil 123 E3
Ferryland, Canada 99 C9
Fertile, U.S.A. 108 B6
Fertília, Italy 34 B1
Fès, Morocco 74 B4
Feschaux, Belgium 17 H5
Feshi, Zaïre 80 F3
Fessenden, U.S.A. 108 B5
Feteşti, Romania 38 E10
Fethiye, Turkey 66 D3
Fetlar, U.K. 14 A8
Feuerthalen, Switz. 23 A7
Feuilles →, Canada 97 C12
Feurs, France 27 C8
Fezzan, Libya 73 C8
Ffestiniog, U.K. 12 E4
Fiambalá, Argentina 126 B2
Fianarantsoa, Madag. 85 C8
Fianarantsoa □, Madag. 85 B8
Fianga, Cameroon 73 G8
Fichtelgebirge, Germany 19 E7
Ficksburg, S. Africa 85 D4
Fidenza, Italy 32 D7
Fiditi, Nigeria 79 D5
Field, Canada 98 C3
Field →, Australia 90 C2
Field I., Australia 88 B5
Fieri, Albania 39 J2
Fiesch, Switz. 22 D6
Fife □, U.K. 14 E5
Fife Ness, U.K. 14 E6
Fifth Cataract, Sudan 76 D3
Figeac, France 26 D6
Figline Valdarno, Italy 33 E8
Figtree, Zimbabwe 83 G2
Figueira Castelo Rodrigo, Portugal 30 E4
Figueira da Foz, Portugal 30 E2
Figueiró dos Vinhos, Portugal 30 F2
Figueras, Spain 28 C7
Figuig, Morocco 75 B4
Fihaonana, Madag. 85 B8
Fiherenana, Madag. 85 B8
Fiherenana →, Madag. 85 C7
Fiji ■, Pac. Oc. 87 C8
Fika, Nigeria 79 C7
Filabres, Sierra de los, Spain 29 H2
Filadélfia, Bolivia 124 C4
Filadélfia, Brazil 122 C2
Filadélfia, Italy 35 D9
Filer, U.S.A. 110 E6
Filey, U.K. 12 C7
Filfla, Malta 37 D1
Filiaşi, Romania 38 E6
Filiátes, Greece 39 K3
Filiatrá, Greece 39 M4
Filicudi, Italy 35 D7
Filiourí →, Greece 39 H8
Filipstad, Sweden 9 G16
Filisur, Switz. 23 C9
Fillmore, Canada 101 D8
Fillmore, Calif., U.S.A. 113 L8
Fillmore, Utah, U.S.A. 111 G7
Filottrano, Italy 33 E10
Finale Lígure, Italy 32 D5
Finale nell' Emília, Italy 33 D8
Fiñana, Spain 29 H2
Finch, Canada 107 A9
Findhorn →, U.K. 14 D5
Findlay, U.S.A. 104 E4
Finger L., Canada 101 C10
Fíngoè, Mozam. 83 E3
Finike, Turkey 66 D4
Finistère □, France 24 D2
Finisterre, Spain 30 C1
Finisterre, C., Spain 30 C1
Finke, Australia 90 D1
Finke →, Australia 91 D2
Finland ■, Europe 8 E22
Finland, G. of, Europe 9 G21
Finlay →, Canada 100 B3
Finley, Australia 91 F4
Finley, U.S.A. 108 B6
Finn →, Ireland 15 B4
Finnigan, Mt., Australia 90 B4
Finniss, C., Australia 91 E1
Finnmark, Norway 8 B20
Finnsnes, Norway 8 B18
Finspång, Sweden 9 G16
Finsteraarhorn, Switz. 22 C6
Finsterwalde, Germany 18 D9
Finsterwolde, Neths. 16 B10
Fiora →, Italy 33 F8
Fiorenzuola d'Arda, Italy 32 D6
Fīq, Syria 69 C4
Firat = Furāt, Nahr al →, Asia 64 D5
Fire River, Canada 98 C3
Firebag →, Canada 101 B6
Firebaugh, U.S.A. 112 J6
Firedrake L., Canada 101 A8
Firenze, Italy 33 E8
Firk →, Iraq 64 D5
Firmi, France 26 D6
Firminy, France 27 C8
Firozabad, India 63 F8
Firozpur, India 62 D6
Fīrūzābād, Iran 65 D7
Fīrūzkūh, Iran 65 C7
Firvale, Canada 100 C3
Fish →, Namibia 84 D2
Fish →, S. Africa 84 E3
Fisher, Australia 89 F5
Fisher B., Canada 101 C9
Fishguard, U.K. 13 F3
Fishing L., Canada 101 C9
Fismes, France 25 C10
Fitchburg, U.S.A. 107 D13
Fitero, Spain 28 C3
Fitri, L., Chad 73 F8
Fitz Roy, Argentina 128 C3
Fitzgerald, Canada 100 B6
Fitzgerald, U.S.A. 105 K4
Fitzmaurice →, Australia 88 B5
Fitzroy →, Queens., Australia 90 C5
Fitzroy →, W. Austral., Australia 88 C3
Fitzroy Crossing, Australia 88 C4
Fitzwilliam I., Canada 106 A3
Fiume = Rijeka, Croatia 33 C11
Fiumefreddo Brúzio, Italy 35 C9
Five Points, U.S.A. 112 J6
Fivizzano, Italy 32 D7
Fizi, Zaïre 82 C2
Fjellerup, Denmark 11 H4
Fjerritslev, Denmark 11 G3
Fkih ben Salah, Morocco 74 B3
Flå, Norway 10 A4
Flagler, U.S.A. 108 F3
Flagstaff, U.S.A. 111 J8
Flaherty I., Canada 98 A4
Flåm, Norway 9 F12
Flambeau →, U.S.A. 108 C9
Flamborough Hd., U.K. 12 C7
Flaming Gorge Dam, U.S.A. 110 F9
Flaming Gorge Reservoir, U.S.A. 110 F9
Flamingo, Teluk, Indonesia 57 F9
Flanders = West-Vlaanderen □, Belgium 17 G2
Flandre Occidentale = West-Vlaanderen □, Belgium 17 G2
Flandre Orientale = Oost-Vlaanderen □, Belgium 17 F3
Flandreau, U.S.A. 108 C6
Flanigan, U.S.A. 112 E7
Flannan Is., U.K. 14 C1
Flåsjön, Sweden 8 D16
Flat →, Canada 100 A3
Flat River, U.S.A. 109 G9
Flathead L., U.S.A. 110 C6
Flattery, C., Australia 90 A4
Flattery, C., U.S.A. 112 B2
Flavy-le-Martel, France 25 C10
Flawil, Switz. 23 B8
Flaxton, U.S.A. 108 A3
Fleetwood, U.K. 12 D4
Flekkefjord, Norway 9 G12
Flémalle, Belgium 17 G6
Flemington, U.S.A. 106 E7
Flensburg, Germany 18 A5
Flensburger Förde, Germany 11 K3
Flers, France 24 D6
Flesherton, Canada 106 B4
Flesko, Tanjung, Indonesia 57 D6
Fleurance, France 26 E4
Fleurier, Switz. 22 C3
Fleurus, Belgium 17 H5
Flevoland □, Neths. 16 C7
Flims, Switz. 23 C8
Flin Flon, Canada 101 C8
Flinders →, Australia 90 B3
Flinders B., Australia 89 F2
Flinders Group, Australia 90 A3
Flinders I., Australia 90 F4
Flinders Ranges, Australia 91 E2
Flinders Reefs, Australia 90 B4
Flint, U.K. 12 D4
Flint, U.S.A. 104 D4
Flint →, U.S.A. 105 K3
Flint I., Kiribati 93 J12
Flinton, Australia 91 D4
Flintshire □, U.K. 12 D4
Flix, Spain 28 D5
Flixecourt, France 25 B9
Flobecq, Belgium 17 G3
Flodden, U.K. 12 B5
Floodwood, U.S.A. 108 B8
Flora, Norway 10 A5
Flora, U.S.A. 104 F1
Florac, France 26 D7
Florala, U.S.A. 105 K2
Florânia, Brazil 122 C4
Floreffe, Belgium 17 H5
Florence = Firenze, Italy 33 E8
Florence, Ala., U.S.A. 105 H2
Florence, Ariz., U.S.A. 111 K8
Florence, Colo., U.S.A. 108 F2
Florence, Oreg., U.S.A. 110 E1
Florence, S.C., U.S.A. 105 H6
Florence, L., Australia 91 D2
Florennes, Belgium 17 H5
Florensac, France 26 E7
Florenville, Belgium 17 J6
Flores, Brazil 122 C4
Flores, Guatemala 116 C2
Flores, Indonesia 57 F6
Flores I., Canada 100 D3
Flores Sea, Indonesia 57 F6
Floresta, Brazil 122 C4
Floreşti, Moldova 41 J5
Floresville, U.S.A. 109 L5
Floriano, Brazil 122 C3
Florianópolis, Brazil 127 B6
Florida, Cuba 116 B4
Florida, Uruguay 127 C4
Florida □, U.S.A. 105 L5
Florida, Straits of, U.S.A. 116 B3
Florida B., U.S.A. 116 A3
Florida Keys, U.S.A. 103 F10
Florídia, Italy 35 E8
Floridsdorf, Austria 21 G6
Flórina, Greece 39 J4
Florø, Norway 9 F11
Flower Station, Canada 107 A8
Flower's Cove, Canada 99 B8
Floydada, U.S.A. 109 J4
Fluk, Indonesia 57 E7
Flumen →, Spain 28 D4
Flumendosa →, Italy 34 C2
Fluminimaggiore, Italy 34 C1
Flushing = Vlissingen, Neths. 17 F3
Fluviá →, Spain 28 C8
Flying Fish, C., Antarctica 5 D15
Foam Lake, Canada 101 C8
Foča, Bos.-H. 21 M8
Foça, Turkey 66 C2
Focşani, Romania 38 D10
Fogang, China 53 F9
Foggaret el Arab, Algeria 75 C5
Foggaret ez Zoua, Algeria 75 C5
Fóggia, Italy 35 A8
Foggo, Nigeria 79 C6
Foglia →, Italy 33 E9
Fogo, Canada 99 C9
Fogo I., Canada 99 C9
Fohnsdorf, Austria 21 H4
Föhr, Germany 18 A4
Foia, Portugal 31 H2
Foix, France 26 F5
Fokino, Russia 42 D2
Folda, Nord-Trøndelag, Norway 8 D14
Folda, Nordland, Norway 8 C16
Foleyet, Canada 98 C3
Folgefonni, Norway 9 F12
Foligno, Italy 33 F9
Folkestone, U.K. 13 F9
Folkston, U.S.A. 105 K5
Follett, U.S.A. 109 G4
Follónica, Italy 32 F7
Follónica, G. di, Italy 32 F7
Folsom Res., U.S.A. 112 G5
Fond-du-Lac, Canada 101 B7
Fond du Lac, U.S.A. 108 D10
Fond-du-Lac →, Canada 101 B7
Fonda, U.S.A. 107 D10
Fondi, Italy 34 A6
Fonfría, Spain 30 D4
Fongen, Norway 10 A5
Fonni, Italy 34 B2
Fonsagrada, Spain 30 B3
Fonseca, G. de, Cent. Amer. 116 D2
Fontaine-Française, France 25 E12
Fontainebleau, France 25 D9
Fontana, U.S.A. 113 L9
Fontana, L., Argentina 128 B2
Fontas →, Canada 100 B4
Fonte Boa, Brazil 120 D4
Fontem, Cameroon 79 D6
Fontenay-le-Comte, France 26 B3
Fontur, Iceland 8 C6
Fonyód, Hungary 21 J7
Foochow = Fuzhou, China 53 D12
Foping, China 50 H4
Foppiano, Italy 32 B5
Forbach, France 25 C13
Forbes, Australia 91 E4
Forbesganj, India 63 F12
Forcados, Nigeria 79 D6
Forcados →, Nigeria 79 D6
Forcall →, Spain 28 E4
Forcalquier, France 27 E9
Forchheim, Germany 19 F7
Forclaz, Col de la, Switz. 22 D4
Ford City, Calif., U.S.A. 113 K7
Ford City, Pa., U.S.A. 106 F5
Førde, Norway 9 F11
Ford's Bridge, Australia 91 D4
Fordyce, U.S.A. 109 J8
Forécariah, Guinea 78 D2
Forel, Mt., Greenland 4 C6
Foremost, Canada 100 D6
Forenza, Italy 35 B8
Forest, Belgium 17 G4
Forest, Canada 106 C3
Forest, U.S.A. 109 J10
Forest City, Iowa, U.S.A. 108 D8
Forest City, N.C., U.S.A. 105 H5
Forest City, Pa., U.S.A. 107 E9
Forest Grove, U.S.A. 112 E3
Forestburg, Canada 100 C6
Foresthill, U.S.A. 112 F6
Forestier Pen., Australia 90 G4
Forestville, Canada 99 C6
Forestville, Calif., U.S.A. 112 G4
Forestville, Wis., U.S.A. 104 C2
Forez, Mts. du, France 26 C7
Forfar, U.K. 14 E6
Forges-les-Eaux, France 25 C8
Forks, U.S.A. 112 C2
Forlì, Italy 33 D9
Forman, U.S.A. 108 B6
Formazza, Italy 32 B5
Formby Pt., U.K. 12 D4
Formentera, Spain 36 C7
Formentor, C. de, Spain 36 B10
Former Yugoslav Republic of Macedonia = Macedonia ■, Europe 39 H4
Fórmia, Italy 34 A6
Formiga, Brazil 123 F2
Formigine, Italy 32 D7
Formiguères, France 26 F6
Formosa = Taiwan ■, Asia 53 F13
Formosa, Argentina 126 B4
Formosa, Brazil 123 E2
Formosa □, Argentina 126 B3
Formosa, Serra, Brazil 125 C6
Formosa Bay, Kenya 82 C5
Formosa Strait, Asia 53 E12
Formoso →, Brazil 123 D2
Fornells, Spain 36 A11
Fornos de Algodres, Portugal 30 E3
Fornovo di Taro, Italy 32 D7
Føroyar, Atl. Oc. 8 F9
Forres, U.K. 14 D5
Forrest, Vic., Australia 91 F3
Forrest, W. Austral., Australia 89 F4
Forrest, Mt., Australia 89 D4
Forrest City, U.S.A. 109 H9
Forrières, Belgium 17 H6
Forsa, Sweden 10 C10
Forsayth, Australia 90 B3
Forsmo, Sweden 10 A11
Forssa, Finland 9 F20
Forst, Germany 18 D10
Forster, Australia 91 E5
Forsyth, Ga., U.S.A. 105 J4
Forsyth, Mont., U.S.A. 110 C10
Fort Albany, Canada 98 B3
Fort Apache, U.S.A. 111 K9
Fort Assiniboine, Canada 100 C6
Fort Augustus, U.K. 14 D4
Fort Beaufort, S. Africa 84 E4
Fort Benton, U.S.A. 110 C8
Fort Bragg, U.S.A. 110 G2
Fort Bridger, U.S.A. 110 F8
Fort Chipewyan, Canada 101 B6
Fort Collins, U.S.A. 108 E2
Fort-Coulonge, Canada 98 C4
Fort Davis, U.S.A. 109 K3
Fort-de-France, Martinique 117 D7
Fort de Possel = Possel, C.A.R. 80 C3
Fort Defiance, U.S.A. 111 J9
Fort Dodge, U.S.A. 108 D7
Fort Edward, U.S.A. 107 C11
Fort Frances, Canada 101 D10
Fort Garland, U.S.A. 111 H11
Fort George = Chisasibi, Canada 98 B4
Fort Good-Hope, Canada 96 B7
Fort Hancock, U.S.A. 111 L11
Fort Hertz = Putao, Burma 61 F20
Fort Hope, Canada 98 B2
Fort Irwin, U.S.A. 113 K10
Fort Jameson = Chipata, Zambia 83 E3
Fort Kent, U.S.A. 99 C6
Fort Klamath, U.S.A. 110 E3
Fort-Lamy = Ndjamena, Chad 73 F7
Fort Laramie, U.S.A. 108 D2
Fort Lauderdale, U.S.A. 105 M5
Fort Liard, Canada 100 A4
Fort Liberté, Haiti 117 C5
Fort Lupton, U.S.A. 108 E2
Fort Mackay, Canada 100 B6
Fort McKenzie, Canada 99 A6
Fort Macleod, Canada 100 D6
Fort MacMahon, Algeria 75 C5
Fort McMurray, Canada 100 B6
Fort McPherson, Canada 96 B6
Fort Madison, U.S.A. 108 E9
Fort Meade, U.S.A. 105 M5
Fort Miribel, Algeria 75 C5
Fort Morgan, U.S.A. 108 E3
Fort Myers, U.S.A. 105 M5
Fort Nelson, Canada 100 B4
Fort Nelson →, Canada 100 B4
Fort Norman = Tulita, Canada 96 B7
Fort Payne, U.S.A. 105 H3
Fort Peck, U.S.A. 110 B10
Fort Peck Dam, U.S.A. 110 C10
Fort Peck L., U.S.A. 110 C10
Fort Pierce, U.S.A. 105 M5
Fort Pierre, U.S.A. 108 C4
Fort Pierre Bordes = Ti-n-Zaouatene, Algeria 75 E5
Fort Plain, U.S.A. 107 D10
Fort Portal, Uganda 82 B3
Fort Providence, Canada 100 A5
Fort Qu'Appelle, Canada 101 C8
Fort Resolution, Canada 100 A6
Fort Rixon, Zimbabwe 83 G2
Fort Rosebery = Mansa, Zambia 83 E2
Fort Ross, U.S.A. 112 G3
Fort Rupert = Waskaganish, Canada 98 B4
Fort St. James, Canada 100 C4
Fort St. John, Canada 100 B4
Fort Sandeman, Pakistan 62 D3
Fort Saskatchewan, Canada 100 C6
Fort Scott, U.S.A. 109 G7
Fort Severn, Canada 98 A2
Fort Shevchenko, Kazakstan 43 H10
Fort Simpson, Canada 100 A4
Fort Smith, Canada 100 B6
Fort Smith, U.S.A. 109 H7
Fort Stanton, U.S.A. 111 K11
Fort Stockton, U.S.A. 109 K3
Fort Sumner, U.S.A. 109 H2
Fort Trinquet = Bir Mogrein, Mauritania 74 C2
Fort Valley, U.S.A. 105 J4
Fort Vermilion, Canada 100 B5
Fort Walton Beach, U.S.A. 105 K2
Fort Wayne, U.S.A. 104 E3
Fort William, U.K. 14 E3
Fort Worth, U.S.A. 109 J6
Fort Yates, U.S.A. 108 B4
Fort Yukon, U.S.A. 96 B5
Fortaleza, Bolivia 124 C4
Fortaleza, Brazil 122 B4
Forteau, Canada 99 B8
Forth →, U.K. 14 E5
Forth, Firth of, U.K. 14 E6
Forthassa Rharbia, Algeria 75 B4
Fortín Coronel Eugenio Garay, Paraguay 125 E5
Fortín Garrapatal, Paraguay 125 E5
Fortín General Pando, Paraguay 125 D6
Fortín Madrejón, Paraguay 125 E6
Fortín Uno, Argentina 128 A3
Fortore →, Italy 33 G12
Fortrose, U.K. 14 D4
Fortuna, Spain 29 G3
Fortuna, Calif., U.S.A. 110 F1
Fortuna, N. Dak., U.S.A. 108 A3
Fortune B., Canada 99 C8
Fos-sur-Mer, France 27 E8
Foshan, China 53 F9
Fosna, Norway 8 E14
Fosnavåg, Norway 9 E11
Fossacésia, Italy 33 F11
Fossano, Italy 32 D4
Fosses-la-Ville, Belgium 17 H5
Fossil, U.S.A. 110 D3
Fossilbrook, Australia 90 B3
Fossombrone, Italy 33 E9
Fosston, U.S.A. 108 B7
Foster, Canada 107 A12
Foster →, Canada 101 B7
Fosters Ra., Australia 90 C1
Fostoria, U.S.A. 104 E4
Fougamou, Gabon 80 E2
Fougères, France 24 D5
Foul Pt., Sri Lanka 60 Q12
Foula, U.K. 14 A6
Foulness I., U.K. 13 F8
Foulpointe, Madag. 85 B8
Foum Assaka, Morocco 74 C2
Foum Zguid, Morocco 74 B3
Foumban, Cameroon 79 D7
Foundiougne, Senegal 78 C1
Fountain, Colo., U.S.A. 108 F2
Fountain, Utah, U.S.A. 110 G8
Fountain Springs, U.S.A. 113 K8
Fourchambault, France 25 E10
Fourchu, Canada 99 C7
Fouriesburg, S. Africa 84 D4
Fourmies, France 25 B11
Foúrnoi, Greece 39 M9
Fours, France 25 F10
Fouta Djalon, Guinea 78 C2
Foux, Cap-à-, Haiti 117 C5
Foveaux Str., N.Z. 87 M2
Fowey, U.K. 13 G3
Fowler, Calif., U.S.A. 111 H4
Fowler, Colo., U.S.A. 108 F2
Fowler, Kans., U.S.A. 109 G4
Fowlers B., Australia 89 F5
Fowlerton, U.S.A. 109 L5
Fowman, Iran 67 D13
Fox →, Canada 101 B10
Fox Valley, Canada 101 C7
Foxe Basin, Canada 97 B12
Foxe Chan., Canada 97 B11
Foxe Pen., Canada 97 B12
Foxhol, Neths. 16 B9
Foxpark, U.S.A. 110 F10
Foxton, N.Z. 87 J5
Foyle, Lough, U.K. 15 A4
Foynes, Ireland 15 D2
Foz, Spain 30 B3
Fóz do Cunene, Angola 84 B1
Foz do Gregório, Brazil 124 B3
Foz do Iguaçu, Brazil 127 B5
Foz do Riosinho, Brazil 124 B3
Frackville, U.S.A. 107 F8
Fraga, Spain 28 D5
Fraire, Belgium 17 H5
Frameries, Belgium 17 H3
Framingham, U.S.A. 107 D13
Franca, Brazil 123 F2
Francavilla al Mare, Italy 33 F11
Francavilla Fontana, Italy 35 B10
France ■, Europe 7 F6
Frances, Australia 91 F3
Frances →, Canada 100 A3
Frances L., Canada 100 A3
Francés Viejo, C., Dom. Rep. 117 C6
Franceville, Gabon 80 E2
Franche-Comté, France 25 F12
Franches Montagnes, Switz. 22 B4
Francisco de Orellana, Ecuador 120 D2
Francisco I. Madero, Coahuila, Mexico 114 B4
Francisco I. Madero, Durango, Mexico 114 C4
Francisco Sá, Brazil 123 E3
Francistown, Botswana 85 C4
Francofonte, Italy 35 E7

François, Canada 99 C8
François L., Canada 100 C3
Francorchamps, Belgium 17 H7
Franeker, Neths. 16 B7
Frankado, Djibouti 77 E5
Frankenberg, Germany 18 D4
Frankenthal, Germany 19 F4
Frankenwald, Germany 19 E7
Frankfort, S. Africa 85 D4
Frankfort, Ind., U.S.A. 104 E2
Frankfort, Kans., U.S.A. 108 F6
Frankfort, Ky., U.S.A. 104 F3
Frankfort, Mich., U.S.A. 104 C2
Frankfurt, Brandenburg, Germany 18 C10
Frankfurt, Hessen, Germany 19 E4
Fränkische Alb, Germany 19 F7
Fränkische Rezal →, Germany 19 F7
Fränkische Saale →, Germany 19 E5
Fränkische Schweiz, Germany 19 F7
Frankland →, Australia 89 G2
Franklin, Ky., U.S.A. 105 G2
Franklin, La., U.S.A. 109 L9
Franklin, Mass., U.S.A. 107 D13
Franklin, N.H., U.S.A. 107 C13
Franklin, Nebr., U.S.A. 108 E5
Franklin, Pa., U.S.A. 106 E5
Franklin, Tenn., U.S.A. 105 H2
Franklin, Va., U.S.A. 105 G7
Franklin, W. Va., U.S.A. 104 F6
Franklin B., Canada 96 B7
Franklin D. Roosevelt L., U.S.A. 110 B4
Franklin I., Antarctica 5 D11
Franklin L., U.S.A. 110 F6
Franklin Mts., Canada 96 B7
Franklin Str., Canada 96 A10
Franklinton, U.S.A. 109 K9
Franklinville, U.S.A. 106 D6
Franks Pk., U.S.A. 110 E9
Frankston, Australia 91 F4
Fränsta, Sweden 10 B10
Frantsa Iosifa, Zemlya, Russia 44 A6
Franz, Canada 98 C3
Franz Josef Land = Frantsa Iosifa, Zemlya, Russia 44 A6
Franzburg, Germany 18 A8
Frascati, Italy 34 A5
Fraser →, B.C., Canada 100 D4
Fraser →, Nfld., Canada 99 A7
Fraser, Mt., Australia 89 E2
Fraser I., Australia 91 D5
Fraser Lake, Canada 100 C4
Fraserburg, S. Africa 84 E3
Fraserburgh, U.K. 14 D6
Fraserdale, Canada 98 C3
Frasne, France 25 F13
Frauenfeld, Switz. 23 A7
Fray Bentos, Uruguay 126 C4
Frazier Downs, Australia 88 C3
Frechilla, Spain 30 C6
Fredericia, Denmark 11 J3
Frederick, Md., U.S.A. 104 F7
Frederick, Okla., U.S.A. 109 H5
Frederick, S. Dak., U.S.A. 108 C5
Frederick Sd., U.S.A. 100 B2
Fredericksburg, Tex., U.S.A. 109 K5
Fredericksburg, Va., U.S.A. 104 F7
Fredericktown, U.S.A. 109 G9
Frederico I. Madero, Presa, Mexico 114 B3
Fredericton, Canada 99 C6
Fredericton Junc., Canada 99 C6
Frederikshåb, Greenland 4 C5
Frederikshavn, Denmark 11 G4
Frederikssund, Denmark 11 J6
Frederiksted, Virgin Is. 117 C7
Fredonia, Ariz., U.S.A. 111 H7
Fredonia, Kans., U.S.A. 109 G7
Fredonia, N.Y., U.S.A. 106 D5
Fredrikstad, Norway 10 E4
Free State □, S. Africa 84 D4
Freehold, U.S.A. 107 F10
Freel Peak, U.S.A. 112 G7
Freeland, U.S.A. 107 E9
Freels, C., Canada 99 C9
Freeman, Calif., U.S.A. 113 K9
Freeman, S. Dak., U.S.A. 108 D6
Freeport, Bahamas 116 A4
Freeport, Canada 99 D6
Freeport, Ill., U.S.A. 108 D10
Freeport, N.Y., U.S.A. 107 F11
Freeport, Tex., U.S.A. 109 L7
Freetown, S. Leone 78 D2
Frégate, L., Canada 98 B5
Fregenal de la Sierra, Spain 31 G4
Fregene, Italy 34 A5
Fréhel, C., France 24 D4
Freiberg, Germany 18 E9
Freibourg = Fribourg, Switz. 22 C4
Freiburg, Baden-W., Germany 19 H3
Freiburg, Niedersachsen, Germany 18 B5
Freiburger Alpen, Switz. 22 C4
Freire, Chile 128 A2
Freirina, Chile 126 B1
Freising, Germany 19 G7
Freistadt, Austria 20 G4
Freital, Germany 18 E9
Fréjus, France 27 E10
Fremantle, Australia 89 F2
Fremont, Calif., U.S.A. 111 H2
Fremont, Mich., U.S.A. 104 D3
Fremont, Nebr., U.S.A. 108 E6
Fremont, Ohio, U.S.A. 104 E4
Fremont →, U.S.A. 111 G8
Fremont L., U.S.A. 110 E9
French Camp, U.S.A. 112 H5
French Creek →, U.S.A. 106 E5
French Guiana ■, S. Amer. 121 C7
French Pass, N.Z. 87 J4
French Polynesia ■, Pac. Oc. 93 J13
Frenchglen, U.S.A. 110 E4
Frenchman Butte, Canada 101 C7
Frenchman Cr. →, Mont., U.S.A. 110 B10
Frenchman Cr. →, Nebr., U.S.A. 108 E4
Frenda, Algeria 75 A5
Fresco →, Brazil 125 B7
Freshfield, C., Antarctica 5 C10
Fresnay-sur-Sarthe, France 24 D7
Fresnillo, Mexico 114 C4
Fresno, U.S.A. 111 H4
Fresno Alhandiga, Spain 30 E5
Fresno Reservoir, U.S.A. 110 B9
Freudenstadt, Germany 19 G4
Freux, Belgium 17 J6
Frévent, France 25 B9
Frew →, Australia 90 C2
Frewena, Australia 90 B2
Freycinet Pen., Australia 90 G4
Freyming-Merlebach, France 25 C13
Freyung, Germany 19 G9
Fria, Guinea 78 C2
Fria, C., Namibia 84 B1
Friant, U.S.A. 112 J7
Frías, Argentina 126 B2
Fribourg, Switz. 22 C4
Fribourg □, Switz. 22 C4
Frick, Switz. 22 A6
Friday Harbor, U.S.A. 112 B3
Friedberg, Bayern, Germany 19 G6
Friedberg, Hessen, Germany 19 E4
Friedland, Germany 18 B9
Friedrichshafen, Germany 19 H5
Friedrichskoog, Germany 18 A4
Friedrichstadt, Germany 18 A5
Friendly Is. = Tonga ■, Pac. Oc. 87 D11
Friesack, Germany 18 C8
Friesche Wad, Neths. 16 B7
Friesland □, Neths. 16 B7
Friesoythe, Germany 18 B3
Frillesås, Sweden 11 G6
Frio →, U.S.A. 109 L5
Frio, C., Brazil 118 F6
Friona, U.S.A. 109 H3
Frisian Is., Europe 18 B2
Fristad, Sweden 11 G7
Fritch, U.S.A. 109 H4
Fritsla, Sweden 11 G6
Fritzlar, Germany 18 D5
Friuli-Venézia Giulia □, Italy 33 B10
Frobisher B., Canada 97 B13
Frobisher Bay = Iqaluit, Canada 97 B13
Frobisher L., Canada 101 B7
Frohavet, Norway 8 E13
Froid, U.S.A. 108 A2
Froid-Chapelle, Belgium 17 H4
Frolovo, Russia 42 F6
Fromberg, U.S.A. 110 D9
Frome, U.K. 13 F5
Frome, L., Australia 91 E2
Frome Downs, Australia 91 E2
Frómista, Spain 30 C6
Front Range, U.S.A. 110 G11
Front Royal, U.S.A. 104 F6
Fronteira, Portugal 31 F3
Fronteiras, Brazil 122 C3
Frontera, Canary Is. 36 G2
Frontera, Mexico 115 D6
Frontignan, France 26 E7
Frosinone, Italy 34 A6
Frosolone, Italy 35 A7
Frostburg, U.S.A. 104 F6
Frostisen, Norway 8 B17
Frouard, France 25 D13
Frøya, Norway 8 E13
Fruges, France 25 B9
Frumoasa, Romania 38 C8
Frunze = Bishkek, Kyrgyzstan 44 E8
Frutal, Brazil 123 F2
Frutigen, Switz. 22 C5
Frýdek-Místek, Czech. 20 F8
Frýdlant, Czech. 20 E5
Fu Jiang →, China 52 C6
Fu Xian, Liaoning, China 51 E11
Fu Xian, Shaanxi, China 50 F5
Fu'an, China 53 D12
Fubian, China 52 B4
Fucécchio, Italy 32 E7
Fucheng, China 50 F9
Fuchou = Fuzhou, China 53 D12
Fuchū, Japan 49 G6
Fuchuan, China 53 E8
Fuchun Jiang →, China 53 B13
Fúcino, Conca del, Italy 33 F10
Fuding, China 53 D13
Fuencaliente, Canary Is. 36 F2
Fuencaliente, Spain 31 G6
Fuencaliente, Pta., Canary Is. 36 F2
Fuengirola, Spain 31 J6
Fuente Alamo, Albacete, Spain 29 G3
Fuente Álamo, Murcia, Spain 29 H3
Fuente de Cantos, Spain 31 G4
Fuente del Maestre, Spain 31 G4
Fuente el Fresno, Spain 31 F7
Fuente Ovejuna, Spain 31 G5
Fuentes de Andalucía, Spain 31 H5
Fuentes de Ebro, Spain 28 D4
Fuentes de León, Spain 31 G4
Fuentes de Oñoro, Spain 30 E4
Fuentesaúco, Spain 30 D5
Fuerte →, Mexico 114 B3
Fuerte Olimpo, Paraguay 126 A4
Fuerteventura, Canary Is. 36 F6
Fufeng, China 50 G4
Fuga I., Phil. 55 B4
Fugong, China 52 D2
Fugou, China 50 G8
Fugu, China 50 E6
Fuhai, China 54 B3
Fuḥaymī, Iraq 67 E10
Fuji, Japan 49 G9
Fuji-San, Japan 49 G9
Fuji-yoshida, Japan 49 G9
Fujian □, China 53 E12
Fujinomiya, Japan 49 G9
Fujisawa, Japan 49 G9
Fukien = Fujian □, China 53 E12
Fukuchiyama, Japan 49 G7
Fukue-Shima, Japan 49 H4
Fukui, Japan 49 F8
Fukui □, Japan 49 G8
Fukuoka, Japan 49 H5
Fukuoka □, Japan 49 H5
Fukushima, Japan 48 F10
Fukushima □, Japan 48 F10
Fukuyama, Japan 49 G6
Fulda, Germany 18 E5
Fulda →, Germany 18 D5
Fuling, China 52 C6
Fullerton, Calif., U.S.A. 113 M9
Fullerton, Nebr., U.S.A. 108 E5
Fulongquan, China 51 B13
Fulton, Mo., U.S.A. 108 F9
Fulton, N.Y., U.S.A. 107 C8
Fulton, Tenn., U.S.A. 105 G1
Fuluälven →, Sweden 10 C7
Fulufjället, Sweden 10 C6
Fumay, France 25 C11
Fumel, France 26 D4
Fumin, China 52 E4
Funabashi, Japan 49 G10
Funchal, Madeira 36 D3
Fundación, Colombia 120 A3
Fundão, Brazil 123 E3
Fundão, Portugal 30 E3
Fundy, B. of, Canada 99 D6
Funing, Hebei, China 51 E10
Funing, Jiangsu, China 51 H10
Funing, Yunnan, China 52 F5
Funiu Shan, China 50 H7
Funsi, Ghana 78 C4
Funtua, Nigeria 79 C6
Fuping, Hebei, China 50 E8
Fuping, Shaanxi, China 50 G5
Fuqing, China 53 E12
Fuquan, China 52 D6
Fur, Denmark 11 H3
Furano, Japan 48 C11
Furāt, Nahr al →, Asia 64 D5
Fūrg, Iran 65 D7
Furkapass, Switz. 23 C7
Furmanov, Russia 42 B5
Furmanovo, Kazakstan 42 F9
Furnás, Spain 36 B8
Furnas, Represa de, Brazil 123 F2
Furneaux Group, Australia 90 G4
Furness, U.K. 12 C4
Furqlus, Syria 69 A6
Fürstenau, Germany 18 C3
Fürstenberg, Germany 18 B9
Fürstenfeld, Austria 21 H6
Fürstenfeldbruck, Germany 19 G7
Fürstenwalde, Germany 18 C10
Fürth, Germany 19 F6
Furth im Wald, Germany 19 F8
Furtwangen, Germany 19 G4
Furukawa, Japan 48 E10
Furusund, Sweden 10 E12
Fury and Hecla Str., Canada 97 B11
Fusagasuga, Colombia 120 C3
Fuscaldo, Italy 35 C9
Fushan, Shandong, China 51 F11
Fushan, Shanxi, China 50 G6
Fushun, Liaoning, China 51 D12
Fushun, Sichuan, China 52 C5
Fusio, Switz. 23 D7
Fusong, China 51 C14
Füssen, Germany 19 H6
Fusui, China 52 F6
Futrono, Chile 128 B2
Futuna, Wall. & F. Is. 87 B8
Fuwa, Egypt 76 H7
Fuxin, China 51 C11
Fuyang, Anhui, China 50 H8
Fuyang, Zhejiang, China 53 B12
Fuyang He →, China 50 E9
Fuying Dao, China 53 D13
Fuyu, China 51 B13
Fuyuan, Heilongjiang, China 54 B8
Fuyuan, Yunnan, China 52 E5
Fuzhou, China 53 D12
Fylde, U.K. 12 D5
Fyn, Denmark 11 J4
Fyne, L., U.K. 14 F3
Fyns Amtskommune □, Denmark 11 J4
Fyresvatn, Norway 10 E2

G

Gaanda, Nigeria 79 C7
Gabarin, Nigeria 79 C7
Gabas →, France 26 E3
Gabela, Angola 80 G2
Gabès, Tunisia 75 B7
Gabès, G. de, Tunisia 75 B7
Gabgaba, W. →, Egypt 76 C3
Gabon ■, Africa 80 E2
Gaborone, Botswana 84 C4
Gabriels, U.S.A. 107 B10
Gābrīk, Iran 65 E8
Gabrovo, Bulgaria 38 G8
Gacé, France 24 D7
Gāch Sār, Iran 65 B6
Gachsārān, Iran 65 D6
Gacko, Bos.-H. 21 M8
Gadag, India 60 M9
Gadamai, Sudan 77 D4
Gadap, Pakistan 62 G2
Gadarwara, India 63 H8
Gadebusch, Germany 18 B7
Gadein, Sudan 77 F2
Gadhada, India 62 J4
Gadmen, Switz. 23 C6
Gádor, Sierra de, Spain 29 J2
Gadsden, Ala., U.S.A. 105 H2
Gadsden, Ariz., U.S.A. 111 K6
Gadwal, India 60 L10
Gadyach = Hadyach, Ukraine 41 G8
Găeşti, Romania 38 E8
Gaeta, Italy 34 A6
Gaeta, G. di, Italy 34 A6
Gaffney, U.S.A. 105 H5
Gafsa, Tunisia 75 B6
Gagarin, Russia 42 C2
Gagetown, Canada 99 C6
Gagino, Russia 42 C7
Gagliano del Capo, Italy 35 C11
Gagnoa, Ivory C. 78 D3
Gagnon, Canada 99 B6
Gagnon, L., Canada 101 A6
Gagra, Georgia 43 J5
Gahini, Rwanda 82 C3
Gahmar, India 63 G10
Gai Xian, China 51 D12
Gaïdhouronísi, Greece 37 E7
Gail, U.S.A. 109 J4
Gail →, Austria 21 J3
Gaillac, France 26 E5
Gaillimh = Galway, Ireland 15 C2
Gaillon, France 24 C8
Gaimán, Argentina 128 B3
Gaines, U.S.A. 106 E7
Gainesville, Fla., U.S.A. 105 L4
Gainesville, Ga., U.S.A. 105 H4
Gainesville, Mo., U.S.A. 109 G8
Gainesville, Tex., U.S.A. 109 J6
Gainsborough, U.K. 12 D7
Gairdner, L., Australia 91 E2
Gairloch, L., U.K. 14 D3
Gais, Switz. 23 B8
Gakuch, Pakistan 63 A5
Galán, Cerro, Argentina 126 B2
Galana →, Kenya 82 C5
Galangue, Angola 81 G3
Galápagos, Pac. Oc. 118 D1
Galashiels, U.K. 14 F6
Galaţi, Romania 38 D11
Galatia, Turkey 66 C5
Galatina, Italy 35 B11
Galátone, Italy 35 B11
Galax, U.S.A. 105 G5
Galaxídhion, Greece 39 L5
Galbraith, Australia 90 B3
Galcaio, Somali Rep. 68 F4
Galdhøpiggen, Norway 10 C2
Galeana, Mexico 114 C4
Galela, Indonesia 57 D7
Galera, Spain 29 H2
Galera, Pta., Chile 128 A2
Galera Point, Trin. & Tob. 117 D7
Galesburg, U.S.A. 108 E9
Galeton, U.S.A. 106 E7
Galheirão →, Brazil 123 D2
Galheiros, Brazil 123 D2
Gali, Georgia 43 J5
Galich, Russia 42 A6
Galiche, Bulgaria 38 F6
Galicia □, Spain 30 C3
Galilee = Hagalil, Israel 69 C4
Galilee, L., Australia 90 C4
Galilee, Sea of = Yam Kinneret, Israel 69 C4
Galinoporni, Cyprus 37 D13
Galion, U.S.A. 106 F2
Galite, Is. de la, Tunisia 75 A6
Galiuro Mts., U.S.A. 111 K8
Gallabat, Sudan 77 E4
Gallarate, Italy 32 C5
Gallardon, France 25 D8
Gallatin, U.S.A. 105 G2
Galle, Sri Lanka 60 R12
Gállego →, Spain 28 D4
Gallegos →, Argentina 128 D3
Galley Hd., Ireland 15 E3
Galliate, Italy 32 C5
Gallinas, Pta., Colombia 120 A3
Gallipoli = Gelibolu, Turkey 66 B2
Gallípoli, Italy 35 B11
Gallipolis, U.S.A. 104 F4
Gällivare, Sweden 8 C19
Gallo, C., Italy 34 D6
Gallocanta, L. de, Spain 28 E3
Galloway, U.K. 14 G4
Galloway, Mull of, U.K. 14 G4
Gallup, U.S.A. 111 J9
Gallur, Spain 28 D3
Galong, Australia 91 E4
Galoya, Sri Lanka 60 Q12
Galt, U.S.A. 112 G5
Galtström, Sweden 10 B11
Galtür, Austria 19 J6
Galty Mts., Ireland 15 D3
Galtymore, Ireland 15 D3
Galva, U.S.A. 108 E9
Galvarino, Chile 128 A2
Galve de Sorbe, Spain 28 D1
Galveston, U.S.A. 109 L7
Galveston B., U.S.A. 109 L7
Gálvez, Argentina 126 C3
Gálvez, Spain 31 F6
Galway, Ireland 15 C2
Galway □, Ireland 15 C2
Galway B., Ireland 15 C2
Gam →, Vietnam 58 B5
Gamagori, Japan 49 G8
Gamari, L., Ethiopia 77 E5
Gamawa, Nigeria 79 C7
Gamay, Phil. 55 E6
Gambaga, Ghana 79 C4
Gambat, Pakistan 62 F3
Gambela, Ethiopia 77 F3
Gambia ■, W. Afr. 78 C1
Gambia →, W. Afr. 78 C1
Gambier, C., Australia 88 B5
Gambier Is., Australia 91 F2
Gamboli, Pakistan 62 E3
Gamboma, Congo 80 E3
Gamerco, U.S.A. 111 J9
Gamlakarleby = Kokkola, Finland 8 E20
Gammon →, Canada 101 C9
Gammouda, Tunisia 75 A6
Gamu-Gofa □, Ethiopia 77 F4
Gan, France 26 E3
Gan Gan, Argentina 128 B3
Gan Goriama, Mts., Cameroon 79 D7
Gan Jiang →, China 53 C10
Ganado, Ariz., U.S.A. 111 J9
Ganado, Tex., U.S.A. 109 L6
Gananoque, Canada 98 D4
Ganāveh, Iran 65 D6
Gäncä, Azerbaijan 43 K8
Gand = Gent, Belgium 17 F3
Ganda, Angola 81 G2
Gandak →, India 63 G11
Gandava, Pakistan 62 E2
Gander, Canada 99 C9
Gander L., Canada 99 C9
Ganderowe Falls, Zimbabwe 83 F2
Gandesa, Spain 28 D5
Gandhi Sagar, India 62 G6
Gandi, Nigeria 79 C6
Gandía, Spain 29 G4
Gandino, Italy 32 C6
Gando, Pta., Canary Is. 36 G4
Gandole, Nigeria 79 D7
Gandu, Brazil 123 D4
Ganedidalem = Gani, Indonesia 57 E7
Ganetti, Sudan 76 D3
Ganga →, India 63 H14
Ganga, Mouths of the, India 63 J13
Ganganagar, India 62 E5
Gangapur, India 62 F7
Gangara, Niger 79 C6
Gangaw, Burma 61 H19
Gangdisê Shan, China 61 D12
Ganges = Ganga →, India 63 H14
Ganges, France 26 E7
Gangoh, India 62 E7
Gangtok, India 61 F16
Gangu, China 50 G3
Gangyao, China 51 B14
Gani, Indonesia 57 E7
Ganj, India 63 F8
Gannat, France 26 B7
Gannett Peak, U.S.A. 110 E9
Gannvalley, U.S.A. 108 C5
Ganquan, China 50 F5
Gänserdorf, Austria 21 G6
Ganshui, China 52 C6
Gansu □, China 50 G3
Ganta, Liberia 78 D3
Gantheaume, C., Australia 91 F2
Gantheaume B., Australia 89 E1
Gantsevichi = Hantsavichy, Belarus 41 F4
Ganyem, Indonesia 57 E10
Ganyu, China 51 G10
Ganyushkino, Kazakstan 43 G9
Ganzhou, China 53 E10
Gao, Mali 79 B5
Gao Xian, China 52 C5
Gao'an, China 53 C10

Gaohe, *China* 53 F9
Gaohebu, *China* 53 B11
Gaokeng, *China* 53 D9
Gaolan Dao, *China* 53 G9
Gaoligong Shan, *China* 52 E2
Gaomi, *China* 51 F10
Gaoping, *China* 50 G7
Gaotang, *China* 50 F9
Gaoua, *Burkina Faso* 78 C4
Gaoual, *Guinea* 78 C2
Gaoxiong = Kaohsiung, *Taiwan* 53 F13
Gaoyang, *China* 50 E8
Gaoyou, *China* 53 A12
Gaoyou Hu, *China* 51 H10
Gaoyuan, *China* 51 F9
Gaozhou, *China* 53 G8
Gap, *France* 27 D10
Gapan, *Phil.* 55 D4
Gar, *China* 54 C2
Garabogazköl Aylagy, *Turkmenistan* 44 E6
Garachico, *Canary Is.* 36 F3
Garachiné, *Panama* 116 E4
Garafía, *Canary Is.* 36 F2
Garajonay, *Canary Is.* 36 F2
Garanhuns, *Brazil* 122 C4
Garawe, *Liberia* 78 E3
Garba Tula, *Kenya* 82 B4
Garber, *U.S.A.* 109 G6
Garberville, *U.S.A.* 110 F2
Garça, *Brazil* 123 F2
Garças →, *Mato Grosso, Brazil* 125 D7
Garças →, *Pernambuco, Brazil* 122 C4
Garcias, *Brazil* 125 E7
Gard, *Somali Rep.* 68 F4
Gard □, *France* 27 D8
Gard →, *France* 27 E8
Garda, L. di, *Italy* 32 C7
Gardanne, *France* 27 E9
Garde L., *Canada* 101 A7
Gardelegen, *Germany* 18 C7
Garden City, *Kans., U.S.A.* 109 G4
Garden City, *Tex., U.S.A.* 109 K4
Garden Grove, *U.S.A.* 113 M9
Gardēz, *Afghan.* 62 C3
Gardiner, *U.S.A.* 110 D8
Gardiners I., *U.S.A.* 107 E12
Gardner, *U.S.A.* 107 D13
Gardner Canal, *Canada* 100 C3
Gardnerville, *U.S.A.* 112 G7
Gare Tigre, *Fr. Guiana* 121 C7
Garéssio, *Italy* 32 D5
Garey, *U.S.A.* 113 L6
Garfield, *U.S.A.* 110 C5
Gargan, Mt., *France* 26 C5
Gargano, Mte., *Italy* 35 A8
Gargouna, *Mali* 79 B5
Garhshankar, *India* 62 D7
Garibaldi Prov. Park, *Canada* 100 D4
Garies, *S. Africa* 84 E2
Garigliano →, *Italy* 34 A6
Garissa, *Kenya* 82 C4
Garissa □, *Kenya* 82 C5
Garkida, *Nigeria* 79 C7
Garko, *Nigeria* 79 C6
Garland, *Tex., U.S.A.* 109 J6
Garland, *Utah, U.S.A.* 110 F7
Garlasco, *Italy* 32 C5
Garm, *Tajikistan* 44 F8
Garmāb, *Iran* 65 C8
Garmisch-Partenkirchen, *Germany* 19 H7
Garmsār, *Iran* 65 C7
Garner, *U.S.A.* 108 D8
Garnett, *U.S.A.* 108 F7
Garo Hills, *India* 63 G14
Garoe, *Somali Rep.* 68 F4
Garonne →, *France* 26 C3
Garonne, Canal Latéral à la →, *France* 26 D4
Garoua, *Cameroon* 79 D7
Garrel, *Germany* 18 C3
Garrigue, *France* 26 E7
Garrison, *Mont., U.S.A.* 110 C7
Garrison, *N. Dak., U.S.A.* 108 B4
Garrison, *Tex., U.S.A.* 109 K7
Garrison Res. = Sakakawea, L., *U.S.A.* 108 B3
Garrovillas, *Spain* 31 F4
Garrucha, *Spain* 29 H3
Garry →, *U.K.* 14 E5
Garry, L., *Canada* 96 B9
Garsen, *Kenya* 82 C5
Garson L., *Canada* 101 B6
Gartempe →, *France* 26 B4
Gartz, *Germany* 18 B10
Garu, *Ghana* 79 C4
Garub, *Namibia* 84 D2
Garut, *Indonesia* 57 G12
Garvão, *Portugal* 31 H2
Garvie Mts., *N.Z.* 87 L2
Garwa = Garoua, *Cameroon* 79 D7
Garwa, *India* 63 G10
Garwolin, *Poland* 20 D11
Gary, *U.S.A.* 104 E2
Garz, *Germany* 18 A9
Garzê, *China* 52 B3
Garzón, *Colombia* 120 C2
Gas-San, *Japan* 48 E10
Gasan Kuli = Esenguly, *Turkmenistan* 44 F6
Gascogne, *France* 26 E4
Gascogne, G. de, *Europe* 28 B2
Gascony = Gascogne, *France* 26 E4
Gascoyne →, *Australia* 89 D1
Gascoyne Junc. T.O., *Australia* 89 E2
Gascueña, *Spain* 28 E2
Gash, Wadi →, *Ethiopia* 77 D4
Gashaka, *Nigeria* 79 D7
Gasherbrum, *Pakistan* 63 B7
Gashua, *Nigeria* 79 C7
Gaspé, *Canada* 99 C7
Gaspé, C. de, *Canada* 99 C7
Gaspé, Pén. de, *Canada* 99 C6
Gaspésie, Parc Prov. de la, *Canada* 99 C6
Gassaway, *U.S.A.* 104 F5
Gasselte, *Neths.* 16 C9
Gasselternijveen, *Neths.* 16 C9
Gássino Torinese, *Italy* 32 C4
Gassol, *Nigeria* 79 D7
Gasteiz = Vitoria, *Spain* 28 C2
Gastonia, *U.S.A.* 105 H5
Gastoúni, *Greece* 39 M4
Gastoúri, *Greece* 39 K2
Gastre, *Argentina* 128 B3
Gata, C., *Cyprus* 37 E12
Gata, C. de, *Spain* 29 J2
Gata, Sierra de, *Spain* 30 E4
Gataga →, *Canada* 100 B3
Gătaia, *Romania* 38 D4
Gatchina, *Russia* 40 C6
Gates, *U.S.A.* 106 C7
Gateshead, *U.K.* 12 C6
Gatesville, *U.S.A.* 109 K6
Gaths, *Zimbabwe* 83 G3
Gatico, *Chile* 126 A1
Gâtinais, *France* 25 D9
Gâtine, Hauteurs de, *France* 26 B3
Gatineau →, *Canada* 98 C4
Gatineau, Parc de la, *Canada* 98 C4
Gattaran, *Phil.* 55 B4
Gattinara, *Italy* 32 C5
Gatun, L., *Panama* 116 E4
Gatyana, *S. Africa* 85 E4
Gau, *Fiji* 87 D8
Gaucín, *Spain* 31 J5
Gauer L., *Canada* 101 B9
Gauhati, *India* 63 F14
Gauja →, *Latvia* 9 H21
Gaula →, *Norway* 8 E14
Gaurain-Ramecroix, *Belgium* 17 G3
Gausta, *Norway* 10 E2
Gauteng □, *S. Africa* 85 D4
Gāv Koshī, *Iran* 65 D8
Gavá, *Spain* 28 D6
Gāvakān, *Iran* 65 D7
Gavarnie, *France* 26 F3
Gavāter, *Iran* 65 E9
Gāvbandī, *Iran* 65 E7
Gavdhopoúla, *Greece* 37 E6
Gávdhos, *Greece* 37 E6
Gavere, *Belgium* 17 G3
Gavião, *Portugal* 31 F3
Gaviota, *U.S.A.* 113 L6
Gävle, *Sweden* 9 F17
Gävleborgs län □, *Sweden* 10 C10
Gavorrano, *Italy* 32 F7
Gavray, *France* 24 D5
Gavrilov Yam, *Russia* 42 B4
Gawachab, *Namibia* 84 D2
Gawilgarh Hills, *India* 60 J10
Gawler, *Australia* 91 E2
Gaxun Nur, *China* 54 B5
Gaya, *India* 63 G11
Gaya, *Niger* 79 C5
Gaya, *Nigeria* 79 C6
Gaylord, *U.S.A.* 104 C3
Gayndah, *Australia* 91 D5
Gaysin = Haysyn, *Ukraine* 41 H5
Gayvoron = Hayvoron, *Ukraine* 41 H5
Gaza, *Gaza Strip* 69 D3
Gaza □, *Mozam.* 85 C5
Gaza Strip □, *Asia* 69 D3
Gazaoua, *Niger* 79 C6
Gāzbor, *Iran* 65 D8
Gazi, *Zaïre* 82 B1
Gaziantep, *Turkey* 66 D7
Gazipaşa, *Turkey* 66 D5
Gazli, *Uzbekistan* 44 E7
Gbarnga, *Liberia* 78 D3
Gbekebo, *Nigeria* 79 D5
Gboko, *Nigeria* 79 D6
Gbongan, *Nigeria* 79 D5
Gcuwa, *S. Africa* 85 E4
Gdańsk, *Poland* 20 A8
Gdańska, Zatoka, *Poland* 20 A9
Gdov, *Russia* 9 G22
Gdynia, *Poland* 20 A8
Gebe, *Indonesia* 57 D7
Gebeit Mine, *Sudan* 76 C4
Gebze, *Turkey* 66 B3
Gecha, *Ethiopia* 77 F4
Gedaref, *Sudan* 77 E4
Gede, Tanjung, *Indonesia* 56 F3
Gedinne, *Belgium* 17 J5
Gediz, *Turkey* 66 C3
Gediz →, *Turkey* 66 C2
Gedo, *Ethiopia* 77 F4
Gèdre, *France* 26 F4
Gedser, *Denmark* 11 K5
Gedser Odde, *Denmark* 11 K5
Geegully Cr. →, *Australia* 88 C3
Geel, *Belgium* 17 F5
Geelong, *Australia* 91 F3
Geelvink Chan., *Australia* 89 E1
Geer →, *Belgium* 17 G7
Geesthacht, *Germany* 18 B6
Geffen, *Neths.* 16 E6
Geidam, *Nigeria* 79 C7
Geikie →, *Canada* 101 B8
Geili, *Sudan* 77 D3
Geilo, *Norway* 10 D2
Geisingen, *Germany* 19 H4
Geislingen, *Germany* 19 G5
Geita, *Tanzania* 82 C3
Geita □, *Tanzania* 82 C3
Gejiu, *China* 52 F4
Gel →, *Sudan* 77 F2
Gel River, *Sudan* 77 F2
Gela, *Italy* 35 E7
Gela, G. di, *Italy* 35 F7
Geladi, *Ethiopia* 68 F4
Gelderland □, *Neths.* 16 D8
Geldermalsen, *Neths.* 16 E6
Geldern, *Germany* 18 D2
Geldrop, *Neths.* 17 F7
Geleen, *Neths.* 17 G7
Gelehun, *S. Leone* 78 D2
Gelendost, *Turkey* 66 C4
Gelendzhik, *Russia* 43 H4
Gelibolu, *Turkey* 66 B2
Gelidonya Burnu, *Turkey* 66 D4
Gelnhausen, *Germany* 19 E5
Gelsenkirchen, *Germany* 18 D3
Gelting, *Germany* 18 A5
Gemas, *Malaysia* 59 L4
Gembloux, *Belgium* 17 G5
Gemena, *Zaïre* 80 D3
Gemerek, *Turkey* 66 C7
Gemert, *Neths.* 17 E7
Gemlik, *Turkey* 66 B3
Gemona del Friuli, *Italy* 33 B10
Gemsa, *Egypt* 76 B3
Gemünden, *Germany* 19 E5
Genale, *Ethiopia* 77 F4
Genappe, *Belgium* 17 G4
Genç, *Turkey* 67 C9
Gençay, *France* 26 B4
Gendringen, *Neths.* 16 E8
Gendt, *Neths.* 16 E7
Geneina, Gebel, *Egypt* 76 J8
Genemuiden, *Neths.* 16 C8
General Acha, *Argentina* 126 D3
General Alvear, *Buenos Aires, Argentina* 126 D3
General Alvear, *Mendoza, Argentina* 126 D2
General Artigas, *Paraguay* 126 B4
General Belgrano, *Argentina* 126 D4
General Cabrera, *Argentina* 126 C3
General Carrera, L., *Chile* 128 C2
General Cepeda, *Mexico* 114 B4
General Conesa, *Argentina* 128 B4
General Guido, *Argentina* 126 D4
General Juan Madariaga, *Argentina* 126 D4
General La Madrid, *Argentina* 126 D3
General Lorenzo Vintter, *Argentina* 128 B4
General MacArthur, *Phil.* 55 F6
General Martin Miguel de Güemes, *Argentina* 126 A3
General Paz, *Argentina* 126 B4
General Pico, *Argentina* 126 D3
General Pinedo, *Argentina* 126 B3
General Pinto, *Argentina* 126 C3
General Sampaio, *Brazil* 122 B4
General Santos, *Phil.* 55 H6
General Toshevo, *Bulgaria* 38 F11
General Trevino, *Mexico* 115 B5
General Trías, *Mexico* 114 B3
General Viamonte, *Argentina* 126 D3
General Villegas, *Argentina* 126 D3
General Vintter, L., *Argentina* 128 B2
Generoso, Mte., *Switz.* 23 E8
Genesee, *Idaho, U.S.A.* 110 C5
Genesee, *Pa., U.S.A.* 106 E7
Genesee →, *U.S.A.* 106 C7
Geneseo, *Ill., U.S.A.* 108 E9
Geneseo, *Kans., U.S.A.* 108 F5
Geneseo, *N.Y., U.S.A.* 106 D7
Geneva = Genève, *Switz.* 22 D2
Geneva, *Ala., U.S.A.* 105 K3
Geneva, *N.Y., U.S.A.* 106 D7
Geneva, *Nebr., U.S.A.* 108 E6
Geneva, *Ohio, U.S.A.* 106 E4
Geneva, L. = Léman, L., *Europe* 22 D3
Geneva, L., *U.S.A.* 104 D1
Genève, *Switz.* 22 D2
Genève □, *Switz.* 22 D2
Gengenbach, *Germany* 19 G4
Gengma, *China* 52 F2
Genichesk = Henichesk, *Ukraine* 41 J8
Genil →, *Spain* 31 H5
Génissiat, Barr. de, *France* 27 B9
Genk, *Belgium* 17 G7
Genlis, *France* 25 E12
Gennargentu, Mti. del, *Italy* 34 C2
Gennep, *Neths.* 17 E7
Gennes, *France* 24 E6
Genoa = Génova, *Italy* 32 D5
Genoa, *Australia* 91 F4
Genoa, *N.Y., U.S.A.* 107 D8
Genoa, *Nebr., U.S.A.* 108 E6
Genoa, *Nev., U.S.A.* 112 F7
Genoa →, *Argentina* 128 B2
Génova, *Italy* 32 D5
Génova, G. di, *Italy* 32 E6
Gent, *Belgium* 17 F3
Gentbrugge, *Belgium* 17 F3
Genthin, *Germany* 18 C8
Gentio do Ouro, *Brazil* 122 D3
Geographe B., *Australia* 89 F2
Geographe Chan., *Australia* 89 D1
Geokchay = Göyçay, *Azerbaijan* 43 K8
Georga, Zemlya, *Russia* 44 A5
George, *S. Africa* 84 E3
George →, *Canada* 99 A6
George, L., *N.S.W., Australia* 91 F4
George, L., *S. Austral., Australia* 91 F3
George, L., *W. Austral., Australia* 88 D3
George, L., *Uganda* 82 B3
George, L., *Fla., U.S.A.* 105 L5
George, L., *N.Y., U.S.A.* 107 C11
George Gill Ra., *Australia* 88 D5
George River = Kangiqsualujjuaq, *Canada* 97 C13
George Sound, *N.Z.* 87 L1
George Town, *Bahamas* 116 B4
George Town, *Malaysia* 59 K3
George V Land, *Antarctica* 5 C10
George VI Sound, *Antarctica* 5 D17
George West, *U.S.A.* 109 L5
Georgetown, *Australia* 90 B3
Georgetown, *Ont., Canada* 98 D4
Georgetown, *P.E.I., Canada* 99 C7
Georgetown, *Cayman Is.* 116 C3
Georgetown, *Gambia* 78 C2
Georgetown, *Guyana* 121 B6
Georgetown, *Calif., U.S.A.* 112 G6
Georgetown, *Colo., U.S.A.* 110 G11
Georgetown, *Ky., U.S.A.* 104 F3
Georgetown, *S.C., U.S.A.* 105 J6
Georgetown, *Tex., U.S.A.* 109 K6
Georgia □, *U.S.A.* 105 J4
Georgia ■, *Asia* 43 J6
Georgia, Str. of, *Canada* 100 D4
Georgian B., *Canada* 98 C3
Georgina →, *Australia* 90 C2
Georgina Downs, *Australia* 90 C2
Georgiu-Dezh = Liski, *Russia* 42 E4
Georgiyevsk, *Russia* 43 H6
Gera, *Germany* 18 E8
Geraardsbergen, *Belgium* 17 G3
Geral, Serra, *Bahia, Brazil* 123 D3
Geral, Serra, *Goiás, Brazil* 122 D2
Geral, Serra, *Sta. Catarina, Brazil* 127 B6
Geral de Goiás, Serra, *Brazil* 123 D2
Geral do Paranã Serra, *Brazil* 123 E2
Geraldine, *U.S.A.* 110 C8
Geraldton, *Australia* 89 E1
Geraldton, *Canada* 98 C2
Gérardmer, *France* 25 D13
Gercüş, *Turkey* 67 D9
Gerede, *Turkey* 66 B5
Gereshk, *Afghan.* 60 D4
Gérgal, *Spain* 29 H2
Gerik, *Malaysia* 59 K3
Gering, *U.S.A.* 108 E3
Gerlach, *U.S.A.* 110 F4
Gerlachovka, *Slovak Rep.* 20 F10
Gerlogubi, *Ethiopia* 68 F4
Germansen Landing, *Canada* 100 B4
Germany ■, *Europe* 18 E6
Germersheim, *Germany* 19 F4
Germī, *Iran* 67 C13
Germiston, *S. Africa* 85 D4
Gernsheim, *Germany* 19 F4
Gero, *Japan* 49 G8
Gerolstein, *Germany* 19 E2
Gerolzhofen, *Germany* 19 F6
Gerona, *Spain* 28 D7
Gerona □, *Spain* 28 C7
Gérouville, *Belgium* 17 J6
Gerrard, *Canada* 100 C5
Gers □, *France* 26 E4
Gers →, *France* 26 D4
Gersfeld, *Germany* 18 E5
Gerze, *Turkey* 66 B6
Geseke, *Germany* 18 D4
Geser, *Indonesia* 57 E8
Gesso →, *Italy* 32 D4
Gestro, Wabi →, *Ethiopia* 77 G5
Gesves, *Belgium* 17 H6
Getafe, *Spain* 30 E7
Gethsémani, *Canada* 99 B7
Gettysburg, *Pa., U.S.A.* 104 F7
Gettysburg, *S. Dak., U.S.A.* 108 C5
Getz Ice Shelf, *Antarctica* 5 D14
Geul →, *Neths.* 17 G7
Gevaş, *Turkey* 67 C10
Gévaudan, *France* 26 D7
Gevgelija, *Macedonia* 39 H5
Gévora →, *Spain* 31 G4
Gex, *France* 27 B10
Geyser, *U.S.A.* 110 C8
Geyserville, *U.S.A.* 112 G4
Geyve, *Turkey* 66 B4
Ghâbat el Arab = Wang Kai, *Sudan* 77 F2
Ghaghara →, *India* 63 G11
Ghalla, Wadi el →, *Sudan* 77 E2
Ghallamane, *Mauritania* 74 D3
Ghana ■, *W. Afr.* 79 D4
Ghansor, *India* 63 H9
Ghanzi, *Botswana* 84 C3
Ghanzi □, *Botswana* 84 C3
Gharb el Istiwa'iya □, *Sudan* 77 F2
Gharbîya, Es Sahrâ el, *Egypt* 76 B2
Ghard Abû Muharik, *Egypt* 76 B2
Ghardaïa, *Algeria* 75 B5
Ghârib, G., *Egypt* 76 J8
Gharyān, *Libya* 75 B7
Gharyān □, *Libya* 75 B7
Ghat, *Libya* 75 D7
Ghatal, *India* 63 H12
Ghatampur, *India* 63 F9
Ghaṭṭī, *Si. Arabia* 64 D3
Ghawdex = Gozo, *Malta* 37 C1
Ghazal, Bahr el →, *Chad* 73 F8
Ghazâl, Bahr el →, *Sudan* 77 F3
Ghazaouet, *Algeria* 75 A4
Ghaziabad, *India* 62 E7
Ghazipur, *India* 63 G10
Ghaznī, *Afghan.* 62 C3
Ghaznī □, *Afghan.* 60 C6
Ghedi, *Italy* 32 C7
Ghèlinsor, *Somali Rep.* 68 F4
Ghent = Gent, *Belgium* 17 F3
Gheorghe Gheorghiu-Dej = Oneşti, *Romania* 38 C9
Gheorgheni, *Romania* 38 C8
Ghergani, *Romania* 38 E8
Gherla, *Romania* 38 B6
Ghilarza, *Italy* 34 B1
Ghisonaccia, *France* 27 F13
Ghisoni, *France* 27 F13
Ghizao, *Afghan.* 62 C1
Ghizar →, *Pakistan* 63 A5
Ghogha, *India* 62 J5
Ghot Ogrein, *Egypt* 76 A2
Ghotaru, *India* 62 F4
Ghotki, *Pakistan* 62 E3
Ghowr □, *Afghan.* 60 C4
Ghudaf, W. al →, *Iraq* 67 F10
Ghudāmis, *Libya* 75 B6
Ghughri, *India* 63 H9
Ghugus, *India* 60 K11
Ghulam Mohammad Barrage, *Pakistan* 62 G3
Ghūrīān, *Afghan.* 60 B2
Gia Dinh, *Vietnam* 59 G6
Gia Lai = Pleiku, *Vietnam* 58 F7
Gia Nghia, *Vietnam* 59 G6
Gia Ngoc, *Vietnam* 58 E7
Gia Vuc, *Vietnam* 58 E7
Gian, *Phil.* 57 C7
Giannutri, *Italy* 32 F8
Giant Forest, *U.S.A.* 112 J8
Giant Mts. = Krkonoše, *Czech.* 20 E5
Giants Causeway, *U.K.* 15 A5
Giarabub = Al Jaghbūb, *Libya* 73 C9
Giarre, *Italy* 35 E8
Giaveno, *Italy* 32 C4
Gibara, *Cuba* 116 B4
Gibb River, *Australia* 88 C4
Gibbon, *U.S.A.* 108 E5
Gibe →, *Ethiopia* 77 F4
Gibellina, *Italy* 34 E6
Gibraléon, *Spain* 31 H4
Gibraltar ■, *Europe* 31 J5
Gibraltar, Str. of, *Medit. S.* 31 K5
Gibson Desert, *Australia* 88 D4
Gibsons, *Canada* 100 D4
Gibsonville, *U.S.A.* 112 F6
Giddings, *U.S.A.* 109 K6
Gidole, *Ethiopia* 77 F4
Gien, *France* 25 E9
Giessen, *Germany* 18 E4
Gieten, *Neths.* 16 B9
Gīfān, *Iran* 65 B8
Gifatin, Geziret, *Egypt* 76 B3
Gifford Creek, *Australia* 88 D2
Gifhorn, *Germany* 18 C6
Gifu, *Japan* 49 G8
Gifu □, *Japan* 49 G8
Gigant, *Russia* 43 G5
Giganta, Sa. de la, *Mexico* 114 B2
Gigen, *Bulgaria* 38 F7
Gigha, *U.K.* 14 F3
Giglio, *Italy* 32 F7
Gignac, *France* 26 E7
Gigüela →, *Spain* 29 F1
Gijón, *Spain* 30 B5
Gil I., *Canada* 100 C3
Gila →, *U.S.A.* 111 K6
Gila Bend, *U.S.A.* 111 K7
Gila Bend Mts., *U.S.A.* 111 K7
Gīlān □, *Iran* 65 B6
Gilbert →, *Australia* 90 B3
Gilbert Is., *Kiribati* 92 G9
Gilbert Plains, *Canada* 101 C8
Gilbert River, *Australia* 90 B3
Gilberton, *Australia* 90 B3
Gilbués, *Brazil* 122 C2
Gilf el Kebîr, Hadabat el, *Egypt* 76 C2
Gilford I., *Canada* 100 C3
Gilgandra, *Australia* 91 E4
Gilgil, *Kenya* 82 C4
Gilgit, *India* 63 B6
Gilgit →, *Pakistan* 63 B6
Giljeva Planina, *Serbia, Yug.* 21 M10

Gillam, *Canada* 101 B10
Gilleleje, *Denmark* 11 H6
Gillen, L., *Australia* 89 E3
Gilles, L., *Australia* 91 E2
Gillette, *U.S.A.* 108 C2
Gilliat, *Australia* 90 C3
Gillingham, *U.K.* 13 F8
Gilly, *Belgium* 17 H4
Gilmer, *U.S.A.* 109 J7
Gilmore, *Australia* 91 F4
Gilmore, L., *Australia* 89 F3
Gilmour, *Canada* 98 D4
Gilo →, *Ethiopia* 77 F3
Gilort →, *Romania* 38 E6
Gilroy, *U.S.A.* 111 H3
Gilze, *Neths.* 17 E5
Gimbi, *Ethiopia* 77 F4
Gimigliano, *Italy* 35 D9
Gimli, *Canada* 101 C9
Gimone →, *France* 26 E5
Gimont, *France* 26 E4
Gin Gin, *Australia* 91 D5
Ginâh, *Egypt* 76 B3
Gindie, *Australia* 90 C4
Gingin, *Australia* 89 F2
Gîngiova, *Romania* 38 F6
Ginir, *Ethiopia* 68 F3
Ginosa, *Italy* 35 B9
Ginzo de Limia, *Spain* 30 C3
Giohar, *Somali Rep.* 68 G4
Gióia, G. di, *Italy* 35 D8
Gióia del Colle, *Italy* 35 B9
Gióia Táuro, *Italy* 35 D8
Gioiosa Iónica, *Italy* 35 D9
Gióna, Óros, *Greece* 39 L5
Giovi, Passo dei, *Italy* 32 D5
Giovinazzo, *Italy* 35 A9
Gir Hills, *India* 62 J4
Girab, *India* 62 F4
Girâfi, W. →, *Egypt* 69 F3
Giraltovce, *Slovak Rep.* 20 F11
Girard, *Kans., U.S.A.* 109 G7
Girard, *Ohio, U.S.A.* 106 E4
Girard, *Pa., U.S.A.* 106 D4
Girardot, *Colombia* 120 C3
Girdle Ness, *U.K.* 14 D6
Giresun, *Turkey* 67 B8
Girga, *Egypt* 76 B3
Giridih, *India* 63 G12
Girifalco, *Italy* 35 D9
Girilambone, *Australia* 91 E4
Girne = Kyrenia, *Cyprus* 66 E5
Giro, *Nigeria* 79 C5
Giromagny, *France* 25 E13
Girona = Gerona, *Spain* 28 D7
Gironde □, *France* 26 D3
Gironde →, *France* 26 C2
Gironella, *Spain* 28 C6
Giru, *Australia* 90 B4
Girvan, *U.K.* 14 F4
Gisborne, *N.Z.* 87 H7
Gisenyi, *Rwanda* 82 C2
Gislaved, *Sweden* 9 H15
Gisors, *France* 25 C8
Gistel, *Belgium* 17 F1
Giswil, *Switz.* 22 C6
Gitega, *Burundi* 82 C2
Gits, *Belgium* 17 F2
Giuba →, *Somali Rep.* 68 G3
Giubiasco, *Switz.* 23 D8
Giugliano in Campania, *Italy* 35 B7
Giulianova, *Italy* 33 F10
Giurgeni, *Romania* 38 E10
Giurgiu, *Romania* 38 F8
Give, *Denmark* 11 J3
Givet, *France* 25 B11
Givors, *France* 27 C8
Givry, *Belgium* 17 H4
Givry, *France* 25 F11
Giyon, *Ethiopia* 77 F4
Giza = El Gîza, *Egypt* 76 H7
Gizhiga, *Russia* 45 C17
Gizhiginskaya Guba, *Russia* 45 C16
Giżycko, *Poland* 20 A11
Gizzeria, *Italy* 35 D9
Gjegjani, *Albania* 39 H3
Gjerstad, *Norway* 10 F3
Gjirokastra, *Albania* 39 J3
Gjoa Haven, *Canada* 96 B10
Gjøl, *Denmark* 11 G3
Gjøvik, *Norway* 10 D4
Glace Bay, *Canada* 99 C8
Glacier Bay, *U.S.A.* 100 B1
Glacier Nat. Park, *Canada* 100 C5
Glacier Park, *U.S.A.* 110 B7
Glacier Peak, *U.S.A.* 110 B3
Gladewater, *U.S.A.* 109 J7
Gladstone, *Queens., Australia* 90 C5
Gladstone, *S. Austral., Australia* 91 E2
Gladstone, *W. Austral., Australia* 89 E1
Gladstone, *Canada* 101 C9
Gladstone, *U.S.A.* 104 C2
Gladwin, *U.S.A.* 104 D3
Gladys L., *Canada* 100 B2
Glåma = Glomma →, *Norway* 10 E4
Gláma, *Iceland* 8 D2
Glamis, *U.S.A.* 113 N11
Glamoč, *Bos.-H.* 33 D13
Glan, *Sweden* 11 F10
Glanerbrug, *Neths.* 16 D9
Glarner Alpen, *Switz.* 23 C8
Glärnisch, *Switz.* 23 C7
Glarus, *Switz.* 23 B8
Glarus □, *Switz.* 23 C8
Glasco, *Kans., U.S.A.* 108 F6
Glasco, *N.Y., U.S.A.* 107 D11
Glasgow, *U.K.* 14 F4
Glasgow, *Ky., U.S.A.* 104 G3
Glasgow, *Mont., U.S.A.* 110 B10
Glastonbury, *U.K.* 13 F5
Glastonbury, *U.S.A.* 107 E12
Glatt →, *Switz.* 23 B7
Glattfelden, *Switz.* 23 A7
Glauchau, *Germany* 18 E8
Glazov, *Russia* 42 A11
Gleiwitz = Gliwice, *Poland* 20 E8
Glen, *U.S.A.* 107 B13
Glen Affric, *U.K.* 14 D4
Glen Canyon Dam, *U.S.A.* 111 H8
Glen Canyon National Recreation Area, *U.S.A.* 111 H8
Glen Coe, *U.K.* 14 E4
Glen Cove, *U.S.A.* 107 F11
Glen Garry, *U.K.* 14 D3
Glen Innes, *Australia* 91 D5
Glen Lyon, *U.S.A.* 107 E8
Glen Mor, *U.K.* 14 D4
Glen Moriston, *U.K.* 14 D4
Glen Orchy, *U.K.* 14 E4
Glen Spean, *U.K.* 14 E4
Glen Ullin, *U.S.A.* 108 B4
Glénan, Is. de, *France* 24 E2
Glenburgh, *Australia* 89 E2
Glencoe, *Canada* 106 D3
Glencoe, *S. Africa* 85 D5
Glencoe, *U.S.A.* 108 C7
Glendale, *Ariz., U.S.A.* 111 K7
Glendale, *Calif., U.S.A.* 113 L8
Glendale, *Oreg., U.S.A.* 110 E2
Glendale, *Zimbabwe* 83 F3
Glendive, *U.S.A.* 108 B2
Glendo, *U.S.A.* 108 D2
Glenelg, *Australia* 91 E2
Glenelg →, *Australia* 91 F3
Glenflorrie, *Australia* 88 D2
Glengarriff, *Ireland* 15 E2
Glengyle, *Australia* 90 C2
Glenmora, *U.S.A.* 109 K8
Glenmorgan, *Australia* 91 D4
Glenn, *U.S.A.* 112 F4
Glenns Ferry, *U.S.A.* 110 E6
Glenorchy, *Australia* 90 G4
Glenore, *Australia* 90 B3
Glenormiston, *Australia* 90 C2
Glenreagh, *Australia* 91 E5
Glenrock, *U.S.A.* 110 E11
Glenrothes, *U.K.* 14 E5
Glens Falls, *U.S.A.* 107 C11
Glenties, *Ireland* 15 B3
Glenville, *U.S.A.* 104 F5
Glenwood, *Alta., Canada* 100 D6
Glenwood, *Nfld., Canada* 99 C9
Glenwood, *Ark., U.S.A.* 109 H8
Glenwood, *Hawaii, U.S.A.* 102 J17
Glenwood, *Iowa, U.S.A.* 108 E7
Glenwood, *Minn., U.S.A.* 108 C7
Glenwood, *Wash., U.S.A.* 112 D5
Glenwood Springs, *U.S.A.* 110 G10
Gletsch, *Switz.* 23 C6
Glettinganes, *Iceland* 8 D7
Glina, *Croatia* 33 C13
Glittertind, *Norway* 10 C2
Gliwice, *Poland* 20 E8
Globe, *U.S.A.* 111 K8
Glödnitz, *Austria* 21 J4
Głogów, *Poland* 20 D6
Glomma →, *Norway* 10 E4
Glorieuses, Is., *Ind. Oc.* 85 A8
Glossop, *U.K.* 12 D6
Gloucester, *Australia* 91 E5
Gloucester, *U.K.* 13 F5
Gloucester, *U.S.A.* 107 D14
Gloucester I., *Australia* 90 B4
Gloucestershire □, *U.K.* 13 F5
Gloversville, *U.S.A.* 107 C10
Glovertown, *Canada* 99 C9
Główno, *Poland* 20 D9
Głubczyce, *Poland* 20 E7
Glubokiy, *Russia* 43 F5
Glubokoye = Hlybokaye, *Belarus* 40 E4
Głuchołazy, *Poland* 20 E7
Glücksburg, *Germany* 18 A5
Glückstadt, *Germany* 18 B5
Glukhov = Hlukhiv, *Ukraine* 41 G7
Glusk, *Belarus* 41 F5
Glyngøre, *Denmark* 11 H2
Gmünd, *Kärnten, Austria* 21 J3
Gmünd, *Niederösterreich, Austria* 20 G5
Gnarp, *Sweden* 10 B11
Gnesta, *Sweden* 10 E11
Gniew, *Poland* 20 B8
Gniezno, *Poland* 20 C7
Gnoien, *Germany* 18 B8
Gnowangerup, *Australia* 89 F2
Go Cong, *Vietnam* 59 G6
Gō-no-ura, *Japan* 49 H4
Go Quao, *Vietnam* 59 H5
Goa, *India* 60 M8
Goa □, *India* 60 M8
Goalen Hd., *Australia* 91 F5
Goalpara, *India* 61 F17
Goalundo Ghat, *Bangla.* 63 H13
Goaso, *Ghana* 78 D4
Goat Fell, *U.K.* 14 F3
Goba, *Ethiopia* 68 F2
Goba, *Mozam.* 85 D5
Gobabis, *Namibia* 84 C2
Gobernador Gregores, *Argentina* 128 C2
Gobi, *Asia* 50 C5
Gobō, *Japan* 49 H7
Gobo, *Sudan* 77 F3
Goch, *Germany* 18 D2
Gochas, *Namibia* 84 C2
Godavari →, *India* 61 L13
Godavari Point, *India* 61 L13
Godbout, *Canada* 99 C6
Godda, *India* 63 G12
Godegård, *Sweden* 11 F9
Goderich, *Canada* 98 D3
Goderville, *France* 24 C7
Godhavn, *Greenland* 4 C5
Godhra, *India* 62 H5
Gödöllö, *Hungary* 21 H9
Godoy Cruz, *Argentina* 126 C2
Gods →, *Canada* 101 B10
Gods L., *Canada* 101 C10
Godthåb, *Greenland* 97 B14
Godwin Austen = K2, *Pakistan* 63 B7
Goeie Hoop, Kaap die = Good Hope, C. of, *S. Africa* 84 E2
Goéland, L. au, *Canada* 98 C4
Goeree, *Neths.* 16 E4
Goes, *Neths.* 17 F3
Gogama, *Canada* 98 C3
Gogango, *Australia* 90 C5
Gogebic, L., *U.S.A.* 108 B10
Gogra = Ghaghara →, *India* 63 G11
Gogriâl, *Sudan* 77 F2
Goiana, *Brazil* 122 C5
Goianésia, *Brazil* 123 E2
Goiânia, *Brazil* 123 E2
Goiás, *Brazil* 123 E1
Goiás □, *Brazil* 122 D2
Goiatuba, *Brazil* 123 E2
Goio-Ere, *Brazil* 127 A5
Goirle, *Neths.* 17 E6
Góis, *Portugal* 30 E2
Gojam □, *Ethiopia* 77 E4
Gojeb, Wabi →, *Ethiopia* 77 F4
Gojō, *Japan* 49 G7
Gojra, *Pakistan* 62 D5
Gokarannath, *India* 63 F9
Gökçeada, *Turkey* 66 B1
Gökırmak →, *Turkey* 66 B6
Göksu →, *Turkey* 66 D6
Göksun, *Turkey* 66 C7
Gokteik, *Burma* 61 H20
Gokurt, *Pakistan* 62 E2
Gola, *India* 63 E9
Golakganj, *India* 63 F13
Golan Heights = Hagolan, *Syria* 69 B4
Golāshkerd, *Iran* 65 E8
Golaya Pristen = Hola Pristan, *Ukraine* 41 J7
Gölbaşı, *Adiyaman, Turkey* 66 D7
Gölbaşı, *Ankara, Turkey* 66 C5
Golchikha, *Russia* 4 B12
Golconda, *U.S.A.* 110 F5
Gölcük, *Kocaeli, Turkey* 66 B3
Gölcük, *Niğde, Turkey* 66 C6
Gold Beach, *U.S.A.* 110 E1
Gold Coast, *Australia* 91 D5
Gold Coast, *W. Afr.* 79 E4
Gold Hill, *U.S.A.* 110 E2
Goldach, *Switz.* 23 B8
Goldau, *Switz.* 23 B7
Goldberg, *Germany* 18 B8
Golden, *Canada* 100 C5
Golden, *U.S.A.* 108 F2
Golden B., *N.Z.* 87 J4
Golden Gate, *U.S.A.* 110 H2
Golden Hinde, *Canada* 100 D3
Golden Lake, *Canada* 106 A7
Golden Prairie, *Canada* 101 C7
Golden Vale, *Ireland* 15 D3
Goldendale, *U.S.A.* 110 D3
Goldfield, *U.S.A.* 111 H5
Goldfields, *Canada* 101 B7
Goldsand L., *Canada* 101 B8
Goldsboro, *U.S.A.* 105 H7
Goldsmith, *U.S.A.* 109 K3
Goldsworthy, *Australia* 88 D2
Goldthwaite, *U.S.A.* 109 K5
Golegã, *Portugal* 31 F2
Golęniów, *Poland* 20 B4
Golestānak, *Iran* 65 D7
Goleta, *U.S.A.* 113 L7
Golfito, *Costa Rica* 116 E3
Golfo Aranci, *Italy* 34 B2
Gölgeli Dağları, *Turkey* 66 D3
Goliad, *U.S.A.* 109 L6
Golija, *Serbia, Yug.* 21 M10
Gölköy, *Turkey* 66 B7
Golo →, *France* 27 F13
Golpāyegān, *Iran* 65 C6
Gölpazarı, *Turkey* 66 B4
Golra, *Pakistan* 62 C5
Golspie, *U.K.* 14 D5
Golyama Kamchiya →, *Bulgaria* 38 F10
Goma, *Rwanda* 82 C2
Goma, *Zaïre* 82 C2
Gomati →, *India* 63 G10
Gombari, *Zaïre* 82 B2
Gombe, *Nigeria* 79 C7
Gombe →, *Tanzania* 82 C3
Gombi, *Nigeria* 79 C7
Gomel = Homyel, *Belarus* 41 F6
Gomera, *Canary Is.* 36 F2
Gómez Palacio, *Mexico* 114 B4
Gomīshān, *Iran* 65 B7
Gommern, *Germany* 18 C7
Gomogomo, *Indonesia* 57 F8
Gomoh, *India* 61 H15
Gompa = Ganta, *Liberia* 78 D3
Goms, *Switz.* 22 D6
Gonābād, *Iran* 65 C8
Gonaïves, *Haiti* 117 C5
Gonâve, G. de la, *Haiti* 117 C5
Gonâve, I. de la, *Haiti* 117 C5
Gonbab-e Kāvūs, *Iran* 65 B7
Gonda, *India* 63 F9
Gondal, *India* 62 J4
Gonder, *Ethiopia* 77 E4
Gonder □, *Ethiopia* 77 E4
Gondia, *India* 60 J12
Gondola, *Mozam.* 83 F3
Gondomar, *Portugal* 30 D2
Gondomar, *Spain* 30 C2
Gondrecourt-le-Château, *France* 25 D12
Gönen, *Turkey* 66 B2
Gong Xian, *China* 52 C5
Gong'an, *China* 53 B9
Gongcheng, *China* 53 E8
Gongga Shan, *China* 52 C3
Gongguan, *China* 52 G7
Gonghe, *China* 54 C5
Gongola →, *Nigeria* 79 D7
Gongolgon, *Australia* 91 E4
Gongshan, *China* 52 D2
Gongtan, *China* 52 C7
Goniadz, *Poland* 20 B12
Goniri, *Nigeria* 79 C7
Gonjo, *China* 52 B2
Gonnesa, *Italy* 34 C1
Gónnos, *Greece* 39 K5
Gonnosfanádiga, *Italy* 34 C1
Gonzaga, *Phil.* 55 B5
Gonzales, *Calif., U.S.A.* 111 H3
Gonzales, *Tex., U.S.A.* 109 L6
González Chaves, *Argentina* 126 D3
Good Hope, C. of, *S. Africa* 84 E2
Gooderham, *Canada* 98 D4
Goodeve, *Canada* 101 C8
Gooding, *U.S.A.* 110 E6
Goodland, *U.S.A.* 108 F4
Goodnight, *U.S.A.* 109 H4
Goodooga, *Australia* 91 D4
Goodsoil, *Canada* 101 C7
Goodsprings, *U.S.A.* 111 J6
Goole, *U.K.* 12 D7
Goolgowi, *Australia* 91 E4
Goomalling, *Australia* 89 F2
Goombalie, *Australia* 91 D4
Goonda, *Mozam.* 83 F3
Goondiwindi, *Australia* 91 D5
Goongarrie, L., *Australia* 89 F3
Goonyella, *Australia* 90 C4
Goor, *Neths.* 16 D9
Gooray, *Australia* 91 D5
Goose →, *Canada* 99 B7
Goose L., *U.S.A.* 110 F3
Gop, *India* 60 H6
Gopalganj, *India* 63 F11
Goppenstein, *Switz.* 22 D5
Göppingen, *Germany* 19 G5
Gor, *Spain* 29 H2
Góra, *Poland* 20 D6
Gorakhpur, *India* 63 F10
Gorbatov, *Russia* 42 B6
Gorbea, Peña, *Spain* 28 B2
Gorda, *U.S.A.* 112 K5
Gorda, Pta., *Canary Is.* 36 F2
Gorda, Pta., *Nic.* 116 D3
Gordan B., *Australia* 88 B5
Gordon, *U.S.A.* 108 D3
Gordon →, *Australia* 90 G4
Gordon, I., *Chile* 128 D3
Gordon Downs, *Australia* 88 C4
Gordon L., *Alta., Canada* 101 B6
Gordon L., *N.W.T., Canada* 100 A6
Gordonvale, *Australia* 90 B4
Gore, *Australia* 91 D5
Goré, *Chad* 73 G8
Gore, *Ethiopia* 77 F4
Gore, *N.Z.* 87 M2
Gore Bay, *Canada* 98 C3
Görele, *Turkey* 67 B8
Goreme, *Turkey* 66 C6
Gorey, *Ireland* 15 D5
Gorg, *Iran* 65 D8
Gorgān, *Iran* 65 B7
Gorgona, isola, *Italy* 32 E6
Gorgora, *Ethiopia* 77 E4
Gorham, *U.S.A.* 107 B13
Gori, *Georgia* 43 J7
Gorinchem, *Neths.* 16 E5
Gorinhatã, *Brazil* 123 E2
Goris, *Armenia* 67 C12
Goritsy, *Russia* 42 B3
Gorízia, *Italy* 33 C10
Gorki = Horki, *Belarus* 40 E6
Gorki = Nizhniy Novgorod, *Russia* 42 B7
Gorkiy = Nizhniy Novgorod, *Russia* 42 B7
Gorkovskoye Vdkhr., *Russia* 42 B6
Gørlev, *Denmark* 11 J5
Gorlice, *Poland* 20 F11
Görlitz, *Germany* 18 D10
Gorlovka = Horlivka, *Ukraine* 41 H10
Gorman, *Calif., U.S.A.* 113 L8
Gorman, *Tex., U.S.A.* 109 J5
Gorna Dzhumayo = Blagoevgrad, *Bulgaria* 39 G6
Gorna Oryakhovitsa, *Bulgaria* 38 F8
Gornja Radgona, *Slovenia* 33 B13
Gornja Tuzla, *Bos.-H.* 21 L8
Gornji Grad, *Slovenia* 33 B11
Gornji Milanovac, *Serbia, Yug.* 21 M10
Gornji Vakuf, *Bos.-H.* 21 M7
Gorno-Altay □, *Russia* 44 D9
Gorno-Altaysk, *Russia* 44 D9
Gorno Slinkino = Gornopravdinsk, *Russia* 44 C8
Gornopravdinsk, *Russia* 44 C8
Gornyatskiy, *Russia* 43 F5
Gornyi, *Russia* 48 B6
Gornyy, *Russia* 42 E9
Gorodenka = Horodenka, *Ukraine* 41 H3
Gorodets, *Russia* 42 B6
Gorodishche = Horodyshche, *Ukraine* 41 H6
Gorodishche, *Russia* 42 D7
Gorodnya = Horodnya, *Ukraine* 41 G6
Gorodok = Haradok, *Belarus* 40 E6
Gorodok = Horodok, *Ukraine* 41 H2
Gorodovikovsk, *Russia* 43 G5
Gorokhov = Horokhiv, *Ukraine* 41 G3
Gorokhovets, *Russia* 42 B6
Gorom Gorom, *Burkina Faso* 79 C4
Goromonzi, *Zimbabwe* 83 F3
Gorongose →, *Mozam.* 85 C5
Gorongoza, *Mozam.* 83 F3
Gorongoza, Sa. da, *Mozam.* 83 F3
Gorontalo, *Indonesia* 57 D6
Goronyo, *Nigeria* 79 C6
Gorredijk, *Neths.* 16 C8
Gorron, *France* 24 D6
Gorshechnoye, *Russia* 42 E4
Gorssel, *Neths.* 16 D8
Gort, *Ireland* 15 C3
Gortis, *Greece* 37 D6
Goryachiy Klyuch, *Russia* 43 H4
Gorzkowice, *Poland* 20 D9
Gorzów Śląski, *Poland* 20 D8
Gorzów Wielkopolski, *Poland* 20 C5
Göschenen, *Switz.* 23 C7
Gosford, *Australia* 91 E5
Goshen, *Calif., U.S.A.* 112 J7
Goshen, *Ind., U.S.A.* 104 E3
Goshen, *N.Y., U.S.A.* 107 E10
Goshogawara, *Japan* 48 D10
Goslar, *Germany* 18 D6
Gospič, *Croatia* 33 D12
Gosport, *U.K.* 13 G6
Gossau, *Switz.* 23 B8
Gosse →, *Australia* 90 B1
Gostivar, *Macedonia* 39 H3
Gostyń, *Poland* 20 D7
Gostynin, *Poland* 20 C9
Göta älv →, *Sweden* 11 G5
Göta kanal, *Sweden* 9 G16
Götaland, *Sweden* 9 G15
Göteborg, *Sweden* 11 G5
Götene, *Sweden* 11 F7
Gotha, *Germany* 18 E6
Gothenburg = Göteborg, *Sweden* 11 G5
Gothenburg, *U.S.A.* 108 E4
Gotland, *Sweden* 9 H18
Gotse Delchev, *Bulgaria* 39 H6
Gotska Sandön, *Sweden* 9 G18
Gōtsu, *Japan* 49 G6
Göttingen, *Germany* 18 D5
Gottwald = Zmiyev, *Ukraine* 41 H9
Gottwaldov = Zlin, *Czech.* 20 F7
Goubangzi, *China* 51 D11
Gouda, *Neths.* 16 D5
Goúdhoura, Ákra, *Greece* 37 E8
Goudiry, *Senegal* 78 C2
Gough I., *Atl. Oc.* 2 G9
Gouin, Rés., *Canada* 98 C5
Gouitafla, *Ivory C.* 78 D3
Goulburn, *Australia* 91 E4
Goulburn Is., *Australia* 90 A1
Goulia, *Ivory C.* 78 C3
Goulimine, *Morocco* 74 C3
Goulmina, *Morocco* 74 B4
Gounou-Gaya, *Chad* 73 G8
Goúra, *Greece* 39 M5
Gouraya, *Algeria* 75 A5
Gourdon, *France* 26 D5
Gouré, *Niger* 79 C7
Gouri, *Chad* 73 E8
Gourits →, *S. Africa* 84 E3
Gourma Rharous, *Mali* 79 B4
Goúrnais, *Greece* 37 D7
Gournay-en-Bray, *France* 25 C8
Gourock Ra., *Australia* 91 F4
Goursi, *Burkina Faso* 78 C4
Gouvêa, *Brazil* 123 E3
Gouverneur, *U.S.A.* 107 B9
Gouviá, *Greece* 37 A3
Gouzon, *France* 26 B6

Govan, *Canada* 101 C8
Governador Valadares, *Brazil* 123 E3
Governor's Harbour, *Bahamas* 116 A4
Gowan Ra., *Australia* 90 C4
Gowanda, *U.S.A.* 106 D6
Gowd-e Zirreh, *Afghan.* .. 60 E3
Gower, *U.K.* 13 F3
Gowna, L., *Ireland* 15 C4
Goya, *Argentina* 126 B4
Göyçay, *Azerbaijan* 43 K8
Goyder Lagoon, *Australia* 91 D2
Goyllarisquisga, *Peru* 124 C2
Göynük, *Turkey* 66 B4
Goz Beïda, *Chad* 73 F9
Goz Regeb, *Sudan* 77 D4
Gozo, *Malta* 37 C1
Graaff-Reinet, *S. Africa* .. 84 E3
Grabow, *Germany* 18 B7
Grabs, *Switz.* 23 B8
Gračac, *Croatia* 33 D12
Gračanica, *Bos.-H.* 21 L8
Graçay, *France* 25 E8
Grace, *U.S.A.* 110 E8
Graceville, *U.S.A.* 108 C6
Gracias a Dios, C., *Honduras* 116 C3
Graciosa, I., *Canary Is.* .. 36 E6
Gradaús, *Brazil* 122 C1
Gradaús, Serra dos, *Brazil* 122 C1
Gradets, *Bulgaria* 38 G9
Grado, *Italy* 33 C10
Grado, *Spain* 30 B4
Gradule, *Australia* 91 D4
Grady, *U.S.A.* 109 H3
Graeca, Lacul, *Romania* .. 38 E9
Grafenau, *Germany* 19 G9
Gräfenberg, *Germany* 19 F7
Grafton, *Australia* 91 D5
Grafton, *U.S.A.* 108 A6
Gragnano, *Italy* 35 B7
Graham, *Canada* 98 C1
Graham, *N.C., U.S.A.* ... 105 G6
Graham, *Tex., U.S.A.* 109 J5
Graham →, *Canada* 100 B4
Graham, Mt., *U.S.A.* 111 K9
Graham Bell, Os., *Russia* . 44 A7
Graham I., *Canada* 100 C2
Graham Land, *Antarctica* . 5 C17
Grahamdale, *Canada* 101 C9
Grahamstown, *S. Africa* .. 84 E4
Graïba, *Tunisia* 75 B7
Graide, *Belgium* 17 J6
Graie, Alpi, *Europe* 32 C4
Grain Coast, *W. Afr.* 78 E3
Grajaú, *Brazil* 122 C2
Grajaú →, *Brazil* 122 B3
Grajewo, *Poland* 20 B12
Gramada, *Bulgaria* 38 F5
Gramat, *France* 26 D5
Grammichele, *Italy* 35 E7
Grampian Highlands = Grampian Mts., *U.K.* ... 14 E5
Grampian Mts., *U.K.* 14 E5
Gran →, *Surinam* 121 C6
Gran Altiplanicie Central, *Argentina* 128 C3
Gran Canaria, *Canary Is.* . 36 F4
Gran Chaco, *S. Amer.* ... 126 B3
Gran Paradiso, *Italy* 32 C4
Gran Sasso d'Italia, *Italy* . 33 F10
Granada, *Nic.* 116 D2
Granada, *Spain* 29 H1
Granada, *U.S.A.* 109 F3
Granada □, *Spain* 31 H7
Granadilla de Abona, *Canary Is.* 36 F3
Granard, *Ireland* 15 C4
Granbury, *U.S.A.* 109 J6
Granby, *Canada* 98 C5
Grand →, *Mo., U.S.A.* .. 108 F8
Grand →, *S. Dak., U.S.A.* 108 C4
Grand Bahama, *Bahamas* . 116 A4
Grand Bank, *Canada* 99 C8
Grand Bassam, *Ivory C.* .. 78 D4
Grand Béréby, *Ivory C.* .. 78 E3
Grand-Bourg, *Guadeloupe* 117 C7
Grand Canal = Yun Ho →, *China* 51 E9
Grand Canyon, *U.S.A.* ... 111 H7
Grand Canyon National Park, *U.S.A.* 111 H7
Grand Cayman, *Cayman Is.* 116 C3
Grand Cess, *Liberia* 78 E3
Grand Coulee, *U.S.A.* ... 110 C4
Grand Coulee Dam, *U.S.A.* 110 C4
Grand Erg Occidental, *Algeria* 75 B5
Grand Erg Oriental, *Algeria* 75 C6
Grand Falls, *Canada* 99 C8
Grand Forks, *Canada* 100 D5
Grand Forks, *U.S.A.* 108 B6
Grand-Fougeray, *France* .. 24 E5
Grand Haven, *U.S.A.* 104 D2
Grand I., *U.S.A.* 104 B2
Grand Island, *U.S.A.* 108 E5
Grand Isle, *U.S.A.* 109 L10
Grand Junction, *U.S.A.* .. 111 G9
Grand L., *N.B., Canada* .. 99 C6
Grand L., *Nfld., Canada* . 99 C8
Grand L., *Nfld., Canada* . 99 B7
Grand L., *U.S.A.* 109 L8
Grand Lac Victoria, *Canada* 98 C4
Grand Lahou, *Ivory C.* ... 78 D3
Grand Lake, *U.S.A.* 110 F11
Grand-Leez, *Belgium* 17 G5
Grand-Lieu, L. de, *France* 24 E5
Grand Manan I., *Canada* . 99 D6
Grand Marais, *Canada* ... 108 B9
Grand Marais, *U.S.A.* 104 B3
Grand-Mère, *Canada* 98 C5
Grand Popo, *Benin* 79 D5
Grand Portage, *U.S.A.* ... 98 C2
Grand Prairie, *U.S.A.* 109 J6
Grand Rapids, *Canada* ... 101 C9
Grand Rapids, *Mich., U.S.A.* 104 D2
Grand Rapids, *Minn., U.S.A.* 108 B8
Grand St.-Bernard, Col du, *Europe* 22 E4
Grand Santi, *Fr. Guiana* .. 121 C7
Grand Teton, *U.S.A.* 110 E8
Grand Valley, *U.S.A.* 110 G9
Grand View, *Canada* 101 C8
Grandas de Salime, *Spain* . 30 B4
Grande →, *Jujuy, Argentina* 126 A2
Grande →, *Mendoza, Argentina* 126 D2
Grande →, *Bolivia* 125 D5
Grande →, *Bahia, Brazil* 122 D3
Grande →, *Minas Gerais, Brazil* 123 F1
Grande →, *Spain* 29 F4
Grande →, *Venezuela* ... 121 B5
Grande, B., *Argentina* 128 D3
Grande, I., *Brazil* 123 F3
Grande, Rio →, *U.S.A.* . 109 N6
Grande, Serra, *Piauí, Brazil* 122 C2
Grande, Serra, *Tocantins, Brazil* 122 D2
Grande Baie, *Canada* 99 C5
Grande Baleine, R. de la →, *Canada* 98 A4
Grande Cache, *Canada* ... 100 C5
Grande de Santiago →, *Mexico* 114 C3
Grande Dixence, Barr. de la, *Switz.* 22 D4
Grande-Entrée, *Canada* .. 99 C7
Grande Prairie, *Canada* .. 100 B5
Grande-Rivière, *Canada* .. 99 C7
Grande Sauldre →, *France* 25 E9
Grande-Vallée, *Canada* ... 99 C6
Grandes-Bergeronnes, *Canada* 99 C6
Grandfalls, *U.S.A.* 109 K3
Grandoe Mines, *Canada* .. 100 B3
Grândola, *Portugal* 31 G2
Grandpré, *France* 25 C11
Grandson, *Switz.* 22 C3
Grandview, *U.S.A.* 110 C4
Grandvilliers, *France* 25 C8
Graneros, *Chile* 126 C1
Grangemouth, *U.K.* 14 E5
Granger, *Wash., U.S.A.* .. 110 C3
Granger, *Wyo., U.S.A.* ... 110 F9
Grangeville, *U.S.A.* 110 D5
Granite City, *U.S.A.* 108 F9
Granite Falls, *U.S.A.* 108 C7
Granite Mt., *U.S.A.* 113 M10
Granite Peak, *Australia* ... 89 E3
Granite Peak, *U.S.A.* 110 D9
Granity, *N.Z.* 87 J3
Granja, *Brazil* 122 B3
Granja de Moreruela, *Spain* 30 D5
Granja de Torrehermosa, *Spain* 31 G5
Granollers, *Spain* 28 D7
Gransee, *Germany* 18 B9
Grant, *U.S.A.* 108 E4
Grant, Mt., *U.S.A.* 110 G4
Grant City, *U.S.A.* 108 E7
Grant I., *Australia* 88 B5
Grant Range, *U.S.A.* 111 G6
Grantham, *U.K.* 12 E7
Grantown-on-Spey, *U.K.* . 14 D5
Grants, *U.S.A.* 111 J10
Grants Pass, *U.S.A.* 110 E2
Grantsburg, *U.S.A.* 108 C8
Grantsville, *U.S.A.* 110 F7
Granville, *France* 24 D5
Granville, *N. Dak., U.S.A.* 108 A4
Granville, *N.Y., U.S.A.* .. 104 D9
Granville L., *Canada* 101 B8
Grao de Gandía, *Spain* ... 29 F4
Grapeland, *U.S.A.* 109 K7
Gras, L. de, *Canada* 96 B8
Graskop, *S. Africa* 85 C5
Grass →, *Canada* 101 B9
Grass Range, *U.S.A.* 110 C9
Grass River Prov. Park, *Canada* 101 C8
Grass Valley, *Calif., U.S.A.* 112 F6
Grass Valley, *Oreg., U.S.A.* 110 D3
Grassano, *Italy* 35 B9
Grasse, *France* 27 E10
Grassmere, *Australia* 91 E3
Graubünden □, *Switz.* ... 23 C9
Graulhet, *France* 26 E5
Graus, *Spain* 28 C5
Gravatá, *Brazil* 122 C4
Grave, *Neths.* 16 E7
Grave, Pte. de, *France* ... 26 C2
's-Graveland, *Neths.* 16 D6
Gravelbourg, *Canada* 101 D7
Gravelines, *France* 25 B9
's-Gravendeel, *Neths.* 16 E5
's-Gravenhage, *Neths.* 16 D4
Gravenhurst, *Canada* 106 B5
's-Gravenpolder, *Neths.* .. 17 F3
's-Gravensande, *Neths.* ... 16 D4
Gravesend, *Australia* 91 D5
Gravesend, *U.K.* 13 F8
Gravina di Púglia, *Italy* ... 35 B9
Gravois, Pointe-à-, *Haiti* .. 117 C5
Gravone →, *France* 27 G12
Gray, *France* 25 E12
Grayling, *U.S.A.* 104 C3
Grayling →, *Canada* 100 B3
Grays Harbor, *U.S.A.* 110 C1
Grays L., *U.S.A.* 110 E8
Grays River, *U.S.A.* 112 D3
Grayson, *Canada* 101 C8
Grayvoron, *Russia* 42 E2
Graz, *Austria* 21 H5
Grazalema, *Spain* 31 J5
Greasy L., *Canada* 100 A4
Great Abaco I., *Bahamas* . 116 A4
Great Artesian Basin, *Australia* 90 C3
Great Australian Bight, *Australia* 89 F5
Great Bahama Bank, *Bahamas* 116 B4
Great Barrier I., *N.Z.* 87 G5
Great Barrier Reef, *Australia* 90 B4
Great Barrington, *U.S.A.* . 107 D11
Great Basin, *U.S.A.* 110 G5
Great Bear →, *Canada* .. 96 B7
Great Bear L., *Canada* ... 96 B7
Great Belt = Store Bælt, *Denmark* 11 J5
Great Bend, *Kans., U.S.A.* 108 F5
Great Bend, *Pa., U.S.A.* . 107 E9
Great Blasket I., *Ireland* .. 15 D1
Great Britain, *Europe* 6 E5
Great Central, *Canada* ... 100 D3
Great Dividing Ra., *Australia* 90 C4
Great Driffield = Driffield, *U.K.* 12 C7
Great Exuma I., *Bahamas* 116 B4
Great Falls, *Canada* 101 C9
Great Falls, *U.S.A.* 110 C8
Great Fish = Groot Vis →, *S. Africa* 84 E4
Great Guana Cay, *Bahamas* 116 B4
Great Harbour Deep, *Canada* 99 B8
Great I., *Canada* 101 B9
Great Inagua I., *Bahamas* 117 B5
Great Indian Desert = Thar Desert, *India* 62 F4
Great Karoo, *S. Africa* ... 84 E3
Great Lake, *Australia* 90 G4
Great Malvern, *U.K.* 13 E5
Great Ormes Head, *U.K.* . 12 D4
Great Ouse →, *U.K.* 12 E8
Great Palm I., *Australia* .. 90 B4
Great Plains, *N. Amer.* ... 102 A6
Great Ruaha →, *Tanzania* 82 D4
Great Saint Bernard P. = Grand St.-Bernard, Col du, *Europe* 22 E4
Great Salt L., *U.S.A.* 110 F7
Great Salt Lake Desert, *U.S.A.* 110 F7
Great Salt Plains L., *U.S.A.* 109 G5
Great Sandy Desert, *Australia* 88 D3
Great Sangi = Sangihe, P., *Indonesia* 57 D7
Great Scarcies →, *S. Leone* 78 D2
Great Slave L., *Canada* .. 100 A5
Great Smoky Mts. Nat. Pk., *U.S.A.* 105 H4
Great Stour = Stour →, *U.K.* 13 F9
Great Victoria Desert, *Australia* 89 E4
Great Wall, *China* 50 E5
Great Whernside, *U.K.* ... 12 C6
Great Yarmouth, *U.K.* ... 12 E9
Greater Antilles, *W. Indies* 117 C5
Greater London □, *U.K.* . 13 F7
Greater Manchester □, *U.K.* 12 D5
Greater Sunda Is., *Indonesia* 56 F4
Grebbestad, *Sweden* 11 F5
Grebenka = Hrebenka, *Ukraine* 41 G7
Greco, C., *Cyprus* 37 E13
Greco, Mte., *Italy* 34 A6
Gredos, Sierra de, *Spain* .. 30 E5
Greece, *U.S.A.* 106 C7
Greece ■, *Europe* 39 K6
Greeley, *Colo., U.S.A.* ... 108 E2
Greeley, *Nebr., U.S.A.* ... 108 E5
Green →, *Ky., U.S.A.* ... 104 G2
Green →, *Utah, U.S.A.* .. 111 G9
Green B., *U.S.A.* 104 C2
Green Bay, *U.S.A.* 104 C2
Green C., *Australia* 91 F5
Green Cove Springs, *U.S.A.* 105 L5
Green River, *U.S.A.* 111 G8
Greenbank, *U.S.A.* 112 B4
Greenbush, *Mich., U.S.A.* 106 B1
Greenbush, *Minn., U.S.A.* 108 A6
Greencastle, *U.S.A.* 104 F2
Greene, *U.S.A.* 107 D9
Greenfield, *Calif., U.S.A.* 112 J5
Greenfield, *Calif., U.S.A.* 113 K8
Greenfield, *Ind., U.S.A.* .. 104 F3
Greenfield, *Iowa, U.S.A.* . 108 E7
Greenfield, *Mass., U.S.A.* 107 D12
Greenfield, *Mo., U.S.A.* .. 109 G8
Greenfield Park, *Canada* . 107 A11
Greenland ■, *N. Amer.* .. 4 C5
Greenland Sea, *Arctic* 4 B7
Greenock, *U.K.* 14 F4
Greenore, *Ireland* 15 B5
Greenore Pt., *Ireland* 15 D5
Greenough →, *Australia* . 89 E1
Greenport, *U.S.A.* 107 E12
Greensboro, *Ga., U.S.A.* . 105 J4
Greensboro, *N.C., U.S.A.* 105 G6
Greensburg, *Ind., U.S.A.* . 104 F3
Greensburg, *Kans., U.S.A.* 109 G5
Greensburg, *Pa., U.S.A.* . 106 F5
Greenville, *Liberia* 78 D3
Greenville, *Ala., U.S.A.* . 105 K2
Greenville, *Calif., U.S.A.* . 112 E6
Greenville, *Ill., U.S.A.* ... 108 F10
Greenville, *Maine, U.S.A.* 99 C6
Greenville, *Mich., U.S.A.* 104 D3
Greenville, *Miss., U.S.A.* . 109 J9
Greenville, *N.C., U.S.A.* . 105 H7
Greenville, *Ohio, U.S.A.* . 104 E3
Greenville, *Pa., U.S.A.* .. 106 E4
Greenville, *S.C., U.S.A.* . 105 H4
Greenville, *Tenn., U.S.A.* 105 G4
Greenville, *Tex., U.S.A.* . 109 J6
Greenwater Lake Prov. Park, *Canada* 101 C8
Greenwich, *U.K.* 13 F8
Greenwich, *Conn., U.S.A.* 107 E11
Greenwich, *N.Y., U.S.A.* . 107 C11
Greenwich, *Ohio, U.S.A.* . 106 E2
Greenwood, *Canada* 100 D5
Greenwood, *Miss., U.S.A.* 109 J9
Greenwood, *S.C., U.S.A.* 105 H4
Greenwood, Mt., *Australia* 88 B5
Gregório →, *Brazil* 124 B3
Gregory, *U.S.A.* 108 D5
Gregory →, *Australia* 90 B2
Gregory, L., *S. Austral., Australia* 91 D2
Gregory, L., *W. Austral., Australia* 89 E2
Gregory Downs, *Australia* 90 B2
Gregory L., *Australia* 88 D4
Gregory Ra., *Queens., Australia* 90 B3
Gregory Ra., *W. Austral., Australia* 88 D3
Greiffenberg, *Germany* ... 18 B9
Greifswald, *Germany* 18 A9
Greifswalder Bodden, *Germany* 18 A9
Grein, *Austria* 21 G4
Greiz, *Germany* 18 E8
Gremikha, *Russia* 44 C4
Grenå, *Denmark* 11 H4
Grenada, *U.S.A.* 109 J10
Grenada ■, *W. Indies* 117 D7
Grenade, *France* 26 E5
Grenadines, *W. Indies* 117 D7
Grenchen, *Switz.* 22 B4
Grenen, *Denmark* 11 G4
Grenfell, *Australia* 91 E4
Grenfell, *Canada* 101 C8
Grenoble, *France* 27 C9
Grenora, *U.S.A.* 108 A3
Grenville, C., *Australia* ... 90 A3
Grenville Chan., *Canada* . 100 C3
Gréoux-les-Bains, *France* . 27 E9
Gresham, *U.S.A.* 112 E4
Gresik, *Indonesia* 57 G15
Grëssoney St. Jean, *Italy* . 32 C4
Gretna Green, *U.K.* 14 F5
Grevelingen Krammer, *Neths.* 16 E4
Greven, *Germany* 18 C3
Grevená, *Greece* 39 J4
Grevenbroich, *Germany* .. 18 D2
Grevenmacher, *Lux.* 17 J8
Grevesmühlen, *Germany* . 18 B7
Grevie, *Sweden* 11 H6
Grey →, *N.Z.* 87 K3
Grey, C., *Australia* 90 A2
Grey Ra., *Australia* 91 D3
Grey Res., *Canada* 99 C8
Greybull, *U.S.A.* 110 D9
Greymouth, *N.Z.* 87 K3
Greytown, *N.Z.* 87 J5
Greytown, *S. Africa* 85 D5
Gribanovskiy, *Russia* 42 E5
Gribbell I., *Canada* 100 C3
Gridley, *U.S.A.* 112 F5
Griekwastad, *S. Africa* ... 84 D3
Griffin, *U.S.A.* 105 J3
Griffith, *Australia* 91 E4
Grijpskerk, *Neths.* 16 B8
Grillby, *Sweden* 10 E11
Grimari, *C.A.R.* 73 G9
Grimaylov = Hrymayliv, *Ukraine* 41 H4
Grimbergen, *Belgium* 17 G4
Grimes, *U.S.A.* 112 F5
Grimma, *Germany* 18 D8
Grimmen, *Germany* 18 A9
Grimsby, *Canada* 106 C5
Grimsby, *U.K.* 12 D7
Grimselpass, *Switz.* 23 C6
Grímsey, *Iceland* 8 C5
Grimshaw, *Canada* 100 B5
Grimstad, *Norway* 11 F2
Grindelwald, *Switz.* 22 C6
Grindsted, *Denmark* 11 J2
Grindu, *Romania* 38 E9
Grinnell, *U.S.A.* 108 E8
Griñón, *Spain* 30 E7
Grintavec, *Slovenia* 33 B11
Grip, *Norway* 10 A1
Gris-Nez, C., *France* 25 B8
Grisolles, *France* 26 E5
Grisons = Graubünden □, *Switz.* 23 C9
Grivegnée, *Belgium* 17 G7
Grmeč Planina, *Bos.-H.* .. 33 D13
Groais I., *Canada* 99 B8
Groblersdal, *S. Africa* 85 D4
Grobming, *Austria* 21 H3
Grodno = Hrodna, *Belarus* 40 F2
Grodzisk Mázowiecki, *Poland* 20 C10
Grodzisk Wielkopolski, *Poland* 20 C6
Grodzyanka = Hrodzyanka, *Belarus* ... 40 F5
Groenlo, *Neths.* 16 D9
Groesbeck, *U.S.A.* 109 K6
Groesbeek, *Neths.* 16 E7
Groix, *France* 24 E3
Groix, I. de, *France* 24 E3
Grójec, *Poland* 20 D10
Grolloo, *Neths.* 16 C9
Gronau, *Niedersachsen, Germany* 18 C5
Gronau, *Nordrhein-Westfalen, Germany* 18 C3
Grong, *Norway* 8 D15
Groningen, *Neths.* 16 B9
Groningen, *Surinam* 121 B6
Groningen □, *Neths.* 16 B9
Groninger Wad, *Neths.* ... 16 B9
Gronsveld, *Neths.* 17 G7
Groom, *U.S.A.* 109 H4
Groot →, *S. Africa* 84 E3
Groot Berg →, *S. Africa* . 84 E2
Groot-Brakrivier, *S. Africa* 84 E3
Groot-Kei →, *S. Africa* .. 85 E4
Groot Vis →, *S. Africa* .. 84 E4
Groote Eylandt, *Australia* 90 A2
Grootebroek, *Neths.* 16 C6
Grootfontein, *Namibia* ... 84 B2
Grootlaagte →, *Africa* ... 84 C3
Grootvloer, *S. Africa* 84 E3
Gros C., *Canada* 100 A6
Grosa, Pta., *Spain* 36 B8
Grósio, *Italy* 32 B7
Grosne →, *France* 27 B8
Gross Glockner, *Austria* .. 21 H2
Grossenbrode, *Germany* ... 18 A7
Grossenhain, *Germany* ... 18 D9
Grosseto, *Italy* 32 F8
Groswater B., *Canada* 99 B8
Grote Gette →, *Neths.* .. 17 G6
Grote Nete →, *Belgium* .. 17 F5
Groton, *Conn., U.S.A.* ... 107 E12
Groton, *S. Dak., U.S.A.* . 108 C5
Grottáglie, *Italy* 35 B10
Grottaminarda, *Italy* 35 A8
Grottammare, *Italy* 33 F10
Grouard Mission, *Canada* . 100 B5
Grouin, Pte. du, *France* .. 24 D5
Groundhog →, *Canada* .. 98 C3
Grouse Creek, *U.S.A.* 110 F7
Grouw, *Neths.* 16 B7
Grove City, *U.S.A.* 106 E4
Groveland, *U.S.A.* 112 H6
Grover City, *U.S.A.* 113 K6
Groveton, *N.H., U.S.A.* .. 107 B13
Groveton, *Tex., U.S.A.* .. 109 K7
Grožnjan, *Croatia* 33 C10
Groznyy, *Russia* 43 J7
Grubbenvorst, *Neths.* 17 F8
Grudziądz, *Poland* 20 B8
Gruissan, *France* 26 E7
Grumo Áppula, *Italy* 35 A9
Grünberg, *Germany* 18 E4
Grundy Center, *U.S.A.* ... 108 D8
Gruver, *U.S.A.* 109 G4
Gruyères, *Switz.* 22 C4
Gryazi, *Russia* 42 D4
Gryazovets, *Russia* 40 C11
Gstaad, *Switz.* 22 D4
Gua, *India* 61 H14
Gua Musang, *Malaysia* ... 59 K3
Guacanayabo, G. de, *Cuba* 116 B4
Guacara, *Venezuela* 120 A4
Guachípas →, *Argentina* . 126 B2
Guachiría →, *Colombia* .. 120 B3
Guadajoz →, *Spain* 31 H6
Guadalajara, *Mexico* 114 C4
Guadalajara, *Spain* 28 E1
Guadalajara □, *Spain* ... 28 E2
Guadalcanal, *Solomon Is.* . 92 H8
Guadalcanal, *Spain* 31 G5
Guadalén →, *Spain* 31 G7
Guadales, *Argentina* 126 C2
Guadalete →, *Spain* 31 J4
Guadalhorce →, *Spain* ... 31 J6
Guadalimar →, *Spain* ... 29 G1
Guadalmena →, *Spain* ... 29 G2
Guadalmez →, *Spain* ... 31 G5
Guadalope →, *Spain* 28 D4
Guadalquivir →, *Spain* .. 31 J4

Guadalupe = Guadeloupe ■, *W. Indies* 117 C7
Guadalupe, *Brazil* 122 C3
Guadalupe, *Mexico* 113 N10
Guadalupe, *Spain* 31 F5
Guadalupe, *U.S.A.* 113 L6
Guadalupe →, *Mexico* 113 N10
Guadalupe →, *U.S.A.* 109 L6
Guadalupe, Sierra de, *Spain* 31 F5
Guadalupe Bravos, *Mexico* 114 A3
Guadalupe I., *Pac. Oc.* 94 G8
Guadalupe Peak, *U.S.A.* 111 L11
Guadalupe y Calvo, *Mexico* 114 B3
Guadarrama, Sierra de, *Spain* 30 E6
Guadauta, *Georgia* 43 J5
Guadeloupe ■, *W. Indies* 117 C7
Guadeloupe Passage, *W. Indies* 117 C7
Guadiamar →, *Spain* 31 J4
Guadiana →, *Portugal* 31 H3
Guadiana Menor →, *Spain* 29 H1
Guadiaro →, *Spain* 31 J5
Guadiato →, *Spain* 31 H5
Guadiela →, *Spain* 28 E2
Guadix, *Spain* 29 H1
Guafo, Boca del, *Chile* 128 B2
Guafo, I., *Chile* 128 B2
Guainía □, *Colombia* 120 C4
Guainía →, *Colombia* 120 C4
Guaíra, *Brazil* 127 A5
Guaitecas, Is., *Chile* 128 B2
Guajará-Mirim, *Brazil* 125 C4
Guajira □, *Colombia* 120 A3
Guajira, Pen. de la, *Colombia* 120 A3
Gualaceo, *Ecuador* 120 D2
Gualán, *Guatemala* 116 C2
Gualdo Tadino, *Italy* 33 E9
Gualeguay, *Argentina* 126 C4
Gualeguaychú, *Argentina* 126 C4
Gualicho, Salina, *Argentina* 128 B3
Gualjaina, *Argentina* 128 B2
Guam ■, *Pac. Oc.* 92 F6
Guamá, *Brazil* 122 B2
Guamá →, *Brazil* 122 B2
Guamblin, I., *Chile* 128 B1
Guaminí, *Argentina* 126 D3
Guamote, *Ecuador* 120 D2
Guampí, Sierra de, *Venezuela* 121 B4
Guamúchil, *Mexico* 114 B3
Guan Xian, *China* 52 B4
Guanabacoa, *Cuba* 116 B3
Guanacaste, Cordillera del, *Costa Rica* 116 D2
Guanaceví, *Mexico* 114 B3
Guanahani = San Salvador, *Bahamas* 117 B5
Guanajay, *Cuba* 116 B3
Guanajuato, *Mexico* 114 C4
Guanajuato □, *Mexico* 114 C4
Guanambi, *Brazil* 123 D3
Guanare, *Venezuela* 120 B4
Guanare →, *Venezuela* 120 B4
Guandacol, *Argentina* 126 B2
Guane, *Cuba* 116 B3
Guang'an, *China* 52 B6
Guangchang, *China* 53 D11
Guangde, *China* 53 B12
Guangdong □, *China* 53 F9
Guangfeng, *China* 53 C12
Guanghan, *China* 52 B5
Guanghua, *China* 53 A8
Guangji, *China* 53 C10
Guangling, *China* 50 E8
Guangning, *China* 53 F9
Guangrao, *China* 51 F10
Guangshun, *China* 52 D6
Guangwu, *China* 50 F3
Guangxi Zhuangzu Zizhiqu □, *China* 52 E7
Guangyuan, *China* 52 A5
Guangze, *China* 53 D11
Guangzhou, *China* 53 F9
Guanhães, *Brazil* 123 E3
Guanipa →, *Venezuela* 121 B5
Guanling, *China* 52 E5
Guannan, *China* 51 G10
Guanta, *Venezuela* 121 A5
Guantánamo, *Cuba* 117 B4
Guantao, *China* 50 F8
Guanyang, *China* 53 E8
Guanyun, *China* 51 G10
Guapí, *Colombia* 120 C2
Guápiles, *Costa Rica* 116 D3
Guaporé →, *Brazil* 125 C4
Guaqui, *Bolivia* 124 D4
Guara, Sierra de, *Spain* 28 C4
Guarabira, *Brazil* 122 C4
Guaranda, *Ecuador* 120 D2
Guarapari, *Brazil* 123 F3
Guarapuava, *Brazil* 123 G1
Guaratinguetá, *Brazil* 127 A6
Guaratuba, *Brazil* 127 B6
Guarda, *Portugal* 30 E3
Guarda □, *Portugal* 30 E3
Guardafui, C. = Asir, Ras, *Somali Rep.* 68 E5
Guardamar del Segura, *Spain* 29 G4
Guardavalle, *Italy* 35 D9
Guardiagrele, *Italy* 33 F11
Guardo, *Spain* 30 C6
Guareña, *Spain* 31 G4
Guareña →, *Spain* 30 D5
Guaria □, *Paraguay* 126 B4
Guárico □, *Venezuela* 120 B4
Guarrojo →, *Colombia* 120 C3
Guarujá, *Brazil* 127 A6
Guarus, *Brazil* 123 F3
Guasave, *Mexico* 114 B3
Guascama, Pta., *Colombia* 120 C2
Guasdualito, *Venezuela* 120 B3
Guasipati, *Venezuela* 121 B5
Guastalla, *Italy* 32 D7
Guatemala, *Guatemala* 116 D1
Guatemala ■, *Cent. Amer.* 116 C1
Guatire, *Venezuela* 120 A4
Guaviare □, *Colombia* 120 C3
Guaviare →, *Colombia* 120 C4
Guaxupé, *Brazil* 127 A6
Guayabero →, *Colombia* 120 C3
Guayama, *Puerto Rico* 117 C6
Guayaneco, Arch., *Chile* 128 C1
Guayaquil, *Ecuador* 120 D2
Guayaquil, G. de, *Ecuador* 120 D1
Guayaramerín, *Bolivia* 125 C4
Guayas →, *Ecuador* 120 D2
Guaymas, *Mexico* 114 B2
Guazhou, *China* 53 A12
Guba, *Zaïre* 83 E2
Gûbâl, Madîq, *Egypt* 76 B3
Gubat, *Phil.* 55 E6
Gúbbio, *Italy* 33 E9
Gubio, *Nigeria* 79 C7
Gubkin, *Russia* 42 E3
Gudata = Guadauta, *Georgia* 43 J5
Gudbrandsdalen, *Norway* 9 F14
Guddu Barrage, *Pakistan* 60 E6
Gudenå →, *Denmark* 11 H3
Gudermes, *Russia* 43 J8
Gudivada, *India* 61 L12
Gudur, *India* 60 M11
Guebwiller, *France* 25 E14
Guecho, *Spain* 28 B2
Guékédou, *Guinea* 78 D2
Guelma, *Algeria* 75 A6
Guelph, *Canada* 98 D3
Guemar, *Algeria* 75 B6
Guéméné-Penfao, *France* 24 E5
Guéméné-sur-Scorff, *France* 24 D3
Guéné, *Benin* 79 C5
Güepi, *Peru* 120 D2
Guer, *France* 24 E4
Güer Aike, *Argentina* 128 D3
Guérande, *France* 24 E4
Guercif, *Morocco* 75 B4
Guéréda, *Chad* 73 F9
Guéret, *France* 26 B5
Guérigny, *France* 25 E10
Guerneville, *U.S.A.* 112 G4
Guernica, *Spain* 28 B2
Guernsey, *U.K.* 13 H5
Guernsey, *U.S.A.* 108 D2
Guerrara, *Oasis, Algeria* 75 B5
Guerrara, *Saoura, Algeria* 75 C4
Guerrero □, *Mexico* 115 D5
Guerzim, *Algeria* 75 C4
Gueugnon, *France* 27 B8
Gueydan, *U.S.A.* 109 K8
Gügher, *Iran* 65 D8
Guglionesi, *Italy* 35 A7
Gui Jiang →, *China* 53 F8
Gui Xian, *China* 52 F7
Guia, *Canary Is.* 36 F4
Guia de Isora, *Canary Is.* 36 F3
Guia Lopes da Laguna, *Brazil* 127 A4
Guiana, *S. Amer.* 118 C4
Guichi, *China* 53 B11
Guider, *Cameroon* 79 D7
Guidimouni, *Niger* 79 C6
Guiding, *China* 52 D6
Guidong, *China* 53 D9
Guiglo, *Ivory C.* 78 D3
Guijá, *Mozam.* 85 C5
Guijo de Coria, *Spain* 30 E4
Guildford, *U.K.* 13 F7
Guilford, *U.S.A.* 99 C6
Guilin, *China* 53 E8
Guillaumes, *France* 27 D10
Guillestre, *France* 27 D10
Guilvinec, *France* 24 E2
Güimar, *Canary Is.* 36 F3
Guimarães, *Brazil* 122 B3
Guimarães, *Portugal* 30 D2
Guimaras, *Phil.* 55 F5
Guinda, *U.S.A.* 112 G4
Guinea, *Africa* 70 F4
Guinea ■, *W. Afr.* 78 C2
Guinea, Gulf of, *Atl. Oc.* 79 E5
Guinea-Bissau ■, *Africa* 78 C2
Güines, *Cuba* 116 B3
Guingamp, *France* 24 D3
Guipavas, *France* 24 D2
Guiping, *China* 53 F8
Guipúzcoa □, *Spain* 28 B2
Guir, O. →, *Algeria* 75 B4
Guiratinga, *Brazil* 125 D7
Güiria, *Venezuela* 121 A5
Guiscard, *France* 25 C10
Guise, *France* 25 C10
Guitiriz, *Spain* 30 B3
Guiuan, *Phil.* 55 F6
Guixi, *China* 53 C11
Guiyang, *Guizhou, China* 52 D6
Guiyang, *Hunan, China* 53 E9
Guizhou □, *China* 52 D6
Gujan-Mestras, *France* 26 D2
Gujarat □, *India* 62 H4
Gujiang, *China* 53 D10
Gujranwala, *Pakistan* 62 C6
Gujrat, *Pakistan* 62 C6
Gukovo, *Russia* 43 F5
Gulbarga, *India* 60 L10
Gulbene, *Latvia* 9 H22
Gulf, The, *Asia* 65 E6
Gulfport, *U.S.A.* 109 K10
Gulgong, *Australia* 91 E4
Gulin, *China* 52 C5
Gulistan, *Pakistan* 62 D2
Gull Lake, *Canada* 101 C7
Gullegem, *Belgium* 17 G2
Güllük, *Turkey* 66 D2
Gulma, *Nigeria* 79 C5
Gulmarg, *India* 63 B6
Gülnar, *Turkey* 66 D5
Gulpen, *Neths.* 17 G7
Gülşehir, *Turkey* 66 C6
Gulshad, *Kazakstan* 44 E8
Gulsvik, *Norway* 10 D3
Gulu, *Uganda* 82 B3
Gulwe, *Tanzania* 82 D4
Gulyaypole = Hulyaypole, *Ukraine* 41 J9
Gum Lake, *Australia* 91 E3
Gumal →, *Pakistan* 62 D4
Gumbaz, *Pakistan* 62 D3
Gumel, *Nigeria* 79 C6
Gumiel de Hizán, *Spain* 28 D1
Gumlu, *Australia* 90 B4
Gumma □, *Japan* 49 F9
Gummersbach, *Germany* 18 D3
Gummi, *Nigeria* 79 C6
Gümüşhaciköy, *Turkey* 66 B6
Gümüşhane, *Turkey* 67 B8
Gumzai, *Indonesia* 57 F8
Guna, *Ethiopia* 77 E4
Guna, *India* 62 G7
Gundagai, *Australia* 91 F4
Gundelfingen, *Germany* 19 G6
Gundih, *Indonesia* 57 G14
Güneydoğu Toroslar, *Turkey* 67 C9
Gungu, *Zaïre* 80 F3
Gunisao →, *Canada* 101 C9
Gunisao L., *Canada* 101 C9
Gunnbjørn Fjeld, *Greenland* 4 C6
Gunnedah, *Australia* 91 E5
Gunningbar Cr. →, *Australia* 91 E4
Gunnison, *Colo., U.S.A.* 111 G10
Gunnison, *Utah, U.S.A.* 110 G8
Gunnison →, *U.S.A.* 111 G9
Gunpowder, *Australia* 90 B2
Guntakal, *India* 60 M10
Guntersville, *U.S.A.* 105 H2
Guntong, *Malaysia* 59 K3
Guntur, *India* 61 L12
Gunungapi, *Indonesia* 57 F7
Gunungsitoli, *Indonesia* 56 D1
Günz →, *Germany* 19 G6
Gunza, *Angola* 80 G2
Günzburg, *Germany* 19 G6
Gunzenhausen, *Germany* 19 F6
Guo He →, *China* 51 H9
Guoyang, *China* 50 H9
Gupis, *Pakistan* 63 A5
Gura Humorului, *Romania* 38 B8
Gurag, *Ethiopia* 77 F4
Gurdaspur, *India* 62 C6
Gurdon, *U.S.A.* 109 J8
Gurgaon, *India* 62 E7
Gürgentepe, *Turkey* 66 B7
Gurgueia →, *Brazil* 122 C3
Gurha, *India* 62 G4
Guri, Embalse de, *Venezuela* 121 B5
Gurjaani, *Georgia* 43 K7
Gurk →, *Austria* 21 J4
Gurkha, *Nepal* 63 E11
Gurley, *Australia* 91 D4
Gürpınar, *Turkey* 67 C10
Gurué, *Mozam.* 83 F4
Gurun, *Malaysia* 59 K3
Gürün, *Turkey* 66 C7
Gurupá, *Brazil* 121 D7
Gurupá, I. Grande de, *Brazil* 121 D7
Gurupi, *Brazil* 123 D2
Gurupi →, *Brazil* 122 B2
Gurupi, Serra do, *Brazil* 122 C2
Guryev = Atyraū, *Kazakstan* 44 E6
Gus-Khrustalnyy, *Russia* 42 C5
Gusau, *Nigeria* 79 C6
Gusev, *Russia* 9 J20
Gushan, *China* 51 E12
Gushgy, *Turkmenistan* 44 F7
Gushi, *China* 53 A10
Gushiago, *Ghana* 79 D4
Gusinje, *Montenegro, Yug.* 21 N9
Gusinoozersk, *Russia* 45 D11
Gúspini, *Italy* 34 C1
Gustanj, *Slovenia* 33 B11
Gustine, *U.S.A.* 111 H3
Güstrow, *Germany* 18 B8
Gusum, *Sweden* 11 F10
Guta = Kalárovo, *Slovak Rep.* 21 H7
Gütersloh, *Germany* 18 D4
Gutha, *Australia* 89 E2
Guthalongra, *Australia* 90 B4
Guthrie, *U.S.A.* 109 H6
Gutian, *China* 53 D12
Gutiérrez, *Bolivia* 125 D5
Guttannen, *Switz.* 23 C6
Guttenberg, *U.S.A.* 108 D9
Guyana ■, *S. Amer.* 121 B6
Guyane française ■ = French Guiana ■, *S. Amer.* 121 C7
Guyang, *China* 50 D6
Guyenne, *France* 26 D4
Guymon, *U.S.A.* 109 G4
Guyra, *Australia* 91 E5
Guyuan, *Hebei, China* 50 D8
Guyuan, *Ningxia Huizu, China* 50 F4
Guzhang, *China* 52 C7
Guzhen, *China* 51 H9
Guzmán, L. de, *Mexico* 114 A3
Gvardeysk, *Russia* 9 J19
Gvardeyskoye, *Ukraine* 41 K8
Gwa, *Burma* 61 L19
Gwaai, *Zimbabwe* 83 F2
Gwabegar, *Australia* 91 E4
Gwadabawa, *Nigeria* 79 C6
Gwādar, *Pakistan* 60 G3
Gwagwada, *Nigeria* 79 C6
Gwalia, *Australia* 89 E3
Gwalior, *India* 62 F8
Gwanda, *Zimbabwe* 83 G2
Gwandu, *Nigeria* 79 C5
Gwane, *Zaïre* 82 B2
Gwaram, *Nigeria* 79 C7
Gwarzo, *Nigeria* 79 C6
Gweebarra B., *Ireland* 15 B3
Gweedore, *Ireland* 15 A3
Gweru, *Zimbabwe* 83 F2
Gwi, *Nigeria* 79 D6
Gwinn, *U.S.A.* 104 B2
Gwio Kura, *Nigeria* 79 C7
Gwol, *Ghana* 78 C4
Gwoza, *Nigeria* 79 C7
Gwydir →, *Australia* 91 D4
Gwynedd □, *U.K.* 12 E3
Gyandzha = Gäncä, *Azerbaijan* 43 K8
Gyaring Hu, *China* 54 C4
Gydanskiy P-ov., *Russia* 44 C8
Gympie, *Australia* 91 D5
Gyoma, *Hungary* 21 J10
Gyöngyös, *Hungary* 21 H9
Györ, *Hungary* 21 H7
Gypsum Pt., *Canada* 100 A6
Gypsumville, *Canada* 101 C9
Gyula, *Hungary* 21 J11
Gyumri, *Armenia* 43 K6
Gyzylarbat, *Turkmenistan* 44 F6
Gzhatsk = Gagarin, *Russia* 42 C2

H

Ha 'Arava →, *Israel* 69 E4
Ha Coi, *Vietnam* 58 B6
Ha Dong, *Vietnam* 58 B5
Ha Giang, *Vietnam* 58 A5
Ha Tien, *Vietnam* 59 G5
Ha Tinh, *Vietnam* 58 C5
Ha Trung, *Vietnam* 58 C5
Haacht, *Belgium* 17 G5
Haag, *Germany* 19 G8
Haaksbergen, *Neths.* 16 D9
Haaltert, *Belgium* 17 G4
Haamstede, *Neths.* 17 E3
Haapsalu, *Estonia* 9 G20
Haarlem, *Neths.* 16 D5
Haast →, *N.Z.* 87 K2
Haast Bluff, *Australia* 88 D5
Haastrecht, *Neths.* 16 E5
Hab Nadi Chauki, *Pakistan* 62 G2
Habaswein, *Kenya* 82 B4
Habay, *Canada* 100 B5
Habay-la-Neuve, *Belgium* 17 J7
Ḩabbānīyah, *Iraq* 67 F10
Ḩabbānīyah, Hawr al, *Iraq* 67 F10
Haboro, *Japan* 48 B10
Haccourt, *Belgium* 17 G7
Hachenburg, *Germany* 18 E3
Hachijō-Jima, *Japan* 49 H9
Hachinohe, *Japan* 48 D10
Hachiōji, *Japan* 49 G9
Hachŏn, *N. Korea* 51 D15
Hachy, *Belgium* 17 J7
Hacıbektaş, *Turkey* 66 C6
Hacılar, *Turkey* 66 C6
Hackensack, *U.S.A.* 107 F10
Hadali, *Pakistan* 62 C5
Hadarba, Ras, *Sudan* 76 C4
Hadarom □, *Israel* 69 E3
Haddington, *U.K.* 14 F6
Hadejia, *Nigeria* 79 C7
Hadejia →, *Nigeria* 79 C7
Haden, *Australia* 91 D5
Hadera, *Israel* 69 C3
Hadera, N. →, *Israel* 69 C3
Haderslev, *Denmark* 11 J3
Hadhramaut = Hadramawt, *Yemen* 68 D4
Hadım, *Turkey* 66 D5
Hadjeb El Aïoun, *Tunisia* 75 A6
Hadong, *S. Korea* 51 G14
Hadramawt, *Yemen* 68 D4
Hadrānīyah, *Iraq* 64 C4
Hadrian's Wall, *U.K.* 12 C5
Hadsten, *Denmark* 11 H4
Hadsund, *Denmark* 11 H4
Hadyach, *Ukraine* 41 G8
Haeju, *N. Korea* 51 E13
Haenam, *S. Korea* 51 G14
Haerhpin = Harbin, *China* 51 B14
Hafar al Bāţin, *Si. Arabia* 64 D5
Hafik, *Turkey* 66 C7
Ḩafīrat al 'Aydā, *Si. Arabia* 64 E3
Hafizabad, *Pakistan* 62 C5
Haflong, *India* 61 G18
Hafnarfjörður, *Iceland* 8 D3
Hafun, Ras, *Somali Rep.* 68 E5
Hagalil, *Israel* 69 C4
Hagen, *Germany* 18 D3
Hagenow, *Germany* 18 B7
Hagerman, *U.S.A.* 109 J2
Hagerstown, *U.S.A.* 104 F7
Hagetmau, *France* 26 E3
Hagfors, *Sweden* 9 F15
Häggenås, *Sweden* 10 A8
Hagi, *Japan* 49 G5
Hagolan, *Syria* 69 B4
Hagondange-Briey, *France* 25 C13
Hags Hd., *Ireland* 15 D2
Hague, C. de la, *France* 24 C5
Hague, The = 's-Gravenhage, *Neths.* 16 D4
Haguenau, *France* 25 D14
Hai □, *Tanzania* 82 C4
Hai Duong, *Vietnam* 58 B6
Hai'an, *Guangdong, China* 53 G8
Hai'an, *Jiangsu, China* 53 A13
Haicheng, *Fujian, China* 53 E11
Haicheng, *Liaoning, China* 51 D12
Haidar Khel, *Afghan.* 62 C3
Haifa = Hefa, *Israel* 69 C3
Haifeng, *China* 53 F10
Haig, *Australia* 89 F4
Haiger, *Germany* 18 E4
Haikang, *China* 53 G8
Haikou, *China* 54 D6
Ḩā'il, *Si. Arabia* 64 E4
Hailar, *China* 54 B6
Hailey, *U.S.A.* 110 E6
Haileybury, *Canada* 98 C4
Hailin, *China* 51 B15
Hailing Dao, *China* 53 G8
Hailong, *China* 51 C13
Hailun, *China* 54 B7
Hailuoto, *Finland* 8 D21
Haimen, *Guangdong, China* 53 F11
Haimen, *Jiangsu, China* 53 B13
Haimen, *Zhejiang, China* 53 C13
Hainan □, *China* 54 E5
Hainaut □, *Belgium* 17 H4
Haines, *U.S.A.* 110 D5
Haines City, *U.S.A.* 105 L5
Haines Junction, *Canada* 100 A1
Haining, *China* 53 B13
Haiphong, *Vietnam* 54 D5
Haiti ■, *W. Indies* 117 C5
Haiya Junction, *Sudan* 76 D4
Haiyan, *China* 53 B13
Haiyang, *China* 51 F11
Haiyuan, *Guangxi Zhuangzu, China* 52 F6
Haiyuan, *Ningxia Huizu, China* 50 F3
Haizhou, *China* 51 G10
Haizhou Wan, *China* 51 G10
Hajar Bangar, *Sudan* 73 F9
Hajdúböszörmény, *Hungary* 21 H11
Hajdúszobaszló, *Hungary* 21 H11
Hajipur, *India* 63 G11
Ḩājjī Muḩsin, *Iraq* 64 C5
Ḩājjīābād, *Eşfahan, Iran* 65 C7
Ḩājjīābād, *Hormozgān, Iran* 65 D7
Hakansson, Mts., *Zaïre* 83 D2
Håkantorp, *Sweden* 11 F6
Hakkâri, *Turkey* 67 D10
Hakkâri Dağları, *Turkey* 67 C10
Hakken-Zan, *Japan* 49 G7
Hakodate, *Japan* 48 D10
Haku-San, *Japan* 49 F8
Hakui, *Japan* 49 F8
Hala, *Pakistan* 60 G6
Ḩalab, *Syria* 66 D7
Ḩalabjah, *Iraq* 67 E11
Halaib, *Sudan* 76 C4
Halanzy, *Belgium* 17 J7
Hālat 'Ammār, *Si. Arabia* 64 D3
Halbā, *Lebanon* 69 A5
Halberstadt, *Germany* 18 D7
Halcombe, *N.Z.* 87 J5
Halcon, Mt., *Phil.* 57 B6
Halden, *Norway* 10 E5
Haldensleben, *Germany* 18 C7
Haldia, *India* 61 H16
Haldwani, *India* 63 E8
Hale →, *Australia* 90 C2
Haleakala Crater, *U.S.A.* 102 H16
Halen, *Belgium* 17 G6
Haleyville, *U.S.A.* 105 H2
Half Assini, *Ghana* 78 D4
Halfway →, *Canada* 100 B4
Haliburton, *Canada* 98 C4
Halifax, *Australia* 90 B4
Halifax, *Canada* 99 D7
Halifax, *U.K.* 12 D6
Halifax B., *Australia* 90 B4
Halifax I., *Namibia* 84 D2
Halīl →, *Iran* 65 E8
Hall, *Austria* 19 H7
Hall Beach, *Canada* 97 B11
Hall Pt., *Australia* 88 C3
Halland, *Sweden* 9 H15
Hallands län □, *Sweden* 11 H6
Hallands Väderö, *Sweden* 11 H6

Hallandsås, *Sweden* 11 H7
Halle, *Belgium* 17 G4
Halle, *Nordrhein-Westfalen, Germany* 18 C4
Halle, *Sachsen-Anhalt, Germany* 18 D7
Hällefors, *Sweden* 9 G16
Hallein, *Austria* 21 H3
Hällekis, *Sweden* 11 F7
Hallett, *Australia* 91 E2
Hallettsville, *U.S.A.* 109 L6
Hällevadsholm, *Sweden* 11 F5
Halliday, *U.S.A.* 108 B3
Halliday L., *Canada* 101 A7
Hallim, *S. Korea* 51 H14
Hallingdalselva →, *Norway* 9 F13
Hallock, *U.S.A.* 101 D9
Halls Creek, *Australia* 88 C4
Hallsberg, *Sweden* 9 G16
Hallstahammar, *Sweden* 10 E10
Hallstead, *U.S.A.* 107 E9
Halmahera, *Indonesia* 57 D7
Halmeu, *Romania* 38 B6
Halmstad, *Sweden* 11 H6
Halq el Oued, *Tunisia* 75 A7
Hals, *Denmark* 11 H4
Halsafjorden, *Norway* 10 A2
Hälsingborg = Helsingborg, *Sweden* 11 H6
Hälsingland, *Sweden* 9 F16
Halstad, *U.S.A.* 108 B6
Haltdalen, *Norway* 10 B5
Haltern, *Germany* 18 D3
Halti, *Finland* 8 B19
Halul, *Qatar* 65 E7
Ḥalvān, *Iran* 65 C8
Ham, *France* 25 C10
Ham Tan, *Vietnam* 59 G6
Ham Yen, *Vietnam* 58 A5
Hamab, *Namibia* 84 D2
Hamad, *Sudan* 77 D3
Hamada, *Japan* 49 G6
Hamadān, *Iran* 67 E13
Hamadān □, *Iran* 65 C6
Hamadia, *Algeria* 75 A5
Hamāh, *Syria* 66 E7
Hamamatsu, *Japan* 49 G8
Hamar, *Norway* 10 D5
Hamâta, Gebel, *Egypt* 76 C3
Hambantota, *Sri Lanka* 60 R12
Hamber Prov. Park, *Canada* 100 C5
Hamburg, *Germany* 18 B5
Hamburg, *Ark., U.S.A.* 109 J9
Hamburg, *Iowa, U.S.A.* 108 E7
Hamburg, *N.Y., U.S.A.* 106 D6
Hamburg, *Pa., U.S.A.* 107 F9
Hamburg □, *Germany* 18 B6
Ḥamḍ, W. al →, *Si. Arabia* 64 E3
Hamden, *U.S.A.* 107 E12
Häme, *Finland* 9 F20
Hämeenlinna, *Finland* 9 F21
Hamélé, *Ghana* 78 C4
Hamelin Pool, *Australia* 89 E1
Hameln, *Germany* 18 C5
Hamer Koke, *Ethiopia* 77 F4
Hamerkaz □, *Israel* 69 C3
Hamersley Ra., *Australia* 88 D2
Hamhung, *N. Korea* 51 E14
Hami, *China* 54 B4
Hamilton, *Australia* 91 F3
Hamilton, *Canada* 98 D4
Hamilton, *N.Z.* 87 G5
Hamilton, *U.K.* 14 F4
Hamilton, *Mo., U.S.A.* 108 F8
Hamilton, *Mont., U.S.A.* 110 C6
Hamilton, *N.Y., U.S.A.* 107 D9
Hamilton, *Ohio, U.S.A.* 104 F3
Hamilton, *Tex., U.S.A.* 109 K5
Hamilton →, *Australia* 90 C2
Hamilton City, *U.S.A.* 112 F4
Hamilton Hotel, *Australia* 90 C3
Hamilton Inlet, *Canada* 99 B8
Hamina, *Finland* 9 F22
Hamiota, *Canada* 101 C8
Hamlet, *U.S.A.* 105 H6
Hamley Bridge, *Australia* 91 E2
Hamlin = Hameln, *Germany* 18 C5
Hamlin, *N.Y., U.S.A.* 106 C7
Hamlin, *Tex., U.S.A.* 109 J4
Hamm, *Germany* 18 D3
Hammam Bouhadjar, *Algeria* 75 A4
Hammamet, *Tunisia* 75 A7
Hammamet, G. de, *Tunisia* 75 A7
Hammarstrand, *Sweden* 10 A10
Hamme, *Belgium* 17 F4
Hamme-Mille, *Belgium* 17 G5
Hammel, *Denmark* 11 H3
Hammelburg, *Germany* 19 E5
Hammerfest, *Norway* 8 A20
Hammond, *Ind., U.S.A.* 104 E2
Hammond, *La., U.S.A.* 109 K9
Hammonton, *U.S.A.* 104 F8
Hamoir, *Belgium* 17 H7
Hamont, *Belgium* 17 F7
Hamoyet, Jebel, *Sudan* 76 D4
Hampden, *N.Z.* 87 L3
Hampshire □, *U.K.* 13 F6
Hampshire Downs, *U.K.* 13 F6
Hampton, *Ark., U.S.A.* 109 J8
Hampton, *Iowa, U.S.A.* 108 D8
Hampton, *N.H., U.S.A.* 107 D14
Hampton, *S.C., U.S.A.* 105 J5
Hampton, *Va., U.S.A.* 104 G7
Hampton Tableland, *Australia* 89 F4
Hamrat esh Sheykh, *Sudan* 77 E2
Hamur, *Turkey* 67 C10
Hamyang, *S. Korea* 51 G14
Han Jiang →, *China* 53 F11
Han Shui →, *China* 53 B10
Hana, *U.S.A.* 102 H17
Hanak, *Si. Arabia* 64 E3
Hanamaki, *Japan* 48 E10
Hanang, *Tanzania* 82 C4
Hanau, *Germany* 19 E4
Hanbogd, *Mongolia* 50 C4
Hancheng, *China* 50 G6
Hanchuan, *China* 53 B9
Hancock, *Mich., U.S.A.* 108 B10
Hancock, *Minn., U.S.A.* 108 C7
Hancock, *N.Y., U.S.A.* 107 E9
Handa, *Japan* 49 G8
Handa, *Somali Rep.* 68 E5
Handan, *China* 50 F8
Handen, *Sweden* 10 E12
Handeni, *Tanzania* 82 D4
Handeni □, *Tanzania* 82 D4
Handub, *Sudan* 76 D4
Handwara, *India* 63 B6
Handzame, *Belgium* 17 F2
Hanegev, *Israel* 69 E3
Haney, *Canada* 100 D4
Hanford, *U.S.A.* 111 H4
Hang Chat, *Thailand* 58 C2
Hang Dong, *Thailand* 58 C2
Hangang →, *S. Korea* 51 F14
Hangayn Nuruu, *Mongolia* 54 B4
Hangchou = Hangzhou, *China* 53 B13
Hanggin Houqi, *China* 50 D4
Hanggin Qi, *China* 50 E5
Hangu, *China* 51 E9
Hangzhou, *China* 53 B13
Hangzhou Wan, *China* 53 B13
Hanhongor, *Mongolia* 50 C3
Ḥanīdh, *Si. Arabia* 65 E6
Ḥanīsh, *Yemen* 68 E3
Hanjiang, *China* 53 E12
Hankinson, *U.S.A.* 108 B6
Hanko, *Finland* 9 G20
Hankou, *China* 53 B10
Hanksville, *U.S.A.* 111 G8
Hanle, *India* 63 C8
Hanmer Springs, *N.Z.* 87 K4
Hann →, *Australia* 88 C4
Hann, Mt., *Australia* 88 C4
Hanna, *Canada* 100 C6
Hannaford, *U.S.A.* 108 B5
Hannah, *U.S.A.* 108 A5
Hannah B., *Canada* 98 B4
Hannibal, *U.S.A.* 108 F9
Hannik, *Sudan* 76 D3
Hannover, *Germany* 18 C5
Hannut, *Belgium* 17 G6
Hanoi, *Vietnam* 54 D5
Hanover = Hannover, *Germany* 18 C5
Hanover, *Canada* 106 B3
Hanover, *S. Africa* 84 E3
Hanover, *N.H., U.S.A.* 107 C12
Hanover, *Ohio, U.S.A.* 106 F2
Hanover, *Pa., U.S.A.* 104 F7
Hanover, I., *Chile* 128 D2
Hanshou, *China* 53 C8
Hansi, *India* 62 E6
Hanson, L., *Australia* 91 E2
Hantsavichy, *Belarus* 41 F4
Hanyang, *China* 53 B10
Hanyin, *China* 52 A7
Hanyuan, *China* 52 C4
Hanzhong, *China* 50 H4
Hanzhuang, *China* 51 G9
Haora, *India* 63 H13
Haoxue, *China* 53 B9
Haparanda, *Sweden* 8 D21
Hapert, *Neths.* 17 F6
Happy, *U.S.A.* 109 H4
Happy Camp, *U.S.A.* 110 F2
Happy Valley-Goose Bay, *Canada* 99 B7
Hapsu, *N. Korea* 51 D15
Hapur, *India* 62 E7
Ḥaql, *Si. Arabia* 69 F3
Haquira, *Peru* 124 C3
Har, *Indonesia* 57 F8
Har-Ayrag, *Mongolia* 50 B5
Har Hu, *China* 54 C4
Har Us Nuur, *Mongolia* 54 B4
Har Yehuda, *Israel* 69 D3
Ḥaraḍ, *Si. Arabia* 68 C4
Haradok, *Belarus* 40 E6
Haranomachi, *Japan* 48 F10
Harardera, *Somali Rep.* 68 G4
Harare, *Zimbabwe* 83 F3
Harat, *Eritrea* 77 D4
Harazé, *Chad* 73 F8
Harbin, *China* 51 B14
Harbiye, *Turkey* 66 D7
Harboør, *Denmark* 11 H2
Harbor Beach, *U.S.A.* 104 D4
Harbor Springs, *U.S.A.* 104 C3
Harbour Breton, *Canada* 99 C8
Harbour Grace, *Canada* 99 C9
Harburg, *Germany* 18 B5
Hårby, *Denmark* 11 J4
Harda, *India* 62 H7
Hardangerfjorden, *Norway* 9 F12
Hardangervidda, *Norway* 9 F12
Hardap Dam, *Namibia* 84 C2
Hardegarijp, *Neths.* 16 B7
Hardenberg, *Neths.* 16 C9
Harderwijk, *Neths.* 16 D7
Hardey →, *Australia* 88 D2
Hardin, *U.S.A.* 110 D10
Harding, *S. Africa* 85 E4
Harding Ra., *Australia* 88 C3
Hardisty, *Canada* 100 C6
Hardman, *U.S.A.* 110 D4
Hardoi, *India* 63 F9
Hardwar = Haridwar, *India* 62 E8
Hardwick, *U.S.A.* 107 B12
Hardy, *U.S.A.* 109 G9
Hardy, Pen., *Chile* 128 E3
Hare B., *Canada* 99 B8
Hareid, *Norway* 9 E12
Harelbeke, *Belgium* 17 G2
Haren, *Germany* 18 C3
Haren, *Neths.* 16 B9
Harer, *Ethiopia* 68 F3
Harerge □, *Ethiopia* 77 F5
Hareto, *Ethiopia* 77 F4
Harfleur, *France* 24 C7
Hargeisa, *Somali Rep.* 68 F3
Hari →, *Indonesia* 56 E2
Haria, *Canary Is.* 36 E6
Haricha, Hamada el, *Mali* 74 D4
Haridwar, *India* 62 E8
Haringhata →, *Bangla.* 61 J16
Haringvliet, *Neths.* 16 E4
Harīrūd →, *Asia* 60 A2
Härjedalen, *Sweden* 9 E15
Harlan, *Iowa, U.S.A.* 108 E7
Harlan, *Ky., U.S.A.* 105 G4
Harlech, *U.K.* 12 E3
Harlem, *U.S.A.* 110 B9
Harlingen, *Neths.* 16 B6
Harlingen, *U.S.A.* 109 M6
Harlowton, *U.S.A.* 110 C9
Harmånger, *Sweden* 10 C11
Harmil, *Eritrea* 77 D5
Harney Basin, *U.S.A.* 110 E4
Harney L., *U.S.A.* 110 E4
Harney Peak, *U.S.A.* 108 D3
Härnön, *Sweden* 10 B12
Härnösand, *Sweden* 10 B11
Haro, *Spain* 28 C2
Harp L., *Canada* 99 A7
Harper, *Liberia* 78 E3
Harplinge, *Sweden* 11 H6
Harrand, *Pakistan* 62 E4
Harriman, *U.S.A.* 105 H3
Harrington Harbour, *Canada* 99 B8
Harris, *U.K.* 14 D2
Harris, Sd. of, *U.K.* 14 D1
Harris L., *Australia* 91 E2
Harrisburg, *Ill., U.S.A.* 109 G10
Harrisburg, *Nebr., U.S.A.* 108 E3
Harrisburg, *Oreg., U.S.A.* 110 D2
Harrisburg, *Pa., U.S.A.* 106 F8
Harrismith, *S. Africa* 85 D4
Harrison, *Ark., U.S.A.* 109 G8
Harrison, *Idaho, U.S.A.* 110 C5
Harrison, *Nebr., U.S.A.* 108 D3
Harrison, C., *Canada* 99 B8
Harrison Bay, *U.S.A.* 96 A4
Harrison L., *Canada* 100 D4
Harrisonburg, *U.S.A.* 104 F6
Harrisonville, *U.S.A.* 108 F7
Harriston, *Canada* 98 D3
Harrisville, *U.S.A.* 106 B1
Harrogate, *U.K.* 12 D6
Harrow, *U.K.* 13 F7
Harsefeld, *Germany* 18 B5
Harsīn, *Iran* 67 E12
Harskamp, *Neths.* 16 D7
Harstad, *Norway* 8 B17
Hart, *U.S.A.* 104 D2
Hart, L., *Australia* 91 E2
Hartbees →, *S. Africa* 84 D3
Hartberg, *Austria* 21 H5
Hartford, *Conn., U.S.A.* 107 E12
Hartford, *Ky., U.S.A.* 104 G2
Hartford, *S. Dak., U.S.A.* 108 D6
Hartford, *Wis., U.S.A.* 108 D10
Hartford City, *U.S.A.* 104 E3
Hartland, *Canada* 99 C6
Hartland Pt., *U.K.* 13 F3
Hartlepool, *U.K.* 12 C6
Hartlepool □, *U.K.* 12 C6
Hartley Bay, *Canada* 100 C3
Hartmannberge, *Namibia* 84 B1
Hartney, *Canada* 101 D8
Harts →, *S. Africa* 84 D3
Hartselle, *U.S.A.* 105 H2
Hartshorne, *U.S.A.* 109 H7
Hartsville, *U.S.A.* 105 H5
Hartwell, *U.S.A.* 105 H4
Harunabad, *Pakistan* 62 E5
Harvand, *Iran* 65 D7
Harvey, *Australia* 89 F2
Harvey, *Ill., U.S.A.* 104 E2
Harvey, *N. Dak., U.S.A.* 108 B5
Harwich, *U.K.* 13 F9
Haryana □, *India* 62 E7
Haryn →, *Belarus* 41 F4
Harz, *Germany* 18 D6
Harzé, *Belgium* 17 H7
Harzgerode, *Germany* 18 D7
Hasaheisa, *Sudan* 77 E3
Hasan Kīādeh, *Iran* 65 B6
Ḥasanābād, *Iran* 65 C7
Hasanpur, *India* 62 E8
Haselünne, *Germany* 18 C3
Hashimoto, *Japan* 49 G7
Hashtjerd, *Iran* 65 C6
Håsjö, *Sweden* 10 A10
Haskell, *Okla., U.S.A.* 109 H7
Haskell, *Tex., U.S.A.* 109 J5
Haslach, *Germany* 19 G4
Haslev, *Denmark* 11 J5
Hasparren, *France* 26 E2
Hassa, *Turkey* 66 D7
Hasselt, *Belgium* 17 G6
Hasselt, *Neths.* 16 C8
Hassene, Adrar, *Algeria* 75 D5
Hassfurt, *Germany* 19 E6
Hassi bou Khelala, *Algeria* 75 B4
Hassi Djafou, *Algeria* 75 B5
Hassi el Abiod, *Algeria* 75 B5
Hassi el Biod, *Algeria* 75 C6
Hassi el Hadjar, *Algeria* 75 B5
Hassi Imoulaye, *Algeria* 75 C6
Hassi Inifel, *Algeria* 75 C5
Hassi Messaoud, *Algeria* 75 B6
Hassi Tartrat, *Algeria* 75 B6
Hassi Zerzour, *Morocco* 74 B4
Hässleholm, *Sweden* 9 H15
Hastière-Lavaux, *Belgium* 17 H5
Hastings, *N.Z.* 87 H6
Hastings, *U.K.* 13 G8
Hastings, *Mich., U.S.A.* 104 D3
Hastings, *Minn., U.S.A.* 108 C8
Hastings, *Nebr., U.S.A.* 108 E5
Hastings Ra., *Australia* 91 E5
Hat Yai, *Thailand* 59 J3
Hatanbulag, *Mongolia* 50 C5
Hatay = Antalya, *Turkey* 66 D4
Hatch, *U.S.A.* 111 K10
Hatches Creek, *Australia* 90 C2
Hatchet L., *Canada* 101 B8
Haţeg, *Romania* 38 D5
Haţeg, Mţii., *Romania* 38 D6
Hatert, *Neths.* 16 E7
Hateruma-Shima, *Japan* 49 M1
Hatfield P.O., *Australia* 91 E3
Hatgal, *Mongolia* 54 A5
Hathras, *India* 62 F8
Hatia, *Bangla.* 61 H17
Hato de Corozal, *Colombia* 120 B3
Hato Mayor, *Dom. Rep.* 117 C6
Hattah, *Australia* 91 E3
Hattem, *Neths.* 16 D8
Hatteras, C., *U.S.A.* 105 H8
Hattiesburg, *U.S.A.* 109 K10
Hatvan, *Hungary* 21 H9
Hau Bon = Cheo Reo, *Vietnam* 58 F7
Hau Duc, *Vietnam* 58 E7
Haug, *Norway* 10 D4
Haugastøl, *Norway* 10 D1
Haugesund, *Norway* 9 G11
Haukipudas, *Finland* 8 D21
Haulerwijk, *Neths.* 16 B8
Haultain →, *Canada* 101 B7
Hauraki G., *N.Z.* 87 G5
Haut Atlas, *Morocco* 74 B3
Haut-Rhin □, *France* 25 E14
Haut Zaïre □, *Zaïre* 82 B2
Haute-Corse □, *France* 27 F13
Haute-Garonne □, *France* 26 E5
Haute-Loire □, *France* 26 C7
Haute-Marne □, *France* 25 D12
Haute-Saône □, *France* 25 E13
Haute-Savoie □, *France* 27 C10
Haute-Vienne □, *France* 26 C5
Hauterive, *Canada* 99 C6
Hautes-Alpes □, *France* 27 D10
Hautes Fagnes = Hohe Venn, *Belgium* 17 H8
Hautes-Pyrénées □, *France* 26 F4
Hauteville-Lompnès, *France* 27 C9
Hautmont, *France* 25 B10
Hautrage, *Belgium* 17 H3
Hauts-de-Seine □, *France* 25 D9
Hauts Plateaux, *Algeria* 75 B4
Hauzenberg, *Germany* 19 G9
Havana = La Habana, *Cuba* 116 B3
Havana, *U.S.A.* 108 E9
Havant, *U.K.* 13 G7
Havasu, L., *U.S.A.* 113 L12
Havel →, *Germany* 18 C8
Havelange, *Belgium* 17 H6
Havelian, *Pakistan* 62 B5
Havelock, *N.B., Canada* 99 C6
Havelock, *Ont., Canada* 98 D4
Havelock, *N.Z.* 87 J4
Havelte, *Neths.* 16 C8
Haverfordwest, *U.K.* 13 F3
Haverhill, *U.S.A.* 107 D13
Havering, *U.K.* 13 F8
Haverstraw, *U.S.A.* 107 E11
Håverud, *Sweden* 11 F6
Havlíčkův Brod, *Czech.* 20 F5
Havneby, *Denmark* 11 J2
Havre, *U.S.A.* 110 B9
Havre-Aubert, *Canada* 99 C7
Havre-St.-Pierre, *Canada* 99 B7
Havza, *Turkey* 66 B6
Haw →, *U.S.A.* 105 H6
Hawaii □, *U.S.A.* 102 H16
Hawaii I., *Pac. Oc.* 102 J17
Hawaiian Is., *Pac. Oc.* 102 H17
Hawaiian Ridge, *Pac. Oc.* 93 E11
Hawarden, *Canada* 101 C7
Hawarden, *U.S.A.* 108 D6
Hawea, L., *N.Z.* 87 L2
Hawera, *N.Z.* 87 H5
Hawick, *U.K.* 14 F6
Hawk Junction, *Canada* 98 C3
Hawke B., *N.Z.* 87 H6
Hawker, *Australia* 91 E2
Hawkesbury, *Canada* 98 C5
Hawkesbury I., *Canada* 100 C3
Hawkesbury Pt., *Australia* 90 A1
Hawkinsville, *U.S.A.* 105 J4
Hawkwood, *Australia* 91 D5
Hawley, *U.S.A.* 108 B6
Hawrān, *Syria* 69 C5
Ḥawrān, W. →, *Iraq* 67 F10
Hawsh Mūssá, *Lebanon* 69 B4
Hawthorne, *U.S.A.* 110 G4
Hawzen, *Ethiopia* 77 E4
Haxtun, *U.S.A.* 108 E3
Hay, *Australia* 91 E3
Hay →, *Australia* 90 C2
Hay →, *Canada* 100 A5
Hay, C., *Australia* 88 B4
Hay L., *Canada* 100 B5
Hay Lakes, *Canada* 100 C6
Hay-on-Wye, *U.K.* 13 E4
Hay River, *Canada* 100 A5
Hay Springs, *U.S.A.* 108 D3
Haya, *Indonesia* 57 E7
Hayachine-San, *Japan* 48 E10
Hayange, *France* 25 C13
Hayden, *Ariz., U.S.A.* 111 K8
Hayden, *Colo., U.S.A.* 110 F10
Haydon, *Australia* 90 B3
Hayes, *U.S.A.* 108 C4
Hayes →, *Canada* 101 B10
Haymana, *Turkey* 66 C5
Haynesville, *U.S.A.* 109 J8
Hayrabolu, *Turkey* 66 B2
Hays, *Canada* 100 C6
Hays, *U.S.A.* 108 F5
Haysyn, *Ukraine* 41 H5
Hayvoron, *Ukraine* 41 H5
Hayward, *Calif., U.S.A.* 112 H4
Hayward, *Wis., U.S.A.* 108 B9
Haywards Heath, *U.K.* 13 F7
Hazafon □, *Israel* 69 C4
Hazarām, Kūh-e, *Iran* 65 D8
Hazard, *U.S.A.* 104 G4
Hazaribag, *India* 63 H11
Hazaribag Road, *India* 63 G11
Hazebrouck, *France* 25 B9
Hazelton, *Canada* 100 B3
Hazelton, *U.S.A.* 108 B4
Hazen, *N. Dak., U.S.A.* 108 B4
Hazen, *Nev., U.S.A.* 110 G4
Hazerswoude, *Neths.* 16 D5
Hazlehurst, *Ga., U.S.A.* 105 K4
Hazlehurst, *Miss., U.S.A.* 109 K9
Hazleton, *U.S.A.* 107 F9
Hazlett, L., *Australia* 88 D4
Hazor, *Israel* 69 B4
He Xian, *Anhui, China* 53 B12
He Xian, *Guangxi Zhuangzu, China* 53 E8
Head of Bight, *Australia* 89 F5
Headlands, *Zimbabwe* 83 F3
Healdsburg, *U.S.A.* 112 G4
Healdton, *U.S.A.* 109 H6
Healesville, *Australia* 91 F4
Heanor, *U.K.* 12 D6
Heard I., *Ind. Oc.* 3 G13
Hearne, *U.S.A.* 109 K6
Hearne B., *Canada* 101 A9
Hearne L., *Canada* 100 A6
Hearst, *Canada* 98 C3
Heart →, *U.S.A.* 108 B4
Heart's Content, *Canada* 99 C9
Heath →, *Bolivia* 124 C4
Heath Pt., *Canada* 99 C7
Heath Steele, *Canada* 99 C6
Heavener, *U.S.A.* 109 H7
Hebbronville, *U.S.A.* 109 M5
Hebei □, *China* 50 E9
Hebel, *Australia* 91 D4
Heber, *U.S.A.* 113 N11
Heber Springs, *U.S.A.* 109 H9
Hebert, *Canada* 101 C7
Hebgen L., *U.S.A.* 110 D8
Hebi, *China* 50 G8
Hebrides, *U.K.* 14 D1
Hebron = Al Khalīl, *West Bank* 69 D4
Hebron, *Canada* 97 C13
Hebron, *N. Dak., U.S.A.* 108 B3
Hebron, *Nebr., U.S.A.* 108 E6
Hecate Str., *Canada* 100 C2
Hechi, *China* 52 E7
Hechingen, *Germany* 19 G4
Hechtel, *Belgium* 17 F6
Hechuan, *China* 52 B6
Hecla, *U.S.A.* 108 C5
Hecla I., *Canada* 101 C9
Heddal, *Norway* 10 E3
Hédé, *France* 24 D5
Hede, *Sweden* 10 B7
Hedemora, *Sweden* 9 F16
Hedley, *U.S.A.* 109 H4
Hedmark fylke □, *Norway* 10 C5
Hedrum, *Norway* 10 E4
Heeg, *Neths.* 16 C7
Heegermeer, *Neths.* 16 C7
Heemskerk, *Neths.* 16 C5
Heemstede, *Neths.* 16 D5
Heer, *Neths.* 17 G7
Heerde, *Neths.* 16 D8
's Heerenburg, *Neths.* 16 E8
Heerenveen, *Neths.* 16 C7
Heerhugowaard, *Neths.* 16 C5
Heerlen, *Neths.* 17 G7
Heers, *Belgium* 17 G6
Heesch, *Neths.* 16 E7
Heestert, *Belgium* 17 G2

Heeze, *Neths.* 17 F7
Ḥefa, *Israel* 69 C3
Ḥefa □, *Israel* 69 C4
Hefei, *China* 53 B11
Hegang, *China* 54 B8
Hegyalja, *Hungary* 21 G11
Heichengzhen, *China* 50 F4
Heide, *Germany* 18 A5
Heidelberg, *Germany* 19 F4
Heidelberg, *S. Africa* 84 E3
Heidenheim, *Germany* 19 G6
Heijing, *China* 52 E3
Heilbron, *S. Africa* 85 D4
Heilbronn, *Germany* 19 F5
Heiligenblut, *Austria* 21 H2
Heiligenhafen, *Germany* 18 A6
Heiligenstadt, *Germany* 18 D6
Heilongjiang □, *China* 51 B14
Heilunkiang = Heilongjiang □, *China* 51 B14
Heimaey, *Iceland* 8 E3
Heino, *Neths.* 16 D8
Heinola, *Finland* 9 F22
Heinsch, *Belgium* 17 J7
Heinze Is., *Burma* 61 M20
Heishan, *China* 51 D12
Heishui, *Liaoning, China* 51 C10
Heishui, *Sichuan, China* 52 A4
Heist, *Belgium* 17 F2
Heist-op-den-Berg, *Belgium* 17 F5
Hejaz = Al Ḥijāz, *Si. Arabia* 68 B2
Hejian, *China* 50 E9
Hejiang, *China* 52 C5
Hejin, *China* 50 G6
Hekelgem, *Belgium* 17 G4
Hekımhan, *Turkey* 66 C7
Hekla, *Iceland* 8 E4
Hekou, *Gansu, China* 50 F2
Hekou, *Guangdong, China* 53 F9
Hekou, *Yunnan, China* 54 D5
Helagsfjället, *Sweden* 10 B6
Helan Shan, *China* 50 E3
Helchteren, *Belgium* 17 F6
Helden, *Neths.* 17 F7
Helechosa, *Spain* 31 F6
Helena, *Ark., U.S.A.* 109 H9
Helena, *Mont., U.S.A.* 110 C7
Helendale, *U.S.A.* 113 L9
Helensburgh, *U.K.* 14 E4
Helensville, *N.Z.* 87 G5
Helgeland, *Norway* 8 C15
Helgeroa, *Norway* 10 F3
Helgoland, *Germany* 18 A3
Heligoland = Helgoland, *Germany* 18 A3
Heligoland B. = Deutsche Bucht, *Germany* 18 A4
Heliopolis, *Egypt* 76 H7
Hella, *Iceland* 8 E3
Hellebæk, *Denmark* 11 H6
Hellendoorn, *Neths.* 16 D8
Hellevoetsluis, *Neths.* 16 E4
Hellín, *Spain* 29 G3
Helmand □, *Afghan.* 60 D4
Helmand →, *Afghan.* 60 D2
Helme →, *Germany* 18 D7
Helmond, *Neths.* 17 F7
Helmsdale, *U.K.* 14 C5
Helmstedt, *Germany* 18 C7
Helnæs, *Denmark* 11 J4
Helong, *China* 51 C15
Helper, *U.S.A.* 110 G8
Helsingborg, *Sweden* 11 H6
Helsinge, *Denmark* 11 H6
Helsingfors = Helsinki, *Finland* 9 F21
Helsingør, *Denmark* 11 H6
Helsinki, *Finland* 9 F21
Helston, *U.K.* 13 G2
Helvellyn, *U.K.* 12 C4
Helvoirt, *Neths.* 17 E6
Helwân, *Egypt* 76 J7
Hemet, *U.S.A.* 113 M10
Hemingford, *U.S.A.* 108 D3
Hemphill, *U.S.A.* 109 K8
Hempstead, *U.S.A.* 109 K6
Hemse, *Sweden* 9 H18
Hemsö, *Sweden* 10 B12
Henan □, *China* 50 G8
Henares →, *Spain* 28 E1
Henashi-Misaki, *Japan* 48 D9
Hendaye, *France* 26 E2
Hendek, *Turkey* 66 B4
Henderson, *Argentina* 126 D3
Henderson, *Ky., U.S.A.* 104 G2
Henderson, *N.C., U.S.A.* 105 G6
Henderson, *Nev., U.S.A.* 113 J12
Henderson, *Tenn., U.S.A.* 105 H1
Henderson, *Tex., U.S.A.* 109 J7
Hendersonville, *U.S.A.* 105 H4
Hendījān, *Iran* 65 D6
Hendon, *Australia* 91 D5
Heng Xian, *China* 52 F7
Hengcheng, *China* 50 E4
Hengdaohezi, *China* 51 B15
Hengelo, *Gelderland, Neths.* 16 D8
Hengelo, *Overijssel, Neths.* 16 D9
Hengfeng, *China* 53 C10
Hengshan, *Hunan, China* 53 D9
Hengshan, *Shaanxi, China* 50 F5
Hengshui, *China* 50 F8
Hengyang, *Hunan, China* 53 D9
Hengyang, *Hunan, China* 53 D9
Henichesk, *Ukraine* 41 J8
Hénin-Beaumont, *France* 25 B9
Henlopen, C., *U.S.A.* 104 F8
Hennan, *Sweden* 10 B9
Hennebont, *France* 24 E3
Hennenman, *S. Africa* 84 D4
Hennessey, *U.S.A.* 109 G6
Hennigsdorf, *Germany* 18 C9
Henrichemont, *France* 25 E9
Henrietta, *U.S.A.* 109 J5
Henrietta, Ostrov, *Russia* 45 B16
Henrietta Maria, C., *Canada* 98 A3
Henry, *U.S.A.* 108 E10
Henryetta, *U.S.A.* 109 H6
Hensall, *Canada* 106 C3
Hentiyn Nuruu, *Mongolia* 54 B5
Henty, *Australia* 91 F4
Henzada, *Burma* 61 L19
Heping, *China* 53 E10
Heppner, *U.S.A.* 110 D4
Hepu, *China* 52 G7
Hepworth, *Canada* 106 B3
Heqing, *China* 52 D3
Hequ, *China* 50 E6
Héraðsflói, *Iceland* 8 D6
Héraðsvötn →, *Iceland* 8 D4
Herald Cays, *Australia* 90 B4
Herāt, *Afghan.* 60 B3
Herāt □, *Afghan.* 60 B3
Hérault □, *France* 26 E7
Hérault →, *France* 26 E7
Herbault, *France* 24 E8
Herbert →, *Australia* 90 B4
Herbert Downs, *Australia* 90 C2
Herberton, *Australia* 90 B4
Herbignac, *France* 24 E4
Herborn, *Germany* 18 E4
Herby, *Poland* 20 E8
Hercegnovi, *Montenegro, Yug.* 21 N8
Herðubreið, *Iceland* 8 D5
Hereford, *U.K.* 13 E5
Hereford, *U.S.A.* 109 H3
Hereford and Worcester □, *U.K.* 13 E5
Herefoss, *Norway* 11 F2
Herent, *Belgium* 17 G5
Herentals, *Belgium* 17 F5
Herenthout, *Belgium* 17 F5
Herfølge, *Denmark* 11 J6
Herford, *Germany* 18 C4
Héricourt, *France* 25 E13
Herington, *U.S.A.* 108 F6
Herisau, *Switz.* 23 B8
Hérisson, *France* 26 B6
Herk →, *Belgium* 17 G6
Herkenbosch, *Neths.* 17 F8
Herkimer, *U.S.A.* 107 D10
Herlong, *U.S.A.* 112 E6
Herm, *U.K.* 24 C4
Hermagor-Pressegger See, *Austria* 21 J3
Herman, *U.S.A.* 108 C6
Hermann, *U.S.A.* 108 F9
Hermannsburg, *Germany* 18 C6
Hermannsburg Mission, *Australia* 88 D5
Hermanus, *S. Africa* 84 E2
Herment, *France* 26 C6
Hermidale, *Australia* 91 E4
Hermiston, *U.S.A.* 110 D4
Hermitage, *N.Z.* 87 K3
Hermite, I., *Chile* 128 E3
Hermon, Mt. = Ash Shaykh, J., *Lebanon* 69 B4
Hermosillo, *Mexico* 114 B2
Hernád →, *Hungary* 21 H11
Hernandarias, *Paraguay* 127 B5
Hernandez, *U.S.A.* 112 J6
Hernando, *Argentina* 126 C3
Hernando, *U.S.A.* 109 H10
Herne, *Belgium* 17 G4
Herne, *Germany* 17 E10
Herne Bay, *U.K.* 13 F9
Herning, *Denmark* 11 H2
Heroica = Caborca, *Mexico* 114 A2
Heroica Nogales = Nogales, *Mexico* 114 A2
Heron Bay, *Canada* 98 C2
Herradura, Pta. de la, *Canary Is.* 36 F5
Herreid, *U.S.A.* 108 C4
Herrera, *Spain* 31 H6
Herrera de Alcántar, *Spain* 31 F3
Herrera de Pisuerga, *Spain* 30 C6
Herrera del Duque, *Spain* 31 F5
Herrick, *Australia* 90 G4
Herrin, *U.S.A.* 109 G10
Herrljunga, *Sweden* 11 F7
Hersbruck, *Germany* 19 F7
Herseaux, *Belgium* 17 G2
Herselt, *Belgium* 17 F5
Hersonissos, *Greece* 37 D7
Herstal, *Belgium* 17 G7
Hertford, *U.K.* 13 F7
Hertfordshire □, *U.K.* 13 F7
's-Hertogenbosch, *Neths.* 17 E6
Hertzogville, *S. Africa* 84 D4
Hervás, *Spain* 30 E5
Herve, *Belgium* 17 G7
Herwijnen, *Neths.* 16 E6
Herzberg, *Brandenburg, Germany* 18 D9
Herzberg, *Niedersachsen, Germany* 18 D6
Herzele, *Belgium* 17 G3
Herzliyya, *Israel* 69 C3
Herzogenbuchsee, *Switz.* 22 B5
Ḥeşār, *Fārs, Iran* 65 D6
Ḥeşār, *Markazī, Iran* 65 C6
Hesdin, *France* 25 B9
Hesel, *Germany* 18 B3
Heshui, *China* 50 G5
Heshun, *China* 50 F7
Hesperange, *Lux.* 17 J8
Hesperia, *U.S.A.* 113 L9
Hesse = Hessen □, *Germany* 18 E5
Hessen □, *Germany* 18 E5
Hetch Hetchy Aqueduct, *U.S.A.* 112 H5
Hettinger, *U.S.A.* 108 C3
Hettstedt, *Germany* 18 D7
Heugem, *Neths.* 17 G7
Heule, *Belgium* 17 G2
Heusden, *Belgium* 17 F6
Heusden, *Neths.* 16 E6
Hève, C. de la, *France* 24 C7
Heverlee, *Belgium* 17 G5
Hewett, C., *Canada* 97 A13
Hexham, *U.K.* 12 C5
Hexi, *Yunnan, China* 52 E4
Hexi, *Zhejiang, China* 53 D12
Hexigten Qi, *China* 51 C9
Ḥeydarābād, *Iran* 65 D7
Heyfield, *Australia* 91 F4
Heysham, *U.K.* 12 C5
Heythuysen, *Neths.* 17 F7
Heyuan, *China* 53 F10
Heywood, *Australia* 91 F3
Heze, *China* 50 G8
Hezhang, *China* 52 D5
Hi Vista, *U.S.A.* 113 L9
Hialeah, *U.S.A.* 105 N5
Hiawatha, *Kans., U.S.A.* 108 F7
Hiawatha, *Utah, U.S.A.* 110 G8
Hibbing, *U.S.A.* 108 B8
Hibbs B., *Australia* 90 G4
Hibernia Reef, *Australia* 88 B3
Hickory, *U.S.A.* 105 H5
Hicks, Pt., *Australia* 91 F4
Hicksville, *U.S.A.* 107 F11
Hida, *Romania* 38 B6
Hida-Gawa →, *Japan* 49 G8
Hida-Sammyaku, *Japan* 49 F8
Hidaka-Sammyaku, *Japan* 48 C11
Hidalgo, *Mexico* 115 C5
Hidalgo □, *Mexico* 115 C5
Hidalgo, Presa M., *Mexico* 114 B3
Hidalgo, Pta. del, *Canary Is.* 36 F3
Hidalgo del Parral, *Mexico* 114 B3
Hiddensee, *Germany* 18 A9
Hidrolândia, *Brazil* 123 E2
Hieflau, *Austria* 21 H4
Hiendelaencina, *Spain* 28 D1
Hierro, *Canary Is.* 36 G1
Higashiajima-San, *Japan* 48 F10
Higashiōsaka, *Japan* 49 G7
Higgins, *U.S.A.* 109 G4
Higgins Corner, *U.S.A.* 112 F5
Higginsville, *Australia* 89 F3
High Atlas = Haut Atlas, *Morocco* 74 B3
High I., *Canada* 99 A7
High Island, *U.S.A.* 109 L7
High Level, *Canada* 100 B5
High Point, *U.S.A.* 105 H6
High Prairie, *Canada* 100 B5
High River, *Canada* 100 C6
High Springs, *U.S.A.* 105 L4
High Tatra = Tatry, *Slovak Rep.* 20 F9
High Veld, *Africa* 70 J6
High Wycombe, *U.K.* 13 F7
Highbury, *Australia* 90 B3
Highland □, *U.K.* 14 D4
Highland Park, *U.S.A.* 104 D2
Highmore, *U.S.A.* 108 C5
Highrock L., *Canada* 101 B7
Higüay, *Dom. Rep.* 117 C6
Hihya, *Egypt* 76 H7
Hiiumaa, *Estonia* 9 G20
Híjar, *Spain* 28 D4
Ḥijāz □, *Si. Arabia* 68 C2
Hijken, *Neths.* 16 C8
Hijo = Tagum, *Phil.* 55 H6
Hikari, *Japan* 49 H5
Hiko, *U.S.A.* 111 H6
Hikone, *Japan* 49 G8
Hikurangi, *N.Z.* 87 F5
Hikurangi, Mt., *N.Z.* 87 H6
Hildburghausen, *Germany* 19 E6
Hildesheim, *Germany* 18 C5
Hill →, *Australia* 89 F2
Hill City, *Idaho, U.S.A.* 110 E6
Hill City, *Kans., U.S.A.* 108 F5
Hill City, *Minn., U.S.A.* 108 B8
Hill City, *S. Dak., U.S.A.* 108 D3
Hill Island L., *Canada* 101 A7
Hillared, *Sweden* 11 G7
Hillcrest Center, *U.S.A.* 113 K8
Hillegom, *Neths.* 16 D5
Hillerød, *Denmark* 11 J6
Hillingdon, *U.K.* 13 F7
Hillman, *U.S.A.* 104 C4
Hillmond, *Canada* 101 C7
Hillsboro, *Kans., U.S.A.* 108 F6
Hillsboro, *N. Dak., U.S.A.* 108 B6
Hillsboro, *N.H., U.S.A.* 107 C13
Hillsboro, *N. Mex., U.S.A.* 111 K10
Hillsboro, *Oreg., U.S.A.* 112 E4
Hillsboro, *Tex., U.S.A.* 109 J6
Hillsborough, *Grenada* 117 D7
Hillsdale, *Mich., U.S.A.* 104 E3
Hillsdale, *N.Y., U.S.A.* 107 D11
Hillside, *Australia* 88 D2
Hillsport, *Canada* 98 C2
Hillston, *Australia* 91 E4
Hilo, *U.S.A.* 102 J17
Hilton, *U.S.A.* 106 C7
Hilvan, *Turkey* 67 D8
Hilvarenbeek, *Neths.* 17 F6
Hilversum, *Neths.* 16 D6
Himachal Pradesh □, *India* 62 D7
Himalaya, *Asia* 63 E11
Himamaylan, *Phil.* 55 F5
Himara, *Albania* 39 J2
Himatnagar, *India* 60 H8
Himeji, *Japan* 49 G7
Himi, *Japan* 49 F8
Himmerland, *Denmark* 11 H3
Ḥimş, *Syria* 69 A5
Ḥimş □, *Syria* 69 A5
Hinche, *Haiti* 117 C5
Hinchinbrook I., *Australia* 90 B4
Hinckley, *U.K.* 13 E6
Hinckley, *U.S.A.* 110 G7
Hindås, *Sweden* 11 G6
Hindaun, *India* 62 F7
Hindmarsh, L., *Australia* 91 F3
Hindsholm, *Denmark* 11 J4
Hindu Bagh, *Pakistan* 62 D2
Hindu Kush, *Asia* 60 B7
Hindubagh, *Pakistan* 60 D5
Hindupur, *India* 60 N10
Hines Creek, *Canada* 100 B5
Hinganghat, *India* 60 J11
Hingeon, *Belgium* 17 G5
Hingham, *U.S.A.* 110 B8
Hingoli, *India* 60 K10
Hinigaran, *Phil.* 55 F5
Hinis, *Turkey* 67 C9
Hinna = Imi, *Ethiopia* 68 F3
Hinna, *Nigeria* 79 C7
Hinnøya, *Norway* 8 B16
Hinojosa del Duque, *Spain* 31 G5
Hinsdale, *U.S.A.* 110 B10
Hinterrhein →, *Switz.* 23 C8
Hinton, *Canada* 100 C5
Hinton, *U.S.A.* 104 G5
Hinwil, *Switz.* 23 B7
Hınzır Burnu, *Turkey* 66 D6
Hippolytushoef, *Neths.* 16 C5
Hirado, *Japan* 49 H4
Hirakud Dam, *India* 61 J13
Hiratsuka, *Japan* 49 G9
Hirfanlı Baraji, *Turkey* 66 C5
Hirhafok, *Algeria* 75 D6
Hîrlău, *Romania* 38 B9
Hiroo, *Japan* 48 C11
Hirosaki, *Japan* 48 D10
Hiroshima, *Japan* 49 G6
Hiroshima □, *Japan* 49 G6
Hirsholmene, *Denmark* 11 G4
Hirson, *France* 25 C11
Hîrşova, *Romania* 38 E10
Hirtshals, *Denmark* 11 G3
Hisar, *India* 62 E6
Hisb →, *Iraq* 64 D5
Ḥismá, *Si. Arabia* 64 D3
Hispaniola, *W. Indies* 117 C5
Hīt, *Iraq* 67 F10
Hita, *Japan* 49 H5
Hitachi, *Japan* 49 F10
Hitchin, *U.K.* 13 F7
Hitoyoshi, *Japan* 49 H5
Hitra, *Norway* 8 E13
Hitzacker, *Germany* 18 B7
Ḥiyyon, N. →, *Israel* 69 E4
Hjalmar L., *Canada* 101 A7
Hjälmare kanal, *Sweden* 10 E9
Hjälmaren, *Sweden* 10 E9
Hjartdal, *Norway* 10 E2
Hjerkinn, *Norway* 10 B3
Hjørring, *Denmark* 11 G3
Hjortkvarn, *Sweden* 11 F9
Hlinsko, *Czech.* 20 F5
Hluhluwe, *S. Africa* 85 D5
Hlukhiv, *Ukraine* 41 G7
Hlyboka, *Ukraine* 41 H3
Hlybokaye, *Belarus* 40 E4
Ho, *Ghana* 79 D5
Ho Chi Minh City = Phanh Bho Ho Chi Minh, *Vietnam* 59 G6
Ho Thuong, *Vietnam* 58 C5
Hoa Binh, *Vietnam* 58 B5
Hoa Da, *Vietnam* 59 G7
Hoa Hiep, *Vietnam* 59 G5
Hoai Nhon, *Vietnam* 58 E7
Hoang Lien Son, *Vietnam* 58 A4
Hoare B., *Canada* 97 B13
Hobart, *Australia* 90 G4
Hobart, *U.S.A.* 109 H5
Hobbs, *U.S.A.* 109 J3
Hobbs Coast, *Antarctica* 5 D14
Hobo, *Colombia* 120 C2
Hoboken, *Belgium* 17 F4
Hoboken, *U.S.A.* 107 F10
Hobro, *Denmark* 11 H3
Hobscheid, *Lux.* 17 J7
Hoburgen, *Sweden* 9 H18
Hochdorf, *Switz.* 23 B6
Hochschwab, *Austria* 21 H5
Höchstadt, *Germany* 19 F6
Hockenheim, *Germany* 19 F4
Hodaka-Dake, *Japan* 49 F8
Hodgson, *Canada* 101 C9
Hódmezövásárhely, *Hungary* 21 J10
Hodna, Chott el, *Algeria* 75 A5
Hodna, Monts du, *Algeria* 75 A5
Hodonín, *Czech.* 20 G7
Hoeamdong, *N. Korea* 51 C16
Hœdic, I. de, *France* 24 E4
Hoegaarden, *Belgium* 17 G5
Hoek van Holland, *Neths.* 16 E4
Hoeksche Waard, *Neths.* 16 E4
Hoenderloo, *Neths.* 16 D7
Hoengsŏng, *S. Korea* 51 F14
Hoensbroek, *Neths.* 17 G7
Hoeryong, *N. Korea* 51 C15
Hoeselt, *Belgium* 17 G6
Hoeven, *Neths.* 17 E5
Hoeyang, *N. Korea* 51 E14
Hof, *Germany* 19 E7
Hofgeismar, *Germany* 18 D5
Hofmeyr, *S. Africa* 84 E4
Höfn, *Iceland* 8 D6
Hofors, *Sweden* 9 F17
Hofsjökull, *Iceland* 8 D4
Hōfu, *Japan* 49 G5
Hogan Group, *Australia* 90 F4
Hogansville, *U.S.A.* 105 J3
Hogeland, *U.S.A.* 110 B9
Hoggar = Ahaggar, *Algeria* 75 D6
Högsäter, *Sweden* 11 F6
Hogsty Reef, *Bahamas* 117 B5
Hoh →, *U.S.A.* 112 C2
Hoh Xil Shan, *China* 54 C3
Hohe Rhön, *Germany* 19 E5
Hohe Tauern, *Austria* 21 H2
Hohe Venn, *Belgium* 17 H8
Hohenau, *Austria* 20 G6
Hohenems, *Austria* 19 H5
Hohenstein-Ernstthal, *Germany* 18 E8
Hohenwald, *U.S.A.* 105 H2
Hohenwestedt, *Germany* 18 A5
Hohhot, *China* 50 D6
Hóhlakas, *Greece* 37 D9
Hohoe, *Ghana* 79 D5
Hoi An, *Vietnam* 58 E7
Hoi Xuan, *Vietnam* 58 B5
Hoisington, *U.S.A.* 108 F5
Højer, *Denmark* 11 K2
Hōjō, *Japan* 49 H6
Hökerum, *Sweden* 11 G7
Hokianga Harbour, *N.Z.* 87 F4
Hokitika, *N.Z.* 87 K3
Hokkaidō □, *Japan* 48 C11
Hokksund, *Norway* 10 E3
Hol-Hol, *Djibouti* 77 E5
Hola Pristan, *Ukraine* 41 J7
Holbæk, *Denmark* 11 J5
Holbrook, *Australia* 91 F4
Holbrook, *U.S.A.* 111 J8
Holden, *Canada* 100 C6
Holden, *U.S.A.* 110 G7
Holdenville, *U.S.A.* 109 H6
Holderness, *U.K.* 12 D7
Holdfast, *Canada* 101 C7
Holdich, *Argentina* 128 C3
Holdrege, *U.S.A.* 108 E5
Holguín, *Cuba* 116 B4
Hollabrunn, *Austria* 20 G6
Hollams Bird I., *Namibia* 84 C1
Holland, *U.S.A.* 104 D2
Hollandia = Jayapura, *Indonesia* 57 E10
Hollandsch Diep, *Neths.* 17 E5
Hollandsch IJssel →, *Neths.* 16 E5
Hollfeld, *Germany* 19 F7
Hollidaysburg, *U.S.A.* 106 F6
Hollis, *U.S.A.* 109 H5
Hollister, *Calif., U.S.A.* 111 H3
Hollister, *Idaho, U.S.A.* 110 E6
Hollum, *Neths.* 16 B7
Holly, *U.S.A.* 108 F3
Holly Hill, *U.S.A.* 105 L5
Holly Springs, *U.S.A.* 109 H10
Hollywood, *Calif., U.S.A.* 111 J4
Hollywood, *Fla., U.S.A.* 105 N5
Holm, *Sweden* 10 B10
Holman Island, *Canada* 96 A8
Hólmavík, *Iceland* 8 D3
Holmes Reefs, *Australia* 90 B4
Holmestrand, *Norway* 10 E4
Holmsbu, *Norway* 10 E4
Holmsjön, *Sweden* 10 B9
Holmsland Klit, *Denmark* 11 J2
Holmsund, *Sweden* 8 E19
Holroyd →, *Australia* 90 A3
Holstebro, *Denmark* 11 H2
Holsworthy, *U.K.* 13 G3
Holte, *Denmark* 11 J6
Holten, *Neths.* 16 D8
Holton, *Canada* 99 B8
Holton, *U.S.A.* 108 F7
Holtville, *U.S.A.* 113 N11
Holwerd, *Neths.* 16 B7
Holy Cross, *U.S.A.* 96 B4
Holy I., *Angl., U.K.* 12 D3
Holy I., *Northumb., U.K.* 12 B6
Holyhead, *U.K.* 12 D3
Holyoke, *Colo., U.S.A.* 108 E3
Holyoke, *Mass., U.S.A.* 107 D12
Holyrood, *Canada* 99 C9
Holzkirchen, *Germany* 19 H7
Holzminden, *Germany* 18 D5
Homa Bay, *Kenya* 82 C3
Homa Bay □, *Kenya* 82 C3
Homalin, *Burma* 61 G19
Homand, *Iran* 65 C8
Homberg, *Germany* 18 D5
Hombori, *Mali* 79 B4
Homburg, *Germany* 19 F3

Home B., *Canada* 97 B13
Home Hill, *Australia* 90 B4
Homedale, *U.S.A.* 110 E5
Homer, *Alaska, U.S.A.* 96 C4
Homer, *La., U.S.A.* 109 J8
Homestead, *Australia* 90 C4
Homestead, *Fla., U.S.A.* 105 N5
Homestead, *Oreg., U.S.A.* 110 D5
Homewood, *U.S.A.* 112 F6
Hominy, *U.S.A.* 109 G6
Homoine, *Mozam.* 85 C6
Homoljske Planina, *Serbia, Yug.* 21 L11
Homorod, *Romania* 38 C8
Homs = Ḥimş, *Syria* 69 A5
Homyel, *Belarus* 41 F6
Hon Chong, *Vietnam* 59 G5
Hon Me, *Vietnam* 58 C5
Hon Quan, *Vietnam* 59 G6
Honan = Henan □, *China* 50 G8
Honbetsu, *Japan* 48 C11
Honcut, *U.S.A.* 112 F5
Honda, *Colombia* 120 B3
Honda Bay, *Phil.* 55 G3
Hondeklipbaai, *S. Africa* 84 E2
Hondo, *Japan* 49 H5
Hondo, *U.S.A.* 109 L5
Hondo →, *Belize* 115 D7
Honduras ■, *Cent. Amer.* 116 D2
Honduras, G. de, *Caribbean* 116 C2
Hønefoss, *Norway* 9 F14
Honesdale, *U.S.A.* 107 E9
Honey L., *U.S.A.* 112 E6
Honfleur, *France* 24 C7
Hong Gai, *Vietnam* 58 B6
Hong He →, *China* 50 H8
Hong Kong ■, *Asia* 53 F10
Hong'an, *China* 53 B10
Hongchŏn, *S. Korea* 51 F14
Honghai Wan, *China* 53 F10
Honghu, *China* 53 C9
Hongjiang, *China* 52 D7
Hongliu He →, *China* 50 F5
Hongor, *Mongolia* 50 B7
Hongsa, *Laos* 58 C3
Hongshui He →, *China* 52 F7
Hongsŏng, *S. Korea* 51 F14
Hongtong, *China* 50 F6
Honguedo, Détroit d', *Canada* 99 C7
Hongwon, *N. Korea* 51 E14
Hongya, *China* 52 C4
Hongyuan, *China* 52 A4
Hongze Hu, *China* 51 H10
Honiara, *Solomon Is.* 92 H7
Honiton, *U.K.* 13 G4
Honjō, *Japan* 48 E10
Honkorâb, Ras, *Egypt* 76 C4
Honningsvåg, *Norway* 8 A21
Honolulu, *U.S.A.* 102 H16
Honshū, *Japan* 49 G9
Hontoria del Pinar, *Spain* 28 D1
Hood, Mt., *U.S.A.* 110 D3
Hood, Pt., *Australia* 89 F2
Hood River, *U.S.A.* 110 D3
Hoodsport, *U.S.A.* 112 C3
Hooge, *Germany* 18 A4
Hoogerheide, *Neths.* 17 F4
Hoogeveen, *Neths.* 16 C8
Hoogeveensche Vaart, *Neths.* 16 C8
Hoogezand, *Neths.* 16 B9
Hooghly → = Hugli →, *India* 63 J13
Hooghly-Chinsura = Chunchura, *India* 63 H13
Hoogkerk, *Neths.* 16 B9
Hoogledе, *Belgium* 17 G2
Hoogstraten, *Belgium* 17 F5
Hoogvliet, *Neths.* 16 E4
Hook Hd., *Ireland* 15 D5
Hook I., *Australia* 90 C4
Hook of Holland = Hoek van Holland, *Neths.* 16 E4
Hooker, *U.S.A.* 109 G4
Hooker Creek, *Australia* 88 C5
Hoopeston, *U.S.A.* 104 E2
Hoopstad, *S. Africa* 84 D4
Hoorn, *Neths.* 16 C6
Hoover Dam, *U.S.A.* 113 K12
Hooversville, *U.S.A.* 106 F6
Hop Bottom, *U.S.A.* 107 E9
Hopa, *Turkey* 67 B9
Hope, *Canada* 100 D4
Hope, *Ariz., U.S.A.* 113 M13
Hope, *Ark., U.S.A.* 109 J8
Hope, *N. Dak., U.S.A.* 108 B6
Hope, L., *Australia* 91 D2
Hope, Pt., *U.S.A.* 96 B3
Hope Town, *Bahamas* 116 A4
Hopedale, *Canada* 99 A7
Hopefield, *S. Africa* 84 E2
Hopei = Hebei □, *China* 50 E9
Hopelchén, *Mexico* 115 D7
Hopetoun, *Vic., Australia* 91 F3
Hopetoun, *W. Austral., Australia* 89 F3
Hopetown, *S. Africa* 84 D3
Hopkins, *U.S.A.* 108 E7
Hopkins, L., *Australia* 88 D4
Hopkinsville, *U.S.A.* 105 G2
Hopland, *U.S.A.* 112 G3
Hoptrup, *Denmark* 11 J3
Hoquiam, *U.S.A.* 112 D3
Horasan, *Turkey* 67 B10
Horcajo de Santiago, *Spain* 28 F1
Horden Hills, *Australia* 88 D5
Horezu, *Romania* 38 D6
Horgen, *Switz.* 23 B7
Horinger, *China* 50 D6
Horki, *Belarus* 40 E6
Horlick Mts., *Antarctica* 5 E15
Horlivka, *Ukraine* 41 H10
Hormoz, *Iran* 65 E7
Hormoz, Jaz. ye, *Iran* 65 E8
Hormuz, Str. of, *The Gulf* 65 E8
Horn, *Iceland* 8 C2
Horn, *Neths.* 17 F7
Horn →, *Canada* 100 A5
Horn, Cape = Hornos, C. de, *Chile* 128 E3
Horn Head, *Ireland* 15 A3
Horn I., *Australia* 90 A3
Horn I., *U.S.A.* 105 K1
Horn Mts., *Canada* 100 A5
Hornachuelos, *Spain* 31 H5
Hornavan, *Sweden* 8 C17
Hornbæk, *Denmark* 11 H6
Hornbeck, *U.S.A.* 109 K8
Hornbrook, *U.S.A.* 110 F2
Hornburg, *Germany* 18 C6
Horncastle, *U.K.* 12 D7
Hornell, *U.S.A.* 106 D7
Hornell L., *Canada* 100 A5
Hornepayne, *Canada* 98 C3
Hornitos, *U.S.A.* 112 H6
Hornos, C. de, *Chile* 128 E3
Hornoy, *France* 25 C8
Hornsby, *Australia* 91 E5
Hornsea, *U.K.* 12 D7
Hornslandet, *Sweden* 10 C11
Hornslet, *Denmark* 11 H4
Hornu, *Belgium* 17 H3
Hörnum, *Germany* 18 A4
Horobetsu, *Japan* 48 C10
Horodenka, *Ukraine* 41 H3
Horodnya, *Ukraine* 41 G6
Horodok, *Khmelnytskyy, Ukraine* 41 H4
Horodok, *Lviv, Ukraine* 41 H2
Horodyshche, *Ukraine* 41 H6
Horokhiv, *Ukraine* 41 G3
Horqin Youyi Qianqi, *China* 51 A12
Horqueta, *Paraguay* 126 A4
Horred, *Sweden* 11 G6
Horse Creek, *U.S.A.* 108 E3
Horse Is., *Canada* 99 B8
Horsefly L., *Canada* 100 C4
Horsens, *Denmark* 11 J3
Horsens Fjord, *Denmark* 11 J4
Horsham, *Australia* 91 F3
Horsham, *U.K.* 13 F7
Horst, *Neths.* 17 F8
Horten, *Norway* 10 E4
Hortobágy →, *Hungary* 21 H11
Horton, *U.S.A.* 108 F7
Horton →, *Canada* 96 B7
Horw, *Switz.* 23 B6
Horwood, L., *Canada* 98 C3
Hosaina, *Ethiopia* 77 F4
Hose, Gunung-Gunung, *Malaysia* 56 D4
Ḥoseynābād, *Khuzestān, Iran* 65 C6
Ḥoseynābād, *Kordestān, Iran* 67 E12
Hoshangabad, *India* 62 H7
Hoshiarpur, *India* 62 D6
Hosingen, *Lux.* 17 H8
Hosmer, *U.S.A.* 108 C5
Hospental, *Switz.* 23 C7
Hospet, *India* 60 M10
Hospitalet de Llobregat, *Spain* 28 D7
Hoste, I., *Chile* 128 E3
Hostens, *France* 26 D3
Hot, *Thailand* 58 C2
Hot Creek Range, *U.S.A.* 110 G5
Hot Springs, *Ark., U.S.A.* 109 H8
Hot Springs, *S. Dak., U.S.A.* 108 D3
Hotagen, *Sweden* 8 E16
Hotan, *China* 54 C2
Hotazel, *S. Africa* 84 D3
Hotchkiss, *U.S.A.* 111 G10
Hotham, C., *Australia* 88 B5
Hoting, *Sweden* 8 D17
Hotte, Massif de la, *Haiti* 117 C5
Hottentotsbaai, *Namibia* 84 D1
Hotton, *Belgium* 17 H6
Houat, I. de, *France* 24 E4
Houck, *U.S.A.* 111 J9
Houdan, *France* 25 D8
Houdeng-Goegnies, *Belgium* 17 H4
Houei Sai, *Laos* 58 B3
Houffalize, *Belgium* 17 H7
Houghton, *U.S.A.* 108 B10
Houghton L., *U.S.A.* 104 C3
Houghton-le-Spring, *U.K.* 12 C6
Houhora Heads, *N.Z.* 87 F4
Houille →, *Belgium* 17 H5
Houlton, *U.S.A.* 99 C6
Houma, *U.S.A.* 109 L9
Houndé, *Burkina Faso* 78 C4
Hourtin, *France* 26 C2
Hourtin-Carcans, Étang d', *France* 26 C2
Houston, *Canada* 100 C3
Houston, *Mo., U.S.A.* 109 G9
Houston, *Tex., U.S.A.* 109 L7
Houten, *Neths.* 16 D6
Houthalen, *Belgium* 17 F6
Houthem, *Belgium* 17 G1
Houthulst, *Belgium* 17 G2
Houtman Abrolhos, *Australia* 89 E1
Houyet, *Belgium* 17 H6
Hov, *Denmark* 11 J4
Hova, *Sweden* 11 F8
Høvåg, *Norway* 11 F2
Hovd, *Mongolia* 54 B4
Hove, *U.K.* 13 G7
Hoveyzeh, *Iran* 65 D6
Hövsgöl, *Mongolia* 50 C5
Hövsgöl Nuur, *Mongolia* 54 A5
Howakil, *Eritrea* 77 D5
Howar, Wadi →, *Sudan* 77 D2
Howard, *Australia* 91 D5
Howard, *Kans., U.S.A.* 109 G6
Howard, *Pa., U.S.A.* 106 E7
Howard, *S. Dak., U.S.A.* 108 C6
Howard I., *Australia* 90 A2
Howard L., *Canada* 101 A7
Howe, *U.S.A.* 110 E7
Howe, C., *Australia* 91 F5
Howell, *U.S.A.* 104 D4
Howick, *Canada* 107 A11
Howick, *S. Africa* 85 D5
Howick Group, *Australia* 90 A4
Howitt, L., *Australia* 91 D2
Howland I., *Pac. Oc.* 92 G10
Howley, *Canada* 99 C8
Howrah = Haora, *India* 63 H13
Howth Hd., *Ireland* 15 C5
Höxter, *Germany* 18 D5
Hoy, *U.K.* 14 C5
Hoya, *Germany* 18 C5
Høyanger, *Norway* 9 F12
Hoyerswerda, *Germany* 18 D10
Hoyos, *Spain* 30 E4
Hpungan Pass, *Burma* 61 F20
Hradec Králové, *Czech.* 20 E5
Hranice, *Czech.* 20 F7
Hrazdan, *Armenia* 43 K7
Hrebenka, *Ukraine* 41 G7
Hrodna, *Belarus* 40 F2
Hrodzyanka, *Belarus* 40 F5
Hron →, *Slovak Rep.* 21 H8
Hrubieszów, *Poland* 20 E13
Hrvatska = Croatia ■, *Europe* 33 C13
Hrymayliv, *Ukraine* 41 H4
Hsenwi, *Burma* 61 H20
Hsiamen = Xiamen, *China* 53 E12
Hsian = Xi'an, *China* 50 G5
Hsinchu, *Taiwan* 53 E13
Hsinhailien = Lianyungang, *China* 51 G10
Hsüchou = Xuzhou, *China* 51 G9
Hu Xian, *China* 50 G5
Hua Hin, *Thailand* 58 F2
Hua Xian, *Henan, China* 50 G8
Hua Xian, *Shaanxi, China* 50 G5
Hua'an, *China* 53 E11
Huacaya, *Bolivia* 125 E5
Huacheng, *China* 53 E10
Huachinera, *Mexico* 114 A3
Huacho, *Peru* 124 C2
Huachón, *Peru* 124 C2
Huade, *China* 50 D7
Huadian, *China* 51 C14
Huai He →, *China* 53 A12
Huai Yot, *Thailand* 59 J2
Huai'an, *Hebei, China* 50 D8
Huai'an, *Jiangsu, China* 51 H10
Huaibei, *China* 50 G9
Huaide, *China* 51 C13
Huaidezhen, *China* 51 C13
Huaihua, *China* 52 D7
Huaiji, *China* 53 F9
Huainan, *China* 53 A11
Huaining, *China* 53 B11
Huairen, *China* 50 E7
Huairou, *China* 50 D9
Huaiyang, *China* 50 H8
Huaiyuan, *Anhui, China* 51 H9
Huaiyuan, *Guangxi Zhuangzu, China* 52 E7
Huajianzi, *China* 51 D13
Huajuapan de Leon, *Mexico* 115 D5
Hualapai Peak, *U.S.A.* 111 J7
Hualien, *Taiwan* 53 E13
Huallaga →, *Peru* 124 B2
Huallanca, *Peru* 124 B2
Huamachuco, *Peru* 124 B2
Huambo, *Angola* 81 G3
Huan Jiang →, *China* 50 G5
Huan Xian, *China* 50 F4
Huancabamba, *Peru* 124 B2
Huancane, *Peru* 124 D4
Huancapi, *Peru* 124 C3
Huancavelica, *Peru* 124 C2
Huancavelica □, *Peru* 124 C3
Huancayo, *Peru* 124 C2
Huanchaca, *Bolivia* 124 E4
Huanchaca, Serranía de, *Bolivia* 125 C5
Huang Hai = Yellow Sea, *China* 51 G12
Huang He →, *China* 51 F10
Huang Xian, *China* 51 F11
Huangchuan, *China* 53 A10
Huanggang, *China* 53 B10
Huangling, *China* 50 G5
Huangliu, *China* 54 E5
Huanglong, *China* 50 G5
Huanglongtan, *China* 53 A8
Huangmei, *China* 53 B10
Huangpi, *China* 53 B10
Huangping, *China* 52 D6
Huangshi, *China* 53 B10
Huangsongdian, *China* 51 C14
Huangyan, *China* 53 C13
Huangyangsi, *China* 53 D8
Huaning, *China* 52 E4
Huanjiang, *China* 52 E7
Huanta, *Peru* 124 C3
Huantai, *China* 51 F9
Huánuco, *Peru* 124 B2
Huánuco □, *Peru* 124 B2
Huanuni, *Bolivia* 124 D4
Huanzo, Cordillera de, *Peru* 124 C3
Huaping, *China* 52 D3
Huaral, *Peru* 124 C2
Huaraz, *Peru* 124 B2
Huari, *Peru* 124 B2
Huarmey, *Peru* 124 C2
Huarochiri, *Peru* 124 C2
Huarocondo, *Peru* 124 C3
Huarong, *China* 53 C9
Huascarán, *Peru* 124 B2
Huascarán, Nevado, *Peru* 124 B2
Huasco, *Chile* 126 B1
Huasco →, *Chile* 126 B1
Huasna, *U.S.A.* 113 K6
Huatabampo, *Mexico* 114 B3
Huauchinango, *Mexico* 115 C5
Huautla de Jiménez, *Mexico* 115 D5
Huaxi, *China* 52 D6
Huay Namota, *Mexico* 114 C4
Huayin, *China* 50 G6
Huayllay, *Peru* 124 C2
Huayuan, *China* 52 C7
Huazhou, *China* 53 G8
Hubbard, *U.S.A.* 109 K6
Hubbart Pt., *Canada* 101 B10
Hubei □, *China* 53 B9
Hubli-Dharwad = Dharwad, *India* 60 M9
Huchang, *N. Korea* 51 D14
Hückelhoven, *Germany* 18 D2
Huddersfield, *U.K.* 12 D6
Hudi, *Sudan* 76 D3
Hudiksvall, *Sweden* 10 C11
Hudson, *Canada* 101 C10
Hudson, *Mass., U.S.A.* 107 D13
Hudson, *Mich., U.S.A.* 104 E3
Hudson, *N.Y., U.S.A.* 107 D11
Hudson, *Wis., U.S.A.* 108 C8
Hudson, *Wyo., U.S.A.* 110 E9
Hudson →, *U.S.A.* 107 F10
Hudson Bay, *N.W.T., Canada* 97 C11
Hudson Bay, *Sask., Canada* 101 C8
Hudson Falls, *U.S.A.* 107 C11
Hudson Mts., *Antarctica* 5 D16
Hudson Str., *Canada* 97 B13
Hudson's Hope, *Canada* 100 B4
Hue, *Vietnam* 58 D6
Huebra →, *Spain* 30 D4
Huechucuicui, Pta., *Chile* 128 B2
Huedin, *Romania* 38 C6
Huehuetenango, *Guatemala* 116 C1
Huejúcar, *Mexico* 114 C4
Huelgoat, *France* 24 D3
Huelma, *Spain* 29 H1
Huelva, *Spain* 31 H4
Huelva □, *Spain* 31 H4
Huelva →, *Spain* 31 H5
Huentelauquén, *Chile* 126 C1
Huércal Overa, *Spain* 29 H3
Huerta, Sa. de la, *Argentina* 126 C2
Huertas, C. de las, *Spain* 29 G4
Huerva →, *Spain* 28 D4
Huesca, *Spain* 28 C4
Huesca □, *Spain* 28 C5
Huéscar, *Spain* 29 H2
Huetamo, *Mexico* 114 D4
Huete, *Spain* 28 E2
Hugh →, *Australia* 90 D1
Hughenden, *Australia* 90 C3
Hughes, *Australia* 89 F4
Hugli →, *India* 63 J13
Hugo, *U.S.A.* 108 F3
Hugoton, *U.S.A.* 109 G4
Hui Xian, *Gansu, China* 50 H4
Hui Xian, *Henan, China* 50 G7
Hui'an, *China* 53 E12
Hui'anbu, *China* 50 F4
Huichang, *China* 53 E10
Huichapán, *Mexico* 115 C5
Huidong, *China* 52 D4
Huifa He →, *China* 51 C14
Huila □, *Colombia* 120 C2
Huila, Nevado del, *Colombia* 120 C2
Huilai, *China* 53 F11
Huili, *China* 52 D4
Huimin, *China* 51 F9
Huinan, *China* 51 C14
Huinca Renancó, *Argentina* 126 C3
Huining, *China* 50 G3
Huinong, *China* 50 E4
Huise, *Belgium* 17 G3
Huishui, *China* 52 D6
Huisne →, *France* 24 E7
Huissen, *Neths.* 16 E7
Huiting, *China* 50 G9
Huitong, *China* 52 D7
Huixtla, *Mexico* 115 D6
Huize, *China* 52 D4
Huizen, *Neths.* 16 D6
Huizhou, *China* 53 F10
Hukawng Valley, *Burma* 61 F20
Hukou, *China* 53 C11
Hukuntsi, *Botswana* 84 C3
Hula, *Ethiopia* 77 F4
Hulan, *China* 54 B7
Ḥulayfā', *Si. Arabia* 64 E4
Huld, *Mongolia* 50 B3
Hulin He →, *China* 51 B12
Hull = Kingston upon Hull, *U.K.* 12 D7
Hull, *Canada* 98 C4
Hull →, *U.K.* 12 D7
Hulst, *Neths.* 17 F4
Hulun Nur, *China* 54 B6
Hulyaypole, *Ukraine* 41 J9
Humahuaca, *Argentina* 126 A2
Humaitá, *Brazil* 125 B5
Humaitá, *Paraguay* 126 B4
Humansdorp, *S. Africa* 84 E3
Humbe, *Angola* 84 B1
Humber →, *U.K.* 12 D7
Humbert River, *Australia* 88 C5
Humble, *U.S.A.* 109 L8
Humboldt, *Canada* 101 C7
Humboldt, *Iowa, U.S.A.* 108 D7
Humboldt, *Tenn., U.S.A.* 109 H10
Humboldt →, *U.S.A.* 110 F4
Humboldt Gletscher, *Greenland* 4 B4
Hume, *U.S.A.* 112 J8
Hume, L., *Australia* 91 F4
Humenné, *Slovak Rep.* 20 G11
Humphreys, Mt., *U.S.A.* 112 H8
Humphreys Peak, *U.S.A.* 111 J8
Humpolec, *Czech.* 20 F5
Humptulips, *U.S.A.* 112 C3
Hūn, *Libya* 73 C8
Hun Jiang →, *China* 51 D13
Húnaflói, *Iceland* 8 D3
Hunan □, *China* 53 D9
Hunchun, *China* 51 C16
Hundested, *Denmark* 11 J5
Hundred Mile House, *Canada* 100 C4
Hunedoara, *Romania* 38 D5
Hünfeld, *Germany* 18 E5
Hung Yen, *Vietnam* 58 B6
Hungary ■, *Europe* 21 H9
Hungary, Plain of, *Europe* 6 F10
Hungerford, *Australia* 91 D3
Hŭngnam, *N. Korea* 51 E14
Huni Valley, *Ghana* 78 D4
Hunsberge, *Namibia* 84 D2
Hunsrück, *Germany* 19 F3
Hunstanton, *U.K.* 12 E8
Hunte →, *Germany* 18 C4
Hunter, *N. Dak., U.S.A.* 108 B6
Hunter, *N.Y., U.S.A.* 107 D10
Hunter I., *Australia* 90 G3
Hunter I., *Canada* 100 C3
Hunter Ra., *Australia* 91 E5
Hunters Road, *Zimbabwe* 83 F2
Hunterville, *N.Z.* 87 H5
Huntingburg, *U.S.A.* 104 F2
Huntingdon, *Canada* 98 C5
Huntingdon, *U.K.* 13 E7
Huntingdon, *U.S.A.* 106 F6
Huntington, *Ind., U.S.A.* 104 E3
Huntington, *N.Y., U.S.A.* 107 F11
Huntington, *Oreg., U.S.A.* 110 D5
Huntington, *Utah, U.S.A.* 110 G8
Huntington, *W. Va., U.S.A.* 104 F4
Huntington Beach, *U.S.A.* 113 M8
Huntington Park, *U.S.A.* 111 K4
Huntly, *N.Z.* 87 G5
Huntly, *U.K.* 14 D6
Huntsville, *Canada* 98 C4
Huntsville, *Ala., U.S.A.* 105 H2
Huntsville, *Tex., U.S.A.* 109 K7
Hunyani →, *Zimbabwe* 83 F3
Hunyuan, *China* 50 E7
Hunza →, *India* 63 B6
Huo Xian, *China* 50 F6
Huong Hoa, *Vietnam* 58 D6
Huong Khe, *Vietnam* 58 C5
Huonville, *Australia* 90 G4
Huoqiu, *China* 53 A11
Huoshan, *Anhui, China* 53 A12
Huoshan, *Anhui, China* 53 B11
Hupeh = Hubei □, *China* 53 B9
Ḩūr, *Iran* 65 D8
Hure Qi, *China* 51 C11
Hurezani, *Romania* 38 E6
Hurghada, *Egypt* 76 B3
Hurley, *N. Mex., U.S.A.* 111 K9
Hurley, *Wis., U.S.A.* 108 B9
Huron, *Calif., U.S.A.* 112 J6
Huron, *Ohio, U.S.A.* 106 E2
Huron, *S. Dak., U.S.A.* 108 C5
Huron, L., *U.S.A.* 106 B2
Hurricane, *U.S.A.* 111 H7
Hurso, *Ethiopia* 77 F5
Hurum, *Norway* 10 C2
Hurunui →, *N.Z.* 87 K4
Hurup, *Denmark* 11 H2
Húsavík, *Iceland* 8 C5
Huşi, *Romania* 38 C11
Huskvarna, *Sweden* 9 H16
Hussar, *Canada* 100 C6
Hustadvika, *Norway* 8 E12
Husum, *Germany* 18 A5
Husum, *Sweden* 10 A13
Hutchinson, *Kans., U.S.A.* 109 F6

Hutchinson, *Minn., U.S.A.* 108 C7
Huttig, *U.S.A.* 109 J8
Hutton, Mt., *Australia* 91 D4
Huttwil, *Switz.* 22 B5
Huwun, *Ethiopia* 77 G5
Huy, *Belgium* 17 G6
Hvammstangi, *Iceland* 8 D3
Hvar, *Croatia* 33 E13
Hvarski Kanal, *Croatia* 33 E13
Hvítá →, *Iceland* 8 D3
Hwachon-chosuji, *S. Korea* 51 E14
Hwang Ho = Huang He →, *China* 51 F10
Hwange, *Zimbabwe* 83 F2
Hwange Nat. Park, *Zimbabwe* 84 B4
Hyannis, *U.S.A.* 108 E4
Hyargas Nuur, *Mongolia* 54 B4
Hybo, *Sweden* 10 C10
Hyde Park, *Guyana* 121 B6
Hyden, *Australia* 89 F2
Hyderabad, *India* 60 L11
Hyderabad, *Pakistan* 62 G3
Hyères, *France* 27 E10
Hyères, Is. d', *France* 27 F10
Hyesan, *N. Korea* 51 D15
Hyland →, *Canada* 100 B3
Hyltebruk, *Sweden* 11 H7
Hymia, *India* 63 C8
Hyndman Peak, *U.S.A.* 110 E6
Hyōgo □, *Japan* 49 G7
Hyrum, *U.S.A.* 110 F8
Hysham, *U.S.A.* 110 C10
Hythe, *U.K.* 13 F9
Hyūga, *Japan* 49 H5
Hyvinge = Hyvinkää, *Finland* 9 F21
Hyvinkää, *Finland* 9 F21

I

I-n-Échaï, *Mali* 74 D4
I-n-Gall, *Niger* 79 B6
Iabès, Erg, *Algeria* 75 C4
Iaco →, *Brazil* 124 B4
Iaçu, *Brazil* 123 D3
Iakora, *Madag.* 85 C8
Iaşi, *Romania* 38 B10
Iauaretê, *Colombia* 120 C4
Iba, *Phil.* 55 D3
Ibadan, *Nigeria* 79 D5
Ibagué, *Colombia* 120 C2
Ibaiti, *Brazil* 123 F1
Iballja, *Albania* 38 G3
Ibăneşti, *Romania* 38 C7
Ibar →, *Serbia, Yug.* 21 M10
Ibaraki □, *Japan* 49 F10
Ibarra, *Ecuador* 120 C2
Ibba, *Sudan* 77 G2
Ibba, Bahr el →, *Sudan* 77 F2
Ibbenbüren, *Germany* 18 C3
Ibembo, *Zaïre* 82 B1
Ibera, L., *Argentina* 126 B4
Iberian Peninsula, *Europe* 6 H5
Iberico, Sistema, *Spain* 28 E2
Iberville, *Canada* 98 C5
Iberville, Lac d', *Canada* 98 A5
Ibi, *Nigeria* 79 D6
Ibiá, *Brazil* 123 E2
Ibicaraí, *Brazil* 123 D4
Ibicuí, *Brazil* 123 D4
Ibicuy, *Argentina* 126 C4
Ibioapaba, Sa. da, *Brazil* 122 B3
Ibipetuba, *Brazil* 122 D3
Ibitiara, *Brazil* 123 D3
Ibiza, *Spain* 36 C7
Íblei, Monti, *Italy* 35 E7
Ibo, *Mozam.* 83 E5
Ibonma, *Indonesia* 57 E8
Ibotirama, *Brazil* 123 D3
Ibrāhīm →, *Lebanon* 69 A4
Ibshawâi, *Egypt* 76 J7
Ibu, *Indonesia* 57 D7
Iburg, *Germany* 18 C4
Ibusuki, *Japan* 49 J5
Icá, *Peru* 124 C2
Ica □, *Peru* 124 C2
Iça →, *Brazil* 124 A4
Icabarú, *Venezuela* 121 C5
Icabarú →, *Venezuela* 121 C5
Içana, *Brazil* 120 C4
Içana →, *Brazil* 120 C4
Icatu, *Brazil* 122 B3
Içel = Mersin, *Turkey* 66 D6
Iceland ■, *Europe* 8 D4
Icha, *Russia* 45 D16
Ich'ang = Yichang, *China* 53 B8
Ichchapuram, *India* 61 K14
Ichihara, *Japan* 49 G10
Ichikawa, *Japan* 49 G9
Ichilo →, *Bolivia* 125 D5
Ichinohe, *Japan* 48 D10
Ichinomiya, *Japan* 49 G8
Ichinoseki, *Japan* 48 E10
Ichnya, *Ukraine* 41 G7
Ichŏn, *S. Korea* 51 F14
Icht, *Morocco* 74 C3
Ichtegem, *Belgium* 17 F2
Icó, *Brazil* 122 C4
Icod, *Canary Is.* 36 F3
Icoraci, *Brazil* 122 B2
Icy Str., *U.S.A.* 100 B1
Ida Grove, *U.S.A.* 108 D7
Ida Valley, *Australia* 89 E3
Idabel, *U.S.A.* 109 J7
Idaga Hamus, *Ethiopia* 77 E4
Idah, *Nigeria* 79 D6
Idaho □, *U.S.A.* 110 D6
Idaho City, *U.S.A.* 110 E6
Idaho Falls, *U.S.A.* 110 E7
Idaho Springs, *U.S.A.* 110 G11
Idanha-a-Nova, *Portugal* 30 F3
Idar-Oberstein, *Germany* 19 F3
Idd el Ghanam, *Sudan* 73 F9
Iddan, *Somali Rep.* 68 F4
Idehan, *Libya* 75 C7
Idehan Marzūq, *Libya* 73 D7
Idelès, *Algeria* 75 D6
Idfû, *Egypt* 76 C3
Ídhi Óros, *Greece* 37 D6
Ídhra, *Greece* 39 M6
Idi, *Indonesia* 56 C1
Idiofa, *Zaïre* 80 E3
Idku, Bahra el, *Egypt* 76 H7
Idlib, *Syria* 66 E7
Idria, *U.S.A.* 112 J6
Idrija, *Slovenia* 33 B11
Idritsa, *Russia* 40 D5
Idstein, *Germany* 19 E4
Idutywa, *S. Africa* 85 E4
Ieper, *Belgium* 17 G1
Ierápetra, *Greece* 37 E7
Ierissós, *Greece* 39 J6
Ierzu, *Italy* 34 C2
Iesi, *Italy* 33 E10
Ifach, Punta, *Spain* 29 G5
'Ifāl, W. al →, *Si. Arabia* 64 D2
Ifanadiana, *Madag.* 85 C8
Ife, *Nigeria* 79 D5
Iférouâne, *Niger* 79 B6
Iffley, *Australia* 90 B3
Ifni, *Morocco* 74 C2
Ifon, *Nigeria* 79 D6
Iforas, Adrar des, *Mali* 79 B5
Ifould, L., *Australia* 89 F5
Ifrane, *Morocco* 74 B3
Iganga, *Uganda* 82 B3
Igara Paraná →, *Colombia* 120 D3
Igarapava, *Brazil* 123 F2
Igarapé Açu, *Brazil* 122 B2
Igarapé-Mirim, *Brazil* 122 B2
Igarka, *Russia* 44 C9
Igatimi, *Paraguay* 127 A4
Igbetti, *Nigeria* 79 D5
Igbo-Ora, *Nigeria* 79 D5
Igboho, *Nigeria* 79 D5
Iğdır, *Turkey* 67 C11
Iggesund, *Sweden* 10 C11
Ighil Izane, *Algeria* 75 A5
Iglésias, *Italy* 34 C1
Igli, *Algeria* 75 B4
Igloolik, *Canada* 97 B11
Igma, Gebel el, *Egypt* 76 J8
Ignace, *Canada* 98 C1
Iğneada Burnu, *Turkey* 66 B3
Igra, *Russia* 42 B11
Iguaçu →, *Brazil* 127 B5
Iguaçu, Cat. del, *Brazil* 127 B5
Iguaçu Falls = Iguaçu, Cat. del, *Brazil* 127 B5
Iguala, *Mexico* 115 D5
Igualada, *Spain* 28 D6
Iguape, *Brazil* 123 F2
Iguassu = Iguaçu →, *Brazil* 127 B5
Iguatu, *Brazil* 122 C4
Iguéla, *Gabon* 80 E1
Igunga □, *Tanzania* 82 C3
Iheya-Shima, *Japan* 49 L3
Ihiala, *Nigeria* 79 D6
Ihosy, *Madag.* 85 C8
Ihotry, L., *Madag.* 85 C7
Ii, *Finland* 8 D21
Ii-Shima, *Japan* 49 L3
Iida, *Japan* 49 G8
Iijoki →, *Finland* 8 D21
Iisalmi, *Finland* 8 E22
Iiyama, *Japan* 49 F9
Iizuka, *Japan* 49 H5
Ijâfene, *Mauritania* 74 D3
Ijebu-Igbo, *Nigeria* 79 D5
Ijebu-Ode, *Nigeria* 79 D5
IJmuiden, *Neths.* 16 D5
IJssel →, *Neths.* 16 C7
IJsselmeer, *Neths.* 16 C6
IJsselmuiden, *Neths.* 16 C7
IJsselstein, *Neths.* 16 D6
Ijuí →, *Brazil* 127 B4
IJzendijke, *Neths.* 17 F3
IJzer →, *Belgium* 17 F1
Ikale, *Nigeria* 79 D6
Ikare, *Nigeria* 79 D6
Ikaría, *Greece* 39 M9
Ikast, *Denmark* 11 H3
Ikeda, *Japan* 49 G6
Ikeja, *Nigeria* 79 D5
Ikela, *Zaïre* 80 E4
Ikerre-Ekiti, *Nigeria* 79 D6
Ikhtiman, *Bulgaria* 38 G6
Iki, *Japan* 49 H4
Ikimba L., *Tanzania* 82 C3
Ikire, *Nigeria* 79 D5
İkizdere, *Turkey* 67 B9
Ikom, *Nigeria* 79 D6
Ikopa →, *Madag.* 85 B8
Ikot Ekpene, *Nigeria* 79 D6
Ikungu, *Tanzania* 82 C3
Ikurun, *Nigeria* 79 D5
Ila, *Nigeria* 79 D5
Ilagan, *Phil.* 55 C4
Īlām, *Iran* 67 F12
Ilam, *Nepal* 63 F12
Ilan, *Taiwan* 53 E13
Ilanskiy, *Russia* 45 D10
Ilanz, *Switz.* 23 C8
Ilaro, *Nigeria* 79 D5
Iława, *Poland* 20 B9
Ilbilbie, *Australia* 90 C4
Ile-à-la-Crosse, *Canada* 101 B7
Ile-à-la-Crosse, Lac, *Canada* 101 B7
Île-de-France, *France* 25 D9
Ilebo, *Zaïre* 80 E4
Ileje □, *Tanzania* 83 D3
Ilek, *Russia* 44 D6
Ilek →, *Russia* 44 D6
Ilero, *Nigeria* 79 D5
Ilesha, *Kwara, Nigeria* 79 D5
Ilesha, *Oyo, Nigeria* 79 D5
Ilford, *Canada* 101 B9
Ilfracombe, *Australia* 90 C3
Ilfracombe, *U.K.* 13 F3
Ilgaz, *Turkey* 66 B5
Ilgaz Dağları, *Turkey* 66 B5
Ilgın, *Turkey* 66 C4
Ilha Grande, *Brazil* 121 D4
Ilha Grande, B. da, *Brazil* 123 F3
Ílhavo, *Portugal* 30 E2
Ilhéus, *Brazil* 123 D4
Ili →, *Kazakstan* 44 E8
Iliç, *Turkey* 67 C8
Ilich, *Kazakstan* 44 E7
Ilichevsk, *Azerbaijan* 67 C11
Iliff, *U.S.A.* 108 E3
Iligan, *Phil.* 55 G6
Iligan Bay, *Phil.* 55 G6
Ilíki, L., *Greece* 39 L6
Ilin I., *Phil.* 55 E4
Iliodhrómia, *Greece* 39 K6
Ilion, *U.S.A.* 107 D9
Ilirska-Bistrica, *Slovenia* 33 C11
Ilkeston, *U.K.* 12 E6
Illampu = Ancohuma, Nevada, *Bolivia* 124 D4
Illana B., *Phil.* 55 H5
Illapel, *Chile* 126 C1
Ille-et-Vilaine □, *France* 24 D5
Ille-sur-Têt, *France* 26 F6
Iller →, *Germany* 19 G5
Illescas, *Spain* 30 E7
Illetas, *Spain* 36 B9
Illichivsk, *Ukraine* 41 J6
Illiers-Combray, *France* 24 D8
Illimani, *Bolivia* 124 D4
Illinois □, *U.S.A.* 103 C9
Illinois →, *U.S.A.* 103 C8
Illium = Troy, *Turkey* 66 C2
Illizi, *Algeria* 75 C6
Illora, *Spain* 31 H7
Ilm →, *Germany* 18 D7
Ilmajoki, *Finland* 9 E20
Ilmen, Ozero, *Russia* 40 C6
Ilmenau, *Germany* 18 E6
Ilo, *Peru* 124 D3
Ilobu, *Nigeria* 79 D5
Iloilo, *Phil.* 55 F5
Ilora, *Nigeria* 79 D5
Ilorin, *Nigeria* 79 D5
Ilovatka, *Russia* 42 E7
Ilovlya, *Russia* 43 F7
Ilovlya →, *Russia* 43 F7
Ilubabor □, *Ethiopia* 77 F3
Ilva Mică, *Romania* 38 B7
Ilwaco, *U.S.A.* 112 D2
Ilwaki, *Indonesia* 57 F7
Ilyichevsk = Illichivsk, *Ukraine* 41 J6
Imabari, *Japan* 49 G6
Imaloto →, *Madag.* 85 C8
Imamoğlu, *Turkey* 66 D6
Imandra, Ozero, *Russia* 44 C4
Imari, *Japan* 49 H4
Imasa, *Sudan* 76 D4
Imatra, *Finland* 40 B5
Imbâbah, *Egypt* 76 H7
Imbabura □, *Ecuador* 120 C2
Imbaimadai, *Guyana* 121 B5
Imbler, *U.S.A.* 110 D5
Imdahane, *Morocco* 74 B3
imeni 26 Bakinskikh Komissarov = Neftçala, *Azerbaijan* 67 C13
Imeni Poliny Osipenko, *Russia* 45 D14
Imeri, Serra, *Brazil* 120 C4
Imerimandroso, *Madag.* 85 B8
Imesan, *Mauritania* 74 D1
Imi, *Ethiopia* 68 F3
Imishly = Imişli, *Azerbaijan* 43 L9
Imişli, *Azerbaijan* 43 L9
Imitek, *Morocco* 74 C3
Imlay, *U.S.A.* 110 F4
Imlay City, *U.S.A.* 106 C1
Immenstadt, *Germany* 19 H6
Immingham, *U.K.* 12 D7
Immokalee, *U.S.A.* 105 M5
Imo □, *Nigeria* 79 D6
Imola, *Italy* 33 D8
Imotski, *Croatia* 21 M7
Imperatriz, *Amazonas, Brazil* 124 B4
Imperatriz, *Maranhão, Brazil* 122 C2
Impéria, *Italy* 32 E5
Imperial, *Canada* 101 C7
Imperial, *Peru* 124 C2
Imperial, *Calif., U.S.A.* 113 N11
Imperial, *Nebr., U.S.A.* 108 E4
Imperial Beach, *U.S.A.* 113 N9
Imperial Dam, *U.S.A.* 113 N12
Imperial Reservoir, *U.S.A.* 113 N12
Imperial Valley, *U.S.A.* 113 N11
Imperieuse Reef, *Australia* 88 C2
Impfondo, *Congo* 80 D3
Imphal, *India* 61 G18
Imphy, *France* 26 B7
Imranlı, *Turkey* 67 C8
Imroz = Gökçeada, *Turkey* 66 B1
Imst, *Austria* 19 H6
Imuruan B., *Phil.* 57 B5
In Belbel, *Algeria* 75 C5
In Delimane, *Mali* 79 B5
In Rhar, *Algeria* 75 C5
In Salah, *Algeria* 75 C5
In Tallak, *Mali* 79 B5
Ina, *Japan* 49 G8
Inajá, *Brazil* 122 C4
Inangahua Junction, *N.Z.* 87 J3
Inanwatan, *Indonesia* 57 E8
Iñapari, *Peru* 124 C4
Inari, *Finland* 8 B22
Inarijärvi, *Finland* 8 B22
Inawashiro-Ko, *Japan* 48 F10
Inca, *Spain* 36 B9
Incaguasi, *Chile* 126 B1
İnce Burun, *Turkey* 66 A6
İncekum Burnu, *Turkey* 66 D5
Inchon, *S. Korea* 51 F14
Incio, *Spain* 30 C3
Incirliova, *Turkey* 66 D2
Incomáti →, *Mozam.* 85 D5
Inda Silase, *Ethiopia* 77 E4
Indalsälven →, *Sweden* 10 B11
Indaw, *Burma* 61 G20
Indbir, *Ethiopia* 77 F4
Independence, *Calif., U.S.A.* 111 H4
Independence, *Iowa, U.S.A.* 108 D9
Independence, *Kans., U.S.A.* 109 G7
Independence, *Mo., U.S.A.* 108 F7
Independence, *Oreg., U.S.A.* 110 D2
Independence Fjord, *Greenland* 4 A6
Independence Mts., *U.S.A.* 110 F5
Independência, *Brazil* 122 C3
Independenţa, *Romania* 38 D10
Index, *U.S.A.* 112 C5
India ■, *Asia* 60 K11
Indian →, *U.S.A.* 105 M5
Indian Cabins, *Canada* 100 B5
Indian Harbour, *Canada* 99 B8
Indian Head, *Canada* 101 C8
Indian Ocean 46 K11
Indian Springs, *U.S.A.* 113 J11
Indiana, *U.S.A.* 106 F5
Indiana □, *U.S.A.* 104 E3
Indianapolis, *U.S.A.* 104 F2
Indianola, *Iowa, U.S.A.* 108 E8
Indianola, *Miss., U.S.A.* 109 J9
Indiapora, *Brazil* 123 E1
Indiga, *Russia* 44 C5
Indigirka →, *Russia* 45 B15
Inđija, *Serbia, Yug.* 21 K10
Indio, *U.S.A.* 113 M10
Indonesia ■, *Asia* 56 F5
Indore, *India* 62 H6
Indramayu, *Indonesia* 57 G13
Indravati →, *India* 61 K12
Indre □, *France* 25 F8
Indre →, *France* 24 E7
Indre-et-Loire □, *France* 24 E7
Indus →, *Pakistan* 62 G2
Indus, Mouth of the, *Pakistan* 62 H2
İnebolu, *Turkey* 66 B5
İnegöl, *Turkey* 66 B3
Inés, Mt., *Argentina* 128 C3
Ineu, *Romania* 38 C4
Inezgane, *Morocco* 74 B3
Infantes, *Spain* 29 G1
Infiernillo, Presa del, *Mexico* 114 D4
Infiesto, *Spain* 30 B5
Ingapirca, *Ecuador* 120 D2
Ingelmunster, *Belgium* 17 G2
Ingende, *Zaïre* 80 E3
Ingeniero Jacobacci, *Argentina* 128 B3
Ingenio, *Canary Is.* 36 G4
Ingenio Santa Ana, *Argentina* 126 B2
Ingersoll, *Canada* 106 C4
Ingham, *Australia* 90 B4
Ingleborough, *U.K.* 12 C5
Inglewood, *Queens., Australia* 91 D5
Inglewood, *Vic., Australia* 91 F3
Inglewood, *N.Z.* 87 H5
Inglewood, *U.S.A.* 113 M8
Ingólfshöfði, *Iceland* 8 E5
Ingolstadt, *Germany* 19 G7
Ingomar, *U.S.A.* 110 C10
Ingonish, *Canada* 99 C7
Ingore, *Guinea-Biss.* 78 C1
Ingraj Bazar, *India* 63 G13
Ingrid Christensen Coast, *Antarctica* 5 C6
Ingul → = Inhul →, *Ukraine* 41 J7
Ingulec = Inhulec, *Ukraine* 41 J7
Ingulets → = Inhulets →, *Ukraine* 41 J7
Inguri → = Enguri →, *Georgia* 43 J5
Ingushetia □, *Russia* 43 J7
Ingwavuma, *S. Africa* 85 D5
Inhaca, I., *Mozam.* 85 D5
Inhafenga, *Mozam.* 85 C5
Inhambane, *Mozam.* 85 C6
Inhambane □, *Mozam.* 85 C5
Inhambupe, *Brazil* 123 D4
Inhaminga, *Mozam.* 83 F4
Inharrime, *Mozam.* 85 C6
Inharrime →, *Mozam.* 85 C6
Inhul →, *Ukraine* 41 J7
Inhulec, *Ukraine* 41 J7
Inhulets →, *Ukraine* 41 J7
Inhuma, *Brazil* 122 C3
Inhumas, *Brazil* 123 E2
Iniesta, *Spain* 29 F3
Ining = Yining, *China* 44 E9
Inini □, *Fr. Guiana* 121 C7
Inírida →, *Colombia* 120 C4
Inishbofin, *Ireland* 15 C1
Inishmore, *Ireland* 15 C2
Inishowen Pen., *Ireland* 15 A4
Injune, *Australia* 91 D4
Inklin, *Canada* 100 B2
Inklin →, *Canada* 100 B2
Inkom, *U.S.A.* 110 E7
Inle L., *Burma* 61 J20
Inn →, *Austria* 19 G9
Innamincka, *Australia* 91 D3
Inner Hebrides, *U.K.* 14 D2
Inner Mongolia = Nei Monggol Zizhiqu □, *China* 50 C6
Inner Sound, *U.K.* 14 D3
Innerkip, *Canada* 106 C4
Innerkirchen, *Switz.* 22 C6
Innerste →, *Germany* 18 C5
Innetalling I., *Canada* 98 A4
Innisfail, *Australia* 90 B4
Innisfail, *Canada* 100 C6
In'no-shima, *Japan* 49 G6
Innsbruck, *Austria* 19 H7
Inny →, *Ireland* 15 C4
Inocência, *Brazil* 123 E1
Inongo, *Zaïre* 80 E3
Inoucdjouac = Inukjuak, *Canada* 97 C12
Inowrocław, *Poland* 20 C8
Inpundong, *N. Korea* 51 D14
Inquisivi, *Bolivia* 124 D4
Ins, *Switz.* 22 B4
Inscription, C., *Australia* 89 E1
Insein, *Burma* 61 L20
Însurăţei, *Romania* 38 E10
Intendente Alvear, *Argentina* 126 D3
Interior, *U.S.A.* 108 D4
Interlaken, *Switz.* 25 F14
International Falls, *U.S.A.* 108 A8
Intiyaco, *Argentina* 126 B3
Intragna, *Switz.* 23 D7
Intutu, *Peru* 120 D3
Inukjuak, *Canada* 97 C12
Inútil, B., *Chile* 128 D2
Inuvik, *Canada* 96 B6
Inveraray, *U.K.* 14 E3
Inverbervie, *U.K.* 14 E6
Invercargill, *N.Z.* 87 M2
Inverclyde □, *U.K.* 14 F4
Inverell, *Australia* 91 D5
Invergordon, *U.K.* 14 D4
Invermere, *Canada* 100 C5
Inverness, *Canada* 99 C7
Inverness, *U.K.* 14 D4
Inverness, *U.S.A.* 105 L4
Inverurie, *U.K.* 14 D6
Inverway, *Australia* 88 C4
Investigator Group, *Australia* 91 E1
Investigator Str., *Australia* 91 F2
Inya, *Russia* 44 D9
Inyanga, *Zimbabwe* 83 F3
Inyangani, *Zimbabwe* 83 F3
Inyantue, *Zimbabwe* 83 F2
Inyo Mts., *U.S.A.* 111 H5
Inyokern, *U.S.A.* 113 K9
Inza, *Russia* 42 D8
Inzhavino, *Russia* 42 D6
Iō-Jima, *Japan* 49 J5
Ioánnina, *Greece* 39 K3
Iola, *U.S.A.* 109 G7
Ion Corvin, *Romania* 38 E10
Iona, *U.K.* 14 E2
Ione, *Calif., U.S.A.* 112 G6
Ione, *Wash., U.S.A.* 110 B5
Ionia, *U.S.A.* 104 D3
Ionian Is. = Iónioi Nísoi, *Greece* 39 L3
Ionian Sea, *Medit. S.* 6 H9
Iónioi Nísoi, *Greece* 39 L3
Íos, *Greece* 39 N8
Iowa □, *U.S.A.* 108 D8
Iowa City, *U.S.A.* 108 E9
Iowa Falls, *U.S.A.* 108 D8
Ipala, *Tanzania* 82 C3
Ipameri, *Brazil* 123 E2
Iparía, *Peru* 124 B3
Ipáti, *Greece* 39 L5
Ipatinga, *Brazil* 123 E3
Ipatovo, *Russia* 43 H6
Ipel →, *Europe* 21 G9
Ipiales, *Colombia* 120 C2
Ipiaú, *Brazil* 123 D4

Ipin = Yibin, *China* 52 C5
Ipirá, *Brazil* 123 D4
Ipiranga, *Brazil* 120 D4
Ipixuna, *Brazil* 124 B3
Ipixuna →, *Amazonas, Brazil* 124 B3
Ipixuna →, *Amazonas, Brazil* 125 B5
Ipoh, *Malaysia* 59 K3
Iporá, *Brazil* 123 D1
Ippy, *C.A.R.* 73 G9
Ipsala, *Turkey* 66 B2
Ipsárion Óros, *Greece* 39 J7
Ipswich, *Australia* 91 D5
Ipswich, *U.K.* 13 E9
Ipswich, *Mass., U.S.A.* 107 D14
Ipswich, *S. Dak., U.S.A.* 108 C5
Ipu, *Brazil* 122 B3
Ipueiras, *Brazil* 122 B3
Ipupiara, *Brazil* 123 D3
Iqaluit, *Canada* 97 B13
Iquique, *Chile* 124 E3
Iquitos, *Peru* 120 D3
Irabu-Jima, *Japan* 49 M2
Iracoubo, *Fr. Guiana* 121 B7
Īrafshān, *Iran* 65 E9
Irahuan, *Phil.* 55 G3
Iráklia, *Greece* 39 N8
Iráklion, *Greece* 37 D7
Iráklion □, *Greece* 37 D7
Irala, *Paraguay* 127 B5
Iramba □, *Tanzania* 82 C3
Iran ■, *Asia* 65 C7
Iran, Gunung-Gunung, *Malaysia* 56 D4
Iran, Plateau of, *Asia* 46 F9
Iran Ra. = Iran, Gunung-Gunung, *Malaysia* 56 D4
Īrānshahr, *Iran* 65 E9
Irapa, *Venezuela* 121 A5
Irapuato, *Mexico* 114 C4
Iraq ■, *Asia* 67 F10
Irarrar, O. →, *Mali* 75 D5
Irati, *Brazil* 127 B5
Irbid, *Jordan* 69 C4
Irbid □, *Jordan* 69 C5
Irebu, *Zaïre* 80 E3
Irecê, *Brazil* 122 D3
Iregua →, *Spain* 28 C7
Ireland ■, *Europe* 15 D4
Ireland's Eye, *Ireland* 15 C5
Irele, *Nigeria* 79 D6
Ireng →, *Brazil* 121 C6
Iret, *Russia* 45 C16
Irgiz, Bolshaya →, *Russia* 42 D9
Irhârharene, *Algeria* 75 C6
Irharrhar, O. →, *Algeria* 75 C6
Irherm, *Morocco* 74 B3
Irhil Mgoun, *Morocco* 74 B3
Irhyangdong, *N. Korea* 51 D15
Iri, *S. Korea* 51 G14
Irian Jaya □, *Indonesia* 57 E9
Irié, *Guinea* 78 D3
Iriga, *Phil.* 55 E5
Iringa, *Tanzania* 82 D4
Iringa □, *Tanzania* 82 D4
Iriomote-Jima, *Japan* 49 M1
Iriona, *Honduras* 116 C2
Iriri →, *Brazil* 121 D7
Iriri Novo →, *Brazil* 125 B7
Irish Republic ■, *Europe* 15 D4
Irish Sea, *U.K.* 12 D3
Irkineyeva, *Russia* 45 D10
Irkutsk, *Russia* 45 D11
Irma, *Canada* 101 C6
Irō-Zaki, *Japan* 49 G9
Iroise, Mer d', *France* 24 D2
Iron Baron, *Australia* 91 E2
Iron Gate = Portile de Fier, *Europe* 38 E5
Iron Knob, *Australia* 91 E2
Iron Mountain, *U.S.A.* 104 C1
Iron Ra., *Australia* 90 A3
Iron River, *U.S.A.* 108 B10
Ironbridge, *U.K.* 13 E5
Irondequoit, *U.S.A.* 106 C7
Ironstone Kopje, *Botswana* 84 D3
Ironton, *Mo., U.S.A.* 109 G9
Ironton, *Ohio, U.S.A.* 104 F4
Ironwood, *U.S.A.* 108 B9
Iroquois Falls, *Canada* 98 C3
Irosin, *Phil.* 55 E6
Irpin, *Ukraine* 41 G6
Irrara Cr. →, *Australia* 91 D4
Irrawaddy □, *Burma* 61 L19
Irrawaddy →, *Burma* 61 M19
Irsina, *Italy* 35 B9
Irtysh →, *Russia* 44 C7
Irumu, *Zaïre* 82 B2
Irún, *Spain* 28 B3
Irunea = Pamplona, *Spain* 28 C3
Irurzun, *Spain* 28 C3
Irvine, *Canada* 101 D6
Irvine, *U.K.* 14 F4
Irvine, *Calif., U.S.A.* 113 M9
Irvine, *Ky., U.S.A.* 104 G4
Irvinestown, *U.K.* 15 B4
Irving, *U.S.A.* 109 J6
Irvona, *U.S.A.* 106 F6
Irwin →, *Australia* 89 E1
Irymple, *Australia* 91 E3
Is-sur-Tille, *France* 25 E12
Isa, *Nigeria* 79 C6
Isaac →, *Australia* 90 C4
Isabel, *U.S.A.* 108 C4
Isabela, I., *Mexico* 114 C3
Isabella, *Phil.* 55 H5
Isabella, Cord., *Nic.* 116 D2
Isabella Ra., *Australia* 88 D3
Ísafjarðardjúp, *Iceland* 8 C2
Ísafjörður, *Iceland* 8 C2
Isagarh, *India* 62 G7
Isahaya, *Japan* 49 H5
Isaka, *Tanzania* 82 C3
Isakly, *Russia* 42 C10
Isana = Içana →, *Brazil* 120 C4
Isangi, *Zaïre* 80 D4
Isar →, *Germany* 19 G8
Isarco →, *Italy* 33 B8
Ísari, *Greece* 39 M5
Isbergues, *France* 25 B9
Iscayachi, *Bolivia* 125 E4
Íschia, *Italy* 34 B6
Iscuandé, *Colombia* 120 C2
Isdell →, *Australia* 88 C3
Ise, *Japan* 49 G8
Ise-Wan, *Japan* 49 G8
Isefjord, *Denmark* 11 J5
Iseltwald, *Switz.* 22 C5
Isenthal, *Switz.* 23 C7
Iseo, *Italy* 32 C7
Iseo, L. d', *Italy* 32 C7
Iseramagazi, *Tanzania* 82 C3
Isère □, *France* 27 C9
Isère →, *France* 27 D8
Iserlohn, *Germany* 18 D3
Isérnia, *Italy* 35 A7
Iseyin, *Nigeria* 79 D5
Isherton, *Guyana* 121 C6
Ishigaki-Shima, *Japan* 49 M2
Ishikari-Gawa →, *Japan* 48 C10
Ishikari-Sammyaku, *Japan* 48 C11
Ishikari-Wan, *Japan* 48 C10
Ishikawa □, *Japan* 49 F8
Ishim, *Russia* 44 D7
Ishim →, *Russia* 44 D8
Ishinomaki, *Japan* 48 E10
Ishioka, *Japan* 49 F10
Ishkuman, *Pakistan* 63 A5
Ishpeming, *U.S.A.* 104 B2
Isigny-sur-Mer, *France* 24 C5
Isil Kul, *Russia* 44 D8
Isiolo, *Kenya* 82 B4
Isiolo □, *Kenya* 82 B4
Isiro, *Zaïre* 82 B2
Isisford, *Australia* 90 C3
İskenderun, *Turkey* 66 D7
İskenderun Körfezi, *Turkey* 66 D6
İskilip, *Turkey* 66 B6
Iskŭr →, *Bulgaria* 38 F7
Iskut →, *Canada* 100 B2
Isla →, *U.K.* 14 E5
Isla Cristina, *Spain* 31 H3
Isla Vista, *U.S.A.* 113 L7
İslâhiye, *Turkey* 66 D7
Islamabad, *Pakistan* 62 C5
Islamkot, *Pakistan* 62 G4
Island →, *Canada* 100 A4
Island Falls, *Canada* 98 C3
Island Falls, *U.S.A.* 99 C6
Island L., *Canada* 101 C10
Island Lagoon, *Australia* 91 E2
Island Pond, *U.S.A.* 107 B13
Islands, B. of, *Canada* 99 C8
Islay, *U.K.* 14 F2
Isle →, *France* 26 D3
Isle aux Morts, *Canada* 99 C8
Isle of Wight □, *U.K.* 13 G6
Isle Royale, *U.S.A.* 108 A10
Isleta, *U.S.A.* 111 J10
Isleton, *U.S.A.* 112 G5
Ismail = Izmayil, *Ukraine* 41 K5
Ismâ'ilîya, *Egypt* 76 H8
Ismaning, *Germany* 19 G7
Ismay, *U.S.A.* 108 B2
Isna, *Egypt* 76 B3
Isogstalo, *India* 63 B8
Isola del Gran Sasso d'Italia, *Italy* 33 F10
Ísola del Liri, *Italy* 34 A6
Ísola della Scala, *Italy* 32 C8
Ísola di Capo Rizzuto, *Italy* 35 D10
Isparta, *Turkey* 66 D4
Isperikh, *Bulgaria* 38 F9
Íspica, *Italy* 35 F7
Israel ■, *Asia* 69 D3
Issano, *Guyana* 121 B6
Issia, *Ivory C.* 78 D3
Issoire, *France* 26 C7
Issoudun, *France* 25 F8
Issyk-Kul = Ysyk-Köl, *Kyrgyzstan* 46 E11
Issyk-Kul, Ozero = Ysyk-Köl, Ozero, *Kyrgyzstan* 44 E8
Ist, *Croatia* 33 D11
Istaihah, *U.A.E.* 65 F7
Istanbul, *Turkey* 66 B3
Istmina, *Colombia* 120 B2
Istok, *Serbia, Yug.* 21 N10
Istokpoga, L., *U.S.A.* 105 M5
Istra, *Croatia* 33 C11
Istranca Dağları, *Turkey* 66 B2
Istres, *France* 27 E8
Istria = Istra, *Croatia* 33 C11
Itá, *Paraguay* 126 B4
Itabaiana, *Paraíba, Brazil* 122 C4
Itabaiana, *Sergipe, Brazil* 122 D4
Itabaianinha, *Brazil* 122 D4
Itaberaba, *Brazil* 123 D3
Itaberaí, *Brazil* 123 E2
Itabira, *Brazil* 123 E3
Itabirito, *Brazil* 123 F3
Itaboca, *Brazil* 121 D5
Itabuna, *Brazil* 123 D4
Itacajá, *Brazil* 122 C2
Itacaunas →, *Brazil* 122 C2
Itacoatiara, *Brazil* 121 D6
Itacuaí →, *Brazil* 124 A3
Itaguaçu, *Brazil* 123 E3
Itaguari →, *Brazil* 123 D3
Itaguatins, *Brazil* 122 C2
Itaim →, *Brazil* 122 C3
Itainópolis, *Brazil* 122 C3
Itaipú, Reprêsa de, *Brazil* 127 B5
Itaituba, *Brazil* 121 D6
Itajaí, *Brazil* 127 B6
Itajubá, *Brazil* 123 F2
Itajuípe, *Brazil* 123 D4
Itaka, *Tanzania* 83 D3
Italy ■, *Europe* 7 G8
Itamataré, *Brazil* 122 B2
Itambacuri, *Brazil* 123 E3
Itambé, *Brazil* 123 E3
Itampolo, *Madag.* 85 C7
Itanhauã →, *Brazil* 121 D5
Itanhém, *Brazil* 123 E3
Itapaci, *Brazil* 123 D2
Itapagé, *Brazil* 122 B4
Itaparica, I. de, *Brazil* 123 D4
Itapebi, *Brazil* 123 E4
Itapecuru-Mirim, *Brazil* 122 B3
Itaperuna, *Brazil* 123 F3
Itapetinga, *Brazil* 123 E3
Itapetininga, *Brazil* 127 A6
Itapeva, *Brazil* 127 A6
Itapicuru →, *Bahia, Brazil* 122 D4
Itapicuru →, *Maranhão, Brazil* 122 B3
Itapinima, *Brazil* 125 B5
Itapipoca, *Brazil* 122 B4
Itapiranga, *Brazil* 121 D6
Itapiúna, *Brazil* 122 B4
Itaporanga, *Brazil* 122 C4
Itapuá □, *Paraguay* 127 B4
Itapuranga, *Brazil* 123 E2
Itaquari, *Brazil* 123 F3
Itaquatiara, *Brazil* 121 D6
Itaquí, *Brazil* 126 B4
Itararé, *Brazil* 127 A6
Itarsi, *India* 62 H7
Itarumã, *Brazil* 123 E1
Itatí, *Argentina* 126 B4
Itatira, *Brazil* 122 B4
Itatuba, *Brazil* 125 B5
Itatupa, *Brazil* 121 D7
Itaueira, *Brazil* 122 C3
Itaueira →, *Brazil* 122 C3
Itaúna, *Brazil* 123 F3
Itbayat, *Phil.* 55 A4
Itchen →, *U.K.* 13 G6
Ite, *Peru* 124 D3
Itezhi Tezhi, L., *Zambia* 83 F2
Ithaca = Itháki, *Greece* 39 L3
Ithaca, *U.S.A.* 107 D8
Itháki, *Greece* 39 L3
Itinga, *Brazil* 123 E3
Itiquira, *Brazil* 125 D7
Itiquira →, *Brazil* 125 D6
Itiruçu, *Brazil* 123 D3
Itiúba, *Brazil* 122 D4
Ito, *Japan* 49 G9
Itoigawa, *Japan* 49 F8
Iton →, *France* 24 C8
Itonamas →, *Bolivia* 125 C5
Itsa, *Egypt* 76 J7
Íttiri, *Italy* 34 B1
Ittoqqortoormiit = Scoresbysund, *Greenland* 4 B6
Itu, *Brazil* 127 A6
Itu, *Nigeria* 79 D6
Ituaçu, *Brazil* 123 D3
Ituango, *Colombia* 120 B2
Ituiutaba, *Brazil* 123 E2
Itumbiara, *Brazil* 123 E2
Ituna, *Canada* 101 C8
Itunge Port, *Tanzania* 83 D3
Ituni, *Guyana* 121 B6
Itupiranga, *Brazil* 122 C2
Iturama, *Brazil* 123 E1
Iturbe, *Argentina* 126 A2
Ituri →, *Zaïre* 82 B2
Iturup, Ostrov, *Russia* 45 E15
Ituverava, *Brazil* 123 F2
Ituxi →, *Brazil* 125 B5
Ituyuro →, *Argentina* 126 A3
Itzehoe, *Germany* 18 B5
Ivaí →, *Brazil* 127 A5
Ivalo, *Finland* 8 B22
Ivalojoki →, *Finland* 8 B22
Ivanava, *Belarus* 41 F3
Ivangorod, *Russia* 40 C5
Ivanhoe, *N.S.W., Australia* 91 E3
Ivanhoe, *W. Austral., Australia* 88 C4
Ivanhoe, *U.S.A.* 112 J7
Ivanhoe L., *Canada* 101 A7
Ivanić Grad, *Croatia* 33 C13
Ivanjica, *Serbia, Yug.* 21 M10
Ivanjšcice, *Croatia* 33 B13
Ivankoyskoye Vdkhr., *Russia* 42 B3
Ivano-Frankivsk, *Ukraine* 41 H3
Ivano-Frankovsk = Ivano-Frankivsk, *Ukraine* 41 H3
Ivanovo = Ivanava, *Belarus* 41 F3
Ivanovo, *Russia* 42 B5
Ivato, *Madag.* 85 C8
Ivatsevichy, *Belarus* 41 F3
Ivaylovgrad, *Bulgaria* 39 H9
Ivinheima →, *Brazil* 127 A5
Ivohibe, *Madag.* 85 C8
Ivolândia, *Brazil* 123 E1
Ivory Coast ■, *Africa* 78 D3
Ivrea, *Italy* 32 C4
Ivujivik, *Canada* 97 B12
Iwahig, *Phil.* 56 C5
Iwaizumi, *Japan* 48 E10
Iwaki, *Japan* 49 F10
Iwakuni, *Japan* 49 G6
Iwamizawa, *Japan* 48 C10
Iwanai, *Japan* 48 C10
Iwata, *Japan* 49 G8
Iwate □, *Japan* 48 E10
Iwate-San, *Japan* 48 E10
Iwo, *Nigeria* 79 D5
Ixiamas, *Bolivia* 124 C4
Ixopo, *S. Africa* 85 E5
Ixtepec, *Mexico* 115 D5
Ixtlán del Río, *Mexico* 114 C4
Iyo, *Japan* 49 H6
Izabal, L. de, *Guatemala* 116 C2
Izamal, *Mexico* 115 C7
Izberbash, *Russia* 43 J8
Izegem, *Belgium* 17 G2
Izena-Shima, *Japan* 49 L3
Izhevsk, *Russia* 44 D6
Izmayil, *Ukraine* 41 K5
İzmir, *Turkey* 66 C2
İzmit, *Turkey* 66 B3
Iznajar, *Spain* 31 H6
Iznalloz, *Spain* 29 H1
İznik, *Turkey* 66 B3
İznik Gölü, *Turkey* 66 B3
Izobil'nyy, *Russia* 43 H5
Izola, *Slovenia* 33 C10
Izozog, Bañados de, *Bolivia* 125 D5
Izra, *Syria* 69 C5
Iztochni Rodopi, *Bulgaria* 39 H8
Izu-Shotō, *Japan* 49 G10
Izumi-sano, *Japan* 49 G7
Izumo, *Japan* 49 G6
Izyaslav, *Ukraine* 41 G4
Izyum, *Ukraine* 41 H9

J

J.F. Rodrigues, *Brazil* 122 B1
Jaba, *Ethiopia* 77 F4
Jabal el Awliya, *Sudan* 77 D3
Jabal Lubnān, *Lebanon* 69 B4
Jabalón →, *Spain* 31 G6
Jabalpur, *India* 63 H8
Jabbūl, *Syria* 64 B3
Jablah, *Syria* 66 E6
Jablanac, *Croatia* 33 D11
Jablonec, *Czech.* 20 E5
Jabłonowo, *Poland* 20 B9
Jaboatão, *Brazil* 122 C4
Jaboticabal, *Brazil* 127 A6
Jaburu, *Brazil* 125 B5
Jaca, *Spain* 28 C4
Jacaré →, *Brazil* 122 D3
Jacareí, *Brazil* 127 A6
Jacarèzinho, *Brazil* 127 A6
Jaciara, *Brazil* 125 D7
Jacinto, *Brazil* 123 E3
Jaciparaná, *Brazil* 125 B5
Jackman, *U.S.A.* 99 C5
Jacksboro, *U.S.A.* 109 J5
Jackson, *Australia* 91 D4
Jackson, *Ala., U.S.A.* 105 K2
Jackson, *Calif., U.S.A.* 112 G6
Jackson, *Ky., U.S.A.* 104 G4
Jackson, *Mich., U.S.A.* 104 D3
Jackson, *Minn., U.S.A.* 108 D7
Jackson, *Miss., U.S.A.* 109 J9
Jackson, *Mo., U.S.A.* 109 G10
Jackson, *Ohio, U.S.A.* 104 F4
Jackson, *Tenn., U.S.A.* 105 H1
Jackson, *Wyo., U.S.A.* 110 E8
Jackson B., *N.Z.* 87 K2
Jackson L., *U.S.A.* 110 E8
Jacksons, *N.Z.* 87 K3
Jacksonville, *Ala., U.S.A.* 105 J3
Jacksonville, *Calif., U.S.A.* 112 H6
Jacksonville, *Fla., U.S.A.* 105 K5
Jacksonville, *Ill., U.S.A.* 108 F9
Jacksonville, *N.C., U.S.A.* 105 H7
Jacksonville, *Oreg., U.S.A.* 110 E2
Jacksonville, *Tex., U.S.A.* 109 K7
Jacksonville Beach, *U.S.A.* 105 K5
Jacmel, *Haiti* 117 C5
Jacob Lake, *U.S.A.* 111 H7
Jacobabad, *Pakistan* 62 E3
Jacobina, *Brazil* 122 D3
Jacques-Cartier, Mt., *Canada* 99 C6
Jacqueville, *Ivory C.* 78 D4
Jacuí →, *Brazil* 127 C5
Jacumba, *U.S.A.* 113 N10
Jacundá →, *Brazil* 122 B1
Jade, *Germany* 18 B4
Jadebusen, *Germany* 18 B4
Jadoigne, *Belgium* 17 G5
Jadotville = Likasi, *Zaïre* 83 E2
Jadraque, *Spain* 28 E2
Jādū, *Libya* 75 B7
Jaén, *Peru* 124 B2
Jaén, *Spain* 31 H7
Jaén □, *Spain* 31 H7
Jafène, *Africa* 74 D3
Jaffa = Tel Aviv-Yafo, *Israel* 69 C3
Jaffa, C., *Australia* 91 F2
Jaffna, *Sri Lanka* 60 Q12
Jagadhri, *India* 62 D7
Jagadishpur, *India* 63 G11
Jagdalpur, *India* 61 K12
Jagersfontein, *S. Africa* 84 D4
Jagraon, *India* 60 D9
Jagst →, *Germany* 19 F5
Jagtial, *India* 60 K11
Jaguaquara, *Brazil* 123 D4
Jaguariaíva, *Brazil* 127 A6
Jaguaribe, *Brazil* 122 C4
Jaguaribe →, *Brazil* 122 B4
Jaguaruana, *Brazil* 122 B4
Jagüey Grande, *Cuba* 116 B3
Jahangirabad, *India* 62 E8
Jahrom, *Iran* 65 D7
Jaicós, *Brazil* 122 C3
Jailolo, *Indonesia* 57 D7
Jailolo, Selat, *Indonesia* 57 D7
Jaipur, *India* 62 F6
Jājarm, *Iran* 65 B8
Jajce, *Bos.-H.* 21 L7
Jakarta, *Indonesia* 57 G12
Jakobstad = Pietarsaari, *Finland* 8 E20
Jakupica, *Macedonia* 39 H4
Jal, *U.S.A.* 109 J3
Jalalabad, *Afghan.* 62 B4
Jalalabad, *India* 63 F8
Jalalpur Jattan, *Pakistan* 62 C6
Jalama, *U.S.A.* 113 L6
Jalapa, *Guatemala* 116 D2
Jalapa Enríquez, *Mexico* 115 D5
Jalasjärvi, *Finland* 9 E20
Jalaun, *India* 63 F8
Jales, *Brazil* 123 F1
Jaleswar, *Nepal* 63 F11
Jalgaon, *Maharashtra, India* 60 J10
Jalgaon, *Maharashtra, India* 60 J9
Jalhay, *Belgium* 17 G7
Jalībah, *Iraq* 64 D5
Jalingo, *Nigeria* 79 D7
Jalisco □, *Mexico* 114 C4
Jalkot, *Pakistan* 63 B5
Jallas →, *Spain* 30 C1
Jalna, *India* 60 K9
Jalón →, *Spain* 28 D3
Jalpa, *Mexico* 114 C4
Jalpaiguri, *India* 61 F16
Jaluit I., *Pac. Oc.* 92 G8
Jalūlā, *Iraq* 67 E11
Jamaari, *Nigeria* 79 C6
Jamaica ■, *W. Indies* 116 C4
Jamalpur, *Bangla.* 61 G16
Jamalpur, *India* 63 G12
Jamalpurganj, *India* 63 H13
Jamanxim →, *Brazil* 125 A6
Jamari, *Brazil* 125 B5
Jamari →, *Brazil* 125 B5
Jambe, *Indonesia* 57 E8
Jambes, *Belgium* 17 H5
Jambi, *Indonesia* 56 E2
Jambi □, *Indonesia* 56 E2
Jambusar, *India* 62 H5
James →, *U.S.A.* 108 D6
James B., *Canada* 97 C11
James Ras., *Australia* 88 D5
James Ross I., *Antarctica* 5 C18
Jamestown, *Australia* 91 E2
Jamestown, *S. Africa* 84 E4
Jamestown, *Ky., U.S.A.* 104 G3
Jamestown, *N. Dak., U.S.A.* 108 B5
Jamestown, *N.Y., U.S.A.* 106 D5
Jamestown, *Pa., U.S.A.* 106 E4
Jamestown, *Tenn., U.S.A.* 105 G3
Jamīlābād, *Iran* 65 C6
Jamiltepec, *Mexico* 115 D5
Jamkhandi, *India* 60 L9
Jammerbugt, *Denmark* 11 G3
Jammu, *India* 62 C6
Jammu & Kashmir □, *India* 63 B7
Jamnagar, *India* 62 H4
Jamoigne, *Belgium* 17 J6
Jampur, *Pakistan* 62 E4
Jamrud, *Pakistan* 62 C4
Jämsä, *Finland* 9 F21
Jamshedpur, *India* 63 H12
Jamtara, *India* 63 H12
Jämtland, *Sweden* 8 E15
Jämtlands län □, *Sweden* 10 B7
Jan L., *Canada* 101 C8
Jan Mayen, *Arctic* 4 B7
Janakkala, *Finland* 9 F21
Janaúba, *Brazil* 123 E3
Janaucu, I., *Brazil* 122 A1
Jand, *Pakistan* 62 C5
Janda, L. de la, *Spain* 31 J5
Jandaia, *Brazil* 123 E1
Jandaq, *Iran* 65 C7
Jandia, *Canary Is.* 36 F5
Jandia, Pta. de, *Canary Is.* 36 F5
Jandiatuba →, *Brazil* 120 D4
Jandola, *Pakistan* 62 C4
Jandowae, *Australia* 91 D5
Jandrain-Jandrenouilles, *Belgium* 17 G5
Jándula →, *Spain* 31 G6
Janesville, *U.S.A.* 108 D10
Janga, *Ghana* 79 C4
Jango, *Brazil* 125 E6
Janīn, *West Bank* 69 C4
Janjina, *Croatia* 21 N7
Janos, *Mexico* 114 A3
Jánosháza, *Hungary* 21 H7
Janów Podlaski, *Poland* 20 C13
Januária, *Brazil* 123 E3
Janub Dârfûr □, *Sudan* 77 E2

Janub Kordofân □, *Sudan* 77 E3
Janubio, *Canary Is.* 36 F6
Janville, *France* 25 D8
Janzé, *France* 24 E5
Jaora, *India* 62 H6
Japan ■, *Asia* 49 G8
Japan, Sea of, *Asia* 48 E7
Japan Trench, *Pac. Oc.* 46 F18
Japen = Yapen, *Indonesia* 57 E9
Japurá →, *Brazil* 120 D4
Jaque, *Panama* 120 B2
Jarābulus, *Syria* 67 D8
Jaraguá, *Brazil* 123 E2
Jaraguari, *Brazil* 125 E7
Jaraicejo, *Spain* 31 F5
Jaraiz, *Spain* 30 E5
Jarama →, *Spain* 28 E1
Jaramānah, *Syria* 66 F7
Jaramillo, *Argentina* 128 C3
Jarandilla, *Spain* 30 E5
Jaranwala, *Pakistan* 62 D5
Jarash, *Jordan* 69 C4
Jarauçu →, *Brazil* 121 D7
Jardim, *Brazil* 126 A4
Jardín →, *Spain* 29 G2
Jardines de la Reina, Is., *Cuba* 116 B4
Jargalang, *China* 51 C12
Jargalant = Hovd, *Mongolia* 54 B4
Jargeau, *France* 25 E9
Jari →, *Brazil* 121 D7
Jarīr, W. al →, *Si. Arabia* 64 E4
Jarmen, *Germany* 18 B9
Jarnac, *France* 26 C3
Jarny, *France* 25 C12
Jarocin, *Poland* 20 D7
Jarosław, *Poland* 20 E12
Järpås, *Sweden* 11 F6
Järpen, *Sweden* 10 A7
Jarrahdale, *Australia* 89 F2
Jarres, Plaine des, *Laos* 58 C4
Jarso, *Ethiopia* 77 F4
Jartai, *China* 50 E3
Jaru, *Brazil* 125 C5
Jaru →, *Brazil* 125 C5
Jarud Qi, *China* 51 B11
Järvenpää, *Finland* 9 F21
Jarvis, *Canada* 106 D4
Jarvis I., *Pac. Oc.* 93 H12
Jarwa, *India* 63 F10
Jaša Tomić, *Serbia, Yug.* 21 K10
Jāsimīyah, *Iraq* 67 F11
Jasin, *Malaysia* 59 L4
Jāsk, *Iran* 65 E8
Jasło, *Poland* 20 F11
Jason, Is., *Falk. Is.* 128 D4
Jasper, *Alta., Canada* 100 C5
Jasper, *Ont., Canada* 107 B9
Jasper, *Ala., U.S.A.* 105 J2
Jasper, *Fla., U.S.A.* 105 K4
Jasper, *Minn., U.S.A.* 108 D6
Jasper, *Tex., U.S.A.* 109 K8
Jasper Nat. Park, *Canada* 100 C5
Jastrebarsko, *Croatia* 33 C12
Jastrzębie Zdrój, *Poland* 20 F8
Jászárokszállás, *Hungary* 21 H10
Jászberény, *Hungary* 21 H9
Jászladány, *Hungary* 21 H10
Jataí, *Brazil* 123 E1
Jatapu →, *Brazil* 121 D6
Jati, *Pakistan* 62 G3
Jatibarang, *Indonesia* 57 G13
Jatinegara, *Indonesia* 57 G12
Játiva, *Spain* 29 G4
Jatobal, *Brazil* 122 B2
Jaú, *Brazil* 127 A6
Jaú →, *Brazil* 121 D5
Jauaperí →, *Brazil* 121 D5
Jauche, *Belgium* 17 G5
Jauja, *Peru* 124 C2
Jaunpur, *India* 63 G10
Jauru →, *Brazil* 125 D6
Java = Jawa, *Indonesia* 57 G14
Java Sea, *Indonesia* 56 E3
Java Trench, *Ind. Oc.* 92 H2
Jávea, *Spain* 29 G5
Javhlant = Ulyasutay, *Mongolia* 54 B4
Javier, I., *Chile* 128 C2
Javron, *France* 24 D6
Jawa, *Indonesia* 57 G14
Jawor, *Poland* 20 D6
Jaworzno, *Poland* 20 E9
Jay, *U.S.A.* 109 G7
Jaya, Puncak, *Indonesia* 57 E9
Jayanca, *Peru* 124 B2
Jayanti, *India* 61 F16
Jayapura, *Indonesia* 57 E10
Jayawijaya, Pegunungan, *Indonesia* 57 E9
Jaynagar, *India* 61 F15
Jayrūd, *Syria* 66 F7
Jayton, *U.S.A.* 109 J4
Jazīreh-ye Shīf, *Iran* 65 D6
Jazminal, *Mexico* 114 C4
Jazzīn, *Lebanon* 69 B4
Jean, *U.S.A.* 113 K11
Jean Marie River, *Canada* 100 A4
Jean Rabel, *Haiti* 117 C5
Jeanerette, *U.S.A.* 109 L9
Jeanette, Ostrov, *Russia* 45 B16
Jeannette, *U.S.A.* 106 F5
Jebba, *Morocco* 74 A4
Jebba, *Nigeria* 79 D5
Jebel, Bahr el →, *Sudan* 77 F3
Jebel Qerri, *Sudan* 77 D3
Jeberos, *Peru* 124 B2
Jedburgh, *U.K.* 14 F6
Jedda = Jiddah, *Si. Arabia* 68 C2
Jędrzejów, *Poland* 20 E10
Jedway, *Canada* 100 C2
Jeetzel →, *Germany* 18 B7
Jefferson, *Iowa, U.S.A.* 108 D7
Jefferson, *Ohio, U.S.A.* 106 E4
Jefferson, *Tex., U.S.A.* 109 J7
Jefferson, *Wis., U.S.A.* 108 D10
Jefferson, Mt., *Nev., U.S.A.* 110 G5
Jefferson, Mt., *Oreg., U.S.A.* 110 D3
Jefferson City, *Mo., U.S.A.* 108 F8
Jefferson City, *Tenn., U.S.A.* 105 G4
Jeffersonville, *U.S.A.* 104 F3
Jega, *Nigeria* 79 C5
Jēkabpils, *Latvia* 9 H21
Jelenia Góra, *Poland* 20 E5
Jelgava, *Latvia* 9 H20
Jelli, *Sudan* 77 F3
Jellicoe, *Canada* 98 C2
Jemaja, *Indonesia* 56 D3
Jemaluang, *Malaysia* 59 L4
Jemappes, *Belgium* 17 H3
Jember, *Indonesia* 57 H15
Jembongan, *Malaysia* 56 C5
Jemeppe, *Belgium* 17 G7
Jemnice, *Czech.* 20 F5
Jena, *Germany* 18 E7
Jena, *U.S.A.* 109 K8
Jendouba, *Tunisia* 75 A6
Jenkins, *U.S.A.* 104 G4
Jenner, *U.S.A.* 112 G3
Jennings, *U.S.A.* 109 K8
Jennings →, *Canada* 100 B2
Jeparit, *Australia* 91 F3
Jequié, *Brazil* 123 D3
Jequitaí →, *Brazil* 123 E3
Jequitinhonha, *Brazil* 123 E3
Jequitinhonha →, *Brazil* 123 E4
Jerada, *Morocco* 75 B4
Jerantut, *Malaysia* 59 L4
Jérémie, *Haiti* 117 C5
Jeremoabo, *Brazil* 122 D4
Jerez, Punta, *Mexico* 115 C5
Jerez de García Salinas, *Mexico* 114 C4
Jerez de la Frontera, *Spain* 31 J4
Jerez de los Caballeros, *Spain* 31 G4
Jericho = Arīḩā, *Syria* 64 C3
Jericho = El Arīḩā, *West Bank* 69 D4
Jericho, *Australia* 90 C4
Jerichow, *Germany* 18 C8
Jerilderie, *Australia* 91 F4
Jermyn, *U.S.A.* 107 E9
Jerome, *U.S.A.* 111 J8
Jersey, *U.K.* 13 H5
Jersey City, *U.S.A.* 107 F10
Jersey Shore, *U.S.A.* 106 E7
Jerseyville, *U.S.A.* 108 F9
Jerusalem, *Israel* 69 D4
Jervis B., *Australia* 91 F5
Jesenice, *Slovenia* 33 B11
Jesenké, *Slovak Rep.* 21 G10
Jesselton = Kota Kinabalu, *Malaysia* 56 C5
Jessnitz, *Germany* 18 D8
Jessore, *Bangla.* 61 H16
Jesup, *U.S.A.* 105 K5
Jesús, *Peru* 124 B2
Jesús Carranza, *Mexico* 115 D5
Jesús María, *Argentina* 126 C3
Jetmore, *U.S.A.* 109 F5
Jetpur, *India* 62 J4
Jette, *Belgium* 17 G4
Jevnaker, *Norway* 10 D4
Jewett, *Ohio, U.S.A.* 106 F3
Jewett, *Tex., U.S.A.* 109 K6
Jewett City, *U.S.A.* 107 E13
Jeyḩūnābād, *Iran* 65 C6
Jeypore, *India* 61 K13
Jeziorany, *Poland* 20 B10
Jhajjar, *India* 62 E7
Jhal Jhao, *Pakistan* 60 F4
Jhalawar, *India* 62 G7
Jhang Maghiana, *Pakistan* 62 D5
Jhansi, *India* 63 G8
Jharia, *India* 63 H12
Jharsuguda, *India* 61 J14
Jhelum, *Pakistan* 62 C5
Jhelum →, *Pakistan* 62 D5
Jhunjhunu, *India* 62 E6
Ji Xian, *Hebei, China* 50 F8
Ji Xian, *Henan, China* 50 G8
Ji Xian, *Shanxi, China* 50 F6
Jia Xian, *Henan, China* 50 H7
Jia Xian, *Shaanxi, China* 50 E6
Jiading, *China* 53 B13
Jiahe, *China* 53 E9
Jialing Jiang →, *China* 52 C6
Jiamusi, *China* 54 B8
Ji'an, *Jiangxi, China* 53 D10
Ji'an, *Jilin, China* 51 D14
Jianchang, *China* 51 D11
Jianchangying, *China* 51 D10
Jianchuan, *China* 52 D2
Jiande, *China* 53 C12
Jiangbei, *China* 52 C6
Jiangcheng, *China* 52 F3
Jiangdi, *China* 52 D4
Jiange, *China* 52 A5
Jiangjin, *China* 52 C6
Jiangkou, *China* 52 D7
Jiangle, *China* 53 D11
Jiangling, *China* 53 B9
Jiangmen, *China* 53 F9
Jiangshan, *China* 53 C12
Jiangsu □, *China* 51 H10
Jiangxi □, *China* 53 D10
Jiangyin, *China* 53 B13
Jiangyong, *China* 53 E8
Jiangyou, *China* 52 B5
Jianhe, *China* 52 D7
Jianli, *China* 53 C9
Jianning, *China* 53 D11
Jian'ou, *China* 53 D12
Jianshi, *China* 52 B7
Jianshui, *China* 52 F4
Jianyang, *Fujian, China* 53 D12
Jianyang, *Sichuan, China* 52 B5
Jiao Xian, *China* 51 F11
Jiaohe, *Hebei, China* 50 E9
Jiaohe, *Jilin, China* 51 C14
Jiaoling, *China* 53 E11
Jiaozhou Wan, *China* 51 F11
Jiaozuo, *China* 50 G7
Jiashan, *China* 53 A11
Jiawang, *China* 51 G9
Jiaxiang, *China* 50 G9
Jiaxing, *China* 53 B13
Jiayi = Chiai, *Taiwan* 53 F13
Jiayu, *China* 53 C9
Jibão, Serra do, *Brazil* 123 D3
Jibiya, *Nigeria* 79 C6
Jibou, *Romania* 38 B6
Jibuti = Djibouti ■, *Africa* 68 E3
Jicarón, I., *Panama* 116 E3
Jičín, *Czech.* 20 E5
Jiddah, *Si. Arabia* 68 C2
Jido, *India* 61 E19
Jieshou, *China* 50 H8
Jiexiu, *China* 50 F6
Jieyang, *China* 53 F11
Jigawa □, *Nigeria* 79 C6
Jiggalong, *Australia* 88 D3
Jihlava, *Czech.* 20 F5
Jijel, *Algeria* 75 A6
Jijiga, *Ethiopia* 68 F3
Jijona, *Spain* 29 G4
Jikamshi, *Nigeria* 79 C6
Jilin, *China* 51 C14
Jilin □, *China* 51 C13
Jiloca →, *Spain* 28 D3
Jilong = Chilung, *Taiwan* 53 E13
Jima, *Ethiopia* 77 F4
Jimbolia, *Romania* 38 D3
Jimena de la Frontera, *Spain* 31 J5
Jiménez, *Mexico* 114 B4
Jimo, *China* 51 F11
Jin Jiang →, *China* 53 C10
Jin Xian, *Hebei, China* 50 E8
Jin Xian, *Liaoning, China* 51 E11
Jinan, *China* 50 F9
Jincheng, *China* 50 G7
Jinchuan, *China* 52 B4
Jind, *India* 62 E7
Jindabyne, *Australia* 91 F4
Jindrichuv Hradeç, *Czech.* 20 F5
Jing He →, *China* 50 G5
Jing Shan, *China* 53 B8
Jing Xian, *Anhui, China* 53 B12
Jing Xian, *Hunan, China* 52 D7
Jing'an, *China* 53 C10
Jingbian, *China* 50 F5
Jingchuan, *China* 50 G4
Jingde, *China* 53 B12
Jingdezhen, *China* 53 C11
Jingdong, *China* 52 E3
Jinggu, *China* 52 F3
Jinghai, *China* 50 E9
Jinghong, *China* 52 F3
Jingjiang, *China* 53 A13
Jingle, *China* 50 E6
Jingmen, *China* 53 B9
Jingning, *China* 50 G3
Jingpo Hu, *China* 51 C15
Jingshan, *China* 53 B9
Jingtai, *China* 50 F3
Jingxi, *China* 52 F6
Jingxing, *China* 50 E8
Jingyang, *China* 50 G5
Jingyu, *China* 51 C14
Jingyuan, *China* 50 F3
Jingziguan, *China* 50 H6
Jinhua, *China* 53 C12
Jining, *Nei Mongol Zizhiqu, China* 50 D7
Jining, *Shandong, China* 50 G9
Jinja, *Uganda* 82 B3
Jinjang, *Malaysia* 59 L3
Jinji, *China* 50 F4
Jinjiang, *Fujian, China* 53 E12
Jinjiang, *Yunnan, China* 52 D3
Jinjie, *China* 52 F6
Jinjini, *Ghana* 78 D4
Jinkou, *China* 53 B10
Jinmen Dao, *China* 53 E12
Jinnah Barrage, *Pakistan* 60 C7
Jinning, *China* 52 E4
Jinotega, *Nic.* 116 D2
Jinotepe, *Nic.* 116 D2
Jinping, *Guizhou, China* 52 D7
Jinping, *Yunnan, China* 52 F4
Jinsha, *China* 52 D6
Jinsha Jiang →, *China* 52 C5
Jinshan, *China* 53 B13
Jinshi, *China* 53 C8
Jintan, *China* 53 B12
Jinxi, *Jiangxi, China* 53 D11
Jinxi, *Liaoning, China* 51 D11
Jinxian, *China* 53 C11
Jinxiang, *China* 50 G9
Jinyun, *China* 53 C13
Jinzhai, *China* 53 B10
Jinzhou, *China* 51 D11
Jiparaná →, *Brazil* 125 B5
Jipijapa, *Ecuador* 120 D1
Jiquilpan, *Mexico* 114 D4
Jishan, *China* 50 G6
Jishou, *China* 52 C7
Jishui, *China* 53 D10
Jisr ash Shughūr, *Syria* 66 E7
Jitarning, *Australia* 89 F2
Jitra, *Malaysia* 59 J3
Jiu →, *Romania* 38 F6
Jiudengkou, *China* 50 E4
Jiujiang, *Guangdong, China* 53 F9
Jiujiang, *Jiangxi, China* 53 C10
Jiuling Shan, *China* 53 C10
Jiulong, *China* 52 C3
Jiuquan, *China* 54 C4
Jiutai, *China* 51 B13
Jiuxiangcheng, *China* 50 H8
Jiuxincheng, *China* 50 E8
Jiuyuhang, *China* 53 B12
Jixi, *Anhui, China* 53 B12
Jixi, *Heilongjiang, China* 51 B16
Jiyang, *China* 51 F9
Jīzān, *Si. Arabia* 68 D3
Jize, *China* 50 F8
Jizera →, *Czech.* 20 E4
Jizō-Zaki, *Japan* 49 G6
Jizzakh, *Uzbekistan* 44 E7
Joaçaba, *Brazil* 127 B5
Joaíma, *Brazil* 123 E3
João, *Brazil* 122 B1
João Amaro, *Brazil* 123 D3
João Câmara, *Brazil* 122 C4
João Pessoa, *Brazil* 122 C5
João Pinheiro, *Brazil* 123 E2
Joaquim Távora, *Brazil* 123 F2
Joaquín V. González, *Argentina* 126 B3
Jobourg, Nez de, *France* 24 C5
Jódar, *Spain* 29 H1
Jodhpur, *India* 62 F5
Jœuf, *France* 25 C13
Jofane, *Mozam.* 85 C5
Jõgeva, *Estonia* 9 G22
Joggins, *Canada* 99 C7
Jogjakarta = Yogyakarta, *Indonesia* 57 G14
Johannesburg, *S. Africa* 85 D4
Johannesburg, *U.S.A.* 113 K9
John Day, *U.S.A.* 110 D4
John Day →, *U.S.A.* 110 D3
John H. Kerr Reservoir, *U.S.A.* 105 G6
John o' Groats, *U.K.* 14 C5
Johnnie, *U.S.A.* 113 J10
John's Ra., *Australia* 90 C1
Johnson, *U.S.A.* 109 G4
Johnson City, *N.Y., U.S.A.* 107 D9
Johnson City, *Tenn., U.S.A.* 105 G4
Johnson City, *Tex., U.S.A.* 109 K5
Johnsonburg, *U.S.A.* 106 E6
Johnsondale, *U.S.A.* 113 K8
Johnson's Crossing, *Canada* 100 A2
Johnston, L., *Australia* 89 F3
Johnston Falls = Mambilima Falls, *Zambia* 83 E2
Johnston I., *Pac. Oc.* 93 F11
Johnstone Str., *Canada* 100 C3
Johnstown, *N.Y., U.S.A.* 107 C10
Johnstown, *Pa., U.S.A.* 106 F6
Johor Baharu, *Malaysia* 59 M4
Jõhvi, *Estonia* 9 G22
Joigny, *France* 25 E10
Joinvile, *Brazil* 127 B6
Joinville, *France* 25 D12
Joinville I., *Antarctica* 5 C18
Jojutla, *Mexico* 115 D5
Jokkmokk, *Sweden* 8 C18
Jökulsá á Bru →, *Iceland* 8 D6
Jökulsá á Fjöllum →, *Iceland* 8 C5
Jolfā, *Āzarbājān-e Sharqī, Iran* 67 C11
Jolfā, *Eşfahan, Iran* 65 C6
Joliet, *U.S.A.* 104 E1
Joliette, *Canada* 98 C5
Jolo, *Phil.* 55 J4
Jolon, *U.S.A.* 112 K5
Jomalig, *Phil.* 55 D5
Jombang, *Indonesia* 57 G15
Jomda, *China* 52 B2
Jome, *Indonesia* 57 E7
Jomfruland, *Norway* 11 F3
Jönåker, *Sweden* 11 F10
Jonava, *Lithuania* 9 J21
Jones Sound, *Canada* 4 B3
Jonesboro, *Ark., U.S.A.* 109 H9
Jonesboro, *Ill., U.S.A.* 109 G10
Jonesboro, *La., U.S.A.* 109 J8
Jonesport, *U.S.A.* 99 D6
Jonglei, *Sudan* 77 F3
Jonglei □, *Sudan* 77 F3
Joniškis, *Lithuania* 9 H20
Jönköping, *Sweden* 9 H16
Jonquière, *Canada* 99 C5
Jonsberg, *Sweden* 11 F10
Jonsered, *Sweden* 11 G6
Jonzac, *France* 26 C3
Joplin, *U.S.A.* 109 G7
Jordan, *U.S.A.* 110 C10
Jordan ■, *Asia* 69 E5
Jordan →, *Asia* 69 D4
Jordan Valley, *U.S.A.* 110 E5
Jordânia, *Brazil* 123 E3
Jorge, C., *Chile* 128 D1
Jorhat, *India* 61 F19
Jörn, *Sweden* 8 D19
Jorong, *Indonesia* 56 E4
Jørpeland, *Norway* 9 G11
Jorquera →, *Chile* 126 B2
Jos, *Nigeria* 79 D6
José Batlle y Ordóñez, *Uruguay* 127 C4
José de San Martín, *Argentina* 128 B2
Joseph, *U.S.A.* 110 D5
Joseph, L., *Nfld., Canada* 99 B6
Joseph, L., *Ont., Canada* 106 A5
Joseph Bonaparte G., *Australia* 88 B4
Joseph City, *U.S.A.* 111 J8
Joshua Tree, *U.S.A.* 113 L10
Joshua Tree National Monument, *U.S.A.* 113 M10
Josselin, *France* 24 E4
Jostedalsbreen, *Norway* 9 F12
Jotunheimen, *Norway* 10 C2
Jourdanton, *U.S.A.* 109 L5
Joure, *Neths.* 16 C7
Joussard, *Canada* 100 B5
Joutseno, *Finland* 40 B5
Jovellanos, *Cuba* 116 B3
Joyeuse, *France* 27 D8
Józefów, *Poland* 20 C11
Ju Xian, *China* 51 F10
Juan Aldama, *Mexico* 114 C4
Juan Bautista Alberdi, *Argentina* 126 C3
Juan de Fuca Str., *Canada* 112 B2
Juan de Nova, *Ind. Oc.* 85 B7
Juan Fernández, Arch. de, *Pac. Oc.* 118 G2
Juan José Castelli, *Argentina* 126 B3
Juan L. Lacaze, *Uruguay* 126 C4
Juanjuí, *Peru* 124 B2
Juankoski, *Finland* 8 E23
Juárez, *Argentina* 126 D4
Juárez, *Mexico* 113 N11
Juárez, Sierra de, *Mexico* 114 A1
Juatinga, Ponta de, *Brazil* 123 F3
Juàzeiro, *Brazil* 122 C3
Juàzeiro do Norte, *Brazil* 122 C4
Jubayl, *Lebanon* 69 A4
Jubbah, *Si. Arabia* 64 D4
Jubbulpore = Jabalpur, *India* 63 H8
Jübek, *Germany* 18 A5
Jubga, *Russia* 43 H4
Jubilee L., *Australia* 89 E4
Juby, C., *Morocco* 74 C2
Júcar →, *Spain* 29 F4
Júcaro, *Cuba* 116 B4
Juchitán, *Mexico* 115 D5
Judaea = Har Yehuda, *Israel* 69 D3
Judenburg, *Austria* 21 H4
Judith →, *U.S.A.* 110 C9
Judith, Pt., *U.S.A.* 107 E13
Judith Gap, *U.S.A.* 110 C9
Jufari →, *Brazil* 121 D5
Jugoslavia = Yugoslavia ■, *Europe* 21 M10
Juigalpa, *Nic.* 116 D2
Juillac, *France* 26 C5
Juist, *Germany* 18 B2
Juiz de Fora, *Brazil* 123 F3
Jujuy □, *Argentina* 126 A2
Julesburg, *U.S.A.* 108 E3
Juli, *Peru* 124 D4
Julia Cr. →, *Australia* 90 C3
Julia Creek, *Australia* 90 C3
Juliaca, *Peru* 124 D3
Julian, *U.S.A.* 113 M10
Julian Alps = Julijske Alpe, *Slovenia* 33 B11
Julianakanaal, *Neths.* 17 F7
Julianatop, *Surinam* 121 C6
Julianehåb, *Greenland* 4 C5
Jülich, *Germany* 18 E2
Julierpass, *Switz.* 23 D9
Julijske Alpe, *Slovenia* 33 B11
Julimes, *Mexico* 114 B3
Jullundur, *India* 62 D6
Julu, *China* 50 F8
Jumbo, *Zimbabwe* 83 F3
Jumbo Pk., *U.S.A.* 113 J12
Jumentos Cays, *Bahamas* 117 B4
Jumet, *Belgium* 17 H4
Jumilla, *Spain* 29 G3
Jumla, *Nepal* 63 E10
Jumna = Yamuna →, *India* 63 G9
Junagadh, *India* 62 J4
Junction, *Tex., U.S.A.* 109 K5
Junction, *Utah, U.S.A.* 111 G7
Junction B., *Australia* 90 A1
Junction City, *Kans., U.S.A.* 108 F6
Junction City, *Oreg., U.S.A.* 110 D2
Junction Pt., *Australia* 90 A1
Jundah, *Australia* 90 C3
Jundiaí, *Brazil* 127 A6
Juneau, *U.S.A.* 96 C6

Junee, *Australia* 91 E4
Jungfrau, *Switz.* 22 C5
Junggar Pendi, *China* 54 B3
Junglinster, *Lux.* 17 J8
Jungshahi, *Pakistan* 62 G2
Juniata →, *U.S.A.* 106 F7
Junín, *Argentina* 126 C3
Junín, *Peru* 124 C2
Junín □, *Peru* 124 C3
Junín de los Andes, *Argentina* 128 A2
Jūniyah, *Lebanon* 69 B4
Juntura, *U.S.A.* 110 E4
Juparanã, L., *Brazil* 123 E3
Jupiter →, *Canada* 99 C7
Juquiá, *Brazil* 123 F2
Jur, Nahr el →, *Sudan* 77 F2
Jura = Jura, Mts. du, *Europe* 25 F13
Jura = Schwäbische Alb, *Germany* 19 G5
Jura, *U.K.* 14 F3
Jura □, *France* 25 F12
Jura, Mts. du, *Europe* 25 F13
Jura, Sd. of, *U.K.* 14 F3
Jura Suisse, *Switz.* 22 B3
Jurado, *Colombia* 120 B2
Jurbarkas, *Lithuania* 9 J20
Jurilovca, *Romania* 38 E11
Jūrmala, *Latvia* 9 H20
Jurong, *China* 53 B12
Juruá →, *Brazil* 120 D4
Juruena, *Brazil* 125 C6
Juruena →, *Brazil* 125 B6
Juruti, *Brazil* 121 D6
Jussey, *France* 25 E12
Justo Daract, *Argentina* 126 C2
Jutaí, *Brazil* 124 B4
Jutaí →, *Brazil* 120 D4
Jüterbog, *Germany* 18 D9
Juticalpa, *Honduras* 116 D2
Jutland = Jylland, *Denmark* 11 H3
Jutphaas, *Neths.* 16 D6
Juventud, I. de la, *Cuba* 116 B3
Juvigny-sous-Andaine, *France* 24 D6
Juvisy-sur-Orge, *France* 25 D9
Juwain, *Afghan.* 60 D2
Jūy Zar, *Iran* 67 F12
Juye, *China* 50 G9
Juzennecourt, *France* 25 D11
Jvari, *Georgia* 43 J6
Jylland, *Denmark* 11 H3
Jyväskylä, *Finland* 9 E21

K

K2, *Pakistan* 63 B7
Kaap Plateau, *S. Africa* 84 D3
Kaapkruis, *Namibia* 84 C1
Kaapstad = Cape Town, *S. Africa* 84 E2
Kaatsheuvel, *Neths.* 17 E6
Kabaena, *Indonesia* 57 F6
Kabala, *S. Leone* 78 D2
Kabale, *Uganda* 82 C3
Kabalo, *Zaïre* 82 D2
Kabambare, *Zaïre* 82 C2
Kabango, *Zaïre* 83 D2
Kabanjahe, *Indonesia* 56 D1
Kabankalan, *Phil.* 55 G5
Kabara, *Mali* 78 B4
Kabardinka, *Russia* 43 H4
Kabardino-Balkar Republic = Kabardino Balkaria □, *Russia* 43 J6
Kabardino Balkaria □, *Russia* 43 J6
Kabare, *Indonesia* 57 E8
Kabarega Falls, *Uganda* 82 B3
Kabasalan, *Phil.* 55 H5
Kabba, *Nigeria* 79 D6
Kabin Buri, *Thailand* 58 F3
Kabinakagami L., *Canada* 98 C3
Kabīr, Zab al →, *Iraq* 67 D10
Kabkabīyah, *Sudan* 73 F9
Kabna, *Sudan* 76 D3
Kabompo, *Zambia* 83 E1
Kabompo →, *Zambia* 81 G4
Kabondo, *Zaïre* 83 D2
Kabongo, *Zaïre* 82 D2
Kabou, *Togo* 79 D5
Kaboudia, Rass, *Tunisia* 75 A7
Kabra, *Australia* 90 C5
Kabūd Gonbad, *Iran* 65 B8
Kabugao, *Phil.* 55 B4
Kābul, *Afghan.* 62 B3
Kābul □, *Afghan.* 60 B6
Kabul →, *Pakistan* 62 C5
Kabunga, *Zaïre* 82 C2
Kaburuang, *Indonesia* 57 D7
Kabushiya, *Sudan* 77 D3
Kabwe, *Zambia* 83 E2
Kačanik, *Serbia, Yug.* 21 N11
Kachchh, Gulf of, *India* 62 H3
Kachchh, Rann of, *India* 62 G4
Kachebera, *Zambia* 83 E3
Kachin □, *Burma* 61 F20
Kachira, L., *Uganda* 82 C3
Kachiry, *Kazakstan* 44 D8
Kachisi, *Ethiopia* 77 F4
Kachot, *Cambodia* 59 G4
Kaçkar, *Turkey* 67 B9
Kadan Kyun, *Burma* 56 B1
Kadanai →, *Afghan.* 62 D1
Kadarkút, *Hungary* 21 J7
Kade, *Ghana* 79 D4
Kadi, *India* 62 H5
Kadina, *Australia* 91 E2
Kadınhanı, *Turkey* 66 C5
Kadirli, *Turkey* 66 D7
Kadiyevka = Stakhanov, *Ukraine* 41 H10
Kadoka, *U.S.A.* 108 D4
Kadom, *Russia* 42 C6
Kadoma, *Zimbabwe* 83 F2
Kâdugli, *Sudan* 77 E2
Kaduna, *Nigeria* 79 C6
Kaduna □, *Nigeria* 79 C6
Kaduy, *Russia* 40 C9
Kaédi, *Mauritania* 78 B2
Kaelé, *Cameroon* 79 C7
Kaeng Khoï, *Thailand* 58 E3
Kaesŏng, *N. Korea* 51 F14
Kāf, *Si. Arabia* 64 D3
Kafakumba, *Zaïre* 80 F4
Kafan = Kapan, *Armenia* 67 C12
Kafanchan, *Nigeria* 79 D6
Kafareti, *Nigeria* 79 C7
Kaffrine, *Senegal* 78 C1
Kafia Kingi, *Sudan* 73 G9
Kafinda, *Zambia* 83 E3
Kafirévs, Ákra, *Greece* 39 L7
Kafr el Dauwâr, *Egypt* 76 H7
Kafr el Sheikh, *Egypt* 76 H7
Kafue, *Zambia* 83 F2
Kafue →, *Zambia* 81 H5
Kafue Flats, *Zambia* 83 F2
Kafue Nat. Park, *Zambia* 83 F2
Kafulwe, *Zambia* 83 D2
Kaga, *Afghan.* 62 B4
Kaga Bandoro, *C.A.R.* 73 G8
Kagan, *Uzbekistan* 44 F7
Kagawa □, *Japan* 49 G6
Kagera □, *Tanzania* 82 C3
Kagera →, *Uganda* 82 C3
Kağizman, *Turkey* 67 B10
Kagoshima, *Japan* 49 J5
Kagoshima □, *Japan* 49 J5
Kagul = Cahul, *Moldova* 41 K5
Kahak, *Iran* 65 B6
Kahama, *Tanzania* 82 C3
Kahama □, *Tanzania* 82 C3
Kahang, *Malaysia* 59 L4
Kahayan →, *Indonesia* 56 E4
Kahe, *Tanzania* 82 C4
Kahemba, *Zaïre* 80 F3
Kahil, Djebel bou, *Algeria* 75 B5
Kahniah →, *Canada* 100 B4
Kahnūj, *Iran* 65 E8
Kahoka, *U.S.A.* 108 E9
Kahoolawe, *U.S.A.* 102 H16
Kahramanmaraş, *Turkey* 66 D7
Kâhta, *Turkey* 67 D8
Kahuta, *Pakistan* 62 C5
Kai, Kepulauan, *Indonesia* 57 F8
Kai Besar, *Indonesia* 57 F8
Kai Is. = Kai, Kepulauan, *Indonesia* 57 F8
Kai Kecil, *Indonesia* 57 F8
Kai Xian, *China* 52 B7
Kaiama, *Nigeria* 79 D5
Kaiapoi, *N.Z.* 87 K4
Kaieteur Falls, *Guyana* 121 B6
Kaifeng, *China* 50 G8
Kaihua, *China* 53 C12
Kaikohe, *N.Z.* 87 F4
Kaikoura, *N.Z.* 87 K4
Kaikoura Ra., *N.Z.* 87 J4
Kailahun, *S. Leone* 78 D2
Kaili, *China* 52 D6
Kailu, *China* 51 C11
Kailua Kona, *U.S.A.* 102 J17
Kaimana, *Indonesia* 57 E8
Kaimanawa Mts., *N.Z.* 87 H5
Kaimganj, *India* 63 F8
Kaimur Hills, *India* 63 G9
Kaingaroa Forest, *N.Z.* 87 H6
Kainji Res., *Nigeria* 79 C5
Kainuu, *Finland* 8 D23
Kaipara Harbour, *N.Z.* 87 G5
Kaiping, *China* 53 F9
Kaipokok B., *Canada* 99 B8
Kairana, *India* 62 E7
Kaironi, *Indonesia* 57 E8
Kairouan, *Tunisia* 75 A7
Kaiserslautern, *Germany* 19 F3
Kaitaia, *N.Z.* 87 F4
Kaitangata, *N.Z.* 87 M2
Kaithal, *India* 62 E7
Kaitu →, *Pakistan* 62 C4
Kaiwi Channel, *U.S.A.* 102 H16
Kaiyang, *China* 52 D6
Kaiyuan, *Liaoning, China* 51 C13
Kaiyuan, *Yunnan, China* 52 F4
Kajaani, *Finland* 8 D22
Kajabbi, *Australia* 90 B3
Kajana = Kajaani, *Finland* 8 D22
Kajang, *Malaysia* 59 L3
Kajaran, *Armenia* 67 C12
Kajiado, *Kenya* 82 C4
Kajiado □, *Kenya* 82 C4
Kajo Kaji, *Sudan* 77 G3
Kaka, *Sudan* 77 E3
Kakabeka Falls, *Canada* 98 C2
Kakamas, *S. Africa* 84 D3
Kakamega, *Kenya* 82 B3
Kakamega □, *Kenya* 82 B3
Kakanj, *Bos.-H.* 21 L8
Kakanui Mts., *N.Z.* 87 L3
Kake, *Japan* 49 G6
Kakegawa, *Japan* 49 G9
Kakeroma-Jima, *Japan* 49 K4
Kakhib, *Russia* 43 J8
Kakhovka, *Ukraine* 41 J7
Kakhovske Vdskh., *Ukraine* 41 J7
Kakinada, *India* 61 L13
Kakisa →, *Canada* 100 A5
Kakisa L., *Canada* 100 A5
Kakogawa, *Japan* 49 G7
Kakwa →, *Canada* 100 C5
Kāl Gūsheh, *Iran* 65 D8
Kal Safīd, *Iran* 67 E12
Kala, *Nigeria* 79 C7
Kalaa-Kebira, *Tunisia* 75 A7
Kalabagh, *Pakistan* 62 C4
Kalabahi, *Indonesia* 57 F6
Kalabáka, *Greece* 39 K4
Kalabo, *Zambia* 81 G4
Kalach, *Russia* 42 E5
Kalach na Donu, *Russia* 43 F6
Kaladan →, *Burma* 61 J18
Kaladar, *Canada* 106 B7
Kalahari, *Africa* 84 C3
Kalahari Gemsbok Nat. Park, *S. Africa* 84 D3
Kalajoki, *Finland* 8 D20
Kālak, *Iran* 65 E8
Kalakamati, *Botswana* 85 C4
Kalakan, *Russia* 45 D12
Kalakh, *Syria* 64 C3
K'alak'unlun Shank'ou, *Pakistan* 63 B7
Kalam, *Pakistan* 63 B5
Kalama, *U.S.A.* 112 E4
Kalama, *Zaïre* 82 C2
Kalámai, *Greece* 39 M5
Kalamariá, *Greece* 39 J5
Kalamata = Kalámai, *Greece* 39 M5
Kalamazoo, *U.S.A.* 104 D3
Kalamazoo →, *U.S.A.* 104 D2
Kalambo Falls, *Tanzania* 83 D3
Kálamos, *Greece* 39 L3
Kalannie, *Australia* 89 F2
Kalāntarī, *Iran* 65 C7
Kalao, *Indonesia* 57 F6
Kalaotoa, *Indonesia* 57 F6
Kälarne, *Sweden* 10 B10
Kalárovo, *Slovak Rep.* 21 H7
Kalasin, *Thailand* 58 D4
Kalat, *Pakistan* 60 E5
Kalāteh, *Iran* 65 B7
Kalāteh-ye-Ganj, *Iran* 65 E8
Kálathos, *Greece* 39 N11
Kalaus →, *Russia* 43 H7
Kalávrita, *Greece* 39 L5
Kalbarri, *Australia* 89 E1
Kale, *Turkey* 66 D3
Kalecik, *Turkey* 66 B5
Kalegauk Kyun, *Burma* 61 M20
Kalehe, *Zaïre* 82 C2
Kalema, *Tanzania* 82 C3
Kalemie, *Zaïre* 82 D2
Kalety, *Poland* 20 E8
Kalewa, *Burma* 61 H19
Kalgan = Zhangjiakou, *China* 50 D8
Kalgoorlie-Boulder, *Australia* 89 F3
Kaliakra, Nos, *Bulgaria* 38 F11
Kalianda, *Indonesia* 56 F3
Kalibo, *Phil.* 55 F5
Kaliganj, *Bangla.* 63 H13
Kalima, *Zaïre* 82 C2
Kalimantan, *Indonesia* 56 E4
Kalimantan Barat □, *Indonesia* 56 E4
Kalimantan Selatan □, *Indonesia* 56 E5
Kalimantan Tengah □, *Indonesia* 56 E4
Kalimantan Timur □, *Indonesia* 56 D5
Kálimnos, *Greece* 39 N10
Kalimpong, *India* 63 F13
Kalinin = Tver, *Russia* 42 B2
Kaliningrad, *Russia* 9 J19
Kalininsk, *Russia* 42 E7
Kalinkavichy, *Belarus* 41 F5
Kalinkovichi = Kalinkavichy, *Belarus* 41 F5
Kalinovik, *Bos.-H.* 21 M8
Kalipetrovo, *Bulgaria* 38 E10
Kaliro, *Uganda* 82 B3
Kalispell, *U.S.A.* 110 B6
Kalisz, *Poland* 20 D8
Kaliua, *Tanzania* 82 D3
Kalix, *Sweden* 8 D20
Kalix →, *Sweden* 8 D20
Kalka, *India* 62 D7
Kalkan, *Turkey* 66 D3
Kalkaska, *U.S.A.* 104 C3
Kalkfeld, *Namibia* 84 C2
Kalkfontein, *Botswana* 84 C3
Kalkrand, *Namibia* 84 C2
Kållandsö, *Sweden* 11 F7
Kallavesi, *Finland* 8 E22
Kallithéa, *Greece* 39 M6
Kallonís, Kólpos, *Greece* 39 K9
Kallsjön, *Sweden* 8 E15
Kalmalo, *Nigeria* 79 C6
Kalmar, *Sweden* 9 H17
Kalmthout, *Belgium* 17 F4
Kalmyk Republic = Kalmykia □, *Russia* 43 G8
Kalmykia □, *Russia* 43 G8
Kalmykovo, *Kazakstan* 44 E6
Kalna, *India* 63 H13
Kalocsa, *Hungary* 21 J9
Kalokhorio, *Cyprus* 37 E12
Kaloko, *Zaïre* 82 D2
Kalol, *Gujarat, India* 62 H5
Kalol, *Gujarat, India* 62 H5
Kalolímnos, *Greece* 39 M10
Kalomo, *Zambia* 83 F2
Kalpi, *India* 63 F8
Kaltbrunn, *Switz.* 23 B8
Kaltern = Caldaro, *Italy* 33 B8
Kaltungo, *Nigeria* 79 D7
Kalu, *Pakistan* 62 G2
Kaluga, *Russia* 42 C3
Kalulushi, *Zambia* 83 E2
Kalundborg, *Denmark* 11 J5
Kalush, *Ukraine* 41 H3
Kałuszyn, *Poland* 20 C11
Kalutara, *Sri Lanka* 60 R11
Kalyazin, *Russia* 42 B3
Kama, *Zaïre* 82 C2
Kama →, *Russia* 44 D6
Kamachumu, *Tanzania* 82 C3
Kamaishi, *Japan* 48 E10
Kamalia, *Pakistan* 62 D5
Kaman, *Turkey* 66 C5
Kamapanda, *Zambia* 83 E1
Kamaran, *Yemen* 68 D3
Kamativi, *Zimbabwe* 83 F2
Kamba, *Nigeria* 79 C5
Kambalda, *Australia* 89 F3
Kambar, *Pakistan* 62 F3
Kambia, *S. Leone* 78 D2
Kambolé, *Zambia* 83 D3
Kambos, *Cyprus* 37 D11
Kambove, *Zaïre* 83 E2
Kamchatka, P-ov., *Russia* 45 D16
Kamchatka Pen. = Kamchatka, P-ov., *Russia* 45 D16
Kamen, *Russia* 44 D9
Kamen-Rybolov, *Russia* 48 B6
Kamenjak, Rt., *Croatia* 33 D10
Kamenka = Kaminka, *Ukraine* 41 H7
Kamenka, *Kazakstan* 42 E10
Kamenka, *Russia* 42 D6
Kamenka, *Russia* 42 E4
Kamenka Bugskaya = Kamyanka-Buzka, *Ukraine* 41 G3
Kamenka Dneprovskaya = Kamyanka-Dniprovska, *Ukraine* 41 J8
Kamennomostskiy, *Russia* 43 H5
Kamenolomini, *Russia* 43 G5
Kamensk-Shakhtinskiy, *Russia* 43 F5
Kamensk Uralskiy, *Russia* 44 D7
Kamenskiy, *Russia* 42 E7
Kamenskoye, *Russia* 45 C17
Kamenyak, *Bulgaria* 38 F9
Kamenz, *Germany* 18 D10
Kameoka, *Japan* 49 G7
Kamiah, *U.S.A.* 110 C5
Kamień Pomorski, *Poland* 20 B4
Kamieskroon, *S. Africa* 84 E2
Kamilukuak, L., *Canada* 101 A8
Kamin-Kashyrskyy, *Ukraine* 41 G3
Kamina, *Zaïre* 83 D1
Kaminak L., *Canada* 101 A9
Kaminka, *Ukraine* 41 H7
Kaminoyama, *Japan* 48 E10
Kamiros, *Greece* 37 C9
Kamituga, *Zaïre* 82 C2
Kamloops, *Canada* 100 C4
Kamnik, *Slovenia* 33 B11
Kamo, *Armenia* 43 K7
Kamo, *Japan* 48 F9
Kamoa Mts., *Guyana* 121 C6
Kamoke, *Pakistan* 62 C6
Kamp →, *Austria* 21 G5
Kampala, *Uganda* 82 B3
Kampar, *Malaysia* 59 K3
Kampar →, *Indonesia* 56 D2
Kampen, *Neths.* 16 C7
Kamperland, *Neths.* 17 E3
Kamphaeng Phet, *Thailand* 58 D2
Kampolombo, L., *Zambia* 83 E2
Kampong To, *Thailand* 59 J3
Kampot, *Cambodia* 59 G5
Kampti, *Burkina Faso* 78 C4
Kampuchea = Cambodia ■, *Asia* 58 F5
Kampung →, *Indonesia* 57 F9
Kampung Air Putih, *Malaysia* 59 K4
Kampung Jerangau, *Malaysia* 59 K4
Kampung Raja, *Malaysia* 59 K4
Kampungbaru = Tolitoli, *Indonesia* 57 D6
Kamrau, Teluk, *Indonesia* 57 E8
Kamsack, *Canada* 101 C8
Kamskoye Ustye, *Russia* 42 C9
Kamuchawie L., *Canada* 101 B8
Kamui-Misaki, *Japan* 48 C10
Kamyanets-Podilskyy, *Ukraine* 41 H4
Kamyanka-Buzka, *Ukraine* 41 G3
Kamyanka-Dniprovska, *Ukraine* 41 J8
Kāmyārān, *Iran* 67 E12
Kamyshin, *Russia* 42 E7
Kamyzyak, *Russia* 43 G9
Kanaaupscow, *Canada* 98 B4
Kanab, *U.S.A.* 111 H7
Kanab →, *U.S.A.* 111 H7
Kanagi, *Japan* 48 D10
Kanairiktok →, *Canada* 99 A7
Kanália, *Greece* 39 K5
Kananga, *Zaïre* 80 F4
Kanarraville, *U.S.A.* 111 H7
Kanash, *Russia* 42 C8
Kanaskat, *U.S.A.* 112 C5
Kanawha →, *U.S.A.* 104 F4
Kanazawa, *Japan* 49 F8
Kanchanaburi, *Thailand* 58 E2
Kanchenjunga, *Nepal* 63 F13
Kanchipuram, *India* 60 N11
Kanda Kanda, *Zaïre* 80 F4
Kandahar = Qandahār, *Afghan.* 60 D4
Kandalaksha, *Russia* 44 C4
Kandalu, *Afghan.* 60 E3
Kandangan, *Indonesia* 56 E5
Kandanos, *Greece* 37 D5
Kander →, *Switz.* 22 C5
Kandersteg, *Switz.* 22 D5
Kandhíla, *Greece* 39 M5
Kandhkot, *Pakistan* 62 E3
Kandhla, *India* 62 E7
Kandi, *Benin* 79 C5
Kandi, *India* 63 H13
Kandıra, *Turkey* 66 B4
Kandla, *India* 62 H4
Kandos, *Australia* 91 E4
Kandy, *Sri Lanka* 60 R12
Kane, *U.S.A.* 106 E6
Kane Basin, *Greenland* 4 B4
Kanevskaya, *Russia* 43 G4
Kanfanar, *Croatia* 33 C10
Kangaba, *Mali* 78 C3
Kangal, *Turkey* 66 C7
Kangān, *Fārs, Iran* 65 E7
Kangān, *Hormozgān, Iran* 65 E8
Kangar, *Malaysia* 59 J3
Kangaroo I., *Australia* 91 F2
Kangasala, *Finland* 9 F21
Kangāvar, *Iran* 67 E12
Kangding, *China* 52 B3
Kăngdong, *N. Korea* 51 E14
Kangean, Kepulauan, *Indonesia* 56 F5
Kangean Is. = Kangean, Kepulauan, *Indonesia* 56 F5
Kanggye, *N. Korea* 51 D14
Kanggyŏng, *S. Korea* 51 F14
Kanghwa, *S. Korea* 51 F14
Kangiqsualujjuaq, *Canada* 97 C13
Kangiqsujuaq, *Canada* 97 B12
Kangirsuk, *Canada* 97 B13
Kangnŭng, *S. Korea* 51 F15
Kango, *Gabon* 80 D2
Kangping, *China* 51 C12
Kangto, *India* 61 F18
Kani, *Ivory C.* 78 D3
Kaniama, *Zaïre* 82 D1
Kaniapiskau →, *Canada* 99 A6
Kaniapiskau L., *Canada* 99 B6
Kanin, Poluostrov, *Russia* 44 C5
Kanin Nos, Mys, *Russia* 44 C5
Kanin Pen. = Kanin, Poluostrov, *Russia* 44 C5
Kaniva, *Australia* 91 F3
Kanjiža, *Serbia, Yug.* 21 J10
Kanjut Sar, *Pakistan* 63 A6
Kankaanpää, *Finland* 9 F20
Kankakee, *U.S.A.* 104 E2
Kankakee →, *U.S.A.* 104 E1
Kankan, *Guinea* 78 C3
Kankendy = Xankändi, *Azerbaijan* 67 C12
Kanker, *India* 61 J12
Kankunskiy, *Russia* 45 D13
Kannapolis, *U.S.A.* 105 H5
Kannauj, *India* 63 F8
Kannod, *India* 60 H10
Kano, *Nigeria* 79 C6
Kano □, *Nigeria* 79 C6
Kan'onji, *Japan* 49 G6
Kanoroba, *Ivory C.* 78 D3
Kanowit, *Malaysia* 56 D4
Kanowna, *Australia* 89 F3
Kanoya, *Japan* 49 J5
Kanpetlet, *Burma* 61 J18
Kanpur, *India* 63 F9
Kansas □, *U.S.A.* 108 F6
Kansas →, *U.S.A.* 108 F7
Kansas City, *Kans., U.S.A.* 108 F7
Kansas City, *Mo., U.S.A.* 108 F7
Kansenia, *Zaïre* 83 E2
Kansk, *Russia* 45 D10
Kansŏng, *S. Korea* 51 E15
Kansu = Gansu □, *China* 50 G3
Kantang, *Thailand* 59 J2
Kantché, *Niger* 79 C6
Kanté, *Togo* 79 D5
Kantemirovka, *Russia* 42 F4
Kantharalak, *Thailand* 58 E5
Kantō □, *Japan* 49 F9
Kantō-Sanchi, *Japan* 49 G9
Kanturk, *Ireland* 15 D3
Kanuma, *Japan* 49 F9
Kanus, *Namibia* 84 D2
Kanye, *Botswana* 84 C4
Kanzenze, *Zaïre* 83 E2
Kanzi, Ras, *Tanzania* 82 D4
Kaohsiung, *Taiwan* 53 F13
Kaokoveld, *Namibia* 84 B1
Kaolack, *Senegal* 78 C1
Kaoshan, *China* 51 B13
Kapadvanj, *India* 62 H5

Kapan, *Armenia* 67 C12
Kapanga, *Zaïre* 80 F4
Kapchagai = Qapshaghay, *Kazakstan* 44 E8
Kapellen, *Belgium* 17 F4
Kapéllo, Ákra, *Greece* 39 N6
Kapema, *Zaïre* 83 E2
Kapfenberg, *Austria* 21 H5
Kapiri Mposhi, *Zambia* 83 E2
Kapiskau →, *Canada* 98 B3
Kapit, *Malaysia* 56 D4
Kapiti I., *N.Z.* 87 J5
Kaplice, *Czech.* 20 G4
Kapoe, *Thailand* 59 H2
Kapoeta, *Sudan* 77 G3
Kapos →, *Hungary* 21 J8
Kaposvár, *Hungary* 21 J7
Kapowsin, *U.S.A.* 112 D4
Kappeln, *Germany* 18 A5
Kapps, *Namibia* 84 C2
Kaprije, *Croatia* 33 E12
Kaprijke, *Belgium* 17 F3
Kapsan, *N. Korea* 51 D15
Kapsukas = Marijampolė, *Lithuania* 9 J20
Kapuas →, *Indonesia* 56 E3
Kapuas Hulu, Pegunungan, *Malaysia* 56 D4
Kapuas Hulu Ra. = Kapuas Hulu, Pegunungan, *Malaysia* 56 D4
Kapulo, *Zaïre* 83 D2
Kapunda, *Australia* 91 E2
Kapuni, *N.Z.* 87 H5
Kapurthala, *India* 62 D6
Kapuskasing, *Canada* 98 C3
Kapuskasing →, *Canada* 98 C3
Kapustin Yar, *Russia* 43 F7
Kaputar, *Australia* 91 E5
Kaputir, *Kenya* 82 B4
Kapuvár, *Hungary* 21 H7
Kara, *Russia* 44 C7
Kara Bogaz Gol, Zaliv = Garabogazköl Aylagy, *Turkmenistan* 44 E6
Kara Kalpak Republic □ = Karakalpakstan □, *Uzbekistan* 44 E6
Kara Kum, *Turkmenistan* 44 F6
Kara Sea, *Russia* 44 B7
Karabiğa, *Turkey* 66 B2
Karabük, *Turkey* 66 B5
Karaburun, *Turkey* 66 C2
Karaburuni, *Albania* 39 J2
Karabutak = Qarabutaq, *Kazakstan* 44 E7
Karacabey, *Turkey* 66 B3
Karacasu, *Turkey* 66 D3
Karachala = Qaraçala, *Azerbaijan* 43 L9
Karachayevsk, *Russia* 43 J5
Karachev, *Russia* 42 D2
Karachey-Cherkessia □, *Russia* 43 J5
Karachi, *Pakistan* 62 G2
Karad, *India* 60 L9
Karadeniz Boğazı, *Turkey* 66 B3
Karaga, *Ghana* 79 D4
Karaganda = Qaraghandy, *Kazakstan* 44 E8
Karagayly, *Kazakstan* 44 E8
Karaginskiy, Ostrov, *Russia* 45 D17
Karagüney Dağları, *Turkey* 66 B6
Karagwe □, *Tanzania* 82 C3
Karaikal, *India* 60 P11
Karaikkudi, *India* 60 P11
Karaisali, *Turkey* 66 D6
Karaj, *Iran* 65 C6
Karak, *Malaysia* 59 L4
Karakalpakstan □, *Uzbekistan* 44 E6
Karakas, *Kazakstan* 44 E9
Karakelong, *Indonesia* 57 D7
Karakitang, *Indonesia* 57 D7
Karaklis = Vanadzor, *Armenia* 43 K7
Karakoçan, *Turkey* 67 C9
Karakoram Pass, *Pakistan* 63 B7
Karakoram Ra., *Pakistan* 63 B7
Karakurt, *Turkey* 67 B10
Karalon, *Russia* 45 D12
Karaman, *Turkey* 66 D5
Karamay, *China* 54 B3
Karambu, *Indonesia* 56 E5
Karamea Bight, *N.Z.* 87 J3
Karamsad, *India* 62 H5
Karand, *Iran* 67 E12
Karanganyar, *Indonesia* 57 G13
Karapınar, *Turkey* 66 D5
Karasburg, *Namibia* 84 D2
Karasino, *Russia* 44 C9
Karasjok, *Norway* 8 B21
Karasu, *Turkey* 66 B4
Karasuk, *Russia* 44 D8
Karasuyama, *Japan* 49 F10
Karataş, *Turkey* 66 D6
Karataş Burnu, *Turkey* 66 D6
Karatau = Qarataū, *Kazakstan* 44 E8
Karatau, Khrebet, *Kazakstan* 44 E7
Karauli, *India* 62 F7
Karavostasi, *Cyprus* 37 D11
Karawang, *Indonesia* 57 G12
Karawanken, *Europe* 21 J4
Karayazı, *Turkey* 67 C10
Karazhal, *Kazakstan* 44 E8
Karbalā, *Iraq* 67 F11
Kårböle, *Sweden* 10 C9
Karcag, *Hungary* 21 H10
Karcha →, *Pakistan* 63 B7
Karda, *Russia* 45 D11
Kardhámila, *Greece* 39 L9
Kardhítsa, *Greece* 39 K4
Kärdla, *Estonia* 9 G20
Kareeberge, *S. Africa* 84 E3
Kareima, *Sudan* 76 D3
Karelia □, *Russia* 44 C4
Karelian Republic □ = Karelia □, *Russia* 44 C4
Kärevändar, *Iran* 65 E9
Kargasok, *Russia* 44 D9
Kargat, *Russia* 44 D9
Kargı, *Turkey* 66 B6
Kargil, *India* 63 B7
Kargopol, *Russia* 40 B10
Karguéri, *Niger* 79 C7
Karia ba Mohammed, *Morocco* 74 B3
Karīān, *Iran* 65 E8
Kariba, *Zimbabwe* 83 F2
Kariba, L., *Zimbabwe* 83 F2
Kariba Dam, *Zimbabwe* 83 F2
Kariba Gorge, *Zambia* 83 F2
Karibib, *Namibia* 84 C2
Karimata, Kepulauan, *Indonesia* 56 E3
Karimata, Selat, *Indonesia* 56 E3
Karimata Is. = Karimata, Kepulauan, *Indonesia* 56 E3
Karimnagar, *India* 60 K11
Karimunjawa, Kepulauan, *Indonesia* 56 F4
Karin, *Somali Rep.* 68 E4
Karīt, *Iran* 65 C8
Kariya, *Japan* 49 G8
Karjala, *Finland* 40 A5
Karkaralinsk = Qarqaraly, *Kazakstan* 44 E8
Karkinitska Zatoka, *Ukraine* 41 K7
Karkinitskiy Zaliv = Karkinitska Zatoka, *Ukraine* 41 K7
Karkur Tohl, *Egypt* 76 C2
Karl Liebknecht, *Russia* 42 E2
Karl-Marx-Stadt = Chemnitz, *Germany* 18 E8
Karla, L. = Voiviïs Límni, *Greece* 39 K5
Karlivka, *Ukraine* 41 H8
Karlobag, *Croatia* 33 D12
Karlovac, *Croatia* 33 C12
Karlovka = Karlivka, *Ukraine* 41 H8
Karlovo, *Bulgaria* 38 G7
Karlovy Vary, *Czech.* 20 E2
Karlsbad = Karlovy Vary, *Czech.* 20 E2
Karlsborg, *Sweden* 11 F8
Karlshamn, *Sweden* 9 H16
Karlskoga, *Sweden* 9 G16
Karlskrona, *Sweden* 9 H16
Karlsruhe, *Germany* 19 F4
Karlstad, *Sweden* 9 G15
Karlstad, *U.S.A.* 108 A6
Karlstadt, *Germany* 19 F5
Karnal, *India* 62 E7
Karnali →, *Nepal* 63 E9
Karnaphuli Res., *Bangla.* 61 H18
Karnataka □, *India* 60 N10
Karnes City, *U.S.A.* 109 L6
Karnische Alpen, *Europe* 21 J3
Karo, *Mali* 78 C4
Karoi, *Zimbabwe* 83 F2
Karonga, *Malawi* 83 D3
Karoonda, *Australia* 91 F2
Karora, *Sudan* 76 D4
Káros, *Greece* 39 N8
Karousádhes, *Greece* 39 K2
Karpasia □, *Cyprus* 37 D13
Kárpathos, *Greece* 39 P10
Kárpathos, Stenón, *Greece* 39 P10
Karpuz Burnu = Apostolos Andreas, C., *Cyprus* 66 E6
Karrebæk, *Denmark* 11 J5
Kars, *Turkey* 67 B10
Karsakpay, *Kazakstan* 44 E7
Karsha, *Kazakstan* 42 F10
Karshi = Qarshi, *Uzbekistan* 44 F7
Karsiyang, *India* 63 F13
Karst, *Croatia* 33 C11
Kartaly, *Russia* 44 D7
Kartapur, *India* 62 D6
Karthaus, *U.S.A.* 106 E6
Kartuzy, *Poland* 20 A8
Karufa, *Indonesia* 57 E8
Karumba, *Australia* 90 B3
Karumo, *Tanzania* 82 C3
Karumwa, *Tanzania* 82 C3
Karungu, *Kenya* 82 C3
Karup, *Denmark* 11 H3
Karviná, *Czech.* 20 F8
Karwar, *India* 60 M9
Karwi, *India* 63 G9
Kaş, *Turkey* 66 D3
Kasache, *Malawi* 83 E3
Kasai →, *Zaïre* 80 E3
Kasai Oriental □, *Zaïre* 82 C1
Kasaji, *Zaïre* 83 E1
Kasama, *Zambia* 83 E3
Kasan-dong, *N. Korea* 51 D14
Kasane, *Namibia* 84 B3
Kasanga, *Tanzania* 83 D3
Kasangulu, *Zaïre* 80 E3
Kasaragod, *India* 60 N9
Kasba L., *Canada* 101 A8
Kasba Tadla, *Morocco* 74 B3
Kāseh Garān, *Iran* 64 C5
Kasempa, *Zambia* 83 E2
Kasenga, *Zaïre* 83 E2
Kasese, *Uganda* 82 B3
Kasewa, *Zambia* 83 E2
Kasganj, *India* 63 F8
Kashabowie, *Canada* 98 C1
Kāshān, *Iran* 65 C6
Kashi, *China* 54 C2
Kashimbo, *Zaïre* 83 E2
Kashin, *Russia* 42 B3
Kashipur, *India* 63 E8
Kashira, *Russia* 42 C4
Kashiwazaki, *Japan* 49 F9
Kashk-e Kohneh, *Afghan.* 60 B3
Kāshmar, *Iran* 65 C8
Kashmir, *Asia* 63 C7
Kashmor, *Pakistan* 62 E3
Kashpirovka, *Russia* 42 D9
Kashun Noerh = Gaxun Nur, *China* 54 B5
Kasimov, *Russia* 42 C5
Kasinge, *Zaïre* 82 D2
Kasiruta, *Indonesia* 57 E7
Kaskaskia →, *U.S.A.* 108 G10
Kaskattama →, *Canada* 101 B10
Kaskinen, *Finland* 9 E19
Kaslo, *Canada* 100 D5
Kasmere L., *Canada* 101 B8
Kasongo, *Zaïre* 82 C2
Kasongo Lunda, *Zaïre* 80 F3
Kásos, *Greece* 39 P9
Kásos, Stenón, *Greece* 39 P9
Kaspi, *Georgia* 43 K7
Kaspiysk, *Russia* 43 J8
Kaspiyskiy, *Russia* 43 H8
Kassab ed Doleib, *Sudan* 77 E3
Kassaba, *Egypt* 76 C2
Kassalâ, *Sudan* 77 D4
Kassalâ □, *Sudan* 77 D4
Kassel, *Germany* 18 D5
Kassinger, *Sudan* 76 D3
Kassiópi, *Greece* 37 A3
Kassue, *Indonesia* 57 F9
Kastamonu, *Turkey* 66 B5
Kastav, *Croatia* 33 C11
Kastélli, *Greece* 37 D5
Kastéllion, *Greece* 37 D7
Kastellou, Ákra, *Greece* 39 P10
Kasterlee, *Belgium* 17 F5
Kastóri, *Greece* 39 M5
Kastoría, *Greece* 39 J4
Kastornoye, *Russia* 42 E4
Kástron, *Greece* 39 K8
Kastsyukovichy, *Belarus* 40 F7
Kasulu, *Tanzania* 82 C3
Kasulu □, *Tanzania* 82 C3
Kasumi, *Japan* 49 G7
Kasumkent, *Russia* 43 K9
Kasungu, *Malawi* 83 E3
Kasur, *Pakistan* 62 D6
Kata, *Russia* 45 D11
Kataba, *Zambia* 83 F2
Katako Kombe, *Zaïre* 82 C1
Katákolon, *Greece* 39 M4
Katale, *Tanzania* 82 C3
Katamatite, *Australia* 91 F4
Katanda, *Kivu, Zaïre* 82 C2
Katanda, *Shaba, Zaïre* 82 D1
Katanga = Shaba □, *Zaïre* 82 D2
Katangi, *India* 60 J11
Katangli, *Russia* 45 D15
Katavi Swamp, *Tanzania* 82 D3
Kateríni, *Greece* 39 J5
Katha, *Burma* 61 G20
Katherîna, Gebel, *Egypt* 76 J8
Katherine, *Australia* 88 B5
Kathiawar, *India* 62 H4
Kathikas, *Cyprus* 37 E11
Kati, *Mali* 78 C3
Katihar, *India* 63 G12
Katima Mulilo, *Zambia* 84 B3
Katimbira, *Malawi* 83 E3
Katingan = Mendawai →, *Indonesia* 56 E4
Katiola, *Ivory C.* 78 D3
Katmandu, *Nepal* 63 F11
Kato Akhaïa, *Greece* 39 L4
Káto Arkhánai, *Greece* 37 D7
Káto Khorió, *Greece* 37 D7
Kato Pyrgos, *Cyprus* 37 D11
Káto Stavros, *Greece* 39 J6
Katompe, *Zaïre* 82 D2
Katonga →, *Uganda* 82 B3
Katoomba, *Australia* 91 E5
Katowice, *Poland* 20 E9
Katrine, L., *U.K.* 14 E4
Katrineholm, *Sweden* 10 E10
Katsepe, *Madag.* 85 B8
Katsina, *Nigeria* 79 C6
Katsina □, *Nigeria* 79 C6
Katsina Ala →, *Nigeria* 79 D6
Katsumoto, *Japan* 49 H4
Katsuura, *Japan* 49 G10
Katsuyama, *Japan* 49 F8
Kattaviá, *Greece* 37 D9
Kattegat, *Denmark* 11 H5
Katumba, *Zaïre* 82 D2
Katungu, *Kenya* 82 C5
Katwa, *India* 63 H13
Katwijk-aan-Zee, *Neths.* 16 D4
Kauai, *U.S.A.* 102 H15
Kauai Channel, *U.S.A.* 102 H15
Kaub, *Germany* 19 E3
Kaufbeuren, *Germany* 19 H6
Kaufman, *U.S.A.* 109 J6
Kauhajoki, *Finland* 9 E20
Kaukauna, *U.S.A.* 104 C1
Kaukauveld, *Namibia* 84 C3
Kaunas, *Lithuania* 9 J20
Kaura Namoda, *Nigeria* 79 C6
Kautokeino, *Norway* 8 B20
Kavacha, *Russia* 45 C17
Kavadarci, *Macedonia* 39 H5
Kavaja, *Albania* 39 H2
Kavak, *Turkey* 66 B7
Kavalerovo, *Russia* 48 B7
Kavali, *India* 60 M12
Kaválla, *Greece* 39 J7
Kavār, *Iran* 65 D7
Kavarna, *Bulgaria* 38 F11
Kavkaz, *Russia* 43 H3
Kavos, *Greece* 37 B4
Kaw, *Fr. Guiana* 121 C7
Kawa, *Sudan* 77 E3
Kawagama L., *Canada* 106 A6
Kawagoe, *Japan* 49 G9
Kawaguchi, *Japan* 49 G9
Kawaihae, *U.S.A.* 102 H17
Kawambwa, *Zambia* 83 D2
Kawanoe, *Japan* 49 G6
Kawardha, *India* 63 J9
Kawasaki, *Japan* 49 G9
Kawene, *Canada* 98 C1
Kawerau, *N.Z.* 87 H6
Kawhia Harbour, *N.Z.* 87 H5
Kawio, Kepulauan, *Indonesia* 57 D7
Kawnro, *Burma* 61 H21
Kawthoolei = Kawthule □, *Burma* 61 L20
Kawthule □, *Burma* 61 L20
Kaya, *Burkina Faso* 79 C4
Kayah □, *Burma* 61 K20
Kayan →, *Indonesia* 56 D5
Kaycee, *U.S.A.* 110 E10
Kayeli, *Indonesia* 57 E7
Kayenta, *U.S.A.* 111 H8
Kayes, *Mali* 78 C2
Kayima, *S. Leone* 78 D2
Kayl, *Lux.* 17 K8
Kayoa, *Indonesia* 57 D7
Kayomba, *Zambia* 83 E1
Kayoro, *Ghana* 79 C4
Kayrunnera, *Australia* 91 E3
Kaysatskoye, *Russia* 42 F8
Kayseri, *Turkey* 66 C6
Kaysville, *U.S.A.* 110 F8
Kayuagung, *Indonesia* 56 E2
Kazachye, *Russia* 45 B14
Kazakstan ■, *Asia* 44 E7
Kazan, *Russia* 42 C9
Kazan-Rettō, *Pac. Oc.* 92 E6
Kazanlŭk, *Bulgaria* 38 G8
Kazanskaya, *Russia* 42 F5
Kazatin = Kozyatyn, *Ukraine* 41 H5
Kazbek, *Russia* 43 J7
Kāzerūn, *Iran* 65 D6
Kazi Magomed = Qazimämmäd, *Azerbaijan* 43 K9
Kazincbarcika, *Hungary* 21 G10
Kaztalovka, *Kazakstan* 42 F9
Kazumba, *Zaïre* 80 F4
Kazuno, *Japan* 48 D10
Kazym →, *Russia* 44 C7
Kcynia, *Poland* 20 C7
Ké-Macina, *Mali* 78 C3
Kéa, *Greece* 39 M7
Keams Canyon, *U.S.A.* 111 J8
Kearney, *U.S.A.* 108 E5
Keban, *Turkey* 67 C8
Keban Baraji, *Turkey* 67 C8
Kebbi □, *Nigeria* 79 C6
Kébi, *Ivory C.* 78 D3
Kebili, *Tunisia* 75 B6
Kebnekaise, *Sweden* 8 C18
Kebri Dehar, *Ethiopia* 68 F3
Kebumen, *Indonesia* 57 G13
Kecel, *Hungary* 21 J9
Kechika →, *Canada* 100 B3
Kecskemét, *Hungary* 21 J9
Kedada, *Ethiopia* 77 F4
Kedgwick, *Canada* 99 C6
Kédhros Óros, *Greece* 37 D6
Kedia Hill, *Botswana* 84 C3
Kediniai, *Lithuania* 9 J21
Kediri, *Indonesia* 57 G15
Kédougou, *Senegal* 78 C2
Kedzierzyn, *Poland* 20 E8
Keeler, *U.S.A.* 112 J9
Keeley L., *Canada* 101 C7
Keeling Is. = Cocos Is., *Ind. Oc.* 92 J1
Keene, *Calif., U.S.A.* 113 K8
Keene, *N.H., U.S.A.* 107 D12
Keeper Hill, *Ireland* 15 D3
Keer-Weer, C., *Australia* 90 A3
Keerbergen, *Belgium* 17 F5
Keeseville, *U.S.A.* 107 B11
Keeten Mastgat, *Neths.* 17 E4
Keetmanshoop, *Namibia* 84 D2
Keewatin, *U.S.A.* 108 B8
Keewatin □, *Canada* 101 A9
Keewatin →, *Canada* 101 B8
Kefa □, *Ethiopia* 77 F4
Kefallinía, *Greece* 39 L3
Kefamenanu, *Indonesia* 57 F6
Keffi, *Nigeria* 79 D6
Keflavík, *Iceland* 8 D2
Keg River, *Canada* 100 B5
Kegaska, *Canada* 99 B7
Kehl, *Germany* 19 G3
Keighley, *U.K.* 12 D6
Keila, *Estonia* 9 G21
Keimoes, *S. Africa* 84 D3
Keita, *Niger* 79 C6
Keitele, *Finland* 8 E22
Keith, *Australia* 91 F3
Keith, *U.K.* 14 D6
Keith Arm, *Canada* 96 B7
Kejser Franz Joseph Fjord = Kong Franz Joseph Fd., *Greenland* 4 B6
Kekri, *India* 62 G6
Kël, *Russia* 45 C13
Kelamet, *Eritrea* 77 D4
Kelan, *China* 50 E6
Kelang, *Malaysia* 59 L3
Kelantan →, *Malaysia* 59 J4
Kelheim, *Germany* 19 G7
Kelibia, *Tunisia* 75 A7
Kelkit, *Turkey* 67 B8
Kelkit →, *Turkey* 66 B7
Kellé, *Congo* 80 E2
Keller, *U.S.A.* 110 B4
Kellerberrin, *Australia* 89 F2
Kellett, C., *Canada* 4 B1
Kelleys I., *U.S.A.* 106 E2
Kellogg, *U.S.A.* 110 C5
Kells = Ceanannus Mor, *Ireland* 15 C5
Kélo, *Chad* 73 G8
Kelokedhara, *Cyprus* 37 E11
Kelowna, *Canada* 100 D5
Kelsey Bay, *Canada* 100 C3
Kelseyville, *U.S.A.* 112 G4
Kelso, *N.Z.* 87 L2
Kelso, *U.K.* 14 F6
Kelso, *U.S.A.* 112 D4
Keluang, *Malaysia* 59 L4
Kelvington, *Canada* 101 C8
Kem, *Russia* 44 C4
Kem-Kem, *Morocco* 74 B4
Kema, *Indonesia* 57 D7
Kemah, *Turkey* 67 C8
Kemaliye, *Turkey* 67 C8
Kemano, *Canada* 100 C3
Kemasik, *Malaysia* 59 K4
Kembolcha, *Ethiopia* 77 E4
Kemer, *Turkey* 66 D4
Kemerovo, *Russia* 44 D9
Kemi, *Finland* 8 D21
Kemi älv = Kemijoki →, *Finland* 8 D21
Kemijärvi, *Finland* 8 C22
Kemijoki →, *Finland* 8 D21
Kemmel, *Belgium* 17 G1
Kemmerer, *U.S.A.* 110 F8
Kemmuna = Comino, *Malta* 37 C1
Kemp, L., *U.S.A.* 109 J5
Kemp Land, *Antarctica* 5 C5
Kempsey, *Australia* 91 E5
Kempt, L., *Canada* 98 C5
Kempten, *Germany* 19 H6
Kemptville, *Canada* 98 C4
Kenadsa, *Algeria* 75 B4
Kendal, *Indonesia* 56 F4
Kendal, *U.K.* 12 C5
Kendall, *Australia* 91 E5
Kendall →, *Australia* 90 A3
Kendallville, *U.S.A.* 104 E3
Kendari, *Indonesia* 57 E6
Kendawangan, *Indonesia* 56 E4
Kende, *Nigeria* 79 C5
Kendenup, *Australia* 89 F2
Kendrapara, *India* 61 J15
Kendrew, *S. Africa* 84 E3
Kendrick, *U.S.A.* 110 C5
Kene Thao, *Laos* 58 D3
Kenedy, *U.S.A.* 109 L6
Kenema, *S. Leone* 78 D2
Keng Kok, *Laos* 58 D5
Keng Tawng, *Burma* 61 J21
Keng Tung, *Burma* 61 J21
Kenge, *Zaïre* 80 E3
Kengeja, *Tanzania* 82 D4
Kenhardt, *S. Africa* 84 D3
Kenitra, *Morocco* 74 B3
Kenli, *China* 51 F10
Kenmare, *Ireland* 15 E2
Kenmare, *U.S.A.* 108 A3
Kenmare →, *Ireland* 15 E2
Kennebec, *U.S.A.* 108 D5
Kennedy, *Zimbabwe* 83 F2
Kennedy Ra., *Australia* 89 D2
Kennedy Taungdeik, *Burma* 61 H18
Kenner, *U.S.A.* 109 L9
Kennet →, *U.K.* 13 F7
Kenneth Ra., *Australia* 88 D2
Kennett, *U.S.A.* 109 G9
Kennewick, *U.S.A.* 110 C4
Kénogami, *Canada* 99 C5
Kenogami →, *Canada* 98 B3
Kenora, *Canada* 101 D10
Kenosha, *U.S.A.* 104 D2
Kensington, *Canada* 99 C7
Kensington, *U.S.A.* 108 F5
Kensington Downs, *Australia* 90 C3
Kent, *Ohio, U.S.A.* 106 E3
Kent, *Oreg., U.S.A.* 110 D3
Kent, *Tex., U.S.A.* 109 K2

Kent, *Wash., U.S.A.* 112 C4
Kent □, *U.K.* 13 F8
Kent Group, *Australia* 90 F4
Kent Pen., *Canada* 96 B9
Kentau, *Kazakstan* 44 E7
Kentland, *U.S.A.* 104 E2
Kenton, *U.S.A.* 104 E4
Kentucky □, *U.S.A.* 104 G3
Kentucky →, *U.S.A.* 104 F3
Kentucky L., *U.S.A.* 105 G2
Kentville, *Canada* 99 C7
Kentwood, *U.S.A.* 109 K9
Kenya ■, *Africa* 82 B4
Kenya, Mt., *Kenya* 82 C4
Keo Neua, Deo, *Vietnam* 58 C5
Keokuk, *U.S.A.* 108 E9
Kep, *Cambodia* 59 G5
Kep, *Vietnam* 58 B6
Kepi, *Indonesia* 57 F9
Kępno, *Poland* 20 D7
Kerala □, *India* 60 P10
Kerama-Rettō, *Japan* 49 L3
Keran, *Pakistan* 63 B5
Kerang, *Australia* 91 F3
Keraudren, C., *Australia* 88 C2
Kerava, *Finland* 9 F21
Kerch, *Ukraine* 41 K9
Kerchenskiy Proliv, *Black Sea* 41 K9
Kerchoual, *Mali* 79 B5
Kerempe Burnu, *Turkey* 66 A5
Keren, *Eritrea* 77 D4
Kerewan, *Gambia* 78 C1
Kerguelen, *Ind. Oc.* 3 G13
Keri Kera, *Sudan* 77 E3
Kericho, *Kenya* 82 C4
Kericho □, *Kenya* 82 C4
Kerinci, *Indonesia* 56 E2
Kerkdriel, *Neths.* 16 E6
Kerkenna, Is., *Tunisia* 75 B7
Kerki, *Turkmenistan* 44 F7
Kérkira, *Greece* 37 A3
Kerkrade, *Neths.* 17 G8
Kerma, *Sudan* 76 D3
Kermadec Is., *Pac. Oc.* 92 K10
Kermadec Trench, *Pac. Oc.* 92 L10
Kermān, *Iran* 65 D8
Kerman, *U.S.A.* 112 J6
Kermān □, *Iran* 65 D8
Kermānshāh = Bākhtarān, *Iran* 67 E12
Kerme Körfezi, *Turkey* 66 D2
Kermit, *U.S.A.* 109 K3
Kern →, *U.S.A.* 113 K7
Kerns, *Switz.* 23 C6
Kernville, *U.S.A.* 113 K8
Keroh, *Malaysia* 59 K3
Kerrobert, *Canada* 101 C7
Kerrville, *U.S.A.* 109 K5
Kerry □, *Ireland* 15 D2
Kerry Hd., *Ireland* 15 D2
Kersa, *Ethiopia* 77 F5
Kerteminde, *Denmark* 11 J4
Kertosono, *Indonesia* 57 G15
Kerulen →, *Asia* 54 B6
Kerzaz, *Algeria* 75 C4
Kerzers, *Switz.* 22 C4
Kesagami →, *Canada* 98 B4
Kesagami L., *Canada* 98 B3
Keşan, *Turkey* 66 B2
Kesch, Piz, *Switz.* 23 C9
Kesennuma, *Japan* 48 E10
Keshit, *Iran* 65 D8
Keşiş Dağ, *Turkey* 67 C8
Keskin, *Turkey* 66 C5
Kessel, *Belgium* 17 F5
Kessel, *Neths.* 17 F8
Kessel-Lo, *Belgium* 17 G5
Kestell, *S. Africa* 85 D4
Kestenga, *Russia* 44 C4
Kesteren, *Neths.* 16 E7
Keswick, *U.K.* 12 C4
Keszthely, *Hungary* 21 J7
Ket →, *Russia* 44 D9
Keta, *Ghana* 79 D5
Ketapang, *Indonesia* 56 E4
Ketchikan, *U.S.A.* 96 C6
Ketchum, *U.S.A.* 110 E6
Kete Krachi, *Ghana* 79 D4
Ketef, Khalîg Umm el, *Egypt* 76 C4
Ketelmeer, *Neths.* 16 C7
Keti Bandar, *Pakistan* 62 G2
Ketri, *India* 62 E6
Kętrzyn, *Poland* 20 A11
Kettering, *U.K.* 13 E7
Kettering, *U.S.A.* 104 F3
Kettle →, *Canada* 101 B11
Kettle Falls, *U.S.A.* 110 B4
Kettleman City, *U.S.A.* 112 J7
Keuruu, *Finland* 9 E21
Kevin, *U.S.A.* 110 B8
Kewanee, *U.S.A.* 108 E10
Kewaunee, *U.S.A.* 104 C2
Keweenaw B., *U.S.A.* 104 B1
Keweenaw Pen., *U.S.A.* 104 B2
Keweenaw Pt., *U.S.A.* 104 B2
Key Harbour, *Canada* 98 C3
Key West, *U.S.A.* 103 F10
Keyser, *U.S.A.* 104 F6
Keystone, *U.S.A.* 108 D3
Kezhma, *Russia* 45 D11
Kežmarok, *Slovak Rep.* 20 F10
Khabarovo, *Russia* 44 C7
Khabarovsk, *Russia* 45 E14
Khabr, *Iran* 65 D8
Khābūr →, *Syria* 67 E9
Khachmas = Xaçmaz, *Azerbaijan* 43 K9
Khachrod, *India* 62 H6
Khadari, W. el →, *Sudan* 77 E2
Khadro, *Pakistan* 62 F3
Khadyzhensk, *Russia* 43 H4
Khadzhilyangar, *India* 63 B8
Khagaria, *India* 63 G12
Khaipur, *Bahawalpur, Pakistan* 62 E5
Khaipur, *Hyderabad, Pakistan* 62 F3
Khair, *India* 62 F7
Khairabad, *India* 63 F9
Khairagarh, *India* 63 J9
Khairpur, *Pakistan* 60 F6
Khakassia □, *Russia* 44 D9
Khakhea, *Botswana* 84 C3
Khalafābād, *Iran* 65 D6
Khalfallah, *Algeria* 75 B5
Khalilabad, *India* 63 F10
Khalīlī, *Iran* 65 E7
Khalkhāl, *Iran* 67 D13
Khálki, *Greece* 39 K5
Khalkís, *Greece* 39 L6
Khalmer-Sede = Tazovskiy, *Russia* 44 C8
Khalmer Yu, *Russia* 44 C7
Khalturin, *Russia* 44 D5
Khalūf, *Oman* 68 C6
Kham Keut, *Laos* 58 C5
Khamas Country, *Botswana* 84 C4
Khambat, G. of, *India* 62 J5
Khambhaliya, *India* 62 H3
Khambhat, *India* 62 H5
Khamilonísion, *Greece* 39 P9
Khamīr, *Iran* 65 E7
Khamir, *Yemen* 68 D3
Khamsa, *Egypt* 69 E1
Khān Abū Shāmat, *Syria* 69 B5
Khān Azād, *Iraq* 64 C5
Khān Mujiddah, *Iraq* 64 C4
Khān Shaykhūn, *Syria* 66 E7
Khān Yūnis, *Gaza Strip* 69 D3
Khānaqīn, *Iraq* 67 E11
Khānbāghī, *Iran* 65 B7
Khandrá, *Greece* 39 P9
Khandwa, *India* 60 J10
Khandyga, *Russia* 45 C14
Khāneh, *Iran* 64 B5
Khanewal, *Pakistan* 62 D4
Khanh Duong, *Vietnam* 58 F7
Khaniá, *Greece* 37 D6
Khaniá □, *Greece* 37 D6
Khaníon, Kólpos, *Greece* 37 D5
Khanka, Ozero, *Asia* 45 E14
Khankendy = Xankändi, *Azerbaijan* 67 C12
Khanna, *India* 62 D7
Khanpur, *Pakistan* 62 E4
Khanty-Mansiysk, *Russia* 44 C7
Khapalu, *Pakistan* 63 B7
Khapcheranga, *Russia* 45 E12
Kharabali, *Russia* 43 G8
Kharagpur, *India* 63 H12
Khárakas, *Greece* 37 D7
Kharan Kalat, *Pakistan* 60 E4
Kharānaq, *Iran* 65 C7
Kharda, *India* 60 K9
Khardung La, *India* 63 B7
Khârga, El Wâhât el, *Egypt* 76 B3
Khargon, *India* 60 J9
Kharit, Wadi el →, *Egypt* 76 C3
Khārk, Jazireh, *Iran* 65 D6
Kharkiv, *Ukraine* 41 H9
Kharkov = Kharkiv, *Ukraine* 41 H9
Kharmanli, *Bulgaria* 39 H8
Kharovsk, *Russia* 40 C11
Kharta, *Turkey* 66 B3
Khartoum = El Khartûm, *Sudan* 77 D3
Khasan, *Russia* 48 C5
Khasavyurt, *Russia* 43 J8
Khāsh, *Iran* 60 E2
Khashm el Girba, *Sudan* 77 E4
Khashuri, *Georgia* 43 J6
Khaskovo, *Bulgaria* 39 H8
Khatanga, *Russia* 45 B11
Khatanga →, *Russia* 45 B11
Khatauli, *India* 62 E7
Khātūnābād, *Iran* 65 C6
Khatyrka, *Russia* 45 C18
Khaybar, Harrat, *Si. Arabia* 64 E4
Khāzimiyah, *Iraq* 64 C4
Khazzân Jabal el Awliyâ, *Sudan* 77 D3
Khe Bo, *Vietnam* 58 C5
Khe Long, *Vietnam* 58 B5
Khed Brahma, *India* 60 G8
Khekra, *India* 62 E7
Khemarak Phouminville, *Cambodia* 59 G4
Khemis Miliana, *Algeria* 75 A5
Khemissèt, *Morocco* 74 B3
Khemmarat, *Thailand* 58 D5
Khenāmān, *Iran* 65 D8
Khenchela, *Algeria* 75 A6
Khenifra, *Morocco* 74 B3
Kherrata, *Algeria* 75 A6
Kherson, *Ukraine* 41 J7
Khersónisos Akrotíri, *Greece* 37 D6
Kheta →, *Russia* 45 B11
Khilok, *Russia* 45 D12
Khimki, *Russia* 42 C3
Khíos, *Greece* 39 L9
Khirbat Qanāfār, *Lebanon* 69 B4
Khiuma = Hiiumaa, *Estonia* 9 G20
Khiva, *Uzbekistan* 44 E7
Khīyāv, *Iran* 64 B5
Khlong Khlung, *Thailand* 58 D2
Khmelnik, *Ukraine* 41 H4
Khmelnitskiy = Khmelnytskyy, *Ukraine* 41 H4
Khmelnytskyy, *Ukraine* 41 H4
Khmer Rep. = Cambodia ■, *Asia* 58 F5
Khoai, Hon, *Vietnam* 59 H5
Khodoriv, *Ukraine* 41 H3
Khodzent = Khudzhand, *Tajikistan* 44 E7
Khojak P., *Afghan.* 60 D5
Khok Kloi, *Thailand* 59 H2
Khok Pho, *Thailand* 59 J3
Kholm, *Russia* 40 D6
Kholmsk, *Russia* 45 E15
Khomas Hochland, *Namibia* 84 C2
Khomeyn, *Iran* 65 C6
Khon Kaen, *Thailand* 58 D4
Khong, *Laos* 58 E5
Khong Sedone, *Laos* 58 E5
Khonuu, *Russia* 45 C15
Khoper →, *Russia* 42 F6
Khor el 'Atash, *Sudan* 77 E3
Khóra, *Greece* 39 M4
Khóra Sfakíon, *Greece* 37 D6
Khorāsān □, *Iran* 65 C8
Khorat = Nakhon Ratchasima, *Thailand* 58 E4
Khorat, Cao Nguyen, *Thailand* 58 E4
Khorb el Ethel, *Algeria* 74 C3
Khorixas, *Namibia* 84 C1
Khorol, *Ukraine* 41 H7
Khorramābād, *Khorāsān, Iran* 65 C8
Khorramābād, *Lorestān, Iran* 67 F13
Khorrāmshahr, *Iran* 65 D6
Khorugh, *Tajikistan* 44 F8
Khosravī, *Iran* 65 D6
Khosrowābād, *Khuzestān, Iran* 65 D6
Khosrowābād, *Kordestān, Iran* 67 E12
Khosūyeh, *Iran* 65 D7
Khotyn, *Ukraine* 41 H4
Khouribga, *Morocco* 74 B3
Khowai, *Bangla.* 61 G17
Khoyniki, *Belarus* 41 G5
Khrami →, *Georgia* 43 K7
Khrenovoye, *Russia* 42 E5
Khristianá, *Greece* 39 N8
Khrysokhou B., *Cyprus* 37 D11
Khu Khan, *Thailand* 58 E5
Khudzhand, *Tajikistan* 44 E7
Khuff, *Si. Arabia* 64 E5
Khūgīānī, *Afghan.* 62 D1
Khulna, *Bangla.* 61 H16
Khulna □, *Bangla.* 61 H16
Khulo, *Georgia* 43 K6
Khumago, *Botswana* 84 C3
Khūnsorkh, *Iran* 65 E8
Khūr, *Iran* 65 C8
Khurai, *India* 62 G8
Khurayş, *Si. Arabia* 65 E6
Khūrīyā Mūrīyā, Jazā 'ir, *Oman* 68 D6
Khurja, *India* 62 E7
Khūsf, *Iran* 65 C8
Khush, *Afghan.* 60 C3
Khushab, *Pakistan* 62 C5
Khust, *Ukraine* 41 H2
Khuzdar, *Pakistan* 62 F2
Khūzestān □, *Iran* 65 D6
Khvājeh, *Iran* 64 B5
Khvalynsk, *Russia* 42 D9
Khvānsār, *Iran* 65 D7
Khvatovka, *Russia* 42 D8
Khvor, *Iran* 65 C7
Khvorgū, *Iran* 65 E8
Khvormūj, *Iran* 65 D6
Khvoy, *Iran* 67 C11
Khvoynaya, *Russia* 40 C8
Khyber Pass, *Afghan.* 62 B4
Kiabukwa, *Zaïre* 83 D1
Kiama, *Australia* 91 E5
Kiamba, *Phil.* 55 H6
Kiambi, *Zaïre* 82 D2
Kiambu, *Kenya* 82 C4
Kiangsi = Jiangxi □, *China* 53 D10
Kiangsu = Jiangsu □, *China* 51 H10
Kibæk, *Denmark* 11 H2
Kibanga Port, *Uganda* 82 B3
Kibangou, *Congo* 80 E2
Kibara, *Tanzania* 82 C3
Kibare, Mts., *Zaïre* 82 D2
Kibombo, *Zaïre* 82 C2
Kibondo, *Tanzania* 82 C3
Kibondo □, *Tanzania* 82 C3
Kibumbu, *Burundi* 82 C2
Kibungu, *Rwanda* 82 C3
Kibuye, *Burundi* 82 C2
Kibuye, *Rwanda* 82 C2
Kibwesa, *Tanzania* 82 D2
Kibwezi, *Kenya* 82 C4
Kichiga, *Russia* 45 D17
Kicking Horse Pass, *Canada* 100 C5
Kidal, *Mali* 79 B5
Kidderminster, *U.K.* 13 E5
Kidete, *Tanzania* 82 D4
Kidira, *Senegal* 78 C2
Kidnappers, C., *N.Z.* 87 H6
Kidston, *Australia* 90 B3
Kidugallo, *Tanzania* 82 D4
Kiel, *Germany* 18 A6
Kiel Canal = Nord-Ostsee-Kanal →, *Germany* 18 A5
Kielce, *Poland* 20 E10
Kieldrecht, *Belgium* 17 F4
Kieler Bucht, *Germany* 18 A6
Kien Binh, *Vietnam* 59 H5
Kien Tan, *Vietnam* 59 G5
Kienge, *Zaïre* 83 E2
Kiessé, *Niger* 79 C5
Kiev = Kyyiv, *Ukraine* 41 G6
Kiffa, *Mauritania* 78 B2
Kifisiá, *Greece* 39 L6
Kifissós →, *Greece* 39 L6
Kifrī, *Iraq* 67 E11
Kigali, *Rwanda* 82 C3
Kigarama, *Tanzania* 82 C3
Kigoma □, *Tanzania* 82 D2
Kigoma-Ujiji, *Tanzania* 82 C2
Kigomasha, Ras, *Tanzania* 82 C4
Kihee, *Australia* 91 D3
Kihnu, *Estonia* 9 G21
Kii-Sanchi, *Japan* 49 G7
Kii-Suidō, *Japan* 49 H7
Kikaiga-Shima, *Japan* 49 K4
Kikinda, *Serbia, Yug.* 21 K10
Kikládhes, *Greece* 39 M7
Kikwit, *Zaïre* 80 E3
Kílalki, *Greece* 39 N10
Kilauea Crater, *U.S.A.* 102 J17
Kilchberg, *Switz.* 23 B7
Kilcoy, *Australia* 91 D5
Kildare, *Ireland* 15 C5
Kildare □, *Ireland* 15 C5
Kilgore, *U.S.A.* 109 J7
Kilifi, *Kenya* 82 C4
Kilifi □, *Kenya* 82 C4
Kilimanjaro, *Tanzania* 82 C4
Kilimanjaro □, *Tanzania* 82 C4
Kilimli, *Turkey* 66 B4
Kilindini, *Kenya* 82 C4
Kilis, *Turkey* 66 D7
Kiliya, *Ukraine* 41 K5
Kilju, *N. Korea* 51 D15
Kilkee, *Ireland* 15 D2
Kilkenny, *Ireland* 15 D4
Kilkenny □, *Ireland* 15 D4
Kilkieran B., *Ireland* 15 C2
Kilkís, *Greece* 39 J5
Killala, *Ireland* 15 B2
Killala B., *Ireland* 15 B2
Killaloe, *Ireland* 15 D3
Killaloe Sta., *Canada* 106 A7
Killam, *Canada* 100 C6
Killarney, *Australia* 91 D5
Killarney, *Canada* 98 C3
Killarney, *Ireland* 15 D2
Killarney, Lakes of, *Ireland* 15 E2
Killary Harbour, *Ireland* 15 C2
Killdeer, *Canada* 101 D7
Killdeer, *U.S.A.* 108 B3
Killeen, *U.S.A.* 109 K6
Killiecrankie, Pass of, *U.K.* 14 E5
Killin, *U.K.* 14 E4
Killíni, *Ilía, Greece* 39 M4
Killíni, *Korinthía, Greece* 39 M5
Killybegs, *Ireland* 15 B3
Kilmarnock, *U.K.* 14 F4
Kilmez, *Russia* 42 B10
Kilmez →, *Russia* 42 B10
Kilmore, *Australia* 91 F3
Kilondo, *Tanzania* 83 D3
Kilosa, *Tanzania* 82 D4
Kilosa □, *Tanzania* 82 D4
Kilrush, *Ireland* 15 D2
Kilwa □, *Tanzania* 83 D4
Kilwa Kisiwani, *Tanzania* 83 D4
Kilwa Kivinje, *Tanzania* 83 D4
Kilwa Masoko, *Tanzania* 83 D4
Kim, *U.S.A.* 109 G3
Kimaam, *Indonesia* 57 F9
Kimamba, *Tanzania* 82 D4
Kimba, *Australia* 91 E2
Kimball, *Nebr., U.S.A.* 108 E3
Kimball, *S. Dak., U.S.A.* 108 D5
Kimberley, *Canada* 100 D5
Kimberley, *S. Africa* 84 D3
Kimberley Downs, *Australia* 88 C3
Kimberly, *U.S.A.* 110 E6
Kimchaek, *N. Korea* 51 D15
Kimchŏn, *S. Korea* 51 F15
Kími, *Greece* 39 L7
Kimje, *S. Korea* 51 G14
Kimmirut, *Canada* 97 B13
Kímolos, *Greece* 39 N7
Kimovsk, *Russia* 42 C3
Kimparana, *Mali* 78 C4
Kimry, *Russia* 42 B3
Kimsquit, *Canada* 100 C3
Kimstad, *Sweden* 11 F9
Kinabalu, Gunong, *Malaysia* 56 C5
Kínaros, *Greece* 39 N9
Kinaskan L., *Canada* 100 B2
Kinbasket L., *Canada* 100 C5
Kincaid, *Canada* 101 D7
Kincardine, *Canada* 98 D3
Kinda, *Zaïre* 83 D2
Kinder Scout, *U.K.* 12 D6
Kindersley, *Canada* 101 C7
Kindia, *Guinea* 78 C2
Kindu, *Zaïre* 82 C2
Kinel, *Russia* 42 D10
Kineshma, *Russia* 42 B6
Kinesi, *Tanzania* 82 C3
King, L., *Australia* 89 F2
King, Mt., *Australia* 90 D4
King City, *U.S.A.* 111 H3
King Cr. →, *Australia* 90 C2
King Edward →, *Australia* 88 B4
King Frederick VI Land = Kong Frederik VI.s Kyst, *Greenland* 4 C5
King George B., *Falk. Is.* 128 D4
King George I., *Antarctica* 5 C18
King George Is., *Canada* 97 C11
King I. = Kadan Kyun, *Burma* 56 B1
King I., *Australia* 90 F3
King I., *Canada* 100 C3
King Leopold Ras., *Australia* 88 C4
King Sd., *Australia* 88 C3
King William I., *Canada* 96 B10
King William's Town, *S. Africa* 84 E4
Kingaroy, *Australia* 91 D5
Kingfisher, *U.S.A.* 109 H6
Kingirbān, *Iraq* 64 C5
Kingisepp = Kuressaare, *Estonia* 9 G20
Kingisepp, *Russia* 40 C5
Kingman, *Ariz., U.S.A.* 113 K12
Kingman, *Kans., U.S.A.* 109 G5
Kingoonya, *Australia* 91 E2
Kings →, *U.S.A.* 111 H4
Kings Canyon National Park, *U.S.A.* 111 H4
King's Lynn, *U.K.* 12 E8
Kings Mountain, *U.S.A.* 105 H5
King's Peak, *U.S.A.* 110 F8
Kingsbridge, *U.K.* 13 G4
Kingsburg, *U.S.A.* 111 H4
Kingscote, *Australia* 91 F2
Kingscourt, *Ireland* 15 C5
Kingsley, *U.S.A.* 108 D7
Kingsport, *U.S.A.* 105 G4
Kingston, *Canada* 98 D4
Kingston, *Jamaica* 116 C4
Kingston, *N.Z.* 87 L2
Kingston, *N.Y., U.S.A.* 107 E10
Kingston, *Pa., U.S.A.* 107 E9
Kingston, *R.I., U.S.A.* 107 E13
Kingston Pk., *U.S.A.* 113 K11
Kingston South East, *Australia* 91 F2
Kingston upon Hull, *U.K.* 12 D7
Kingston upon Hull □, *U.K.* 12 D7
Kingston-upon-Thames, *U.K.* 13 F7
Kingstown, *St. Vincent* 117 D7
Kingstree, *U.S.A.* 105 J6
Kingsville, *Canada* 98 D3
Kingsville, *U.S.A.* 109 M6
Kingussie, *U.K.* 14 D4
Kınık, *Turkey* 66 C2
Kinistino, *Canada* 101 C7
Kinkala, *Congo* 80 E2
Kinki □, *Japan* 49 H8
Kinleith, *N.Z.* 87 H5
Kinmount, *Canada* 106 B6
Kinna, *Sweden* 11 G6
Kinnaird, *Canada* 100 D5
Kinnairds Hd., *U.K.* 14 D7
Kinnared, *Sweden* 11 G7
Kinnarodden, *Norway* 6 A11
Kino, *Mexico* 114 B2
Kinoje →, *Canada* 98 B3
Kinomoto, *Japan* 49 G8
Kinoni, *Uganda* 82 C3
Kinrooi, *Belgium* 17 F7
Kinross, *U.K.* 14 E5
Kinsale, *Ireland* 15 E3
Kinsale, Old Hd. of, *Ireland* 15 E3
Kinsha = Chang Jiang →, *China* 53 B13
Kinshasa, *Zaïre* 80 E3
Kinsley, *U.S.A.* 109 G5
Kinston, *U.S.A.* 105 H7
Kintampo, *Ghana* 79 D4
Kintap, *Indonesia* 56 E5
Kintore Ra., *Australia* 88 D4
Kintyre, *U.K.* 14 F3
Kintyre, Mull of, *U.K.* 14 F3
Kinushseo →, *Canada* 98 A3
Kinuso, *Canada* 100 B5
Kinyangiri, *Tanzania* 82 C3
Kinzig →, *Germany* 19 G3
Kinzua, *U.S.A.* 106 E6
Kinzua Dam, *U.S.A.* 106 E5
Kiosk, *Canada* 98 C4
Kiowa, *Kans., U.S.A.* 109 G5
Kiowa, *Okla., U.S.A.* 109 H7
Kipahigan L., *Canada* 101 B8
Kipanga, *Tanzania* 82 D4
Kiparissía, *Greece* 39 M4
Kiparissiakós Kólpos, *Greece* 39 M4
Kipembawe, *Tanzania* 82 D3
Kipengere Ra., *Tanzania* 83 D3
Kipili, *Tanzania* 82 D3
Kipini, *Kenya* 82 C5
Kipling, *Canada* 101 C8
Kippure, *Ireland* 15 C5

Kipushi, *Zaïre* 83 E2
Kiratpur, *India* 62 E8
Kirchberg, *Switz.* 22 B5
Kirchhain, *Germany* 18 E4
Kirchheim, *Germany* 19 G5
Kirchheim-Bolanden, *Germany* 19 F4
Kirensk, *Russia* 45 D11
Kirgella Rocks, *Australia* 89 F3
Kirghizia ■ = Kyrgyzstan ■, *Asia* 44 E8
Kirghizstan = Kyrgyzstan ■, *Asia* 44 E8
Kiri, *Zaïre* 80 E3
Kiribati ■, *Pac. Oc.* 92 H10
Kırıkhan, *Turkey* 66 D7
Kırıkkale, *Turkey* 66 C5
Kirillov, *Russia* 40 C10
Kirin = Jilin, *China* 51 C14
Kirin = Jilin □, *China* 51 C13
Kirishi, *Russia* 40 C7
Kiritimati, *Kiribati* 93 G12
Kırka, *Turkey* 66 C4
Kirkcaldy, *U.K.* 14 E5
Kirkcudbright, *U.K.* 14 G4
Kirkee, *India* 60 K8
Kirkenær, *Norway* 10 D6
Kirkenes, *Norway* 8 B23
Kirkintilloch, *U.K.* 14 F4
Kirkjubæjarklaustur, *Iceland* 8 E4
Kirkkonummi, *Finland* 9 F21
Kirkland, *U.S.A.* 111 J7
Kirkland Lake, *Canada* 98 C3
Kırklareli, *Turkey* 66 B2
Kirksville, *U.S.A.* 108 E8
Kirkūk, *Iraq* 67 E11
Kirkwall, *U.K.* 14 C6
Kirkwood, *S. Africa* 84 E4
Kirn, *Germany* 19 F3
Kirov, *Russia* 42 C2
Kirov, *Russia* 44 D5
Kirovabad = Gäncä, *Azerbaijan* 43 K8
Kirovakan = Vanadzor, *Armenia* 43 K7
Kirovograd = Kirovohrad, *Ukraine* 41 H7
Kirovohrad, *Ukraine* 41 H7
Kirovsk = Babadayhan, *Turkmenistan* 44 F7
Kirovsk, *Russia* 44 C4
Kirovskiy, *Russia* 43 H9
Kirovskiy, *Kamchatka, Russia* 45 D16
Kirovskiy, *Primorsk, Russia* 48 B6
Kirriemuir, *U.K.* 14 E6
Kirsanov, *Russia* 42 D6
Kırşehir, *Turkey* 66 C6
Kirtachi, *Niger* 79 C5
Kirthar Range, *Pakistan* 62 F2
Kiruna, *Sweden* 8 C19
Kirundu, *Zaïre* 82 C2
Kirup, *Australia* 89 F2
Kirya, *Russia* 42 C8
Kiryū, *Japan* 49 F9
Kisaga, *Tanzania* 82 C3
Kisalaya, *Nic.* 116 D3
Kisámou, Kólpos, *Greece* 37 D5
Kisanga, *Zaïre* 82 B2
Kisangani, *Zaïre* 82 B2
Kisar, *Indonesia* 57 F7
Kisaran, *Indonesia* 56 D1
Kisarawe, *Tanzania* 82 D4
Kisarawe □, *Tanzania* 82 D4
Kisarazu, *Japan* 49 G9
Kisbér, *Hungary* 21 H8
Kiselevsk, *Russia* 44 D9
Kishanganga -►, *Pakistan* 63 B5
Kishanganj, *India* 63 F13
Kishangarh, *India* 62 F4
Kishi, *Nigeria* 79 D5
Kishinev = Chişinău, *Moldova* 41 J5
Kishiwada, *Japan* 49 G7
Kishtwar, *India* 63 C6
Kisii, *Kenya* 82 C3
Kisii □, *Kenya* 82 C3
Kisiju, *Tanzania* 82 D4
Kisir, *Turkey* 67 B10
Kisizi, *Uganda* 82 C2
Kiska I., *U.S.A.* 96 C1
Kiskatinaw -►, *Canada* 100 B4
Kiskittogisu L., *Canada* 101 C9
Kiskörös, *Hungary* 21 J9
Kiskundorozsma, *Hungary* 21 J10
Kiskunfélegyháza, *Hungary* 21 J9
Kiskunhalas, *Hungary* 21 J9
Kiskunmajsa, *Hungary* 21 J9
Kislovodsk, *Russia* 43 J6
Kismayu = Chisimaio, *Somali Rep.* 71 G8
Kiso-Gawa -►, *Japan* 49 G8
Kiso-Sammyaku, *Japan* 49 G8
Kisofukushima, *Japan* 49 G8
Kisoro, *Uganda* 82 C2
Kispest, *Hungary* 21 H9
Kissidougou, *Guinea* 78 D2
Kissimmee, *U.S.A.* 105 L5
Kissimmee -►, *U.S.A.* 105 M5
Kississing L., *Canada* 101 B8
Kissónerga, *Cyprus* 37 E11
Kistanje, *Croatia* 33 E12
Kisújszállás, *Hungary* 21 H10
Kisumu, *Kenya* 82 C3
Kisvárda, *Hungary* 21 G12
Kiswani, *Tanzania* 82 C4
Kiswere, *Tanzania* 83 D4
Kit Carson, *U.S.A.* 108 F3
Kita, *Mali* 78 C3
Kitab, *Uzbekistan* 44 F7
Kitaibaraki, *Japan* 49 F10
Kitakami, *Japan* 48 E10
Kitakami-Gawa -►, *Japan* 48 E10
Kitakami-Sammyaku, *Japan* 48 E10
Kitakata, *Japan* 48 F9
Kitakyūshū, *Japan* 49 H5
Kitale, *Kenya* 82 B4
Kitami, *Japan* 48 C11
Kitami-Sammyaku, *Japan* 48 B11
Kitangiri, L., *Tanzania* 82 C3
Kitaya, *Tanzania* 83 E5
Kitchener, *Australia* 89 F3
Kitchener, *Canada* 98 D3
Kitee, *Finland* 40 A6
Kitega = Gitega, *Burundi* 82 C2
Kitengo, *Zaïre* 82 D1
Kiteto □, *Tanzania* 82 C4
Kitgum, *Uganda* 82 B3
Kíthira, *Greece* 39 N7
Kíthnos, *Greece* 39 M7
Kiti, *Cyprus* 37 E12
Kiti, C., *Cyprus* 37 E12
Kitikmeot □, *Canada* 96 A9
Kitimat, *Canada* 100 C3
Kitinen -►, *Finland* 8 C22
Kitiyab, *Sudan* 77 D3
Kítros, *Greece* 39 J5
Kitsuki, *Japan* 49 H5
Kittakittaooloo, L., *Australia* 91 D2
Kittanning, *U.S.A.* 106 F5
Kittatinny Mts., *U.S.A.* 107 E10
Kittery, *U.S.A.* 105 D10
Kittilä, *Finland* 8 C21
Kitui, *Kenya* 82 C4
Kitui □, *Kenya* 82 C4
Kitwe, *Zambia* 83 E2
Kitzbühel, *Austria* 19 H8
Kitzingen, *Germany* 19 F6
Kivarli, *India* 62 G5
Kivertsi, *Ukraine* 41 G3
Kividhes, *Cyprus* 37 E11
Kivu □, *Zaïre* 82 C2
Kivu, L., *Zaïre* 82 C2
Kiyev = Kyyiv, *Ukraine* 41 G6
Kiyevskoye Vdkhr. = Kyyivske Vdskh., *Ukraine* 41 G6
Kiziguru, *Rwanda* 82 C3
Kızıl Irmak -►, *Turkey* 66 B6
Kizil Jilga, *India* 63 B8
Kizil Yurt, *Russia* 43 J8
Kızılcahamam, *Turkey* 66 B5
Kızılhisar, *Turkey* 66 D3
Kızılırmak, *Turkey* 66 B5
Kızıltepe, *Turkey* 67 D9
Kizimkazi, *Tanzania* 82 D4
Kizlyar, *Russia* 43 J8
Kizyl-Arvat = Gyzylarbat, *Turkmenistan* 44 F6
Kjellerup, *Denmark* 11 H3
Kjölur, *Iceland* 8 D4
Kladanj, *Bos.-H.* 21 L8
Kladno, *Czech.* 20 E4
Kladovo, *Serbia, Yug.* 21 L12
Klaeng, *Thailand* 58 F3
Klagenfurt, *Austria* 21 J4
Klagshamn, *Sweden* 11 J6
Klagstorp, *Sweden* 11 J7
Klaipėda, *Lithuania* 9 J19
Klaksvík, *Færoe Is.* 8 E9
Klamath -►, *U.S.A.* 110 F1
Klamath Falls, *U.S.A.* 110 E3
Klamath Mts., *U.S.A.* 110 F2
Klanjec, *Croatia* 33 B12
Klappan -►, *Canada* 100 B3
Klarälven -►, *Sweden* 9 G15
Klaten, *Indonesia* 57 G14
Klatovy, *Czech.* 20 F3
Klausen = Chiusa, *Italy* 33 B8
Klawer, *S. Africa* 84 E2
Klawock, *U.S.A.* 100 B2
Klazienaveen, *Neths.* 16 C10
Kleczew, *Poland* 20 C8
Kleena Kleene, *Canada* 100 C4
Klein, *U.S.A.* 110 C9
Klein-Karas, *Namibia* 84 D2
Kleine Gette -►, *Belgium* 17 G6
Kleine Nete -►, *Belgium* 17 F5
Klekovača, *Bos.-H.* 33 D13
Klenovec, *Macedonia* 39 H3
Klenovec, *Slovak Rep.* 20 G9
Klerksdorp, *S. Africa* 84 D4
Kletnya, *Russia* 40 F7
Kletsk = Klyetsk, *Belarus* 41 F4
Kletskiy, *Russia* 43 F6
Kleve, *Germany* 18 D2
Klickitat, *U.S.A.* 110 D3
Klickitat -►, *U.S.A.* 112 E5
Klidhes, *Cyprus* 37 D13
Klimovichi, *Belarus* 40 F6
Klin, *Russia* 42 B3
Klinaklini -►, *Canada* 100 C3
Klintsy, *Russia* 41 F7
Klipdale, *S. Africa* 84 E2
Klipplaat, *S. Africa* 84 E3
Klitmøller, *Denmark* 11 G2
Kljajićevo, *Serbia, Yug.* 21 K9
Ključ, *Bos.-H.* 33 D13
Kłobuck, *Poland* 20 E8
Kłodzko, *Poland* 20 E6
Kloetinge, *Neths.* 17 F3
Klondike, *Canada* 96 B6
Kloosterzande, *Neths.* 17 F4
Klosterneuburg, *Austria* 21 G6
Klosters, *Switz.* 23 C9
Kloten, *Switz.* 23 B7
Klötze, *Germany* 18 C7
Klouto, *Togo* 79 D5
Kluane L., *Canada* 96 B6
Kluczbork, *Poland* 20 E8
Klundert, *Neths.* 17 E5
Klyetsk, *Belarus* 41 F4
Klyuchevskaya, Gora, *Russia* 45 D17
Knaresborough, *U.K.* 12 C6
Knee L., *Man., Canada* 101 B10
Knee L., *Sask., Canada* 101 B7
Kneïss, Is., *Tunisia* 75 B7
Knesselare, *Belgium* 17 F2
Knezha, *Bulgaria* 38 F7
Knić, *Serbia, Yug.* 21 M10
Knight Inlet, *Canada* 100 C3
Knighton, *U.K.* 13 E4
Knights Ferry, *U.S.A.* 112 H6
Knights Landing, *U.S.A.* 112 G5
Knin, *Croatia* 33 D13
Knittelfeld, *Austria* 21 H4
Knjaževac, *Serbia, Yug.* 21 M12
Knob, C., *Australia* 89 F2
Knockmealdown Mts., *Ireland* 15 D4
Knokke, *Belgium* 17 F2
Knossós, *Greece* 37 D7
Knox, *U.S.A.* 104 E2
Knox, C., *Canada* 100 C2
Knox City, *U.S.A.* 109 J5
Knox Coast, *Antarctica* 5 C8
Knoxville, *Iowa, U.S.A.* 108 E8
Knoxville, *Tenn., U.S.A.* 105 H4
Knutshø, *Norway* 10 B3
Knysna, *S. Africa* 84 E3
Knyszyn, *Poland* 20 B12
Ko Kha, *Thailand* 58 C2
Ko Tao, *Thailand* 59 G2
Koartac = Quaqtaq, *Canada* 97 B13
Koba, *Aru, Indonesia* 57 F8
Koba, *Bangka, Indonesia* 56 E3
Kobarid, *Slovenia* 33 B10
Kobayashi, *Japan* 49 J5
Kobdo = Hovd, *Mongolia* 54 B4
Kōbe, *Japan* 49 G7
Kobelyaky, *Ukraine* 41 H8
København, *Denmark* 11 J6
Kōbi-Sho, *Japan* 49 M1
Koblenz, *Germany* 19 E3
Koblenz, *Switz.* 22 A6
Kobo, *Ethiopia* 77 E4
Kobroor, Kepulauan, *Indonesia* 57 F8
Kobryn, *Belarus* 41 F3
Kobuleti, *Georgia* 43 K5
Kobyłka, *Poland* 20 C11
Kobylkino, *Russia* 42 C6
Kocaeli = İzmit, *Turkey* 66 B3
Kočani, *Macedonia* 39 H5
Koceljevo, *Serbia, Yug.* 21 L9
Kočevje, *Slovenia* 33 C11
Koch Bihar, *India* 61 F16
Kochang, *S. Korea* 51 G14
Kochas, *India* 63 G10
Kocher -►, *Germany* 19 F5
Kocheya, *Russia* 45 D13
Kōchi, *Japan* 49 H6
Kōchi □, *Japan* 49 H6
Kochiu = Gejiu, *China* 52 F4
Kodiak, *U.S.A.* 96 C4
Kodiak I., *U.S.A.* 96 C4
Kodinar, *India* 62 J4
Kodori -►, *Georgia* 43 J5
Koekelare, *Belgium* 17 F1
Koersel, *Belgium* 17 F6
Koes, *Namibia* 84 D2
Koffiefontein, *S. Africa* 84 D4
Kofiau, *Indonesia* 57 E7
Koforidua, *Ghana* 79 D4
Kōfu, *Japan* 49 G9
Koga, *Japan* 49 F9
Kogaluk -►, *Canada* 99 A7
Kogan, *Australia* 91 D5
Køge, *Denmark* 9 J15
Kogi □, *Nigeria* 79 D6
Kogin Baba, *Nigeria* 79 D7
Koh-i-Bābā, *Afghan.* 60 B5
Koh-i-Khurd, *Afghan.* 62 C1
Kohat, *Pakistan* 62 C4
Kohima, *India* 61 G19
Kohkīlūyeh va Būyer Aḥmadi □, *Iran* 65 D6
Kohler Ra., *Antarctica* 5 D15
Kohtla-Järve, *Estonia* 9 G22
Koillismaa, *Finland* 8 D23
Koin-dong, *N. Korea* 51 D14
Kojō, *N. Korea* 51 E14
Kojonup, *Australia* 89 F2
Kojūr, *Iran* 65 B6
Koka, *Sudan* 76 C3
Kokand = Qŭqon, *Uzbekistan* 44 E8
Kokanee Glacier Prov. Park, *Canada* 100 D5
Kokas, *Indonesia* 57 E8
Kokchetav = Kökshetaū, *Kazakstan* 44 D7
Kokemäenjoki -►, *Finland* 9 F19
Kokerite, *Guyana* 121 B6
Kokhma, *Russia* 42 B5
Kokkola, *Finland* 8 E20
Koko, *Nigeria* 79 C5
Koko Kyunzu, *Burma* 61 M18
Kokolopozo, *Ivory C.* 78 D3
Kokomo, *U.S.A.* 104 E2
Kokonau, *Indonesia* 57 E9
Kokoro, *Niger* 79 C5
Koksan, *N. Korea* 51 E14
Kökshetaū, *Kazakstan* 44 D7
Koksoak -►, *Canada* 97 C13
Kokstad, *S. Africa* 85 E4
Kokubu, *Japan* 49 J5
Kokuora, *Russia* 45 B15
Kola, *Indonesia* 57 F8
Kola, *Russia* 44 C4
Kola Pen. = Kolskiy Poluostrov, *Russia* 44 C4
Kolahoi, *India* 63 B6
Kolahun, *Liberia* 78 D2
Kolaka, *Indonesia* 57 E6
Kolar, *India* 60 N11
Kolar Gold Fields, *India* 60 N11
Kolari, *Finland* 8 C20
Kolayat, *India* 60 F8
Kolby Kås, *Denmark* 11 J4
Kolchugino = Leninsk-Kuznetskiy, *Russia* 44 D9
Kolchugino, *Russia* 42 B4
Kolda, *Senegal* 78 C2
Kolding, *Denmark* 11 J3
Kole, *Zaïre* 80 E4
Koléa, *Algeria* 75 A5
Kolepom = Yos Sudarso, Pulau, *Indonesia* 57 F9
Kolguyev, Ostrov, *Russia* 44 C5
Kolham, *Neths.* 16 B9
Kolhapur, *India* 60 L9
Kolia, *Ivory C.* 78 D3
Kolín, *Czech.* 20 E5
Kolind, *Denmark* 11 H4
Kolkas Rags, *Latvia* 9 H20
Kölleda, *Germany* 18 D7
Kollum, *Neths.* 16 B8
Kolmanskop, *Namibia* 84 D2
Köln, *Germany* 18 E2
Koło, *Poland* 20 C8
Kołobrzeg, *Poland* 20 A5
Kolokani, *Mali* 78 C3
Kolomna, *Russia* 42 C4
Kolomyya, *Ukraine* 41 H3
Kolondiéba, *Mali* 78 C3
Kolonodale, *Indonesia* 57 E6
Kolosib, *India* 61 G18
Kolpashevo, *Russia* 44 D9
Kolpino, *Russia* 40 C6
Kolpny, *Russia* 42 D3
Kolskiy Poluostrov, *Russia* 44 C4
Kolubara -►, *Serbia, Yug.* 21 L10
Koluszki, *Poland* 20 D9
Kolwezi, *Zaïre* 83 E2
Kolyma -►, *Russia* 45 C17
Kolymskoye Nagorye, *Russia* 45 C16
Kôm Ombo, *Egypt* 76 C3
Komandorskiye Is. = Komandorskiye Ostrova, *Russia* 45 D17
Komandorskiye Ostrova, *Russia* 45 D17
Komárno, *Slovak Rep.* 21 H8
Komárom, *Hungary* 21 H8
Komatipoort, *S. Africa* 85 D5
Komatou Yialou, *Cyprus* 37 D13
Komatsu, *Japan* 49 F8
Komatsujima, *Japan* 49 H7
Kombissiri, *Burkina Faso* 79 C4
Kombori, *Burkina Faso* 78 C4
Komen, *Slovenia* 33 C10
Komenda, *Ghana* 79 D4
Komi □, *Russia* 44 C6
Komiža, *Croatia* 33 E13
Komló, *Hungary* 21 J8
Kommunarsk = Alchevsk, *Ukraine* 41 H10
Kommunizma, Pik, *Tajikistan* 44 F8
Komodo, *Indonesia* 57 F5
Komoé, *Ivory C.* 78 D4
Komono, *Congo* 80 E2
Komoran, Pulau, *Indonesia* 57 F9
Komoro, *Japan* 49 F9
Komotini, *Greece* 39 H8
Kompasberg, *S. Africa* 84 E3
Kompong Bang, *Cambodia* 59 F5
Kompong Cham, *Cambodia* 59 F5
Kompong Chhnang, *Cambodia* 59 F5
Kompong Chikreng, *Cambodia* 58 F5
Kompong Kleang, *Cambodia* 58 F5
Kompong Luong, *Cambodia* 59 G5
Kompong Pranak, *Cambodia* 58 F5
Kompong Som, *Cambodia* 59 G4
Kompong Som, Chhung, *Cambodia* 59 G4
Kompong Speu, *Cambodia* 59 G5
Kompong Sralao, *Cambodia* 58 E5
Kompong Thom, *Cambodia* 58 F5
Kompong Trabeck, *Cambodia* 58 F5
Kompong Trabeck, *Cambodia* 59 G5
Kompong Trach, *Cambodia* 59 G5
Kompong Tralach, *Cambodia* 59 G5
Komrat = Comrat, *Moldova* 41 J5
Komsberg, *S. Africa* 84 E3
Komsomolets, Ostrov, *Russia* 45 A10
Komsomolsk, *Russia* 42 B5
Komsomolsk, *Russia* 45 D14
Komsomolskiy, *Russia* 42 C7
Konakovo, *Russia* 42 B3
Konarhá □, *Afghan.* 60 B7
Konārī, *Iran* 65 D6
Konawa, *U.S.A.* 109 H6
Konch, *India* 63 G8
Kondakovo, *Russia* 45 C16
Konde, *Tanzania* 82 C4
Kondinin, *Australia* 89 F2
Kondoa, *Tanzania* 82 C4
Kondoa □, *Tanzania* 82 D4
Kondókali, *Greece* 37 A3
Kondopaga, *Russia* 40 A8
Kondratyevo, *Russia* 45 D10
Kondrovo, *Russia* 42 C2
Konduga, *Nigeria* 79 C7
Köneürgench, *Turkmenistan* 44 E6
Konevo, *Russia* 40 A10
Kong, *Ivory C.* 78 D4
Kong -►, *Cambodia* 58 F5
Kong, Koh, *Cambodia* 59 G4
Kong Christian IX.s Land, *Greenland* 4 C6
Kong Christian X.s Land, *Greenland* 4 B6
Kong Franz Joseph Fd., *Greenland* 4 B6
Kong Frederik IX.s Land, *Greenland* 4 C5
Kong Frederik VI.s Kyst, *Greenland* 4 C5
Kong Frederik VIII.s Land, *Greenland* 4 B6
Kong Oscar Fjord, *Greenland* 4 B6
Kongeå -►, *Denmark* 11 J3
Kongju, *S. Korea* 51 F14
Konglu, *Burma* 61 F20
Kongolo, *Kasai Or., Zaïre* 82 D1
Kongolo, *Shaba, Zaïre* 82 D2
Kongor, *Sudan* 77 F3
Kongoussi, *Burkina Faso* 79 C4
Kongsberg, *Norway* 10 E3
Kongsvinger, *Norway* 10 D6
Kongwa, *Tanzania* 82 D4
Koni, *Zaïre* 83 E2
Koni, Mts., *Zaïre* 83 E2
Königsberg = Kaliningrad, *Russia* 9 J19
Königslutter, *Germany* 18 C6
Königswusterhausen, *Germany* 18 C9
Konin, *Poland* 20 C8
Kónitsa, *Greece* 39 J3
Köniz, *Switz.* 22 C4
Konjice, *Slovenia* 33 B12
Konkiep, *Namibia* 84 D2
Konkouré -►, *Guinea* 78 D2
Könnern, *Germany* 18 D7
Kono, *S. Leone* 78 D2
Konolfingen, *Switz.* 22 C5
Kononongo, *Ghana* 79 D4
Konosha, *Russia* 40 B11
Kōnosu, *Japan* 49 F9
Konotop, *Ukraine* 41 G7
Konqi He -►, *China* 54 B4
Końskie, *Poland* 20 D10
Konstantinovka = Kostyantynivka, *Ukraine* 41 H9
Konstantinovsk, *Russia* 43 G5
Konstanz, *Germany* 19 H5
Kont, *Iran* 65 E9
Kontagora, *Nigeria* 79 C6
Kontich, *Belgium* 17 F4
Kontum, *Vietnam* 58 E7
Kontum, Plateau du, *Vietnam* 58 E7
Konya, *Turkey* 66 D5
Konya Ovası, *Turkey* 66 C5
Konz, *Germany* 19 F2
Konza, *Kenya* 82 C4
Kookynie, *Australia* 89 E3
Kooline, *Australia* 88 D2
Kooloonong, *Australia* 91 E3
Koolyanobbing, *Australia* 89 F2
Koondrook, *Australia* 91 F3
Koonibba, *Australia* 91 E1
Koorawatha, *Australia* 91 E4
Koorda, *Australia* 89 F2
Kooskia, *U.S.A.* 110 C6
Kootenai -►, *Canada* 110 B5
Kootenay L., *Canada* 100 D5
Kootenay Nat. Park, *Canada* 100 C5
Kootjieskolk, *S. Africa* 84 E3
Kopanovka, *Russia* 43 G8
Kopaonik, *Serbia, Yug.* 21 M11
Kópavogur, *Iceland* 8 D3
Koper, *Slovenia* 33 C10
Kopervik, *Norway* 9 G11
Kopeysk, *Russia* 44 D7
Kopi, *Australia* 91 E2
Köping, *Sweden* 10 E10
Kopiste, *Croatia* 33 F13
Köpmanholmen, *Sweden* 10 A12
Koppang, *Norway* 10 C5
Kopperå, *Norway* 10 A5
Koppies, *S. Africa* 85 D4
Koprivnica, *Croatia* 33 B13

Kopychyntsi, *Ukraine* 41 H3
Korab, *Macedonia* 39 H3
Korakiána, *Greece* 37 A3
Korba, *India* 63 H10
Korbach, *Germany* 18 D4
Korbu, G., *Malaysia* 59 K3
Korça, *Albania* 39 J3
Korce = Korça, *Albania* 39 J3
Korčula, *Croatia* 33 F14
Korčulanski Kanal, *Croatia* 33 E13
Kord Küy, *Iran* 65 B7
Kord Sheykh, *Iran* 65 D7
Kordestān □, *Iran* 64 C5
Kordofân, *Sudan* 73 F10
Korea, North ■, *Asia* 51 E14
Korea, South ■, *Asia* 51 F15
Korea Bay, *Korea* 51 E13
Korea Strait, *Asia* 51 G15
Korenevo, *Russia* 42 E2
Korenovsk, *Russia* 43 H4
Korets, *Ukraine* 41 G4
Korgan, *Turkey* 66 B7
Korgus, *Sudan* 76 D3
Korhogo, *Ivory C.* 78 D3
Koribundu, *S. Leone* 78 D2
Korim, *Indonesia* 57 E9
Korinthiakós Kólpos, *Greece* 39 L5
Kórinthos, *Greece* 39 M5
Korioumé, *Mali* 78 B4
Koríssa, Límni, *Greece* 37 B3
Kōriyama, *Japan* 48 F10
Korkuteli, *Turkey* 66 D4
Kormakiti, C., *Cyprus* 37 D11
Körmend, *Hungary* 21 H6
Kornat, *Croatia* 33 E12
Korneshty = Corneşti, *Moldova* 41 J5
Kornsjø, *Norway* 10 F5
Kornstad, *Norway* 10 B1
Koro, *Fiji* 87 C8
Koro, *Ivory C.* 78 D3
Koro, *Mali* 78 C4
Koro Sea, *Fiji* 87 C9
Korocha, *Russia* 42 E3
Köroğlu Dağları, *Turkey* 66 B5
Korogwe, *Tanzania* 82 D4
Korogwe □, *Tanzania* 82 D4
Koroit, *Australia* 91 F3
Koronadal, *Phil.* 55 H6
Koronowo, *Poland* 20 B7
Koror, *Pac. Oc.* 57 C8
Körös →, *Hungary* 21 J10
Korosten, *Ukraine* 41 G5
Korostyshev, *Ukraine* 41 G5
Korotoyak, *Russia* 42 E4
Korraraika, Helodranon' i, *Madag.* 85 B7
Korsakov, *Russia* 45 E15
Korshunovo, *Russia* 45 D12
Korsør, *Denmark* 9 J14
Korsun Shevchenkovskiy, *Ukraine* 41 H6
Korsze, *Poland* 20 A11
Kortemark, *Belgium* 17 F2
Kortessem, *Belgium* 17 G6
Korti, *Sudan* 76 D3
Kortrijk, *Belgium* 17 G2
Korwai, *India* 62 G8
Koryakskoye Nagorye, *Russia* 45 C18
Koryŏng, *S. Korea* 51 G15
Koryukovka, *Ukraine* 41 G7
Kos, *Greece* 39 N10
Kosa, *Ethiopia* 77 F4
Kosaya Gora, *Russia* 42 C3
Kościan, *Poland* 20 C6
Kościerzyna, *Poland* 20 A7
Kosciusko, *U.S.A.* 109 J10
Kosciusko, Mt., *Australia* 91 F4
Kosciusko I., *U.S.A.* 100 B2
Kösély →, *Hungary* 21 H11
Kosha, *Sudan* 76 C3
K'oshih = Kashi, *China* 54 C2
Koshiki-Rettō, *Japan* 49 J4
Kosi, *India* 62 F7
Košice, *Slovak Rep.* 20 G11
Kosjerić, *Serbia, Yug.* 21 M9
Koskhinoú, *Greece* 37 C10
Kosŏng, *N. Korea* 51 E15
Kosovska-Mitrovica = Titova-Mitrovica, *Serbia, Yug.* 21 N10
Kostajnica, *Croatia* 33 C13
Kostanjevica, *Slovenia* 33 C12
Kostelec, *Czech.* 20 E6
Koster, *S. Africa* 84 D4
Kôstî, *Sudan* 77 E3
Kostopil, *Ukraine* 41 G4
Kostroma, *Russia* 42 B5
Kostromskoye Vdkhr., *Russia* 42 B5
Kostyantynivka, *Ukraine* 41 H9
Kostyukovichi = Kastsyukovichy, *Belarus* 40 F7
Koszalin, *Poland* 20 A6
Köszeg, *Hungary* 21 H6
Kot Addu, *Pakistan* 62 D4
Kot Moman, *Pakistan* 62 C5
Kota, *India* 62 G6
Kota Baharu, *Malaysia* 59 J4
Kota Belud, *Malaysia* 56 C5
Kota Kinabalu, *Malaysia* 56 C5
Kota Tinggi, *Malaysia* 59 M4
Kotaagung, *Indonesia* 56 F2
Kotabaru, *Indonesia* 56 E5
Kotabumi, *Indonesia* 56 E2
Kotagede, *Indonesia* 57 G14
Kotamobagu, *Indonesia* 57 D6
Kotaneelee →, *Canada* 100 A4
Kotawaringin, *Indonesia* 56 E4
Kotcho L., *Canada* 100 B4
Kotelnich, *Russia* 42 A9
Kotelnikovo, *Russia* 43 G6
Kotelnyy, Ostrov, *Russia* 45 B14
Köthen, *Germany* 18 D7
Kothi, *India* 63 G9
Kotiro, *Pakistan* 62 F2
Kotka, *Finland* 9 F22
Kotlas, *Russia* 44 C5
Kotli, *Pakistan* 62 C5
Kotmul, *Pakistan* 63 B6
Kotonkoro, *Nigeria* 79 C6
Kotor, *Montenegro, Yug.* 21 N8
Kotoriba, *Croatia* 33 B13
Kotovo, *Russia* 42 E7
Kotovsk, *Russia* 42 D5
Kotovsk, *Ukraine* 41 J5
Kotputli, *India* 62 F7
Kotri, *Pakistan* 62 G3
Kótronas, *Greece* 39 N5
Kottayam, *India* 60 Q10
Kotturu, *India* 60 M10
Kotuy →, *Russia* 45 B11
Kotzebue, *U.S.A.* 96 B3
Kouango, *C.A.R.* 80 C4
Koudekerke, *Neths.* 17 F3
Koudougou, *Burkina Faso* 78 C4
Koufonísi, *Greece* 37 E8
Kougaberge, *S. Africa* 84 E3
Kouibli, *Ivory C.* 78 D3
Kouilou →, *Congo* 80 E2
Kouki, *C.A.R.* 80 C3
Koula Moutou, *Gabon* 80 E2
Koulen, *Cambodia* 58 F5
Koulikoro, *Mali* 78 C3
Kouloúra, *Greece* 37 A3
Koúm-bournoú, Ákra, *Greece* 37 C10
Koumala, *Australia* 90 C4
Koumankou, *Mali* 78 C3
Koumbia, *Burkina Faso* 78 C4
Koumbia, *Guinea* 78 C2
Koumboum, *Guinea* 78 C2
Koumpenntoum, *Senegal* 78 C2
Koumra, *Chad* 73 G8
Koundara, *Guinea* 78 C2
Kounradskiy, *Kazakstan* 44 E8
Kountze, *U.S.A.* 109 K7
Koupéla, *Burkina Faso* 79 C4
Kouris →, *Cyprus* 37 E11
Kourou, *Fr. Guiana* 121 B7
Kouroussa, *Guinea* 78 C3
Koussané, *Mali* 78 C2
Kousseri, *Cameroon* 73 F7
Koutiala, *Mali* 78 C3
Kouto, *Ivory C.* 78 D3
Kouvé, *Togo* 79 D5
Kouvola, *Finland* 9 F22
Kovačica, *Serbia, Yug.* 21 K10
Kovel, *Ukraine* 41 G3
Kovin, *Serbia, Yug.* 21 L10
Kovrov, *Russia* 42 B5
Kowanyama, *Australia* 90 B3
Kowkash, *Canada* 98 B2
Kowloon, *H.K.* 53 F10
Kowŏn, *N. Korea* 51 E14
Köyceğiz, *Turkey* 66 D3
Koyuk, *U.S.A.* 96 B3
Koyukuk →, *U.S.A.* 96 B4
Koyulhisar, *Turkey* 66 B7
Koza, *Japan* 49 L3
Kozan, *Turkey* 66 D6
Kozáni, *Greece* 39 J4
Kozara, *Bos.-H.* 33 D14
Kozarac, *Bos.-H.* 33 D13
Kozelets, *Ukraine* 41 G6
Kozelsk, *Russia* 42 C2
Kozhikode = Calicut, *India* 60 P9
Kozje, *Slovenia* 33 B12
Kozlovets, *Bulgaria* 38 F8
Kozlovka, *Russia* 42 C9
Kozlu, *Turkey* 66 B4
Kozluk, *Turkey* 67 C9
Koźmin, *Poland* 20 D7
Kozmodemyansk, *Russia* 42 B8
Kozyatyn, *Ukraine* 41 H5
Kpabia, *Ghana* 79 D4
Kpalimé, *Togo* 79 D5
Kpandae, *Ghana* 79 D4
Kpessi, *Togo* 79 D5
Kra, Isthmus of = Kra, Kho Khot, *Thailand* 59 G2
Kra, Kho Khot, *Thailand* 59 G2
Kra Buri, *Thailand* 59 G2
Krabbendijke, *Neths.* 17 F4
Krabi, *Thailand* 59 H2
Kragan, *Indonesia* 57 G14
Kragerø, *Norway* 10 F3
Kragujevac, *Serbia, Yug.* 21 L10
Krajina, *Bos.-H.* 33 D13
Krakatau = Rakata, Pulau, *Indonesia* 56 F3
Krakor, *Cambodia* 58 F5
Kraków, *Poland* 20 E9
Kraksaan, *Indonesia* 57 G15
Kråkstad, *Norway* 10 E4
Kralanh, *Cambodia* 58 F4
Králiky, *Czech.* 20 E6
Kraljevo, *Serbia, Yug.* 21 M10
Kralovice, *Czech.* 20 F3
Kralupy, *Czech.* 20 E4
Kramatorsk, *Ukraine* 41 H9
Kramfors, *Sweden* 10 B11
Kramis, C., *Algeria* 75 A5
Krångede, *Sweden* 10 A10
Kranj, *Slovenia* 33 B11
Kranjska Gora, *Slovenia* 33 B10
Krankskop, *S. Africa* 85 D5
Krapina, *Croatia* 33 B12
Krapina →, *Croatia* 33 C12
Krapkowice, *Poland* 20 E7
Kraskino, *Russia* 45 E14
Krāslava, *Latvia* 40 E4
Kraslice, *Czech.* 20 E2
Krasnaya Gorbatka, *Russia* 42 C5
Krasnaya Polyana, *Russia* 43 J5
Kraśnik, *Poland* 20 E12
Kraśnik Fabryczny, *Poland* 20 E12
Krasnoarmeisk, *Ukraine* 41 H9
Krasnoarmeysk, *Russia* 42 E7
Krasnoarmeyskiy, *Russia* 43 G6
Krasnodar, *Russia* 43 H4
Krasnodon, *Ukraine* 41 H10
Krasnogorskiy, *Russia* 42 B9
Krasnograd = Krasnohrad, *Ukraine* 41 H8
Krasnogvardeyskoye, *Russia* 43 H5
Krasnogvardyesk, *Ukraine* 41 K8
Krasnohrad, *Ukraine* 41 H8
Krasnokutsk, *Ukraine* 41 G8
Krasnolesnyy, *Russia* 42 E4
Krasnoperekopsk, *Ukraine* 41 J7
Krasnorechenskiy, *Russia* 48 B7
Krasnoselkupsk, *Russia* 44 C9
Krasnoslobodsk, *Russia* 42 C6
Krasnoslobodsk, *Russia* 43 F7
Krasnoturinsk, *Russia* 44 D7
Krasnoufimsk, *Russia* 44 D6
Krasnouralsk, *Russia* 44 D7
Krasnovodsk = Türkmenbashi, *Turkmenistan* 44 E6
Krasnoyarsk, *Russia* 45 D10
Krasnoye = Krasnyy, *Russia* 40 E6
Krasnozavodsk, *Russia* 42 B4
Krasny Sulin, *Russia* 43 G5
Krasnystaw, *Poland* 20 E13
Krasnyy, *Russia* 40 E6
Krasnyy Kholm, *Russia* 42 A3
Krasnyy Kut, *Russia* 42 E8
Krasnyy Liman, *Ukraine* 41 H9
Krasnyy Luch, *Ukraine* 41 H10
Krasnyy Profintern, *Russia* 42 B5
Krasnyy Yar, *Russia* 42 D10
Krasnyy Yar, *Russia* 42 E7
Krasnyy Yar, *Russia* 43 G9
Krasnyye Baki, *Russia* 42 B7
Krasnyyoskolske Vdskh., *Ukraine* 41 H9
Kraszna →, *Hungary* 21 G12
Kratie, *Cambodia* 58 F6
Krau, *Indonesia* 57 E10
Kravanh, Chuor Phnum, *Cambodia* 59 G4
Krefeld, *Germany* 18 D2
Krémaston, Límni, *Greece* 39 L4
Kremenchug = Kremenchuk, *Ukraine* 41 H7
Kremenchuk, *Ukraine* 41 H7
Kremenchuksk Vdskh., *Ukraine* 41 H7
Kremenets, *Ukraine* 41 G3
Kremennaya, *Ukraine* 41 H10
Kremges = Svitlovodsk, *Ukraine* 41 H7
Kremikovtsi, *Bulgaria* 38 G6
Kremmen, *Germany* 18 C9
Kremmling, *U.S.A.* 110 F10
Krems, *Austria* 21 G5
Kremsmünster, *Austria* 21 G4
Kretinga, *Lithuania* 9 J19
Krettamia, *Algeria* 74 C4
Krettsy, *Russia* 40 C7
Kreuzberg, *Germany* 19 E5
Kreuzlingen, *Switz.* 23 A8
Kribi, *Cameroon* 79 E6
Krichem, *Bulgaria* 38 G7
Krichev = Krychaw, *Belarus* 40 F6
Krim, *Slovenia* 33 C11
Krimpen, *Neths.* 16 E5
Kriós, Ákra, *Greece* 37 D5
Krishna →, *India* 61 M12
Krishnanagar, *India* 63 H13
Kristiansand, *Norway* 9 G13
Kristianstad, *Sweden* 9 H16
Kristiansund, *Norway* 10 A1
Kristiinankaupunki, *Finland* 9 E19
Kristinehamn, *Sweden* 9 G16
Kristinestad = Kristiinankaupunki, *Finland* 9 E19
Kríti, *Greece* 37 D7
Kritsá, *Greece* 37 D7
Kriva →, *Macedonia* 38 G4
Kriva Palanka, *Macedonia* 38 G5
Krivaja →, *Bos.-H.* 21 L8
Krivoy Rog = Kryvyy Rih, *Ukraine* 41 J7
Križevci, *Croatia* 33 B13
Krk, *Croatia* 33 C11
Krka →, *Slovenia* 33 C12
Krkonoše, *Czech.* 20 E5
Krnov, *Czech.* 20 E7
Krobia, *Poland* 20 D6
Krokeaí, *Greece* 39 N5
Krokodil →, *Mozam.* 85 D5
Krokom, *Sweden* 10 A8
Krolevets, *Ukraine* 41 G7
Kroměříz, *Czech.* 20 F7
Krommenie, *Neths.* 16 D5
Kromy, *Russia* 42 D2
Kronach, *Germany* 19 E7
Kronprins Olav Kyst, *Antarctica* 5 C5
Kronshtadt, *Russia* 40 C5
Kroonstad, *S. Africa* 84 D4
Kröpelin, *Germany* 18 A7
Kropotkin, *Irkutsk, Russia* 45 D12
Kropotkin, *Krasnodar, Russia* 43 H5
Kropp, *Germany* 18 A5
Krościenko, *Poland* 20 F10
Krosno, *Poland* 20 F11
Krosno Odrzańskie, *Poland* 20 C5
Krotoszyn, *Poland* 20 D7
Krotovka, *Russia* 42 D10
Kroussón, *Greece* 37 D6
Krško, *Slovenia* 33 C12
Kruger Nat. Park, *S. Africa* 85 C5
Krugersdorp, *S. Africa* 85 D4
Kruiningen, *Neths.* 17 F4
Kruisfontein, *S. Africa* 84 E3
Kruishoutem, *Belgium* 17 G3
Kruisland, *Neths.* 17 E4
Kruja, *Albania* 39 H2
Krulevshchina = Krulyewshchyna, *Belarus* 40 E4
Krulyewshchyna, *Belarus* 40 E4
Kruma, *Albania* 38 G3
Krumbach, *Germany* 19 G6
Krung Thep = Bangkok, *Thailand* 58 F3
Krupanj, *Serbia, Yug.* 21 L9
Krupinica →, *Slovak Rep.* 21 G8
Krupki, *Belarus* 40 E5
Kruševac, *Serbia, Yug.* 21 M11
Kruzof I., *U.S.A.* 100 B1
Krychaw, *Belarus* 40 F6
Krymsk, *Russia* 43 H4
Krymskiy Poluostrov = Krymskyy Pivostriv, *Ukraine* 41 K8
Krymskyy Pivostriv, *Ukraine* 41 K8
Krynica Morska, *Poland* 20 A9
Krynki, *Poland* 20 B13
Kryvyy Rih, *Ukraine* 41 J7
Krzywiń, *Poland* 20 D6
Krzyz, *Poland* 20 C6
Ksabi, *Morocco* 74 B4
Ksar Chellala, *Algeria* 75 A5
Ksar el Boukhari, *Algeria* 75 A5
Ksar el Kebir, *Morocco* 74 B3
Ksar es Souk = Ar Rachidiya, *Morocco* 74 B4
Ksar Rhilane, *Tunisia* 75 B6
Ksour, Mts. des, *Algeria* 75 B4
Kstovo, *Russia* 42 B7
Kuala, *Indonesia* 56 D3
Kuala Berang, *Malaysia* 59 K4
Kuala Dungun, *Malaysia* 59 K4
Kuala Kangsar, *Malaysia* 59 K3
Kuala Kelawang, *Malaysia* 59 L4
Kuala Kerai, *Malaysia* 59 K4
Kuala Kubu Baharu, *Malaysia* 59 L3
Kuala Lipis, *Malaysia* 59 K4
Kuala Lumpur, *Malaysia* 59 L3
Kuala Nerang, *Malaysia* 59 J3
Kuala Pilah, *Malaysia* 59 L4
Kuala Rompin, *Malaysia* 59 L4
Kuala Selangor, *Malaysia* 59 L3
Kuala Terengganu, *Malaysia* 59 K4
Kualajelai, *Indonesia* 56 E4
Kualakapuas, *Indonesia* 56 E4
Kualakurun, *Indonesia* 56 E4
Kualapembuang, *Indonesia* 56 E4
Kualasimpang, *Indonesia* 56 D1
Kuancheng, *China* 51 D10
Kuandang, *Indonesia* 57 D6
Kuandian, *China* 51 D13
Kuangchou = Guangzhou, *China* 53 F9
Kuantan, *Malaysia* 59 L4
Kuba = Quba, *Azerbaijan* 43 K9
Kuban →, *Russia* 43 H3
Kubenskoye, Ozero, *Russia* 40 C10
Kubokawa, *Japan* 49 H6
Kubrat, *Bulgaria* 38 F9
Kučevo, *Serbia, Yug.* 21 L11
Kucha Gompa, *India* 63 B7
Kuchaman, *India* 62 F6
Kuchino-eruba-Jima, *Japan* 49 J5
Kuchino-Shima, *Japan* 49 K4
Kuchinotsu, *Japan* 49 H5
Kucing, *Malaysia* 56 D4
Kuçova, *Albania* 39 J2
Kud →, *Pakistan* 62 F2
Kuda, *India* 60 H7
Kudat, *Malaysia* 56 C5
Kudus, *Indonesia* 57 G14
Kudymkar, *Russia* 44 D6
Kueiyang = Guiyang, *China* 52 D6
Kufra Oasis = Al Kufrah, *Libya* 73 D9
Kufstein, *Austria* 19 H8
Kugluktuk, *Canada* 96 B8
Kugong I., *Canada* 98 A4
Küh-e-Hazārām, *Iran* 65 D8
Kūhak, *Iran* 60 F3
Kūhbonān, *Iran* 65 D8
Kūhestak, *Iran* 65 E8
Kūhīn, *Iran* 65 C6
Kūhīrī, *Iran* 65 E9
Kuhnsdorf, *Austria* 21 J4
Kūhpāyeh, *Eşfahan, Iran* 65 C7
Kūhpāyeh, *Kermān, Iran* 65 D8
Kui Buri, *Thailand* 59 F2
Kuinre, *Neths.* 16 C7
Kuito, *Angola* 81 G3
Kujang, *N. Korea* 51 E14
Kuji, *Japan* 48 D10
Kujū-San, *Japan* 49 H5
Kukawa, *Nigeria* 79 C7
Kukerin, *Australia* 89 F2
Kukmor, *Russia* 42 B10
Kukup, *Malaysia* 59 M4
Kukvidze, *Russia* 42 E6
Kula, *Serbia, Yug.* 21 K9
Kula, *Turkey* 66 C3
Kulai, *Malaysia* 59 M4
Kulal, Mt., *Kenya* 82 B4
Kulaly, Ostrov, *Kazakstan* 43 H10
Kulasekarappattinam, *India* 60 Q11
Kuldiga, *Latvia* 9 H19
Kuldja = Yining, *China* 44 E9
Kuldu, *Sudan* 77 E2
Kulebaki, *Russia* 42 C6
Kulen Vakuf, *Bos.-H.* 33 D13
Kulgam, *India* 63 C6
Kulim, *Malaysia* 59 K3
Kulin, *Australia* 89 F2
Kulja, *Australia* 89 F2
Kulm, *U.S.A.* 108 B5
Kulmbach, *Germany* 19 E7
Kŭlob, *Tajikistan* 44 F7
Kulp, *Turkey* 67 C9
Kulsary, *Kazakstan* 44 E6
Kulti, *India* 63 H12
Kulu, *Turkey* 66 C5
Kulumbura, *Australia* 88 B4
Kulunda, *Russia* 44 D8
Kulungar, *Afghan.* 62 C3
Külvand, *Iran* 65 D7
Kulwin, *Australia* 91 F3
Kulyab = Kŭlob, *Tajikistan* 44 F7
Kum Tekei, *Kazakstan* 44 E8
Kuma →, *Russia* 43 H8
Kumaganum, *Nigeria* 79 C7
Kumagaya, *Japan* 49 F9
Kumai, *Indonesia* 56 E4
Kumamba, Kepulauan, *Indonesia* 57 E9
Kumamoto, *Japan* 49 H5
Kumamoto □, *Japan* 49 H5
Kumanovo, *Macedonia* 38 G4
Kumara, *N.Z.* 87 K3
Kumarl, *Australia* 89 F3
Kumasi, *Ghana* 78 D4
Kumayri = Gyumri, *Armenia* 43 K6
Kumba, *Cameroon* 79 E6
Kumbakonam, *India* 60 P11
Kumbarilla, *Australia* 91 D5
Kumbo, *Cameroon* 79 D7
Kŭmchŏn, *N. Korea* 51 E14
Kumdok, *India* 63 C8
Kume-Shima, *Japan* 49 L3
Kumeny, *Russia* 42 A9
Kŭmhwa, *S. Korea* 51 E14
Kumi, *Uganda* 82 B3
Kumla, *Sweden* 9 G16
Kumluca, *Turkey* 66 D4
Kummerower See, *Germany* 18 B8
Kumo, *Nigeria* 79 C7
Kumon Bum, *Burma* 61 F20
Kumylzhenskaya, *Russia* 42 F6
Kunama, *Australia* 91 F4
Kunashir, Ostrov, *Russia* 45 E15
Kunda, *Estonia* 9 G22
Kundla, *India* 62 J4
Kungala, *Australia* 91 D5
Kungälv, *Sweden* 11 G5
Kunghit I., *Canada* 100 C2
Kungrad = Qŭnghirot, *Uzbekistan* 44 E6
Kungsbacka, *Sweden* 11 G6
Kungur, *Russia* 44 D6
Kungurri, *Australia* 90 C4
Kunhar →, *Pakistan* 63 B5
Kunhegyes, *Hungary* 21 H10
Kuningan, *Indonesia* 57 G13
Kunlong, *Burma* 61 H21
Kunlun Shan, *Asia* 54 C3
Kunming, *China* 52 E4
Kunrade, *Neths.* 17 G7
Kunsan, *S. Korea* 51 G14
Kunshan, *China* 53 B13
Kununurra, *Australia* 88 C4
Kunwarara, *Australia* 90 C5
Kunya-Urgench = Köneürgench, *Turkmenistan* 44 E6
Künzelsau, *Germany* 19 F5
Kuopio, *Finland* 8 E22
Kupa →, *Croatia* 33 C13
Kupang, *Indonesia* 57 F6
Kupres, *Bos.-H.* 21 L7
Kupyansk, *Ukraine* 41 H9
Kupyansk-Uzlovoi, *Ukraine* 41 H9
Kuqa, *China* 54 B3
Kür →, *Azerbaijan* 67 C13
Kura = Kür →, *Azerbaijan* 67 C13
Kuranda, *Australia* 90 B4
Kurashiki, *Japan* 49 G6
Kurayoshi, *Japan* 49 G6
Kürdämir, *Azerbaijan* 43 K9

Kurdistan, *Asia* 67 D10
Kŭrdzhali, *Bulgaria* 39 H8
Kure, *Japan* 49 G6
Küre, *Turkey* 66 B5
Küre Dağları, *Turkey* 66 B6
Kuressaare, *Estonia* 9 G20
Kurgaldzhinskiy, *Kazakstan* 44 D8
Kurgan, *Russia* 44 D7
Kurganinsk, *Russia* 43 H5
Kurgannaya = Kurganinsk, *Russia* 43 H5
Kuria Maria Is. = Khūrīyā Mūrīyā, Jazā 'ir, *Oman* 68 D6
Kuridala, *Australia* 90 C3
Kurigram, *Bangla.* 61 G16
Kurikka, *Finland* 9 E20
Kuril Is. = Kurilskiye Ostrova, *Russia* 45 E15
Kuril Trench, *Pac. Oc.* 46 E19
Kurilsk, *Russia* 45 E15
Kurilskiye Ostrova, *Russia* 45 E15
Kuringen, *Belgium* 17 G6
Kurino, *Japan* 49 J5
Kurinskaya Kosa, *Azerbaijan* 67 C13
Kurkur, *Egypt* 76 C3
Kurlovskiy, *Russia* 42 C5
Kurmuk, *Sudan* 77 E3
Kurnool, *India* 60 M10
Kuro-Shima, *Kagoshima, Japan* 49 J4
Kuro-Shima, *Okinawa, Japan* 49 M2
Kurow, *N.Z.* 87 L3
Kurrajong, *Australia* 91 E5
Kurram →, *Pakistan* 62 C4
Kurri Kurri, *Australia* 91 E5
Kursavka, *Russia* 43 H6
Kurshskiy Zaliv, *Russia* 9 J19
Kursk, *Russia* 42 E3
Kuršumlija, *Serbia, Yug.* 21 M11
Kurşunlu, *Turkey* 66 B5
Kurtalan, *Turkey* 67 D9
Kuru, Bahr el →, *Sudan* 77 F2
Kurucaşile, *Turkey* 66 B5
Kuruktag, *China* 54 B3
Kuruman, *S. Africa* 84 D3
Kuruman →, *S. Africa* 84 D3
Kurume, *Japan* 49 H5
Kurunegala, *Sri Lanka* 60 R12
Kurupukari, *Guyana* 121 C6
Kurya, *Russia* 45 C11
Kus Gölü, *Turkey* 66 B2
Kuşadası, *Turkey* 66 D2
Kusatsu, *Japan* 49 F9
Kusawa L., *Canada* 100 A1
Kusel, *Germany* 19 F3
Kushchevskaya, *Russia* 43 G4
Kushikino, *Japan* 49 J5
Kushima, *Japan* 49 J5
Kushimoto, *Japan* 49 H7
Kushiro, *Japan* 48 C12
Kushiro →, *Japan* 48 C12
Kūshk, *Iran* 65 D8
Kushka = Gushgy, *Turkmenistan* 44 F7
Kūshkī, *Īlām, Iran* 64 C5
Kūshkī, *Khorāsān, Iran* 65 B8
Kūshkū, *Iran* 65 E7
Kushol, *India* 63 C7
Kushtia, *Bangla.* 61 H16
Kushum →, *Kazakstan* 42 F10
Kuskokwim →, *U.S.A.* 96 B3
Kuskokwim B., *U.S.A.* 96 C3
Küsnacht, *Switz.* 23 B7
Kussharo-Ko, *Japan* 48 C12
Küssnacht, *Switz.* 23 B6
Kustanay = Qostanay, *Kazakstan* 44 D7
Kut, Ko, *Thailand* 59 G4
Kütahya, *Turkey* 66 C4
Kutaisi, *Georgia* 43 J6
Kutaraja = Banda Aceh, *Indonesia* 56 C1
Kutch, Gulf of = Kachchh, Gulf of, *India* 62 H3
Kutch, Rann of = Kachchh, Rann of, *India* 62 G4
Kutina, *Croatia* 33 C13
Kutiyana, *India* 62 J4
Kutkashen, *Azerbaijan* 43 K8
Kutná Hora, *Czech.* 20 F5
Kutno, *Poland* 20 C9
Kuttabul, *Australia* 90 C4
Kutu, *Zaïre* 80 E3
Kutum, *Sudan* 77 E1
Kuujjuaq, *Canada* 97 C13
Kuŭp-tong, *N. Korea* 51 D14
Kuurne, *Belgium* 17 G2
Kuusamo, *Finland* 8 D23
Kuusankoski, *Finland* 9 F22
Kuvshinovo, *Russia* 42 B2
Kuwait = Al Kuwayt, *Kuwait* 64 D5
Kuwait ■, *Asia* 64 D5
Kuwana, *Japan* 49 G8
Kuybyshev = Samara, *Russia* 42 D10
Kuybyshev, *Russia* 44 D8
Kuybyshevo, *Ukraine* 41 J9
Kuybyshevskoye Vdkhr., *Russia* 42 C9
Kuye He →, *China* 50 E6
Kūyeh, *Iran* 64 B5
Kūysanjaq, *Iraq* 67 D11
Kuyumba, *Russia* 45 C10
Kuzey Anadolu Dağları, *Turkey* 66 B7
Kuznetsk, *Russia* 42 D8
Kvænangen, *Norway* 8 A19
Kvaløy, *Norway* 8 B18
Kvam, *Norway* 10 C3
Kvareli = Qvareli, *Georgia* 43 K7
Kvarner, *Croatia* 33 D11
Kvarnerič, *Croatia* 33 D11
Kviteseid, *Norway* 10 E2
Kwabhaca, *S. Africa* 85 E4
Kwadacha →, *Canada* 100 B3
Kwakhanai, *Botswana* 84 C3
Kwakoegron, *Surinam* 121 B6
Kwale, *Kenya* 82 C4
Kwale, *Nigeria* 79 D6
Kwale □, *Kenya* 82 C4
KwaMashu, *S. Africa* 85 D5
Kwamouth, *Zaïre* 80 E3
Kwando →, *Africa* 84 B3
Kwangdaeri, *N. Korea* 51 D14
Kwangju, *S. Korea* 51 G14
Kwango →, *Zaïre* 71 G5
Kwangsi-Chuang = Guangxi Zhuangzu Zizhiqu □, *China* 52 E7
Kwangtung = Guangdong □, *China* 53 F9
Kwara □, *Nigeria* 79 D5
Kwataboahegan →, *Canada* 98 B3
Kwatisore, *Indonesia* 57 E8
KwaZulu Natal □, *S. Africa* 85 D5
Kweichow = Guizhou □, *China* 52 D6
Kwekwe, *Zimbabwe* 83 F2
Kwimba □, *Tanzania* 82 C3
Kwinana New Town, *Australia* 89 F2
Kwoka, *Indonesia* 57 E8
Kyabé, *Chad* 73 G8
Kyabra Cr. →, *Australia* 91 D3
Kyabram, *Australia* 91 F4
Kyaikto, *Burma* 58 D1
Kyakhta, *Russia* 45 D11
Kyancutta, *Australia* 91 E2
Kyangin, *Burma* 61 K19
Kyaukpadaung, *Burma* 61 J19
Kyaukpyu, *Burma* 61 K18
Kyaukse, *Burma* 61 J20
Kyburz, *U.S.A.* 112 G6
Kyenjojo, *Uganda* 82 B3
Kyle Dam, *Zimbabwe* 83 G3
Kyle of Lochalsh, *U.K.* 14 D3
Kyll →, *Germany* 19 F2
Kyllburg, *Germany* 19 E2
Kymijoki →, *Finland* 9 F22
Kyneton, *Australia* 91 F3
Kynuna, *Australia* 90 C3
Kyō-ga-Saki, *Japan* 49 G7
Kyoga, L., *Uganda* 82 B3
Kyogle, *Australia* 91 D5
Kyongju, *S. Korea* 51 G15
Kyongpyaw, *Burma* 61 L19
Kyŏngsŏng, *N. Korea* 51 D15
Kyōto, *Japan* 49 G7
Kyōto □, *Japan* 49 G7
Kyparissovouno, *Cyprus* 37 D12
Kyperounda, *Cyprus* 37 E11
Kyren, *Russia* 45 D11
Kyrenia, *Cyprus* 66 E5
Kyrgyzstan ■, *Asia* 44 E8
Kyritz, *Germany* 18 C8
Kyrönjoki →, *Finland* 8 E19
Kyrtylakh, *Russia* 45 C13
Kystatyam, *Russia* 45 C13
Kythréa, *Cyprus* 37 D12
Kyulyunken, *Russia* 45 C14
Kyunhla, *Burma* 61 H19
Kyuquot, *Canada* 100 C3
Kyurdamir = Kürdämir, *Azerbaijan* 43 K9
Kyūshū, *Japan* 49 H5
Kyūshū □, *Japan* 49 H5
Kyūshū-Sanchi, *Japan* 49 H5
Kyustendil, *Bulgaria* 38 G5
Kyusyur, *Russia* 45 B13
Kywong, *Australia* 91 E4
Kyyiv, *Ukraine* 41 G6
Kyyivske Vdskh., *Ukraine* 41 G6
Kyzyl, *Russia* 45 D10
Kyzyl Kum, *Uzbekistan* 44 E7
Kyzyl-Kyya, *Kyrgyzstan* 44 E8
Kzyl-Orda = Qyzylorda, *Kazakstan* 44 E7

L

La Albuera, *Spain* 31 G4
La Albufera, *Spain* 29 F4
La Alcarria, *Spain* 28 E2
La Algaba, *Spain* 31 H4
La Almarcha, *Spain* 28 F2
La Almunia de Doña Godina, *Spain* 28 D3
La Asunción, *Venezuela* 121 A5
La Banda, *Argentina* 126 B3
La Bañeza, *Spain* 30 C5
La Barca, *Mexico* 114 C4
La Barge, *U.S.A.* 110 E8
La Bassée, *France* 25 B9
La Bastide-Puylaurent, *France* 26 D7
La Baule, *France* 24 E4
La Belle, *U.S.A.* 105 M5
La Biche →, *Canada* 100 B4
La Bisbal, *Spain* 28 D8
La Blanquilla, *Venezuela* 121 A5
La Bomba, *Mexico* 114 A1
La Bresse, *France* 25 D13
La Bureba, *Spain* 28 C1
La Cal →, *Bolivia* 125 D6
La Calera, *Chile* 126 C1
La Campiña, *Spain* 31 H6
La Canal, *Spain* 36 C7
La Cañiza, *Spain* 30 C2
La Capelle, *France* 25 C10
La Carlota, *Argentina* 126 C3
La Carlota, *Phil.* 55 F5
La Carolina, *Spain* 31 G7
La Cavalerie, *France* 26 D7
La Ceiba, *Honduras* 116 C2
La Chaise-Dieu, *France* 26 C7
La Chaize-le-Vicomte, *France* 24 F5
La Chapelle d'Angillon, *France* 25 E9
La Chapelle-Glain, *France* 24 E5
La Charité-sur-Loire, *France* 25 E10
La Chartre-sur-le-Loir, *France* 24 E7
La Châtaigneraie, *France* 26 B3
La Châtre, *France* 26 B5
La Chaux de Fonds, *Switz.* 22 B3
La Chorrera, *Colombia* 120 D3
La Ciotat, *France* 27 E9
La Clayette, *France* 27 B8
La Cocha, *Argentina* 126 B2
La Concepción = Ri-Aba, *Eq. Guin.* 79 E6
La Concepción, *Venezuela* 120 A3
La Concordia, *Mexico* 115 D6
La Conner, *U.S.A.* 110 B2
La Coruña, *Spain* 30 B2
La Coruña □, *Spain* 30 B2
La Côte, *Switz.* 22 D2
La Côte-St.-André, *France* 27 C9
La Courtine-le-Trucq, *France* 26 C6
La Crau, *France* 27 E8
La Crete, *Canada* 100 B5
La Crosse, *Kans., U.S.A.* 108 F5
La Crosse, *Wis., U.S.A.* 108 D9
La Cruz, *Costa Rica* 116 D2
La Cruz, *Mexico* 114 C3
La Dorada, *Colombia* 120 B3
La Ensenada, *Chile* 128 B2
La Escondida, *Mexico* 114 C5
La Esmeralda, *Paraguay* 126 A3
La Esperanza, *Argentina* 128 B3
La Esperanza, *Cuba* 116 B3
La Esperanza, *Honduras* 116 D2
La Estrada, *Spain* 30 C2
La Fayette, *U.S.A.* 105 H3
La Fé, *Cuba* 116 B3
La Fère, *France* 25 C10
La Ferté-Bernard, *France* 24 D7
La Ferté-Macé, *France* 24 D6
La Ferté-St.-Aubin, *France* 25 E8
La Ferté-sous-Jouarre, *France* 25 D10
La Ferté-Vidame, *France* 24 D7
La Flèche, *France* 24 E6
La Follette, *U.S.A.* 105 G3
La Fregeneda, *Spain* 30 E4
La Fría, *Venezuela* 120 B3
La Fuente de San Esteban, *Spain* 30 E4
La Gineta, *Spain* 29 F2
La Gloria, *Colombia* 120 B3
La Gran Sabana, *Venezuela* 121 B5
La Grand-Combe, *France* 27 D8
La Grande, *U.S.A.* 110 D4
La Grande-Motte, *France* 27 E8
La Grange, *Calif., U.S.A.* 112 H6
La Grange, *Ga., U.S.A.* 105 J3
La Grange, *Ky., U.S.A.* 104 F3
La Grange, *Tex., U.S.A.* 109 L6
La Grita, *Venezuela* 120 B3
La Guaira, *Venezuela* 120 A4
La Guardia, *Spain* 30 D2
La Gudiña, *Spain* 30 C3
La Güera, *Mauritania* 74 D1
La Guerche-de-Bretagne, *France* 24 E5
La Guerche-sur-l'Aubois, *France* 25 F9
La Habana, *Cuba* 116 B3
La Harpe, *U.S.A.* 108 E9
La Haye-du-Puits, *France* 24 C5
La Horqueta, *Venezuela* 121 B5
La Horra, *Spain* 30 D7
La Independencia, *Mexico* 115 D6
La Isabela, *Dom. Rep.* 117 C5
La Jara, *U.S.A.* 111 H11
La Joya, *Peru* 124 D3
La Junquera, *Spain* 28 C7
La Junta, *U.S.A.* 109 F3
La Laguna, *Canary Is.* 36 F3
La Libertad, *Guatemala* 116 C1
La Libertad, *Mexico* 114 B2
La Libertad □, *Peru* 124 B2
La Ligua, *Chile* 126 C1
La Línea de la Concepción, *Spain* 31 J5
La Loche, *Canada* 101 B7
La Londe-les-Maures, *France* 27 E10
La Lora, *Spain* 30 C7
La Loupe, *France* 24 D8
La Louvière, *Belgium* 17 H4
La Machine, *France* 25 F10
La Maddalena, *Italy* 34 A2
La Malbaie, *Canada* 99 C5
La Mancha, *Spain* 29 F2
La Mariña, *Spain* 30 B3
La Mesa, *Calif., U.S.A.* 113 N9
La Mesa, *N. Mex., U.S.A.* 111 K10
La Misión, *Mexico* 114 A1
La Mothe-Achard, *France* 24 F5
La Motte, *France* 27 D10
La Motte-Chalançon, *France* 27 D9
La Moure, *U.S.A.* 108 B5
La Muela, *Spain* 28 D3
La Mure, *France* 27 D9
La Negra, *Chile* 126 A1
La Neuveville, *Switz.* 22 B4
La Oliva, *Canary Is.* 36 F6
La Oraya, *Peru* 124 C2
La Orotava, *Canary Is.* 36 F3
La Pacaudière, *France* 26 B7
La Palma, *Canary Is.* 36 F2
La Palma, *Panama* 116 E4
La Palma del Condado, *Spain* 31 H4
La Paloma, *Chile* 126 C1
La Pampa □, *Argentina* 126 D2
La Paragua, *Venezuela* 121 B5
La Paz, *Entre Ríos, Argentina* 126 C4
La Paz, *San Luis, Argentina* 126 C2
La Paz, *Bolivia* 124 D4
La Paz, *Honduras* 116 D2
La Paz, *Mexico* 114 C2
La Paz, *Phil.* 55 D4
La Paz □, *Bolivia* 124 D4
La Paz Centro, *Nic.* 116 D2
La Pedrera, *Colombia* 120 D4
La Perouse Str., *Asia* 48 B11
La Pesca, *Mexico* 115 C5
La Piedad, *Mexico* 114 C4
La Pine, *U.S.A.* 110 E3
La Plant, *U.S.A.* 108 C4
La Plata, *Argentina* 126 D4
La Plata, *Colombia* 120 C2
La Plata, L., *Argentina* 128 B2
La Pobla de Lillet, *Spain* 28 C6
La Pola de Gordón, *Spain* 30 C5
La Porte, *U.S.A.* 104 E2
La Puebla, *Spain* 28 F8
La Puebla de Cazalla, *Spain* 31 H5
La Puebla de los Infantes, *Spain* 31 H5
La Puebla de Montalbán, *Spain* 30 F6
La Puerta, *Spain* 29 G2
La Punt, *Switz.* 23 C9
La Purísima, *Mexico* 114 B2
La Push, *U.S.A.* 112 C2
La Quiaca, *Argentina* 126 A2
La Rambla, *Spain* 31 H6
La Reine, *Canada* 98 C4
La Réole, *France* 26 D3
La Restinga, *Canary Is.* 36 G2
La Rioja, *Argentina* 126 B2
La Rioja □, *Argentina* 126 B2
La Rioja □, *Spain* 28 C2
La Robla, *Spain* 30 C5
La Roche, *Switz.* 22 C4
La Roche-Bernard, *France* 24 E4
La Roche-Canillac, *France* 26 C5
La Roche-en-Ardenne, *Belgium* 17 H7
La Roche-sur-Yon, *France* 24 F5
La Rochefoucauld, *France* 26 C4
La Rochelle, *France* 26 B2
La Roda, *Albacete, Spain* 29 F2
La Roda, *Sevilla, Spain* 31 H6
La Romana, *Dom. Rep.* 117 C6
La Ronge, *Canada* 101 B7
La Rumorosa, *Mexico* 113 N10
La Sabina, *Spain* 36 C7
La Sagra, *Spain* 29 H2
La Salle, *U.S.A.* 108 E10
La Sanabria, *Spain* 30 C4
La Santa, *Canary Is.* 36 E6
La Sarraz, *Switz.* 22 C3
La Sarre, *Canada* 98 C4
La Scie, *Canada* 99 C8
La Selva, *Spain* 28 D7
La Selva Beach, *U.S.A.* 112 J5
La Serena, *Chile* 126 B1
La Serena, *Spain* 31 G5
La Seyne-sur-Mer, *France* 27 E9
La Sila, *Italy* 35 C9
La Solana, *Spain* 29 G1
La Souterraine, *France* 26 B5
La Spézia, *Italy* 32 D6
La Suze-sur-Sarthe, *France* 24 E7
La Tagua, *Colombia* 120 C3
La Teste, *France* 26 D2
La Tortuga, *Venezuela* 117 D6
La Tour-du-Pin, *France* 27 C9
La Tranche-sur-Mer, *France* 24 F5
La Tremblade, *France* 26 C2
La Tuque, *Canada* 98 C5
La Unión, *Chile* 128 B2
La Unión, *Colombia* 120 C2
La Unión, *El Salv.* 116 D2
La Unión, *Mexico* 114 D4
La Unión, *Peru* 124 B2
La Unión, *Spain* 29 H4
La Urbana, *Venezuela* 120 B4
La Vecilla, *Spain* 30 C5
La Vega, *Dom. Rep.* 117 C5
La Vega, *Peru* 124 C2
La Vela, *Venezuela* 120 A4
La Veleta, *Spain* 31 H7
La Venta, *Mexico* 115 D6
La Ventura, *Mexico* 114 C4
La Venturosa, *Colombia* 120 B4
La Victoria, *Venezuela* 120 A4
La Voulte-sur-Rhône, *France* 27 D8
La Zarza, *Spain* 31 H4
Laaber →, *Germany* 19 G8
Laage, *Germany* 18 B8
Laba →, *Russia* 43 H4
Labason, *Phil.* 55 G5
Labastide-Murat, *France* 26 D5
Labastide-Rouairoux, *France* 26 E6
Labbézenga, *Mali* 79 B5
Labe = Elbe →, *Europe* 18 B4
Labé, *Guinea* 78 C2
Laberec →, *Slovak Rep.* 20 G11
Laberge, L., *Canada* 100 A1
Labin, *Croatia* 33 C11
Labinsk, *Russia* 43 H5
Labis, *Malaysia* 59 L4
Labo, *Phil.* 55 D5
Laboe, *Germany* 18 A6
Labouheyre, *France* 26 D3
Laboulaye, *Argentina* 126 C3
Labra, Peña, *Spain* 30 B6
Labrador, Coast of □, *Canada* 99 B7
Labrador City, *Canada* 99 B6
Lábrea, *Brazil* 125 B5
Labrède, *France* 26 D3
Labuan, Pulau, *Malaysia* 56 C5
Labuha, *Indonesia* 57 E7
Labuhan, *Indonesia* 57 G11
Labuhanbajo, *Indonesia* 57 F6
Labuissière, *Belgium* 17 H4
Labuk, Telok, *Malaysia* 56 C5
Labyrinth, L., *Australia* 91 E2
Labytnangi, *Russia* 44 C7
Lac Allard, *Canada* 99 B7
Lac Bouchette, *Canada* 99 C5
Lac du Flambeau, *U.S.A.* 108 B10
Lac Édouard, *Canada* 98 C5
Lac La Biche, *Canada* 100 C6
Lac la Martre = Wha Ti, *Canada* 96 B8
Lac-Mégantic, *Canada* 99 C5
Lac Seul, Res., *Canada* 98 B1
Lac Thien, *Vietnam* 58 F7
Lacanau, *France* 26 D2
Lacanau, Étang de, *France* 26 D2
Lacantúm →, *Mexico* 115 D6
Lacara →, *Spain* 31 G4
Lacaune, *France* 26 E6
Lacaune, Mts. de, *France* 26 E6
Laccadive Is. = Lakshadweep Is., *Ind. Oc.* 46 H11
Lacepede B., *Australia* 91 F2
Lacepede Is., *Australia* 88 C3
Lacerdónia, *Mozam.* 83 F4
Lacey, *U.S.A.* 112 C4
Lachay, Pta., *Peru* 124 C2
Lachen, *Switz.* 23 B7
Lachhmangarh, *India* 62 F6
Lachi, *Pakistan* 62 C4
Lachine, *Canada* 98 C5
Lachlan →, *Australia* 91 E3
Lachute, *Canada* 98 C5
Lackawanna, *U.S.A.* 106 D6
Lacolle, *Canada* 107 A11
Lacombe, *Canada* 100 C6
Lacona, *U.S.A.* 107 C8
Láconi, *Italy* 34 C2
Laconia, *U.S.A.* 107 C13
Lacq, *France* 26 E3
Lacrosse, *U.S.A.* 110 C5
Ladakh Ra., *India* 63 B8
Ladário, *Brazil* 125 D6
Ládhon →, *Greece* 39 M4
Ladik, *Turkey* 66 B6
Ladismith, *S. Africa* 84 E3
Lādīz, *Iran* 65 D9
Ladnun, *India* 62 F6
Ladoga, L. = Ladozhskoye Ozero, *Russia* 40 B6
Ladon, *France* 25 D9
Ladozhskoye Ozero, *Russia* 40 B6
Ladrillero, G., *Chile* 128 C1
Lady Grey, *S. Africa* 84 E4
Ladybrand, *S. Africa* 84 D4
Ladysmith, *Canada* 100 D4
Ladysmith, *S. Africa* 85 D4
Ladysmith, *U.S.A.* 108 C9
Lae, *Papua N. G.* 92 H6
Laem Ngop, *Thailand* 59 F4
Laem Pho, *Thailand* 59 J3
Læsø, *Denmark* 11 G4
Læsø Rende, *Denmark* 11 G4
Lafayette, *Colo., U.S.A.* 108 F2
Lafayette, *Ind., U.S.A.* 104 E2
Lafayette, *La., U.S.A.* 109 K9
Lafayette, *Tenn., U.S.A.* 105 G3
Laferte →, *Canada* 100 A5
Lafia, *Nigeria* 79 D6
Lafiagi, *Nigeria* 79 D6
Lafleche, *Canada* 101 D7
Lafon, *Sudan* 77 F3
Laforsen, *Sweden* 10 C9
Lagan →, *Sweden* 11 H7

Lagan →, *U.K.* 15 B6
Lagarfljót →, *Iceland* 8 D6
Lagarto, *Brazil* 122 D4
Lage, *Germany* 18 D4
Lage, *Spain* 30 B2
Lage-Mierde, *Neths.* 17 F6
Lågen →, *Oppland, Norway* 9 F14
Lågen →, *Vestfold, Norway* 9 G14
Lägerdorf, *Germany* 18 B5
Laghouat, *Algeria* 75 B5
Lagnieu, *France* 27 C9
Lagny, *France* 25 D9
Lago, *Italy* 35 C9
Lago Posadas, *Argentina* 128 C2
Lago Ranco, *Chile* 128 B2
Lagôa, *Portugal* 31 H2
Lagoaça, *Portugal* 30 D4
Lagodekhi, *Georgia* 43 K8
Lagónegro, *Italy* 35 B8
Lagonoy Gulf, *Phil.* 55 E5
Lagos, *Nigeria* 79 D5
Lagos, *Portugal* 31 H2
Lagos de Moreno, *Mexico* 114 C4
Lagrange, *Australia* 88 C3
Lagrange B., *Australia* 88 C3
Laguardia, *Spain* 28 C2
Laguépie, *France* 26 D5
Laguna, *Brazil* 127 B6
Laguna, *U.S.A.* 111 J10
Laguna Beach, *U.S.A.* 113 M9
Laguna de la Janda, *Spain* 31 J5
Laguna Limpia, *Argentina* 126 B4
Laguna Madre, *U.S.A.* 115 B5
Lagunas, *Chile* 126 A2
Lagunas, *Peru* 124 B2
Lagunillas, *Bolivia* 125 D5
Lahad Datu, *Malaysia* 57 C5
Lahan Sai, *Thailand* 58 E4
Lahanam, *Laos* 58 D5
Laharpur, *India* 63 F9
Lahat, *Indonesia* 56 E2
Lahewa, *Indonesia* 56 D1
Lahiang Lahiang, *Phil.* 55 H4
Lāhījān, *Iran* 65 B6
Lahn →, *Germany* 19 E3
Laholm, *Sweden* 11 H7
Laholmsbukten, *Sweden* 11 H6
Lahontan Reservoir, *U.S.A.* 110 G4
Lahore, *Pakistan* 62 D6
Lahr, *Germany* 19 G3
Lahti, *Finland* 9 F21
Lahtis = Lahti, *Finland* 9 F21
Laï, *Chad* 73 G8
Lai Chau, *Vietnam* 58 A4
Lai'an, *China* 53 A12
Laibin, *China* 52 F7
Laidley, *Australia* 91 D5
Laifeng, *China* 52 C7
L'Aigle, *France* 24 D7
Laignes, *France* 25 E11
L'Aiguillon-sur-Mer, *France* 26 B2
Laikipia □, *Kenya* 82 B4
Laingsburg, *S. Africa* 84 E3
Lainio älv →, *Sweden* 8 C20
Lairg, *U.K.* 14 C4
Laishui, *China* 50 E8
Laiwu, *China* 51 F9
Laixi, *China* 51 F11
Laiyang, *China* 51 F11
Laiyuan, *China* 50 E8
Laizhou Wan, *China* 51 F10
Laja →, *Mexico* 114 C4
Lajere, *Nigeria* 79 C7
Lajes, *Rio Grande do N., Brazil* 122 C4
Lajes, *Sta. Catarina, Brazil* 127 B5
Lajinha, *Brazil* 123 F3
Lajkovac, *Serbia, Yug.* 21 L10
Lajosmizse, *Hungary* 21 H9
Lak Sao, *Laos* 58 C5
Lakaband, *Pakistan* 62 D3
Lake Alpine, *U.S.A.* 112 G7
Lake Andes, *U.S.A.* 108 D5
Lake Anse, *U.S.A.* 104 B1
Lake Arthur, *U.S.A.* 109 K8
Lake Cargelligo, *Australia* 91 E4
Lake Charles, *U.S.A.* 109 K8
Lake City, *Colo., U.S.A.* 111 G10
Lake City, *Fla., U.S.A.* 105 K4
Lake City, *Iowa, U.S.A.* 108 D7
Lake City, *Mich., U.S.A.* 104 C3
Lake City, *Minn., U.S.A.* 108 C8
Lake City, *Pa., U.S.A.* 106 D4
Lake City, *S.C., U.S.A.* 105 J6
Lake George, *U.S.A.* 107 C11
Lake Grace, *Australia* 89 F2
Lake Harbour = Kimmirut, *Canada* 97 B13
Lake Havasu City, *U.S.A.* 113 L12
Lake Hughes, *U.S.A.* 113 L8
Lake Isabella, *U.S.A.* 113 K8
Lake King, *Australia* 89 F2
Lake Lenore, *Canada* 101 C8
Lake Louise, *Canada* 100 C5
Lake Mead National Recreation Area, *U.S.A.* 113 K12
Lake Mills, *U.S.A.* 108 D8
Lake Nash, *Australia* 90 C2
Lake Providence, *U.S.A.* 109 J9
Lake River, *Canada* 98 B3
Lake Superior Prov. Park, *Canada* 98 C3
Lake Village, *U.S.A.* 109 J9
Lake Wales, *U.S.A.* 105 M5
Lake Worth, *U.S.A.* 105 M5
Lakefield, *Canada* 98 D4
Lakeland, *Australia* 90 B3
Lakeland, *U.S.A.* 105 L5
Lakemba, *Fiji* 87 D9
Lakeport, *U.S.A.* 112 F4
Lakes Entrance, *Australia* 91 F4
Lakeside, *Ariz., U.S.A.* 111 J9
Lakeside, *Calif., U.S.A.* 113 N10
Lakeside, *Nebr., U.S.A.* 108 D3
Lakeview, *U.S.A.* 110 E3
Lakewood, *Colo., U.S.A.* 108 F2
Lakewood, *N.J., U.S.A.* 107 F10
Lakewood, *Ohio, U.S.A.* 106 E3
Lakewood Center, *U.S.A.* 112 C4
Lakhaniá, *Greece* 37 D9
Lakhonpheng, *Laos* 58 E5
Lakhpat, *India* 62 H3
Läki, *Azerbaijan* 43 K8
Lakin, *U.S.A.* 109 G4
Lakitusaki →, *Canada* 98 B3
Lákkoi, *Greece* 37 D5
Lakonikós Kólpos, *Greece* 39 N5
Lakor, *Indonesia* 57 F7
Lakota, *Ivory C.* 78 D3
Lakota, *U.S.A.* 108 A5
Laksefjorden, *Norway* 8 A22
Lakselv, *Norway* 8 A21
Lakshadweep Is., *Ind. Oc.* 46 H11
Lakshmikantapur, *India* 63 H13
Lala Ghat, *India* 61 G18
Lala Musa, *Pakistan* 62 C5
Lalago, *Tanzania* 82 C3
Lalapanzi, *Zimbabwe* 83 F3
Lalganj, *India* 63 G11
Lalibela, *Ethiopia* 77 E4
Lalin, *China* 51 B14
Lalín, *Spain* 30 C2
Lalin He →, *China* 51 B13
Lalinde, *France* 26 D4
Lalitapur = Patan, *Nepal* 61 F14
Lalitpur, *India* 63 G8
Lam, *Vietnam* 58 B6
Lam Pao Res., *Thailand* 58 D4
Lama Kara, *Togo* 79 D5
Lamaing, *Burma* 61 M20
Lamar, *Colo., U.S.A.* 108 F3
Lamar, *Mo., U.S.A.* 109 G7
Lamarque, *Argentina* 128 A3
Lamas, *Peru* 124 B2
Lamastre, *France* 27 D8
Lamballe, *France* 24 D4
Lambaréné, *Gabon* 80 E2
Lambasa, *Fiji* 87 C8
Lambay I., *Ireland* 15 C5
Lambayeque □, *Peru* 124 B2
Lambert, *U.S.A.* 108 B2
Lambert Glacier, *Antarctica* 5 D6
Lamberts Bay, *S. Africa* 84 E2
Lambesc, *France* 27 E9
Lámbia, *Greece* 39 M4
Lambro →, *Italy* 32 C6
Lame, *Nigeria* 79 C6
Lame Deer, *U.S.A.* 110 D10
Lamego, *Portugal* 30 D3
Lamèque, *Canada* 99 C7
Lameroo, *Australia* 91 F3
Lamesa, *U.S.A.* 109 J4
Lamía, *Greece* 39 L5
Lamitan, *Phil.* 55 H5
Lammermuir Hills, *U.K.* 14 F6
Lamon Bay, *Phil.* 55 D5
Lamont, *Canada* 100 C6
Lamont, *U.S.A.* 113 K8
Lampa, *Peru* 124 D3
Lampang, *Thailand* 58 C2
Lampasas, *U.S.A.* 109 K5
Lampaul, *France* 24 D1
Lampazos de Naranjo, *Mexico* 114 B4
Lampeter, *U.K.* 13 E3
Lampione, *Medit. S.* 75 A7
Lampman, *Canada* 101 D8
Lamprey, *Canada* 101 B10
Lampung □, *Indonesia* 56 F2
Lamu, *Kenya* 82 C5
Lamu □, *Kenya* 82 C5
Lamud, *Peru* 124 B2
Lamy, *U.S.A.* 111 J11
Lan Xian, *China* 50 E6
Lanai I., *U.S.A.* 102 H16
Lanak La, *India* 63 B8
Lanaken, *Belgium* 17 G7
Lanak'o Shank'ou = Lanak La, *India* 63 B8
Lanao, L., *Phil.* 55 H6
Lanark, *Canada* 107 A8
Lanark, *U.K.* 14 F5
Lancang, *China* 52 F2
Lancang Jiang →, *China* 52 G3
Lancashire □, *U.K.* 12 D5
Lancaster, *Canada* 107 A10
Lancaster, *U.K.* 12 C5
Lancaster, *Calif., U.S.A.* 113 L8
Lancaster, *Ky., U.S.A.* 104 G3
Lancaster, *N.H., U.S.A.* 107 B13
Lancaster, *N.Y., U.S.A.* 106 D6
Lancaster, *Pa., U.S.A.* 107 F8
Lancaster, *S.C., U.S.A.* 105 H5
Lancaster, *Wis., U.S.A.* 108 D9
Lancaster Sd., *Canada* 97 A11
Lancer, *Canada* 101 C7
Lanchow = Lanzhou, *China* 50 F2
Lanciano, *Italy* 33 F11
Lanco, *Chile* 128 A2
Lancones, *Peru* 124 A1
Lancun, *China* 51 F11
Łancut, *Poland* 20 E12
Lancy, *Switz.* 22 D2
Landau, *Bayern, Germany* 19 G8
Landau, *Rhld-Pfz., Germany* 19 F4
Landeck, *Austria* 19 H6
Landen, *Belgium* 17 G6
Lander, *U.S.A.* 110 E9
Lander →, *Australia* 88 D5
Landerneau, *France* 24 D2
Landeryd, *Sweden* 11 G7
Landes, *France* 26 D3
Landes □, *France* 26 E3
Landete, *Spain* 28 F3
Landi Kotal, *Pakistan* 62 B4
Landivisiau, *France* 24 D2
Landor, *Australia* 89 E2
Landquart, *Switz.* 23 C9
Landquart →, *Switz.* 23 C9
Landrecies, *France* 25 B10
Land's End, *U.K.* 13 G2
Landsberg, *Germany* 19 G6
Landsborough Cr. →, *Australia* 90 C3
Landshut, *Germany* 19 G8
Landskrona, *Sweden* 11 J6
Landstuhl, *Germany* 19 F3
Landvetter, *Sweden* 11 G6
Laneffe, *Belgium* 17 H5
Lanesboro, *U.S.A.* 107 E9
Lanett, *U.S.A.* 105 J3
Lang Bay, *Canada* 100 D4
Lang Qua, *Vietnam* 58 A5
Lang Shan, *China* 50 D4
Lang Son, *Vietnam* 58 B6
Lang Suan, *Thailand* 59 H2
La'nga Co, *China* 61 D12
Lángadhás, *Greece* 39 J6
Langádhia, *Greece* 39 M5
Långan →, *Sweden* 10 A8
Langar, *Iran* 65 C9
Langara I., *Canada* 100 C2
Langatabbetje, *Surinam* 121 C7
Langdai, *China* 52 D5
Langdon, *U.S.A.* 108 A5
Langdorp, *Belgium* 17 G5
Langeac, *France* 26 C7
Langeais, *France* 24 E7
Langeb Baraka →, *Sudan* 76 D4
Langeberg, *S. Africa* 84 E3
Langeberge, *S. Africa* 84 D3
Langeland, *Denmark* 11 K4
Langemark, *Belgium* 17 G1
Langen, *Germany* 19 F4
Langenburg, *Canada* 101 C8
Langeneß, *Germany* 18 A4
Langenthal, *Switz.* 22 B5
Langeoog, *Germany* 18 B3
Langeskov, *Denmark* 11 J4
Langesund, *Norway* 10 F3
Länghem, *Sweden* 11 G7
Langhirano, *Italy* 32 D7
Langholm, *U.K.* 14 F6
Langhus, *Norway* 10 E4
Langjökull, *Iceland* 8 D3
Langkawi, P., *Malaysia* 59 J2
Langklip, *S. Africa* 84 D3
Langkon, *Malaysia* 56 C5
Langlade, *St- P. & M.* 99 C8
Langlois, *U.S.A.* 110 E1
Langnau, *Switz.* 22 C5
Langogne, *France* 26 D7
Langon, *France* 26 D3
Langøya, *Norway* 8 B16
Langres, *France* 25 E12
Langres, Plateau de, *France* 25 E12
Langsa, *Indonesia* 56 D1
Långsele, *Sweden* 10 A11
Langtry, *U.S.A.* 109 L4
Langu, *Thailand* 59 J2
Languedoc, *France* 26 E7
Langwies, *Switz.* 23 C9
Langxi, *China* 53 B12
Langxiangzhen, *China* 50 E9
Langzhong, *China* 52 B5
Lanigan, *Canada* 101 C7
Lankao, *China* 50 G8
Länkäran, *Azerbaijan* 67 C13
Lannemezan, *France* 26 E4
Lannilis, *France* 24 D2
Lannion, *France* 24 D3
L'Annonciation, *Canada* 98 C5
Lanouaille, *France* 26 C5
Lanping, *China* 52 D2
Lansdale, *U.S.A.* 107 F9
Lansdowne, *Australia* 91 E5
Lansdowne, *Canada* 107 B8
Lansdowne House, *Canada* 98 B2
L'Anse, *U.S.A.* 98 C2
L'Anse au Loup, *Canada* 99 B8
Lansford, *U.S.A.* 107 F9
Lanshan, *China* 53 E9
Lansing, *U.S.A.* 104 D3
Lanslebourg-Mont-Cenis, *France* 27 C10
Lanta Yai, Ko, *Thailand* 59 J2
Lantian, *China* 50 G5
Lanus, *Argentina* 126 C4
Lanusei, *Italy* 34 C2
Lanuza, *Phil.* 55 G7
Lanxi, *China* 53 C12
Lanzarote, *Canary Is.* 36 E6
Lanzhou, *China* 50 F2
Lanzo Torinese, *Italy* 32 C4
Lao →, *Italy* 35 C8
Lao Bao, *Laos* 58 D6
Lao Cai, *Vietnam* 58 A4
Laoag, *Phil.* 55 B4
Laoang, *Phil.* 55 E6
Laoha He →, *China* 51 C11
Laois □, *Ireland* 15 D4
Laon, *France* 25 C10
Laona, *U.S.A.* 104 C1
Laos ■, *Asia* 58 D5
Lapa, *Brazil* 127 B6
Lapalisse, *France* 26 B7
Laparan, *Phil.* 57 C6
Lapeer, *U.S.A.* 104 D4
Lapithos, *Cyprus* 37 D12
Lapland = Lappland, *Europe* 8 B21
Laporte, *U.S.A.* 107 E8
Lapovo, *Serbia, Yug.* 21 L11
Lappeenranta, *Finland* 9 F23
Lappland, *Europe* 8 B21
Laprida, *Argentina* 126 D3
Lapseki, *Turkey* 66 B2
Laptev Sea, *Russia* 45 B13
Lapua, *Finland* 8 E20
Lăpuşul →, *Romania* 38 B6
L'Aquila, *Italy* 33 F10
Lār, *Āzarbājān-e Sharqī, Iran* 64 B5
Lār, *Fārs, Iran* 65 E7
Lara □, *Venezuela* 120 A4
Larabanga, *Ghana* 78 D4
Laracha, *Spain* 30 B2
Larache, *Morocco* 74 A3
Laragne-Montéglin, *France* 27 D9
Laramie, *U.S.A.* 108 E2
Laramie Mts., *U.S.A.* 108 E2
Laranjeiras, *Brazil* 122 D4
Laranjeiras do Sul, *Brazil* 127 B5
Larantuka, *Indonesia* 57 F6
Larap, *Phil.* 55 D5
Larat, *Indonesia* 57 F8
L'Arbresle, *France* 27 C8
Larde, *Mozam.* 83 F4
Larder Lake, *Canada* 98 C4
Lardhos, Ákra, *Greece* 37 C10
Lardhos, Órmos, *Greece* 37 C10
Laredo, *Spain* 28 B1
Laredo, *U.S.A.* 109 M5
Laredo Sd., *Canada* 100 C3
Laren, *Neths.* 16 D6
Largentière, *France* 27 D8
L'Argentière-la-Bessée, *France* 27 D10
Largo, *U.S.A.* 105 M4
Largs, *U.K.* 14 F4
Lari, *Italy* 32 E7
Lariang, *Indonesia* 57 E5
Larimore, *U.S.A.* 108 B6
Lārīn, *Iran* 65 C7
Larino, *Italy* 35 A7
Lárisa, *Greece* 39 K5
Larkana, *Pakistan* 62 F3
Larnaca, *Cyprus* 66 E5
Larnaca Bay, *Cyprus* 37 E12
Larne, *U.K.* 15 B6
Larned, *U.S.A.* 108 F5
Larochette, *Belgium* 17 J8
Laroquebrou, *France* 26 D6
Larrimah, *Australia* 88 C5
Larsen Ice Shelf, *Antarctica* 5 C17
Larvik, *Norway* 10 E4
Laryak, *Russia* 44 C8
Larzac, Causse du, *France* 26 E7
Las Alpujarras, *Spain* 29 J1
Las Animas, *U.S.A.* 108 F3
Las Anod, *Somali Rep.* 68 F4
Las Blancos, *Spain* 29 H4
Las Brenãs, *Argentina* 126 B3
Las Cabezas de San Juan, *Spain* 31 J5
Las Chimeneas, *Mexico* 113 N10
Las Coloradas, *Argentina* 128 A2
Las Cruces, *U.S.A.* 111 K10
Las Flores, *Argentina* 126 D4
Las Heras, *Argentina* 126 C2
Las Horquetas, *Argentina* 128 C2
Las Khoreh, *Somali Rep.* 68 E4
Las Lajas, *Argentina* 128 A2
Las Lomas, *Peru* 124 A1
Las Lomitas, *Argentina* 126 A3
Las Marismas, *Spain* 31 H4
Las Mercedes, *Venezuela* 120 B4
Las Navas de la Concepción, *Spain* 31 H5
Las Navas de Tolosa, *Spain* 31 G7
Las Navas del Marqués, *Spain* 30 E6
Las Palmas, *Argentina* 126 B4
Las Palmas, *Canary Is.* 36 F4
Las Palmas →, *Mexico* 113 N10
Las Piedras, *Uruguay* 127 C4
Las Pipinas, *Argentina* 126 D4
Las Plumas, *Argentina* 128 B3
Las Rosas, *Argentina* 126 C3
Las Tablas, *Panama* 116 E3
Las Termas, *Argentina* 126 B3
Las Truchas, *Mexico* 114 D4
Las Varillas, *Argentina* 126 C3
Las Vegas, *N. Mex., U.S.A.* 111 J11
Las Vegas, *Nev., U.S.A.* 113 J11
Lascano, *Uruguay* 127 C5
Lashburn, *Canada* 101 C7
Lashio, *Burma* 61 H20
Lashkar, *India* 62 F8
Łasin, *Poland* 20 B9
Lasíthi, *Greece* 37 D7
Lasíthi □, *Greece* 37 D7
Laško, *Slovenia* 33 B12
Lassance, *Brazil* 123 E3
Lassay, *France* 24 D6
Lassen Pk., *U.S.A.* 110 F3
Last Mountain L., *Canada* 101 C7
Lastchance Cr. →, *U.S.A.* 112 E5
Lastoursville, *Gabon* 80 E2
Lastovo, *Croatia* 33 F13
Lastovski Kanal, *Croatia* 33 F13
Lat Yao, *Thailand* 58 E2
Latacunga, *Ecuador* 120 D2
Latakia = Al Lādhiqīyah, *Syria* 66 E6
Latchford, *Canada* 98 C4
Laterza, *Italy* 35 B9
Latham, *Australia* 89 E2
Lathen, *Germany* 18 C3
Lathrop Wells, *U.S.A.* 113 J10
Latiano, *Italy* 35 B10
Latina, *Italy* 34 A5
Latisana, *Italy* 33 C10
Latium = Lazio □, *Italy* 33 F9
Laton, *U.S.A.* 112 J7
Latorica →, *Slovak Rep.* 21 G11
Latouche Treville, C., *Australia* 88 C3
Latrobe, *Australia* 90 G4
Latrobe, *U.S.A.* 106 F5
Latrónico, *Italy* 35 B9
Latvia ■, *Europe* 9 H20
Lau Group, *Fiji* 87 C9
Lauca →, *Bolivia* 124 D4
Lauchhammer, *Germany* 18 D9
Lauenburg, *Germany* 18 B6
Läufelfingen, *Switz.* 22 B5
Laufen, *Switz.* 22 B5
Lauffen, *Germany* 19 F5
Laujar, *Spain* 29 J2
Laukaa, *Finland* 9 E21
Launceston, *Australia* 90 G4
Launceston, *U.K.* 13 G3
Laune →, *Ireland* 15 D2
Laupheim, *Germany* 19 G5
Laura, *Australia* 90 B3
Laureana di Borrello, *Italy* 35 D9
Laurel, *Miss., U.S.A.* 109 K10
Laurel, *Mont., U.S.A.* 110 D9
Laurencekirk, *U.K.* 14 E6
Laurens, *U.S.A.* 105 H4
Laurentian Plateau, *Canada* 99 B6
Laurentides, Parc Prov. des, *Canada* 99 C5
Lauria, *Italy* 35 B8
Laurie L., *Canada* 101 B8
Laurinburg, *U.S.A.* 105 H6
Laurium, *U.S.A.* 104 B1
Lausanne, *Switz.* 22 C3
Laut, *Indonesia* 56 D3
Laut Kecil, Kepulauan, *Indonesia* 56 E5
Lautaro, *Chile* 128 A2
Lauterbach, *Germany* 18 E5
Lauterbrunnen, *Switz.* 22 C5
Lauterecken, *Germany* 19 F3
Lautoka, *Fiji* 87 C7
Lauwe, *Belgium* 17 G2
Lauwers, *Neths.* 16 A8
Lauwers Zee, *Neths.* 16 B8
Lauzon, *Canada* 99 C5
Lava Hot Springs, *U.S.A.* 110 E7
Lavadores, *Spain* 30 C2
Lavagna, *Italy* 32 D6
Laval, *France* 24 D6
Lavalle, *Argentina* 126 B2
Lávara, *Greece* 39 H9
Lavardac, *France* 26 D4
Lavaur, *France* 26 E5
Lavaux, *Switz.* 22 D3
Lavelanet, *France* 26 F5
Lavello, *Italy* 35 A8
Laverne, *U.S.A.* 109 G5
Laverton, *Australia* 89 E3
Lavos, *Portugal* 30 E2
Lavras, *Brazil* 123 F3
Lavre, *Portugal* 31 G2
Lavrentiya, *Russia* 45 C19
Lávrion, *Greece* 39 M7
Lávris, *Greece* 37 D6
Lavumisa, *Swaziland* 85 D5
Lawas, *Malaysia* 56 D5
Lawele, *Indonesia* 57 F6
Lawn Hill, *Australia* 90 B2
Lawng Pit, *Burma* 61 G20
Lawqah, *Si. Arabia* 64 D4
Lawra, *Ghana* 78 C4
Lawrence, *N.Z.* 87 L2
Lawrence, *Kans., U.S.A.* 108 F7
Lawrence, *Mass., U.S.A.* 107 D13
Lawrenceburg, *Ind., U.S.A.* 104 F3
Lawrenceburg, *Tenn., U.S.A.* 105 H2
Lawrenceville, *U.S.A.* 105 J4
Laws, *U.S.A.* 112 H8
Lawton, *U.S.A.* 109 H5
Lawu, *Indonesia* 57 G14
Laxford, L., *U.K.* 14 C3
Lay →, *France* 26 B2
Laylān, *Iraq* 64 C5
Layon →, *France* 24 E6
Laysan I., *Pac. Oc.* 93 E11
Laytonville, *U.S.A.* 110 G2
Lazarevskoye, *Russia* 43 J4
Lazio □, *Italy* 33 F9
Lazo, *Russia* 48 C6
Le Barcarès, *France* 26 F7
Le Beausset, *France* 27 E9

Le Blanc, *France* 26 B5
Le Bleymard, *France* 26 D7
Le Bourgneuf-la-Fôret, *France* 24 D6
Le Bouscat, *France* 26 D3
Le Brassus, *Switz.* 22 C2
Le Bugue, *France* 26 D4
Le Canourgue, *France* 26 D7
Le Cateau, *France* 25 B10
Le Chambon-Feugerolles, *France* 27 C8
Le Château-d'Oléron, *France* 26 C2
Le Châtelard, *Switz.* 22 D3
Le Châtelet, *France* 26 B6
Le Châtelet-en-Brie, *France* 25 D9
Le Chesne, *France* 25 C11
Le Cheylard, *France* 27 D8
Le Conquet, *France* 24 D2
Le Creusot, *France* 25 F11
Le Croisic, *France* 24 E4
Le Donjon, *France* 26 B7
Le Dorat, *France* 26 B5
Le François, *Martinique* 117 D7
Le Grand-Lucé, *France* 24 E7
Le Grand-Pressigny, *France* 24 F7
Le Havre, *France* 24 C7
Le Lavandou, *France* 27 E10
Le Lion-d'Angers, *France* 24 E6
Le Locle, *Switz.* 22 B3
Le Louroux-Béconnais, *France* 24 E6
Le Luc, *France* 27 E10
Le Madonie, *Italy* 34 E6
Le Maire, Estr. de, *Argentina* 128 D4
Le Mans, *France* 24 E7
Le Mars, *U.S.A.* 108 D6
Le Mêle-sur-Sarthe, *France* 24 D7
Le Merlerault, *France* 24 D7
Le Monastier-sur-Gazeille, *France* 26 D7
Le Monêtier-les-Bains, *France* 27 D10
Le Mont d'Or, *France* 25 F13
Le Mont-Dore, *France* 26 C6
Le Mont-St.-Michel, *France* 24 D5
Le Moule, *Guadeloupe* 117 C7
Le Muy, *France* 27 E10
Le Palais, *France* 24 E3
Le Perthus, *France* 26 F6
Le Pont, *Switz.* 22 C2
Le Pouldu, *France* 24 E3
Le Puy-en-Velay, *France* 26 C7
Le Quesnoy, *France* 25 B10
Le Roy, *U.S.A.* 109 F7
Le Sentier, *Switz.* 22 C2
Le Sueur, *U.S.A.* 108 C8
Le Teil, *France* 27 D8
Le Teilleul, *France* 24 D6
Le Theil, *France* 24 D7
Le Thillot, *France* 25 E13
Le Thuy, *Vietnam* 58 D6
Le Touquet-Paris-Plage, *France* 25 B8
Le Tréport, *France* 24 B8
Le Val-d'Ajol, *France* 25 E13
Le Verdon-sur-Mer, *France* 26 C2
Le Vigan, *France* 26 E7
Lea →, *U.K.* 13 F7
Leach, *Cambodia* 59 F4
Lead, *U.S.A.* 108 C3
Leader, *Canada* 101 C7
Leadhills, *U.K.* 14 F5
Leadville, *U.S.A.* 111 G10
Leaf →, *U.S.A.* 109 K10
Leakey, *U.S.A.* 109 L5
Leamington, *Canada* 98 D3
Leamington, *U.S.A.* 110 G7
Leamington Spa = Royal Leamington Spa, *U.K.* 13 E6
Le'an, *China* 53 D10
Leandro Norte Alem, *Argentina* 127 B4
Learmonth, *Australia* 88 D1
Leask, *Canada* 101 C7
Leavenworth, *Kans., U.S.A.* 108 F7
Leavenworth, *Wash., U.S.A.* 110 C3
Łeba, *Poland* 20 A7
Lebak, *Phil.* 55 H6
Lebam, *U.S.A.* 112 D3
Lebanon, *Ind., U.S.A.* 104 E2
Lebanon, *Kans., U.S.A.* 108 F5
Lebanon, *Ky., U.S.A.* 104 G3
Lebanon, *Mo., U.S.A.* 109 G8
Lebanon, *Oreg., U.S.A.* 110 D2
Lebanon, *Pa., U.S.A.* 107 F8
Lebanon, *Tenn., U.S.A.* 105 G2
Lebanon ■, *Asia* 69 B4
Lebbeke, *Belgium* 17 G4
Lebec, *U.S.A.* 113 L8
Lebedyan, *Russia* 42 D4
Lebedyn, *Ukraine* 41 G8
Lebomboberge, *S. Africa* 85 C5
Lębork, *Poland* 20 A7
Lebrija, *Spain* 31 J4
Lebu, *Chile* 126 D1
Lecce, *Italy* 35 B11
Lecco, *Italy* 32 C6
Lecco, L. di, *Italy* 32 C6
Lécera, *Spain* 28 D4
Lech, *Austria* 19 H6
Lech →, *Germany* 19 G6
Lechang, *China* 53 E9
Lechtaler Alpen, *Austria* 19 H6
Lectoure, *France* 26 E4
Łęczyca, *Poland* 20 C9
Ledbury, *U.K.* 13 E5
Lede, *Belgium* 17 G3
Ledeberg, *Belgium* 17 F3
Ledesma, *Spain* 30 D5
Ledong, *China* 58 C7
Leduc, *Canada* 100 C6
Ledyczek, *Poland* 20 B6
Lee, *U.S.A.* 107 D11
Lee →, *Ireland* 15 E3
Lee Vining, *U.S.A.* 112 H7
Leech L., *U.S.A.* 108 B7
Leedey, *U.S.A.* 109 H5
Leeds, *U.K.* 12 D6
Leeds, *U.S.A.* 105 J2
Leek, *Neths.* 16 B8
Leek, *U.K.* 12 D5
Leende, *Neths.* 17 F7
Leer, *Germany* 18 B3
Leerdam, *Neths.* 16 E6
Leersum, *Neths.* 16 E6
Leesburg, *U.S.A.* 105 L5
Leesville, *U.S.A.* 109 K8
Leeton, *Australia* 91 E4
Leetonia, *U.S.A.* 106 F4
Leeu Gamka, *S. Africa* 84 E3
Leeuwarden, *Neths.* 16 B7
Leeuwin, C., *Australia* 89 F2
Leeward Is., *Atl. Oc.* 117 C7
Lefka, *Cyprus* 37 D11
Lefkoniko, *Cyprus* 37 D12
Lefors, *U.S.A.* 109 H4
Lefroy, L., *Australia* 89 F3
Legal, *Canada* 100 C6
Leganés, *Spain* 30 E7
Legazpi, *Phil.* 55 E5
Legendre I., *Australia* 88 D2
Leghorn = Livorno, *Italy* 32 E7
Legionowo, *Poland* 20 C10
Léglise, *Belgium* 17 J7
Legnago, *Italy* 33 C8
Legnano, *Italy* 32 C5
Legnica, *Poland* 20 D6
Legrad, *Croatia* 33 B13
Legume, *Australia* 91 D5
Leh, *India* 63 B7
Lehi, *U.S.A.* 110 F8
Lehighton, *U.S.A.* 107 F9
Lehrte, *Germany* 18 C5
Lehututu, *Botswana* 84 C3
Lei Shui →, *China* 53 D9
Leiah, *Pakistan* 62 D4
Leibnitz, *Austria* 21 J5
Leibo, *China* 52 C4
Leicester, *U.K.* 13 E6
Leicestershire □, *U.K.* 13 E6
Leichhardt →, *Australia* 90 B2
Leichhardt Ra., *Australia* 90 C4
Leiden, *Neths.* 16 D5
Leiderdorp, *Neths.* 16 D5
Leidschendam, *Neths.* 16 D4
Leie →, *Belgium* 25 A10
Leignon, *Belgium* 17 H6
Leine →, *Germany* 18 C5
Leinster, *Australia* 89 E3
Leinster □, *Ireland* 15 C4
Leinster, Mt., *Ireland* 15 D5
Leipzig, *Germany* 18 D8
Leiria, *Portugal* 31 F2
Leiria □, *Portugal* 31 F2
Leirvik, *Norway* 9 G11
Leisler, Mt., *Australia* 88 D4
Leith, *U.K.* 14 F5
Leith Hill, *U.K.* 13 F7
Leitha →, *Europe* 21 H7
Leitrim, *Ireland* 15 B3
Leitrim □, *Ireland* 15 B3
Leiyang, *China* 53 D9
Leiza, *Spain* 28 B3
Leizhou Bandao, *China* 54 D6
Leizhou Wan, *China* 53 G8
Lek →, *Neths.* 16 E5
Leka, *Norway* 8 D14
Leke, *Belgium* 17 F1
Lekkerkerk, *Neths.* 16 E5
Leksula, *Indonesia* 57 E7
Lékva Ori, *Greece* 37 D6
Leland, *U.S.A.* 109 J9
Leland Lakes, *Canada* 101 A6
Leleque, *Argentina* 128 B2
Lelystad, *Neths.* 16 D6
Lema, *Nigeria* 79 C5
Léman, L., *Europe* 22 D3
Lemelerveld, *Neths.* 16 D8
Lemera, *Zaïre* 82 C2
Lemery, *Phil.* 55 E4
Lemgo, *Germany* 18 C4
Lemhi Ra., *U.S.A.* 110 D7
Lemmer, *Neths.* 16 C7
Lemmon, *U.S.A.* 108 C3
Lemon Grove, *U.S.A.* 113 N9
Lemoore, *U.S.A.* 111 H4
Lempdes, *France* 26 C7
Lemsid, *W. Sahara* 74 C2
Lemvig, *Denmark* 11 H2
Lena →, *Russia* 45 B13
Lencloître, *France* 24 F7
Lençóis, *Brazil* 123 D3
Léndas, *Greece* 37 E6
Lendeh, *Iran* 65 D6
Lendelede, *Belgium* 17 G2
Lendinara, *Italy* 33 C8
Lengerich, *Germany* 18 C3
Lenggong, *Malaysia* 59 K3
Lenggries, *Germany* 19 H7
Lengua de Vaca, Pta., *Chile* 126 C1
Lenina, Kanal →, *Russia* 43 J7
Leninabad = Khudzhand, *Tajikistan* 44 E7
Leninakan = Gyumri, *Armenia* 43 K6
Leningrad = Sankt-Peterburg, *Russia* 40 C6
Lenino, *Ukraine* 41 K8
Leninogorsk, *Kazakstan* 44 D9
Leninsk, *Russia* 43 F7
Leninsk-Kuznetskiy, *Russia* 44 D9
Leninskoye, *Russia* 42 A8
Leninskoye, *Russia* 45 E14
Lenk, *Switz.* 22 D4
Lenkoran = Länkäran, *Azerbaijan* 67 C13
Lenmalu, *Indonesia* 57 E8
Lenne →, *Germany* 18 D3
Lennox, I., *Chile* 128 E3
Lennoxville, *Canada* 107 A13
Leno, *Italy* 32 C7
Lenoir, *U.S.A.* 105 H5
Lenoir City, *U.S.A.* 105 H3
Lenora, *U.S.A.* 108 F4
Lenore L., *Canada* 101 C8
Lenox, *U.S.A.* 107 D11
Lens, *Belgium* 17 G3
Lens, *France* 25 B9
Lens St. Remy, *Belgium* 17 G6
Lensk, *Russia* 45 C12
Lent, *Neths.* 16 E7
Lentekhi, *Georgia* 43 J6
Lentini, *Italy* 35 E8
Lenwood, *U.S.A.* 113 L9
Lenzburg, *Switz.* 22 B6
Lenzen, *Germany* 18 B7
Lenzerheide, *Switz.* 23 C9
Léo, *Burkina Faso* 78 C4
Leoben, *Austria* 21 H5
Leodhas = Lewis, *U.K.* 14 C2
Leola, *U.S.A.* 108 C5
Leominster, *U.K.* 13 E5
Leominster, *U.S.A.* 107 D13
Léon, *France* 26 E2
León, *Mexico* 114 C4
León, *Nic.* 116 D2
León, *Spain* 30 C5
Leon, *U.S.A.* 108 E8
León □, *Spain* 30 C5
León, Montañas de, *Spain* 30 C4
Leonardtown, *U.S.A.* 104 F7
Leone, Mte., *Switz.* 22 D6
Leonforte, *Italy* 35 E7
Leongatha, *Australia* 91 F4
Leonídhion, *Greece* 39 M5
Leonora, *Australia* 89 E3
Léopold II, Lac = Mai-Ndombe, L., *Zaïre* 80 E3
Leopoldina, *Brazil* 123 F3
Leopoldo Bulhões, *Brazil* 123 E2
Leopoldsburg, *Belgium* 17 F6
Léopoldville = Kinshasa, *Zaïre* 80 E3
Leoti, *U.S.A.* 108 F4
Leova, *Moldova* 41 J5
Leoville, *Canada* 101 C7
Lépa, L. do, *Angola* 84 B2
Lepe, *Spain* 31 H3
Lepel = Lyepyel, *Belarus* 40 E5
Lepikha, *Russia* 45 C13
Leping, *China* 53 C11
Lepontine, Alpi, *Italy* 23 D6
Leppävirta, *Finland* 9 E22
Lequeitio, *Spain* 28 B2
Lercara Friddi, *Italy* 34 E6
Lerdo, *Mexico* 114 B4
Léré, *Chad* 73 G7
Lere, *Nigeria* 79 D6
Leribe, *Lesotho* 85 D4
Lérici, *Italy* 32 D6
Lérida, *Spain* 28 D5
Lérida □, *Spain* 28 C6
Lérins, Is. de, *France* 27 E11
Lerma, *Spain* 30 C7
Léros, *Greece* 39 M9
Lérouville, *France* 25 D12
Lerwick, *U.K.* 14 A7
Les Abrets, *France* 27 C9
Les Andelys, *France* 24 C8
Les Arcs, *France* 27 E10
Les Baux-de-Provence, *France* 27 E8
Les Bois, *Switz.* 22 B3
Les Cayes, *Haiti* 117 C5
Les Diablerets, *Switz.* 22 D4
Les Échelles, *France* 27 C9
Les Essarts, *France* 24 F5
Les Étroits, *Canada* 99 C6
Les Eyzies-de-Tayac-Sireuil, *France* 26 D5
Les Herbiers, *France* 24 F5
Les Minquiers, *Chan. Is.* 24 D4
Les Ponts-de-Cé, *France* 24 E6
Les Riceys, *France* 25 E11
Les Sables-d'Olonne, *France* 26 B2
Les Vans, *France* 27 D8
Les Verrières, *Switz.* 22 C2
Lesbos = Lésvos, *Greece* 39 K9
Leshan, *China* 52 C4
Lésina, L. di, *Italy* 33 G12
Lesja, *Norway* 10 B2
Lesjaverk, *Norway* 10 B2
Leskov I., *Antarctica* 5 B1
Leskovac, *Serbia, Yug.* 21 M11
Leslie, *U.S.A.* 109 H8
Lesneven, *France* 24 D2
Lešnica, *Serbia, Yug.* 21 L9
Lesnoye, *Russia* 42 A2
Lesopilnoye, *Russia* 48 A7
Lesotho ■, *Africa* 85 D4
Lesozavodsk, *Russia* 45 E14
Lesparre-Médoc, *France* 26 C3
Lessay, *France* 24 C5
Lesse →, *Belgium* 17 H5
Lesser Antilles, *W. Indies* 117 C7
Lesser Slave L., *Canada* 100 B5
Lesser Sunda Is., *Indonesia* 57 F6
Lessines, *Belgium* 17 G3
Lester, *U.S.A.* 112 C5
Lestock, *Canada* 101 C8
Lesuer I., *Australia* 88 B4
Lésvos, *Greece* 39 K9
Leszno, *Poland* 20 D6
Letchworth, *U.K.* 13 F7
Letea, Ostrov, *Romania* 38 D12
Lethbridge, *Canada* 100 D6
Lethem, *Guyana* 121 C6
Leti, Kepulauan, *Indonesia* 57 F7
Leti Is. = Leti, Kepulauan, *Indonesia* 57 F7
Letiahau →, *Botswana* 84 C3
Leticia, *Colombia* 120 D4
Leting, *China* 51 E10
Letjiesbos, *S. Africa* 84 E3
Letlhakeng, *Botswana* 84 C3
Letpadan, *Burma* 61 L19
Letpan, *Burma* 61 K19
Letterkenny, *Ireland* 15 B4
Leu, *Romania* 38 E7
Leucadia, *U.S.A.* 113 M9
Leucate, *France* 26 F7
Leucate, Étang de, *France* 26 F7
Leuk, *Switz.* 22 D5
Leukerbad, *Switz.* 22 D5
Leupegem, *Belgium* 17 G3
Leuser, G., *Indonesia* 56 D1
Leutkirch, *Germany* 19 H6
Leuven, *Belgium* 17 G5
Leuze, *Hainaut, Belgium* 17 G3
Leuze, *Namur, Belgium* 17 G5
Lev Tolstoy, *Russia* 42 D4
Levádhia, *Greece* 39 L5
Levan, *U.S.A.* 110 G8
Levanger, *Norway* 8 E14
Levant, I. du, *France* 27 E10
Lévanto, *Italy* 32 D6
Levanzo, *Italy* 34 E5
Levelland, *U.S.A.* 109 J3
Leven, *U.K.* 14 E6
Leven, L., *U.K.* 14 E5
Leven, Toraka, *Madag.* 85 A8
Levens, *France* 27 E11
Leveque C., *Australia* 88 C3
Leverano, *Italy* 35 B10
Leverkusen, *Germany* 18 D2
Levet, *France* 25 F9
Levice, *Slovak Rep.* 21 G8
Levico, *Italy* 33 C8
Levie, *France* 27 G13
Levier, *France* 25 F13
Levin, *N.Z.* 87 J5
Lévis, *Canada* 99 C5
Levis, L., *Canada* 100 A5
Levítha, *Greece* 39 M9
Levittown, *N.Y., U.S.A.* 107 F11
Levittown, *Pa., U.S.A.* 107 F10
Levkás, *Greece* 39 L3
Levkímmi, *Greece* 37 B4
Levkímmi, Ákra, *Greece* 37 B4
Levkôsia = Nicosia, *Cyprus* 66 E5
Levoča, *Slovak Rep.* 20 F10
Levroux, *France* 25 F8
Levski, *Bulgaria* 38 F8
Levskigrad = Karlovo, *Bulgaria* 38 G7
Lewellen, *U.S.A.* 108 E3
Lewes, *U.K.* 13 G8
Lewes, *U.S.A.* 104 F8
Lewis, *U.K.* 14 C2
Lewis →, *U.S.A.* 112 E4
Lewis, Butt of, *U.K.* 14 C2
Lewis Ra., *Australia* 88 D4
Lewis Range, *U.S.A.* 110 C7
Lewisburg, *Pa., U.S.A.* 106 F8
Lewisburg, *Tenn., U.S.A.* 105 H2
Lewisporte, *Canada* 99 C8
Lewiston, *Idaho, U.S.A.* 110 C5
Lewiston, *Maine, U.S.A.* 105 C11
Lewistown, *Mont., U.S.A.* 110 C9
Lewistown, *Pa., U.S.A.* 106 F7
Lexington, *Ill., U.S.A.* 108 E10
Lexington, *Ky., U.S.A.* 104 F3
Lexington, *Miss., U.S.A.* 109 J9
Lexington, *Mo., U.S.A.* 108 F8
Lexington, *N.C., U.S.A.* 105 H5
Lexington, *Nebr., U.S.A.* 108 E5
Lexington, *Ohio, U.S.A.* 106 F2
Lexington, *Oreg., U.S.A.* 110 D4
Lexington, *Tenn., U.S.A.* 105 H1
Lexington Park, *U.S.A.* 104 F7
Leye, *China* 52 E6
Leyre →, *France* 26 D2
Leysin, *Switz.* 22 D4
Leyte, *Phil.* 55 F6
Leyte Gulf, *Phil.* 55 F6
Lezay, *France* 26 B4
Lezha, *Albania* 39 H2
Lezhi, *China* 52 B5
Lézignan-Corbières, *France* 26 E6
Lezoux, *France* 26 C7
Lgov, *Russia* 42 E2
Lhasa, *China* 54 D4
Lhazê, *China* 54 D3
Lhokkruet, *Indonesia* 56 D1
Lhokseumawe, *Indonesia* 56 C1
Lhuntsi Dzong, *India* 61 F17
Li, *Thailand* 58 D2
Li Shui →, *China* 53 C9
Li Xian, *Gansu, China* 50 G3
Li Xian, *Hebei, China* 50 E8
Li Xian, *Hunan, China* 53 C8
Li Xian, *Sichuan, China* 52 B4
Liádhoi, *Greece* 39 N9
Lian Xian, *China* 53 E9
Liancheng, *China* 53 E11
Lianga, *Phil.* 55 G7
Liangcheng, *Nei Mongol Zizhiqu, China* 50 D7
Liangcheng, *Shandong, China* 51 G10
Liangdang, *China* 50 H4
Lianghekou, *China* 52 C7
Liangping, *China* 52 B6
Lianhua, *China* 53 D9
Lianjiang, *Fujian, China* 53 D12
Lianjiang, *Guangdong, China* 53 G8
Lianping, *China* 53 E10
Lianshan, *China* 53 E9
Lianshanguan, *China* 51 D12
Lianshui, *China* 51 H10
Lianyuan, *China* 53 D8
Lianyungang, *China* 51 G10
Liao He →, *China* 51 D11
Liaocheng, *China* 50 F8
Liaodong Bandao, *China* 51 E12
Liaodong Wan, *China* 51 D11
Liaoning □, *China* 51 D12
Liaoyang, *China* 51 D12
Liaoyuan, *China* 51 C13
Liaozhong, *China* 51 D12
Liapádhes, *Greece* 39 K2
Liard →, *Canada* 100 A4
Liari, *Pakistan* 62 G2
Líbano, *Colombia* 120 C2
Libau = Liepāja, *Latvia* 9 H19
Libby, *U.S.A.* 110 B6
Libenge, *Zaïre* 80 D3
Liberal, *Kans., U.S.A.* 109 G4
Liberal, *Mo., U.S.A.* 109 G7
Liberdade, *Brazil* 124 C3
Liberdade →, *Brazil* 125 B7
Liberec, *Czech.* 20 E5
Liberia, *Costa Rica* 116 D2
Liberia ■, *W. Afr.* 78 D3
Libertad, *Venezuela* 120 B4
Liberty, *Mo., U.S.A.* 108 F7
Liberty, *Tex., U.S.A.* 109 K7
Libin, *Belgium* 17 J6
Lîbîya, Sahrâ', *Africa* 73 C9
Libo, *China* 52 E6
Libobo, Tanjung, *Indonesia* 57 E7
Libode, *S. Africa* 85 E4
Libonda, *Zambia* 81 G4
Libourne, *France* 26 D3
Libramont, *Belgium* 17 J6
Libreville, *Gabon* 80 D1
Libya ■, *N. Afr.* 73 C8
Libyan Desert = Lîbîya, Sahrâ', *Africa* 73 C9
Libyan Plateau = Ed-Déffa, *Egypt* 76 A2
Licantén, *Chile* 126 D1
Licata, *Italy* 34 E6
Lice, *Turkey* 67 C9
Licheng, *China* 50 F7
Lichfield, *U.K.* 12 E6
Lichinga, *Mozam.* 83 E4
Lichtaart, *Belgium* 17 F5
Lichtenburg, *S. Africa* 84 D4
Lichtenfels, *Germany* 19 E7
Lichtenvoorde, *Neths.* 16 E9
Lichtervelde, *Belgium* 17 F2
Lichuan, *Hubei, China* 52 B7
Lichuan, *Jiangxi, China* 53 D11
Licosa, Punta, *Italy* 35 B7
Lida, *Belarus* 9 K21
Lida, *U.S.A.* 111 H5
Lidingö, *Sweden* 10 E12
Lidköping, *Sweden* 11 F7
Lido, *Italy* 33 C9
Lido, *Niger* 79 C5
Lido di Roma = Óstia, Lido di, *Italy* 34 A5
Lidzbark Warminski, *Poland* 20 A10
Liebenwalde, *Germany* 18 C9
Lieberose, *Germany* 18 D10
Liebig, Mt., *Australia* 88 D5
Liechtenstein ■, *Europe* 23 B9
Liederkerke, *Belgium* 17 G4
Liège, *Belgium* 17 G7
Liège □, *Belgium* 17 G7
Liegnitz = Legnica, *Poland* 20 D6
Liempde, *Neths.* 17 E6
Lienart, *Zaïre* 82 B2
Lienyünchiangshih = Lianyungang, *China* 51 G10
Lienz, *Austria* 21 J2
Liepāja, *Latvia* 9 H19
Lier, *Belgium* 17 F5
Lierneux, *Belgium* 17 H7
Lieshout, *Neths.* 17 E7
Liestal, *Switz.* 22 B5
Liévin, *France* 25 B9
Lièvre →, *Canada* 98 C4
Liezen, *Austria* 21 H4

Liffey →, Ireland 15 C5
Lifford, Ireland 15 B4
Liffré, France 24 D5
Lifjell, Norway 10 E2
Lifudzin, Russia 48 B7
Ligao, Phil. 55 E5
Lightning Ridge, Australia 91 D4
Lignano Sabbiadoro, Italy 33 C10
Ligny-en-Barrois, France 25 D12
Ligny-le-Châtel, France 25 E10
Ligoúrion, Greece 39 M6
Ligueil, France 24 E7
Liguria □, Italy 32 D6
Ligurian Sea, Medit. S. 32 E5
Lihou Reefs and Cays, Australia 90 B5
Lihue, U.S.A. 102 H15
Lijiang, China 52 D3
Likasi, Zaïre 83 E2
Likati, Zaïre 80 D4
Likhoslavl, Russia 42 B2
Likhovskoy, Russia 43 F5
Likoma I., Malawi 83 E3
Likumburu, Tanzania 83 D4
L'Île-Bouchard, France 24 E7
L'Ile-Rousse, France 27 F12
Liling, China 53 D9
Lille, Belgium 17 F5
Lille, France 25 B10
Lille Bælt, Denmark 11 J3
Lillebonne, France 24 C7
Lillehammer, Norway 10 C4
Lillers, France 25 B9
Lillesand, Norway 11 F2
Lilleshall, U.K. 13 E5
Lillestrøm, Norway 10 E5
Lillian Point, Mt., Australia 89 E4
Lillo, Spain 28 F1
Lillooet →, Canada 100 D4
Lilongwe, Malawi 83 E3
Liloy, Phil. 57 C6
Lim →, Bos.-H. 21 M9
Lima, Indonesia 57 E7
Lima, Peru 124 C2
Lima, Mont., U.S.A. 110 D7
Lima, Ohio, U.S.A. 104 E3
Lima □, Peru 124 C2
Lima →, Portugal 30 D2
Limages, Canada 107 A9
Liman, Russia 43 H8
Limassol, Cyprus 66 E5
Limavady, U.K. 15 A5
Limavady □, U.K. 15 B5
Limay →, Argentina 128 A3
Limay Mahuida, Argentina 126 D2
Limbang, Brunei 56 D5
Limbara, Mte., Italy 34 B2
Limbaži, Latvia 9 H21
Limbdi, India 62 H4
Limbe, Cameroon 79 E6
Limbourg, Belgium 17 G7
Limbri, Australia 91 E5
Limbunya, Australia 88 C4
Limburg, Germany 19 E4
Limburg □, Belgium 17 F6
Limburg □, Neths. 17 F7
Limeira, Brazil 127 A6
Limerick, Ireland 15 D3
Limerick □, Ireland 15 D3
Limestone, U.S.A. 106 D6
Limestone →, Canada 101 B10
Limfjorden, Denmark 11 H3
Limia = Lima →, Portugal 30 D2
Limingen, Norway 8 D15
Limmared, Sweden 11 G7
Limmat →, Switz. 23 B6
Limmen, Neths. 16 C5
Limmen Bight, Australia 90 A2
Limmen Bight →, Australia 90 B2
Límni, Greece 39 L6
Límnos, Greece 39 K8
Limoeiro, Brazil 122 C4
Limoeiro do Norte, Brazil 122 C4
Limoges, France 26 C5
Limón, Costa Rica 116 D3
Limon, U.S.A. 108 F3
Limone Piemonte, Italy 32 D4
Limousin, France 26 C5
Limousin, Plateaux du, France 26 C5
Limoux, France 26 E6
Limpopo →, Africa 85 D5
Limuru, Kenya 82 C4
Lin Xian, China 50 F6
Lin'an, China 53 B12
Linapacan I., Phil. 55 F3
Linapacan Str., Phil. 55 F3
Linares, Chile 126 D1
Linares, Colombia 120 C2
Linares, Mexico 115 C5
Linares, Spain 29 G1
Linares □, Chile 126 D1
Línas Mte., Italy 34 C1
Lincang, China 52 F3
Lincheng, China 50 F8
Linchuan, China 53 D11
Lincoln, Argentina 126 C3
Lincoln, N.Z. 87 K4
Lincoln, U.K. 12 D7
Lincoln, Calif., U.S.A. 112 G5
Lincoln, Ill., U.S.A. 108 E10
Lincoln, Kans., U.S.A. 108 F5
Lincoln, Maine, U.S.A. 99 C6
Lincoln, N.H., U.S.A. 107 B13
Lincoln, N. Mex., U.S.A. 111 K11
Lincoln, Nebr., U.S.A. 108 E6
Lincoln Hav = Lincoln Sea, Arctic 4 A5
Lincoln Sea, Arctic 4 A5
Lincolnshire □, U.K. 12 D7
Lincolnshire Wolds, U.K. 12 D7
Lincolnton, U.S.A. 105 H5
L'Incudine, France 27 G13
Lind, U.S.A. 110 C4
Linda, U.S.A. 112 F5
Lindau, Germany 19 H5
Linde →, Neths. 16 C7
Linden, Guyana 121 B6
Linden, Calif., U.S.A. 112 G5
Linden, Tex., U.S.A. 109 J7
Lindenheuvel, Neths. 17 G7
Lindenhurst, U.S.A. 107 F11
Linderöd, Sweden 11 J7
Linderödsåsen, Sweden 11 J7
Lindesnes, Norway 9 H12
Líndhos, Greece 66 D3
Lindi, Tanzania 83 D4
Lindi □, Tanzania 83 D4
Lindi →, Zaïre 82 B2
Lindoso, Portugal 30 D2
Lindow, Germany 18 C8
Lindsay, Canada 98 D4
Lindsay, Calif., U.S.A. 111 H4
Lindsay, Okla., U.S.A. 109 H6
Lindsborg, U.S.A. 108 F6
Linfen, China 50 F6
Ling Xian, Hunan, China 53 D9
Ling Xian, Shandong, China 50 F9
Lingao, China 58 C7
Lingayen, Phil. 57 A6
Lingayen G., Phil. 55 C4
Lingbi, China 51 H9
Lingchuan, Guangxi Zhuangzu, China 53 E8
Lingchuan, Shanxi, China 50 G7
Lingen, Germany 18 C3
Lingga, Indonesia 56 E2
Lingga, Kepulauan, Indonesia 56 E2
Lingga Arch. = Lingga, Kepulauan, Indonesia 56 E2
Lingle, U.S.A. 108 D2
Lingling, China 53 D8
Lingqiu, China 50 E8
Lingshan, China 52 F7
Lingshi, China 50 F6
Lingshou, China 50 E8
Lingshui, China 58 C8
Lingtai, China 50 G4
Linguéré, Senegal 78 B1
Lingwu, China 50 E4
Lingyuan, China 51 D10
Lingyun, China 52 E6
Linh Cam, Vietnam 58 C5
Linhai, China 53 C13
Linhares, Brazil 123 E3
Linhe, China 50 D4
Linjiang, China 51 D14
Linköping, Sweden 11 F9
Linkou, China 51 B16
Linli, China 53 C8
Linlithgow, U.K. 14 F5
Linnhe, L., U.K. 14 E3
Linosa, I., Medit. S. 75 A7
Linqi, China 50 G7
Linqing, China 50 F8
Linqu, China 51 F10
Linru, China 50 G7
Lins, Brazil 127 A6
Linshui, China 52 B6
Lintao, China 50 G2
Linth →, Switz. 19 H5
Linthal, Switz. 23 C8
Lintlaw, Canada 101 C8
Linton, Canada 99 C5
Linton, Ind., U.S.A. 104 F2
Linton, N. Dak., U.S.A. 108 B4
Lintong, China 50 G5
Linville, Australia 91 D5
Linwood, Canada 106 C4
Linwu, China 53 E9
Linxi, China 51 C10
Linxia, China 54 C5
Linxiang, China 53 C9
Linyanti →, Africa 84 B4
Linyi, China 51 G10
Linz, Austria 21 G4
Linz, Germany 18 E3
Linzhenzhen, China 50 F5
Linzi, China 51 F10
Lion, G. du, France 27 E8
Lionárisso, Cyprus 37 D13
Lioni, Italy 35 B8
Lions, G. of = Lion, G. du, France 27 E8
Lion's Den, Zimbabwe 83 F3
Lion's Head, Canada 98 D3
Liozno = Lyozna, Belarus 40 E6
Lipa, Phil. 55 E4
Lipali, Mozam. 83 F4
Lípari, Italy 35 D7
Lípari, Is. = Eólie, Ís., Italy 35 D7
Lipcani, Moldova 41 H4
Lipetsk, Russia 42 D4
Liping, China 52 D7
Lipkany = Lipcani, Moldova 41 H4
Lipljan, Serbia, Yug. 21 N11
Lipno, Poland 20 C9
Lipova, Romania 38 C4
Lipovcy Manzovka, Russia 48 B6
Lipovets, Ukraine 41 H5
Lippe →, Germany 18 D2
Lippstadt, Germany 18 D4
Lipscomb, U.S.A. 109 G4
Lipsko, Poland 20 D11
Lipsói, Greece 39 M9
Liptovsky Svaty Milkulaš, Slovak Rep. 20 F9
Liptrap C., Australia 91 F4
Lipu, China 53 E8
Lira, Uganda 82 B3
Liri →, Italy 34 A6
Liria, Spain 28 F4
Lisala, Zaïre 80 D4
Lisboa, Portugal 31 G1
Lisboa □, Portugal 31 G1
Lisbon = Lisboa, Portugal 31 G1
Lisbon, N. Dak., U.S.A. 108 B6
Lisbon, N.H., U.S.A. 107 B13
Lisbon, Ohio, U.S.A. 106 F4
Lisburn, U.K. 15 B5
Lisburne, C., U.S.A. 96 B3
Liscannor, B., Ireland 15 D2
Liscia →, Italy 34 A2
Lishe Jiang →, China 52 E3
Lishi, China 50 F6
Lishu, China 51 C13
Lishui, Jiangsu, China 53 B12
Lishui, Zhejiang, China 53 C12
Lisianski I., Pac. Oc. 92 E10
Lisichansk = Lysychansk, Ukraine 41 H10
Lisieux, France 24 C7
Liski, Russia 42 E4
L'Isle-Adam, France 25 C9
L'Isle-Jourdain, Gers, France 26 E5
L'Isle-Jourdain, Vienne, France 26 B4
L'Isle-sur-le-Doubs, France 25 E13
Lisle-sur-Tarn, France 26 E5
Lismore, Australia 91 D5
Lismore, Ireland 15 D4
Lisse, Neths. 16 D5
List, Germany 18 A4
Lista, Norway 9 G12
Lister, Mt., Antarctica 5 D11
Liston, Australia 91 D5
Listowel, Canada 98 D3
Listowel, Ireland 15 D2
Lit-et-Mixe, France 26 D2
Litang, Guangxi Zhuangzu, China 52 F7
Litang, Sichuan, China 52 B3
Litang, Malaysia 57 C5
Litang Qu →, China 52 C3
Litani →, Lebanon 69 B4
Litchfield, Calif., U.S.A. 112 E6
Litchfield, Conn., U.S.A. 107 E11
Litchfield, Ill., U.S.A. 108 F10
Litchfield, Minn., U.S.A. 108 C7
Lithgow, Australia 91 E5
Líthinon, Ákra, Greece 37 E6
Lithuania ■, Europe 9 J20
Litija, Slovenia 33 B11
Litókhoron, Greece 39 J5
Litoměřice, Czech. 20 E4
Little Abaco I., Bahamas 116 A4
Little Barrier I., N.Z. 87 G5
Little Belt Mts., U.S.A. 110 C8
Little Blue →, U.S.A. 108 F6
Little Cadotte →, Canada 100 B5
Little Cayman, I., Cayman Is. 116 C3
Little Churchill →, Canada 101 B9
Little Colorado →, U.S.A. 111 H8
Little Current, Canada 98 C3
Little Current →, Canada 98 B3
Little Falls, Minn., U.S.A. 108 C7
Little Falls, N.Y., U.S.A. 107 C10
Little Fork →, U.S.A. 108 A8
Little Grand Rapids, Canada 101 C9
Little Humboldt →, U.S.A. 110 F5
Little Inagua I., Bahamas 117 B5
Little Karoo, S. Africa 84 E3
Little Lake, U.S.A. 113 K9
Little Laut Is. = Laut Kecil, Kepulauan, Indonesia 56 E5
Little Minch, U.K. 14 D2
Little Missouri →, U.S.A. 108 B3
Little Ouse →, U.K. 13 E8
Little Rann, India 62 H4
Little Red →, U.S.A. 109 H9
Little River, N.Z. 87 K4
Little Rock, U.S.A. 109 H8
Little Ruaha →, Tanzania 82 D4
Little Sable Pt., U.S.A. 104 D2
Little Sioux →, U.S.A. 108 E6
Little Smoky →, Canada 100 C5
Little Snake →, U.S.A. 110 F9
Little Valley, U.S.A. 106 D6
Little Wabash →, U.S.A. 104 G1
Littlefield, U.S.A. 109 J3
Littlefork, U.S.A. 108 A8
Littlehampton, U.K. 13 G7
Littleton, U.S.A. 107 B13
Liu He →, China 51 D11
Liu Jiang →, China 52 F7
Liuba, China 50 H4
Liucheng, China 52 E7
Liugou, China 51 D10
Liuhe, China 51 C13
Liuheng Dao, China 53 C14
Liukang Tenggaja, Indonesia 57 F5
Liuli, Tanzania 83 E3
Liuwa Plain, Zambia 81 G4
Liuyang, China 53 C9
Liuzhou, China 52 E7
Liuzhuang, China 51 H11
Livadherón, Greece 39 J4
Livadhia, Cyprus 37 E12
Livarot, France 24 D7
Live Oak, Calif., U.S.A. 112 F5
Live Oak, Fla., U.S.A. 105 K4
Liveras, Cyprus 37 D11
Liveringa, Australia 88 C3
Livermore, U.S.A. 112 H5
Livermore, Mt., U.S.A. 109 K2
Liverpool, Australia 91 E5
Liverpool, Canada 99 D7
Liverpool, U.K. 12 D5
Liverpool Plains, Australia 91 E5
Liverpool Ra., Australia 91 E5
Livingston, Guatemala 116 C2
Livingston, Calif., U.S.A. 112 H6
Livingston, Mont., U.S.A. 110 D8
Livingston, Tex., U.S.A. 109 K7
Livingstone, Zambia 83 F2
Livingstone Mts., Tanzania 83 D3
Livingstonia, Malawi 83 E3
Livny, Russia 42 D3
Livonia, U.S.A. 104 D4
Livorno, Italy 32 E7
Livramento, Brazil 127 C4
Livramento do Brumado, Brazil 123 D3
Livron-sur-Drôme, France 27 D8
Liwale, Tanzania 83 D4
Liwale □, Tanzania 83 D4
Lixi, China 52 D3
Liyang, China 53 B12
Lizard I., Australia 90 A4
Lizard Pt., U.K. 13 H2
Lizarda, Brazil 122 C2
Lizzano, Italy 35 B10
Ljubija, Bos.-H. 33 D13
Ljubljana, Slovenia 33 B11
Ljubno, Slovenia 33 B11
Ljubuški, Bos.-H. 21 M7
Ljung, Sweden 11 F7
Ljungan →, Sweden 10 B11
Ljungaverk, Sweden 10 B10
Ljungby, Sweden 9 H15
Ljusdal, Sweden 10 C10
Ljusnan →, Sweden 9 F17
Ljusne, Sweden 9 F17
Ljutomer, Slovenia 33 B13
Llagostera, Spain 28 D7
Llamellín, Peru 124 B2
Llancanelo, Salina, Argentina 126 D2
Llandeilo, U.K. 13 F3
Llandovery, U.K. 13 F4
Llandrindod Wells, U.K. 13 E4
Llandudno, U.K. 12 D4
Llanelli, U.K. 13 F3
Llanes, Spain 30 B6
Llangollen, U.K. 12 E4
Llanidloes, U.K. 13 E4
Llano, U.S.A. 109 K5
Llano →, U.S.A. 109 K5
Llano Estacado, U.S.A. 109 J3
Llanos, S. Amer. 118 C3
Llanquihue □, Chile 128 B2
Llanquihue, L., Chile 128 B1
Llebetx, C., Spain 36 B9
Lleida = Lérida, Spain 28 D5
Llentrisca, C., Spain 36 C7
Llera, Mexico 115 C5
Llerena, Spain 31 G4
Llica, Bolivia 124 D4
Llico, Chile 126 C1
Llobregat →, Spain 28 D7
Lloret de Mar, Spain 28 D7
Lloyd B., Australia 90 A3
Lloyd L., Canada 101 B7
Lloydminster, Canada 101 C6
Lluchmayor, Spain 36 B9
Llullaillaco, Volcán, S. Amer. 126 A2
Lo, Belgium 17 G1
Lo →, Vietnam 58 B5
Loa, U.S.A. 111 G8
Loa →, Chile 126 A1
Loano, Italy 32 D5
Lobatse, Botswana 84 D4
Löbau, Germany 18 D10
Lobbes, Belgium 17 H4
Lobenstein, Germany 18 E7
Lobería, Argentina 126 D4
Lobito, Angola 81 G2
Lobón, Canal de, Spain 31 G4
Lobos, Argentina 126 D4
Lobos, I., Mexico 114 B2
Lobos, I. de, Canary Is. 36 F6
Lobos de Tierra, I., Peru 124 B1
Loc Binh, Vietnam 58 B6
Loc Ninh, Vietnam 59 G6
Locarno, Switz. 23 D7
Loch Garman = Wexford, Ireland 15 D5
Lochaber, U.K. 14 E4
Lochcarron, U.K. 14 D3
Lochem, Neths. 16 D8
Loches, France 24 E8
Lochgelly, U.K. 14 E5
Lochgilphead, U.K. 14 E3
Lochinver, U.K. 14 C3
Lochnagar, Australia 90 C4
Lochnagar, U.K. 14 E5
Łochów, Poland 20 C11
Lochy →, U.K. 14 E3
Lock, Australia 91 E2
Lock Haven, U.S.A. 106 E7
Lockeford, U.S.A. 112 G5
Lockeport, Canada 99 D6
Lockerbie, U.K. 14 F5
Lockhart, U.S.A. 109 L6
Lockhart, L., Australia 89 F2
Lockney, U.S.A. 109 H4
Lockport, U.S.A. 106 C6
Locminé, France 24 E4
Locri, Italy 35 D9
Locronan, France 24 D2
Loctudy, France 24 E2
Lod, Israel 69 D3
Lodeinoye Pole, Russia 40 B7
Lodève, France 26 E7
Lodge Grass, U.S.A. 110 D10
Lodgepole, U.S.A. 108 E3
Lodgepole Cr. →, U.S.A. 108 E2
Lodhran, Pakistan 62 E4
Lodi, Italy 32 C6
Lodi, U.S.A. 112 G5
Lodja, Zaïre 82 C1
Lodosa, Spain 28 C2
Lödöse, Sweden 11 F6
Lodwar, Kenya 82 B4
Łódź, Poland 20 D9
Loei, Thailand 58 D3
Loenen, Neths. 16 D8
Loengo, Zaïre 82 C2
Loeriesfontein, S. Africa 84 E2
Lofoten, Norway 8 B15
Lofsdalen, Sweden 10 B7
Lofsen →, Sweden 10 B7
Logan, Kans., U.S.A. 108 F5
Logan, Ohio, U.S.A. 104 F4
Logan, Utah, U.S.A. 110 F8
Logan, W. Va., U.S.A. 104 G5
Logan, Mt., Canada 96 B5
Logan Pass, U.S.A. 100 D6
Logandale, U.S.A. 113 J12
Logansport, Ind., U.S.A. 104 E2
Logansport, La., U.S.A. 109 K8
Logo, Sudan 77 F3
Logone →, Chad 73 F8
Logroño, Spain 28 C2
Logrosán, Spain 31 F5
Løgstør, Denmark 11 H3
Lohardaga, India 63 H11
Lohja, Finland 9 F21
Lohr, Germany 19 F5
Loi-kaw, Burma 61 K20
Loimaa, Finland 9 F20
Loir →, France 24 E6
Loir-et-Cher □, France 24 E8
Loire □, France 27 C8
Loire →, France 24 E4
Loire-Atlantique □, France 24 E5
Loiret □, France 25 E9
Loitz, Germany 18 B9
Loja, Ecuador 124 A2
Loja, Spain 31 H6
Loja □, Ecuador 120 D2
Loji, Indonesia 57 E7
Loka, Sudan 77 G3
Lokandu, Zaïre 82 C2
Løken, Norway 10 E5
Lokeren, Belgium 17 F3
Lokhvitsa, Ukraine 41 G7
Lokichokio, Kenya 82 B3
Lokitaung, Kenya 82 B4
Lokkan tekojärvi, Finland 8 C22
Løkken, Denmark 11 G3
Løkken, Norway 10 A3
Loknya, Russia 40 D6
Lokoja, Nigeria 79 D6
Lokolama, Zaïre 80 E3
Lokot, Russia 42 D2
Lol →, Sudan 77 F2
Lola, Guinea 78 D3
Lola, Mt., U.S.A. 112 F6
Lolibai, Gebel, Sudan 77 G3
Lolimi, Sudan 77 G3
Loliondo, Tanzania 82 C4
Lolland, Denmark 11 K5
Lollar, Germany 18 E4
Lolo, U.S.A. 110 C6
Lolodorf, Cameroon 79 E7
Lom, Bulgaria 38 F6
Lom →, Bulgaria 38 F6
Lom Kao, Thailand 58 D3
Lom Sak, Thailand 58 D3
Loma, U.S.A. 110 C8
Loma Linda, U.S.A. 113 L9
Lomami →, Zaïre 82 B1
Lomas de Zamóra, Argentina 126 C4
Lombadina, Australia 88 C3
Lombárdia □, Italy 32 C6
Lombardy = Lombárdia □, Italy 32 C6
Lombez, France 26 E4
Lomblen, Indonesia 57 F6
Lombok, Indonesia 56 F5
Lomé, Togo 79 D5
Lomela, Zaïre 80 E4
Lomela →, Zaïre 80 E4
Lomello, Italy 32 C5
Lometa, U.S.A. 109 K5
Lomié, Cameroon 80 D2
Lomma, Sweden 11 J7
Lomme →, Belgium 17 H6
Lommel, Belgium 17 F6
Lomond, Canada 100 C6

Lomond, L., U.K. 14 E4
Lomphat, Cambodia 58 F6
Lompobatang, Indonesia 57 F5
Lompoc, U.S.A. 113 L6
Lomsegga, Norway 10 C2
Łomza, Poland 20 B12
Loncoche, Chile 128 A2
Loncopuè, Argentina 128 A2
Londa, India 60 M9
Londerzeel, Belgium 17 G4
Londiani, Kenya 82 C4
Londinières, France 24 C8
London, Canada 98 D3
London, U.K. 13 F7
London, Ky., U.S.A. 104 G3
London, Ohio, U.S.A. 104 F4
London, Greater □, U.K. 13 F7
Londonderry, U.K. 15 B4
Londonderry □, U.K. 15 B4
Londonderry, C., Australia 88 B4
Londonderry, I., Chile 128 E2
Londrina, Brazil 127 A5
Lone Pine, U.S.A. 111 H4
Long Beach, Calif., U.S.A. 113 M8
Long Beach, N.Y., U.S.A. 107 F11
Long Beach, Wash., U.S.A. 112 D2
Long Branch, U.S.A. 107 F11
Long Creek, U.S.A. 110 D4
Long Eaton, U.K. 12 E6
Long I., Australia 90 C4
Long I., Bahamas 117 B4
Long I., U.S.A. 107 F11
Long Island Sd., U.S.A. 107 E12
Long L., Canada 98 C2
Long Lake, U.S.A. 107 C10
Long Pine, U.S.A. 108 D5
Long Point B., Canada 106 D4
Long Pt., Nfld., Canada 99 C8
Long Pt., Ont., Canada 106 D4
Long Range Mts., Canada 99 C8
Long Reef, Australia 88 B4
Long Str. = Longa, Proliv, Russia 4 C16
Long Thanh, Vietnam 59 G6
Long Xian, China 50 G4
Long Xuyen, Vietnam 59 G5
Longá, Greece 39 N4
Longa, Proliv, Russia 4 C16
Long'an, China 52 F6
Longarone, Italy 33 B9
Longchang, China 52 C5
Longchi, China 52 C4
Longchuan, Guangdong, China 53 E10
Longchuan, Yunnan, China 52 E1
Longde, China 50 G4
Longeau, France 25 E12
Longford, Australia 90 G4
Longford, Ireland 15 C4
Longford □, Ireland 15 C4
Longguan, China 50 D8
Longhua, China 51 D9
Longhui, China 53 D8
Longido, Tanzania 82 C4
Longiram, Indonesia 56 E5
Longkou, Jiangxi, China 53 D10
Longkou, Shandong, China 51 F11
Longlac, Canada 98 C2
Longli, China 52 D6
Longlier, Belgium 17 J6
Longlin, China 52 E5
Longling, China 52 E2
Longmen, China 53 F10
Longming, China 52 F6
Longmont, U.S.A. 108 E2
Longnan, China 53 E10
Longnawan, Indonesia 56 D4
Longobucco, Italy 35 C9
Longquan, China 53 C12
Longreach, Australia 90 C3
Longshan, China 52 C7
Longsheng, China 53 E8
Longton, Australia 90 C4
Longtown, U.K. 13 F5
Longué-Jumelles, France 24 E6
Longueau, France 25 C9
Longueuil, Canada 107 A11
Longuyon, France 25 C12
Longview, Canada 100 C6
Longview, Tex., U.S.A. 109 J7
Longview, Wash., U.S.A. 112 D4
Longvilly, Belgium 17 H7
Longwy, France 25 C12
Longxi, China 50 G3
Longyou, China 53 C12
Longzhou, China 52 F6
Lonigo, Italy 33 C8
Löningen, Germany 18 C3
Lonja →, Croatia 33 C13
Lonoke, U.S.A. 109 H9
Lonquimay, Chile 128 A2
Lons-le-Saunier, France 25 F12
Lønstrup, Denmark 11 G3
Lookout, C., Canada 98 A3
Lookout, C., U.S.A. 105 H7
Loolmalasin, Tanzania 82 C4
Loon →, Alta., Canada 100 B5
Loon →, Man., Canada 101 B8
Loon Lake, Canada 101 C7
Loon-op-Zand, Neths. 17 E6
Loongana, Australia 89 F4
Loop Hd., Ireland 15 D2
Loosduinen, Neths. 16 D4
Lop Buri, Thailand 58 E3
Lop Nor = Lop Nur, China 54 B4
Lop Nur, China 54 B4
Lopare, Bos.-H. 21 L8
Lopatin, Russia 43 J8
Lopatina, G., Russia 45 D15
Lopaye, Sudan 77 F3
Lopera, Spain 31 H6
Lopez, Phil. 55 E5
Lopez, C., Gabon 80 E1
Loppersum, Neths. 16 B9
Lopphavet, Norway 8 A19
Lora →, Afghan. 60 D4
Lora, Hamun-i-, Pakistan 60 E4
Lora Cr. →, Australia 91 D2
Lora del Río, Spain 31 H5
Lorain, U.S.A. 106 E2
Loralai, Pakistan 62 D3
Lorca, Spain 29 H3
Lord Howe I., Pac. Oc. 92 L7
Lord Howe Ridge, Pac. Oc. 92 L8
Lordsburg, U.S.A. 111 K9
Loreto, Bolivia 125 D5
Loreto, Brazil 122 C2
Loreto, Italy 33 E10
Loreto, Mexico 114 B2
Loreto □, Peru 120 D3
Loreto Aprutino, Italy 33 F10
Lorgues, France 27 E10
Lorica, Colombia 120 B2
Lorient, France 24 E3
Lorn, U.K. 14 E3
Lorn, Firth of, U.K. 14 E3
Lorne, Australia 91 F3
Lorovouno, Cyprus 37 D11
Lörrach, Germany 19 H3
Lorraine, France 25 D12
Lorrainville, Canada 98 C4
Los, Îles de, Guinea 78 D2
Los Alamos, Calif., U.S.A. 113 L6
Los Alamos, N. Mex., U.S.A. 111 J10
Los Altos, U.S.A. 112 H4
Los Andes, Chile 126 C1
Los Angeles, Chile 126 D1
Los Angeles, U.S.A. 113 L8
Los Angeles Aqueduct, U.S.A. 113 K9
Los Antiguos, Argentina 128 C2
Los Banos, U.S.A. 111 H3
Los Barrios, Spain 31 J5
Los Blancos, Argentina 126 A3
Los Cristianos, Canary Is. 36 F3
Los Gatos, U.S.A. 112 H5
Los Hermanos, Venezuela 117 D7
Los Islotes, Canary Is. 36 E6
Los Lagos, Chile 128 A2
Los Llanos de Aridane, Canary Is. 36 F2
Los Lomas, Peru 124 A1
Los Lunas, U.S.A. 111 J10
Los Menucos, Argentina 128 B3
Los Mochis, Mexico 114 B3
Los Monegros, Spain 28 D4
Los Monos, Argentina 128 C3
Los Olivos, U.S.A. 113 L6
Los Palacios, Cuba 116 B3
Los Palacios y Villafranca, Spain 31 H5
Los Reyes, Mexico 114 D4
Los Ríos □, Ecuador 120 D2
Los Roques, Venezuela 120 A4
Los Santos de Maimona, Spain 31 G4
Los Teques, Venezuela 120 A4
Los Testigos, Venezuela 121 A5
Los Vilos, Chile 126 C1
Los Yébenes, Spain 31 F7
Losada →, Colombia 120 C3
Loshkalakh, Russia 45 C15
Lošinj, Croatia 33 D11
Losser, Neths. 16 D10
Lossiemouth, U.K. 14 D5
Lot □, France 26 D5
Lot →, France 26 D4
Lot-et-Garonne □, France 26 D4
Lota, Chile 126 D1
Løten, Norway 10 D5
Loṭfābād, Iran 65 B8
Lothair, S. Africa 85 D5
Lothiers, France 25 F8
Lötschbergtunnel, Switz. 22 D5
Lottefors, Sweden 10 C10
Lotung, Taiwan 53 E13
Lotzwil, Switz. 22 B5
Loubomo, Congo 80 E2
Loudéac, France 24 D4
Loudi, China 53 D8
Loudon, U.S.A. 105 H3
Loudonville, U.S.A. 106 F2
Loudun, France 24 E7
Loué, France 24 E6
Loue →, France 25 E12
Louga, Senegal 78 B1
Loughborough, U.K. 12 E6
Loughrea, Ireland 15 C3
Loughros More B., Ireland 15 B3
Louhans, France 27 B9
Louis Trichardt, S. Africa 85 C4
Louis XIV, Pte., Canada 98 B4
Louisa, U.S.A. 104 F4
Louisbourg, Canada 99 C8
Louise I., Canada 100 C2
Louiseville, Canada 98 C5
Louisiade Arch., Papua N. G. 92 J7
Louisiana, U.S.A. 108 F9
Louisiana □, U.S.A. 109 K9
Louisville, Ky., U.S.A. 104 F3
Louisville, Miss., U.S.A. 109 J10
Loulay, France 26 B3
Loulé, Portugal 31 H2
Louny, Czech. 20 E3
Loup City, U.S.A. 108 E5
Lourdes, France 26 E3
Lourdes-du-Blanc-Sablon, Canada 99 B8
Lourenço, Brazil 121 C7
Lourenço-Marques = Maputo, Mozam. 85 D5
Loures, Portugal 31 G1
Lourinhã, Portugal 31 F1
Lousã, Portugal 30 E2
Louth, Australia 91 E4
Louth, Ireland 15 C5
Louth, U.K. 12 D7
Louth □, Ireland 15 C5
Louvain = Leuven, Belgium 17 G5
Louveigné, Belgium 17 G7
Louviers, France 24 C8
Louwsburg, S. Africa 85 D5
Lovat →, Russia 40 C6
Love, Canada 101 C8
Lovech, Bulgaria 38 F7
Loveland, U.S.A. 108 E2
Lovell, U.S.A. 110 D9
Lovelock, U.S.A. 110 F4
Lóvere, Italy 32 C7
Loviisa, Finland 9 F22
Loving, U.S.A. 109 J2
Lovington, U.S.A. 109 J3
Lovios, Spain 30 D2
Lovisa = Loviisa, Finland 9 F22
Lovran, Croatia 33 C11
Low Pt., Australia 89 F4
Low Tatra = Nízké Tatry, Slovak Rep. 20 G9
Lowa, Zaïre 82 C2
Lowa →, Zaïre 82 C2
Lowell, U.S.A. 107 D13
Lower Arrow L., Canada 100 D5
Lower California = Baja California, Mexico 114 A1
Lower Hutt, N.Z. 87 J5
Lower L., U.S.A. 110 F3
Lower Lake, U.S.A. 112 G4
Lower Post, Canada 100 B3
Lower Red L., U.S.A. 108 B7
Lower Saxony = Niedersachsen □, Germany 18 C5
Lower Tunguska = Tunguska, Nizhnyaya →, Russia 45 C9
Lowestoft, U.K. 13 E9
Łowicz, Poland 20 C9
Lowville, U.S.A. 107 C9
Loxton, Australia 91 E3
Loxton, S. Africa 84 E3
Loyalton, U.S.A. 112 F6
Loyalty Is. = Loyauté, Is., N. Cal. 92 K8
Loyang = Luoyang, China 50 G7
Loyauté, Is., N. Cal. 92 K8
Loyev = Loyew, Belarus 41 G6
Loyew, Belarus 41 G6
Loyoro, Uganda 82 B3
Lož, Slovenia 33 C11
Lozère □, France 26 D7
Loznica, Serbia, Yug. 21 L9
Lozova, Ukraine 41 H9
Luachimo, Angola 80 F4
Luacono, Angola 80 G4
Lualaba →, Zaïre 82 B5
Luampa, Zambia 83 F1
Lu'an, China 53 B11
Luan Chau, Vietnam 58 B4
Luan He →, China 51 E10
Luan Xian, China 51 E10
Luancheng, Guangxi Zhuangzu, China 52 F7
Luancheng, Hebei, China 50 F8
Luanda, Angola 80 F2
Luang Prabang, Laos 58 C4
Luang Thale, Thailand 59 J3
Luangwa, Zambia 83 F3
Luangwa →, Zambia 83 E3
Luangwa Valley, Zambia 83 E3
Luanne, China 51 D9
Luanping, China 51 D9
Luanshya, Zambia 83 E2
Luapula □, Zambia 83 E2
Luapula →, Africa 83 D2
Luarca, Spain 30 B4
Luashi, Zaïre 83 E1
Luau, Angola 80 G4
Lubalo, Angola 80 F3
Lubań, Poland 20 D5
Lubana, Ozero = Lubānas Ezers, Latvia 9 H22
Lubānas Ezers, Latvia 9 H22
Lubang, Phil. 55 E4
Lubang Is., Phil. 57 B6
Lubartów, Poland 20 D12
Lubawa, Poland 20 B9
Lubbeek, Belgium 17 G5
Lübben, Germany 18 D9
Lübbenau, Germany 18 D9
Lubbock, U.S.A. 109 J4
Lübeck, Germany 18 B6
Lübecker Bucht, Germany 18 A7
Lubefu, Zaïre 82 C1
Lubefu →, Zaïre 82 C1
Lubero = Luofu, Zaïre 82 C2
Lubicon L., Canada 100 B5
Lublin, Poland 20 D12
Lubliniec, Poland 20 E8
Lubnān, J., Lebanon 69 B4
Lubny, Ukraine 41 G7
Lubon, Poland 20 C6
Lubongola, Zaïre 82 C2
Lubsko, Poland 20 D4
Lübtheen, Germany 18 B7
Lubuagan, Phil. 55 C4
Lubudi →, Zaïre 83 D2
Lubuk Antu, Malaysia 56 D4
Lubuklinggau, Indonesia 56 E2
Lubuksikaping, Indonesia 56 D2
Lubumbashi, Zaïre 83 E2
Lubunda, Zaïre 82 D2
Lubungu, Zambia 83 E2
Lubutu, Zaïre 82 C2
Luc An Chau, Vietnam 58 A5
Luc-en-Diois, France 27 D9
Lucan, Canada 106 C3
Lucban, Phil. 55 D4
Lucca, Italy 32 E7
Luce Bay, U.K. 14 G4
Lucea, Jamaica 116 C4
Lucedale, U.S.A. 105 K1
Lucena, Phil. 55 E4
Lucena, Spain 31 H6
Lucena del Cid, Spain 28 E4
Lučenec, Slovak Rep. 21 G9
Lucens, Switz. 22 C3
Lucera, Italy 35 A8
Lucerne = Luzern, Switz. 23 B6
Lucerne, U.S.A. 112 F4
Lucerne Valley, U.S.A. 113 L10
Lucero, Mexico 114 A3
Luchena →, Spain 29 H3
Lucheng, China 50 F7
Lucheringo →, Mozam. 83 E4
Luchiang, Taiwan 53 E13
Lüchow, Germany 18 C7
Luchuan, China 53 F8
Lucie →, Surinam 121 C6
Lucira, Angola 81 G2
Luckau, Germany 18 D9
Luckenwalde, Germany 18 C9
Lucknow, India 63 F9
Luçon, France 26 B2
Lüda = Dalian, China 51 E11
Luda Kamchiya →, Bulgaria 38 F10
Ludbreg, Croatia 33 B13
Lüdenscheid, Germany 18 D3
Lüderitz, Namibia 84 D2
Ludewe □, Tanzania 83 D3
Ludhiana, India 62 D6
Ludian, China 52 D4
Luding Qiao, China 52 C4
Lüdinghausen, Germany 18 D3
Ludington, U.S.A. 104 D2
Ludlow, U.K. 13 E5
Ludlow, Calif., U.S.A. 113 L10
Ludlow, Vt., U.S.A. 107 C12
Ludus, Romania 38 C7
Ludvika, Sweden 9 F16
Ludwigsburg, Germany 19 G5
Ludwigshafen, Germany 19 F4
Ludwigslust, Germany 18 B7
Ludza, Latvia 40 D4
Luebo, Zaïre 80 F4
Lueki, Zaïre 82 C2
Luena, Zaïre 83 D2
Luena, Zambia 83 E3
Luepa, Venezuela 121 B5
Lüeyang, China 50 H4
Lufeng, Guangdong, China 53 F10
Lufeng, Yunnan, China 52 E4
Lufira →, Zaïre 83 D2
Lufkin, U.S.A. 109 K7
Lufupa, Zaïre 83 E1
Luga, Russia 40 C5
Luga →, Russia 40 C5
Lugano, Switz. 23 D7
Lugano, L. di, Switz. 23 E8
Lugansk = Luhansk, Ukraine 41 H10
Lugard's Falls, Kenya 82 C4
Lugela, Mozam. 83 F4
Lugenda →, Mozam. 83 E4
Lugh Ganana, Somali Rep. 68 G3
Lugnaquilla, Ireland 15 D5
Lugnvik, Sweden 10 B11
Lugo, Italy 33 D8
Lugo, Spain 30 B3
Lugo □, Spain 30 C3
Lugoj, Romania 38 D4
Lugones, Spain 30 B5
Lugovoy, Kazakstan 44 E8
Luhansk, Ukraine 41 H10
Luhe, China 53 A12
Luhe →, Germany 18 B6
Luhuo, China 52 B3
Luiana, Angola 84 B3
Luimneach = Limerick, Ireland 15 D3
Luino, Italy 32 C5
Luís Correia, Brazil 122 B3
Luís Gonçalves, Brazil 122 C1
Luitpold Coast, Antarctica 5 D1
Luiza, Zaïre 80 F4
Luizi, Zaïre 82 D2
Luján, Argentina 126 C4
Lujiang, China 53 B11
Lukanga Swamp, Zambia 83 E2
Lukenie →, Zaïre 80 E3
Lukhisaral, India 63 G12
Lŭki, Bulgaria 39 H7
Lukolela, Equateur, Zaïre 80 E3
Lukolela, Kasai Or., Zaïre 82 D1
Lukosi, Zimbabwe 83 F2
Lukovit, Bulgaria 38 F7
Łuków, Poland 20 D12
Lukoyanov, Russia 42 C7
Lule älv →, Sweden 8 D19
Luleå, Sweden 8 D20
Lüleburgaz, Turkey 66 B2
Luliang, China 52 E4
Luling, U.S.A. 109 L6
Lulong, China 51 E10
Lulonga →, Zaïre 80 D3
Lulua →, Zaïre 80 E4
Luluabourg = Kananga, Zaïre 80 F4
Lumai, Angola 81 G4
Lumajang, Indonesia 57 H15
Lumbala N'guimbo, Angola 81 G4
Lumberton, Miss., U.S.A. 109 K10
Lumberton, N.C., U.S.A. 105 H6
Lumberton, N. Mex., U.S.A. 111 H10
Lumbres, France 25 B9
Lumbwa, Kenya 82 C4
Lummen, Belgium 17 G6
Lumsden, N.Z. 87 L2
Lumut, Malaysia 59 K3
Lumut, Tg., Indonesia 56 E3
Luna, Phil. 55 C4
Lunan, China 52 E4
Lunavada, India 62 H5
Lunca, Romania 38 B8
Lund, Sweden 11 J7
Lund, U.S.A. 110 G6
Lundazi, Zambia 83 E3
Lunderskov, Denmark 11 J3
Lundi →, Zimbabwe 83 G3
Lundu, Malaysia 56 D3
Lundy, U.K. 13 F3
Lune →, U.K. 12 C5
Lüneburg, Germany 18 B6
Lüneburg Heath = Lüneburger Heide, Germany 18 C6
Lüneburger Heide, Germany 18 C6
Lunel, France 27 E8
Lünen, Germany 18 D3
Lunenburg, Canada 99 D7
Lunéville, France 25 D13
Lunga →, Zambia 83 E2
Lungern, Switz. 22 C6
Lungi Airport, S. Leone 78 D2
Lunglei, India 61 H18
Luni, India 62 F5
Luni →, India 62 G4
Luninets = Luninyets, Belarus 41 F4
Luning, U.S.A. 110 G4
Lunino, Russia 42 D7
Luninyets, Belarus 41 F4
Lunner, Norway 10 D4
Lunsemfwa →, Zambia 83 E3
Lunsemfwa Falls, Zambia 83 E2
Lunteren, Neths. 16 D7
Luo He →, China 50 G6
Luocheng, China 52 E7
Luochuan, China 50 G5
Luoci, China 52 E4
Luodian, China 52 E6
Luoding, China 53 F8
Luofu, Zaïre 82 C2
Luohe, China 50 H8
Luojiang, China 52 B5
Luonan, China 50 G6
Luoning, China 50 G6
Luoshan, China 53 A10
Luotian, China 53 B10
Luoyang, China 50 G7
Luoyuan, China 53 D12
Luozi, Zaïre 80 E2
Luozigou, China 51 C16
Lupanshui, China 52 D5
Lupeni, Romania 38 D6
Lupilichi, Mozam. 83 E4
Lupoing, China 52 E5
Luquan, China 52 E4
Luque, Paraguay 126 B4
Luque, Spain 31 H6
Luray, U.S.A. 104 F6
Lure, France 25 E13
Luremo, Angola 80 F3
Lurgan, U.K. 15 B5
Luri, France 27 F13
Luribay, Bolivia 124 D4
Lurin, Peru 124 C2
Lusaka, Zambia 83 F2
Lusambo, Zaïre 82 C1
Lusangaye, Zaïre 82 C2
Luseland, Canada 101 C7
Lushan, Henan, China 50 H7
Lushan, Sichuan, China 52 B4
Lushi, China 50 G6
Lushnja, Albania 39 J2
Lushoto, Tanzania 82 C4
Lushoto □, Tanzania 82 C4
Lushui, China 52 E2
Lüshun, China 51 E11
Lusignan, France 26 B4
Lusigny-sur-Barse, France 25 D11
Lusk, U.S.A. 108 D2
Lussac-les-Châteaux, France 26 B4
Lussanvira, Brazil 123 F1
Luta = Dalian, China 51 E11
Luton, U.K. 13 F7
Lutong, Malaysia 56 D4

Lutry, *Switz.* 22 C3
Lutselke, *Canada* 101 A6
Lutsk, *Ukraine* 41 G3
Lützow Holmbukta, *Antarctica* 5 C4
Lutzputs, *S. Africa* 84 D3
Luverne, *U.S.A.* 108 D6
Luvua, *Zaïre* 83 D2
Luvua →, *Zaïre* 82 D2
Luwegu →, *Tanzania* 83 D4
Luwuk, *Indonesia* 57 E6
Luxembourg, *Lux.* 17 J8
Luxembourg □, *Belgium* 17 J7
Luxembourg ■, *Europe* 17 J8
Luxeuil-les-Bains, *France* 25 E13
Luxi, *Hunan, China* 53 C8
Luxi, *Yunnan, China* 52 E4
Luxi, *Yunnan, China* 52 E2
Luxor = El Uqsur, *Egypt* 76 B3
Luy →, *France* 26 E2
Luy-de-Béarn →, *France* 26 E3
Luy-de-France →, *France* 26 E3
Luyi, *China* 50 H8
Luyksgestel, *Neths.* 17 F6
Luz-St.-Sauveur, *France* 26 F4
Luzern, *Switz.* 23 B6
Luzern □, *Switz.* 22 B5
Luzhai, *China* 52 E7
Luzhou, *China* 52 C5
Luziânia, *Brazil* 123 E2
Luzilândia, *Brazil* 122 B3
Luzon, *Phil.* 55 D4
Luzy, *France* 25 F10
Luzzi, *Italy* 35 C9
Lviv, *Ukraine* 41 H3
Lvov = Lviv, *Ukraine* 41 H3
Lyakhavichy, *Belarus* 41 F4
Lyakhovskiye, Ostrova, *Russia* 45 B15
Lyaki = Läki, *Azerbaijan* 43 K8
Lyallpur = Faisalabad, *Pakistan* 62 D5
Lycaonia, *Turkey* 66 D5
Lychen, *Germany* 18 B9
Lychkova, *Russia* 40 D7
Lycia, *Turkey* 66 D3
Lycksele, *Sweden* 8 D18
Lydda = Lod, *Israel* 69 D3
Lydenburg, *S. Africa* 85 D5
Lydia, *Turkey* 66 C3
Lyell, *N.Z.* 87 J4
Lyell I., *Canada* 100 C2
Lyepyel, *Belarus* 40 E5
Lygnern, *Sweden* 11 G6
Lyman, *U.S.A.* 110 F8
Lyme Regis, *U.K.* 13 G5
Lymington, *U.K.* 13 G6
Łyna →, *Poland* 9 J19
Lynchburg, *U.S.A.* 104 G6
Lynd →, *Australia* 90 B3
Lynd Ra., *Australia* 91 D4
Lynden, *Canada* 106 C4
Lynden, *U.S.A.* 112 B4
Lyndhurst, *Queens., Australia* 90 B3
Lyndhurst, *S. Austral., Australia* 91 E2
Lyndon →, *Australia* 89 D1
Lyndonville, *N.Y., U.S.A.* 106 C6
Lyndonville, *Vt., U.S.A.* 107 B12
Lyngdal, *Norway* 10 E3
Lyngen, *Norway* 8 B19
Lynher Reef, *Australia* 88 C3
Lynn, *U.S.A.* 107 D14
Lynn Canal, *U.S.A.* 100 B1
Lynn Lake, *Canada* 101 B8
Lynnwood, *U.S.A.* 112 C4
Lynton, *U.K.* 13 F4
Lyntupy, *Belarus* 9 J22
Lynx L., *Canada* 101 A7
Lyø, *Denmark* 11 J4
Lyon, *France* 27 C8
Lyonnais, *France* 27 C8
Lyons = Lyon, *France* 27 C8
Lyons, *Colo., U.S.A.* 108 E2
Lyons, *Ga., U.S.A.* 105 J4
Lyons, *Kans., U.S.A.* 108 F5
Lyons, *N.Y., U.S.A.* 106 C8
Lyozna, *Belarus* 40 E6
Lyrestad, *Sweden* 11 F8
Lys = Leie →, *Belgium* 25 A10
Lysekil, *Sweden* 11 F5
Lyskovo, *Russia* 42 B7
Lyss, *Switz.* 22 B4
Lysychansk, *Ukraine* 41 H10
Lytle, *U.S.A.* 109 L5
Lyttelton, *N.Z.* 87 K4
Lytton, *Canada* 100 C4
Lyuban, *Russia* 40 C6
Lyubertsy, *Russia* 42 C3
Lyubim, *Russia* 42 A5
Lyuboml, *Ukraine* 41 G3
Lyubotyn, *Ukraine* 41 H8
Lyubytino, *Russia* 40 C7
Lyudinovo, *Russia* 42 D2

M

Ma →, *Vietnam* 58 C5
Ma'adaba, *Jordan* 69 E4
Maamba, *Zambia* 84 B4
Ma'ān, *Jordan* 69 E4
Ma'ān □, *Jordan* 69 F5
Maanselkä, *Finland* 8 C23
Ma'anshan, *China* 53 B12
Maarheeze, *Neths.* 17 F7
Maarianhamina, *Finland* 9 F18
Maarn, *Neths.* 16 D6
Ma'arrat an Nu'mān, *Syria* 66 E7
Maarssen, *Neths.* 16 D6
Maartensdijk, *Neths.* 16 D6
Maas →, *Neths.* 16 E5
Maasbracht, *Belgium* 17 F7
Maasbree, *Neths.* 17 F8
Maasdam, *Neths.* 16 E5
Maasdijk, *Neths.* 16 E4
Maaseik, *Belgium* 17 F7
Maasland, *Neths.* 16 E4
Maasniel, *Neths.* 17 F8
Maassluis, *Neths.* 16 E4
Maastricht, *Neths.* 17 G7
Maave, *Mozam.* 85 C5
Mabaruma, *Guyana* 121 B6
Mabel L., *Canada* 100 C5
Mabenge, *Zaïre* 82 B1
Mabian, *China* 52 C4
Mablethorpe, *U.K.* 12 D8
Maboma, *Zaïre* 82 B2
Mabrouk, *Mali* 79 B4
Mabton, *U.S.A.* 110 C3
Mac Bac, *Vietnam* 59 H6
Macachín, *Argentina* 126 D3
Macaé, *Brazil* 123 F3
Macaíba, *Brazil* 122 C4
Macajuba, *Brazil* 123 D3
McAlester, *U.S.A.* 109 H7
McAllen, *U.S.A.* 109 M5
Macamic, *Canada* 98 C4
Macao = Macau ■, *China* 53 F9
Macão, *Portugal* 31 F3
Macapá, *Brazil* 121 C7
Macará, *Ecuador* 120 D2
Macarani, *Brazil* 123 E3
Macarena, Serranía de la, *Colombia* 120 C3
McArthur →, *Australia* 90 B2
McArthur, Port, *Australia* 90 B2
McArthur River, *Australia* 90 B2
Macas, *Ecuador* 120 D2
Macate, *Peru* 124 B2
Macau, *Brazil* 122 C4
Macau ■, *China* 53 F9
Macaúbas, *Brazil* 123 D3
Macaya →, *Colombia* 120 C3
McBride, *Canada* 100 C4
McCall, *U.S.A.* 110 D5
McCamey, *U.S.A.* 109 K3
McCammon, *U.S.A.* 110 E7
McCauley I., *Canada* 100 C2
McCleary, *U.S.A.* 112 C3
Macclesfield, *U.K.* 12 D5
McClintock, *Canada* 101 B10
M'Clintock Chan., *Canada* 96 A9
McClintock Ra., *Australia* 88 C4
McCloud, *U.S.A.* 110 F2
McCluer I., *Australia* 88 B5
McClure, *U.S.A.* 106 F7
McClure, L., *U.S.A.* 112 H6
M'Clure Str., *Canada* 4 B2
McClusky, *U.S.A.* 108 B4
McComb, *U.S.A.* 109 K9
McConaughy, L., *U.S.A.* 108 E4
McCook, *U.S.A.* 108 E4
McCullough Mt., *U.S.A.* 113 K11
McCusker →, *Canada* 101 B7
McDame, *Canada* 100 B3
McDermitt, *U.S.A.* 110 F5
Macdonald, L., *Australia* 88 D4
McDonald Is., *Ind. Oc.* 3 G13
Macdonnell Ranges, *Australia* 88 D5
McDouall Peak, *Australia* 91 D1
Macdougall L., *Canada* 96 B10
MacDowell L., *Canada* 98 B1
Macduff, *U.K.* 14 D6
Maceda, *Spain* 30 C3
Macedonia ■, *Europe* 39 H4
Maceió, *Brazil* 122 C4
Maceira, *Portugal* 31 F2
Macenta, *Guinea* 78 D3
Macerata, *Italy* 33 E10
McFarland, *U.S.A.* 113 K7
McFarlane →, *Canada* 101 B7
Macfarlane, L., *Australia* 91 E2
McGehee, *U.S.A.* 109 J9
McGill, *U.S.A.* 110 G6
Macgillycuddy's Reeks, *Ireland* 15 D2
MacGregor, *Canada* 101 D9
McGregor, *U.S.A.* 108 D9
McGregor →, *Canada* 100 B4
McGregor Ra., *Australia* 91 D3
Mach, *Pakistan* 60 E5
Māch Kowr, *Iran* 65 E9
Machacalis, *Brazil* 123 E3
Machado = Jiparaná →, *Brazil* 125 B5
Machagai, *Argentina* 126 B3
Machakos, *Kenya* 82 C4
Machakos □, *Kenya* 82 C4
Machala, *Ecuador* 120 D2
Machanga, *Mozam.* 85 C6
Machattie, L., *Australia* 90 C2
Machava, *Mozam.* 85 D5
Machece, *Mozam.* 83 F4
Machecoul, *France* 24 F5
Machelen, *Belgium* 17 G4
Macheng, *China* 53 B10
Machevna, *Russia* 45 C18
Machezo, *Spain* 31 F6
Machias, *U.S.A.* 99 D6
Machichaco, C., *Spain* 28 B2
Machichi →, *Canada* 101 B10
Machico, *Madeira* 36 D3
Machilipatnam, *India* 61 L12
Machiques, *Venezuela* 120 A3
Machupicchu, *Peru* 124 C3
Machynlleth, *U.K.* 13 E4
McIlwraith Ra., *Australia* 90 A3
Măcin, *Romania* 38 D11
Macina, *Mali* 78 C4
McIntosh, *U.S.A.* 108 C4
McIntosh L., *Canada* 101 B8
Macintosh Ra., *Australia* 89 E4
Macintyre →, *Australia* 91 D5
Macizo Galaico, *Spain* 30 C3
Mackay, *Australia* 90 C4
Mackay, *U.S.A.* 110 E7
MacKay →, *Canada* 100 B6
Mackay, L., *Australia* 88 D4
McKay Ra., *Australia* 88 D3
McKeesport, *U.S.A.* 106 F5
McKenna, *U.S.A.* 112 D4
Mackenzie, *Canada* 100 B4
Mackenzie, *Guyana* 121 B6
McKenzie, *U.S.A.* 105 G1
Mackenzie →, *Australia* 90 C4
Mackenzie →, *Canada* 96 B6
McKenzie →, *U.S.A.* 110 D2
Mackenzie Bay, *Canada* 4 B1
Mackenzie City = Linden, *Guyana* 121 B6
Mackenzie Highway, *Canada* 100 B5
Mackenzie Mts., *Canada* 96 B6
Mackinaw City, *U.S.A.* 104 C3
McKinlay, *Australia* 90 C3
McKinlay →, *Australia* 90 C3
McKinley, Mt., *U.S.A.* 96 B4
McKinley Sea, *Arctic* 4 A7
McKinney, *U.S.A.* 109 J6
Mackinnon Road, *Kenya* 82 C4
Macksville, *Australia* 91 E5
McLaughlin, *U.S.A.* 108 C4
Maclean, *Australia* 91 D5
McLean, *U.S.A.* 109 H4
McLeansboro, *U.S.A.* 108 F10
Maclear, *S. Africa* 85 E4
Macleay →, *Australia* 91 E5
McLennan, *Canada* 100 B5
MacLeod, B., *Canada* 101 A7
McLeod, L., *Australia* 89 D1
MacLeod Lake, *Canada* 100 C4
McLoughlin, Mt., *U.S.A.* 110 E2
McLure, *Canada* 100 C4
McMechen, *U.S.A.* 106 G4
McMillan, L., *U.S.A.* 109 J2
McMinnville, *Oreg., U.S.A.* 110 D2
McMinnville, *Tenn., U.S.A.* 105 H3
McMorran, *Canada* 101 C7
McMurdo Sd., *Antarctica* 5 D11
McMurray = Fort McMurray, *Canada* 100 B6
McMurray, *U.S.A.* 112 B4
McNary, *U.S.A.* 111 J9
MacNutt, *Canada* 101 C8
Macodoene, *Mozam.* 85 C6
Macomb, *U.S.A.* 108 E9
Macomer, *Italy* 34 B1
Mâcon, *France* 27 B8
Macon, *Ga., U.S.A.* 105 J4
Macon, *Miss., U.S.A.* 105 J1
Macon, *Mo., U.S.A.* 108 F8
Macondo, *Angola* 81 G4
Macossa, *Mozam.* 83 F3
Macoun L., *Canada* 101 B8
Macovane, *Mozam.* 85 C6
McPherson, *U.S.A.* 108 F6
McPherson Pk., *U.S.A.* 113 L7
McPherson Ra., *Australia* 91 D5
Macquarie Harbour, *Australia* 90 G4
Macquarie Is., *Pac. Oc.* 92 N7
MacRobertson Land, *Antarctica* 5 D6
Macroom, *Ireland* 15 E3
Macroy, *Australia* 88 D2
MacTier, *Canada* 106 A5
Macubela, *Mozam.* 83 F4
Macugnaga, *Italy* 32 C4
Macuiza, *Mozam.* 83 F3
Macujer, *Colombia* 120 C3
Macusani, *Peru* 124 C3
Macuse, *Mozam.* 83 F4
Macuspana, *Mexico* 115 D6
Macusse, *Angola* 84 B3
McVille, *U.S.A.* 108 B5
Madadeni, *S. Africa* 85 D5
Madagali, *Nigeria* 79 C7
Madagascar ■, *Africa* 85 C8
Madā'in Sālih, *Si. Arabia* 64 E3
Madama, *Niger* 73 D7
Madame I., *Canada* 99 C7
Madaoua, *Niger* 79 C6
Madara, *Nigeria* 79 C7
Madaripur, *Bangla.* 61 H17
Madauk, *Burma* 61 L20
Madawaska, *Canada* 106 A7
Madawaska →, *Canada* 98 C4
Madaya, *Burma* 61 H20
Madbar, *Sudan* 77 F3
Maddaloni, *Italy* 35 A7
Made, *Neths.* 17 E5
Madeira, *Atl. Oc.* 36 D3
Madeira →, *Brazil* 121 D6
Madeleine, Is. de la, *Canada* 99 C7
Maden, *Turkey* 67 C8
Madera, *U.S.A.* 111 H3
Madha, *India* 60 L9
Madhubani, *India* 63 F12
Madhya Pradesh □, *India* 62 J7
Madian, *China* 53 A11
Madidi →, *Bolivia* 124 C4
Madikeri, *India* 60 N9
Madill, *U.S.A.* 109 H6
Madimba, *Zaïre* 80 E3
Ma'din, *Syria* 67 E8
Madīnat ash Sha'b, *Yemen* 68 E3
Madingou, *Congo* 80 E2
Madirovalo, *Madag.* 85 B8
Madison, *Calif., U.S.A.* 112 G5
Madison, *Fla., U.S.A.* 105 K4
Madison, *Ind., U.S.A.* 104 F3
Madison, *Nebr., U.S.A.* 108 E6
Madison, *Ohio, U.S.A.* 106 E3
Madison, *S. Dak., U.S.A.* 108 D6
Madison, *Wis., U.S.A.* 108 D10
Madison →, *U.S.A.* 110 D8
Madisonville, *Ky., U.S.A.* 104 G2
Madisonville, *Tex., U.S.A.* 109 K7
Madista, *Botswana* 84 C4
Madiun, *Indonesia* 57 G14
Madley, *U.K.* 13 E5
Madol, *Sudan* 77 F2
Madon →, *France* 25 D13
Madona, *Latvia* 9 H22
Madras = Tamil Nadu □, *India* 60 P10
Madras, *India* 60 N12
Madras, *U.S.A.* 110 D3
Madre, L., *Mexico* 115 B5
Madre, Laguna, *U.S.A.* 109 M6
Madre, Sierra, *Phil.* 55 C5
Madre de Dios □, *Peru* 124 C3
Madre de Dios →, *Bolivia* 124 C4
Madre de Dios, I., *Chile* 128 D1
Madre del Sur, Sierra, *Mexico* 115 D5
Madre Occidental, Sierra, *Mexico* 114 B3
Madre Oriental, Sierra, *Mexico* 114 C4
Madri, *India* 62 G5
Madrid, *Spain* 30 E7
Madrid □, *Spain* 30 E7
Madridejos, *Spain* 31 F7
Madrigal de las Altas Torres, *Spain* 30 D6
Madrona, Sierra, *Spain* 31 G6
Madroñera, *Spain* 31 F5
Madu, *Sudan* 77 E2
Madura, Selat, *Indonesia* 57 G15
Madura Motel, *Australia* 89 F4
Madurai, *India* 60 Q11
Madurantakam, *India* 60 N11
Madzhalis, *Russia* 43 J8
Mae Chan, *Thailand* 58 B2
Mae Hong Son, *Thailand* 58 C2
Mae Khlong →, *Thailand* 58 F3
Mae Phrik, *Thailand* 58 D2
Mae Ramat, *Thailand* 58 D2
Mae Rim, *Thailand* 58 C2
Mae Sot, *Thailand* 58 D2
Mae Suai, *Thailand* 58 C2
Mae Tha, *Thailand* 58 C2
Maebashi, *Japan* 49 F9
Maella, *Spain* 28 D5
Măeruş, *Romania* 38 D8
Maesteg, *U.K.* 13 F4
Maestra, Sierra, *Cuba* 116 B4
Maestrazgo, Mts. del, *Spain* 28 E4
Maevatanana, *Madag.* 85 B8
Mafeking = Mafikeng, *S. Africa* 84 D4
Mafeking, *Canada* 101 C8
Maféré, *Ivory C.* 78 D4
Mafeteng, *Lesotho* 84 D4
Maffe, *Belgium* 17 H6
Maffra, *Australia* 91 F4
Mafia I., *Tanzania* 82 D4
Mafikeng, *S. Africa* 84 D4
Mafra, *Brazil* 127 B6
Mafra, *Portugal* 31 G1
Mafungabusi Plateau, *Zimbabwe* 83 F2
Magadan, *Russia* 45 D16
Magadi, *Kenya* 82 C4
Magadi, L., *Kenya* 82 C4
Magaliesburg, *S. Africa* 85 D4
Magallanes □, *Chile* 128 D2
Magallanes, Estrecho de, *Chile* 128 D2
Magangué, *Colombia* 120 B3
Magaria, *Niger* 79 C6
Magburaka, *S. Leone* 78 D2
Magdalen Is. = Madeleine, Is. de la, *Canada* 99 C7
Magdalena, *Argentina* 126 D4
Magdalena, *Bolivia* 125 C5
Magdalena, *Malaysia* 56 D5
Magdalena, *Mexico* 114 A2
Magdalena, *U.S.A.* 111 J10
Magdalena □, *Colombia* 120 A3
Magdalena →, *Colombia* 120 A3
Magdalena →, *Mexico* 114 A2
Magdalena, B., *Mexico* 114 C2
Magdalena, I., *Chile* 128 B2
Magdalena, Llano de la, *Mexico* 114 C2
Magdeburg, *Germany* 18 C7
Magdelaine Cays, *Australia* 90 B5
Magdub, *Sudan* 77 E2
Magee, *U.S.A.* 109 K10
Magee, I., *U.K.* 15 B6
Magelang, *Indonesia* 57 G14
Magellan's Str. = Magallanes, Estrecho de, *Chile* 128 D2
Magenta, *Italy* 32 C5
Magenta, L., *Australia* 89 F2
Magerøya, *Norway* 8 A21
Maggia, *Switz.* 23 D7
Maggia →, *Switz.* 23 D7
Maggiorasca, Mte., *Italy* 32 D6
Maggiore, L., *Italy* 32 C5
Maghama, *Mauritania* 78 B2
Magherafelt, *U.K.* 15 B5
Maghnia, *Algeria* 75 B4
Magione, *Italy* 33 E9
Magistralnyy, *Russia* 45 D11
Magliano in Toscana, *Italy* 33 F8
Máglie, *Italy* 35 B11
Magnac-Laval, *France* 26 B5
Magnetic Pole (North) = North Magnetic Pole, *Canada* 4 B2
Magnetic Pole (South) = South Magnetic Pole, *Antarctica* 5 C9
Magnitogorsk, *Russia* 44 D6
Magnolia, *Ark., U.S.A.* 109 J8
Magnolia, *Miss., U.S.A.* 109 K9
Magnor, *Norway* 10 E6
Magny-en-Vexin, *France* 25 C8
Magog, *Canada* 99 C5
Magoro, *Uganda* 82 B3
Magosa = Famagusta, *Cyprus* 66 E5
Magouládhes, *Greece* 37 A3
Magoye, *Zambia* 83 F2
Magpie L., *Canada* 99 B7
Magrath, *Canada* 100 D6
Magro →, *Spain* 29 F4
Magrur, Wadi →, *Sudan* 77 D2
Magu □, *Tanzania* 82 C3
Maguan, *China* 52 F5
Maguarinho, C., *Brazil* 122 B2
Mağusa = Famagusta, *Cyprus* 66 E5
Maguse L., *Canada* 101 A9
Maguse Pt., *Canada* 101 A10
Magwe, *Burma* 61 J19
Maha Sarakham, *Thailand* 58 D4
Mahābād, *Iran* 67 D11
Mahabharat Lekh, *Nepal* 63 E9
Mahabo, *Madag.* 85 C7
Mahadeo Hills, *India* 62 H8
Mahagi, *Zaïre* 82 B3
Mahaicony, *Guyana* 121 B6
Mahajamba →, *Madag.* 85 B8
Mahajamba, Helodranon' i, *Madag.* 85 B8
Mahajan, *India* 62 E5
Mahajanga, *Madag.* 85 B8
Mahajanga □, *Madag.* 85 B8
Mahajilo →, *Madag.* 85 B8
Mahakam →, *Indonesia* 56 E5
Mahalapye, *Botswana* 84 C4
Maḩallāt, *Iran* 65 C6
Māhān, *Iran* 65 D8
Mahanadi →, *India* 61 J15
Mahanoro, *Madag.* 85 B8
Mahanoy City, *U.S.A.* 107 F8
Maharashtra □, *India* 60 J9
Maharès, *Tunisia* 75 B7
Mahari Mts., *Tanzania* 82 D2
Mahasham, W. →, *Egypt* 69 E3
Mahasolo, *Madag.* 85 B8
Mahattat ash Shīdīyah, *Jordan* 69 F4
Mahattat 'Unayzah, *Jordan* 69 E4
Mahaxay, *Laos* 58 D5
Mahbes, *W. Sahara* 74 C3
Mahbubnagar, *India* 60 L10
Maḩḑah, *Oman* 65 E7
Mahdia, *Guyana* 121 B6
Mahdia, *Tunisia* 75 A7
Mahe, *India* 63 C8
Mahenge, *Tanzania* 83 D4
Maheno, *N.Z.* 87 L3
Mahesana, *India* 62 H5
Mahia Pen., *N.Z.* 87 H6
Mahilyow, *Belarus* 40 F6
Mahirija, *Morocco* 75 B4
Mahmiya, *Sudan* 77 D3
Mahmud Kot, *Pakistan* 62 D4
Mahmudia, *Romania* 38 D12
Mahnomen, *U.S.A.* 108 B7
Mahoba, *India* 63 G8
Mahón, *Spain* 36 B11
Mahone Bay, *Canada* 99 D7
Mahuta, *Nigeria* 79 C5
Mai-Ndombe, L., *Zaïre* 80 E3
Mai-Sai, *Thailand* 58 B2
Maicao, *Colombia* 120 A3
Maîche, *France* 25 E13
Maici →, *Brazil* 125 B5
Maicurú →, *Brazil* 121 D7
Máida, *Italy* 35 D9
Maidan Khula, *Afghan.* 62 C3
Maidenhead, *U.K.* 13 F7
Maidi, *Yemen* 77 D5
Maidstone, *Canada* 101 C7
Maidstone, *U.K.* 13 F8
Maiduguri, *Nigeria* 79 C7
Maignelay, *France* 25 C9
Maigo, *Phil.* 55 G5
Maigualida, Sierra, *Venezuela* 121 B4
Maigudo, *Ethiopia* 77 F4

Maijdi, *Bangla.* 61 H17
Maikala Ra., *India* 61 J12
Mailly-le-Camp, *France* 25 D11
Mailsi, *Pakistan* 62 E5
Main →, *Germany* 19 F4
Main →, *U.K.* 15 B5
Main Centre, *Canada* 101 C7
Mainburg, *Germany* 19 G7
Maine, *France* 24 E6
Maine □, *U.S.A.* 99 C6
Maine →, *Ireland* 15 D2
Maine-et-Loire □, *France* 24 E6
Maïne-Soroa, *Niger* 79 C7
Maingkwan, *Burma* 61 F20
Mainit, L., *Phil.* 55 G6
Mainland, *Orkney, U.K.* 14 C5
Mainland, *Shet., U.K.* 14 A7
Mainpuri, *India* 63 F8
Maintenon, *France* 25 D8
Maintirano, *Madag.* 85 B7
Mainvault, *Belgium* 17 G3
Mainz, *Germany* 19 F4
Maipú, *Argentina* 126 D4
Maiquetía, *Venezuela* 120 A4
Maira →, *Italy* 32 D4
Mairabari, *India* 61 F18
Mairipotaba, *Brazil* 123 E2
Maisí, *Cuba* 117 B5
Maisi, Pta. de, *Cuba* 117 B5
Maisse, *France* 25 D9
Maissin, *Belgium* 17 J6
Maitland, *N.S.W., Australia* 91 E5
Maitland, *S. Austral., Australia* 91 E2
Maitland →, *Canada* 106 C3
Maiyema, *Nigeria* 79 C5
Maiyuan, *China* 53 E11
Maiz, Is. del, *Nic.* 116 D3
Maizuru, *Japan* 49 G7
Majagual, *Colombia* 120 B3
Majalengka, *Indonesia* 57 G13
Majari →, *Brazil* 121 C5
Majene, *Indonesia* 57 E5
Majes →, *Peru* 124 D3
Maji, *Ethiopia* 77 F4
Majiang, *China* 52 D6
Major, *Canada* 101 C7
Majorca = Mallorca, *Spain* 36 B10
Majuriã, *Brazil* 125 B5
Maka, *Senegal* 78 C2
Makak, *Cameroon* 79 E7
Makale, *Indonesia* 57 E5
Makamba, *Burundi* 82 C2
Makari, *Cameroon* 80 B2
Makarikari = Makgadikgadi Salt Pans, *Botswana* 84 C4
Makarovo, *Russia* 45 D11
Makarska, *Croatia* 21 M7
Makaryev, *Russia* 42 B6
Makasar = Ujung Pandang, *Indonesia* 57 F5
Makasar, Selat, *Indonesia* 57 E5
Makasar, Str. of = Makasar, Selat, *Indonesia* 57 E5
Makat, *Kazakstan* 44 E6
Makedonija = Macedonia ■, *Europe* 39 H4
Makena, *U.S.A.* 102 H16
Makeni, *S. Leone* 78 D2
Makeyevka = Makiyivka, *Ukraine* 41 H9
Makgadikgadi Salt Pans, *Botswana* 84 C4
Makhachkala, *Russia* 43 J8
Makharadze = Ozurgeti, *Georgia* 43 K5
Makhmūr, *Iraq* 67 E10
Makian, *Indonesia* 57 D7
Makindu, *Kenya* 82 C4
Makinsk, *Kazakstan* 44 D8
Makiyivka, *Ukraine* 41 H9
Makkah, *Si. Arabia* 68 C2
Makkovik, *Canada* 99 A8
Makkum, *Neths.* 16 B6
Makó, *Hungary* 21 J10
Makokou, *Gabon* 80 D2
Makongo, *Zaïre* 82 B2
Makoro, *Zaïre* 82 B2
Makoua, *Congo* 80 E3
Makrá, *Greece* 39 N8
Makrai, *India* 60 H10
Makran Coast Range, *Pakistan* 60 G4
Makrana, *India* 62 F6
Makriyialos, *Greece* 37 D7
Maksimkin Yar, *Russia* 44 D9
Maktar, *Tunisia* 75 A6
Mākū, *Iran* 67 C11
Makumbi, *Zaïre* 80 F4
Makunda, *Botswana* 84 C3
Makurazaki, *Japan* 49 J5
Makurdi, *Nigeria* 79 D6
Makūyeh, *Iran* 65 D7
Makwassie, *S. Africa* 84 D4
Mal B., *Ireland* 15 D2
Mal i Nemërçkës, *Albania* 39 J3
Mala, *Peru* 124 C2
Mala, Pta., *Panama* 116 E3
Mala Belozërka, *Ukraine* 41 J8
Mala Kapela, *Croatia* 33 D12
Mala Vyska, *Ukraine* 41 H6
Malabang, *Phil.* 55 H6
Malabar Coast, *India* 60 P9
Malabo = Rey Malabo, *Eq. Guin.* 79 E6
Malabon, *Phil.* 55 D4
Malacca, Str. of, *Indonesia* 59 L3
Malacky, *Slovak Rep.* 21 G7
Malad City, *U.S.A.* 110 E7
Maladzyechna, *Belarus* 40 E4
Málaga, *Colombia* 120 B3
Málaga, *Spain* 31 J6
Malaga, *U.S.A.* 109 J2
Málaga □, *Spain* 31 J6
Malagarasi, *Tanzania* 82 D3
Malagarasi →, *Tanzania* 82 D2
Malagón, *Spain* 31 F7
Malagón →, *Spain* 31 H3
Malaimbandy, *Madag.* 85 C8
Malakâl, *Sudan* 77 F3
Malakand, *Pakistan* 62 B4
Malakoff, *U.S.A.* 109 J7
Malamyzh, *Russia* 45 E14
Malang, *Indonesia* 57 G15
Malangen, *Norway* 8 B18
Malanje, *Angola* 80 F3
Mälaren, *Sweden* 10 E11
Malargüe, *Argentina* 126 D2
Malartic, *Canada* 98 C4
Malaryta, *Belarus* 41 G3
Malatya, *Turkey* 67 C8
Malawi ■, *Africa* 83 E3
Malawi, L., *Africa* 83 E3
Malay Pen., *Asia* 59 J3
Malaya Belozërka = Mala Belozërka, *Ukraine* 41 J8
Malaya Vishera, *Russia* 40 C7
Malaya Viska = Mala Vyska, *Ukraine* 41 H6
Malaybalay, *Phil.* 55 G6
Malāyer, *Iran* 67 E13
Malaysia ■, *Asia* 56 D4
Malazgirt, *Turkey* 67 C10
Malbon, *Australia* 90 C3
Malbooma, *Australia* 91 E1
Malbork, *Poland* 20 A9
Malcésine, *Italy* 32 C7
Malchin, *Germany* 18 B8
Malchow, *Germany* 18 B8
Malcolm, *Australia* 89 E3
Malcolm, Pt., *Australia* 89 F3
Maldegem, *Belgium* 17 F2
Malden, *Mass., U.S.A.* 107 D13
Malden, *Mo., U.S.A.* 109 G10
Malden I., *Kiribati* 93 H12
Maldives ■, *Ind. Oc.* 46 J11
Maldonado, *Uruguay* 127 C5
Maldonado, Punta, *Mexico* 115 D5
Malè, *Italy* 32 B7
Maléa, Ákra, *Greece* 39 N6
Malegaon, *India* 60 J9
Malei, *Mozam.* 83 F4
Malek Kandī, *Iran* 67 D12
Malela, *Zaïre* 82 C2
Malema, *Mozam.* 83 E4
Máleme, *Greece* 37 D5
Malerkotla, *India* 62 D6
Máles, *Greece* 37 D7
Malesherbes, *France* 25 D9
Malestroit, *France* 24 E4
Malfa, *Italy* 35 D7
Malgobek, *Russia* 43 J7
Malgomaj, *Sweden* 8 D17
Malgrat, *Spain* 28 D7
Malha, *Sudan* 77 D2
Malheur →, *U.S.A.* 110 D5
Malheur L., *U.S.A.* 110 E4
Mali, *Guinea* 78 C2
Mali ■, *Africa* 78 B4
Mali →, *Burma* 61 G20
Mali Kanal, *Serbia, Yug.* 21 K9
Malibu, *U.S.A.* 113 L8
Malik, *Indonesia* 57 E6
Malili, *Indonesia* 57 E6
Malimba, Mts., *Zaïre* 82 D2
Malin Hd., *Ireland* 15 A4
Malindi, *Kenya* 82 C5
Malines = Mechelen, *Belgium* 17 F4
Malino, *Indonesia* 57 D6
Malinyi, *Tanzania* 83 D4
Malipo, *China* 52 F5
Maliqi, *Albania* 39 J3
Malita, *Phil.* 57 C7
Malkara, *Turkey* 66 B2
Małkinia Górna, *Poland* 20 C12
Malko Tŭrnovo, *Bulgaria* 39 H10
Mallacoota, *Australia* 91 F4
Mallacoota Inlet, *Australia* 91 F4
Mallaig, *U.K.* 14 E3
Mallawan, *India* 63 F9
Mallawi, *Egypt* 76 B3
Malleco □, *Chile* 128 A2
Mallemort, *France* 27 E9
Málles Venosta, *Italy* 32 B7
Mállia, *Greece* 37 D7
Mallión, Kólpos, *Greece* 37 D7
Mallorca, *Spain* 36 B10
Mallorytown, *Canada* 107 B9
Mallow, *Ireland* 15 D3
Malmberget, *Sweden* 8 C19
Malmédy, *Belgium* 17 H8
Malmesbury, *S. Africa* 84 E2
Malmö, *Sweden* 11 J6
Malmöhus län □, *Sweden* 11 J7
Malmslätt, *Sweden* 11 F9
Malmyzh, *Russia* 42 B10
Maloarkhangelsk, *Russia* 42 D3
Maloca, *Brazil* 121 C6
Maloja, *Switz.* 23 D9
Maloja, P., *Switz.* 23 D9
Malolos, *Phil.* 57 B6
Malombe L., *Malawi* 83 E4
Malone, *U.S.A.* 107 B10
Malong, *China* 52 E4
Måløy, *Norway* 9 F11
Maloyaroslovets, *Russia* 42 C3
Malpartida, *Spain* 31 F4
Malpaso, *Canary Is.* 36 G1
Malpica, *Spain* 30 B2
Mals = Málles Venosta, *Italy* 32 B7
Malta, *Brazil* 122 C4
Malta, *Idaho, U.S.A.* 110 E7
Malta, *Mont., U.S.A.* 110 B10
Malta ■, *Europe* 37 D1
Malta Channel, *Medit. S.* 34 F6
Maltahöhe, *Namibia* 84 C2
Malters, *Switz.* 22 B6
Malton, *Canada* 106 C5
Malton, *U.K.* 12 C7
Maluku, *Indonesia* 57 E7
Maluku □, *Indonesia* 57 E7
Maluku Sea = Molucca Sea, *Indonesia* 57 E6
Malumfashi, *Nigeria* 79 C6
Malvan, *India* 60 L8
Malvern, *U.S.A.* 109 H8
Malvern Hills, *U.K.* 13 E5
Malvik, *Norway* 10 A4
Malvinas, Is. = Falkland Is. □, *Atl. Oc.* 128 D5
Malya, *Tanzania* 82 C3
Malyn, *Ukraine* 41 G5
Malyy Lyakhovskiy, Ostrov, *Russia* 45 B15
Malyy Nimnyr, *Russia* 45 D13
Mama, *Russia* 45 D12
Mamadysh, *Russia* 42 C10
Mamanguape, *Brazil* 122 C4
Mamasa, *Indonesia* 57 E5
Mambasa, *Zaïre* 82 B2
Mamberamo →, *Indonesia* 57 E9
Mambilima Falls, *Zambia* 83 E2
Mambirima, *Zaïre* 83 E2
Mambo, *Tanzania* 82 C4
Mambrui, *Kenya* 82 C5
Mamburao, *Phil.* 55 E4
Mameigwess L., *Canada* 98 B2
Mamer, *Lux.* 17 J8
Mamers, *France* 24 D7
Mamfe, *Cameroon* 79 D6
Mamiña, *Chile* 124 E4
Mámmola, *Italy* 35 D9
Mammoth, *U.S.A.* 111 K8
Mamoré →, *Bolivia* 125 C4
Mamou, *Guinea* 78 C2
Mampatá, *Guinea-Biss.* 78 C2
Mampong, *Ghana* 79 D4
Mamuil Malal, Paso, *S. Amer.* 128 A2
Mamuju, *Indonesia* 57 E5
Man, *Ivory C.* 78 D3
Man, I. of, *U.K.* 12 C3
Man Na, *Burma* 61 H20
Mana, *Fr. Guiana* 121 B7
Mana →, *Fr. Guiana* 121 B7
Måna →, *Norway* 10 E2
Manaar, G. of = Mannar, G. of, *Asia* 60 Q11
Manabí □, *Ecuador* 120 D1
Manacacías →, *Colombia* 120 C3
Manacapuru, *Brazil* 121 D5
Manacapuru →, *Brazil* 121 D5
Manacor, *Spain* 36 B10
Manado, *Indonesia* 57 D6
Manage, *Belgium* 17 G4
Managua, *Nic.* 116 D2
Managua, L., *Nic.* 116 D2
Manakara, *Madag.* 85 C8
Manama = Al Manāmah, *Bahrain* 65 E6
Manambao →, *Madag.* 85 B7
Manambato, *Madag.* 85 A8
Manambolo →, *Madag.* 85 B7
Manambolosy, *Madag.* 85 B8
Mananara, *Madag.* 85 B8
Mananara →, *Madag.* 85 C8
Mananjary, *Madag.* 85 C8
Manantenina, *Madag.* 85 C8
Manaos = Manaus, *Brazil* 121 D6
Manapire →, *Venezuela* 120 B4
Manapouri, *N.Z.* 87 L1
Manapouri, L., *N.Z.* 87 L1
Manas, *China* 54 B3
Manas →, *India* 61 F17
Manaslu, *Nepal* 63 E11
Manasquan, *U.S.A.* 107 F10
Manassa, *U.S.A.* 111 H11
Manaung, *Burma* 61 K18
Manaus, *Brazil* 121 D6
Manavgat, *Turkey* 66 D4
Manawan L., *Canada* 101 B8
Manay, *Phil.* 55 H7
Manbij, *Syria* 66 D7
Mancelona, *U.S.A.* 104 C3
Mancha Real, *Spain* 31 H7
Manche □, *France* 24 C5
Manchester, *U.K.* 12 D5
Manchester, *Calif., U.S.A.* 112 G3
Manchester, *Conn., U.S.A.* 107 E12
Manchester, *Ga., U.S.A.* 105 J3
Manchester, *Iowa, U.S.A.* 108 D9
Manchester, *Ky., U.S.A.* 104 G4
Manchester, *N.H., U.S.A.* 107 D13
Manchester, *N.Y., U.S.A.* 106 D7
Manchester, *Vt., U.S.A.* 107 C11
Manchester L., *Canada* 101 A7
Manchuria = Dongbei, *China* 51 D13
Manchurian Plain, *China* 46 E16
Manciano, *Italy* 33 F8
Mancifa, *Ethiopia* 77 F5
Mancora, Pta., *Peru* 124 A1
Mand →, *Iran* 65 D7
Manda, *Chunya, Tanzania* 82 D3
Manda, *Ludewe, Tanzania* 83 E3
Mandabé, *Madag.* 85 C7
Mandaguari, *Brazil* 127 A5
Mandah, *Mongolia* 50 B5
Mandal, *Norway* 9 G12
Mandalay, *Burma* 61 J20
Mandale = Mandalay, *Burma* 61 J20
Mandalgovi, *Mongolia* 50 B4
Mandalī, *Iraq* 67 F11
Mandan, *U.S.A.* 108 B4
Mandaon, *Phil.* 55 E5
Mandar, Teluk, *Indonesia* 57 E5
Mandas, *Italy* 34 C2
Mandaue, *Phil.* 55 F5
Mandelieu-la-Napoule, *France* 27 E10
Mandera, *Kenya* 82 B5
Mandera □, *Kenya* 82 B5
Manderfeld, *Belgium* 17 H8
Mandi, *India* 62 D7
Mandimba, *Mozam.* 83 E4
Mandioli, *Indonesia* 57 E7
Mandioré, L., *S. Amer.* 125 D6
Mandla, *India* 63 H9
Mandø, *Denmark* 11 J2
Mandoto, *Madag.* 85 B8
Mandoúdhion, *Greece* 39 L6
Mandra, *Pakistan* 62 C5
Mandrare →, *Madag.* 85 D8
Mandritsara, *Madag.* 85 B8
Mandsaur, *India* 62 G6
Mandurah, *Australia* 89 F2
Mandúria, *Italy* 35 B10
Mandvi, *India* 62 H3
Mandya, *India* 60 N10
Mandzai, *Pakistan* 62 D2
Mané, *Burkina Faso* 79 C4
Maneh, *Iran* 65 B8
Manengouba, Mts., *Cameroon* 79 D6
Maneroo, *Australia* 90 C3
Maneroo Cr. →, *Australia* 90 C3
Manfalût, *Egypt* 76 B3
Manfred, *Australia* 91 E3
Manfredónia, *Italy* 35 A8
Manfredónia, G. di, *Italy* 35 A9
Manga, *Brazil* 123 D3
Manga, *Burkina Faso* 79 C4
Manga, *Niger* 79 C7
Mangabeiras, Chapada das, *Brazil* 122 D2
Mangalia, *Romania* 38 F11
Mangalore, *India* 60 N9
Manganeses, *Spain* 30 D5
Mangaweka, *N.Z.* 87 H5
Manggar, *Indonesia* 56 E3
Manggawitu, *Indonesia* 57 E8
Mangkalihat, Tanjung, *Indonesia* 57 D5
Mangla Dam, *Pakistan* 63 C5
Manglares, C., *Colombia* 120 C2
Manglaur, *India* 62 E7
Mangnai, *China* 54 C4
Mango, *Togo* 79 C5
Mangoche, *Malawi* 83 E4
Mangoky →, *Madag.* 85 C7
Mangole, *Indonesia* 57 E7
Mangombe, *Zaïre* 82 C2
Mangonui, *N.Z.* 87 F4
Mangualde, *Portugal* 30 E3
Mangueigne, *Chad* 73 F9
Mangueira, L. da, *Brazil* 127 C5
Manguéni, Hamada, *Niger* 75 D7
Mangum, *U.S.A.* 109 H5
Mangyshlak Poluostrov, *Kazakstan* 44 E6
Manhattan, *U.S.A.* 108 F6
Manhiça, *Mozam.* 85 D5
Manhuaçu, *Brazil* 123 F3
Manhumirim, *Brazil* 123 F3
Maní, *Colombia* 120 C3
Mania →, *Madag.* 85 B8
Maniago, *Italy* 33 B9
Manica, *Mozam.* 85 B5
Manica e Sofala □, *Mozam.* 85 B5
Manicaland □, *Zimbabwe* 83 F3
Manicoré, *Brazil* 125 B5
Manicoré →, *Brazil* 125 B5
Manicouagan →, *Canada* 99 C6
Manīfah, *Si. Arabia* 65 E6
Manifold, *Australia* 90 C5
Manifold, C., *Australia* 90 C5
Maniganggo, *China* 52 B2
Manigotagan, *Canada* 101 C9
Manihiki, *Cook Is.* 93 J11
Manika, Plateau de la, *Zaïre* 83 E2
Manila, *Phil.* 55 D4
Manila, *U.S.A.* 110 F9
Manila B., *Phil.* 55 D4
Manilla, *Australia* 91 E5
Manimpé, *Mali* 78 C3
Maningrida, *Australia* 90 A1
Manipur □, *India* 61 G18
Manipur →, *Burma* 61 H19
Manisa, *Turkey* 66 C2
Manistee, *U.S.A.* 104 C2
Manistee →, *U.S.A.* 104 C2
Manistique, *U.S.A.* 104 C2
Manito L., *Canada* 101 C7
Manitoba □, *Canada* 101 B9
Manitoba, L., *Canada* 101 C9
Manitou, *Canada* 101 D9
Manitou I., *U.S.A.* 98 C2
Manitou Is., *U.S.A.* 104 C2
Manitou L., *Canada* 99 B6
Manitou Springs, *U.S.A.* 108 F2
Manitoulin I., *Canada* 98 C3
Manitowaning, *Canada* 98 C3
Manitowoc, *U.S.A.* 104 C2
Manitsauá-Missu →, *Brazil* 125 C7
Manizales, *Colombia* 120 B2
Manja, *Madag.* 85 C7
Manjacaze, *Mozam.* 85 C5
Manjakandriana, *Madag.* 85 B8
Manjhand, *Pakistan* 62 G3
Manjil, *Iran* 65 B6
Manjimup, *Australia* 89 F2
Manjra →, *India* 60 K10
Mankato, *Kans., U.S.A.* 108 F5
Mankato, *Minn., U.S.A.* 108 C8
Mankayane, *Swaziland* 85 D5
Mankono, *Ivory C.* 78 D3
Mankota, *Canada* 101 D7
Manlay, *Mongolia* 50 B4
Manlleu, *Spain* 28 C7
Manly, *Australia* 91 E5
Manmad, *India* 60 J9
Mann Ras., *Australia* 89 E5
Manna, *Indonesia* 56 E2
Mannahill, *Australia* 91 E3
Mannar, *Sri Lanka* 60 Q11
Mannar, G. of, *Asia* 60 Q11
Mannar I., *Sri Lanka* 60 Q11
Männedorf, *Switz.* 23 B7
Mannheim, *Germany* 19 F4
Manning, *Canada* 100 B5
Manning, *Oreg., U.S.A.* 112 E3
Manning, *S.C., U.S.A.* 105 J5
Manning Prov. Park, *Canada* 100 D4
Mannington, *U.S.A.* 104 F5
Mannu →, *Italy* 34 C2
Mannu, C., *Italy* 34 B1
Mannum, *Australia* 91 E2
Mano, *S. Leone* 78 D2
Manoa, *Bolivia* 125 B4
Manokwari, *Indonesia* 57 E8
Manombo, *Madag.* 85 C7
Manono, *Zaïre* 82 D2
Manosque, *France* 27 E9
Manouane, L., *Canada* 99 B5
Manpojin, *N. Korea* 51 D14
Manresa, *Spain* 28 D6
Mansa, *Gujarat, India* 62 H5
Mansa, *Punjab, India* 62 E6
Mansa, *Zambia* 83 E2
Mansehra, *Pakistan* 62 B5
Mansel I., *Canada* 97 B11
Mansfield, *Australia* 91 F4
Mansfield, *U.K.* 12 D6
Mansfield, *La., U.S.A.* 109 J8
Mansfield, *Mass., U.S.A.* 107 D13
Mansfield, *Ohio, U.S.A.* 106 F2
Mansfield, *Pa., U.S.A.* 106 E7
Mansfield, *Wash., U.S.A.* 110 C4
Mansidão, *Brazil* 122 D3
Mansilla de las Mulas, *Spain* 30 C5
Mansle, *France* 26 C4
Manso →, *Brazil* 123 D2
Mansoa, *Guinea-Biss.* 78 C1
Manson Creek, *Canada* 100 B4
Mansoura, *Algeria* 75 A5
Manta, *Ecuador* 120 D1
Manta, B. de, *Ecuador* 120 D1
Mantalingajan, Mt., *Phil.* 55 G2
Mantare, *Tanzania* 82 C3
Manteca, *U.S.A.* 111 H3
Mantecal, *Venezuela* 120 B4
Mantena, *Brazil* 123 E3
Manteo, *U.S.A.* 105 H8
Mantes-la-Jolie, *France* 25 D8
Manthani, *India* 60 K11
Manthelan, *France* 24 E7
Manti, *U.S.A.* 110 G8
Mantiqueira, Serra da, *Brazil* 123 F3
Manton, *U.S.A.* 104 C3
Mantorp, *Sweden* 11 F9
Mántova, *Italy* 32 C7
Mänttä, *Finland* 9 E21
Mantua = Mántova, *Italy* 32 C7
Manturovo, *Russia* 42 A7
Manu, *Peru* 124 C3
Manu →, *Peru* 124 C3
Manua Is., *Amer. Samoa* 87 B14
Manuae, *Cook Is.* 93 J12
Manuel Alves →, *Brazil* 123 D2
Manuel Alves Grande →, *Brazil* 122 C2
Manuel Urbano, *Brazil* 124 B4
Manui, *Indonesia* 57 E6
Manuripi →, *Bolivia* 124 C4
Manville, *U.S.A.* 108 D2
Many, *U.S.A.* 109 K8
Manyara, L., *Tanzania* 82 C4
Manych →, *Russia* 43 G5
Manych-Gudilo, Ozero, *Russia* 43 G6
Manyonga →, *Tanzania* 82 C3
Manyoni, *Tanzania* 82 D3
Manyoni □, *Tanzania* 82 D3
Manzai, *Pakistan* 62 C4
Manzala, Bahra el, *Egypt* 76 H7
Manzanares, *Spain* 29 F1

Manzaneda, Cabeza de, Spain 30 C3
Manzanillo, Cuba 116 B4
Manzanillo, Mexico 114 D4
Manzanillo, Pta., Panama 116 E4
Manzano Mts., U.S.A. 111 J10
Manzarīyeh, Iran 65 C6
Manzhouli, China 54 B6
Manzini, Swaziland 85 D5
Mao, Chad 73 F8
Maoke, Pegunungan, Indonesia 57 E9
Maolin, China 51 C12
Maoming, China 53 G8
Maowen, China 52 B4
Maoxing, China 51 B13
Mapam Yumco, China 54 C3
Mapastepec, Mexico 115 D6
Mapia, Kepulauan, Indonesia 57 D8
Mapimí, Mexico 114 B4
Mapimí, Bolsón de, Mexico 114 B4
Maping, China 53 B9
Mapinga, Tanzania 82 D4
Mapinhane, Mozam. 85 C6
Mapire, Venezuela 121 B5
Maple Creek, Canada 101 D7
Maple Valley, U.S.A. 112 C4
Mapleton, U.S.A. 110 D2
Mapuera →, Brazil 121 D6
Maputo, Mozam. 85 D5
Maputo, B. de, Mozam. 85 D5
Maqiaohe, China 51 B16
Maqnā, Si. Arabia 64 D2
Maqteïr, Mauritania 74 D2
Maquela do Zombo, Angola 80 F3
Maquinchao, Argentina 128 B3
Maquoketa, U.S.A. 108 D9
Mar, Serra do, Brazil 127 B6
Mar Chiquita, L., Argentina 126 C3
Mar del Plata, Argentina 126 D4
Mar Menor, Spain 29 H4
Mara, Guyana 121 B6
Mara, Tanzania 82 C3
Mara □, Tanzania 82 C3
Maraã, Brazil 120 D4
Marabá, Brazil 122 C2
Maracá, I. de, Brazil 121 C7
Maracaibo, Venezuela 120 A3
Maracaibo, L. de, Venezuela 120 B3
Maracaju, Brazil 127 A4
Maracajú, Serra de, Brazil 125 E6
Maracanã, Brazil 122 B2
Maracás, Brazil 123 D3
Maracay, Venezuela 120 A4
Marādah, Libya 73 C8
Maradi, Niger 79 C6
Maradun, Nigeria 79 C6
Marāgheh, Iran 67 D12
Maragogipe, Brazil 123 D4
Marāh, Si. Arabia 64 E5
Marajó, B. de, Brazil 122 B2
Marajó, I. de, Brazil 122 B2
Marākand, Iran 64 B5
Maralal, Kenya 82 B4
Maralinga, Australia 89 F5
Marama, Australia 91 F3
Marampa, S. Leone 78 D2
Maran, Malaysia 59 L4
Marana, U.S.A. 111 K8
Maranboy, Australia 88 B5
Maranchón, Spain 28 D2
Marand, Iran 67 C11
Marang, Malaysia 59 K4
Maranguape, Brazil 122 B4
Maranhão = São Luís, Brazil 122 B3
Maranhão □, Brazil 122 B2
Marano, L. di, Italy 33 C10
Maranoa →, Australia 91 D4
Marañón →, Peru 124 A3
Marão, Mozam. 85 C5
Marapi →, Brazil 121 C6
Marari, Brazil 124 B4
Maraş = Kahramanmaraş, Turkey 66 D7
Mărăşeşti, Romania 38 D10
Maratea, Italy 35 C8
Marateca, Portugal 31 G2
Marathasa □, Cyprus 37 E11
Marathókambos, Greece 39 M9
Marathon, Australia 90 C3
Marathon, Canada 98 C2
Marathón, Greece 39 L6
Marathon, N.Y., U.S.A. 107 D8
Marathon, Tex., U.S.A. 109 K3
Marathóvouno, Cyprus 37 D12
Maratua, Indonesia 57 D5
Maraú, Brazil 123 D4
Maravatío, Mexico 114 D4
Marawi City, Phil. 55 G6
Marāwih, U.A.E. 65 E7
Marbella, Spain 31 J6
Marble Bar, Australia 88 D2
Marble Falls, U.S.A. 109 K5
Marblehead, U.S.A. 107 D14
Marburg, Germany 18 E4
Marby, Sweden 10 A8
Marcal →, Hungary 21 H7
Marcapata, Peru 124 C3
Marcaria, Italy 32 C7
March, U.K. 13 E8
Marchand = Rommani, Morocco 74 B3
Marche, France 26 B5
Marche □, Italy 33 E10
Marche-en-Famenne, Belgium 17 H6
Marchena, Spain 31 H5
Marches = Marche □, Italy 33 E10
Marciana Marina, Italy 32 F7
Marcianise, Italy 35 A7
Marcigny, France 27 B8
Marcillat-en-Combraille, France 26 B6
Marcinelle, Belgium 17 H4
Marck, France 25 B8
Marckolsheim, France 25 D14
Marcona, Peru 124 D2
Marcos Juárez, Argentina 126 C3
Marcus I. = Minami-Tori-Shima, Pac. Oc. 92 E7
Marcus Necker Ridge, Pac. Oc. 92 F9
Marcy, Mt., U.S.A. 107 B11
Mardan, Pakistan 62 B5
Mardie, Australia 88 D2
Mardin, Turkey 67 D9
Marechal Deodoro, Brazil 122 C4
Maree, L., U.K. 14 D3
Mareeba, Australia 90 B4
Marek = Stanke Dimitrov, Bulgaria 38 G6
Marek, Indonesia 57 E6
Maremma, Italy 32 F8
Maréna, Mali 78 C3
Marenberg, Slovenia 33 B12
Marengo, U.S.A. 108 E8
Marennes, France 26 C2
Marenyi, Kenya 82 C4
Marerano, Madag. 85 C7
Maréttimo, Italy 34 E5
Mareuil-sur-Lay, France 26 B2
Marfa, U.S.A. 109 K2
Marfa Pt., Malta 37 D1
Marganets = Marhanets, Ukraine 41 J8
Margaret →, Australia 88 C4
Margaret Bay, Canada 100 C3
Margaret L., Canada 100 B5
Margaret River, Australia 88 C4
Margarita, I. de, Venezuela 121 A5
Margarítion, Greece 39 K3
Margaritovo, Russia 48 C7
Margate, S. Africa 85 E5
Margate, U.K. 13 F9
Margelan = Marghilon, Uzbekistan 44 E8
Margeride, Mts. de la, France 26 D7
Margherita di Savola, Italy 35 A9
Marghilon, Uzbekistan 44 E8
Margosatubig, Phil. 55 H5
Marguerite, Canada 100 C4
Marhanets, Ukraine 41 J8
Marhoum, Algeria 75 B4
Mari El □, Russia 42 B8
Mari Republic □ = Mari El □, Russia 42 B8
María Elena, Chile 126 A2
María Grande, Argentina 126 C4
Maria I., N. Terr., Australia 90 A2
Maria I., Tas., Australia 90 G4
Maria van Diemen, C., N.Z. 87 F4
Mariager, Denmark 11 H4
Mariager Fjord, Denmark 11 H4
Mariakani, Kenya 82 C4
Marian L., Canada 100 A5
Mariana Trench, Pac. Oc. 46 H18
Marianao, Cuba 116 B3
Marianna, Ark., U.S.A. 109 H9
Marianna, Fla., U.S.A. 105 K3
Mariánské Lázně, Czech. 20 F2
Marias →, U.S.A. 110 C8
Mariato, Punta, Panama 116 E3
Mariazell, Austria 21 H5
Ma'rib, Yemen 68 D4
Maribo, Denmark 11 K5
Maribor, Slovenia 33 B12
Marico →, Africa 84 C4
Maricopa, Ariz., U.S.A. 111 K7
Maricopa, Calif., U.S.A. 113 K7
Maricourt, Canada 97 C12
Marîdî, Sudan 77 G2
Marîdî, Wadi →, Sudan 77 F2
Marié →, Brazil 120 D4
Marie Byrd Land, Antarctica 5 D14
Marie-Galante, Guadeloupe 117 C7
Mariecourt = Kangiqsujuaq, Canada 97 B12
Mariefred, Sweden 10 E11
Marienbad = Mariánské Lázně, Czech. 20 F2
Marienberg, Germany 18 E9
Marienberg, Neths. 16 D9
Marienbourg, Belgium 17 H5
Mariental, Namibia 84 C2
Marienville, U.S.A. 106 E5
Mariestad, Sweden 11 F7
Marietta, Ga., U.S.A. 105 J3
Marietta, Ohio, U.S.A. 104 F5
Marieville, Canada 107 A11
Marignane, France 27 E9
Marihatag, Phil. 55 G7
Mariinsk, Russia 44 D9
Mariinskiy Posad, Russia 42 B8
Marijampolė, Lithuania 9 J20
Marília, Brazil 127 A5
Marillana, Australia 88 D2
Marín, Spain 30 C2
Marina, U.S.A. 112 J5
Marina di Cirò, Italy 35 C10
Marina Plains, Australia 90 A3
Marinduque, Phil. 55 E5
Marine City, U.S.A. 104 D4
Marineo, Italy 34 E6
Marinette, U.S.A. 104 C2
Maringá, Brazil 127 A5
Marinha Grande, Portugal 31 F2
Marion, Ala., U.S.A. 105 J2
Marion, Ill., U.S.A. 109 G10
Marion, Ind., U.S.A. 104 E3
Marion, Iowa, U.S.A. 108 D9
Marion, Kans., U.S.A. 108 F6
Marion, Mich., U.S.A. 104 C3
Marion, N.C., U.S.A. 105 H4
Marion, Ohio, U.S.A. 104 E4
Marion, S.C., U.S.A. 105 H6
Marion, Va., U.S.A. 105 G5
Marion, L., U.S.A. 105 J5
Maripa, Venezuela 121 B4
Maripasoula, Fr. Guiana 121 C7
Mariposa, U.S.A. 111 H4
Mariscal Estigarribia, Paraguay 126 A3
Maritime Alps = Maritimes, Alpes, Europe 27 D11
Maritimes, Alpes, Europe 27 D11
Maritsa = Évros →, Bulgaria 66 B2
Maritsa, Greece 37 C10
Mariupol, Ukraine 41 J9
Marīvān, Iran 67 E12
Markam, China 52 C2
Markazī □, Iran 65 C6
Markdale, Canada 106 B4
Marke, Belgium 17 G2
Marked Tree, U.S.A. 109 H9
Markelsdorfer Huk, Germany 18 A6
Marken, Neths. 16 D6
Markermeer, Neths. 16 C6
Market Drayton, U.K. 12 E5
Market Harborough, U.K. 13 E7
Markham, Canada 106 C5
Markham, Mt., Antarctica 5 E11
Markham L., Canada 101 A8
Marki, Poland 20 C11
Markleeville, U.S.A. 112 G7
Markoupoulon, Greece 39 M6
Markovo, Russia 45 C17
Markoye, Burkina Faso 79 C5
Marks, Russia 42 E8
Marksville, U.S.A. 109 K8
Markt Schwaben, Germany 19 G7
Marktredwitz, Germany 19 E8
Marla, Australia 91 D1
Marlboro, U.S.A. 107 D13
Marlborough, Australia 90 C4
Marlborough Downs, U.K. 13 F6
Marle, France 25 C10
Marlin, U.S.A. 109 K6
Marlow, Germany 18 A8
Marlow, U.S.A. 109 H6
Marly-le-Grand, Switz. 22 C4
Marmagao, India 60 M8
Marmande, France 26 D4
Marmara, Turkey 66 B2
Marmara, Sea of = Marmara Denizi, Turkey 66 B3
Marmara Denizi, Turkey 66 B3
Marmaris, Turkey 66 D3
Marmarth, U.S.A. 108 B3
Marmelos →, Brazil 125 B5
Marmion, Mt., Australia 89 E2
Marmion L., Canada 98 C1
Marmolada, Mte., Italy 33 B8
Marmolejo, Spain 31 G6
Marmora, Canada 98 D4
Marnay, France 25 E12
Marne, Germany 18 B5
Marne □, France 25 D11
Marne →, France 25 D9
Marneuli, Georgia 43 K7
Maroa, Venezuela 120 C4
Maroala, Madag. 85 B8
Maroantsetra, Madag. 85 B8
Maromandia, Madag. 85 A8
Marondera, Zimbabwe 83 F3
Maroni →, Fr. Guiana 121 B7
Maronne →, France 26 C5
Maroochydore, Australia 91 D5
Maroona, Australia 91 F3
Maros →, Hungary 21 J10
Marosakoa, Madag. 85 B8
Marostica, Italy 33 C8
Maroua, Cameroon 79 C7
Marovoay, Madag. 85 B8
Marowijne □, Surinam 121 C7
Marowijne →, Surinam 121 B7
Marquard, S. Africa 84 D4
Marqueira, Portugal 31 G1
Marquesas Is. = Marquises, Is., Pac. Oc. 93 H14
Marquette, U.S.A. 104 B2
Marquise, France 25 B8
Marquises, Is., Pac. Oc. 93 H14
Marra, Gebel, Sudan 77 F2
Marracuene, Mozam. 85 D5
Marradi, Italy 33 D8
Marrakech, Morocco 74 B3
Marrawah, Australia 90 G3
Marrecas, Serra das, Brazil 122 C3
Marree, Australia 91 D2
Marrilla, Australia 88 D1
Marrimane, Mozam. 85 C5
Marromeu, Mozam. 85 B6
Marroquí, Punta, Spain 31 K5
Marrowie Cr. →, Australia 91 E4
Marrubane, Mozam. 83 F4
Marrum, Neths. 16 B7
Marrupa, Mozam. 83 E4
Marsá Matrûh, Egypt 76 A2
Marsá Susah, Libya 73 B9
Marsabit, Kenya 82 B4
Marsabit □, Kenya 82 B4
Marsala, Italy 34 E5
Marsalforn, Malta 37 C1
Marsberg, Germany 18 D4
Marsciano, Italy 33 F9
Marsden, Australia 91 E4
Marsdiep, Neths. 16 C5
Marseillan, France 26 E7
Marseille, France 27 E9
Marseilles = Marseille, France 27 E9
Marsh I., U.S.A. 109 L9
Marsh L., U.S.A. 108 C6
Marshall, Liberia 78 D2
Marshall, Ark., U.S.A. 109 H8
Marshall, Mich., U.S.A. 104 D3
Marshall, Minn., U.S.A. 108 C7
Marshall, Mo., U.S.A. 108 F8
Marshall, Tex., U.S.A. 109 J7
Marshall →, Australia 90 C2
Marshall Is. ■, Pac. Oc. 92 G9
Marshalltown, U.S.A. 108 D8
Marshfield, Mo., U.S.A. 109 G8
Marshfield, Wis., U.S.A. 108 C9
Marshūn, Iran 65 B6
Màrsico Nuovo, Italy 35 B8
Märsta, Sweden 10 E11
Marstal, Denmark 11 K4
Marstrand, Sweden 11 G5
Mart, U.S.A. 109 K6
Marta →, Italy 33 F8
Martaban, Burma 61 L20
Martaban, G. of, Burma 61 L20
Martano, Italy 35 B11
Martapura, Kalimantan, Indonesia 56 E4
Martapura, Sumatera, Indonesia 56 E2
Marte, Nigeria 79 C7
Martel, France 26 D5
Martelange, Belgium 17 J7
Martés, Sierra, Spain 29 F4
Martha's Vineyard, U.S.A. 107 E14
Martigné-Ferchaud, France 24 E5
Martigny, Switz. 22 D4
Martigues, France 27 E9
Martil, Morocco 74 A3
Martin, Slovak Rep. 20 F8
Martin, S. Dak., U.S.A. 108 D4
Martin, Tenn., U.S.A. 109 G10
Martín →, Spain 28 D4
Martin L., U.S.A. 105 J3
Martina, Switz. 23 C10
Martina Franca, Italy 35 B10
Martinborough, N.Z. 87 J5
Martinez, U.S.A. 112 G4
Martinho Campos, Brazil 123 E2
Martinique ■, W. Indies 117 D7
Martinique Passage, W. Indies 117 C7
Martínon, Greece 39 L6
Martinópolis, Brazil 127 A5
Martins Ferry, U.S.A. 106 F4
Martinsburg, Pa., U.S.A. 106 F6
Martinsburg, W. Va., U.S.A. 104 F7
Martinsville, Ind., U.S.A. 104 F2
Martinsville, Va., U.S.A. 105 G6
Marton, N.Z. 87 J5
Martorell, Spain 28 D6
Martos, Spain 31 H7
Martuni, Armenia 43 K7
Maru, Nigeria 79 C6
Marudi, Malaysia 56 D4
Ma'ruf, Afghan. 60 D5
Marugame, Japan 49 G6
Marúggio, Italy 35 B10
Maruim, Brazil 122 D4
Marulan, Australia 91 E5
Marum, Neths. 16 B8
Marunga, Angola 84 B3
Marungu, Mts., Zaïre 82 D2
Marvast, Iran 65 D7
Marvejols, France 26 D7
Marwar, India 62 G5
Mary, Turkmenistan 44 F7
Mary Frances L., Canada 101 A7
Mary Kathleen, Australia 90 C2
Maryborough = Port Laoise, Ireland 15 C4
Maryborough, Queens., Australia 91 D5
Maryborough, Vic., Australia 91 F3
Maryfield, Canada 101 D8
Maryland □, U.S.A. 104 F7
Maryland Junction, Zimbabwe 83 F3
Maryport, U.K. 12 C4
Mary's Harbour, Canada 99 B8
Marystown, Canada 99 C8
Marysvale, U.S.A. 111 G7
Marysville, Canada 100 D5
Marysville, Calif., U.S.A. 112 F5
Marysville, Kans., U.S.A. 108 F6
Marysville, Mich., U.S.A. 106 D2
Marysville, Ohio, U.S.A. 104 E4
Marysville, Wash., U.S.A. 112 B4
Maryvale, Australia 91 D5
Maryville, U.S.A. 105 H4
Marzo, Punta, Colombia 120 B2
Marzūq, Libya 73 C7
Masahunga, Tanzania 82 C3
Masai, Malaysia 59 M4
Masai Steppe, Tanzania 82 C4
Masaka, Uganda 82 C3
Masalembo, Kepulauan, Indonesia 56 F4
Masalima, Kepulauan, Indonesia 56 F5
Masallı, Azerbaijan 67 C13
Masamba, Indonesia 57 E6
Masan, S. Korea 51 G15
Masanasa, Spain 29 F4
Masasi, Tanzania 83 E4
Masasi □, Tanzania 83 E4
Masaya, Nic. 116 D2
Masba, Nigeria 79 C7
Masbate, Phil. 55 E5
Mascara, Algeria 75 A5
Mascota, Mexico 114 C4
Masela, Indonesia 57 F7
Maseru, Lesotho 84 D4
Mashaba, Zimbabwe 83 G3
Mashābih, Si. Arabia 64 E3
Mashan, China 52 F7
Masherbrum, Pakistan 63 B7
Mashhad, Iran 65 B8
Mashi, Nigeria 79 C6
Mashīz, Iran 65 D8
Mashkel, Hamun-i-, Pakistan 60 E3
Mashki Chāh, Pakistan 60 E3
Mashonaland Central □, Zimbabwe 85 B5
Mashonaland East □, Zimbabwe 85 B5
Mashonaland West □, Zimbabwe 85 B4
Mashtaga = Maştağa, Azerbaijan 43 K10
Masi Manimba, Zaïre 80 E3
Masindi, Uganda 82 B3
Masindi Port, Uganda 82 B3
Masisea, Peru 124 B3
Masisi, Zaïre 82 C2
Masjed Soleyman, Iran 65 D6
Mask, L., Ireland 15 C2
Maslinica, Croatia 33 E13
Masnou, Spain 28 D7
Masoala, Tanjon' i, Madag. 85 B9
Masoarivo, Madag. 85 B7
Masohi, Indonesia 57 E7
Masomeloka, Madag. 85 C8
Mason, Nev., U.S.A. 112 G7
Mason, Tex., U.S.A. 109 K5
Mason City, U.S.A. 108 D8
Maspalomas, Canary Is. 36 G4
Maspalomas, Pta., Canary Is. 36 G4
Masqat, Oman 68 C6
Massa, Italy 32 D7
Massa, O. →, Morocco 74 B3
Massa Maríttima, Italy 32 E7
Massachusetts □, U.S.A. 107 D12
Massachusetts B., U.S.A. 107 D14
Massafra, Italy 35 B10
Massaguet, Chad 73 F8
Massakory, Chad 73 F8
Massanella, Spain 36 B9
Massangena, Mozam. 85 C5
Massapê, Brazil 122 B3
Massarosa, Italy 32 E7
Massat, France 26 F5
Massawa = Mitsiwa, Eritrea 77 D4
Massena, U.S.A. 107 B10
Massénya, Chad 73 F8
Masset, Canada 100 C2
Massiac, France 26 C7
Massif Central, France 26 D7
Massillon, U.S.A. 106 F3
Massinga, Mozam. 85 C6
Masson, Canada 107 A9
Masson I., Antarctica 5 C7
Maştağa, Azerbaijan 43 K10
Mastanli = Momchilgrad, Bulgaria 39 H8
Masterton, N.Z. 87 J5
Mástikho, Ákra, Greece 39 L9
Mastuj, Pakistan 63 A5
Mastung, Pakistan 60 E5
Mastūrah, Si. Arabia 76 C4
Masty, Belarus 40 F3
Masuda, Japan 49 G5
Masvingo, Zimbabwe 83 G3
Masvingo □, Zimbabwe 83 G3
Maswa □, Tanzania 82 C3
Maşyāf, Syria 66 E7
Mata de São João, Brazil 123 D4
Matabeleland North □, Zimbabwe 83 F2
Matabeleland South □, Zimbabwe 83 G2
Mataboor, Indonesia 57 E9
Matachel →, Spain 31 G4
Matachewan, Canada 98 C3
Matacuni →, Venezuela 121 C4
Matad, Mongolia 54 B6
Matadi, Zaïre 80 F2
Matagalpa, Nic. 116 D2
Matagami, Canada 98 C4
Matagami, L., Canada 98 C4

Matagorda, *U.S.A.* 109 L7
Matagorda B., *U.S.A.* 109 L6
Matagorda I., *U.S.A.* 109 L6
Matak, P., *Indonesia* 59 L6
Matakana, *Australia* 91 E4
Mátala, *Greece* 37 E6
Matalaque, *Peru* 124 D3
Matam, *Senegal* 78 B2
Matameye, *Niger* 79 C6
Matamoros, *Campeche, Mexico* 115 D6
Matamoros, *Coahuila, Mexico* 114 B4
Matamoros, *Puebla, Mexico* 115 D5
Matamoros, *Tamaulipas, Mexico* 115 B5
Ma'ṭan as Sarra, *Libya* 73 D9
Matandu →, *Tanzania* 83 D3
Matane, *Canada* 99 C6
Matang, *China* 52 F5
Matankari, *Niger* 79 C5
Matanzas, *Cuba* 116 B3
Matapan, C. = Taínaron, Ákra, *Greece* 39 N5
Matapédia, *Canada* 99 C6
Matara, *Sri Lanka* 60 S12
Mataram, *Indonesia* 56 F5
Matarani, *Peru* 124 D3
Mataranka, *Australia* 88 B5
Matarma, Râs, *Egypt* 69 E1
Mataró, *Spain* 28 D7
Matarraña →, *Spain* 28 D5
Matatiele, *S. Africa* 85 E4
Mataura, *N.Z.* 87 M2
Mategua, *Bolivia* 125 C5
Matehuala, *Mexico* 114 C4
Mateira, *Brazil* 123 E1
Mateke Hills, *Zimbabwe* 83 G3
Matélica, *Italy* 33 E10
Matera, *Italy* 35 B9
Mátészalka, *Hungary* 21 H12
Matetsi, *Zimbabwe* 83 F2
Mateur, *Tunisia* 75 A6
Matfors, *Sweden* 10 B11
Matha, *France* 26 C3
Matheson Island, *Canada* 101 C9
Mathis, *U.S.A.* 109 L6
Mathura, *India* 62 F7
Mati, *Phil.* 55 H7
Mati →, *Albania* 39 H2
Matías Romero, *Mexico* 115 D5
Matibane, *Mozam.* 83 E5
Matima, *Botswana* 84 C3
Matiri Ra., *N.Z.* 87 J4
Matlock, *U.K.* 12 D6
Matmata, *Tunisia* 75 B6
Matna, *Sudan* 77 E4
Mato →, *Venezuela* 121 B4
Mato, Serrania de, *Venezuela* 120 B4
Mato Grosso □, *Brazil* 125 C6
Mato Grosso, Planalto do, *Brazil* 125 C7
Mato Grosso, Plateau of, *Brazil* 118 E5
Mato Grosso do Sul □, *Brazil* 125 D7
Matochkin Shar, *Russia* 44 B6
Matopo Hills, *Zimbabwe* 83 G2
Matopos, *Zimbabwe* 83 G2
Matosinhos, *Portugal* 30 D2
Matour, *France* 27 B8
Matsena, *Nigeria* 79 C7
Matsesta, *Russia* 43 J4
Matsu Tao, *Taiwan* 53 E13
Matsue, *Japan* 49 G6
Matsumae, *Japan* 48 D10
Matsumoto, *Japan* 49 F9
Matsusaka, *Japan* 49 G8
Matsuura, *Japan* 49 H4
Matsuyama, *Japan* 49 H6
Mattagami →, *Canada* 98 B3
Mattancheri, *India* 60 Q10
Mattawa, *Canada* 98 C4
Mattawamkeag, *U.S.A.* 99 C6
Matterhorn, *Switz.* 22 E5
Matthew Town, *Bahamas* 117 B5
Matthew's Ridge, *Guyana* 121 B5
Mattice, *Canada* 98 C3
Mattituck, *U.S.A.* 107 F12
Mattmar, *Sweden* 10 A7
Matuba, *Mozam.* 85 C5
Matucana, *Peru* 124 C2
Matun, *Afghan.* 62 C3
Maturín, *Venezuela* 121 B5
Matveyev Kurgan, *Russia* 43 G4
Mau, *India* 63 G10
Mau Escarpment, *Kenya* 82 C4
Mau Ranipur, *India* 63 G8
Maubeuge, *France* 25 B10
Maubourguet, *France* 26 E4
Maud, Pt., *Australia* 88 D1
Maude, *Australia* 91 E3
Maudin Sun, *Burma* 61 M19
Maués, *Brazil* 121 D6
Mauganj, *India* 61 G12
Maui, *U.S.A.* 102 H16
Maulamyaing = Moulmein, *Burma* 61 L20
Maule □, *Chile* 126 D1
Mauléon-Licharre, *France* 26 E3
Maullín, *Chile* 128 B2
Maumee, *U.S.A.* 104 E4
Maumee →, *U.S.A.* 104 E4
Maumere, *Indonesia* 57 F6
Maun, *Botswana* 84 B3
Mauna Kea, *U.S.A.* 102 J17
Mauna Loa, *U.S.A.* 102 J17
Maungmagan Kyunzu, *Burma* 61 M20
Maupin, *U.S.A.* 110 D3
Maure-de-Bretagne, *France* 24 E5
Maurepas, L., *U.S.A.* 109 K9
Maures, *France* 27 E10
Mauriac, *France* 26 C6
Maurice, L., *Australia* 89 E5
Maurienne, *France* 27 C10
Mauritania ■, *Africa* 74 D3
Mauritius ■, *Ind. Oc.* 70 J9
Mauron, *France* 24 D4
Maurs, *France* 26 D6
Mauston, *U.S.A.* 108 D9
Mauterndorf, *Austria* 21 H3
Mauvezin, *France* 26 E4
Mauzé-sur-le-Mignon, *France* 26 B3
Mavaca →, *Venezuela* 121 C4
Mavinga, *Angola* 81 H4
Mavli, *India* 62 G5
Mavrova, *Albania* 39 J2
Mavuradonha Mts., *Zimbabwe* 83 F3
Mawa, *Zaïre* 82 B2
Mawana, *India* 62 E7
Mawand, *Pakistan* 62 E3
Mawk Mai, *Burma* 61 J20
Mawlaik, *Burma* 61 H19
Mawquq, *Si. Arabia* 64 E4
Mawson Coast, *Antarctica* 5 C6
Max, *U.S.A.* 108 B4
Maxcanú, *Mexico* 115 C6
Maxesibeni, *S. Africa* 85 E4
Maxhamish L., *Canada* 100 B4
Maxixe, *Mozam.* 85 C6
Maxville, *Canada* 107 A10
Maxwell, *U.S.A.* 112 F4
Maxwelton, *Australia* 90 C3
May Downs, *Australia* 90 C4
May Pen, *Jamaica* 116 C4
Maya, *Spain* 28 B3
Maya →, *Russia* 45 D14
Maya Mts., *Belize* 115 D7
Mayaguana, *Bahamas* 117 B5
Mayagüez, *Puerto Rico* 117 C6
Mayahi, *Niger* 79 C6
Mayals, *Spain* 28 D5
Mayāmey, *Iran* 65 B7
Mayang, *China* 52 D7
Mayarí, *Cuba* 117 B4
Maybell, *U.S.A.* 110 F9
Maychew, *Ethiopia* 77 E4
Maydān, *Iraq* 67 E11
Maydena, *Australia* 90 G4
Mayen, *Germany* 19 E3
Mayenne, *France* 24 D6
Mayenne □, *France* 24 D6
Mayenne →, *France* 24 E6
Mayer, *U.S.A.* 111 J7
Mayerthorpe, *Canada* 100 C5
Mayfield, *U.S.A.* 105 G1
Mayhill, *U.S.A.* 111 K11
Maykop, *Russia* 43 H5
Maymyo, *Burma* 58 A1
Maynard, *U.S.A.* 112 C4
Maynard Hills, *Australia* 89 E2
Mayne →, *Australia* 90 C3
Maynooth, *Ireland* 15 C5
Mayo, *Canada* 96 B6
Mayo □, *Ireland* 15 C2
Mayo →, *Argentina* 128 C3
Mayo →, *Peru* 124 B2
Mayo L., *Canada* 96 B6
Mayon Volcano, *Phil.* 55 E5
Mayor I., *N.Z.* 87 G6
Mayorga, *Spain* 30 C5
Mayotte, I., *Mayotte* 71 H8
Mayraira Pt., *Phil.* 55 B4
Mayskiy, *Russia* 43 J7
Mayson L., *Canada* 101 B7
Maysville, *U.S.A.* 104 F4
Mayu, *Indonesia* 57 D7
Mayville, *N. Dak., U.S.A.* 108 B6
Mayville, *N.Y., U.S.A.* 106 D5
Mayya, *Russia* 45 C14
Mazabuka, *Zambia* 83 F2
Mazagán = El Jadida, *Morocco* 74 B3
Mazagão, *Brazil* 121 D7
Mazamet, *France* 26 E6
Mazán, *Peru* 120 D3
Māzandarān □, *Iran* 65 B7
Mazapil, *Mexico* 114 C4
Mazar, O. →, *Algeria* 75 B5
Mazara del Vallo, *Italy* 34 E5
Mazarredo, *Argentina* 128 C3
Mazarrón, *Spain* 29 H3
Mazarrón, G. de, *Spain* 29 H3
Mazaruni →, *Guyana* 121 B6
Mazatán, *Mexico* 114 B2
Mazatenango, *Guatemala* 116 D1
Mazatlán, *Mexico* 114 C3
Mažeikiai, *Lithuania* 9 H20
Māzhān, *Iran* 65 C8
Mazīnān, *Iran* 65 B8
Mazoe, *Mozam.* 83 F3
Mazoe →, *Mozam.* 83 F3
Mazowe, *Zimbabwe* 83 F3
Mazrûb, *Sudan* 77 E2
Mazu Dao, *China* 53 D12
Mazurian Lakes = Mazurski, Pojezierze, *Poland* 20 B10
Mazurski, Pojezierze, *Poland* 20 B10
Mazyr, *Belarus* 41 F5
Mazzarino, *Italy* 35 E7
Mbaba, *Senegal* 78 C1
Mbabane, *Swaziland* 85 D5
Mbagne, *Mauritania* 78 B2
M'bahiakro, *Ivory C.* 78 D4
Mbaïki, *C.A.R.* 80 D3
Mbala, *Zambia* 83 D3
Mbale, *Uganda* 82 B3
Mbalmayo, *Cameroon* 79 E7
Mbamba Bay, *Tanzania* 83 E3
Mbandaka, *Zaïre* 80 D3
Mbanga, *Cameroon* 79 E6
Mbanza Congo, *Angola* 80 F2
Mbanza Ngungu, *Zaïre* 80 F2
Mbarara, *Uganda* 82 C3
Mbashe →, *S. Africa* 85 E4
Mbatto, *Ivory C.* 78 D4
Mbenkuru →, *Tanzania* 83 D4
Mberengwa, *Zimbabwe* 83 G2
Mberengwa, Mt., *Zimbabwe* 83 G2
Mberubu, *Nigeria* 79 D6
Mbesuma, *Zambia* 83 D3
Mbeya, *Tanzania* 83 D3
Mbeya □, *Tanzania* 82 D3
Mbinga, *Tanzania* 83 E4
Mbinga □, *Tanzania* 83 E3
Mbini □, *Eq. Guin.* 80 D2
Mboki, *C.A.R.* 77 F2
Mboro, *Senegal* 78 B1
Mboune, *Senegal* 78 C2
Mbour, *Senegal* 78 C1
Mbout, *Mauritania* 78 B2
Mbozi □, *Tanzania* 83 D3
Mbuji-Mayi, *Zaïre* 82 D1
Mbulu, *Tanzania* 82 C4
Mbulu □, *Tanzania* 82 C4
Mburucuyá, *Argentina* 126 B4
Mcherrah, *Algeria* 74 C4
Mchinja, *Tanzania* 83 D4
Mchinji, *Malawi* 83 E3
Mdennah, *Mauritania* 74 D3
Mead, L., *U.S.A.* 113 J12
Meade, *U.S.A.* 109 G4
Meadow, *Australia* 89 E1
Meadow Lake, *Canada* 101 C7
Meadow Lake Prov. Park, *Canada* 101 C7
Meadow Valley Wash →, *U.S.A.* 113 J12
Meadville, *U.S.A.* 106 E4
Meaford, *Canada* 98 D3
Mealhada, *Portugal* 30 E2
Mealy Mts., *Canada* 99 B8
Meander River, *Canada* 100 B5
Meares, C., *U.S.A.* 110 D2
Mearim →, *Brazil* 122 B3
Meath □, *Ireland* 15 C5
Meath Park, *Canada* 101 C7
Meaulne, *France* 26 B6
Meaux, *France* 25 D9
Mebechi-Gawa →, *Japan* 48 D10
Mecanhelas, *Mozam.* 83 F4
Mecaya →, *Colombia* 120 C2
Mecca = Makkah, *Si. Arabia* 68 C2
Mecca, *U.S.A.* 113 M10
Mechanicsburg, *U.S.A.* 106 F8
Mechanicville, *U.S.A.* 107 D11
Mechara, *Ethiopia* 77 F5
Mechelen, *Antwerpen, Belgium* 17 F4
Mechelen, *Limburg, Belgium* 17 G7
Mecheria, *Algeria* 75 B4
Mechernich, *Germany* 18 E2
Mechetinskaya, *Russia* 43 G5
Mechra Benâbbou, *Morocco* 74 B3
Mecitözü, *Turkey* 66 B6
Mecklenburg-Vorpommern □, *Germany* 18 B8
Mecklenburger Bucht, *Germany* 18 A7
Meconta, *Mozam.* 83 E4
Meda, *Australia* 88 C3
Meda, *Portugal* 30 E3
Medan, *Indonesia* 56 D1
Médanos, *Argentina* 128 A4
Medanosa, Pta., *Argentina* 128 C3
Medéa, *Algeria* 75 A5
Medeiros Neto, *Brazil* 123 E3
Medel, Pic, *Switz.* 23 C7
Medellín, *Colombia* 120 B2
Medelpad, *Sweden* 9 E17
Medemblik, *Neths.* 16 C6
Médenine, *Tunisia* 75 B7
Mederdra, *Mauritania* 78 B1
Medford, *Mass., U.S.A.* 107 D13
Medford, *Oreg., U.S.A.* 110 E2
Medford, *Wis., U.S.A.* 108 C9
Medgidia, *Romania* 38 E11
Medi, *Sudan* 77 F3
Media Agua, *Argentina* 126 C2
Media Luna, *Argentina* 126 C2
Mediaş, *Romania* 38 C7
Medical Lake, *U.S.A.* 110 C5
Medicina, *Italy* 33 D8
Medicine Bow, *U.S.A.* 110 F10
Medicine Bow Pk., *U.S.A.* 110 F10
Medicine Bow Ra., *U.S.A.* 110 F10
Medicine Hat, *Canada* 101 D6
Medicine Lake, *U.S.A.* 108 A2
Medicine Lodge, *U.S.A.* 109 G5
Medina = Al Madīnah, *Si. Arabia* 64 E3
Medina, *Brazil* 123 E3
Medina, *Colombia* 120 C3
Medina, *N. Dak., U.S.A.* 108 B5
Medina, *N.Y., U.S.A.* 106 C6
Medina, *Ohio, U.S.A.* 106 E3
Medina →, *U.S.A.* 109 L5
Medina de Ríoseco, *Spain* 30 D5
Medina del Campo, *Spain* 30 D6
Medina L., *U.S.A.* 109 L5
Medina-Sidonia, *Spain* 31 J5
Medinaceli, *Spain* 28 D2
Medinipur, *India* 63 H12
Mediterranean Sea, *Europe* 6 H7
Medjerda, O. →, *Tunisia* 75 A7
Medley, *Canada* 101 C6
Médoc, *France* 26 C3
Medstead, *Canada* 101 C7
Medulin, *Croatia* 33 D10
Medveda, *Serbia, Yug.* 21 N11
Medvedevo, *Russia* 42 B8
Medveditsa →, *Russia* 42 F6
Medveditsa →, *Russia* 42 B3
Medvedok, *Russia* 42 B10
Medvezhi, Ostrava, *Russia* 45 B17
Medvezhyegorsk, *Russia* 44 C4
Medway →, *U.K.* 13 F8
Medzilaborce, *Slovak Rep.* 20 F11
Meeberrie, *Australia* 89 E2
Meekatharra, *Australia* 89 E2
Meeker, *U.S.A.* 110 F10
Meer, *Belgium* 17 F5
Meerane, *Germany* 18 E8
Meerbeke, *Belgium* 17 G4
Meerhout, *Belgium* 17 F6
Meerle, *Belgium* 17 F5
Meersburg, *Germany* 19 H5
Meerssen, *Neths.* 17 G7
Meerut, *India* 62 E7
Meeteetse, *U.S.A.* 110 D9
Meeuwen, *Belgium* 17 F7
Mega, *Ethiopia* 77 G4
Megálo Petalí, *Greece* 39 M7
Megalópolis, *Greece* 39 M5
Meganísi, *Greece* 39 L3
Mégara, *Greece* 39 M6
Megève, *France* 27 C10
Meghalaya □, *India* 61 G17
Meghezez, *Ethiopia* 77 F4
Mégiscane, L., *Canada* 98 C4
Megra, *Russia* 40 B9
Mehadia, *Romania* 38 E5
Mehaigne →, *Belgium* 17 G6
Mehaïguene, O. →, *Algeria* 75 B5
Meheisa, *Sudan* 76 D3
Mehndawal, *India* 63 F10
Mehr Jān, *Iran* 65 C7
Mehrābād, *Iran* 67 D12
Mehrān, *Iran* 67 F12
Mehrīz, *Iran* 65 D7
Mehun-sur-Yèvre, *France* 25 E9
Mei Jiang →, *China* 53 E11
Mei Xian, *Guangdong, China* 53 E11
Mei Xian, *Shaanxi, China* 50 G4
Meia Ponte →, *Brazil* 123 E2
Meicheng, *China* 53 C12
Meichengzhen, *China* 53 C8
Meichuan, *China* 53 B10
Meiganga, *Cameroon* 80 C2
Meijel, *Neths.* 17 F7
Meiktila, *Burma* 61 J19
Meilen, *Switz.* 23 B7
Meiningen, *Germany* 18 E6
Meio →, *Brazil* 123 D3
Meira, Sierra de, *Spain* 30 B3
Meiringen, *Switz.* 22 C6
Meishan, *China* 52 B4
Meissen, *Germany* 18 D9
Meissner, *Germany* 18 D5
Meitan, *China* 52 D6
Mejillones, *Chile* 126 A1
Meka, *Australia* 89 E2
Mékambo, *Gabon* 80 D2
Mekdela, *Ethiopia* 77 E4
Mekele, *Ethiopia* 77 E4
Mekhtar, *Pakistan* 60 D6
Meknès, *Morocco* 74 B3
Meko, *Nigeria* 79 D5
Mekong →, *Asia* 59 H6
Mekongga, *Indonesia* 57 E6
Mekvari = Kür →, *Azerbaijan* 67 C13
Melagiri Hills, *India* 60 N10
Melah, Sebkhet el, *Algeria* 75 C4
Melaka, *Malaysia* 59 L4
Melalap, *Malaysia* 56 C5
Mélambes, *Greece* 37 D6
Melanesia, *Pac. Oc.* 92 H7
Melbourne, *Australia* 91 F3
Melbourne, *U.S.A.* 105 L5
Melchor Múzquiz, *Mexico* 114 B4
Melchor Ocampo, *Mexico* 114 C4
Méldola, *Italy* 33 D9
Meldorf, *Germany* 18 A5
Melegnano, *Italy* 32 C6
Melenci, *Serbia, Yug.* 21 K10
Melenki, *Russia* 42 C5
Mélèzes →, *Canada* 97 C12
Melfi, *Chad* 73 F8
Melfi, *Italy* 35 B8
Melfort, *Canada* 101 C8
Melfort, *Zimbabwe* 83 F3
Melgaço, *Madeira* 30 C2
Melgar de Fernamental, *Spain* 30 C6
Melhus, *Norway* 10 A4
Melick, *Neths.* 17 F8
Melide, *Switz.* 23 E7
Meligalá, *Greece* 39 M4
Melilla, *N. Afr.* 75 A4
Melipilla, *Chile* 126 C1
Mélissa, Ákra, *Greece* 37 D6
Melita, *Canada* 101 D8
Mélito di Porto Salvo, *Italy* 35 E8
Melitopol, *Ukraine* 41 J8
Melk, *Austria* 21 G5
Mellansel, *Sweden* 8 E18
Melle, *Belgium* 17 G3
Melle, *France* 26 B3
Melle, *Germany* 18 C4
Mellégue, O. →, *Tunisia* 75 A6
Mellen, *U.S.A.* 108 B9
Mellerud, *Sweden* 11 F6
Mellette, *U.S.A.* 108 C5
Mellid, *Spain* 30 C2
Mellieha, *Malta* 37 D1
Mellit, *Sudan* 77 E2
Mellizo Sur, Cerro, *Chile* 128 C2
Mellrichstadt, *Germany* 19 E6
Melnik, *Bulgaria* 39 H6
Mělník, *Czech.* 20 E4
Melo, *Uruguay* 127 C5
Melolo, *Indonesia* 57 F6
Melouprey, *Cambodia* 58 F5
Melrhir, Chott, *Algeria* 75 B6
Melrose, *N.S.W., Australia* 91 E4
Melrose, *W. Austral., Australia* 89 E3
Melrose, *U.K.* 14 F6
Melrose, *U.S.A.* 109 H3
Mels, *Switz.* 23 B8
Melsele, *Belgium* 17 F4
Melstone, *U.S.A.* 110 C10
Melsungen, *Germany* 18 D5
Melton Mowbray, *U.K.* 12 E7
Melun, *France* 25 D9
Melut, *Sudan* 77 E3
Melville, *Canada* 101 C8
Melville, C., *Australia* 90 A3
Melville, L., *Canada* 99 B8
Melville B., *Australia* 90 A2
Melville I., *Australia* 88 B5
Melville I., *Canada* 4 B2
Melville Pen., *Canada* 97 B11
Melvin →, *Canada* 100 B5
Memaliaj, *Albania* 39 J2
Memba, *Mozam.* 83 E5
Memboro, *Indonesia* 57 F5
Membrilla, *Spain* 29 G1
Memel = Klaìpėda, *Lithuania* 9 J19
Memel, *S. Africa* 85 D4
Memmingen, *Germany* 19 H6
Mempawah, *Indonesia* 56 D3
Memphis, *Tenn., U.S.A.* 109 H10
Memphis, *Tex., U.S.A.* 109 H4
Mena, *Ukraine* 41 G7
Mena, *U.S.A.* 109 H7
Mena →, *Ethiopia* 77 F5
Menai Strait, *U.K.* 12 D3
Ménaka, *Mali* 79 B5
Menaldum, *Neths.* 16 B7
Menan = Chao Phraya →, *Thailand* 58 F3
Menarandra →, *Madag.* 85 D7
Menard, *U.S.A.* 109 K5
Menasha, *U.S.A.* 104 C1
Menate, *Indonesia* 56 E4
Mendawai →, *Indonesia* 56 E4
Mende, *France* 26 D7
Mendebo, *Ethiopia* 77 F4
Mendez, *Mexico* 115 B5
Mendhar, *India* 63 C6
Mendi, *Ethiopia* 77 F4
Mendip Hills, *U.K.* 13 F5
Mendocino, *U.S.A.* 110 G2
Mendocino, C., *U.S.A.* 110 F1
Mendota, *Calif., U.S.A.* 111 H3
Mendota, *Ill., U.S.A.* 108 E10
Mendoza, *Argentina* 126 C2
Mendoza □, *Argentina* 126 C2
Mendrisio, *Switz.* 23 E7
Mene Grande, *Venezuela* 120 B3
Menemen, *Turkey* 66 C2
Menen, *Belgium* 17 G2
Menéndez, L., *Argentina* 128 B2
Menfi, *Italy* 34 E5
Mengcheng, *China* 53 A11
Mengdingjie, *China* 52 F2
Mengeš, *Slovenia* 33 B11
Menggala, *Indonesia* 56 E3
Menghai, *China* 52 G3
Mengíbar, *Spain* 31 H7
Mengjin, *China* 50 G7
Mengla, *China* 52 G3
Menglian, *China* 52 F2
Mengoub, *Algeria* 74 C3
Mengshan, *China* 53 E8
Mengyin, *China* 51 G9
Mengzhe, *China* 52 F3
Mengzi, *China* 52 F4
Menihek L., *Canada* 99 B6
Menin = Menen, *Belgium* 17 G2
Menindee, *Australia* 91 E3
Menindee L., *Australia* 91 E3
Meningie, *Australia* 91 F2
Menlo Park, *U.S.A.* 112 H4
Menominee, *U.S.A.* 104 C2
Menominee →, *U.S.A.* 104 C2
Menomonie, *U.S.A.* 108 C9

Menongue, *Angola* 81 G3
Menorca, *Spain* 36 B11
Mentakab, *Malaysia* 59 L4
Mentawai, Kepulauan, *Indonesia* 56 E1
Menton, *France* 27 E11
Mentor, *U.S.A.* 106 E3
Menzel-Bourguiba, *Tunisia* 75 A6
Menzel Chaker, *Tunisia* 75 B7
Menzel-Temime, *Tunisia* 75 A7
Menzies, *Australia* 89 E3
Me'ona, *Israel* 69 B4
Meoqui, *Mexico* 114 B3
Mepaco, *Mozam.* 83 F3
Meppel, *Neths.* 16 C8
Meppen, *Germany* 18 C3
Mequinenza, *Spain* 28 D5
Mer, *France* 24 E8
Mer Rouge, *U.S.A.* 109 J9
Merabéllou, Kólpos, *Greece* 37 D7
Meramangye, L., *Australia* 89 E5
Meran = Merano, *Italy* 33 B8
Merano, *Italy* 33 B8
Merate, *Italy* 32 C6
Merauke, *Indonesia* 57 F10
Merbabu, *Indonesia* 57 G14
Merbein, *Australia* 91 E3
Merca, *Somali Rep.* 68 G3
Mercadal, *Spain* 36 B11
Mercato Saraceno, *Italy* 33 E9
Merced, *U.S.A.* 111 H3
Merced Pk., *U.S.A.* 112 H7
Mercedes, *Buenos Aires, Argentina* 126 C4
Mercedes, *Corrientes, Argentina* 126 B4
Mercedes, *San Luis, Argentina* 126 C2
Mercedes, *Uruguay* 126 C4
Merceditas, *Chile* 126 B1
Mercer, *N.Z.* 87 G5
Mercer, *U.S.A.* 106 E4
Merchtem, *Belgium* 17 G4
Mercier, *Bolivia* 124 C4
Mercury, *U.S.A.* 113 J11
Mercy C., *Canada* 97 B13
Merdrignac, *France* 24 D4
Mere, *Belgium* 17 G3
Meredith, C., *Falk. Is.* 128 D4
Meredith, L., *U.S.A.* 109 H4
Merefa, *Ukraine* 41 H9
Merelbeke, *Belgium* 17 G3
Méréville, *France* 25 D9
Merga = Nukheila, *Sudan* 76 D2
Mergui Arch. = Myeik Kyunzu, *Burma* 59 G1
Mérida, *Mexico* 115 C7
Mérida, *Spain* 31 G4
Mérida, *Venezuela* 120 B3
Mérida □, *Venezuela* 120 B3
Mérida, Cord. de, *Venezuela* 120 B3
Meriden, *U.S.A.* 107 E12
Meridian, *Calif., U.S.A.* 112 F5
Meridian, *Idaho, U.S.A.* 110 E5
Meridian, *Miss., U.S.A.* 105 J1
Meridian, *Tex., U.S.A.* 109 K6
Mering, *Germany* 19 G7
Meriruma, *Brazil* 121 C7
Merkel, *U.S.A.* 109 J4
Merksem, *Belgium* 17 F4
Merksplas, *Belgium* 17 F5
Mermaid Reef, *Australia* 88 C2
Mern, *Denmark* 11 J6
Merowe, *Sudan* 76 D3
Merredin, *Australia* 89 F2
Merrick, *U.K.* 14 F4
Merrickville, *Canada* 107 B9
Merrill, *Oreg., U.S.A.* 110 E3
Merrill, *Wis., U.S.A.* 108 C10
Merriman, *U.S.A.* 108 D4
Merritt, *Canada* 100 C4
Merriwa, *Australia* 91 E5
Merriwagga, *Australia* 91 E4
Merry I., *Canada* 98 A4
Merrygoen, *Australia* 91 E4
Merryville, *U.S.A.* 109 K8
Mersa Fatma, *Eritrea* 68 E3
Mersch, *Lux.* 17 J8
Merseburg, *Germany* 18 D7
Mersey —►, *U.K.* 12 D5
Merseyside □, *U.K.* 12 D5
Mersin, *Turkey* 66 D6
Mersing, *Malaysia* 59 L4
Merta, *India* 62 F6
Mertert, *Lux.* 17 J8
Merthyr Tydfil, *U.K.* 13 F4
Merthyr Tydfil □, *U.K.* 13 F4
Mértola, *Portugal* 31 H3
Mertzig, *Lux.* 17 J8
Mertzon, *U.S.A.* 109 K4
Méru, *France* 25 C9
Meru, *Kenya* 82 B4
Meru, *Tanzania* 82 C4
Meru □, *Kenya* 82 B4
Merville, *France* 25 B9
Méry-sur-Seine, *France* 25 D10
Merzifon, *Turkey* 66 B6
Merzig, *Germany* 19 F2
Merzouga, Erg Tin, *Algeria* 75 D7
Mesa, *U.S.A.* 111 K8
Mesach Mellet, *Libya* 75 D7
Mesagne, *Italy* 35 B10
Mesanagrós, *Greece* 37 C9
Mesaoría □, *Cyprus* 37 D12
Mesarás, Kólpos, *Greece* 37 D6
Meschede, *Germany* 18 D4
Mescit, *Turkey* 67 B9
Mesfinto, *Ethiopia* 77 E4
Mesgouez, L., *Canada* 98 B4
Meshchovsk, *Russia* 42 C2
Meshed = Mashhad, *Iran* 65 B8
Meshoppen, *U.S.A.* 107 E8
Meshra er Req, *Sudan* 77 F2
Mesick, *U.S.A.* 104 C3
Mesilinka —►, *Canada* 100 B4
Mesilla, *U.S.A.* 111 K10
Meslay-du-Maine, *France* 24 E6
Mesocco, *Switz.* 23 D8
Mesolóngion, *Greece* 39 L4
Mesopotamia = Al Jazirah, *Iraq* 67 E10
Mesoraca, *Italy* 35 C9
Mesquite, *U.S.A.* 111 H6
Mess Cr. —►, *Canada* 100 B2
Messac, *France* 24 E5
Messad, *Algeria* 75 B5
Messalo —►, *Mozam.* 83 E4
Méssaména, *Cameroon* 79 E7
Messancy, *Belgium* 17 J7
Messier, Canal, *Chile* 128 C2
Messina, *Italy* 35 D8
Messina, *S. Africa* 85 C5
Messina, Str. di, *Italy* 35 D8
Messíni, *Greece* 39 M5
Messiniakós Kólpos, *Greece* 39 N5
Messkirch, *Germany* 19 H5
Messonghi, *Greece* 37 B3
Mesta —►, *Bulgaria* 39 H7
Mestanza, *Spain* 31 G6
Mestre, *Italy* 33 C9
Mestre, Espigão, *Brazil* 123 D2
Městys Zelezná Ruda, *Czech.* 20 F3
Mesudiye, *Turkey* 66 B7
Meta □, *Colombia* 120 C3
Meta —►, *S. Amer.* 120 B4
Metairie, *U.S.A.* 109 L9
Metaline Falls, *U.S.A.* 110 B5
Metán, *Argentina* 126 B3
Metangula, *Mozam.* 83 E3
Metáuro —►, *Italy* 33 E10
Metema, *Ethiopia* 77 E4
Metengobalame, *Mozam.* 83 E3
Méthana, *Greece* 39 M6
Methven, *N.Z.* 87 K3
Methy L., *Canada* 101 B7
Metil, *Mozam.* 83 F4
Metlakatla, *U.S.A.* 100 B2
Metlaoui, *Tunisia* 75 B6
Metlika, *Slovenia* 33 C12
Metropolis, *U.S.A.* 109 G10
Mettet, *Belgium* 17 H5
Mettur Dam, *India* 60 P10
Metz, *France* 25 C13
Meulaboh, *Indonesia* 56 D1
Meulan, *France* 25 C8
Meung-sur-Loire, *France* 25 E8
Meureudu, *Indonesia* 56 C1
Meurthe —►, *France* 25 D13
Meurthe-et-Moselle □, *France* 25 D13
Meuse □, *France* 25 C12
Meuse —►, *Europe* 17 G7
Meuselwitz, *Germany* 18 D8
Mexborough, *U.K.* 12 D6
Mexia, *U.S.A.* 109 K6
Mexiana, I., *Brazil* 122 A2
Mexicali, *Mexico* 114 A1
Mexican Plateau, *Mexico* 94 G9
México, *Mexico* 115 D5
Mexico, *Maine, U.S.A.* 107 B14
Mexico, *Mo., U.S.A.* 108 F9
México □, *Mexico* 114 D5
Mexico ■, *Cent. Amer.* 114 C4
Mexico, G. of, *Cent. Amer.* 115 C7
Meyenburg, *Germany* 18 B8
Meymac, *France* 26 C6
Meymaneh, *Afghan.* 60 B4
Meyrargues, *France* 27 E9
Meyrueis, *France* 26 D7
Meyssac, *France* 26 C5
Mezdra, *Bulgaria* 38 F6
Mèze, *France* 26 E7
Mezen, *Russia* 44 C5
Mezen —►, *Russia* 44 C5
Mézene, *France* 27 D8
Mezha —►, *Russia* 40 E6
Mézidon, *France* 24 C6
Mézilhac, *France* 27 D8
Mézin, *France* 26 D4
Mezőberény, *Hungary* 21 J11
Mezőkövácsháza, *Hungary* 21 J10
Mezőkövesd, *Hungary* 21 H10
Mézos, *France* 26 D2
Mezőtúr, *Hungary* 21 J10
Mezquital, *Mexico* 114 C4
Mezzolombardo, *Italy* 32 B8
Mgeta, *Tanzania* 83 D4
Mglin, *Russia* 41 F7
Mhlaba Hills, *Zimbabwe* 83 F3
Mhow, *India* 62 H6
Miahuatlán, *Mexico* 115 D5
Miajadas, *Spain* 31 F5
Miallo, *Australia* 90 B4
Miami, *Ariz., U.S.A.* 111 K8
Miami, *Fla., U.S.A.* 105 N5
Miami, *Tex., U.S.A.* 109 H4
Miami —►, *U.S.A.* 104 F3
Miami Beach, *U.S.A.* 105 N5
Mian Xian, *China* 50 H4
Mianchi, *China* 50 G6
Mīāndowāb, *Iran* 67 D12
Miandrivazo, *Madag.* 85 B8
Mīāneh, *Iran* 67 D12
Mianning, *China* 52 C4
Mianwali, *Pakistan* 62 C4
Mianyang, *Hubei, China* 53 B9
Mianyang, *Sichuan, China* 52 B5
Mianzhu, *China* 52 B5
Miaoli, *Taiwan* 53 E13
Miarinarivo, *Madag.* 85 B8
Miass, *Russia* 44 D7
Miastko, *Poland* 20 A6
Michelstadt, *Germany* 19 F5
Michigan □, *U.S.A.* 104 C3
Michigan, L., *U.S.A.* 104 C2
Michigan City, *U.S.A.* 104 E2
Michikamau L., *Canada* 99 B7
Michipicoten, *Canada* 98 C3
Michipicoten I., *Canada* 98 C2
Michoacan □, *Mexico* 114 D4
Michurin, *Bulgaria* 38 G10
Michurinsk, *Russia* 42 D5
Miclere, *Australia* 90 C4
Mico, Pta., *Nic.* 116 D3
Micronesia, Federated States of ■, *Pac. Oc.* 92 G7
Midai, P., *Indonesia* 59 L6
Midale, *Canada* 101 D8
Middagsfjället, *Sweden* 10 A6
Middelbeers, *Neths.* 17 F6
Middelburg, *Neths.* 17 F3
Middelburg, *Eastern Cape, S. Africa* 84 E3
Middelburg, *Mpumalanga, S. Africa* 85 D4
Middelfart, *Denmark* 11 J3
Middelharnis, *Neths.* 16 E4
Middelkerke, *Belgium* 17 F1
Middelrode, *Neths.* 17 E6
Middelwit, *S. Africa* 84 C4
Middle Alkali L., *U.S.A.* 110 F3
Middle Fork Feather —►, *U.S.A.* 112 F5
Middle I., *Australia* 89 F3
Middle Loup —►, *U.S.A.* 108 E5
Middleboro, *U.S.A.* 107 E14
Middleburg, *N.Y., U.S.A.* 107 D10
Middleburg, *Pa., U.S.A.* 106 F7
Middlebury, *U.S.A.* 107 B11
Middleport, *U.S.A.* 104 F4
Middlesboro, *U.S.A.* 105 G4
Middlesbrough, *U.K.* 12 C6
Middlesbrough □, *U.K.* 12 C6
Middlesex, *Belize* 116 C2
Middlesex, *U.S.A.* 107 F10
Middleton, *Australia* 90 C3
Middleton, *Canada* 99 D6
Middletown, *Calif., U.S.A.* 112 G4
Middletown, *Conn., U.S.A.* 107 E12
Middletown, *N.Y., U.S.A.* 107 E10
Middletown, *Ohio, U.S.A.* 104 F3
Middletown, *Pa., U.S.A.* 107 F8
Midelt, *Morocco* 74 B4
Midi, Canal du —►, *France* 26 E5
Midi d'Ossau, Pic du, *France* 26 F3
Midland, *Canada* 98 D4
Midland, *Calif., U.S.A.* 113 M12
Midland, *Mich., U.S.A.* 104 D3
Midland, *Pa., U.S.A.* 106 F4
Midland, *Tex., U.S.A.* 109 K3
Midlands □, *Zimbabwe* 83 F2
Midleton, *Ireland* 15 E3
Midlothian, *U.S.A.* 109 J6
Midlothian □, *U.K.* 14 F5
Midongy, Tangorombohitr' i, *Madag.* 85 C8
Midongy Atsimo, *Madag.* 85 C8
Midou —►, *France* 26 E3
Midouze —►, *France* 26 E3
Midsayap, *Phil.* 55 H6
Midu, *China* 52 E3
Midway Is., *Pac. Oc.* 92 E10
Midway Wells, *U.S.A.* 113 N11
Midwest, *U.S.A.* 103 B9
Midwest, *Wyo., U.S.A.* 110 E10
Midwest City, *U.S.A.* 109 H6
Midwolda, *Neths.* 16 B9
Midyat, *Turkey* 67 D9
Mie □, *Japan* 49 G8
Miechów, *Poland* 20 E10
Międzychód, *Poland* 20 C5
Międzyrzec Podlaski, *Poland* 20 D12
Międzyrzecz, *Poland* 20 C5
Miélan, *France* 26 E4
Mielec, *Poland* 20 E11
Mienga, *Angola* 84 B2
Miercurea Ciuc, *Romania* 38 C8
Mieres, *Spain* 30 B5
Mierlo, *Neths.* 17 F7
Mieso, *Ethiopia* 77 F5
Mifflintown, *U.S.A.* 106 F7
Mifraz H̱efa, *Israel* 69 C4
Migdāl, *Israel* 69 C4
Migennes, *France* 25 E10
Migliarino, *Italy* 33 D8
Miguel Alemán, Presa, *Mexico* 115 D5
Miguel Alves, *Brazil* 122 B3
Miguel Calmon, *Brazil* 122 D3
Mihaliççık, *Turkey* 66 C4
Mihara, *Japan* 49 G6
Mijares —►, *Spain* 28 F4
Mijas, *Spain* 31 J6
Mikese, *Tanzania* 82 D4
Mikha-Tskhakaya = Senaki, *Georgia* 43 J6
Mikhailovka = Mykhaylivka, *Ukraine* 41 J8
Mikhaylov, *Russia* 42 C4
Mikhaylovgrad, *Bulgaria* 38 F6
Mikhaylovka, *Russia* 42 E6
Mikhnevo, *Russia* 42 C3
Mikínai, *Greece* 39 M5
Mikkeli, *Finland* 9 F22
Mikkwa —►, *Canada* 100 B6
Mikniya, *Sudan* 77 D3
Mikołajki, *Poland* 20 B11
Míkonos, *Greece* 39 M8
Mikrón Dhérion, *Greece* 39 H9
Mikulov, *Czech.* 20 G6
Mikumi, *Tanzania* 82 D4
Milaca, *U.S.A.* 108 C8
Milagro, *Ecuador* 120 D2
Milagros, *Phil.* 55 E5
Milan = Milano, *Italy* 32 C6
Milan, *Mo., U.S.A.* 108 E8
Milan, *Tenn., U.S.A.* 105 H1
Milang, *Australia* 91 E2
Milange, *Mozam.* 83 F4
Milano, *Italy* 32 C6
Milâs, *Turkey* 66 D2
Mílatos, *Greece* 37 D7
Milazzo, *Italy* 35 D8
Milbank, *U.S.A.* 108 C6
Milden, *Canada* 101 C7
Mildmay, *Canada* 106 B3
Mildura, *Australia* 91 E3
Mile, *China* 52 E4
Miléai, *Greece* 39 K6
Miles, *Australia* 91 D5
Miles, *U.S.A.* 109 K4
Miles City, *U.S.A.* 108 B2
Milestone, *Canada* 101 D8
Mileto, *Italy* 35 D9
Miletto, Mte., *Italy* 35 A7
Miletus, *Turkey* 66 D2
Mileura, *Australia* 89 E2
Milford, *Calif., U.S.A.* 112 E6
Milford, *Conn., U.S.A.* 107 E11
Milford, *Del., U.S.A.* 104 F8
Milford, *Mass., U.S.A.* 107 D13
Milford, *Pa., U.S.A.* 107 E10
Milford, *Utah, U.S.A.* 111 G7
Milford Haven, *U.K.* 13 F2
Milford Sd., *N.Z.* 87 L1
Milgun, *Australia* 89 D2
Milḥ, Baḥr al, *Iraq* 67 F10
Miliana, *Aïn Salah, Algeria* 75 C5
Miliana, *Médéa, Algeria* 75 A5
Miling, *Australia* 89 F2
Militello in Val di Catánia, *Italy* 35 E7
Milk —►, *U.S.A.* 110 B10
Milk, Wadi el —►, *Sudan* 76 D3
Milk River, *Canada* 100 D6
Mill, *Neths.* 17 E7
Mill City, *U.S.A.* 110 D2
Mill I., *Antarctica* 5 C8
Mill Valley, *U.S.A.* 112 H4
Millau, *France* 26 D7
Millbridge, *Canada* 106 B7
Millbrook, *Canada* 106 B6
Mille Lacs, L. des, *Canada* 98 C1
Mille Lacs L., *U.S.A.* 108 B8
Milledgeville, *U.S.A.* 105 J4
Millen, *U.S.A.* 105 J5
Miller, *U.S.A.* 108 C5
Millerovo, *Russia* 43 F5
Millersburg, *Ohio, U.S.A.* 106 F3
Millersburg, *Pa., U.S.A.* 106 F8
Millerton, *U.S.A.* 107 E11
Millerton L., *U.S.A.* 112 J7
Millevaches, Plateau de, *France* 26 C6
Millicent, *Australia* 91 F3
Millingen, *Neths.* 16 E8
Millinocket, *U.S.A.* 99 C6
Millmerran, *Australia* 91 D5
Mills L., *Canada* 100 A5
Millsboro, *U.S.A.* 106 G4
Milltown Malbay, *Ireland* 15 D2
Millville, *U.S.A.* 104 F8
Millwood L., *U.S.A.* 109 J8
Milly-la-Forêt, *France* 25 D9
Milna, *Croatia* 33 E13
Milne —►, *Australia* 90 C2
Milne Inlet, *Canada* 97 A11
Milnor, *U.S.A.* 108 B6
Milo, *Canada* 100 C6
Mílos, *Greece* 39 N7
Miloševo, *Serbia, Yug.* 21 K10
Milparinka P.O., *Australia* 91 D3
Miltenberg, *Germany* 19 F5
Milton, *Canada* 106 C5
Milton, *N.Z.* 87 M2
Milton, *U.K.* 14 D4
Milton, *Calif., U.S.A.* 112 G6
Milton, *Fla., U.S.A.* 105 K2
Milton, *Pa., U.S.A.* 106 F8
Milton-Freewater, *U.S.A.* 110 D4
Milton Keynes, *U.K.* 13 E7
Miltou, *Chad* 73 F8
Milverton, *Canada* 106 C4
Milwaukee, *U.S.A.* 104 D2
Milwaukee Deep, *Atl. Oc.* 117 C6
Milwaukie, *U.S.A.* 112 E4
Mim, *Ghana* 78 D4
Mimizan, *France* 26 D2
Mimoso, *Brazil* 123 E2
Min Chiang —►, *China* 53 E12
Min Jiang —►, *China* 52 C5
Min Xian, *China* 50 G3
Mina, *U.S.A.* 111 G4
Mina Pirquitas, *Argentina* 126 A2
Mīnā Su'ud, *Si. Arabia* 65 D6
Mīnā'al Aḥmadī, *Kuwait* 65 D6
Mīnāb, *Iran* 65 E8
Minago —►, *Canada* 101 C9
Minaki, *Canada* 101 D10
Minamata, *Japan* 49 H5
Minami-Tori-Shima, *Pac. Oc.* 92 E7
Minas, *Uruguay* 127 C4
Minas, Sierra de las, *Guatemala* 116 C2
Minas Basin, *Canada* 99 C7
Minas de Rio Tinto, *Spain* 31 H4
Minas de San Quintín, *Spain* 31 G6
Minas Gerais □, *Brazil* 123 E2
Minas Novas, *Brazil* 123 E3
Minatitlán, *Mexico* 115 D6
Minbu, *Burma* 61 J19
Mincio —►, *Italy* 32 C7
Mindanao, *Phil.* 55 H6
Mindanao Sea = Bohol Sea, *Phil.* 57 C6
Mindanao Trench, *Pac. Oc.* 55 F7
Mindel —►, *Germany* 19 G6
Mindelheim, *Germany* 19 G6
Minden, *Canada* 106 B6
Minden, *Germany* 18 C4
Minden, *La., U.S.A.* 109 J8
Minden, *Nev., U.S.A.* 112 G7
Mindiptana, *Indonesia* 57 F10
Mindoro, *Phil.* 55 E4
Mindoro Str., *Phil.* 55 E4
Mindouli, *Congo* 80 E2
Mine, *Japan* 49 G5
Minehead, *U.K.* 13 F4
Mineiros, *Brazil* 125 D7
Mineola, *U.S.A.* 109 J7
Mineral King, *U.S.A.* 112 J8
Mineral Wells, *U.S.A.* 109 J5
Mineralnyye Vody, *Russia* 43 H6
Minersville, *Pa., U.S.A.* 107 F8
Minersville, *Utah, U.S.A.* 111 G7
Minerva, *U.S.A.* 106 F3
Minervino Murge, *Italy* 35 A9
Minetto, *U.S.A.* 107 C8
Mingäçevir, *Azerbaijan* 43 K8
Mingäçevir Su Anbarı, *Azerbaijan* 43 K8
Mingan, *Canada* 99 B7
Mingechaur = Mingäçevir, *Azerbaijan* 43 K8
Mingechaurskoye Vdkhr. = Mingäçevir Su Anbarı, *Azerbaijan* 43 K8
Mingela, *Australia* 90 B4
Mingenew, *Australia* 89 E2
Mingera Cr. —►, *Australia* 90 C2
Minggang, *China* 53 A10
Mingin, *Burma* 61 H19
Minglanilla, *Spain* 28 F3
Minglun, *China* 52 E7
Mingorria, *Spain* 30 E6
Mingt'iehkaitafan = Mintaka Pass, *Pakistan* 63 A6
Mingxi, *China* 53 D11
Mingyuegue, *China* 51 C15
Minho = Miño —►, *Spain* 30 D2
Minhou, *China* 53 E12
Minićevo, *Serbia, Yug.* 21 M12
Minidoka, *U.S.A.* 110 E7
Minigwal, L., *Australia* 89 E3
Minilya, *Australia* 89 D1
Minilya —►, *Australia* 89 D1
Minipi, L., *Canada* 99 B7
Mink L., *Canada* 100 A5
Minna, *Nigeria* 79 D6
Minneapolis, *Kans., U.S.A.* 108 F6
Minneapolis, *Minn., U.S.A.* 108 C8
Minnedosa, *Canada* 101 C9
Minnesota □, *U.S.A.* 108 B7
Minnesund, *Norway* 10 D5
Minnie Creek, *Australia* 89 D2
Minnipa, *Australia* 91 E2
Minnitaki L., *Canada* 98 C1
Mino, *Japan* 49 G8
Miño —►, *Spain* 30 D2
Minorca = Menorca, *Spain* 36 B11
Minore, *Australia* 91 E4
Minot, *U.S.A.* 108 A4
Minqin, *China* 50 E2
Minqing, *China* 53 D12
Minsen, *Germany* 18 B3
Minsk, *Belarus* 40 F4
Mińsk Mazowiecki, *Poland* 20 C11
Mintaka Pass, *Pakistan* 63 A6
Minto, *U.S.A.* 96 B5
Minton, *Canada* 101 D8
Minturn, *U.S.A.* 110 G10
Minturno, *Italy* 34 A6
Minûf, *Egypt* 76 H7
Minusinsk, *Russia* 45 D10
Minutang, *India* 61 E20
Minvoul, *Gabon* 80 D2
Minya el Qamh, *Egypt* 76 H7
Mionica, *Serbia, Yug.* 21 L10
Mir, *Niger* 79 C7
Mīr Kūh, *Iran* 65 E8
Mīr Shahdād, *Iran* 65 E8
Mira, *Italy* 33 C9
Mira, *Portugal* 30 E2
Mira —►, *Colombia* 120 C2
Mira —►, *Portugal* 31 H2
Mira por vos Cay, *Bahamas* 117 B5
Mirabella Eclano, *Italy* 35 A7
Miracema do Norte, *Brazil* 122 C2

Mirador, *Brazil* 122 C3
Miraflores, *Colombia* 120 C3
Miraj, *India* 60 L9
Miram Shah, *Pakistan* 62 C4
Miramar, *Argentina* 126 D4
Miramar, *Mozam.* 85 C6
Miramas, *France* 27 E8
Mirambeau, *France* 26 C3
Miramichi B., *Canada* 99 C7
Miramont-de-Guyenne, *France* 26 D4
Miranda, *Brazil* 125 E6
Miranda □, *Venezuela* 120 A4
Miranda →, *Brazil* 125 D6
Miranda de Ebro, *Spain* 28 C2
Miranda do Corvo, *Spain* 30 E2
Miranda do Douro, *Portugal* 30 D4
Mirande, *France* 26 E4
Mirandela, *Portugal* 30 D3
Mirando City, *U.S.A.* 109 M5
Mirándola, *Italy* 32 D8
Mirandópolis, *Brazil* 127 A5
Mirango, *Malawi* 83 E3
Mirani, *Australia* 90 C4
Mirano, *Italy* 33 C9
Mirassol, *Brazil* 127 A6
Mirbāţ, *Oman* 68 D5
Mirear, *Egypt* 76 C4
Mirebeau, *Côte-d'Or, France* 25 E12
Mirebeau, *Vienne, France* 24 F7
Mirecourt, *France* 25 D13
Mirgorod = Myrhorod, *Ukraine* 41 H7
Miri, *Malaysia* 56 D4
Miriam Vale, *Australia* 90 C5
Mirim, L., *S. Amer.* 127 C5
Mirimire, *Venezuela* 120 A4
Miriti, *Brazil* 125 B6
Mirnyy, *Russia* 45 C12
Mirond L., *Canada* 101 B8
Mirpur, *Pakistan* 63 C5
Mirpur Bibiwari, *Pakistan* 62 E2
Mirpur Khas, *Pakistan* 62 G3
Mirpur Sakro, *Pakistan* 62 G2
Mirria, *Niger* 79 C6
Mirror, *Canada* 100 C6
Mîrşani, *Romania* 38 E6
Miryang, *S. Korea* 51 G15
Mirzaani, *Georgia* 43 K8
Mirzapur, *India* 63 G10
Mirzapur-cum-Vindhyachal = Mirzapur, *India* 63 G10
Misantla, *Mexico* 115 D5
Misawa, *Japan* 48 D10
Miscou I., *Canada* 99 C7
Mish'āb, Ra'as al, *Si. Arabia* 65 D6
Mishagua →, *Peru* 124 C3
Mishan, *China* 54 B8
Mishawaka, *U.S.A.* 104 E2
Mishbih, Gebel, *Egypt* 76 C3
Mishima, *Japan* 49 G9
Misilmeri, *Italy* 34 D6
Misión, *Mexico* 113 N10
Misión Fagnano, *Argentina* 128 D3
Misiones □, *Argentina* 127 B5
Misiones □, *Paraguay* 126 B4
Miskah, *Si. Arabia* 64 E4
Miskitos, Cayos, *Nic.* 116 D3
Miskolc, *Hungary* 21 G10
Misoke, *Zaïre* 82 C2
Misool, *Indonesia* 57 E8
Misrātah, *Libya* 73 B8
Missanabie, *Canada* 98 C3
Missão Velha, *Brazil* 122 C4
Missinaibi →, *Canada* 98 B3
Missinaibi L., *Canada* 98 C3
Mission, *S. Dak., U.S.A.* 108 D4
Mission, *Tex., U.S.A.* 109 M5
Mission City, *Canada* 100 D4
Mission Viejo, *U.S.A.* 113 M9
Missisa L., *Canada* 98 B2
Missisagi →, *Canada* 98 C3
Mississippi □, *U.S.A.* 109 J10
Mississippi →, *U.S.A.* 109 L10
Mississippi L., *Canada* 107 A8
Mississippi River Delta, *U.S.A.* 109 L9
Mississippi Sd., *U.S.A.* 109 K10
Missoula, *U.S.A.* 110 C6
Missour, *Morocco* 74 B4
Missouri □, *U.S.A.* 108 F8
Missouri →, *U.S.A.* 108 F9
Missouri Valley, *U.S.A.* 108 E7
Mist, *U.S.A.* 112 E3
Mistake B., *Canada* 101 A10
Mistassini →, *Canada* 99 C5
Mistassini L., *Canada* 98 B5
Mistastin L., *Canada* 99 A7
Mistatim, *Canada* 101 C8
Mistelbach, *Austria* 20 G6
Misterbianco, *Italy* 35 E8
Mistretta, *Italy* 35 E7
Misty L., *Canada* 101 B8
Misurata = Misrātah, *Libya* 73 B8
Mît Ghamr, *Egypt* 76 H7
Mitatib, *Sudan* 77 D4
Mitchell, *Australia* 91 D4
Mitchell, *Canada* 106 C3
Mitchell, *Ind., U.S.A.* 104 F2
Mitchell, *Nebr., U.S.A.* 108 E3
Mitchell, *Oreg., U.S.A.* 110 D3
Mitchell, *S. Dak., U.S.A.* 108 D5
Mitchell →, *Australia* 90 B3
Mitchell, Mt., *U.S.A.* 105 H4
Mitchell Ras., *Australia* 90 A2
Mitchelstown, *Ireland* 15 D3
Mitha Tiwana, *Pakistan* 62 C5
Mitilíni, *Greece* 39 K9
Mito, *Japan* 49 F10
Mitrofanovka, *Russia* 42 F4
Mitrovica = Titova-Mitrovica, *Serbia, Yug.* 21 N10
Mitsinjo, *Madag.* 85 B8
Mitsiwa, *Eritrea* 77 D4
Mitsiwa Channel, *Eritrea* 77 D5
Mitsukaidō, *Japan* 49 F9
Mittagong, *Australia* 91 E5
Mittelland, *Switz.* 22 C4
Mittellandkanal →, *Germany* 18 C3
Mittenwalde, *Germany* 18 C9
Mitterteich, *Germany* 19 F8
Mittweida, *Germany* 18 E8
Mitú, *Colombia* 120 C3
Mituas, *Colombia* 120 C4
Mitumba, *Tanzania* 82 D3
Mitumba, Chaîne des, *Zaïre* 82 D2
Mitumba Mts. = Mitumba, Chaîne des, *Zaïre* 82 D2
Mitwaba, *Zaïre* 83 D2
Mityana, *Uganda* 82 B3
Mitzic, *Gabon* 80 D2
Mixteco →, *Mexico* 115 D5
Miyagi □, *Japan* 48 E10
Miyâh, W. el →, *Egypt* 76 B3
Miyah, W. el →, *Syria* 64 C3
Miyake-Jima, *Japan* 49 G9
Miyako, *Japan* 48 E10
Miyako-Jima, *Japan* 49 M2
Miyako-Rettō, *Japan* 49 M2
Miyakonojō, *Japan* 49 J5
Miyanoura-Dake, *Japan* 49 J5
Miyazaki, *Japan* 49 J5
Miyazaki □, *Japan* 49 H5
Miyazu, *Japan* 49 G7
Miyet, Bahr el = Dead Sea, *Asia* 69 D4
Miyi, *China* 52 D4
Miyoshi, *Japan* 49 G6
Miyun, *China* 50 D9
Miyun Shuiku, *China* 51 D9
Mizdah, *Libya* 75 B7
Mizen Hd., *Cork, Ireland* 15 E2
Mizen Hd., *Wick., Ireland* 15 D5
Mizhi, *China* 50 F6
Mizil, *Romania* 38 E9
Mizoram □, *India* 61 H18
Mizpe Ramon, *Israel* 69 E3
Mizusawa, *Japan* 48 E10
Mjöbäck, *Sweden* 11 G6
Mjölby, *Sweden* 11 F9
Mjörn, *Sweden* 11 G6
Mjøsa, *Norway* 10 D5
Mkata, *Tanzania* 82 D4
Mkokotoni, *Tanzania* 82 D4
Mkomazi, *Tanzania* 82 C4
Mkomazi →, *S. Africa* 85 E5
Mkulwe, *Tanzania* 83 D3
Mkumbi, Ras, *Tanzania* 82 D4
Mkushi, *Zambia* 83 E2
Mkushi River, *Zambia* 83 E2
Mkuze, *S. Africa* 85 D5
Mladá Boleslav, *Czech.* 20 E4
Mladenovac, *Serbia, Yug.* 21 L10
Mlala Hills, *Tanzania* 82 D3
Mlange, *Malawi* 83 F4
Mlava →, *Serbia, Yug.* 21 L11
Mława, *Poland* 20 B10
Mliniště, *Bos.-H.* 33 D13
Mljet, *Croatia* 21 N7
Młynary, *Poland* 20 A9
Mmabatho, *S. Africa* 84 D4
Mme, *Cameroon* 79 D7
Mo i Rana, *Norway* 8 C16
Moa, *Indonesia* 57 F7
Moa →, *S. Leone* 78 D2
Moab, *U.S.A.* 111 G9
Moabi, *Gabon* 80 E2
Moaco →, *Brazil* 124 B4
Moala, *Fiji* 87 D8
Moalie Park, *Australia* 91 D3
Moaña, *Spain* 30 C2
Moba, *Zaïre* 82 D2
Mobārakābād, *Iran* 65 D7
Mobārakīyeh, *Iran* 65 C6
Mobaye, *C.A.R.* 80 D4
Mobayi, *Zaïre* 80 D4
Moberly, *U.S.A.* 108 F8
Moberly →, *Canada* 100 B4
Mobile, *U.S.A.* 105 K1
Mobile B., *U.S.A.* 105 K2
Mobridge, *U.S.A.* 108 C4
Mobutu Sese Seko, L. = Albert L., *Africa* 82 B3
Moc Chau, *Vietnam* 58 B5
Moc Hoa, *Vietnam* 59 G5
Mocabe Kasari, *Zaïre* 83 D2
Mocajuba, *Brazil* 122 B2
Moçambique, *Mozam.* 83 F5
Moçâmedes = Namibe, *Angola* 81 H2
Mocapra →, *Venezuela* 120 B4
Mocha, I., *Chile* 128 A2
Mochudi, *Botswana* 84 C4
Mocimboa da Praia, *Mozam.* 83 E5
Moclips, *U.S.A.* 112 C2
Mocoa, *Colombia* 120 C2
Mococa, *Brazil* 127 A6
Mocorito, *Mexico* 114 B3
Moctezuma, *Mexico* 114 B3
Moctezuma →, *Mexico* 115 C5
Mocuba, *Mozam.* 83 F4
Mocúzari, Presa, *Mexico* 114 B3
Modane, *France* 27 C10
Modasa, *India* 62 H5
Modave, *Belgium* 17 H6
Modder →, *S. Africa* 84 D3
Modderrivier, *S. Africa* 84 D3
Módena, *Italy* 32 D7
Modena, *U.S.A.* 111 H7
Modesto, *U.S.A.* 111 H3
Módica, *Italy* 35 F7
Modigliana, *Italy* 33 D8
Modo, *Sudan* 77 F3
Modra, *Slovak Rep.* 21 G7
Moe, *Australia* 91 F4
Moebase, *Mozam.* 83 F4
Moëlan-sur-Mer, *France* 24 E3
Moengo, *Surinam* 121 B7
Moergestel, *Neths.* 17 E6
Moers, *Germany* 17 F9
Moësa →, *Switz.* 23 D8
Moffat, *U.K.* 14 F5
Moga, *India* 62 D6
Mogadishu = Muqdisho, *Somali Rep.* 68 G4
Mogador = Essaouira, *Morocco* 74 B3
Mogadouro, *Portugal* 30 D4
Mogalakwena →, *S. Africa* 85 C4
Mogami →, *Japan* 48 E10
Mogán, *Canary Is.* 36 G4
Mogaung, *Burma* 61 G20
Møgeltønder, *Denmark* 11 K2
Mogente, *Spain* 29 G4
Mogho, *Ethiopia* 77 G5
Mogi das Cruzes, *Brazil* 127 A6
Mogi-Guaçu →, *Brazil* 127 A6
Mogi-Mirim, *Brazil* 127 A6
Mogielnica, *Poland* 20 D10
Mogilev = Mahilyow, *Belarus* 40 F6
Mogilev-Podolskiy = Mohyliv-Podilskyy, *Ukraine* 41 H4
Mogilno, *Poland* 20 C7
Mogincual, *Mozam.* 83 F5
Mogliano Véneto, *Italy* 33 C9
Mogocha, *Russia* 45 D12
Mogoi, *Indonesia* 57 E8
Mogok, *Burma* 61 H20
Moguer, *Spain* 31 H4
Mogumber, *Australia* 89 F2
Mohács, *Hungary* 21 K8
Mohales Hoek, *Lesotho* 84 E4
Mohall, *U.S.A.* 108 A4
Moḥammadābād, *Iran* 65 B8
Mohammadia, *Algeria* 75 A5
Mohammedia, *Morocco* 74 B3
Mohave, L., *U.S.A.* 113 K12
Mohawk →, *U.S.A.* 107 D11
Möhne →, *Germany* 18 D3
Moholm, *Sweden* 11 F8
Mohoro, *Tanzania* 82 D4
Mohyliv-Podilskyy, *Ukraine* 41 H4
Moia, *Sudan* 77 F2
Moidart, L., *U.K.* 14 E3
Moinești, *Romania* 38 C9
Moirans, *France* 27 C9
Moirans-en-Montagne, *France* 27 B9
Moíres, *Greece* 37 D6
Moisaküla, *Estonia* 9 G21
Moisie, *Canada* 99 B6
Moisie →, *Canada* 99 B6
Moissac, *France* 26 D5
Moïssala, *Chad* 73 G8
Moita, *Portugal* 31 G2
Mojácar, *Spain* 29 H3
Mojados, *Spain* 30 D6
Mojave, *U.S.A.* 113 K8
Mojave Desert, *U.S.A.* 113 L10
Mojiang, *China* 52 F3
Mojo, *Bolivia* 126 A2
Mojo, *Ethiopia* 77 F4
Mojokerto, *Indonesia* 57 G15
Mojos, Llanos de, *Bolivia* 125 D5
Moju →, *Brazil* 122 B2
Mokai, *N.Z.* 87 H5
Mokambo, *Zaïre* 83 E2
Mokameh, *India* 63 G11
Mokelumne →, *U.S.A.* 112 G5
Mokelumne Hill, *U.S.A.* 112 G6
Mokhós, *Greece* 37 D7
Mokhotlong, *Lesotho* 85 D4
Moknine, *Tunisia* 75 A7
Mokokchung, *India* 61 F19
Mokra Gora, *Serbia, Yug.* 21 N10
Mokronog, *Slovenia* 33 C12
Moksha →, *Russia* 42 C6
Mokshan, *Russia* 42 D7
Mol, *Belgium* 17 F6
Mola, C. de la, *Spain* 28 F9
Mola di Bari, *Italy* 35 A10
Moláoi, *Greece* 39 N5
Molat, *Croatia* 33 D11
Molchanovo, *Russia* 44 D9
Mold, *U.K.* 12 D4
Moldavia, *Romania* 38 C10
Moldavia ■ = Moldova ■, *Europe* 41 J5
Molde, *Norway* 8 E12
Moldova ■, *Europe* 41 J5
Moldova Nouă, *Romania* 38 E4
Moldoveana, *Romania* 38 D7
Molepolole, *Botswana* 84 C4
Moléson, *Switz.* 22 C4
Molfetta, *Italy* 35 A9
Molina de Aragón, *Spain* 28 E3
Moline, *U.S.A.* 108 E9
Molinella, *Italy* 33 D8
Molinos, *Argentina* 126 B2
Moliro, *Zaïre* 82 D3
Molise □, *Italy* 33 G11
Moliterno, *Italy* 35 B8
Mollahat, *Bangla.* 63 H13
Mölle, *Sweden* 11 H6
Molledo, *Spain* 30 B6
Mollendo, *Peru* 124 D3
Mollerin, L., *Australia* 89 F2
Mollerusa, *Spain* 28 D5
Mollina, *Spain* 31 H6
Mölln, *Germany* 18 B6
Mölltorp, *Sweden* 11 F8
Mölndal, *Sweden* 11 G6
Molochansk, *Ukraine* 41 J8
Molochnoye, Ozero, *Ukraine* 41 J8
Molodechno = Maladzyechna, *Belarus* 40 E4
Molokai, *U.S.A.* 102 H16
Molong, *Australia* 91 E4
Molopo →, *Africa* 84 D3
Mólos, *Greece* 39 L5
Molotov = Perm, *Russia* 44 D6
Moloundou, *Cameroon* 80 D3
Molsheim, *France* 25 D14
Molson L., *Canada* 101 C9
Molteno, *S. Africa* 84 E4
Molu, *Indonesia* 57 F8
Molucca Sea, *Indonesia* 57 E6
Moluccas = Maluku, *Indonesia* 57 E7
Moma, *Mozam.* 83 F4
Moma, *Zaïre* 82 C1
Mombaça, *Brazil* 122 C4
Mombasa, *Kenya* 82 C4
Mombetsu, *Japan* 48 B11
Mombuey, *Spain* 30 C4
Momchilgrad, *Bulgaria* 39 H8
Momi, *Zaïre* 82 C2
Momignies, *Belgium* 17 H4
Mompós, *Colombia* 120 B3
Møn, *Denmark* 11 K6
Mon →, *Burma* 61 J19
Mona, Canal de la, *W. Indies* 117 C6
Mona, Isla, *Puerto Rico* 117 C6
Mona, Pta., *Costa Rica* 116 E3
Mona, Pta., *Spain* 31 J7
Monach Is., *U.K.* 14 D1
Monaco ■, *Europe* 27 E11
Monadhliath Mts., *U.K.* 14 D4
Monagas □, *Venezuela* 121 B5
Monaghan, *Ireland* 15 B5
Monaghan □, *Ireland* 15 B5
Monahans, *U.S.A.* 109 K3
Monapo, *Mozam.* 83 E5
Monarch Mt., *Canada* 100 C3
Monastir = Bitola, *Macedonia* 39 H4
Monastir, *Tunisia* 75 A7
Moncada, *Phil.* 55 D4
Moncada, *Spain* 28 F4
Moncalieri, *Italy* 32 D4
Moncalvo, *Italy* 32 C5
Moncão, *Portugal* 30 C2
Moncarapacho, *Portugal* 31 H3
Moncayo, Sierra del, *Spain* 28 D3
Mönchengladbach, *Germany* 18 D2
Monchique, *Portugal* 31 H2
Monclova, *Mexico* 114 B4
Moncontour, *France* 24 D4
Moncoutant, *France* 26 B3
Moncton, *Canada* 99 C7
Mondego →, *Portugal* 30 E2
Mondego, C., *Portugal* 30 E2
Mondeodo, *Indonesia* 57 E6
Mondolfo, *Italy* 33 E10
Mondoñedo, *Spain* 30 B3
Mondovì, *Italy* 32 D4
Mondovi, *U.S.A.* 108 C9
Mondragon, *France* 27 D8
Mondragon, *Phil.* 55 E6
Mondragone, *Italy* 34 A6
Mondrain I., *Australia* 89 F3
Monduli □, *Tanzania* 82 C4
Monemvasía, *Greece* 39 N6
Monessen, *U.S.A.* 106 F5
Monesterio, *Spain* 31 G4
Monestier-de-Clermont, *France* 27 D9
Monett, *U.S.A.* 109 G8
Monfalcone, *Italy* 33 C10
Monflanquin, *France* 26 D4
Monforte, *Portugal* 31 F3
Monforte de Lemos, *Spain* 30 C3
Mong Hsu, *Burma* 61 J21
Mong Kung, *Burma* 61 J20
Mong Nai, *Burma* 61 J20
Mong Pawk, *Burma* 61 H21
Mong Ton, *Burma* 61 J21
Mong Wa, *Burma* 61 J22
Mong Yai, *Burma* 61 H21
Mongalla, *Sudan* 77 F3
Mongers, L., *Australia* 89 E2
Monghyr = Munger, *India* 63 G12
Mongibello = Etna, *Italy* 35 E8
Mongo, *Chad* 73 F8
Mongolia ■, *Asia* 45 E10
Mongonu, *Nigeria* 79 C7
Mongororo, *Chad* 73 F9
Mongu, *Zambia* 81 H4
Môngua, *Angola* 84 B2
Monistrol-d'Allier, *France* 26 D7
Monistrol-sur-Loire, *France* 27 C8
Monkey Bay, *Malawi* 83 E4
Monkey River, *Belize* 115 D7
Monkira, *Australia* 90 C3
Monkoto, *Zaïre* 80 E4
Monmouth, *U.K.* 13 F5
Monmouth, *U.S.A.* 108 E9
Monmouthshire □, *U.K.* 13 F5
Mono L., *U.S.A.* 111 H4
Monolith, *U.S.A.* 113 K8
Monólithos, *Greece* 37 C9
Monongahela, *U.S.A.* 106 F5
Monópoli, *Italy* 35 B10
Monor, *Hungary* 21 H9
Monóvar, *Spain* 29 G4
Monqoumba, *C.A.R.* 80 D3
Monreal del Campo, *Spain* 28 E3
Monreale, *Italy* 34 D6
Monroe, *Ga., U.S.A.* 105 J4
Monroe, *La., U.S.A.* 109 J8
Monroe, *Mich., U.S.A.* 104 E4
Monroe, *N.C., U.S.A.* 105 H5
Monroe, *N.Y., U.S.A.* 107 E10
Monroe, *Utah, U.S.A.* 111 G7
Monroe, *Wash., U.S.A.* 112 C5
Monroe, *Wis., U.S.A.* 108 D10
Monroe City, *U.S.A.* 108 F9
Monroeville, *Ala., U.S.A.* 105 K2
Monroeville, *Pa., U.S.A.* 106 F5
Monrovia, *Liberia* 78 D2
Mons, *Belgium* 17 H3
Monsaraz, *Portugal* 31 G3
Monse, *Indonesia* 57 E6
Monsefú, *Peru* 124 B2
Monségur, *France* 26 D4
Monsélice, *Italy* 33 C8
Monster, *Neths.* 16 D4
Mont Cenis, Col du, *France* 27 C10
Mont-de-Marsan, *France* 26 E3
Mont-Joli, *Canada* 99 C6
Mont-Laurier, *Canada* 98 C4
Mont-St.-Michel, Le = Le Mont-St.-Michel, *France* 24 D5
Mont-sous-Vaudrey, *France* 25 F12
Mont-sur-Marchienne, *Belgium* 17 H4
Mont Tremblant Prov. Park, *Canada* 98 C5
Montabaur, *Germany* 18 E3
Montagnac, *France* 26 E7
Montagnana, *Italy* 33 C8
Montagu, *S. Africa* 84 E3
Montagu I., *Antarctica* 5 B1
Montague, *Canada* 99 C7
Montague, *U.S.A.* 110 F2
Montague, I., *Mexico* 114 A2
Montague Ra., *Australia* 89 E2
Montague Sd., *Australia* 88 B4
Montaigu, *France* 24 F5
Montalbán, *Spain* 28 E4
Montalbano di Elicona, *Italy* 35 D8
Montalbano Iónico, *Italy* 35 B9
Montalbo, *Spain* 28 F2
Montalcino, *Italy* 33 E8
Montalegre, *Portugal* 30 D3
Montalto di Castro, *Italy* 33 F8
Montalto Uffugo, *Italy* 35 C9
Montalvo, *U.S.A.* 113 L7
Montamarta, *Spain* 30 D5
Montaña, *Peru* 124 B3
Montana, *Switz.* 22 D4
Montana □, *U.S.A.* 110 C9
Montaña Clara, I., *Canary Is.* 36 E6
Montánchez, *Spain* 31 F4
Montañita, *Colombia* 120 C2
Montargis, *France* 25 E9
Montauban, *France* 26 D5
Montauk, *U.S.A.* 107 E13
Montauk Pt., *U.S.A.* 107 E13
Montbard, *France* 25 E11
Montbéliard, *France* 25 E13
Montblanch, *Spain* 28 D6
Montbrison, *France* 27 C8
Montcalm, Pic de, *France* 26 F5
Montceau-les-Mines, *France* 25 F11
Montchanin, *France* 27 B8
Montclair, *U.S.A.* 107 F10
Montcornet, *France* 25 C11
Montcuq, *France* 26 D5
Montdidier, *France* 25 C9
Monte Albán, *Mexico* 115 D5
Monte Alegre, *Brazil* 121 D7
Monte Alegre de Goiás, *Brazil* 123 D2
Monte Alegre de Minas, *Brazil* 123 E2
Monte Azul, *Brazil* 123 E3
Monte Bello Is., *Australia* 88 D2
Monte-Carlo, *Monaco* 27 E11
Monte Carmelo, *Brazil* 123 E2
Monte Caseros, *Argentina* 126 C4
Monte Comán, *Argentina* 126 C2
Monte Cristi, *Dom. Rep.* 117 C5
Monte Dinero, *Argentina* 128 D3
Monte Lindo →, *Paraguay* 126 A4
Monte Quemado, *Argentina* 126 B3
Monte Redondo, *Portugal* 30 F2
Monte Rio, *U.S.A.* 112 G4
Monte San Giovanni Campano, *Italy* 34 A6
Monte San Savino, *Italy* 33 E8

Monte Sant' Ángelo, Italy 35 A8
Monte Santu, C. di, Italy 34 B2
Monte Vista, U.S.A. 111 H10
Monteagudo, Argentina 127 B5
Monteagudo, Bolivia 125 D5
Montealegre, Spain 29 G3
Montebello, Canada 98 C5
Montebelluna, Italy 33 C9
Montebourg, France 24 C5
Montecastrilli, Italy 33 F9
Montecatini Terme, Italy 32 E7
Montecito, U.S.A. 113 L7
Montecristi, Ecuador 120 D1
Montecristo, Italy 32 F7
Montefalco, Italy 33 F9
Montefiascone, Italy 33 F9
Montefrío, Spain 31 H6
Montegnée, Belgium 17 G7
Montego Bay, Jamaica 116 C4
Montegranaro, Italy 33 E10
Monteiro, Brazil 122 C4
Montejicar, Spain 29 H1
Montejinnie, Australia 88 C5
Montelíbano, Colombia 120 B2
Montélimar, France 27 D8
Montella, Italy 35 B8
Montellano, Spain 31 J5
Montello, U.S.A. 108 D10
Montelupo Fiorentino, Italy 32 E8
Montemor-o-Novo, Portugal 31 G2
Montemor-o-Velho, Portugal 30 E2
Montemorelos, Mexico 115 B5
Montendre, France 26 C3
Montenegro, Brazil 127 B5
Montenegro □, Yugoslavia 21 N9
Montenero di Bisáccia, Italy 33 G11
Montepuez, Mozam. 83 E4
Montepuez →, Mozam. 83 E5
Montepulciano, Italy 33 E8
Montereale, Italy 33 F10
Montereau-Fault-Yonne, France 25 D9
Monterey, U.S.A. 111 H3
Monterey B., U.S.A. 112 J5
Montería, Colombia 120 B2
Montero, Bolivia 125 D5
Monteros, Argentina 126 B2
Monterotondo, Italy 33 F9
Monterrey, Mexico 114 B4
Montes Altos, Brazil 122 C2
Montes Claros, Brazil 123 E3
Montesano, U.S.A. 112 D3
Montesárchio, Italy 35 A7
Montescaglioso, Italy 35 B9
Montesilvano Marina, Italy 33 F11
Montevarchi, Italy 33 E8
Montevideo, Uruguay 127 C4
Montevideo, U.S.A. 108 C7
Montezuma, U.S.A. 108 E8
Montfaucon, France 25 C12
Montfaucon-en-Velay, France 27 C8
Montfort, France 24 D5
Montfort, Neths. 17 F7
Montfort-l'Amaury, France 25 D8
Montgenèvre, France 27 D10
Montgomery = Sahiwal, Pakistan 62 D5
Montgomery, U.K. 13 E4
Montgomery, Ala., U.S.A. 105 J2
Montgomery, W. Va., U.S.A. 104 F5
Montguyon, France 26 C3
Monthey, Switz. 22 D3
Monticelli d'Ongina, Italy 32 C6
Monticello, Ark., U.S.A. 109 J9
Monticello, Fla., U.S.A. 105 K4
Monticello, Ind., U.S.A. 104 E2
Monticello, Iowa, U.S.A. 108 D9
Monticello, Ky., U.S.A. 105 G3
Monticello, Minn., U.S.A. 108 C8
Monticello, Miss., U.S.A. 109 K9
Monticello, N.Y., U.S.A. 107 E10
Monticello, Utah, U.S.A. 111 H9
Montichiari, Italy 32 C7
Montier-en-Der, France 25 D11
Montignac, France 26 C5
Montignies-sur-Sambre, Belgium 17 H4
Montigny, France 25 C13
Montigny-sur-Aube, France 25 E11
Montijo, Spain 31 G4
Montijo, Presa de, Spain 31 G4
Montilla, Spain 31 H6
Montlhéry, France 25 D9
Montluçon, France 26 B6
Montmagny, Canada 99 C5
Montmarault, France 26 B6
Montmartre, Canada 101 C8
Montmédy, France 25 C12
Montmélian, France 27 C10
Montmirail, France 25 D10
Montmoreau-St.-Cybard, France 26 C4
Montmorency, Canada 99 C5
Montmorillon, France 26 B4
Montmort, France 25 D10
Monto, Australia 90 C5
Montoir-sur-le-Loir, France 24 E7
Montório al Vomano, Italy 33 F10
Montoro, Spain 31 G6
Montour Falls, U.S.A. 106 D8
Montpelier, Idaho, U.S.A. 110 E8
Montpelier, Ohio, U.S.A. 104 E3
Montpelier, Vt., U.S.A. 107 B12
Montpellier, France 26 E7
Montpezat-de-Quercy, France 26 D5
Montpon-Ménestérol, France 26 D4
Montréal, Canada 98 C5
Montréal, France 26 E6
Montreal L., Canada 101 C7
Montreal Lake, Canada 101 C7
Montredon-Labessonnié, France 26 E6
Montréjeau, France 26 E4
Montrésor, France 24 E8
Montreuil, France 25 B8
Montreuil-Bellay, France 24 E6
Montreux, Switz. 22 D3
Montrevault, France 24 E5
Montrevel-en-Bresse, France 27 B9
Montrichard, France 24 E8
Montrose, U.K. 14 E6
Montrose, Colo., U.S.A. 111 G10
Montrose, Pa., U.S.A. 107 E9
Monts, Pte. des, Canada 99 C6
Monts-sur-Guesnes, France 24 F7
Montsalvy, France 26 D6
Montsant, Sierra de, Spain 28 D5
Montsauche, France 25 E11
Montsech, Sierra del, Spain 28 C5
Montseny, Spain 28 D2
Montserrat, Spain 28 D6
Montserrat ■, W. Indies 117 C7
Montuenga, Spain 30 D6
Montuiri, Spain 36 B9
Monveda, Zaïre 80 D4
Monywa, Burma 61 H19
Monza, Italy 32 C6
Monze, Zambia 83 F2
Monze, C., Pakistan 62 G2
Monzón, Spain 28 D5
Mooi River, S. Africa 85 D4
Mook, Neths. 16 E7
Moolawatana, Australia 91 D2
Mooliabeenee, Australia 89 F2
Mooloogool, Australia 89 E2
Moomin Cr. →, Australia 91 D4
Moonah →, Australia 90 C2
Moonbeam, Canada 98 C3
Moonda, L., Australia 90 D3
Moonie, Australia 91 D5
Moonie →, Australia 91 D4
Moonta, Australia 91 E2
Moora, Australia 89 F2
Mooraberree, Australia 90 D3
Moorarie, Australia 89 E2
Moorcroft, U.S.A. 108 C2
Moore →, Australia 89 F2
Moore, L., Australia 89 E2
Moore Reefs, Australia 90 B4
Moorefield, U.S.A. 104 F6
Moores Res., U.S.A. 107 B13
Mooresville, U.S.A. 105 H5
Moorfoot Hills, U.K. 14 F5
Moorhead, U.S.A. 108 B6
Mooroopna, Australia 91 F4
Moorpark, U.S.A. 113 L8
Moorreesburg, S. Africa 84 E2
Moorslede, Belgium 17 G2
Moosburg, Germany 19 G7
Moose →, Canada 98 B3
Moose Factory, Canada 98 B3
Moose I., Canada 101 C9
Moose Jaw, Canada 101 C7
Moose Jaw →, Canada 101 C7
Moose Lake, Canada 101 C8
Moose Lake, U.S.A. 108 B8
Moose Mountain Cr. →, Canada 101 D8
Moose Mountain Prov. Park, Canada 101 D8
Moose River, Canada 98 B3
Moosehead L., U.S.A. 99 C6
Moosomin, Canada 101 C8
Moosonee, Canada 98 B3
Moosup, U.S.A. 107 E13
Mopeia Velha, Mozam. 83 F4
Mopipi, Botswana 84 C3
Mopoi, C.A.R. 82 A2
Mopti, Mali 78 C4
Moqatta, Sudan 77 E4
Moquegua, Peru 124 D3
Moquegua □, Peru 124 D3
Mór, Hungary 21 H8
Móra, Portugal 31 G2
Mora, Sweden 9 F16
Mora, Minn., U.S.A. 108 C8
Mora, N. Mex., U.S.A. 111 J11
Mora de Ebro, Spain 28 D5
Mora de Rubielos, Spain 28 E4
Mora la Nueva, Spain 28 D5
Morača →, Montenegro, Yug. 21 N9
Morada Nova, Brazil 122 C4
Morada Nova de Minas, Brazil 123 E2
Moradabad, India 63 E8
Morafenobe, Madag. 85 B7
Morąg, Poland 20 B9
Moral de Calatrava, Spain 29 G1
Moraleja, Spain 30 E4
Morales, Colombia 120 C2
Moramanga, Madag. 85 B8
Moran, Kans., U.S.A. 109 G7
Moran, Wyo., U.S.A. 110 E8
Moranbah, Australia 90 C4
Morano Cálabro, Italy 35 C9
Morant Cays, Jamaica 116 C4
Morant Pt., Jamaica 116 C4
Morar, L., U.K. 14 E3
Moratalla, Spain 29 G3
Moratuwa, Sri Lanka 60 R11
Morava →, Slovak Rep. 20 G6
Moravia, U.S.A. 108 E8
Moravian Hts. = Ceskomoravská Vrchovina, Czech. 20 F5
Moravica →, Serbia, Yug. 21 M10
Moravice →, Czech. 20 F7
Moraviţa, Romania 21 K11
Moravská Třebová, Czech. 20 F6
Morawa, Australia 89 E2
Morawhanna, Guyana 121 B6
Moray □, U.K. 14 D5
Moray Firth, U.K. 14 D5
Morbach, Germany 19 F3
Morbegno, Italy 32 B6
Morbi, India 62 H4
Morbihan □, France 24 E4
Morcenx, France 26 D3
Mordelles, France 24 D5
Morden, Canada 101 D9
Mordovian Republic □ = Mordvinia □, Russia 42 C7
Mordovo, Russia 42 D5
Mordvinia □, Russia 42 C7
Møre og Romsdal fylke □, Norway 10 B2
Morea, Australia 91 F3
Morea, Greece 6 H10
Moreau →, U.S.A. 108 C4
Morecambe, U.K. 12 C5
Morecambe B., U.K. 12 C5
Moree, Australia 91 D4
Morehead, U.S.A. 104 F4
Morehead City, U.S.A. 105 H7
Morelia, Mexico 114 D4
Morella, Australia 90 C3
Morella, Spain 28 E4
Morelos, Mexico 114 B3
Morelos □, Mexico 115 D5
Morena, Sierra, Spain 31 G7
Morenci, U.S.A. 111 K9
Moreni, Romania 38 E8
Moreno Valley, U.S.A. 113 M10
Morero, Bolivia 125 C4
Moreru →, Brazil 125 C6
Moresby I., Canada 100 C2
Morestel, France 27 C9
Moret-sur-Loing, France 25 D9
Moreton, Australia 90 A3
Moreton I., Australia 91 D5
Moreuil, France 25 C9
Morey, Spain 36 B10
Morez, France 27 B10
Morgan, Australia 91 E2
Morgan, U.S.A. 110 F8
Morgan City, U.S.A. 109 L9
Morgan Hill, U.S.A. 112 H5
Morganfield, U.S.A. 104 G2
Morganton, U.S.A. 105 H5
Morgantown, U.S.A. 104 F6
Morgat, France 24 D2
Morgenzon, S. Africa 85 D4
Morges, Switz. 22 C2
Morghak, Iran 65 D8
Morhange, France 25 D13
Mori, Italy 32 C7
Morialmée, Belgium 17 H5
Morice L., Canada 100 C3
Morichal, Colombia 120 C3
Morichal Largo →, Venezuela 121 B5
Moriki, Nigeria 79 C6
Morinville, Canada 100 C6
Morioka, Japan 48 E10
Moris, Mexico 114 B3
Morlaàs, France 26 E3
Morlaix, France 24 D3
Morlanwelz, Belgium 17 H4
Mormanno, Italy 35 C8
Mormant, France 25 D9
Mornington, Vic., Australia 91 F4
Mornington, W. Austral., Australia 88 C4
Mornington, I., Chile 128 C1
Mornington I., Australia 90 B2
Mórnos →, Greece 39 L4
Moro, Sudan 77 E3
Moro G., Phil. 55 H5
Morocco ■, N. Afr. 74 B3
Morococha, Peru 124 C2
Morogoro, Tanzania 82 D4
Morogoro □, Tanzania 82 D4
Moroleón, Mexico 114 C4
Morombe, Madag. 85 C7
Moron, Argentina 126 C4
Morón, Cuba 116 B4
Mörön →, Mongolia 54 B6
Morón de Almazán, Spain 28 D2
Morón de la Frontera, Spain 31 H5
Morona →, Peru 120 D2
Morona-Santiago □, Ecuador 120 D2
Morondava, Madag. 85 C7
Morondo, Ivory C. 78 D3
Morongo Valley, U.S.A. 113 L10
Moronou, Ivory C. 78 D4
Morotai, Indonesia 57 D7
Moroto, Uganda 82 B3
Moroto Summit, Kenya 82 B3
Morozovsk, Russia 43 F5
Morpeth, U.K. 12 B6
Morphou, Cyprus 66 E5
Morphou Bay, Cyprus 37 D11
Morrilton, U.S.A. 109 H8
Morrinhos, Ceara, Brazil 122 B3
Morrinhos, Minas Gerais, Brazil 123 E2
Morrinsville, N.Z. 87 G5
Morris, Canada 101 D9
Morris, Ill., U.S.A. 104 E1
Morris, Minn., U.S.A. 108 C7
Morris, Mt., Australia 89 E5
Morrisburg, Canada 98 D4
Morrison, U.S.A. 108 E10
Morristown, Ariz., U.S.A. 111 K7
Morristown, N.J., U.S.A. 107 F10
Morristown, S. Dak., U.S.A. 108 C4
Morristown, Tenn., U.S.A. 105 G4
Morro, Pta., Chile 126 B1
Morro Bay, U.S.A. 111 J3
Morro del Jable, Canary Is. 36 F5
Morro do Chapéu, Brazil 123 D3
Morro Jable, Pta. de, Canary Is. 36 F5
Morros, Brazil 122 B3
Morrosquillo, G. de, Colombia 116 E4
Morrumbene, Mozam. 85 C6
Mors, Denmark 11 H2
Morshansk, Russia 42 D5
Mörsil, Sweden 10 A7
Mortagne →, France 25 D13
Mortagne-au-Perche, France 24 D7
Mortagne-sur-Gironde, France 26 C3
Mortagne-sur-Sèvre, France 24 F6
Mortain, France 24 D6
Mortara, Italy 32 C5
Morteau, France 25 E13
Morteros, Argentina 126 C3
Mortes, R. das →, Brazil 123 D1
Mortlake, Australia 91 F3
Morton, Tex., U.S.A. 109 J3
Morton, Wash., U.S.A. 112 D4
Mortsel, Belgium 17 F4
Morundah, Australia 91 E4
Moruya, Australia 91 F5
Morvan, France 25 E11
Morven, Australia 91 D4
Morvern, U.K. 14 E3
Morwell, Australia 91 F4
Mosalsk, Russia 42 C2
Mosbach, Germany 19 F5
Moščenice, Croatia 33 C11
Mosciano Sant' Ángelo, Italy 33 F10
Moscos Is., Burma 58 E1
Moscow = Moskva, Russia 42 C3
Moscow, U.S.A. 110 C5
Mosel →, Europe 19 E3
Moselle = Mosel →, Europe 19 E3
Moselle □, France 25 D13
Moses Lake, U.S.A. 110 C4
Mosgiel, N.Z. 87 L3
Moshi, Tanzania 82 C4
Moshi □, Tanzania 82 C4
Moshupa, Botswana 84 C4
Mosjøen, Norway 8 D15
Moskenesøya, Norway 8 C15
Moskenstraumen, Norway 8 C15
Moskva, Russia 42 C3
Moskva →, Russia 42 C4
Moslavačka Gora, Croatia 33 C13
Mosomane, Botswana 84 C4
Moson-magyaróvar, Hungary 21 H7
Mospino, Ukraine 41 J9
Mosquera, Colombia 120 C2
Mosquero, U.S.A. 109 H3
Mosqueruela, Spain 28 E4
Mosquitia, Honduras 116 C3
Mosquitos, G. de los, Panama 116 E3
Moss, Norway 10 E4
Moss Vale, Australia 91 E5
Mossaka, Congo 80 E3
Mossâmedes, Brazil 123 E1
Mossbank, Canada 101 D7
Mossburn, N.Z. 87 L2
Mosselbaai, S. Africa 84 E3
Mossendjo, Congo 80 E2
Mosses, Col des, Switz. 22 D4
Mossgiel, Australia 91 E3
Mossman, Australia 90 B4
Mossoró, Brazil 122 C4
Mossuril, Mozam. 83 E5
Mossy →, Canada 101 C8
Most, Czech. 20 E3
Mosta, Malta 37 D1
Moşţafáābād, Iran 65 C7
Mostaganem, Algeria 75 A5
Mostar, Bos.-H. 21 M7
Mostardas, Brazil 127 C5
Mostefa, Rass, Tunisia 75 A7
Mostiska = Mostyska, Ukraine 41 H2
Móstoles, Spain 30 E7
Mosty = Masty, Belarus 40 F3
Mostyska, Ukraine 41 H2
Mosul = Al Mawşil, Iraq 67 D10
Mosulpo, S. Korea 51 H14
Mota del Cuervo, Spain 28 F2
Mota del Marqués, Spain 30 D5
Motagua →, Guatemala 116 C2
Motala, Sweden 11 F9
Motherwell, U.K. 14 F5
Motihari, India 63 F11
Motilla del Palancar, Spain 28 F3
Motnik, Slovenia 33 B11
Motocurunya, Venezuela 121 C5
Motovun, Croatia 33 C10
Motozintla de Mendoza, Mexico 115 D6
Motril, Spain 29 J1
Motru →, Romania 38 E6
Mott, U.S.A. 108 B3
Móttola, Italy 35 B10
Motueka, N.Z. 87 J4
Motueka →, N.Z. 87 J4
Motul, Mexico 115 C7
Mouanda, Gabon 80 E2
Mouchalagane →, Canada 99 B6
Mouding, China 52 E3
Moudjeria, Mauritania 78 B2
Moudon, Switz. 22 C3
Mouila, Gabon 80 E2
Moulamein, Australia 91 F3
Moulianá, Greece 37 D7
Moulins, France 26 B7
Moulmein, Burma 61 L20
Moulouya, O. →, Morocco 75 A4
Moulton, U.S.A. 109 L6
Moultrie, U.S.A. 105 K4
Moultrie, L., U.S.A. 105 J5
Mound City, Mo., U.S.A. 108 E7
Mound City, S. Dak., U.S.A. 108 C4
Moúnda, Ákra, Greece 39 L3
Moundou, Chad 73 G8
Moundsville, U.S.A. 106 G4
Moung, Cambodia 58 F4
Mount Airy, U.S.A. 105 G5
Mount Albert, Canada 106 B5
Mount Amherst, Australia 88 C4
Mount Angel, U.S.A. 110 D2
Mount Augustus, Australia 88 D2
Mount Barker, S. Austral., Australia 91 F2
Mount Barker, W. Austral., Australia 89 F2
Mount Carmel, U.S.A. 104 F2
Mount Clemens, U.S.A. 98 D3
Mount Coolon, Australia 90 C4
Mount Darwin, Zimbabwe 83 F3
Mount Desert I., U.S.A. 99 D6
Mount Dora, U.S.A. 105 L5
Mount Douglas, Australia 90 C4
Mount Eba, Australia 91 E2
Mount Edgecumbe, U.S.A. 100 B1
Mount Elizabeth, Australia 88 C4
Mount Fletcher, S. Africa 85 E4
Mount Forest, Canada 98 D3
Mount Gambier, Australia 91 F3
Mount Garnet, Australia 90 B4
Mount Hope, N.S.W., Australia 91 E4
Mount Hope, S. Austral., Australia 91 E2
Mount Hope, U.S.A. 104 G5
Mount Horeb, U.S.A. 108 D10
Mount Howitt, Australia 91 D3
Mount Isa, Australia 90 C2
Mount Keith, Australia 89 E3
Mount Laguna, U.S.A. 113 N10
Mount Larcom, Australia 90 C5
Mount Lofty Ra., Australia 91 E2
Mount McKinley National Park, U.S.A. 96 B5
Mount Magnet, Australia 89 E2
Mount Margaret, Australia 91 D3
Mount Maunganui, N.Z. 87 G6
Mount Molloy, Australia 90 B4
Mount Monger, Australia 89 F3
Mount Morgan, Australia 90 C5
Mount Morris, U.S.A. 106 D7
Mount Mulligan, Australia 90 B3
Mount Narryer, Australia 89 E2
Mount Olympus = Uludağ, Turkey 66 B3
Mount Oxide Mine, Australia 90 B2
Mount Pearl, Canada 99 C9
Mount Perry, Australia 91 D5
Mount Phillips, Australia 88 D2
Mount Pleasant, Iowa, U.S.A. 108 E9
Mount Pleasant, Mich., U.S.A. 104 D3
Mount Pleasant, Pa., U.S.A. 106 F5
Mount Pleasant, S.C., U.S.A. 105 J6
Mount Pleasant, Tenn., U.S.A. 105 H2
Mount Pleasant, Tex., U.S.A. 109 J7
Mount Pleasant, Utah, U.S.A. 110 G8
Mount Pocono, U.S.A. 107 E9
Mount Rainier National Park, U.S.A. 112 D5
Mount Revelstoke Nat. Park, Canada 100 C5
Mount Robson Prov. Park, Canada 100 C5
Mount Sandiman, Australia 89 D2
Mount Shasta, U.S.A. 110 F2
Mount Signal, U.S.A. 113 N11
Mount Sterling, Ill., U.S.A. 108 F9
Mount Sterling, Ky., U.S.A. 104 F4
Mount Surprise, Australia 90 B3

Mount Union, U.S.A. 106 F7
Mount Vernon, Australia 88 D2
Mount Vernon, Ind., U.S.A. 108 F10
Mount Vernon, N.Y., U.S.A. 107 F11
Mount Vernon, Ohio, U.S.A. 106 F2
Mount Vernon, Wash., U.S.A. 112 B4
Mountain Center, U.S.A. 113 M10
Mountain City, Nev., U.S.A. 110 F6
Mountain City, Tenn., U.S.A. 105 G5
Mountain Grove, U.S.A. 109 G8
Mountain Home, Ark., U.S.A. 109 G8
Mountain Home, Idaho, U.S.A. 110 E6
Mountain Iron, U.S.A. 108 B8
Mountain Park, Canada 100 C5
Mountain Pass, U.S.A. 113 K11
Mountain View, Ark., U.S.A. 109 H8
Mountain View, Calif., U.S.A. 111 H2
Mountainair, U.S.A. 111 J10
Mountmellick, Ireland 15 C4
Moura, Australia 90 C4
Moura, Brazil 121 D5
Moura, Portugal 31 G3
Mourão, Portugal 31 G3
Mourdi, Dépression du, Chad 73 E9
Mourdiah, Mali 78 C3
Mourenx-Ville-Nouvelle, France 26 E3
Mouri, Ghana 79 D4
Mourilyan, Australia 90 B4
Mourmelon-le-Grand, France 25 C11
Mourne →, U.K. 15 B4
Mourne Mts., U.K. 15 B5
Mournies, Greece 37 D6
Mouscron, Belgium 17 G2
Moussoro, Chad 73 F8
Mouthe, France 25 F13
Moutier, Switz. 22 B4
Moûtiers, France 27 C10
Moutohara, N.Z. 87 H6
Moutong, Indonesia 57 D6
Mouy, France 25 C9
Mouzáki, Greece 39 K4
Movas, Mexico 114 B3
Moville, Ireland 15 A4
Moxhe, Belgium 17 G6
Moxotó →, Brazil 122 C4
Moy →, Ireland 15 B3
Moyale, Kenya 68 G2
Moyamba, S. Leone 78 D2
Moyen Atlas, Morocco 74 B3
Moyle □, U.K. 15 A5
Moyo, Indonesia 56 F5
Moyobamba, Peru 124 B2
Moyyero →, Russia 45 C11
Moyynty, Kazakstan 44 E8
Mozambique = Moçambique, Mozam. 83 F5
Mozambique ■, Africa 83 F4
Mozambique Chan., Africa 85 B7
Mozdok, Russia 43 J7
Mozdūrān, Iran 65 B9
Mozhaysk, Russia 42 C3
Mozhga, Russia 42 B11
Mozhnābād, Iran 65 C9
Mozirje, Slovenia 33 B11
Mozyr = Mazyr, Belarus 41 F5
Mpanda, Tanzania 82 D3
Mpanda □, Tanzania 82 D3
Mpésoba, Mali 78 C3
Mpika, Zambia 83 E3
Mpulungu, Zambia 83 D3
Mpumalanga, S. Africa 85 D5
Mpumalanga □, S. Africa 85 B5
Mpwapwa, Tanzania 82 D4
Mpwapwa □, Tanzania 82 D4
Mqinvartsveri = Kazbek, Russia 43 J7
Mrągowo, Poland 20 B11
Mramor, Serbia, Yug. 21 M11
Mrimina, Morocco 74 C3
Mrkonjić Grad, Bos.-H. 21 L7
Mrkopalj, Croatia 33 C11
Msab, Oued en →, Algeria 75 B6
Msaken, Tunisia 75 A7
Msambansovu, Zimbabwe 83 F3
M'sila, Algeria 75 A5
Msoro, Zambia 83 E3
Msta →, Russia 40 C6
Mstislavl = Mstsislaw, Belarus 40 E6
Mstsislaw, Belarus 40 E6
Mtama, Tanzania 83 E4
Mtilikwe →, Zimbabwe 83 G3
Mtsensk, Russia 42 D3
Mtskheta, Georgia 43 K7
Mtubatuba, S. Africa 85 D5
Mtwara-Mikindani, Tanzania 83 E5
Mu Gia, Deo, Vietnam 58 D5
Mu Us Shamo, China 50 E5
Muaná, Brazil 122 B2
Muang Chiang Rai, Thailand 58 C2
Muang Lamphun, Thailand 58 C2
Muang Pak Beng, Laos 58 C3
Muar, Malaysia 59 L4
Muarabungo, Indonesia 56 E2
Muaraenim, Indonesia 56 E2
Muarajuloi, Indonesia 56 E4
Muarakaman, Indonesia 56 E5
Muaratebo, Indonesia 56 E2
Muaratembesi, Indonesia 56 E2
Muaratewe, Indonesia 56 E4
Mubarakpur, India 63 F10
Mubarraz = Al Mubarraz, Si. Arabia 65 E6
Mubende, Uganda 82 B3
Mubi, Nigeria 79 C7
Mubur, P., Indonesia 59 L6
Mucajaí →, Brazil 121 C5
Mucajaí, Serra do, Brazil 121 C5
Muchachos, Roque de los, Canary Is. 36 F2
Mücheln, Germany 18 D7
Muchinga Mts., Zambia 83 E3
Muchkapskiy, Russia 42 E6
Muck, U.K. 14 E2
Muckadilla, Australia 91 D4
Muco →, Colombia 120 C3
Muconda, Angola 80 G4
Mucuim →, Brazil 125 B5
Mucur, Turkey 66 C6
Mucura, Brazil 121 D5
Mucuri, Brazil 123 E4
Mucurici, Brazil 123 E3
Mucusso, Angola 84 B3
Muda, Canary Is. 36 F6
Mudan Jiang →, China 51 A15
Mudanjiang, China 51 B15
Mudanya, Turkey 66 B3
Muddy Cr. →, U.S.A. 111 H8
Mudgee, Australia 91 E4
Mudjatik →, Canada 101 B7
Mudurnu, Turkey 66 B4
Muecate, Mozam. 83 E4
Muêda, Mozam. 83 E4
Mueller Ra., Australia 88 C4
Muende, Mozam. 83 E3
Muerto, Mar, Mexico 115 D6
Muertos, Punta de los, Spain 29 J3
Mufindi □, Tanzania 83 D4
Mufu Shan, China 53 C10
Mufulira, Zambia 83 E2
Mufumbiro Range, Africa 82 C2
Mugardos, Spain 30 B2
Muge, Portugal 31 F2
Muge →, Portugal 31 F2
Múggia, Italy 33 C10
Mughayrā', Si. Arabia 64 D3
Mugi, Japan 49 H7
Mugia, Spain 30 B1
Mugila, Mts., Zaïre 82 D2
Muğla, Turkey 66 D3
Müglizh, Bulgaria 38 G8
Mugu, Nepal 63 E10
Muhammad, Râs, Egypt 76 B3
Muhammad Qol, Sudan 76 C4
Muhammadabad, India 63 F10
Muhesi →, Tanzania 82 D4
Muheza □, Tanzania 82 C4
Mühldorf, Germany 19 G8
Mühlhausen, Germany 18 D6
Mühlig Hofmann fjell, Antarctica 5 D3
Muhos, Finland 8 D22
Muhu, Estonia 9 G20
Muhutwe, Tanzania 82 C3
Muiden, Neths. 16 D6
Muikamachi, Japan 49 F9
Muine Bheag, Ireland 15 D5
Muiños, Spain 30 D3
Muir, L., Australia 89 F2
Mukacheve, Ukraine 41 H2
Mukachevo = Mukacheve, Ukraine 41 H2
Mukah, Malaysia 56 D4
Mukawwa, Geziret, Egypt 76 C4
Mukdahan, Thailand 58 D5
Mukden = Shenyang, China 51 D12
Mukhtolovo, Russia 42 C6
Mukhtuya = Lensk, Russia 45 C12
Mukinbudin, Australia 89 F2
Mukishi, Zaïre 83 D1
Mukomuko, Indonesia 56 E2
Mukomwenze, Zaïre 82 D2
Muktsar, India 62 D6
Mukur, Afghan. 62 C2
Mukutawa →, Canada 101 C9
Mukwela, Zambia 83 F2
Mula, Spain 29 G3
Mulange, Zaïre 82 C2
Mulchén, Chile 126 D1
Mulde →, Germany 18 D8
Mule Creek, U.S.A. 108 D2
Muleba, Tanzania 82 C3
Muleba □, Tanzania 82 C3
Mulegns, Switz. 23 C9
Muleshoe, U.S.A. 109 H3
Mulgathing, Australia 91 E1
Mulgrave, Canada 99 C7
Mulhacén, Spain 29 H1
Mülheim, Germany 18 D2
Mulhouse, France 25 E14
Muli, China 52 D3
Muling, China 51 B16
Mull, U.K. 14 E3
Mullaittvu, Sri Lanka 60 Q12
Mullen, U.S.A. 108 D4
Mullengudgery, Australia 91 E4
Mullens, U.S.A. 104 G5
Muller, Pegunungan, Indonesia 56 D4
Mullet Pen., Ireland 15 B1
Mullewa, Australia 89 E2
Müllheim, Germany 19 H3
Mulligan →, Australia 90 C2
Mullin, U.S.A. 109 K5
Mullingar, Ireland 15 C4
Mullins, U.S.A. 105 H6
Mullumbimby, Australia 91 D5
Mulobezi, Zambia 83 F2
Multan, Pakistan 62 D4
Multrå, Sweden 10 A11
Mulumbe, Mts., Zaïre 83 D2
Mulungushi Dam, Zambia 83 E2
Mulvane, U.S.A. 109 G6
Mulwad, Sudan 76 D3
Mulwala, Australia 91 F4
Mumbaī = Bombay, India 60 K8
Mumbwa, Zambia 83 E2
Mumra, Russia 43 H8
Mun →, Thailand 58 E5
Muna, Indonesia 57 F6
Munamagi, Estonia 9 H22
Münchberg, Germany 19 E7
Müncheberg, Germany 18 C10
München, Germany 19 G7
Munchen-Gladbach = Mönchengladbach, Germany 18 D2
Muncho Lake, Canada 100 B3
Munchŏn, N. Korea 51 E14
Münchwilen, Switz. 23 B7
Muncie, U.S.A. 104 E3
Muncoonie, L., Australia 90 D2
Mundala, Indonesia 57 E10
Mundare, Canada 100 C6
Munday, U.S.A. 109 J5
Münden, Germany 18 D5
Mundiwindi, Australia 88 D3
Mundo →, Spain 29 G2
Mundo Novo, Brazil 123 D3
Mundra, India 62 H3
Mundrabilla, Australia 89 F4
Munducurus, Brazil 121 D6
Munera, Spain 29 F2
Mungallala, Australia 91 D4
Mungallala Cr. →, Australia 91 D4
Mungana, Australia 90 B3
Mungaoli, India 62 G8
Mungari, Mozam. 83 F3
Mungbere, Zaïre 82 B2
Munger, India 63 G12
Mungindi, Australia 91 D4
Munhango, Angola 81 G3
Munich = München, Germany 19 G7
Munising, U.S.A. 104 B2
Munka-Ljungby, Sweden 11 H6
Munkedal, Sweden 11 F5
Munku-Sardyk, Russia 45 D11
Münnerstadt, Germany 19 E6
Muñoz Gamero, Pen., Chile 128 D2
Munroe L., Canada 101 B9
Munsan, S. Korea 51 F14
Münsingen, Switz. 22 C5
Munster, France 25 D14
Munster, Niedersachsen, Germany 18 C6
Münster, Nordrhein-Westfalen, Germany 18 D3
Münster, Switz. 23 D6
Munster □, Ireland 15 D3
Muntadgin, Australia 89 F2
Muntele Mare, Romania 38 C6
Muntok, Indonesia 56 E3
Munyama, Zambia 83 F2
Munzur Dağları, Turkey 67 C8
Muong Beng, Laos 58 B3
Muong Boum, Vietnam 58 A4
Muong Et, Laos 58 B5
Muong Hai, Laos 58 B3
Muong Hiem, Laos 58 B4
Muong Houn, Laos 58 B3
Muong Hung, Vietnam 58 B4
Muong Kau, Laos 58 E5
Muong Khao, Laos 58 C4
Muong Khoua, Laos 58 B4
Muong Liep, Laos 58 C3
Muong May, Laos 58 E6
Muong Ngeun, Laos 58 B3
Muong Ngoi, Laos 58 B4
Muong Nhie, Vietnam 58 A4
Muong Nong, Laos 58 D6
Muong Ou Tay, Laos 58 A3
Muong Oua, Laos 58 C3
Muong Peun, Laos 58 B4
Muong Phalane, Laos 58 D5
Muong Phieng, Laos 58 C3
Muong Phine, Laos 58 D6
Muong Sai, Laos 58 B3
Muong Saiapoun, Laos 58 C3
Muong Sen, Vietnam 58 C5
Muong Sing, Laos 58 B3
Muong Son, Laos 58 B4
Muong Soui, Laos 58 C4
Muong Va, Laos 58 B4
Muong Xia, Vietnam 58 B5
Muonio, Finland 8 C20
Muonionjoki →, Finland 8 C20
Muotathal, Switz. 23 C7
Mupa, Angola 81 H3
Muping, China 51 F11
Muqaddam, Wadi →, Sudan 76 D3
Muqdisho, Somali Rep. 68 G4
Mur-de-Bretagne, France 24 D4
Mura →, Slovenia 33 B13
Muradiye, Turkey 67 C10
Murakami, Japan 48 E9
Murallón, Cuerro, Chile 128 C2
Muralto, Switz. 23 D7
Muranda, Rwanda 82 C2
Murang'a, Kenya 82 C4
Murashi, Russia 44 D5
Murat, France 26 C6
Murat →, Turkey 67 C9
Muratlı, Turkey 66 B2
Muravera, Italy 34 C2
Murayama, Japan 48 E10
Murban, U.A.E. 65 F7
Murça, Portugal 30 D3
Murchison →, Australia 89 E1
Murchison, Mt., Antarctica 5 D11
Murchison Falls = Kabarega Falls, Uganda 82 B3
Murchison House, Australia 89 E1
Murchison Ra., Australia 90 C1
Murchison Rapids, Malawi 83 F3
Murcia, Spain 29 G3
Murcia □, Spain 29 H3
Murdo, U.S.A. 108 D4
Murdoch Pt., Australia 90 A3
Mureş →, Romania 38 C3
Mureşul = Mureş →, Romania 38 C3
Muret, France 26 E5
Murfatlar, Romania 38 E11
Murfreesboro, U.S.A. 105 H2
Murg, Switz. 23 B8
Murg →, Germany 19 G4
Murgab = Murghob, Tajikistan 44 F8
Murgenthal, Switz. 22 B5
Murghob, Tajikistan 44 F8
Murgon, Australia 91 D5
Murgoo, Australia 89 E2
Muri, Switz. 23 B6
Muria, Indonesia 57 G14
Muriaé, Brazil 123 F3
Murias de Paredes, Spain 30 C4
Murici, Brazil 122 C4
Muriel Mine, Zimbabwe 83 F3
Müritz-see, Germany 18 B8
Murka, Kenya 82 C4
Murmansk, Russia 44 C4
Murmerwoude, Neths. 16 B8
Murnau, Germany 19 H7
Muro, France 27 F12
Muro, Spain 36 B10
Muro, C. de, France 27 G12
Muro Lucano, Italy 35 B8
Murom, Russia 42 C6
Muroran, Japan 48 C10
Muros, Spain 30 C1
Muros y de Noya, Ría de, Spain 30 C2
Muroto, Japan 49 H7
Muroto-Misaki, Japan 49 H7
Murphy, U.S.A. 110 E5
Murphys, U.S.A. 112 G6
Murphysboro, U.S.A. 109 G10
Murrat, Sudan 76 D2
Murray, Ky., U.S.A. 105 G1
Murray, Utah, U.S.A. 110 F8
Murray →, Australia 91 F2
Murray →, Canada 100 B4
Murray, L., U.S.A. 105 H5
Murray Bridge, Australia 91 F2
Murray Downs, Australia 90 C1
Murray Harbour, Canada 99 C7
Murraysburg, S. Africa 84 E3
Murree, Pakistan 62 C5
Murrieta, U.S.A. 113 M9
Murrin Murrin, Australia 89 E3
Murrumbidgee →, Australia 91 E3
Murrumburrah, Australia 91 E4
Murrurundi, Australia 91 E5
Murshid, Sudan 76 C3
Murshidabad, India 63 G13
Murska Sobota, Slovenia 33 B13
Murten, Switz. 22 C4
Murtensee, Switz. 22 C4
Murtle L., Canada 100 C5
Murtoa, Australia 91 F3
Murtosa, Portugal 30 E2
Muru →, Brazil 124 B3
Murungu, Tanzania 82 C3
Murwara, India 63 H9
Murwillumbah, Australia 91 D5
Mürz →, Austria 21 H5
Mürzzuschlag, Austria 21 H5
Muş, Turkey 67 C9
Musa, G., Egypt 76 J8
Musa Khel, Pakistan 62 D3
Mūsá Qal'eh, Afghan. 60 C4
Musaffargarh, Pakistan 60 D7
Musala, Bulgaria 38 G6
Musala, Indonesia 56 D1
Musan, N. Korea 51 C15
Musangu, Zaïre 83 E1
Musasa, Tanzania 82 C3
Musay'īd, Qatar 65 E6
Muscat = Masqat, Oman 68 C6
Muscat & Oman = Oman ■, Asia 68 C6
Muscatine, U.S.A. 108 E9
Musel, Spain 30 B5
Musgrave, Australia 90 A3
Musgrave Ras., Australia 89 E5
Mushie, Zaïre 80 E3
Mushin, Nigeria 79 D5
Musi →, Indonesia 56 E2
Muskeg →, Canada 100 A4
Muskegon, U.S.A. 104 D2
Muskegon →, U.S.A. 104 D2
Muskegon Heights, U.S.A. 104 D2
Muskogee, U.S.A. 109 H7
Muskwa →, Canada 100 B4
Muslīmiyah, Syria 64 B3
Musmar, Sudan 76 D4
Musofu, Zambia 83 E2
Musoma, Tanzania 82 C3
Musoma □, Tanzania 82 C3
Musquaro, L., Canada 99 B7
Musquodoboit Harbour, Canada 99 D7
Musselburgh, U.K. 14 F5
Musselkanaal, Neths. 16 C10
Musselshell →, U.S.A. 110 C10
Mussidan, France 26 C4
Mussomeli, Italy 34 E6
Musson, Belgium 17 J7
Mussoorie, India 62 D8
Mussuco, Angola 84 B2
Mustafakemalpaşa, Turkey 66 B3
Mustang, Nepal 63 E10
Musters, L., Argentina 128 C3
Musudan, N. Korea 51 D15
Muswellbrook, Australia 91 E5
Mût, Egypt 76 B2
Mut, Turkey 66 D5
Mutanda, Mozam. 85 C5
Mutanda, Zambia 83 E2
Mutare, Zimbabwe 83 F3
Muting, Indonesia 57 F10
Mutoray, Russia 45 C11
Mutshatsha, Zaïre 83 E1
Mutsu, Japan 48 D10
Mutsu-Wan, Japan 48 D10
Muttaburra, Australia 90 C3
Mutuáli, Mozam. 83 E4
Mutunópolis, Brazil 123 D2
Muweilih, Egypt 69 E3
Muxima, Angola 80 F2
Muy Muy, Nic. 116 D2
Muyinga, Burundi 82 C3
Muynak, Uzbekistan 44 E6
Muzaffarabad, Pakistan 63 B5
Muzaffargarh, Pakistan 62 D4
Muzaffarnagar, India 62 E7
Muzaffarpur, India 63 F11
Muzhi, Russia 44 C7
Muzillac, France 24 E4
Muzon, C., U.S.A. 100 C2
Muztag, China 54 C3
Mvôlô, Sudan 77 F2
Mvuma, Zimbabwe 83 F3
Mvurwi, Zimbabwe 83 F3
Mwadui, Tanzania 82 C3
Mwambo, Tanzania 83 E5
Mwandi, Zambia 83 F1
Mwanza, Tanzania 82 C3
Mwanza, Zaïre 82 D2
Mwanza, Zambia 83 F1
Mwanza □, Tanzania 82 C3
Mwaya, Tanzania 83 D3
Mweelrea, Ireland 15 C2
Mweka, Zaïre 80 E4
Mwenezi, Zimbabwe 83 G3
Mwenezi →, Mozam. 83 G3
Mwenga, Zaïre 82 C2
Mweru, L., Zambia 83 D2
Mweza Range, Zimbabwe 83 G3
Mwilambwe, Zaïre 82 D5
Mwimbi, Tanzania 83 D3
Mwinilunga, Zambia 83 E1
My Tho, Vietnam 59 G6
Mya, O. →, Algeria 75 B5
Myajlar, India 62 F4
Myanaung, Burma 61 K19
Myanmar = Burma ■, Asia 61 J20
Myaungmya, Burma 61 L19
Myeik Kyunzu, Burma 59 G1
Myerstown, U.S.A. 107 F8
Myingyan, Burma 61 J19
Myitkyina, Burma 61 G20
Myjava, Slovak Rep. 20 G7
Mykhaylivka, Ukraine 41 J8
Mykines, Færoe Is. 8 E9
Mykolayiv, Ukraine 41 J7
Mymensingh, Bangla. 61 G17
Mynydd Du, U.K. 13 F4
Mýrdalsjökull, Iceland 8 E4
Myrhorod, Ukraine 41 H7
Myroodah, Australia 88 C3
Myrtle Beach, U.S.A. 105 J6
Myrtle Creek, U.S.A. 110 E2
Myrtle Point, U.S.A. 110 E1
Myrtou, Cyprus 37 D12
Mysen, Norway 10 E5
Mysia, Turkey 66 C2
Myslenice, Poland 20 F9
Myślibórz, Poland 20 C4
Mysłowice, Poland 20 E9
Mysore = Karnataka □, India 60 N10
Mysore, India 60 N10
Mystic, U.S.A. 107 E13
Myszków, Poland 20 E9
Mythen, Switz. 23 B7
Mytishchi, Russia 42 C3
Myton, U.S.A. 110 F8
Mývatn, Iceland 8 D5
Mzimba, Malawi 83 E3
Mzimkulu →, S. Africa 85 E5
Mzimvubu →, S. Africa 85 E4
Mzuzu, Malawi 83 E3

N

N' Dioum, *Senegal* 78 B2
Na Hearadh = Harris, *U.K.* 14 D2
Na Noi, *Thailand* 58 C3
Na Phao, *Laos* 58 D5
Na Sam, *Vietnam* 58 A6
Na San, *Vietnam* 58 B5
Naab →, *Germany* 19 F8
Naaldwijk, *Neths.* 16 E4
Na'am, *Sudan* 77 F2
Naantali, *Finland* 9 F19
Naarden, *Neths.* 16 D6
Naas, *Ireland* 15 C5
Nababiep, *S. Africa* 84 D2
Nabadwip = Navadwip, *India* 63 H13
Nabari, *Japan* 49 G8
Nabawa, *Australia* 89 E1
Nabberu, L., *Australia* 89 E3
Nabburg, *Germany* 19 F8
Naberezhnyye Chelny, *Russia* 42 C11
Nabeul, *Tunisia* 75 A7
Nabha, *India* 62 D7
Nabīd, *Iran* 65 D8
Nabire, *Indonesia* 57 E9
Nabisar, *Pakistan* 62 G3
Nabisipi →, *Canada* 99 B7
Nabiswera, *Uganda* 82 B3
Nablus = Nābulus, *West Bank* 69 C4
Naboomspruit, *S. Africa* 85 C4
Nabua, *Phil.* 55 E5
Nābulus, *West Bank* 69 C4
Nacala, *Mozam.* 83 E5
Nacala-Velha, *Mozam.* 83 E5
Nacaome, *Honduras* 116 D2
Nacaroa, *Mozam.* 83 E4
Naches, *U.S.A.* 110 C3
Naches →, *U.S.A.* 112 D6
Nachingwea, *Tanzania* 83 E4
Nachingwea □, *Tanzania* 83 E4
Nachna, *India* 62 F4
Náchod, *Czech.* 20 E6
Nacimiento Reservoir, *U.S.A.* 112 K6
Nacka, *Sweden* 10 E12
Nackara, *Australia* 91 E2
Naco, *Mexico* 114 A3
Naco, *U.S.A.* 111 L9
Nacogdoches, *U.S.A.* 109 K7
Nácori Chico, *Mexico* 114 B3
Nacozari, *Mexico* 114 A3
Nadi, *Sudan* 76 D3
Nadiad, *India* 62 H5
Nădlac, *Romania* 38 C3
Nador, *Morocco* 75 A4
Nadur, *Malta* 37 C1
Nadūshan, *Iran* 65 C7
Nadvirna, *Ukraine* 41 H3
Nadvornaya = Nadvirna, *Ukraine* 41 H3
Nadym, *Russia* 44 C8
Nadym →, *Russia* 44 C8
Nærbø, *Norway* 9 G11
Næstved, *Denmark* 11 J5
Nafada, *Nigeria* 79 C7
Näfels, *Switz.* 23 B8
Naftshahr, *Iran* 67 E11
Nafud Desert = An Nafūd, *Si. Arabia* 64 D4
Nafūsah, Jabal, *Libya* 75 B7
Nag Hammâdi, *Egypt* 76 B3
Naga, *Phil.* 55 E5
Naga, Kreb en, *Africa* 74 D3
Nagagami →, *Canada* 98 C3
Nagahama, *Japan* 49 G8
Nagai, *Japan* 48 E10
Nagaland □, *India* 61 F19
Nagano, *Japan* 49 F9
Nagano □, *Japan* 49 F9
Nagaoka, *Japan* 49 F9
Nagappattinam, *India* 60 P11
Nagar Parkar, *Pakistan* 62 G4
Nagasaki, *Japan* 49 H4
Nagasaki □, *Japan* 49 H4
Nagato, *Japan* 49 G5
Nagaur, *India* 62 F5
Nagercoil, *India* 60 Q10
Nagina, *India* 63 E8
Nagīneh, *Iran* 65 C8
Nagir, *Pakistan* 63 A6
Nagold, *Germany* 19 G4
Nagold →, *Germany* 19 G4
Nagoorin, *Australia* 90 C5
Nagorno-Karabakh, *Azerbaijan* 67 C12
Nagornyy, *Russia* 45 D13
Nagoya, *Japan* 49 G8
Nagpur, *India* 60 J11
Nagua, *Dom. Rep.* 117 C6
Nagykanizsa, *Hungary* 21 J7
Nagykörös, *Hungary* 21 H9
Nagyléta, *Hungary* 21 H11
Naha, *Japan* 49 L3
Nahanni Butte, *Canada* 100 A4
Nahanni Nat. Park, *Canada* 100 A3
Nahariyya, *Israel* 66 F6
Nahāvand, *Iran* 67 E13
Nahe →, *Germany* 19 F3
Nahîya, W. →, *Egypt* 76 J7
Nahlin, *Canada* 100 B2
Nahuel Huapi, L., *Argentina* 128 B2
Naicá, *Mexico* 114 B3
Naicam, *Canada* 101 C8
Nā'ifah, *Si. Arabia* 68 D5
Naila, *Germany* 19 E7
Nain, *Canada* 99 A7
Nā'īn, *Iran* 65 C7
Naini Tal, *India* 63 E8
Nainpur, *India* 60 H12
Naintré, *France* 24 F7
Naipu, *Romania* 38 E8
Naira, *Indonesia* 57 E7
Nairn, *U.K.* 14 D5
Nairobi, *Kenya* 82 C4
Naissaar, *Estonia* 9 G21
Naivasha, *Kenya* 82 C4
Naivasha, L., *Kenya* 82 C4
Najac, *France* 26 D5
Najafābād, *Iran* 65 C6
Nájera, *Spain* 28 C2
Najerilla →, *Spain* 28 C2
Najibabad, *India* 62 E8
Najin, *N. Korea* 51 C16
Najmah, *Si. Arabia* 65 E6
Naju, *S. Korea* 51 G14
Nakadōri-Shima, *Japan* 49 H4
Nakalagba, *Zaïre* 82 B2
Nakaminato, *Japan* 49 F10
Nakamura, *Japan* 49 H6
Nakano, *Japan* 49 F9
Nakano-Shima, *Japan* 49 K4
Nakashibetsu, *Japan* 48 C12
Nakfa, *Eritrea* 77 D4
Nakhichevan = Naxçıvan, *Azerbaijan* 67 C11
Nakhichevan Republic □ = Naxçıvan □, *Azerbaijan* 67 C11
Nakhl, *Egypt* 69 F2
Nakhl-e Taqī, *Iran* 65 E7
Nakhodka, *Russia* 45 E14
Nakhon Nayok, *Thailand* 58 E3
Nakhon Pathom, *Thailand* 58 F3
Nakhon Phanom, *Thailand* 58 D5
Nakhon Ratchasima, *Thailand* 58 E4
Nakhon Sawan, *Thailand* 58 E3
Nakhon Si Thammarat, *Thailand* 59 H3
Nakhon Thai, *Thailand* 58 D3
Nakina, *B.C., Canada* 100 B2
Nakina, *Ont., Canada* 98 B2
Nakło nad Noteią, *Poland* 20 B7
Nakodar, *India* 62 D6
Nakskov, *Denmark* 11 K5
Näkten, *Sweden* 10 B8
Naktong →, *S. Korea* 51 G15
Nakuru, *Kenya* 82 C4
Nakuru □, *Kenya* 82 C4
Nakuru, L., *Kenya* 82 C4
Nakusp, *Canada* 100 C5
Nal →, *Pakistan* 62 G1
Nalchik, *Russia* 43 J6
Nälden, *Sweden* 10 A8
Näldsjön, *Sweden* 10 A8
Nalerigu, *Ghana* 79 C4
Nalgonda, *India* 60 L11
Nalhati, *India* 63 G12
Nalinnes, *Belgium* 17 H4
Nallamalai Hills, *India* 60 M11
Nallıhan, *Turkey* 66 B4
Nalón →, *Spain* 30 B4
Nālūt, *Libya* 75 B7
Nam Can, *Vietnam* 59 H5
Nam Co, *China* 54 C4
Nam Dinh, *Vietnam* 58 B6
Nam Du, Hon, *Vietnam* 59 H5
Nam Ngum Dam, *Laos* 58 C4
Nam-Phan, *Vietnam* 59 G6
Nam Phong, *Thailand* 58 D4
Nam Tha, *Laos* 58 B3
Nam Tok, *Thailand* 58 E2
Namacunde, *Angola* 84 B2
Namacurra, *Mozam.* 85 B6
Namak, Daryācheh-ye, *Iran* 65 C7
Namak, Kavir-e, *Iran* 65 C8
Namaland, *Namibia* 84 C2
Namangan, *Uzbekistan* 44 E8
Namapa, *Mozam.* 83 E4
Namaqualand, *S. Africa* 84 D2
Namasagali, *Uganda* 82 B3
Namber, *Indonesia* 57 E8
Nambour, *Australia* 91 D5
Nambucca Heads, *Australia* 91 E5
Namche Bazar, *Nepal* 63 F12
Namchonjŏm, *N. Korea* 51 E14
Namêche, *Belgium* 17 H6
Namecunda, *Mozam.* 83 E4
Nameh, *Indonesia* 56 D5
Nameponda, *Mozam.* 83 F4
Nametil, *Mozam.* 83 F4
Namew L., *Canada* 101 C8
Namib Desert = Namibwoestyn, *Namibia* 84 C2
Namibe, *Angola* 81 H2
Namibe □, *Angola* 84 B1
Namibia ■, *Africa* 84 C2
Namibwoestyn, *Namibia* 84 C2
Namīn, *Iran* 67 C13
Namlea, *Indonesia* 57 E7
Namoi →, *Australia* 91 E4
Namous, O. en →, *Algeria* 75 B4
Nampa, *U.S.A.* 110 E5
Nampō-Shotō, *Japan* 49 J10
Nampula, *Mozam.* 83 F4
Namrole, *Indonesia* 57 E7
Namse Shankou, *China* 61 E13
Namsen →, *Norway* 8 D14
Namsos, *Norway* 8 D14
Namtsy, *Russia* 45 C13
Namtu, *Burma* 61 H20
Namtumbo, *Tanzania* 83 E4
Namu, *Canada* 100 C3
Namur, *Belgium* 17 H5
Namur □, *Belgium* 17 H6
Namutoni, *Namibia* 84 B2
Namwala, *Zambia* 83 F2
Namwŏn, *S. Korea* 51 G14
Namysłów, *Poland* 20 D7
Nan, *Thailand* 58 C3
Nan →, *Thailand* 58 E3
Nan Xian, *China* 53 C9
Nanaimo, *Canada* 100 D4
Nanam, *N. Korea* 51 D15
Nanan, *China* 53 E12
Nanango, *Australia* 91 D5
Nan'ao, *China* 53 F11
Nanao, *Japan* 49 F8
Nanbu, *China* 52 B6
Nanchang, *China* 53 C10
Nancheng, *China* 53 D11
Nanching = Nanjing, *China* 53 A12
Nanchong, *China* 52 B6
Nanchuan, *China* 52 C6
Nancy, *France* 25 D13
Nanda Devi, *India* 63 D8
Nandan, *China* 52 E6
Nandan, *Japan* 49 G7
Nanded, *India* 60 K10
Nandewar Ra., *Australia* 91 E5
Nandi, *Fiji* 87 C7
Nandi □, *Kenya* 82 B4
Nandurbar, *India* 60 J9
Nandyal, *India* 60 M11
Nanfeng, *Guangdong, China* 53 F8
Nanfeng, *Jiangxi, China* 53 D11
Nanga, *Australia* 89 E1
Nanga-Eboko, *Cameroon* 79 E7
Nanga Parbat, *Pakistan* 63 B6
Nangade, *Mozam.* 83 E4
Nangapinoh, *Indonesia* 56 E4
Nangarhār □, *Afghan.* 60 B7
Nangatayap, *Indonesia* 56 E4
Nangeya Mts., *Uganda* 82 B3
Nangis, *France* 25 D10
Nangong, *China* 50 F8
Nanhua, *China* 52 E3
Nanhuang, *China* 51 F11
Nanhui, *China* 53 B13
Nanjeko, *Zambia* 83 F1
Nanji Shan, *China* 53 D13
Nanjian, *China* 52 E3
Nanjiang, *China* 52 A6
Nanjing, *Fujian, China* 53 E11
Nanjing, *Jiangsu, China* 53 A12
Nanjirinji, *Tanzania* 83 D4
Nankana Sahib, *Pakistan* 62 D5
Nankang, *China* 53 E10
Nanking = Nanjing, *China* 53 A12
Nankoku, *Japan* 49 H6
Nanling, *China* 53 B12
Nanning, *China* 52 F7
Nannup, *Australia* 89 F2
Nanpan Jiang →, *China* 52 E6
Nanpara, *India* 63 F9
Nanpi, *China* 50 E9
Nanping, *Fujian, China* 53 D12
Nanping, *Henan, China* 53 C9
Nanri Dao, *China* 53 E12
Nanripe, *Mozam.* 83 E4
Nansei-Shotō = Ryūkyū-rettō, *Japan* 49 M2
Nansen Sd., *Canada* 4 A3
Nansio, *Tanzania* 82 C3
Nant, *France* 26 D7
Nantes, *France* 24 E5
Nanteuil-le-Haudouin, *France* 25 C9
Nantiat, *France* 26 B5
Nanticoke, *U.S.A.* 107 E8
Nanton, *Canada* 100 C6
Nantong, *China* 53 A13
Nantua, *France* 27 B9
Nantucket I., *U.S.A.* 94 E12
Nanuque, *Brazil* 123 E3
Nanusa, Kepulauan, *Indonesia* 57 D7
Nanutarra, *Australia* 88 D2
Nanxiong, *China* 53 E10
Nanyang, *China* 50 H7
Nanyi Hu, *China* 53 B12
Nanyuan, *China* 50 E9
Nanyuki, *Kenya* 82 B4
Nanzhang, *China* 53 B8
Nao, C. de la, *Spain* 29 G5
Naococane L., *Canada* 99 B5
Naoetsu, *Japan* 49 F9
Náousa, *Greece* 39 J5
Naozhou Dao, *China* 53 G8
Napa, *U.S.A.* 112 G4
Napa →, *U.S.A.* 112 G4
Napanee, *Canada* 98 D4
Napanoch, *U.S.A.* 107 E10
Nape, *Laos* 58 C5
Nape Pass = Keo Neua, Deo, *Vietnam* 58 C5
Napf, *Switz.* 22 B5
Napier, *N.Z.* 87 H6
Napier Broome B., *Australia* 88 B4
Napier Downs, *Australia* 88 C3
Napier Pen., *Australia* 90 A2
Naples = Nápoli, *Italy* 35 B7
Naples, *U.S.A.* 105 M5
Napo, *China* 52 F5
Napo □, *Ecuador* 120 D2
Napo →, *Peru* 120 D3
Napoleon, *N. Dak., U.S.A.* 108 B5
Napoleon, *Ohio, U.S.A.* 104 E3
Nápoli, *Italy* 35 B7
Nápoli, G. di, *Italy* 35 B7
Napopo, *Zaïre* 82 B2
Nappa Merrie, *Australia* 91 D3
Naqâda, *Egypt* 76 B3
Naqadeh, *Iran* 67 D11
Naqqāsh, *Iran* 65 C6
Nara, *Japan* 49 G7
Nara, *Mali* 78 B3
Nara □, *Japan* 49 G8
Nara Canal, *Pakistan* 62 G3
Nara Visa, *U.S.A.* 109 H3
Naracoorte, *Australia* 91 F3
Naradhan, *Australia* 91 E4
Narasapur, *India* 61 L12
Narathiwat, *Thailand* 59 J3
Narayanganj, *Bangla.* 61 H17
Narayanpet, *India* 60 L10
Narbonne, *France* 26 E7
Narcea →, *Spain* 30 B4
Nardīn, *Iran* 65 B7
Nardò, *Italy* 35 B11
Narembeen, *Australia* 89 F2
Nares Str., *Arctic* 94 A13
Naretha, *Australia* 89 F3
Narew →, *Poland* 20 C10
Nari →, *Pakistan* 62 E2
Narin, *Afghan.* 60 A6
Narindra, Helodranon' i, *Madag.* 85 A8
Narino □, *Colombia* 120 C2
Narita, *Japan* 49 G10
Narmada →, *India* 62 J5
Narman, *Turkey* 67 B9
Narmland, *Sweden* 9 F15
Narnaul, *India* 62 E7
Narni, *Italy* 33 F9
Naro, *Ghana* 78 C4
Naro, *Italy* 34 E6
Naro Fominsk, *Russia* 42 C3
Narodnaya, *Russia* 46 C9
Narok, *Kenya* 82 C4
Narok □, *Kenya* 82 C4
Narón, *Spain* 30 B2
Narooma, *Australia* 91 F5
Narowal, *Pakistan* 62 C6
Narrabri, *Australia* 91 E4
Narran →, *Australia* 91 D4
Narrandera, *Australia* 91 E4
Narraway →, *Canada* 100 B5
Narrogin, *Australia* 89 F2
Narromine, *Australia* 91 E4
Narsimhapur, *India* 63 H8
Nartkala, *Russia* 43 J6
Naruto, *Japan* 49 G7
Narva, *Estonia* 40 C5
Narva →, *Russia* 9 G22
Narvik, *Norway* 8 B17
Narvskoye Vdkhr., *Russia* 40 C5
Narwana, *India* 62 E7
Naryan-Mar, *Russia* 44 C6
Naryilco, *Australia* 91 D3
Narym, *Russia* 44 D9
Narymskoye, *Kazakstan* 44 E9
Naryn, *Kyrgyzstan* 44 E8
Nasa, *Norway* 8 C16
Nasarawa, *Nigeria* 79 D6
Năsăud, *Romania* 38 B7
Naseby, *N.Z.* 87 L3
Naselle, *U.S.A.* 112 D3
Naser, Buheirat en, *Egypt* 76 C3
Nashua, *Iowa, U.S.A.* 108 D8
Nashua, *Mont., U.S.A.* 110 B10
Nashua, *N.H., U.S.A.* 107 D13
Nashville, *Ark., U.S.A.* 109 J8
Nashville, *Ga., U.S.A.* 105 K4
Nashville, *Tenn., U.S.A.* 105 G2
Našice, *Croatia* 21 K8
Nasielsk, *Poland* 20 C10
Nasik, *India* 60 K8
Nasipit, *Phil.* 55 G6
Nasirabad, *India* 62 F6
Naskaupi →, *Canada* 99 B7
Naso, *Italy* 35 D7
Naṣriān-e Pā'īn, *Iran* 64 C5
Nass →, *Canada* 100 B3
Nassau, *Bahamas* 116 A4
Nassau, *U.S.A.* 107 D11
Nassau, B., *Chile* 128 E3
Nasser, L. = Naser, Buheirat en, *Egypt* 76 C3
Nasser City = Kôm Ombo, *Egypt* 76 C3
Nassian, *Ivory C.* 78 D4
Nässjö, *Sweden* 9 H16
Nasugbu, *Phil.* 55 D4
Näsviken, *Sweden* 10 C10
Nat Kyizin, *Burma* 61 M20
Nata, *Botswana* 84 C4
Natagaima, *Colombia* 120 C2
Natal, *Brazil* 122 C4
Natal, *Canada* 100 D6
Natal, *Indonesia* 56 D1
Natalinci, *Serbia, Yug.* 21 L10
Naṭanz, *Iran* 65 C6
Natashquan, *Canada* 99 B7
Natashquan →, *Canada* 99 B7
Natchez, *U.S.A.* 109 K9
Natchitoches, *U.S.A.* 109 K8
Naters, *Switz.* 22 D5
Nathalia, *Australia* 91 F4
Nathdwara, *India* 62 G5
Nati, Pta., *Spain* 36 A10
Natimuk, *Australia* 91 F3
Nation →, *Canada* 100 B4
National City, *U.S.A.* 113 N9
Natitingou, *Benin* 79 C5
Natividad, I., *Mexico* 114 B1
Natoma, *U.S.A.* 108 F5
Natron, L., *Tanzania* 82 C4
Natrona Heights, *U.S.A.* 106 F5
Natrûn, W. el →, *Egypt* 76 H7
Natuna Besar, Kepulauan, *Indonesia* 59 L7
Natuna Is. = Natuna Besar, Kepulauan, *Indonesia* 59 L7
Natuna Selatan, Kepulauan, *Indonesia* 59 L7
Natural Bridge, *U.S.A.* 107 B9
Naturaliste, C., *Australia* 90 G4
Nau Qala, *Afghan.* 62 B3
Naubinway, *U.S.A.* 98 C2
Naucelle, *France* 26 D6
Nauders, *Austria* 19 J6
Nauen, *Germany* 18 C8
Naugatuck, *U.S.A.* 107 E11
Naumburg, *Germany* 18 D7
Nā'ūr at Tunayb, *Jordan* 69 D4
Nauru ■, *Pac. Oc.* 92 H8
Naushahra = Nowshera, *Pakistan* 60 B8
Nauta, *Peru* 120 D3
Nautanwa, *India* 61 F13
Nautla, *Mexico* 115 C5
Nava, *Mexico* 114 B4
Nava del Rey, *Spain* 30 D5
Navacerrada, Puerto de, *Spain* 30 E7
Navadwip, *India* 63 H13
Navahermosa, *Spain* 31 F6
Navahrudak, *Belarus* 40 F3
Navajo Reservoir, *U.S.A.* 111 H10
Navalcarnero, *Spain* 30 E6
Navalmoral de la Mata, *Spain* 30 F5
Navalvillar de Pela, *Spain* 31 F5
Navan = An Uaimh, *Ireland* 15 C5
Navapolatsk, *Belarus* 40 E5
Navarino, I., *Chile* 128 E3
Navarra □, *Spain* 28 C3
Navarre, *U.S.A.* 106 F3
Navarrenx, *France* 26 E3
Navarro →, *U.S.A.* 112 F3
Navasota, *U.S.A.* 109 K6
Navassa, *W. Indies* 117 C4
Nave, *Italy* 32 C7
Naver →, *U.K.* 14 C4
Navia, *Spain* 30 B4
Navia →, *Spain* 30 B4
Navia de Suarna, *Spain* 30 C4
Navidad, *Chile* 126 C1
Navlya, *Russia* 42 D2
Navoi = Nawoiy, *Uzbekistan* 44 E7
Navojoa, *Mexico* 114 B3
Navolato, *Mexico* 114 C3
Návpaktos, *Greece* 39 L4
Návplion, *Greece* 39 M5
Navrongo, *Ghana* 79 C4
Navsari, *India* 60 J8
Nawa Kot, *Pakistan* 62 E4
Nawabganj, *Ut. P., India* 63 F9
Nawabganj, *Ut. P., India* 63 E8
Nawabshah, *Pakistan* 62 F3
Nawada, *India* 63 G11
Nawakot, *Nepal* 63 F11
Nawalgarh, *India* 62 F6
Nawanshahr, *India* 63 C6
Nawi, *Sudan* 76 D3
Nawoiy, *Uzbekistan* 44 E7
Naxçıvan, *Azerbaijan* 67 C11
Naxçıvan □, *Azerbaijan* 67 C11
Náxos, *Greece* 39 M8
Nay, *France* 26 E3
Nāy Band, *Iran* 65 E7
Naya →, *Colombia* 120 C2
Nayakhan, *Russia* 45 C16
Nayarit □, *Mexico* 114 C4
Nayé, *Senegal* 78 C2
Nayong, *China* 52 D5
Nayoro, *Japan* 48 B11
Nayyāl, W. →, *Si. Arabia* 64 D3
Nazaré, *Bahia, Brazil* 123 D4
Nazaré, *Pará, Brazil* 125 B7
Nazaré, *Tocantins, Brazil* 122 C2
Nazaré, *Portugal* 31 F1
Nazareth = Nazerat, *Israel* 69 C4
Nazas, *Mexico* 114 B4
Nazas →, *Mexico* 114 B4
Naze, The, *U.K.* 13 F9
Nazerat, *Israel* 69 C4
Nāzīk, *Iran* 67 C11
Nazilli, *Turkey* 66 D3
Nazir Hat, *Bangla.* 61 H17
Nazko, *Canada* 100 C4
Nazko →, *Canada* 100 C4
Nazret, *Ethiopia* 77 F4
Nchanga, *Zambia* 83 E2
Ncheu, *Malawi* 83 E3
Ndala, *Tanzania* 82 C3
Ndalatando, *Angola* 80 F2
Ndali, *Benin* 79 D5
Ndareda, *Tanzania* 82 C4
Ndélé, *C.A.R.* 73 G9
Ndendé, *Gabon* 80 E2
Ndjamena, *Chad* 73 F7
Ndjolé, *Gabon* 80 E2
Ndola, *Zambia* 83 E2

Ndoto Mts., Kenya 82 B4
Nduguti, Tanzania 82 C3
Nea →, Norway 10 A5
Néa Flippiás, Greece 39 K3
Neagh, Lough, U.K. 15 B5
Neah Bay, U.S.A. 112 B2
Neale, L., Australia 88 D5
Neápolis, Kozan, Greece 39 J4
Neápolis, Kríti, Greece 37 D7
Neápolis, Lakonia, Greece 39 N6
Near Is., U.S.A. 96 C1
Neath, U.K. 13 F4
Neath Port Talbot □, U.K. 13 F4
Nebbou, Burkina Faso 79 C4
Nebine Cr. →, Australia 91 D4
Nebitdag, Turkmenistan 44 F6
Nebolchy, Russia 40 C7
Nebraska □, U.S.A. 108 E5
Nebraska City, U.S.A. 108 E7
Nébrodi, Monti, Italy 35 E7
Necedah, U.S.A. 108 C9
Nechako →, Canada 100 C4
Neches →, U.S.A. 109 L8
Neckar →, Germany 19 F4
Necochea, Argentina 126 D4
Nedelišće, Croatia 33 B13
Neder Rijn →, Neths. 16 E8
Nederbrakel, Belgium 17 G3
Nederweert, Neths. 17 F7
Nédha →, Greece 39 M4
Nedroma, Algeria 75 A4
Neede, Neths. 16 D9
Needles, U.S.A. 113 L12
Needles, The, U.K. 13 G6
Ñeembucú □, Paraguay 126 B4
Neemuch = Nimach, India 62 G6
Neenah, U.S.A. 104 C1
Neepawa, Canada 101 C9
Neer, Neths. 17 F7
Neerpelt, Belgium 17 F6
Nefta, Tunisia 75 B6
Neftah Sidi Boubekeur, Algeria 75 A5
Neftçala, Azerbaijan 67 C13
Neftegorsk, Russia 43 H4
Neftekumsk, Russia 43 H7
Neftenbach, Switz. 23 A7
Negapatam = Nagappattinam, India 60 P11
Negaunee, U.S.A. 104 B2
Negele, Ethiopia 68 F2
Negev Desert = Hanegev, Israel 69 E3
Negombo, Sri Lanka 60 R11
Negotin, Serbia, Yug. 21 L12
Negra, Peña, Spain 30 C4
Negra, Pta., Mauritania 74 D1
Negra, Pta., Peru 124 B1
Negra Pt., Phil. 57 A6
Negrais, C. = Maudin Sun, Burma 61 M19
Negreira, Spain 30 C2
Négrine, Algeria 75 B6
Negro →, Argentina 128 B4
Negro →, Bolivia 125 C5
Negro →, Brazil 121 D6
Negro →, Uruguay 127 C4
Negros, Phil. 55 G5
Nehalem →, U.S.A. 112 E3
Nehāvand, Iran 65 C6
Nehbandān, Iran 65 D9
Neheim, Germany 18 D3
Nehoiaşu, Romania 38 D9
Nei Monggol Zizhiqu □, China 50 C6
Neidpath, Canada 101 C7
Neihart, U.S.A. 110 C8
Neijiang, China 52 C5
Neilton, U.S.A. 110 C2
Neiqiu, China 50 F8
Neira de Jusá, Spain 30 C3
Neiva, Colombia 120 C2
Neixiang, China 50 H6
Nejanilini L., Canada 101 B9
Nejo, Ethiopia 77 F4
Nekā, Iran 65 B7
Nekemte, Ethiopia 77 F4
Nêkheb, Egypt 76 B3
Neksø, Denmark 9 J16
Nelas, Portugal 30 E3
Nelia, Australia 90 C3
Nelidovo, Russia 40 D7
Neligh, U.S.A. 108 D5
Nelkan, Russia 45 D14
Nellore, India 60 M11
Nelma, Russia 45 E14
Nelson, Canada 100 D5
Nelson, N.Z. 87 J4
Nelson, U.K. 12 D5
Nelson, U.S.A. 111 J7
Nelson →, Canada 101 C9
Nelson, C., Australia 91 F3
Nelson, Estrecho, Chile 128 D2
Nelson Forks, Canada 100 B4
Nelson House, Canada 101 B9
Nelson L., Canada 101 B8
Nelspoort, S. Africa 84 E3
Nelspruit, S. Africa 85 D5
Néma, Mauritania 78 B3
Neman, Russia 9 J20
Neman →, Lithuania 9 J19
Nemeiben L., Canada 101 B7
Nemira, Romania 38 C9
Nemours, France 25 D9
Nemunas = Neman →, Lithuania 9 J19
Nemuro, Japan 48 C12
Nemuro-Kaikyō, Japan 48 C12
Nemuy, Russia 45 D14
Nen Jiang →, China 51 B13
Nenagh, Ireland 15 D3
Nenana, U.S.A. 96 B5
Nenasi, Malaysia 59 L4
Nene →, U.K. 12 E8
Nenjiang, China 54 B7
Neno, Malawi 83 F3
Neodesha, U.S.A. 109 G7
Neópolis, Brazil 122 D4
Neosho, U.S.A. 109 G7
Neosho →, U.S.A. 109 H7
Nepal ■, Asia 63 F11
Nepalganj, Nepal 63 E9
Nephi, U.S.A. 110 G8
Nephin, Ireland 15 B2
Neptune, U.S.A. 107 F10
Néra →, Romania 38 E4
Nérac, France 26 D4
Nerchinsk, Russia 45 D12
Nerchinskiy Zavod, Russia 45 D12
Nereju, Romania 38 D9
Nerekhta, Russia 42 B5
Néret L., Canada 99 B5
Neringa, Lithuania 9 J19
Nerja, Spain 31 J7
Nerl →, Russia 42 B5
Nerpio, Spain 29 G2
Nerva, Spain 31 H4
Nes, Neths. 16 B7
Nesbyen, Norway 10 D3
Nesebûr, Bulgaria 38 G10
Nesland, Norway 10 E1
Neslandsvatn, Norway 10 F3
Nesle, France 25 C9
Nesodden, Norway 10 E4
Nesque →, France 27 E8
Ness, L., U.K. 14 D4
Nesslau, Switz. 23 B8
Nesterov, Ukraine 41 G2
Néstos →, Greece 39 H7
Nesvizh = Nyasvizh, Belarus 41 F4
Netanya, Israel 69 C3
Nète →, Belgium 17 F4
Netherdale, Australia 90 C4
Netherlands ■, Europe 16 E6
Netherlands Antilles ■, W. Indies 120 A4
Neto →, Italy 35 C10
Nettancourt, France 25 D11
Nettilling L., Canada 97 B12
Nettuno, Italy 34 A5
Netzahualcoyotl, Presa, Mexico 115 D6
Neu-Isenburg, Germany 19 E4
Neu-Ulm, Germany 19 G6
Neubrandenburg, Germany 18 B9
Neubukow, Germany 18 A7
Neuburg, Germany 19 G7
Neuchâtel, Switz. 22 C3
Neuchâtel □, Switz. 22 C3
Neuchâtel, Lac de, Switz. 22 C3
Neudau, Austria 21 H6
Neuenegg, Switz. 22 C4
Neuenhaus, Germany 18 C2
Neuf-Brisach, France 25 D14
Neufahrn, Germany 19 G8
Neufchâteau, Belgium 17 J6
Neufchâteau, France 25 D12
Neufchâtel-en-Bray, France 24 C8
Neufchâtel-sur-Aisne, France 25 C11
Neuhaus, Germany 18 B6
Neuhausen, Switz. 23 A7
Neuillé-Pont-Pierre, France 24 E7
Neuilly-St.-Front, France 25 C10
Neukalen, Germany 18 B8
Neumarkt, Germany 19 F7
Neumarkt-Sankt Veit, Germany 19 G8
Neumünster, Germany 18 A5
Neung-sur-Beuvron, France 25 E8
Neunkirchen, Austria 21 H6
Neunkirchen, Germany 19 F3
Neuquén, Argentina 128 A3
Neuquén □, Argentina 126 D2
Neuquén →, Argentina 128 A3
Neuruppin, Germany 18 C8
Neuse →, U.S.A. 105 H7
Neusiedler See, Austria 21 H6
Neuss, Germany 17 F9
Neussargues-Moissac, France 26 C7
Neustadt, Baden-W., Germany 19 H4
Neustadt, Bayern, Germany 19 F8
Neustadt, Bayern, Germany 19 G7
Neustadt, Bayern, Germany 19 F6
Neustadt, Bayern, Germany 19 E7
Neustadt, Brandenburg, Germany 18 C8
Neustadt, Hessen, Germany 18 E5
Neustadt, Niedersachsen, Germany 18 C5
Neustadt, Rhld-Pfz., Germany 19 F4
Neustadt, Schleswig-Holstein, Germany 18 A6
Neustadt, Thüringen, Germany 18 E7
Neustrelitz, Germany 18 B9
Neuvic, France 26 C6
Neuville, Belgium 17 H5
Neuville-aux-Bois, France 25 D9
Neuville-de-Poitou, France 26 B4
Neuville-sur-Saône, France 27 C8
Neuvy-le-Roi, France 24 E7
Neuvy-St.-Sépulchre, France 26 B5
Neuvy-sur-Barangeon, France 25 E9
Neuwerk, Germany 18 B4
Neuwied, Germany 18 E3
Neva →, Russia 40 C6
Nevada, U.S.A. 109 G7
Nevada □, U.S.A. 110 G5
Nevada, Sierra, Spain 29 H1
Nevada, Sierra, U.S.A. 110 G3
Nevada City, U.S.A. 112 F6
Nevado, Cerro, Argentina 126 D2
Nevanka, Russia 45 D10
Nevel, Russia 40 D5
Nevele, Belgium 17 F3
Nevers, France 25 F10
Nevertire, Australia 91 E4
Neville, Canada 101 D7
Nevinnomyssk, Russia 43 H6
Nevis, W. Indies 117 C7
Nevrokop = Gotse Delchev, Bulgaria 39 H6
Nevşehir, Turkey 66 C6
New →, Guyana 121 C6
New Albany, Ind., U.S.A. 104 F3
New Albany, Miss., U.S.A. 109 H10
New Albany, Pa., U.S.A. 107 E8
New Amsterdam, Guyana 121 B6
New Angledool, Australia 91 D4
New Bedford, U.S.A. 107 E14
New Bern, U.S.A. 105 H7
New Bethlehem, U.S.A. 106 E5
New Bloomfield, U.S.A. 106 F7
New Boston, U.S.A. 109 J7
New Braunfels, U.S.A. 109 L5
New Brighton, N.Z. 87 K4
New Brighton, U.S.A. 106 F4
New Britain, Papua N. G. 92 H7
New Britain, U.S.A. 107 E12
New Brunswick, U.S.A. 107 F10
New Brunswick □, Canada 99 C6
New Bussa, Nigeria 79 D5
New Caledonia ■, Pac. Oc. 92 K8
New Castle, Ind., U.S.A. 104 F3
New Castle, Pa., U.S.A. 106 E4
New City, U.S.A. 107 E11
New Cumberland, U.S.A. 106 F4
New Cuyama, U.S.A. 113 L7
New Delhi, India 62 E7
New Denver, Canada 100 D5
New Don Pedro Reservoir, U.S.A. 112 H6
New England, U.S.A. 108 B3
New England Ra., Australia 91 E5
New Forest, U.K. 13 G6
New Glasgow, Canada 99 C7
New Guinea, Oceania 46 K17
New Hamburg, Canada 106 C4
New Hampshire □, U.S.A. 107 C13
New Hampton, U.S.A. 108 D8
New Hanover, S. Africa 85 D5
New Haven, Conn., U.S.A. 107 E12
New Haven, Mich., U.S.A. 106 D2
New Hazelton, Canada 100 B3
New Hebrides = Vanuatu ■, Pac. Oc. 92 J8
New Iberia, U.S.A. 109 K9
New Ireland, Papua N. G. 92 H7
New Jersey □, U.S.A. 107 F10
New Kensington, U.S.A. 106 F5
New Lexington, U.S.A. 104 F4
New Liskeard, Canada 98 C4
New London, Conn., U.S.A. 107 E12
New London, Minn., U.S.A. 108 C7
New London, Ohio, U.S.A. 106 E2
New London, Wis., U.S.A. 108 C10
New Madrid, U.S.A. 109 G10
New Meadows, U.S.A. 110 D5
New Melones L., U.S.A. 112 H6
New Mexico □, U.S.A. 111 J10
New Milford, Conn., U.S.A. 107 E11
New Milford, Pa., U.S.A. 107 E9
New Norcia, Australia 89 F2
New Norfolk, Australia 90 G4
New Orleans, U.S.A. 109 K9
New Philadelphia, U.S.A. 106 F3
New Plymouth, N.Z. 87 H5
New Plymouth, U.S.A. 110 E5
New Providence, Bahamas 116 A4
New Radnor, U.K. 13 E4
New Richmond, U.S.A. 108 C8
New Roads, U.S.A. 109 K9
New Rochelle, U.S.A. 107 F11
New Rockford, U.S.A. 108 B5
New Ross, Ireland 15 D5
New Salem, U.S.A. 108 B4
New Scone, U.K. 14 E5
New Siberian Is. = Novaya Sibir, Ostrov, Russia 45 B16
New Siberian Is. = Novosibirskiye Ostrova, Russia 45 B15
New Smyrna Beach, U.S.A. 105 L5
New South Wales □, Australia 91 E4
New Springs, Australia 89 E3
New Town, U.S.A. 108 A3
New Ulm, U.S.A. 108 C7
New Waterford, Canada 99 C7
New Westminster, Canada 100 D4
New York □, U.S.A. 107 D9
New York City, U.S.A. 107 F11
New Zealand ■, Oceania 87 J5
Newala, Tanzania 83 E4
Newala □, Tanzania 83 E4
Newark, Del., U.S.A. 104 F8
Newark, N.J., U.S.A. 107 F10
Newark, N.Y., U.S.A. 106 C7
Newark, Ohio, U.S.A. 106 F2
Newark-on-Trent, U.K. 12 D7
Newaygo, U.S.A. 104 D3
Newberg, U.S.A. 110 D2
Newberry, Mich., U.S.A. 104 B3
Newberry, S.C., U.S.A. 105 H5
Newberry Springs, U.S.A. 113 L10
Newbridge = Droichead Nua, Ireland 15 C5
Newbrook, Canada 100 C6
Newburgh, U.S.A. 107 E10
Newbury, U.K. 13 F6
Newbury, U.S.A. 107 B12
Newburyport, U.S.A. 107 D14
Newcastle, Australia 91 E5
Newcastle, Canada 99 C6
Newcastle, S. Africa 85 D4
Newcastle, U.K. 15 B6
Newcastle, Calif., U.S.A. 112 G5
Newcastle, Wyo., U.S.A. 108 D2
Newcastle Emlyn, U.K. 13 E3
Newcastle Ra., Australia 88 C5
Newcastle-under-Lyme, U.K. 12 D5
Newcastle-upon-Tyne, U.K. 12 C6
Newcastle Waters, Australia 90 B1
Newdegate, Australia 89 F2
Newell, U.S.A. 108 C3
Newfoundland □, Canada 99 B8
Newfoundland I., N. Amer. 94 E14
Newhalem, U.S.A. 100 D4
Newhall, U.S.A. 113 L8
Newham, U.K. 13 F8
Newhaven, U.K. 13 G8
Newkirk, U.S.A. 109 G6
Newman, Australia 88 D2
Newman, U.S.A. 112 H5
Newmarket, Canada 106 B5
Newmarket, Ireland 15 D3
Newmarket, U.K. 13 E8
Newmarket, U.S.A. 107 C14
Newnan, U.S.A. 105 J3
Newport, I. of W., U.K. 13 G6
Newport, Newp., U.K. 13 F5
Newport, Ark., U.S.A. 109 H9
Newport, Ky., U.S.A. 104 F3
Newport, N.H., U.S.A. 107 C12
Newport, Oreg., U.S.A. 110 D1
Newport, Pa., U.S.A. 106 F7
Newport, R.I., U.S.A. 107 E13
Newport, Tenn., U.S.A. 105 H4
Newport, Vt., U.S.A. 107 B12
Newport, Wash., U.S.A. 110 B5
Newport □, U.K. 13 F4
Newport Beach, U.S.A. 113 M9
Newport News, U.S.A. 104 G7
Newquay, U.K. 13 G2
Newry, U.K. 15 B5
Newry & Mourne □, U.K. 15 B5
Newton, Iowa, U.S.A. 108 E8
Newton, Mass., U.S.A. 107 D13
Newton, Miss., U.S.A. 109 J10
Newton, N.C., U.S.A. 105 H5
Newton, N.J., U.S.A. 107 E10
Newton, Tex., U.S.A. 109 K8
Newton Abbot, U.K. 13 G4
Newton Boyd, Australia 91 D5
Newton Stewart, U.K. 14 G4
Newtonmore, U.K. 14 D4
Newtown, U.K. 13 E4
Newtownabbey □, U.K. 15 B6
Newtownards, U.K. 15 B6
Newville, U.S.A. 106 F7
Nexon, France 26 C5
Neya, Russia 42 A6
Neyrīz, Iran 65 D7
Neyshābūr, Iran 65 B8
Nezhin = Nizhyn, Ukraine 41 G6
Nezperce, U.S.A. 110 C5
Ngabang, Indonesia 56 D3
Ngabordamlu, Tanjung, Indonesia 57 F8
Ngambé, Cameroon 79 D7
Ngami Depression, Botswana 84 C3
Ngamo, Zimbabwe 83 F2
Nganglong Kangri, China 61 C12
Nganjuk, Indonesia 57 G14
Ngao, Thailand 58 C2
Ngaoundéré, Cameroon 80 C2
Ngapara, N.Z. 87 L3
Ngara, Tanzania 82 C3
Ngara □, Tanzania 82 C3
Ngawi, Indonesia 57 G14
Nghia Lo, Vietnam 58 B5
Ngoma, Malawi 83 E3
Ngomahura, Zimbabwe 83 G3
Ngomba, Tanzania 83 D3
Ngop, Sudan 77 F3
Ngoring Hu, China 54 C4
Ngorkou, Mali 78 B4
Ngorongoro, Tanzania 82 C4
Ngozi, Burundi 82 C2
Ngudu, Tanzania 82 C3
Nguigmi, Niger 73 F7
Ngukurr, Australia 90 A1
Ngunga, Tanzania 82 C3
Nguru, Nigeria 79 C7
Nguru Mts., Tanzania 82 D4
Nguyen Binh, Vietnam 58 A5
Nha Trang, Vietnam 59 F7
Nhacoongo, Mozam. 85 C6
Nhamaabué, Mozam. 83 F4
Nhambiquara, Brazil 125 C6
Nhamundá, Brazil 121 D6
Nhamundá →, Brazil 121 D6
Nhangutazi, L., Mozam. 85 C5
Nhecolândia, Brazil 125 D6
Nhill, Australia 91 F3
Nho Quan, Vietnam 58 B5
Nhulunbuy, Australia 90 A2
Nia-nia, Zaïre 82 B2
Niafounké, Mali 78 B4
Niagara, U.S.A. 104 C1
Niagara Falls, Canada 98 D4
Niagara Falls, U.S.A. 106 C6
Niagara-on-the-Lake, Canada 106 C5
Niah, Malaysia 56 D4
Niamey, Niger 79 C5
Nianforando, Guinea 78 D2
Nianfors, Sweden 10 C10
Niangara, Zaïre 82 B2
Nias, Indonesia 56 D1
Niassa □, Mozam. 83 E4
Nibbiano, Italy 32 D6
Nibe, Denmark 11 H3
Nicaragua ■, Cent. Amer. 116 D2
Nicaragua, L. de, Nic. 116 D2
Nicastro, Italy 35 D9
Nice, France 27 E11
Niceville, U.S.A. 105 K2
Nichinan, Japan 49 J5
Nicholás, Canal, W. Indies 116 B3
Nicholasville, U.S.A. 104 G3
Nichols, U.S.A. 107 D8
Nicholson, Australia 88 C4
Nicholson, U.S.A. 107 E9
Nicholson →, Australia 90 B2
Nicholson Ra., Australia 89 E2
Nickerie □, Surinam 121 C6
Nickerie →, Surinam 121 B6
Nicobar Is., Ind. Oc. 46 J13
Nicoclí, Colombia 120 B2
Nicola, Canada 100 C4
Nicolet, Canada 98 C5
Nicolls Town, Bahamas 116 A4
Nicosia, Cyprus 66 E5
Nicosia, Italy 35 E7
Nicótera, Italy 35 D8
Nicoya, Costa Rica 116 D2
Nicoya, G. de, Costa Rica 116 E3
Nicoya, Pen. de, Costa Rica 116 E2
Nidau, Switz. 22 B4
Nidd →, U.K. 12 C6
Nidda, Germany 18 E5
Nidda →, Germany 19 E4
Nidwalden □, Switz. 23 C6
Nidzica, Poland 20 B10
Niebüll, Germany 18 A4
Nied →, Germany 25 C13
Niederaula, Germany 18 E5
Niederbipp, Switz. 22 B5
Niederbronn-les-Bains, France 25 D14
Niedere Tauern, Austria 21 H4
Niedersachsen □, Germany 18 C5
Niekerkshoop, S. Africa 84 D3
Niel, Belgium 17 F4
Niellé, Ivory C. 78 C3
Niemba, Zaïre 82 D2
Niemen = Neman →, Lithuania 9 J19
Nienburg, Germany 18 C5
Niers →, Germany 18 D2
Niesen, Switz. 22 C5
Niesky, Germany 18 D10
Nieu Bethesda, S. Africa 84 E3
Nieuw-Amsterdam, Neths. 16 C9
Nieuw Amsterdam, Surinam 121 B6
Nieuw Beijerland, Neths. 16 E4
Nieuw-Dordrecht, Neths. 16 C9
Nieuw Loosdrecht, Neths. 16 D6
Nieuw Nickerie, Surinam 121 B6
Nieuw-Schoonebeek, Neths. 16 C10
Nieuw-Vennep, Neths. 16 D5
Nieuw-Vossemeer, Neths. 17 E4
Nieuwe-Niedorp, Neths. 16 C5
Nieuwe-Pekela, Neths. 16 B9
Nieuwe-Schans, Neths. 16 B10
Nieuwendijk, Neths. 16 E5
Nieuwerkerken, Belgium 17 G6
Nieuwkoop, Neths. 16 D5
Nieuwleusen, Neths. 16 C8
Nieuwnamen, Neths. 17 F4
Nieuwolda, Neths. 16 B9
Nieuwoudtville, S. Africa 84 E2
Nieuwpoort, Belgium 17 F1
Nieuwveen, Neths. 16 D5
Nieves, Spain 30 C2
Nieves, Pico de las, Canary Is. 36 G4
Nièvre □, France 25 E10
Niğde, Turkey 66 D6
Nigel, S. Africa 85 D4
Niger □, Nigeria 79 C6
Niger ■, W. Afr. 79 B6
Niger →, W. Afr. 79 D6
Nigeria ■, W. Afr. 79 D6
Nightcaps, N.Z. 87 L2
Nigríta, Greece 39 J6
Nihtaur, India 63 E8
Nii-Jima, Japan 49 G9
Niigata, Japan 48 F9

Niigata □, *Japan* 49 F9
Niihama, *Japan* 49 H6
Niihau, *U.S.A.* 102 H14
Niimi, *Japan* 49 G6
Niitsu, *Japan* 48 F9
Níjar, *Spain* 29 J2
Nijil, *Jordan* 69 E4
Nijkerk, *Neths.* 16 D7
Nijlen, *Belgium* 17 F5
Nijmegen, *Neths.* 16 E7
Nijverdal, *Neths.* 16 D8
Nīk Pey, *Iran* 67 D13
Nike, *Nigeria* 79 D6
Nikiniki, *Indonesia* 57 F6
Nikki, *Benin* 79 D5
Nikkō, *Japan* 49 F9
Nikolayev = Mykolayiv, *Ukraine* 41 J7
Nikolayevsk, *Russia* 42 E7
Nikolayevsk-na-Amur, *Russia* 45 D15
Nikolsk, *Russia* 42 D8
Nikolskoye, *Russia* 45 D17
Nikopol, *Bulgaria* 38 F7
Nikopol, *Ukraine* 41 J8
Niksar, *Turkey* 66 B7
Nīkshahr, *Iran* 65 E9
Nikšić, *Montenegro, Yug.* 21 N8
Nîl, Nahr en →, *Africa* 76 H7
Nîl el Abyad →, *Sudan* 77 D3
Nîl el Azraq →, *Sudan* 77 D3
Niland, *U.S.A.* 113 M11
Nile = Nîl, Nahr en →, *Africa* 76 H7
Nile Delta, *Egypt* 76 H7
Niles, *U.S.A.* 106 E4
Nilo Peçanha, *Brazil* 123 D4
Nimach, *India* 62 G6
Nimbahera, *India* 62 G6
Nîmes, *France* 27 E8
Nimfaíon, Ákra = Pínnes, Ákra, *Greece* 39 J7
Nimmitabel, *Australia* 91 F4
Nimule, *Sudan* 77 G3
Nin, *Croatia* 33 D12
Nīnawá, *Iraq* 67 D10
Nindigully, *Australia* 91 D4
Ninemile, *U.S.A.* 100 B2
Nineveh = Nīnawá, *Iraq* 67 D10
Ning Xian, *China* 50 G4
Ningaloo, *Australia* 88 D1
Ning'an, *China* 51 B15
Ningbo, *China* 53 C13
Ningcheng, *China* 51 D10
Ningde, *China* 53 D12
Ningdu, *China* 53 D10
Ninggang, *China* 53 D9
Ningguo, *China* 53 B12
Ninghai, *China* 53 C13
Ninghua, *China* 53 D11
Ningjin, *China* 50 F8
Ningjing Shan, *China* 52 B2
Ninglang, *China* 52 D3
Ningling, *China* 50 G8
Ningming, *China* 52 F6
Ningnan, *China* 52 D4
Ningpo = Ningbo, *China* 53 C13
Ningqiang, *China* 50 H4
Ningshan, *China* 50 H5
Ningsia Hui A.R. = Ningxia Huizu Zizhiqu □, *China* 50 E3
Ningwu, *China* 50 E7
Ningxia Huizu Zizhiqu □, *China* 50 E3
Ningxiang, *China* 53 C9
Ningyang, *China* 50 G9
Ningyuan, *China* 53 E8
Ninh Binh, *Vietnam* 58 B5
Ninh Giang, *Vietnam* 58 B6
Ninh Hoa, *Vietnam* 58 F7
Ninh Ma, *Vietnam* 58 F7
Ninove, *Belgium* 17 G4
Nioaque, *Brazil* 127 A4
Niobrara, *U.S.A.* 108 D6
Niobrara →, *U.S.A.* 108 D6
Niono, *Mali* 78 C3
Nioro du Rip, *Senegal* 78 C1
Nioro du Sahel, *Mali* 78 B3
Niort, *France* 26 B3
Nipawin, *Canada* 101 C8
Nipawin Prov. Park, *Canada* 101 C8
Nipigon, *Canada* 98 C2
Nipigon, L., *Canada* 98 C2
Nipin →, *Canada* 101 B7
Nipishish L., *Canada* 99 B7
Nipissing L., *Canada* 98 C4
Nipomo, *U.S.A.* 113 K6
Nipton, *U.S.A.* 113 K11
Niquelândia, *Brazil* 123 D2
Nīr, *Iran* 67 C12
Nirasaki, *Japan* 49 G9
Nirmal, *India* 60 K11
Nirmali, *India* 63 F12
Niš, *Serbia, Yug.* 21 M11
Nisa, *Portugal* 31 F3
Nişāb, *Si. Arabia* 64 D5
Nişāb, *Yemen* 68 E4
Nišava →, *Serbia, Yug.* 21 M11
Niscemi, *Italy* 35 E7
Nishinomiya, *Japan* 49 G7
Nishin'omote, *Japan* 49 J5
Nishiwaki, *Japan* 49 G7
Nísíros, *Greece* 39 N10
Niskibi →, *Canada* 98 A2
Nispen, *Neths.* 17 F4
Nisqually →, *U.S.A.* 112 C4
Nissáki, *Greece* 37 A3
Nissan →, *Sweden* 11 H6
Nissedal, *Norway* 10 E2
Nisser, *Norway* 10 E2
Nissum Bredning, *Denmark* 9 H13
Nissum Fjord, *Denmark* 11 H2
Nistelrode, *Neths.* 17 E7
Nistru = Dnister →, *Europe* 41 J6
Nisutlin →, *Canada* 100 A2
Nitchequon, *Canada* 99 B5
Niterói, *Brazil* 123 F3
Nith →, *U.K.* 14 F5
Nitra, *Slovak Rep.* 21 G8
Nittedal, *Norway* 10 D4
Nittenau, *Germany* 19 F8
Niuafo'ou, *Tonga* 87 B11
Niue, *Cook Is.* 93 J11
Niulan Jiang →, *China* 52 D4
Niut, *Indonesia* 56 D4
Niutou Shan, *China* 53 C13
Niuzhuang, *China* 51 D12
Nivala, *Finland* 8 E21
Nivelles, *Belgium* 17 G4
Nivernais, *France* 25 E10
Nixon, *U.S.A.* 109 L6
Nizamabad, *India* 60 K11
Nizamghat, *India* 61 E19
Nizhne Kolymsk, *Russia* 45 C17
Nizhne-Vartovsk, *Russia* 44 C8
Nizhneangarsk, *Russia* 45 D11
Nizhnegorskiy = Nyzhnohirskyy, *Ukraine* 41 K8
Nizhnekamsk, *Russia* 42 C10
Nizhneudinsk, *Russia* 45 D10
Nizhneyansk, *Russia* 45 B14
Nizhniy Chir, *Russia* 43 F6
Nizhniy Lomov, *Russia* 42 D6
Nizhniy Novgorod, *Russia* 42 B7
Nizhniy Tagil, *Russia* 44 D6
Nizhyn, *Ukraine* 41 G6
Nizip, *Turkey* 66 D7
Nízké Tatry, *Slovak Rep.* 20 G9
Nizza Monferrato, *Italy* 32 D5
Njakwa, *Malawi* 83 E3
Njanji, *Zambia* 83 E3
Njinjo, *Tanzania* 83 D4
Njombe, *Tanzania* 83 D3
Njombe □, *Tanzania* 83 D3
Njombe →, *Tanzania* 82 D4
Nkambe, *Cameroon* 79 D7
Nkana, *Zambia* 83 E2
Nkawkaw, *Ghana* 79 D4
Nkayi, *Zimbabwe* 83 F2
Nkhata Bay, *Malawi* 80 G6
Nkhota Kota, *Malawi* 83 E3
Nkongsamba, *Cameroon* 79 E6
Nkurenkuru, *Namibia* 84 B2
Nkwanta, *Ghana* 78 D4
Nmai →, *Burma* 61 G20
Noakhali = Maijdi, *Bangla.* 61 H17
Noatak, *U.S.A.* 96 B3
Nobel, *Canada* 106 A4
Nobeoka, *Japan* 49 H5
Noblejas, *Spain* 28 F1
Noblesville, *U.S.A.* 104 E3
Noce →, *Italy* 32 B8
Nocera Inferiore, *Italy* 35 B7
Nocera Terinese, *Italy* 35 C9
Nocera Umbra, *Italy* 33 E9
Noci, *Italy* 35 B10
Nockatunga, *Australia* 91 D3
Nocona, *U.S.A.* 109 J6
Noda, *Japan* 49 G9
Noel, *U.S.A.* 109 G7
Nogales, *Mexico* 114 A2
Nogales, *U.S.A.* 111 L8
Nōgata, *Japan* 49 H5
Nogent-en-Bassigny, *France* 25 D12
Nogent-le-Rotrou, *France* 24 D7
Nogent-sur-Seine, *France* 25 D10
Noggerup, *Australia* 89 F2
Noginsk, *Moskva, Russia* 42 C4
Noginsk, *Sib., Russia* 45 C10
Nogoa →, *Australia* 90 C4
Nogoyá, *Argentina* 126 C4
Nogueira de Ramuin, *Spain* 30 C3
Noguera Pallaresa →, *Spain* 28 D5
Noguera Ribagorzana →, *Spain* 28 D5
Nohar, *India* 62 E6
Noire, Montagne, *France* 26 E6
Noire, Mt., *France* 24 D3
Noirétable, *France* 26 C7
Noirmoutier, I. de, *France* 24 F4
Noirmoutier-en-l'Ile, *France* 24 F4
Nojane, *Botswana* 84 C3
Nojima-Zaki, *Japan* 49 G9
Nok Kundi, *Pakistan* 60 E3
Nokaneng, *Botswana* 84 B3
Nokhtuysk, *Russia* 45 C12
Nokia, *Finland* 9 F20
Nokomis, *Canada* 101 C8
Nokomis L., *Canada* 101 B8
Nol, *Sweden* 11 G6
Nola, *C.A.R.* 80 D3
Nola, *Italy* 35 B7
Nolay, *France* 25 F11
Noli, C. di, *Italy* 32 D5
Nolinsk, *Russia* 42 B9
Noma Omuramba →, *Namibia* 84 B3
Noman L., *Canada* 101 A7
Nombre de Dios, *Panama* 116 E4
Nome, *U.S.A.* 96 B3
Nomo-Zaki, *Japan* 49 H4
Nonacho L., *Canada* 101 A7
Nonancourt, *France* 24 D8
Nonant-le-Pin, *France* 24 D7
Nonda, *Australia* 90 C3
Nong Chang, *Thailand* 58 E2
Nong Het, *Laos* 58 C4
Nong Khai, *Thailand* 58 D4
Nong'an, *China* 51 B13
Nongoma, *S. Africa* 85 D5
Nonoava, *Mexico* 114 B3
Nonthaburi, *Thailand* 58 F3
Nontron, *France* 26 C4
Nonza, *France* 27 F13
Noonamah, *Australia* 88 B5
Noonan, *U.S.A.* 108 A3
Noondoo, *Australia* 91 D4
Noonkanbah, *Australia* 88 C3
Noord-Bergum, *Neths.* 16 B8
Noord Brabant □, *Neths.* 17 E6
Noord Holland □, *Neths.* 16 D5
Noordbeveland, *Neths.* 17 E3
Noordeloos, *Neths.* 16 E5
Noordhollandsch Kanaal, *Neths.* 16 C5
Noordhorn, *Neths.* 16 B8
Noordoostpolder, *Neths.* 16 C7
Noordwijk aan Zee, *Neths.* 16 D4
Noordwijk-Binnen, *Neths.* 16 D4
Noordwijkerhout, *Neths.* 16 D5
Noordzee Kanaal, *Neths.* 16 D5
Noorwolde, *Neths.* 16 C8
Nootka, *Canada* 100 D3
Nootka I., *Canada* 100 D3
Nóqui, *Angola* 80 F2
Nora, *Eritrea* 77 D5
Noranda, *Canada* 98 C4
Nórcia, *Italy* 33 F10
Norco, *U.S.A.* 113 M9
Nord □, *France* 25 B10
Nord-Ostsee-Kanal →, *Germany* 18 A5
Nordagutu, *Norway* 10 E3
Nordaustlandet, *Svalbard* 4 B9
Nordborg, *Denmark* 11 J3
Nordby, *Århus, Denmark* 11 J4
Nordby, *Ribe, Denmark* 11 J2
Norddeich, *Germany* 18 B3
Nordegg, *Canada* 100 C5
Norden, *Germany* 18 B3
Nordenham, *Germany* 18 B4
Norderhov, *Norway* 10 D4
Norderney, *Germany* 18 B3
Nordfjord, *Norway* 9 F11
Nordfriesische Inseln, *Germany* 18 A4
Nordhausen, *Germany* 18 D6
Nordhorn, *Germany* 18 C3
Norðoyar, *Færoe Is.* 8 E9
Nordjyllands Amtskommune □, *Denmark* 11 H4
Nordkapp, *Norway* 8 A21
Nordkapp, *Svalbard* 4 A9
Nordkinn = Kinnarodden, *Norway* 6 A11
Nordkinn-halvøya, *Norway* 8 A22
Nördlingen, *Germany* 19 G6
Nordrhein-Westfalen □, *Germany* 18 D3
Nordstrand, *Germany* 18 A4
Nordvik, *Russia* 45 B12
Nore, *Norway* 10 D3
Norefjell, *Norway* 10 D3
Norembega, *Canada* 98 C3
Noresund, *Norway* 10 D3
Norfolk, *Nebr., U.S.A.* 108 D6
Norfolk, *Va., U.S.A.* 104 G7
Norfolk □, *U.K.* 12 E9
Norfolk Broads, *U.K.* 12 E9
Norfolk I., *Pac. Oc.* 92 K8
Norfork Res., *U.S.A.* 109 G8
Norg, *Neths.* 16 B8
Norilsk, *Russia* 45 C9
Norley, *Australia* 91 D3
Norma, Mt., *Australia* 90 C3
Normal, *U.S.A.* 108 E10
Norman, *U.S.A.* 109 H6
Norman →, *Australia* 90 B3
Norman Wells, *Canada* 96 B7
Normanby →, *Australia* 90 A3
Normandie, *France* 24 D7
Normandie, Collines de, *France* 24 D6
Normandin, *Canada* 98 C5
Normandy = Normandie, *France* 24 D7
Normanhurst, Mt., *Australia* 89 E3
Normanton, *Australia* 90 B3
Norquay, *Canada* 101 C8
Norquinco, *Argentina* 128 B2
Norrbotten □, *Sweden* 8 C19
Nørre Åby, *Denmark* 11 J3
Nørre Nebel, *Denmark* 11 J2
Norre Vorupør, *Denmark* 11 H2
Nørresundby, *Denmark* 11 G3
Norris, *U.S.A.* 110 D8
Norristown, *U.S.A.* 107 F9
Norrköping, *Sweden* 11 F10
Norrland, *Sweden* 9 E16
Norrtälje, *Sweden* 10 E12
Norseman, *Australia* 89 F3
Norsholm, *Sweden* 11 F9
Norsk, *Russia* 45 D14
Norte, Pta., *Argentina* 128 B4
Norte, Pta. del, *Canary Is.* 36 G2
Norte de Santander □, *Colombia* 120 B3
Nortelândia, *Brazil* 125 C6
North Adams, *U.S.A.* 107 D11
North Ayrshire □, *U.K.* 14 F4
North Battleford, *Canada* 101 C7
North Bay, *Canada* 98 C4
North Belcher Is., *Canada* 98 A4
North Bend, *Canada* 100 D4
North Bend, *Oreg., U.S.A.* 110 E1
North Bend, *Pa., U.S.A.* 106 E7
North Bend, *Wash., U.S.A.* 112 C5
North Berwick, *U.K.* 14 E6
North Berwick, *U.S.A.* 107 C14
North C., *Canada* 99 C7
North C., *N.Z.* 87 F4
North Canadian →, *U.S.A.* 109 H7
North Cape = Nordkapp, *Norway* 8 A21
North Cape = Nordkapp, *Svalbard* 4 A9
North Caribou L., *Canada* 98 B1
North Carolina □, *U.S.A.* 105 H5
North Channel, *Canada* 98 C3
North Channel, *U.K.* 14 G3
North Charleston, *U.S.A.* 105 J6
North Chicago, *U.S.A.* 104 D2
North Dakota □, *U.S.A.* 108 B5
North Dandalup, *Australia* 89 F2
North Down □, *U.K.* 15 B6
North Downs, *U.K.* 13 F8
North East, *U.S.A.* 106 D5
North East Frontier Agency = Arunachal Pradesh □, *India* 61 E19
North East Lincolnshire □, *U.K.* 12 D7
North East Providence Chan., *W. Indies* 116 A4
North Eastern □, *Kenya* 82 B5
North Esk →, *U.K.* 14 E6
North European Plain, *Europe* 6 E10
North Foreland, *U.K.* 13 F9
North Fork, *U.S.A.* 112 H7
North Fork American →, *U.S.A.* 112 G5
North Fork Feather →, *U.S.A.* 112 F5
North Frisian Is. = Nordfriesische Inseln, *Germany* 18 A4
North Henik L., *Canada* 101 A9
North Highlands, *U.S.A.* 112 G5
North Horr, *Kenya* 82 B4
North I., *Kenya* 82 B4
North I., *N.Z.* 87 H5
North Kingsville, *U.S.A.* 106 E4
North Knife →, *Canada* 101 B10
North Koel →, *India* 63 G10
North Korea ■, *Asia* 51 E14
North Lakhimpur, *India* 61 F19
North Lanarkshire □, *U.K.* 14 F5
North Las Vegas, *U.S.A.* 113 J11
North Lincolnshire □, *U.K.* 12 D7
North Little Rock, *U.S.A.* 109 H8
North Loup →, *U.S.A.* 108 E5
North Magnetic Pole, *Canada* 4 B2
North Minch, *U.K.* 14 C3
North Nahanni →, *Canada* 100 A4
North Olmsted, *U.S.A.* 106 E3
North Ossetia □, *Russia* 43 J7
North Pagai, I. = Pagai Utara, *Indonesia* 56 E2
North Palisade, *U.S.A.* 111 H4
North Platte, *U.S.A.* 108 E4
North Platte →, *U.S.A.* 108 E4
North Pole, *Arctic* 4 A
North Portal, *Canada* 101 D8
North Powder, *U.S.A.* 110 D5
North Pt., *Canada* 99 C7
North Rhine Westphalia □ = Nordrhein-Westfalen □, *Germany* 18 D3
North Ronaldsay, *U.K.* 14 B6
North Saskatchewan →, *Canada* 101 C7
North Sea, *Europe* 6 D6
North Somerset □, *U.K.* 13 F5
North Sporades = Voríai Sporádhes, *Greece* 39 K6
North Sydney, *Canada* 99 C7
North Taranaki Bight, *N.Z.* 87 H5
North Thompson →, *Canada* 100 C4
North Tonawanda, *U.S.A.* 106 C6
North Troy, *U.S.A.* 107 B12
North Truchas Pk., *U.S.A.* 111 J11
North Twin I., *Canada* 98 B3
North Tyne →, *U.K.* 12 C5
North Uist, *U.K.* 14 D1
North Vancouver, *Canada* 100 D4
North Vernon, *U.S.A.* 104 F3
North Wabasca L., *Canada* 100 B6
North Walsham, *U.K.* 12 E9
North-West □, *S. Africa* 84 D4
North West C., *Australia* 88 D1
North West Christmas I. Ridge, *Pac. Oc.* 93 G11
North West Frontier □, *Pakistan* 62 C4
North West Highlands, *U.K.* 14 D3
North West Providence Channel, *W. Indies* 116 A4
North West River, *Canada* 99 B7
North West Territories □, *Canada* 96 B9
North Western □, *Zambia* 83 E2
North York Moors, *U.K.* 12 C7
North Yorkshire □, *U.K.* 12 C6
Northallerton, *U.K.* 12 C6
Northam, *S. Africa* 84 C4
Northampton, *Australia* 89 E1
Northampton, *U.K.* 13 E7
Northampton, *Mass., U.S.A.* 107 D12
Northampton, *Pa., U.S.A.* 107 F9
Northampton Downs, *Australia* 90 C4
Northamptonshire □, *U.K.* 13 E7
Northbridge, *U.S.A.* 107 D13
Northcliffe, *Australia* 89 F2
Northeim, *Germany* 18 D6
Northern □, *Malawi* 83 E3
Northern □, *Uganda* 82 B3
Northern □, *Zambia* 83 E3
Northern Cape □, *S. Africa* 84 D3
Northern Circars, *India* 61 L13
Northern Indian L., *Canada* 101 B9
Northern Ireland □, *U.K.* 15 B5
Northern Light, L., *Canada* 98 C1
Northern Marianas ■, *Pac. Oc.* 92 F6
Northern Province □, *S. Leone* 78 D2
Northern Territory □, *Australia* 88 D5
Northern Transvaal □, *S. Africa* 85 C4
Northfield, *U.S.A.* 108 C8
Northland □, *N.Z.* 87 F4
Northome, *U.S.A.* 108 B7
Northport, *Ala., U.S.A.* 105 J2
Northport, *Mich., U.S.A.* 104 C3
Northport, *Wash., U.S.A.* 110 B5
Northumberland □, *U.K.* 12 B5
Northumberland, C., *Australia* 91 F3
Northumberland Is., *Australia* 90 C4
Northumberland Str., *Canada* 99 C7
Northwich, *U.K.* 12 D5
Northwood, *Iowa, U.S.A.* 108 D8
Northwood, *N. Dak., U.S.A.* 108 B6
Norton, *U.S.A.* 108 F5
Norton, *Zimbabwe* 83 F3
Norton Sd., *U.S.A.* 96 B3
Nortorf, *Germany* 18 A5
Norwalk, *Calif., U.S.A.* 113 M8
Norwalk, *Conn., U.S.A.* 107 E11
Norwalk, *Ohio, U.S.A.* 106 E2
Norway, *U.S.A.* 104 C2
Norway ■, *Europe* 8 E14
Norway House, *Canada* 101 C9
Norwegian Sea, *Atl. Oc.* 4 C8
Norwich, *Canada* 106 D4
Norwich, *U.K.* 12 E9
Norwich, *Conn., U.S.A.* 107 E12
Norwich, *N.Y., U.S.A.* 107 D9
Norwood, *Canada* 106 B7
Noshiro, *Japan* 48 D10
Nosivka, *Ukraine* 41 G6
Nosok, *Russia* 44 B9
Nosovka = Nosivka, *Ukraine* 41 G6
Noss Hd., *U.K.* 14 C5
Nossa Senhora da Glória, *Brazil* 122 D4
Nossa Senhora das Dores, *Brazil* 122 D4
Nossa Senhora do Livramento, *Brazil* 125 D6
Nossebro, *Sweden* 11 F6
Nossob →, *S. Africa* 84 D3
Nosy Bé, *Madag.* 81 G9
Nosy Boraha, *Madag.* 85 B8
Nosy Mitsio, *Madag.* 81 G9
Nosy Varika, *Madag.* 85 C8
Noteć →, *Poland* 20 C5
Notigi Dam, *Canada* 101 B9
Notikewin →, *Canada* 100 B5
Notios Evvoïkos Kólpos, *Greece* 39 L7
Noto, *Italy* 35 F8
Noto, G. di, *Italy* 35 F8
Notodden, *Norway* 10 E3
Notre-Dame, *Canada* 99 C7
Notre Dame B., *Canada* 99 C8
Notre Dame de Koartac = Quaqtaq, *Canada* 97 B13
Notre Dame d'Ivugivic = Ivujivik, *Canada* 97 B12
Notsé, *Togo* 79 D5
Nottaway →, *Canada* 98 B4
Nøtterøy, *Norway* 10 E4
Nottingham, *U.K.* 12 E6
Nottinghamshire □, *U.K.* 12 D7
Nottoway →, *U.S.A.* 104 G7
Notwane →, *Botswana* 84 C4
Nouâdhibou, *Mauritania* 74 D1
Nouâdhibou, Ras, *Mauritania* 74 D1
Nouakchott, *Mauritania* 78 B1
Nouméa, *N. Cal.* 92 K8
Noupoort, *S. Africa* 84 E3

Nouveau Comptoir = Wemindji, *Canada* 98 B4
Nouvelle-Calédonie = New Caledonia ■, *Pac. Oc.* 92 K8
Nouzonville, *France* 25 C11
Nová Baňa, *Slovak Rep.* 21 G8
Nová Bystřice, *Czech.* 20 F5
Nova Casa Nova, *Brazil* 122 C3
Nova Cruz, *Brazil* 122 C4
Nova Era, *Brazil* 123 E3
Nova Esperança, *Brazil* 127 A5
Nova Friburgo, *Brazil* 123 F3
Nova Gaia = Cambundi-Catembo, *Angola* 80 G3
Nova Gradiška, *Croatia* 21 K7
Nova Granada, *Brazil* 123 F2
Nova Iguaçu, *Brazil* 123 F3
Nova Iorque, *Brazil* 122 C3
Nova Kakhovka, *Ukraine* 41 J7
Nova Lamego, *Guinea-Biss.* 78 C2
Nova Lima, *Brazil* 127 A7
Nova Lisboa = Huambo, *Angola* 81 G3
Nova Lusitânia, *Mozam.* 83 F3
Nova Mambone, *Mozam.* 85 C6
Nova Odesa, *Ukraine* 41 J6
Nova Ponte, *Brazil* 123 E2
Nova Scotia □, *Canada* 99 C7
Nova Sofala, *Mozam.* 85 C5
Nova Venécia, *Brazil* 123 E3
Nova Vida, *Brazil* 125 C5
Nova Zagora, *Bulgaria* 38 G8
Novaleksandrovskaya = Novoaleksandrovsk, *Russia* 43 H5
Novannenskiy = Novoannenskiy, *Russia* 42 E6
Novara, *Italy* 32 C5
Novato, *U.S.A.* 112 G4
Novaya Kakhovka = Nova Kakhovka, *Ukraine* 41 J7
Novaya Kazanka, *Kazakstan* 43 F9
Novaya Ladoga, *Russia* 40 B7
Novaya Lyalya, *Russia* 44 D7
Novaya Sibir, Ostrov, *Russia* 45 B16
Novaya Zemlya, *Russia* 44 B6
Novelda, *Spain* 29 G4
Novellara, *Italy* 32 D7
Noventa Vicentina, *Italy* 33 C8
Novgorod, *Russia* 40 C6
Novgorod-Severskiy = Novhorod-Siverskyy, *Ukraine* 41 G7
Novhorod-Siverskyy, *Ukraine* 41 G7
Novi Bečej, *Serbia, Yug.* 21 K10
Novi Grad, *Croatia* 33 C10
Novi Krichim, *Bulgaria* 38 G7
Novi Lígure, *Italy* 32 D5
Novi Pazar, *Bulgaria* 38 F10
Novi Pazar, *Serbia, Yug.* 21 M10
Novi Sad, *Serbia, Yug.* 21 K9
Novi Vinodolski, *Croatia* 33 C11
Novigrad, *Croatia* 33 D12
Noville, *Belgium* 17 H7
Novo Acôrdo, *Brazil* 122 D2
Novo Aripuanã, *Brazil* 121 E5
Nôvo Cruzeiro, *Brazil* 123 E3
Nôvo Hamburgo, *Brazil* 127 B5
Novo Horizonte, *Brazil* 123 F2
Novo Mesto, *Slovenia* 33 C12
Novo Remanso, *Brazil* 122 C3
Novoaleksandrovsk, *Russia* 43 H5
Novoannenskiy, *Russia* 42 E6
Novoataysk, *Russia* 44 D9
Novoazovsk, *Ukraine* 41 J10
Novocheboksarsk, *Russia* 42 B8
Novocherkassk, *Russia* 43 G5
Novodevichye, *Russia* 42 D9
Novogrudok = Navahrudak, *Belarus* 40 F3
Novohrad-Volynskyy, *Ukraine* 41 G4
Novokachalinsk, *Russia* 48 B6
Novokazalinsk = Zhangaqazaly, *Kazakstan* 44 E7
Novokhopersk, *Russia* 42 E5
Novokuybyshevsk, *Russia* 42 D9
Novokuznetsk, *Russia* 44 D9
Novomirgorod, *Ukraine* 41 H6
Novomoskovsk, *Russia* 42 C4
Novomoskovsk, *Ukraine* 41 H8
Novopolotsk = Navapolatsk, *Belarus* 40 E5
Novorossiysk, *Russia* 43 H3
Novorybnoye, *Russia* 45 B11
Novorzhev, *Russia* 40 D5
Novoselytsya, *Ukraine* 41 H4
Novoshakhtinsk, *Russia* 43 G4
Novosibirsk, *Russia* 44 D9
Novosibirskiye Ostrova, *Russia* 45 B15
Novosil, *Russia* 42 D3
Novosokolniki, *Russia* 40 D6
Novotitarovskaya, *Russia* 43 H4
Novotroitsk, *Russia* 44 D6
Novoukrayinka, *Ukraine* 41 H6
Novouljanovsk, *Russia* 42 C9
Novouzensk, *Russia* 42 E9
Novovolynsk, *Ukraine* 41 G3
Novovoronezhskiy, *Russia* 42 E4
Novozybkov, *Russia* 41 F6
Novska, *Croatia* 21 K6
Novy Bug = Novyy Buh, *Ukraine* 41 J7
Nový Bydzov, *Czech.* 20 E5
Novy Dwór Mazowiecki, *Poland* 20 C10
Novyy Afon, *Georgia* 43 J5
Novyy Buh, *Ukraine* 41 J7
Novyy Oskol, *Russia* 42 E3
Novyy Port, *Russia* 44 C8
Now Shahr, *Iran* 65 B6
Nowa Deba, *Poland* 20 E11
Nowa Ruda, *Poland* 20 E6
Nowa Sól, *Poland* 20 D5
Nowbarān, *Iran* 65 C6
Nowe, *Poland* 20 B8
Nowghāb, *Iran* 65 C8
Nowgong, *India* 61 F18
Nowogard, *Poland* 20 B5
Nowogród, *Poland* 20 B11
Nowra, *Australia* 91 E5
Nowshera, *Pakistan* 60 B8
Nowy Korczyn, *Poland* 20 E10
Nowy Sącz, *Poland* 20 F10
Noxen, *U.S.A.* 107 E8
Noxon, *U.S.A.* 110 C6
Noya, *Spain* 30 C2
Noyant, *France* 24 E7
Noyers, *France* 25 E10
Noyes I., *U.S.A.* 100 B2
Noyon, *France* 25 C9
Noyon, *Mongolia* 50 C2
Nozay, *France* 24 E5
Nsa, O. en →, *Algeria* 75 B6
Nsanje, *Malawi* 83 F4
Nsawam, *Ghana* 79 D4
Nsomba, *Zambia* 83 E2
Nsukka, *Nigeria* 79 D6
Nu Jiang →, *China* 52 C1
Nu Shan, *China* 52 D2
Nuba Mts. = Nubah, Jibalan, *Sudan* 77 E3
Nubah, Jibalan, *Sudan* 77 E3
Nubia, *Africa* 70 D7
Nubian Desert = Nûbîya, Es Sahrâ En, *Sudan* 76 C3
Nûbîya, Es Sahrâ En, *Sudan* 76 C3
Ñuble □, *Chile* 126 D1
Nuboai, *Indonesia* 57 E9
Nubra →, *India* 63 B7
Nueces →, *U.S.A.* 109 M6
Nueltin L., *Canada* 101 A9
Nuenen, *Neths.* 17 F7
Nueva, I., *Chile* 128 E3
Nueva Antioquia, *Colombia* 120 B4
Nueva Asunción □, *Paraguay* 126 A3
Nueva Esparta □, *Venezuela* 121 A5
Nueva Gerona, *Cuba* 116 B3
Nueva Imperial, *Chile* 128 A2
Nueva Palmira, *Uruguay* 126 C4
Nueva Rosita, *Mexico* 114 B4
Nueva San Salvador, *El Salv.* 116 D2
Nuéve de Julio, *Argentina* 126 D3
Nuevitas, *Cuba* 116 B4
Nuevo, G., *Argentina* 128 B4
Nuevo Guerrero, *Mexico* 115 B5
Nuevo Laredo, *Mexico* 115 B5
Nuevo León □, *Mexico* 114 C4
Nuevo Mundo, Cerro, *Bolivia* 124 E4
Nuevo Rocafuerte, *Ecuador* 120 D2
Nugget Pt., *N.Z.* 87 M2
Nugrus, Gebel, *Egypt* 76 C3
Nuhaka, *N.Z.* 87 H6
Nuits-St.-Georges, *France* 25 E11
Nukey Bluff, *Australia* 91 E2
Nukheila, *Sudan* 76 D2
Nukhuyb, *Iraq* 67 F10
Nuku'alofa, *Tonga* 87 E11
Nukus, *Uzbekistan* 44 E6
Nuland, *Neths.* 16 E6
Nulato, *U.S.A.* 96 B4
Nules, *Spain* 28 F4
Nullagine →, *Australia* 88 D3
Nullarbor, *Australia* 89 F5
Nullarbor Plain, *Australia* 89 F4
Numalla, L., *Australia* 91 D3
Numan, *Nigeria* 79 D7
Numansdorp, *Neths.* 16 E4
Numata, *Japan* 49 F9
Numatinna →, *Sudan* 77 F2
Numazu, *Japan* 49 G9
Numbulwar, *Australia* 90 A2
Numfoor, *Indonesia* 57 E8
Numurkah, *Australia* 91 F4
Nunaksaluk I., *Canada* 99 A7
Nuneaton, *U.K.* 13 E6
Nungo, *Mozam.* 83 E4
Nungwe, *Tanzania* 82 C3
Nunivak I., *U.S.A.* 96 B3
Nunkun, *India* 63 C7
Nunspeet, *Neths.* 16 D7
Nùoro, *Italy* 34 B2
Nuquí, *Colombia* 120 B2
Nūrābād, *Iran* 65 E8
Nure →, *Italy* 32 C6
Nuremberg = Nürnberg, *Germany* 19 F7
Nuri, *Mexico* 114 B3
Nurina, *Australia* 89 F4
Nuriootpa, *Australia* 91 E2
Nurlat, *Russia* 42 C10
Nurmes, *Finland* 8 E23
Nürnberg, *Germany* 19 F7
Nurran, L. = Terewah, L., *Australia* 91 D4
Nurrari Lakes, *Australia* 89 E5
Nurri, *Italy* 34 C2
Nusa Barung, *Indonesia* 57 H15
Nusa Kambangan, *Indonesia* 57 G13
Nusa Tenggara Barat □, *Indonesia* 56 F5
Nusa Tenggara Timur □, *Indonesia* 57 F6
Nusaybin, *Turkey* 67 D9
Nushki, *Pakistan* 62 E2
Nutak, *Canada* 97 C13
Nuth, *Neths.* 17 G7
Nutwood Downs, *Australia* 90 B1
Nuuk = Godthåb, *Greenland* 97 B14
Nuwakot, *Nepal* 63 E10
Nuweiba', *Egypt* 76 B3
Nuweveldberge, *S. Africa* 84 E3
Nuyts, C., *Australia* 89 F5
Nuyts Arch., *Australia* 91 E1
Nxau-Nxau, *Botswana* 84 B3
Nyaake, *Liberia* 78 E3
Nyack, *U.S.A.* 107 E11
Nyadal, *Sweden* 10 B11
Nyah West, *Australia* 91 F3
Nyahanga, *Tanzania* 82 C3
Nyahua, *Tanzania* 82 D3
Nyahururu, *Kenya* 82 B4
Nyainqentanglha Shan, *China* 54 C4
Nyakanazi, *Tanzania* 82 C3
Nyakrom, *Ghana* 79 D4
Nyâlâ, *Sudan* 77 E1
Nyamandhlovu, *Zimbabwe* 83 F2
Nyambiti, *Tanzania* 82 C3
Nyamwaga, *Tanzania* 82 C3
Nyandekwa, *Tanzania* 82 C3
Nyanding →, *Sudan* 77 F3
Nyandoma, *Russia* 40 B11
Nyangana, *Namibia* 84 B3
Nyanguge, *Tanzania* 82 C3
Nyankpala, *Ghana* 79 D4
Nyanza, *Burundi* 82 C2
Nyanza, *Rwanda* 82 C2
Nyanza □, *Kenya* 82 C3
Nyarling →, *Canada* 100 A6
Nyasa, L. = Malawi, L., *Africa* 83 E3
Nyasvizh, *Belarus* 41 F4
Nyazura, *Zimbabwe* 83 F3
Nyazwidzi →, *Zimbabwe* 83 F3
Nyborg, *Denmark* 11 J4
Nybro, *Sweden* 9 H16
Nyda, *Russia* 44 C8
Nyeri, *Kenya* 82 C4
Nyerol, *Sudan* 77 F3
Nyhem, *Sweden* 10 B9
Nyiel, *Sudan* 77 F3
Nyinahin, *Ghana* 78 D4
Nyírbátor, *Hungary* 21 H12
Nyíregyháza, *Hungary* 21 H11
Nykøbing, *Storstrøm, Denmark* 11 K5
Nykøbing, *Vestsjælland, Denmark* 11 J5
Nykøbing, *Viborg, Denmark* 11 H2
Nyköping, *Sweden* 11 F11
Nykvarn, *Sweden* 10 E11
Nyland, *Sweden* 10 A11
Nylstroom, *S. Africa* 85 C4
Nymagee, *Australia* 91 E4
Nymburk, *Czech.* 20 E5
Nynäshamn, *Sweden* 10 F11
Nyngan, *Australia* 91 E4
Nyoman = Neman →, *Lithuania* 9 J19
Nyon, *Switz.* 22 D2
Nyong →, *Cameroon* 79 E6
Nyons, *France* 27 D9
Nyord, *Denmark* 11 J6
Nyou, *Burkina Faso* 79 C4
Nysa, *Poland* 20 E7
Nysa →, *Europe* 18 C10
Nyssa, *U.S.A.* 110 E5
Nysted, *Denmark* 11 K5
Nyunzu, *Zaïre* 82 D2
Nyurbe, *Russia* 45 C12
Nyzhnohirskyy, *Ukraine* 41 K8
Nzega, *Tanzania* 82 C3
Nzega □, *Tanzania* 82 C3
N'Zérékoré, *Guinea* 78 D3
Nzeto, *Angola* 80 F2
Nzilo, Chutes de, *Zaïre* 83 E2
Nzubuka, *Tanzania* 82 C3

O

Ō-Shima, *Nagasaki, Japan* 49 G4
Ō-Shima, *Shizuoka, Japan* 49 G9
Oacoma, *U.S.A.* 108 D5
Oahe, L., *U.S.A.* 108 C4
Oahe Dam, *U.S.A.* 108 C4
Oahu, *U.S.A.* 102 H16
Oak Creek, *U.S.A.* 110 F10
Oak Harbor, *U.S.A.* 112 B4
Oak Hill, *U.S.A.* 104 G5
Oak Park, *U.S.A.* 104 E2
Oak Ridge, *U.S.A.* 105 G3
Oak View, *U.S.A.* 113 L7
Oakan-Dake, *Japan* 48 C12
Oakbank, *Australia* 91 E3
Oakdale, *Calif., U.S.A.* 111 H3
Oakdale, *La., U.S.A.* 109 K8
Oakengates, *U.K.* 12 E5
Oakes, *U.S.A.* 108 B5
Oakesdale, *U.S.A.* 110 C5
Oakey, *Australia* 91 D5
Oakham, *U.K.* 12 E7
Oakhurst, *U.S.A.* 112 H7
Oakland, *Calif., U.S.A.* 111 H2
Oakland, *Oreg., U.S.A.* 110 E2
Oakland City, *U.S.A.* 104 F2
Oakley, *Idaho, U.S.A.* 110 E7
Oakley, *Kans., U.S.A.* 108 F4
Oakover →, *Australia* 88 D3
Oakridge, *U.S.A.* 110 E2
Oakville, *U.S.A.* 112 D3
Oamaru, *N.Z.* 87 L3
Oasis, *Calif., U.S.A.* 113 M10
Oasis, *Nev., U.S.A.* 112 H9
Oates Land, *Antarctica* 5 C11
Oatman, *U.S.A.* 113 K12
Oaxaca, *Mexico* 115 D5
Oaxaca □, *Mexico* 115 D5
Ob →, *Russia* 44 C7
Oba, *Canada* 98 C3
Obala, *Cameroon* 79 E7
Obama, *Japan* 49 G7
Oban, *U.K.* 14 E3
Obbia, *Somali Rep.* 68 F4
Obdam, *Neths.* 16 C5
Obed, *Canada* 100 C5
Ober-Aagau, *Switz.* 22 B5
Obera, *Argentina* 127 B4
Oberalppass, *Switz.* 23 C7
Oberalpstock, *Switz.* 23 C7
Oberammergau, *Germany* 19 H7
Oberdrauburg, *Austria* 21 J2
Oberengadin, *Switz.* 23 C9
Oberentfelden, *Switz.* 22 B6
Oberhausen, *Germany* 18 D2
Oberkirch, *Germany* 19 G4
Oberland, *Switz.* 22 C5
Oberlin, *Kans., U.S.A.* 108 F4
Oberlin, *La., U.S.A.* 109 K8
Oberlin, *Ohio, U.S.A.* 106 E2
Obernai, *France* 25 D14
Oberndorf, *Germany* 19 G4
Oberon, *Australia* 91 E4
Oberpfälzer Wald, *Germany* 19 F8
Obersiggenthal, *Switz.* 23 B6
Oberstdorf, *Germany* 19 H6
Oberwil, *Switz.* 22 A5
Obi, Kepulauan, *Indonesia* 57 E7
Obi Is. = Obi, Kepulauan, *Indonesia* 57 E7
Obiaruku, *Nigeria* 79 D6
Óbidos, *Brazil* 121 D6
Óbidos, *Portugal* 31 F1
Obihiro, *Japan* 48 C11
Obilatu, *Indonesia* 57 E7
Obilnoye, *Russia* 43 G7
Obing, *Germany* 19 H8
Öbisfelde, *Germany* 18 C6
Objat, *France* 26 C5
Obluchye, *Russia* 45 E14
Obninsk, *Russia* 42 C3
Obo, *C.A.R.* 82 A2
Obo, *Ethiopia* 77 G4
Oboa, Mt., *Uganda* 82 B3
Obock, *Djibouti* 77 E5
Oborniki, *Poland* 20 C6
Oboyan, *Russia* 42 E3
Obozerskaya = Obozerskiy, *Russia* 44 C5
Obozerskiy, *Russia* 44 C5
Obrovac, *Croatia* 33 D12
Obruk, *Turkey* 66 C5
Observatory Inlet, *Canada* 100 B3
Obshchi Syrt, *Russia* 6 E16
Obskaya Guba, *Russia* 44 C8
Obuasi, *Ghana* 79 D4
Obubra, *Nigeria* 79 D6
Obwalden □, *Switz.* 22 C6
Obzor, *Bulgaria* 38 G10
Ocala, *U.S.A.* 105 L4
Ocamo →, *Venezuela* 121 C4
Ocampo, *Mexico* 114 B3
Ocaña, *Colombia* 120 B3
Ocaña, *Spain* 28 F1
Ocanomowoc, *U.S.A.* 108 D10
Ocate, *U.S.A.* 109 G2
Occidental, Cordillera, *Colombia* 120 C3
Occidental, Cordillera, *Peru* 124 C3
Ocean City, *N.J., U.S.A.* 104 F8
Ocean City, *Wash., U.S.A.* 112 C2
Ocean I. = Banaba, *Kiribati* 92 H8
Ocean Park, *U.S.A.* 112 D2
Oceano, *U.S.A.* 113 K6
Oceanport, *U.S.A.* 107 F10
Oceanside, *U.S.A.* 113 M9
Ochagavia, *Spain* 28 C3
Ochakiv, *Ukraine* 41 J6
Ochamchira, *Georgia* 43 J5
Ochamps, *Belgium* 17 J6
Ochil Hills, *U.K.* 14 E5
Ochre River, *Canada* 101 C9
Ochsenfurt, *Germany* 19 F6
Ochsenhausen, *Germany* 19 G5
Ocilla, *U.S.A.* 105 K4
Ocmulgee →, *U.S.A.* 105 K4
Ocna Sibiului, *Romania* 38 D7
Ocnița, *Moldova* 41 H4
Ocoña, *Peru* 124 D3
Ocoña →, *Peru* 124 D3
Oconee →, *U.S.A.* 105 K4
Oconto, *U.S.A.* 104 C2
Oconto Falls, *U.S.A.* 104 C1
Ocosingo, *Mexico* 115 D6
Ocotal, *Nic.* 116 D2
Ocotlán, *Mexico* 114 C4
Ocquier, *Belgium* 17 H6
Ocreza →, *Portugal* 31 F3
Octave, *U.S.A.* 111 J7
Octeville, *France* 24 C5
Ocumare del Tuy, *Venezuela* 120 A4
Ocuri, *Bolivia* 125 D4
Oda, *Ghana* 79 D4
Ōda, *Japan* 49 G6
Odâ, *Sudan* 76 C4
Ódáðahraun, *Iceland* 8 D5
Ödåkra, *Sweden* 11 H6
Odate, *Japan* 48 D10
Odawara, *Japan* 49 G9
Odda, *Norway* 9 F12
Odder, *Denmark* 11 J4
Oddur, *Somali Rep.* 68 G3
Ödeborg, *Sweden* 11 F5
Odei →, *Canada* 101 B9
Odemira, *Portugal* 31 H2
Ödemiş, *Turkey* 66 C3
Odendaalsrus, *S. Africa* 84 D4
Odense, *Denmark* 11 J4
Odenwald, *Germany* 19 F5
Oder →, *Germany* 18 B10
Oderzo, *Italy* 33 C9
Odesa, *Ukraine* 41 J6
Odessa = Odesa, *Ukraine* 41 J6
Odessa, *Canada* 107 B8
Odessa, *Tex., U.S.A.* 109 K3
Odessa, *Wash., U.S.A.* 110 C4
Odiakwe, *Botswana* 84 C4
Odiel →, *Spain* 31 H4
Odienné, *Ivory C.* 78 D3
Odintsovo, *Russia* 42 C3
Odiongan, *Phil.* 55 E4
Odobeşti, *Romania* 38 D10
O'Donnell, *U.S.A.* 109 J4
Odoorn, *Neths.* 16 C9
Odorheiu Secuiesc, *Romania* 38 C8
Odoyevo, *Russia* 42 D3
Odra = Oder →, *Germany* 18 B10
Odra →, *Poland* 20 B4
Odra →, *Spain* 30 C6
Odžaci, *Serbia, Yug.* 21 K9
Odzi, *Zimbabwe* 85 B5
Oedelem, *Belgium* 17 F2
Oegstgeest, *Neths.* 16 D4
Oeiras, *Brazil* 122 C3
Oeiras, *Portugal* 31 G1
Oelrichs, *U.S.A.* 108 D3
Oelsnitz, *Germany* 18 E8
Oelwein, *U.S.A.* 108 D9
Oenpelli, *Australia* 88 B5
Of, *Turkey* 67 B9
Ofanto →, *Italy* 35 A9
Offa, *Nigeria* 79 D5
Offaly □, *Ireland* 15 C4
Offenbach, *Germany* 19 E4
Offenburg, *Germany* 19 G3
Offerdal, *Sweden* 10 A8
Offida, *Italy* 33 F10
Offranville, *France* 24 C8
Ofidhousa, *Greece* 39 N9
Ofotfjorden, *Norway* 8 B17
Ōfunato, *Japan* 48 E10
Oga, *Japan* 48 E9
Oga-Hantō, *Japan* 48 E9
Ogahalla, *Canada* 98 B2
Ōgaki, *Japan* 49 G8
Ogallala, *U.S.A.* 108 E4
Ogasawara Gunto, *Pac. Oc.* 46 G18
Ogbomosho, *Nigeria* 79 D5
Ogden, *Iowa, U.S.A.* 108 D8
Ogden, *Utah, U.S.A.* 110 F7
Ogdensburg, *U.S.A.* 107 B9
Ogeechee →, *U.S.A.* 105 K5
Ogilby, *U.S.A.* 113 N12
Oglio →, *Italy* 32 C7
Ogmore, *Australia* 90 C4
Ognon →, *France* 25 E12
Ogoja, *Nigeria* 79 D6
Ogoki →, *Canada* 98 B2
Ogoki L., *Canada* 98 B2
Ogoki Res., *Canada* 98 B2
Ogooué →, *Gabon* 80 E1
Ogosta →, *Bulgaria* 38 F6
Ogowe = Ogooué →, *Gabon* 80 E1
Ogr = Sharafa, *Sudan* 77 E2
Ogre, *Latvia* 9 H21
Ogrein, *Sudan* 76 D3
Ogulin, *Croatia* 33 C12
Ogun □, *Nigeria* 79 D5
Oguta, *Nigeria* 79 D6
Ogwashi-Uku, *Nigeria* 79 D6
Ogwe, *Nigeria* 79 E6
Ohai, *N.Z.* 87 L2
Ohakune, *N.Z.* 87 H5
Ohanet, *Algeria* 75 C6
Ohata, *Japan* 48 D10
Ohau, L., *N.Z.* 87 L2
Ohey, *Belgium* 17 H6
Ohio □, *U.S.A.* 104 E3
Ohio →, *U.S.A.* 104 G1
Ohre →, *Czech.* 20 E4
Ohre →, *Germany* 18 C7

Ohrid, *Macedonia* 39 H3
Ohridsko Jezero, *Macedonia* 39 H3
Ohrigstad, *S. Africa* 85 C5
Öhringen, *Germany* 19 F5
Oiapoque →, *Brazil* 121 C7
Oikou, *China* 51 E9
Oil City, *U.S.A.* 106 E5
Oildale, *U.S.A.* 113 K7
Oirschot, *Neths.* 17 E6
Oise □, *France* 25 C9
Oise →, *France* 25 D9
Oisterwijk, *Neths.* 17 E6
Ōita, *Japan* 49 H5
Ōita □, *Japan* 49 H5
Oiticica, *Brazil* 122 C3
Ojai, *U.S.A.* 113 L7
Ojinaga, *Mexico* 114 B4
Ojiya, *Japan* 49 F9
Ojos del Salado, Cerro, *Argentina* 126 B2
Oka →, *Russia* 42 B7
Okaba, *Indonesia* 57 F9
Okahandja, *Namibia* 84 C2
Okahukura, *N.Z.* 87 H5
Okanagan L., *Canada* 100 C5
Okandja, *Gabon* 80 E2
Okanogan, *U.S.A.* 110 B4
Okanogan →, *U.S.A.* 110 B4
Okaputa, *Namibia* 84 C2
Okara, *Pakistan* 62 D5
Okarito, *N.Z.* 87 K3
Okaukuejo, *Namibia* 84 B2
Okavango Swamps, *Botswana* 84 B3
Okaya, *Japan* 49 F9
Okayama, *Japan* 49 G6
Okayama □, *Japan* 49 G6
Okazaki, *Japan* 49 G8
Oke-Iho, *Nigeria* 79 D5
Okeechobee, *U.S.A.* 105 M5
Okeechobee, L., *U.S.A.* 105 M5
Okefenokee Swamp, *U.S.A.* 105 K4
Okehampton, *U.K.* 13 G3
Okene, *Nigeria* 79 D6
Oker →, *Germany* 18 C6
Okha, *Russia* 45 D15
Ókhi Óros, *Greece* 39 L7
Okhotsk, *Russia* 45 D15
Okhotsk, Sea of, *Asia* 45 D15
Okhotskiy Perevoz, *Russia* 45 C14
Okhtyrka, *Ukraine* 41 G8
Oki-Shotō, *Japan* 49 F6
Okiep, *S. Africa* 84 D2
Okigwi, *Nigeria* 79 D6
Okija, *Nigeria* 79 D6
Okinawa □, *Japan* 49 L3
Okinawa-Guntō, *Japan* 49 L3
Okinawa-Jima, *Japan* 49 L4
Okino-erabu-Shima, *Japan* 49 L4
Okitipupa, *Nigeria* 79 D5
Oklahoma □, *U.S.A.* 109 H6
Oklahoma City, *U.S.A.* 109 H6
Okmulgee, *U.S.A.* 109 H7
Oknitsa = Ocniţa, *Moldova* 41 H4
Okolo, *Uganda* 82 B3
Okolona, *U.S.A.* 109 H10
Okrika, *Nigeria* 79 E6
Oktabrsk = Oktyabrsk, *Kazakstan* 44 E6
Oktyabrsk, *Kazakstan* 44 E6
Oktyabrsk, *Russia* 42 D9
Oktyabrskiy = Aktsyabrski, *Belarus* 41 F5
Oktyabrskiy, *Russia* 43 G5
Oktyabrskoy Revolyutsii, Os., *Russia* 45 B10
Oktyabrskoye = Zhovtneve, *Ukraine* 41 J7
Oktyabrskoye, *Russia* 44 C7
Okulovka, *Russia* 40 C7
Okuru, *N.Z.* 87 K2
Okushiri-Tō, *Japan* 48 C9
Okuta, *Nigeria* 79 D5
Okwa →, *Botswana* 84 C3
Ola, *U.S.A.* 109 H8
Ólafsfjörður, *Iceland* 8 C4
Ólafsvík, *Iceland* 8 D2
Olancha, *U.S.A.* 113 J8
Olancha Pk., *U.S.A.* 113 J8
Olanchito, *Honduras* 116 C2
Öland, *Sweden* 9 H17
Olargues, *France* 26 E6
Olary, *Australia* 91 E3
Olascoaga, *Argentina* 126 D3
Olathe, *U.S.A.* 108 F7
Olavarría, *Argentina* 126 D3
Oława, *Poland* 20 E7
Ólbia, *Italy* 34 B2
Ólbia, G. di, *Italy* 34 B2
Old Bahama Chan. = Bahama, Canal Viejo de, *W. Indies* 116 B4
Old Baldy Pk. = San Antonio, Mt., *U.S.A.* 113 L9
Old Cork, *Australia* 90 C3
Old Crow, *Canada* 96 B6
Old Dale, *U.S.A.* 113 L11
Old Dongola, *Sudan* 76 D3
Old Fletton, *U.K.* 13 E7
Old Forge, *N.Y., U.S.A.* 107 C10
Old Forge, *Pa., U.S.A.* 107 E9
Old Fort →, *Canada* 101 B6
Old Shinyanga, *Tanzania* 82 C3
Old Speck Mt., *U.S.A.* 107 B14
Old Town, *U.S.A.* 99 D6
Old Wives L., *Canada* 101 C7
Oldbury, *U.K.* 13 F5
Oldcastle, *Ireland* 15 C4
Oldeani, *Tanzania* 82 C4
Oldenburg, *Niedersachsen, Germany* 18 B4
Oldenburg, *Schleswig-Holstein, Germany* 18 A6
Oldenzaal, *Neths.* 16 D9
Oldham, *U.K.* 12 D5
Oldman →, *Canada* 100 D6
Olds, *Canada* 100 C6
Olean, *U.S.A.* 106 D6
Oléggio, *Italy* 32 C5
Oleiros, *Portugal* 30 F3
Olekma →, *Russia* 45 C13
Olekminsk, *Russia* 45 C13
Oleksandriya, *Ukraine* 41 H7
Oleksandriya, *Ukraine* 41 G4
Oleksandrovka, *Ukraine* 41 H7
Olema, *U.S.A.* 112 G4
Olen, *Belgium* 17 F5
Olenek, *Russia* 45 C12
Olenek →, *Russia* 45 B13
Olenino, *Russia* 42 B1
Oléron, I. d', *France* 26 C2
Oleśnica, *Poland* 20 D7
Olesno, *Poland* 20 E8
Olevsk, *Ukraine* 41 G4
Olga, *Russia* 45 E14
Olga, L., *Canada* 98 C4
Olga, Mt., *Australia* 89 E5
Ølgod, *Denmark* 11 J2
Olhão, *Portugal* 31 H3
Olib, *Croatia* 33 D11
Oliena, *Italy* 34 B2
Oliete, *Spain* 28 D4
Olifants →, *Africa* 85 C5
Olifantshoek, *S. Africa* 84 D3
Ólimbos, *Greece* 39 P10
Ólimbos, Óros, *Greece* 39 J5
Olímpia, *Brazil* 127 A6
Olinda, *Brazil* 122 C5
Olindiná, *Brazil* 122 D4
Olite, *Spain* 28 C3
Oliva, *Argentina* 126 C3
Oliva, *Spain* 29 G4
Oliva, Punta del, *Spain* 30 B5
Oliva de la Frontera, *Spain* 31 G4
Olivares, *Spain* 28 F2
Olivehurst, *U.S.A.* 112 F5
Oliveira, *Brazil* 123 F3
Oliveira de Azemeis, *Portugal* 30 E2
Oliveira dos Brejinhos, *Brazil* 123 D3
Olivenza, *Spain* 31 G3
Oliver, *Canada* 100 D5
Oliver L., *Canada* 101 B8
Olivone, *Switz.* 23 C7
Olkhovka, *Russia* 42 F7
Olkusz, *Poland* 20 E9
Ollagüe, *Chile* 126 A2
Olloy, *Belgium* 17 H5
Olmedo, *Spain* 30 D6
Olmos, *Peru* 124 B2
Olney, *Ill., U.S.A.* 104 F1
Olney, *Tex., U.S.A.* 109 J5
Oloma, *Cameroon* 79 E7
Olomane →, *Canada* 99 B7
Olomouc, *Czech.* 20 F7
Olonets, *Russia* 40 B7
Olongapo, *Phil.* 55 D4
Oloron, Gave d' →, *France* 26 E2
Oloron-Ste.-Marie, *France* 26 E3
Olot, *Spain* 28 C7
Olovo, *Bos.-H.* 21 L8
Olovyannaya, *Russia* 45 D12
Oloy →, *Russia* 45 C16
Olpe, *Germany* 18 D3
Olshanka, *Ukraine* 41 H6
Olshany, *Ukraine* 41 G8
Olst, *Neths.* 16 D8
Olsztyn, *Poland* 20 B10
Olt →, *Romania* 38 F7
Olten, *Switz.* 22 B5
Olteniţa, *Romania* 38 E9
Olton, *U.S.A.* 109 H3
Oltu, *Turkey* 67 B9
Olur, *Turkey* 67 B10
Olutanga, *Phil.* 55 H5
Olvega, *Spain* 28 D3
Olvera, *Spain* 31 J5
Olymbos, *Cyprus* 37 D12
Olympia, *Greece* 39 M4
Olympia, *U.S.A.* 112 D4
Olympic Mts., *U.S.A.* 112 C3
Olympic Nat. Park, *U.S.A.* 112 C3
Olympus, *Cyprus* 66 E5
Olympus, Mt. = Ólimbos, Óros, *Greece* 39 J5
Olympus, Mt., *U.S.A.* 112 C3
Olyphant, *U.S.A.* 107 E9
Om →, *Russia* 44 D8
Om Hajer, *Eritrea* 77 E4
Om Koi, *Thailand* 58 D2
Ōma, *Japan* 48 D10
Ōmachi, *Japan* 49 F8
Ōmae-Zaki, *Japan* 49 G9
Ōmagari, *Japan* 48 E10
Omagh, *U.K.* 15 B4
Omagh □, *U.K.* 15 B4
Omaha, *U.S.A.* 108 E7
Omak, *U.S.A.* 110 B4
Omalos, *Greece* 37 D5
Oman ■, *Asia* 68 C6
Oman, G. of, *Asia* 65 E8
Omaruru, *Namibia* 84 C2
Omaruru →, *Namibia* 84 C1
Omate, *Peru* 124 D3
Ombai, Selat, *Indonesia* 57 F6
Omboué, *Gabon* 80 E1
Ombrone →, *Italy* 32 F8
Omdurmân, *Sudan* 77 D3
Omegna, *Italy* 32 C5
Omeonga, *Zaïre* 82 C1
Ometepe, I. de, *Nic.* 116 D2
Ometepec, *Mexico* 115 D5
Ominato, *Japan* 48 D10
Omineca →, *Canada* 100 B4
Omiš, *Croatia* 33 E13
Omišalj, *Croatia* 33 C11
Omitara, *Namibia* 84 C2
Ōmiya, *Japan* 49 G9
Omme Å →, *Denmark* 11 J2
Ommen, *Neths.* 16 C8
Ömnögovĭ □, *Mongolia* 50 C3
Omo →, *Ethiopia* 77 F4
Omodhos, *Cyprus* 37 E11
Omolon →, *Russia* 45 C16
Omono-Gawa →, *Japan* 48 E10
Omsk, *Russia* 44 D8
Omsukchan, *Russia* 45 C16
Ōmu, *Japan* 48 B11
Omul, Vf., *Romania* 38 D8
Ōmura, *Japan* 49 H4
Omuramba Omatako →, *Namibia* 81 H4
Omurtag, *Bulgaria* 38 F9
Ōmuta, *Japan* 49 H5
On, *Belgium* 17 H6
Oña, *Spain* 28 C1
Onaga, *U.S.A.* 108 F6
Onalaska, *U.S.A.* 108 D9
Onamia, *U.S.A.* 108 B8
Onancock, *U.S.A.* 104 G8
Onang, *Indonesia* 57 E5
Onaping L., *Canada* 98 C3
Oñate, *Spain* 28 B2
Onavas, *Mexico* 114 B3
Onawa, *U.S.A.* 108 D6
Onaway, *U.S.A.* 104 C3
Oncócua, *Angola* 84 B1
Onda, *Spain* 28 F4
Ondaejin, *N. Korea* 51 D15
Ondangua, *Namibia* 84 B2
Ondárroa, *Spain* 28 B2
Ondas →, *Brazil* 123 D3
Ondava →, *Slovak Rep.* 20 G11
Onderdijk, *Neths.* 16 C6
Ondjiva, *Angola* 84 B2
Ondo, *Nigeria* 79 D5
Ondo □, *Nigeria* 79 D6
Öndörhaan, *Mongolia* 54 B6
Öndörshil, *Mongolia* 50 B5
Öndverðarnes, *Iceland* 8 D1
Onega, *Russia* 44 C4
Onega →, *Russia* 6 C13
Onega, G. of = Onezhskaya Guba, *Russia* 44 C4
Onega, L. = Onezhskoye Ozero, *Russia* 40 B8
Onehunga, *N.Z.* 87 G5
Oneida, *U.S.A.* 107 C9
Oneida L., *U.S.A.* 107 C9
O'Neill, *U.S.A.* 108 D5
Onekotan, Ostrov, *Russia* 45 E16
Onema, *Zaïre* 82 C1
Oneonta, *Ala., U.S.A.* 105 J2
Oneonta, *N.Y., U.S.A.* 107 D9
Oneşti, *Romania* 38 C9
Onezhskaya Guba, *Russia* 44 C4
Onezhskoye Ozero, *Russia* 40 B8
Ongarue, *N.Z.* 87 H5
Ongerup, *Australia* 89 F2
Ongjin, *N. Korea* 51 F13
Ongkharak, *Thailand* 58 E3
Ongniud Qi, *China* 51 C10
Ongoka, *Zaïre* 82 C2
Ongole, *India* 60 M12
Ongon, *Mongolia* 50 B7
Onguren, *Russia* 45 D11
Onhaye, *Belgium* 17 H5
Oni, *Georgia* 43 J6
Onida, *U.S.A.* 108 C4
Onilahy →, *Madag.* 85 C7
Onitsha, *Nigeria* 79 D6
Onoda, *Japan* 49 G5
Onpyŏng-ni, *S. Korea* 51 H14
Ons, Is. d', *Spain* 30 C2
Onsala, *Sweden* 11 G6
Onslow, *Australia* 88 D2
Onslow B., *U.S.A.* 105 H7
Onstwedde, *Neths.* 16 B10
Ontake-San, *Japan* 49 G8
Ontaneda, *Spain* 30 B7
Ontario, *Calif., U.S.A.* 113 L9
Ontario, *Oreg., U.S.A.* 110 D5
Ontario □, *Canada* 98 B2
Ontario, L., *U.S.A.* 98 D4
Onteniente, *Spain* 29 G4
Ontonagon, *U.S.A.* 108 B10
Ontur, *Spain* 29 G3
Onyx, *U.S.A.* 113 K8
Oodnadatta, *Australia* 91 D2
Ooldea, *Australia* 89 F5
Ooltgensplaat, *Neths.* 17 E4
Oombulgurri, *Australia* 88 C4
Oona River, *Canada* 100 C2
Oordegem, *Belgium* 17 G3
Oorindi, *Australia* 90 C3
Oost-Vlaanderen □, *Belgium* 17 F3
Oost-Vlieland, *Neths.* 16 B6
Oostakker, *Belgium* 17 F3
Oostburg, *Neths.* 17 F3
Oostduinkerke, *Belgium* 17 F1
Oostelijk-Flevoland, *Neths.* 16 C7
Oostende, *Belgium* 17 F1
Oosterbeek, *Neths.* 16 E7
Oosterdijk, *Neths.* 16 C6
Oosterend, *Friesland, Neths.* 16 B6
Oosterend, *Noord-Holland, Neths.* 16 B5
Oosterhout, *Neths.* 17 E5
Oosterschelde, *Neths.* 17 E4
Oosterwolde, *Neths.* 16 B8
Oosterzele, *Belgium* 17 G3
Oostkamp, *Belgium* 17 F2
Oostmalle, *Belgium* 17 F5
Oostrozebekke, *Belgium* 17 G2
Oostvleteven, *Belgium* 17 G1
Oostvoorne, *Neths.* 16 E4
Oostzaan, *Neths.* 16 D5
Ootacamund, *India* 60 P10
Ootmarsum, *Neths.* 16 D9
Ootsa L., *Canada* 100 C3
Opala, *Russia* 45 D16
Opala, *Zaïre* 82 C1
Opanake, *Sri Lanka* 60 R12
Opasatika, *Canada* 98 C3
Opasquia, *Canada* 101 C10
Opatija, *Croatia* 33 C11
Opava, *Czech.* 20 F7
Opeinde, *Neths.* 16 B8
Opelousas, *U.S.A.* 109 K8
Opémisca, L., *Canada* 98 C5
Opglabbeek, *Belgium* 17 F7
Opheim, *U.S.A.* 110 B10
Ophthalmia Ra., *Australia* 88 D2
Opi, *Nigeria* 79 D6
Opinaca →, *Canada* 98 B4
Opinaca L., *Canada* 98 B4
Opiskotish, L., *Canada* 99 B6
Oploo, *Neths.* 17 E7
Opmeer, *Neths.* 16 C5
Opobo, *Nigeria* 79 E6
Opochka, *Russia* 40 D5
Opoczno, *Poland* 20 D10
Opol, *Phil.* 55 G6
Opole, *Poland* 20 E7
Oporto = Porto, *Portugal* 30 D2
Opotiki, *N.Z.* 87 H6
Opp, *U.S.A.* 105 K2
Oppdal, *Norway* 9 E13
Oppenheim, *Germany* 19 F4
Opperdoes, *Neths.* 16 C6
Óppido Mamertina, *Italy* 35 D8
Oppland fylke □, *Norway* 10 C3
Oppstad, *Norway* 10 D5
Oprtalj, *Croatia* 33 C10
Opua, *N.Z.* 87 F5
Opunake, *N.Z.* 87 H4
Opuzen, *Croatia* 21 M7
Ora, *Cyprus* 37 E12
Ora, *Italy* 33 B8
Ora Banda, *Australia* 89 F3
Oracle, *U.S.A.* 111 K8
Oradea, *Romania* 38 B4
Öræfajökull, *Iceland* 8 D5
Orahovac, *Serbia, Yug.* 21 N10
Orai, *India* 63 G8
Oraison, *France* 27 E9
Oral = Zhayyq →, *Kazakstan* 44 E6
Oral, *Kazakstan* 42 E10
Oran, *Algeria* 75 A4
Oran, *Argentina* 126 A3
Orange = Oranje →, *S. Africa* 84 D2
Orange, *Australia* 91 E4
Orange, *France* 27 D8
Orange, *Calif., U.S.A.* 113 M9
Orange, *Mass., U.S.A.* 107 D12
Orange, *Tex., U.S.A.* 109 K8
Orange, *Va., U.S.A.* 104 F6
Orange, C., *Brazil* 121 C7
Orange Cove, *U.S.A.* 112 J7
Orange Free State □ = Free State □, *S. Africa* 84 D4
Orange Grove, *U.S.A.* 109 M6
Orange Walk, *Belize* 115 D7
Orangeburg, *U.S.A.* 105 J5
Orangeville, *Canada* 98 D3
Orani, *Phil.* 55 D4
Oranienburg, *Germany* 18 C9
Oranje →, *S. Africa* 84 D2
Oranje Vrystaat □ = Free State □, *S. Africa* 84 D4
Oranjemund, *Namibia* 84 D2
Oranjerivier, *S. Africa* 84 D3
Oras, *Phil.* 55 E6
Orăştie, *Romania* 38 D6
Oraşul Stalin = Braşov, *Romania* 38 D8
Orava →, *Slovak Rep.* 20 F9
Oravita, *Romania* 38 D4
Orb →, *France* 26 E7
Orba →, *Italy* 32 D5
Ørbæk, *Denmark* 11 J4
Orbe, *Switz.* 22 C3
Orbec, *France* 24 C7
Orbetello, *Italy* 33 F8
Órbigo →, *Spain* 30 C5
Orbost, *Australia* 91 F4
Orce, *Spain* 29 H2
Orce →, *Spain* 29 H2
Orchies, *France* 25 B10
Orchila, I., *Venezuela* 120 A4
Orco →, *Italy* 32 C4
Orcopampa, *Peru* 124 D3
Orcutt, *U.S.A.* 113 L6
Ord →, *Australia* 88 C4
Ord, Mt., *Australia* 88 C4
Ordenes, *Spain* 30 B2
Orderville, *U.S.A.* 111 H7
Ording = St-Peter-Ording, *Germany* 18 A4
Ordos = Mu Us Shamo, *China* 50 E5
Ordu, *Turkey* 66 B7
Ordubad, *Azerbaijan* 67 C12
Orduña, *Álava, Spain* 28 C7
Orduña, *Granada, Spain* 29 H1
Ordway, *U.S.A.* 108 F3
Ordzhonikidze = Vladikavkaz, *Russia* 43 J7
Ordzhonikidze, *Ukraine* 41 J8
Ore, *Zaïre* 82 B2
Ore Mts. = Erzgebirge, *Germany* 18 E9
Orealla, *Guyana* 121 B6
Orebić, *Croatia* 21 M7
Örebro, *Sweden* 9 G16
Oregon, *U.S.A.* 108 D10
Oregon □, *U.S.A.* 110 E3
Oregon City, *U.S.A.* 112 E4
Orekhov = Orikhiv, *Ukraine* 41 J8
Orekhovo-Zuyevo, *Russia* 42 C4
Orel, *Russia* 42 D3
Orel →, *Ukraine* 41 H8
Orellana, Canal de, *Spain* 31 F5
Orellana, Pantano de, *Spain* 31 F5
Orellana la Vieja, *Spain* 31 F5
Orem, *U.S.A.* 110 F8
Ören, *Turkey* 66 D2
Orenburg, *Russia* 44 D6
Orense, *Spain* 30 C3
Orense □, *Spain* 30 C3
Orepuki, *N.Z.* 87 M1
Orestiás, *Greece* 39 H9
Øresund, *Europe* 11 J6
Orford Ness, *U.K.* 13 E9
Orgañà, *Spain* 28 C6
Organos, Pta. de los, *Canary Is.* 36 F2
Orgaz, *Spain* 31 F7
Orgeyev = Orhei, *Moldova* 41 J5
Orgon, *France* 27 E9
Orhaneli, *Turkey* 66 C3
Orhangazi, *Turkey* 66 B3
Orhei, *Moldova* 41 J5
Orhon Gol →, *Mongolia* 54 A5
Ória, *Italy* 35 B10
Orient, *Australia* 91 D3
Oriental, Cordillera, *Bolivia* 125 D4
Oriental, Cordillera, *Colombia* 120 B3
Oriente, *Argentina* 126 D3
Origny-Ste.-Benoîte, *France* 25 C10
Orihuela, *Spain* 29 G4
Orihuela del Tremedal, *Spain* 28 E3
Orikhiv, *Ukraine* 41 J8
Oriku, *Albania* 39 J2
Orinduik, *Guyana* 121 C5
Orinoco →, *Venezuela* 121 B5
Orissa □, *India* 61 K14
Orissaare, *Estonia* 9 G20
Oristano, *Italy* 34 C1
Oristano, G. di, *Italy* 34 C1
Orituco →, *Venezuela* 120 B4
Orizaba, *Mexico* 115 D5
Orizona, *Brazil* 123 E2
Orjen, *Bos.-H.* 21 N8
Orjiva, *Spain* 29 J1
Orkanger, *Norway* 10 A3
Örkelljunga, *Sweden* 11 H7
Örkény, *Hungary* 21 H9
Orkla →, *Norway* 10 A3
Orkney, *S. Africa* 84 D4
Orkney □, *U.K.* 14 C6
Orkney Is., *U.K.* 14 C6
Orland, *U.S.A.* 112 F4
Orlando, *U.S.A.* 105 L5
Orlando, C. d', *Italy* 35 D7
Orléanais, *France* 25 E9
Orléans, *France* 25 E8
Orleans, *U.S.A.* 107 B12
Orléans, I. d', *Canada* 99 C5
Orlice →, *Czech.* 20 E6
Orlov, *Slovak Rep.* 20 F10
Orlov Gay, *Russia* 42 E9
Ormara, *Pakistan* 60 G4
Ormea, *Italy* 32 D4
Ormília, *Greece* 39 J6
Ormoc, *Phil.* 55 F6
Ormond, *N.Z.* 87 H6
Ormond Beach, *U.S.A.* 105 L5
Ormož, *Slovenia* 33 B13
Ormstown, *Canada* 107 A11
Ornans, *France* 25 E13
Orne □, *France* 24 D7
Orne →, *France* 24 C6
Ørnhøj, *Denmark* 11 H2
Ornö, *Sweden* 10 E12
Örnsköldsvik, *Sweden* 10 A12
Oro, *N. Korea* 51 D14
Oro →, *Mexico* 114 B3
Oro Grande, *U.S.A.* 113 L9
Orobie, Alpi, *Italy* 32 B6

Orocué, *Colombia* 120 C3
Orodo, *Nigeria* 79 D6
Orogrande, *U.S.A.* 111 K10
Orol, *Spain* 30 B3
Orol Dengizi = Aral Sea, *Asia* 44 E7
Oromocto, *Canada* 99 C6
Oron, *Nigeria* 79 E6
Oron, *Switz.* 22 C3
Orono, *Canada* 106 C6
Oropesa, *Spain* 30 F5
Oroquieta, *Phil.* 55 G5
Orós, *Brazil* 122 C4
Orosei, G. di, *Italy* 34 B2
Orosháza, *Hungary* 21 J10
Orotukan, *Russia* 45 C16
Oroville, *Calif., U.S.A.* 112 F5
Oroville, *Wash., U.S.A.* 110 B4
Oroville, L., *U.S.A.* 112 F5
Orroroo, *Australia* 91 E2
Orrville, *U.S.A.* 106 F3
Orsara di Púglia, *Italy* 35 A8
Orsha, *Belarus* 40 E6
Orsières, *Switz.* 22 D4
Orsk, *Russia* 44 D6
Ørslev, *Denmark* 11 J5
Orsogna, *Italy* 33 F11
Orşova, *Romania* 38 E5
Ørsted, *Denmark* 11 H4
Orta, L. d', *Italy* 32 C5
Orta Nova, *Italy* 35 A8
Ortaca, *Turkey* 66 D3
Ortaköy, *Çorum, Turkey* 66 B6
Ortaköy, *Niğde, Turkey* 66 C6
Orte, *Italy* 33 F9
Ortegal, C., *Spain* 30 B3
Orteguaza →, *Colombia* 120 C2
Orthez, *France* 26 E3
Ortho, *Belgium* 17 H7
Ortigueira, *Spain* 30 B3
Orting, *U.S.A.* 112 C4
Ortles, *Italy* 32 B7
Ortón →, *Bolivia* 124 C4
Ortona, *Italy* 33 F11
Orūmīyeh, *Iran* 67 D11
Orūmīyeh, Daryācheh-ye, *Iran* 67 D11
Orune, *Italy* 34 B2
Oruro, *Bolivia* 124 D4
Oruro □, *Bolivia* 124 D4
Orust, *Sweden* 11 F5
Oruzgān □, *Afghan.* 60 C5
Orvault, *France* 24 E5
Orvieto, *Italy* 33 F9
Orwell, *U.S.A.* 106 E4
Orwell →, *U.K.* 13 E9
Oryakhovo, *Bulgaria* 38 F6
Orzinuovi, *Italy* 32 C6
Orzysz, *Poland* 20 B11
Osa, Pen. de, *Costa Rica* 116 E3
Osage, *Iowa, U.S.A.* 108 D8
Osage, *Wyo., U.S.A.* 108 D2
Osage →, *U.S.A.* 108 F9
Osage City, *U.S.A.* 108 F7
Ōsaka, *Japan* 49 G7
Osan, *S. Korea* 51 F14
Osawatomie, *U.S.A.* 108 F7
Osborne, *U.S.A.* 108 F5
Osceola, *Ark., U.S.A.* 109 H10
Osceola, *Iowa, U.S.A.* 108 E8
Oschatz, *Germany* 18 D9
Oschersleben, *Germany* 18 C7
Óschiri, *Italy* 34 B2
Oscoda, *U.S.A.* 106 B1
Ösel = Saaremaa, *Estonia* 9 G20
Osery, *Russia* 42 C4
Osh, *Kyrgyzstan* 44 E8
Oshawa, *Canada* 98 D4
Oshkosh, *Nebr., U.S.A.* 108 E3
Oshkosh, *Wis., U.S.A.* 108 C10
Oshmyany = Ashmyany, *Belarus* 9 J21
Oshnovīyeh, *Iran* 64 B5
Oshogbo, *Nigeria* 79 D5
Oshtorīnān, *Iran* 67 E13
Oshwe, *Zaïre* 80 E3
Osijek, *Croatia* 21 K8
Ósilo, *Italy* 34 B1
Osimo, *Italy* 33 E10
Osintorf, *Belarus* 40 E6
Osipenko = Berdyansk, *Ukraine* 41 J9
Osipovichi = Asipovichy, *Belarus* 40 F5
Osizweni, *S. Africa* 85 D5
Oskaloosa, *U.S.A.* 108 E8
Oskarshamn, *Sweden* 9 H17
Oskélanéo, *Canada* 98 C4
Öskemen, *Kazakstan* 44 E9
Oskol →, *Ukraine* 41 H9
Oslo, *Norway* 10 E4
Oslob, *Phil.* 55 G5
Oslofjorden, *Norway* 10 E4
Osmanabad, *India* 60 K10
Osmancık, *Turkey* 66 B6
Osmaniye, *Turkey* 66 D7
Ösmo, *Sweden* 10 F11
Osnabrück, *Germany* 18 C4
Osor, *Italy* 33 D11
Osorio, *Brazil* 127 B5
Osorno, *Chile* 128 B2
Osorno, *Spain* 30 C6
Osorno □, *Chile* 128 B2
Osorno, Vol., *Chile* 128 B2
Osoyoos, *Canada* 100 D5
Osøyri, *Norway* 9 F11
Ospika →, *Canada* 100 B4
Osprey Reef, *Australia* 90 A4
Oss, *Neths.* 16 E7
Ossa, Mt., *Australia* 90 G4
Óssa, Oros, *Greece* 39 K5
Ossa de Montiel, *Spain* 29 G2
Ossabaw I., *U.S.A.* 105 K5
Osse →, *France* 26 D4
Ossendrecht, *Neths.* 17 F4
Ossining, *U.S.A.* 107 E11
Ossipee, *U.S.A.* 107 C13
Ossokmanuan L., *Canada* 99 B7
Ossora, *Russia* 45 D17
Ostashkov, *Russia* 42 B1
Oste →, *Germany* 18 B5
Ostend = Oostende, *Belgium* 17 F1
Oster, *Ukraine* 41 G6
Osterburg, *Germany* 18 C7
Osterburken, *Germany* 19 F5
Österdalälven, *Sweden* 9 F16
Østerdalen, *Norway* 9 F14
Östergötlands län □, *Sweden* 11 F9
Osterholz-Scharmbeck, *Germany* 18 B4
Østerild, *Denmark* 11 G2
Ostermundigen, *Switz.* 22 C4
Östersund, *Sweden* 10 A8
Østfold fylke □, *Norway* 10 E5
Ostfriesische Inseln, *Germany* 18 B3
Ostfriesland, *Germany* 18 B3
Óstia, Lido di, *Italy* 34 A5
Ostíglia, *Italy* 33 C8
Ostra, *Italy* 33 E10
Ostrava, *Czech.* 20 F8
Ostróda, *Poland* 20 B9
Ostrogozhsk, *Russia* 42 E4
Ostrogróg Sźamotuły, *Poland* 20 C6
Ostroh, *Ukraine* 41 G4
Ostrołęka, *Poland* 20 B11
Ostrov, *Bulgaria* 38 F7
Ostrov, *Romania* 38 E10
Ostrov, *Russia* 40 D5
Ostrów Mazowiecka, *Poland* 20 C11
Ostrów Wielkopolski, *Poland* 20 D7
Ostrowiec-Świętokrzyski, *Poland* 20 E11
Ostrzeszów, *Poland* 20 D7
Ostseebad Kühlungsborn, *Germany* 18 A7
Ostuni □, *Austria* 19 J8
Ostuni, *Italy* 35 B10
Osum →, *Bulgaria* 38 F7
Osumi →, *Albania* 39 J3
Ōsumi-Kaikyō, *Japan* 49 J5
Ōsumi-Shotō, *Japan* 49 J5
Osun □, *Nigeria* 79 D5
Osuna, *Spain* 31 H5
Oswego, *U.S.A.* 107 C8
Oswestry, *U.K.* 12 E4
Oświęcim, *Poland* 20 E9
Otago □, *N.Z.* 87 L2
Otago Harbour, *N.Z.* 87 L3
Ōtake, *Japan* 49 G6
Otaki, *N.Z.* 87 J5
Otaru, *Japan* 48 C10
Otaru-Wan = Ishikari-Wan, *Japan* 48 C10
Otava →, *Czech.* 20 F4
Otavalo, *Ecuador* 120 C2
Otavi, *Namibia* 84 B2
Otchinjau, *Angola* 84 B1
Otelec, *Romania* 38 D3
Otero de Rey, *Spain* 30 B3
Othello, *U.S.A.* 110 C4
Othonoí, *Greece* 39 K2
Óthris, Óros, *Greece* 39 K5
Otira Gorge, *N.Z.* 87 K3
Otis, *U.S.A.* 108 E3
Otjiwarongo, *Namibia* 84 C2
Otočac, *Croatia* 33 D12
Otoineppu, *Japan* 48 B11
Otorohanga, *N.Z.* 87 H5
Otoskwin →, *Canada* 98 B2
Otosquen, *Canada* 101 C8
Otra →, *Norway* 9 G13
Otradnyy, *Russia* 42 D10
Otranto, *Italy* 35 B11
Otranto, C. d', *Italy* 35 B11
Otranto, Str. of, *Italy* 35 B11
Otse, *S. Africa* 84 D4
Ōtsu, *Japan* 49 G7
Ōtsuki, *Japan* 49 G9
Otta, *Norway* 10 C3
Ottawa = Outaouais →, *Canada* 98 C5
Ottawa, *Canada* 98 C4
Ottawa, *Ill., U.S.A.* 108 E10
Ottawa, *Kans., U.S.A.* 108 F7
Ottawa Is., *Canada* 97 C11
Ottélé, *Cameroon* 79 E7
Otter L., *Canada* 101 B8
Otter Rapids, *Ont., Canada* 98 B3
Otter Rapids, *Sask., Canada* 101 B8
Otterndorf, *Germany* 18 B4
Otterup, *Denmark* 11 J4
Otterville, *Canada* 106 D4
Ottignies, *Belgium* 17 G5
Otto Beit Bridge, *Zimbabwe* 83 F2
Ottosdal, *S. Africa* 84 D4
Ottsjön, *Sweden* 10 A7
Ottumwa, *U.S.A.* 108 E8
Otu, *Nigeria* 79 D5
Otukpa, *Nigeria* 79 D6
Oturkpo, *Nigeria* 79 D6
Otway, B., *Chile* 128 D2
Otway, C., *Australia* 91 F3
Otwock, *Poland* 20 C11
Ötz, *Austria* 19 H6
Ötz →, *Austria* 19 H6
Ötztaler Alpen, *Austria* 19 J7
Ou →, *Laos* 58 B4
Ou Neua, *Laos* 58 A3
Ou-Sammyaku, *Japan* 48 E10
Ouachita →, *U.S.A.* 109 K9
Ouachita, L., *U.S.A.* 109 H8
Ouachita Mts., *U.S.A.* 109 H7
Ouadâne, *Mauritania* 74 D2
Ouadda, *C.A.R.* 73 G9
Ouagadougou, *Burkina Faso* 79 C4
Ouahigouya, *Burkina Faso* 78 C4
Ouahila, *Algeria* 74 C3
Ouahran = Oran, *Algeria* 75 A4
Oualâta, *Mauritania* 78 B3
Ouallene, *Algeria* 75 D5
Ouanda Djallé, *C.A.R.* 73 G9
Ouango, *C.A.R.* 80 D4
Ouarâne, *Mauritania* 74 D2
Ouargla, *Algeria* 75 B6
Ouarkziz, Djebel, *Algeria* 74 C3
Ouarzazate, *Morocco* 74 B3
Ouatagouna, *Mali* 79 B5
Oubangi →, *Zaïre* 80 E3
Oubarakai, O. →, *Algeria* 75 C6
Ouche →, *France* 25 E12
Oud-Beijerland, *Neths.* 16 E4
Oud-Gastel, *Neths.* 17 E4
Oud Turnhout, *Belgium* 17 F6
Ouddorp, *Neths.* 16 E3
Oude-Pekela, *Neths.* 16 B10
Oude Rijn →, *Neths.* 16 D4
Oudega, *Neths.* 16 B8
Oudenaarde, *Belgium* 17 G3
Oudenbosch, *Neths.* 17 E5
Oudenburg, *Belgium* 17 F2
Ouderkerk, *Utrecht, Neths.* 16 D5
Ouderkerk, *Zuid-Holland, Neths.* 16 E5
Oudeschild, *Neths.* 16 B5
Oudewater, *Neths.* 16 D5
Oudkarspel, *Neths.* 16 C5
Oudon, *France* 24 E5
Oudon →, *France* 24 E6
Oudtshoorn, *S. Africa* 84 E3
Oued Zem, *Morocco* 74 B3
Ouellé, *Ivory C.* 78 D4
Ouenza, *Algeria* 75 A6
Ouessa, *Burkina Faso* 78 C4
Ouessant, I. d', *France* 24 D1
Ouesso, *Congo* 80 D3
Ouest, Pte., *Canada* 99 C7
Ouezzane, *Morocco* 74 B3
Ouffet, *Belgium* 17 H6
Ouidah, *Benin* 79 D5
Ouistreham, *France* 24 C6
Oujda, *Morocco* 75 B4
Oujeft, *Mauritania* 74 D2
Oulainen, *Finland* 8 D21
Ould Yenjé, *Mauritania* 78 B2
Ouled Djellal, *Algeria* 75 B6
Ouled Naïl, Mts. des, *Algeria* 75 B5
Oulmès, *Morocco* 74 B3
Oulu, *Finland* 8 D21
Oulujärvi, *Finland* 8 D22
Oulujoki →, *Finland* 8 D21
Oulx, *Italy* 32 C3
Oum Chalouba, *Chad* 73 E9
Oum-el-Bouaghi, *Algeria* 75 A6
Oum el Ksi, *Algeria* 74 C3
Oum-er-Rbia, O. →, *Morocco* 74 B3
Oumè, *Ivory C.* 78 D3
Ounane, Dj., *Algeria* 75 C6
Ounasjoki →, *Finland* 8 C21
Ounguati, *Namibia* 84 C2
Ounianga-Kébir, *Chad* 73 E9
Ounianga Sérir, *Chad* 73 E9
Our →, *Lux.* 17 J8
Ouray, *U.S.A.* 111 G10
Ourcq →, *France* 25 C10
Ourém, *Brazil* 122 B2
Ourense = Orense, *Spain* 30 C3
Ouricuri, *Brazil* 122 C3
Ourinhos, *Brazil* 127 A6
Ourique, *Portugal* 31 H2
Ouro Fino, *Brazil* 127 A6
Ouro Prêto, *Brazil* 123 F3
Ouro Sogui, *Senegal* 78 B2
Oursi, *Burkina Faso* 79 C4
Ourthe →, *Belgium* 17 H7
Ouse, *Australia* 90 G4
Ouse →, *E. Susx., U.K.* 13 G8
Ouse →, *N. Yorks., U.K.* 12 C8
Oust, *France* 26 F5
Oust →, *France* 24 E4
Outaouais →, *Canada* 98 C5
Outardes →, *Canada* 99 C6
Outat Oulad el Haj, *Morocco* 75 B4
Outer Hebrides, *U.K.* 14 D1
Outer I., *Canada* 99 B8
Outes, *Spain* 30 C2
Outjo, *Namibia* 84 C2
Outlook, *Canada* 101 C7
Outlook, *U.S.A.* 108 A2
Outokumpu, *Finland* 8 E23
Outreau, *France* 25 B8
Ouvèze →, *France* 27 E8
Ouyen, *Australia* 91 F3
Ouzouer-le-Marché, *France* 25 E8
Ovada, *Italy* 32 D5
Ovalau, *Fiji* 87 C8
Ovalle, *Chile* 126 C1
Ovamboland, *Namibia* 84 B2
Ovar, *Portugal* 30 E2
Ovejas, *Colombia* 120 B2
Overdinkel, *Neths.* 16 D10
Overflakkee, *Neths.* 16 E4
Overijse, *Belgium* 17 G5
Overijssel □, *Neths.* 16 D9
Overijsselsch Kanaal →, *Neths.* 16 C8
Overland Park, *U.S.A.* 108 F7
Overpelt, *Belgium* 17 F6
Overton, *U.S.A.* 113 J12
Övertorneå, *Sweden* 8 C20
Ovid, *U.S.A.* 108 E3
Ovidiopol, *Ukraine* 41 J6
Oviedo, *Spain* 30 B5
Oviedo □, *Spain* 30 B5
Oviken, *Sweden* 10 A8
Oviksfjällen, *Sweden* 10 B7
Oviši, *Latvia* 9 H19
Övör Hangay □, *Mongolia* 50 B2
Ovoro, *Nigeria* 79 D6
Øvre Årdal, *Norway* 9 F12
Ovruch, *Ukraine* 41 G5
Owaka, *N.Z.* 87 M2
Owambo = Ovamboland, *Namibia* 84 B2
Owase, *Japan* 49 G8
Owatonna, *U.S.A.* 108 C8
Owbeh, *Afghan.* 60 B3
Owego, *U.S.A.* 107 D8
Owen Falls Dam, *Uganda* 82 B3
Owen Sound, *Canada* 98 D3
Owendo, *Gabon* 80 D1
Owens →, *U.S.A.* 112 J9
Owens L., *U.S.A.* 113 J9
Owensboro, *U.S.A.* 104 G2
Owensville, *U.S.A.* 108 F9
Owerri, *Nigeria* 79 D6
Owl →, *Canada* 101 B10
Owo, *Nigeria* 79 D6
Owosso, *U.S.A.* 104 D3
Owyhee, *U.S.A.* 110 F5
Owyhee →, *U.S.A.* 110 E5
Owyhee, L., *U.S.A.* 110 E5
Oxapampa, *Peru* 124 C2
Öxarfjörður, *Iceland* 8 C5
Oxelösund, *Sweden* 11 F11
Oxford, *N.Z.* 87 K4
Oxford, *U.K.* 13 F6
Oxford, *Miss., U.S.A.* 109 H10
Oxford, *N.C., U.S.A.* 105 G6
Oxford, *Ohio, U.S.A.* 104 F3
Oxford L., *Canada* 101 C9
Oxfordshire □, *U.K.* 13 F6
Oxley, *Australia* 91 E3
Oxnard, *U.S.A.* 113 L7
Oxus = Amudarya →, *Uzbekistan* 44 E6
Oya, *Malaysia* 56 D4
Oyama, *Japan* 49 F9
Oyapock →, *Fr. Guiana* 121 C7
Oyem, *Gabon* 80 D2
Oyen, *Canada* 101 C6
Øyeren, *Norway* 10 E5
Oykel →, *U.K.* 14 D4
Oymyakon, *Russia* 45 C15
Oyo, *Nigeria* 79 D5
Oyo □, *Nigeria* 79 D5
Oyón, *Peru* 124 C2
Oyonnax, *France* 27 B9
Oyster Bay, *U.S.A.* 107 F11
Ōyūbari, *Japan* 48 C11
Özalp, *Turkey* 67 C10
Ozamiz, *Phil.* 55 G5
Ozark, *Ala., U.S.A.* 105 K3
Ozark, *Ark., U.S.A.* 109 H8
Ozark, *Mo., U.S.A.* 109 G8
Ozark Plateau, *U.S.A.* 109 G9
Ozarks, L. of the, *U.S.A.* 108 F8
Ózd, *Hungary* 21 G10
Ozernoye, *Russia* 42 E10
Ozette L., *U.S.A.* 112 B2
Ozieri, *Italy* 34 B2
Ozinki, *Russia* 42 E9
Ozona, *U.S.A.* 109 K4
Ozorków, *Poland* 20 D9
Ozuluama, *Mexico* 115 C5
Ozurgeti, *Georgia* 43 K5

P

Pa, *Burkina Faso* 78 C4
Pa-an, *Burma* 61 L20
Pa Mong Dam, *Thailand* 58 D4
Paal, *Belgium* 17 F6
Paamiut = Frederikshåb, *Greenland* 4 C5
Paar →, *Germany* 19 G6
Paarl, *S. Africa* 84 E2
Paauilo, *U.S.A.* 102 H17
Pab Hills, *Pakistan* 62 F2
Pabianice, *Poland* 20 D9
Pabna, *Bangla.* 61 G16
Pabo, *Uganda* 82 B3
Pacaás Novos, Serra dos, *Brazil* 125 C5
Pacaipampa, *Peru* 124 B2
Pacaja →, *Brazil* 122 B1
Pacajus, *Brazil* 122 B4
Pacaraima, Sierra, *Venezuela* 121 C5
Pacarán, *Peru* 124 C2
Pacaraos, *Peru* 124 C2
Pacasmayo, *Peru* 124 B2
Paceco, *Italy* 34 E5
Pachacamac, *Peru* 124 C2
Pachhar, *India* 62 G7
Pachino, *Italy* 35 F8
Pachitea →, *Peru* 124 B3
Pachiza, *Peru* 124 B2
Pacho, *Colombia* 120 B3
Pachpadra, *India* 60 G8
Pachuca, *Mexico* 115 C5
Pacific, *Canada* 100 C3
Pacific-Antarctic Ridge, *Pac. Oc.* 93 M16
Pacific Grove, *U.S.A.* 111 H3
Pacific Ocean, *Pac. Oc.* 93 G14
Pacifica, *U.S.A.* 112 H4
Pacitan, *Indonesia* 57 H14
Packwood, *U.S.A.* 112 D5
Pacuí →, *Brazil* 123 E2
Pacy-sur-Eure, *France* 24 C8
Padaido, Kepulauan, *Indonesia* 57 E9
Padang, *Indonesia* 56 E2
Padangpanjang, *Indonesia* 56 E2
Padangsidempuan, *Indonesia* 56 D1
Padauari →, *Brazil* 121 D5
Padborg, *Denmark* 11 K3
Padcaya, *Bolivia* 125 E5
Paddockwood, *Canada* 101 C7
Paderborn, *Germany* 18 D4
Padilla, *Bolivia* 125 D5
Padloping Island, *Canada* 97 B13
Pádova, *Italy* 33 C8
Padra, *India* 62 H5
Padrauna, *India* 63 F10
Padre I., *U.S.A.* 109 M6
Padro, Mte., *France* 27 F12
Padrón, *Spain* 30 C2
Padstow, *U.K.* 13 G3
Padua = Pádova, *Italy* 33 C8
Paducah, *Ky., U.S.A.* 104 G1
Paducah, *Tex., U.S.A.* 109 H4
Padul, *Spain* 31 H7
Padula, *Italy* 35 B8
Paengnyong-do, *S. Korea* 51 F13
Paeroa, *N.Z.* 87 G5
Paesana, *Italy* 32 D4
Pafúri, *Mozam.* 85 C5
Pag, *Croatia* 33 D11
Paga, *Ghana* 79 C4
Pagadian, *Phil.* 55 H5
Pagai Selatan, P., *Indonesia* 56 E2
Pagai Utara, *Indonesia* 56 E2
Pagalu = Annobón, *Atl. Oc.* 70 G4
Pagastikós Kólpos, *Greece* 39 K6
Pagatan, *Indonesia* 56 E5
Page, *Ariz., U.S.A.* 111 H8
Page, *N. Dak., U.S.A.* 108 B6
Paglieta, *Italy* 33 F11
Pagny-sur-Moselle, *France* 25 D13
Pago Pago, *Amer. Samoa* 87 B13
Pagosa Springs, *U.S.A.* 111 H10
Pagwa River, *Canada* 98 B2
Pahala, *U.S.A.* 102 J17
Pahang →, *Malaysia* 59 L4
Pahiatua, *N.Z.* 87 J5
Pahokee, *U.S.A.* 105 M5
Pahrump, *U.S.A.* 113 J11
Pahute Mesa, *U.S.A.* 112 H10
Pai, *Thailand* 58 C2
Paia, *U.S.A.* 102 H16
Paicines, *U.S.A.* 112 J5
Paide, *Estonia* 9 G21
Paignton, *U.K.* 13 G4
Paiho, *Taiwan* 53 F13
Paiján, *Peru* 124 B2
Päijänne, *Finland* 9 F21
Paimbœuf, *France* 24 E4
Paimpol, *France* 24 D3
Painan, *Indonesia* 56 E2
Painesville, *U.S.A.* 106 E3
Paint Hills = Wemindji, *Canada* 98 B4
Paint L., *Canada* 101 B9
Paint Rock, *U.S.A.* 109 K5
Painted Desert, *U.S.A.* 111 J8
Paintsville, *U.S.A.* 104 G4
País Vasco □, *Spain* 28 C2
Paisley, *Canada* 106 B3
Paisley, *U.K.* 14 F4
Paisley, *U.S.A.* 110 E3
Paita, *Peru* 124 B1
Paiva →, *Portugal* 30 D2
Paizhou, *China* 53 B9
Pajares, *Spain* 30 B5
Pajares, Puerto de, *Spain* 30 C5
Pak Lay, *Laos* 58 C3
Pak Phanang, *Thailand* 59 H3
Pak Sane, *Laos* 58 C4
Pak Song, *Laos* 58 E6
Pak Suong, *Laos* 58 C4
Pakaraima Mts., *Guyana* 121 B5
Pákhnes, *Greece* 37 D6
Pakistan ■, *Asia* 62 E3
Pakkading, *Laos* 58 C4
Pakokku, *Burma* 61 J19
Pakpattan, *Pakistan* 62 D5
Pakrac, *Croatia* 21 K7

Paks, *Hungary* 21 J8
Pakse, *Laos* 58 E5
Paktīā □, *Afghan.* 60 C6
Pakwach, *Uganda* 82 B3
Pala, *Chad* 73 G8
Pala, *U.S.A.* 113 M9
Pala, *Zaïre* 82 D2
Palabek, *Uganda* 82 B3
Palacios, *U.S.A.* 109 L6
Palafrugell, *Spain* 28 D8
Palagiano, *Italy* 35 B10
Palagonía, *Italy* 35 E7
Palagruža, *Croatia* 33 F13
Palaiókastron, *Greece* 37 D8
Palaiokhóra, *Greece* 37 D5
Palam, *India* 60 K10
Palamás, *Greece* 39 K5
Palamós, *Spain* 28 D8
Palampur, *India* 62 C7
Palana, *Australia* 90 F4
Palana, *Russia* 45 D16
Palanan, *Phil.* 55 C5
Palanan Pt., *Phil.* 55 C5
Palandri, *Pakistan* 63 C5
Palanga, *Lithuania* 9 J19
Palangkaraya, *Indonesia* 56 E4
Palani Hills, *India* 60 P10
Palanpur, *India* 62 G5
Palanro, *Indonesia* 57 E5
Palapye, *Botswana* 84 C4
Palas, *Pakistan* 63 B5
Palatka, *Russia* 45 C16
Palatka, *U.S.A.* 105 L5
Palau ■, *Pac. Oc.* 46 J17
Palawan, *Phil.* 55 G3
Palayankottai, *India* 60 Q10
Palazzo, Pte., *France* 27 F12
Palazzo San Gervásio, *Italy* 35 B8
Palazzolo Acréide, *Italy* 35 E7
Palca, *Chile* 124 D4
Paldiski, *Estonia* 9 G21
Paleleh, *Indonesia* 57 D6
Palembang, *Indonesia* 56 E2
Palena →, *Chile* 128 B2
Palena, L., *Chile* 128 B2
Palencia, *Spain* 30 C6
Palencia □, *Spain* 30 C6
Paleokastrítsa, *Greece* 37 A3
Paleometokho, *Cyprus* 37 D12
Palermo, *Colombia* 120 C2
Palermo, *Italy* 34 D6
Palermo, *U.S.A.* 110 G3
Palestine, *Asia* 69 D4
Palestine, *U.S.A.* 109 K7
Palestrina, *Italy* 34 A5
Paletwa, *Burma* 61 J18
Palghat, *India* 60 P10
Palgrave, Mt., *Australia* 88 D2
Pali, *India* 62 G5
Palinuro, C., *Italy* 35 B8
Palisade, *U.S.A.* 108 E4
Paliseul, *Belgium* 17 J6
Palitana, *India* 62 J4
Palizada, *Mexico* 115 D6
Palizzi Marina, *Italy* 35 E8
Palk Bay, *Asia* 60 Q11
Palk Strait, *Asia* 60 Q11
Palkānah, *Iraq* 64 C5
Palla Road = Dinokwe, *Botswana* 84 C4
Pallanza = Verbánia, *Italy* 32 C5
Pallasovka, *Russia* 42 E8
Pallisa, *Uganda* 82 B3
Pallu, *India* 62 E6
Palm Bay, *U.S.A.* 105 L5
Palm Beach, *U.S.A.* 105 M6
Palm Desert, *U.S.A.* 113 M10
Palm Is., *Australia* 90 B4
Palm Springs, *U.S.A.* 113 M10
Palma, *Mozam.* 83 E5
Palma →, *Brazil* 123 D2
Palma, B. de, *Spain* 36 B9
Palma de Mallorca, *Spain* 36 B9
Palma del Río, *Spain* 31 H5
Palma di Montechiaro, *Italy* 34 E6
Palma Soriano, *Cuba* 116 B4
Palmanova, *Italy* 33 C10
Palmares, *Brazil* 122 C4
Palmarito, *Venezuela* 120 B3
Palmarola, *Italy* 34 B5
Palmas, *Brazil* 127 B5
Palmas, C., *Liberia* 78 E3
Pálmas, G. di, *Italy* 34 C1
Palmas de Monte Alto, *Brazil* 123 D3
Palmdale, *U.S.A.* 113 L8
Palmeira, *Brazil* 123 G2
Palmeira dos Índios, *Brazil* 122 C4
Palmeirais, *Brazil* 122 C3
Palmeiras →, *Brazil* 123 D2
Palmeirinhas, Pta. das, *Angola* 80 F2
Palmela, *Portugal* 31 G2
Palmelo, *Brazil* 123 E2
Palmer, *U.S.A.* 96 B5
Palmer →, *Australia* 90 B3
Palmer Arch., *Antarctica* 5 C17
Palmer Lake, *U.S.A.* 108 F2
Palmer Land, *Antarctica* 5 D18
Palmerston, *Canada* 106 C4
Palmerston, *N.Z.* 87 L3
Palmerston North, *N.Z.* 87 J5
Palmerton, *U.S.A.* 107 F9
Palmetto, *U.S.A.* 105 M4
Palmi, *Italy* 35 D8
Palmira, *Argentina* 126 C2
Palmira, *Colombia* 120 C2
Palmyra = Tudmur, *Syria* 67 E8
Palmyra, *Mo., U.S.A.* 108 F9
Palmyra, *N.Y., U.S.A.* 106 C7
Palmyra Is., *Pac. Oc.* 93 G11
Palo Alto, *U.S.A.* 111 H2
Palo del Colle, *Italy* 35 A9
Palo Verde, *U.S.A.* 113 M12
Palombara Sabina, *Italy* 33 F9
Palompon, *Phil.* 55 F6
Palopo, *Indonesia* 57 E6
Palos, C. de, *Spain* 29 H4
Palos Verdes, *U.S.A.* 113 M8
Palos Verdes, Pt., *U.S.A.* 113 M8
Palouse, *U.S.A.* 110 C5
Palpa, *Peru* 124 C2
Palparara, *Australia* 90 C3
Pålsboda, *Sweden* 10 E9
Palu, *Indonesia* 57 E5
Palu, *Turkey* 67 C9
Paluan, *Phil.* 57 B6
Palwal, *India* 62 E7
Pama, *Burkina Faso* 79 C5
Pamanukan, *Indonesia* 57 G12
Pamekasan, *Indonesia* 57 G15
Pamiers, *France* 26 E5
Pamirs, *Tajikistan* 44 F8
Pamlico →, *U.S.A.* 105 H7
Pamlico Sd., *U.S.A.* 105 H8
Pampa, *U.S.A.* 109 H4
Pampa de Agma, *Argentina* 128 B3
Pampa de las Salinas, *Argentina* 126 C2
Pampa Grande, *Bolivia* 125 D5
Pampa Hermosa, *Peru* 124 B2
Pampanua, *Indonesia* 57 E6
Pamparato, *Italy* 32 D4
Pampas, *Argentina* 126 D3
Pampas, *Peru* 124 C3
Pampas →, *Peru* 124 C3
Pamphylia, *Turkey* 66 D4
Pamplona, *Colombia* 120 B3
Pamplona, *Spain* 28 C3
Pampoenpoort, *S. Africa* 84 E3
Pan Xian, *China* 52 E5
Pana, *U.S.A.* 108 F10
Panabo, *Phil.* 55 H6
Panaca, *U.S.A.* 111 H6
Panagyurishte, *Bulgaria* 38 G7
Panaitan, *Indonesia* 57 G11
Panaji, *India* 60 M8
Panamá, *Panama* 116 E4
Panama ■, *Cent. Amer.* 116 E4
Panamá, G. de, *Panama* 116 E4
Panama Canal, *Panama* 116 E4
Panama City, *U.S.A.* 105 K3
Panamint Range, *U.S.A.* 113 J9
Panamint Springs, *U.S.A.* 113 J9
Panão, *Peru* 124 B2
Panaon I., *Phil.* 55 F6
Panare, *Thailand* 59 J3
Panarea, *Italy* 35 D8
Panaro →, *Italy* 32 D8
Panarukan, *Indonesia* 57 G15
Panay, *Phil.* 55 F5
Panay, G., *Phil.* 57 B6
Pancake Range, *U.S.A.* 111 G6
Pančevo, *Serbia, Yug.* 21 L10
Pancorbo, Paso, *Spain* 28 C1
Pandan, *Antique, Phil.* 55 F5
Pandan, *Catanduanes, Phil.* 55 D6
Pandegelang, *Indonesia* 57 G12
Pandharpur, *India* 60 L9
Pandilla, *Spain* 28 D1
Pando, *Uruguay* 127 C4
Pando □, *Bolivia* 124 C4
Pando, L. = Hope, L., *Australia* 91 D2
Pandokrátor, *Greece* 37 A3
Pandora, *Costa Rica* 116 E3
Panevėžys, *Lithuania* 9 J21
Panfilov, *Kazakstan* 44 E8
Panfilovo, *Russia* 42 E6
Pang-Long, *Burma* 61 H21
Pang-Yang, *Burma* 61 H21
Panga, *Zaïre* 82 B2
Pangalanes, Canal des, *Madag.* 85 C8
Pangani, *Tanzania* 82 D4
Pangani □, *Tanzania* 82 D4
Pangani →, *Tanzania* 82 D4
Pangfou = Bengbu, *China* 51 H9
Pangil, *Zaïre* 82 C2
Pangkah, Tanjung, *Indonesia* 57 G15
Pangkajene, *Indonesia* 57 E5
Pangkalanbrandan, *Indonesia* 56 D1
Pangkalanbuun, *Indonesia* 56 E4
Pangkalansusu, *Indonesia* 56 D1
Pangkalpinang, *Indonesia* 56 E3
Pangkoh, *Indonesia* 56 E4
Pangnirtung, *Canada* 97 B13
Pangrango, *Indonesia* 57 G12
Panguipulli, *Chile* 128 A2
Panguitch, *U.S.A.* 111 H7
Pangutaran Group, *Phil.* 55 H4
Panhandle, *U.S.A.* 109 H4
Pani Mines, *India* 62 H5
Pania-Mutombo, *Zaïre* 82 D1
Panipat, *India* 62 E7
Panjal Range, *India* 62 C7
Panjgur, *Pakistan* 60 F4
Panjim = Panaji, *India* 60 M8
Panjinad Barrage, *Pakistan* 60 E7
Panjwai, *Afghan.* 62 D1
Pankshin, *Nigeria* 79 D6
Panmunjŏm, *N. Korea* 51 F14
Panna, *India* 63 G9
Panna Hills, *India* 63 G9
Pano Lefkara, *Cyprus* 37 E12
Pano Panayia, *Cyprus* 37 E11
Panorama, *Brazil* 127 A5
Pánormon, *Greece* 37 D6
Panshan, *China* 51 D12
Panshi, *China* 51 C14
Pantar, *Indonesia* 57 F6
Pante Macassar, *Indonesia* 57 F6
Pantelleria, *Italy* 34 F5
Pantón, *Spain* 30 C3
Pánuco, *Mexico* 115 C5
Panyam, *Nigeria* 79 D6
Panyu, *China* 53 F9
Pao →, *Anzoátegui, Venezuela* 121 B5
Pao →, *Apure, Venezuela* 120 B4
Páola, *Italy* 35 C9
Paola, *Malta* 37 D2
Paola, *U.S.A.* 108 F7
Paonia, *U.S.A.* 111 G10
Paoting = Baoding, *China* 50 E8
Paot'ou = Baotou, *China* 50 D6
Paoua, *C.A.R.* 73 G8
Pápa, *Hungary* 21 H7
Papagayo →, *Mexico* 115 D5
Papagayo, G. de, *Costa Rica* 116 D2
Papakura, *N.Z.* 87 G5
Papantla, *Mexico* 115 C5
Papar, *Malaysia* 56 C5
Pápas, Ákra, *Greece* 39 L4
Papenburg, *Germany* 18 B3
Paphlagonia, *Turkey* 66 B5
Paphos, *Cyprus* 66 E5
Papien Chiang = Da →, *Vietnam* 58 B5
Papigochic →, *Mexico* 114 B3
Paposo, *Chile* 126 B1
Papoutsa, *Cyprus* 37 E12
Papua New Guinea ■, *Oceania* 92 H6
Papuča, *Croatia* 33 D12
Papudo, *Chile* 126 C1
Papuk, *Croatia* 21 K7
Papun, *Burma* 61 K20
Papunya, *Australia* 88 D5
Pará = Belém, *Brazil* 122 B2
Pará □, *Brazil* 125 A7
Pará □, *Surinam* 121 B6
Parábita, *Italy* 35 B11
Paraburdoo, *Australia* 88 D2
Paracale, *Phil.* 55 D5
Paracas, Pen., *Peru* 124 C2
Paracatu, *Brazil* 123 E2
Paracatu →, *Brazil* 123 E2
Paracel Is., *S. China Sea* 56 A4
Parachilna, *Australia* 91 E2
Parachinar, *Pakistan* 62 C4
Paraćin, *Serbia, Yug.* 21 M11
Paracuru, *Brazil* 122 B4
Parada, Punta, *Peru* 124 D2
Paradas, *Spain* 31 H5
Paradela, *Spain* 30 C3
Paradhísi, *Greece* 37 C10
Paradip, *India* 61 J15
Paradise, *Calif., U.S.A.* 112 F5
Paradise, *Mont., U.S.A.* 110 C6
Paradise, *Nev., U.S.A.* 113 J11
Paradise →, *Canada* 99 B8
Paradise Valley, *U.S.A.* 110 F5
Parado, *Indonesia* 57 F5
Paragould, *U.S.A.* 109 G9
Paraguá →, *Bolivia* 125 C5
Paragua →, *Venezuela* 121 B5
Paraguaçu →, *Brazil* 123 D4
Paraguaçu Paulista, *Brazil* 127 A5
Paraguaipoa, *Venezuela* 120 A3
Paraguaná, Pen. de, *Venezuela* 120 A3
Paraguarí, *Paraguay* 126 B4
Paraguarí □, *Paraguay* 126 B4
Paraguay ■, *S. Amer.* 126 A4
Paraguay →, *Paraguay* 126 B4
Paraíba = João Pessoa, *Brazil* 122 C5
Paraíba □, *Brazil* 122 C4
Paraíba do Sul →, *Brazil* 123 F3
Parainen, *Finland* 9 F20
Paraiso, *Mexico* 115 D6
Parak, *Iran* 65 E7
Parakhino Paddubye, *Russia* 40 C7
Parakou, *Benin* 79 D5
Paralimni, *Cyprus* 37 D12
Paramaribo, *Surinam* 121 B6
Parambu, *Brazil* 122 C3
Paramillo, Nudo del, *Colombia* 120 B2
Paramirim, *Brazil* 123 D3
Paramirim →, *Brazil* 123 D3
Paramithiá, *Greece* 39 K3
Paramushir, Ostrov, *Russia* 45 D16
Paran →, *Israel* 69 E4
Paraná, *Argentina* 126 C3
Paranã, *Brazil* 123 D2
Paraná □, *Brazil* 127 A5
Paraná →, *Argentina* 126 C4
Paranaguá, *Brazil* 127 B6
Paranaíba →, *Brazil* 123 F1
Paranapanema →, *Brazil* 127 A5
Paranapiacaba, Serra do, *Brazil* 127 A6
Paranavaí, *Brazil* 127 A5
Parang, *Jolo, Phil.* 55 J4
Parang, *Mindanao, Phil.* 57 C6
Parangaba, *Brazil* 122 B4
Parapóla, *Greece* 39 N6
Paraspóri, Ákra, *Greece* 39 P10
Paratinga, *Brazil* 123 D3
Paratoo, *Australia* 91 E2
Parattah, *Australia* 90 G4
Paraúna, *Brazil* 123 E1
Paray-le-Monial, *France* 27 B8
Parbati →, *India* 62 G7
Parbhani, *India* 60 K10
Parchim, *Germany* 18 B7
Parczew, *Poland* 20 D12
Pardes Hanna, *Israel* 69 C3
Pardilla, *Spain* 30 D7
Pardo →, *Bahia, Brazil* 123 E4
Pardo →, *Mato Grosso, Brazil* 127 A5
Pardo →, *Minas Gerais, Brazil* 123 E3
Pardo →, *São Paulo, Brazil* 123 F2
Pardubice, *Czech.* 20 E5
Pare, *Indonesia* 57 G15
Pare □, *Tanzania* 82 C4
Pare Mts., *Tanzania* 82 C4
Parecis, Serra dos, *Brazil* 125 C6
Paredes de Nava, *Spain* 30 C6
Pareh, *Iran* 64 B5
Parelhas, *Brazil* 122 C4
Paren, *Russia* 45 C17
Parent, *Canada* 98 C5
Parent, L., *Canada* 98 C4
Parentis-en-Born, *France* 26 D2
Parepare, *Indonesia* 57 E5
Parfino, *Russia* 40 D6
Pargo, Pta. do, *Madeira* 36 D2
Paria, G. de, *Venezuela* 121 A5
Paria, Pen. de, *Venezuela* 121 A5
Pariaguán, *Venezuela* 121 B5
Pariaman, *Indonesia* 56 E2
Paricatuba, *Brazil* 121 D5
Paricutín, Cerro, *Mexico* 114 D4
Parigi, *Java, Indonesia* 57 G13
Parigi, *Sulawesi, Indonesia* 57 E6
Parika, *Guyana* 121 B6
Parikkala, *Finland* 40 B5
Parima, Serra, *Brazil* 121 C5
Parinari, *Peru* 124 A3
Pariñas, Pta., *S. Amer.* 118 D2
Parîngul Mare, *Romania* 38 D6
Parintins, *Brazil* 121 D6
Pariparit Kyun, *Burma* 61 M18
Paris, *Canada* 98 D3
Paris, *France* 25 D9
Paris, *Idaho, U.S.A.* 110 E8
Paris, *Ky., U.S.A.* 104 F3
Paris, *Tenn., U.S.A.* 105 G1
Paris, *Tex., U.S.A.* 109 J7
Paris, Ville de □, *France* 25 D9
Parish, *U.S.A.* 107 C8
Pariti, *Indonesia* 57 F6
Park, *U.S.A.* 112 B4
Park City, *U.S.A.* 110 F8
Park Falls, *U.S.A.* 108 C9
Park Range, *U.S.A.* 110 G10
Park Rapids, *U.S.A.* 108 B7
Park River, *U.S.A.* 108 A6
Park Rynie, *S. Africa* 85 E5
Parkā Bandar, *Iran* 65 E8
Parkano, *Finland* 9 E20
Parker, *Ariz., U.S.A.* 113 L12
Parker, *S. Dak., U.S.A.* 108 D6
Parker Dam, *U.S.A.* 113 L12
Parkersburg, *U.S.A.* 104 F5
Parkerview, *Canada* 101 C8
Parkes, *Australia* 91 E4
Parkfield, *U.S.A.* 112 K6
Parkland, *U.S.A.* 112 C4
Parkside, *Canada* 101 C7
Parkston, *U.S.A.* 108 D5
Parksville, *Canada* 100 D4
Parma, *Italy* 32 D7
Parma, *Idaho, U.S.A.* 110 E5
Parma, *Ohio, U.S.A.* 106 E3
Parma →, *Italy* 32 D7
Parnaguá, *Brazil* 122 D3
Parnaíba, *Piauí, Brazil* 122 B3
Parnaíba, *São Paulo, Brazil* 125 D7
Parnaíba →, *Brazil* 122 B3
Parnamirim, *Brazil* 122 C4
Parnarama, *Brazil* 122 C3
Parnassós, *Greece* 39 L5
Párnis, *Greece* 39 L6
Párnon Óros, *Greece* 39 M5
Parnu, *Estonia* 9 G21
Paroo →, *Australia* 91 E3
Páros, *Greece* 39 M8
Parowan, *U.S.A.* 111 H7
Parpaillon, *France* 27 D10
Parral, *Chile* 126 D1
Parramatta, *Australia* 91 E5
Parras, *Mexico* 114 B4
Parrett →, *U.K.* 13 F5
Parris I., *U.S.A.* 105 J5
Parrsboro, *Canada* 99 C7
Parry Is., *Canada* 4 B2
Parry Sound, *Canada* 98 C3
Parsberg, *Germany* 19 F7
Parshall, *U.S.A.* 108 B3
Parsnip →, *Canada* 100 B4
Parsons, *U.S.A.* 109 G7
Parsons Ra., *Australia* 90 A2
Partanna, *Italy* 34 E5
Parthenay, *France* 24 F6
Partinico, *Italy* 34 D6
Paru →, *Brazil* 121 D7
Parú →, *Venezuela* 120 C4
Paru de Oeste →, *Brazil* 121 C6
Parucito →, *Venezuela* 120 B4
Paruro, *Peru* 124 C3
Parvān □, *Afghan.* 60 B6
Parvatipuram, *India* 61 K13
Parys, *S. Africa* 84 D4
Pas-de-Calais □, *France* 25 B9
Pasadena, *Calif., U.S.A.* 113 L8
Pasadena, *Tex., U.S.A.* 109 L7
Pasaje, *Ecuador* 120 D2
Pasaje →, *Argentina* 126 B3
Pasay, *Phil.* 55 D4
Pascagoula, *U.S.A.* 109 K10
Pascagoula →, *U.S.A.* 109 K10
Paşcani, *Romania* 38 B9
Pasco, *U.S.A.* 110 C4
Pasco □, *Peru* 124 C2
Pasco, Cerro de, *Peru* 124 C2
Pascua, I. de, *Pac. Oc.* 93 K17
Pasewalk, *Germany* 18 B10
Pasfield L., *Canada* 101 B7
Pasha →, *Russia* 40 B7
Pashiwari, *Pakistan* 63 B6
Pashmakli = Smolyan, *Bulgaria* 39 H7
Pasinler, *Turkey* 67 C9
Pasirian, *Indonesia* 57 H15
Paskūh, *Iran* 65 E9
Pasley, C., *Australia* 89 F3
Pašman, *Croatia* 33 E12
Pasni, *Pakistan* 60 G3
Paso Cantinela, *Mexico* 113 N11
Paso de Indios, *Argentina* 128 B3
Paso de los Libres, *Argentina* 126 B4
Paso de los Toros, *Uruguay* 126 C4
Paso Flores, *Argentina* 128 B2
Paso Robles, *U.S.A.* 111 J3
Pasorapa, *Bolivia* 125 D5
Paspébiac, *Canada* 99 C6
Pasrur, *Pakistan* 62 C6
Passage West, *Ireland* 15 E3
Passaic, *U.S.A.* 107 F10
Passau, *Germany* 19 G9
Passendale, *Belgium* 17 G2
Passero, C., *Italy* 35 F8
Passo Fundo, *Brazil* 127 B5
Passos, *Brazil* 123 F2
Passow, *Germany* 18 B10
Passwang, *Switz.* 22 B5
Passy, *France* 27 C10
Pastavy, *Belarus* 9 J22
Pastaza □, *Ecuador* 120 D2
Pastaza →, *Peru* 120 D2
Pastęk, *Poland* 20 A9
Pasto, *Colombia* 120 C2
Pastos Bons, *Brazil* 122 C3
Pastrana, *Spain* 28 E2
Pasuruan, *Indonesia* 57 G15
Patagonia, *Argentina* 128 C2
Patagonia, *U.S.A.* 111 L8
Patambar, *Iran* 65 D9
Patan, *India* 60 H8
Patan, *Maharashtra, India* 62 H5
Patan, *Nepal* 61 F14
Patani, *Indonesia* 57 D7
Pataudi, *India* 62 E7
Patay, *France* 25 D8
Patchewollock, *Australia* 91 F3
Patchogue, *U.S.A.* 107 F11
Patea, *N.Z.* 87 H5
Pategi, *Nigeria* 79 D6
Patensie, *S. Africa* 84 E3
Paternò, *Italy* 35 E7
Pateros, *U.S.A.* 110 B4
Paterson, *U.S.A.* 107 F10
Paterson Ra., *Australia* 88 D3
Paterswolde, *Neths.* 16 B9
Pathankot, *India* 62 C6
Pathfinder Reservoir, *U.S.A.* 110 E10
Pathiu, *Thailand* 59 G2
Pathum Thani, *Thailand* 58 E3
Pati, *Indonesia* 57 G14
Patía, *Colombia* 120 C2
Patía →, *Colombia* 120 C2
Patiala, *India* 62 D7
Patine Kouka, *Senegal* 78 C2
Pativilca, *Peru* 124 C2
Patkai Bum, *India* 61 F19
Pátmos, *Greece* 39 M9
Patna, *India* 63 G11
Patnos, *Turkey* 67 C10
Patonga, *Uganda* 82 B3
Patos, *Brazil* 122 C4
Patos, L. dos, *Brazil* 127 C5
Patos de Minas, *Brazil* 123 E2
Patquía, *Argentina* 126 C2
Pátrai, *Greece* 39 L4
Patraikós Kólpos, *Greece* 39 L4
Patras = Pátrai, *Greece* 39 L4
Patricio Lynch, I., *Chile* 128 C1
Patrocínio, *Brazil* 123 E2
Patta, *Kenya* 82 C5
Pattada, *Italy* 34 B2
Pattani, *Thailand* 59 J3
Patten, *U.S.A.* 99 C6
Patterson, *Calif., U.S.A.* 111 H3
Patterson, *La., U.S.A.* 109 L9
Patterson, Mt., *U.S.A.* 112 G7
Patti, *India* 62 D6
Patti, *Italy* 35 D7
Pattoki, *Pakistan* 62 D5
Patton, *U.S.A.* 106 F6
Patu, *Brazil* 122 C4
Patuakhali, *Bangla.* 61 H17
Patuca →, *Honduras* 116 C3

Patuca, Punta, *Honduras* 116 C3
Pâturages, *Belgium* 17 H3
Pátzcuaro, *Mexico* 114 D4
Pau, *France* 26 E3
Pau, Gave de →, *France* 26 E2
Pau d' Arco, *Brazil* 122 C2
Pau dos Ferros, *Brazil* 122 C4
Paucartambo, *Peru* 124 C3
Pauillac, *France* 26 C3
Pauini, *Brazil* 124 B4
Pauini →, *Brazil* 121 D5
Pauk, *Burma* 61 J19
Paul I., *Canada* 99 A7
Paul Isnard, *Fr. Guiana* 121 C7
Paulhan, *France* 26 E7
Paulis = Isiro, *Zaïre* 82 B2
Paulista, *Brazil* 122 C5
Paulistana, *Brazil* 122 C3
Paullina, *U.S.A.* 108 D7
Paulo Afonso, *Brazil* 122 C4
Paulo de Faria, *Brazil* 123 F2
Paulpietersburg, *S. Africa* 85 D5
Pauls Valley, *U.S.A.* 109 H6
Pauma Valley, *U.S.A.* 113 M10
Pausa, *Peru* 124 D3
Pauto →, *Colombia* 120 B3
Pāveh, *Iran* 67 E12
Pavelets, *Russia* 42 D4
Pavia, *Italy* 32 C6
Pāvilosta, *Latvia* 9 H19
Pavlikeni, *Bulgaria* 38 F8
Pavlodar, *Kazakstan* 44 D8
Pavlograd = Pavlohrad, *Ukraine* 41 H8
Pavlohrad, *Ukraine* 41 H8
Pavlovo, *Oka, Russia* 42 C6
Pavlovo, *Sakha, Russia* 45 C12
Pavlovsk, *Russia* 42 E5
Pavlovskaya, *Russia* 43 G4
Pavlovskiy-Posad, *Russia* 42 C4
Pavullo nel Frignano, *Italy* 32 D7
Pawhuska, *U.S.A.* 109 G6
Pawling, *U.S.A.* 107 E11
Pawnee, *U.S.A.* 109 G6
Pawnee City, *U.S.A.* 108 E6
Pawtucket, *U.S.A.* 107 E13
Paximádhia, *Greece* 37 D6
Paxoí, *Greece* 39 K3
Paxton, *Ill., U.S.A.* 104 E1
Paxton, *Nebr., U.S.A.* 108 E4
Payakumbuh, *Indonesia* 56 E2
Payerne, *Switz.* 22 C3
Payette, *U.S.A.* 110 D5
Paymogo, *Spain* 31 H3
Payne Bay = Kangirsuk, *Canada* 97 B13
Paynes Find, *Australia* 89 E2
Paynesville, *Liberia* 78 D2
Paynesville, *U.S.A.* 108 C7
Paysandú, *Uruguay* 126 C4
Payson, *Ariz., U.S.A.* 111 J8
Payson, *Utah, U.S.A.* 110 F8
Paz →, *Guatemala* 116 D1
Paz, B. la, *Mexico* 114 C2
Pāzanān, *Iran* 65 D6
Pazar, *Turkey* 67 B9
Pazarcık, *Turkey* 66 D7
Pazardzhik, *Bulgaria* 38 G7
Pazaryolu, *Turkey* 67 B9
Pazin, *Croatia* 33 C10
Pazña, *Bolivia* 124 D4
Pčinja →, *Macedonia* 39 H4
Pe Ell, *U.S.A.* 112 D3
Peabody, *U.S.A.* 107 D14
Peace →, *Canada* 100 B6
Peace Point, *Canada* 100 B6
Peace River, *Canada* 100 B5
Peach Springs, *U.S.A.* 111 J7
Peak, The = Kinder Scout, *U.K.* 12 D6
Peak Downs, *Australia* 90 C4
Peak Downs Mine, *Australia* 90 C4
Peak Hill, *N.S.W., Australia* 91 E4
Peak Hill, *W. Austral., Australia* 89 E2
Peak Ra., *Australia* 90 C4
Peake, *Australia* 91 F2
Peake Cr. →, *Australia* 91 D2
Peale, Mt., *U.S.A.* 111 G9
Pearblossom, *U.S.A.* 113 L9
Pearl →, *U.S.A.* 109 K10
Pearl City, *U.S.A.* 102 H16
Pearsall, *U.S.A.* 109 L5
Pearse I., *Canada* 100 C2
Peary Land, *Greenland* 4 A6
Pease →, *U.S.A.* 109 H5
Pebane, *Mozam.* 83 F4
Pebas, *Peru* 120 D3
Pebble, I., *Falk. Is.* 128 D5
Pebble Beach, *U.S.A.* 112 J5
Peć, *Serbia, Yug.* 21 N10
Peçanha, *Brazil* 123 E3
Péccioli, *Italy* 32 E7
Pechea, *Romania* 38 D10
Pechenga, *Russia* 44 C4
Pechenizhyn, *Ukraine* 41 H3
Pechiguera, Pta., *Canary Is.* 36 F6
Pechnezhskoye Vdkhr., *Ukraine* 41 G9
Pechora →, *Russia* 44 C6
Pechorskaya Guba, *Russia* 44 C6
Pecica, *Romania* 38 C4
Pečka, *Serbia, Yug.* 21 L9
Pécora, C., *Italy* 34 C1
Pečory, *Russia* 9 H22
Pecos, *U.S.A.* 109 K3
Pecos →, *U.S.A.* 109 L3
Pécs, *Hungary* 21 J8
Pedder, L., *Australia* 90 G4
Peddie, *S. Africa* 85 E4
Pédernales, *Dom. Rep.* 117 C5
Pedieos →, *Cyprus* 37 D12
Pedirka, *Australia* 91 D2
Pedra Azul, *Brazil* 123 E3
Pedra Grande, Recifes de, *Brazil* 123 E4
Pedras Negras, *Brazil* 125 C5
Pedreiras, *Brazil* 122 B3
Pedro Afonso, *Brazil* 122 C2
Pedro Cays, *Jamaica* 116 C4
Pedro Chico, *Colombia* 120 C3
Pedro de Valdivia, *Chile* 126 A2
Pedro Juan Caballero, *Paraguay* 127 A4
Pedro Muñoz, *Spain* 29 F2
Pedrógão Grande, *Portugal* 30 F2
Peebinga, *Australia* 91 E3
Peebles, *U.K.* 14 F5
Peekskill, *U.S.A.* 107 E11
Peel, *U.K.* 12 C3
Peel →, *Australia* 91 E5
Peel →, *Canada* 96 B6
Peene →, *Germany* 18 A9
Peera Peera Poolanna L., *Australia* 91 D2
Peers, *Canada* 100 C5
Pegasus Bay, *N.Z.* 87 K4
Pegnitz, *Germany* 19 F7
Pegnitz →, *Germany* 19 F6
Pego, *Spain* 29 G4
Pegu, *Burma* 61 L20
Pegu Yoma, *Burma* 61 K19
Pehuajó, *Argentina* 126 D3
Pei Xian, *China* 50 G9
Peichiang, *Taiwan* 53 F13
Peine, *Chile* 126 A2
Peine, *Germany* 18 C6
Peip'ing = Beijing, *China* 50 E9
Peipus, L. = Chudskoye, Oz., *Russia* 9 G22
Peissenberg, *Germany* 19 H7
Peitz, *Germany* 18 D10
Peixe, *Brazil* 123 D2
Peixe →, *Brazil* 123 F1
Peixoto de Azeredo →, *Brazil* 125 C6
Peize, *Neths.* 16 B8
Pek →, *Serbia, Yug.* 21 L11
Pekalongan, *Indonesia* 57 G13
Pekan, *Malaysia* 59 L4
Pekanbaru, *Indonesia* 56 D2
Pekin, *U.S.A.* 108 E10
Peking = Beijing, *China* 50 E9
Pelabuhan Kelang, *Malaysia* 59 L3
Pelabuhan Ratu, Teluk, *Indonesia* 57 G12
Pelabuhanratu, *Indonesia* 57 G12
Pélagos, *Greece* 39 K7
Pelaihari, *Indonesia* 56 E4
Pelat, Mt., *France* 27 D10
Peleaga, Vf., *Romania* 38 D5
Pelechuco, *Bolivia* 124 C4
Pelée, Mt., *Martinique* 117 D7
Pelee, Pt., *Canada* 98 D3
Pelee I., *Canada* 98 D3
Pelejo, *Peru* 124 B2
Pelekech, *Kenya* 82 B4
Peleng, *Indonesia* 57 E6
Pelham, *U.S.A.* 105 K3
Pelhřimov, *Czech.* 20 F5
Pelican L., *Canada* 101 C8
Pelican Narrows, *Canada* 101 B8
Pelican Rapids, *Canada* 101 C8
Pelkosenniemi, *Finland* 8 C22
Pella, *S. Africa* 84 D2
Pella, *U.S.A.* 108 E8
Péllaro, *Italy* 35 D8
Pello, *Finland* 8 C21
Pellworm, *Germany* 18 A4
Pelly →, *Canada* 96 B6
Pelly Bay, *Canada* 97 B11
Pelly L., *Canada* 96 B9
Peloponnese = Pelopónnisos □, *Greece* 39 M5
Pelopónnisos □, *Greece* 39 M5
Peloritani, Monti, *Italy* 35 D8
Peloro, C., *Italy* 35 D8
Pelorus Sd., *N.Z.* 87 J4
Pelotas, *Brazil* 127 C5
Pelvoux, Massif du, *France* 27 D10
Pemalang, *Indonesia* 57 G13
Pematangsiantar, *Indonesia* 56 D1
Pemba, *Mozam.* 83 E5
Pemba, *Zambia* 83 F2
Pemba Channel, *Tanzania* 82 D4
Pemba I., *Tanzania* 82 D4
Pemberton, *Australia* 89 F2
Pemberton, *Canada* 100 C4
Pembina, *U.S.A.* 108 A6
Pembina →, *U.S.A.* 101 D9
Pembine, *U.S.A.* 104 C2
Pembroke, *Canada* 98 C4
Pembroke, *U.K.* 13 F3
Pembroke, *U.S.A.* 105 J5
Pembrokeshire □, *U.K.* 13 F3
Pen-y-Ghent, *U.K.* 12 C5
Peña, Sierra de la, *Spain* 28 C4
Peña de Francia, Sierra de, *Spain* 30 E4
Penafiel, *Portugal* 30 D2
Peñafiel, *Spain* 30 D6
Peñaflor, *Spain* 31 H5
Peñalara, Pico, *Spain* 30 E7
Penalva, *Brazil* 122 B2
Penamacôr, *Portugal* 30 E3
Penang = Pinang, *Malaysia* 59 K3
Penápolis, *Brazil* 127 A6
Peñaranda de Bracamonte, *Spain* 30 E5
Peñarroya-Pueblonuevo, *Spain* 31 G5
Peñas, C. de, *Spain* 30 B5
Penas, G. de, *Chile* 128 C2
Peñas, Pta., *Venezuela* 121 A5
Peñas de San Pedro, *Spain* 29 G2
Peñas del Chache, *Canary Is.* 36 E6
Peñausende, *Spain* 30 D5
Pench'i = Benxi, *China* 51 D12
Pend Oreille →, *U.S.A.* 110 B5
Pend Oreille L., *U.S.A.* 110 C5
Pendembu, *S. Leone* 78 D2
Pendências, *Brazil* 122 C4
Pender B., *Australia* 88 C3
Pendleton, *Calif., U.S.A.* 113 M9
Pendleton, *Oreg., U.S.A.* 110 D4
Penedo, *Brazil* 122 D4
Penetanguishene, *Canada* 98 D4
Peng Xian, *China* 52 B4
Pengalengan, *Indonesia* 57 G12
Penge, *Kasai Or., Zaïre* 82 D1
Penge, *Kivu, Zaïre* 82 C2
Penglai, *China* 51 F11
Pengshui, *China* 52 C7
Penguin, *Australia* 90 G4
Pengxi, *China* 52 B5
Pengze, *China* 53 C11
Penhalonga, *Zimbabwe* 83 F3
Peniche, *Portugal* 31 F1
Penicuik, *U.K.* 14 F5
Penida, *Indonesia* 56 F5
Peninsular Malaysia □, *Malaysia* 59 L4
Peñíscola, *Spain* 28 E5
Penitente, Serra dos, *Brazil* 122 C2
Penmarch, *France* 24 E2
Penmarch, Pte. de, *France* 24 E2
Penn Hills, *U.S.A.* 106 F5
Penn Yan, *U.S.A.* 106 D7
Pennabilli, *Italy* 33 E9
Pennant, *Canada* 101 C7
Penne, *Italy* 33 F10
Penner →, *India* 60 M12
Pennine, Alpi, *Alps* 32 B4
Pennines, *U.K.* 12 C5
Pennington, *U.S.A.* 112 F5
Pennino, Mte., *Italy* 33 E9
Pennsylvania □, *U.S.A.* 104 E6
Penny, *Canada* 100 C4
Peno, *Russia* 42 B1
Penola, *Australia* 91 F3
Penong, *Australia* 89 F5
Penonomé, *Panama* 116 E3
Penrith, *Australia* 91 E5
Penrith, *U.K.* 12 C5
Pensacola, *U.S.A.* 105 K2
Pensacola Mts., *Antarctica* 5 E1
Pense, *Canada* 101 C8
Penshurst, *Australia* 91 F3
Pentecoste, *Brazil* 122 B4
Penticton, *Canada* 100 D5
Pentland, *Australia* 90 C4
Pentland Firth, *U.K.* 14 C5
Pentland Hills, *U.K.* 14 F5
Penylan L., *Canada* 101 A7
Penza, *Russia* 42 D7
Penzance, *U.K.* 13 G2
Penzberg, *Germany* 19 H7
Penzhino, *Russia* 45 C17
Penzhinskaya Guba, *Russia* 45 C17
Penzlin, *Germany* 18 B9
Peoria, *Ariz., U.S.A.* 111 K7
Peoria, *Ill., U.S.A.* 108 E10
Pepingen, *Belgium* 17 G4
Pepinster, *Belgium* 17 G7
Pera Hd., *Australia* 90 A3
Perabumulih, *Indonesia* 56 E2
Perakhóra, *Greece* 39 L5
Perales de Alfambra, *Spain* 28 E3
Perales del Puerto, *Spain* 30 E4
Peralta, *Spain* 28 C3
Pérama, *Kérkira, Greece* 37 A3
Pérama, *Kríti, Greece* 37 D6
Peräpohjola, *Finland* 8 C22
Percé, *Canada* 99 C7
Perche, *France* 24 D8
Perche, Collines du, *France* 24 D7
Percival Lakes, *Australia* 88 D4
Percy, *France* 24 D5
Percy Is., *Australia* 90 C5
Perdido →, *Argentina* 128 B3
Perdido, Mte., *Spain* 26 F4
Perdu, Mt. = Perdido, Mte., *Spain* 26 F4
Pereira, *Colombia* 120 C2
Pereira Barreto, *Brazil* 123 F1
Perekerten, *Australia* 91 E3
Perelazovskiy, *Russia* 43 F6
Perené →, *Peru* 124 C3
Perenjori, *Australia* 89 E2
Pereslavl-Zalesskiy, *Russia* 42 B4
Pereyaslav-Khmelnytskyy, *Ukraine* 41 G6
Pérez, I., *Mexico* 115 C7
Pergamino, *Argentina* 126 C3
Pergau →, *Malaysia* 59 K3
Pérgine Valsugana, *Italy* 33 B8
Pérgola, *Italy* 33 E9
Perham, *U.S.A.* 108 B7
Perhentian, Kepulauan, *Malaysia* 59 K4
Periam, *Romania* 38 C3
Péribonca →, *Canada* 99 C5
Péribonca, L., *Canada* 99 B5
Perico, *Argentina* 126 A2
Pericos, *Mexico* 114 B3
Périers, *France* 24 C5
Périgord, *France* 26 D4
Périgueux, *France* 26 C4
Perijá, Sierra de, *Colombia* 120 B3
Peristéra, *Greece* 39 K6
Peristerona →, *Cyprus* 37 D12
Perito Moreno, *Argentina* 128 C2
Peritoró, *Brazil* 122 B3
Perković, *Croatia* 33 E13
Perlas, Arch. de las, *Panama* 116 E4
Perlas, Punta de, *Nic.* 116 D3
Perleberg, *Germany* 18 B7
Perm, *Russia* 44 D6
Pernambuco = Recife, *Brazil* 122 C5
Pernambuco □, *Brazil* 122 C4
Pernatty Lagoon, *Australia* 91 E2
Pernik, *Bulgaria* 38 G6
Peron, C., *Australia* 89 E1
Peron Is., *Australia* 88 B5
Peron Pen., *Australia* 89 E1
Péronne, *France* 25 C9
Péronnes, *Belgium* 17 H4
Perosa Argentina, *Italy* 32 D4
Perow, *Canada* 100 C3
Perpendicular Pt., *Australia* 91 E5
Perpignan, *France* 26 F6
Perris, *U.S.A.* 113 M9
Perros-Guirec, *France* 24 D3
Perry, *Fla., U.S.A.* 105 K4
Perry, *Ga., U.S.A.* 105 J4
Perry, *Iowa, U.S.A.* 108 E7
Perry, *Maine, U.S.A.* 105 C12
Perry, *Okla., U.S.A.* 109 G6
Perryton, *U.S.A.* 109 G4
Perryville, *U.S.A.* 109 G10
Perşembe, *Turkey* 66 B7
Perseverancia, *Bolivia* 125 C5
Pershotravensk, *Ukraine* 41 G4
Persia = Iran ■, *Asia* 65 C7
Persian Gulf = Gulf, The, *Asia* 65 E6
Perstorp, *Sweden* 11 H7
Pertek, *Turkey* 67 C8
Perth, *Australia* 89 F2
Perth, *Canada* 98 D4
Perth, *U.K.* 14 E5
Perth & Kinross □, *U.K.* 14 E5
Perth Amboy, *U.S.A.* 107 F10
Pertuis, *France* 27 E9
Peru, *Ill., U.S.A.* 108 E10
Peru, *Ind., U.S.A.* 104 E2
Peru ■, *S. Amer.* 120 D2
Peru-Chile Trench, *Pac. Oc.* 93 K20
Perúgia, *Italy* 33 E9
Perušić, *Croatia* 33 D12
Péruwelz, *Belgium* 17 G3
Pervomaysk, *Russia* 42 C6
Pervomaysk, *Ukraine* 41 H6
Pervouralsk, *Russia* 44 D6
Perwez, *Belgium* 17 G5
Pes, Pta. del, *Spain* 36 C7
Pésaro, *Italy* 33 E9
Pescara, *Italy* 33 F11
Pescara →, *Italy* 33 F11
Peschanokopskoye, *Russia* 43 G5
Péscia, *Italy* 32 E7
Pescina, *Italy* 33 G10
Peseux, *Switz.* 22 C3
Peshawar, *Pakistan* 62 B4
Peshtigo, *U.S.A.* 104 C2
Peski, *Russia* 42 E6
Pêso da Régua, *Portugal* 30 D3
Pesqueira, *Brazil* 122 C4
Pessac, *France* 26 D3
Pessoux, *Belgium* 17 H6
Pestovo, *Russia* 40 C8
Pestravka, *Russia* 42 D9
Petah Tiqwa, *Israel* 69 C3
Petaling Jaya, *Malaysia* 59 L3
Petaloudhes, *Greece* 37 C10
Petaluma, *U.S.A.* 112 G4
Petange, *Lux.* 17 J7
Petatlán, *Mexico* 114 D4
Petauke, *Zambia* 83 E3
Petawawa, *Canada* 98 C4
Petegem, *Belgium* 17 G3
Petén Itzá, L., *Guatemala* 116 C2
Peter I.s Øy, *Antarctica* 5 C16
Peter Pond L., *Canada* 101 B7
Peterbell, *Canada* 98 C3
Peterborough, *Australia* 91 E2
Peterborough, *Canada* 97 D12
Peterborough, *U.K.* 13 E7
Peterborough, *U.S.A.* 107 D13
Peterhead, *U.K.* 14 D7
Petermann Bjerg, *Greenland* 94 B17
Peter's Mine, *Guyana* 121 B6
Petersburg, *Alaska, U.S.A.* 100 B2
Petersburg, *Ind., U.S.A.* 104 F2
Petersburg, *Va., U.S.A.* 104 G7
Petersburg, *W. Va., U.S.A.* 104 F6
Petford, *Australia* 90 B3
Petília Policastro, *Italy* 35 C9
Petit Bois I., *U.S.A.* 105 K1
Petit-Cap, *Canada* 99 C7
Petit Goâve, *Haiti* 117 C5
Petit Lac Manicouagan, *Canada* 99 B6
Petit Saint Bernard, Col du, *Italy* 32 C3
Petitcodiac, *Canada* 99 C6
Petite Baleine →, *Canada* 98 A4
Petite Saguenay, *Canada* 99 C5
Petitsikapau, L., *Canada* 99 B6
Petlad, *India* 62 H5
Peto, *Mexico* 115 C7
Petone, *N.Z.* 87 J5
Petoskey, *U.S.A.* 104 C3
Petra, *Jordan* 69 E4
Petra, *Spain* 36 B10
Petra, Ostrova, *Russia* 4 B13
Petra Velikogo, Zaliv, *Russia* 48 C5
Petralia Sottana, *Italy* 35 E7
Petrel, *Spain* 29 G4
Petreto-Bicchisano, *France* 27 G12
Petrich, *Bulgaria* 39 H6
Petrijanec, *Croatia* 33 B13
Petrikov = Pyetrikaw, *Belarus* 41 F5
Petrinja, *Croatia* 33 C13
Petrodvorets, *Russia* 40 C5
Petrograd = Sankt-Peterburg, *Russia* 40 C6
Petrolândia, *Brazil* 122 C4
Petrolia, *Canada* 98 D3
Petrolina, *Brazil* 122 C3
Petropavl, *Kazakstan* 44 D7
Petropavlovsk = Petropavl, *Kazakstan* 44 D7
Petropavlovsk-Kamchatskiy, *Russia* 45 D16
Petropavlovskiy = Akhtubinsk, *Russia* 43 F8
Petrópolis, *Brazil* 123 F3
Petroşani, *Romania* 38 D6
Petrova Gora, *Croatia* 33 C12
Petrovac, *Montenegro, Yug.* 21 N8
Petrovsk, *Russia* 42 D7
Petrovsk-Zabaykalskiy, *Russia* 45 D11
Petrovskaya, *Russia* 43 H3
Petrovskoye = Svetlograd, *Russia* 43 H6
Petrozavodsk, *Russia* 40 B8
Petrus Steyn, *S. Africa* 85 D4
Petrusburg, *S. Africa* 84 D4
Peumo, *Chile* 126 C1
Peureulak, *Indonesia* 56 D1
Pevek, *Russia* 45 C18
Peveragno, *Italy* 32 D4
Peyrehorade, *France* 26 E2
Peyruis, *France* 27 D9
Pézenas, *France* 26 E7
Pfaffenhofen, *Germany* 19 G7
Pfäffikon, *Switz.* 23 B7
Pfarrkirchen, *Germany* 19 G8
Pfeffenhausen, *Germany* 19 G7
Pforzheim, *Germany* 19 G4
Pfullendorf, *Germany* 19 H5
Pfungstadt, *Germany* 19 F4
Phagwara, *India* 60 D9
Phaistós, *Greece* 37 D6
Phala, *Botswana* 84 C4
Phalera = Phulera, *India* 62 F6
Phalodi, *India* 62 F5
Phalsbourg, *France* 25 D14
Phan, *Thailand* 58 C2
Phan Rang, *Vietnam* 59 G7
Phan Ri = Hoa Da, *Vietnam* 59 G7
Phan Thiet, *Vietnam* 59 G7
Phanat Nikhom, *Thailand* 58 F3
Phangan, Ko, *Thailand* 59 H3
Phangnga, *Thailand* 59 H2
Phanh Bho Ho Chi Minh, *Vietnam* 59 G6
Phanom Sarakham, *Thailand* 58 F3
Pharenda, *India* 63 F10
Phatthalung, *Thailand* 59 J3
Phayao, *Thailand* 58 C2
Phelps, *N.Y., U.S.A.* 106 D7
Phelps, *Wis., U.S.A.* 108 B10
Phelps L., *Canada* 101 B8
Phenix City, *U.S.A.* 105 J3
Phet Buri, *Thailand* 58 F2
Phetchabun, *Thailand* 58 D3
Phetchabun, Thiu Khao, *Thailand* 58 E3
Phetchaburi = Phet Buri, *Thailand* 58 F2
Phi Phi, Ko, *Thailand* 59 J2
Phiafay, *Laos* 58 E6
Phibun Mangsahan, *Thailand* 58 E5
Phichai, *Thailand* 58 D3
Phichit, *Thailand* 58 D3
Philadelphia, *Miss., U.S.A.* 109 J10
Philadelphia, *N.Y., U.S.A.* 107 B9
Philadelphia, *Pa., U.S.A.* 107 F9
Philip, *U.S.A.* 108 C4
Philippeville, *Belgium* 17 H5
Philippi L., *Australia* 90 C2
Philippines ■, *Asia* 55 F5
Philippolis, *S. Africa* 84 E4
Philippopolis = Plovdiv, *Bulgaria* 38 G7
Philipsburg, *Mont., U.S.A.* 110 C7
Philipsburg, *Pa., U.S.A.* 106 F6

Philipstown = Daingean, *Ireland* 15 C4
Philipstown, *S. Africa* 84 E3
Phillip I., *Australia* 91 F4
Phillips, *Tex., U.S.A.* 109 H4
Phillips, *Wis., U.S.A.* 108 C9
Phillipsburg, *Kans., U.S.A.* 108 F5
Phillipsburg, *N.J., U.S.A.* 107 F9
Phillott, *Australia* 91 D4
Philmont, *U.S.A.* 107 D11
Philomath, *U.S.A.* 110 D2
Phimai, *Thailand* 58 E4
Phitsanulok, *Thailand* 58 D3
Phnom Dangrek, *Thailand* 58 E5
Phnom Penh, *Cambodia* 59 G5
Phoenix, *Ariz., U.S.A.* 111 K7
Phoenix, *N.Y., U.S.A.* 107 C8
Phoenix Is., *Kiribati* 92 H10
Phoenixville, *U.S.A.* 107 F9
Phon, *Thailand* 58 E4
Phon Tiou, *Laos* 58 D5
Phong →, *Thailand* 58 D4
Phong Saly, *Laos* 58 B4
Phong Tho, *Vietnam* 58 A4
Phonhong, *Laos* 58 C4
Phonum, *Thailand* 59 H2
Phosphate Hill, *Australia* 90 C2
Photharam, *Thailand* 58 F2
Phra Chedi Sam Ong, *Thailand* 58 E2
Phra Nakhon Si Ayutthaya, *Thailand* 58 E3
Phra Thong, Ko, *Thailand* 59 H2
Phrae, *Thailand* 58 C3
Phrom Phiram, *Thailand* 58 D3
Phrygia, *Turkey* 66 C4
Phu Dien, *Vietnam* 58 C5
Phu Loi, *Laos* 58 B4
Phu Ly, *Vietnam* 58 B5
Phu Tho, *Vietnam* 58 B5
Phuc Yen, *Vietnam* 58 B5
Phuket, *Thailand* 59 J2
Phuket, Ko, *Thailand* 59 J2
Phulera, *India* 62 F6
Phumiphon, Khuan, *Thailand* 58 D2
Phun Phin, *Thailand* 59 H2
Piacá, *Brazil* 122 C2
Piacenza, *Italy* 32 C6
Piaçubaçu, *Brazil* 122 D4
Piádena, *Italy* 32 C7
Pialba, *Australia* 91 D5
Pian Cr. →, *Australia* 91 E4
Piana, *France* 27 F12
Pianella, *Italy* 33 F11
Pianoro, *Italy* 33 D8
Pianosa, *Puglia, Italy* 33 F12
Pianosa, *Toscana, Italy* 32 F7
Piapot, *Canada* 101 D7
Piare →, *Italy* 33 C9
Pias, *Portugal* 31 G3
Piaseczno, *Poland* 20 C11
Piatã, *Brazil* 123 D3
Piatra, *Romania* 38 F8
Piatra Neamţ, *Romania* 38 C9
Piauí □, *Brazil* 122 C3
Piaui →, *Brazil* 122 C3
Piave →, *Italy* 33 C9
Piazza Ármerina, *Italy* 35 E7
Pibor →, *Sudan* 77 F3
Pibor Post, *Sudan* 77 F3
Pica, *Chile* 124 E4
Picardie, *France* 25 C9
Picardie, Plaine de, *France* 25 C9
Picardy = Picardie, *France* 25 C9
Picayune, *U.S.A.* 109 K10
Picerno, *Italy* 35 B8
Pichilemu, *Chile* 126 C1
Pichincha, □, *Ecuador* 120 D2
Pickerel L., *Canada* 98 C1
Pickle Lake, *Canada* 98 B1
Pico Truncado, *Argentina* 128 C3
Picos, *Brazil* 122 C3
Picos Ancares, Sierra de, *Spain* 30 C4
Picota, *Peru* 124 B2
Picquigny, *France* 25 C9
Picton, *Australia* 91 E5
Picton, *Canada* 98 D4
Picton, *N.Z.* 87 J5
Picton, I., *Chile* 128 E3
Pictou, *Canada* 99 C7
Picture Butte, *Canada* 100 D6
Picuí, *Brazil* 122 C4
Picún Leufú, *Argentina* 128 A3
Pidurutalagala, *Sri Lanka* 60 R12
Piedecuesta, *Colombia* 120 B3
Piedicavallo, *Italy* 32 C4
Piedmont = Piemonte □, *Italy* 32 D4
Piedmont, *U.S.A.* 105 J3
Piedmont Plateau, *U.S.A.* 105 J5
Piedmonte d'Alife, *Italy* 35 A7
Piedra →, *Spain* 28 D3
Piedra del Anguila, *Argentina* 128 B2
Piedra Lais, *Venezuela* 120 C4
Piedrabuena, *Spain* 31 F6
Piedrahita, *Spain* 30 E5
Piedras, R. de las →, *Peru* 124 C4
Piedras Negras, *Mexico* 114 B4
Pieksämäki, *Finland* 9 E22
Piemonte □, *Italy* 32 D4
Pierce, *U.S.A.* 110 C6
Piercefield, *U.S.A.* 107 B10
Pierre, *U.S.A.* 108 C4
Pierre Bénite, Barrage de la, *France* 27 C8
Pierre-de-Bresse, *France* 27 B9
Pierrefeu-du-Var, *France* 27 E10
Pierrefonds, *France* 25 C9
Pierrefontaine-les-Varans, *France* 25 E13
Pierrefort, *France* 26 D6
Pierrelatte, *France* 27 D8
Piešťany, *Slovak Rep.* 20 G7
Piesting →, *Austria* 21 G6
Piet Retief, *S. Africa* 85 D5
Pietarsaari, *Finland* 8 E20
Pietermaritzburg, *S. Africa* 85 D5
Pietersburg, *S. Africa* 85 C4
Pietraperzia, *Italy* 35 E7
Pietrasanta, *Italy* 32 E7
Pietrosul, *Romania* 38 B8
Pietrosul, *Romania* 38 B7
Pieve di Cadore, *Italy* 33 B9
Pieve di Teco, *Italy* 32 D4
Pievepélago, *Italy* 32 D7
Pigádhia, *Greece* 39 P10
Pigeon, *U.S.A.* 104 D4
Piggott, *U.S.A.* 109 G9
Pigna, *Italy* 32 E4
Pigüe, *Argentina* 126 D3
Pihani, *India* 63 F9
Pihlajavesi, *Finland* 9 F23
Pijnacker, *Neths.* 16 D4
Pikalevo, *Russia* 40 C8
Pikes Peak, *U.S.A.* 108 F2
Piketberg, *S. Africa* 84 E2
Pikeville, *U.S.A.* 104 G4
Pikou, *China* 51 E12
Pikwitonei, *Canada* 101 B9
Piła, *Poland* 20 B6
Pila, *Spain* 29 G3
Pilani, *India* 62 E6
Pilar, *Brazil* 122 C4
Pilar, *Paraguay* 126 B4
Pilas Group, *Phil.* 57 C6
Pilaya →, *Bolivia* 125 E5
Pilcomayo →, *Paraguay* 126 B4
Pilibhit, *India* 63 E8
Pilica →, *Poland* 20 D11
Pilkhawa, *India* 62 E7
Pillaro, *Ecuador* 120 D2
Pílos, *Greece* 39 N4
Pilot Mound, *Canada* 101 D9
Pilot Point, *U.S.A.* 109 J6
Pilot Rock, *U.S.A.* 110 D4
Pilsen = Plzeň, *Czech.* 20 F3
Pilštanj, *Slovenia* 33 B12
Pima, *U.S.A.* 111 K9
Pimba, *Australia* 91 E2
Pimenta Bueno, *Brazil* 125 C5
Pimentel, *Peru* 124 B2
Pina, *Spain* 28 D4
Pinamalayan, *Phil.* 55 E4
Pinang, *Malaysia* 59 K3
Pinar, C. del, *Spain* 36 B10
Pinar del Río, *Cuba* 116 B3
Pinarbaşi, *Turkey* 66 C7
Pınarhisar, *Turkey* 66 B2
Pinchang, *China* 52 B6
Pincher Creek, *Canada* 100 D6
Pinchi L., *Canada* 100 C4
Pinckneyville, *U.S.A.* 108 F10
Pîncota, *Romania* 38 C4
Pind Dadan Khan, *Pakistan* 62 C5
Pindar, *Australia* 89 E2
Pindaré →, *Brazil* 122 B3
Pindaré Mirim, *Brazil* 122 B2
Pindi Gheb, *Pakistan* 62 C5
Pindiga, *Nigeria* 79 D7
Pindobal, *Brazil* 122 B2
Pindos Óros, *Greece* 39 K4
Pindus Mts. = Pindos Óros, *Greece* 39 K4
Pine, *U.S.A.* 111 J8
Pine →, *Canada* 101 B7
Pine, C., *Canada* 99 C9
Pine Bluff, *U.S.A.* 109 H8
Pine City, *U.S.A.* 108 C8
Pine Falls, *Canada* 101 C9
Pine Flat L., *U.S.A.* 112 J7
Pine Pass, *Canada* 100 B4
Pine Point, *Canada* 100 A6
Pine Ridge, *U.S.A.* 108 D3
Pine River, *Canada* 101 C8
Pine River, *U.S.A.* 108 B7
Pine Valley, *U.S.A.* 113 N10
Pinecrest, *U.S.A.* 112 G6
Pinedale, *U.S.A.* 112 J7
Pinega →, *Russia* 44 C5
Pinehill, *Australia* 90 C4
Pinerolo, *Italy* 32 D4
Pineto, *Italy* 33 F11
Pinetop, *U.S.A.* 111 J9
Pinetown, *S. Africa* 85 D5
Pinetree, *U.S.A.* 110 E11
Pineville, *Ky., U.S.A.* 105 G4
Pineville, *La., U.S.A.* 109 K8
Piney, *France* 25 D11
Ping →, *Thailand* 58 E3
Pingaring, *Australia* 89 F2
Pingba, *China* 52 D6
Pingchuan, *China* 52 D3
Pingding, *China* 50 F7
Pingdingshan, *China* 50 H7
Pingdong, *Taiwan* 53 F13
Pingdu, *China* 51 F10
Pingelly, *Australia* 89 F2
Pingguo, *China* 52 F6
Pinghe, *China* 53 E11
Pinghu, *China* 53 B13
Pingjiang, *China* 53 C9
Pingle, *China* 53 E8
Pingli, *China* 52 A7
Pingliang, *China* 50 G4
Pinglu, *China* 50 E7
Pingluo, *China* 50 E4
Pingnan, *Fujian, China* 53 D12
Pingnan, *Guangxi Zhuangzu, China* 53 F8
Pingquan, *China* 51 D10
Pingrup, *Australia* 89 F2
Pingtan, *China* 53 E12
Pingtang, *China* 52 E6
P'ingtung, *Taiwan* 53 F13
Pingwu, *China* 50 H3
Pingxiang, *Guangxi Zhuangzu, China* 52 F6
Pingxiang, *Jiangxi, China* 53 D9
Pingyao, *China* 50 F7
Pingyi, *China* 51 G9
Pingyin, *China* 50 F9
Pingyuan, *Guangdong, China* 53 E10
Pingyuan, *Shandong, China* 50 F9
Pingyuanjie, *China* 52 F4
Pinhal, *Brazil* 127 A6
Pinheiro, *Brazil* 122 B2
Pinhel, *Portugal* 30 E3
Pinhuá →, *Brazil* 125 B4
Pini, *Indonesia* 56 D1
Piniós →, *Ilía, Greece* 39 M4
Piniós →, *Trikkala, Greece* 39 K5
Pinjarra, *Australia* 89 F2
Pink →, *Canada* 101 B8
Pinnacles, *Australia* 89 E3
Pinnacles, *U.S.A.* 112 J5
Pinnaroo, *Australia* 91 F3
Pinneberg, *Germany* 18 B5
Pínnes, Ákra, *Greece* 39 J7
Pino Hachado, Paso, *S. Amer.* 128 A2
Pinon Hills, *U.S.A.* 113 L9
Pinos, *Mexico* 114 C4
Pinos, Mt., *U.S.A.* 113 L7
Pinos Pt., *U.S.A.* 111 H3
Pinos Puente, *Spain* 31 H7
Pinotepa Nacional, *Mexico* 115 D5
Pinrang, *Indonesia* 57 E5
Pinsk, *Belarus* 41 F4
Pintados, *Chile* 124 E4
Pintumba, *Australia* 89 F5
Pinyang, *China* 53 D13
Pinyug, *Russia* 44 C5
Pinzolo, *Italy* 32 B7
Pio XII, *Brazil* 122 B2
Pioche, *U.S.A.* 111 H6
Piombino, *Italy* 32 F7
Piombino, Canale di, *Italy* 32 F7
Pioner, Os., *Russia* 45 B10
Pionki, *Poland* 20 D11
Piorini →, *Brazil* 121 D5
Piorini, L., *Brazil* 121 D5
Piotrków Trybunalski, *Poland* 20 D9
Piove di Sacco, *Italy* 33 C9
Pīp, *Iran* 65 E9
Pipar, *India* 62 F5
Piparia, *India* 62 H8
Pipestone, *U.S.A.* 108 D6
Pipestone →, *Canada* 98 B2
Pipestone Cr. →, *Canada* 101 D8
Pipmuacan, Rés., *Canada* 99 C5
Pippingarra, *Australia* 88 D2
Pipriac, *France* 24 E5
Piqua, *U.S.A.* 104 E3
Piquet Carneiro, *Brazil* 122 C4
Piquiri →, *Brazil* 127 A5
Pīr Sohrāb, *Iran* 65 E9
Piracanjuba, *Brazil* 123 E2
Piracicaba, *Brazil* 127 A6
Piracuruca, *Brazil* 122 B3
Piræus = Piraiévs, *Greece* 39 M6
Piraiévs, *Greece* 39 M6
Piráino, *Italy* 35 D7
Pirajuí, *Brazil* 127 A6
Piran, *Slovenia* 33 C10
Piranè, *Argentina* 126 B4
Piranhas, *Brazil* 122 C4
Pirano = Piran, *Slovenia* 33 C10
Pirapemas, *Brazil* 122 B3
Pirapora, *Brazil* 123 E3
Piray →, *Bolivia* 125 D5
Pires do Rio, *Brazil* 123 E2
Pírgos, *Ilía, Greece* 39 M4
Pírgos, *Messinia, Greece* 39 N5
Pirgovo, *Bulgaria* 38 F8
Piriac-sur-Mer, *France* 24 E4
Piribebuy, *Paraguay* 126 B4
Pirin Planina, *Bulgaria* 39 H6
Pirineos, *Spain* 28 C6
Piripiri, *Brazil* 122 B3
Piritu, *Venezuela* 120 B4
Pirmasens, *Germany* 19 F3
Pirna, *Germany* 18 E9
Pirot, *Serbia, Yug.* 21 M12
Piru, *Indonesia* 57 E7
Piru, *U.S.A.* 113 L8
Piryatin = Pyryatyn, *Ukraine* 41 G7
Pisa, *Italy* 32 E7
Pisac, *Peru* 124 C3
Pisagua, *Chile* 124 D3
Pisarovina, *Croatia* 33 C12
Pisciotta, *Italy* 35 B8
Pisco, *Peru* 124 C2
Písek, *Czech.* 20 F4
Pishan, *China* 54 C2
Pishin Lora →, *Pakistan* 62 E1
Pisidia, *Turkey* 66 D4
Pising, *Indonesia* 57 F6
Pismo Beach, *U.S.A.* 113 K6
Pissis, Cerro, *Argentina* 126 B2
Pissos, *France* 26 D3
Pissouri, *Cyprus* 37 E11
Pisticci, *Italy* 35 B9
Pistóia, *Italy* 32 E7
Pistol B., *Canada* 101 A10
Pisuerga →, *Spain* 30 D6
Pisz, *Poland* 20 B11
Pitalito, *Colombia* 120 C2
Pitanga, *Brazil* 123 F1
Pitangui, *Brazil* 123 E3
Pitarpunga, L., *Australia* 91 E3
Pitcairn I., *Pac. Oc.* 93 K14
Pite älv →, *Sweden* 8 D19
Piteå, *Sweden* 8 D19
Piterka, *Russia* 42 E8
Piteşti, *Romania* 38 E7
Pithapuram, *India* 61 L13
Pithara, *Australia* 89 F2
Píthion, *Greece* 39 H9
Pithiviers, *France* 25 D9
Pitigliano, *Italy* 33 F8
Pitkyaranta, *Russia* 40 B6
Pitlochry, *U.K.* 14 E5
Pitrufquén, *Chile* 128 A2
Pitsilia □, *Cyprus* 37 E12
Pitt I., *Canada* 100 C3
Pittem, *Belgium* 17 F2
Pittsburg, *Kans., U.S.A.* 109 G7
Pittsburg, *Tex., U.S.A.* 109 J7
Pittsburgh, *U.S.A.* 106 F5
Pittsfield, *Ill., U.S.A.* 108 F9
Pittsfield, *Mass., U.S.A.* 107 D11
Pittsfield, *N.H., U.S.A.* 107 C13
Pittston, *U.S.A.* 107 E9
Pittsworth, *Australia* 91 D5
Pituri →, *Australia* 90 C2
Piuí, *Brazil* 123 F2
Pium, *Brazil* 122 D2
Piura, *Peru* 124 B1
Piura □, *Peru* 124 A2
Pivijay, *Colombia* 120 A3
Pixley, *U.S.A.* 112 K7
Piyai, *Greece* 39 K4
Pizarro, *Colombia* 120 C2
Pizol, *Switz.* 23 C8
Pizzo, *Italy* 35 D9
Placentia, *Canada* 99 C9
Placentia B., *Canada* 99 C9
Placer, *Phil.* 55 F5
Placerville, *U.S.A.* 112 G6
Placetas, *Cuba* 116 B4
Plaffeien, *Switz.* 22 C4
Plain Dealing, *U.S.A.* 109 J8
Plainfield, *U.S.A.* 107 F10
Plains, *Kans., U.S.A.* 109 G4
Plains, *Mont., U.S.A.* 110 C6
Plains, *Tex., U.S.A.* 109 J3
Plainview, *Nebr., U.S.A.* 108 D6
Plainview, *Tex., U.S.A.* 109 H4
Plainville, *U.S.A.* 108 F5
Plainwell, *U.S.A.* 104 D3
Plaisance, *France* 26 E4
Pláka, *Greece* 39 J8
Pláka, Ákra, *Greece* 37 D8
Plakhino, *Russia* 44 C9
Plana Cays, *Bahamas* 117 B5
Planada, *U.S.A.* 112 H6
Plancoët, *France* 24 D4
Plandište, *Serbia, Yug.* 21 K11
Planeta Rica, *Colombia* 120 B2
Planina, *Slovenia* 33 B12
Planina, *Slovenia* 33 C11
Plankinton, *U.S.A.* 108 D5
Plano, *U.S.A.* 109 J6
Plant City, *U.S.A.* 105 L4
Plaquemine, *U.S.A.* 109 K9
Plasencia, *Spain* 30 E4
Plaški, *Croatia* 33 C12
Plaster City, *U.S.A.* 113 N11
Plaster Rock, *Canada* 99 C6
Plastun, *Russia* 48 B8
Plata, Río de la, *S. Amer.* 126 C4
Platani →, *Italy* 34 E6
Plátanos, *Greece* 37 D5
Plateau □, *Nigeria* 79 D6
Plateau du Coteau du Missouri, *U.S.A.* 108 B4
Plato, *Colombia* 120 B3
Platta, Piz, *Switz.* 23 D9
Platte, *U.S.A.* 108 D5
Platte →, *Mo., U.S.A.* 108 F7
Platte →, *Nebr., U.S.A.* 94 E10
Platteville, *U.S.A.* 108 E2
Plattling, *Germany* 19 G8
Plattsburgh, *U.S.A.* 107 B11
Plattsmouth, *U.S.A.* 108 E7
Plau, *Germany* 18 B8
Plauen, *Germany* 18 E8
Plavinas, *Latvia* 9 H21
Plavnica, *Montenegro, Yug.* 21 N9
Plavsk, *Russia* 42 D3
Playa Blanca, *Canary Is.* 36 F6
Playa Blanca Sur, *Canary Is.* 36 F6
Playa de las Americas, *Canary Is.* 36 F3
Playa de Mogán, *Canary Is.* 36 G4
Playa del Inglés, *Canary Is.* 36 G4
Playa Esmerelda, *Canary Is.* 36 F5
Playgreen L., *Canada* 101 C9
Pleasant Bay, *Canada* 99 C7
Pleasant Hill, *Calif., U.S.A.* 112 H4
Pleasant Hill, *Mo., U.S.A.* 108 F7
Pleasanton, *U.S.A.* 109 L5
Pleasantville, *U.S.A.* 104 F8
Pléaux, *France* 26 C6
Pleiku, *Vietnam* 58 F7
Plélan-le-Grand, *France* 24 D4
Plémet-la-Pierre, *France* 24 D4
Pléneuf-Val-André, *France* 24 D4
Pleniţa, *Romania* 38 E6
Plenty →, *Australia* 90 C2
Plenty, B. of, *N.Z.* 87 G6
Plentywood, *U.S.A.* 108 A2
Plessisville, *Canada* 99 C5
Plestin-les-Grèves, *France* 24 D3
Pleszew, *Poland* 20 D7
Pleternica, *Croatia* 21 K7
Pletipi L., *Canada* 99 B5
Pleven, *Bulgaria* 38 F7
Plevlja, *Montenegro, Yug.* 21 M9
Płock, *Poland* 20 C9
Plöcken Passo, *Italy* 33 B9
Ploegsteert, *Belgium* 17 G1
Ploemeur, *France* 24 E3
Ploërmel, *France* 24 E4
Ploieşti, *Romania* 38 E9
Plombières-les-Bains, *France* 25 E13
Plomin, *Croatia* 33 C11
Plön, *Germany* 18 A6
Plöner See, *Germany* 18 A6
Plonge, Lac la, *Canada* 101 B7
Płońsk, *Poland* 20 C10
Ploty, *Poland* 20 B5
Plouaret, *France* 24 D3
Plouay, *France* 24 E3
Ploudalmézeau, *France* 24 D2
Plougasnou, *France* 24 D3
Plouha, *France* 24 D4
Plouhinec, *France* 24 E2
Plovdiv, *Bulgaria* 38 G7
Plum, *U.S.A.* 106 F5
Plum I., *U.S.A.* 107 E12
Plumas, *U.S.A.* 112 F7
Plummer, *U.S.A.* 110 C5
Plumtree, *Zimbabwe* 83 G2
Plunge, *Lithuania* 9 J19
Pluvigner, *France* 24 E3
Plymouth, *U.K.* 13 G3
Plymouth, *Calif., U.S.A.* 112 G6
Plymouth, *Ind., U.S.A.* 104 E2
Plymouth, *Mass., U.S.A.* 107 E14
Plymouth, *N.C., U.S.A.* 105 H7
Plymouth, *N.H., U.S.A.* 107 C13
Plymouth, *Pa., U.S.A.* 107 E9
Plymouth, *Wis., U.S.A.* 104 D2
Plynlimon = Pumlumon Fawr, *U.K.* 13 E4
Plyusa, *Russia* 40 C5
Plyusa →, *Russia* 40 C5
Plyussa = Plyusa, *Russia* 40 C5
Plyussa → = Plyusa →, *Russia* 40 C5
Plzeň, *Czech.* 20 F3
Pniewy, *Poland* 20 C6
Pô, *Burkina Faso* 79 C4
Po →, *Italy* 33 D9
Po, Foci del, *Italy* 33 D9
Po Hai = Bo Hai, *China* 51 E10
Po Hai, *China* 46 F15
Pobé, *Benin* 79 D5
Pobeda, *Russia* 45 C15
Pobedino, *Russia* 45 E15
Pobedy Pik, *Kyrgyzstan* 44 E8
Pobiedziska, *Poland* 20 C7
Pobla de Segur, *Spain* 28 C5
Pobladura de Valle, *Spain* 30 C5
Pocahontas, *Ark., U.S.A.* 109 G9
Pocahontas, *Iowa, U.S.A.* 108 D7
Pocatello, *U.S.A.* 110 E7
Pochep, *Russia* 41 F7
Pochinki, *Russia* 42 C7
Pochinok, *Russia* 40 E7
Pochutla, *Mexico* 115 D5
Poci, *Venezuela* 121 B5
Pocinhos, *Brazil* 122 C4
Pocito Casas, *Mexico* 114 B2
Poções, *Brazil* 123 D3
Pocomoke City, *U.S.A.* 104 F8
Poconé, *Brazil* 125 D6
Poços de Caldas, *Brazil* 127 A6
Poddebice, *Poland* 20 D8
Poděbrady, *Czech.* 20 E5
Podensac, *France* 26 D3
Podgorica, *Montenegro, Yug.* 21 N9
Podilska Vysochyna, *Ukraine* 41 H4
Podkamennaya Tunguska →, *Russia* 45 C10
Podlapac, *Croatia* 33 D12
Podolsk, *Russia* 42 C3
Podor, *Senegal* 78 B1
Podporozhy, *Russia* 40 B8
Podravska Slatina, *Croatia* 21 K7
Podujevo, *Serbia, Yug.* 21 N11
Poel, *Germany* 18 B7
Pofadder, *S. Africa* 84 D2
Pogamasing, *Canada* 98 C3
Poggiardo, *Italy* 35 B11
Poggibonsi, *Italy* 33 E8
Pogoanele, *Romania* 38 E9
Pogradeci, *Albania* 39 J3
Pogranitšnyi, *Russia* 48 B5

Poh, Indonesia 57 E6
Pohang, S. Korea 51 F15
Pohjanmaa, Finland 8 E20
Pohnpei, Pac. Oc. 92 G7
Pohorelá, Slovak Rep. 20 G10
Pohorje, Slovenia 33 B12
Poiana Mare, Romania 38 F6
Poinsett, C., Antarctica 5 C8
Point Edward, Canada 98 D3
Point Pedro, Sri Lanka 60 Q12
Point Pleasant, N.J., U.S.A. 107 F10
Point Pleasant, W. Va., U.S.A. 104 F4
Pointe-à-la Hache, U.S.A. 109 L10
Pointe-à-Pitre, Guadeloupe 117 C7
Pointe Noire, Congo 80 E2
Poirino, Italy 32 D4
Poisonbush Ra., Australia 88 D3
Poissy, France 25 D9
Poitiers, France 24 F7
Poitou, France 26 B3
Poitou, Seuil du, France 26 B4
Poix de Picardie, France 25 C8
Poix-Terron, France 25 C11
Pojoaque Valley, U.S.A. 111 J11
Pokaran, India 60 F7
Pokataroo, Australia 91 D4
Pokhvistnevo, Russia 42 D11
Poko, Sudan 77 F3
Poko, Zaïre 82 B2
Pokrov, Russia 42 C4
Pokrovsk = Engels, Russia 42 E8
Pokrovsk, Russia 45 C13
Pokrovskoye, Russia 43 G4
Pol, Spain 30 B3
Pola = Pula, Croatia 33 D10
Pola, Russia 40 D7
Pola de Allande, Spain 30 B4
Pola de Lena, Spain 30 B5
Pola de Siero, Spain 30 B5
Pola de Somiedo, Spain 30 B4
Polacca, U.S.A. 111 J8
Polan, Iran 65 E9
Poland ■, Europe 20 C9
Polanów, Poland 20 A6
Polatlı, Turkey 66 C5
Polatsk, Belarus 40 E5
Polcura, Chile 126 D1
Polden Hills, U.K. 13 F5
Polessk, Russia 9 J19
Polesye = Pripet Marshes, Europe 41 F5
Polgar, Hungary 21 H11
Pŏlgyo-ri, S. Korea 51 G14
Poli, Cameroon 80 C2
Políaigos, Greece 39 N7
Policastro, G. di, Italy 35 C8
Police, Poland 20 B4
Polignano a Mare, Italy 35 B10
Poligny, France 25 F12
Políkhnitas, Greece 39 K9
Polillo Is., Phil. 55 D4
Polillo Strait, Phil. 55 D4
Polis, Cyprus 37 D11
Polístena, Italy 35 D9
Políyiros, Greece 39 J6
Polk, U.S.A. 106 E5
Polla, Italy 35 B8
Pollachi, India 60 P10
Pollensa, Spain 36 B10
Pollensa, B. de, Spain 36 B10
Póllica, Italy 35 B8
Pollino, Mte., Italy 35 C9
Pollock, U.S.A. 108 C4
Polna, Russia 40 C5
Polnovat, Russia 44 C7
Polo, U.S.A. 108 E10
Pology, Ukraine 41 J9
Polonne, Ukraine 41 G4
Polonnoye = Polonne, Ukraine 41 G4
Polson, U.S.A. 110 C6
Poltava, Ukraine 41 H8
Põltsamaa, Estonia 9 G21
Polunochnoye, Russia 44 C7
Põlva, Estonia 9 G22
Polynesia, Pac. Oc. 93 H11
Polynésie française = French Polynesia ■, Pac. Oc. 93 J13
Pomarance, Italy 32 E7
Pomárico, Italy 35 B9
Pomaro, Mexico 114 D4
Pombal, Brazil 122 C4
Pombal, Portugal 30 F2
Pómbia, Greece 37 D6
Pomeroy, Ohio, U.S.A. 104 F4
Pomeroy, Wash., U.S.A. 110 C5
Pomichna, Ukraine 41 H6
Pomona, U.S.A. 113 L9
Pomorie, Bulgaria 38 G10
Pomos, Cyprus 37 D11
Pomos, C., Cyprus 37 D11
Pompano Beach, U.S.A. 105 M5
Pompei, Italy 35 B7
Pompey, France 25 D13
Pompeys Pillar, U.S.A. 110 D10
Ponape = Pohnpei, Pac. Oc. 92 G7
Ponask, L., Canada 98 B1
Ponass L., Canada 101 C8
Ponca, U.S.A. 108 D6
Ponca City, U.S.A. 109 G6
Ponce, Puerto Rico 117 C6
Ponchatoula, U.S.A. 109 K9
Poncheville, L., Canada 98 B4
Poncin, France 27 B9
Pond, U.S.A. 113 K7
Pond Inlet, Canada 97 A12
Pondicherry, India 60 P11
Pondrôme, Belgium 17 H6
Ponds, I. of, Canada 99 B8
Ponferrada, Spain 30 C4
Pongo, Wadi →, Sudan 77 F2
Poniatowa, Poland 20 D12
Ponikva, Slovenia 33 B12
Ponnani, India 60 P9
Ponnyadaung, Burma 61 J19
Ponoka, Canada 100 C6
Ponorogo, Indonesia 57 G14
Ponoy →, Russia 44 C5
Pons, France 26 C3
Pons, Spain 28 D6
Ponsul →, Portugal 31 F3
Pont-à-Celles, Belgium 17 G4
Pont-à-Mousson, France 25 D13
Pont-Audemer, France 24 C7
Pont-Aven, France 24 E3
Pont Canavese, Italy 32 C4
Pont-de-Roide, France 25 E13
Pont-de-Salars, France 26 D6
Pont-de-Vaux, France 25 F11
Pont-de-Veyle, France 27 B8
Pont-l'Abbé, France 24 E2
Pont-l'Évêque, France 24 C7
Pont-St.-Esprit, France 27 D8
Pont-Saint-Martin, Italy 32 C4
Pont-sur-Yonne, France 25 D10
Ponta de Pedras, Brazil 122 B2
Ponta do Sol, Madeira 36 D2
Ponta Grossa, Brazil 127 B5
Ponta Pora, Brazil 127 A4
Pontacq, France 26 E3
Pontailler-sur-Saône, France 25 E12
Pontal →, Brazil 122 C3
Pontalina, Brazil 123 E2
Pontarlier, France 25 F13
Pontassieve, Italy 33 E8
Pontaubault, France 24 D5
Pontaumur, France 26 C6
Pontcharra, France 27 C10
Pontchartrain L., U.S.A. 109 K9
Pontchâteau, France 24 E4
Ponte Alta, Serra do, Brazil 123 E2
Ponte Alta do Norte, Brazil 122 D2
Ponte Branca, Brazil 125 D7
Ponte da Barca, Portugal 30 D2
Ponte de Sor, Portugal 31 F3
Ponte dell'Ólio, Italy 32 D6
Ponte di Legno, Italy 32 B7
Ponte do Lima, Portugal 30 D2
Ponte do Pungué, Mozam. 83 F3
Ponte-Leccia, France 27 F13
Ponte nelle Alpi, Italy 33 B9
Ponte Nova, Brazil 123 F3
Ponte San Pietro, Italy 32 C6
Pontebba, Italy 33 B10
Pontecorvo, Italy 34 A6
Pontedera, Italy 32 E7
Pontefract, U.K. 12 D6
Ponteix, Canada 101 D7
Pontelandolfo, Italy 35 A7
Pontevedra, Spain 30 C2
Pontevedra □, Spain 30 C2
Pontevedra, R. de →, Spain 30 C2
Pontevico, Italy 32 C7
Pontiac, Ill., U.S.A. 108 E10
Pontiac, Mich., U.S.A. 104 D4
Pontian Kecil, Malaysia 59 M4
Pontianak, Indonesia 56 E3
Pontine Is. = Ponziane, Ísole, Italy 34 B5
Pontine Mts. = Kuzey Anadolu Dağları, Turkey 66 B7
Pontínia, Italy 34 A6
Pontivy, France 24 D4
Pontoise, France 25 C9
Ponton →, Canada 100 B5
Pontorson, France 24 D5
Pontrémoli, Italy 32 D6
Pontresina, Switz. 23 D9
Pontrieux, France 24 D3
Pontypool, Canada 106 B6
Pontypool, U.K. 13 F4
Pontypridd, U.K. 13 F4
Ponza, Italy 34 B5
Ponziane, Ísole, Italy 34 B5
Poochera, Australia 91 E1
Poole, U.K. 13 G6
Pooley I., Canada 100 C3
Poona = Pune, India 60 K8
Pooncarie, Australia 91 E3
Poopelloe L., Australia 91 E3
Poopó, Bolivia 124 D4
Poopó, L. de, Bolivia 124 D4
Popanyinning, Australia 89 F2
Popayán, Colombia 120 C2
Poperinge, Belgium 17 G1
Popigay, Russia 45 B12
Popilta, L., Australia 91 E3
Popio L., Australia 91 E3
Poplar, U.S.A. 108 A2
Poplar →, Man., Canada 101 C9
Poplar →, N.W.T., Canada 100 A4
Poplar Bluff, U.S.A. 109 G9
Poplarville, U.S.A. 109 K10
Popocatépetl, Volcán, Mexico 115 D5
Popokabaka, Zaïre 80 F3
Pópoli, Italy 33 F10
Popovača, Croatia 33 C13
Popovo, Bulgaria 38 F9
Poppel, Belgium 17 F6
Poprád, Slovak Rep. 20 F10
Poprád →, Slovak Rep. 20 F10
Porali →, Pakistan 62 G2
Porangaba, Brazil 124 B3
Porangatu, Brazil 123 D2
Porbandar, India 62 J3
Porce →, Colombia 120 B3
Porcher I., Canada 100 C2
Porco, Bolivia 125 D4
Porcos →, Brazil 123 D2
Porcuna, Spain 31 H6
Porcupine →, Canada 101 B8
Porcupine →, U.S.A. 96 B5
Pordenone, Italy 33 C9
Poreč, Croatia 33 C10
Porecatu, Brazil 123 F1
Poretskoye, Russia 42 C8
Pori, Finland 9 F19
Porkhov, Russia 40 D5
Porlamar, Venezuela 121 A5
Porlezza, Italy 32 B6
Porma →, Spain 30 C5
Pornic, France 24 E4
Poronaysk, Russia 45 E15
Póros, Greece 39 M6
Poroshiri-Dake, Japan 48 C11
Poroto Mts., Tanzania 83 D3
Porpoise B., Antarctica 5 C9
Porquerolles, I. de, France 27 F10
Porrentruy, Switz. 22 B4
Porreras, Spain 36 B10
Porretta, Passo di, Italy 32 D7
Porsangen, Norway 8 A21
Porsgrunn, Norway 10 E3
Port Adelaide, Australia 91 E2
Port Alberni, Canada 100 D4
Port Alfred, Canada 99 C5
Port Alfred, S. Africa 84 E4
Port Alice, Canada 100 C3
Port Allegany, U.S.A. 106 E6
Port Allen, U.S.A. 109 K9
Port Alma, Australia 90 C5
Port Angeles, U.S.A. 112 B3
Port Antonio, Jamaica 116 C4
Port Aransas, U.S.A. 109 M6
Port Arthur = Lüshun, China 51 E11
Port Arthur, Australia 90 G4
Port Arthur, U.S.A. 109 L8
Port au Port B., Canada 99 C8
Port-au-Prince, Haiti 117 C5
Port Augusta, Australia 91 E2
Port Augusta West, Australia 91 E2
Port Austin, U.S.A. 98 D3
Port Bell, Uganda 82 B3
Port Bergé Vaovao, Madag. 85 B8
Port Blandford, Canada 99 C9
Port Bou, Spain 28 C8
Port Bouët, Ivory C. 78 D4
Port Bradshaw, Australia 90 A2
Port Broughton, Australia 91 E2
Port Burwell, Canada 98 D3
Port Canning, India 63 H13
Port-Cartier, Canada 99 B6
Port Chalmers, N.Z. 87 L3
Port Chester, U.S.A. 107 F11
Port Clements, Canada 100 C2
Port Clinton, U.S.A. 104 E4
Port Colborne, Canada 98 D4
Port Coquitlam, Canada 100 D4
Port Credit, Canada 106 C5
Port Curtis, Australia 90 C5
Port Dalhousie, Canada 106 C5
Port Darwin, Australia 88 B5
Port Darwin, Falk. Is. 128 D5
Port Davey, Australia 90 G4
Port-de-Bouc, France 27 E8
Port-de-Paix, Haiti 117 C5
Port Dickson, Malaysia 59 L3
Port Douglas, Australia 90 B4
Port Dover, Canada 106 D4
Port Edward, Canada 100 C2
Port Elgin, Canada 98 D3
Port Elizabeth, S. Africa 84 E4
Port Ellen, U.K. 14 F2
Port-en-Bessin, France 24 C6
Port Erin, U.K. 12 C3
Port Essington, Australia 88 B5
Port Etienne = Nouâdhibou, Mauritania 74 D1
Port Fairy, Australia 91 F3
Port Fouâd = Bûr Fuad, Egypt 76 H8
Port Gamble, U.S.A. 112 C4
Port-Gentil, Gabon 80 E1
Port Gibson, U.S.A. 109 K9
Port Glasgow, U.K. 14 F4
Port Harcourt, Nigeria 79 E6
Port Hardy, Canada 100 C3
Port Harrison = Inukjuak, Canada 97 C12
Port Hawkesbury, Canada 99 C7
Port Hedland, Australia 88 D2
Port Henry, U.S.A. 107 B11
Port Hood, Canada 99 C7
Port Hope, Canada 98 D4
Port Hueneme, U.S.A. 113 L7
Port Huron, U.S.A. 104 D4
Port Iliç, Azerbaijan 67 C13
Port Isabel, U.S.A. 109 M6
Port Jefferson, U.S.A. 107 F11
Port Jervis, U.S.A. 107 E10
Port-Joinville, France 24 F4
Port Katon, Russia 43 G4
Port Kelang = Pelabuhan Kelang, Malaysia 59 L3
Port Kembla, Australia 91 E5
Port Kenny, Australia 91 E1
Port-la-Nouvelle, France 26 E7
Port Lairge = Waterford, Ireland 15 D4
Port Laoise, Ireland 15 C4
Port Lavaca, U.S.A. 109 L6
Port-Leucate, France 26 F7
Port Lincoln, Australia 91 E2
Port Loko, S. Leone 78 D2
Port Louis, France 24 E3
Port Lyautey = Kenitra, Morocco 74 B3
Port MacDonnell, Australia 91 F3
Port Macquarie, Australia 91 E5
Port Maria, Jamaica 116 C4
Port Mellon, Canada 100 D4
Port-Menier, Canada 99 C7
Port Morant, Jamaica 116 C4
Port Moresby, Papua N. G. 92 H6
Port Mourant, Guyana 121 B6
Port Mouton, Canada 99 D7
Port Musgrave, Australia 90 A3
Port-Navalo, France 24 E4
Port Nelson, Canada 101 B10
Port Nolloth, S. Africa 84 D2
Port Nouveau-Québec = Kangiqsualujjuaq, Canada 97 C13
Port O'Connor, U.S.A. 109 L6
Port of Spain, Trin. & Tob. 117 D7
Port Orchard, U.S.A. 112 C4
Port Orford, U.S.A. 110 E1
Port Pegasus, N.Z. 87 M1
Port Perry, Canada 98 D4
Port Phillip B., Australia 91 F3
Port Pirie, Australia 91 E2
Port Radium = Echo Bay, Canada 96 B8
Port Renfrew, Canada 100 D4
Port Roper, Australia 90 A2
Port Rowan, Canada 98 D3
Port Safaga = Bûr Safâga, Egypt 76 B3
Port Said = Bûr Sa'îd, Egypt 76 H8
Port St. Joe, U.S.A. 105 L3
Port St. Johns, S. Africa 85 E4
Port-St.-Louis-du-Rhône, France 27 E8
Port San Vicente, Phil. 55 B5
Port Sanilac, U.S.A. 98 D3
Port Saunders, Canada 99 B8
Port Severn, Canada 106 B5
Port Shepstone, S. Africa 85 E5
Port Simpson, Canada 100 C2
Port Stanley = Stanley, Falk. Is. 128 D5
Port Stanley, Canada 98 D3
Port Sudan = Bûr Sûdân, Sudan 76 D4
Port-sur-Saône, France 25 E13
Port Talbot, U.K. 13 F4
Port Taufîq = Bûr Taufîq, Egypt 76 J8
Port Townsend, U.S.A. 112 B4
Port-Vendres, France 26 F7
Port Wakefield, Australia 91 E2
Port Washington, U.S.A. 104 D2
Port Weld, Malaysia 59 K3
Portachuelo, Bolivia 125 D5
Portadown, U.K. 15 B5
Portage, U.S.A. 108 D10
Portage La Prairie, Canada 101 D9
Portageville, U.S.A. 109 G10
Portalegre, Portugal 31 F3
Portalegre □, Portugal 31 F3
Portales, U.S.A. 109 H3
Portarlington, Ireland 15 C4
Porteirinha, Brazil 123 E3
Portel, Brazil 122 B1
Portel, Portugal 31 G3
Porter L., N.W.T., Canada 101 A7
Porter L., Sask., Canada 101 B7
Porterville, S. Africa 84 E2
Porterville, U.S.A. 111 H4
Porthcawl, U.K. 13 F4
Porthill, U.S.A. 110 B5
Portile de Fier, Europe 38 E5
Portimão, Portugal 31 H2
Portland, N.S.W., Australia 91 E4
Portland, Vic., Australia 91 F3
Portland, Canada 107 B8
Portland, Conn., U.S.A. 107 E12
Portland, Maine, U.S.A. 99 D5
Portland, Mich., U.S.A. 104 D3
Portland, Oreg., U.S.A. 112 E4
Portland, I. of, U.K. 13 G5
Portland B., Australia 91 F3
Portland Bill, U.K. 13 G5
Portland Prom., Canada 97 C12
Portlands Roads, Australia 90 A3
Portneuf, Canada 99 C5
Pôrto, Brazil 122 B3
Porto, France 27 F12
Porto, Portugal 30 D2
Porto □, Portugal 30 D2
Porto, G. de, France 27 F12
Pôrto Acre, Brazil 124 B4
Pôrto Alegre, Pará, Brazil 121 D7
Pôrto Alegre, Rio Grande do S., Brazil 127 C5
Porto Amboim = Gunza, Angola 80 G2
Porto Argentera, Italy 32 D4
Porto Azzurro, Italy 32 F7
Porto Botte, Italy 34 C1
Pôrto Cajueiro, Brazil 125 C6
Porto Civitanova, Italy 33 E10
Porto Cristo, Spain 36 B10
Pôrto da Fôlha, Brazil 122 C4
Pôrto de Móz, Brazil 121 D7
Pôrto de Pedras, Brazil 122 C4
Pôrto des Meinacos, Brazil 125 C7
Porto Empédocle, Italy 34 E6
Pôrto Esperança, Brazil 125 D6
Pôrto Esperidão, Brazil 125 D6
Pôrto Franco, Brazil 122 C2
Porto Garibaldi, Italy 33 D9
Pôrto Grande, Brazil 121 C7
Pôrto Jofre, Brazil 125 D6
Pórto Lágo, Greece 39 J8
Porto Mendes, Brazil 127 A5
Porto Moniz, Madeira 36 D2
Pôrto Murtinho, Brazil 125 E6
Pôrto Nacional, Brazil 122 D2
Porto Novo, Benin 79 D5
Porto Petro, Spain 36 B10
Porto Recanati, Italy 33 E10
Porto San Giórgio, Italy 33 E10
Pôrto Santana, Brazil 121 D7
Porto Santo, Madeira 72 B1
Porto Santo Stéfano, Italy 32 F8
Pôrto São José, Brazil 127 A5
Pôrto Seguro, Brazil 123 E4
Porto Tolle, Italy 33 D9
Porto Tórres, Italy 34 B1
Pôrto União, Brazil 127 B5
Pôrto Válter, Brazil 124 B3
Porto-Vecchio, France 27 G13
Pôrto Velho, Brazil 125 B5
Portobelo, Panama 116 E4
Portoferráio, Italy 32 F7
Portogruaro, Italy 33 C9
Portola, U.S.A. 112 F6
Portomaggiore, Italy 33 D8
Portoscuso, Italy 34 C1
Portovénere, Italy 32 D6
Portoviejo, Ecuador 120 D1
Portpatrick, U.K. 14 G3
Portree, U.K. 14 D2
Portrush, U.K. 15 A5
Portsall, France 24 D2
Portsmouth, Domin. 117 C7
Portsmouth, U.K. 13 G6
Portsmouth, N.H., U.S.A. 107 C14
Portsmouth, Ohio, U.S.A. 104 F4
Portsmouth, R.I., U.S.A. 107 E13
Portsmouth, Va., U.S.A. 104 G7
Portsoy, U.K. 14 D6
Porttipahtan tekojärvi, Finland 8 B22
Portugal ■, Europe 30 F3
Portugalete, Spain 28 B1
Portuguesa □, Venezuela 120 B4
Portumna, Ireland 15 C3
Portville, U.S.A. 106 D6
Porvenir, Bolivia 124 C4
Porvenir, Chile 128 D2
Porvoo, Finland 9 F21
Porzuna, Spain 31 F6
Posada →, Italy 34 B2
Posadas, Argentina 127 B4
Posadas, Spain 31 H5
Poschiavo, Switz. 23 D10
Posets, Spain 28 C5
Poshan = Boshan, China 51 F9
Posht-e-Badam, Iran 65 C7
Posídhion, Ákra, Greece 39 K6
Poso, Indonesia 57 E6
Posoegroenoe, Surinam 121 C6
Posong, S. Korea 51 G14
Posse, Brazil 123 D2
Possel, C.A.R. 80 C3
Possession I., Antarctica 5 D11
Pössneck, Germany 18 E7
Post, U.S.A. 109 J4
Post Falls, U.S.A. 110 C5
Postavy = Pastavy, Belarus 9 J22
Poste Maurice Cortier, Algeria 75 D5
Postmasburg, S. Africa 84 D3
Postojna, Slovenia 33 C11
Poston, U.S.A. 113 M12
Potchefstroom, S. Africa 84 D4
Poté, Brazil 123 E3
Poteau, U.S.A. 109 H7
Poteet, U.S.A. 109 L5
Potelu, Lacul, Romania 38 F7
Potenza, Italy 35 B8
Potenza →, Italy 33 E10
Potenza Picena, Italy 33 E10
Poteriteri, L., N.Z. 87 M1
Potes, Spain 30 B6
Potgietersrus, S. Africa 85 C4
Poti, Georgia 43 J5
Potiraguá, Brazil 123 E4
Potiskum, Nigeria 79 C7
Potomac →, U.S.A. 104 F7
Potosí, Bolivia 125 D4
Potosí □, Bolivia 124 E4
Potosi Mt., U.S.A. 113 K11
Pototan, Phil. 55 F5
Potrerillos, Chile 126 B2
Potsdam, Germany 18 C9
Potsdam, U.S.A. 107 B10
Pottenstein, Germany 19 F7
Potter, U.S.A. 108 E3

Pottery Hill = Abû Ballas, Egypt 76 C2
Pottstown, U.S.A. 107 F9
Pottsville, U.S.A. 107 F8
Pottuvil, Sri Lanka 60 R12
P'otzu, Taiwan 53 F13
Pouancé, France 24 E5
Pouce Coupé, Canada 100 B4
Poughkeepsie, U.S.A. 107 E11
Pouilly-sur-Loire, France 25 E9
Poulaphouca Res., Ireland 15 C5
Poulsbo, U.S.A. 112 C4
Pourri, Mt., France 27 C10
Pouso Alegre, Mato Grosso, Brazil 125 C6
Pouso Alegre, Minas Gerais, Brazil 127 A6
Pouzauges, France 24 F6
Povenets, Russia 44 C4
Poverty B., N.Z. 87 H7
Póvoa de Lanhosa, Portugal 30 D2
Póvoa de Varzim, Portugal 30 D2
Povorino, Russia 42 E6
Powassan, Canada 98 C4
Poway, U.S.A. 113 N9
Powder →, U.S.A. 108 B2
Powder River, U.S.A. 110 E10
Powell, U.S.A. 110 D9
Powell L., U.S.A. 111 H8
Powell River, Canada 100 D4
Powers, Mich., U.S.A. 104 C2
Powers, Oreg., U.S.A. 110 E1
Powers Lake, U.S.A. 108 A3
Powys □, U.K. 13 E4
Poxoreu, Brazil 125 D7
Poyang Hu, China 53 C11
Poyarkovo, Russia 45 E13
Poza de la Sal, Spain 28 C1
Poza Rica, Mexico 115 C5
Pozanti, Turkey 66 D6
Požarevac, Serbia, Yug. 21 L11
Poznań, Poland 20 C6
Pozo, U.S.A. 113 K6
Pozo Alcón, Spain 29 H2
Pozo Almonte, Chile 124 E4
Pozo Colorado, Paraguay 126 A4
Pozo del Dátil, Mexico 114 B2
Pozoblanco, Spain 31 G6
Pozuzo, Peru 124 C2
Pozzallo, Italy 35 F7
Pozzuoli, Italy 35 B7
Pra →, Ghana 79 D4
Prachin Buri, Thailand 58 E3
Prachuap Khiri Khan, Thailand 59 G2
Pradelles, France 26 D7
Pradera, Colombia 120 C2
Prades, France 26 F6
Prado, Brazil 123 E4
Prado del Rey, Spain 31 J5
Præstø, Denmark 11 J6
Pragersko, Slovenia 33 B12
Prague = Praha, Czech. 20 E4
Praha, Czech. 20 E4
Prahecq, France 26 B3
Prahova →, Romania 38 E8
Prahovo, Serbia, Yug. 21 L12
Praia, C. Verde Is. 71 E1
Praid, Romania 38 C8
Prainha, Amazonas, Brazil 125 B5
Prainha, Pará, Brazil 121 D7
Prairie, Australia 90 C3
Prairie →, U.S.A. 109 H5
Prairie City, U.S.A. 110 D4
Prairie du Chien, U.S.A. 108 D9
Prairies, Canada 96 C9
Pramánda, Greece 39 K4
Pran Buri, Thailand 58 F2
Prang, Ghana 79 D4
Prapat, Indonesia 56 D1
Prasonísi, Ákra, Greece 37 D9
Prata, Brazil 123 E2
Pratapgarh, India 62 G6
Prática di Mare, Italy 34 A5
Prätigau, Switz. 23 C9
Prato, Italy 32 E8
Prátola Peligna, Italy 33 F10
Pratovécchio, Italy 33 E8
Prats-de-Mollo-la-Preste, France 26 F6
Pratt, U.S.A. 109 G5
Pratteln, Switz. 22 A5
Prattville, U.S.A. 105 J2
Pravdinsk, Russia 42 B6
Pravia, Spain 30 B4
Praya, Indonesia 56 F5
Pré-en-Pail, France 24 D6
Pré-Saint-Didier, Italy 32 C4
Precordillera, Argentina 126 C2
Predáppio, Italy 33 D8
Predazzo, Italy 33 B8
Predejane, Serbia, Yug. 21 N12
Preeceville, Canada 101 C8
Préfailles, France 24 E4
Pregonero, Venezuela 120 B3
Pregrada, Croatia 33 B12
Preiļi, Latvia 9 H22
Preko, Croatia 33 D12
Prelate, Canada 101 C7
Prelog, Croatia 33 B13
Premier, Canada 100 B3
Premont, U.S.A. 109 M5
Premuda, Croatia 33 D11
Prenjasi, Albania 39 H3
Prentice, U.S.A. 108 C9
Prenzlau, Germany 18 B9
Preobrazheniye, Russia 48 C6
Preparis North Channel, Ind. Oc. 61 M18
Preparis South Channel, Ind. Oc. 61 M18
Přerov, Czech. 20 F7
Presanella, Italy 32 B7
Prescott, Canada 98 D4
Prescott, Ariz., U.S.A. 111 J7
Prescott, Ark., U.S.A. 109 J8
Preservation Inlet, N.Z. 87 M1
Preševo, Serbia, Yug. 21 N11
Presho, U.S.A. 108 D4
Presicce, Italy 35 C11
Presidencia de la Plaza, Argentina 126 B4
Presidencia Roque Saenz Peña, Argentina 126 B3
Presidente Epitácio, Brazil 123 F1
Presidente Hayes □, Paraguay 126 A4
Presidente Hermes, Brazil 125 C5
Presidente Prudente, Brazil 127 A5
Presidio, Mexico 114 B4
Presidio, U.S.A. 109 L2
Preslav, Bulgaria 38 F9
Prešov, Slovak Rep. 20 F11
Prespa, L. = Prespansko Jezero, Macedonia 39 J4
Prespansko Jezero, Macedonia 39 J4
Presque Isle, U.S.A. 99 C6
Prestbury, U.K. 13 F5
Prestea, Ghana 78 D4
Presteigne, U.K. 13 E5
Presto, Bolivia 125 D5
Preston, Canada 106 C4
Preston, U.K. 12 D5
Preston, Idaho, U.S.A. 110 E8
Preston, Minn., U.S.A. 108 D8
Preston, Nev., U.S.A. 110 G6
Preston, C., Australia 88 D2
Prestonpans, U.K. 14 F6
Prestwick, U.K. 14 F4
Prêto →, Amazonas, Brazil 121 D5
Prêto →, Bahia, Brazil 122 D3
Prêto do Igapó-Açu →, Brazil 121 D6
Pretoria, S. Africa 85 D4
Preuilly-sur-Claise, France 24 F7
Préveza, Greece 39 L3
Priazovskoye, Ukraine 41 J8
Pribilof Is., Bering S. 4 D17
Priboj, Serbia, Yug. 21 M9
Příbram, Czech. 20 F4
Price, U.S.A. 110 G8
Price I., Canada 100 C3
Prichard, U.S.A. 105 K1
Priego, Spain 28 E2
Priego de Córdoba, Spain 31 H6
Priekule, Latvia 9 H19
Prien, Germany 19 H8
Prienai, Lithuania 9 J20
Prieska, S. Africa 84 D3
Priest →, U.S.A. 110 B5
Priest L., U.S.A. 110 B5
Priest Valley, U.S.A. 112 J6
Priestly, Canada 100 C3
Prievidza, Slovak Rep. 20 G8
Prijedor, Bos.-H. 33 D13
Prikaspiyskaya Nizmennost = Caspian Depression, Eurasia 43 G9
Prikubanskaya Nizmennost, Russia 43 H4
Prilep, Macedonia 39 H4
Priluki = Pryluky, Ukraine 41 G7
Prime Seal I., Australia 90 G4
Primeira Cruz, Brazil 122 B3
Primorsk, Russia 40 B5
Primorsko-Akhtarsk, Russia 43 G4
Primorskoye, Ukraine 41 J9
Primrose L., Canada 101 C7
Prince Albert, Canada 101 C7
Prince Albert, S. Africa 84 E3
Prince Albert Mts., Antarctica 5 D11
Prince Albert Nat. Park, Canada 101 C7
Prince Albert Pen., Canada 96 A8
Prince Albert Sd., Canada 96 A8
Prince Alfred, C., Canada 4 B1
Prince Charles I., Canada 97 B12
Prince Charles Mts., Antarctica 5 D6
Prince Edward I. □, Canada 99 C7
Prince Edward Is., Ind. Oc. 3 G11
Prince George, Canada 100 C4
Prince of Wales, C., U.S.A. 94 C3
Prince of Wales I., Australia 90 A3
Prince of Wales I., Canada 96 A10
Prince of Wales I., U.S.A. 100 B2
Prince Patrick I., Canada 4 B2
Prince Regent Inlet, Canada 4 B3
Prince Rupert, Canada 100 C2
Princenhage, Neths. 17 F5
Princesa Isabel, Brazil 122 C4
Princess Charlotte B., Australia 90 A3
Princess May Ras., Australia 88 C4
Princess Royal I., Canada 100 C3
Princeton, Canada 100 D4
Princeton, Calif., U.S.A. 112 F4
Princeton, Ill., U.S.A. 108 E10
Princeton, Ind., U.S.A. 104 F2
Princeton, Ky., U.S.A. 104 G2
Princeton, Mo., U.S.A. 108 E8
Princeton, N.J., U.S.A. 107 F10
Princeton, W. Va., U.S.A. 104 G5
Principe, I. de, Atl. Oc. 70 F4
Principe Chan., Canada 100 C2
Principe da Beira, Brazil 125 C5
Prineville, U.S.A. 110 D3
Prins Harald Kyst, Antarctica 5 D4
Prinsesse Astrid Kyst, Antarctica 5 D3
Prinsesse Ragnhild Kyst, Antarctica 5 D4
Prinzapolca, Nic. 116 D3
Prior, C., Spain 30 B2
Priozersk, Russia 40 B6
Pripet → = Prypyat →, Europe 41 G6
Pripet Marshes, Europe 41 F5
Pripyat Marshes = Pripet Marshes, Europe 41 F5
Pripyats = Prypyat →, Europe 41 G6
Prislop, Pasul, Romania 38 B8
Pristen, Russia 42 E3
Priština, Serbia, Yug. 21 N11
Pritzwalk, Germany 18 B8
Privas, France 27 D8
Priverno, Italy 34 A6
Privolzhsk, Russia 42 B5
Privolzhskaya Vozvyshennost, Russia 42 E7
Privolzhskiy, Russia 42 E8
Privolzhye, Russia 42 D9
Priyutnoye, Russia 43 G6
Prizren, Serbia, Yug. 21 N10
Prizzi, Italy 34 E6
Prnjavor, Bos.-H. 21 L7
Probolinggo, Indonesia 57 G15
Procida, Italy 35 B7
Proddatur, India 60 M11
Prodhromos, Cyprus 37 E11
Proença-a-Nova, Portugal 31 F3
Prof. Van Blommestein Meer, Surinam 121 C6
Profítis Ilías, Greece 37 C9
Profondeville, Belgium 17 H5
Progreso, Mexico 115 C7
Prokhladnyy, Russia 43 J7
Prokletije, Albania 38 G2
Prokopyevsk, Russia 44 D9
Prokuplje, Serbia, Yug. 21 M11
Proletarsk, Russia 43 G5
Proletarskaya = Proletarsk, Russia 43 G5
Prome = Pyè, Burma 61 K19
Prophet →, Canada 100 B4
Propriá, Brazil 122 D4
Propriano, France 27 G12
Proserpine, Australia 90 C4
Prosser, U.S.A. 110 C4
Prostějov, Czech. 20 F7
Proston, Australia 91 D5
Protection, U.S.A. 109 G5
Próti, Greece 39 M4
Provadiya, Bulgaria 38 F10
Proven, Belgium 17 G1
Provence, France 27 E9
Providence, Ky., U.S.A. 104 G2
Providence, R.I., U.S.A. 107 E13
Providence Bay, Canada 98 C3
Providence Mts., U.S.A. 111 J6
Providencia, Ecuador 120 D2
Providencia, I. de, Colombia 116 D3
Provideniya, Russia 45 C19
Provins, France 25 D10
Provo, U.S.A. 110 F8
Provost, Canada 101 C6
Prozor, Bos.-H. 21 M7
Prudentópolis, Brazil 123 G1
Prud'homme, Canada 101 C7
Prudnik, Poland 20 E7
Prüm, Germany 19 E2
Pruszcz Gdański, Poland 20 A8
Pruszków, Poland 20 C10
Prut →, Romania 38 D11
Pruzhany, Belarus 41 F3
Prvič, Croatia 33 D11
Prydz B., Antarctica 5 C6
Pryluky, Ukraine 41 G7
Pryor, U.S.A. 109 G7
Prypyat →, Europe 41 G6
Przasnysz, Poland 20 B10
Przedbórz, Poland 20 D9
Przemyśl, Poland 20 F12
Przeworsk, Poland 20 E12
Przewóz, Poland 20 D4
Przhevalsk, Kyrgyzstan 44 E8
Przysuchla, Poland 20 D10
Psakhná, Greece 39 L6
Psará, Greece 39 L8
Psel →, Ukraine 41 H7
Pserimos, Greece 39 N10
Psíra, Greece 37 D7
Pskov, Russia 40 D5
Pskovskoye, Ozero, Russia 9 H22
Psunj, Croatia 21 K7
Pszczyna, Poland 20 F8
Pteleón, Greece 39 K5
Ptich = Ptsich →, Belarus 41 F5
Ptolemaís, Greece 39 J4
Ptsich →, Belarus 41 F5
Ptuj, Slovenia 33 B12
Ptujska Gora, Slovenia 33 B12
Pu Xian, China 50 F6
Pua, Thailand 58 C3
Puán, Argentina 126 D3
Pu'an, China 52 E5
Puan, S. Korea 51 G14
Pubei, China 52 F7
Pucacuro →, Peru 120 D3
Pucallpa, Peru 124 B3
Pucará, Bolivia 125 D5
Pucará, Peru 124 D3
Pucarani, Bolivia 124 D4
Pucheng, China 53 D12
Pučišće, Croatia 33 E13
Pucka, Zatoka, Poland 20 A8
Pudasjärvi, Finland 8 D22
Puding, China 52 D5
Pudozh, Russia 40 B9
Pudukkottai, India 60 P11
Puebla, Mexico 115 D5
Puebla □, Mexico 115 D5
Puebla de Alcocer, Spain 31 G5
Puebla de Don Fadrique, Spain 29 H2
Puebla de Don Rodrigo, Spain 31 F6
Puebla de Guzmán, Spain 31 H3
Puebla de Sanabria, Spain 30 C4
Puebla de Trives, Spain 30 C3
Puebla del Caramiñal, Spain 30 C2
Pueblo, U.S.A. 108 F2
Pueblo Hundido, Chile 126 B1
Pueblo Nuevo, Venezuela 120 B3
Puelches, Argentina 126 D2
Puelén, Argentina 126 D2
Puente Alto, Chile 126 C1
Puente del Arzobispo, Spain 30 F5
Puente-Genil, Spain 31 H6
Puente la Reina, Spain 28 C3
Puenteareas, Spain 30 C2
Puentedeume, Spain 30 B2
Puentes de Garcia Rodriguez, Spain 30 B3
Pu'er, China 52 F3
Puerco →, U.S.A. 111 J10
Puerto, Canary Is. 36 F2
Puerto Acosta, Bolivia 124 D4
Puerto Aisén, Chile 128 C2
Puerto Ángel, Mexico 115 D5
Puerto Arista, Mexico 115 D6
Puerto Armuelles, Panama 116 E3
Puerto Ayacucho, Venezuela 120 B4
Puerto Barrios, Guatemala 116 C2
Puerto Bermejo, Argentina 126 B4
Puerto Bermúdez, Peru 124 C3
Puerto Bolívar, Ecuador 120 D2
Puerto Cabello, Venezuela 120 A4
Puerto Cabezas, Nic. 116 D3
Puerto Cabo Gracias á Dios, Nic. 116 D3
Puerto Capaz = Jebba, Morocco 74 A4
Puerto Carreño, Colombia 120 B4
Puerto Castilla, Honduras 116 C2
Puerto Chicama, Peru 124 B2
Puerto Coig, Argentina 128 D3
Puerto Cortes, Costa Rica 116 E3
Puerto Cortés, Honduras 116 C2
Puerto Cumarebo, Venezuela 120 A4
Puerto de Alcudia, Spain 36 B10
Puerto de Andraitx, Spain 36 B9
Puerto de Cabrera, Spain 36 B9
Puerto de Gran Tarajal, Canary Is. 36 F5
Puerto de la Cruz, Canary Is. 36 F3
Puerto de Pozo Negro, Canary Is. 36 F6
Puerto de Sóller, Spain 36 B9
Puerto del Carmen, Canary Is. 36 F6
Puerto del Rosario, Canary Is. 36 F6
Puerto Deseado, Argentina 128 C3
Puerto Guaraní, Paraguay 125 E6
Puerto Heath, Bolivia 124 C4
Puerto Huitoto, Colombia 120 C3
Puerto Inca, Peru 124 B3
Puerto Juárez, Mexico 115 C7
Puerto La Cruz, Venezuela 121 A5
Puerto Leguízamo, Colombia 120 D3
Puerto Limón, Colombia 120 C3
Puerto Lobos, Argentina 128 B3
Puerto López, Colombia 120 C3
Puerto Lumbreras, Spain 29 H3
Puerto Madryn, Argentina 128 B3
Puerto Maldonado, Peru 124 C4
Puerto Manotí, Cuba 116 B4
Puerto Mazarrón, Spain 29 H3
Puerto Mercedes, Colombia 120 C3
Puerto Miraña, Colombia 120 D3
Puerto Montt, Chile 128 B2
Puerto Morelos, Mexico 115 C7
Puerto Nariño, Colombia 120 C4
Puerto Natales, Chile 128 D2
Puerto Nuevo, Colombia 120 B4
Puerto Nutrias, Venezuela 120 B4
Puerto Ordaz, Venezuela 121 B5
Puerto Padre, Cuba 116 B4
Puerto Páez, Venezuela 120 B4
Puerto Peñasco, Mexico 114 A2
Puerto Pinasco, Paraguay 126 A4
Puerto Pirámides, Argentina 128 B4
Puerto Plata, Dom. Rep. 117 C5
Puerto Pollensa, Spain 36 B10
Puerto Portillo, Peru 124 B3
Puerto Princesa, Phil. 55 G3
Puerto Quellón, Chile 128 B2
Puerto Quepos, Costa Rica 116 E3
Puerto Real, Spain 31 J4
Puerto Rico, Bolivia 124 C4
Puerto Rico, Canary Is. 36 G4
Puerto Rico ■, W. Indies 117 C6
Puerto Rico Trench, Atl. Oc. 117 C6
Puerto Saavedra, Chile 128 A2
Puerto Sastre, Paraguay 126 A4
Puerto Siles, Bolivia 125 C4
Puerto Suárez, Bolivia 125 D6
Puerto Tejada, Colombia 120 C2
Puerto Umbría, Colombia 120 C2
Puerto Vallarta, Mexico 114 C3
Puerto Varas, Chile 128 B2
Puerto Villazón, Bolivia 125 C5
Puerto Wilches, Colombia 120 B3
Puertollano, Spain 31 G6
Puertomarín, Spain 30 C3
Puesto Cunambo, Peru 120 D2
Pueyrredón, L., Argentina 128 C2
Pugachev, Russia 42 D9
Puge, China 52 D4
Puge, Tanzania 82 C3
Puget Sound, U.S.A. 110 C2
Puget-Théniers, France 27 E10
Púglia □, Italy 35 B9
Pugŏdong, N. Korea 51 C16
Pugu, Tanzania 82 D4
Pūgūnzī, Iran 65 E8
Pui, Romania 38 D6
Puica, Peru 124 C3
Puig Mayor, Spain 36 B9
Puigcerdá, Spain 28 C6
Puigmal, Spain 28 C7
Puigpuñent, Spain 36 B9
Puisaye, Collines de la, France 25 E10
Puiseaux, France 25 D9
Pujilí, Ecuador 120 D2
Pujon-chosuji, N. Korea 51 D14
Puka, Albania 38 G2
Pukaki L., N.Z. 87 L3
Pukapuka, Cook Is. 93 J11
Pukatawagan, Canada 101 B8
Pukchin, N. Korea 51 D13
Pukchŏng, N. Korea 51 D15
Pukekohe, N.Z. 87 G5
Pukou, China 53 A12
Pula, Croatia 33 D10
Pula, Italy 34 D2
Pulacayo, Bolivia 124 E4
Pulaski, N.Y., U.S.A. 107 C8
Pulaski, Tenn., U.S.A. 105 H2
Pulaski, Va., U.S.A. 104 G5
Puławy, Poland 20 D11
Pulga, U.S.A. 112 F5
Pulicat, L., India 60 N12
Pullman, U.S.A. 110 C5
Pulog, Phil. 55 C4
Pułtusk, Poland 20 C11
Pülümür, Turkey 67 C8
Pumlumon Fawr, U.K. 13 E4
Puna, Bolivia 125 D4
Puná, I., Ecuador 120 D1
Punakha, Bhutan 61 F16
Punasar, India 62 F5
Punata, Bolivia 125 D4
Punch, India 63 C6
Pune, India 60 K8
Pungsan, N. Korea 51 D15
Pungue, Ponte de, Mozam. 83 F3
Puning, China 53 F11
Punjab □, India 62 D6
Punjab □, Pakistan 62 E6
Puno, Peru 124 D3
Punta Alta, Argentina 128 A4
Punta Arenas, Chile 128 D2
Punta Cardón, Venezuela 120 A3
Punta Coles, Peru 124 D3
Punta de Bombón, Peru 124 D3
Punta de Díaz, Chile 126 B1
Punta Delgado, Argentina 128 B4
Punta Gorda, Belize 115 D7
Punta Gorda, U.S.A. 105 M5
Punta Prieta, Mexico 114 B2
Punta Prima, Spain 36 B11
Puntabie, Australia 91 E1
Puntarenas, Costa Rica 116 E3
Punto Fijo, Venezuela 120 A3
Punxsatawney, U.S.A. 106 F5
Puqi, China 53 C9
Puquio, Peru 124 C3
Pur →, Russia 44 C8
Purace, Vol., Colombia 120 C2
Puralia = Puruliya, India 63 H12
Purbeck, Isle of, U.K. 13 G5
Purcell, U.S.A. 109 H6
Purchena Tetica, Spain 29 H2
Puri, India 61 K14
Purificación, Colombia 120 C3
Purmerend, Neths. 16 C5
Purnia, India 63 G12
Purukcahu, Indonesia 56 E4
Puruliya, India 63 H12
Purus →, Brazil 121 D5
Puruvesi, Finland 40 B5
Pŭrvomay, Bulgaria 38 G8
Purwakarta, Indonesia 57 G12

Purwodadi, *Jawa, Indonesia* 57 G14
Purwodadi, *Jawa, Indonesia* 57 G13
Purwokerto, *Indonesia* 57 G13
Purworejo, *Indonesia* 57 G14
Puryŏng, *N. Korea* 51 C15
Pusan, *S. Korea* 51 G15
Pushchino, *Russia* 45 D16
Pushkin, *Russia* 40 C6
Pushkino, *Russia* 42 E8
Pushkino, *Russia* 42 B3
Püspökladány, *Hungary* 21 H11
Pustoshka, *Russia* 40 D5
Putahow L., *Canada* 101 B8
Putao, *Burma* 61 F20
Putaruru, *N.Z.* 87 H5
Putbus, *Germany* 18 A9
Puthein Myit →, *Burma* 61 M19
Putian, *China* 53 E12
Putignano, *Italy* 35 B10
Putina, *Peru* 124 C4
Puting, Tanjung, *Indonesia* 56 E4
Putlitz, *Germany* 18 B8
Putna →, *Romania* 38 D10
Putnam, *U.S.A.* 107 E13
Putorana, Gory, *Russia* 45 C10
Putre, *Chile* 124 D4
Puttalam, *Sri Lanka* 60 Q11
Putte, *Neths.* 17 F4
Putten, *Neths.* 16 D7
Puttgarden, *Germany* 18 A7
Putumayo →, *S. Amer.* 120 D4
Putuo, *China* 53 C14
Putussibau, *Indonesia* 56 D4
Puurs, *Belgium* 17 F4
Puy-de-Dôme, *France* 26 C6
Puy-de-Dôme □, *France* 26 C7
Puy-Guillaume, *France* 26 C7
Puy-l'Évêque, *France* 26 D5
Puyallup, *U.S.A.* 112 C4
Puyang, *China* 50 G8
Puyehue, *Chile* 128 B2
Puylaurens, *France* 26 E6
Puyo, *Ecuador* 120 D2
Pūzeh Rīg, *Iran* 65 E8
Pwani □, *Tanzania* 82 D4
Pweto, *Zaïre* 83 D2
Pwllheli, *U.K.* 12 E3
Pyana →, *Russia* 42 C8
Pyapon, *Burma* 61 L19
Pyasina →, *Russia* 45 B9
Pyatigorsk, *Russia* 43 H6
Pyatykhatky, *Ukraine* 41 H7
Pyè, *Burma* 61 K19
Pyetrikaw, *Belarus* 41 F5
Pyhäjoki, *Finland* 8 D21
Pyinmana, *Burma* 61 K20
Pyla, C., *Cyprus* 37 E12
Pyŏktong, *N. Korea* 51 D13
Pyŏnggang, *N. Korea* 51 E14
P'yŏngtaek, *S. Korea* 51 F14
P'yŏngyang, *N. Korea* 51 E13
Pyote, *U.S.A.* 109 K3
Pyramid L., *U.S.A.* 110 G4
Pyramid Pk., *U.S.A.* 113 J10
Pyramids, *Egypt* 76 J7
Pyrénées, *Europe* 26 F4
Pyrénées-Atlantiques □, *France* 26 E3
Pyrénées-Orientales □, *France* 26 F6
Pyryatyn, *Ukraine* 41 G7
Pyrzyce, *Poland* 20 B4
Pytalovo, *Russia* 40 D4
Pyttegga, *Norway* 10 B1
Pyu, *Burma* 61 K20

Q

Qaanaaq = Thule, *Greenland* 4 B4
Qabirri →, *Azerbaijan* 43 K8
Qachasnek, *S. Africa* 85 E4
Qādib, *Yemen* 68 E5
Qa'el Jafr, *Jordan* 69 E5
Qa'emābād, *Iran* 65 D9
Qā'emshahr, *Iran* 65 B7
Qagan Nur, *China* 50 C8
Qahar Youyi Zhongqi, *China* 50 D7
Qahremānshahr = Bākhtarān, *Iran* 67 E12
Qaidam Pendi, *China* 54 C4
Qajarīyeh, *Iran* 65 D6
Qala, Ras il, *Malta* 37 C1
Qala-i-Jadid, *Afghan.* 62 D2
Qala Yangi, *Afghan.* 62 B2
Qal'at al Akhḍar, *Si. Arabia* 64 E3
Qal'at Dīzah, *Iraq* 67 D11
Qal'at Sukkar, *Iraq* 67 G12
Qal'eh Darreh, *Iran* 64 B5
Qal'eh Shaharak, *Afghan.* 60 B4
Qalyûb, *Egypt* 76 H7
Qamar, Ghubbat al, *Yemen* 68 D5
Qamdo, *China* 52 B1
Qamruddin Karez, *Pakistan* 62 D3
Qandahār, *Afghan.* 60 D4
Qandahār □, *Afghan.* 60 D4
Qapān, *Iran* 65 B7
Qapshaghay, *Kazakstan* 44 E8
Qaqortoq = Julianehåb, *Greenland* 4 C5
Qâra, *Egypt* 76 B2
Qara Qash →, *India* 63 B8
Qarabutaq, *Kazakstan* 44 E7
Qaraçala, *Azerbaijan* 43 L9
Qaraghandy, *Kazakstan* 44 E8
Qārah, *Si. Arabia* 64 D4
Qarataū, *Kazakstan* 44 E8
Qardud, *Sudan* 77 E2
Qareh →, *Iran* 67 C12
Qareh Tekān, *Iran* 65 B6
Qarqan, *China* 54 C3
Qarqan He →, *China* 54 C3
Qarqaraly, *Kazakstan* 44 E8
Qarrasa, *Sudan* 77 E3
Qarshi, *Uzbekistan* 44 F7
Qartabā, *Lebanon* 69 A4
Qaryat al Gharab, *Iraq* 64 D5
Qaryat al 'Ulyā, *Si. Arabia* 64 E5
Qasr 'Amra, *Jordan* 64 D3
Qaṣr-e Qand, *Iran* 65 E9
Qasr Farâfra, *Egypt* 76 B2
Qatanā, *Syria* 69 B5
Qatar ■, *Asia* 65 E6
Qatlīsh, *Iran* 65 B8
Qattâra, *Egypt* 76 A2
Qattâra, Munkhafed el, *Egypt* 76 B2
Qattâra Depression = Qattâra, Munkhafed el, *Egypt* 76 B2
Qawām al Ḥamzah, *Iraq* 64 D5
Qāyen, *Iran* 65 C8
Qazaqstan = Kazakstan ■, *Asia* 44 E7
Qazimämmäd, *Azerbaijan* 43 K9
Qazvin, *Iran* 65 B6
Qena, *Egypt* 76 B3
Qena, W. →, *Egypt* 76 B3
Qeqertarsuaq = Disko, *Greenland* 4 C5
Qeqertarsuaq = Godhavn, *Greenland* 4 C5
Qeshlāq, *Iran* 67 E12
Qeshm, *Iran* 65 E8
Qezi'ot, *Israel* 69 E3
Qi Xian, *China* 50 G8
Qian Gorlos, *China* 51 B13
Qian Xian, *China* 50 G5
Qiancheng, *China* 52 D7
Qianjiang, *Guangxi Zhuangzu, China* 52 F7
Qianjiang, *Hubei, China* 53 B9
Qianjiang, *Sichuan, China* 52 C7
Qianshan, *China* 53 B11
Qianwei, *China* 52 C4
Qianxi, *China* 52 D6
Qianyang, *Hunan, China* 53 D8
Qianyang, *Shaanxi, China* 50 G4
Qianyang, *Zhejiang, China* 53 B12
Qiaojia, *China* 52 D4
Qibā', *Si. Arabia* 64 E5
Qichun, *China* 53 B10
Qidong, *Hunan, China* 53 D9
Qidong, *Jiangsu, China* 53 B13
Qijiang, *China* 52 C6
Qila Safed, *Pakistan* 60 E2
Qila Saifullāh, *Pakistan* 62 D3
Qilian Shan, *China* 54 C4
Qimen, *China* 53 C11
Qin He →, *China* 50 G7
Qin Jiang →, *China* 53 D10
Qin Ling = Qinling Shandi, *China* 50 H5
Qin'an, *China* 50 G3
Qing Xian, *China* 50 E9
Qingcheng, *China* 51 F9
Qingdao, *China* 51 F11
Qingfeng, *China* 50 G8
Qinghai □, *China* 54 C4
Qinghai Hu, *China* 54 C5
Qinghecheng, *China* 51 D13
Qinghemen, *China* 51 D11
Qingjian, *China* 50 F6
Qingjiang, *Jiangsu, China* 51 H10
Qingjiang, *Jiangxi, China* 53 C10
Qingliu, *China* 53 D11
Qinglong, *China* 52 E5
Qingping, *China* 52 D6
Qingpu, *China* 53 B13
Qingshui, *China* 50 G4
Qingshuihe, *China* 50 E6
Qingtian, *China* 53 C13
Qingtongxia Shuiku, *China* 50 F3
Qingxi, *China* 52 D7
Qingxu, *China* 50 F7
Qingyang, *Anhui, China* 53 B11
Qingyang, *Gansu, China* 50 F4
Qingyi Jiang →, *China* 52 C4
Qingyuan, *Guangdong, China* 53 F9
Qingyuan, *Liaoning, China* 51 C13
Qingyuan, *Zhejiang, China* 53 D12
Qingyun, *China* 51 F9
Qingzhen, *China* 52 D6
Qinhuangdao, *China* 51 E10
Qinling Shandi, *China* 50 H5
Qinshui, *China* 50 G7
Qinyang, *China* 50 G7
Qinyuan, *China* 50 F7
Qinzhou, *China* 52 G7
Qionghai, *China* 58 C8
Qionglai, *China* 52 B4
Qionglai Shan, *China* 52 B4
Qiongshan, *China* 58 C8
Qiongzhou Haixia, *China* 58 B8
Qiqihar, *China* 45 E13
Qiraîya, W. →, *Egypt* 69 E3
Qiryat Ata, *Israel* 69 C4
Qiryat Gat, *Israel* 69 D3
Qiryat Mal'akhi, *Israel* 69 D3
Qiryat Shemona, *Israel* 69 B4
Qiryat Yam, *Israel* 69 C4
Qishan, *China* 50 G4
Qitai, *China* 54 B3
Qiubei, *China* 52 E5
Qixia, *China* 51 F11
Qiyang, *China* 53 D8
Qızılağac Körfäzi, *Azerbaijan* 67 C13
Qojūr, *Iran* 64 B5
Qom, *Iran* 65 C6
Qomsheh, *Iran* 65 D6
Qorveh, *Iran* 67 E12
Qostanay, *Kazakstan* 44 D7
Qoṭūr, *Iran* 67 C11
Qu Jiang →, *China* 52 B6
Qu Xian, *Sichuan, China* 52 B6
Qu Xian, *Zhejiang, China* 53 C12
Quairading, *Australia* 89 F2
Quakenbrück, *Germany* 18 C3
Quakertown, *U.S.A.* 107 F9
Qualeup, *Australia* 89 F2
Quambatook, *Australia* 91 F3
Quambone, *Australia* 91 E4
Quamby, *Australia* 90 C3
Quan Long, *Vietnam* 59 H5
Quanah, *U.S.A.* 109 H5
Quandialla, *Australia* 91 E4
Quang Ngai, *Vietnam* 58 E7
Quang Yen, *Vietnam* 58 B6
Quannan, *China* 53 E10
Quantock Hills, *U.K.* 13 F4
Quanzhou, *Fujian, China* 53 E12
Quanzhou, *Guangxi Zhuangzu, China* 53 E8
Quaqtaq, *Canada* 97 B13
Quaraí, *Brazil* 126 C4
Quarré-les-Tombes, *France* 25 E10
Quartu Sant'Elena, *Italy* 34 C2
Quartzsite, *U.S.A.* 113 M12
Quatsino, *Canada* 100 C3
Quatsino Sd., *Canada* 100 C3
Quba, *Azerbaijan* 43 K9
Qūchān, *Iran* 65 B8
Queanbeyan, *Australia* 91 F4
Québec, *Canada* 99 C5
Québec □, *Canada* 99 B6
Quedlinburg, *Germany* 18 D7
Queen Alexandra Ra., *Antarctica* 5 E11
Queen Charlotte, *Canada* 100 C2
Queen Charlotte Bay, *Falk. Is.* 128 D4
Queen Charlotte Is., *Canada* 100 C2
Queen Charlotte Str., *Canada* 100 C3
Queen Elizabeth Is., *Canada* 94 B10
Queen Elizabeth Nat. Park, *Uganda* 82 C3
Queen Mary Land, *Antarctica* 5 D7
Queen Maud G., *Canada* 96 B9
Queen Maud Land, *Antarctica* 5 D3
Queen Maud Mts., *Antarctica* 5 E13
Queens Chan., *Australia* 88 C4
Queenscliff, *Australia* 91 F3
Queensland □, *Australia* 90 C3
Queenstown, *Australia* 90 G4
Queenstown, *N.Z.* 87 L2
Queenstown, *S. Africa* 84 E4
Queets, *U.S.A.* 112 C2
Queguay Grande →, *Uruguay* 126 C4
Queimadas, *Brazil* 122 D4
Quela, *Angola* 80 F3
Quelimane, *Mozam.* 83 F4
Quelpart = Cheju Do, *S. Korea* 51 H14
Quemado, *N. Mex., U.S.A.* 111 J9
Quemado, *Tex., U.S.A.* 109 L4
Quemoy = Chinmen, *Taiwan* 53 E13
Quemú-Quemú, *Argentina* 126 D3
Quequén, *Argentina* 126 D4
Querco, *Peru* 124 C3
Querétaro, *Mexico* 114 C4
Querétaro □, *Mexico* 114 C5
Querfurt, *Germany* 18 D7
Quesada, *Spain* 29 H1
Queshan, *China* 50 H8
Quesnel, *Canada* 100 C4
Quesnel →, *Canada* 100 C4
Quesnel L., *Canada* 100 C4
Questa, *U.S.A.* 111 H11
Questembert, *France* 24 E4
Quetena, *Bolivia* 124 E4
Quetico Prov. Park, *Canada* 98 C1
Quetrequile, *Argentina* 128 B3
Quetta, *Pakistan* 62 D2
Quevedo, *Ecuador* 120 D2
Quezaltenango, *Guatemala* 116 D1
Quezon City, *Phil.* 55 D4
Qufār, *Si. Arabia* 64 E4
Qui Nhon, *Vietnam* 58 F7
Quibaxe, *Angola* 80 F2
Quibdo, *Colombia* 120 B2
Quiberon, *France* 24 E3
Quíbor, *Venezuela* 120 B4
Quick, *Canada* 100 C3
Quickborn, *Germany* 18 B5
Quiet L., *Canada* 100 A2
Quiévrain, *Belgium* 17 H3
Quiindy, *Paraguay* 126 B4
Quila, *Mexico* 114 C3
Quilán, C., *Chile* 128 B2
Quilcene, *U.S.A.* 112 C4
Quilengues, *Angola* 81 G2
Quilimarí, *Chile* 126 C1
Quilino, *Argentina* 126 C3
Quillabamba, *Peru* 124 C3
Quillacollo, *Bolivia* 124 D4
Quillagua, *Chile* 126 A2
Quillaicillo, *Chile* 126 C1
Quillan, *France* 26 F6
Quillebeuf-sur-Seine, *France* 24 C7
Quillota, *Chile* 126 C1
Quilmes, *Argentina* 126 C4
Quilon, *India* 60 Q10
Quilpie, *Australia* 91 D3
Quilpué, *Chile* 126 C1
Quilua, *Mozam.* 83 F4
Quime, *Bolivia* 124 D4
Quimilí, *Argentina* 126 B3
Quimper, *France* 24 D2
Quimperlé, *France* 24 E3
Quinault →, *U.S.A.* 112 C2
Quincemil, *Peru* 124 C3
Quincy, *Calif., U.S.A.* 112 F6
Quincy, *Fla., U.S.A.* 105 K3
Quincy, *Ill., U.S.A.* 108 F9
Quincy, *Mass., U.S.A.* 107 D14
Quincy, *Wash., U.S.A.* 110 C4
Quines, *Argentina* 126 C2
Quinga, *Mozam.* 83 F5
Quingey, *France* 25 E12
Quintana de la Serena, *Spain* 31 G5
Quintana Roo □, *Mexico* 115 D7
Quintanar de la Orden, *Spain* 28 F1
Quintanar de la Sierra, *Spain* 28 D2
Quintanar del Rey, *Spain* 29 F3
Quintero, *Chile* 126 C1
Quintin, *France* 24 D4
Quinto, *Spain* 28 D4
Quinyambie, *Australia* 91 E3
Quípar →, *Spain* 29 G3
Quipungo, *Angola* 81 G2
Quirihue, *Chile* 126 D1
Quirindi, *Australia* 91 E5
Quiroga, *Spain* 30 C3
Quiruvilca, *Peru* 124 B2
Quissac, *France* 27 E8
Quissanga, *Mozam.* 83 E5
Quitilipi, *Argentina* 126 B3
Quitman, *Ga., U.S.A.* 105 K4
Quitman, *Miss., U.S.A.* 105 J1
Quitman, *Tex., U.S.A.* 109 J7
Quito, *Ecuador* 120 D2
Quixadá, *Brazil* 122 B4
Quixaxe, *Mozam.* 83 F5
Quixeramobim, *Brazil* 122 C4
Qujing, *China* 52 E4
Qul'ân, Jazâ'ir, *Egypt* 76 C4
Qumbu, *S. Africa* 85 E4
Quneitra, *Syria* 69 B4
Qŭnghirot, *Uzbekistan* 44 E6
Quoin I., *Australia* 88 B4
Quoin Pt., *S. Africa* 84 E2
Quondong, *Australia* 91 E3
Quorn, *Australia* 91 E2
Qŭqon, *Uzbekistan* 44 E8
Qurein, *Sudan* 77 E3
Qurnat as Sawdā', *Lebanon* 69 A5
Qûs, *Egypt* 76 B3
Qusar, *Azerbaijan* 43 K9
Qusaybah, *Iraq* 67 E9
Quseir, *Egypt* 76 B3
Qūshchī, *Iran* 67 D11
Quthing, *Lesotho* 85 E4
Qūṭīābād, *Iran* 67 E13
Quwo, *China* 50 G6
Quyang, *China* 50 E8
Quynh Nhai, *Vietnam* 58 B4
Quzi, *China* 50 F4
Qvareli, *Georgia* 43 K7
Qytet Stalin = Kuçova, *Albania* 39 J2
Qyzylorda, *Kazakstan* 44 E7

R

Ra, Ko, *Thailand* 59 H2
Råå, *Sweden* 11 J6
Raahe, *Finland* 8 D21
Raalte, *Neths.* 16 D8
Raamsdonksveer, *Neths.* 17 E5
Raasay, *U.K.* 14 D2
Raasay, Sd. of, *U.K.* 14 D2
Rab, *Croatia* 33 D11
Raba, *Indonesia* 57 F5
Rába →, *Hungary* 21 H7
Rabaçal →, *Portugal* 30 D3
Rabah, *Nigeria* 79 C6
Rabai, *Kenya* 82 C4
Rabastens, *France* 26 E5
Rabastens-de-Bigorre, *France* 26 E4
Rabat, *Malta* 37 D1
Rabat, *Morocco* 74 B3
Rabaul, *Papua N. G.* 92 H7
Rabbit →, *Canada* 100 B3
Rabbit Lake, *Canada* 101 C7
Rabbitskin →, *Canada* 100 A4
Rabka, *Poland* 20 F9
Rābor, *Iran* 65 D8
Rácale, *Italy* 35 C11
Racalmuto, *Italy* 34 E6
Racconigi, *Italy* 32 D4
Race, C., *Canada* 99 C9
Rach Gia, *Vietnam* 59 G5
Raciąż, *Poland* 20 C10
Racibórz, *Poland* 20 E8
Racine, *U.S.A.* 104 D2
Rackerby, *U.S.A.* 112 F5
Radama, Nosy, *Madag.* 85 A8
Radama, Saikanosy, *Madag.* 85 A8
Rădăuţi, *Romania* 38 B8
Radbuza →, *Czech.* 20 F3
Radeburg, *Germany* 18 D9
Radeče, *Slovenia* 33 B12
Radekhiv, *Ukraine* 41 G3
Radekhov = Radekhiv, *Ukraine* 41 G3
Radford, *U.S.A.* 104 G5
Radhanpur, *India* 62 H4
Radiska →, *Macedonia* 39 H3
Radisson, *Canada* 101 C7
Radium Hot Springs, *Canada* 100 C5
Radna, *Romania* 38 C4
Radnor Forest, *U.K.* 13 E4
Radolfzell, *Germany* 19 H4
Radom, *Poland* 20 D11
Radomir, *Bulgaria* 38 G6
Radomsko, *Poland* 20 D9
Radomyshl, *Ukraine* 41 G5
Radoviš, *Macedonia* 39 H5
Radovljica, *Slovenia* 33 B11
Radstock, *U.K.* 13 F5
Radstock, C., *Australia* 91 E1
Răducăneni, *Romania* 38 C10
Radviliškis, *Lithuania* 9 J20
Radville, *Canada* 101 D8
Rae, *Canada* 100 A5
Rae Bareli, *India* 63 F9
Rae Isthmus, *Canada* 97 B11
Raeren, *Belgium* 17 G8
Raeside, L., *Australia* 89 E3
Raetihi, *N.Z.* 87 H5
Rafaela, *Argentina* 126 C3
Rafah, *Gaza Strip* 69 D3
Rafai, *C.A.R.* 82 B1
Raffadali, *Italy* 34 E6
Rafḥā, *Si. Arabia* 64 D4
Rafsanjān, *Iran* 65 D8
Raft Pt., *Australia* 88 C3
Ragachow, *Belarus* 41 F6
Ragag, *Sudan* 77 E1
Ragama, *Sri Lanka* 60 R11
Ragged, Mt., *Australia* 89 F3
Raglan, *Australia* 90 C5
Raglan, *N.Z.* 87 G5
Ragunda, *Sweden* 10 A10
Ragusa, *Italy* 35 F7
Raha, *Indonesia* 57 E6
Rahad, Nahr ed →, *Sudan* 77 E3
Rahad al Bardī, *Sudan* 73 F9
Rahaeng = Tak, *Thailand* 58 D2
Rahden, *Germany* 18 C4
Raheita, *Eritrea* 77 E5
Raḥīmah, *Si. Arabia* 65 E6
Rahimyar Khan, *Pakistan* 62 E4
Rāhjerd, *Iran* 65 C6
Raichur, *India* 60 L10
Raiganj, *India* 63 G13
Raigarh, *India* 61 J13
Raijua, *Indonesia* 57 F6
Railton, *Australia* 90 G4
Rainbow Lake, *Canada* 100 B5
Rainier, *U.S.A.* 112 D4
Rainier, Mt., *U.S.A.* 112 D5
Rainy L., *Canada* 101 D10
Rainy River, *Canada* 101 D10
Raippaluoto, *Finland* 8 E19
Raipur, *India* 61 J12
Raisio, *Finland* 9 F20
Raj Nandgaon, *India* 61 J12
Raja, Ujung, *Indonesia* 56 D1
Raja Ampat, Kepulauan, *Indonesia* 57 E7
Rajahmundry, *India* 61 L12
Rajang →, *Malaysia* 56 D4
Rajapalaiyam, *India* 60 Q10
Rajasthan □, *India* 62 F5
Rajasthan Canal, *India* 62 E5
Rajauri, *India* 63 C6
Rajgarh, *Mad. P., India* 62 G7
Rajgarh, *Raj., India* 62 E6
Rajhenburg, *Slovenia* 33 B12
Rajkot, *India* 62 H4
Rajmahal Hills, *India* 63 G12
Rajpipla, *India* 60 J8
Rajpura, *India* 62 D7
Rajshahi, *Bangla.* 61 G16
Rajshahi □, *Bangla.* 63 G13
Rakaia, *N.Z.* 87 K4
Rakaia →, *N.Z.* 87 K4
Rakan, Ra's, *Qatar* 65 E6
Rakaposhi, *Pakistan* 63 A6
Rakata, Pulau, *Indonesia* 56 F3
Rakhiv, *Ukraine* 41 H3
Rakhni, *Pakistan* 62 D3
Rakitnoye, *Russia* 48 B7
Rakkestad, *Norway* 10 E5
Rakops, *Botswana* 84 C3
Rákospalota, *Hungary* 21 H9

Rakovica, Croatia 33 D12
Rakovník, Czech. 20 E3
Rakovski, Bulgaria 38 G7
Rakvere, Estonia 9 G22
Raleigh, U.S.A. 105 H6
Raleigh B., U.S.A. 105 H7
Ralja, Serbia, Yug. 21 L10
Ralls, U.S.A. 109 J4
Ram →, Canada 100 A4
Râm Allâh, West Bank 69 D4
Ram Hd., Australia 91 F4
Rama, Nic. 116 D3
Ramacca, Italy 35 E7
Ramales de la Victoria, Spain 28 B1
Ramalho, Serra do, Brazil 123 D3
Raman, Thailand 59 J3
Ramanathapuram, India 60 Q11
Ramanetaka, B. de, Madag. 85 A8
Ramat Gan, Israel 69 C3
Ramatlhabama, S. Africa 84 D4
Ramban, India 63 C6
Rambervillers, France 25 D13
Rambipuji, Indonesia 57 H15
Rambouillet, France 25 D8
Ramea, Canada 99 C8
Ramechhap, Nepal 63 F12
Ramelau, Indonesia 57 F7
Ramenskoye, Russia 42 C4
Ramgarh, Bihar, India 63 H11
Ramgarh, Raj., India 62 F6
Ramgarh, Raj., India 62 F4
Rāmhormoz, Iran 65 D6
Ramīān, Iran 65 B7
Ramingining, Australia 90 A2
Ramla, Israel 69 D3
Ramlu, Eritrea 77 E5
Ramme, Denmark 11 H2
Ramnad = Ramanathapuram, India 60 Q11
Ramnagar, India 63 C6
Ramnäs, Sweden 10 E10
Ramon, Russia 42 E4
Ramona, U.S.A. 113 M10
Ramore, Canada 98 C3
Ramotswa, Botswana 84 C4
Rampur, H.P., India 62 D7
Rampur, Mad. P., India 62 H5
Rampur, Ut. P., India 63 E8
Rampur Hat, India 63 G12
Rampura, India 62 G6
Ramree I. = Ramree Kyun, Burma 61 K18
Ramree Kyun, Burma 61 K18
Rāmsar, Iran 65 B6
Ramsel, Belgium 17 F5
Ramsey, Canada 98 C3
Ramsey, U.K. 12 C3
Ramsgate, U.K. 13 F9
Ramsjö, Sweden 10 B9
Ramtek, India 60 J11
Ramvik, Sweden 10 B11
Ranaghat, India 63 H13
Ranahu, Pakistan 62 G3
Ranau, Malaysia 56 C5
Rancagua, Chile 126 C1
Rance, Belgium 17 H4
Rance →, France 24 D5
Rance, Barrage de la, France 24 D4
Rancharia, Brazil 123 F1
Rancheria →, Canada 100 A3
Ranchester, U.S.A. 110 D10
Ranchi, India 63 H11
Rancho Cucamonga, U.S.A. 113 L9
Ranco, L., Chile 128 B2
Randan, France 26 B7
Randazzo, Italy 35 E7
Randers, Denmark 11 H4
Randers Fjord, Denmark 11 H4
Randfontein, S. Africa 85 D4
Randle, U.S.A. 112 D5
Randolph, Mass., U.S.A. 107 D13
Randolph, N.Y., U.S.A. 106 D6
Randolph, Utah, U.S.A. 110 F8
Randolph, Vt., U.S.A. 107 C12
Randsfjorden, Norway 10 D4
Råne älv →, Sweden 8 D20
Rangae, Thailand 59 J3
Rangaunu B., N.Z. 87 F4
Rångedala, Sweden 11 G7
Rangeley, U.S.A. 107 B14
Rangely, U.S.A. 110 F9
Ranger, U.S.A. 109 J5
Rangia, India 61 F17
Rangiora, N.Z. 87 K4
Rangitaiki →, N.Z. 87 G6
Rangitata →, N.Z. 87 K3
Rangkasbitung, Indonesia 57 G12
Rangon →, Burma 61 L20
Rangoon, Burma 61 L20
Rangpur, Bangla. 61 G16
Rangsit, Thailand 58 F3
Ranibennur, India 60 M9
Raniganj, India 63 H12
Raniwara, India 60 G8
Rāniyah, Iraq 64 B5
Ranken →, Australia 90 C2
Rankin, U.S.A. 109 K4
Rankin Inlet, Canada 96 B10
Rankins Springs, Australia 91 E4
Rannoch, L., U.K. 14 E4
Rannoch Moor, U.K. 14 E4
Ranobe, Helodranon' i, Madag. 85 C7
Ranohira, Madag. 85 C8
Ranomafana, Toamasina, Madag. 85 B8
Ranomafana, Toliara, Madag. 85 C8
Ranong, Thailand 59 H2
Rānsa, Iran 65 C6
Ransiki, Indonesia 57 E8
Rantau, Indonesia 56 E5
Rantauprapat, Indonesia 56 D1
Rantemario, Indonesia 57 E5
Rantoul, U.S.A. 104 E1
Ranum, Denmark 11 H3
Raon l'Étape, France 25 D13
Raoui, Erg er, Algeria 75 C4
Raoyang, China 50 E8
Rapa, Pac. Oc. 93 K13
Rapallo, Italy 32 D6
Rāpch, Iran 65 E8
Rapid →, Canada 100 B3
Rapid City, U.S.A. 108 D3
Rapid River, U.S.A. 104 C2
Rapides des Joachims, Canada 98 C4
Rapla, Estonia 9 G21
Rapperswil, Switz. 23 B7
Rapu Rapu I., Phil. 55 E6
Rarotonga, Cook Is. 93 K12
Ra's al 'Ayn, Syria 67 D9
Ra's al Khaymah, U.A.E. 65 E8
Ra's al-Unuf, Libya 73 B8
Ra's an Naqb, Jordan 69 F4
Ras Bânâs, Egypt 76 C4
Ras Dashen, Ethiopia 77 E4
Ras el Ma, Algeria 75 B4
Râs Ghârib, Egypt 76 J8
Ras Mallap, Egypt 76 J8
Râs Timirist, Mauritania 78 B1
Rasa, Punta, Argentina 128 B4
Rasca, Pta. de la, Canary Is. 36 G3
Raseiniai, Lithuania 9 J20
Rashad, Sudan 77 E3
Rashîd, Egypt 76 H7
Rashîd, Masabb, Egypt 76 H7
Rasht, Iran 67 D13
Rasi Salai, Thailand 58 E5
Raška, Serbia, Yug. 21 M10
Rason L., Australia 89 E3
Raşova, Romania 38 E10
Rasra, India 63 G10
Rass el Oued, Algeria 75 A6
Rasskazovo, Russia 42 D5
Rastatt, Germany 19 G4
Rat Buri, Thailand 58 F2
Rat Islands, U.S.A. 96 C1
Rat River, Canada 100 A6
Ratangarh, India 62 E6
Raţāwī, Iraq 64 D5
Rath, India 63 G8
Rath Luirc, Ireland 15 D3
Rathdrum, Ireland 15 D5
Rathenow, Germany 18 C8
Rathkeale, Ireland 15 D3
Rathlin I., U.K. 15 A5
Rathlin O'Birne I., Ireland 15 B3
Ratibor = Racibórz, Poland 20 E8
Ratlam, India 62 H6
Ratnagiri, India 60 L8
Raton, U.S.A. 109 G2
Rattaphum, Thailand 59 J3
Rattray Hd., U.K. 14 D7
Ratz, Mt., Canada 100 B2
Ratzeburg, Germany 18 B6
Raub, Malaysia 59 L3
Rauch, Argentina 126 D4
Raufarhöfn, Iceland 8 C6
Raufoss, Norway 10 D4
Raukumara Ra., N.Z. 87 H6
Raul Soares, Brazil 123 F3
Rauland, Norway 10 E2
Rauma, Finland 9 F19
Rauma →, Norway 10 B1
Raurkela, India 63 H11
Rausu-Dake, Japan 48 B12
Rava-Ruska, Ukraine 41 G2
Rava Russkaya = Rava-Ruska, Ukraine 41 G2
Ravānsar, Iran 67 E12
Ravanusa, Italy 34 E6
Rāvar, Iran 65 D8
Ravels, Belgium 17 F6
Ravena, U.S.A. 107 D11
Ravenna, Italy 33 D9
Ravenna, Nebr., U.S.A. 108 E5
Ravenna, Ohio, U.S.A. 106 E3
Ravensburg, Germany 19 H5
Ravenshoe, Australia 90 B4
Ravenstein, Neths. 16 E7
Ravensthorpe, Australia 89 F3
Ravenswood, Australia 90 C4
Ravenswood, U.S.A. 104 F5
Ravi →, Pakistan 62 D4
Ravna Gora, Croatia 33 C11
Rawa Mazowiecka, Poland 20 D10
Rawalpindi, Pakistan 62 C5
Rawāndūz, Iraq 67 D11
Rawang, Malaysia 59 L3
Rawdon, Canada 98 C5
Rawene, N.Z. 87 F4
Rawicz, Poland 20 D6
Rawlinna, Australia 89 F4
Rawlins, U.S.A. 110 F10
Rawlinson Ra., Australia 89 D4
Rawson, Argentina 128 B3
Ray, U.S.A. 108 A3
Ray, C., Canada 99 C8
Rayadurg, India 60 M10
Rayagada, India 61 K13
Raychikhinsk, Russia 45 E13
Rāyen, Iran 65 D8
Raymond, Canada 100 D6
Raymond, Calif., U.S.A. 112 H7
Raymond, Wash., U.S.A. 112 D3
Raymondville, U.S.A. 109 M6
Raymore, Canada 101 C8
Rayne, U.S.A. 109 K8
Rayón, Mexico 114 B2
Rayong, Thailand 58 F3
Rayville, U.S.A. 109 J9
Raz, Pte. du, France 24 D2
Razan, Iran 67 E13
Ražana, Serbia, Yug. 21 L9
Ražanj, Serbia, Yug. 21 M11
Razdel'naya = Rozdilna, Ukraine 41 J6
Razdolnoye, Russia 48 C5
Razdolnoye, Ukraine 41 K7
Razeh, Iran 65 C6
Razelm, Lacul, Romania 38 E12
Razgrad, Bulgaria 38 F9
Razmak, Pakistan 62 C3
Ré, I. de, France 26 B2
Reading, U.K. 13 F7
Reading, U.S.A. 107 F9
Real, Cordillera, Bolivia 124 D4
Realicó, Argentina 126 D3
Réalmont, France 26 E6
Reata, Mexico 114 B4
Rebais, France 25 D10
Rebecca, L., Australia 89 F3
Rebi, Indonesia 57 F8
Rebiana, Libya 73 D9
Rebun-Tō, Japan 48 B10
Recanati, Italy 33 E10
Recaş, Romania 38 D4
Recherche, Arch. of the, Australia 89 F3
Recht, Belgium 17 H8
Rechytsa, Belarus 41 F6
Recife, Brazil 122 C5
Recklinghausen, Germany 17 E10
Reconquista, Argentina 126 B4
Recreio, Brazil 125 B6
Recreo, Argentina 126 B2
Recuay, Peru 124 B2
Red →, La., U.S.A. 109 K9
Red →, N. Dak., U.S.A. 108 A6
Red Bank, U.S.A. 107 F10
Red Bay, Canada 99 B8
Red Bluff, U.S.A. 110 F2
Red Bluff L., U.S.A. 109 K3
Red Cliffs, Australia 91 E3
Red Cloud, U.S.A. 108 E5
Red Deer, Canada 100 C6
Red Deer →, Alta., Canada 101 C6
Red Deer →, Man., Canada 101 C8
Red Deer L., Canada 101 C8
Red Indian L., Canada 99 C8
Red Lake, Canada 101 C10
Red Lake Falls, U.S.A. 108 B6
Red Lodge, U.S.A. 110 D9
Red Mountain, U.S.A. 113 K9
Red Oak, U.S.A. 108 E7
Red Rock, Canada 98 C2
Red Rock, L., U.S.A. 108 E8
Red Rocks Pt., Australia 89 F4
Red Sea, Asia 68 C2
Red Slate Mt., U.S.A. 112 H8
Red Sucker L., Canada 101 C10
Red Tower Pass = Turnu Roşu, P., Romania 38 D7
Red Wing, U.S.A. 108 C8
Rédange, Lux. 17 J7
Redbridge, U.K. 13 F8
Redcar, U.K. 12 C6
Redcar & Cleveland □, U.K. 12 C6
Redcliff, Canada 101 C6
Redcliffe, Australia 91 D5
Redcliffe, Mt., Australia 89 E3
Reddersburg, S. Africa 84 D4
Redding, U.S.A. 110 F2
Redditch, U.K. 13 E6
Redenção, Brazil 122 B4
Redfield, U.S.A. 108 C5
Redkino, Russia 42 B3
Redknife →, Canada 100 A5
Redlands, U.S.A. 113 M9
Redmond, Australia 89 F2
Redmond, Oreg., U.S.A. 110 D3
Redmond, Wash., U.S.A. 112 C4
Redon, France 24 E4
Redonda, Antigua 117 C7
Redondela, Spain 30 C2
Redondo, Portugal 31 G3
Redondo Beach, U.S.A. 113 M8
Redrock Pt., Canada 100 A5
Redruth, U.K. 13 G2
Redvers, Canada 101 D8
Redwater, Canada 100 C6
Redwood, U.S.A. 107 B9
Redwood City, U.S.A. 111 H2
Redwood Falls, U.S.A. 108 C7
Ree, L., Ireland 15 C4
Reed, L., Canada 101 C8
Reed City, U.S.A. 104 D3
Reeder, U.S.A. 108 B3
Reedley, U.S.A. 111 H4
Reedsburg, U.S.A. 108 D9
Reedsport, U.S.A. 110 E1
Reefton, N.Z. 87 K3
Refahiye, Turkey 67 C8
Refugio, U.S.A. 109 L6
Rega →, Poland 20 A5
Regalbuto, Italy 35 E7
Regen, Germany 19 G9
Regen →, Germany 19 F8
Regeneração, Brazil 122 C3
Regensburg, Germany 19 F8
Regensdorf, Switz. 23 B6
Réggio di Calábria, Italy 35 D8
Réggio nell'Emília, Italy 32 D7
Regina, Canada 101 C8
Régina, Fr. Guiana 121 C7
Registro, Brazil 127 A6
Reguengos de Monsaraz, Portugal 31 G3
Rehar →, India 63 H10
Rehoboth, Namibia 84 C2
Rehovot, Israel 69 D3
Rei-Bouba, Cameroon 73 G7
Reichenbach, Germany 18 E8
Reichenbach, Switz. 22 C5
Reid, Australia 89 F4
Reid River, Australia 90 B4
Reiden, Switz. 22 B5
Reidsville, U.S.A. 105 G6
Reigate, U.K. 13 F7
Reillo, Spain 28 F3
Reims, France 25 C11
Reina Adelaida, Arch., Chile 128 D2
Reinach, Aargau, Switz. 22 B6
Reinach, Basel, Switz. 22 B5
Reinbeck, U.S.A. 108 D8
Reindeer →, Canada 101 B8
Reindeer I., Canada 101 C9
Reindeer L., Canada 101 B8
Reinga, C., N.Z. 87 F4
Reinosa, Spain 30 B6
Reinosa, Paso, Spain 30 C6
Reitdiep, Neths. 16 B8
Reitz, S. Africa 85 D4
Reivilo, S. Africa 84 D3
Rejmyre, Sweden 11 F9
Reka →, Slovenia 33 C11
Rekinniki, Russia 45 C17
Reliance, Canada 101 A7
Remad, Oued →, Algeria 75 B4
Rémalard, France 24 D7
Remarkable, Mt., Australia 91 E2
Rembang, Indonesia 57 G14
Remchi, Algeria 75 A4
Remedios, Colombia 120 B3
Remedios, Panama 116 E3
Remeshk, Iran 65 E8
Remich, Lux. 17 J8
Rémire, Fr. Guiana 121 C7
Remiremont, France 25 D13
Remo, Ethiopia 77 F5
Remontnoye, Russia 43 G6
Remoulins, France 27 E8
Remscheid, Germany 18 D3
Ren Xian, China 50 F8
Renascença, Brazil 120 D4
Rende, Italy 35 C9
Rendeux, Belgium 17 H7
Rendína, Greece 39 K4
Rendsburg, Germany 18 A5
Rene, Russia 45 C19
Renfrew, Canada 98 C4
Renfrew, U.K. 14 F4
Renfrewshire □, U.K. 14 F4
Rengat, Indonesia 56 E2
Rengo, Chile 126 C1
Renhua, China 53 E9
Renhuai, China 52 D6
Reni, Ukraine 41 K5
Renk, Sudan 77 E3
Renkum, Neths. 16 E7
Renmark, Australia 91 E3
Rennell Sd., Canada 100 C2
Renner Springs T.O., Australia 90 B1
Rennes, France 24 D5
Rennes, Bassin de, France 24 E5
Reno, U.S.A. 112 F7
Reno →, Italy 33 D9
Renovo, U.S.A. 106 E7
Renqiu, China 50 E9
Rensselaer, Ind., U.S.A. 104 E2
Rensselaer, N.Y., U.S.A. 107 D11
Rentería, Spain 28 B3
Renton, U.S.A. 112 C4
Réo, Burkina Faso 78 C4
Reotipur, India 63 G10
Republic, Mich., U.S.A. 104 B2
Republic, Wash., U.S.A. 110 B4
Republican →, U.S.A. 108 F6
Republican City, U.S.A. 108 E5
Republiek, Surinam 121 B6
Repulse Bay, Canada 97 B11
Requena, Peru 124 B3
Requena, Spain 29 F3
Resadiye = Datça, Turkey 66 D2
Reşadiye, Turkey 66 B7
Resele, Sweden 10 A11
Reserve, Canada 101 C8
Reserve, U.S.A. 111 K9
Resht = Rasht, Iran 67 D13
Resistencia, Argentina 126 B4
Reşiţa, Romania 38 D4
Resolution I., Canada 97 B13
Resolution I., N.Z. 87 L1
Resplandes, Brazil 122 C2
Resplendor, Brazil 123 E3
Ressano Garcia, Mozam. 85 D5
Reston, Canada 101 D8
Retalhuleu, Guatemala 116 D1
Reteag, Romania 38 B7
Retenue, L. de, Zaïre 83 E2
Retford, U.K. 12 D7
Rethel, France 25 C11
Rethem, Germany 18 C5
Réthímnon, Greece 37 D6
Réthímnon □, Greece 37 D6
Retiche, Alpi, Switz. 23 D10
Retie, Belgium 17 F6
Retiers, France 24 E5
Retortillo, Spain 30 E4
Reuland, Belgium 17 H8
Réunion ■, Ind. Oc. 70 J9
Reus, Spain 28 D6
Reusel, Neths. 17 F6
Reuss →, Switz. 23 B6
Reutlingen, Germany 19 G5
Reutte, Austria 19 H6
Reuver, Neths. 17 F8
Reval = Tallinn, Estonia 9 G21
Revel, France 26 E6
Revelganj, India 63 G11
Revelstoke, Canada 100 C5
Reventazón, Peru 124 B1
Revigny-sur-Ornain, France 25 D11
Revilla Gigedo, Is., Pac. Oc. 94 H8
Revillagigedo I., U.S.A. 100 B2
Revin, France 25 C11
Revuè →, Mozam. 83 F3
Rewa, India 63 G9
Rewa →, Guyana 121 C6
Rewari, India 62 E7
Rexburg, U.S.A. 110 E8
Rey, Iran 65 C6
Rey, Rio del →, Nigeria 79 E6
Rey Malabo, Eq. Guin. 79 E6
Reyðarfjörður, Iceland 8 D6
Reyes, Bolivia 124 C4
Reyes, Pt., U.S.A. 112 H3
Reyhanlı, Turkey 66 D7
Reykjahlið, Iceland 8 D5
Reykjanes, Iceland 8 E2
Reykjavík, Iceland 8 D3
Reynolds, Canada 101 D9
Reynolds Ra., Australia 88 D5
Reynoldsville, U.S.A. 106 E6
Reynosa, Mexico 115 B5
Rēzekne, Latvia 9 H22
Rezvān, Iran 65 E8
Rharis, O. →, Algeria 75 C6
Rhayader, U.K. 13 E4
Rheden, Neths. 16 D8
Rhein, Canada 101 C8
Rhein →, Europe 16 E8
Rhein-Main-Donau-Kanal, Germany 19 F7
Rheinbach, Germany 18 E2
Rheine, Germany 18 C3
Rheineck, Switz. 23 B9
Rheinfelden, Switz. 22 A5
Rheinland-Pfalz □, Germany 19 E2
Rheinsberg, Germany 18 B8
Rheinwaldhorn, Switz. 23 D8
Rhenen, Neths. 16 E7
Rheriss, Oued →, Morocco 74 B4
Rheydt, Germany 18 D2
Rhin = Rhein →, Europe 16 E8
Rhinau, France 25 D14
Rhine = Rhein →, Europe 16 E8
Rhineland-Palatinate □ = Rheinland-Pfalz □, Germany 19 E2
Rhinelander, U.S.A. 108 C10
Rhino Camp, Uganda 82 B3
Rhir, Cap, Morocco 74 B3
Rhisnes, Belgium 17 G5
Rho, Italy 32 C6
Rhode Island □, U.S.A. 107 E13
Rhodes = Ródhos, Greece 37 C10
Rhodesia = Zimbabwe ■, Africa 83 F2
Rhodope Mts. = Rhodopi Planina, Bulgaria 39 H7
Rhodopi Planina, Bulgaria 39 H7
Rhön = Hohe Rhön, Germany 19 E5
Rhondda, U.K. 13 F4
Rhondda Cynon Taff □, U.K. 13 F4
Rhône □, France 27 C8
Rhône →, France 27 E8
Rhum, U.K. 14 E2
Rhyl, U.K. 12 D4
Rhymney, U.K. 13 F4
Ri-Aba, Eq. Guin. 79 E6
Riachão, Brazil 122 C2
Riacho de Santana, Brazil 123 D3
Rialma, Brazil 123 E2
Riaño, Spain 30 C5
Rians, France 27 E9
Riansares →, Spain 28 F1
Riasi, India 63 C6
Riau □, Indonesia 56 D2
Riau, Kepulauan, Indonesia 56 D2
Riau Arch. = Riau, Kepulauan, Indonesia 56 D2
Riaza, Spain 28 D1
Riaza →, Spain 28 D1
Riba de Saelices, Spain 28 E2
Ribadavia, Spain 30 C2
Ribadeo, Spain 30 B3
Ribadesella, Spain 30 B5

Ribamar, *Brazil* 122 B3
Ribas, *Spain* 28 C7
Ribas do Rio Pardo, *Brazil* 125 E7
Ribble →, *U.K.* 12 C5
Ribe, *Denmark* 11 J2
Ribeauvillé, *France* 25 D14
Ribécourt, *France* 25 C9
Ribeira, *Spain* 30 C2
Ribeira Brava, *Madeira* 36 D2
Ribeira do Pombal, *Brazil* 122 D4
Ribeirão Prêto, *Brazil* 127 A6
Ribeiro Gonçalves, *Brazil* 122 C2
Ribemont, *France* 25 C10
Ribera, *Italy* 34 E6
Ribérac, *France* 26 C4
Riberalta, *Bolivia* 125 C4
Ribnica, *Slovenia* 33 C11
Rîbniţa, *Moldova* 41 J5
Ribnitz-Damgarten, *Germany* 18 A8
Riccarton, *N.Z.* 87 K4
Riccia, *Italy* 35 A7
Riccione, *Italy* 33 D9
Rice, *U.S.A.* 113 L12
Rice L., *Canada* 106 B6
Rice Lake, *U.S.A.* 108 C9
Rich, *Morocco* 74 B4
Rich Hill, *U.S.A.* 109 F7
Richards Bay, *S. Africa* 85 D5
Richards L., *Canada* 101 B7
Richardson →, *Canada* 101 B6
Richardson Springs, *U.S.A.* 112 F5
Richardton, *U.S.A.* 108 B3
Riche, C., *Australia* 89 F2
Richelieu, *France* 24 E7
Richey, *U.S.A.* 108 B2
Richfield, *Idaho, U.S.A.* 110 E6
Richfield, *Utah, U.S.A.* 111 G8
Richford, *U.S.A.* 107 B12
Richibucto, *Canada* 99 C7
Richland, *Ga., U.S.A.* 105 J3
Richland, *Oreg., U.S.A.* 110 D5
Richland, *Wash., U.S.A.* 110 C4
Richland Center, *U.S.A.* 108 D9
Richlands, *U.S.A.* 104 G5
Richmond, *N.S.W., Australia* 91 E5
Richmond, *Queens., Australia* 90 C3
Richmond, *N.Z.* 87 J4
Richmond, *U.K.* 12 C6
Richmond, *Calif., U.S.A.* 112 H4
Richmond, *Ind., U.S.A.* 104 F3
Richmond, *Ky., U.S.A.* 104 G3
Richmond, *Mich., U.S.A.* 106 D2
Richmond, *Mo., U.S.A.* 108 F8
Richmond, *Tex., U.S.A.* 109 L7
Richmond, *Utah, U.S.A.* 110 F8
Richmond, *Va., U.S.A.* 104 G7
Richmond Ra., *Australia* 91 D5
Richmond-upon-Thames, *U.K.* 13 F7
Richterswil, *Switz.* 23 B7
Richton, *U.S.A.* 105 K1
Richwood, *U.S.A.* 104 F5
Ricla, *Spain* 28 D3
Ridder = Leninogorsk, *Kazakstan* 44 D9
Ridderkerk, *Neths.* 16 E5
Riddes, *Switz.* 22 D4
Ridgecrest, *U.S.A.* 113 K9
Ridgedale, *Canada* 101 C8
Ridgefield, *U.S.A.* 112 E4
Ridgeland, *U.S.A.* 105 J5
Ridgelands, *Australia* 90 C5
Ridgetown, *Canada* 98 D3
Ridgewood, *U.S.A.* 107 F10
Ridgway, *U.S.A.* 106 E6
Riding Mountain Nat. Park, *Canada* 101 C8
Ridley, Mt., *Australia* 89 F3
Ried, *Austria* 21 G3
Riedlingen, *Germany* 19 G5
Riel, *Neths.* 17 E6
Rienza →, *Italy* 33 B8
Riesa, *Germany* 18 D9
Riesco, I., *Chile* 128 D2
Riesi, *Italy* 35 E7
Riet →, *S. Africa* 84 D3
Rieti, *Italy* 33 F9
Rieupeyroux, *France* 26 D6
Riez, *France* 27 E10
Riffe L., *U.S.A.* 112 D4
Rifle, *U.S.A.* 110 G10
Rift Valley □, *Kenya* 82 B4
Rig Rig, *Chad* 73 F7
Riga, *Latvia* 9 H21
Riga, G. of, *Latvia* 9 H20
Rigān, *Iran* 65 D8
Rīgas Jūras Līcis = Riga, G. of, *Latvia* 9 H20
Rigaud, *Canada* 107 A10
Rigby, *U.S.A.* 110 E8
Rigestān □, *Afghan.* 60 D4
Riggins, *U.S.A.* 110 D5
Rignac, *France* 26 D6
Rigolet, *Canada* 99 B8
Riihimäki, *Finland* 9 F21
Riiser-Larsen-halvøya, *Antarctica* 5 C4
Rijau, *Nigeria* 79 C6
Rijeka, *Croatia* 33 C11
Rijen, *Neths.* 17 E5
Rijkevorsel, *Belgium* 17 F5
Rijn →, *Neths.* 16 D4
Rijnsberg, *Neths.* 16 D4
Rijsbergen, *Neths.* 17 E5
Rijssen, *Neths.* 16 D9
Rijswijk, *Neths.* 16 D4
Rike, *Ethiopia* 77 E4
Rikuzentakada, *Japan* 48 E10
Rila Planina, *Bulgaria* 38 G6
Riley, *U.S.A.* 110 E4
Rima →, *Nigeria* 79 C6
Rimah, Wadi ar →, *Si. Arabia* 64 E4
Rimavská Sobota, *Slovak Rep.* 21 G10
Rimbey, *Canada* 100 C6
Rimbo, *Sweden* 10 E12
Rimi, *Nigeria* 79 C6
Rímini, *Italy* 33 D9
Rîmnicu Sărat, *Romania* 38 D10
Rîmnicu Vîlcea, *Romania* 38 D7
Rimouski, *Canada* 99 C6
Rimrock, *U.S.A.* 112 D5
Rinca, *Indonesia* 57 F5
Rincón de Romos, *Mexico* 114 C4
Rinconada, *Argentina* 126 A2
Ringarum, *Sweden* 11 F10
Ringe, *Denmark* 11 J4
Ringim, *Nigeria* 79 C6
Ringkøbing, *Denmark* 11 H2
Ringling, *U.S.A.* 110 C8
Ringsaker, *Norway* 10 D4
Ringsted, *Denmark* 11 J5
Ringvassøy, *Norway* 8 B18
Rinjani, *Indonesia* 56 F5
Rinteln, *Germany* 18 C5
Río, Punta del, *Spain* 29 J2
Rio Branco, *Brazil* 124 B4
Río Branco, *Uruguay* 127 C5
Rio Brilhante, *Brazil* 127 A5
Río Bueno, *Chile* 128 B2
Río Chico, *Venezuela* 120 A4
Rio Claro, *Brazil* 127 A6
Rio Claro, *Trin. & Tob.* 117 D7
Río Colorado, *Argentina* 128 A4
Río Cuarto, *Argentina* 126 C3
Rio das Pedras, *Mozam.* 85 C6
Rio de Contas, *Brazil* 123 D3
Rio de Janeiro, *Brazil* 123 F3
Rio de Janeiro □, *Brazil* 123 F3
Rio do Prado, *Brazil* 123 E3
Rio do Sul, *Brazil* 127 B6
Río Gallegos, *Argentina* 128 D3
Río Grande, *Argentina* 128 D3
Río Grande, *Bolivia* 124 E4
Rio Grande, *Brazil* 127 C5
Río Grande, *Mexico* 114 C4
Río Grande, *Nic.* 116 D3
Rio Grande →, *U.S.A.* 109 N6
Rio Grande City, *U.S.A.* 109 M5
Río Grande del Norte →, *N. Amer.* 103 E7
Rio Grande do Norte □, *Brazil* 122 C4
Rio Grande do Sul □, *Brazil* 127 C5
Río Hato, *Panama* 116 E3
Río Lagartos, *Mexico* 115 C7
Rio Largo, *Brazil* 122 C4
Rio Maior, *Portugal* 31 F2
Rio Marina, *Italy* 32 F7
Río Mayo, *Argentina* 128 C2
Río Mulatos, *Bolivia* 124 D4
Río Muni = Mbini □, *Eq. Guin.* 80 D2
Rio Negro, *Brazil* 127 B6
Rio Negro, *Chile* 128 B2
Rio Negro, Pantanal do, *Brazil* 125 D6
Rio Pardo, *Brazil* 127 C5
Río Pico, *Argentina* 128 B2
Rio Real, *Brazil* 123 D4
Río Segundo, *Argentina* 126 C3
Río Tercero, *Argentina* 126 C3
Rio Tinto, *Brazil* 122 C4
Rio Tinto, *Portugal* 30 D2
Rio Verde, *Brazil* 123 E1
Río Verde, *Mexico* 115 C5
Rio Verde de Mato Grosso, *Brazil* 125 D7
Rio Vista, *U.S.A.* 112 G5
Ríobamba, *Ecuador* 120 D2
Ríohacha, *Colombia* 120 A3
Rioja, *Peru* 124 B2
Riom, *France* 26 C7
Riom-ès-Montagnes, *France* 26 C6
Rion-des-Landes, *France* 26 E3
Rionegro, *Colombia* 120 B2
Rionero in Vúlture, *Italy* 35 B8
Rioni →, *Georgia* 43 J5
Rios, *Spain* 30 D3
Ríosucio, *Caldas, Colombia* 120 B2
Ríosucio, *Choco, Colombia* 120 B2
Riou L., *Canada* 101 B7
Rioz, *France* 25 E13
Riozinho →, *Brazil* 120 D4
Riparia, Dora →, *Italy* 32 C4
Ripatransone, *Italy* 33 F10
Ripley, *Canada* 106 B3
Ripley, *Calif., U.S.A.* 113 M12
Ripley, *N.Y., U.S.A.* 106 D5
Ripley, *Tenn., U.S.A.* 109 H10
Ripoll, *Spain* 28 C7
Ripon, *U.K.* 12 C6
Ripon, *Calif., U.S.A.* 112 H5
Ripon, *Wis., U.S.A.* 104 D1
Riposto, *Italy* 35 E8
Risalpur, *Pakistan* 62 B4
Risan, *Montenegro, Yug.* 21 N8
Risaralda □, *Colombia* 120 B2
Riscle, *France* 26 E3
Rishā', W. ar →, *Si. Arabia* 64 E5
Rishiri-Tō, *Japan* 48 B10
Rishon le Ẕiyyon, *Israel* 69 D3
Risle →, *France* 24 C7
Rison, *U.S.A.* 109 J8
Risør, *Norway* 11 F3
Rissani, *Morocco* 74 B4
Riti, *Nigeria* 79 D6
Rittman, *U.S.A.* 106 F3
Ritzville, *U.S.A.* 110 C4
Riva Bella, *France* 24 C6
Riva del Garda, *Italy* 32 C7
Rivadavia, *Buenos Aires, Argentina* 126 D3
Rivadavia, *Mendoza, Argentina* 126 C2
Rivadavia, *Salta, Argentina* 126 A3
Rivadavia, *Chile* 126 B1
Rivarolo Canavese, *Italy* 32 C4
Rivas, *Nic.* 116 D2
Rive-de-Gier, *France* 27 C8
River Cess, *Liberia* 78 D3
Rivera, *Uruguay* 127 C4
Riverdale, *U.S.A.* 112 J7
Riverhead, *U.S.A.* 107 F12
Riverhurst, *Canada* 101 C7
Riverina, *Australia* 89 E3
Rivers, *Canada* 101 C8
Rivers □, *Nigeria* 79 E6
Rivers, L. of the, *Canada* 101 D7
Rivers Inlet, *Canada* 100 C3
Riversdale, *S. Africa* 84 E3
Riverside, *Calif., U.S.A.* 113 M9
Riverside, *Wyo., U.S.A.* 110 F10
Riversleigh, *Australia* 90 B2
Riverton, *Australia* 91 E2
Riverton, *Canada* 101 C9
Riverton, *N.Z.* 87 M1
Riverton, *U.S.A.* 110 E9
Riverton Heights, *U.S.A.* 112 C4
Rives, *France* 27 C9
Rivesaltes, *France* 26 F6
Riviera, *Europe* 32 E5
Riviera di Levante, *Italy* 32 D6
Riviera di Ponente, *Italy* 32 D5
Rivière-à-Pierre, *Canada* 99 C5
Rivière-au-Renard, *Canada* 99 C7
Rivière-du-Loup, *Canada* 99 C6
Rivière-Pentecôte, *Canada* 99 C6
Rivière-Pilote, *Martinique* 117 D7
Rivne, *Ukraine* 41 G4
Rívoli, *Italy* 32 C4
Rivoli B., *Australia* 91 F3
Rixensart, *Belgium* 17 G5
Riyadh = Ar Riyāḍ, *Si. Arabia* 64 E5
Rize, *Turkey* 67 B9
Rizhao, *China* 51 G10
Rizokarpaso, *Cyprus* 66 E6
Rizzuto, C., *Italy* 35 D10
Rjukan, *Norway* 10 E2
Roa, *Norway* 10 D4
Roa, *Spain* 30 D7
Road Town, *Virgin Is.* 117 C7
Roag, L., *U.K.* 14 C2
Roanne, *France* 27 B8
Roanoke, *Ala., U.S.A.* 105 J3
Roanoke, *Va., U.S.A.* 104 G6
Roanoke →, *U.S.A.* 105 H7
Roanoke I., *U.S.A.* 105 H8
Roanoke Rapids, *U.S.A.* 105 G7
Roatán, *Honduras* 116 C2
Robbins I., *Australia* 90 G4
Robe →, *Australia* 88 D2
Robe →, *Ireland* 15 C2
Röbel, *Germany* 18 B8
Robert Lee, *U.S.A.* 109 K4
Roberts, *U.S.A.* 110 E7
Robertsganj, *India* 63 G10
Robertson, *S. Africa* 84 E2
Robertson I., *Antarctica* 5 C18
Robertson Ra., *Australia* 88 D3
Robertsport, *Liberia* 78 D2
Robertstown, *Australia* 91 E2
Roberval, *Canada* 99 C5
Robeson Chan., *Greenland* 4 A4
Robinson →, *Australia* 90 B2
Robinson Ra., *Australia* 89 E2
Robinson River, *Australia* 90 B2
Robinvale, *Australia* 91 E3
Roblin, *Canada* 101 C8
Roboré, *Bolivia* 125 D6
Robson, Mt., *Canada* 100 C5
Robstown, *U.S.A.* 109 M6
Roca, C. da, *Portugal* 6 H4
Roca Partida, I., *Mexico* 114 D2
Rocas, I., *Brazil* 122 B5
Rocca d'Aspidé, *Italy* 35 B8
Rocca San Casciano, *Italy* 33 D8
Roccalbegna, *Italy* 33 F8
Roccastrada, *Italy* 33 F8
Roccella Iónica, *Italy* 35 D9
Rocha, *Uruguay* 127 C5
Rochdale, *U.K.* 12 D5
Rochechouart, *France* 26 C4
Rochedo, *Brazil* 125 D7
Rochefort, *Belgium* 17 H6
Rochefort, *France* 26 C3
Rochefort-en-Terre, *France* 24 E4
Rochelle, *U.S.A.* 108 E10
Rocher River, *Canada* 100 A6
Rocherath, *Belgium* 17 H8
Rocheservière, *France* 24 F5
Rochester, *Canada* 100 C6
Rochester, *U.K.* 13 F8
Rochester, *Ind., U.S.A.* 104 E2
Rochester, *Minn., U.S.A.* 108 C8
Rochester, *N.H., U.S.A.* 107 C14
Rochester, *N.Y., U.S.A.* 106 C7
Rociana, *Spain* 31 H4
Rociu, *Romania* 38 E8
Rock →, *Canada* 100 A3
Rock Hill, *U.S.A.* 105 H5
Rock Island, *U.S.A.* 108 E9
Rock Rapids, *U.S.A.* 108 D6
Rock River, *U.S.A.* 110 F11
Rock Sound, *Bahamas* 116 B4
Rock Springs, *Mont., U.S.A.* 110 C10
Rock Springs, *Wyo., U.S.A.* 110 F9
Rock Valley, *U.S.A.* 108 D6
Rockall, *Atl. Oc.* 6 D3
Rockanje, *Neths.* 16 E4
Rockdale, *Tex., U.S.A.* 109 K6
Rockdale, *Wash., U.S.A.* 112 C5
Rockefeller Plateau, *Antarctica* 5 E14
Rockford, *U.S.A.* 108 D10
Rockglen, *Canada* 101 D7
Rockhampton, *Australia* 90 C5
Rockhampton Downs, *Australia* 90 B2
Rockingham, *Australia* 89 F2
Rockingham B., *Australia* 90 B4
Rockingham Forest, *U.K.* 13 E7
Rocklake, *U.S.A.* 108 A5
Rockland, *Canada* 107 A9
Rockland, *Idaho, U.S.A.* 110 E7
Rockland, *Maine, U.S.A.* 99 D6
Rockland, *Mich., U.S.A.* 108 B10
Rocklin, *U.S.A.* 112 G5
Rockmart, *U.S.A.* 105 H3
Rockport, *Mo., U.S.A.* 108 E7
Rockport, *Tex., U.S.A.* 109 L6
Rocksprings, *U.S.A.* 109 K4
Rockville, *Conn., U.S.A.* 107 E12
Rockville, *Md., U.S.A.* 104 F7
Rockwall, *U.S.A.* 109 J6
Rockwell City, *U.S.A.* 108 D7
Rockwood, *U.S.A.* 105 H3
Rocky Ford, *U.S.A.* 108 F3
Rocky Gully, *Australia* 89 F2
Rocky Lane, *Canada* 100 B5
Rocky Mount, *U.S.A.* 105 H7
Rocky Mountain House, *Canada* 100 C6
Rocky Mts., *N. Amer.* 100 C4
Rockyford, *Canada* 100 C6
Rocroi, *France* 25 C11
Rod, *Pakistan* 60 E3
Rødberg, *Norway* 10 D2
Rødby, *Denmark* 11 K5
Rødbyhavn, *Denmark* 11 K5
Roddickton, *Canada* 99 B8
Rødding, *Denmark* 11 J3
Rødekro, *Denmark* 11 J3
Roden, *Neths.* 16 B8
Rødenes, *Norway* 10 E5
Rodenkirchen, *Germany* 18 B4
Roderick I., *Canada* 100 C3
Rodez, *France* 26 D6
Rodholívas, *Greece* 39 J6
Rodhopoú, *Greece* 37 D5
Ródhos, *Greece* 37 C10
Rodi Gargánico, *Italy* 35 A8
Rodna, *Romania* 38 B7
Rodney, *Canada* 106 D3
Rodney, C., *N.Z.* 87 G5
Rodniki, *Russia* 42 B5
Rodriguez, *Ind. Oc.* 3 E13
Roe →, *U.K.* 15 A5
Roebling, *U.S.A.* 107 F10
Roebourne, *Australia* 88 D2
Roebuck B., *Australia* 88 C3
Roebuck Plains, *Australia* 88 C3
Roer →, *Neths.* 17 F7
Roermond, *Neths.* 17 F7
Roes Welcome Sd., *Canada* 97 B11
Roeselare, *Belgium* 17 G2
Rœulx, *Belgium* 17 G4
Rogachev = Ragachow, *Belarus* 41 F6
Rogagua, L., *Bolivia* 124 C4
Rogaška Slatina, *Slovenia* 33 B12
Rogatec, *Slovenia* 33 B12
Rogatyn, *Ukraine* 41 H3
Rogdhia, *Greece* 37 D7
Rogers, *U.S.A.* 109 G7
Rogers City, *U.S.A.* 104 C4
Rogerson, *U.S.A.* 110 E6
Rogersville, *U.S.A.* 105 G4
Roggan River, *Canada* 98 B4
Roggel, *Neths.* 17 F7
Roggeveldberge, *S. Africa* 84 E3
Roggiano Gravina, *Italy* 35 C9
Rogliano, *France* 27 F13
Rogliano, *Italy* 35 C9
Rogoaguado, L., *Bolivia* 125 C4
Rogue →, *U.S.A.* 110 E1
Rohan, *France* 24 D4
Róhda, *Greece* 37 A3
Rohnert Park, *U.S.A.* 112 G4
Rohrbach-lès-Bitche, *France* 25 C14
Rohri, *Pakistan* 62 F3
Rohri Canal, *Pakistan* 62 F3
Rohtak, *India* 62 E7
Roi Et, *Thailand* 58 D4
Roisel, *France* 25 C10
Roja, *Latvia* 9 H20
Rojas, *Argentina* 126 C3
Rojo, C., *Mexico* 115 C5
Rokan →, *Indonesia* 56 D2
Rokeby, *Australia* 90 A3
Rokiškis, *Lithuania* 9 J21
Rokitno, *Russia* 42 E2
Rolândia, *Brazil* 127 A5
Rolde, *Neths.* 16 C9
Rolette, *U.S.A.* 108 A5
Rolla, *Kans., U.S.A.* 109 G4
Rolla, *Mo., U.S.A.* 109 G9
Rolla, *N. Dak., U.S.A.* 108 A5
Rollag, *Norway* 10 D3
Rolle, *Switz.* 22 D2
Rolleston, *Australia* 90 C4
Rollingstone, *Australia* 90 B4
Rom, *Sudan* 77 F3
Roma, *Australia* 91 D4
Roma, *Italy* 34 A5
Roma, *Sweden* 9 H18
Roman, *Romania* 38 C9
Roman, *Russia* 45 C12
Roman-Kosh, Gora, *Ukraine* 41 K8
Romanche →, *France* 27 C9
Romang, *Indonesia* 57 F7
Românï, *Egypt* 69 E1
Romania ■, *Europe* 38 D8
Romano, Cayo, *Cuba* 116 B4
Romano di Lombárdia, *Italy* 32 C6
Romanovka = Basarabeasca, *Moldova* 41 J5
Romans-sur-Isère, *France* 27 C9
Romanshorn, *Switz.* 23 A8
Romblon, *Phil.* 55 E5
Rombo □, *Tanzania* 82 C4
Rome = Roma, *Italy* 34 A5
Rome, *Ga., U.S.A.* 105 H3
Rome, *N.Y., U.S.A.* 107 C9
Romeleåsen, *Sweden* 11 J7
Romenay, *France* 27 B9
Romerike, *Norway* 10 D5
Romilly-sur-Seine, *France* 25 D10
Romîni, *Romania* 38 E7
Rommani, *Morocco* 74 B3
Romney, *U.S.A.* 104 F6
Romney Marsh, *U.K.* 13 F8
Romny, *Ukraine* 41 G7
Rømø, *Denmark* 11 J2
Romodan, *Ukraine* 41 G7
Romodanovo, *Russia* 42 C7
Romont, *Switz.* 22 C3
Romorantin-Lanthenay, *France* 25 E8
Romsdalen, *Norway* 10 B2
Ron, *Vietnam* 58 D6
Rona, *U.K.* 14 D3
Ronan, *U.S.A.* 110 C6
Roncador, Cayos, *Caribbean* 116 D3
Roncador, Serra do, *Brazil* 123 D1
Roncesvalles, Paso, *Spain* 28 B3
Ronceverte, *U.S.A.* 104 G5
Ronciglione, *Italy* 33 F9
Ronco →, *Italy* 33 D9
Ronda, *Spain* 31 J5
Ronda, Serranía de, *Spain* 31 J5
Rondane, *Norway* 10 C3
Rondón, *Colombia* 120 B3
Rondônia, *Brazil* 125 C5
Rondônia □, *Brazil* 125 C5
Rondonópolis, *Brazil* 125 D7
Rong Jiang →, *China* 52 E7
Rong Xian, *Guangxi Zhuangzu, China* 53 F8
Rong Xian, *Sichuan, China* 52 C5
Rong'an, *China* 52 E7
Rongchang, *China* 52 C5
Ronge, L. la, *Canada* 101 B7
Rongjiang, *China* 52 E7
Rongshui, *China* 52 E7
Rønne, *Denmark* 9 J16
Ronne Ice Shelf, *Antarctica* 5 D18
Ronsard, C., *Australia* 89 D1
Ronse, *Belgium* 17 G3
Ronuro →, *Brazil* 125 C7
Roodepoort, *S. Africa* 85 D4
Roodeschool, *Neths.* 16 B9
Roof Butte, *U.S.A.* 111 H9
Roompot, *Neths.* 17 E3
Roorkee, *India* 62 E7
Roosendaal, *Neths.* 17 E4
Roosevelt, *Minn., U.S.A.* 108 A7
Roosevelt, *Utah, U.S.A.* 110 F8
Roosevelt →, *Brazil* 125 B5
Roosevelt, Mt., *Canada* 100 B3
Roosevelt I., *Antarctica* 5 D12
Roosevelt Res., *U.S.A.* 111 K8
Roper →, *Australia* 90 A2
Ropesville, *U.S.A.* 109 J3
Roque Pérez, *Argentina* 126 D4
Roquefort, *France* 26 D3
Roquemaure, *France* 27 D8
Roquetas, *Spain* 28 E5
Roquevaire, *France* 27 E9
Roraima □, *Brazil* 121 C5
Roraima, Mt., *Venezuela* 121 B5
Rorketon, *Canada* 101 C9
Røros, *Norway* 10 B5
Rorschach, *Switz.* 23 B8
Rosa, *Zambia* 83 D3
Rosa, C., *Algeria* 75 A6
Rosa, Monte, *Europe* 22 E5
Rosal, *Spain* 30 D2
Rosal de la Frontera, *Spain* 31 H3
Rosalia, *U.S.A.* 110 C5
Rosamond, *U.S.A.* 113 L8

Rosans, *France* 27 D9
Rosario, *Argentina* 126 C3
Rosário, *Brazil* 122 B3
Rosario, *Baja Calif., Mexico* 114 A1
Rosario, *Sinaloa, Mexico* 114 C3
Rosario, *Paraguay* 126 A4
Rosario, Villa del, *Venezuela* 120 A3
Rosario de la Frontera, *Argentina* 126 B3
Rosario de Lerma, *Argentina* 126 A2
Rosario del Tala, *Argentina* 126 C4
Rosário do Sul, *Brazil* 127 C5
Rosário Oeste, *Brazil* 125 C6
Rosarito, *Mexico* 113 N9
Rosarno, *Italy* 35 D8
Rosas, *Spain* 28 C8
Rosas, G. de, *Spain* 28 C8
Roscoe, *U.S.A.* 108 C5
Roscoff, *France* 24 D3
Roscommon, *Ireland* 15 C3
Roscommon, *U.S.A.* 104 C3
Roscommon □, *Ireland* 15 C3
Roscrea, *Ireland* 15 D4
Rose →, *Australia* 90 A2
Rose Blanche, *Canada* 99 C8
Rose Harbour, *Canada* 100 C2
Rose Pt., *Canada* 100 C2
Rose Valley, *Canada* 101 C8
Roseau, *Domin.* 117 C7
Roseau, *U.S.A.* 108 A7
Rosebery, *Australia* 90 G4
Rosebud, *U.S.A.* 109 K6
Roseburg, *U.S.A.* 110 E2
Rosedale, *Australia* 90 C5
Rosedale, *U.S.A.* 109 J9
Rosée, *Belgium* 17 H5
Roseland, *U.S.A.* 112 G4
Rosemary, *Canada* 100 C6
Rosenberg, *U.S.A.* 109 L7
Rosendaël, *France* 25 A9
Rosenheim, *Germany* 19 H8
Roseto degli Abruzzi, *Italy* 33 F11
Rosetown, *Canada* 101 C7
Rosetta = Rashîd, *Egypt* 76 H7
Roseville, *U.S.A.* 112 G5
Rosewood, *N. Terr., Australia* 88 C4
Rosewood, *Queens., Australia* 91 D5
Roshkhvār, *Iran* 65 C8
Rosières-en-Santerre, *France* 25 C9
Rosignano Maríttimo, *Italy* 32 E7
Rosignol, *Guyana* 121 B6
Roşiori de Vede, *Romania* 38 E8
Rositsa, *Bulgaria* 38 F10
Rositsa →, *Bulgaria* 38 F8
Roskilde, *Denmark* 11 J6
Roskilde Amtskommune □, *Denmark* 11 J6
Roskilde Fjord, *Denmark* 11 J6
Roslavl, *Russia* 40 F7
Roslyn, *Australia* 91 E4
Rosmaninhal, *Portugal* 31 F3
Rosmead, *S. Africa* 84 E4
Røsnæs, *Denmark* 11 J4
Rosolini, *Italy* 35 F7
Rosporden, *France* 24 E3
Ross, *Australia* 90 G4
Ross, *N.Z.* 87 K3
Ross I., *Antarctica* 5 D11
Ross Ice Shelf, *Antarctica* 5 E12
Ross L., *U.S.A.* 110 B3
Ross-on-Wye, *U.K.* 13 F5
Ross Sea, *Antarctica* 5 D11
Rossa, *Switz.* 23 D8
Rossan Pt., *Ireland* 15 B3
Rossano Cálabro, *Italy* 35 C9
Rossburn, *Canada* 101 C8
Rosseau, *Canada* 106 A5
Rossignol, L., *Canada* 98 B5
Rossignol Res., *Canada* 99 D6
Rossland, *Canada* 100 D5
Rosslare, *Ireland* 15 D5
Rosslau, *Germany* 18 D8
Rosso, *Mauritania* 78 B1
Rosso, C., *France* 27 F12
Rossosh, *Russia* 42 E4
Rossport, *Canada* 98 C2
Rossum, *Neths.* 16 E6
Røssvatnet, *Norway* 8 D16
Rossville, *Australia* 90 B4
Røst, *Norway* 8 C15
Rosthern, *Canada* 101 C7
Rostock, *Germany* 18 A8
Rostov, *Don, Russia* 43 G4
Rostov, *Yarosl., Russia* 42 B4
Rostrenen, *France* 24 D3
Roswell, *Ga., U.S.A.* 105 H3
Roswell, *N. Mex., U.S.A.* 109 J2
Rosyth, *U.K.* 14 E5
Rota, *Spain* 31 J4
Rotälven →, *Sweden* 10 C8
Rotan, *U.S.A.* 109 J4
Rotem, *Belgium* 17 F7
Rotenburg, *Germany* 18 B5
Roth, *Germany* 19 F7
Rothaargebirge, *Germany* 18 E4
Rothenburg, *Switz.* 23 B6
Rothenburg ob der Tauber, *Germany* 19 F6
Rother →, *U.K.* 13 G8
Rotherham, *U.K.* 12 D6
Rothes, *U.K.* 14 D5
Rothesay, *Canada* 99 C6
Rothesay, *U.K.* 14 F3
Rothrist, *Switz.* 22 B5
Roti, *Indonesia* 57 F6
Roto, *Australia* 91 E4
Rotondella, *Italy* 35 B9
Rotoroa, L., *N.Z.* 87 J4
Rotorua, *N.Z.* 87 H6
Rotorua, L., *N.Z.* 87 H6
Rotselaar, *Belgium* 17 G5
Rott →, *Germany* 19 G9
Rotten →, *Switz.* 22 D5
Rottenburg, *Germany* 19 G4
Rotterdam, *Neths.* 16 E5
Rottnest I., *Australia* 89 F2
Rottumeroog, *Neths.* 16 A9
Rottweil, *Germany* 19 G4
Rotuma, *Fiji* 92 J9
Roubaix, *France* 25 B10
Rouen, *France* 24 C8
Rouergue, *France* 26 D5
Rouillac, *France* 26 C3
Rouleau, *Canada* 101 C8
Round Mountain, *U.S.A.* 110 G5
Round Mt., *Australia* 91 E5
Roundup, *U.S.A.* 110 C9
Roura, *Fr. Guiana* 121 C7
Rousay, *U.K.* 14 B5
Rouses Point, *U.S.A.* 107 B11
Roussillon, *Isère, France* 27 C8
Roussillon, *Pyrénées-Or., France* 26 F6
Rouveen, *Neths.* 16 C8
Rouxville, *S. Africa* 84 E4
Rouyn, *Canada* 98 C4
Rovaniemi, *Finland* 8 C21
Rovato, *Italy* 32 C7
Rovenki, *Ukraine* 41 H10
Rovereto, *Italy* 32 C8
Rovigo, *Italy* 33 C8
Rovinari, *Romania* 38 E6
Rovinj, *Croatia* 33 C10
Rovira, *Colombia* 120 C2
Rovno = Rivne, *Ukraine* 41 G4
Rovnoye, *Russia* 42 E8
Rovuma →, *Tanzania* 83 E5
Row'ān, *Iran* 65 C6
Rowena, *Australia* 91 D4
Rowley Shoals, *Australia* 88 C2
Roxa, *Guinea-Biss.* 78 C1
Roxas, *Capiz, Phil.* 55 F5
Roxas, *Isabela, Phil.* 55 C4
Roxas, *Mindoro, Phil.* 55 E4
Roxboro, *U.S.A.* 105 G6
Roxborough Downs, *Australia* 90 C2
Roxburgh, *N.Z.* 87 L2
Roxen, *Sweden* 11 F9
Roy, *Mont., U.S.A.* 110 C9
Roy, *N. Mex., U.S.A.* 109 H2
Roy Hill, *Australia* 88 D2
Roya, Peña, *Spain* 28 E4
Royal Leamington Spa, *U.K.* 13 E6
Royal Tunbridge Wells, *U.K.* 13 F8
Royan, *France* 26 C2
Roye, *France* 25 C9
Røyken, *Norway* 10 E4
Rožaj, *Montenegro, Yug.* 21 N10
Rozay-en-Brie, *France* 25 D9
Rozdilna, *Ukraine* 41 J6
Rozhyshche, *Ukraine* 41 G3
Rožňava, *Slovak Rep.* 20 G10
Rozoy-sur-Serre, *France* 25 C11
Rtishchevo, *Russia* 42 D6
Rúa, *Spain* 30 C3
Ruacaná, *Angola* 84 B1
Ruahine Ra., *N.Z.* 87 H6
Ruapehu, *N.Z.* 87 H5
Ruapuke I., *N.Z.* 87 M2
Ruâq, W. →, *Egypt* 69 F2
Rub' al Khali, *Si. Arabia* 68 D4
Rubeho Mts., *Tanzania* 82 D4
Rubezhnoye = Rubizhne, *Ukraine* 41 H10
Rubh a' Mhail, *U.K.* 14 F2
Rubha Hunish, *U.K.* 14 D2
Rubha Robhanais = Lewis, Butt of, *U.K.* 14 C2
Rubiataba, *Brazil* 123 E2
Rubicon →, *U.S.A.* 112 G5
Rubicone →, *Italy* 33 D9
Rubinéia, *Brazil* 123 F1
Rubino, *Ivory C.* 78 D4
Rubio, *Venezuela* 120 B3
Rubizhne, *Ukraine* 41 H10
Rubtsovsk, *Russia* 44 D9
Ruby L., *U.S.A.* 110 F6
Ruby Mts., *U.S.A.* 110 F6
Rucheng, *China* 53 E9
Rud, *Norway* 10 D4
Rūd Sar, *Iran* 65 B6
Ruda Śląska, *Poland* 20 E8
Rudall, *Australia* 91 E2
Rudall →, *Australia* 88 D3
Ruden, *Germany* 18 A9
Rüdersdorf, *Germany* 18 C9
Rudewa, *Tanzania* 83 E3
Rudkøbing, *Denmark* 11 K4
Rudnik, *Serbia, Yug.* 21 L10
Rudnogorsk, *Russia* 45 D11
Rudnya, *Russia* 40 E6
Rudnyy, *Kazakstan* 44 D7
Rudolf, Ostrov, *Russia* 44 A6
Rudolstadt, *Germany* 18 E7
Rudong, *China* 53 A13
Rudozem, *Bulgaria* 39 H7
Rudyard, *U.S.A.* 104 B3
Rue, *France* 25 B8
Ruelle, *France* 26 C4
Rufa'a, *Sudan* 77 E3
Ruffec, *France* 26 B4
Rufiji □, *Tanzania* 82 D4
Rufiji →, *Tanzania* 82 D4
Rufino, *Argentina* 126 C3
Rufisque, *Senegal* 78 C1
Rufunsa, *Zambia* 83 F2
Rugao, *China* 53 A13
Rugby, *U.K.* 13 E6
Rugby, *U.S.A.* 108 A5
Rügen, *Germany* 18 A9
Rugles, *France* 24 D7
Ruhengeri, *Rwanda* 82 C2
Ruhla, *Germany* 18 E6
Ruhland, *Germany* 18 D9
Ruhnu saar, *Estonia* 9 H20
Ruhr →, *Germany* 18 D2
Ruhuhu →, *Tanzania* 83 E3
Rui Barbosa, *Brazil* 123 D3
Rui'an, *China* 53 D13
Ruichang, *China* 53 C10
Ruidosa, *U.S.A.* 109 L2
Ruidoso, *U.S.A.* 111 K11
Ruili, *China* 52 E1
Ruinen, *Neths.* 16 C8
Ruinerwold, *Neths.* 16 C8
Ruiten A Kanaal →, *Neths.* 16 C10
Ruivo, Pico, *Madeira* 36 D3
Rujm Tal'at al Jamā'ah, *Jordan* 69 E4
Ruk, *Pakistan* 62 F3
Rukwa □, *Tanzania* 82 D3
Rukwa L., *Tanzania* 82 D3
Rulhieres, C., *Australia* 88 B4
Rulles, *Belgium* 17 J7
Rum = Rhum, *U.K.* 14 E2
Rum Cay, *Bahamas* 117 B5
Rum Jungle, *Australia* 88 B5
Ruma, *Serbia, Yug.* 21 K9
Rumāḥ, *Si. Arabia* 64 E5
Rumania = Romania ■, *Europe* 38 D8
Rumaylah, *Iraq* 64 D5
Rumbalara, *Australia* 90 D1
Rumbêk, *Sudan* 77 F2
Rumbeke, *Belgium* 17 G2
Rumelange, *Lux.* 17 K8
Rumford, *U.S.A.* 107 B14
Rumilly, *France* 27 C9
Rumoi, *Japan* 48 C10
Rumonge, *Burundi* 82 C2
Rumsey, *Canada* 100 C6
Rumula, *Australia* 90 B4
Rumuruti, *Kenya* 82 B4
Runan, *China* 50 H8
Runanga, *N.Z.* 87 K3
Runaway, C., *N.Z.* 87 G6
Runcorn, *U.K.* 12 D5
Rungwa, *Tanzania* 82 D3
Rungwa →, *Tanzania* 82 D3
Rungwe, *Tanzania* 83 D3
Rungwe □, *Tanzania* 83 D3
Runka, *Nigeria* 79 C6
Runton Ra., *Australia* 88 D3
Ruokolahti, *Finland* 40 B5
Ruoqiang, *China* 54 C3
Rupa, *India* 61 F18
Rupar, *India* 62 D7
Rupat, *Indonesia* 56 D2
Rupert →, *Canada* 98 B4
Rupert House = Waskaganish, *Canada* 98 B4
Rupununi →, *Guyana* 121 C6
Rur →, *Germany* 18 E2
Rurrenabaque, *Bolivia* 124 C4
Rus →, *Spain* 29 F2
Rusambo, *Zimbabwe* 83 F3
Rusape, *Zimbabwe* 83 F3
Ruschuk = Ruse, *Bulgaria* 38 F8
Ruse, *Bulgaria* 38 F8
Ruşeţu, *Romania* 38 E10
Rushan, *China* 51 F11
Rushden, *U.K.* 13 E7
Rushford, *U.S.A.* 108 D9
Rushville, *Ill., U.S.A.* 108 E9
Rushville, *Ind., U.S.A.* 104 F3
Rushville, *Nebr., U.S.A.* 108 D3
Rushworth, *Australia* 91 F4
Russas, *Brazil* 122 B4
Russell, *Canada* 101 C8
Russell, *U.S.A.* 108 F5
Russell L., *Man., Canada* 101 B8
Russell L., *N.W.T., Canada* 100 A5
Russellkonda, *India* 61 K14
Russellville, *Ala., U.S.A.* 105 H2
Russellville, *Ark., U.S.A.* 109 H8
Russellville, *Ky., U.S.A.* 105 G2
Russi, *Italy* 33 D9
Russia ■, *Eurasia* 45 C11
Russian →, *U.S.A.* 112 G3
Russkaya Polyana, *Kazakstan* 44 D8
Russkoye Ustie, *Russia* 4 B15
Rustam, *Pakistan* 62 B5
Rustam Shahr, *Pakistan* 62 F2
Rustavi, *Georgia* 43 K7
Rustenburg, *S. Africa* 84 D4
Ruston, *U.S.A.* 109 J8
Ruswil, *Switz.* 22 B6
Rutana, *Burundi* 82 C2
Rute, *Spain* 31 H6
Ruteng, *Indonesia* 57 F6
Ruth, *Mich., U.S.A.* 106 C2
Ruth, *Nev., U.S.A.* 110 G6
Rutherford, *U.S.A.* 112 G4
Rutherglen, *U.K.* 14 F4
Rüti, *Switz.* 23 B7
Rutigliano, *Italy* 35 A10
Rutland Plains, *Australia* 90 B3
Rutledge →, *Canada* 101 A6
Rutledge L., *Canada* 101 A6
Rutqa, W. →, *Syria* 67 E9
Rutshuru, *Zaïre* 82 C2
Ruurlo, *Neths.* 16 D8
Ruvo di Púglia, *Italy* 35 A9
Ruvu, *Tanzania* 82 D4
Ruvu →, *Tanzania* 82 D4
Ruvuma □, *Tanzania* 83 E4
Ruwais, *U.A.E.* 65 E7
Ruwenzori, *Africa* 82 B2
Ruyigi, *Burundi* 82 C3
Ruyuan, *China* 53 E9
Ruzayevka, *Russia* 42 C7
Ružomberok, *Slovak Rep.* 20 F9
Rwanda ■, *Africa* 82 C3
Ry, *Denmark* 11 H3
Ryakhovo, *Bulgaria* 38 F9
Ryan, L., *U.K.* 14 G3
Ryazan, *Russia* 42 C4
Ryazhsk, *Russia* 42 D5
Rybache = Rybachye, *Kazakstan* 44 E9
Rybachye = Ysyk-Köl, *Kyrgyzstan* 46 E11
Rybachye, *Kazakstan* 44 E9
Rybinsk, *Russia* 42 A4
Rybinskoye Vdkhr., *Russia* 40 C10
Rybnik, *Poland* 20 E8
Rybnitsa = Rîbniţa, *Moldova* 41 J5
Rybnoye, *Russia* 42 C4
Rychwał, *Poland* 20 C8
Ryde, *U.K.* 13 G6
Ryderwood, *U.S.A.* 112 D3
Rydöbruk, *Sweden* 11 H7
Rydułtowy, *Poland* 20 E8
Rye, *U.K.* 13 G8
Rye →, *U.K.* 12 C7
Rye Patch Reservoir, *U.S.A.* 110 F4
Ryegate, *U.S.A.* 110 C9
Rylsk, *Russia* 42 E2
Rylstone, *Australia* 91 E4
Ryn Peski, *Kazakstan* 43 G9
Ryōthu, *Japan* 48 E9
Rypin, *Poland* 20 B9
Ryūgasaki, *Japan* 49 G10
Ryūkyū Is. = Ryūkyū-rettō, *Japan* 49 M2
Ryūkyū-rettō, *Japan* 49 M2
Rzeszów, *Poland* 20 E11
Rzhev, *Russia* 42 B2

S

Sa, *Thailand* 58 C3
Sa Dec, *Vietnam* 59 G5
Sa'ādatābād, *Fārs, Iran* 65 D7
Sa'ādatābād, *Kermān, Iran* 65 D7
Saale →, *Germany* 18 D7
Saaler Bodden, *Germany* 18 A8
Saalfeld, *Germany* 18 E7
Saane →, *Switz.* 22 B4
Saar →, *Europe* 25 C13
Saarbrücken, *Germany* 19 F2
Saarburg, *Germany* 19 F2
Saaremaa, *Estonia* 9 G20
Saarijärvi, *Finland* 9 E21
Saariselkä, *Finland* 8 B23
Saarland □, *Germany* 25 C13
Saarlouis, *Germany* 19 F2
Saas Fee, *Switz.* 22 D5
Sab 'Ābar, *Syria* 66 F7
Saba, *W. Indies* 117 C7
Šabac, *Serbia, Yug.* 21 L9
Sabadell, *Spain* 28 D7
Sabah □, *Malaysia* 56 C5
Sabak Bernam, *Malaysia* 59 L3
Sabalān, Kūhhā-ye, *Iran* 67 C12
Sábana de la Mar, *Dom. Rep.* 117 C6
Sábanalarga, *Colombia* 120 A3
Sabang, *Indonesia* 56 C1
Sabará, *Brazil* 123 E3
Sabattis, *U.S.A.* 107 B10
Sabáudia, *Italy* 34 A6
Sabaya, *Bolivia* 124 D4
Saberania, *Indonesia* 57 E9
Sabhah, *Libya* 73 C7
Sabie, *S. Africa* 85 D5
Sabinal, *Mexico* 114 A3
Sabinal, *U.S.A.* 109 L5
Sabinal, Punta del, *Spain* 29 J2
Sabinas, *Mexico* 114 B4
Sabinas →, *Mexico* 114 B4
Sabinas Hidalgo, *Mexico* 114 B4
Sabine →, *U.S.A.* 109 L8
Sabine L., *U.S.A.* 109 L8
Sabine Pass, *U.S.A.* 109 L8
Sabinópolis, *Brazil* 123 E3
Sabinov, *Slovak Rep.* 20 F11
Sabirabad, *Azerbaijan* 43 K9
Sabkhet el Bardawîl, *Egypt* 69 D2
Sablayan, *Phil.* 55 E4
Sable, C., *Canada* 99 D6
Sable, C., *U.S.A.* 103 E10
Sable I., *Canada* 99 D8
Sablé-sur-Sarthe, *France* 24 E6
Saboeiro, *Brazil* 122 C4
Sabor →, *Portugal* 30 D3
Sabou, *Burkina Faso* 78 C4
Sabrātah, *Libya* 75 B7
Sabria, *Tunisia* 75 B6
Sabrina Coast, *Antarctica* 5 C9
Sabugal, *Portugal* 30 E3
Sabulubek, *Indonesia* 56 E1
Sabzevār, *Iran* 65 B8
Sabzvārān, *Iran* 65 D8
Sac City, *U.S.A.* 108 D7
Sacedón, *Spain* 28 E2
Sachigo →, *Canada* 98 A2
Sachigo, L., *Canada* 98 B1
Sachkhere, *Georgia* 43 J6
Sachseln, *Switz.* 23 C6
Sachsen □, *Germany* 18 E9
Sachsen-Anhalt □, *Germany* 18 D8
Sacile, *Italy* 33 C9
Sackets Harbor, *U.S.A.* 107 C8
Saco, *Maine, U.S.A.* 105 D10
Saco, *Mont., U.S.A.* 110 B10
Sacramento, *Brazil* 123 E2
Sacramento, *U.S.A.* 112 G5
Sacramento →, *U.S.A.* 112 G5
Sacramento Mts., *U.S.A.* 111 K11
Sacramento Valley, *U.S.A.* 112 G5
Sacratif, C., *Spain* 29 J1
Săcueni, *Romania* 38 B5
Sada, *Spain* 30 B2
Sádaba, *Spain* 28 C3
Sadani, *Tanzania* 82 D4
Sadao, *Thailand* 59 J3
Sadd el Aali, *Egypt* 76 C3
Saddle Mt., *U.S.A.* 112 E3
Sade, *Nigeria* 79 C7
Sadimi, *Zaïre* 83 D1
Sa'dīyah, Hawr as, *Iraq* 67 F12
Sado, *Japan* 48 E9
Sado →, *Portugal* 31 G2
Sadon, *Burma* 61 G20
Sadon, *Russia* 43 J6
Sæby, *Denmark* 11 G4
Saegerstown, *U.S.A.* 106 E4
Saelices, *Spain* 28 F2
Safaga, *Egypt* 76 B3
Şafājah, *Si. Arabia* 64 E3
Säffle, *Sweden* 9 G15
Safford, *U.S.A.* 111 K9
Saffron Walden, *U.K.* 13 E8
Safi, *Morocco* 74 B3
Şafīābād, *Iran* 65 B8
Safīd Dasht, *Iran* 65 C6
Safīd Kūh, *Afghan.* 60 B3
Safonovo, *Russia* 40 E7
Safranbolu, *Turkey* 66 B5
Safwān, *Iraq* 64 D5
Sag Harbor, *U.S.A.* 107 F12
Saga, *Indonesia* 57 E8
Saga, *Japan* 49 H5
Saga □, *Japan* 49 H5
Sagae, *Japan* 48 E10
Sagala, *Mali* 78 C3
Sagar, *India* 60 M9
Sagara, L., *Tanzania* 82 D3
Sagay, *Phil.* 55 F5
Sagil, *Mongolia* 54 A4
Saginaw, *U.S.A.* 104 D4
Saginaw B., *U.S.A.* 104 D4
Şagīr, Zāb aş →, *Iraq* 67 E10
Sagleipie, *Liberia* 78 D3
Saglouc = Salluit, *Canada* 97 B12
Sagŏ-ri, *S. Korea* 51 G14
Sagone, *France* 27 F12
Sagone, G. de, *France* 27 F12
Sagres, *Portugal* 31 J2
Sagua la Grande, *Cuba* 116 B3
Saguache, *U.S.A.* 111 G10
Saguenay →, *Canada* 99 C5
Sagunto, *Spain* 28 F4
Sahaba, *Sudan* 76 D3
Sahagún, *Colombia* 120 B2
Sahagún, *Spain* 30 C5
Saḩam al Jawlān, *Syria* 69 C4
Sahand, Kūh-e, *Iran* 67 D12
Sahara, *Africa* 72 D5
Saharan Atlas = Saharien, Atlas, *Algeria* 75 B5
Saharanpur, *India* 62 E7
Saharien, Atlas, *Algeria* 75 B5
Sahasinaka, *Madag.* 85 C8
Sahaswan, *India* 63 E8
Sahel, Canal du, *Mali* 78 C3
Sahibganj, *India* 63 G12
Sāḩilīyah, *Iraq* 67 F10
Sahiwal, *Pakistan* 62 D5
Şaḩneh, *Iran* 67 E12
Sahtaneh →, *Canada* 100 B4
Sahuaripa, *Mexico* 114 B3
Sahuarita, *U.S.A.* 111 L8
Sahuayo, *Mexico* 114 C4
Sahy, *Slovak Rep.* 21 G8
Sai Buri, *Thailand* 59 J3
Sai-Cinza, *Brazil* 125 B6
Sa'id Bundas, *Sudan* 73 G9
Saïda, *Algeria* 75 B5
Sa'īdābād, *Kermān, Iran* 65 D7
Sa'īdābād, *Semnān, Iran* 65 B7
Saïdia, *Morocco* 75 A4
Sa'īdīyeh, *Iran* 65 B6
Saidpur, *Bangla.* 61 G16
Saidu, *Pakistan* 63 B5
Saignelégier, *Switz.* 22 B3

Saignes, France 26 C6
Saigon = Phanh Bho Ho Chi Minh, Vietnam 59 G6
Saijō, Japan 49 H6
Saikhoa Ghat, India 61 F19
Saiki, Japan 49 H5
Saillans, France 27 D9
Sailolof, Indonesia 57 E8
Saimaa, Finland 9 F23
Saimbeyli, Turkey 66 D7
Şa'in Dezh, Iran 67 D12
St. Abb's Head, U.K. 14 F6
St. Aegyd, Austria 21 H5
St.-Affrique, France 26 E6
St.-Agrève, France 27 C8
St.-Aignan, France 24 E8
St. Alban's, Canada 99 C8
St. Albans, U.K. 13 F7
St. Albans, Vt., U.S.A. 107 B11
St. Albans, W. Va., U.S.A. 104 F5
St. Alban's Head, U.K. 13 G5
St. Albert, Canada 100 C6
St.-Amand-en-Puisaye, France 25 E10
St.-Amand-les-Eaux, France 25 B10
St.-Amand-Mont-Rond, France 26 B6
St.-Amarin, France 25 E14
St.-Amour, France 27 B9
St.-André-de-Cubzac, France 26 D3
St.-André-de-l'Eure, France 24 D8
St.-André-les-Alpes, France 27 E10
St. Andrew's, Canada 99 C8
St. Andrews, U.K. 14 E6
St-Anicet, Canada 107 A10
St. Ann B., Canada 99 C7
St. Anne, U.K. 24 C4
St. Ann's Bay, Jamaica 116 C4
St. Anthony, Canada 99 B8
St. Anthony, U.S.A. 110 E8
St.-Antonin-Noble-Val, France 26 D5
St. Arnaud, Australia 91 F3
St. Arthur, Canada 99 C6
St. Asaph, U.K. 12 D4
St.-Astier, France 26 C4
St.-Aubin, Switz. 22 C3
St.-Aubin-du-Cormier, France 24 D5
St-Augustin-Saguenay, Canada 99 B8
St. Augustine, U.S.A. 105 L5
St. Austell, U.K. 13 G3
St.-Avold, France 25 C13
St.-Barthélemy, I., W. Indies 117 C7
St. Bees Hd., U.K. 12 C4
St.-Benoît-du-Sault, France 26 B5
St.-Bernard, Col du Grand, Europe 22 E4
St.-Bernard, Col du Petit, France 27 C10
St.-Blaise, Switz. 22 B3
St. Boniface, Canada 101 D9
St.-Bonnet, France 27 D10
St.-Brévin-les-Pins, France 24 E4
St.-Brice-en-Coglès, France 24 D5
St. Bride's, Canada 99 C9
St. Brides B., U.K. 13 F2
St.-Brieuc, France 24 D4
St.-Calais, France 24 E7
St.-Cast-le-Guildo, France 24 D4
St. Catharines, Canada 98 D4
St. Catherines I., U.S.A. 105 K5
St. Catherine's Pt., U.K. 13 G6
St.-Céré, France 26 D5
St.-Cergue, Switz. 22 D2
St.-Cernin, France 26 C6
St.-Chamond, France 27 C8
St. Charles, Ill., U.S.A. 104 E1
St. Charles, Mo., U.S.A. 108 F9
St.-Chély-d'Apcher, France 26 D7
St.-Chinian, France 26 E6
St. Christopher = St. Kitts, W. Indies 117 C7
St. Christopher-Nevis ■ = St. Kitts & Nevis ■, W. Indies 117 C7
St.-Ciers-sur-Gironde, France 26 C3
St. Clair, Mich., U.S.A. 106 D2
St. Clair, Pa., U.S.A. 107 F8
St. Clair, L., Canada 98 D3
St. Clairsville, U.S.A. 106 F4
St.-Claud, France 26 C4
St. Claude, Canada 101 D9
St.-Claude, France 27 B9
St. Cloud, Fla., U.S.A. 105 L5
St. Cloud, Minn., U.S.A. 108 C7
St-Coeur de Marie, Canada 99 C5
St. Cricq, C., Australia 89 E1
St. Croix, Virgin Is. 117 C7
St. Croix →, U.S.A. 108 C8
St. Croix Falls, U.S.A. 108 C8
St.-Cyr-sur-Mer, France 27 E9
St. David's, Canada 99 C8
St. David's, U.K. 13 F2
St. David's Head, U.K. 13 F2
St.-Denis, France 25 D9
St.-Denis-d'Orques, France 24 D6
St.-Dié, France 25 D13
St.-Dizier, France 25 D11
St.-Égrève, France 27 C9
St. Elias, Mt., U.S.A. 96 B5
St. Elias Mts., Canada 100 A1
St.-Élie, Fr. Guiana 121 C7
St.-Eloy-les-Mines, France 26 B6
St.-Émilion, France 26 D3
St.-Étienne, France 27 C8
St.-Étienne-de-Tinée, France 27 D10
St. Eugène, Canada 107 A10
St. Eustatius, W. Indies 117 C7
St-Félicien, Canada 98 C5
St.-Florent, France 27 F13
St.-Florent, G. de, France 27 F13
St.-Florent-sur-Cher, France 25 F9
St.-Florentin, France 25 D10
St.-Flour, France 26 C7
St.-Fons, France 27 C8
St. Francis, U.S.A. 108 F4
St. Francis →, U.S.A. 109 H9
St. Francis, C., S. Africa 84 E3
St. Francisville, U.S.A. 109 K9
St-François, L., Canada 107 A10
St.-Fulgent, France 24 F5
St-Gabriel-de-Brandon, Canada 98 C5
St. Gallen = Sankt Gallen, Switz. 23 B8
St.-Gaudens, France 26 E4
St.-Gengoux-le-National, France 27 B8
St.-Geniez-d'Olt, France 26 D6
St. George, Australia 91 D4
St. George, Canada 99 C6
St. George, S.C., U.S.A. 105 J5
St. George, Utah, U.S.A. 111 H7
St. George, C., Canada 99 C8
St. George, C., U.S.A. 105 L3
St. George Ra., Australia 88 C4
St-Georges, Belgium 17 G6
St. George's, Canada 99 C8
St-Georges, Canada 99 C5
St.-Georges, Fr. Guiana 121 C7
St. George's, Grenada 117 D7
St. George's B., Canada 99 C8
St. Georges Basin, Australia 88 C4
St. George's Channel, Europe 15 E6
St.-Georges-de-Didonne, France 26 C3
St. Georges Hd., Australia 91 F5
St.-Gérard, Belgium 17 H5
St.-Germain-de-Calberte, France 26 D7
St.-Germain-des-Fossés, France 26 B7
St.-Germain-du-Plain, France 25 F11
St.-Germain-en-Laye, France 25 D9
St.-Germain-Laval, France 27 C8
St.-Germain-Lembron, France 26 C7
St.-Gervais-d'Auvergne, France 26 B6
St.-Gervais-les-Bains, France 27 C10
St.-Gildas, Pte. de, France 24 E4
St.-Gilles, France 27 E8
St.-Gilles-Croix-de-Vie, France 26 B2
St.-Gingolph, Switz. 22 D3
St.-Girons, France 26 F5
St. Gotthard P. = San Gottardo, P. del, Switz. 23 C7
St.-Gualtier, France 24 F8
St.-Guénolé, France 24 E2
St. Helena, U.S.A. 110 G2
St. Helena ■, Atl. Oc. 71 H3
St. Helena, Mt., U.S.A. 112 G4
St. Helena B., S. Africa 84 E2
St. Helens, Australia 90 G4
St. Helens, U.K. 12 D5
St. Helens, U.S.A. 112 E4
St. Helens, Mt., U.S.A. 112 D4
St. Helier, U.K. 13 H5
St.-Hilaire-du-Harcouët, France 24 D5
St.-Hippolyte, France 25 E13
St.-Hippolyte-du-Fort, France 26 E7
St.-Honoré-les-Bains, France 25 F10
St.-Hubert, Belgium 17 H6
St-Hyacinthe, Canada 98 C5
St. Ignace, U.S.A. 104 C3
St. Ignace I., Canada 98 C2
St. Ignatius, U.S.A. 110 C6
St.-Imier, Switz. 22 B3
St. Ives, Cambs., U.K. 13 E7
St. Ives, Corn., U.K. 13 G2
St.-James, France 24 D5
St. James, U.S.A. 108 D7
St-Jean, Canada 98 C5
St-Jean →, Canada 99 B7
St-Jean, L., Canada 99 C5
St. Jean Baptiste, Canada 101 D9
St.-Jean-d'Angély, France 26 C3
St.-Jean-de-Bournay, France 27 C9
St.-Jean-de-Luz, France 26 E2
St.-Jean-de-Maurienne, France 27 C10
St.-Jean-de-Monts, France 24 F4
St.-Jean-du-Gard, France 26 D7
St.-Jean-en-Royans, France 27 C9
St-Jean-Port-Joli, Canada 99 C5
St-Jérôme, Qué., Canada 98 C5
St-Jérôme, Qué., Canada 99 C5
St. John, Canada 99 C6
St. John, Kans., U.S.A. 109 G5
St. John, N. Dak., U.S.A. 108 A5
St. John →, U.S.A. 99 C6
St. John, C., Canada 99 B8
St. John's, Antigua 117 C7
St. John's, Canada 99 C9
St. Johns, Ariz., U.S.A. 111 J9
St. Johns, Mich., U.S.A. 104 D3
St. Johns →, U.S.A. 105 K5
St. Johnsbury, U.S.A. 107 B12
St. Johnsville, U.S.A. 107 C10
St. Joseph, La., U.S.A. 109 K9
St. Joseph, Mich., U.S.A. 104 D2
St. Joseph, Mo., U.S.A. 108 F7
St. Joseph →, U.S.A. 104 D2
St. Joseph, I., Canada 98 C3
St. Joseph, L., Canada 98 B1
St-Jovite, Canada 98 C5
St.-Juéry, France 26 E6
St.-Julien-Chapteuil, France 27 C8
St.-Julien-du-Sault, France 25 D10
St.-Julien-en-Genevois, France 27 B10
St.-Junien, France 26 C4
St.-Just-en-Chaussée, France 25 C9
St.-Just-en-Chevalet, France 26 C7
St.-Justin, France 26 E3
St. Kilda, N.Z. 87 L3
St. Kitts, W. Indies 117 C7
St. Kitts & Nevis ■, W. Indies 117 C7
St. Laurent, Canada 101 C9
St.-Laurent, Fr. Guiana 121 B7
St.-Laurent-du-Pont, France 27 C9
St.-Laurent-en-Grandvaux, France 27 B9
St. Lawrence, Australia 90 C4
St. Lawrence, Canada 99 C8
St. Lawrence →, Canada 99 C6
St. Lawrence, Gulf of, Canada 99 C7
St. Lawrence I., U.S.A. 96 B3
St.-Léger, Belgium 17 J7
St. Leonard, Canada 99 C6
St.-Léonard-de-Noblat, France 26 C5
St. Lewis →, Canada 99 B8
St.-Lô, France 24 C5
St-Louis, Senegal 78 B1
St. Louis, Mich., U.S.A. 104 D3
St. Louis, Mo., U.S.A. 108 F9
St. Louis →, U.S.A. 108 B8
St.-Loup-sur-Semouse, France 25 E13
St. Lucia ■, W. Indies 117 D7
St. Lucia, L., S. Africa 85 D5
St. Lucia Channel, W. Indies 117 D7
St. Lunaire-Griquet, Canada 99 B8
St. Maarten, W. Indies 117 C7
St.-Maixent-l'École, France 26 B3
St.-Malo, France 24 D4
St.-Malo, G. de, France 24 D4
St.-Mandrier-sur-Mer, France 27 E9
St-Marc, Haiti 117 C5
St.-Marcellin, France 27 C9
St.-Marcouf, Is., France 24 C5
St. Maries, U.S.A. 110 C5
St-Martin, W. Indies 117 C7
St. Martin, L., Canada 101 C9
St.-Martin-de-Ré, France 26 B2
St.-Martin-Vésubie, France 27 D11
St. Martins, Canada 99 C6
St. Martinville, U.S.A. 109 K9
St.-Martory, France 26 E4
St. Mary Pk., Australia 91 E2
St. Marys, Australia 90 G4
St. Marys, Canada 106 C3
St. Mary's, U.K. 13 H1
St. Marys, U.S.A. 106 E6
St. Mary's, C., Canada 99 C9
St. Mary's B., Canada 99 C9
St. Marys Bay, Canada 99 D6
St.-Mathieu, Pte., France 24 D2
St. Matthews, I. = Zadetkyi Kyun, Burma 59 H2
St.-Maur-des-Fossés, France 25 D9
St. Maurice, Switz. 22 D4
St-Maurice →, Canada 98 C5
St.-Médard-de-Guizières, France 26 C3
St.-Méen-le-Grand, France 24 D4
St. Michael's Mount, U.K. 13 G2
St.-Michel-de-Maurienne, France 27 C10
St.-Mihiel, France 25 D12
St.-Nazaire, France 24 E4
St. Neots, U.K. 13 E7
St.-Nicolas-de-Port, France 25 D13
St. Niklass = Sint Niklaas, Belgium 17 F4
St. Niklaus, Switz. 22 D5
St.-Omer, France 25 B9
St-Pacome, Canada 99 C6
St.-Palais-sur-Mer, France 26 C2
St-Pamphile, Canada 99 C6
St.-Pardoux-la-Rivière, France 26 C4
St. Pascal, Canada 99 C6
St. Paul, Canada 100 C6
St. Paul, Minn., U.S.A. 108 C8
St. Paul, Nebr., U.S.A. 108 E5
St. Paul, I., Ind. Oc. 3 F13
St.-Paul-de-Fenouillet, France 26 F6
St. Paul I., Canada 99 C7
St.-Paul-lès-Dax, France 26 E2
St.-Péray, France 27 D8
St.-Père-en-Retz, France 24 E4
St. Peter, U.S.A. 108 C8
St-Peter-Ording, Germany 18 A4
St. Peter Port, U.K. 13 H5
St. Peters, N.S., Canada 99 C7
St. Peters, P.E.I., Canada 99 C7
St. Petersburg = Sankt-Peterburg, Russia 40 C6
St. Petersburg, U.S.A. 105 M4
St.-Philbert-de-Grand-Lieu, France 24 E5
St.-Pierre, St- P. & M. 99 C8
St-Pierre, L., Canada 98 C5
St.-Pierre-d'Oléron, France 26 C2
St.-Pierre-Église, France 24 C5
St.-Pierre-en-Port, France 24 C7
St.-Pierre et Miquelon □, St- P. & M. 99 C8
St.-Pierre-le-Moûtier, France 25 F10
St.-Pierre-sur-Dives, France 24 C6
St.-Pieters Leew, Belgium 17 G4
St.-Pol-de-Léon, France 24 D2
St.-Pol-sur-Mer, France 25 A9
St.-Pol-sur-Ternoise, France 25 B9
St.-Pons, France 26 E6
St.-Pourçain-sur-Sioule, France 26 B7
St.-Quay-Portrieux, France 24 D4
St.-Quentin, France 25 C10
St.-Rambert-d'Albon, France 27 C8
St.-Raphaël, France 27 E10
St. Regis, U.S.A. 110 C6
St.-Rémy-de-Provence, France 27 E8
St.-Renan, France 24 D2
St.-Saëns, France 24 C8
St.-Sauveur-en-Puisaye, France 25 E10
St.-Sauveur-le-Vicomte, France 24 C5
St.-Savin, France 26 B4
St.-Savinien, France 26 C3
St. Sebastien, Tanjon' i, Madag. 85 A8
St.-Seine-l'Abbaye, France 25 E11
St.-Sernin-sur-Rance, France 26 E6
St.-Servan-sur-Mer, France 24 D4
St.-Sever, France 26 E3
St.-Sever-Calvados, France 24 D5
St-Siméon, Canada 99 C6
St. Stephen, Canada 99 C6
St.-Sulpice, France 26 E5
St.-Sulpice-Laurière, France 26 B5
St.-Syprien, France 26 F7
St.-Thégonnec, France 24 D3
St. Thomas, Canada 98 D3
St. Thomas I., Virgin Is. 117 C7
St-Tite, Canada 98 C5
St.-Tropez, France 27 E10
St. Troud = Sint Truiden, Belgium 17 G6
St.-Vaast-la-Hougue, France 24 C5
St.-Valéry-en-Caux, France 24 C7
St.-Valéry-sur-Somme, France 25 B8
St.-Vallier, France 27 C8
St.-Vallier-de-Thiey, France 27 E10
St.-Varent, France 24 F6
St. Vincent, W. Indies 117 D7
St. Vincent, G., Australia 91 F2
St. Vincent & the Grenadines ■, W. Indies 117 D7
St.-Vincent-de-Tyrosse, France 26 E2
St. Vincent Passage, W. Indies 117 D7
St-Vith, Belgium 17 H8
St.-Yrieix-la-Perche, France 26 C5
Ste.-Adresse, France 24 C7
Ste-Agathe-des-Monts, Canada 98 C5
Ste-Anne de Beaupré, Canada 99 C5
Ste-Anne-des-Monts, Canada 99 C6
Ste-Croix, Switz. 22 C3
Ste.-Enimie, France 26 D7
Ste.-Foy-la-Grande, France 26 D4
Ste. Genevieve, U.S.A. 108 G9
Ste.-Hermine, France 26 B2
Ste.-Livrade-sur-Lot, France 26 D4
Ste-Marguerite →, Canada 99 B6
Ste.-Marie, Martinique 117 D7
Ste.-Marie-aux-Mines, France 25 D14
Ste-Marie de la Madeleine, Canada 99 C5
Ste.-Maure-de-Touraine, France 24 E7
Ste.-Maxime, France 27 E10
Ste.-Menehould, France 25 C11
Ste.-Mère-Église, France 24 C5
Ste.-Rose, Guadeloupe 117 C7
Ste. Rose du Lac, Canada 101 C9
Saintes, France 26 C3
Saintes, I. des, Guadeloupe 117 C7
Stes.-Maries-de-la-Mer, France 27 E8
Saintonge, France 26 C3
Saipan, Pac. Oc. 92 F6
Sairang, India 61 H18
Sairecábur, Cerro, Bolivia 126 A2
Saitama □, Japan 49 F9
Sajama, Bolivia 124 D4
Sajum, India 63 C8
Sak →, S. Africa 84 E3
Sakai, Japan 49 G7
Sakaide, Japan 49 G6
Sakaiminato, Japan 49 G6
Sakākah, Si. Arabia 64 D4
Sakakawea, L., U.S.A. 108 B3
Sakami, L., Canada 98 B4
Sâkâne, 'Erg i-n, Mali 74 D4
Sakania, Zaïre 83 E2
Sakarya = Adapazarı, Turkey 66 B4
Sakarya →, Turkey 66 B4
Sakashima-Guntō, Japan 49 M2
Sakata, Japan 48 E9
Sakchu, N. Korea 51 D13
Sakeny →, Madag. 85 C8
Sakété, Benin 79 D5
Sakha □, Russia 45 C13
Sakhalin, Russia 45 D15
Sakhalinskiy Zaliv, Russia 45 D15
Şaki, Azerbaijan 43 K8
Šakiai, Lithuania 9 J20
Sakon Nakhon, Thailand 58 D5
Sakrand, Pakistan 62 F3
Sakrivier, S. Africa 84 E3
Sakskøbing, Denmark 11 K5
Sakuma, Japan 49 G8
Sakurai, Japan 49 G7
Saky, Ukraine 41 K7
Sal →, Russia 43 G5
Sala, Sweden 9 G17
Sala Consilina, Italy 35 B8
Sala-y-Gómez, Pac. Oc. 93 K17
Salaberry-de-Valleyfield, Canada 98 C5
Saladas, Argentina 126 B4
Saladillo, Argentina 126 D4
Salado →, Buenos Aires, Argentina 126 D4
Salado →, La Pampa, Argentina 128 A3
Salado →, Río Negro, Argentina 128 B3
Salado →, Santa Fe, Argentina 126 C3
Salado →, Mexico 114 B5
Salaga, Ghana 79 D4
Sālah, Syria 69 C5
Sálakhos, Greece 37 C9
Salala, Liberia 78 D2
Salala, Sudan 76 C4
Salālah, Oman 68 D5
Salamanca, Chile 126 C1
Salamanca, Spain 30 E5
Salamanca, U.S.A. 106 D6
Salamanca □, Spain 30 E5
Salāmatābād, Iran 64 C5
Salamina, Colombia 120 B2
Salamis, Cyprus 37 D12
Salamís, Greece 39 M6
Salar de Atacama, Chile 126 A2
Salar de Uyuni, Bolivia 124 E4
Sălard, Romania 38 B5
Salas, Spain 30 B4
Salas de los Infantes, Spain 28 C1
Salatiga, Indonesia 57 G14
Salaverry, Peru 124 B2
Salawati, Indonesia 57 E8
Salayar, Indonesia 57 F6
Salazar →, Spain 28 C3
Salbris, France 25 E9
Salcombe, U.K. 13 G4
Saldaña, Spain 30 C6
Saldanha, S. Africa 84 E2
Saldanha B., S. Africa 84 E2
Saldus, Latvia 9 H20
Sale, Australia 91 F4
Salé, Morocco 74 B3
Sale, U.K. 12 D5
Salekhard, Russia 44 C7
Salem, India 60 P11
Salem, Ind., U.S.A. 104 F2
Salem, Mass., U.S.A. 107 D14
Salem, Mo., U.S.A. 109 G9
Salem, N.J., U.S.A. 104 F8
Salem, Ohio, U.S.A. 106 F4
Salem, Oreg., U.S.A. 110 D2
Salem, S. Dak., U.S.A. 108 D6
Salem, Va., U.S.A. 104 G5
Salemi, Italy 34 E5
Salernes, France 27 E10
Salerno, Italy 35 B7
Salerno, G. di, Italy 35 B7
Salford, U.K. 12 D5
Salgir →, Ukraine 41 K8
Salgótarján, Hungary 21 G9
Salgueiro, Brazil 122 C4
Salida, U.S.A. 102 C5
Salies-de-Béarn, France 26 E3
Salihli, Turkey 66 C3
Salihorsk, Belarus 41 F4
Salima, Malawi 81 G6
Salina, Italy 35 D7
Salina, U.S.A. 108 F6
Salina Cruz, Mexico 115 D5
Salinas, Brazil 123 E3
Salinas, Chile 126 A2
Salinas, Ecuador 120 D1

Salinas, *U.S.A.* 111 H3
Salinas →, *Guatemala* 115 D6
Salinas →, *U.S.A.* 111 H3
Salinas, B. de, *Nic.* 116 D2
Salinas, C. de, *Spain* 36 B10
Salinas, Pampa de las, *Argentina* 126 C2
Salinas Ambargasta, *Argentina* 126 B3
Salinas de Hidalgo, *Mexico* 114 C4
Salinas Grandes, *Argentina* 126 B2
Saline →, *Ark., U.S.A.* 109 J8
Saline →, *Kans., U.S.A.* 108 F6
Salines, *Spain* 36 B10
Salinópolis, *Brazil* 122 B2
Salins-les-Bains, *France* 25 F12
Salir, *Portugal* 31 H2
Salisbury = Harare, *Zimbabwe* 83 F3
Salisbury, *Australia* 91 E2
Salisbury, *U.K.* 13 F6
Salisbury, *Md., U.S.A.* 104 F8
Salisbury, *N.C., U.S.A.* 105 H5
Salisbury Plain, *U.K.* 13 F6
Săliște, *Romania* 38 D6
Salitre →, *Brazil* 122 C3
Salka, *Nigeria* 79 C5
Şalkhad, *Syria* 69 C5
Salla, *Finland* 8 C23
Sallent, *Spain* 28 D6
Salles-Curan, *France* 26 D6
Salling, *Denmark* 11 H2
Sallisaw, *U.S.A.* 109 H7
Sallom Junction, *Sudan* 76 D4
Salluit, *Canada* 97 B12
Salmās, *Iran* 67 C11
Salmerón, *Spain* 28 E2
Salmo, *Canada* 100 D5
Salmon, *U.S.A.* 110 D7
Salmon →, *Canada* 100 C4
Salmon →, *U.S.A.* 110 D5
Salmon Arm, *Canada* 100 C5
Salmon Falls, *U.S.A.* 110 E6
Salmon Gums, *Australia* 89 F3
Salmon Res., *Canada* 99 C8
Salmon River Mts., *U.S.A.* 110 D6
Salo, *Finland* 9 F20
Salò, *Italy* 32 C7
Salobreña, *Spain* 31 J7
Salome, *U.S.A.* 113 M13
Salon-de-Provence, *France* 27 E9
Salonica = Thessaloníki, *Greece* 39 J5
Salonta, *Romania* 38 C4
Salor →, *Spain* 31 F3
Salou, C., *Spain* 28 D6
Salpausselkä, *Finland* 9 F22
Salsacate, *Argentina* 126 C2
Salses, *France* 26 F6
Salsk, *Russia* 43 G5
Salso →, *Italy* 34 E6
Salsomaggiore Terme, *Italy* 32 D6
Salt →, *Canada* 100 B6
Salt →, *U.S.A.* 111 K7
Salt Creek, *Australia* 91 F2
Salt Fork Arkansas →, *U.S.A.* 109 G6
Salt Lake City, *U.S.A.* 110 F8
Salt Range, *Pakistan* 62 C5
Salta, *Argentina* 126 A2
Salta □, *Argentina* 126 A2
Saltcoats, *U.K.* 14 F4
Saltee Is., *Ireland* 15 D5
Saltfjellet, *Norway* 8 C16
Saltfjorden, *Norway* 8 C16
Saltholm, *Denmark* 11 J6
Saltillo, *Mexico* 114 B4
Salto, *Argentina* 126 C3
Salto, *Uruguay* 126 C4
Salto da Divisa, *Brazil* 123 E4
Salton City, *U.S.A.* 113 M11
Salton Sea, *U.S.A.* 113 M11
Saltpond, *Ghana* 79 D4
Saltsjöbaden, *Sweden* 10 E12
Saltville, *U.S.A.* 104 G5
Saluda →, *U.S.A.* 105 H5
Salûm, *Egypt* 76 A2
Salûm, Khâlig el, *Egypt* 76 A2
Salur, *India* 61 K13
Salut, Is. du, *Fr. Guiana* 121 B7
Saluzzo, *Italy* 32 D4
Salvación, B., *Chile* 128 D1
Salvador, *Brazil* 123 D4
Salvador, *Canada* 101 C7
Salvador, L., *U.S.A.* 109 L9
Salvaterra, *Brazil* 122 B2
Salvaterra de Magos, *Portugal* 31 F2
Sálvora, I., *Spain* 30 C2
Salween →, *Burma* 61 L20
Salyan, *Azerbaijan* 67 C13
Salyersville, *U.S.A.* 104 G4
Salza →, *Austria* 21 H4
Salzach →, *Austria* 21 G2
Salzburg, *Austria* 21 H3
Salzgitter, *Germany* 18 C6
Salzwedel, *Germany* 18 C7
Sam Neua, *Laos* 58 B5
Sam Ngao, *Thailand* 58 D2
Sam Rayburn Reservoir, *U.S.A.* 109 K7
Sam Son, *Vietnam* 58 C5
Sam Teu, *Laos* 58 C5
Sama, *Russia* 44 C7
Sama de Langreo, *Spain* 30 B5
Samagaltay, *Russia* 45 D10
Samaipata, *Bolivia* 125 D5
Samales Group, *Phil.* 55 J4
Samâlût, *Egypt* 76 J7
Samana, *India* 62 D7
Samana Cay, *Bahamas* 117 B5
Samandağı, *Turkey* 66 D6
Samanga, *Tanzania* 83 D4
Samangwa, *Zaïre* 82 C1
Samani, *Japan* 48 C11
Samar, *Phil.* 55 F6
Samara, *Russia* 42 D10
Samara →, *Russia* 42 D10
Samara →, *Ukraine* 41 H8
Samaria = Shōmrōn, *West Bank* 69 C4
Samariá, *Greece* 37 D5
Samarinda, *Indonesia* 56 E5
Samarkand = Samarqand, *Uzbekistan* 44 F7
Samarqand, *Uzbekistan* 44 F7
Sāmarrā, *Iraq* 67 E10
Samastipur, *India* 63 G11
Samatan, *France* 26 E4
Samaúma, *Brazil* 125 B5
Şamaxi, *Azerbaijan* 43 K9
Samba, *India* 63 C6
Samba, *Zaïre* 82 C2
Sambaíba, *Brazil* 122 C2
Sambalpur, *India* 61 J14
Sambar, Tanjung, *Indonesia* 56 E4
Sambas, *Indonesia* 56 D3
Sambava, *Madag.* 85 A9
Sambawizi, *Zimbabwe* 83 F2
Sambhal, *India* 63 E8
Sambhar, *India* 62 F6
Sambiase, *Italy* 35 D9
Sambir, *Ukraine* 41 H2
Sambonifacio, *Italy* 32 C8
Sambor, *Cambodia* 58 F6
Sambre →, *Europe* 17 H5
Sambuca di Sicília, *Italy* 34 E6
Samburu □, *Kenya* 82 B4
Samchŏk, *S. Korea* 51 F15
Samchonpo, *S. Korea* 51 G15
Same, *Tanzania* 82 C4
Samedan, *Switz.* 23 C9
Samer, *France* 25 B8
Samfya, *Zambia* 83 E2
Sámi, *Greece* 39 L3
Şämkir, *Azerbaijan* 43 K8
Samnah, *Si. Arabia* 64 E3
Samnaun, *Switz.* 23 C10
Samo Alto, *Chile* 126 C1
Samobor, *Croatia* 33 C12
Samoëns, *France* 27 B10
Samokov, *Bulgaria* 38 G6
Samoorombón, B., *Argentina* 126 D4
Samorogouan, *Burkina Faso* 78 C4
Sámos, *Greece* 39 M9
Samoš, *Serbia, Yug.* 21 K10
Samos, *Spain* 30 C3
Samothráki, *Évros, Greece* 39 J8
Samothráki, *Kérkira, Greece* 37 A3
Samoylovka, *Russia* 42 E6
Sampa, *Ghana* 78 D4
Sampacho, *Argentina* 126 C3
Sampang, *Indonesia* 57 G15
Samper de Calanda, *Spain* 28 D4
Sampit, *Indonesia* 56 E4
Sampit, Teluk, *Indonesia* 56 E4
Samrée, *Belgium* 17 H7
Samreng, *Cambodia* 58 E4
Samreng, *Thailand* 58 E3
Samsø, *Denmark* 11 J4
Samsø Bælt, *Denmark* 11 J4
Samsun, *Turkey* 66 B7
Samtredia, *Georgia* 43 J6
Samui, Ko, *Thailand* 59 H3
Samur →, *Russia* 43 K9
Samurskiy Khrebet, *Russia* 43 K8
Samusole, *Zaïre* 83 E1
Samut Prakan, *Thailand* 58 F3
Samut Sakhon, *Thailand* 58 F3
Samut Songkhram →, *Thailand* 58 F3
Samwari, *Pakistan* 62 E2
San, *Mali* 78 C4
San →, *Cambodia* 58 F5
San →, *Poland* 20 E11
San Adrián, C. de, *Spain* 30 B2
San Agustín, *Colombia* 120 C2
San Agustin, C., *Phil.* 55 H7
San Agustín de Valle Fértil, *Argentina* 126 C2
San Ambrosio, *Pac. Oc.* 118 F3
San Andreas, *U.S.A.* 112 G6
San Andrés, I. de, *Caribbean* 116 D3
San Andres Mts., *U.S.A.* 111 K10
San Andrés Tuxtla, *Mexico* 115 D5
San Angelo, *U.S.A.* 109 K4
San Anselmo, *U.S.A.* 112 H4
San Antonio, *Belize* 115 D7
San Antonio, *Chile* 126 C1
San Antonio, *Phil.* 55 D4
San Antonio, *Spain* 36 C7
San Antonio, *N. Mex., U.S.A.* 111 K10
San Antonio, *Tex., U.S.A.* 109 L5
San Antonio, *Venezuela* 120 C4
San Antonio →, *U.S.A.* 109 L6
San Antonio, C., *Argentina* 126 D4
San Antonio, C., *Cuba* 116 B3
San Antonio, C. de, *Spain* 29 G5
San Antonio, Mt., *U.S.A.* 113 L9
San Antonio de los Baños, *Cuba* 116 B3
San Antonio de los Cobres, *Argentina* 126 A2
San Antonio Oeste, *Argentina* 128 B4
San Arcángelo, *Italy* 35 B9
San Ardo, *U.S.A.* 112 J6
San Augustín, *Canary Is.* 36 G4
San Augustine, *U.S.A.* 109 K7
San Bartolomé, *Canary Is.* 36 F6
San Bartolomé de Tirajana, *Canary Is.* 36 G4
San Bartolomeo in Galdo, *Italy* 35 A8
San Benedetto del Tronto, *Italy* 33 F10
San Benedetto Po, *Italy* 32 C7
San Benedicto, I., *Mexico* 114 D2
San Benito, *U.S.A.* 109 M6
San Benito →, *U.S.A.* 112 J5
San Benito Mt., *U.S.A.* 112 J6
San Bernardino, *U.S.A.* 113 L9
San Bernardino, Paso del, *Switz.* 23 D8
San Bernardino Mts., *U.S.A.* 113 L10
San Bernardino Str., *Phil.* 55 E6
San Bernardo, *Chile* 126 C1
San Bernardo, I. de, *Colombia* 120 B2
San Blas, *Mexico* 114 B3
San Blas, Arch. de, *Panama* 116 E4
San Blas, C., *U.S.A.* 105 L3
San Borja, *Bolivia* 124 C4
San Buenaventura, *Bolivia* 124 C4
San Buenaventura, *Mexico* 114 B4
San Carlos = Butuku-Luba, *Eq. Guin.* 79 E6
San Carlos, *Argentina* 126 C2
San Carlos, *Bolivia* 125 D5
San Carlos, *Chile* 126 D1
San Carlos, *Mexico* 114 B4
San Carlos, *Nic.* 116 D3
San Carlos, *Negros, Phil.* 55 F5
San Carlos, *Pangasinan, Phil.* 55 D4
San Carlos, *Spain* 36 B8
San Carlos, *Uruguay* 127 C5
San Carlos, *U.S.A.* 111 K8
San Carlos, *Amazonas, Venezuela* 120 C4
San Carlos, *Cojedes, Venezuela* 120 B4
San Carlos de Bariloche, *Argentina* 128 B2
San Carlos de la Rápita, *Spain* 28 E5
San Carlos del Zulia, *Venezuela* 120 B3
San Carlos L., *U.S.A.* 111 K8
San Cataldo, *Italy* 34 E6
San Celoni, *Spain* 28 D7
San Clemente, *Chile* 126 D1
San Clemente, *Spain* 29 F2
San Clemente, *U.S.A.* 113 M9
San Clemente I., *U.S.A.* 113 N8
San Costanzo, *Italy* 33 E10
San Cristóbal, *Argentina* 126 C3
San Cristóbal, *Colombia* 120 D3
San Cristóbal, *Dom. Rep.* 117 C5
San Cristóbal, *Mexico* 115 D6
San Cristóbal, *Spain* 36 B11
San Cristóbal, *Venezuela* 120 B3
San Damiano d'Asti, *Italy* 32 D5
San Daniele del Friuli, *Italy* 33 B10
San Demétrio Corone, *Italy* 35 C9
San Diego, *Calif., U.S.A.* 113 N9
San Diego, *Tex., U.S.A.* 109 M5
San Diego, C., *Argentina* 128 D3
San Diego de la Unión, *Mexico* 114 C4
San Dimitri, Ras, *Malta* 37 C1
San Doná di Piave, *Italy* 33 C9
San Elpídio a Mare, *Italy* 33 E10
San Estanislao, *Paraguay* 126 A4
San Esteban de Gormaz, *Spain* 28 D1
San Felice sul Panaro, *Italy* 32 D8
San Felipe, *Chile* 126 C1
San Felipe, *Colombia* 120 C4
San Felipe, *Mexico* 114 A2
San Felipe, *Venezuela* 120 A4
San Felipe →, *U.S.A.* 113 M11
San Felíu de Guíxols, *Spain* 28 D8
San Felíu de Llobregat, *Spain* 28 D7
San Félix, *Pac. Oc.* 118 F2
San Fernando, *Chile* 126 C1
San Fernando, *Mexico* 114 B1
San Fernando, *La Union, Phil.* 55 C4
San Fernando, *Pampanga, Phil.* 55 D4
San Fernando, *Baleares, Spain* 36 C7
San Fernando, *Cádiz, Spain* 31 J4
San Fernando, *Trin. & Tob.* 117 D7
San Fernando, *U.S.A.* 113 L8
San Fernando →, *Mexico* 114 C5
San Fernando de Apure, *Venezuela* 120 B4
San Fernando de Atabapo, *Venezuela* 120 C4
San Fernando di Púglia, *Italy* 35 A9
San Francisco, *Argentina* 126 C3
San Francisco, *Bolivia* 125 D4
San Francisco, *U.S.A.* 111 H2
San Francisco →, *U.S.A.* 111 K9
San Francisco, Paso de, *S. Amer.* 126 B2
San Francisco de Macorîs, *Dom. Rep.* 117 C5
San Francisco del Monte de Oro, *Argentina* 126 C2
San Francisco del Oro, *Mexico* 114 B3
San Francisco Javier, *Spain* 36 C7
San Francisco Solano, Pta., *Colombia* 120 B2
San Fratello, *Italy* 35 D7
San Gabriel, *Ecuador* 120 C2
San Gavino Monreale, *Italy* 34 C1
San Gil, *Colombia* 120 B3
San Gimignano, *Italy* 32 E8
San Giórgio di Nogaro, *Italy* 33 C10
San Giórgio Iónico, *Italy* 35 B10
San Giovanni Bianco, *Italy* 32 C6
San Giovanni in Fiore, *Italy* 35 C9
San Giovanni in Persiceto, *Italy* 33 D8
San Giovanni Rotondo, *Italy* 35 A8
San Giovanni Valdarno, *Italy* 33 E8
San Giuliano Terme, *Italy* 32 E7
San Gorgonio Mt., *U.S.A.* 113 L10
San Gottardo, P. del, *Switz.* 23 C7
San Gregorio, *Uruguay* 127 C4
San Gregorio, *U.S.A.* 112 H4
San Guiseppe Iato, *Italy* 34 E6
San Ignacio, *Belize* 115 D7
San Ignacio, *Bolivia* 125 D5
San Ignacio, *Mexico* 114 B2
San Ignacio, *Paraguay* 126 B4
San Ignacio, L., *Mexico* 114 B2
San Ildefonso, C., *Phil.* 55 C5
San Isidro, *Argentina* 126 C4
San Jacinto, *Colombia* 120 B2
San Jacinto, *U.S.A.* 113 M10
San Jaime, *Spain* 36 B11
San Javier, *Misiones, Argentina* 127 B4
San Javier, *Santa Fe, Argentina* 126 C4
San Javier, *Beni, Bolivia* 125 C5
San Javier, *Santa Cruz, Bolivia* 125 D5
San Javier, *Chile* 126 D1
San Javier, *Spain* 29 H4
San Jerónimo, Sa. de, *Colombia* 120 B2
San Jeronimo Taviche, *Mexico* 115 D5
San Joaquín, *Bolivia* 125 C5
San Joaquin, *U.S.A.* 112 J6
San Joaquín, *Venezuela* 120 A4
San Joaquín →, *Bolivia* 125 C5
San Joaquin →, *U.S.A.* 111 G3
San Joaquin Valley, *U.S.A.* 112 J6
San Jordi, *Spain* 36 B9
San Jorge, *Argentina* 126 C3
San Jorge, *Spain* 36 C7
San Jorge, B. de, *Mexico* 114 A2
San Jorge, G., *Argentina* 128 C3
San Jorge, G. de, *Spain* 28 E4
San Jorge, G. of, *Argentina* 118 H4
San José, *Bolivia* 125 D5
San José, *Costa Rica* 116 E3
San José, *Guatemala* 116 D1
San José, *Mexico* 114 C2
San Jose, *Phil.* 55 D4
San José, *Spain* 36 C7
San Jose, *U.S.A.* 111 H3
San Jose →, *U.S.A.* 111 J10
San Jose de Buenovista, *Phil.* 55 E4
San José de Feliciano, *Argentina* 126 C4
San José de Jáchal, *Argentina* 126 C2
San José de Mayo, *Uruguay* 126 C4
San José de Ocune, *Colombia* 120 C3
San José de Uchapiamonas, *Bolivia* 124 C4
San José del Cabo, *Mexico* 114 C3
San José del Guaviare, *Colombia* 120 C3
San José do Anauá, *Brazil* 121 C5
San Juan, *Argentina* 126 C2
San Juan, *Colombia* 120 B2
San Juan, *Mexico* 114 C4
San Juan, *Ica, Peru* 124 D2
San Juan, *Puno, Peru* 124 C4
San Juan, *Phil.* 55 G7
San Juan, *Puerto Rico* 117 C6
San Juan □, *Argentina* 126 C2
San Juan →, *Argentina* 126 C2
San Juan →, *Bolivia* 125 E4
San Juan →, *Colombia* 120 C2
San Juan →, *Nic.* 116 D3
San Juan →, *U.S.A.* 111 H8
San Juan →, *Venezuela* 121 A5
San Juan, C., *Eq. Guin.* 80 D1
San Juan Bautista, *Paraguay* 126 B4
San Juan Bautista, *Spain* 36 B8
San Juan Bautista, *U.S.A.* 111 H3
San Juan Bautista Valle Nacional, *Mexico* 115 D5
San Juan Capistrano, *U.S.A.* 113 M9
San Juan Cr. →, *U.S.A.* 112 J5
San Juan de Guadalupe, *Mexico* 114 C4
San Juan de los Morros, *Venezuela* 120 B4
San Juan del César, *Colombia* 120 A3
San Juan del Norte, *Nic.* 116 D3
San Juan del Norte, B. de, *Nic.* 116 D3
San Juan del Puerto, *Spain* 31 H4
San Juan del Río, *Mexico* 115 C5
San Juan del Sur, *Nic.* 116 D2
San Juan I., *U.S.A.* 112 B3
San Juan Mts., *U.S.A.* 111 H10
San Julián, *Argentina* 128 C3
San Just, Sierra de, *Spain* 28 E4
San Justo, *Argentina* 126 C3
San Kamphaeng, *Thailand* 58 C2
San Lázaro, C., *Mexico* 114 C2
San Lázaro, Sa., *Mexico* 114 C3
San Leandro, *U.S.A.* 111 H2
San Leonardo, *Spain* 28 D1
San Lorenzo, *Argentina* 126 C3
San Lorenzo, *Beni, Bolivia* 125 D4
San Lorenzo, *Tarija, Bolivia* 125 E5
San Lorenzo, *Ecuador* 120 C2
San Lorenzo, *Paraguay* 126 B4
San Lorenzo, *Spain* 36 B10
San Lorenzo, *Venezuela* 120 B3
San Lorenzo →, *Mexico* 114 C3
San Lorenzo, I., *Mexico* 114 B2
San Lorenzo, I., *Peru* 124 C2
San Lorenzo, Mt., *Argentina* 128 C2
San Lorenzo de la Parrilla, *Spain* 28 F2
San Lorenzo de Morunys, *Spain* 28 C6
San Lucas, *Bolivia* 125 E4
San Lucas, *Baja Calif. S., Mexico* 114 C3
San Lucas, *Baja Calif. S., Mexico* 114 B2
San Lucas, *U.S.A.* 112 J5
San Lucas, C., *Mexico* 114 C3
San Lúcido, *Italy* 35 C9
San Luis, *Argentina* 126 C2
San Luis, *Cuba* 116 B3
San Luis, *Guatemala* 116 C2
San Luis, *U.S.A.* 111 H11
San Luis □, *Argentina* 126 C2
San Luis, I., *Mexico* 114 B2
San Luis, L. de, *Bolivia* 125 C5
San Luis, Sierra de, *Argentina* 126 C2
San Luis de la Paz, *Mexico* 114 C4
San Luis Obispo, *U.S.A.* 113 K6
San Luis Potosí, *Mexico* 114 C4
San Luis Potosí □, *Mexico* 114 C4
San Luis Reservoir, *U.S.A.* 112 H5
San Luis Río Colorado, *Mexico* 114 A2
San Marco Argentano, *Italy* 35 C9
San Marco dei Cavoti, *Italy* 35 A7
San Marco in Lámis, *Italy* 35 A8
San Marcos, *Colombia* 120 B2
San Marcos, *Guatemala* 116 D1
San Marcos, *Mexico* 114 B2
San Marcos, *U.S.A.* 109 L6
San Marino ■, *Europe* 33 E9
San Martín, *Argentina* 126 C2
San Martín, *Colombia* 120 C3
San Martin →, *Bolivia* 125 C5
San Martín, L., *Argentina* 128 C2
San Martin de los Andes, *Argentina* 128 B2
San Martín de Valdeiglesias, *Spain* 30 E6
San Martino de Calvi, *Italy* 32 C6
San Mateo, *Phil.* 55 C4
San Mateo, *Baleares, Spain* 36 B7
San Mateo, *Valencia, Spain* 28 E5
San Mateo, *U.S.A.* 111 H2
San Matías, *Bolivia* 125 D6
San Matías, G., *Argentina* 128 B4
San Miguel, *El Salv.* 116 D2
San Miguel, *Panama* 116 E4
San Miguel, *Spain* 36 B7
San Miguel, *U.S.A.* 111 J3
San Miguel, *Venezuela* 120 B4
San Miguel →, *Bolivia* 125 C5
San Miguel →, *S. Amer.* 120 C2
San Miguel de Huachi, *Bolivia* 124 D4
San Miguel de Salinas, *Spain* 29 H4
San Miguel de Tucumán, *Argentina* 126 B2
San Miguel del Monte, *Argentina* 126 D4
San Miguel I., *U.S.A.* 113 L6
San Miniato, *Italy* 32 E7
San Narciso, *Phil.* 55 D4
San Nicolás, *Canary Is.* 36 G4
San Nicolas, *Phil.* 55 B4
San Nicolás de los Arroyas, *Argentina* 126 C3
San Nicolas I., *U.S.A.* 113 M7
San Onofre, *Colombia* 120 B2
San Onofre, *U.S.A.* 113 M9

San Pablo, *Bolivia* 126 A2
San Pablo, *Phil.* 55 D4
San Páolo di Civitate, *Italy* 35 A8
San Pedro, *Buenos Aires, Argentina* 127 B5
San Pedro, *Jujuy, Argentina* 126 A3
San Pedro, *Colombia* 120 C3
San-Pédro, *Ivory C.* 78 E3
San Pedro, *Mexico* 114 C2
San Pedro, *Peru* 124 C3
San Pedro □, *Paraguay* 126 A4
San Pedro →, *Chihuahua, Mexico* 114 B3
San Pedro →, *Michoacan, Mexico* 114 D4
San Pedro →, *Nayarit, Mexico* 114 C3
San Pedro →, *U.S.A.* 111 K8
San Pedro, Pta., *Chile* 126 B1
San Pedro, Sierra de, *Spain* 31 F4
San Pedro Channel, *U.S.A.* 113 M8
San Pedro de Arimena, *Colombia* 120 C3
San Pedro de Atacama, *Chile* 126 A2
San Pedro de Jujuy, *Argentina* 126 A3
San Pedro de las Colonias, *Mexico* 114 B4
San Pedro de Lloc, *Peru* 124 B2
San Pedro de Macorís, *Dom. Rep.* 117 C6
San Pedro del Norte, *Nic.* 116 D3
San Pedro del Paraná, *Paraguay* 126 B4
San Pedro del Pinatar, *Spain* 29 H4
San Pedro Mártir, Sierra, *Mexico* 114 A1
San Pedro Mixtepec, *Mexico* 115 D5
San Pedro Ocampo = Melchor Ocampo, *Mexico* 114 C4
San Pedro Sula, *Honduras* 116 C2
San Pieto, *Italy* 34 C1
San Pietro Vernótico, *Italy* 35 B11
San Quintín, *Mexico* 114 A1
San Rafael, *Argentina* 126 C2
San Rafael, *Calif., U.S.A.* 112 H4
San Rafael, *N. Mex., U.S.A.* 111 J10
San Rafael, *Venezuela* 120 A3
San Rafael Mt., *U.S.A.* 113 L7
San Rafael Mts., *U.S.A.* 113 L7
San Ramón, *Bolivia* 125 C5
San Ramón, *Peru* 124 C2
San Ramón de la Nueva Orán, *Argentina* 126 A3
San Remo, *Italy* 32 E4
San Román, C., *Venezuela* 120 A3
San Roque, *Argentina* 126 B4
San Roque, *Spain* 31 J5
San Rosendo, *Chile* 126 D1
San Saba, *U.S.A.* 109 K5
San Salvador, *Bahamas* 117 B5
San Salvador, *El Salv.* 116 D2
San Salvador, *Spain* 36 B10
San Salvador de Jujuy, *Argentina* 126 A3
San Salvador I., *Bahamas* 117 B5
San Sebastián, *Argentina* 128 D3
San Sebastián, *Spain* 28 B3
San Sebastián, *Venezuela* 120 B4
San Sebastian de la Gomera, *Canary Is.* 36 F2
San Serra, *Spain* 36 B10
San Serverino Marche, *Italy* 33 E10
San Simeon, *U.S.A.* 112 K5
San Simon, *U.S.A.* 111 K9
San Stéfano di Cadore, *Italy* 33 B9
San Telmo, *Mexico* 114 A1
San Telmo, *Spain* 36 B9
San Tiburcio, *Mexico* 114 C4
San Valentin, Mte., *Chile* 128 C2
San Vicente de Alcántara, *Spain* 31 F3
San Vicente de la Barquera, *Spain* 30 B6
San Vicente del Caguán, *Colombia* 120 C3
San Vincenzo, *Italy* 32 E7
San Vito, *Italy* 34 C2
San Vito, C., *Italy* 34 D5
San Vito al Tagliamento, *Italy* 33 C9
San Vito Chietino, *Italy* 33 F11
San Vito dei Normanni, *Italy* 35 B10
San Yanaro, *Colombia* 120 C4
San Ygnacio, *U.S.A.* 109 M5
Saña, *Peru* 124 B2
Sana', *Yemen* 68 D3
Sana →, *Bos.-H.* 33 C13
Sanaba, *Burkina Faso* 78 C4
Şanāfīr, *Si. Arabia* 76 B3
Sanaga →, *Cameroon* 79 E6
Sanaloa, Presa, *Mexico* 114 C3
Sanana, *Indonesia* 57 E7
Sanand, *India* 62 H5
Sanandaj, *Iran* 67 E12
Sanandita, *Bolivia* 126 A3
Sanary-sur-Mer, *France* 27 E9
Sanawad, *India* 62 H7
Sancellas, *Spain* 36 B9
Sancergues, *France* 25 E9
Sancerre, *France* 25 E9
Sancerrois, Collines du, *France* 25 E9
Sancha He →, *China* 52 D6
Sanchahe, *China* 51 B14
Sánchez, *Dom. Rep.* 117 C6
Sanchor, *India* 62 G4
Sanco Pt., *Phil.* 57 C7
Sancoins, *France* 25 F9
Sancti-Spíritus, *Cuba* 116 B4
Sancy, Puy de, *France* 26 C6
Sand →, *S. Africa* 85 C5
Sand Springs, *U.S.A.* 109 G6
Sanda, *Japan* 49 G7
Sandakan, *Malaysia* 56 C5
Sandan = Sambor, *Cambodia* 58 F6
Sandanski, *Bulgaria* 39 H6
Sandaré, *Mali* 78 C2
Sanday, *U.K.* 14 B6
Sandefjord, *Norway* 10 E4
Sanders, *U.S.A.* 111 J9
Sanderson, *U.S.A.* 109 K3
Sandfly L., *Canada* 101 B7
Sandgate, *Australia* 91 D5
Sandía, *Peru* 124 C4
Sandıklı, *Turkey* 66 C4
Sandnes, *Norway* 9 G11
Sandness, *U.K.* 14 A7
Sandnessjøen, *Norway* 8 C15
Sandoa, *Zaïre* 80 F4
Sandona, *Colombia* 120 C2
Sandover →, *Australia* 90 C2
Sandoway, *Burma* 61 K19
Sandoy, *Færoe Is.* 8 F9
Sandpoint, *U.S.A.* 110 B5
Sandringham, *U.K.* 12 E8
Sandslån, *Sweden* 10 A11
Sandspit, *Canada* 100 C2
Sandstone, *Australia* 89 E2
Sandu, *China* 52 E6
Sandusky, *Mich., U.S.A.* 98 D3
Sandusky, *Ohio, U.S.A.* 106 E2
Sandvig, *Sweden* 11 J8
Sandviken, *Sweden* 9 F17
Sandwich, C., *Australia* 90 B4
Sandwich B., *Canada* 99 B8
Sandwich B., *Namibia* 84 C1
Sandwip Chan., *Bangla.* 61 H17
Sandy, *Nev., U.S.A.* 113 K11
Sandy, *Oreg., U.S.A.* 112 E4
Sandy, *Utah, U.S.A.* 110 F8
Sandy Bight, *Australia* 89 F3
Sandy C., *Queens., Australia* 90 C5
Sandy C., *Tas., Australia* 90 G3
Sandy Cay, *Bahamas* 117 B4
Sandy Cr. →, *U.S.A.* 110 F9
Sandy L., *Canada* 98 B1
Sandy Lake, *Canada* 98 B1
Sandy Narrows, *Canada* 101 B8
Sanford, *Fla., U.S.A.* 105 L5
Sanford, *Maine, U.S.A.* 107 C14
Sanford, *N.C., U.S.A.* 105 H6
Sanford →, *Australia* 89 E2
Sanford, Mt., *U.S.A.* 96 B5
Sang-i-Masha, *Afghan.* 62 C2
Sanga, *Mozam.* 83 E4
Sanga →, *Congo* 80 E3
Sanga-Tolon, *Russia* 45 C15
Sangamner, *India* 60 K9
Sangar, *Afghan.* 62 C1
Sangar, *Russia* 45 C13
Sangar Sarai, *Afghan.* 62 B4
Sangasangadalam, *Indonesia* 56 E5
Sangatte, *France* 25 B8
Sangay, *Ecuador* 120 D2
Sange, *Zaïre* 82 D2
Sangeang, *Indonesia* 57 F5
Sanger, *U.S.A.* 111 H4
Sangerhausen, *Germany* 18 D7
Sanggan He →, *China* 50 E9
Sanggau, *Indonesia* 56 D4
Sangihe, Kepulauan, *Indonesia* 57 D7
Sangihe, P., *Indonesia* 57 D7
Sangju, *S. Korea* 51 F15
Sangkapura, *Indonesia* 56 F4
Sangkhla, *Thailand* 58 E2
Sangli, *India* 60 L9
Sangmélina, *Cameroon* 79 E7
Sangonera →, *Spain* 29 H3
Sangre de Cristo Mts., *U.S.A.* 109 G2
Sangro →, *Italy* 33 F11
Sangudo, *Canada* 100 C6
Sangue →, *Brazil* 125 C6
Sangüesa, *Spain* 28 C3
Sanguinaires, Is., *France* 27 G12
Sangzhi, *China* 53 C8
Sanhala, *Ivory C.* 78 C3
Sanje, *Uganda* 82 C3
Sanjiang, *China* 52 E7
Sanjo, *Japan* 48 F9
Sankt Antönien, *Switz.* 23 C9
Sankt Blasien, *Germany* 19 H4
Sankt Gallen, *Switz.* 23 B8
Sankt Gallen □, *Switz.* 23 B8
Sankt Goar, *Germany* 19 E3
Sankt Ingbert, *Germany* 19 F3
Sankt Margrethen, *Switz.* 23 B9
Sankt Moritz, *Switz.* 23 D9
Sankt-Peterburg, *Russia* 40 C6
Sankt Pölten, *Austria* 21 G5
Sankt Valentin, *Austria* 21 G4
Sankt Veit, *Austria* 21 J4
Sankt Wendel, *Germany* 19 F3
Sankuru →, *Zaïre* 80 E4
Sanliurfa, *Turkey* 67 D8
Sanlúcar de Barrameda, *Spain* 31 J4
Sanlúcar la Mayor, *Spain* 31 H4
Sanluri, *Italy* 34 C1
Sanmenxia, *China* 50 G6
Sanming, *China* 53 D11
Sannaspos, *S. Africa* 84 D4
Sannicandro Gargánico, *Italy* 35 A8
Sannidal, *Norway* 10 F3
Sannieshof, *S. Africa* 84 D4
Sannīn, J., *Lebanon* 69 B4
Sanok, *Poland* 20 F12
Sanquhar, *U.K.* 14 F5
Sansanding Dam, *Mali* 78 C3
Sansepolcro, *Italy* 33 E9
Sansha, *China* 53 D13
Sanshui, *China* 53 F9
Sanski Most, *Bos.-H.* 33 D13
Sansui, *China* 52 D7
Santa, *Peru* 124 B2
Sant' Ágata de Goti, *Italy* 35 A7
Sant' Ágata di Militello, *Italy* 35 D7
Santa Ana, *Beni, Bolivia* 125 C4
Santa Ana, *Santa Cruz, Bolivia* 125 D6
Santa Ana, *Santa Cruz, Bolivia* 125 D5
Santa Ana, *Ecuador* 120 D1
Santa Ana, *El Salv.* 116 D2
Santa Ana, *Mexico* 114 A2
Santa Ana, *U.S.A.* 113 M9
Santa Ana →, *Venezuela* 120 B3
Sant' Ángelo Lodigiano, *Italy* 32 C6
Sant' Antíoco, *Italy* 34 C1
Sant' Arcángelo di Romagna, *Italy* 33 D9
Santa Bárbara, *Colombia* 120 B2
Santa Bárbara, *Honduras* 116 D2
Santa Bárbara, *Mexico* 114 B3
Santa Bárbara, *Spain* 28 E5
Santa Barbara, *U.S.A.* 113 L7
Santa Bárbara, *Venezuela* 120 B3
Santa Bárbara, Mt., *Spain* 29 H2
Santa Barbara Channel, *U.S.A.* 113 L7
Santa Barbara I., *U.S.A.* 113 M7
Santa Catalina, *Colombia* 120 A2
Santa Catalina, *Mexico* 114 B2
Santa Catalina, Gulf of, *U.S.A.* 113 N9
Santa Catalina I., *U.S.A.* 113 M8
Santa Catarina □, *Brazil* 127 B6
Santa Catarina, I. de, *Brazil* 127 B6
Santa Caterina Villarmosa, *Italy* 35 E7
Santa Cecília, *Brazil* 127 B5
Santa Clara, *Cuba* 116 B4
Santa Clara, *Calif., U.S.A.* 111 H3
Santa Clara, *Utah, U.S.A.* 111 H7
Santa Clara de Olimar, *Uruguay* 127 C5
Santa Clotilde, *Peru* 120 D3
Santa Coloma de Farners, *Spain* 28 D7
Santa Coloma de Gramanet, *Spain* 28 D7
Santa Comba, *Spain* 30 B2
Santa Croce Camerina, *Italy* 35 F7
Santa Croce di Magliano, *Italy* 35 A7
Santa Cruz, *Argentina* 128 D3
Santa Cruz, *Bolivia* 125 D5
Santa Cruz, *Brazil* 122 C4
Santa Cruz, *Chile* 126 C1
Santa Cruz, *Costa Rica* 116 D2
Santa Cruz, *Madeira* 36 D3
Santa Cruz, *Peru* 124 B2
Santa Cruz, *Phil.* 55 D4
Santa Cruz, *U.S.A.* 111 H2
Santa Cruz, *Venezuela* 121 B5
Santa Cruz □, *Argentina* 128 C3
Santa Cruz □, *Bolivia* 125 D5
Santa Cruz →, *Argentina* 128 D3
Santa Cruz Cabrália, *Brazil* 123 E4
Santa Cruz de la Palma, *Canary Is.* 36 F2
Santa Cruz de Mudela, *Spain* 29 G1
Santa Cruz de Tenerife, *Canary Is.* 36 F3
Santa Cruz del Norte, *Cuba* 116 B3
Santa Cruz del Retamar, *Spain* 30 E6
Santa Cruz del Sur, *Cuba* 116 B4
Santa Cruz do Rio Pardo, *Brazil* 127 A6
Santa Cruz do Sul, *Brazil* 127 B5
Santa Cruz I., *Solomon Is.* 92 J8
Santa Cruz I., *U.S.A.* 113 M7
Santa Domingo, Cay, *Bahamas* 116 B4
Santa Elena, *Argentina* 126 C4
Santa Elena, *Ecuador* 120 D1
Santa Elena, C., *Costa Rica* 116 D2
Sant' Eufémia, G. di, *Italy* 35 D9
Santa Eugenia, Pta., *Mexico* 114 B1
Santa Eulalia, *Spain* 36 C8
Santa Fe, *Argentina* 126 C3
Santa Fe, *Spain* 31 H7
Santa Fe, *U.S.A.* 111 J11
Santa Fé □, *Argentina* 126 C3
Santa Filomena, *Brazil* 122 C2
Santa Galdana, *Spain* 36 B10
Santa Gertrudis, *Spain* 36 B7
Santa Helena, *Brazil* 122 B2
Santa Helena de Goiás, *Brazil* 123 E1
Santa Inês, *Brazil* 123 D4
Santa Inés, *Baleares, Spain* 36 B7
Santa Inés, *Extremadura, Spain* 31 G5
Santa Inés, I., *Chile* 128 D2
Santa Isabel = Rey Malabo, *Eq. Guin.* 79 E6
Santa Isabel, *Argentina* 126 D2
Santa Isabel, *Brazil* 123 D1
Santa Isabel, Pico, *Eq. Guin.* 79 E6
Santa Isabel do Araguaia, *Brazil* 122 C2
Santa Isabel do Morro, *Brazil* 123 D1
Santa Lucía, *Corrientes, Argentina* 126 B4
Santa Lucía, *San Juan, Argentina* 126 C2
Santa Lucía, *Spain* 29 H4
Santa Lucía, *Uruguay* 126 C4
Santa Lucia Range, *U.S.A.* 111 J3
Santa Magdalena, I., *Mexico* 114 C2
Santa Margarita, *Argentina* 126 D3
Santa Margarita, *Mexico* 114 C2
Santa Margarita, *Spain* 36 B10
Santa Margarita, *U.S.A.* 112 K6
Santa Margarita →, *U.S.A.* 113 M9
Santa Margherita, *Italy* 32 D6
Santa María, *Argentina* 126 B2
Santa Maria, *Brazil* 127 B5
Santa Maria, *Phil.* 55 C4
Santa Maria, *Spain* 36 B9
Santa Maria, *Switz.* 23 C10
Santa Maria, *U.S.A.* 113 L6
Santa María →, *Mexico* 114 A3
Santa María, B. de, *Mexico* 114 B3
Santa Maria, C. de, *Portugal* 31 J3
Santa Maria Cápua Vétere, *Italy* 35 A7
Santa Maria da Vitória, *Brazil* 123 D3
Santa María de Ipire, *Venezuela* 121 B4
Santa Maria di Leuca, C., *Italy* 35 C11
Santa Maria do Suaçuí, *Brazil* 123 E3
Santa Maria dos Marmelos, *Brazil* 125 B5
Santa María la Real de Nieva, *Spain* 30 D6
Santa Marta, *Colombia* 120 A3
Santa Marta, *Spain* 31 G4
Santa Marta, Ría de, *Spain* 30 B3
Santa Marta, Sierra Nevada de, *Colombia* 120 A3
Santa Marta Grande, C., *Brazil* 127 B6
Santa Maura = Levkás, *Greece* 39 L3
Santa Monica, *U.S.A.* 113 M8
Santa Olalla, *Huelva, Spain* 31 H4
Santa Olalla, *Toledo, Spain* 30 E6
Sant' Onofrio, *Italy* 35 D9
Santa Pola, *Spain* 29 G4
Santa Ponsa, *Spain* 36 B9
Santa Quitéria, *Brazil* 122 B3
Santa Rita, *U.S.A.* 111 K10
Santa Rita, *Guarico, Venezuela* 120 B4
Santa Rita, *Zulia, Venezuela* 120 A3
Santa Rita do Araquaia, *Brazil* 125 D7
Santa Rosa, *La Pampa, Argentina* 126 D3
Santa Rosa, *San Luis, Argentina* 126 C2
Santa Rosa, *Bolivia* 124 C4
Santa Rosa, *Brazil* 127 B5
Santa Rosa, *Colombia* 120 C4
Santa Rosa, *Ecuador* 120 D2
Santa Rosa, *Peru* 124 C3
Santa Rosa, *Calif., U.S.A.* 112 G4
Santa Rosa, *N. Mex., U.S.A.* 109 H2
Santa Rosa, *Venezuela* 120 C4
Santa Rosa de Cabal, *Colombia* 120 C2
Santa Rosa de Copán, *Honduras* 116 D2
Santa Rosa de Osos, *Colombia* 120 B2
Santa Rosa de Río Primero, *Argentina* 126 C3
Santa Rosa de Viterbo, *Colombia* 120 B3
Santa Rosa del Palmar, *Bolivia* 125 D5
Santa Rosa I., *Calif., U.S.A.* 113 M6
Santa Rosa I., *Fla., U.S.A.* 105 K2
Santa Rosa Range, *U.S.A.* 110 F5
Santa Rosalía, *Mexico* 114 B2
Santa Sofia, *Italy* 33 E8
Santa Sylvina, *Argentina* 126 B3
Santa Tecla = Nueva San Salvador, *El Salv.* 116 D2
Santa Teresa, *Argentina* 126 C3
Santa Teresa, *Brazil* 123 E3
Santa Teresa, *Mexico* 115 B5
Santa Teresa, *Venezuela* 121 C5
Santa Teresa di Riva, *Italy* 35 E8
Santa Teresa Gallura, *Italy* 34 A2
Santa Vitória, *Brazil* 123 E1
Santa Vitória do Palmar, *Brazil* 127 C5
Santa Ynez →, *U.S.A.* 113 L6
Santa Ynez Mts., *U.S.A.* 113 L6
Santa Ysabel, *U.S.A.* 113 M10
Santadi, *Italy* 34 C1
Santai, *China* 52 B5
Santaluz, *Brazil* 122 D4
Santana, *Brazil* 123 D3
Santana, *Madeira* 36 D3
Santana, Coxilha de, *Brazil* 127 C4
Santana do Ipanema, *Brazil* 122 C4
Santana do Livramento, *Brazil* 127 C4
Santanayi, *Spain* 36 B10
Santander, *Colombia* 120 C2
Santander, *Spain* 30 B7
Santander Jiménez, *Mexico* 115 C5
Santaquin, *U.S.A.* 110 G8
Santarém, *Brazil* 121 D7
Santarém, *Portugal* 31 F2
Santarém □, *Portugal* 31 F2
Santaren Channel, *W. Indies* 116 B4
Santee, *U.S.A.* 113 N10
Santéramo in Colle, *Italy* 35 B9
Santerno →, *Italy* 33 D8
Santhià, *Italy* 32 C5
Santiago, *Bolivia* 125 D6
Santiago, *Brazil* 127 B5
Santiago, *Chile* 126 C1
Santiago, *Panama* 116 E3
Santiago, *Peru* 124 C2
Santiago, *Phil.* 55 C4
Santiago □, *Chile* 126 C1
Santiago →, *Mexico* 94 G9
Santiago →, *Peru* 120 D2
Santiago, C., *Chile* 128 D1
Santiago, Punta de, *Eq. Guin.* 79 E6
Santiago, Serranía de, *Bolivia* 125 D6
Santiago de Chuco, *Peru* 124 B2
Santiago de Compostela, *Spain* 30 C2
Santiago de Cuba, *Cuba* 116 C4
Santiago de los Cabelleros, *Dom. Rep.* 117 C5
Santiago del Estero, *Argentina* 126 B3
Santiago del Estero □, *Argentina* 126 B3
Santiago del Teide, *Canary Is.* 36 F3
Santiago do Cacém, *Portugal* 31 G2
Santiago Ixcuintla, *Mexico* 114 C3
Santiago Papasquiaro, *Mexico* 114 B3
Santiaguillo, L. de, *Mexico* 114 C4
Santillana del Mar, *Spain* 30 B6
Säntis, *Switz.* 23 B8
Santisteban del Puerto, *Spain* 29 G1
Santo →, *Peru* 124 B2
Santo Amaro, *Brazil* 123 D4
Santo Anastácio, *Brazil* 127 A5
Santo André, *Brazil* 127 A6
Santo Ângelo, *Brazil* 127 B5
Santo Antonio, *Brazil* 125 D6
Santo Antônio de Jesus, *Brazil* 123 D4
Santo Antônio do Içá, *Brazil* 120 D4
Santo Antônio do Leverger, *Brazil* 125 D6
Santo Corazón, *Bolivia* 125 D6
Santo Domingo, *Dom. Rep.* 117 C6
Santo Domingo, *Baja Calif., Mexico* 114 A1
Santo Domingo, *Baja Calif. S., Mexico* 114 B2
Santo Domingo, *Nic.* 116 D3
Santo Domingo de la Calzada, *Spain* 28 C2
Santo Domingo de los Colorados, *Ecuador* 120 D2
Santo Stéfano di Camastro, *Italy* 35 D7
Santo Stino di Livenza, *Italy* 33 C9
Santo Tirso, *Portugal* 30 D2
Santo Tomás, *Mexico* 114 A1
Santo Tomás, *Peru* 124 C3
Santo Tomé, *Argentina* 127 B4
Santo Tomé de Guayana = Ciudad Guayana, *Venezuela* 121 B5
Santoña, *Spain* 30 B7
Santoríni = Thíra, *Greece* 39 N8
Santos, *Brazil* 127 A6
Santos, Sierra de los, *Spain* 31 G5
Santos Dumont, *Brazil* 123 F3
Santpoort, *Neths.* 16 D5
Sanvignes-les-Mines, *France* 25 F11

Sanyuan, *China* 50 G5
Sanza Pombo, *Angola* 80 F3
São Anastácio, *Brazil* 127 A5
São Bartolomeu de Messines, *Portugal* 31 H2
São Benedito, *Brazil* 122 B3
São Bento, *Brazil* 122 B3
São Bento do Norte, *Brazil* 122 C4
São Bernado de Campo, *Brazil* 123 F2
São Borja, *Brazil* 127 B4
São Bras d'Alportel, *Portugal* 31 H3
São Caitano, *Brazil* 122 C4
São Carlos, *Brazil* 127 A6
São Cristóvão, *Brazil* 122 D4
São Domingos, *Brazil* 123 D2
São Domingos do Maranhão, *Brazil* 122 C3
São Félix, *Brazil* 123 D1
São Francisco, *Brazil* 123 E3
São Francisco →, *Brazil* 122 D4
São Francisco do Maranhão, *Brazil* 122 C3
São Francisco do Sul, *Brazil* 127 B6
São Gabriel, *Brazil* 127 C5
São Gabriel da Palha, *Brazil* 123 E3
São Gonçalo, *Brazil* 123 F3
São Gotardo, *Brazil* 123 E2
Sao Hill, *Tanzania* 83 D4
São João da Boa Vista, *Brazil* 127 A6
São João da Pesqueira, *Portugal* 30 D3
São João da Ponte, *Brazil* 123 E3
São João del Rei, *Brazil* 123 F3
São João do Araguaia, *Brazil* 122 C2
São João do Paraíso, *Brazil* 123 E3
São João do Piauí, *Brazil* 122 C3
São João dos Patos, *Brazil* 122 C3
São Joaquim da Barra, *Brazil* 123 F2
São Jorge, Pta. de, *Madeira* 36 D3
São José, B. de, *Brazil* 122 B3
São José da Laje, *Brazil* 122 C4
São José de Mipibu, *Brazil* 122 C4
São José do Peixe, *Brazil* 122 C3
São José do Rio Prêto, *Brazil* 127 A6
São José dos Campos, *Brazil* 127 A6
São Leopoldo, *Brazil* 127 B5
São Lourenço, *Brazil* 123 F2
São Lourenço →, *Brazil* 125 D6
São Lourenço, Pantanal do, *Brazil* 125 D6
São Lourenço, Pta. de, *Madeira* 36 D3
São Luís, *Brazil* 122 B3
São Luís do Curu, *Brazil* 122 B4
São Luís Gonzaga, *Brazil* 127 B5
São Marcos →, *Brazil* 123 E2
São Marcos, B. de, *Brazil* 122 B3
São Martinho, *Portugal* 30 E2
São Mateus, *Brazil* 123 E4
São Mateus →, *Brazil* 123 E4
São Miguel do Araguaia, *Brazil* 123 D1
São Miguel dos Campos, *Brazil* 122 C4
São Nicolau →, *Brazil* 122 C3
São Paulo, *Brazil* 127 A6
São Paulo □, *Brazil* 127 A6
São Paulo, I., *Atl. Oc.* 2 D8
São Paulo de Olivença, *Brazil* 120 D4
São Pedro do Sul, *Portugal* 30 E2
São Rafael, *Brazil* 122 C4
São Raimundo das Mangabeiras, *Brazil* 122 C2
São Raimundo Nonato, *Brazil* 122 C3
São Romão, *Brazil* 123 E2
São Roque, *Madeira* 36 D3
São Roque, C. de, *Brazil* 122 C4
São Sebastião, I. de, *Brazil* 127 A6
São Sebastião do Paraíso, *Brazil* 127 A6
São Simão, *Brazil* 123 E1
São Teotónio, *Portugal* 31 H2
São Tomé, *Atl. Oc.* 70 F4
São Tomé, *Brazil* 122 C4
São Tomé, C. de, *Brazil* 123 F3
São Tomé & Principe ■, *Africa* 71 F4
São Vicente, *Brazil* 127 A6
São Vicente, *Madeira* 36 D2
São Vicente, C. de, *Portugal* 31 H2
Saona, I., *Dom. Rep.* 117 C6
Saône →, *France* 27 C8
Saône-et-Loire □, *France* 25 F11
Saonek, *Indonesia* 57 E8
Saoura, O. →, *Algeria* 75 C4
Sapanca, *Turkey* 66 B4
Sapão →, *Brazil* 122 D2
Saparua, *Indonesia* 57 E7
Sapé, *Brazil* 122 C4
Sapele, *Nigeria* 79 D6
Sapelo I., *U.S.A.* 105 K5
Sapiéntza, *Greece* 39 N4
Sapone, *Burkina Faso* 79 C4
Saposoa, *Peru* 124 B2
Sapozhok, *Russia* 42 D5
Sappemeer, *Neths.* 16 B9
Sappho, *U.S.A.* 112 B2
Sapporo, *Japan* 48 C10
Sapri, *Italy* 35 B8
Sapudi, *Indonesia* 57 G16
Sapulpa, *U.S.A.* 109 G7
Saqqez, *Iran* 67 D12
Sar Dasht, *Iran* 65 C6
Sar Gachīneh, *Iran* 65 D6
Sar Planina, *Macedonia* 38 G4
Sara, *Burkina Faso* 78 C4
Sara, *Phil.* 55 F5
Sara Buri, *Thailand* 58 E3
Sarāb, *Iran* 67 D12
Sarabadi, *Iraq* 64 C5
Sarada →, *India* 61 F12
Saragossa = Zaragoza, *Spain* 28 D4
Saraguro, *Ecuador* 120 D2
Sarajevo, *Bos.-H.* 21 M8
Saramacca □, *Surinam* 121 C6
Saramacca →, *Surinam* 121 B6
Saran, G., *Indonesia* 56 E4
Saranac Lake, *U.S.A.* 107 B10
Saranda, *Tanzania* 82 D3
Sarandí del Yi, *Uruguay* 127 C4
Sarandí Grande, *Uruguay* 126 C4
Sarangani B., *Phil.* 55 J6
Sarangani Is., *Phil.* 55 J6
Sarangarh, *India* 61 J13
Saransk, *Russia* 42 C7
Sarapul, *Russia* 44 D6
Sarasota, *U.S.A.* 105 M4
Saratoga, *Calif., U.S.A.* 112 H4
Saratoga, *Wyo., U.S.A.* 110 F10
Saratoga Springs, *U.S.A.* 107 C11
Saratov, *Russia* 42 E7
Saravane, *Laos* 58 E6
Sarawak □, *Malaysia* 56 D4
Saray, *Tekirdağ, Turkey* 66 B2
Saray, *Van, Turkey* 67 C11
Saraya, *Senegal* 78 C2
Sarayköy, *Turkey* 66 D3
Sarayönü, *Turkey* 66 C5
Sarbāz, *Iran* 65 E9
Sarbīsheh, *Iran* 65 C8
Sarca →, *Italy* 32 C7
Sarda → = Sarada →, *India* 61 F12
Sardalas, *Libya* 75 C7
Sardarshahr, *India* 62 E6
Sardegna □, *Italy* 34 B2
Sardhana, *India* 62 E7
Sardina, Pta., *Canary Is.* 36 F4
Sardinata, *Colombia* 120 B3
Sardinia = Sardegna □, *Italy* 34 B2
Sardis, *Turkey* 66 C2
Sārdūīyeh = Dar Mazār, *Iran* 65 D8
Saréyamou, *Mali* 78 B4
Sargent, *U.S.A.* 108 E5
Sargodha, *Pakistan* 62 C5
Sarh, *Chad* 73 G8
Sarhro, Djebel, *Morocco* 74 B3
Sārī, *Iran* 65 B7
Sária, *Greece* 39 P10
Sarıgöl, *Turkey* 66 C3
Sarikamiş, *Turkey* 67 B10
Sarıkaya, *Turkey* 66 C6
Sarikei, *Malaysia* 56 D4
Sarina, *Australia* 90 C4
Sariñena, *Spain* 28 D4
Sarita, *U.S.A.* 109 M6
Sariwŏn, *N. Korea* 51 E13
Sariyar Baraji, *Turkey* 66 B4
Sark, *U.K.* 13 H5
Sarkad, *Hungary* 21 J11
Şarkışla, *Turkey* 66 C7
Şarköy, *Turkey* 66 B2
Sarlat-la-Canéda, *France* 26 D5
Sarles, *U.S.A.* 108 A5
Sărmaşu, *Romania* 38 C7
Sarmi, *Indonesia* 57 E9
Sarmiento, *Argentina* 128 C3
Särna, *Sweden* 10 C7
Sarnano, *Italy* 33 E10
Sarnen, *Switz.* 22 C6
Sarnia, *Canada* 98 D3
Sarno, *Italy* 35 B7
Sarny, *Ukraine* 44 D3
Särö, *Sweden* 11 G5
Sarolangun, *Indonesia* 56 E2
Saronikós Kólpos, *Greece* 39 M6
Saronno, *Italy* 32 C6
Saros Körfezi, *Turkey* 66 B2
Sárospatak, *Hungary* 21 G11
Sarpsborg, *Norway* 10 E5
Sarracín, *Spain* 28 C1
Sarralbe, *France* 25 D14
Sarre = Saar →, *Europe* 25 C13
Sarre-Union, *France* 25 D14
Sarrebourg, *France* 25 D14
Sarreguemines, *France* 25 C14
Sarriá, *Spain* 30 C3
Sarrión, *Spain* 28 E4
Sarro, *Mali* 78 C3
Sarstedt, *Germany* 18 C5
Sartène, *France* 27 G12
Sarthe □, *France* 24 E7
Sarthe →, *France* 24 E6
Sartilly, *France* 24 D5
Sartynya, *Russia* 44 C7
Sárvár, *Hungary* 21 H6
Sarvestān, *Iran* 65 D7
Särvfjället, *Sweden* 10 B7
Sárviz →, *Hungary* 21 J8
Sary-Tash, *Kyrgyzstan* 44 F8
Sarych, Mys, *Ukraine* 41 K7
Saryshagan, *Kazakstan* 44 E8
Sarzana, *Italy* 32 D6
Sarzeau, *France* 24 E4
Sas van Gent, *Neths.* 17 F3
Sasabeneh, *Ethiopia* 68 F3
Sasaram, *India* 63 G11
Sasebo, *Japan* 49 H4
Saser, *India* 63 B7
Saskatchewan □, *Canada* 101 C7
Saskatchewan →, *Canada* 101 C8
Saskatoon, *Canada* 101 C7
Saskylakh, *Russia* 45 B12
Sasolburg, *S. Africa* 85 D4
Sasovo, *Russia* 42 C5
Sassandra, *Ivory C.* 78 E3
Sassandra →, *Ivory C.* 78 E3
Sássari, *Italy* 34 B1
Sassenheim, *Neths.* 16 D5
Sassnitz, *Germany* 18 A9
Sasso Marconi, *Italy* 33 D8
Sassocorvaro, *Italy* 33 E9
Sassoferrato, *Italy* 33 E9
Sassuolo, *Italy* 32 D7
Sástago, *Spain* 28 D4
Sastown, *Liberia* 78 E3
Sasumua Dam, *Kenya* 82 C4
Sasyk, Ozero, *Ukraine* 41 K5
Sata-Misaki, *Japan* 49 J5
Satadougou, *Mali* 78 C2
Satakunta, *Finland* 9 F20
Satanta, *U.S.A.* 109 G4
Satara, *India* 60 L8
Satilla →, *U.S.A.* 105 K5
Satipo, *Peru* 124 C3
Satmala Hills, *India* 60 J9
Satna, *India* 63 G9
Šator, *Bos.-H.* 33 D13
Sátoraljaújhely, *Hungary* 21 G11
Satpura Ra., *India* 62 J7
Satrup, *Germany* 18 A5
Satsuna-Shotō, *Japan* 49 K5
Sattahip, *Thailand* 58 F3
Satu Mare, *Romania* 38 B5
Satui, *Indonesia* 56 E5
Satun, *Thailand* 59 J3
Saturnina →, *Brazil* 125 C6
Sauce, *Argentina* 126 C4
Sauceda, *Mexico* 114 B4
Saucillo, *Mexico* 114 B3
Sauda, *Norway* 9 G12
Saúde, *Brazil* 122 D3
Sauðarkrókur, *Iceland* 8 D4
Saudi Arabia ■, *Asia* 68 B3
Sauer →, *Germany* 17 J9
Saugeen →, *Canada* 106 B3
Saugerties, *U.S.A.* 107 D11
Saugues, *France* 26 D7
Sauherad, *Norway* 10 E3
Saujon, *France* 26 C3
Sauk Centre, *U.S.A.* 108 C7
Sauk Rapids, *U.S.A.* 108 C7
Saül, *Fr. Guiana* 121 C7
Saulgau, *Germany* 19 G5
Saulieu, *France* 25 E11
Sault, *France* 27 D9
Sault Ste. Marie, *Canada* 98 C3
Sault Ste. Marie, *U.S.A.* 104 B3
Saumlaki, *Indonesia* 57 F8
Saumur, *France* 24 E6
Saunders C., *N.Z.* 87 L3
Saunders I., *Antarctica* 5 B1
Saunders Point, *Australia* 89 E4
Sauri, *Nigeria* 79 C6
Saurimo, *Angola* 80 F4
Sausalito, *U.S.A.* 112 H4
Sautatá, *Colombia* 120 B2
Sauveterre-de-Béarn, *France* 26 E3
Sauzé-Vaussais, *France* 26 B4
Savá, *Honduras* 116 C2
Sava →, *Serbia, Yug.* 21 L10
Savage, *U.S.A.* 108 B2
Savage I. = Niue, *Cook Is.* 93 J11
Savai'i, *W. Samoa* 87 A12
Savalou, *Benin* 79 D5
Savane, *Mozam.* 83 F4
Savanna, *U.S.A.* 108 D9
Savanna la Mar, *Jamaica* 116 C4
Savannah, *Ga., U.S.A.* 105 J5
Savannah, *Mo., U.S.A.* 108 F7
Savannah, *Tenn., U.S.A.* 105 H1
Savannah →, *U.S.A.* 105 J5
Savannakhet, *Laos* 58 D5
Savant L., *Canada* 98 B1
Savant Lake, *Canada* 98 B1
Savanur, *India* 60 M9
Savé, *Benin* 79 D5
Save →, *France* 26 E5
Save →, *Mozam.* 85 C5
Sāveh, *Iran* 65 C6
Savelugu, *Ghana* 79 D4
Savenay, *France* 24 E5
Saverdun, *France* 26 E5
Saverne, *France* 25 D14
Savièse, *Switz.* 22 D4
Savigliano, *Italy* 32 D4
Savigny-sur-Braye, *France* 24 E7
Saviñao, *Spain* 30 C3
Savio →, *Italy* 33 D9
Savo, *Finland* 8 E22
Savognin, *Switz.* 23 C9
Savoie □, *France* 27 C10
Savona, *Italy* 32 D5
Savonlinna, *Finland* 40 B5
Şavşat, *Turkey* 67 B10
Sawahlunto, *Indonesia* 56 E2
Sawai, *Indonesia* 57 E7
Sawai Madhopur, *India* 62 F7
Sawang Daen Din, *Thailand* 58 D4
Sawankhalok, *Thailand* 58 D2
Sawara, *Japan* 49 G10
Sawatch Mts., *U.S.A.* 111 G10
Sawel Mt., *U.K.* 15 B4
Sawi, *Thailand* 59 G2
Sawmills, *Zimbabwe* 83 F2
Sawu, *Indonesia* 57 F6
Sawu Sea, *Indonesia* 57 F6
Saxby →, *Australia* 90 B3
Saxon, *Switz.* 22 D4
Saxony, Lower = Niedersachsen □, *Germany* 18 C5
Saxton, *U.S.A.* 106 F6
Say, *Niger* 79 C5
Saya, *Nigeria* 79 D5
Sayabec, *Canada* 99 C6
Sayaboury, *Laos* 58 C3
Sayán, *Peru* 124 C2
Sayan, Vostochnyy, *Russia* 45 D10
Sayan, Zapadnyy, *Russia* 45 D10
Saydā, *Lebanon* 69 B4
Sayhan-Ovoo, *Mongolia* 50 B2
Sayhandulaan, *Mongolia* 50 B5
Sayḥut, *Yemen* 68 D5
Saykhin, *Kazakstan* 43 F8
Saynshand, *Mongolia* 50 B6
Sayre, *Okla., U.S.A.* 109 H5
Sayre, *Pa., U.S.A.* 107 E8
Sayula, *Mexico* 114 D4
Sazin, *Pakistan* 63 B5
Sazlika →, *Bulgaria* 39 H8
Sbeïtla, *Tunisia* 75 A6
Scaër, *France* 24 D3
Scafell Pike, *U.K.* 12 C4
Scalea, *Italy* 35 C8
Scalpay, *U.K.* 14 D2
Scandia, *Canada* 100 C6
Scandiano, *Italy* 32 D7
Scandinavia, *Europe* 6 C8
Scansano, *Italy* 33 F8
Scapa Flow, *U.K.* 14 C5
Scappoose, *U.S.A.* 112 E4
Scarborough, *Trin. & Tob.* 117 D7
Scarborough, *U.K.* 12 C7
Scebeli, Wabi →, *Somali Rep.* 68 G3
Šćedro, *Croatia* 33 E13
Scenic, *U.S.A.* 108 D3
Schaalsee, *Germany* 18 B6
Schaan, *Liech.* 23 B9
Schaesberg, *Neths.* 17 G8
Schaffen, *Belgium* 17 G6
Schaffhausen, *Switz.* 23 A7
Schaffhausen □, *Switz.* 23 A7
Schagen, *Neths.* 16 C5
Schaijk, *Neths.* 16 E7
Schalkhaar, *Neths.* 16 D8
Schalkwijk, *Neths.* 16 E6
Schangnau, *Switz.* 22 C5
Schänis, *Switz.* 23 B8
Schärding, *Austria* 20 G3
Scharhörn, *Germany* 18 B4
Scharnitz, *Austria* 19 H7
Scheessel, *Germany* 18 B5
Schefferville, *Canada* 99 B6
Schelde →, *Belgium* 17 F4
Schell Creek Ra., *U.S.A.* 110 G6
Schenectady, *U.S.A.* 107 D11
Scherfede, *Germany* 18 D5
Scherpenheuvel, *Belgium* 17 G5
Scherpenisse, *Neths.* 17 E4
Scherpenzeel, *Neths.* 16 D7
Schesaplana, *Switz.* 23 B9
Schesslitz, *Germany* 19 F7
Scheveningen, *Neths.* 16 D4
Schiedam, *Neths.* 16 E4
Schiermonnikoog, *Neths.* 16 B8
Schiers, *Switz.* 23 C9
Schifferstadt, *Germany* 19 F4
Schifflange, *Lux.* 17 K8
Schijndel, *Neths.* 17 E6
Schiltigheim, *France* 25 D14
Schio, *Italy* 33 C8
Schipbeek, *Neths.* 16 D8
Schipluiden, *Neths.* 16 E4
Schirmeck, *France* 25 D14
Schlanders = Silandro, *Italy* 32 B7
Schlei →, *Germany* 18 A5
Schleiden, *Germany* 18 E2
Schleiz, *Germany* 18 E7
Schleswig, *Germany* 18 A5
Schleswig-Holstein □, *Germany* 18 A5
Schlieren, *Switz.* 23 B6
Schlüchtern, *Germany* 19 E5
Schmalkalden, *Germany* 18 E6
Schmölln, *Brandenburg, Germany* 18 B10
Schmölln, *Thüringen, Germany* 18 E8
Schneeberg, *Austria* 21 H5
Schneeberg, *Germany* 18 E8
Schoenberg, *Belgium* 17 H8
Schofield, *U.S.A.* 108 C10
Scholls, *U.S.A.* 112 E4
Schönberg, *Mecklenburg-Vorpommern, Germany* 18 B6
Schönberg, *Schleswig-Holstein, Germany* 18 A6
Schönebeck, *Germany* 18 C7
Schönenwerd, *Switz.* 22 B5
Schongau, *Germany* 19 H6
Schöningen, *Germany* 18 C6
Schoondijke, *Neths.* 17 F3
Schoonebeek, *Neths.* 16 C9
Schoonhoven, *Neths.* 16 E5
Schoorl, *Neths.* 16 C5
Schortens, *Germany* 18 B3
Schoten, *Belgium* 17 F5
Schouten I., *Australia* 90 G4
Schouten Is. = Supiori, *Indonesia* 57 E9
Schouwen, *Neths.* 17 E3
Schramberg, *Germany* 19 G4
Schrankogl, *Austria* 19 H7
Schreckhorn, *Switz.* 22 C6
Schreiber, *Canada* 98 C2
Schrobenhausen, *Germany* 19 G7
Schruns, *Austria* 19 H5
Schuler, *Canada* 101 C6
Schuls, *Switz.* 23 C10
Schumacher, *Canada* 98 C3
Schüpfen, *Switz.* 22 B4
Schüpfheim, *Switz.* 22 C6
Schurz, *U.S.A.* 110 G4
Schuyler, *U.S.A.* 108 E6
Schuylkill Haven, *U.S.A.* 107 F8
Schwabach, *Germany* 19 F7
Schwäbisch Gmünd, *Germany* 19 G5
Schwäbisch Hall, *Germany* 19 F5
Schwäbische Alb, *Germany* 19 G5
Schwabmünchen, *Germany* 19 G6
Schwanden, *Switz.* 23 C8
Schwandorf, *Germany* 19 F8
Schwaner, Pegunungan, *Indonesia* 56 E4
Schwarmstedt, *Germany* 18 C5
Schwärze, *Germany* 18 C9
Schwarze Elster →, *Germany* 18 D8
Schwarzenberg, *Germany* 18 E8
Schwarzenburg, *Switz.* 22 C4
Schwarzwald, *Germany* 19 H4
Schwaz, *Austria* 19 H7
Schwedt, *Germany* 18 B10
Schweinfurt, *Germany* 19 E6
Schweizer Mittelland, *Switz.* 22 C4
Schweizer-Reneke, *S. Africa* 84 D4
Schwenningen = Villingen-Schwenningen, *Germany* 19 G4
Schwerin, *Germany* 18 B7
Schweriner See, *Germany* 18 B7
Schwetzingen, *Germany* 19 F4
Schwyz, *Switz.* 23 B7
Schwyz □, *Switz.* 23 B7
Sciacca, *Italy* 34 E6
Scicli, *Italy* 35 F7
Scilla, *Italy* 35 D8
Scilly, Isles of, *U.K.* 13 H1
Ścinawa, *Poland* 20 D6
Scioto →, *U.S.A.* 104 F4
Scobey, *U.S.A.* 108 A2
Scone, *Australia* 91 E5
Scórdia, *Italy* 35 E7
Scoresbysund, *Greenland* 4 B6
Scorno, Punta dello, *Italy* 34 A1
Scotia, *Calif., U.S.A.* 110 F1
Scotia, *N.Y., U.S.A.* 107 D11
Scotia Sea, *Antarctica* 5 B18
Scotland, *U.S.A.* 108 D6
Scotland □, *U.K.* 14 E5
Scotland Neck, *U.S.A.* 105 G7
Scott, C., *Australia* 88 B4
Scott City, *U.S.A.* 108 F4
Scott Glacier, *Antarctica* 5 C8
Scott I., *Antarctica* 5 C11
Scott Inlet, *Canada* 97 A12
Scott Is., *Canada* 100 C3
Scott L., *Canada* 101 B7
Scott Reef, *Australia* 88 B3
Scottburgh, *S. Africa* 85 E5
Scottdale, *U.S.A.* 106 F5
Scottsbluff, *U.S.A.* 108 E3
Scottsboro, *U.S.A.* 105 H2
Scottsburg, *U.S.A.* 104 F3
Scottsdale, *Australia* 90 G4
Scottsdale, *U.S.A.* 111 K7
Scottsville, *Ky., U.S.A.* 105 G2
Scottsville, *N.Y., U.S.A.* 106 C7
Scottville, *U.S.A.* 104 D2
Scranton, *U.S.A.* 107 E9
Scugog, L., *Canada* 106 B6
Scunthorpe, *U.K.* 12 D7
Scuol, *Switz.* 23 C10
Scusciuban, *Somali Rep.* 68 E5
Scutari = Üsküdar, *Turkey* 39 H11
Seabra, *Brazil* 123 D3
Seabrook, L., *Australia* 89 F2
Seaford, *U.S.A.* 104 F8
Seaforth, *Canada* 98 D3
Seagraves, *U.S.A.* 109 J3
Seal →, *Canada* 101 B10
Seal Cove, *Canada* 99 C8
Seal L., *Canada* 99 B7
Sealy, *U.S.A.* 109 L6
Searchlight, *U.S.A.* 113 K12
Searcy, *U.S.A.* 109 H9
Searles L., *U.S.A.* 113 K9
Seaside, *Calif., U.S.A.* 112 J5
Seaside, *Oreg., U.S.A.* 112 E3
Seaspray, *Australia* 91 F4
Seattle, *U.S.A.* 112 C4
Seaview Ra., *Australia* 90 B4

Sebastián Vizcaíno, B., Mexico 114 B2
Sebastopol = Sevastopol, Ukraine 41 K7
Sebastopol, U.S.A. 112 G4
Sebderat, Eritrea 77 D4
Sebdou, Algeria 75 B4
Seben, Turkey 66 B4
Sebewaing, U.S.A. 104 D4
Sebezh, Russia 40 D5
Sebha = Sabhah, Libya 73 C7
Sébi, Mali 78 B4
Şebinkarahisar, Turkey 67 B8
Sebiş, Romania 38 C5
Sebkhet Te-n-Dghâmcha, Mauritania 78 B1
Sebkra Azzel Mati, Algeria 75 C5
Sebkra Mekerghene, Algeria 75 C5
Sebnitz, Germany 18 E10
Sebou, Oued →, Morocco 74 B3
Sebring, Fla., U.S.A. 105 M5
Sebring, Ohio, U.S.A. 106 F3
Sebringville, Canada 106 C3
Sebta = Ceuta, N. Afr. 74 A3
Sebuku, Indonesia 56 E5
Sebuku, Teluk, Malaysia 56 D5
Secchia →, Italy 32 C8
Sechelt, Canada 100 D4
Sechura, Peru 124 B1
Sechura, Desierto de, Peru 124 B1
Seclin, France 25 B10
Secondigny, France 24 F6
Secretary I., N.Z. 87 L1
Secunderabad, India 60 L11
Sécure →, Bolivia 125 D5
Sedalia, U.S.A. 108 F8
Sedan, Australia 91 E2
Sedan, France 25 C11
Sedan, U.S.A. 109 G6
Sedano, Spain 28 C1
Seddon, N.Z. 87 J5
Seddonville, N.Z. 87 J4
Sedeh, Fārs, Iran 65 D7
Sedeh, Khorāsān, Iran 65 C8
Sederot, Israel 69 D3
Sedgewick, Canada 100 C6
Sedhiou, Senegal 78 C1
Sedičany, Czech. 20 F4
Sedico, Italy 33 B9
Sedley, Canada 101 C8
Sedova, Pik, Russia 44 B6
Sedrata, Algeria 75 A6
Sedro Woolley, U.S.A. 112 B4
Sedrun, Switz. 23 C7
Seebad Ahlbeck, Germany 18 B10
Seehausen, Germany 18 C7
Seeheim, Namibia 84 D2
Seekoei →, S. Africa 84 E4
Seelow, Germany 18 C10
Sées, France 24 D7
Seesen, Germany 18 D6
Sefadu, S. Leone 78 D2
Seferihisar, Turkey 66 C2
Séfeto, Mali 78 C3
Sefrou, Morocco 74 B4
Sefwi Bekwai, Ghana 78 D4
Segamat, Malaysia 59 L4
Segarcea, Romania 38 E6
Segbwema, S. Leone 78 D2
Seget, Indonesia 57 E8
Seggueur, O. →, Algeria 75 B5
Segonzac, France 26 C3
Segorbe, Spain 28 F4
Ségou, Mali 78 C3
Segovia = Coco →, Cent. Amer. 116 D3
Segovia, Colombia 120 B3
Segovia, Spain 30 E6
Segovia □, Spain 30 E6
Segré, France 24 E6
Segre →, Spain 28 D5
Séguéla, Ivory C. 78 D3
Seguin, U.S.A. 109 L6
Segundo →, Argentina 126 C3
Segura →, Spain 29 G4
Segura, Sierra de, Spain 29 G2
Seh Qal'eh, Iran 65 C8
Sehitwa, Botswana 84 C3
Sehore, India 62 H7
Sehwan, Pakistan 62 F2
Şeica Mare, Romania 38 C7
Seiland, Norway 8 A20
Seiling, U.S.A. 109 G5
Seille →, Moselle, France 25 C13
Seille →, Saône-et-Loire, France 27 B8
Seilles, Belgium 17 G6
Sein, I. de, France 24 D2
Seinäjoki, Finland 9 E20
Seine →, France 24 C7
Seine, B. de la, France 24 C6
Seine-et-Marne □, France 25 D9
Seine-Maritime □, France 24 C7
Seine-St.-Denis □, France 25 D9
Seistan, Iran 65 D9
Sejerø, Denmark 11 J5
Sejerø Bugt, Denmark 11 J5
Seka, Ethiopia 77 F4
Sekayu, Indonesia 56 E2
Seke, Tanzania 82 C3
Sekenke, Tanzania 82 C3
Sekondi-Takoradi, Ghana 78 E4
Seksna, Russia 40 C10
Sekuma, Botswana 84 C3
Selah, U.S.A. 110 C3
Selama, Malaysia 59 K3
Selárgius, Italy 34 C2
Selaru, Indonesia 57 F8
Selb, Germany 19 E8
Selby, U.K. 12 D6
Selby, U.S.A. 108 C4
Selca, Croatia 33 E13
Selçuk, Turkey 66 D2
Selden, U.S.A. 108 F4
Sele →, Italy 35 B7
Selemdzha →, Russia 45 D13
Selenga = Selenge Mörön →, Asia 54 A5
Selenge Mörön →, Asia 54 A5
Selenica, Albania 39 J2
Selenter See, Germany 18 A6
Sélestat, France 25 D14
Seletan, Tg., Indonesia 56 E4
Selfridge, U.S.A. 108 B4
Sélibabi, Mauritania 78 B2
Seliger, Ozero, Russia 42 B1
Seligman, U.S.A. 111 J7
Şelim, Turkey 67 B10
Selîma, El Wâhât el, Sudan 76 C2
Selinda Spillway, Botswana 84 B3
Selinoús, Greece 39 M4
Selizharovo, Russia 42 B1
Seljord, Norway 10 E2
Selkirk, Canada 101 C9
Selkirk, U.K. 14 F6
Selkirk I., Canada 101 C9
Selkirk Mts., Canada 100 C5
Selles-sur-Cher, France 25 E8
Selliá, Greece 37 D6
Sellières, France 25 F12
Sells, U.S.A. 111 L8
Sellye, Hungary 21 K7
Selma, Ala., U.S.A. 105 J2
Selma, Calif., U.S.A. 111 H4
Selma, N.C., U.S.A. 105 H6
Selmer, U.S.A. 105 H1
Selongey, France 25 E12
Selowandoma Falls, Zimbabwe 83 G3
Selpele, Indonesia 57 E8
Selsey Bill, U.K. 13 G7
Seltso, Russia 42 D2
Seltz, France 25 D15
Selu, Indonesia 57 F8
Sélune →, France 24 D5
Selva, Argentina 126 B3
Selva, Italy 33 B8
Selva, Spain 28 D6
Selvas, Brazil 124 B4
Selwyn, Australia 90 C3
Selwyn L., Canada 101 A8
Selwyn Ra., Australia 90 C3
Selyatyn, Ukraine 38 B8
Semani →, Albania 39 J2
Semara, W. Sahara 74 C2
Semarang, Indonesia 57 G14
Semau, Indonesia 57 F6
Sembabule, Uganda 82 C3
Şemdinli, Turkey 67 D11
Sémé, Senegal 78 B2
Semeih, Sudan 77 E3
Semenov, Russia 42 B7
Semenovka, Ukraine 41 H7
Semenovka, Ukraine 41 F7
Semeru, Indonesia 57 H15
Semey, Kazakstan 44 D9
Semikarakorskiy, Russia 43 G5
Semiluki, Russia 42 E4
Seminoe Reservoir, U.S.A. 110 E10
Seminole, Okla., U.S.A. 109 H6
Seminole, Tex., U.S.A. 109 J3
Semiozernoye, Kazakstan 44 D7
Semipalatinsk = Semey, Kazakstan 44 D9
Semirara Is., Phil. 55 F4
Semisopochnoi I., U.S.A. 96 C2
Semitau, Indonesia 56 D4
Semiyarka, Kazakstan 44 D8
Semiyarskoye = Semiyarka, Kazakstan 44 D8
Semmering P., Austria 21 H5
Semnān, Iran 65 C7
Semnān □, Iran 65 C7
Semois →, Europe 17 J5
Semporna, Malaysia 57 D5
Semuda, Indonesia 56 E4
Semur-en-Auxois, France 25 E11
Sena, Bolivia 124 C4
Senā, Iran 65 D6
Sena, Mozam. 83 F3
Sena →, Bolivia 124 C4
Sena Madureira, Brazil 124 B4
Senador Pompeu, Brazil 122 C4
Senaja, Malaysia 56 C5
Senaki, Georgia 43 J6
Senanga, Zambia 84 B3
Senatobia, U.S.A. 109 H10
Sendafa, Ethiopia 77 F4
Sendai, Kagoshima, Japan 49 J5
Sendai, Miyagi, Japan 48 E10
Sendai-Wan, Japan 48 E10
Sendenhorst, Germany 18 D3
Seneca, Oreg., U.S.A. 110 D4
Seneca, S.C., U.S.A. 105 H4
Seneca Falls, U.S.A. 107 D8
Seneca L., U.S.A. 106 D8
Seneffe, Belgium 17 G4
Senegal ■, W. Afr. 78 C2
Senegal →, W. Afr. 78 B1
Senegambia, Africa 70 E2
Senekal, S. Africa 85 D4
Senftenberg, Germany 18 D10
Senga Hill, Zambia 83 D3
Senge Khambab = Indus →, Pakistan 62 G2
Sengerema □, Tanzania 82 C3
Sengiley, Russia 42 D9
Sengkang, Indonesia 57 E6
Sengua →, Zimbabwe 83 F2
Senguerr →, Argentina 128 C3
Senhor-do-Bonfim, Brazil 122 D3
Senica, Slovak Rep. 20 G7
Senigállia, Italy 33 E10
Senio →, Italy 33 D9
Senirkent, Turkey 66 C4
Senise, Italy 35 B9
Senj, Croatia 33 D11
Senja, Norway 8 B17
Senlis, France 25 C9
Senmonorom, Cambodia 58 F6
Sennâr, Sudan 77 E3
Senne →, Belgium 17 G4
Senneterre, Canada 98 C4
Senniquelle, Liberia 78 D3
Senno, Belarus 40 E5
Sennori, Italy 34 B1
Seno, Laos 58 D5
Senonches, France 24 D8
Senorbì, Italy 34 C2
Senožeče, Slovenia 33 C11
Sens, France 25 D10
Senta, Serbia, Yug. 21 K10
Sentani, Indonesia 57 E10
Sentery, Zaïre 82 D2
Sentinel, U.S.A. 111 K7
Sentolo, Indonesia 57 G14
Senya Beraku, Ghana 79 D4
Seo de Urgel, Spain 28 C6
Seohara, India 63 E8
Seoni, India 63 H8
Seoul = Sŏul, S. Korea 51 F14
Separation Point, Canada 99 B8
Sepīdān, Iran 65 D7
Sepo-ri, N. Korea 51 E14
Sepone, Laos 58 D6
Sept-Îles, Canada 99 B6
Septemvri, Bulgaria 38 G7
Sepúlveda, Spain 30 D7
Sequeros, Spain 30 E4
Sequim, U.S.A. 112 B3
Sequoia National Park, U.S.A. 111 H4
Serafimovich, Russia 42 F6
Seraing, Belgium 17 G7
Seraja, Indonesia 59 L7
Serakhis →, Cyprus 37 D11
Seram, Indonesia 57 E7
Seram Laut, Kepulauan, Indonesia 57 E8
Seram Sea, Indonesia 57 E7
Serang, Indonesia 57 G12
Serasan, Indonesia 59 L7
Seravezza, Italy 32 E7
Serbia □, Yugoslavia 21 M11
Serdo, Ethiopia 77 E5
Serdobsk, Russia 42 D7
Seredka, Russia 40 C5
Şereflikoçhisar, Turkey 66 C5
Seregno, Italy 32 C6
Seremban, Malaysia 59 L3
Serengeti □, Tanzania 82 C3
Serengeti Plain, Tanzania 82 C3
Serenje, Zambia 83 E3
Sereth = Siret →, Romania 38 D11
Sergach, Russia 42 C7
Serge →, Spain 28 D5
Sergipe □, Brazil 122 D4
Sergiyev Posad, Russia 42 B4
Seria, Brunei 56 D4
Serian, Malaysia 56 D4
Seriate, Italy 32 C6
Seribu, Kepulauan, Indonesia 56 F3
Sérifontaine, France 25 C8
Sérifos, Greece 39 M7
Sérignan, France 26 E7
Serik, Turkey 66 D4
Seringapatam Reef, Australia 88 B3
Sermaize-les-Bains, France 25 D11
Sermata, Indonesia 57 F7
Sérmide, Italy 33 C8
Sernovodsk, Russia 42 D10
Sernur, Russia 42 B9
Serny Zavod, Turkmenistan 44 F6
Serón, Spain 29 H2
Serós, Spain 28 D5
Serov, Russia 44 D7
Serowe, Botswana 84 C4
Serpa, Portugal 31 H3
Serpeddi, Punta, Italy 34 C2
Serpentara, Isola, Italy 34 C2
Serpentine, Australia 89 F2
Serpentine Lakes, Australia 89 E4
Serpis →, Spain 29 G4
Serpukhov, Russia 42 C3
Serra do Navio, Brazil 121 C7
Serra San Bruno, Italy 35 D9
Serra Talhada, Brazil 122 C4
Serracapriola, Italy 35 A8
Serradilla, Spain 30 F4
Sérrai, Greece 39 H6
Serramanna, Italy 34 C1
Serrat, C., Tunisia 75 A6
Serre-Ponçon, L. de, France 27 D10
Serres, France 27 D9
Serrezuela, Argentina 126 C2
Serrinha, Brazil 123 D4
Serrita, Brazil 122 C4
Sersale, Italy 35 C9
Sertã, Portugal 30 F2
Sertânia, Brazil 122 C4
Sertanópolis, Brazil 127 A5
Sêrtar, China 52 A3
Sertig, Switz. 23 C9
Serua, Indonesia 57 F8
Serui, Indonesia 57 E9
Serule, Botswana 84 C4
Sérvia, Greece 39 J4
Sese Is., Uganda 82 C3
Sesepe, Indonesia 57 E7
Sesfontein, Namibia 84 B1
Sesheke, Zambia 84 B3
Sesia →, Italy 32 C5
Sesimbra, Portugal 31 G1
Sessa Aurunca, Italy 34 A6
S'estañol, Spain 36 B9
Sesto San Giovanni, Italy 32 C6
Sestri Levante, Italy 32 D6
Sestriere, Italy 32 D3
Sestroretsk, Russia 40 B6
Sestrunj, Croatia 33 D12
Sestu, Italy 34 C2
Sesvenna, Switz. 23 C10
Setana, Japan 48 C9
Sète, France 26 E7
Sete Lagôas, Brazil 123 E3
Sétif, Algeria 75 A6
Seto, Japan 49 G8
Setonaikai, Japan 49 G6
Settat, Morocco 74 B3
Setté-Cama, Gabon 80 E1
Séttimo Tor, Italy 32 C4
Setting L., Canada 101 B9
Settle, U.K. 12 C5
Settlement Pt., Bahamas 105 M6
Setto Calende, Italy 32 C5
Setúbal, Portugal 31 G2
Setúbal □, Portugal 31 G2
Setúbal, B. de, Portugal 31 G2
Seugne →, France 26 C3
Seulimeum, Indonesia 56 C1
Seuzach, Switz. 23 A7
Sevan, Armenia 43 K7
Sevan, Ozero = Sevana Lich, Armenia 43 K7
Sevana Lich, Armenia 43 K7
Sevastopol, Ukraine 41 K7
Sevelen, Switz. 23 B8
Seven Emu, Australia 90 B2
Seven Sisters, Canada 100 C3
Sevenum, Neths. 17 F8
Sever →, Spain 31 F3
Sévérac-le-Château, France 26 D7
Severn →, Canada 98 A2
Severn →, U.K. 13 F5
Severn L., Canada 98 B1
Severnaya Zemlya, Russia 45 B10
Severo-Kurilsk, Russia 45 D16
Severo-Yeniseyskiy, Russia 45 C10
Severodonetsk = Syeverodonetsk, Ukraine 41 H10
Severodvinsk, Russia 44 C4
Sevier, U.S.A. 111 G7
Sevier →, U.S.A. 111 G7
Sevier L., U.S.A. 110 G7
Sevilla, Colombia 120 C2
Sevilla, Spain 31 H5
Sevilla □, Spain 31 H5
Seville = Sevilla, Spain 31 H5
Sevnica, Slovenia 33 B12
Sèvre-Nantaise →, France 24 E5
Sèvre-Niortaise →, France 26 B3
Sevsk, Russia 42 D2
Seward, Alaska, U.S.A. 96 B5
Seward, Nebr., U.S.A. 108 E6
Seward Pen., U.S.A. 96 B3
Sewell, Chile 126 C1
Sewer, Indonesia 57 F8
Sewickley, U.S.A. 106 F4
Sexbierum, Neths. 16 B6
Sexsmith, Canada 100 B5
Seychelles ■, Ind. Oc. 71 G9
Seyðisfjörður, Iceland 8 D6
Seydişehir, Turkey 66 D4
Seydvān, Iran 67 C11
Seyhan Barajı, Turkey 66 D6
Seyitgazi, Turkey 66 C4
Seym →, Ukraine 41 G7
Seymchan, Russia 45 C16
Seymour, Australia 91 F4
Seymour, S. Africa 85 E4
Seymour, Conn., U.S.A. 107 E11
Seymour, Ind., U.S.A. 104 F3
Seymour, Tex., U.S.A. 109 J5
Seymour, Wis., U.S.A. 104 C1
Seyne, France 27 D10
Seyssel, France 27 C9
Sežana, Slovenia 33 C10
Sézanne, France 25 D10
Sezze, Italy 34 A6
Sfax, Tunisia 75 B7
Sfîntu Gheorghe, Romania 38 D8
Sfîntu Gheorghe, Braţul →, Romania 38 E12
Sha Xi →, China 53 D12
Sha Xian, China 53 D11
Shaanxi □, China 50 G5
Shaba □, Zaïre 82 D2
Shabunda, Zaïre 82 C2
Shache, China 54 C2
Shackleton Ice Shelf, Antarctica 5 C8
Shackleton Inlet, Antarctica 5 E11
Shādegān, Iran 65 D6
Shadi, China 53 D10
Shadi, India 63 C7
Shadrinsk, Russia 44 D7
Shaffa, Nigeria 79 C7
Shafter, Calif., U.S.A. 113 K7
Shafter, Tex., U.S.A. 109 L2
Shaftesbury, U.K. 13 F5
Shagamu, Nigeria 79 D5
Shagram, Pakistan 63 A5
Shah Bunder, Pakistan 62 G2
Shahabad, Punjab, India 62 D7
Shahabad, Raj., India 62 G7
Shahabad, Ut. P., India 63 F8
Shahadpur, Pakistan 62 G3
Shahba, Syria 69 C5
Shahdād, Iran 65 D8
Shahdadkot, Pakistan 62 F2
Shahe, China 50 F8
Shahganj, India 63 F10
Shahgarh, India 60 F6
Shaḩḩāt, Libya 73 B9
Shahjahanpur, India 63 F8
Shahpur, India 62 H7
Shahpur, Pakistan 62 E3
Shahpura, India 63 H9
Shahr Kord, Iran 65 C6
Shāhrakht, Iran 65 C9
Shahrig, Pakistan 62 D2
Shahukou, China 50 D7
Shaikhabad, Afghan. 62 B3
Shajapur, India 62 H7
Shakargarh, Pakistan 62 C6
Shakawe, Botswana 84 B3
Shaker Heights, U.S.A. 106 E3
Shakhty, Russia 43 G5
Shakhunya, Russia 42 B8
Shaki, Nigeria 79 D5
Shala, L., Ethiopia 77 F4
Shali, Russia 43 J7
Shallow Lake, Canada 106 B3
Shalqar, Kazakstan 44 E6
Shalskiy, Russia 40 B8
Shaluli Shan, China 52 B2
Shām, Iran 65 E8
Shamâl Dârfûr □, Sudan 77 D2
Shamâl Kordofân □, Sudan 77 D2
Shamanovo, Russia 45 C15
Shamattawa, Canada 101 B10
Shamattawa →, Canada 98 A2
Shambe, Sudan 77 F3
Shambu, Ethiopia 77 F4
Shamīl, Iran 65 E8
Shamkhor = Şämkir, Azerbaijan 43 K8
Shāmkūh, Iran 65 C8
Shamli, India 62 E7
Shamo = Gobi, Asia 50 C5
Shamo, L., Ethiopia 77 F4
Shamokin, U.S.A. 107 F8
Shamrock, U.S.A. 109 H4
Shamva, Zimbabwe 83 F3
Shan □, Burma 61 J21
Shan Xian, China 50 G9
Shanan →, Ethiopia 77 F5
Shanchengzhen, China 51 C13
Shāndak, Iran 65 D9
Shandon, U.S.A. 112 K6
Shandong □, China 51 F10
Shandong Bandao, China 51 F11
Shang Xian, China 50 H5
Shangalowe, Zaïre 83 E2
Shangani →, Zimbabwe 83 F2
Shangbancheng, China 51 D10
Shangcai, China 53 A10
Shangcheng, China 53 B10
Shangchuan Dao, China 53 G9
Shangdu, China 50 D7
Shanggao, China 53 C10
Shanghai, China 53 B13
Shanghang, China 53 E11
Shanghe, China 51 F9
Shangjin, China 53 A8
Shanglin, China 52 F7
Shangnan, China 50 H6
Shangqiu, China 50 G8
Shangrao, China 53 C11
Shangshui, China 50 H8
Shangsi, China 52 F6
Shangyou, China 53 E10
Shangzhi, China 51 B14
Shanhetun, China 51 B14
Shani, Nigeria 79 C7
Shaniko, U.S.A. 110 D3
Shannon, N.Z. 87 J5
Shannon →, Ireland 15 D2
Shansi = Shanxi □, China 50 F7
Shantar, Ostrov Bolshoy, Russia 45 D14
Shantipur, India 63 H13
Shantou, China 53 F11
Shantung = Shandong □, China 51 F10
Shanxi □, China 50 F7
Shanyang, China 50 H5
Shanyin, China 50 E7
Shaoguan, China 53 E9
Shaowu, China 53 D11
Shaoxing, China 53 C13
Shaoyang, Hunan, China 53 D8
Shaoyang, Hunan, China 53 D8
Shapinsay, U.K. 14 B6
Shaqra', Si. Arabia 64 E5
Shaqrā', Yemen 68 E4
Sharafa, Sudan 77 E2
Sharafkhāneh, Iran 67 C11
Sharbot Lake, Canada 107 B8
Shari, Japan 48 C12

Sharjah = Ash Shāriqah, *U.A.E.* 65 E7
Shark B., *Australia* 89 E1
Sharm el Sheikh, *Egypt* 76 B3
Sharon, *Mass., U.S.A.* 107 D13
Sharon, *Pa., U.S.A.* 106 E4
Sharon Springs, *U.S.A.* 108 F4
Sharp Pt., *Australia* 90 A3
Sharpe L., *Canada* 101 C10
Sharpsville, *U.S.A.* 106 E4
Sharq el Istiwa'iya □, *Sudan* 77 F3
Sharya, *Russia* 42 A7
Shasha, *Ethiopia* 77 F4
Shashemene, *Ethiopia* 77 F4
Shashi, *Botswana* 85 C4
Shashi, *China* 53 B9
Shashi →, *Africa* 83 G2
Shasta, Mt., *U.S.A.* 110 F2
Shasta L., *U.S.A.* 110 F2
Shatsk, *Russia* 42 C5
Shatt al'Arab →, *Iraq* 65 D6
Shattuck, *U.S.A.* 109 G5
Shatura, *Russia* 42 C4
Shaumyani = Shulaveri, *Georgia* 43 K7
Shaunavon, *Canada* 101 D7
Shaver L., *U.S.A.* 112 H7
Shaw →, *Australia* 88 D2
Shaw I., *Australia* 90 C4
Shawan, *China* 54 B3
Shawanaga, *Canada* 106 A4
Shawano, *U.S.A.* 104 C1
Shawinigan, *Canada* 98 C5
Shawnee, *U.S.A.* 109 H6
Shaybārā, *Si. Arabia* 64 E3
Shayib el Banat, Gebel, *Egypt* 76 B3
Shaykh Sa'īd, *Iraq* 67 F12
Shchekino, *Russia* 42 C3
Shcherbakov = Rybinsk, *Russia* 42 A4
Shchigry, *Russia* 42 E3
Shchors, *Ukraine* 41 G6
Shchuchinsk, *Kazakstan* 44 D8
She Xian, *Anhui, China* 53 C12
She Xian, *Hebei, China* 50 F7
Shea, *Guyana* 121 C6
Shebekino, *Russia* 42 E3
Shebele = Scebeli, Wabi →, *Somali Rep.* 68 G3
Sheboygan, *U.S.A.* 104 D2
Shediac, *Canada* 99 C7
Sheelin, L., *Ireland* 15 C4
Sheep Haven, *Ireland* 15 A4
Sheerness, *U.K.* 13 F8
Sheet Harbour, *Canada* 99 D7
Sheffield, *U.K.* 12 D6
Sheffield, *Ala., U.S.A.* 105 H2
Sheffield, *Mass., U.S.A.* 107 D11
Sheffield, *Pa., U.S.A.* 106 E5
Sheffield, *Tex., U.S.A.* 109 K4
Sheho, *Canada* 101 C8
Shehojele, *Ethiopia* 77 E4
Shehong, *China* 52 B5
Shehuen →, *Argentina* 128 C3
Sheikhpura, *India* 63 G11
Shek Hasan, *Ethiopia* 77 E4
Shekhupura, *Pakistan* 62 D5
Sheki = Şaki, *Azerbaijan* 43 K8
Shelburne, *N.S., Canada* 99 D6
Shelburne, *Ont., Canada* 98 D3
Shelburne, *U.S.A.* 107 B11
Shelburne B., *Australia* 90 A3
Shelburne Falls, *U.S.A.* 107 D12
Shelby, *Mich., U.S.A.* 104 D2
Shelby, *Mont., U.S.A.* 110 B8
Shelby, *N.C., U.S.A.* 105 H5
Shelby, *Ohio, U.S.A.* 106 F2
Shelbyville, *Ill., U.S.A.* 108 F10
Shelbyville, *Ind., U.S.A.* 104 F3
Shelbyville, *Tenn., U.S.A.* 105 H2
Sheldon, *U.S.A.* 108 D7
Sheldrake, *Canada* 99 B7
Shelikhova, Zaliv, *Russia* 45 D16
Shell Lake, *Canada* 101 C7
Shell Lakes, *Australia* 89 E4
Shellbrook, *Canada* 101 C7
Shellharbour, *Australia* 91 E5
Shelling Rocks, *Ireland* 15 E1
Shelon →, *Russia* 40 C6
Shelton, *Conn., U.S.A.* 107 E11
Shelton, *Wash., U.S.A.* 112 C3
Shemakha = Şamaxi, *Azerbaijan* 43 K9
Shen Xian, *China* 50 F8
Shenandoah, *Iowa, U.S.A.* 108 E7
Shenandoah, *Pa., U.S.A.* 107 F8
Shenandoah, *Va., U.S.A.* 104 F6
Shenandoah →, *U.S.A.* 104 F7
Shenchi, *China* 50 E7
Shendam, *Nigeria* 79 D6
Shendî, *Sudan* 77 D3
Sheng Xian, *China* 53 C13
Shengfang, *China* 50 E9
Shëngjergji, *Albania* 39 H3
Shëngjini, *Albania* 39 H2
Shenjingzi, *China* 51 B13
Shenmu, *China* 50 E6
Shennongjia, *China* 53 B8
Shenqiu, *China* 50 H8
Shenqiucheng, *China* 50 H8
Shensi = Shaanxi □, *China* 50 G5
Shenyang, *China* 51 D12
Shenzhen, *China* 53 F10
Sheopur Kalan, *India* 60 G10
Shepetivka, *Ukraine* 41 G4
Shepetovka = Shepetivka, *Ukraine* 41 G4
Shepparton, *Australia* 91 F4
Sheqi, *China* 50 H7
Sher Qila, *Pakistan* 63 A6
Sherborne, *U.K.* 13 G5
Sherbro I., *S. Leone* 78 D2
Sherbrooke, *Canada* 99 C5
Shereik, *Sudan* 76 D3
Sheridan, *Ark., U.S.A.* 109 H8
Sheridan, *Wyo., U.S.A.* 110 D10
Sherkot, *India* 63 E8
Sherman, *U.S.A.* 109 J6
Sherridon, *Canada* 101 B8
Sherwood, *N. Dak., U.S.A.* 108 A4
Sherwood, *Tex., U.S.A.* 109 K4
Sherwood Forest, *U.K.* 12 D6
Sheslay, *Canada* 100 B2
Sheslay →, *Canada* 100 B2
Shethanei L., *Canada* 101 B9
Shetland □, *U.K.* 14 A7
Shetland Is., *U.K.* 14 A7
Shewa □, *Ethiopia* 77 F4
Shewa Gimira, *Ethiopia* 77 F4
Sheyenne, *U.S.A.* 108 B5
Sheyenne →, *U.S.A.* 108 B6
Shibām, *Yemen* 68 D4
Shibata, *Japan* 48 F9
Shibecha, *Japan* 48 C12
Shibetsu, *Japan* 48 B11
Shibîn el Kôm, *Egypt* 76 H7
Shibîn el Qanâtir, *Egypt* 76 H7
Shibing, *China* 52 D7
Shibogama L., *Canada* 98 B2
Shibushi, *Japan* 49 J5
Shicheng, *China* 53 D11
Shickshock Mts. = Chic-Chocs, Mts., *Canada* 99 C6
Shidao, *China* 51 F12
Shidian, *China* 52 E2
Shido, *Japan* 49 G7
Shiel, L., *U.K.* 14 E3
Shield, C., *Australia* 90 A2
Shiga □, *Japan* 49 G8
Shigaib, *Sudan* 73 E9
Shigu, *China* 52 D2
Shiguaigou, *China* 50 D6
Shihchiachuangi = Shijiazhuang, *China* 50 E8
Shijiazhuang, *China* 50 E8
Shijiu Hu, *China* 53 B12
Shikarpur, *India* 62 E8
Shikarpur, *Pakistan* 62 F3
Shikoku □, *Japan* 49 H6
Shikoku-Sanchi, *Japan* 49 H6
Shilabo, *Ethiopia* 68 F3
Shiliguri, *India* 61 F16
Shilka, *Russia* 45 D12
Shilka →, *Russia* 45 D13
Shillelagh, *Ireland* 15 D5
Shillong, *India* 61 G17
Shilo, *West Bank* 69 C4
Shilong, *China* 53 F9
Shilou, *China* 50 F6
Shilovo, *Russia* 42 C5
Shimabara, *Japan* 49 H5
Shimada, *Japan* 49 G9
Shimane □, *Japan* 49 G6
Shimanovsk, *Russia* 45 D13
Shimen, *China* 53 C8
Shimenjie, *China* 53 C11
Shimian, *China* 52 C4
Shimizu, *Japan* 49 G9
Shimodate, *Japan* 49 F9
Shimoga, *India* 60 N9
Shimoni, *Kenya* 82 C4
Shimonoseki, *Japan* 49 H5
Shimpuru Rapids, *Angola* 84 B2
Shimsk, *Russia* 40 C6
Shin, L., *U.K.* 14 C4
Shin-Tone →, *Japan* 49 G10
Shinan, *China* 52 F7
Shinano →, *Japan* 49 F9
Shīndand, *Afghan.* 60 C3
Shingleton, *U.S.A.* 98 C2
Shingū, *Japan* 49 H7
Shinjō, *Japan* 48 E10
Shinkafe, *Nigeria* 79 C6
Shinshār, *Syria* 69 A5
Shinyanga, *Tanzania* 82 C3
Shinyanga □, *Tanzania* 82 C3
Shiogama, *Japan* 48 E10
Shiojiri, *Japan* 49 F8
Ship I., *U.S.A.* 109 K10
Shipehenski Prokhod, *Bulgaria* 38 G8
Shiping, *China* 52 F4
Shipki La, *India* 60 D11
Shippegan, *Canada* 99 C7
Shippensburg, *U.S.A.* 106 F7
Shiprock, *U.S.A.* 111 H9
Shiqian, *China* 52 D7
Shiqma, N. →, *Israel* 69 D3
Shiquan, *China* 50 H5
Shīr Kūh, *Iran* 65 D7
Shiragami-Misaki, *Japan* 48 D10
Shirakawa, *Fukushima, Japan* 49 F10
Shirakawa, *Gifu, Japan* 49 F8
Shirane-San, *Gumma, Japan* 49 F9
Shirane-San, *Yamanashi, Japan* 49 G9
Shiraoi, *Japan* 48 C10
Shīrāz, *Iran* 65 D7
Shirbin, *Egypt* 76 H7
Shire →, *Africa* 83 F4
Shiretoko-Misaki, *Japan* 48 B12
Shirinab →, *Pakistan* 62 D2
Shiriya-Zaki, *Japan* 48 D10
Shiroishi, *Japan* 48 E10
Shīrvān, *Iran* 65 B8
Shirwa, L. = Chilwa, L., *Malawi* 83 F4
Shishou, *China* 53 C9
Shitai, *China* 53 B11
Shivpuri, *India* 62 G7
Shixian, *China* 51 C15
Shixing, *China* 53 E10
Shiyan, *China* 53 A8
Shiyata, *Egypt* 76 B2
Shizhu, *China* 52 C7
Shizong, *China* 52 E5
Shizuishan, *China* 50 E4
Shizuoka, *Japan* 49 G9
Shizuoka □, *Japan* 49 G9
Shklov = Shklow, *Belarus* 40 E6
Shklow, *Belarus* 40 E6
Shkoder = Shkodra, *Albania* 38 G2
Shkodra, *Albania* 38 G2
Shkumbini →, *Albania* 39 H2
Shmidta, O., *Russia* 45 A10
Shō-Gawa →, *Japan* 49 F8
Shoal Lake, *Canada* 101 C8
Shōdo-Shima, *Japan* 49 G7
Shoeburyness, *U.K.* 13 F8
Sholapur = Solapur, *India* 60 L9
Shologontsy, *Russia* 45 C12
Shōmrōn, *West Bank* 69 C4
Shoshone, *Calif., U.S.A.* 113 K10
Shoshone, *Idaho, U.S.A.* 110 E6
Shoshone L., *U.S.A.* 110 D8
Shoshone Mts., *U.S.A.* 110 G5
Shoshong, *Botswana* 84 C4
Shoshoni, *U.S.A.* 110 E9
Shostka, *Ukraine* 41 G7
Shou Xian, *China* 53 A11
Shouchang, *China* 53 C12
Shouguang, *China* 51 F10
Shouning, *China* 53 D12
Shouyang, *China* 50 F7
Show Low, *U.S.A.* 111 J9
Shpola, *Ukraine* 41 H6
Shreveport, *U.S.A.* 109 J8
Shrewsbury, *U.K.* 12 E5
Shrirampur, *India* 63 H13
Shropshire □, *U.K.* 13 E5
Shu, *Kazakstan* 44 E8
Shu →, *Kazakstan* 46 E10
Shuangbai, *China* 52 E3
Shuangcheng, *China* 51 B14
Shuangfeng, *China* 53 D9
Shuanggou, *China* 51 G9
Shuangjiang, *China* 52 F2
Shuangliao, *China* 51 C12
Shuangshanzi, *China* 51 D10
Shuangyang, *China* 51 C13
Shuangyashan, *China* 54 B8
Shucheng, *China* 53 B11
Shugozero, *Russia* 40 C8
Shuguri Falls, *Tanzania* 83 D4
Shuiji, *China* 53 D12
Shuiye, *China* 50 F8
Shujalpur, *India* 62 H7
Shukpa Kunzang, *India* 63 B8
Shulan, *China* 51 B14
Shulaveri, *Georgia* 43 K7
Shule, *China* 54 C2
Shumagin Is., *U.S.A.* 96 C4
Shumerlya, *Russia* 42 C8
Shumikha, *Russia* 44 D7
Shunchang, *China* 53 D11
Shunde, *China* 53 F9
Shungay, *Kazakstan* 43 F8
Shungnak, *U.S.A.* 96 B4
Shuo Xian, *China* 50 E7
Shūr →, *Iran* 65 D7
Shūr Āb, *Iran* 65 C6
Shūr Gaz, *Iran* 65 D8
Shūrāb, *Iran* 65 C8
Shūrjestān, *Iran* 65 D7
Shurugwi, *Zimbabwe* 83 F3
Shūsf, *Iran* 65 D9
Shūsh, *Iran* 67 F13
Shūshtar, *Iran* 65 D6
Shuswap L., *Canada* 100 C5
Shuya, *Russia* 42 B5
Shuyang, *China* 51 G10
Shūzū, *Iran* 65 D7
Shwebo, *Burma* 61 H19
Shwegu, *Burma* 61 G20
Shweli →, *Burma* 61 H20
Shymkent, *Kazakstan* 44 E7
Shyok, *India* 63 B8
Shyok →, *Pakistan* 63 B6
Si Chon, *Thailand* 59 H2
Si Kiang = Xi Jiang →, *China* 53 F9
Si-ngan = Xi'an, *China* 50 G5
Si Prachan, *Thailand* 58 E3
Si Racha, *Thailand* 58 F3
Si Xian, *China* 51 H9
Siahan Range, *Pakistan* 60 F4
Siaksriindrapura, *Indonesia* 56 D2
Sialkot, *Pakistan* 62 C6
Siam = Thailand ■, *Asia* 58 E4
Siantan, P., *Indonesia* 59 L6
Siàpo →, *Venezuela* 120 C4
Siāreh, *Iran* 65 D9
Siargao, *Phil.* 55 G7
Siari, *Pakistan* 63 B7
Siasi, *Phil.* 57 C6
Siasi I., *Phil.* 55 J4
Siátista, *Greece* 39 J4
Siau, *Indonesia* 57 D7
Šiauliai, *Lithuania* 9 J20
Siaya □, *Kenya* 82 B3
Siazan = Siyäzän, *Azerbaijan* 43 K9
Sibâi, Gebel el, *Egypt* 76 B3
Sibari, *Italy* 35 C9
Şibayi, L., *S. Africa* 85 D5
Šibenik, *Croatia* 33 E12
Siberia, *Russia* 4 D13
Siberut, *Indonesia* 56 E1
Sibi, *Pakistan* 62 E2
Sibil, *Indonesia* 57 E10
Sibiti, *Congo* 80 E2
Sibiu, *Romania* 38 D7
Sibley, *Iowa, U.S.A.* 108 D7
Sibley, *La., U.S.A.* 109 J8
Sibolga, *Indonesia* 56 D1
Sibret, *Belgium* 17 J7
Sibsagar, *India* 61 F19
Sibu, *Malaysia* 56 D4
Sibuco, *Phil.* 55 H5
Sibuguey B., *Phil.* 55 H5
Sibut, *C.A.R.* 73 G8
Sibutu, *Phil.* 57 D5
Sibutu Group, *Phil.* 55 J3
Sibutu Passage, *E. Indies* 57 D5
Sibuyan, *Phil.* 55 E5
Sibuyan Sea, *Phil.* 55 E5
Sicamous, *Canada* 100 C5
Sichuan □, *China* 52 B5
Sicilia, *Italy* 35 E7
Sicilia □, *Italy* 35 E7
Sicilia, Canale di, *Italy* 34 E5
Sicilian Channel = Sicilia, Canale di, *Italy* 34 E5
Sicily = Sicilia, *Italy* 35 E7
Sicuani, *Peru* 124 C3
Siculiana, *Italy* 34 E6
Sidamo □, *Ethiopia* 77 G4
Sidaouet, *Niger* 79 B6
Sidári, *Greece* 37 A3
Siddeburen, *Neths.* 16 B9
Siddhapur, *India* 62 H5
Siddipet, *India* 60 K11
Sidéradougou, *Burkina Faso* 78 C4
Siderno, *Italy* 35 D9
Sídheros, Ákra, *Greece* 37 D8
Sidhirókastron, *Greece* 39 H6
Sîdi Abd el Rahmân, *Egypt* 76 H6
Sîdi Barrâni, *Egypt* 76 A2
Sidi-bel-Abbès, *Algeria* 75 A4
Sidi Bennour, *Morocco* 74 B3
Sidi Haneish, *Egypt* 76 A2
Sidi Kacem, *Morocco* 74 B3
Sidi Omar, *Egypt* 76 A1
Sidi Slimane, *Morocco* 74 B3
Sidi Smaïl, *Morocco* 74 B3
Sidlaw Hills, *U.K.* 14 E5
Sidley, Mt., *Antarctica* 5 D14
Sidmouth, *U.K.* 13 G4
Sidmouth, C., *Australia* 90 A3
Sidney, *Canada* 100 D4
Sidney, *Mont., U.S.A.* 108 B2
Sidney, *N.Y., U.S.A.* 107 D9
Sidney, *Nebr., U.S.A.* 108 E3
Sidney, *Ohio, U.S.A.* 104 E3
Sidoarjo, *Indonesia* 57 G15
Sidon = Saydā, *Lebanon* 69 B4
Sidra, G. of = Surt, Khalīj, *Libya* 73 B8
Sidra, G. of, *Libya* 70 C5
Siedlce, *Poland* 20 C12
Sieg →, *Germany* 18 E3
Siegburg, *Germany* 18 E3
Siegen, *Germany* 18 E4
Siem Pang, *Cambodia* 58 E6
Siem Reap, *Cambodia* 58 F4
Siena, *Italy* 33 E8
Sieradz, *Poland* 20 D8
Sierck-les-Bains, *France* 25 C13
Sierpc, *Poland* 20 C9
Sierpe, Bocas de la, *Venezuela* 121 B5
Sierra Blanca, *U.S.A.* 111 L11
Sierra Blanca Peak, *U.S.A.* 111 K11
Sierra City, *U.S.A.* 112 F6
Sierra Colorada, *Argentina* 128 B3
Sierra de Yeguas, *Spain* 31 H6
Sierra Gorda, *Chile* 126 A2
Sierra Grande, *Argentina* 128 B3
Sierra Leone ■, *W. Afr.* 78 D2
Sierra Madre, *Mexico* 115 D6
Sierra Mojada, *Mexico* 114 B4
Sierraville, *U.S.A.* 112 F6
Sierre, *Switz.* 22 D5
Sífnos, *Greece* 39 N7
Sifton, *Canada* 101 C8
Sifton Pass, *Canada* 100 B3
Sig, *Algeria* 75 A4
Sigdal, *Norway* 10 D3
Sigean, *France* 26 E6
Sighetu-Marmatiei, *Romania* 38 B6
Sighişoara, *Romania* 38 C7
Sigli, *Indonesia* 56 C1
Siglufjörður, *Iceland* 8 C4
Sigmaringen, *Germany* 19 G5
Signakhi = Tsnori, *Georgia* 43 K7
Signal, *U.S.A.* 113 L13
Signal Pk., *U.S.A.* 113 M12
Signau, *Switz.* 22 C5
Signy-l'Abbaye, *France* 25 C11
Sigsig, *Ecuador* 120 D2
Sigtuna, *Sweden* 10 E11
Sigüenza, *Spain* 28 D2
Siguiri, *Guinea* 78 C3
Sigulda, *Latvia* 9 H21
Sigurd, *U.S.A.* 111 G8
Sihanoukville = Kompong Som, *Cambodia* 59 G4
Sihaus, *Peru* 124 B2
Sihui, *China* 53 F9
Siikajoki →, *Finland* 8 D21
Siilinjärvi, *Finland* 8 E22
Siirt, *Turkey* 67 D9
Sijarira Ra., *Zimbabwe* 83 F2
Sikao, *Thailand* 59 J2
Sikar, *India* 62 F6
Sikasso, *Mali* 78 C3
Sikeston, *U.S.A.* 109 G10
Sikhote Alin, Khrebet, *Russia* 45 E14
Sikhote Alin Ra. = Sikhote Alin, Khrebet, *Russia* 45 E14
Sikiá., *Greece* 39 J6
Síkinos, *Greece* 39 N8
Sikkani Chief →, *Canada* 100 B4
Sikkim □, *India* 61 F16
Sikotu-Ko, *Japan* 48 C10
Sil →, *Spain* 30 C3
Silacayoapan, *Mexico* 115 D5
Silandro, *Italy* 32 B7
Silay, *Phil.* 55 F5
Silba, *Croatia* 33 D11
Silchar, *India* 61 G18
Silcox, *Canada* 101 B10
Şile, *Turkey* 66 B3
Silenrieux, *Belgium* 17 H4
Siler City, *U.S.A.* 105 H6
Silesia = Śląsk, *Poland* 20 E6
Silet, *Algeria* 75 D5
Silgarhi Doti, *Nepal* 63 E9
Silghat, *India* 61 F18
Silifke, *Turkey* 66 D5
Siliguri = Shiliguri, *India* 61 F16
Siling Co, *China* 54 C3
Silíqua, *Italy* 34 C1
Silistra, *Bulgaria* 38 E10
Silivri, *Turkey* 66 B3
Siljan, *Sweden* 9 F16
Silkeborg, *Denmark* 11 H3
Sillajhuay, Cordillera, *Chile* 124 D4
Sillamäe, *Estonia* 9 G22
Sillé-le-Guillaume, *France* 24 D6
Sillustani, *Peru* 124 D3
Siloam Springs, *U.S.A.* 109 G7
Silopi, *Turkey* 67 D10
Silsbee, *U.S.A.* 109 K7
Šilute, *Lithuania* 9 J19
Silva Porto = Kuito, *Angola* 81 G3
Silvan, *Turkey* 67 C9
Silvaplana, *Switz.* 23 D9
Silver City, *N. Mex., U.S.A.* 111 K9
Silver City, *Nev., U.S.A.* 110 G4
Silver Cr. →, *U.S.A.* 110 E4
Silver Creek, *U.S.A.* 106 D5
Silver L., *Calif., U.S.A.* 112 G6
Silver L., *Calif., U.S.A.* 113 K10
Silver Lake, *U.S.A.* 110 E3
Silver Streams, *S. Africa* 84 D3
Silverton, *Colo., U.S.A.* 111 H10
Silverton, *Tex., U.S.A.* 109 H4
Silves, *Portugal* 31 H2
Silvi Marina, *Italy* 33 F11
Silvia, *Colombia* 120 C2
Silvies →, *U.S.A.* 110 E4
Silvolde, *Neths.* 16 E8
Silvretta-Gruppe, *Switz.* 23 C10
Silwa Bahari, *Egypt* 76 C3
Silz, *Austria* 19 H6
Sim, C., *Morocco* 74 B3
Simanggang, *Malaysia* 56 D4
Simao, *China* 52 F3
Simão Dias, *Brazil* 122 D4
Simard, L., *Canada* 98 C4
Şimareh →, *Iran* 67 F12
Simav, *Turkey* 66 C3
Simba, *Tanzania* 82 C4
Simbach, *Germany* 19 G9
Simbirsk, *Russia* 42 C9
Simbo, *Tanzania* 82 C2
Simcoe, *Canada* 98 D3
Simcoe, L., *Canada* 98 D4
Simenga, *Russia* 45 C11
Simeto →, *Italy* 35 E8
Simeulue, *Indonesia* 56 D1
Simferopol, *Ukraine* 41 K8
Sími, *Greece* 66 D2
Simi Valley, *U.S.A.* 113 L8
Simikot, *Nepal* 63 E9
Simití, *Colombia* 120 B3
Simla, *India* 62 D7
Şimleu-Silvaniei, *Romania* 38 B5
Simme →, *Switz.* 22 C4
Simmern, *Germany* 19 F3
Simmie, *Canada* 101 D7
Simmler, *U.S.A.* 113 K7
Simões, *Brazil* 122 C3
Simojoki →, *Finland* 8 D21
Simojovel, *Mexico* 115 D6
Simonette →, *Canada* 100 B5
Simonstown, *S. Africa* 84 E2
Simplício Mendes, *Brazil* 122 C3
Simplon, *Switz.* 22 D6
Simplon P., *Switz.* 22 D6
Simplon Tunnel, *Switz.* 22 D6
Simpson Desert, *Australia* 90 D2
Simpungdong, *N. Korea* 51 D15
Simrishamn, *Sweden* 9 J16

Simunjan, Malaysia 56 D4
Simushir, Ostrov, Russia 45 E16
Sinabang, Indonesia 56 D1
Sinadogo, Somali Rep. 68 F4
Sinai = Es Sînâ', Egypt 76 J8
Sinai, Mt. = Mûsa, G., Egypt 76 J8
Sinai Peninsula, Egypt 69 F2
Sinaia, Romania 38 D8
Sinaloa □, Mexico 114 C3
Sinaloa de Levya, Mexico 114 B3
Sinalunga, Italy 33 E8
Sinan, China 52 D7
Sinarádhes, Greece 37 A3
Sīnāwan, Libya 75 B7
Sincan, Turkey 66 B5
Sincé, Colombia 120 B2
Sincelejo, Colombia 120 B2
Sinchang, N. Korea 51 D15
Sinchang-ni, N. Korea 51 E14
Sinclair, U.S.A. 110 F10
Sinclair Mills, Canada 100 C4
Sincorá, Serra do, Brazil 123 D3
Sind, Pakistan 62 G3
Sind □, Pakistan 62 F3
Sind →, India 63 B6
Sind Sagar Doab, Pakistan 62 D4
Sindal, Denmark 11 G4
Sindangan, Phil. 55 G5
Sindangbarang, Indonesia 57 G12
Sinde, Zambia 83 F2
Sinegorskiy, Russia 43 G5
Sinelnikovo = Synelnykove, Ukraine 41 H8
Sines, Portugal 31 H2
Sines, C. de, Portugal 31 H2
Sineu, Spain 36 B10
Sinfra, Ivory C. 78 D3
Sing Buri, Thailand 58 E3
Singa, Sudan 77 E3
Singapore ■, Asia 59 M4
Singapore, Straits of, Asia 59 M5
Singaraja, Indonesia 56 F5
Singen, Germany 19 H4
Singida, Tanzania 82 C3
Singida □, Tanzania 82 D3
Singitikós Kólpos, Greece 39 J6
Singkaling Hkamti, Burma 61 G19
Singkawang, Indonesia 56 D3
Singleton, Australia 91 E5
Singleton, Mt., N. Terr., Australia 88 D5
Singleton, Mt., W. Austral., Australia 89 E2
Singoli, India 62 G6
Singora = Songkhla, Thailand 59 J3
Singosan, N. Korea 51 E14
Sinhung, N. Korea 51 D14
Sînî □, Egypt 69 F2
Siniscóla, Italy 34 B2
Sinj, Croatia 33 E13
Sinjai, Indonesia 57 F6
Sinjār, Iraq 67 D9
Sinkat, Sudan 76 D4
Sinkiang Uighur = Xinjiang Uygur Zizhiqu □, China 54 B3
Sinmak, N. Korea 51 E14
Sínnai, Italy 34 C2
Sinni →, Italy 35 B9
Sinnuris, Egypt 76 J7
Sinoe, L., Romania 38 E11
Sinop, Turkey 66 A6
Sinpo, N. Korea 51 E15
Sins, Switz. 23 B6
Sinsk, Russia 45 C13
Sint-Amandsberg, Belgium 17 F3
Sint Annaland, Neths. 17 E4
Sint Annaparoch, Neths. 16 B7
Sint-Denijs, Belgium 17 G2
Sint Eustatius, I., Neth. Ant. 117 C7
Sint-Genesius-Rode, Belgium 17 G4
Sint-Gillis-Waas, Belgium 17 F4
Sint-Huibrechts-Lille, Belgium 17 F6
Sint-Katelinje-Waver, Belgium 17 F5
Sint-Kruis, Belgium 17 F2
Sint-Laureins, Belgium 17 F3
Sint Maarten, I., W. Indies 117 C7
Sint-Michiels, Belgium 17 F2
Sint Nicolaasga, Neths. 16 C7
Sint Niklaas, Belgium 17 F4
Sint Oedenrode, Neths. 17 E6
Sint Pancras, Neths. 16 C5
Sint Philipsland, Neths. 17 E4
Sint Truiden, Belgium 17 G6
Sint Willebrord, Neths. 17 E5
Sîntana, Romania 38 C4
Sintang, Indonesia 56 D4
Sintjohannesga, Neths. 16 C7
Sinton, U.S.A. 109 L6
Sintra, Portugal 31 G1
Sinŭiju, N. Korea 51 D13
Sinyukha →, Ukraine 41 H6
Siocon, Phil. 55 H5
Siófok, Hungary 21 J8
Sioma, Zambia 84 B3
Sion, Switz. 22 D4
Sioux City, U.S.A. 108 D6
Sioux Falls, U.S.A. 108 D6
Sioux Lookout, Canada 98 B1
Sipalay, Phil. 55 G5
Siping, China 51 C13
Sipiwesk L., Canada 101 B9
Sipura, Indonesia 56 E1
Siquia →, Nic. 116 D3
Siquijor, Phil. 55 G5
Siquirres, Costa Rica 116 D3
Siquisique, Venezuela 120 A4
Sir Edward Pellew Group, Australia 90 B2
Sir Graham Moore Is., Australia 88 B4
Sira →, Norway 9 G12
Siracusa, Italy 35 E8
Sirajganj, Bangla. 63 G13
Sirakoro, Mali 78 C3
Şiran, Turkey 67 B8
Sirasso, Ivory C. 78 D3
Sīrdān, Iran 67 D13
Sirdaryo = Syrdarya →, Kazakstan 44 E7
Sirer, Spain 36 C7
Siret, Romania 38 B9
Siret →, Romania 38 D11
Şiria, Romania 38 C4
Sirino, Mte., Italy 35 B8
Sírna, Greece 39 N9
Sirnach, Switz. 23 B7
Şirnak, Turkey 67 D10
Sirohi, India 62 G5
Sironj, India 62 G7
Síros, Greece 39 M7
Sirretta Pk., U.S.A. 113 K8
Sirsa, India 62 E6
Siruela, Spain 31 G5
Sisak, Croatia 33 C13
Sisaket, Thailand 58 E5
Sisante, Spain 29 F2
Sisargas, Is., Spain 30 B2
Sishen, S. Africa 84 D3
Sishui, Henan, China 50 G7
Sishui, Shandong, China 51 G9
Sisipuk L., Canada 101 B8
Sisophon, Cambodia 58 F4
Sissach, Switz. 22 B5
Sisseton, U.S.A. 108 C6
Sissonne, France 25 C10
Sīstān va Balūchestān □, Iran 65 E9
Sisteron, France 27 D9
Sisters, U.S.A. 110 D3
Sitamarhi, India 63 F11
Sitapur, India 63 F9
Siteki, Swaziland 85 D5
Sitges, Spain 28 D6
Sitía, Greece 37 D8
Sítio da Abadia, Brazil 123 D2
Sitka, U.S.A. 96 C6
Sitoti, Botswana 84 C3
Sitra, Egypt 76 B2
Sittang Myit →, Burma 61 L20
Sittard, Neths. 17 G7
Sittensen, Germany 18 B5
Sittona, Eritrea 77 E4
Sittwe, Burma 61 J18
Siuna, Nic. 116 D3
Siuri, India 63 H12
Sivana, India 62 E8
Sīvand, Iran 65 D7
Sivas, Turkey 66 C7
Siverek, Turkey 67 D8
Sivrihisar, Turkey 66 C4
Sivry, Belgium 17 H4
Siwa, Egypt 76 B2
Siwa, El Wâhât es, Egypt 76 B2
Siwa Oasis, Egypt 70 D6
Siwalik Range, Nepal 63 F10
Siwan, India 63 F11
Siyâl, Jazâ'ir, Egypt 76 C4
Siyäzän, Azerbaijan 43 K9
Sizewell, U.K. 13 E9
Siziwang Qi, China 50 D6
Sjælland, Denmark 11 J5
Sjællands Odde, Denmark 11 J5
Själevad, Sweden 10 A12
Sjenica, Serbia, Yug. 21 M10
Sjoa, Norway 10 C3
Sjöbo, Sweden 11 J7
Sjösa, Sweden 11 F11
Sjumen = Šumen, Bulgaria 38 F9
Skadovsk, Ukraine 41 J7
Skaftafell, Iceland 8 D5
Skagafjörður, Iceland 8 D4
Skagastølstindane, Norway 9 F12
Skagaströnd, Iceland 8 D3
Skagen, Denmark 11 G4
Skagerrak, Denmark 11 G3
Skagit →, U.S.A. 112 B4
Skagway, U.S.A. 100 B1
Skala-Podilska, Ukraine 41 H4
Skala Podolskaya = Skala-Podilska, Ukraine 41 H4
Skalat, Ukraine 41 H3
Skalni Dol = Kamenyak, Bulgaria 38 F9
Skals, Denmark 11 H3
Skanderborg, Denmark 11 H3
Skåne, Sweden 9 J15
Skanör, Sweden 11 J6
Skara, Sweden 9 G15
Skardu, Pakistan 63 B6
Skarrild, Denmark 11 J2
Skarzysko-Kamienna, Poland 20 D10
Skebokvarn, Sweden 10 E10
Skeena →, Canada 100 C2
Skeena Mts., Canada 100 B3
Skegness, U.K. 12 D8
Skeldon, Guyana 121 B6
Skellefte älv →, Sweden 8 D19
Skellefteå, Sweden 8 D19
Skelleftehamn, Sweden 8 D19
Skender Vakuf, Bos.-H. 21 L7
Skene, Sweden 11 G6
Skerries, The, U.K. 12 D3
Skhoinoúsa, Greece 39 N8
Ski, Norway 10 E4
Skíathos, Greece 39 K6
Skibbereen, Ireland 15 E2
Skiddaw, U.K. 12 C4
Skien, Norway 10 E3
Skierniewice, Poland 20 D10
Skikda, Algeria 75 A6
Skilloura, Cyprus 37 D12
Skinári, Ákra, Greece 39 M3
Skipton, Australia 91 F3
Skipton, U.K. 12 D5
Skirmish Pt., Australia 90 A1
Skíros, Greece 39 L7
Skivarp, Sweden 11 J7
Skive, Denmark 11 H3
Skjálfandafljót →, Iceland 8 D5
Skjálfandi, Iceland 8 C5
Skjeberg, Norway 10 E5
Skjern, Denmark 11 J2
Škofja Loka, Slovenia 33 B11
Skoghall, Sweden 9 G15
Skole, Ukraine 41 H2
Skópelos, Greece 39 K6
Skopí, Greece 37 D8
Skopin, Russia 42 D4
Skopje, Macedonia 39 G4
Skórcz, Poland 20 B8
Skövde, Sweden 9 G15
Skovorodino, Russia 45 D13
Skowhegan, U.S.A. 99 D6
Skownan, Canada 101 C9
Skradin, Croatia 33 E12
Skreanäs, Sweden 11 H6
Skull, Ireland 15 E2
Skultorp, Sweden 11 F7
Skunk →, U.S.A. 108 E9
Skuodas, Lithuania 9 H19
Skurup, Sweden 11 J7
Skutskär, Sweden 10 D11
Skvyra, Ukraine 41 H5
Skwierzyna, Poland 20 C5
Skye, U.K. 14 D2
Skykomish, U.S.A. 110 C3
Skyros = Skíros, Greece 39 L7
Slættaratindur, Færoe Is. 8 E9
Slagelse, Denmark 11 J5
Slagharen, Neths. 16 C9
Slamet, Indonesia 56 F3
Slaney →, Ireland 15 D5
Slangerup, Denmark 11 J6
Slano, Croatia 21 N7
Slantsy, Russia 40 C5
Śląsk, Poland 20 E6
Slate Is., Canada 98 C2
Slatina, Romania 38 E7
Slaton, U.S.A. 109 J4
Slave →, Canada 100 A6
Slave Coast, W. Afr. 79 D5
Slave Lake, Canada 100 B6
Slave Pt., Canada 100 A5
Slavgorod, Russia 44 D8
Slavonska Požega, Croatia 21 K7
Slavonski Brod, Croatia 21 K8
Slavuta, Ukraine 41 G4
Slavyanka, Russia 48 C5
Slavyansk = Slovyansk, Ukraine 41 H9
Slavyansk-na-Kubani, Russia 43 H4
Slawharad, Belarus 40 F6
Sławno, Poland 20 A6
Sławoborze, Poland 20 B5
Sleaford, U.K. 12 E7
Sleaford B., Australia 91 E2
Sleat, Sd. of, U.K. 14 D3
Sleeper Is., Canada 97 C11
Sleepy Eye, U.S.A. 108 C7
Sleidinge, Belgium 17 F3
Sleman, Indonesia 57 G14
Slemon L., Canada 100 A5
Slidell, U.S.A. 109 K10
Sliedrecht, Neths. 16 E5
Sliema, Malta 37 D2
Slieve Aughty, Ireland 15 C3
Slieve Bloom, Ireland 15 C4
Slieve Donard, U.K. 15 B6
Slieve Gullion, U.K. 15 B5
Slieve Mish, Ireland 15 D2
Slievenamon, Ireland 15 D4
Sligeach = Sligo, Ireland 15 B3
Sligo, Ireland 15 B3
Sligo □, Ireland 15 B3
Sligo B., Ireland 15 B3
Slijpe, Belgium 17 F1
Slikkerveer, Neths. 16 E5
Slite, Sweden 9 H18
Sliven, Bulgaria 38 G9
Slivnitsa, Bulgaria 38 G6
Sljeme, Croatia 33 C12
Sloan, U.S.A. 113 K11
Sloansville, U.S.A. 107 D10
Slobozia, Romania 38 E10
Slocan, Canada 100 D5
Slochteren, Neths. 16 B9
Slöinge, Sweden 11 H6
Slonim, Belarus 41 F3
Slotermeer, Neths. 16 C7
Slough, U.K. 13 F7
Sloughhouse, U.S.A. 112 G5
Slovak Rep. ■, Europe 20 G9
Slovakia = Slovak Rep. ■, Europe 20 G9
Slovakian Ore Mts. = Slovenské Rudohorie, Slovak Rep. 20 G9
Slovenia ■, Europe 33 C11
Slovenija = Slovenia ■, Europe 33 C11
Slovenj Gradec, Slovenia 33 B12
Slovenska Bistrica, Slovenia 33 B12
Slovenská Republika = Slovak Rep. ■, Europe 20 G9
Slovenské Rudohorie, Slovak Rep. 20 G9
Slovyansk, Ukraine 41 H9
Słubice, Poland 20 C4
Sluch →, Ukraine 41 G4
Sluis, Neths. 17 F2
Slunj, Croatia 33 C12
Słupca, Poland 20 C7
Słupsk, Poland 20 A7
Slurry, S. Africa 84 D4
Slutsk, Belarus 41 F4
Slyne Hd., Ireland 15 C1
Slyudyanka, Russia 45 D11
Småland, Sweden 9 H16
Smålandsfarvandet, Denmark 11 J5
Smålandsstenar, Sweden 11 G7
Smalltree L., Canada 101 A7
Smara, Morocco 72 B3
Smarhon, Belarus 40 E4
Smarje, Slovenia 33 B12
Smartt Syndicate Dam, S. Africa 84 E3
Smartville, U.S.A. 112 F5
Smeaton, Canada 101 C8
Smederevo, Serbia, Yug. 21 L10
Smederevska Palanka, Serbia, Yug. 21 L10
Smela = Smila, Ukraine 41 H6
Smethport, U.S.A. 106 E6
Smidovich, Russia 45 E14
Smila, Ukraine 41 H6
Smilde, Neths. 16 C8
Smiley, Canada 101 C7
Smith, Canada 100 B6
Smith →, Canada 100 B3
Smith Arm, Canada 96 B7
Smith Center, U.S.A. 108 F5
Smith Sund, Greenland 4 B4
Smithburne →, Australia 90 B3
Smithers, Canada 100 C3
Smithfield, S. Africa 85 E4
Smithfield, N.C., U.S.A. 105 H6
Smithfield, Utah, U.S.A. 110 F8
Smiths Falls, Canada 98 D4
Smithton, Australia 90 G4
Smithtown, Australia 91 E5
Smithville, Canada 106 C5
Smithville, U.S.A. 109 K6
Smoky →, Canada 100 B5
Smoky Bay, Australia 91 E1
Smoky Falls, Canada 98 B3
Smoky Hill →, U.S.A. 108 F6
Smoky Lake, Canada 100 C6
Smøla, Norway 10 A2
Smolensk, Russia 40 E7
Smolikas, Óros, Greece 39 J3
Smolník, Slovak Rep. 20 G10
Smolyan, Bulgaria 39 H7
Smooth Rock Falls, Canada 98 C3
Smoothstone L., Canada 101 C7
Smorgon = Smarhon, Belarus 40 E4
Smyadovo, Bulgaria 38 F10
Smyrna = İzmir, Turkey 66 C2
Snæfell, Iceland 8 D6
Snaefell, U.K. 12 C3
Snæfellsjökull, Iceland 8 D2
Snake →, U.S.A. 110 C4
Snake I., Australia 91 F4
Snake L., Canada 101 B7
Snake Range, U.S.A. 110 G6
Snake River Plain, U.S.A. 110 E7
Snarum, Norway 10 D3
Snåsavatnet, Norway 8 D14
Snedsted, Denmark 11 H2
Sneek, Neths. 16 B7
Sneeker-meer, Neths. 16 B7
Sneeuberge, S. Africa 84 E3
Snejbjerg, Denmark 11 H2
Snelling, U.S.A. 112 H6
Snezhnoye, Ukraine 41 J10
Snežnik, Slovenia 33 C11
Snigirevka = Snihurivka, Ukraine 41 J7
Snihurivka, Ukraine 41 J7
Snizort, L., U.K. 14 D2
Snøhetta, Norway 10 B3
Snohomish, U.S.A. 112 C4
Snoul, Cambodia 59 F6
Snow Hill, U.S.A. 104 F8
Snow Lake, Canada 101 C8
Snow Mt., U.S.A. 112 F4
Snowbird L., Canada 101 A8
Snowdon, U.K. 12 D3
Snowdrift →, Canada 101 A6
Snowflake, U.S.A. 111 J8
Snowshoe Pk., U.S.A. 110 B6
Snowtown, Australia 91 E2
Snowville, U.S.A. 110 F7
Snowy →, Australia 91 F4
Snowy Mts., Australia 91 F4
Snug Corner, Bahamas 117 B5
Snyatyn, Ukraine 41 H3
Snyder, Okla., U.S.A. 109 H5
Snyder, Tex., U.S.A. 109 J4
Soacha, Colombia 120 C3
Soahanina, Madag. 85 B7
Soalala, Madag. 85 B8
Soan →, Pakistan 62 C4
Soanierana-Ivongo, Madag. 85 B8
Soap Lake, U.S.A. 110 C4
Sobat, Nahr →, Sudan 77 F3
Sobhapur, India 62 H8
Sobinka, Russia 42 C5
Sobolevo, Russia 45 D16
Sobótka, Poland 20 E6
Sobradinho, Reprêsa de, Brazil 122 C3
Sobrado, Spain 30 B2
Sobral, Brazil 122 B3
Sobreira Formosa, Portugal 31 F3
Soc Giang, Vietnam 58 A6
Soc Trang, Vietnam 59 H5
Soča →, Europe 33 B10
Sochaczew, Poland 20 C10
Soch'e = Shache, China 54 C2
Sochi, Russia 43 J4
Société, Is. de la, Pac. Oc. 93 J12
Society Is. = Société, Is. de la, Pac. Oc. 93 J12
Socompa, Portezuelo de, Chile 126 A2
Socorro, Colombia 120 B3
Socorro, U.S.A. 111 J10
Socorro, I., Mexico 114 D2
Socotra, Ind. Oc. 68 E5
Socúellmos, Spain 29 F2
Soda L., U.S.A. 111 J5
Soda Plains, India 63 B8
Soda Springs, U.S.A. 110 E8
Sodankylä, Finland 8 C22
Söderhamn, Sweden 9 F17
Söderköping, Sweden 9 G17
Södermanland, Sweden 9 G17
Södermanlands län □, Sweden 10 E10
Södertälje, Sweden 10 E11
Sodiri, Sudan 77 E2
Sodo, Ethiopia 77 F4
Sodražica, Slovenia 33 C11
Sodus, U.S.A. 106 C7
Soekmekaar, S. Africa 85 C4
Soest, Germany 18 D4
Soest, Neths. 16 D6
Soestdijk, Neths. 16 D6
Sofádhes, Greece 39 K5
Sofara, Mali 78 C4
Sofia = Sofiya, Bulgaria 38 G6
Sofia →, Madag. 85 B8
Sofievka, Ukraine 41 H7
Sofikón, Greece 39 M6
Sofiya, Bulgaria 38 G6
Sofiysk, Russia 45 D14
Sōfu-Gan, Japan 49 K10
Sogakofe, Ghana 79 D5
Sogamoso, Colombia 120 B3
Soğār, Iran 65 E8
Sögel, Germany 18 C3
Sogndalsfjøra, Norway 9 F12
Søgne, Norway 9 G12
Sognefjorden, Norway 9 F11
Söğüt, Turkey 66 B4
Sŏgwi-po, S. Korea 51 H14
Soh, Iran 65 C6
Sohâg, Egypt 76 B3
Sŏhori, N. Korea 51 D15
Soignies, Belgium 17 G4
Soira, Eritrea 77 E4
Soissons, France 25 C10
Sōja, Japan 49 G6
Sojat, India 62 G5
Sok →, Russia 42 D10
Sokal, Ukraine 41 G3
Söke, Turkey 66 D2
Sokelo, Zaïre 83 D1
Sokhumi, Georgia 43 J5
Sokki, Oued In →, Algeria 75 C5
Sokna, Norway 10 D3
Soknedal, Norway 10 B4
Soko Banja, Serbia, Yug. 21 M11
Sokodé, Togo 79 D5
Sokol, Russia 40 C11
Sokółka, Poland 20 B13
Sokolo, Mali 78 C3
Sokołów Małpolski, Poland 20 E12
Sokołów Podlaski, Poland 20 C12
Sokoto, Nigeria 79 C6
Sokoto □, Nigeria 79 C6
Sokoto →, Nigeria 79 C5
Sol Iletsk, Russia 44 D6
Solai, Kenya 82 B4
Solano, Phil. 55 C4
Solapur, India 60 L9
Solares, Spain 30 B7
Soléa □, Cyprus 37 D12
Solec Kujawski, Poland 20 B8
Soledad, Colombia 120 A3
Soledad, U.S.A. 111 H3
Soledad, Venezuela 121 B5
Solent, The, U.K. 13 G6
Solenzara, France 27 G13
Solesmes, France 25 B10
Solfonn, Norway 9 F12
Solhan, Turkey 67 C9
Soligorsk = Salihorsk, Belarus 41 F4
Solikamsk, Russia 44 D6
Solila, Madag. 85 C8
Solimões = Amazonas →, S. Amer. 121 D7
Solingen, Germany 17 F10

Sollebrunn, *Sweden* 11 F6
Sollefteå, *Sweden* 10 A11
Sollentuna, *Sweden* 10 E11
Sóller, *Spain* 36 B9
Solling, *Germany* 18 D5
Solna, *Sweden* 10 E12
Solnechnogorsk, *Russia* 42 B3
Sologne, *France* 25 E8
Solok, *Indonesia* 56 E2
Sololá, *Guatemala* 116 D1
Solomon, N. Fork →, *U.S.A.* 108 F5
Solomon, S. Fork →, *U.S.A.* 108 F5
Solomon Is. ■, *Pac. Oc.* 92 H7
Solon, *China* 54 B7
Solon Springs, *U.S.A.* 108 B9
Solonópole, *Brazil* 122 C4
Solor, *Indonesia* 57 F6
Solotcha, *Russia* 42 C4
Solothurn, *Switz.* 22 B5
Solothurn □, *Switz.* 22 B5
Solsona, *Spain* 28 D6
Šolta, *Croatia* 33 E13
Solṭānābād, *Khorāsān, Iran* 65 C8
Solṭānābād, *Khorāsān, Iran* 65 B8
Solṭānābād, *Markazī, Iran* 65 C6
Soltau, *Germany* 18 C5
Soltsy, *Russia* 40 C6
Solunska Glava, *Macedonia* 39 H4
Solvang, *U.S.A.* 113 L6
Solvay, *U.S.A.* 107 C8
Sölvesborg, *Sweden* 9 H16
Solway Firth, *U.K.* 12 C4
Solwezi, *Zambia* 83 E2
Sōma, *Japan* 48 F10
Soma, *Turkey* 66 C2
Somali Pen., *Africa* 70 F8
Somali Rep. ■, *Africa* 68 F4
Somalia = Somali Rep. ■, *Africa* 68 F4
Sombernon, *France* 25 E11
Sombor, *Serbia, Yug.* 21 K9
Sombra, *Canada* 106 D2
Sombrerete, *Mexico* 114 C4
Sombrero, *Anguilla* 117 C7
Someren, *Neths.* 17 F7
Somers, *U.S.A.* 110 B6
Somerset, *Canada* 101 D9
Somerset, *Colo., U.S.A.* 111 G10
Somerset, *Ky., U.S.A.* 104 G3
Somerset, *Mass., U.S.A.* 107 E13
Somerset, *Pa., U.S.A.* 106 F5
Somerset □, *U.K.* 13 F5
Somerset East, *S. Africa* 84 E4
Somerset I., *Canada* 96 A10
Somerset West, *S. Africa* 84 E2
Somerton, *U.S.A.* 111 K6
Somerville, *U.S.A.* 107 F10
Someş →, *Romania* 38 B5
Someşul Mare →, *Romania* 38 B7
Somma Lombardo, *Italy* 32 C5
Somma Vesuviana, *Italy* 35 B7
Sommariva, *Australia* 91 D4
Sommatino, *Italy* 34 E6
Somme □, *France* 25 C9
Somme →, *France* 25 B8
Somme, B. de la, *France* 24 B8
Sommelsdijk, *Neths.* 16 E4
Sommepy-Tahure, *France* 25 C11
Sömmerda, *Germany* 18 D7
Sommesous, *France* 25 D11
Sommières, *France* 27 E8
Somoto, *Nic.* 116 D2
Sompolno, *Poland* 20 C8
Somport, Paso, *Spain* 28 C4
Somport, Puerto de, *Spain* 28 C4
Somuncurá, Meseta de, *Argentina* 128 B3
Son, *Neths.* 17 E6
Son, *Norway* 10 E4
Son, *Spain* 30 C2
Son Ha, *Vietnam* 58 E7
Son Hoa, *Vietnam* 58 F7
Son La, *Vietnam* 58 B4
Son Tay, *Vietnam* 58 B5
Soná, *Panama* 116 E3
Sonamarg, *India* 63 B6
Sonamukhi, *India* 63 H12
Sŏnchŏn, *N. Korea* 51 E13
Soncino, *Italy* 32 C6
Sondags →, *S. Africa* 84 E4
Sóndalo, *Italy* 32 B7
Sondar, *India* 63 C6
Sønder Omme, *Denmark* 11 J2
Sønder Tornby, *Denmark* 11 G3
Sønderborg, *Denmark* 11 K3
Sønderjyllands Amtskommune □, *Denmark* 11 J3
Sondershausen, *Germany* 18 D6
Søndre Strømfjord, *Greenland* 97 B14
Sóndrio, *Italy* 32 B6
Sone, *Mozam.* 83 F3
Sonepur, *India* 61 J13
Song, *Thailand* 58 C3
Song Cau, *Vietnam* 58 F7
Song Xian, *China* 50 G7
Songchŏn, *N. Korea* 51 E14
Songea, *Tanzania* 83 E4
Songea □, *Tanzania* 83 E4
Songeons, *France* 25 C8
Songhua Hu, *China* 51 C14
Songhua Jiang →, *China* 54 B8
Songjiang, *China* 53 B13
Songjin, *N. Korea* 51 D15
Songjŏng-ni, *S. Korea* 51 G14
Songkan, *China* 52 C6
Songkhla, *Thailand* 59 J3
Songming, *China* 52 E4
Songnim, *N. Korea* 51 E13
Songpan, *China* 52 A4
Songtao, *China* 52 C7
Songwe, *Zaïre* 82 C2
Songwe →, *Africa* 83 D3
Songxi, *China* 53 D12
Songzi, *China* 53 B8
Sonid Youqi, *China* 50 C7
Sonipat, *India* 62 E7
Sonkovo, *Russia* 42 B3
Sonmiani, *Pakistan* 62 G2
Sonnino, *Italy* 34 A6
Sono →, *Minas Gerais, Brazil* 123 E2
Sono →, *Tocantins, Brazil* 122 C2
Sonogno, *Switz.* 23 D7
Sonora, *Calif., U.S.A.* 111 H3
Sonora, *Tex., U.S.A.* 109 K4
Sonora □, *Mexico* 114 B2
Sonora →, *Mexico* 114 B2
Sonora Desert, *U.S.A.* 113 L12
Sonoyta, *Mexico* 114 A2
Sonqor, *Iran* 67 E12
Sŏnsan, *S. Korea* 51 F15
Sonsonate, *El Salv.* 116 D2
Sonthofen, *Germany* 19 H6
Soochow = Suzhou, *China* 53 B13
Sop Hao, *Laos* 58 B5
Sop Prap, *Thailand* 58 D2
Sopachuy, *Bolivia* 125 D5
Sopi, *Indonesia* 57 D7
Sopo, Nahr →, *Sudan* 77 F2
Sopot, *Poland* 20 A8
Sopotnica, *Macedonia* 39 H4
Sopron, *Hungary* 21 H6
Sop's Arm, *Canada* 99 C8
Sopur, *India* 63 B6
Sør-Rondane, *Antarctica* 5 D4
Sør-Trøndelag fylke □, *Norway* 10 B3
Sora, *Italy* 34 A6
Sorah, *Pakistan* 62 F3
Söråker, *Sweden* 10 B11
Sorano, *Italy* 33 F8
Sorata, *Bolivia* 124 D4
Sorbas, *Spain* 29 H2
Sorel, *Canada* 98 C5
Sörenberg, *Switz.* 22 C6
Soreq, N. →, *Israel* 69 D3
Soresina, *Italy* 32 C6
Sorgono, *Italy* 34 B2
Sorgues, *France* 27 D8
Sorgun, *Turkey* 66 C6
Soria, *Spain* 28 D2
Soria □, *Spain* 28 D2
Soriano, *Uruguay* 126 C4
Soriano nel Cimino, *Italy* 33 F9
Sorkh, Kuh-e, *Iran* 65 C8
Sorø, *Denmark* 11 J5
Soro, *Guinea* 78 C3
Soroca, *Moldova* 41 H5
Sorocaba, *Brazil* 127 A6
Soroki = Soroca, *Moldova* 41 H5
Soron, *India* 63 F8
Sorong, *Indonesia* 57 E8
Soroní, *Greece* 37 C10
Soroti, *Uganda* 82 B3
Sørøya, *Norway* 8 A20
Sørøysundet, *Norway* 8 A20
Sorraia →, *Portugal* 31 G2
Sorrento, *Australia* 91 F3
Sorrento, *Italy* 35 B7
Sorsele, *Sweden* 8 D17
Sorso, *Italy* 34 B1
Sorsogon, *Phil.* 55 E6
Sortavala, *Russia* 40 B6
Sortino, *Italy* 35 E8
Sortland, *Norway* 8 B16
Sorvizhi, *Russia* 42 B9
Sos, *Spain* 28 C3
Sŏsan, *S. Korea* 51 F14
Soscumica, L., *Canada* 98 B4
Sosna →, *Russia* 42 D4
Sosnovka, *Russia* 42 B10
Sosnovka, *Russia* 42 D5
Sosnovka, *Russia* 45 D11
Sosnovyy Bor, *Russia* 40 C5
Sosnowiec, *Poland* 20 E9
Sospel, *France* 27 E11
Šoštanj, *Slovenia* 33 B12
Sŏsura, *N. Korea* 51 C16
Sotkamo, *Finland* 8 D23
Soto la Marina →, *Mexico* 115 C5
Soto y Amío, *Spain* 30 C5
Sotteville-lès-Rouen, *France* 24 C8
Sotuta, *Mexico* 115 C7
Souanké, *Congo* 80 D2
Soúdha, *Greece* 37 D6
Soúdhas, Kólpos, *Greece* 37 D6
Sougne-Remouchamps, *Belgium* 17 H7
Souillac, *France* 26 D5
Souk-Ahras, *Algeria* 75 A6
Souk el Arba du Rharb, *Morocco* 74 B3
Soukhouma, *Laos* 58 E5
Sŏul, *S. Korea* 51 F14
Soulac-sur-Mer, *France* 26 C2
Soultz-sous-Forêts, *France* 25 D14
Soumagne, *Belgium* 17 G7
Sound, The = Øresund, *Europe* 11 J6
Sound, The, *U.K.* 13 G3
Soúnion, Ákra, *Greece* 39 M7
Sour el Ghozlane, *Algeria* 75 A5
Sources, Mt. aux, *Lesotho* 85 D4
Sourdeval, *France* 24 D6
Soure, *Brazil* 122 B2
Soure, *Portugal* 30 E2
Souris, *Man., Canada* 101 D8
Souris, *P.E.I., Canada* 99 C7
Souris →, *Canada* 108 A5
Sousa, *Brazil* 122 C4
Sousel, *Brazil* 122 B1
Sousel, *Portugal* 31 G3
Souss, O. →, *Morocco* 74 B3
Sousse, *Tunisia* 75 A7
Soustons, *France* 26 E2
South Africa ■, *Africa* 84 E3
South Atlantic Ocean 118 H7
South Aulatsivik I., *Canada* 99 A7
South Australia □, *Australia* 91 E2
South Ayrshire □, *U.K.* 14 F4
South Baldy, *U.S.A.* 111 J10
South Bend, *Ind., U.S.A.* 104 E2
South Bend, *Wash., U.S.A.* 112 D3
South Boston, *U.S.A.* 105 G6
South Branch, *Canada* 99 C8
South Brook, *Canada* 99 C8
South Carolina □, *U.S.A.* 105 J5
South Charleston, *U.S.A.* 104 F5
South China Sea, *Asia* 56 C4
South Dakota □, *U.S.A.* 108 C5
South Downs, *U.K.* 13 G7
South East C., *Australia* 90 G4
South East Is., *Australia* 89 F3
South Esk →, *U.K.* 14 E5
South Foreland, *U.K.* 13 F9
South Fork →, *U.S.A.* 110 C7
South Fork, American →, *U.S.A.* 112 G5
South Fork, Feather →, *U.S.A.* 112 F5
South Georgia, *Antarctica* 5 B1
South Gloucestershire □, *U.K.* 13 F5
South Haven, *U.S.A.* 104 D2
South Henik, L., *Canada* 101 A9
South Honshu Ridge, *Pac. Oc.* 92 E6
South Horr, *Kenya* 82 B4
South I., *Kenya* 82 B4
South I., *N.Z.* 87 L3
South Invercargill, *N.Z.* 87 M2
South Knife →, *Canada* 101 B10
South Korea ■, *Asia* 51 F15
South Lake Tahoe, *U.S.A.* 112 G6
South Lanarkshire □, *U.K.* 14 F5
South Loup →, *U.S.A.* 108 E5
South Magnetic Pole, *Antarctica* 5 C9
South Milwaukee, *U.S.A.* 104 D2
South Molton, *U.K.* 13 F4
South Nahanni →, *Canada* 100 A4
South Natuna Is. = Natuna Selatan, Kepulauan, *Indonesia* 59 L7
South Negril Pt., *Jamaica* 116 C4
South Orkney Is., *Antarctica* 5 C18
South Ossetia □, *Georgia* 43 J7
South Pagai, I. = Pagai Selatan, P., *Indonesia* 56 E2
South Pass, *U.S.A.* 110 E9
South Pittsburg, *U.S.A.* 105 H3
South Platte →, *U.S.A.* 108 E4
South Pole, *Antarctica* 5 E
South Porcupine, *Canada* 98 C3
South River, *Canada* 98 C4
South River, *U.S.A.* 107 F10
South Ronaldsay, *U.K.* 14 C6
South Sandwich Is., *Antarctica* 5 B1
South Saskatchewan →, *Canada* 101 C7
South Seal →, *Canada* 101 B9
South Shetland Is., *Antarctica* 5 C18
South Shields, *U.K.* 12 C6
South Sioux City, *U.S.A.* 108 D6
South Taranaki Bight, *N.Z.* 87 H5
South Thompson →, *Canada* 100 C4
South Twin I., *Canada* 98 B4
South Tyne →, *U.K.* 12 C5
South Uist, *U.K.* 14 D1
South West Africa = Namibia ■, *Africa* 84 C2
South West C., *Australia* 90 G4
South Yorkshire □, *U.K.* 12 D6
Southampton, *Canada* 98 D3
Southampton, *U.K.* 13 G6
Southampton, *U.S.A.* 107 F12
Southampton I., *Canada* 97 B11
Southbridge, *N.Z.* 87 K4
Southbridge, *U.S.A.* 107 D12
Southend, *Canada* 101 B8
Southend-on-Sea, *U.K.* 13 F8
Southern □, *Malawi* 83 F4
Southern □, *S. Leone* 78 D2
Southern □, *Uganda* 82 C3
Southern □, *Zambia* 83 F2
Southern Alps, *N.Z.* 87 K3
Southern Cross, *Australia* 89 F2
Southern Hills, *Australia* 89 F3
Southern Indian L., *Canada* 101 B9
Southern Ocean, *Antarctica* 5 C6
Southern Pines, *U.S.A.* 105 H6
Southern Uplands, *U.K.* 14 F5
Southington, *U.S.A.* 107 E12
Southold, *U.S.A.* 107 E12
Southport, *Australia* 91 D5
Southport, *U.K.* 12 D4
Southport, *U.S.A.* 105 J6
Southwest C., *N.Z.* 87 M1
Southwold, *U.K.* 13 E9
Soutpansberg, *S. Africa* 85 C4
Souvigny, *France* 26 B7
Sovetsk, *Kaliningd., Russia* 9 J19
Sovetsk, *Kirov, Russia* 42 B9
Sovetskaya Gavan, *Russia* 45 E15
Sovicille, *Italy* 33 E8
Sovra, *Croatia* 21 N7
Soweto, *S. Africa* 85 D4
Sōya-Kaikyō = La Perouse Str., *Asia* 48 B11
Sōya-Misaki, *Japan* 48 B10
Soyo, *Angola* 80 F2
Sozh →, *Belarus* 41 F6
Sozopol, *Bulgaria* 38 G10
Spa, *Belgium* 17 H7
Spain ■, *Europe* 7 H5
Spakenburg, *Neths.* 16 D6
Spalding, *Australia* 91 E2
Spalding, *U.K.* 12 E7
Spalding, *U.S.A.* 108 E5
Spangler, *U.S.A.* 106 F6
Spaniard's Bay, *Canada* 99 C9
Spanish, *Canada* 98 C3
Spanish Fork, *U.S.A.* 110 F8
Spanish Town, *Jamaica* 116 C4
Sparks, *U.S.A.* 112 F7
Sparta = Spárti, *Greece* 39 M5
Sparta, *Ga., U.S.A.* 105 J4
Sparta, *Wis., U.S.A.* 108 D9
Spartanburg, *U.S.A.* 105 H4
Spartansburg, *U.S.A.* 106 E5
Spartel, C., *Morocco* 74 A3
Spárti, *Greece* 39 M5
Spartivento, C., *Calabria, Italy* 35 E9
Spartivento, C., *Sard., Italy* 34 D1
Spas-Demensk, *Russia* 42 C2
Spas-Klepiki, *Russia* 42 C5
Spassk Dalniy, *Russia* 45 E14
Spassk-Ryazanskiy, *Russia* 42 C5
Spátha, Ákra, *Greece* 37 D5
Spatsizi →, *Canada* 100 B3
Spearfish, *U.S.A.* 108 C3
Spearman, *U.S.A.* 109 G4
Speer, *Switz.* 23 B8
Speers, *Canada* 101 C7
Speightstown, *Barbados* 117 D8
Speke Gulf, *Tanzania* 82 C3
Spekholzerheide, *Neths.* 17 G8
Spencer, *Idaho, U.S.A.* 110 D7
Spencer, *Iowa, U.S.A.* 108 D7
Spencer, *N.Y., U.S.A.* 107 D8
Spencer, *Nebr., U.S.A.* 108 D5
Spencer, *W. Va., U.S.A.* 104 F5
Spencer, C., *Australia* 91 F2
Spencer B., *Namibia* 84 D1
Spencer G., *Australia* 91 E2
Spencerville, *Canada* 107 B9
Spences Bridge, *Canada* 100 C4
Spenser Mts., *N.Z.* 87 K4
Sperkhiós →, *Greece* 39 L5
Sperrin Mts., *U.K.* 15 B5
Spessart, *Germany* 19 E5
Spétsai, *Greece* 39 M6
Spey →, *U.K.* 14 D5
Speyer, *Germany* 19 F4
Speyer →, *Germany* 19 F4
Spezzano Albanese, *Italy* 35 C9
Spiekeroog, *Germany* 18 B3
Spielfeld, *Austria* 33 B12
Spiez, *Switz.* 22 C5
Spijk, *Neths.* 16 B9
Spijkenisse, *Neths.* 16 E4
Spíli, *Greece* 37 D6
Spilimbergo, *Italy* 33 B9
Spin Baldak = Qala-i-Jadid, *Afghan.* 62 D2
Spinalónga, *Greece* 37 D7
Spinazzola, *Italy* 35 B9
Spirit Lake, *Idaho, U.S.A.* 110 C5
Spirit Lake, *Wash., U.S.A.* 112 D4
Spirit River, *Canada* 100 B5
Spiritwood, *Canada* 101 C7
Spišská Nová Ves, *Slovak Rep.* 20 G10
Spithead, *U.K.* 13 G6
Spittal, *Austria* 21 J3
Spitzbergen = Svalbard, *Arctic* 4 B8
Spjelkavik, *Norway* 9 E12
Split, *Croatia* 33 E13
Split L., *Canada* 101 B9
Splitski Kanal, *Croatia* 33 E13
Splügen, *Switz.* 23 C8
Splügenpass, *Switz.* 23 C8
Spofford, *U.S.A.* 109 L4
Spokane, *U.S.A.* 110 C5
Spoleto, *Italy* 33 F9
Spooner, *U.S.A.* 108 C9
Sporyy Navolok, Mys, *Russia* 44 B7
Spragge, *Canada* 98 C3
Sprague, *U.S.A.* 110 C5
Sprague River, *U.S.A.* 110 E3
Spratly Is., *S. China Sea* 56 C4
Spray, *U.S.A.* 110 D4
Spree →, *Germany* 18 C9
Spremberg, *Germany* 18 D10
Sprengisandur, *Iceland* 8 D5
Sprimont, *Belgium* 17 G7
Spring City, *U.S.A.* 110 G8
Spring Garden, *U.S.A.* 112 F6
Spring Mts., *U.S.A.* 111 H6
Spring Valley, *Calif., U.S.A.* 113 N10
Spring Valley, *Minn., U.S.A.* 108 D8
Springbok, *S. Africa* 84 D2
Springdale, *Canada* 99 C8
Springdale, *Ark., U.S.A.* 109 G7
Springdale, *Wash., U.S.A.* 110 B5
Springe, *Germany* 18 C5
Springer, *U.S.A.* 109 G2
Springerville, *U.S.A.* 111 J9
Springfield, *Canada* 106 D4
Springfield, *N.Z.* 87 K3
Springfield, *Colo., U.S.A.* 109 G3
Springfield, *Ill., U.S.A.* 108 F10
Springfield, *Mass., U.S.A.* 107 D12
Springfield, *Mo., U.S.A.* 109 G8
Springfield, *Ohio, U.S.A.* 104 F4
Springfield, *Oreg., U.S.A.* 110 D2
Springfield, *Tenn., U.S.A.* 105 G2
Springfield, *Vt., U.S.A.* 107 C12
Springfontein, *S. Africa* 84 E4
Springhill, *Canada* 99 C7
Springhouse, *Canada* 100 C4
Springhurst, *Australia* 91 F4
Springs, *S. Africa* 85 D4
Springsure, *Australia* 90 C4
Springvale, *Queens., Australia* 90 C3
Springvale, *W. Austral., Australia* 88 C4
Springvale, *U.S.A.* 107 C14
Springville, *Calif., U.S.A.* 112 J8
Springville, *N.Y., U.S.A.* 106 D6
Springville, *Utah, U.S.A.* 110 F8
Springwater, *Canada* 101 C7
Spruce-Creek, *U.S.A.* 106 F6
Spur, *U.S.A.* 109 J4
Spurn Hd., *U.K.* 12 D8
Spuž, *Montenegro, Yug.* 21 N9
Spuzzum, *Canada* 100 D4
Squam L., *U.S.A.* 107 C13
Squamish, *Canada* 100 D4
Square Islands, *Canada* 99 B8
Squillace, G. di, *Italy* 35 D9
Squinzano, *Italy* 35 B11
Squires, Mt., *Australia* 89 E4
Sragen, *Indonesia* 57 G14
Srbac, *Bos.-H.* 21 K7
Srbija = Serbia □, *Yugoslavia* 21 M11
Srbobran, *Serbia, Yug.* 21 K9
Sre Khtum, *Cambodia* 59 F6
Sre Umbell, *Cambodia* 59 G4
Srebrnica, *Bos.-H.* 21 L9
Sredinny Ra. = Sredinnyy Khrebet, *Russia* 45 D16
Sredinnyy Khrebet, *Russia* 45 D16
Središče, *Slovenia* 33 B13
Sredna Gora, *Bulgaria* 38 G7
Sredne Tambovskoye, *Russia* 45 D14
Srednekolymsk, *Russia* 45 C16
Srednevilyuysk, *Russia* 45 C13
Śrem, *Poland* 20 C7
Sremska Mitrovica, *Serbia, Yug.* 21 L9
Srepok →, *Cambodia* 58 F6
Sretensk, *Russia* 45 D12
Sri Lanka ■, *Asia* 60 R12
Srikakulam, *India* 61 K13
Srinagar, *India* 63 B6
Środa Wielkopolski, *Poland* 20 C7
Srpska Itabej, *Serbia, Yug.* 21 K10
Staaten →, *Australia* 90 B3
Staberhuk, *Germany* 18 A7
Stabroek, *Belgium* 17 F4
Stad Delden, *Neths.* 16 D9
Stade, *Germany* 18 B5
Staden, *Belgium* 17 G2
Städjan, *Sweden* 10 C6
Stadskanaal, *Neths.* 16 B9
Stadthagen, *Germany* 18 C5
Stadtlohn, *Germany* 18 D2
Stadtroda, *Germany* 18 E7
Stäfa, *Switz.* 23 B7
Staffa, *U.K.* 14 E2
Stafford, *U.K.* 12 E5
Stafford, *U.S.A.* 109 G5
Stafford Springs, *U.S.A.* 107 E12
Staffordshire □, *U.K.* 12 E5
Stagnone, Isole dello, *Italy* 34 E5
Staines, *U.K.* 13 F7
Stakhanov, *Ukraine* 41 H10
Stalden, *Switz.* 22 D5
Stalingrad = Volgograd, *Russia* 43 F7
Staliniri = Tskhinvali, *Georgia* 43 J7
Stalino = Donetsk, *Ukraine* 41 J9
Stalinogorsk = Novomoskovsk, *Russia* 42 C4
Stalis, *Greece* 37 D7
Stalowa Wola, *Poland* 20 E12
Stalybridge, *U.K.* 12 D5
Stamford, *Australia* 90 C3
Stamford, *U.K.* 13 E7
Stamford, *Conn., U.S.A.* 107 E11
Stamford, *Tex., U.S.A.* 109 J5
Stamps, *U.S.A.* 109 J8
Stanberry, *U.S.A.* 108 E7
Stančevo = Kalipetrovo, *Bulgaria* 38 E10

Standerton, *S. Africa* 85 D4
Standish, *U.S.A.* 104 D4
Stanford, *U.S.A.* 110 C8
Stange, *Norway* 10 D5
Stanger, *S. Africa* 85 D5
Stanislaus →, *U.S.A.* 112 H5
Stanislav = Ivano-Frankivsk, *Ukraine* 41 H3
Stanke Dimitrov, *Bulgaria* 38 G6
Stanley, *Australia* 90 G4
Stanley, *N.B., Canada* 99 C6
Stanley, *Sask., Canada* 101 B8
Stanley, *Falk. Is.* 128 D5
Stanley, *Idaho, U.S.A.* 110 D6
Stanley, *N. Dak., U.S.A.* 108 A3
Stanley, *N.Y., U.S.A.* 106 D7
Stanley, *Wis., U.S.A.* 108 C9
Stanovoy Khrebet, *Russia* 45 D13
Stanovoy Ra. = Stanovoy Khrebet, *Russia* 45 D13
Stans, *Switz.* 23 C6
Stansmore Ra., *Australia* 88 D4
Stanthorpe, *Australia* 91 D5
Stanton, *U.S.A.* 109 J4
Stanwood, *U.S.A.* 112 B4
Staphorst, *Neths.* 16 C8
Staples, *U.S.A.* 108 B7
Stapleton, *U.S.A.* 108 E4
Star City, *Canada* 101 C8
Stara Moravica, *Serbia, Yug.* 21 K9
Stara Planina, *Bulgaria* 38 F6
Stara Zagora, *Bulgaria* 38 G8
Starachowice, *Poland* 20 D11
Staraya Russa, *Russia* 40 D6
Starbuck I., *Kiribati* 93 H12
Stargard Szczeciński, *Poland* 20 B5
Stari Trg, *Slovenia* 33 C12
Staritsa, *Russia* 42 B2
Starke, *U.S.A.* 105 K4
Starkville, *Colo., U.S.A.* 109 G2
Starkville, *Miss., U.S.A.* 105 J1
Starnberg, *Germany* 19 G7
Starnberger See, *Germany* 19 H7
Starobilsk, *Ukraine* 41 H10
Starodub, *Russia* 41 F7
Starogard Gdański, *Poland* 20 B8
Starokonstantinov = Starokonstyantyniv, *Ukraine* 41 H4
Starokonstyantyniv, *Ukraine* 41 H4
Starominskaya, *Russia* 43 G4
Staroshcherbinovskaya, *Russia* 43 G4
Start Pt., *U.K.* 13 G4
Staryy Biryuzyak, *Russia* 43 H8
Staryy Chartoriysk, *Ukraine* 41 G3
Staryy Kheydzhan, *Russia* 45 C15
Staryy Krym, *Ukraine* 41 K8
Staryy Oskol, *Russia* 42 E3
Stassfurt, *Germany* 18 D7
State College, *U.S.A.* 106 F7
Stateline, *U.S.A.* 112 G7
Staten, I. = Estados, I. de Los, *Argentina* 128 D4
Staten, I., *Argentina* 118 J4
Staten I., *U.S.A.* 107 F10
Statesboro, *U.S.A.* 105 J5
Statesville, *U.S.A.* 105 H5
Stauffer, *U.S.A.* 113 L7
Staunton, *Ill., U.S.A.* 108 F10
Staunton, *Va., U.S.A.* 104 F6
Stavanger, *Norway* 9 G11
Staveley, *N.Z.* 87 K3
Stavelot, *Belgium* 17 H7
Stavenhagen, *Germany* 18 B8
Stavenisse, *Neths.* 17 E4
Staveren, *Neths.* 16 C6
Stavern, *Norway* 10 F4
Stavre, *Sweden* 10 B9
Stavropol, *Russia* 43 H6
Stavros, *Cyprus* 37 D11
Stavrós, *Greece* 37 D6
Stavros, Ákra, *Greece* 37 D6
Stavroúpolis, *Greece* 39 H7
Stawell, *Australia* 91 F3
Stawell →, *Australia* 90 C3
Stawiszyn, *Poland* 20 D8
Stayner, *Canada* 106 B4
Steamboat Springs, *U.S.A.* 110 F10
Steckborn, *Switz.* 23 A7
Steele, *U.S.A.* 108 B5
Steelton, *U.S.A.* 106 F8
Steelville, *U.S.A.* 109 G9
Steen River, *Canada* 100 B5
Steenbergen, *Neths.* 17 E4
Steenkool = Bintuni, *Indonesia* 57 E8
Steenvoorde, *France* 25 B9
Steenwijk, *Neths.* 16 C8
Steep Pt., *Australia* 89 E1
Steep Rock, *Canada* 101 C9
Ştefăneşti, *Romania* 38 B10
Stefanie L. = Chew Bahir, *Ethiopia* 77 G4
Stefansson Bay, *Antarctica* 5 C5
Steffisburg, *Switz.* 22 C5
Stege, *Denmark* 11 K6
Steiermark □, *Austria* 21 H5
Steigerwald, *Germany* 19 F6
Steilacoom, *U.S.A.* 112 C4
Stein, *Neths.* 17 G7
Steinbach, *Canada* 101 D9
Steinfort, *Lux.* 17 J7
Steinfurt, *Germany* 18 C3
Steinheim, *Germany* 18 D5
Steinhuder Meer, *Germany* 18 C5
Steinkjer, *Norway* 8 D14
Steinkopf, *S. Africa* 84 D2
Stekene, *Belgium* 17 F4
Stellarton, *Canada* 99 C7
Stellenbosch, *S. Africa* 84 E2
Stellendam, *Neths.* 16 E4
Stelvio, Paso dello, *Italy* 32 B7
Stemshaug, *Norway* 10 A2
Stendal, *Germany* 18 C7
Stene, *Belgium* 17 F1
Stenstorp, *Sweden* 11 F7
Steornabhaigh = Stornoway, *U.K.* 14 C2
Stepanakert = Xankändi, *Azerbaijan* 67 C12
Stepanavan, *Armenia* 43 K7
Stephen, *U.S.A.* 108 A6
Stephens Creek, *Australia* 91 E3
Stephens I., *Canada* 100 C2
Stephenville, *Canada* 99 C8
Stephenville, *U.S.A.* 109 J5
Stepnica, *Poland* 20 B4
Stepnoi = Elista, *Russia* 43 G7
Stepnyak, *Kazakstan* 44 D8
Steppe, *Asia* 46 D9
Sterkstroom, *S. Africa* 84 E4
Sterling, *Colo., U.S.A.* 108 E3
Sterling, *Ill., U.S.A.* 108 E10
Sterling, *Kans., U.S.A.* 108 F5
Sterling City, *U.S.A.* 109 K4
Sterling Run, *U.S.A.* 106 E6
Sterlitamak, *Russia* 44 D6
Sternberg, *Germany* 18 B7
Šternberk, *Czech.* 20 F7
Stérnes, *Greece* 37 D6
Sterzing = Vipiteno, *Italy* 33 B8
Stettin = Szczecin, *Poland* 20 B4
Stettiner Haff, *Germany* 18 B10
Stettler, *Canada* 100 C6
Steubenville, *U.S.A.* 106 F4
Stevens Point, *U.S.A.* 108 C10
Stevenson, *U.S.A.* 112 E5
Stevenson L., *Canada* 101 C9
Stevns Klint, *Denmark* 11 J6
Stewart, *B.C., Canada* 100 B3
Stewart, *N.W.T., Canada* 96 B6
Stewart, *U.S.A.* 112 F7
Stewart, C., *Australia* 90 A1
Stewart, I., *Chile* 128 D2
Stewart I., *N.Z.* 87 M1
Stewarts Point, *U.S.A.* 112 G3
Stewiacke, *Canada* 99 C7
Steynsburg, *S. Africa* 84 E4
Steyr, *Austria* 21 G4
Steytlerville, *S. Africa* 84 E3
Stia, *Italy* 33 E8
Stiens, *Neths.* 16 B7
Stigler, *U.S.A.* 109 H7
Stigliano, *Italy* 35 B9
Stigsnæs, *Denmark* 11 J5
Stigtomta, *Sweden* 11 F10
Stikine →, *Canada* 100 B2
Stilfontein, *S. Africa* 84 D4
Stilís, *Greece* 39 L5
Stillwater, *N.Z.* 87 K3
Stillwater, *Minn., U.S.A.* 108 C8
Stillwater, *N.Y., U.S.A.* 107 D11
Stillwater, *Okla., U.S.A.* 109 G6
Stillwater Range, *U.S.A.* 110 G4
Stilwell, *U.S.A.* 109 H7
Štip, *Macedonia* 39 H5
Stíra, *Greece* 39 L7
Stirling, *Australia* 90 B3
Stirling, *Canada* 100 D6
Stirling, *U.K.* 14 E5
Stirling □, *U.K.* 14 E4
Stirling Ra., *Australia* 89 F2
Stittsville, *Canada* 107 A9
Stjernøya, *Norway* 8 A20
Stjørdalshalsen, *Norway* 8 E14
Stockach, *Germany* 19 H5
Stockerau, *Austria* 21 G6
Stockett, *U.S.A.* 110 C8
Stockholm, *Sweden* 10 E12
Stockholms län □, *Sweden* 10 E12
Stockhorn, *Switz.* 22 C5
Stockport, *U.K.* 12 D5
Stocksbridge, *U.K.* 12 D6
Stockton, *Calif., U.S.A.* 111 H3
Stockton, *Kans., U.S.A.* 108 F5
Stockton, *Mo., U.S.A.* 109 G8
Stockton-on-Tees, *U.K.* 12 C6
Stockton-on-Tees □, *U.K.* 12 C6
Stockvik, *Sweden* 10 B11
Stöde, *Sweden* 10 B10
Stogovo, *Macedonia* 39 H3
Stoke on Trent, *U.K.* 12 D5
Stokes Bay, *Canada* 98 C3
Stokes Pt., *Australia* 90 G3
Stokes Ra., *Australia* 88 C5
Stokksnes, *Iceland* 8 D6
Stokmarknes, *Norway* 8 B16
Stolac, *Bos.-H.* 21 M7
Stolberg, *Germany* 18 E2
Stolbovaya, *Russia* 45 C16
Stolbovoy, Ostrov, *Russia* 45 D17
Stolbtsy = Stowbtsy, *Belarus* 40 F4
Stolin, *Belarus* 41 G4
Stolwijk, *Neths.* 16 E5
Stomíon, *Greece* 37 D5
Ston, *Croatia* 21 N7
Stonehaven, *U.K.* 14 E6
Stonehenge, *Australia* 90 C3
Stonewall, *Canada* 101 C9
Stony L., *Man., Canada* 101 B9
Stony L., *Ont., Canada* 106 B6
Stony Rapids, *Canada* 101 B7
Stony Tunguska = Podkamennaya Tunguska →, *Russia* 45 C10
Stonyford, *U.S.A.* 112 F4
Stopnica, *Poland* 20 E10
Stora Lulevatten, *Sweden* 8 C18
Storavan, *Sweden* 8 D18
Stord, *Norway* 9 G11
Store Bælt, *Denmark* 11 J5
Store Creek, *Australia* 91 E4
Store Heddinge, *Denmark* 11 J6
Støren, *Norway* 10 A4
Storm B., *Australia* 90 G4
Storm Lake, *U.S.A.* 108 D7
Stormberge, *S. Africa* 84 E4
Stormsrivier, *S. Africa* 84 E3
Stornoway, *U.K.* 14 C2
Storozhinets = Storozhynets, *Ukraine* 41 H3
Storozhynets, *Ukraine* 41 H3
Storsjö, *Sweden* 10 B7
Storsjøen, *Hedmark, Norway* 10 D5
Storsjøen, *Hedmark, Norway* 10 C5
Storsjön, *Sweden* 10 B7
Storstrøms Amtskommune □, *Denmark* 11 K5
Storuman, *Sweden* 8 D17
Storuman, sjö, *Sweden* 8 D17
Stoughton, *Canada* 101 D8
Stour →, *Dorset, U.K.* 13 G5
Stour →, *Here. & Worcs., U.K.* 13 E5
Stour →, *Kent, U.K.* 13 F9
Stour →, *Suffolk, U.K.* 13 F9
Stourbridge, *U.K.* 13 E5
Stout, L., *Canada* 101 C10
Stove Pipe Wells Village, *U.S.A.* 113 J9
Stowbtsy, *Belarus* 40 F4
Stowmarket, *U.K.* 13 E9
Strabane, *U.K.* 15 B4
Strabane □, *U.K.* 15 B4
Stracin, *Macedonia* 38 G5
Stradella, *Italy* 32 C6
Strahan, *Australia* 90 G4
Strakonice, *Czech.* 20 F3
Straldzha, *Bulgaria* 38 G9
Stralsund, *Germany* 18 A9
Strand, *S. Africa* 84 E2
Stranda, *Møre og Romsdal, Norway* 9 E12
Stranda, *Nord-Trøndelag, Norway* 8 E14
Strangford L., *U.K.* 15 B6
Strängnäs, *Sweden* 10 E11
Strangsville, *U.S.A.* 106 E3
Stranraer, *U.K.* 14 G3
Strasbourg, *Canada* 101 C8
Strasbourg, *France* 25 D14
Strasburg, *Germany* 18 B9
Strasburg, *U.S.A.* 108 B4
Strassen, *Lux.* 17 J8
Stratford, *Canada* 98 D3
Stratford, *N.Z.* 87 H5
Stratford, *Calif., U.S.A.* 111 H4
Stratford, *Conn., U.S.A.* 107 E11
Stratford, *Tex., U.S.A.* 109 G3
Stratford-upon-Avon, *U.K.* 13 E6
Strath Spey, *U.K.* 14 D5
Strathalbyn, *Australia* 91 F2
Strathcona Prov. Park, *Canada* 100 D3
Strathmore, *Australia* 90 B3
Strathmore, *Canada* 100 C6
Strathmore, *U.K.* 14 E5
Strathmore, *U.S.A.* 112 J7
Strathnaver, *Canada* 100 C4
Strathpeffer, *U.K.* 14 D4
Strathroy, *Canada* 98 D3
Strathy Pt., *U.K.* 14 C4
Stratton, *U.S.A.* 108 F3
Straubing, *Germany* 19 G8
Straumnes, *Iceland* 8 C2
Strausberg, *Germany* 18 C9
Strawberry Reservoir, *U.S.A.* 110 F8
Strawn, *U.S.A.* 109 J5
Strážnice, *Czech.* 20 G7
Streaky B., *Australia* 91 E1
Streaky Bay, *Australia* 91 E1
Streator, *U.S.A.* 108 E10
Streé, *Belgium* 17 H4
Streeter, *U.S.A.* 108 B5
Streetsville, *Canada* 106 C5
Strehaia, *Romania* 38 E6
Strelcha, *Bulgaria* 38 G7
Strelka, *Russia* 45 D10
Streng →, *Cambodia* 58 F4
Strésa, *Italy* 32 C5
Streymoy, *Færoe Is.* 8 E9
Strezhevoy, *Russia* 44 C8
Stříbro, *Czech.* 20 F3
Strijen, *Neths.* 16 E5
Strimón →, *Greece* 39 J6
Strimonikós Kólpos, *Greece* 39 J6
Stroeder, *Argentina* 128 B4
Strofádhes, *Greece* 39 M4
Strömbacka, *Sweden* 10 C10
Strómboli, *Italy* 35 D8
Stromeferry, *U.K.* 14 D3
Stromness, *U.K.* 14 C5
Stromsburg, *U.S.A.* 108 E6
Strömstad, *Sweden* 9 G14
Strömsund, *Sweden* 8 E16
Stróngoli, *Italy* 35 C10
Stronsay, *U.K.* 14 B6
Stroud, *U.K.* 13 F5
Stroud Road, *Australia* 91 E5
Stroudsburg, *U.S.A.* 107 F9
Stroumbi, *Cyprus* 37 E11
Struer, *Denmark* 11 H2
Struga, *Macedonia* 39 H3
Strugi Krasnyye, *Russia* 40 C5
Strumica, *Macedonia* 39 H5
Strumica →, *Europe* 39 H6
Struthers, *Canada* 98 C2
Struthers, *U.S.A.* 106 E4
Stryker, *U.S.A.* 110 B6
Stryy, *Ukraine* 41 H2
Strzegom, *Poland* 20 E6
Strzelce Krajeńskie, *Poland* 20 C5
Strzelecki Cr. →, *Australia* 91 D2
Strzelin, *Poland* 20 E7
Strzelno, *Poland* 20 C8
Strzyżów, *Poland* 20 F11
Stuart, *Fla., U.S.A.* 105 M5
Stuart, *Nebr., U.S.A.* 108 D5
Stuart →, *Canada* 100 C4
Stuart Bluff Ra., *Australia* 88 D5
Stuart L., *Canada* 100 C4
Stuart Ra., *Australia* 91 D1
Stubbekøbing, *Denmark* 11 K6
Stugun, *Sweden* 10 A9
Stull, L., *Canada* 98 B1
Stung Treng, *Cambodia* 58 F5
Stupart →, *Canada* 101 B10
Stupino, *Russia* 42 C4
Sturgeon B., *Canada* 101 C9
Sturgeon Bay, *U.S.A.* 104 C2
Sturgeon Falls, *Canada* 98 C4
Sturgeon L., *Alta., Canada* 100 B5
Sturgeon L., *Ont., Canada* 106 B6
Sturgeon L., *Ont., Canada* 98 B1
Sturgis, *Mich., U.S.A.* 104 E3
Sturgis, *S. Dak., U.S.A.* 108 C3
Sturt Cr. →, *Australia* 88 C4
Sturt Creek, *Australia* 88 C4
Stutterheim, *S. Africa* 84 E4
Stuttgart, *Germany* 19 G5
Stuttgart, *U.S.A.* 109 H9
Stuyvesant, *U.S.A.* 107 D11
Stykkishólmur, *Iceland* 8 D2
Styria = Steiermark □, *Austria* 21 H5
Su Xian, *China* 50 H9
Suakin, *Sudan* 76 D4
Suan, *N. Korea* 51 E14
Suapure →, *Venezuela* 120 B4
Suaqui, *Mexico* 114 B3
Suatá →, *Venezuela* 121 B4
Subang, *Indonesia* 57 G12
Subansiri →, *India* 61 F18
Subayhah, *Si. Arabia* 64 D3
Subi, *Indonesia* 59 L7
Subiaco, *Italy* 33 G10
Subotica, *Serbia, Yug.* 21 J9
Success, *Canada* 101 C7
Suceava, *Romania* 38 B9
Suceava →, *Romania* 38 B9
Sucha-Beskidzka, *Poland* 20 F9
Suchan, *Poland* 20 B5
Suchan, *Russia* 48 C6
Suchitoto, *El Salv.* 116 D2
Suchou = Suzhou, *China* 53 B13
Süchow = Xuzhou, *China* 51 G9
Suchowola, *Poland* 20 B13
Sucio →, *Colombia* 120 B2
Suck →, *Ireland* 15 C3
Sucre, *Bolivia* 125 D4
Sucre, *Colombia* 120 B3
Sucre □, *Colombia* 120 B2
Sucre □, *Venezuela* 121 A5
Sucuaro, *Colombia* 120 C4
Sućuraj, *Croatia* 33 E14
Sucuriju, *Brazil* 122 A2
Sucuriú →, *Brazil* 125 E7
Sud, Pte., *Canada* 99 C7
Sud-Ouest, Pte. du, *Canada* 99 C7
Suda →, *Russia* 40 C9
Sudak, *Ukraine* 41 K8
Sudan, *U.S.A.* 109 H3
Sudan ■, *Africa* 77 E3
Sudbury, *Canada* 98 C3
Sudbury, *U.K.* 13 E8
Sûdd, *Sudan* 77 F2
Suddie, *Guyana* 121 B6
Süderbrarup, *Germany* 18 A5
Süderlügum, *Germany* 18 A4
Süderoogsand, *Germany* 18 A4
Sudeten Mts. = Sudety, *Europe* 20 E6
Sudety, *Europe* 20 E6
Suðuroy, *Færoe Is.* 8 F9
Sudi, *Tanzania* 83 E4
Sudirman, Pegunungan, *Indonesia* 57 E9
Sudogda, *Russia* 42 C5
Sudr, *Egypt* 76 J8
Sudzha, *Russia* 42 E2
Sueca, *Spain* 29 F4
Suedala, *Sweden* 11 J7
Suez = El Suweis, *Egypt* 76 J8
Suez, G. of = Suweis, Khalîg el, *Egypt* 76 J8
Suez Canal = Suweis, Qanâ es, *Egypt* 76 H8
Suffield, *Canada* 101 C6
Suffolk, *U.S.A.* 104 G7
Suffolk □, *U.K.* 13 E9
Sugar City, *U.S.A.* 108 F3
Suğla Gölü, *Turkey* 66 D5
Sugluk = Salluit, *Canada* 97 B12
Sugny, *Belgium* 17 J5
Suhaia, L., *Romania* 38 F8
Suhār, *Oman* 65 E8
Suhbaatar, *Mongolia* 54 A5
Sühbaatar □, *Mongolia* 50 B8
Suhl, *Germany* 18 E6
Suhr, *Switz.* 22 B6
Şuhut, *Turkey* 66 C4
Sui Xian, *Henan, China* 50 G8
Sui Xian, *Henan, China* 53 B9
Suiá Missu →, *Brazil* 125 C7
Suichang, *China* 53 C12
Suichuan, *China* 53 D10
Suide, *China* 50 F6
Suifenhe, *China* 51 B16
Suihua, *China* 54 B7
Suijiang, *China* 52 C4
Suining, *Hunan, China* 53 D8
Suining, *Jiangsu, China* 51 H9
Suining, *Sichuan, China* 52 B5
Suiping, *China* 50 H7
Suippes, *France* 25 C11
Suir →, *Ireland* 15 D4
Suixi, *China* 53 G8
Suiyang, *Guizhou, China* 52 D6
Suiyang, *Heilongjiang, China* 51 B16
Suizhong, *China* 51 D11
Sujangarh, *India* 62 F6
Sukabumi, *Indonesia* 57 G12
Sukadana, *Kalimantan, Indonesia* 56 E3
Sukadana, *Sumatera, Indonesia* 56 F3
Sukagawa, *Japan* 49 F10
Sukaraja, *Indonesia* 56 E4
Sukarnapura = Jayapura, *Indonesia* 57 E10
Sukchŏn, *N. Korea* 51 E13
Sukhinichi, *Russia* 42 C2
Sukhona →, *Russia* 44 D4
Sukhothai, *Thailand* 58 D2
Sukhumi = Sokhumi, *Georgia* 43 J5
Sukkur, *Pakistan* 62 F3
Sukkur Barrage, *Pakistan* 62 F3
Sukumo, *Japan* 49 H6
Sukunka →, *Canada* 100 B4
Sul, Canal do, *Brazil* 122 B2
Sula →, *Ukraine* 41 H7
Sula, Kepulauan, *Indonesia* 57 E7
Sulaco →, *Honduras* 116 C2
Sulaiman Range, *Pakistan* 62 D3
Sulak →, *Russia* 43 J8
Sūlār, *Iran* 65 D6
Sulawesi □, *Indonesia* 57 E6
Sulawesi Sea = Celebes Sea, *Indonesia* 57 D6
Sulechów, *Poland* 20 C5
Sulejów, *Poland* 20 D9
Sulgen, *Switz.* 23 A8
Sulima, *S. Leone* 78 D2
Sulina, *Romania* 38 D12
Sulina, Braţul →, *Romania* 38 D12
Sulingen, *Germany* 18 C4
Sulitjelma, *Norway* 8 C17
Sullana, *Peru* 124 A1
Sullivan, *Ill., U.S.A.* 108 F10
Sullivan, *Ind., U.S.A.* 104 F2
Sullivan, *Mo., U.S.A.* 108 F9
Sullivan Bay, *Canada* 100 C3
Sully-sur-Loire, *France* 25 E9
Sulmona, *Italy* 33 F10
Sulphur, *La., U.S.A.* 109 K8
Sulphur, *Okla., U.S.A.* 109 H6
Sulphur Pt., *Canada* 100 A6
Sulphur Springs, *U.S.A.* 109 J7
Sulphur Springs Draw →, *U.S.A.* 109 J4
Sultan, *Canada* 98 C3
Sultan, *U.S.A.* 112 C5
Sultan Dağları, *Turkey* 66 C4
Sultanpur, *India* 63 F10
Sulu Arch., *Phil.* 55 J4
Sulu Sea, *E. Indies* 55 G4
Sülüklü, *Turkey* 66 C5
Sululta, *Ethiopia* 77 F4
Suluova, *Turkey* 66 B6
Suluq, *Libya* 73 B9
Sulzbach, *Germany* 19 F3
Sulzbach-Rosenberg, *Germany* 19 F7
Sulzberger Ice Shelf, *Antarctica* 5 D10
Sumalata, *Indonesia* 57 D6
Sumampa, *Argentina* 126 B3
Sumatera □, *Indonesia* 56 D2
Sumatra = Sumatera □, *Indonesia* 56 D2
Sumatra, *U.S.A.* 110 C10
Sumba, *Indonesia* 57 F5
Sumba, Selat, *Indonesia* 57 F5
Sumbawa, *Indonesia* 56 F5
Sumbawa Besar, *Indonesia* 56 F5
Sumbawanga □, *Tanzania* 82 D3
Sumbe, *Angola* 80 G2
Sumburgh Hd., *U.K.* 14 B7
Sumdo, *India* 63 B8
Sumé, *Brazil* 122 C4
Sumedang, *Indonesia* 57 G12
Šumen, *Bulgaria* 38 F9

Sumenep, *Indonesia* 57 G15
Sumgait = Sumqayıt, *Azerbaijan* 43 K9
Sumiswald, *Switz.* 22 B5
Summer L., *U.S.A.* 110 E3
Summerland, *Canada* 100 D5
Summerside, *Canada* 99 C7
Summerville, *Ga., U.S.A.* 105 H3
Summerville, *S.C., U.S.A.* 105 J5
Summit Lake, *Canada* 100 C4
Summit Peak, *U.S.A.* 111 H10
Sumner, *Iowa, U.S.A.* 108 D8
Sumner, *Wash., U.S.A.* 112 C4
Sumoto, *Japan* 49 G7
Sumqayıt, *Azerbaijan* 43 K9
Sumter, *U.S.A.* 105 J5
Sumy, *Ukraine* 41 G8
Sun City, *Ariz., U.S.A.* 111 K7
Sun City, *Calif., U.S.A.* 113 M9
Sunagawa, *Japan* 48 C10
Sunan, *N. Korea* 51 E13
Sunart, L., *U.K.* 14 E3
Sunburst, *U.S.A.* 110 B8
Sunbury, *Australia* 91 F3
Sunbury, *U.S.A.* 107 F8
Sunchales, *Argentina* 126 C3
Suncho Corral, *Argentina* 126 B3
Sunchon, *S. Korea* 51 G14
Suncook, *U.S.A.* 107 C13
Sunda, Selat, *Indonesia* 56 F3
Sunda Is., *Indonesia* 46 K14
Sunda Str. = Sunda, Selat, *Indonesia* 56 F3
Sundance, *U.S.A.* 108 C2
Sundarbans, The, *Asia* 61 J16
Sundargarh, *India* 61 H14
Sundays = Sondags →, *S. Africa* 84 E4
Sundbyberg, *Sweden* 10 E11
Sunderland, *Canada* 106 B5
Sunderland, *U.K.* 12 C6
Sundre, *Canada* 100 C6
Sundridge, *Canada* 98 C4
Sunds, *Denmark* 11 H3
Sundsjö, *Sweden* 10 B9
Sundsvall, *Sweden* 10 B11
Sung Hei, *Vietnam* 59 G6
Sungai Kolok, *Thailand* 59 J3
Sungai Lembing, *Malaysia* 59 L4
Sungai Patani, *Malaysia* 59 K3
Sungaigerong, *Indonesia* 56 E2
Sungailiat, *Indonesia* 56 E3
Sungaipakning, *Indonesia* 56 D2
Sungaipenuh, *Indonesia* 56 E2
Sungaitiram, *Indonesia* 56 E5
Sungari = Songhua Jiang →, *China* 54 B8
Sungguminasa, *Indonesia* 57 F5
Sunghua Chiang = Songhua Jiang →, *China* 54 B8
Sungikai, *Sudan* 77 E2
Sungurlu, *Turkey* 66 B6
Sunja, *Croatia* 33 C13
Sunndalsøra, *Norway* 9 E13
Sunnyside, *Utah, U.S.A.* 110 G8
Sunnyside, *Wash., U.S.A.* 110 C3
Sunnyvale, *U.S.A.* 111 H2
Sunray, *U.S.A.* 109 G4
Suntar, *Russia* 45 C12
Sunyani, *Ghana* 78 D4
Suomenselkä, *Finland* 8 E21
Suomussalmi, *Finland* 8 D23
Suoyarvi, *Russia* 40 A7
Supai, *U.S.A.* 111 H7
Supamo →, *Venezuela* 121 B5
Supaul, *India* 63 F12
Supe, *Peru* 124 C2
Superior, *Ariz., U.S.A.* 111 K8
Superior, *Mont., U.S.A.* 110 C6
Superior, *Nebr., U.S.A.* 108 E5
Superior, *Wis., U.S.A.* 108 B8
Superior, L., *U.S.A.* 98 C2
Supetar, *Croatia* 33 E13
Suphan Buri, *Thailand* 58 E3
Suphan Dağı, *Turkey* 67 C10
Supiori, *Indonesia* 57 E9
Supung Sk., *China* 51 D13
Sūq Suwayq, *Si. Arabia* 64 E3
Suqian, *China* 51 H10
Sūr, *Lebanon* 69 B4
Sur, Pt., *U.S.A.* 111 H3
Sura →, *Russia* 42 C8
Surab, *Pakistan* 62 E2
Surabaja = Surabaya, *Indonesia* 57 G15
Surabaya, *Indonesia* 57 G15
Suraia, *Romania* 38 D10
Surakarta, *Indonesia* 57 G14
Surakhany, *Azerbaijan* 43 K10
Surat, *Australia* 91 D4
Surat, *India* 60 J8
Surat Thani, *Thailand* 59 H2
Suratgarh, *India* 62 E5
Surazh, *Belarus* 40 E6
Surazh, *Russia* 41 F7
Surduc Pasul, *Romania* 38 D6
Surdulica, *Serbia, Yug.* 21 N12
Sûre = Sauer →, *Germany* 17 J9
Surendranagar, *India* 62 H4
Surf, *U.S.A.* 113 L6
Surgères, *France* 26 B3
Surgut, *Russia* 44 C8
Surhuisterveen, *Neths.* 16 B8
Suriapet, *India* 60 L11
Surigao, *Phil.* 55 G6
Surigao Strait, *Phil.* 55 F6
Surin, *Thailand* 58 E4
Surin Nua, Ko, *Thailand* 59 H1
Surinam ■, *S. Amer.* 121 C6
Suriname □, *Surinam* 121 B6
Suriname ■ = Surinam ■, *S. Amer.* 121 C6
Suriname →, *Surinam* 121 B6
Sürmaq, *Iran* 65 D7
Sürmene, *Turkey* 67 B9
Surovikino, *Russia* 43 F6
Surprise L., *Canada* 100 B2
Surrey □, *U.K.* 13 F7
Sursee, *Switz.* 22 B6
Sursk, *Russia* 42 D7
Surskoye, *Russia* 42 C8
Surt, *Libya* 73 B8
Surt, Khalīj, *Libya* 73 B8
Surtsey, *Iceland* 8 E3
Surubim, *Brazil* 122 C4
Sürüç, *Turkey* 67 D8
Suruga-Wan, *Japan* 49 G9
Surumu →, *Brazil* 121 C5
Susa, *Italy* 32 C4
Suså →, *Denmark* 11 J5
Sušac, *Croatia* 33 F13
Susak, *Croatia* 33 D11
Susaki, *Japan* 49 H6
Süsangerd, *Iran* 67 G13
Susanino, *Russia* 45 D15
Susanville, *U.S.A.* 110 F3
Susch, *Switz.* 23 C10
Suşehri, *Turkey* 67 B8
Susong, *China* 53 B11
Susquehanna →, *U.S.A.* 107 G8
Susquehanna Depot, *U.S.A.* 107 E9
Susques, *Argentina* 126 A2
Sussex, *Canada* 99 C6
Sussex, *U.S.A.* 107 E10
Sussex, E. □, *U.K.* 13 G8
Sussex, W. □, *U.K.* 13 G7
Susteren, *Neths.* 17 F7
Sustut →, *Canada* 100 B3
Susuman, *Russia* 45 C15
Susunu, *Indonesia* 57 E8
Susurluk, *Turkey* 66 C3
Susuz, *Turkey* 67 B10
Sütçüler, *Turkey* 66 D4
Sutherland, *S. Africa* 84 E3
Sutherland, *U.S.A.* 108 E4
Sutherland Falls, *N.Z.* 87 L1
Sutherlin, *U.S.A.* 110 E2
Sutivan, *Croatia* 33 E13
Sutlej →, *Pakistan* 62 E4
Sutter, *U.S.A.* 112 F5
Sutter Creek, *U.S.A.* 112 G6
Sutton, *Canada* 107 A12
Sutton, *U.S.A.* 108 E6
Sutton →, *Canada* 98 A3
Sutton in Ashfield, *U.K.* 12 D6
Suttor →, *Australia* 90 C4
Suttsu, *Japan* 48 C10
Suva, *Fiji* 87 D8
Suva Reka, *Serbia, Yug.* 21 N10
Suvo Rudište, *Serbia, Yug.* 21 M10
Suvorov, *Russia* 42 C3
Suvorov Is. = Suwarrow Is., *Cook Is.* 93 J11
Suwałki, *Poland* 20 A12
Suwannaphum, *Thailand* 58 E4
Suwannee →, *U.S.A.* 105 L4
Suwanose-Jima, *Japan* 49 K4
Suwarrow Is., *Cook Is.* 93 J11
Suwayq aş Şuqban, *Iraq* 64 D5
Suweis, Khalîg el, *Egypt* 76 J8
Suweis, Qanâ es, *Egypt* 76 H8
Suwŏn, *S. Korea* 51 F14
Suzdal, *Russia* 42 B5
Suzhou, *China* 53 B13
Suzu, *Japan* 49 F8
Suzu-Misaki, *Japan* 49 F8
Suzuka, *Japan* 49 G8
Suzzara, *Italy* 32 C7
Svalbard, *Arctic* 4 B8
Svalöv, *Sweden* 11 J7
Svappavaara, *Sweden* 8 C19
Svarstad, *Norway* 10 E3
Svartisen, *Norway* 8 C15
Svartvik, *Sweden* 10 B11
Svatove, *Ukraine* 41 H10
Svatovo = Svatove, *Ukraine* 41 H10
Svay Chek, *Cambodia* 58 F4
Svay Rieng, *Cambodia* 59 G5
Svealand □, *Sweden* 9 G16
Sveg, *Sweden* 9 E16
Svendborg, *Denmark* 11 J4
Svene, *Norway* 10 E3
Svenljunga, *Sweden* 11 G7
Svenstrup, *Denmark* 11 H3
Sverdlovsk = Yekaterinburg, *Russia* 44 D7
Sverdlovsk, *Ukraine* 41 H10
Sverdrup Is., *Canada* 4 B3
Svetac, *Croatia* 33 E12
Sveti Ivan Zelina, *Croatia* 33 C13
Sveti Jurij, *Slovenia* 33 B12
Sveti Lenart, *Slovenia* 33 B12
Sveti Nikole, *Macedonia* 39 H4
Sveti Trojica, *Slovenia* 33 B12
Svetlaya, *Russia* 48 A9
Svetlogorsk = Svyetlahorsk, *Belarus* 41 F5
Svetlograd, *Russia* 43 H6
Svetlovodsk = Svitlovodsk, *Ukraine* 41 H7
Svetozarevo, *Serbia, Yug.* 21 L11
Svidník, *Slovak Rep.* 20 F11
Svilaja Planina, *Croatia* 33 E13
Svilengrad, *Bulgaria* 39 H9
Svir →, *Russia* 40 B7
Sviritsa, *Russia* 40 B7
Svishtov, *Bulgaria* 38 F8
Svislach, *Belarus* 41 F3
Svitava →, *Czech.* 20 F6
Svitavy, *Czech.* 20 F6
Svitlovodsk, *Ukraine* 41 H7
Svobodnyy, *Russia* 45 D13
Svolvær, *Norway* 8 B16
Svratka →, *Czech.* 20 F6
Svrljig, *Serbia, Yug.* 21 M12
Svyetlahorsk, *Belarus* 41 F5
Swabian Alps = Schwäbische Alb, *Germany* 19 G5
Swainsboro, *U.S.A.* 105 J4
Swakopmund, *Namibia* 84 C1
Swale →, *U.K.* 12 C6
Swalmen, *Neths.* 17 F8
Swan Hill, *Australia* 91 F3
Swan Hills, *Canada* 100 C5
Swan Is., *W. Indies* 116 C3
Swan L., *Canada* 101 C8
Swan River, *Canada* 101 C8
Swanage, *U.K.* 13 G6
Swansea, *Australia* 91 E5
Swansea, *U.K.* 13 F4
Swansea □, *U.K.* 13 F3
Swar →, *Pakistan* 63 B5
Swartberge, *S. Africa* 84 E3
Swartmodder, *S. Africa* 84 D3
Swartruggens, *S. Africa* 84 D4
Swarzędz, *Poland* 20 C7
Swastika, *Canada* 98 C3
Swatow = Shantou, *China* 53 F11
Swaziland ■, *Africa* 85 D5
Sweden ■, *Europe* 9 G16
Swedru, *Ghana* 79 D4
Sweet Home, *U.S.A.* 110 D2
Sweetwater, *Nev., U.S.A.* 112 G7
Sweetwater, *Tex., U.S.A.* 109 J4
Sweetwater →, *U.S.A.* 110 E10
Swellendam, *S. Africa* 84 E3
Świdnica, *Poland* 20 E6
Świdnik, *Poland* 20 D12
Świdwin, *Poland* 20 B5
Świebodzin, *Poland* 20 C5
Świecie, *Poland* 20 B8
Świętokrzyskie, Góry, *Poland* 20 E10
Swift Current, *Canada* 101 C7
Swiftcurrent →, *Canada* 101 C7
Swilly, L., *Ireland* 15 A4
Swindle, I., *Canada* 100 C3
Swindon, *U.K.* 13 F6
Swinemünde = Świnoujście, *Poland* 20 B4
Świnoujście, *Poland* 20 B4
Switzerland ■, *Europe* 22 D6
Swords, *Ireland* 15 C5
Syasstroy, *Russia* 40 B7
Sychevka, *Russia* 42 C2
Sydney, *Australia* 91 E5
Sydney, *Canada* 99 C7
Sydney Mines, *Canada* 99 C7
Sydprøven, *Greenland* 4 C5
Sydra, G. of = Surt, Khalīj, *Libya* 73 B8
Syeverodonetsk, *Ukraine* 41 H10
Syke, *Germany* 18 C4
Syktyvkar, *Russia* 44 C6
Sylacauga, *U.S.A.* 105 J2
Sylarna, *Sweden* 8 E15
Sylhet, *Bangla.* 61 G17
Sylt, *Germany* 18 A4
Sylvan Lake, *Canada* 100 C6
Sylvania, *U.S.A.* 105 J5
Sylvester, *U.S.A.* 105 K4
Sym, *Russia* 44 C9
Symón, *Mexico* 114 C4
Synelnykove, *Ukraine* 41 H8
Synnott Ra., *Australia* 88 C4
Syracuse, *Kans., U.S.A.* 109 F4
Syracuse, *N.Y., U.S.A.* 107 C8
Syrdarya →, *Kazakstan* 44 E7
Syria ■, *Asia* 67 E8
Syrian Desert = Ash Shām, Bādiyat, *Asia* 46 F7
Syul'dzhyukyor, *Russia* 45 C12
Syzran, *Russia* 42 D9
Szaraz →, *Hungary* 21 J10
Szarvas, *Hungary* 21 J10
Szczebrzeszyn, *Poland* 20 E12
Szczecin, *Poland* 20 B4
Szczecinek, *Poland* 20 B6
Szczekocimy, *Poland* 20 E9
Szczytno, *Poland* 20 B11
Szechwan = Sichuan □, *China* 52 B5
Szeged, *Hungary* 21 J10
Szeghalom, *Hungary* 21 H11
Székesfehérvár, *Hungary* 21 H8
Szekszárd, *Hungary* 21 J8
Szendrö, *Hungary* 21 G10
Szentendre, *Hungary* 21 H9
Szentes, *Hungary* 21 J10
Szentgotthárd, *Hungary* 21 J6
Szentlörinc, *Hungary* 21 J8
Szigetvár, *Hungary* 21 J7
Szolnok, *Hungary* 21 H10
Szombathely, *Hungary* 21 H6
Szprotawa, *Poland* 20 D5
Szydłowiec, *Poland* 20 D10
Szypliszki, *Poland* 20 A13

T

't Harde, *Neths.* 16 D7
't Zandt, *Neths.* 16 B9
Ta Khli Khok, *Thailand* 58 E3
Ta Lai, *Vietnam* 59 G6
Tabacal, *Argentina* 126 A3
Tabaco, *Phil.* 55 E5
Tabagné, *Ivory C.* 78 D4
Ţābah, *Si. Arabia* 64 E4
Tabajara, *Brazil* 125 B5
Tabalos, *Peru* 124 B2
Tabarca, I. de, *Spain* 29 G4
Tabarka, *Tunisia* 75 A6
Ţabas, *Khorāsān, Iran* 65 C9
Ţabas, *Khorāsān, Iran* 65 C8
Tabasará, Serranía de, *Panama* 116 E3
Tabasco □, *Mexico* 115 D6
Tabatinga, Serra da, *Brazil* 122 D3
Tabāzīn, *Iran* 65 D8
Tabelbala, Kahal de, *Algeria* 75 C4
Taber, *Canada* 100 D6
Tabernas, *Spain* 29 H2
Tabernes de Valldigna, *Spain* 29 F4
Tabira, *Brazil* 122 C4
Tablas, *Phil.* 55 E5
Tablas Strait, *Phil.* 55 E4
Table B. = Tafelbaai, *S. Africa* 84 E2
Table B., *Canada* 99 B8
Table Mt., *S. Africa* 84 E2
Tableland, *Australia* 88 C4
Tabletop, Mt., *Australia* 90 C4
Tábor, *Czech.* 20 F4
Tabora, *Tanzania* 82 D3
Tabora □, *Tanzania* 82 D3
Tabou, *Ivory C.* 78 E3
Tabrīz, *Iran* 67 C12
Tabuaeran, *Pac. Oc.* 93 G12
Tabuelan, *Phil.* 55 F5
Tabuenca, *Spain* 28 D3
Tabūk, *Si. Arabia* 64 D3
Tacámbaro de Codallos, *Mexico* 114 D4
Tacheng, *China* 54 B3
Tachia, *Taiwan* 53 E13
Tach'ing Shan = Daqing Shan, *China* 50 D6
Táchira □, *Venezuela* 120 B3
Tácina →, *Italy* 35 D9
Tacloban, *Phil.* 55 F6
Tacna, *Peru* 124 D3
Tacna □, *Peru* 124 D3
Tacoma, *U.S.A.* 112 C4
Tacuarembó, *Uruguay* 127 C4
Tacutu →, *Brazil* 121 C5
Tademaït, Plateau du, *Algeria* 75 C5
Tadent, O. →, *Algeria* 75 D6
Tadjerdjeri, O. →, *Algeria* 75 C6
Tadjerouna, *Algeria* 75 B5
Tadjettaret, O. →, *Algeria* 75 D6
Tadjmout, *Oasis, Algeria* 75 B5
Tadjmout, *Saoura, Algeria* 75 C5
Tadjoura, *Djibouti* 68 E3
Tadjoura, Golfe de, *Djibouti* 77 E5
Tadmor, *N.Z.* 87 J4
Tadoule, L., *Canada* 101 B9
Tadoussac, *Canada* 99 C6
Tadzhikistan = Tajikistan ■, *Asia* 44 F8
Taechŏn-ni, *S. Korea* 51 F14
Taegu, *S. Korea* 51 G15
Taegwan, *N. Korea* 51 D13
Taejŏn, *S. Korea* 51 F14
Tafalla, *Spain* 28 C3
Tafar, *Sudan* 77 F2
Tafassasset, O. →, *Algeria* 75 D6
Tafelbaai, *S. Africa* 84 E2
Tafelney, C., *Morocco* 74 B3
Tafermaar, *Indonesia* 57 F8
Taffermit, *Morocco* 74 C3
Tafí Viejo, *Argentina* 126 B2
Tafīhān, *Iran* 65 D7
Tafiré, *Ivory C.* 78 D3
Tafnidilt, *Morocco* 74 C2
Tafraoute, *Morocco* 74 C3
Taft, *Iran* 65 D7
Taft, *Phil.* 55 F6
Taft, *Calif., U.S.A.* 113 K7
Taft, *Tex., U.S.A.* 109 M6
Taga Dzong, *Bhutan* 61 F16
Taganrog, *Russia* 43 G4
Taganrogskiy Zaliv, *Russia* 43 G4
Tagânt, *Mauritania* 78 B2
Tagatay, *Phil.* 55 D4
Tagbilaran, *Phil.* 55 G5
Tággia, *Italy* 32 E4
Taghzout, *Morocco* 74 B4
Tagish, *Canada* 100 A2
Tagish L., *Canada* 100 A2
Tagliacozzo, *Italy* 33 F10
Tagliamento →, *Italy* 33 C10
Táglio di Po, *Italy* 33 D9
Tagna, *Colombia* 120 D3
Tago, *Phil.* 55 G7
Tagomago, I. de, *Spain* 36 B8
Taguatinga, *Brazil* 123 D3
Tagudin, *Phil.* 55 C4
Tagum, *Phil.* 55 H6
Tagus = Tejo →, *Europe* 31 G1
Tahakopa, *N.Z.* 87 M2
Tahala, *Morocco* 74 B4
Tahan, Gunong, *Malaysia* 59 K4
Tahat, *Algeria* 75 D6
Tāherī, *Iran* 65 E7
Tahiti, *Pac. Oc.* 93 J13
Tahoe, L., *U.S.A.* 112 G6
Tahoe City, *U.S.A.* 112 F6
Taholah, *U.S.A.* 112 C2
Tahoua, *Niger* 79 C6
Tahta, *Egypt* 76 B3
Tahtalı Dağları, *Turkey* 66 C7
Tahuamanu →, *Bolivia* 124 C4
Tahulandang, *Indonesia* 57 D7
Tahuna, *Indonesia* 57 D7
Taï, *Ivory C.* 78 D3
Tai Hu, *China* 54 C7
Tai Shan, *China* 51 F9
Tai Xian, *China* 53 A13
Tai'an, *China* 51 F9
Taibei = T'aipei, *Taiwan* 53 E13
Taibique, *Canary Is.* 36 G2
Taibus Qi, *China* 50 D8
T'aichung, *Taiwan* 53 E13
Taieri →, *N.Z.* 87 M3
Taigu, *China* 50 F7
Taihang Shan, *China* 50 G7
Taihape, *N.Z.* 87 H5
Taihe, *Anhui, China* 50 H8
Taihe, *Jiangxi, China* 53 D10
Taihu, *China* 53 B11
Taijiang, *China* 52 D7
Taikang, *China* 50 G8
Tailem Bend, *Australia* 91 F2
Tailfingen, *Germany* 19 G5
Taimyr Peninsula = Taymyr, Poluostrov, *Russia* 45 B11
Tain, *U.K.* 14 D4
T'ainan, *Taiwan* 53 F13
Taínaron, Ákra, *Greece* 39 N5
Taining, *China* 53 D11
Taintignies, *Belgium* 17 G2
Taiobeiras, *Brazil* 123 E3
T'aipei, *Taiwan* 53 E13
Taiping, *China* 53 B12
Taiping, *Malaysia* 59 K3
Taipingzhen, *China* 50 H6
Taipu, *Brazil* 122 C4
Tairbeart = Tarbert, *U.K.* 14 D2
Taishan, *China* 53 F9
Taishun, *China* 53 D12
Taita □, *Kenya* 82 C4
Taita Hills, *Kenya* 82 C4
Taitao, C., *Chile* 128 C1
Taitao, Pen. de, *Chile* 128 C2
T'aitung, *Taiwan* 53 F13
Taivalkoski, *Finland* 8 D23
Taiwan ■, *Asia* 53 F13
Taixing, *China* 53 A13
Taïyetos Óros, *Greece* 39 N5
Taiyiba, *Israel* 69 C4
Taiyuan, *China* 50 F7
Taizhong = T'aichung, *Taiwan* 53 E13
Taizhou, *China* 53 A12
Taizhou Liedao, *China* 53 C13
Ta'izz, *Yemen* 68 E3
Tājābād, *Iran* 65 D7
Tajapuru, Furo do, *Brazil* 122 B1
Tajikistan ■, *Asia* 44 F8
Tajima, *Japan* 49 F9
Tajo = Tejo →, *Europe* 31 G1
Tajrīsh, *Iran* 65 C6
Tājūrā, *Libya* 73 B7
Tak, *Thailand* 58 D2
Takāb, *Iran* 67 D12
Takachiho, *Japan* 49 H5
Takada, *Japan* 49 F9
Takahagi, *Japan* 49 F10
Takaka, *N.Z.* 87 J4
Takamatsu, *Japan* 49 G7
Takaoka, *Japan* 49 F8
Takapuna, *N.Z.* 87 G5
Takasaki, *Japan* 49 F9
Takatsuki, *Japan* 49 G7
Takaungu, *Kenya* 82 C4
Takayama, *Japan* 49 F8
Take-Shima, *Japan* 49 J5
Takefu, *Japan* 49 G8
Takengon, *Indonesia* 56 D1
Takeo, *Cambodia* 59 G5
Takeo, *Japan* 49 H5
Tåkern, *Sweden* 11 F8
Tākestān, *Iran* 65 C6
Taketa, *Japan* 49 H5
Takh, *India* 63 C7
Takhman, *Cambodia* 59 G5
Takikawa, *Japan* 48 C10
Takla L., *Canada* 100 B3
Takla Landing, *Canada* 100 B3
Takla Makan = Taklamakan Shamo, *China* 46 F12
Taklamakan Shamo, *China* 46 F12
Taku →, *Canada* 100 B2
Takum, *Nigeria* 79 D6
Takutu →, *Guyana* 121 C5
Tal Halāl, *Iran* 65 D7
Tala, *Uruguay* 127 C4
Talachyn, *Belarus* 40 E5
Talacogan, *Phil.* 55 G6
Talagante, *Chile* 126 C1
Talaïnt, *Morocco* 74 C3
Talak, *Niger* 79 B6
Talamanca, Cordillera de, *Cent. Amer.* 116 E3
Talara, *Peru* 124 A1

Talas, *Kyrgyzstan* 44 E8
Talas, *Turkey* 66 C6
Talâta, *Egypt* 69 E1
Talata Mafara, *Nigeria* 79 C6
Talaud, Kepulauan, *Indonesia* 57 D7
Talaud Is. = Talaud, Kepulauan, *Indonesia* 57 D7
Talavera de la Reina, *Spain* 30 F6
Talawana, *Australia* 88 D3
Talayan, *Phil.* 55 H6
Talbert, Sillon de, *France* 24 D3
Talbot, C., *Australia* 88 B4
Talbragar →, *Australia* 91 E4
Talca, *Chile* 126 D1
Talca □, *Chile* 126 D1
Talcahuano, *Chile* 126 D1
Talcher, *India* 61 J14
Talcho, *Niger* 79 C5
Taldy Kurgan = Taldyqorghan, *Kazakstan* 44 E8
Taldyqorghan, *Kazakstan* 44 E8
Tālesh, *Iran* 67 D13
Ţalesh, Kūhhā-ye, *Iran* 67 D13
Talguharai, *Sudan* 76 D4
Tali Post, *Sudan* 77 F3
Talibon, *Phil.* 57 B6
Talibong, Ko, *Thailand* 59 J2
Talihina, *U.S.A.* 109 H7
Talisayan, *Phil.* 55 G6
Taliwang, *Indonesia* 56 F5
Tall 'Afar, *Iraq* 67 D10
Tall 'Asūr, *West Bank* 69 D4
Tall Kalakh, *Syria* 69 A5
Talla, *Egypt* 76 J7
Talladega, *U.S.A.* 105 J2
Tallahassee, *U.S.A.* 105 K3
Tallangatta, *Australia* 91 F4
Tallarook, *Australia* 91 F4
Tallering Pk., *Australia* 89 E2
Tallinn, *Estonia* 9 G21
Tallulah, *U.S.A.* 109 J9
Talmest, *Morocco* 74 B3
Talmont, *France* 26 B2
Talne, *Ukraine* 41 H6
Talnoye = Talne, *Ukraine* 41 H6
Talodi, *Sudan* 77 E3
Talovaya, *Russia* 42 E5
Taloyoak, *Canada* 96 B10
Talpa de Allende, *Mexico* 114 C4
Talsi, *Latvia* 9 H20
Talsinnt, *Morocco* 75 B4
Taltal, *Chile* 126 B1
Taltson →, *Canada* 100 A6
Talwood, *Australia* 91 D4
Talyawalka Cr. →, *Australia* 91 E3
Tam Chau, *Vietnam* 59 G5
Tam Ky, *Vietnam* 58 E7
Tam Quan, *Vietnam* 58 E7
Tama, *U.S.A.* 108 E8
Tamala, *Australia* 89 E1
Tamalameque, *Colombia* 120 B3
Tamale, *Ghana* 79 D4
Taman, *Russia* 43 H3
Tamanar, *Morocco* 74 B3
Tamano, *Japan* 49 G6
Tamanrasset, *Algeria* 75 D6
Tamanrasset, O. →, *Algeria* 75 D5
Tamaqua, *U.S.A.* 107 F9
Tamar →, *U.K.* 13 G3
Támara, *Colombia* 120 B3
Tamarang, *Australia* 91 E5
Tamarinda, *Spain* 36 B10
Tamarite de Litera, *Spain* 28 D5
Tamashima, *Japan* 49 G6
Tamaské, *Niger* 79 C6
Tamaulipas □, *Mexico* 115 C5
Tamaulipas, Sierra de, *Mexico* 115 C5
Tamazula, *Mexico* 114 C3
Tamazunchale, *Mexico* 115 C5
Tamba-Dabatou, *Guinea* 78 C2
Tambacounda, *Senegal* 78 C2
Tambelan, Kepulauan, *Indonesia* 56 D3
Tambellup, *Australia* 89 F2
Tambo, *Australia* 90 C4
Tambo, *Peru* 124 C3
Tambo →, *Peru* 124 C3
Tambo de Mora, *Peru* 124 C2
Tambobamba, *Peru* 124 C3
Tambohorano, *Madag.* 85 B7
Tambopata →, *Peru* 124 C4
Tambora, *Indonesia* 56 F5
Tambov, *Russia* 42 D5
Tambre →, *Spain* 30 C2
Tambuku, *Indonesia* 57 G15
Tamburâ, *Sudan* 77 F2
Tâmchekket, *Mauritania* 78 B2
Tame, *Colombia* 120 B3
Tamega →, *Portugal* 30 D2
Tamelelt, *Morocco* 74 B3
Tamenglong, *India* 61 G18
Tamerza, *Tunisia* 75 B6
Tamgak, Mts., *Niger* 72 E6
Tamiahua, L. de, *Mexico* 115 C5
Tamil Nadu □, *India* 60 P10
Tamines, *Belgium* 17 H5
Tamis →, *Serbia, Yug.* 38 E3
Tamluk, *India* 63 H12
Tammerfors = Tampere, *Finland* 9 F20
Tammisaari, *Finland* 9 F20
Tamo Abu, Pegunungan, *Malaysia* 56 D5
Tampa, *U.S.A.* 105 M4
Tampa B., *U.S.A.* 105 M4
Tampere, *Finland* 9 F20
Tampico, *Mexico* 115 C5
Tampin, *Malaysia* 59 L4
Tamri, *Morocco* 74 B3
Tamrida = Qādib, *Yemen* 68 E5
Tamsagbulag, *Mongolia* 54 B6
Tamu, *Burma* 61 G19
Tamuja →, *Spain* 31 F4
Tamworth, *Australia* 91 E5
Tamworth, *U.K.* 13 E6
Tamyang, *S. Korea* 51 G14
Tan An, *Vietnam* 59 G6
Tan-tan, *Morocco* 74 C2
Tana →, *Kenya* 82 C5
Tana →, *Norway* 8 A23
Tana, L., *Ethiopia* 77 E4
Tana River, *Kenya* 82 C4
Tanabe, *Japan* 49 H7
Tanabi, *Brazil* 123 F2
Tanafjorden, *Norway* 8 A23
Tanaga, Pta., *Canary Is.* 36 G1
Tanagro →, *Italy* 35 B8
Tanahbala, *Indonesia* 56 E1
Tanahgrogot, *Indonesia* 56 E5
Tanahjampea, *Indonesia* 57 F6
Tanahmasa, *Indonesia* 56 E1
Tanahmerah, *Indonesia* 57 F10
Tanakura, *Japan* 49 F10
Tanami, *Australia* 88 C4
Tanami Desert, *Australia* 88 C5
Tanana, *U.S.A.* 96 B4
Tanana →, *U.S.A.* 96 B4
Tananarive = Antananarivo, *Madag.* 85 B8
Tanannt, *Morocco* 74 B3
Tánaro →, *Italy* 32 C5
Tanaunella, *Italy* 34 B2
Tanbar, *Australia* 90 D3
Tancarville, *France* 24 C7
Tancheng, *China* 51 G10
Tanchŏn, *N. Korea* 51 D15
Tanda, *Ut. P., India* 63 F10
Tanda, *Ut. P., India* 63 E8
Tanda, *Ivory C.* 78 D4
Tandag, *Phil.* 55 G7
Tandaia, *Tanzania* 83 D3
Tăndărei, *Romania* 38 E10
Tandaué, *Angola* 84 B2
Tandil, *Argentina* 126 D4
Tandil, Sa. del, *Argentina* 126 D4
Tandlianwala, *Pakistan* 62 D5
Tando Adam, *Pakistan* 62 G3
Tandou L., *Australia* 91 E3
Tandsbyn, *Sweden* 10 A8
Tane-ga-Shima, *Japan* 49 J5
Taneatua, *N.Z.* 87 H6
Tanen Tong Dan, *Burma* 58 D2
Tanezrouft, *Algeria* 75 D5
Tang, Koh, *Cambodia* 59 G4
Tang Krasang, *Cambodia* 58 F5
Tanga, *Tanzania* 82 D4
Tanga □, *Tanzania* 82 D4
Tanganyika, L., *Africa* 82 D2
Tanger = Tangier, *Morocco* 74 A3
Tangerang, *Indonesia* 57 G12
Tangerhütte, *Germany* 18 C7
Tangermünde, *Germany* 18 C7
Tanggu, *China* 51 E9
Tanggula Shan, *China* 54 C4
Tanghe, *China* 50 H7
Tangier, *Morocco* 74 A3
Tangorin P.O., *Australia* 90 C3
Tangshan, *China* 51 E10
Tangtou, *China* 51 G10
Tanguiéta, *Benin* 79 C5
Tangxi, *China* 53 C12
Tangyan He →, *China* 52 C7
Tanimbar, Kepulauan, *Indonesia* 57 F8
Tanimbar Is. = Tanimbar, Kepulauan, *Indonesia* 57 F8
Taninges, *France* 27 B10
Tanjay, *Phil.* 55 G5
Tanjong Malim, *Malaysia* 59 L3
Tanjore = Thanjavur, *India* 60 P11
Tanjung, *Indonesia* 56 E5
Tanjungbalai, *Indonesia* 56 D1
Tanjungbatu, *Indonesia* 56 D5
Tanjungkarang Telukbetung, *Indonesia* 56 F3
Tanjungpandan, *Indonesia* 56 E3
Tanjungpinang, *Indonesia* 56 D2
Tanjungpriok, *Indonesia* 57 G12
Tanjungredeb, *Indonesia* 56 D5
Tanjungselor, *Indonesia* 56 D5
Tank, *Pakistan* 62 C4
Tänndalen, *Sweden* 10 B6
Tannis Bugt, *Denmark* 11 G4
Tannu-Ola, *Russia* 45 D10
Tano →, *Ghana* 78 D4
Tanon Str., *Phil.* 55 F5
Tanout, *Niger* 79 C6
Tanquinho, *Brazil* 123 D4
Tanshui, *Taiwan* 53 E13
Tanta, *Egypt* 76 H7
Tantoyuca, *Mexico* 115 C5
Tantung = Dandong, *China* 51 D13
Tanumshede, *Sweden* 11 F5
Tanunda, *Australia* 91 E2
Tanus, *France* 26 D6
Tanzania ■, *Africa* 82 D3
Tanzilla →, *Canada* 100 B2
Tao Ko, *Thailand* 59 G2
Tao'an, *China* 51 B12
Tao'er He →, *China* 51 B13
Taohua Dao, *China* 53 C14
Taolanaro, *Madag.* 85 D8
Taole, *China* 50 E4
Taormina, *Italy* 35 E8
Taos, *U.S.A.* 111 H11
Taoudenni, *Mali* 74 D4
Taoudrart, Adrar, *Algeria* 75 D5
Taounate, *Morocco* 74 B4
Taourirt, *Algeria* 75 C5
Taourirt, *Morocco* 75 B4
Taouz, *Morocco* 74 B4
Taoyuan, *China* 53 C8
T'aoyüan, *Taiwan* 53 E13
Tapa, *Estonia* 9 G21
Tapa Shan = Daba Shan, *China* 52 B7
Tapachula, *Mexico* 115 E6
Tapah, *Malaysia* 59 K3
Tapajós →, *Brazil* 121 D7
Tapaktuan, *Indonesia* 56 D1
Tapanahoni →, *Surinam* 121 C7
Tapanui, *N.Z.* 87 L2
Tapauá, *Brazil* 125 B5
Tapauá →, *Brazil* 125 B5
Tapeta, *Liberia* 78 D3
Taphan Hin, *Thailand* 58 D3
Tapi →, *India* 60 J8
Tapia, *Spain* 30 B4
Tápiószele, *Hungary* 21 H9
Tapiraí, *Brazil* 123 E2
Tapirapé →, *Brazil* 122 D1
Tapirapecó, Serra, *Venezuela* 121 C5
Tapirapuã, *Brazil* 125 C6
Tapoeripa, *Surinam* 121 B6
Tapolca, *Hungary* 21 J7
Tappahannock, *U.S.A.* 104 G7
Tapuaenuku, Mt., *N.Z.* 87 J4
Tapul Group, *Phil.* 55 J4
Tapurucuará, *Brazil* 121 D4
Taqīābād, *Iran* 65 C8
Ţaqţaq, *Iraq* 67 E11
Taquara, *Brazil* 127 B5
Taquari →, *Brazil* 125 D6
Taquaritinga, *Brazil* 123 F2
Tara, *Australia* 91 D5
Tara, *Canada* 106 B3
Tara, *Russia* 44 D8
Tara, *Zambia* 83 F2
Tara →, *Russia* 44 D8
Taraba □, *Nigeria* 79 D7
Tarabagatay, Khrebet, *Kazakstan* 44 E9
Tarabuco, *Bolivia* 125 D5
Tarābulus, *Lebanon* 69 A4
Tarābulus, *Libya* 75 B7
Tarahouahout, *Algeria* 75 D6
Tarajalejo, *Canary Is.* 36 F5
Tarakan, *Indonesia* 56 D5
Tarakit, Mt., *Kenya* 82 B4
Taralga, *Australia* 91 E4
Tarama-Jima, *Japan* 49 M2
Taran, Mys, *Russia* 9 J18
Taranagar, *India* 62 E6
Taranaki □, *N.Z.* 87 H5
Tarancón, *Spain* 28 E1
Taranga, *India* 62 H5
Taranga Hill, *India* 62 H5
Táranto, *Italy* 35 B10
Táranto, G. di, *Italy* 35 B10
Tarapacá, *Colombia* 120 D4
Tarapacá □, *Chile* 126 A2
Tarapoto, *Peru* 124 B2
Taraquá, *Brazil* 120 C4
Tarare, *France* 27 C8
Tararua Ra., *N.Z.* 87 J5
Tarascon, *France* 27 E8
Tarascon-sur-Ariège, *France* 26 F5
Tarashcha, *Ukraine* 41 H6
Tarata, *Peru* 124 D3
Tarauacá, *Brazil* 124 B3
Tarauacá →, *Brazil* 124 B4
Taravo →, *France* 27 G12
Tarawera, *N.Z.* 87 H6
Tarawera L., *N.Z.* 87 H6
Tarazona, *Spain* 28 D3
Tarazona de la Mancha, *Spain* 29 F3
Tarbat Ness, *U.K.* 14 D5
Tarbela Dam, *Pakistan* 62 B5
Tarbert, *Arg. & Bute, U.K.* 14 F3
Tarbert, *W. Isles, U.K.* 14 D2
Tarbes, *France* 26 E4
Tarboro, *U.S.A.* 105 H7
Tarbrax, *Australia* 90 C3
Tarcento, *Italy* 33 B10
Tarcoola, *Australia* 91 E1
Tarcoon, *Australia* 91 E4
Tardets-Sorholus, *France* 26 E3
Tardoire →, *France* 26 C4
Taree, *Australia* 91 E5
Tarentaise, *France* 27 C10
Tarf, Ras, *Morocco* 74 A3
Tarfa, W. el →, *Egypt* 76 J7
Tarfaya, *Morocco* 74 C2
Targon, *France* 26 D3
Targuist, *Morocco* 74 B4
Tarhbalt, *Morocco* 74 B3
Tarhit, *Algeria* 75 B4
Táriba, *Venezuela* 120 B3
Tarifa, *Spain* 31 J5
Tarija, *Bolivia* 126 A3
Tarija □, *Bolivia* 126 A3
Tariku →, *Indonesia* 57 E9
Tarim Basin = Tarim Pendi, *China* 54 C3
Tarim He →, *China* 54 C3
Tarim Pendi, *China* 54 C3
Tarime □, *Tanzania* 82 C3
Taritatu →, *Indonesia* 57 E9
Tarka →, *S. Africa* 84 E4
Tarkastad, *S. Africa* 84 E4
Tarkhankut, Mys, *Ukraine* 41 K7
Tarko Sale, *Russia* 44 C8
Tarkwa, *Ghana* 78 D4
Tarlac, *Phil.* 55 D4
Tarlton Downs, *Australia* 90 C2
Tarm, *Denmark* 11 J2
Tarma, *Peru* 124 C2
Tarn □, *France* 26 E6
Tarn →, *France* 26 D5
Tarn-et-Garonne □, *France* 26 D5
Tarna →, *Hungary* 21 H9
Tårnby, *Denmark* 11 J6
Tarnobrzeg, *Poland* 20 E11
Tarnów, *Poland* 20 F11
Táro →, *Italy* 32 D7
Taroom, *Australia* 91 D4
Taroudannt, *Morocco* 74 B3
Tarp, *Germany* 18 A5
Tarpon Springs, *U.S.A.* 105 L4
Tarquínia, *Italy* 33 F8
Tarragona, *Spain* 28 D6
Tarragona □, *Spain* 28 D6
Tarrasa, *Spain* 28 D7
Tárrega, *Spain* 28 D6
Tarrytown, *U.S.A.* 107 E11
Tarshiha = Me'ona, *Israel* 69 B4
Tarso Emissi, *Chad* 73 D8
Tarsus, *Turkey* 66 D6
Tartagal, *Argentina* 126 A3
Tärtär, *Azerbaijan* 43 K8
Tärtär →, *Azerbaijan* 43 K8
Tartas, *France* 26 E3
Tartu, *Estonia* 9 G22
Ţarţūs, *Syria* 66 E6
Tarumirim, *Brazil* 123 E3
Tarumizu, *Japan* 49 J5
Tarussa, *Russia* 42 C3
Tarutao, Ko, *Thailand* 59 J2
Tarutung, *Indonesia* 56 D1
Tarvísio, *Italy* 33 B10
Tarz Ulli, *Libya* 75 C7
Tasāwah, *Libya* 73 C7
Taschereau, *Canada* 98 C4
Taseko →, *Canada* 100 C4
Tash-Kömür, *Kyrgyzstan* 44 E8
Tash-Kumyr = Tash-Kömür, *Kyrgyzstan* 44 E8
Tashauz = Dashhowuz, *Turkmenistan* 44 E6
Tashi Chho Dzong = Thimphu, *Bhutan* 61 F16
Tashkent = Toshkent, *Uzbekistan* 44 E7
Tashtagol, *Russia* 44 D9
Tasikmalaya, *Indonesia* 57 G13
Tåsjön, *Sweden* 8 D16
Taskan, *Russia* 45 C16
Taşköprü, *Turkey* 66 B6
Tasman B., *N.Z.* 87 J4
Tasman Mts., *N.Z.* 87 J4
Tasman Pen., *Australia* 90 G4
Tasman Sea, *Pac. Oc.* 92 L8
Tasmania □, *Australia* 90 G4
Tăşnad, *Romania* 38 B5
Tassil Tin-Rerhoh, *Algeria* 75 D5
Tassili n-Ajjer, *Algeria* 75 C6
Tassili-Oua-n-Ahaggar, *Algeria* 75 D6
Tasu Sd., *Canada* 100 C2
Tata, *Morocco* 74 C3
Tatabánya, *Hungary* 21 H8
Tatahouine, *Tunisia* 75 B7
Tatar Republic □ = Tatarstan □, *Russia* 42 C10
Tatarbunary, *Ukraine* 41 K5
Tatarsk, *Russia* 44 D8
Tatarstan □, *Russia* 42 C10
Tateyama, *Japan* 49 G9
Tathlina L., *Canada* 100 A5
Tathra, *Australia* 91 F4
Tatinnai L., *Canada* 101 A9
Tatnam, C., *Canada* 101 B10
Tatra = Tatry, *Slovak Rep.* 20 F9
Tatry, *Slovak Rep.* 20 F9
Tatsuno, *Japan* 49 G7
Tatta, *Pakistan* 62 G2
Tatuī, *Brazil* 127 A6
Tatum, *U.S.A.* 109 J3
Tat'ung = Datong, *China* 50 D7
Tatvan, *Turkey* 67 C10
Tauá, *Brazil* 122 C3
Taubaté, *Brazil* 127 A6
Tauberbischofsheim, *Germany* 19 F5
Taucha, *Germany* 18 D8
Taufikia, *Sudan* 77 F3
Taumarunui, *N.Z.* 87 H5
Taumaturgo, *Brazil* 124 B3
Taung, *S. Africa* 84 D3
Taungdwingyi, *Burma* 61 J19
Taunggyi, *Burma* 61 J20
Taungup, *Burma* 61 K19
Taungup Pass, *Burma* 61 K19
Taungup Taunggya, *Burma* 61 K18
Taunsa Barrage, *Pakistan* 62 D4
Taunton, *U.K.* 13 F4
Taunton, *U.S.A.* 107 E13
Taunus, *Germany* 19 E4
Taupo, *N.Z.* 87 H6
Taupo, L., *N.Z.* 87 H5
Tauragė, *Lithuania* 9 J20
Tauranga, *N.Z.* 87 G6
Tauranga Harb., *N.Z.* 87 G6
Taurianova, *Italy* 35 D9
Taurus Mts. = Toros Dağları, *Turkey* 66 D5
Tauste, *Spain* 28 D3
Tauz = Tovuz, *Azerbaijan* 43 K7
Tavannes, *Switz.* 22 B4
Tavas, *Turkey* 66 D3
Tavda, *Russia* 44 D7
Tavda →, *Russia* 44 D7
Taverny, *France* 25 C9
Taveta, *Tanzania* 82 C4
Taveuni, *Fiji* 87 C9
Tavignano →, *France* 27 F13
Tavira, *Portugal* 31 H3
Tavistock, *Canada* 106 C4
Tavistock, *U.K.* 13 G3
Tavolara, *Italy* 34 B2
Távora →, *Portugal* 30 D3
Tavoy, *Burma* 58 E2
Tavşanlı, *Turkey* 66 C3
Taw →, *U.K.* 13 F3
Tawas City, *U.S.A.* 104 C4
Tawau, *Malaysia* 56 D5
Tawitawi, *Phil.* 55 J4
Taxila, *Pakistan* 62 C5
Tay →, *U.K.* 14 E5
Tay, Firth of, *U.K.* 14 E5
Tay, L., *Australia* 89 F3
Tay, L., *U.K.* 14 E4
Tay Ninh, *Vietnam* 59 G6
Tayabamba, *Peru* 124 B2
Tayabas Bay, *Phil.* 55 E4
Taylakova, *Russia* 44 D8
Taylakovy = Taylakova, *Russia* 44 D8
Taylor, *Canada* 100 B4
Taylor, *Nebr., U.S.A.* 108 E5
Taylor, *Pa., U.S.A.* 107 E9
Taylor, *Tex., U.S.A.* 109 K6
Taylor, Mt., *U.S.A.* 111 J10
Taylorville, *U.S.A.* 108 F10
Taymā, *Si. Arabia* 64 E3
Taymyr, Oz., *Russia* 45 B11
Taymyr, Poluostrov, *Russia* 45 B11
Tayport, *U.K.* 14 E6
Tayshet, *Russia* 45 D10
Taytay, *Phil.* 55 F3
Taz →, *Russia* 44 C8
Taza, *Morocco* 74 B4
Tāzah Khurmātū, *Iraq* 67 E11
Tazawa-Ko, *Japan* 48 E10
Tazenakht, *Morocco* 74 B3
Tazin L., *Canada* 101 B7
Tazoult, *Algeria* 75 A6
Tazovskiy, *Russia* 44 C8
Tbilisi, *Georgia* 43 K7
Tchad = Chad ■, *Africa* 73 E8
Tchad, L., *Chad* 73 F7
Tchaourou, *Benin* 79 D5
Tch'eng-tou = Chengdu, *China* 52 B5
Tchentlo L., *Canada* 100 B4
Tchibanga, *Gabon* 80 E2
Tchien, *Liberia* 78 D3
Tchin Tabaraden, *Niger* 79 B6
Tch'ong-k'ing = Chongqing, *China* 52 C6
Tczew, *Poland* 20 A8
Te Anau, L., *N.Z.* 87 L1
Te Aroha, *N.Z.* 87 G5
Te Awamutu, *N.Z.* 87 H5
Te Kuiti, *N.Z.* 87 H5
Te Puke, *N.Z.* 87 G6
Te Waewae B., *N.Z.* 87 M1
Tea →, *Brazil* 120 D4
Tea Tree, *Australia* 90 C1
Teague, *U.S.A.* 109 K6
Teano, *Italy* 35 A7
Teapa, *Mexico* 115 D6
Teba, *Spain* 31 J6
Tebakang, *Malaysia* 56 D4
Teberda, *Russia* 43 J5
Tébessa, *Algeria* 75 A6
Tebicuary →, *Paraguay* 126 B4
Tebingtinggi, *Indonesia* 56 D1
Tébourba, *Tunisia* 75 A6
Téboursouk, *Tunisia* 75 A6
Tebulos, *Georgia* 43 J7
Tecate, *Mexico* 113 N10
Tecer Dağları, *Turkey* 66 C7
Tech →, *France* 26 F7
Techiman, *Ghana* 78 D4
Tecka, *Argentina* 128 B2
Tecomán, *Mexico* 114 D4
Tecopa, *U.S.A.* 113 K10
Tecoripa, *Mexico* 114 B3
Tecuala, *Mexico* 114 C3
Tecuci, *Romania* 38 D10
Tecumseh, *U.S.A.* 104 D4
Tedzhen = Tejen, *Turkmenistan* 44 F7
Tees →, *U.K.* 12 C6
Teesside, *U.K.* 12 C6
Teeswater, *Canada* 106 C3
Tefé, *Brazil* 121 D5
Tefé →, *Brazil* 121 D5
Tefenni, *Turkey* 66 D3
Tegal, *Indonesia* 57 G13
Tegelen, *Neths.* 17 F8
Tegernsee, *Germany* 19 H7
Teggiano, *Italy* 35 B8
Teghra, *India* 63 G11
Tegid, L. = Bala, L., *U.K.* 12 E4

Tegina, *Nigeria* **79 C6**
Tegucigalpa, *Honduras* **116 D2**
Tehachapi, *U.S.A.* **113 K8**
Tehachapi Mts., *U.S.A.* **113 L8**
Tehamiyam, *Sudan* **76 D4**
Tehilla, *Sudan* **76 D4**
Téhini, *Ivory C.* **78 D4**
Tehrān, *Iran* **65 C6**
Tehuacán, *Mexico* **115 D5**
Tehuantepec, *Mexico* **115 D5**
Tehuantepec, G. de, *Mexico* **115 D5**
Tehuantepec, Istmo de, *Mexico* **115 D6**
Teide, *Canary Is.* **36 F3**
Teifi →, *U.K.* **13 E3**
Teign →, *U.K.* **13 G4**
Teignmouth, *U.K.* **13 G4**
Teixeira, *Brazil* **122 C4**
Teixeira Pinto, *Guinea-Biss.* **78 C1**
Tejen, *Turkmenistan* **44 F7**
Tejo →, *Europe* **31 G1**
Tejon Pass, *U.S.A.* **113 L8**
Tekamah, *U.S.A.* **108 E6**
Tekapo, L., *N.Z.* **87 K3**
Tekax, *Mexico* **115 C7**
Tekeli, *Kazakstan* **44 E8**
Tekeze →, *Ethiopia* **77 E4**
Tekija, *Serbia, Yug.* **21 L12**
Tekirdağ, *Turkey* **66 B2**
Tekkali, *India* **61 K14**
Tekke, *Turkey* **66 B7**
Tekman, *Turkey* **67 C9**
Tekoa, *U.S.A.* **110 C5**
Tekouiât, O. →, *Algeria* **75 D5**
Tel Aviv-Yafo, *Israel* **69 C3**
Tel Lakhish, *Israel* **69 D3**
Tel Megiddo, *Israel* **69 C4**
Tela, *Honduras* **116 C2**
Télagh, *Algeria* **75 B4**
Telanaipura = Jambi, *Indonesia* **56 E2**
Telavi, *Georgia* **43 J7**
Telde, *Canary Is.* **36 G4**
Telegraph Creek, *Canada* **100 B2**
Telekhany = Tsyelyakhany, *Belarus* **41 F3**
Telemark, *Norway* **9 G12**
Telemark fylke □, *Norway* **10 E2**
Telén, *Argentina* **126 D2**
Teleng, *Iran* **65 E9**
Teleño, *Spain* **30 C4**
Teleorman →, *Romania* **38 E8**
Teles Pires →, *Brazil* **125 B6**
Telescope Pk., *U.S.A.* **113 J9**
Teletaye, *Mali* **79 B5**
Telford, *U.K.* **12 E5**
Telfs, *Austria* **19 H7**
Télimélé, *Guinea* **78 C2**
Telkwa, *Canada* **100 C3**
Tell City, *U.S.A.* **104 G2**
Tellicherry, *India* **60 P9**
Tellin, *Belgium* **17 H6**
Telluride, *U.S.A.* **111 H10**
Teloloapán, *Mexico* **115 D5**
Telpos Iz, *Russia* **6 C17**
Telsen, *Argentina* **128 B3**
Telšiai, *Lithuania* **9 H20**
Teltow, *Germany* **18 C9**
Teluk Anson, *Malaysia* **59 K3**
Teluk Betung = Tanjungkarang Telukbetung, *Indonesia* **56 F3**
Teluk Intan = Teluk Anson, *Malaysia* **59 K3**
Telukbutun, *Indonesia* **59 K7**
Telukdalem, *Indonesia* **56 D1**
Tema, *Ghana* **79 D5**
Temanggung, *Indonesia* **57 G14**
Temapache, *Mexico* **115 C5**
Temax, *Mexico* **115 C7**
Temba, *S. Africa* **85 D4**
Tembe, *Zaïre* **82 C2**
Temblador, *Venezuela* **121 B5**
Tembleque, *Spain* **28 F1**
Temblor Range, *U.S.A.* **113 K7**
Teme →, *U.K.* **13 E5**
Temecula, *U.S.A.* **113 M9**
Temerloh, *Malaysia* **59 L4**
Temir, *Kazakstan* **44 E6**
Temirtau, *Kazakstan* **44 D8**
Temirtau, *Russia* **44 D9**
Témiscaming, *Canada* **98 C4**
Temma, *Australia* **90 G3**
Temnikov, *Russia* **42 C6**
Temo →, *Italy* **34 B1**
Temora, *Australia* **91 E4**
Temosachic, *Mexico* **114 B3**
Tempe, *U.S.A.* **111 K8**
Tempe Downs, *Australia* **88 D5**
Témpio Pausánia, *Italy* **34 B2**
Tempiute, *U.S.A.* **112 H11**
Temple, *U.S.A.* **109 K6**
Temple B., *Australia* **90 A3**
Templemore, *Ireland* **15 D4**
Templeton, *U.S.A.* **112 K6**
Templeton →, *Australia* **90 C2**
Templeuve, *Belgium* **17 G2**
Templin, *Germany* **18 B9**
Tempoal, *Mexico* **115 C5**
Temryuk, *Russia* **43 H3**
Temse, *Belgium* **17 F4**
Temska →, *Serbia, Yug.* **21 M12**
Temuco, *Chile* **128 A2**
Temuka, *N.Z.* **87 L3**
Ten Boer, *Neths.* **16 B9**
Tena, *Ecuador* **120 D2**
Tenabo, *Mexico* **115 C6**
Tenaha, *U.S.A.* **109 K7**
Tenali, *India* **60 L12**
Tenancingo, *Mexico* **115 D5**
Tenango, *Mexico* **115 D5**
Tenasserim, *Burma* **59 F2**
Tenasserim □, *Burma* **58 F2**
Tenay, *France* **27 C9**
Tenby, *U.K.* **13 F3**
Tenda, Col di, *France* **27 D11**
Tendaho, *Ethiopia* **68 E3**
Tende, *France* **27 D11**
Tendelti, *Sudan* **77 E3**
Tendjedi, Adrar, *Algeria* **75 D6**
Tendrara, *Morocco* **75 B4**
Tendre, Mt., *Switz.* **22 C2**
Tendrovskaya Kosa, *Ukraine* **41 J6**
Teneida, *Egypt* **76 B2**
Tenente Marques →, *Brazil* **125 C6**
Ténéré, *Niger* **79 B7**
Tenerife, *Canary Is.* **36 F3**
Tenerife, Pico, *Canary Is.* **36 G1**
Ténès, *Algeria* **75 A5**
Teng Xian, *Guangxi Zhuangzu, China* **53 F8**
Teng Xian, *Shandong, China* **51 G9**
Tengah □, *Indonesia* **57 E6**
Tengah Kepulauan, *Indonesia* **56 F5**
Tengchong, *China* **52 E2**
Tengchowfu = Penglai, *China* **51 F11**
Tenggara □, *Indonesia* **57 E6**
Tenggarong, *Indonesia* **56 E5**
Tenggol, P., *Malaysia* **59 K4**
Tengiz, Ozero, *Kazakstan* **44 D7**
Tenigerbad, *Switz.* **23 C7**
Tenino, *U.S.A.* **112 D4**
Tenkasi, *India* **60 Q10**
Tenke, *Shaba, Zaïre* **83 E2**
Tenke, *Shaba, Zaïre* **83 E2**
Tenkodogo, *Burkina Faso* **79 C4**
Tenna →, *Italy* **33 E10**
Tennant Creek, *Australia* **90 B1**
Tennessee □, *U.S.A.* **105 H2**
Tennessee →, *U.S.A.* **104 G1**
Tenneville, *Belgium* **17 H7**
Tennille, *U.S.A.* **105 J4**
Tennsift, Oued →, *Morocco* **74 B3**
Teno, Pta. de, *Canary Is.* **36 F3**
Tenom, *Malaysia* **56 C5**
Tenosique, *Mexico* **115 D6**
Tenryū-Gawa →, *Japan* **49 G8**
Tent L., *Canada* **101 A7**
Tenterfield, *Australia* **91 D5**
Teófilo Otoni, *Brazil* **123 E3**
Teotihuacán, *Mexico* **115 D5**
Tepa, *Indonesia* **57 F7**
Tepalcatepec →, *Mexico* **114 D4**
Tepehuanes, *Mexico* **114 B3**
Tepequem, Serra, *Brazil* **121 C5**
Tepetongo, *Mexico* **114 C4**
Tepic, *Mexico* **114 C4**
Tepoca, C., *Mexico* **114 A2**
Tequila, *Mexico* **114 C4**
Ter →, *Spain* **28 C8**
Ter Apel, *Neths.* **16 C10**
Téra, *Niger* **79 C5**
Tera →, *Spain* **30 D5**
Teraina, *Kiribati* **93 G11**
Téramo, *Italy* **33 F10**
Terang, *Australia* **91 F3**
Terborg, *Neths.* **16 E8**
Tercan, *Turkey* **67 C9**
Tercero →, *Argentina* **126 C3**
Terebovlya, *Ukraine* **41 H3**
Terek →, *Russia* **43 J8**
Terenos, *Brazil* **125 E7**
Tereshka →, *Russia* **42 E8**
Teresina, *Brazil* **122 C3**
Teresinha, *Brazil* **121 C7**
Terewah, L., *Australia* **91 D4**
Terges →, *Portugal* **31 H3**
Tergnier, *France* **25 C10**
Terhazza, *Mali* **74 D3**
Terheijden, *Neths.* **17 E5**
Teridgerie Cr. →, *Australia* **91 E4**
Terlizzi, *Italy* **35 A9**
Terme, *Turkey* **66 B7**
Termez = Termiz, *Uzbekistan* **44 F7**
Términi Imerese, *Italy* **34 E6**
Términos, L. de, *Mexico* **115 D6**
Termiz, *Uzbekistan* **44 F7**
Térmoli, *Italy* **33 F12**
Ternate, *Indonesia* **57 D7**
Terneuzen, *Neths.* **17 F3**
Terney, *Russia* **45 E14**
Terni, *Italy* **33 F9**
Ternitz, *Austria* **21 H6**
Ternopil, *Ukraine* **41 H3**
Ternopol = Ternopil, *Ukraine* **41 H3**
Terowie, *N.S.W., Australia* **91 E4**
Terowie, *S. Austral., Australia* **91 E2**
Terra Bella, *U.S.A.* **113 K7**
Terrace, *Canada* **100 C3**
Terrace Bay, *Canada* **98 C2**
Terracina, *Italy* **34 A6**
Terralba, *Italy* **34 C1**
Terranova = Ólbia, *Italy* **34 B2**
Terranuova Bracciolini, *Italy* **33 E8**
Terrasini Favarotta, *Italy* **34 D6**
Terrassa = Tarrasa, *Spain* **28 D7**
Terrasson-la-Villedieu, *France* **26 C5**
Terre Haute, *U.S.A.* **104 F2**
Terrebonne B., *U.S.A.* **109 L9**
Terrecht, *Mali* **75 D4**
Terrell, *U.S.A.* **109 J6**
Terrenceville, *Canada* **99 C9**
Terrick Terrick, *Australia* **90 C4**
Terry, *U.S.A.* **108 B2**
Terschelling, *Neths.* **16 B6**
Tersko-Kumskiy Kanal →, *Russia* **43 H7**
Terter → = Tärtär →, *Azerbaijan* **43 K8**
Teruel, *Spain* **28 E3**
Teruel □, *Spain* **28 E4**
Tervel, *Bulgaria* **38 F10**
Tervola, *Finland* **8 C21**
Teryaweyna L., *Australia* **91 E3**
Tešanj, *Bos.-H.* **21 L7**
Teseney, *Eritrea* **77 D4**
Tesha →, *Russia* **42 C6**
Teshio, *Japan* **48 B10**
Teshio-Gawa →, *Japan* **48 B10**
Tesiyn Gol →, *Mongolia* **54 A4**
Teslin, *Canada* **100 A2**
Teslin →, *Canada* **100 A2**
Teslin L., *Canada* **100 A2**
Tesouro, *Brazil* **125 D7**
Tessalit, *Mali* **79 A5**
Tessaoua, *Niger* **79 C6**
Tessenderlo, *Belgium* **17 F6**
Tessin, *Germany* **18 A8**
Tessit, *Mali* **79 B5**
Test →, *U.K.* **13 F6**
Testa del Gargano, *Italy* **35 A9**
Têt →, *France* **26 F7**
Tetachuck L., *Canada* **100 C3**
Tetas, Pta., *Chile* **126 A1**
Tete, *Mozam.* **83 F3**
Tete □, *Mozam.* **83 F3**
Teterev →, *Ukraine* **41 G6**
Teteringen, *Neths.* **17 E5**
Teterow, *Germany* **18 B8**
Teteven, *Bulgaria* **38 G7**
Tethul →, *Canada* **100 A6**
Tetiyev, *Ukraine* **41 H5**
Teton →, *U.S.A.* **110 C8**
Tétouan, *Morocco* **74 A3**
Tetovo, *Macedonia* **38 G4**
Tetyukhe Pristan, *Russia* **48 B7**
Tetyushi, *Russia* **42 C9**
Teuco →, *Argentina* **126 B3**
Teufen, *Switz.* **23 B8**
Teulada, *Italy* **34 D1**
Teulon, *Canada* **101 C9**
Teun, *Indonesia* **57 F7**
Teutoburger Wald, *Germany* **18 C4**
Tévere →, *Italy* **33 G9**
Teverya, *Israel* **69 C4**
Teviot →, *U.K.* **14 F6**
Tewantin, *Australia* **91 D5**
Tewkesbury, *U.K.* **13 F5**
Texada I., *Canada* **100 D4**
Texarkana, *Ark., U.S.A.* **109 J8**
Texarkana, *Tex., U.S.A.* **109 J7**
Texas, *Australia* **91 D5**
Texas □, *U.S.A.* **109 K5**
Texas City, *U.S.A.* **109 L7**
Texel, *Neths.* **16 B5**
Texhoma, *U.S.A.* **109 G4**
Texline, *U.S.A.* **109 G3**
Texoma, L., *U.S.A.* **109 J6**
Teykovo, *Russia* **42 B5**
Teza →, *Russia* **42 B5**
Tezin, *Afghan.* **62 B3**
Teziutlán, *Mexico* **115 D5**
Tezpur, *India* **61 F18**
Tezzeron L., *Canada* **100 C4**
Tha-anne →, *Canada* **101 A10**
Tha Deua, *Laos* **58 D4**
Tha Deua, *Laos* **58 C3**
Tha Pla, *Thailand* **58 D3**
Tha Rua, *Thailand* **58 E3**
Tha Sala, *Thailand* **59 H2**
Tha Song Yang, *Thailand* **58 D1**
Thaba Putsoa, *Lesotho* **85 D4**
Thabana Ntlenyana, *Lesotho* **85 D4**
Thabazimbi, *S. Africa* **85 C4**
Thai Binh, *Vietnam* **58 B6**
Thai Hoa, *Vietnam* **58 C5**
Thai Muang, *Thailand* **59 H2**
Thai Nguyen, *Vietnam* **58 B5**
Thailand ■, *Asia* **58 E4**
Thailand, G. of, *Asia* **59 G3**
Thakhek, *Laos* **58 D5**
Thal, *Pakistan* **62 C4**
Thal Desert, *Pakistan* **62 D4**
Thala, *Tunisia* **75 A6**
Thala La, *Burma* **61 E20**
Thalabarivat, *Cambodia* **58 F5**
Thalkirch, *Switz.* **23 C8**
Thallon, *Australia* **91 D4**
Thalwil, *Switz.* **23 B7**
Thame →, *U.K.* **13 F6**
Thames, *N.Z.* **87 G5**
Thames →, *Canada* **98 D3**
Thames →, *U.K.* **13 F8**
Thames →, *U.S.A.* **107 E12**
Thamesford, *Canada* **106 C3**
Thamesville, *Canada* **106 D3**
Than Uyen, *Vietnam* **58 B4**
Thane, *India* **60 K8**
Thanesar, *India* **62 D7**
Thanet, I. of, *U.K.* **13 F9**
Thangoo, *Australia* **88 C3**
Thangool, *Australia* **90 C5**
Thanh Hoa, *Vietnam* **58 C5**
Thanh Hung, *Vietnam* **59 H5**
Thanh Pho Ho Chi Minh = Phanh Bho Ho Chi Minh, *Vietnam* **59 G6**
Thanh Thuy, *Vietnam* **58 A5**
Thanjavur, *India* **60 P11**
Thann, *France* **25 E14**
Thaon-les-Vosges, *France* **25 D13**
Thap Sakae, *Thailand* **59 G2**
Thap Than, *Thailand* **58 E2**
Thar Desert, *India* **62 F4**
Tharad, *India* **62 G4**
Thargomindah, *Australia* **91 D3**
Tharrawaddy, *Burma* **61 L19**
Tharthār, Mileh, *Iraq* **67 E10**
Tharthār, W. ath →, *Iraq* **67 E10**
Thásos, *Greece* **39 J7**
That Khe, *Vietnam* **58 A6**
Thatcher, *Ariz., U.S.A.* **111 K9**
Thatcher, *Colo., U.S.A.* **109 G2**
Thaton, *Burma* **61 L20**
Thau, Bassin de, *France* **26 E7**
Thaungdut, *Burma* **61 G19**
Thayer, *U.S.A.* **109 G9**
Thayetmyo, *Burma* **61 K19**
Thayngen, *Switz.* **23 A7**
Thazi, *Burma* **61 J20**
The Alberga →, *Australia* **91 D2**
The Bight, *Bahamas* **117 B4**
The Coorong, *Australia* **91 F2**
The Dalles, *U.S.A.* **110 D3**
The English Company's Is., *Australia* **90 A2**
The Frome →, *Australia* **91 D2**
The Grampians, *Australia* **91 F3**
The Great Divide = Great Dividing Ra., *Australia* **90 C4**
The Hague = 's-Gravenhage, *Neths.* **16 D4**
The Hamilton →, *Australia* **91 D2**
The Macumba →, *Australia* **91 D2**
The Neales →, *Australia* **91 D2**
The Officer →, *Australia* **89 E5**
The Pas, *Canada* **101 C8**
The Range, *Zimbabwe* **83 F3**
The Rock, *Australia* **91 F4**
The Salt L., *Australia* **91 E3**
The Stevenson →, *Australia* **91 D2**
The Warburton →, *Australia* **91 D2**
Thebes = Thívai, *Greece* **39 L6**
Thebes, *Egypt* **76 B3**
Thedford, *Canada* **106 C3**
Thedford, *U.S.A.* **108 E4**
Theebine, *Australia* **91 D5**
Thekulthili L., *Canada* **101 A7**
Thelon →, *Canada* **101 A8**
Thénezay, *France* **24 F6**
Thenia, *Algeria* **75 A5**
Thenon, *France* **26 C5**
Theodore, *Australia* **90 C5**
Thepha, *Thailand* **59 J3**
Thérain →, *France* **25 C9**
Theresa, *U.S.A.* **107 B9**
Thermaïkós Kólpos, *Greece* **39 J5**
Thermopolis, *U.S.A.* **110 E9**
Thermopylae P., *Greece* **39 L5**
Thessalía □, *Greece* **39 L4**
Thessalon, *Canada* **98 C3**
Thessaloníki, *Greece* **39 J5**
Thessaloniki, Gulf of = Thermaïkós Kólpos, *Greece* **39 J5**
Thessaly = Thessalía □, *Greece* **39 L4**
Thetford, *U.K.* **13 E8**
Thetford Mines, *Canada* **99 C5**
Theun →, *Laos* **58 C5**
Theunissen, *S. Africa* **84 D4**
Theux, *Belgium* **17 G7**
Thevenard, *Australia* **91 E1**
Thiámis →, *Greece* **39 K3**
Thiberville, *France* **24 C7**
Thibodaux, *U.S.A.* **109 L9**
Thicket Portage, *Canada* **101 B9**
Thief River Falls, *U.S.A.* **108 A6**
Thiel Mts., *Antarctica* **5 E16**
Thiene, *Italy* **33 C8**
Thiérache, *France* **25 C10**
Thiers, *France* **26 C7**
Thies, *Senegal* **78 C1**
Thiet, *Sudan* **77 F2**
Thika, *Kenya* **82 C4**
Thikombia, *Fiji* **87 B9**
Thille-Boubacar, *Senegal* **78 B1**
Thimphu, *Bhutan* **61 F16**
þingvallavatn, *Iceland* **8 D3**
Thionville, *France* **25 C13**
Thíra, *Greece* **39 N8**
Thirasía, *Greece* **39 N8**
Thirsk, *U.K.* **12 C6**
Thisted, *Denmark* **9 H13**
Thistle I., *Australia* **91 F2**
Thívai, *Greece* **39 L6**
Thiviers, *France* **26 C4**
Thizy, *France* **27 B8**
þjórsá →, *Iceland* **8 E3**
Thlewiaza →, *Man., Canada* **101 B8**
Thlewiaza →, *N.W.T., Canada* **101 A10**
Thmar Puok, *Cambodia* **58 F4**
Tho Vinh, *Vietnam* **58 C5**
Thoa →, *Canada* **101 A7**
Thoen, *Thailand* **58 D2**
Thoeng, *Thailand* **58 C3**
Thoissey, *France* **27 B8**
Tholdi, *Pakistan* **63 B7**
Tholen, *Neths.* **17 E4**
Thomas, *Okla., U.S.A.* **109 H5**
Thomas, *W. Va., U.S.A.* **104 F6**
Thomas, L., *Australia* **91 D2**
Thomaston, *U.S.A.* **105 J3**
Thomasville, *Ala., U.S.A.* **105 K2**
Thomasville, *Ga., U.S.A.* **105 K3**
Thomasville, *N.C., U.S.A.* **105 H5**
Thommen, *Belgium* **17 H8**
Thompson, *Canada* **101 B9**
Thompson, *U.S.A.* **111 G9**
Thompson →, *Canada* **100 C4**
Thompson →, *U.S.A.* **108 F8**
Thompson Falls, *U.S.A.* **110 C6**
Thompson Landing, *Canada* **101 A6**
Thompson Pk., *U.S.A.* **110 F2**
Thomson's Falls = Nyahururu, *Kenya* **82 B4**
Thon Buri, *Thailand* **59 F3**
Thônes, *France* **27 C10**
Thonon-les-Bains, *France* **27 B10**
Thorez, *Ukraine* **41 H10**
þórisvatn, *Iceland* **8 D4**
Thornaby on Tees, *U.K.* **12 C6**
Thornbury, *Canada* **106 B4**
Thorold, *Canada* **106 C5**
þórshöfn, *Iceland* **8 C6**
Thouarcé, *France* **24 E6**
Thouars, *France* **24 F6**
Thouet →, *France* **24 E6**
Thouin, C., *Australia* **88 D2**
Thousand Oaks, *U.S.A.* **113 L8**
Thrace, *Turkey* **66 B2**
Thrakikón Pélagos, *Greece* **39 J8**
Three Forks, *U.S.A.* **110 D8**
Three Hills, *Canada* **100 C6**
Three Hummock I., *Australia* **90 G3**
Three Lakes, *U.S.A.* **108 C10**
Three Points, C., *Ghana* **78 E4**
Three Rivers, *Australia* **89 E2**
Three Rivers, *Calif., U.S.A.* **112 J8**
Three Rivers, *Tex., U.S.A.* **109 L5**
Three Sisters, *U.S.A.* **110 D3**
Throssell, L., *Australia* **89 E3**
Throssell Ra., *Australia* **88 D3**
Thuan Hoa, *Vietnam* **59 H5**
Thubun Lakes, *Canada* **101 A6**
Thueyts, *France* **27 D8**
Thuillies, *Belgium* **17 H4**
Thuin, *Belgium* **17 H4**
Thuir, *France* **26 F6**
Thule, *Greenland* **4 B4**
Thun, *Switz.* **22 C5**
Thundelarra, *Australia* **89 E2**
Thunder B., *U.S.A.* **106 B1**
Thunder Bay, *Canada* **98 C2**
Thunersee, *Switz.* **22 C5**
Thung Song, *Thailand* **59 H2**
Thunkar, *Bhutan* **61 F17**
Thuong Tra, *Vietnam* **58 D6**
Thur →, *Switz.* **23 A8**
Thurgau □, *Switz.* **23 A8**
Thüringen □, *Germany* **18 E7**
Thüringer Wald, *Germany* **18 E7**
Thurles, *Ireland* **15 D4**
Thurloo Downs, *Australia* **91 D3**
Thurn P., *Austria* **19 H8**
Thursday I., *Australia* **90 A3**
Thurso, *Canada* **98 C4**
Thurso, *U.K.* **14 C5**
Thurston I., *Antarctica* **5 D16**
Thury-Harcourt, *France* **24 D6**
Thusis, *Switz.* **23 C8**
Thutade L., *Canada* **100 B3**
Thyborøn, *Denmark* **11 H2**
Thylungra, *Australia* **91 D3**
Thyolo, *Malawi* **83 F4**
Thysville = Mbanza Ngungu, *Zaïre* **80 F2**
Ti-n-Barraouene, O. →, *Africa* **79 B5**
Ti-n-Medjerdam, O. →, *Algeria* **75 C5**
Ti-n-Tarabine, O. →, *Algeria* **75 D6**
Ti-n-Zaouaténe, *Algeria* **75 E5**
Tia, *Australia* **91 E5**
Tiahuanacu, *Bolivia* **124 D4**
Tian Shan, *Asia* **54 B3**
Tianchang, *China* **53 A12**
Tiandong, *China* **52 F6**
Tian'e, *China* **52 E6**
Tianguá, *Brazil* **122 B3**
Tianhe, *China* **52 E7**
Tianjin, *China* **51 E9**
Tiankoura, *Burkina Faso* **78 C4**
Tianlin, *China* **52 E6**
Tianmen, *China* **53 B9**
Tianquan, *China* **52 B4**
Tianshui, *China* **50 G3**
Tiantai, *China* **53 C13**
Tianyang, *China* **52 F6**

Tianzhen, *China* 50 D8
Tianzhu, *China* 52 D7
Tianzhuangtai, *China* 51 D12
Tiaret, *Algeria* 75 A5
Tiassalé, *Ivory C.* 78 D4
Tibagi, *Brazil* 127 A5
Tibagi →, *Brazil* 127 A5
Tibati, *Cameroon* 79 D7
Tiber = Tévere →, *Italy* 33 G9
Tiber Reservoir, *U.S.A.* 110 B8
Tiberias = Teverya, *Israel* 69 C4
Tiberias, L. = Yam Kinneret, *Israel* 69 C4
Tibesti, *Chad* 73 D8
Tibet = Xizang □, *China* 54 C3
Tibet, Plateau of, *Asia* 46 F12
Tibiao, *Phil.* 55 F5
Tibiri, *Niger* 79 C6
Ţibleş, *Romania* 38 B7
Tibnī, *Syria* 67 E8
Tibooburra, *Australia* 91 D3
Tibro, *Sweden* 11 F8
Tibugá, G. de, *Colombia* 120 B2
Tiburón, *Mexico* 114 B2
Ticao I., *Phil.* 55 E5
Tîchît, *Mauritania* 78 B3
Tichla, *Mauritania* 74 D2
Ticho, *Ethiopia* 77 F4
Ticino □, *Switz.* 23 D7
Ticino →, *Italy* 32 C6
Ticonderoga, *U.S.A.* 107 C11
Ticul, *Mexico* 115 C7
Tidaholm, *Sweden* 11 F7
Tiddim, *Burma* 61 H18
Tideridjaouine, Adrar, *Algeria* 75 D5
Tidikelt, *Algeria* 75 C5
Tidjikja, *Mauritania* 78 B2
Tidore, *Indonesia* 57 D7
Tiébissou, *Ivory C.* 78 D3
Tiefencastel, *Switz.* 23 C9
Tiel, *Neths.* 16 E6
Tiel, *Senegal* 78 C1
Tieling, *China* 51 C12
Tielt, *Belgium* 17 F2
Tien Shan = Tian Shan, *Asia* 54 B3
Tien-tsin = Tianjin, *China* 51 E9
Tien Yen, *Vietnam* 58 B6
T'ienching = Tianjin, *China* 51 E9
Tienen, *Belgium* 17 G5
Tiénigbé, *Ivory C.* 78 D3
Tientsin = Tianjin, *China* 51 E9
Tierra Amarilla, *Chile* 126 B1
Tierra Amarilla, *U.S.A.* 111 H10
Tierra Colorada, *Mexico* 115 D5
Tierra de Barros, *Spain* 31 G4
Tierra de Campos, *Spain* 30 C6
Tierra del Fuego □, *Argentina* 128 D3
Tierra del Fuego, I. Gr. de, *Argentina* 128 D3
Tierralta, *Colombia* 120 B2
Tiétar →, *Spain* 30 F4
Tieté →, *Brazil* 127 A5
Tieyon, *Australia* 91 D1
Tifarati, *W. Sahara* 74 C2
Tiffin, *U.S.A.* 104 E4
Tiflèt, *Morocco* 74 B3
Tiflis = Tbilisi, *Georgia* 43 K7
Tifton, *U.S.A.* 105 K4
Tifu, *Indonesia* 57 E7
Tighina, *Moldova* 41 J5
Tigil, *Russia* 45 D16
Tignish, *Canada* 99 C7
Tigray □, *Ethiopia* 77 E4
Tigre →, *Peru* 120 D3
Tigre →, *Venezuela* 121 B5
Tigris = Dijlah, Nahr →, *Asia* 64 D5
Tiguentourine, *Algeria* 75 C6
Tigyaing, *Burma* 61 H20
Tigzerte, O. →, *Morocco* 74 C3
Tîh, Gebel el, *Egypt* 76 J8
Tihodaine, Dunes de, *Algeria* 75 C6
Tijesno, *Croatia* 33 E12
Tījī, *Libya* 75 B7
Tijuana, *Mexico* 113 N9
Tikal, *Guatemala* 116 C2
Tikamgarh, *India* 63 G8
Tikhoretsk, *Russia* 43 H5
Tikhvin, *Russia* 40 C7
Tikkadouine, Adrar, *Algeria* 75 D5
Tiko, *Cameroon* 79 E6
Tikrīt, *Iraq* 67 E10
Tiksi, *Russia* 45 B13
Tilamuta, *Indonesia* 57 D6
Tilburg, *Neths.* 17 E6
Tilbury, *Canada* 98 D3
Tilbury, *U.K.* 13 F8
Tilcara, *Argentina* 126 A2
Tilden, *Nebr., U.S.A.* 108 D6
Tilden, *Tex., U.S.A.* 109 L5
Tilemses, *Niger* 79 B5
Tilemsi, Vallée du, *Mali* 79 B5
Tilhar, *India* 63 F8
Tilia, O. →, *Algeria* 75 C5
Tilichiki, *Russia* 45 C17
Tililane, *Algeria* 75 C4
Tílissos, *Greece* 37 D7
Till →, *U.K.* 12 B5
Tillabéri, *Niger* 79 C5
Tillamook, *U.S.A.* 110 D2
Tillberga, *Sweden* 10 E10
Tillia, *Niger* 79 B5
Tillsonburg, *Canada* 98 D3
Tillyeria □, *Cyprus* 37 D11
Tílos, *Greece* 39 N10
Tilpa, *Australia* 91 E3
Tilrhemt, *Algeria* 75 B5
Tilsit = Sovetsk, *Russia* 9 J19
Tilt →, *U.K.* 14 E5
Tilton, *U.S.A.* 107 C13
Timagami L., *Canada* 98 C3
Timaru, *N.Z.* 87 L3
Timashevo, *Russia* 42 D10
Timashevsk, *Russia* 43 H4
Timau, *Italy* 33 B10
Timau, *Kenya* 82 B4
Timbákion, *Greece* 37 D6
Timbaúba, *Brazil* 122 C4
Timbedgha, *Mauritania* 78 B3
Timber Lake, *U.S.A.* 108 C4
Timber Mt., *U.S.A.* 112 H10
Timbío, *Colombia* 120 C2
Timbiqui, *Colombia* 120 C2
Timboon, *Australia* 91 F3
Timbuktu = Tombouctou, *Mali* 78 B4
Timellouline, *Algeria* 75 C6
Timétrine Montagnes, *Mali* 79 B4
Timfristós, Óros, *Greece* 39 L4
Timhadit, *Morocco* 74 B3
Timi, *Cyprus* 37 E11
Tîmia, *Niger* 79 B6
Timimoun, *Algeria* 75 C5
Timiş = Tamis →, *Serbia, Yug.* 38 E3
Timişoara, *Romania* 38 D4
Timmins, *Canada* 98 C3
Timok →, *Serbia, Yug.* 21 L12
Timon, *Brazil* 122 C3
Timor, *Indonesia* 57 F7
Timor □, *Indonesia* 57 F7
Timor Sea, *Ind. Oc.* 88 B4
Tin Alkoum, *Algeria* 75 D7
Tin Gornai, *Mali* 79 B4
Tin Mt., *U.S.A.* 112 J9
Tîna, Khalîg el, *Egypt* 76 H8
Tinaca Pt., *Phil.* 55 J6
Tinaco, *Venezuela* 120 B4
Tinafak, O. →, *Algeria* 75 C6
Tinajo, *Canary Is.* 36 E6
Tinaquillo, *Venezuela* 120 B4
Tinca, *Romania* 38 C4
Tinchebray, *France* 24 D6
Tindouf, *Algeria* 74 C3
Tinée →, *France* 27 E11
Tineo, *Spain* 30 B4
Tinerhir, *Morocco* 74 B3
Tinfouchi, *Algeria* 74 C3
Ting Jiang →, *China* 53 E11
Tinggi, Pulau, *Malaysia* 59 L5
Tinglev, *Denmark* 11 K3
Tingo Maria, *Peru* 124 B2
Tinh Bien, *Vietnam* 59 G5
Tinharé, I. de, *Brazil* 123 D4
Tinjoub, *Algeria* 72 C3
Tinkurrin, *Australia* 89 F2
Tinnevelly = Tirunelveli, *India* 60 Q10
Tinnoset, *Norway* 10 E3
Tinnsjø, *Norway* 10 E2
Tinogasta, *Argentina* 126 B2
Tínos, *Greece* 39 M8
Tiñoso, C., *Spain* 29 H3
Tinta, *Peru* 124 C3
Tintigny, *Belgium* 17 J7
Tintina, *Argentina* 126 B3
Tintinara, *Australia* 91 F3
Tinto →, *Spain* 31 H4
Tioga, *U.S.A.* 106 E7
Tioman, Pulau, *Malaysia* 59 L5
Tione di Trento, *Italy* 32 B7
Tionesta, *U.S.A.* 106 E5
Tior, *Sudan* 77 F3
Tioulilin, *Algeria* 75 C4
Tipongpani, *India* 61 F19
Tipperary, *Ireland* 15 D3
Tipperary □, *Ireland* 15 D4
Tipton, *U.K.* 13 E5
Tipton, *Calif., U.S.A.* 111 H4
Tipton, *Ind., U.S.A.* 104 E2
Tipton, *Iowa, U.S.A.* 108 E9
Tipton Mt., *U.S.A.* 113 K12
Tiptonville, *U.S.A.* 109 G10
Tiquié →, *Brazil* 120 C4
Tiracambu, Serra do, *Brazil* 122 B2
Tīrān, *Iran* 65 C6
Tīrān, *Si. Arabia* 76 B3
Tirana, *Albania* 39 H2
Tiranë = Tirana, *Albania* 39 H2
Tirano, *Italy* 32 B7
Tiraspol, *Moldova* 41 J5
Tirat Karmel, *Israel* 69 C3
Tiratimine, *Algeria* 75 C5
Tirdout, *Mali* 79 B4
Tire, *Turkey* 66 C2
Tirebolu, *Turkey* 67 B8
Tiree, *U.K.* 14 E2
Tîrgovişte, *Romania* 38 E8
Tîrgu Frumos, *Romania* 38 B10
Tîrgu-Jiu, *Romania* 38 D6
Tîrgu Mureş, *Romania* 38 C7
Tîrgu Neamţ, *Romania* 38 B9
Tîrgu Ocna, *Romania* 38 C9
Tîrgu Secuiesc, *Romania* 38 D9
Tirich Mir, *Pakistan* 60 A7
Tiriolo, *Italy* 35 D9
Tiririca, Serra da, *Brazil* 123 E2
Tiris, *W. Sahara* 74 D2
Tîrnava Mare →, *Romania* 38 C7
Tîrnava Mică →, *Romania* 38 C7
Tîrnăveni, *Romania* 38 C7
Tírnavos, *Greece* 39 K5
Tirodi, *India* 60 J11
Tiros, *Brazil* 123 E2
Tirschenreuth, *Germany* 19 F8
Tirso →, *Italy* 34 C1
Tirso, L. del, *Italy* 34 B1
Tiruchchirappalli, *India* 60 P11
Tirunelveli, *India* 60 Q10
Tirupati, *India* 60 N11
Tiruppur, *India* 60 P10
Tiruvannamalai, *India* 60 N11
Tisa →, *Serbia, Yug.* 21 J10
Tisdale, *Canada* 101 C8
Tishomingo, *U.S.A.* 109 H6
Tisnaren, *Sweden* 10 F9
Tisovec, *Slovak Rep.* 20 G9
Tissemsilt, *Algeria* 75 A5
Tissint, *Morocco* 74 C3
Tissø, *Denmark* 11 J5
Tisza = Tisa →, *Serbia, Yug.* 21 J10
Tiszafüred, *Hungary* 21 H10
Tiszavasvári, *Hungary* 21 H11
Tit, *Ahaggar, Algeria* 75 D6
Tit, *Tademait, Algeria* 75 C5
Tit-Ary, *Russia* 45 B13
Titaguas, *Spain* 28 F3
Titel, *Serbia, Yug.* 21 K10
Tithwal, *Pakistan* 63 B5
Titicaca, L., *S. Amer.* 124 D4
Titiwa, *Nigeria* 79 C7
Titlis, *Switz.* 23 C6
Titograd = Podgorica, *Montenegro, Yug.* 21 N9
Titov Veles, *Macedonia* 39 H4
Titova Korenica, *Croatia* 33 D12
Titova-Mitrovica, *Serbia, Yug.* 21 N10
Titovo Užice, *Serbia, Yug.* 21 M9
Titule, *Zaïre* 82 B2
Titumate, *Colombia* 120 B2
Titusville, *Fla., U.S.A.* 105 L5
Titusville, *Pa., U.S.A.* 106 E5
Tivaouane, *Senegal* 78 C1
Tiveden, *Sweden* 11 F8
Tiverton, *U.K.* 13 G4
Tívoli, *Italy* 33 G9
Tiyo, *Eritrea* 77 E5
Tizga, *Morocco* 74 B3
Ti'zi N'Isli, *Morocco* 74 B3
Tizi-Ouzou, *Algeria* 75 A5
Tizimín, *Mexico* 115 C7
Tiznados →, *Venezuela* 120 B4
Tiznit, *Morocco* 74 C3
Tjeggelvas, *Sweden* 8 C17
Tjeukemeer, *Neths.* 16 C7
Tjirebon = Cirebon, *Indonesia* 57 G13
Tjøme, *Norway* 10 E4
Tjonger Kanaal, *Neths.* 16 C7
Tjörn, *Sweden* 11 G5
Tkibuli = Tqibuli, *Georgia* 43 J6
Tkvarcheli = Tqvarcheli, *Georgia* 43 J5
Tlacotalpan, *Mexico* 115 D5
Tlahualilo, *Mexico* 114 B4
Tlaquepaque, *Mexico* 114 C4
Tlaxcala, *Mexico* 115 D5
Tlaxcala □, *Mexico* 115 D5
Tlaxiaco, *Mexico* 115 D5
Tlell, *Canada* 100 C2
Tlemcen, *Algeria* 75 B4
Tleta Sidi Bouguedra, *Morocco* 74 B3
Tlyarata, *Russia* 43 J8
Tmassah, *Libya* 73 C8
Tnine d'Anglou, *Morocco* 74 C3
To Bong, *Vietnam* 58 F7
Toad →, *Canada* 100 B4
Toamasina, *Madag.* 85 B8
Toamasina □, *Madag.* 85 B8
Toay, *Argentina* 126 D3
Toba, *Japan* 49 G8
Toba Kakar, *Pakistan* 62 D3
Toba Tek Singh, *Pakistan* 62 D5
Tobago, *W. Indies* 117 D7
Tobarra, *Spain* 29 G3
Tobelo, *Indonesia* 57 D7
Tobermorey, *Australia* 90 C2
Tobermory, *Canada* 98 C3
Tobermory, *U.K.* 14 E2
Tobin, *U.S.A.* 112 F5
Tobin, L., *Australia* 88 D4
Tobin L., *Canada* 101 C8
Toblach = Dobbiaco, *Italy* 33 B9
Toboali, *Indonesia* 56 E3
Tobol, *Kazakstan* 44 D7
Tobol →, *Russia* 44 D7
Toboli, *Indonesia* 57 E6
Tobolsk, *Russia* 44 D7
Tobruk = Tubruq, *Libya* 73 B9
Tobyhanna, *U.S.A.* 107 E9
Tobyl = Tobol →, *Russia* 44 D7
Tocache Nuevo, *Peru* 124 B2
Tocantínia, *Brazil* 122 C2
Tocantinópolis, *Brazil* 122 C2
Tocantins □, *Brazil* 122 D2
Tocantins →, *Brazil* 122 B2
Toccoa, *U.S.A.* 105 H4
Toce →, *Italy* 32 C5
Tochigi, *Japan* 49 F9
Tochigi □, *Japan* 49 F9
Tocina, *Spain* 31 H5
Tocopilla, *Chile* 126 A1
Tocumwal, *Australia* 91 F4
Tocuyo →, *Venezuela* 120 A4
Tocuyo de la Costa, *Venezuela* 120 A4
Todd →, *Australia* 90 C2
Todeli, *Indonesia* 57 E6
Todenyang, *Kenya* 82 B4
Todi, *Italy* 33 F9
Tödi, *Switz.* 23 C7
Todos os Santos, B. de, *Brazil* 123 D4
Todos Santos, *Mexico* 114 C2
Todtnau, *Germany* 19 H3
Toecé, *Burkina Faso* 79 C4
Tofield, *Canada* 100 C6
Tofino, *Canada* 100 D3
Töfsingdalens nationalpark, *Sweden* 10 B6
Toftlund, *Denmark* 11 J3
Tofua, *Tonga* 87 D11
Tōgane, *Japan* 49 G10
Togba, *Mauritania* 78 B2
Toggenburg, *Switz.* 23 B8
Togian, Kepulauan, *Indonesia* 57 E6
Togliatti, *Russia* 42 D9
Togo ■, *W. Afr.* 79 D5
Togtoh, *China* 50 D6
Tohma →, *Turkey* 66 C7
Tōhoku □, *Japan* 48 E10
Toinya, *Sudan* 77 F2
Tojikiston = Tajikistan ■, *Asia* 44 F8
Tojo, *Indonesia* 57 E6
Tōjō, *Japan* 49 G6
Toka, *Guyana* 121 C6
Tokachi-Dake, *Japan* 48 C11
Tokachi-Gawa →, *Japan* 48 C11
Tokaj, *Hungary* 21 G11
Tokala, *Indonesia* 57 E6
Tōkamachi, *Japan* 49 F9
Tokanui, *N.Z.* 87 M2
Tokar, *Sudan* 76 D4
Tokara-Rettō, *Japan* 49 K4
Tokarahi, *N.Z.* 87 L3
Tokashiki-Shima, *Japan* 49 L3
Tokat, *Turkey* 66 B7
Tŏkchŏn, *N. Korea* 51 E14
Tokeland, *U.S.A.* 112 D3
Tokelau Is., *Pac. Oc.* 92 H10
Tokmak, *Kyrgyzstan* 44 E8
Tokmak, *Ukraine* 41 J8
Toko Ra., *Australia* 90 C2
Tokoro-Gawa →, *Japan* 48 B12
Tokuno-Shima, *Japan* 49 L4
Tokushima, *Japan* 49 G7
Tokushima □, *Japan* 49 H7
Tokuyama, *Japan* 49 G5
Tōkyō, *Japan* 49 G9
Tolaga Bay, *N.Z.* 87 H7
Tolbukhin = Dobrich, *Bulgaria* 38 F10
Toledo, *Spain* 30 F6
Toledo, *Ohio, U.S.A.* 104 E4
Toledo, *Oreg., U.S.A.* 110 D2
Toledo, *Wash., U.S.A.* 110 C2
Toledo, Montes de, *Spain* 31 F6
Tolentino, *Italy* 33 E10
Tolga, *Algeria* 75 B6
Tolga, *Norway* 10 B5
Toliara, *Madag.* 85 C7
Toliara □, *Madag.* 85 C8
Tolima, *Colombia* 120 C2
Tolima □, *Colombia* 120 C2
Tolitoli, *Indonesia* 57 D6
Tolkamer, *Neths.* 16 E8
Tollhouse, *U.S.A.* 112 H7
Tolmachevo, *Russia* 40 C5
Tolmezzo, *Italy* 33 B10
Tolmin, *Slovenia* 33 B10
Tolo, *Zaïre* 80 E3
Tolo, Teluk, *Indonesia* 57 E6
Tolochin = Talachyn, *Belarus* 40 E5
Tolosa, *Spain* 28 B2
Tolox, *Spain* 31 J6
Toltén, *Chile* 128 A2
Toluca, *Mexico* 115 D5
Tom Burke, *S. Africa* 85 C4
Tom Price, *Australia* 88 D2
Tomah, *U.S.A.* 108 D9
Tomahawk, *U.S.A.* 108 C10
Tomakomai, *Japan* 48 C10
Tomales, *U.S.A.* 112 G4
Tomales B., *U.S.A.* 112 G3
Tomar, *Portugal* 31 F2
Tomarza, *Turkey* 66 C6
Tomás Barrón, *Bolivia* 124 D4
Tomaszów Mazowiecki, *Poland* 20 D9
Tomatlán, *Mexico* 114 D3
Tombador, Serra do, *Brazil* 125 C6
Tombé, *Sudan* 77 F3
Tombigbee →, *U.S.A.* 105 K2
Tombouctou, *Mali* 78 B4
Tombstone, *U.S.A.* 111 L8
Tombua, *Angola* 84 B1
Tomé, *Chile* 126 D1
Tomé-Açu, *Brazil* 122 B2
Tomelilla, *Sweden* 11 J7
Tomelloso, *Spain* 29 F1
Tomingley, *Australia* 91 E4
Tomini, *Indonesia* 57 D6
Tomini, Teluk, *Indonesia* 57 E6
Tominian, *Mali* 78 C4
Tomiño, *Spain* 30 D2
Tomkinson Ras., *Australia* 89 E4
Tommot, *Russia* 45 D13
Tomnavoulin, *U.K.* 14 D5
Tomnop Ta Suos, *Cambodia* 59 G5
Tomo, *Colombia* 120 C4
Tomo →, *Colombia* 120 B4
Tomorit, *Albania* 39 J3
Toms Place, *U.S.A.* 112 H8
Toms River, *U.S.A.* 107 G10
Tomsk, *Russia* 44 D9
Tonalá, *Mexico* 115 D6
Tonale, Passo del, *Italy* 32 B7
Tonalea, *U.S.A.* 111 H8
Tonantins, *Brazil* 120 D4
Tonasket, *U.S.A.* 110 B4
Tonate, *Fr. Guiana* 121 C7
Tonawanda, *U.S.A.* 106 D6
Tonbridge, *U.K.* 13 F8
Tondano, *Indonesia* 57 D6
Tondela, *Portugal* 30 E2
Tønder, *Denmark* 11 K2
Tondi Kiwindi, *Niger* 79 C5
Tondibi, *Mali* 79 B4
Tonekābon, *Iran* 65 B6
Tong Xian, *China* 50 E9
Tonga ■, *Pac. Oc.* 87 D11
Tonga Trench, *Pac. Oc.* 92 J10
Tongaat, *S. Africa* 85 D5
Tong'an, *China* 53 E12
Tongareva, *Cook Is.* 93 H12
Tongatapu, *Tonga* 87 E11
Tongbai, *China* 53 A9
Tongcheng, *Anhui, China* 53 B11
Tongcheng, *Hubei, China* 53 C9
Tongchŏn-ni, *N. Korea* 51 E14
Tongchuan, *China* 50 G5
Tongdao, *China* 52 D7
Tongeren, *Belgium* 17 G6
Tonggu, *China* 53 C10
Tongguan, *China* 50 G6
Tonghai, *China* 52 E4
Tonghua, *China* 51 D13
Tongjiang, *Heilongjiang, China* 54 B8
Tongjiang, *Sichuan, China* 52 B6
Tongjosŏn Man, *N. Korea* 51 E14
Tongking, G. of = Tonkin, G. of, *Asia* 58 B7
Tongliang, *China* 52 C6
Tongliao, *China* 51 C12
Tongling, *China* 53 B11
Tonglu, *China* 53 C12
Tongnae, *S. Korea* 51 G15
Tongnan, *China* 52 B5
Tongobory, *Madag.* 85 C7
Tongoy, *Chile* 126 C1
Tongren, *China* 52 D7
Tongres = Tongeren, *Belgium* 17 G6
Tongsa Dzong, *Bhutan* 61 F17
Tongue, *U.K.* 14 C4
Tongue →, *U.S.A.* 108 B2
Tongwei, *China* 50 G3
Tongxin, *China* 50 F3
Tongyang, *N. Korea* 51 E14
Tongyu, *China* 51 B12
Tongzi, *China* 52 C6
Tonj, *Sudan* 77 F2
Tonk, *India* 62 F6
Tonkawa, *U.S.A.* 109 G6
Tonkin = Bac Phan, *Vietnam* 58 B5
Tonkin, G. of, *Asia* 58 B7
Tonlé Sap, *Cambodia* 58 F4
Tonnay-Charente, *France* 26 C3
Tonneins, *France* 26 D4
Tonnerre, *France* 25 E10
Tönning, *Germany* 18 A4
Tono, *Japan* 48 E10
Tonopah, *U.S.A.* 111 G5
Tonosí, *Panama* 116 E3
Tønsberg, *Norway* 10 E4
Tonya, *Turkey* 67 B8
Tooele, *U.S.A.* 110 F7
Toompine, *Australia* 91 D3
Toonpan, *Australia* 90 B4
Toora, *Australia* 91 F4
Toora-Khem, *Russia* 45 D10
Toowoomba, *Australia* 91 D5
Topalu, *Romania* 38 E11
Topaz, *U.S.A.* 112 G7
Topeka, *U.S.A.* 108 F7
Topki, *Russia* 44 D9
Topl'a →, *Slovak Rep.* 20 G11
Topley, *Canada* 100 C3
Toplica →, *Serbia, Yug.* 21 M11
Topliţa, *Romania* 38 C8
Topocalma, Pta., *Chile* 126 C1
Topock, *U.S.A.* 113 L12
Topola, *Serbia, Yug.* 21 L10
Topol'čany, *Slovak Rep.* 20 G8
Topolnitsa →, *Bulgaria* 38 G7
Topolobampo, *Mexico* 114 B3
Topolovgrad, *Bulgaria* 38 G9
Toppenish, *U.S.A.* 110 C3
Topusko, *Croatia* 33 C12
Toquepala, *Peru* 124 D3
Torá, *Spain* 28 D6
Tora Kit, *Sudan* 77 E3
Toraka Vestale, *Madag.* 85 B7
Torata, *Peru* 124 D3
Torbalı, *Turkey* 66 C2
Torbay, *Canada* 99 C9
Torbay, *U.K.* 13 G4
Tørdal, *Norway* 10 E2
Tordesillas, *Spain* 30 D6
Tordoya, *Spain* 30 B2
Töreboda, *Sweden* 11 F8

Torfaen □, *U.K.* 13 F4
Torgau, *Germany* 18 D8
Torgelow, *Germany* 18 B9
Torhout, *Belgium* 17 F2
Tori, *Ethiopia* 77 F3
Tori-Shima, *Japan* 49 J10
Torigni-sur-Vire, *France* 24 C6
Torija, *Spain* 28 E1
Torin, *Mexico* 114 B2
Toriñana, C., *Spain* 30 B1
Torino, *Italy* 32 C4
Torit, *Sudan* 77 G3
Torkamān, *Iran* 67 D12
Torkovichi, *Russia* 40 C6
Tormes →, *Spain* 30 D4
Tornado Mt., *Canada* 100 D6
Torne älv →, *Sweden* 8 D21
Torneå = Tornio, *Finland* 8 D21
Torneträsk, *Sweden* 8 B18
Tornio, *Finland* 8 D21
Tornionjoki →, *Finland* 8 D21
Tornquist, *Argentina* 126 D3
Toro, *Baleares, Spain* 36 B11
Toro, *Zamora, Spain* 30 D5
Torö, *Sweden* 11 F11
Toro, Cerro del, *Chile* 126 B2
Toro Pk., *U.S.A.* 113 M10
Törökszentmiklós, *Hungary* 21 H10
Toroníos Kólpos, *Greece* 39 J6
Toronto, *Australia* 91 E5
Toronto, *Canada* 98 D4
Toronto, *U.S.A.* 106 F4
Toropets, *Russia* 40 D6
Tororo, *Uganda* 82 B3
Toros Dağları, *Turkey* 66 D5
Torotoro, *Bolivia* 125 D4
Torpshammar, *Sweden* 10 B10
Torquay, *Canada* 101 D8
Torquay, *U.K.* 13 G4
Torquemada, *Spain* 30 C6
Torralba de Calatrava, *Spain* 31 F7
Torrance, *U.S.A.* 113 M8
Torrão, *Portugal* 31 G2
Torre Annunziata, *Italy* 35 B7
Tôrre de Moncorvo, *Portugal* 30 D3
Torre del Greco, *Italy* 35 B7
Torre del Mar, *Spain* 31 J6
Torre-Pacheco, *Spain* 29 H4
Torre Péllice, *Italy* 32 D4
Torreblanca, *Spain* 28 E5
Torrecampo, *Spain* 31 G6
Torrecilla en Cameros, *Spain* 28 C2
Torredembarra, *Spain* 28 D6
Torredonjimeno, *Spain* 31 H7
Torrejoncillo, *Spain* 30 F4
Torrelaguna, *Spain* 28 E1
Torrelavega, *Spain* 30 B6
Torremaggiore, *Italy* 35 A8
Torremolinos, *Spain* 31 J6
Torrens, L., *Australia* 91 E2
Torrens Cr. →, *Australia* 90 C4
Torrens Creek, *Australia* 90 C4
Torrente, *Spain* 29 F4
Torrenueva, *Spain* 29 G1
Torreón, *Mexico* 114 B4
Torreperogil, *Spain* 29 G1
Torres, *Mexico* 114 B2
Torres Novas, *Portugal* 31 F2
Torres Strait, *Australia* 92 H6
Torres Vedras, *Portugal* 31 F1
Torrevieja, *Spain* 29 H4
Torrey, *U.S.A.* 111 G8
Torridge →, *U.K.* 13 G3
Torridon, L., *U.K.* 14 D3
Torrijos, *Spain* 30 F6
Torrington, *Conn., U.S.A.* 107 E11
Torrington, *Wyo., U.S.A.* 108 D2
Torroella de Montgri, *Spain* 28 C8
Torrox, *Spain* 31 J7
Tórshavn, *Færoe Is.* 8 E9
Torsö, *Sweden* 11 F7
Tortola, *Virgin Is.* 117 C7
Tórtoles de Esgueva, *Spain* 30 D6
Tortona, *Italy* 32 D5
Tortoreto, *Italy* 33 F10
Tortorici, *Italy* 35 D7
Tortosa, *Spain* 28 E5
Tortosa, C. de, *Spain* 28 E5
Tortosendo, *Portugal* 30 E3
Tortue, I. de la, *Haiti* 117 B5
Tortum, *Turkey* 67 B9
Ţorūd, *Iran* 65 C7
Torul, *Turkey* 67 B8
Toruń, *Poland* 20 B8
Torup, *Sweden* 11 H7
Tory I., *Ireland* 15 A3
Torysa →, *Slovak Rep.* 20 G11
Torzhok, *Russia* 42 B2
Tosa, *Japan* 49 H6
Tosa-Shimizu, *Japan* 49 H6
Tosa-Wan, *Japan* 49 H6
Toscana □, *Italy* 32 E8
Toscano, Arcipelago, *Italy* 32 F7
Toshkent, *Uzbekistan* 44 E7
Tosno, *Russia* 40 C6
Tossa, *Spain* 28 D7
Tostado, *Argentina* 126 B3
Tostedt, *Germany* 18 B5
Tostón, Pta. de, *Canary Is.* 36 F5
Tosu, *Japan* 49 H5
Tosya, *Turkey* 66 B6
Totana, *Spain* 29 H3
Toten, *Norway* 10 D4
Toteng, *Botswana* 84 C3
Tôtes, *France* 24 C8
Tótkomlós, *Hungary* 21 J10
Totma, *Russia* 44 C5
Totnes, *U.K.* 13 G4
Totness, *Surinam* 121 B6
Totonicapán, *Guatemala* 116 D1
Totora, *Bolivia* 125 D4
Totten Glacier, *Antarctica* 5 C8
Tottenham, *Australia* 91 E4
Tottenham, *Canada* 106 B5
Tottori, *Japan* 49 G7
Tottori □, *Japan* 49 G7
Touat, *Algeria* 75 C5
Touba, *Ivory C.* 78 D3
Toubkal, Djebel, *Morocco* 74 B3
Toucy, *France* 25 E10
Tougan, *Burkina Faso* 78 C4
Touggourt, *Algeria* 75 B6
Tougué, *Guinea* 78 C2
Toukmatine, *Algeria* 75 D6
Toul, *France* 25 D12
Toulepleu, *Ivory C.* 78 D3
Toulon, *France* 27 E9
Toulouse, *France* 26 E5
Toummo, *Niger* 73 D7
Toumodi, *Ivory C.* 78 D3
Tounan, *Taiwan* 53 F13
Tounassine, Hamada, *Algeria* 74 C3
Toungoo, *Burma* 61 K20
Touques →, *France* 24 C7
Touraine, *France* 24 E7
Tourane = Da Nang, *Vietnam* 58 D7
Tourcoing, *France* 25 B10
Tourine, *Mauritania* 74 D2
Tournai, *Belgium* 17 G2
Tournan-en-Brie, *France* 25 D9
Tournay, *France* 26 E4
Tournon, *France* 27 C8
Tournon-St.-Martin, *France* 24 F7
Tournus, *France* 27 B8
Touros, *Brazil* 122 C4
Tours, *France* 24 E7
Touwsrivier, *S. Africa* 84 E3
Tovar, *Venezuela* 120 B3
Tovarkovskiy, *Russia* 42 D4
Tovdal, *Norway* 11 F2
Tovdalselva →, *Norway* 11 F2
Tovuz, *Azerbaijan* 43 K7
Towada, *Japan* 48 D10
Towada-Ko, *Japan* 48 D10
Towamba, *Australia* 91 F4
Towanda, *U.S.A.* 107 E8
Towang, *India* 61 F17
Tower, *U.S.A.* 108 B8
Towerhill Cr. →, *Australia* 90 C3
Towner, *U.S.A.* 108 A4
Townsend, *U.S.A.* 110 C8
Townshend I., *Australia* 90 C5
Townsville, *Australia* 90 B4
Towson, *U.S.A.* 104 F7
Toya-Ko, *Japan* 48 C10
Toyah, *U.S.A.* 109 K3
Toyahvale, *U.S.A.* 109 K3
Toyama, *Japan* 49 F8
Toyama □, *Japan* 49 F8
Toyama-Wan, *Japan* 49 F8
Toyohashi, *Japan* 49 G8
Toyokawa, *Japan* 49 G8
Toyonaka, *Japan* 49 G7
Toyooka, *Japan* 49 G7
Toyota, *Japan* 49 G8
Tozeur, *Tunisia* 75 B6
Tqibuli, *Georgia* 43 J6
Tqvarcheli, *Georgia* 43 J5
Trá Li = Tralee, *Ireland* 15 D2
Tra On, *Vietnam* 59 H5
Trabancos →, *Spain* 30 D5
Traben-Trarbach, *Germany* 19 F3
Trabzon, *Turkey* 67 B8
Tracadie, *Canada* 99 C7
Tracy, *Calif., U.S.A.* 111 H3
Tracy, *Minn., U.S.A.* 108 C7
Tradate, *Italy* 32 C5
Trafalgar, C., *Spain* 31 J4
Traiguén, *Chile* 128 A2
Trail, *Canada* 100 D5
Trainor L., *Canada* 100 A4
Traíra →, *Brazil* 120 D4
Trákhonas, *Cyprus* 37 D12
Tralee, *Ireland* 15 D2
Tralee B., *Ireland* 15 D2
Tramelan, *Switz.* 22 B4
Tramore, *Ireland* 15 D4
Tran Ninh, Cao Nguyen, *Laos* 58 C4
Tranås, *Sweden* 9 G16
Trancas, *Argentina* 126 B2
Trancoso, *Portugal* 30 E3
Tranebjerg, *Denmark* 11 J4
Tranemo, *Sweden* 11 G7
Trang, *Thailand* 59 J2
Trangahy, *Madag.* 85 B7
Trangan, *Indonesia* 57 F8
Trangie, *Australia* 91 E4
Trångsviken, *Sweden* 10 A8
Trani, *Italy* 35 A9
Tranoroa, *Madag.* 85 C8
Tranqueras, *Uruguay* 127 C4
Trans Nzoia □, *Kenya* 82 B3
Transantarctic Mts., *Antarctica* 5 E12
Transcona, *Canada* 101 D9
Transilvania, *Romania* 38 D8
Transilvanian Alps = Carpaţii Meridionali, *Romania* 38 D8
Transylvania = Transilvania, *Romania* 38 D8
Trápani, *Italy* 34 D5
Trapper Pk., *U.S.A.* 110 D6
Traralgon, *Australia* 91 F4
Trarza, *Mauritania* 78 B2
Trasacco, *Italy* 33 G10
Trăscău, Munţii, *Romania* 38 C6
Trasimeno, L., *Italy* 33 E9
Trat, *Thailand* 59 F4
Traun, *Austria* 21 G4
Traunstein, *Germany* 19 H8
Tråvad, *Sweden* 11 F7
Traveller's L., *Australia* 91 E3
Travemünde, *Germany* 18 B6
Travers, Mt., *N.Z.* 87 K4
Traverse City, *U.S.A.* 104 C3
Travnik, *Bos.-H.* 21 L7
Trayning, *Australia* 89 F2
Trazo, *Spain* 30 B2
Trbovlje, *Slovenia* 33 B12
Trébbia →, *Italy* 32 C6
Trebel →, *Germany* 18 B9
Trebinje, *Bos.-H.* 21 N8
Trebisacce, *Italy* 35 C9
Trebišnica →, *Bos.-H.* 21 N8
Trebišov, *Slovak Rep.* 20 G11
Trebižat →, *Bos.-H.* 21 M7
Trebnje, *Slovenia* 33 C12
Třeboň, *Czech.* 20 G4
Trebujena, *Spain* 31 J4
Trecate, *Italy* 32 C5
Trece Martires, *Phil.* 55 D4
Tredegar, *U.K.* 13 F4
Tregaron, *U.K.* 13 E4
Trégastel-Plage, *France* 24 D3
Tregnago, *Italy* 33 C8
Tregrosse Is., *Australia* 90 B5
Tréguier, *France* 24 D3
Trégunc, *France* 24 E3
Treherne, *Canada* 101 D9
Tréia, *Italy* 33 E10
Treignac, *France* 26 C5
Treinta y Tres, *Uruguay* 127 C5
Treis, *Germany* 19 E3
Trelde Næs, *Denmark* 11 J3
Trelew, *Argentina* 128 B3
Trélissac, *France* 26 C4
Trelleborg, *Sweden* 11 J7
Trélon, *France* 25 B11
Tremiti, *Italy* 33 F12
Tremonton, *U.S.A.* 110 F7
Tremp, *Spain* 28 C5
Trenche →, *Canada* 98 C5
Trenčín, *Slovak Rep.* 20 G8
Trenggalek, *Indonesia* 57 H14
Trenque Lauquen, *Argentina* 126 D3
Trent →, *U.K.* 12 D7
Trentino-Alto Adige □, *Italy* 32 B8
Trento, *Italy* 32 B8
Trenton, *Canada* 98 D4
Trenton, *Mo., U.S.A.* 108 E8
Trenton, *N.J., U.S.A.* 107 F10
Trenton, *Nebr., U.S.A.* 108 E4
Trenton, *Tenn., U.S.A.* 109 H10
Trepassey, *Canada* 99 C9
Trepuzzi, *Italy* 35 B11
Tres Arroyos, *Argentina* 126 D3
Três Corações, *Brazil* 123 F2
Três Lagoas, *Brazil* 123 F1
Tres Lagos →, *Argentina* 128 C2
Tres Marías, *Mexico* 114 C3
Três Marias, Reprêsa, *Brazil* 123 E2
Tres Montes, C., *Chile* 128 C1
Tres Pinos, *U.S.A.* 112 J5
Três Pontas, *Brazil* 123 F2
Tres Puentes, *Chile* 126 B1
Tres Puntas, C., *Argentina* 128 C3
Três Rios, *Brazil* 123 F3
Tres Valles, *Mexico* 115 D5
Treska →, *Macedonia* 39 H4
Trespaderne, *Spain* 28 C1
Trets, *France* 27 E9
Treuchtlingen, *Germany* 19 G6
Treuenbrietzen, *Germany* 18 C8
Treviglio, *Italy* 32 C6
Trevinca, Peña, *Spain* 30 C4
Treviso, *Italy* 33 C9
Trévoux, *France* 27 C8
Treysa, *Germany* 18 E5
Trgovište, *Serbia, Yug.* 21 N12
Triabunna, *Australia* 90 G4
Triánda, *Greece* 37 C10
Triang, *Malaysia* 59 L4
Triaucourt-en-Argonne, *France* 25 D12
Tribsees, *Germany* 18 A8
Tribulation, C., *Australia* 90 B4
Tribune, *U.S.A.* 108 F4
Tricárico, *Italy* 35 B9
Tricase, *Italy* 35 C11
Trichinopoly = Tiruchchirappalli, *India* 60 P11
Trichur, *India* 60 P10
Trida, *Australia* 91 E4
Trier, *Germany* 19 F2
Trieste, *Italy* 33 C10
Trieste, G. di, *Italy* 33 C10
Trieux →, *France* 24 D3
Triggiano, *Italy* 35 A9
Triglav, *Slovenia* 33 B10
Trigno →, *Italy* 33 F11
Trigueros, *Spain* 31 H4
Trikhonis, Límni, *Greece* 39 L4
Tríkkala, *Greece* 39 K4
Trikomo, *Cyprus* 37 D12
Trikora, Puncak, *Indonesia* 57 E9
Trilj, *Croatia* 33 E13
Trillo, *Spain* 28 E2
Trim, *Ireland* 15 C5
Trincomalee, *Sri Lanka* 60 Q12
Trindade, *Brazil* 123 E2
Trindade, I., *Atl. Oc.* 2 F8
Trinidad, *Bolivia* 125 C5
Trinidad, *Colombia* 120 B3
Trinidad, *Cuba* 116 B3
Trinidad, *Uruguay* 126 C4
Trinidad, *U.S.A.* 109 G2
Trinidad, *W. Indies* 117 D7
Trinidad →, *Mexico* 115 D5
Trinidad, G., *Chile* 128 C1
Trinidad, I., *Argentina* 128 A4
Trinidad & Tobago ■, *W. Indies* 117 D7
Trinitápoli, *Italy* 35 A9
Trinity, *Canada* 99 C9
Trinity, *U.S.A.* 109 K7
Trinity →, *Calif., U.S.A.* 110 F2
Trinity →, *Tex., U.S.A.* 109 L7
Trinity B., *Canada* 99 C9
Trinity Range, *U.S.A.* 110 F4
Trinkitat, *Sudan* 76 D4
Trino, *Italy* 32 C5
Trion, *U.S.A.* 105 H3
Trionto, C., *Italy* 35 C9
Triora, *Italy* 32 E4
Tripoli = Tarābulus, *Lebanon* 69 A4
Tripoli = Tarābulus, *Libya* 75 B7
Tripolitania, *N. Afr.* 70 C5
Tripp, *U.S.A.* 108 D6
Tripura □, *India* 61 H17
Tripylos, *Cyprus* 37 E11
Trischen, *Germany* 18 A4
Tristan da Cunha, *Atl. Oc.* 71 K2
Trivandrum, *India* 60 Q10
Trivento, *Italy* 35 A7
Trnava, *Slovak Rep.* 21 G7
Trochu, *Canada* 100 C6
Trodely I., *Canada* 98 B4
Trogir, *Croatia* 33 E13
Troglav, *Croatia* 33 E13
Trøgstad, *Norway* 10 E5
Tróia, *Italy* 35 A8
Troilus, L., *Canada* 98 B5
Troina, *Italy* 35 E7
Trois Fourches, Cap des, *Morocco* 75 A4
Trois-Pistoles, *Canada* 99 C6
Trois-Rivières, *Canada* 98 C5
Troisvierges, *Belgium* 17 H8
Troitsk, *Russia* 44 D7
Troitsko Pechorsk, *Russia* 44 C6
Trölladyngja, *Iceland* 8 D5
Trollhättan, *Sweden* 11 F6
Trollheimen, *Norway* 10 B3
Trombetas →, *Brazil* 121 D6
Tromsø, *Norway* 8 B18
Trona, *U.S.A.* 113 K9
Tronador, *Argentina* 128 B2
Trøndelag, *Norway* 8 D14
Trondheim, *Norway* 10 A4
Trondheimsfjorden, *Norway* 8 E14
Trönninge, *Sweden* 11 H6
Trönö, *Sweden* 10 C10
Tronto →, *Italy* 33 F10
Troodos, *Cyprus* 66 E5
Troon, *U.K.* 14 F4
Tropea, *Italy* 35 D8
Tropic, *U.S.A.* 111 H7
Tropoja, *Albania* 38 G3
Trossachs, The, *U.K.* 14 E4
Trostan, *U.K.* 15 A5
Trostberg, *Germany* 19 G8
Trostyanets, *Ukraine* 41 G8
Trotternish, *U.K.* 14 D2
Troup, *U.S.A.* 109 J7
Trout →, *Canada* 100 A5
Trout L., *N.W.T., Canada* 100 A4
Trout L., *Ont., Canada* 101 C10
Trout Lake, *Mich., U.S.A.* 98 C2
Trout Lake, *Wash., U.S.A.* 112 E5
Trout River, *Canada* 99 C8
Trouville-sur-Mer, *France* 24 C7
Trowbridge, *U.K.* 13 F5
Troy, *Turkey* 66 C2
Troy, *Ala., U.S.A.* 105 K3
Troy, *Idaho, U.S.A.* 110 C5
Troy, *Kans., U.S.A.* 108 F7
Troy, *Mo., U.S.A.* 108 F9
Troy, *Mont., U.S.A.* 110 B6
Troy, *N.Y., U.S.A.* 107 D11
Troy, *Ohio, U.S.A.* 104 E3
Troyan, *Bulgaria* 38 G7
Troyes, *France* 25 D11
Trpanj, *Croatia* 21 M7
Trstena, *Slovak Rep.* 20 F9
Trstenik, *Serbia, Yug.* 21 M10
Trubchevsk, *Russia* 41 F7
Trucial States = United Arab Emirates ■, *Asia* 65 F7
Truckee, *U.S.A.* 112 F6
Trudfront, *Russia* 43 H8
Trudovoye, *Russia* 48 C6
Trujillo, *Colombia* 120 C2
Trujillo, *Honduras* 116 C2
Trujillo, *Peru* 124 B2
Trujillo, *Spain* 31 F5
Trujillo, *U.S.A.* 109 H2
Trujillo, *Venezuela* 120 B3
Trujillo □, *Venezuela* 120 B3
Truk, *Pac. Oc.* 92 G7
Trumann, *U.S.A.* 109 H9
Trumbull, Mt., *U.S.A.* 111 H7
Trun, *France* 24 D7
Trun, *Switz.* 23 C7
Trundle, *Australia* 91 E4
Trung-Phan, *Vietnam* 58 E7
Truro, *Canada* 99 C7
Truro, *U.K.* 13 G2
Truskavets, *Ukraine* 41 H2
Truslove, *Australia* 89 F3
Trustrup, *Denmark* 11 H4
Truth or Consequences, *U.S.A.* 111 K10
Trutnov, *Czech.* 20 E5
Truyère →, *France* 26 D6
Tryavna, *Bulgaria* 38 G8
Tryon, *U.S.A.* 105 H4
Tryonville, *U.S.A.* 106 E5
Trzcianka, *Poland* 20 B6
Trzebiatów, *Poland* 20 A5
Trzebiez, *Poland* 20 B4
Trzebinia-Siersza, *Poland* 20 E9
Trzebnica, *Poland* 20 D7
Tržič, *Slovenia* 33 B11
Tsagan Aman, *Russia* 43 G8
Tsaratanana, *Madag.* 85 B8
Tsaratanana, Mt. de, *Madag.* 85 A8
Tsarevo = Michurin, *Bulgaria* 38 G10
Tsau, *Botswana* 84 C3
Tsebrykove, *Ukraine* 41 J6
Tselinograd = Aqmola, *Kazakstan* 44 D8
Tsetserleg, *Mongolia* 54 B5
Tshabong, *Botswana* 84 D3
Tshane, *Botswana* 84 C3
Tshela, *Zaïre* 80 E2
Tshesebe, *Botswana* 85 C4
Tshibeke, *Zaïre* 82 C2
Tshibinda, *Zaïre* 82 C2
Tshikapa, *Zaïre* 80 F4
Tshilenge, *Zaïre* 82 D1
Tshinsenda, *Zaïre* 83 E2
Tshofa, *Zaïre* 82 D2
Tshwane, *Botswana* 84 C3
Tsigara, *Botswana* 84 C4
Tsihombe, *Madag.* 85 D8
Tsimlyansk, *Russia* 43 G6
Tsimlyansk Res. = Tsimlyanskoye Vdkhr., *Russia* 43 F6
Tsimlyanskoye Vdkhr., *Russia* 43 F6
Tsinan = Jinan, *China* 50 F9
Tsineng, *S. Africa* 84 D3
Tsinghai = Qinghai □, *China* 54 C4
Tsingtao = Qingdao, *China* 51 F11
Tsinjomitondraka, *Madag.* 85 B8
Tsiroanomandidy, *Madag.* 85 B8
Tsiteli-Tsqaro, *Georgia* 43 K8
Tsivilsk, *Russia* 42 C8
Tsivory, *Madag.* 85 C8
Tskhinvali, *Georgia* 43 J7
Tsna →, *Russia* 42 C6
Tsnori, *Georgia* 43 K7
Tso Moriri, L., *India* 63 C8
Tsodilo Hill, *Botswana* 84 B3
Tsogttsetsiy, *Mongolia* 50 C3
Tsolo, *S. Africa* 85 E4
Tsomo, *S. Africa* 85 E4
Tsu, *Japan* 49 G8
Tsu L., *Canada* 100 A6
Tsuchiura, *Japan* 49 F10
Tsugaru-Kaikyō, *Japan* 48 D10
Tsumeb, *Namibia* 84 B2
Tsumis, *Namibia* 84 C2
Tsuruga, *Japan* 49 G8
Tsurugi-San, *Japan* 49 H7
Tsuruoka, *Japan* 48 E9
Tsushima, *Gifu, Japan* 49 G8
Tsushima, *Nagasaki, Japan* 49 G4
Tsvetkovo, *Ukraine* 41 H6
Tsyelyakhany, *Belarus* 41 F3
Tua →, *Portugal* 30 D3
Tual, *Indonesia* 57 F8
Tuam, *Ireland* 15 C3
Tuamotu Arch. = Tuamotu Is., *Pac. Oc.* 93 J13
Tuamotu Is., *Pac. Oc.* 93 J13
Tuamotu Ridge, *Pac. Oc.* 93 K14
Tuanfeng, *China* 53 B10
Tuanxi, *China* 52 D6
Tuao, *Phil.* 55 C4
Tuapse, *Russia* 43 H4
Tuatapere, *N.Z.* 87 M1
Tuba City, *U.S.A.* 111 H8
Tuban, *Indonesia* 57 G15
Tubarão, *Brazil* 127 B6
Tūbās, *West Bank* 69 C4
Tubau, *Malaysia* 56 D4
Tubbergen, *Neths.* 16 D9
Tübingen, *Germany* 19 G5
Tubize, *Belgium* 17 G4
Tubruq, *Libya* 73 B9
Tubuai Is., *Pac. Oc.* 93 K12
Tuc Trung, *Vietnam* 59 G6
Tucacas, *Venezuela* 120 A4
Tucano, *Brazil* 122 D4
T'uch'ang, *Taiwan* 53 E13
Tuchodi →, *Canada* 100 B4

Tuchola, *Poland* 20 B7
Tucson, *U.S.A.* 111 K8
Tucumán □, *Argentina* 126 B2
Tucumcari, *U.S.A.* 109 H3
Tucunaré, *Brazil* 125 B6
Tucupido, *Venezuela* 120 B4
Tucupita, *Venezuela* 121 B5
Tucuruí, *Brazil* 122 B2
Tucuruí, Reprêsa de, *Brazil* 122 B2
Tudela, *Spain* 28 C3
Tudela de Duero, *Spain* 30 D6
Tudmur, *Syria* 67 E8
Tudor, L., *Canada* 99 A6
Tudora, *Romania* 38 B9
Tuella →, *Portugal* 30 D3
Tuen, *Australia* 91 D4
Tueré →, *Brazil* 122 B1
Tugela →, *S. Africa* 85 D5
Tuguegarao, *Phil.* 55 C4
Tugur, *Russia* 45 D14
Tuineje, *Canary Is.* 36 F5
Tukangbesi, Kepulauan, *Indonesia* 57 F6
Tukarak I., *Canada* 98 A4
Tukayyid, *Iraq* 64 D5
Tûkh, *Egypt* 76 H7
Tukobo, *Ghana* 78 D4
Tūkrah, *Libya* 73 B9
Tuktoyaktuk, *Canada* 96 B6
Tukums, *Latvia* 9 H20
Tukuyu, *Tanzania* 83 D3
Tula, *Hidalgo, Mexico* 115 C5
Tula, *Tamaulipas, Mexico* 115 C5
Tula, *Nigeria* 79 D7
Tula, *Russia* 42 C3
Tulancingo, *Mexico* 115 C5
Tulare, *U.S.A.* 111 H4
Tulare Lake Bed, *U.S.A.* 111 J4
Tularosa, *U.S.A.* 111 K10
Tulbagh, *S. Africa* 84 E2
Tulcán, *Ecuador* 120 C2
Tulcea, *Romania* 38 D11
Tulchyn, *Ukraine* 41 H5
Tūleh, *Iran* 65 C7
Tulemalu L., *Canada* 101 A9
Tuli, *Indonesia* 57 E6
Tuli, *Zimbabwe* 83 G2
Tulia, *U.S.A.* 109 H4
Tulita, *Canada* 96 B7
Ţülkarm, *West Bank* 69 C4
Tullahoma, *U.S.A.* 105 H2
Tullamore, *Australia* 91 E4
Tullamore, *Ireland* 15 C4
Tulle, *France* 26 C5
Tullibigeal, *Australia* 91 E4
Tullins, *France* 27 C9
Tulln, *Austria* 21 G6
Tullow, *Ireland* 15 D4
Tullus, *Sudan* 77 E1
Tully, *Australia* 90 B4
Ţulmaythah, *Libya* 73 B9
Tulmur, *Australia* 90 C3
Tulnici, *Romania* 38 D9
Tulovo, *Bulgaria* 38 G8
Tulsa, *U.S.A.* 109 G7
Tulsequah, *Canada* 100 B2
Tulu Milki, *Ethiopia* 77 F4
Tulu Welel, *Ethiopia* 77 F3
Tulua, *Colombia* 120 C2
Tulun, *Russia* 45 D11
Tulungagung, *Indonesia* 56 F4
Tum, *Indonesia* 57 E8
Tuma, *Russia* 42 C5
Tuma →, *Nic.* 116 D3
Tumaco, *Colombia* 120 C2
Tumaco, Ensenada, *Colombia* 120 C2
Tumatumari, *Guyana* 121 B6
Tumba, *Sweden* 10 E11
Tumba, L., *Zaïre* 80 E3
Tumbarumba, *Australia* 91 F4
Tumbaya, *Argentina* 126 A2
Túmbes, *Peru* 124 A1
Tumbes □, *Peru* 124 A1
Tumbwe, *Zaïre* 83 E2
Tumby Bay, *Australia* 91 E2
Tumd Youqi, *China* 50 D6
Tumen, *China* 51 C15
Tumen Jiang →, *China* 51 C16
Tumeremo, *Venezuela* 121 B5
Tumiritinga, *Brazil* 123 E3
Tumkur, *India* 60 N10
Tummel, L., *U.K.* 14 E5
Tump, *Pakistan* 60 F3
Tumpat, *Malaysia* 59 J4
Tumu, *Ghana* 78 C4
Tumucumaque, Serra, *Brazil* 121 C7
Tumupasa, *Bolivia* 124 C4
Tumut, *Australia* 91 F4
Tumwater, *U.S.A.* 110 C2
Tunas de Zaza, *Cuba* 116 B4
Tunbridge Wells = Royal Tunbridge Wells, *U.K.* 13 F8
Tunceli, *Turkey* 67 C8
Tuncurry, *Australia* 91 E5
Tunduru, *Tanzania* 83 E4
Tunduru □, *Tanzania* 83 E4
Tundzha →, *Bulgaria* 39 H9
Tunga Pass, *India* 61 E19
Tungabhadra →, *India* 60 M11
Tungaru, *Sudan* 77 E3
Tungla, *Nic.* 116 D3
Tungshih, *Taiwan* 53 E13
Tungsten, *Canada* 100 A3
Tungurahua □, *Ecuador* 120 D2
Tunguska, Nizhnyaya →, *Russia* 45 C9
Tunia, *Colombia* 120 C2
Tunica, *U.S.A.* 109 H9
Tunis, *Tunisia* 75 A7
Tunis, Golfe de, *Tunisia* 75 A7
Tunisia ■, *Africa* 75 B6
Tunja, *Colombia* 120 B3
Tunkhannock, *U.S.A.* 107 E9
Tunliu, *China* 50 F7
Tunnsjøen, *Norway* 8 D15
Tunungayualok I., *Canada* 99 A7
Tunuyán, *Argentina* 126 C2
Tunuyán →, *Argentina* 126 C2
Tunxi, *China* 53 C12
Tuo Jiang →, *China* 52 C5
Tuolumne, *U.S.A.* 111 H3
Tuolumne →, *U.S.A.* 112 H5
Tuoy-Khaya, *Russia* 45 C12
Tūp Āghāj, *Iran* 67 D12
Tupã, *Brazil* 127 A5
Tupaciguara, *Brazil* 123 E2
Tupelo, *U.S.A.* 105 H1
Tupik, *Russia* 42 C1
Tupik, *Russia* 45 D12
Tupinambaranas, *Brazil* 121 D6
Tupirama, *Brazil* 122 C2
Tupiratins, *Brazil* 122 C2
Tupiza, *Bolivia* 126 A2
Tupman, *U.S.A.* 113 K7
Tupper, *Canada* 100 B4
Tupper Lake, *U.S.A.* 107 B10
Tupungato, Cerro, *S. Amer.* 126 C2
Tuquan, *China* 51 B11
Túquerres, *Colombia* 120 C2
Tura, *Russia* 45 C11
Turabah, *Si. Arabia* 64 D4
Turagua, Serranía, *Venezuela* 121 B5
Tūrān, *Iran* 65 C8
Turan, *Russia* 45 D10
Turayf, *Si. Arabia* 64 D3
Turbenthal, *Switz.* 23 B7
Turégano, *Spain* 30 D6
Turek, *Poland* 20 C8
Turen, *Venezuela* 120 B4
Turfan = Turpan, *China* 54 B3
Turfan Depression = Turpan Hami, *China* 54 B3
Tŭrgovishte, *Bulgaria* 38 F9
Turgutlu, *Turkey* 66 C2
Turhal, *Turkey* 66 B7
Turia →, *Spain* 29 F4
Turiaçu, *Brazil* 122 B2
Turiaçu →, *Brazil* 122 B2
Turin = Torino, *Italy* 32 C4
Turin, *Canada* 100 D6
Turkana □, *Kenya* 82 B4
Turkana, L., *Africa* 82 B4
Turkestan = Türkistan, *Kazakstan* 44 E7
Túrkeve, *Hungary* 21 H10
Turkey ■, *Eurasia* 66 C7
Turkey Creek, *Australia* 88 C4
Turki, *Russia* 42 D6
Türkistan, *Kazakstan* 44 E7
Türkmenbashi, *Turkmenistan* 44 E6
Turkmenistan ■, *Asia* 44 F6
Türkoğlu, *Turkey* 66 D7
Turks & Caicos Is. ■, *W. Indies* 117 B5
Turks Island Passage, *W. Indies* 117 B5
Turku, *Finland* 9 F20
Turkwe →, *Kenya* 82 B4
Turlock, *U.S.A.* 111 H3
Turnagain →, *Canada* 100 B3
Turnagain, C., *N.Z.* 87 J6
Turneffe Is., *Belize* 115 D7
Turner, *Australia* 88 C4
Turner, *U.S.A.* 110 B9
Turner Pt., *Australia* 90 A1
Turner Valley, *Canada* 100 C6
Turners Falls, *U.S.A.* 107 D12
Turnhout, *Belgium* 17 F5
Turnor L., *Canada* 101 B7
Tŭrnovo = Veliko Tŭrnovo, *Bulgaria* 38 F8
Turnu Măgurele, *Romania* 38 F7
Turnu Roşu, P., *Romania* 38 D7
Turon, *U.S.A.* 109 G5
Turpan, *China* 54 B3
Turpan Hami, *China* 54 B3
Turriff, *U.K.* 14 D6
Tursāq, *Iraq* 67 F11
Tursi, *Italy* 35 B9
Turtle Head I., *Australia* 90 A3
Turtle L., *Canada* 101 C7
Turtle Lake, *N. Dak., U.S.A.* 108 B4
Turtle Lake, *Wis., U.S.A.* 108 C8
Turtleford, *Canada* 101 C7
Turukhansk, *Russia* 45 C9
Turzovka, *Slovak Rep.* 20 F8
Tuscaloosa, *U.S.A.* 105 J2
Tuscánia, *Italy* 33 F8
Tuscany = Toscana □, *Italy* 32 E8
Tuscola, *Ill., U.S.A.* 104 F1
Tuscola, *Tex., U.S.A.* 109 J5
Tuscumbia, *U.S.A.* 105 H2
Tuskar Rock, *Ireland* 15 D5
Tuskegee, *U.S.A.* 105 J3
Tustin, *U.S.A.* 113 M9
Tustna, *Norway* 10 A2
Tutak, *Turkey* 67 C10
Tutayev, *Russia* 42 B4
Tuticorin, *India* 60 Q11
Tutin, *Serbia, Yug.* 21 N10
Tutóia, *Brazil* 122 B3
Tutong, *Brunei* 56 D4
Tutova →, *Romania* 38 C10
Tutrakan, *Bulgaria* 38 E9
Tutshi L., *Canada* 100 B2
Tuttle, *U.S.A.* 108 B5
Tuttlingen, *Germany* 19 H4
Tutuala, *Indonesia* 57 F7
Tutuila, *Amer. Samoa* 87 B13
Tututepec, *Mexico* 115 D5
Tuva □, *Russia* 45 D10
Tuvalu ■, *Pac. Oc.* 92 H9
Tuxpan, *Mexico* 115 C5
Tuxtla Gutiérrez, *Mexico* 115 D6
Tuy, *Spain* 30 C2
Tuy An, *Vietnam* 58 F7
Tuy Duc, *Vietnam* 59 F6
Tuy Hoa, *Vietnam* 58 F7
Tuy Phong, *Vietnam* 59 G7
Tuya L., *Canada* 100 B2
Tuyen Hoa, *Vietnam* 58 D6
Tuyen Quang, *Vietnam* 58 B5
Tūysarkān, *Iran* 67 E13
Tuz Gölü, *Turkey* 66 C5
Ţūz Khurmātū, *Iraq* 67 E11
Tuzla, *Bos.-H.* 21 L8
Tuzlov →, *Russia* 43 G4
Tuzluca, *Turkey* 67 B10
Tvååker, *Sweden* 11 G6
Tvedestrand, *Norway* 11 F2
Tver, *Russia* 42 B2
Tvŭrditsa, *Bulgaria* 38 G8
Twain, *U.S.A.* 112 E5
Twain Harte, *U.S.A.* 112 G6
Tweed, *Canada* 106 B7
Tweed →, *U.K.* 14 F7
Tweed Heads, *Australia* 91 D5
Tweedsmuir Prov. Park, *Canada* 100 C3
Twello, *Neths.* 16 D8
Twentynine Palms, *U.S.A.* 113 L10
Twillingate, *Canada* 99 C9
Twin Bridges, *U.S.A.* 110 D7
Twin Falls, *U.S.A.* 110 E6
Twin Valley, *U.S.A.* 108 B6
Twisp, *U.S.A.* 110 B3
Twistringen, *Germany* 18 C4
Two Harbors, *U.S.A.* 108 B9
Two Hills, *Canada* 100 C6
Two Rivers, *U.S.A.* 104 C2
Twofold B., *Australia* 91 F4
Tyachiv, *Ukraine* 41 H2
Tychy, *Poland* 20 E8
Tykocin, *Poland* 20 B12
Tyler, *U.S.A.* 103 D7
Tyler, *Minn., U.S.A.* 108 C6
Tyler, *Tex., U.S.A.* 109 J7
Tyligul →, *Ukraine* 41 J6
Tylldal, *Norway* 10 B4
Týn nad Vltavou, *Czech.* 20 F4
Tynda, *Russia* 45 D13
Tyne →, *U.K.* 12 C6
Tyne & Wear □, *U.K.* 12 C6
Tynemouth, *U.K.* 12 B6
Tynset, *Norway* 10 B4
Tyre = Sūr, *Lebanon* 69 B4
Tyrifjorden, *Norway* 10 D4
Tyringe, *Sweden* 11 H7
Tyristrand, *Norway* 10 D4
Tyrnyauz, *Russia* 43 J6
Tyrone, *U.S.A.* 106 F6
Tyrrell →, *Australia* 91 F3
Tyrrell, L., *Australia* 91 F3
Tyrrell Arm, *Canada* 101 A9
Tyrrell L., *Canada* 101 A7
Tyrrhenian Sea, *Medit. S.* 34 B5
Tysfjorden, *Norway* 8 B17
Tystberga, *Sweden* 11 F11
Tyub Karagan, Mys, *Kazakstan* 43 H10
Tyuleni, Ostrova, *Kazakstan* 43 H10
Tyuleniy, *Russia* 43 H8
Tyuleniy, Mys, *Azerbaijan* 43 K10
Tyumen, *Russia* 44 D7
Tywi →, *U.K.* 13 F3
Tywyn, *U.K.* 13 E3
Tzaneen, *S. Africa* 85 C5
Tzermiádhes, *Greece* 37 D7
Tzermíadhes Neápolis, *Greece* 39 P8
Tzoumérka, Óros, *Greece* 39 K4
Tzukong = Zigong, *China* 52 C5
Tzummarum, *Neths.* 16 B7

U

U Taphao, *Thailand* 58 F3
U.S.A. = United States of America ■, *N. Amer.* 102 C7
Uachadi, Sierra, *Venezuela* 121 C4
Uainambi, *Colombia* 120 C4
Uanda, *Australia* 90 C3
Uarsciek, *Somali Rep.* 68 G4
Uasin □, *Kenya* 82 B4
Uato-Udo, *Indonesia* 57 F7
Uatumã →, *Brazil* 121 D6
Uauá, *Brazil* 122 C4
Uaupés, *Brazil* 120 D4
Uaupés →, *Brazil* 120 C4
Uaxactún, *Guatemala* 116 C2
Ubá, *Brazil* 123 F3
Ubaitaba, *Brazil* 123 D4
Ubangi = Oubangi →, *Zaïre* 80 E3
Ubaté, *Colombia* 120 B3
Ubauro, *Pakistan* 62 E3
Ubaye →, *France* 27 D10
Ubayyiḑ, W. al →, *Iraq* 67 F10
Ube, *Japan* 49 H5
Ubeda, *Spain* 29 G1
Uberaba, *Brazil* 123 E2
Uberaba, L., *Brazil* 125 D6
Uberlândia, *Brazil* 123 E2
Überlingen, *Germany* 19 H5
Ubiaja, *Nigeria* 79 D6
Ubolratna Res., *Thailand* 58 D4
Ubombo, *S. Africa* 85 D5
Ubon Ratchathani, *Thailand* 58 E5
Ubondo, *Zaïre* 82 C2
Ubort →, *Belarus* 41 F5
Ubrique, *Spain* 31 J5
Ubundu, *Zaïre* 82 C2
Ucayali →, *Peru* 124 A3
Uccle, *Belgium* 17 G4
Uchi Lake, *Canada* 101 C10
Uchiura-Wan, *Japan* 48 C10
Uchiza, *Peru* 124 B2
Uchte, *Germany* 18 C4
Uchur →, *Russia* 45 D14
Ucluelet, *Canada* 100 D3
Ucuriş, *Romania* 38 C4
Uda →, *Russia* 45 D14
Udaipur, *India* 62 G5
Udaipur Garhi, *Nepal* 63 F12
Udbina, *Croatia* 33 D12
Uddel, *Neths.* 16 D7
Uddevalla, *Sweden* 11 F5
Uddjaur, *Sweden* 8 D17
Uden, *Neths.* 17 E7
Udgir, *India* 60 K10
Udhampur, *India* 63 C6
Udi, *Nigeria* 79 D6
Údine, *Italy* 33 B10
Udmurtia □, *Russia* 44 D6
Udon Thani, *Thailand* 58 D4
Udupi, *India* 60 N9
Udvoy Balkan, *Bulgaria* 38 G9
Udzungwa Range, *Tanzania* 83 D4
Ueckermünde, *Germany* 18 B10
Ueda, *Japan* 49 F9
Uedineniya, Os., *Russia* 4 B12
Uele →, *Zaïre* 80 D4
Uelen, *Russia* 45 C19
Uelzen, *Germany* 18 C6
Uetendorf, *Switz.* 22 C5
Ufa, *Russia* 44 D6
Uffenheim, *Germany* 19 F6
Ugab →, *Namibia* 84 C1
Ugalla →, *Tanzania* 82 D3
Uganda ■, *Africa* 82 B3
Ugchelen, *Neths.* 16 D7
Ugento, *Italy* 35 C11
Ugep, *Nigeria* 79 D6
Ugie, *S. Africa* 85 E4
Ugijar, *Spain* 29 J1
Ugine, *France* 27 C10
Uglegorsk, *Russia* 45 E15
Uglich, *Russia* 42 B4
Ugljane, *Croatia* 33 E13
Ugolyak, *Russia* 45 C13
Ugra →, *Russia* 42 C3
Ugûn Mûsa, *Egypt* 69 F1
Ugŭrchin, *Bulgaria* 38 F7
Uh →, *Slovak Rep.* 21 G11
Uherske Hradiště, *Czech.* 20 F7
Uhrichsville, *U.S.A.* 106 F3
Uibhist a Deas = South Uist, *U.K.* 14 D1
Uibhist a Tuath = North Uist, *U.K.* 14 D1
Uíge, *Angola* 80 F2
Uijŏngbu, *S. Korea* 51 F14
Ŭiju, *N. Korea* 51 D13
Uinta Mts., *U.S.A.* 110 F8
Uitenhage, *S. Africa* 84 E4
Uitgeest, *Neths.* 16 C5
Uithoorn, *Neths.* 16 D5
Uithuizen, *Neths.* 16 B9
Uitkerke, *Belgium* 17 F2
Újfehértó, *Hungary* 21 H11
Ujhani, *India* 63 F8
Uji-guntō, *Japan* 49 J4
Ujjain, *India* 62 H6
Újpest, *Hungary* 21 H9
Újszász, *Hungary* 21 H10
Ujung Pandang, *Indonesia* 57 F5
Uka, *Russia* 45 D17
Ukara I., *Tanzania* 82 C3
Uke-Shima, *Japan* 49 K4
Ukerewe □, *Tanzania* 82 C3
Ukerewe I., *Tanzania* 82 C3
Ukholovo, *Russia* 42 D5
Ukhrul, *India* 61 G19
Ukhta, *Russia* 44 C6
Ukiah, *U.S.A.* 112 F3
Ukki Fort, *India* 63 C7
Ukmerge, *Lithuania* 9 J21
Ukraine ■, *Europe* 41 H7
Ukwi, *Botswana* 84 C3
Ulaanbaatar, *Mongolia* 45 E11
Ulaangom, *Mongolia* 54 A4
Ulamba, *Zaïre* 83 D1
Ulan Bator = Ulaanbaatar, *Mongolia* 45 E11
Ulan Erge, *Russia* 43 G7
Ulan Khol, *Russia* 43 H8
Ulan Ude, *Russia* 45 D11
Ulanga □, *Tanzania* 83 D4
Ulanów, *Poland* 20 E12
Ulaş, *Turkey* 66 C7
Ulaya, *Morogoro, Tanzania* 82 D4
Ulaya, *Tabora, Tanzania* 82 C3
Ulcinj, *Montenegro, Yug.* 39 H2
Ulco, *S. Africa* 84 D3
Ulefoss, *Norway* 9 G13
Ulfborg, *Denmark* 11 H2
Ulft, *Neths.* 16 E8
Ulhasnagar, *India* 60 K8
Uljma, *Serbia, Yug.* 21 K11
Ulla →, *Spain* 30 C2
Ulladulla, *Australia* 91 F5
Ullånger, *Sweden* 10 B12
Ullapool, *U.K.* 14 D3
Ullared, *Sweden* 11 G6
Ulldecona, *Spain* 28 E5
Ullswater, *U.K.* 12 C5
Ullung-do, *S. Korea* 51 F16
Ulm, *Germany* 19 G5
Ulmarra, *Australia* 91 D5
Ulmeni, *Romania* 38 D9
Ulonguè, *Mozam.* 83 E3
Ulricehamn, *Sweden* 9 H15
Ulrum, *Neths.* 16 B8
Ulsan, *S. Korea* 51 G15
Ulsberg, *Norway* 10 B3
Ulster □, *U.K.* 15 B5
Ulubaria, *India* 63 H13
Ulubat Gölü, *Turkey* 66 B3
Ulubey, *Turkey* 66 C3
Uluborlu, *Turkey* 66 C4
Uluçinar, *Turkey* 66 D6
Uludağ, *Turkey* 66 B3
Uludere, *Turkey* 67 D10
Uluguru Mts., *Tanzania* 82 D4
Ulukışla, *Turkey* 66 D6
Ulungur He →, *China* 54 B3
Uluru = Ayers Rock, *Australia* 89 E5
Ulutau, *Kazakstan* 44 E7
Ulvenhout, *Neths.* 17 E5
Ulverston, *U.K.* 12 C4
Ulverstone, *Australia* 90 G4
Ulya, *Russia* 45 D15
Ulyanovsk = Simbirsk, *Russia* 42 C9
Ulyasutay, *Mongolia* 54 B4
Ulysses, *U.S.A.* 109 G4
Umag, *Croatia* 33 C10
Umala, *Bolivia* 124 D4
Uman, *Ukraine* 41 H6
Umaria, *India* 61 H12
Umarkot, *Pakistan* 60 G6
Umatilla, *U.S.A.* 110 D4
Umba, *Russia* 44 C4
Umbértide, *Italy* 33 E9
Umbrella Mts., *N.Z.* 87 L2
Umbria □, *Italy* 33 F9
Ume älv →, *Sweden* 8 E19
Umeå, *Sweden* 8 E19
Umera, *Indonesia* 57 E7
Umfuli →, *Zimbabwe* 83 F2
Umgusa, *Zimbabwe* 83 F2
Umka, *Serbia, Yug.* 21 L10
Umkomaas, *S. Africa* 85 E5
Umm ad Daraj, J., *Jordan* 69 C4
Umm al Qaywayn, *U.A.E.* 65 E7
Umm al Qittayn, *Jordan* 69 C5
Umm Arda, *Sudan* 77 D3
Umm Bāb, *Qatar* 65 E6
Umm Bel, *Sudan* 77 E2
Umm Dubban, *Sudan* 77 D3
Umm el Fahm, *Israel* 69 C4
Umm Koweika, *Sudan* 77 E3
Umm Lajj, *Si. Arabia* 64 E3
Umm Merwa, *Sudan* 76 D3
Umm Ruwaba, *Sudan* 77 E3
Umm Sidr, *Sudan* 77 E2
Ummanz, *Germany* 18 A9
Umnak I., *U.S.A.* 96 C3
Umniati →, *Zimbabwe* 83 F2
Umpqua →, *U.S.A.* 110 E1
Umreth, *India* 62 H5
Umtata, *S. Africa* 85 E4
Umuahia, *Nigeria* 79 D6
Umuarama, *Brazil* 127 A5
Umvukwe Ra., *Zimbabwe* 83 F3
Umzimvubu = Port St. Johns, *S. Africa* 85 E4
Umzingwane →, *Zimbabwe* 83 G2
Umzinto, *S. Africa* 85 E5
Una, *India* 62 J4
Una →, *Bos.-H.* 33 C13
Unac →, *Bos.-H.* 33 D13
Unadilla, *U.S.A.* 107 D9
Unalaska, *U.S.A.* 96 C3
'Unāzah, J., *Asia* 67 F8
Uncastillo, *Spain* 28 C3
Uncía, *Bolivia* 124 D4
Uncompahgre Peak, *U.S.A.* 111 G10
Unden, *Sweden* 11 F8
Underbool, *Australia* 91 F3
Undersaker, *Sweden* 10 A7
Undersvik, *Sweden* 10 C10
Unecha, *Russia* 41 F7
Uneiuxi →, *Brazil* 120 D4
Ungarie, *Australia* 91 E4
Ungarra, *Australia* 91 E2
Ungava B., *Canada* 97 C13
Ungava Pen., *Canada* 97 C12
Ungeny = Ungheni, *Moldova* 41 J4

Unggi, *N. Korea* 51 C16
Ungheni, *Moldova* 41 J4
Ungwatiri, *Sudan* 77 D4
Uni, *Russia* 42 B10
União da Vitória, *Brazil* 127 B5
União dos Palmares, *Brazil* 122 C4
Unije, *Croatia* 33 D11
Unimak I., *U.S.A.* 96 C3
Unini →, *Brazil* 121 D5
Union, *Miss., U.S.A.* 109 J10
Union, *Mo., U.S.A.* 108 F9
Union, *S.C., U.S.A.* 105 H5
Union, Mt., *U.S.A.* 111 J7
Union City, *Calif., U.S.A.* 112 H4
Union City, *N.J., U.S.A.* 107 F10
Union City, *Pa., U.S.A.* 106 E5
Union City, *Tenn., U.S.A.* 109 G10
Union Gap, *U.S.A.* 110 C3
Union Springs, *U.S.A.* 105 J3
Uniondale, *S. Africa* 84 E3
Uniontown, *U.S.A.* 104 F6
Unionville, *U.S.A.* 108 E8
United Arab Emirates ■, *Asia* 65 F7
United Kingdom ■, *Europe* 7 E5
United States of America ■, *N. Amer.* 102 C7
Unity, *Canada* 101 C7
Universales, Mtes., *Spain* 28 E3
Unjha, *India* 62 H5
Unnao, *India* 63 F9
Uno, Ilha, *Guinea-Biss.* 78 C1
Unst, *U.K.* 14 A8
Unstrut →, *Germany* 18 D7
Unter-engadin, *Switz.* 23 C10
Unterägeri, *Switz.* 23 B7
Unterkulm, *Switz.* 22 B6
Unterseen, *Switz.* 22 C5
Unterwaldner Alpen, *Switz.* 23 C6
Unuk →, *Canada* 100 B2
Ünye, *Turkey* 66 B7
Unzha, *Russia* 42 A7
Unzha →, *Russia* 42 B6
Uors, *Switz.* 23 C8
Uozu, *Japan* 49 F8
Upa →, *Czech.* 20 E6
Upata, *Venezuela* 121 B5
Upemba, L., *Zaïre* 83 D2
Upernavik, *Greenland* 4 B5
Upington, *S. Africa* 84 D3
Upleta, *India* 62 J4
Upolu, *W. Samoa* 87 A13
Upper Alkali Lake, *U.S.A.* 110 F3
Upper Arrow L., *Canada* 100 C5
Upper Foster L., *Canada* 101 B7
Upper Hutt, *N.Z.* 87 J5
Upper Klamath L., *U.S.A.* 110 E3
Upper Lake, *U.S.A.* 112 F4
Upper Musquodoboit, *Canada* 99 C7
Upper Red L., *U.S.A.* 108 A7
Upper Sandusky, *U.S.A.* 104 E4
Upper Volta = Burkina Faso ■, *Africa* 78 C4
Upphärad, *Sweden* 11 F6
Uppland, *Sweden* 9 F17
Uppsala, *Sweden* 10 E11
Upshi, *India* 63 C7
Upstart, C., *Australia* 90 B4
Upton, *U.S.A.* 108 C2
Ur, *Iraq* 64 D5
Urabá, G. de, *Colombia* 120 B2
Uracara, *Brazil* 121 D6
Urad Qianqi, *China* 50 D5
Urakawa, *Japan* 48 C11
Ural = Zhayyq →, *Kazakstan* 44 E6
Ural, *Australia* 91 E4
Ural Mts. = Uralskie Gory, *Eurasia* 44 D6
Uralla, *Australia* 91 E5
Uralsk = Oral, *Kazakstan* 42 E10
Uralskie Gory, *Eurasia* 44 D6
Urambo, *Tanzania* 82 D3
Urambo □, *Tanzania* 82 D3
Urandangi, *Australia* 90 C2
Uranium City, *Canada* 101 B7
Uranquinty, *Australia* 91 F4
Uraricaá →, *Brazil* 121 C5
Uraricoera →, *Brazil* 121 C5
Urawa, *Japan* 49 G9
Uray, *Russia* 44 C7
'Uray'irah, *Si. Arabia* 65 E6
Urbana, *Ill., U.S.A.* 104 E1
Urbana, *Ohio, U.S.A.* 104 E4
Urbánia, *Italy* 33 E9
Urbano Santos, *Brazil* 122 B3
Urbel →, *Spain* 28 C1
Urbino, *Italy* 33 E9
Urbión, Picos de, *Spain* 28 C2
Urcos, *Peru* 124 C3
Urda, *Spain* 31 F7
Urdinarrain, *Argentina* 126 C4
Urdos, *France* 26 F3
Urdzhar, *Kazakstan* 44 E9
Ure →, *U.K.* 12 C6
Uren, *Russia* 42 B7
Ures, *Mexico* 114 B2
Urfa = Sanliurfa, *Turkey* 67 D8
Urfahr, *Austria* 21 G4
Urganch, *Uzbekistan* 44 E7
Urgench = Urganch, *Uzbekistan* 44 E7
Uri, *India* 63 B6
Uri □, *Switz.* 23 C7
Uribante →, *Venezuela* 120 B3
Uribe, *Colombia* 120 C3
Uribia, *Colombia* 120 A3
Uriondo, *Bolivia* 126 A3
Urique, *Mexico* 114 B3
Urique →, *Mexico* 114 B3
Urirotstock, *Switz.* 23 C7
Urk, *Neths.* 16 C7
Urla, *Turkey* 66 C2
Urlati, *Romania* 38 E9
Urmia = Orūmīyeh, *Iran* 67 D11
Urmia, L. = Orūmīyeh, Daryācheh-ye, *Iran* 67 D11
Urner Alpen, *Switz.* 23 C7
Uroševac, *Serbia, Yug.* 21 N11
Urrao, *Colombia* 120 B2
Ursus, *Poland* 20 C10
Uruaçu, *Brazil* 123 D2
Uruana, *Brazil* 123 E2
Uruapan, *Mexico* 114 D4
Uruará →, *Brazil* 121 D7
Urubamba, *Peru* 124 C3
Urubamba →, *Peru* 124 C3
Urubaxi →, *Brazil* 121 D5
Urubu →, *Brazil* 121 D6
Uruçara, *Brazil* 121 D6
Uruçuí, *Brazil* 122 C3
Uruçuí, Serra do, *Brazil* 122 C3
Uruçuí Prêto →, *Brazil* 122 C3
Urucuia →, *Brazil* 123 E2
Urucurituba, *Brazil* 121 D6
Uruguai →, *Brazil* 127 B5
Uruguaiana, *Brazil* 126 B4
Uruguay ■, *S. Amer.* 126 C4
Uruguay →, *S. Amer.* 126 C4
Urumchi = Ürümqi, *China* 44 E9
Ürümqi, *China* 44 E9
Urup →, *Russia* 43 H5
Urup, Os., *Russia* 45 E16
Urutaí, *Brazil* 123 E2
Uryupinsk, *Russia* 42 E5
Urzhum, *Russia* 42 B9
Urziceni, *Romania* 38 E9
Uşak, *Turkey* 66 C3
Usakos, *Namibia* 84 C2
Usborne, Mt., *Falk. Is.* 128 D5
Ušće, *Serbia, Yug.* 21 M10
Usedom, *Germany* 18 B9
'Usfān, *Si. Arabia* 76 C4
Ush-Tobe, *Kazakstan* 44 E8
Ushakova, Os., *Russia* 4 A12
Ushant = Ouessant, I. d', *France* 24 D1
Ushashi, *Tanzania* 82 C3
Ushat, *Sudan* 77 F2
Ushibuka, *Japan* 49 H5
Ushuaia, *Argentina* 128 D3
Ushumun, *Russia* 45 D13
Usk →, *U.K.* 13 F5
Üsküdar, *Turkey* 39 H11
Uslar, *Germany* 18 D5
Usman, *Russia* 42 D4
Usoke, *Tanzania* 82 D3
Usolye Sibirskoye, *Russia* 45 D11
Usoro, *Nigeria* 79 D6
Uspallata, P. de, *Argentina* 126 C2
Uspenskiy, *Kazakstan* 44 E8
Usquert, *Neths.* 16 B9
Ussel, *France* 26 C6
Ussuri →, *Asia* 48 A7
Ussuriysk, *Russia* 45 E14
Ussurka, *Russia* 48 B6
Ust-Aldan = Batamay, *Russia* 45 C13
Ust Amginskoye = Khandyga, *Russia* 45 C14
Ust-Bolsheretsk, *Russia* 45 D16
Ust Buzulukskaya, *Russia* 42 E6
Ust Chaun, *Russia* 45 C18
Ust-Donetskiy, *Russia* 43 G5
Ust'-Ilga, *Russia* 45 D11
Ust Ilimpeya = Yukti, *Russia* 45 C11
Ust-Ilimsk, *Russia* 45 D11
Ust Ishim, *Russia* 44 D8
Ust-Kamchatsk, *Russia* 45 D17
Ust-Kamenogorsk = Öskemen, *Kazakstan* 44 E9
Ust-Karenga, *Russia* 45 D12
Ust Khayryuzovo, *Russia* 45 D16
Ust-Kut, *Russia* 45 D11
Ust Kuyga, *Russia* 45 B14
Ust-Labinsk, *Russia* 43 H4
Ust Luga, *Russia* 40 C5
Ust Maya, *Russia* 45 C14
Ust-Mil, *Russia* 45 D14
Ust Muya, *Russia* 45 D12
Ust-Nera, *Russia* 45 C15
Ust-Nyukzha, *Russia* 45 D13
Ust Olenek, *Russia* 45 B12
Ust-Omchug, *Russia* 45 C15
Ust Port, *Russia* 44 C9
Ust Tsilma, *Russia* 44 C6
Ust-Tungir, *Russia* 45 D13
Ust Urt = Ustyurt, Plateau, *Asia* 44 E6
Ust Vorkuta, *Russia* 44 C7
Ustaoset, *Norway* 10 D2
Ustaritz, *France* 26 E2
Uster, *Switz.* 23 B7
Ústí nad Labem, *Czech.* 20 E4
Ústí nad Orlicí, *Czech.* 20 F6
Ustica, *Italy* 34 D6
Ustinov = Izhevsk, *Russia* 44 D6
Ustka, *Poland* 20 A6
Ustrzyki Dolne, *Poland* 20 F12
Ustye, *Russia* 45 D10
Ustyurt, Plateau, *Asia* 44 E6
Ustyuzhna, *Russia* 40 C9
Usu, *China* 54 B3
Usuki, *Japan* 49 H5
Usulután, *El Salv.* 116 D2
Usumacinta →, *Mexico* 115 D6
Usumbura = Bujumbura, *Burundi* 82 C2
Usure, *Tanzania* 82 C3
Uta, *Indonesia* 57 E9
Utah □, *U.S.A.* 110 G8
Utah, L., *U.S.A.* 110 F8
Ute Creek →, *U.S.A.* 109 H3
Utena, *Lithuania* 9 J21
Ütersen, *Germany* 18 B5
Utete, *Tanzania* 82 D4
Uthai Thani, *Thailand* 58 E3
Uthal, *Pakistan* 62 G2
Utiariti, *Brazil* 125 C6
Utica, *N.Y., U.S.A.* 107 C9
Utica, *Ohio, U.S.A.* 106 F2
Utiel, *Spain* 28 F3
Utik L., *Canada* 101 B9
Utikuma L., *Canada* 100 B5
Utinga, *Brazil* 123 D3
Utrecht, *Neths.* 16 D6
Utrecht, *S. Africa* 85 D5
Utrecht □, *Neths.* 16 D6
Utrera, *Spain* 31 H5
Utsjoki, *Finland* 8 B22
Utsunomiya, *Japan* 49 F9
Uttar Pradesh □, *India* 63 F9
Uttaradit, *Thailand* 58 D3
Uttoxeter, *U.K.* 12 E6
Ütze, *Germany* 18 C6
Uummannarsuaq = Farvel, Kap, *Greenland* 4 D5
Uusikaarlepyy, *Finland* 8 E20
Uusikaupunki, *Finland* 9 F19
Uva, *Russia* 42 B11
Uvá →, *Colombia* 120 C3
Uvalde, *U.S.A.* 109 L5
Uvarovo, *Russia* 42 E6
Uvat, *Russia* 44 D7
Uvinza, *Tanzania* 82 D3
Uvira, *Zaïre* 82 C2
Uvs Nuur, *Mongolia* 54 A4
Uwajima, *Japan* 49 H6
Uweinat, Jebel, *Sudan* 76 C1
Uxbridge, *Canada* 106 B5
Uxin Qi, *China* 50 E5
Uxmal, *Mexico* 115 C7
Uyandi, *Russia* 45 C15
Uyo, *Nigeria* 79 D6
Uyuni, *Bolivia* 124 E4
Uzbekistan ■, *Asia* 44 E7
Uzen, Bolshoi →, *Kazakstan* 43 F9
Uzen, Mal →, *Kazakstan* 43 F9
Uzerche, *France* 26 C5
Uzès, *France* 27 D8
Uzh →, *Ukraine* 41 G6
Uzhgorod = Uzhhorod, *Ukraine* 41 H2
Uzhhorod, *Ukraine* 41 H2
Uzlovaya, *Russia* 42 D4
Uzunköprü, *Turkey* 66 B2
Uzwil, *Switz.* 23 B8

V

Vaal →, *S. Africa* 84 D3
Vaal Dam, *S. Africa* 85 D4
Vaals, *Neths.* 17 G8
Vaalwater, *S. Africa* 85 C4
Vaasa, *Finland* 8 E19
Vaassen, *Neths.* 16 D7
Vabre, *France* 26 E6
Vác, *Hungary* 21 H9
Vacaria, *Brazil* 127 B5
Vacaville, *U.S.A.* 112 G5
Vaccarès, Étang de, *France* 27 E8
Vach → = Vakh →, *Russia* 44 C8
Vache, Î.-à-, *Haiti* 117 C5
Vadnagar, *India* 62 H5
Vado Lígure, *Italy* 32 D5
Vadodara, *India* 62 H5
Vadsø, *Norway* 8 A23
Vadstena, *Sweden* 11 F8
Vaduz, *Liech.* 23 B9
Værøy, *Norway* 8 C15
Vágar, *Færoe Is.* 8 E9
Vagney, *France* 25 E13
Vagnhärad, *Sweden* 10 F11
Vagos, *Portugal* 30 E2
Vågsfjorden, *Norway* 8 B17
Váh →, *Slovak Rep.* 21 H8
Vahsel B., *Antarctica* 5 D1
Văi, *Greece* 37 D8
Vaigach, *Russia* 44 B6
Vaiges, *France* 24 D6
Vaihingen, *Germany* 19 G4
Vailly-sur-Aisne, *France* 25 C10
Vaison-la-Romaine, *France* 27 D9
Vakfikebir, *Turkey* 67 B8
Vakh →, *Russia* 44 C8
Vakhtan, *Russia* 42 B8
Val-de-Marne □, *France* 25 D9
Val-d'Oise □, *France* 25 C9
Val d'Or, *Canada* 98 C4
Val Marie, *Canada* 101 D7
Valaam, *Russia* 40 B6
Valadares, *Portugal* 30 D2
Valahia, *Romania* 38 E8
Valais □, *Switz.* 22 D5
Valais, Alpes du, *Switz.* 22 D5
Valandovo, *Macedonia* 39 H5
Valcheta, *Argentina* 128 B3
Valdagno, *Italy* 33 C8
Valdahon, *France* 25 E13
Valday, *Russia* 42 B1
Valdayskaya Vozvyshennost, *Russia* 42 B1
Valdeazogues →, *Spain* 31 G6
Valdemarsvik, *Sweden* 11 F10
Valdepeñas, *Ciudad Real, Spain* 31 G7
Valdepeñas, *Jaén, Spain* 31 H7
Valderaduey →, *Spain* 30 D5
Valderrobres, *Spain* 28 E5
Valdés, Pen., *Argentina* 128 B4
Valdez, *Ecuador* 120 C2
Valdez, *U.S.A.* 96 B5
Valdivia, *Chile* 128 A2
Valdivia, *Colombia* 120 B2
Valdivia □, *Chile* 128 B2
Valdobbiádene, *Italy* 33 C9
Valdosta, *U.S.A.* 105 K4
Valdoviño, *Spain* 30 B2
Valdres, *Norway* 10 D3
Vale, *Georgia* 43 K6
Vale, *U.S.A.* 110 E5
Vale of Glamorgan □, *U.K.* 13 F4
Valea lui Mihai, *Romania* 38 B5
Valença, *Brazil* 123 D4
Valença, *Portugal* 30 C2
Valença do Piauí, *Brazil* 122 C3
Valençay, *France* 25 E8
Valence, *Drôme, France* 27 D8
Valence, *Tarn-et-Garonne, France* 26 D4
Valencia, *Spain* 29 F4
Valencia, *Venezuela* 120 A4
Valencia □, *Spain* 29 F4
Valencia, G. de, *Spain* 29 F5
Valencia de Alcántara, *Spain* 31 F3
Valencia de Don Juan, *Spain* 30 C5
Valencia del Ventoso, *Spain* 31 G4
Valencia Harbour, *Ireland* 15 E1
Valencia I., *Ireland* 15 E1
Valenciennes, *France* 25 B10
Valensole, *France* 27 E9
Valentim, Sa. do, *Brazil* 122 C3
Valentin, *Russia* 48 C7
Valentine, *Nebr., U.S.A.* 108 D4
Valentine, *Tex., U.S.A.* 109 K2
Valenza, *Italy* 32 C5
Valera, *Venezuela* 120 B3
Valga, *Estonia* 9 H22
Valguarnera Caropepe, *Italy* 35 E7
Valier, *U.S.A.* 110 B7
Valinco, G. de, *France* 27 G12
Valjevo, *Serbia, Yug.* 21 L9
Valka, *Latvia* 9 H21
Valkeakoski, *Finland* 9 F20
Valkenburg, *Neths.* 17 G7
Valkenswaard, *Neths.* 17 F6
Vall de Uxó, *Spain* 28 F4
Valla, *Sweden* 10 E10
Valladolid, *Mexico* 115 C7
Valladolid, *Spain* 30 D6
Valladolid □, *Spain* 30 D6
Vallata, *Italy* 35 A8
Valldemosa, *Spain* 36 B9
Valle d'Aosta □, *Italy* 32 C4
Valle de Arán, *Spain* 28 C5
Valle de Cabuérniga, *Spain* 30 B6
Valle de la Pascua, *Venezuela* 120 B4
Valle de las Palmas, *Mexico* 113 N10
Valle de Santiago, *Mexico* 114 C4
Valle de Suchil, *Mexico* 114 C4
Valle de Zaragoza, *Mexico* 114 B3
Valle del Cauca □, *Colombia* 120 C2
Valle Fértil, Sierra del, *Argentina* 126 C2
Valle Hermoso, *Mexico* 115 B5
Vallecas, *Spain* 30 E7
Valledupar, *Colombia* 120 A3
Vallehermoso, *Canary Is.* 36 F2
Vallejo, *U.S.A.* 112 G4
Vallenar, *Chile* 126 B1
Valleraugue, *France* 26 D7
Vallet, *France* 24 E5
Valletta, *Malta* 37 D2
Valley Center, *U.S.A.* 113 M9
Valley City, *U.S.A.* 108 B6
Valley Falls, *U.S.A.* 110 E3
Valley Springs, *U.S.A.* 112 G6
Valley Wells, *U.S.A.* 113 K11
Valleyview, *Canada* 100 B5
Valli di Comácchio, *Italy* 33 D9
Vallimanca, Arroyo, *Argentina* 126 D4
Vallo della Lucánia, *Italy* 35 B8
Vallon-Pont-d'Arc, *France* 27 D8
Vallorbe, *Switz.* 22 C2
Valls, *Spain* 28 D6
Vallsta, *Sweden* 10 C10
Valmaseda, *Spain* 28 B1
Valmiera, *Latvia* 9 H21
Valmont, *France* 24 C7
Valmontone, *Italy* 34 A5
Valmy, *France* 25 C11
Valnera, Mte., *Spain* 28 B1
Valognes, *France* 24 C5
Valona = Vlóra, *Albania* 39 J2
Valongo, *Portugal* 30 D2
Valozhyn, *Belarus* 40 E4
Valpaços, *Portugal* 30 D3
Valparaíso, *Chile* 126 C1
Valparaíso, *Mexico* 114 C4
Valparaiso, *U.S.A.* 104 E2
Valparaíso □, *Chile* 126 C1
Valpovo, *Croatia* 21 K8
Valréas, *France* 27 D8
Vals, *Switz.* 23 C8
Vals →, *S. Africa* 84 D4
Vals, Tanjung, *Indonesia* 57 F9
Vals-les-Bains, *France* 27 D8
Valsad, *India* 60 J8
Valskog, *Sweden* 10 E9
Válta, *Greece* 39 J6
Valtellina, *Italy* 32 B6
Valuyki, *Russia* 42 E4
Valverde, *Canary Is.* 36 G2
Valverde del Camino, *Spain* 31 H4
Valverde del Fresno, *Spain* 30 E4
Vama, *Romania* 38 B8
Vammala, *Finland* 9 F20
Vámos, *Greece* 37 D6
Van, *Turkey* 67 C10
Van, L. = Van Gölü, *Turkey* 67 C10
Van Alstyne, *U.S.A.* 109 J6
Van Bruyssel, *Canada* 99 C5
Van Buren, *Canada* 99 C6
Van Buren, *Ark., U.S.A.* 109 H7
Van Buren, *Maine, U.S.A.* 105 B11
Van Buren, *Mo., U.S.A.* 109 G9
Van Canh, *Vietnam* 58 F7
Van Diemen, C., *N. Terr., Australia* 88 B5
Van Diemen, C., *Queens., Australia* 90 B2
Van Diemen G., *Australia* 88 B5
Van Gölü, *Turkey* 67 C10
Van Horn, *U.S.A.* 109 K2
Van Ninh, *Vietnam* 58 F7
Van Rees, Pegunungan, *Indonesia* 57 E9
Van Tassell, *U.S.A.* 108 D2
Van Wert, *U.S.A.* 104 E3
Van Yen, *Vietnam* 58 B5
Vanadzor, *Armenia* 43 K7
Vanavara, *Russia* 45 C11
Vancouver, *Canada* 100 D4
Vancouver, *U.S.A.* 112 E4
Vancouver, C., *Australia* 89 G2
Vancouver I., *Canada* 100 D3
Vandalia, *Ill., U.S.A.* 108 F10
Vandalia, *Mo., U.S.A.* 108 F9
Vandenburg, *U.S.A.* 113 L6
Vanderbijlpark, *S. Africa* 85 D4
Vandergrift, *U.S.A.* 106 F5
Vanderhoof, *Canada* 100 C4
Vanderkloof Dam, *S. Africa* 84 E3
Vanderlin I., *Australia* 90 B2
Vandyke, *Australia* 90 C4
Vänern, *Sweden* 11 F7
Vänersborg, *Sweden* 11 F6
Vang Vieng, *Laos* 58 C4
Vanga, *Kenya* 82 C4
Vangaindrano, *Madag.* 85 C8
Vanguard, *Canada* 101 D7
Vanier, *Canada* 98 C4
Vankleek Hill, *Canada* 98 C5
Vanna, *Norway* 8 A18
Vännäs, *Sweden* 8 E18
Vannes, *France* 24 E4
Vanoise, Massif de la, *France* 27 C10
Vanrhynsdorp, *S. Africa* 84 E2
Vanrook, *Australia* 90 B3
Vansbro, *Sweden* 9 F16
Vansittart B., *Australia* 88 B4
Vantaa, *Finland* 9 F21
Vanthli, *India* 62 J4
Vanua Levu, *Fiji* 87 C8
Vanua Mbalavu, *Fiji* 87 C9
Vanuatu ■, *Pac. Oc.* 92 J8
Vanwyksvlei, *S. Africa* 84 E3
Vanzylsrus, *S. Africa* 84 D3
Vapnyarka, *Ukraine* 41 H5
Var □, *France* 27 E10
Var →, *France* 27 E11
Vara, *Sweden* 11 F6
Varades, *France* 24 E5
Varáita →, *Italy* 32 D4
Varallo, *Italy* 32 C5
Varanasi, *India* 63 G10
Varanger-halvøya, *Norway* 8 A23
Varangerfjorden, *Norway* 8 A23
Varaždin, *Croatia* 33 B13
Varazze, *Italy* 32 D5
Varberg, *Sweden* 11 G6
Vardar = Axiós →, *Greece* 39 J5
Varde, *Denmark* 11 J2
Varde Å →, *Denmark* 11 J2
Vardø, *Norway* 8 A24
Varel, *Germany* 18 B4
Varella, Mui, *Vietnam* 58 F7
Varėna, *Lithuania* 9 J21
Varennes-sur-Allier, *France* 26 B7
Vareš, *Bos.-H.* 21 L8
Varese, *Italy* 32 C5
Varese Lígure, *Italy* 32 D6
Vårgårda, *Sweden* 11 F6
Vargem Bonita, *Brazil* 123 F2
Vargem Grande, *Brazil* 122 B3
Varginha, *Brazil* 127 A6

Vargön, *Sweden* 11 F6
Variadero, *U.S.A.* 109 H2
Varillas, *Chile* 126 A1
Väring, *Sweden* 11 F8
Varkaus, *Finland* 9 E22
Varna, *Bulgaria* 38 F10
Värnamo, *Sweden* 9 H16
Värö, *Sweden* 11 G6
Vars, *Canada* 107 A9
Varsseveld, *Neths.* 16 E8
Varto, *Turkey* 67 C9
Varvarin, *Serbia, Yug.* 21 M11
Varzaneh, *Iran* 65 C7
Várzea Alegre, *Brazil* 122 C4
Várzea da Palma, *Brazil* 123 E3
Várzea Grande, *Brazil* 125 D6
Varzi, *Italy* 32 D6
Varzo, *Italy* 32 B5
Varzy, *France* 25 E10
Vasa Barris →, *Brazil* 122 D4
Vascão →, *Portugal* 31 H3
Vaşcău, *Romania* 38 C5
Vascongadas = País Vasco □, *Spain* 28 C2
Vasht = Khāsh, *Iran* 60 E2
Vasilevichi, *Belarus* 41 F5
Vasilikón, *Greece* 39 L6
Vasilkov = Vasylkiv, *Ukraine* 41 G6
Vaslui, *Romania* 38 C10
Vassar, *Canada* 101 D9
Vassar, *U.S.A.* 104 D4
Västerås, *Sweden* 10 E10
Västerbotten, *Sweden* 8 D18
Västerdalälven →, *Sweden* 9 F16
Västernorrlands län □, *Sweden* 10 A11
Västervik, *Sweden* 9 H17
Västmanland, *Sweden* 9 G16
Vasto, *Italy* 33 F11
Vasvár, *Hungary* 21 H6
Vasylkiv, *Ukraine* 41 G6
Vatan, *France* 25 E8
Vathí, *Greece* 39 M10
Váthia, *Greece* 39 N5
Vatican City ■, *Europe* 33 G9
Vaticano, C., *Italy* 35 D8
Vatili, *Cyprus* 37 D12
Vatnajökull, *Iceland* 8 D5
Vatnås, *Norway* 10 E3
Vatoa, *Fiji* 87 D9
Vatólakkos, *Greece* 37 D5
Vatoloha, *Madag.* 85 B8
Vatomandry, *Madag.* 85 B8
Vatra-Dornei, *Romania* 38 B8
Vättern, *Sweden* 11 F8
Vättis, *Switz.* 23 C8
Vaucluse □, *France* 27 E9
Vaucouleurs, *France* 25 D12
Vaud □, *Switz.* 22 C2
Vaughn, *Mont., U.S.A.* 110 C8
Vaughn, *N. Mex., U.S.A.* 111 J11
Vaulruz, *Switz.* 22 C3
Vaupés = Uaupés →, *Brazil* 120 C4
Vaupes □, *Colombia* 120 C3
Vauvert, *France* 27 E8
Vauxhall, *Canada* 100 C6
Vava'u, *Tonga* 87 D11
Vavoua, *Ivory C.* 78 D3
Vawkavysk, *Belarus* 41 F3
Vaxholm, *Sweden* 10 E12
Växjö, *Sweden* 9 H16
Vaygach, Ostrov, *Russia* 44 C6
Váyia, Ákra, *Greece* 37 C10
Veadeiros, *Brazil* 123 D2
Vechta, *Germany* 18 C4
Vechte →, *Neths.* 16 C8
Vecsés, *Hungary* 21 H9
Veddige, *Sweden* 11 G6
Vedea →, *Romania* 38 F8
Vedia, *Argentina* 126 C3
Vedra, I. del, *Spain* 36 C7
Vedrin, *Belgium* 17 G5
Veendam, *Neths.* 16 B9
Veenendaal, *Neths.* 16 D7
Veerle, *Belgium* 17 F5
Vefsna →, *Norway* 8 D15
Vega, *Norway* 8 D14
Vega, *U.S.A.* 109 H3
Vegadeo, *Spain* 30 B3
Veghel, *Neths.* 17 E7
Vegorritis, Límni, *Greece* 39 J4
Vegreville, *Canada* 100 C6
Vegusdal, *Norway* 11 F2
Veii, *Italy* 33 F9
Vejen, *Denmark* 11 J3
Vejer de la Frontera, *Spain* 31 J5
Vejle, *Denmark* 11 J3
Vejle Fjord, *Denmark* 11 J3
Vela Luka, *Croatia* 33 F13
Velas, C., *Costa Rica* 116 D2
Velasco, Sierra de, *Argentina* 126 B2
Velay, Mts. du, *France* 26 D7
Velddrif, *S. Africa* 84 E2
Veldegem, *Belgium* 17 F2
Velden, *Neths.* 17 F8
Veldhoven, *Neths.* 17 F6
Velebit Planina, *Croatia* 33 D12
Velebitski Kanal, *Croatia* 33 D11
Veleka →, *Bulgaria* 38 G10
Velenje, *Slovenia* 33 B12
Velestínon, *Greece* 39 K5
Vélez, *Colombia* 120 B3
Vélez Blanco, *Spain* 29 H2
Vélez Málaga, *Spain* 31 J6
Vélez Rubio, *Spain* 29 H2
Velhas →, *Brazil* 123 E3
Velika, *Croatia* 21 K7
Velika Gorica, *Croatia* 33 C13
Velika Kapela, *Croatia* 33 C12
Velika Kladuša, *Bos.-H.* 33 C12
Velika Morava →, *Serbia, Yug.* 21 L11
Velikaya →, *Russia* 40 D5
Velikaya Kema, *Russia* 48 B8
Velikaya Lepetikha, *Ukraine* 41 J7
Velike Lašče, *Slovenia* 33 C11
Velikiye Luki, *Russia* 40 D6
Veliko Tŭrnovo, *Bulgaria* 38 F8
Velikonda Range, *India* 60 M11
Velingrad, *Bulgaria* 39 G6
Velino, Mte., *Italy* 33 F10
Velizh, *Russia* 40 E6
Velke Meziřici, *Czech.* 20 F6
Velletri, *Italy* 34 A5
Vellinge, *Sweden* 11 J7
Vellore, *India* 60 N11
Velp, *Neths.* 16 D7
Velsen-Noord, *Neths.* 16 D5
Velsk, *Russia* 40 B11
Velten, *Germany* 18 C9
Veluwe Meer, *Neths.* 16 D7
Velva, *U.S.A.* 108 A4
Veme, *Norway* 10 D4
Ven, *Sweden* 11 J6
Venaco, *France* 27 F13
Venado Tuerto, *Argentina* 126 C3
Venafro, *Italy* 35 A7
Venarey-les-Laumes, *France* 25 E11
Venaria, *Italy* 32 C4
Venčane, *Serbia, Yug.* 21 L10
Vence, *France* 27 E11
Vendas Novas, *Portugal* 31 G2
Vendée □, *France* 24 F5
Vendée →, *France* 24 F5
Vendéen, Bocage, *France* 26 B2
Vendeuvre-sur-Barse, *France* 25 D11
Vendôme, *France* 24 E8
Vendrell, *Spain* 28 D6
Vendsyssel, *Denmark* 11 G4
Véneta, L., *Italy* 33 C9
Véneto □, *Italy* 33 C8
Venev, *Russia* 42 C4
Venézia, *Italy* 33 C9
Venézia, G. di, *Italy* 33 C10
Venezuela ■, *S. Amer.* 120 B4
Venezuela, G. de, *Venezuela* 120 A3
Vengurla, *India* 60 M8
Venice = Venézia, *Italy* 33 C9
Venkatapuram, *India* 61 K12
Venlo, *Neths.* 17 F8
Vennesla, *Norway* 9 G12
Venraij, *Neths.* 17 E7
Venta de Cardeña, *Spain* 31 G6
Venta de San Rafael, *Spain* 30 E6
Ventana, Punta de la, *Mexico* 114 C3
Ventana, Sa. de la, *Argentina* 126 D3
Ventersburg, *S. Africa* 84 D4
Venterstad, *S. Africa* 84 E4
Ventimíglia, *Italy* 32 E4
Ventnor, *U.K.* 13 G6
Ventotene, *Italy* 34 B6
Ventoux, Mt., *France* 27 D9
Ventspils, *Latvia* 9 H19
Venturí →, *Venezuela* 120 C4
Ventucopa, *U.S.A.* 113 L7
Ventura, *U.S.A.* 113 L7
Venus B., *Australia* 91 F4
Veøy, *Norway* 10 B1
Vera, *Argentina* 126 B3
Vera, *Spain* 29 H3
Veracruz, *Mexico* 115 D5
Veracruz □, *Mexico* 115 D5
Veraval, *India* 62 J4
Verbánia, *Italy* 32 C5
Verbicaro, *Italy* 35 C8
Verbier, *Switz.* 22 D4
Vercelli, *Italy* 32 C5
Verchovchevo, *Ukraine* 41 H8
Verdalsøra, *Norway* 8 E14
Verde →, *Argentina* 128 B3
Verde →, *Goiás, Brazil* 123 E1
Verde →, *Goiás, Brazil* 123 E1
Verde →, *Mato Grosso, Brazil* 125 C6
Verde →, *Mato Grosso do Sul, Brazil* 125 E7
Verde →, *Chihuahua, Mexico* 114 B3
Verde →, *Oaxaca, Mexico* 115 D5
Verde →, *Veracruz, Mexico* 114 C4
Verde →, *Paraguay* 126 A4
Verde, Cay, *Bahamas* 116 B4
Verde Grande →, *Brazil* 123 E3
Verde Island Pass, *Phil.* 55 E4
Verde Pequeno →, *Brazil* 123 D3
Verden, *Germany* 18 C5
Verdi, *U.S.A.* 112 F7
Verdigre, *U.S.A.* 108 D5
Verdon →, *France* 27 E9
Verdun, *France* 25 C12
Verdun-sur-le-Doubs, *France* 25 F12
Vereeniging, *S. Africa* 85 D4
Vérendrye, Parc Prov. de la, *Canada* 98 C4
Verga, C., *Guinea* 78 C2
Vergato, *Italy* 32 D8
Vergemont, *Australia* 90 C3
Vergemont Cr. →, *Australia* 90 C3
Vergennes, *U.S.A.* 107 B11
Vergt, *France* 26 C4
Verín, *Spain* 30 D3
Veriña, *Spain* 30 B5
Verkhnedvinsk = Vyerkhnyadzvinsk, *Belarus* 40 E4
Verkhnevilyuysk, *Russia* 45 C13
Verkhneye Kalinino, *Russia* 45 D11
Verkhniy Baskunchak, *Russia* 43 F8
Verkhnyaya Amga, *Russia* 45 D13
Verkhovye, *Russia* 42 D3
Verkhoyansk, *Russia* 45 C14
Verkhoyansk Ra. = Verkhoyanskiy Khrebet, *Russia* 45 C13
Verkhoyanskiy Khrebet, *Russia* 45 C13
Verlo, *Canada* 101 C7
Verma, *Norway* 10 B2
Vermenton, *France* 25 E10
Vermilion, *Canada* 101 C6
Vermilion →, *Alta., Canada* 101 C6
Vermilion →, *Qué., Canada* 98 C5
Vermilion, B., *U.S.A.* 109 L9
Vermilion Bay, *Canada* 101 D10
Vermilion Chutes, *Canada* 100 B6
Vermilion L., *U.S.A.* 108 B8
Vermillion, *U.S.A.* 108 D6
Vermont □, *U.S.A.* 107 C12
Vernal, *U.S.A.* 110 F9
Vernalis, *U.S.A.* 112 H5
Vernayaz, *Switz.* 22 D4
Verner, *Canada* 98 C3
Verneuil-sur-Avre, *France* 24 D7
Verneukpan, *S. Africa* 84 D3
Vernier, *Switz.* 22 D2
Vernon, *Canada* 100 C5
Vernon, *France* 24 C8
Vernon, *U.S.A.* 109 H5
Vernonia, *U.S.A.* 112 E3
Vero Beach, *U.S.A.* 105 M5
Véroia, *Greece* 39 J5
Verolanuova, *Italy* 32 C7
Véroli, *Italy* 34 A6
Verona, *Italy* 32 C8
Versailles, *France* 25 D9
Versalles, *Bolivia* 125 C5
Versoix, *Switz.* 22 D2
Vert, C., *Senegal* 78 C1
Vertou, *France* 24 E5
Vertus, *France* 25 D11
Verulam, *S. Africa* 85 D5
Verviers, *Belgium* 17 G7
Vervins, *France* 25 C10
Verzej, *Slovenia* 33 B13
Vescavoto, *France* 27 F13
Vesdre →, *Belgium* 17 G7
Veselí nad Lužnicí, *Czech.* 20 F4
Veselovskoye Vdkhr., *Russia* 43 G5
Veshenskaya, *Russia* 42 F5
Vesle →, *France* 25 C10
Vesoul, *France* 25 E13
Vessigebro, *Sweden* 11 H6
Vester Torup, *Denmark* 11 G3
Vesterålen, *Norway* 8 B16
Vestersche Veld, *Neths.* 16 C8
Vestfjorden, *Norway* 8 C15
Vestmannaeyjar, *Iceland* 8 E3
Vestmarka, *Norway* 10 E5
Vestone, *Italy* 32 C7
Vestsjællands Amtskommune □, *Denmark* 11 J5
Vestspitsbergen, *Svalbard* 4 B8
Vestvågøy, *Norway* 8 B15
Vesuvio, *Italy* 35 B7
Vesuvius, Mt. = Vesuvio, *Italy* 35 B7
Vesyegonsk, *Russia* 40 C9
Veszprém, *Hungary* 21 H7
Vésztő, *Hungary* 21 J11
Vetlanda, *Sweden* 9 H16
Vetluga, *Russia* 42 B7
Vetlugu →, *Russia* 42 B8
Vetluzhskiy, *Russia* 42 B7
Vetluzhskiy, *Russia* 42 A7
Vetovo, *Bulgaria* 38 F9
Vetralia, *Italy* 33 F9
Vettore, Mte., *Italy* 33 F10
Veurne, *Belgium* 17 F1
Vevey, *Switz.* 22 D3
Veynes, *France* 27 D9
Veys, *Iran* 65 D6
Vézelise, *France* 25 D13
Vézère →, *France* 26 D4
Vezirköprü, *Turkey* 66 B6
Vi Thanh, *Vietnam* 59 H5
Viacha, *Bolivia* 124 D4
Viadana, *Italy* 32 D7
Viamão, *Brazil* 127 C5
Viana, *Brazil* 122 B3
Viana, *Spain* 28 C2
Viana del Bollo, *Spain* 30 C3
Viana do Alentejo, *Portugal* 31 G3
Viana do Castelo, *Portugal* 30 D2
Vianden, *Belgium* 17 J8
Vianen, *Neths.* 16 E6
Vianna do Castelo □, *Portugal* 30 D2
Vianópolis, *Brazil* 123 E2
Viar →, *Spain* 31 H5
Viaréggio, *Italy* 32 E7
Viaur →, *France* 26 D5
Vibank, *Canada* 101 C8
Vibo Valéntia, *Italy* 35 D9
Viborg, *Denmark* 11 H3
Vibraye, *France* 24 D7
Vic, Étang de, *France* 26 E7
Vic-en-Bigorre, *France* 26 E4
Vic-Fézensac, *France* 26 E4
Vic-sur-Cère, *France* 26 D6
Vicenza, *Italy* 33 C8
Vich, *Spain* 28 D7
Vichada □, *Colombia* 120 C4
Vichada →, *Colombia* 120 C4
Vichuga, *Russia* 42 B5
Vichy, *France* 26 B7
Vicksburg, *Ariz., U.S.A.* 113 M13
Vicksburg, *Mich., U.S.A.* 104 D3
Vicksburg, *Miss., U.S.A.* 109 J9
Vico, L. di, *Italy* 33 F9
Vico del Gargano, *Italy* 35 A8
Viçosa, *Brazil* 122 C4
Viçosa do Ceará, *Brazil* 122 B3
Vicosoprano, *Switz.* 23 D9
Victor, *India* 62 J4
Victor, *Colo., U.S.A.* 108 F2
Victor, *N.Y., U.S.A.* 106 D7
Victor Harbor, *Australia* 91 F2
Victoria, *Argentina* 126 C3
Victoria, *Canada* 100 D4
Victoria, *Chile* 128 A2
Victoria, *Guinea* 78 C2
Victoria, *Malaysia* 56 C5
Victoria, *Malta* 37 C1
Victoria, *Phil.* 55 D4
Victoria, *Kans., U.S.A.* 108 F5
Victoria, *Tex., U.S.A.* 109 L6
Victoria □, *Australia* 91 F3
Victoria →, *Australia* 88 C4
Victoria, Grand L., *Canada* 98 C4
Victoria, L., *Africa* 82 C3
Victoria, L., *Australia* 91 E3
Victoria Beach, *Canada* 101 C9
Victoria de Durango, *Mexico* 114 C4
Victoria de las Tunas, *Cuba* 116 B4
Victoria Falls, *Zimbabwe* 83 F2
Victoria Harbour, *Canada* 98 D4
Victoria I., *Canada* 96 A8
Victoria Ld., *Antarctica* 5 D11
Victoria Nile →, *Uganda* 82 B3
Victoria Res., *Canada* 99 C8
Victoria River Downs, *Australia* 88 C5
Victoria Taungdeik, *Burma* 61 J18
Victoria West, *S. Africa* 84 E3
Victorias, *Phil.* 55 F5
Victoriaville, *Canada* 99 C5
Victorica, *Argentina* 126 D2
Victorville, *U.S.A.* 113 L9
Vicuña, *Chile* 126 C1
Vicuña Mackenna, *Argentina* 126 C3
Vidal, *U.S.A.* 113 L12
Vidal Junction, *U.S.A.* 113 L12
Vidalia, *U.S.A.* 105 J4
Vidauban, *France* 27 E10
Vídho, *Greece* 37 A3
Vidigueira, *Portugal* 31 G3
Vidin, *Bulgaria* 38 F5
Vidio, C., *Spain* 30 B4
Vidisha, *India* 62 H7
Vidzy, *Belarus* 9 J22
Viechtach, *Germany* 19 F8
Viedma, *Argentina* 128 B4
Viedma, L., *Argentina* 128 C2
Vieira, *Portugal* 30 D2
Viella, *Spain* 28 C5
Vielsalm, *Belgium* 17 H7
Vienenburg, *Germany* 18 D6
Vieng Pou Kha, *Laos* 58 B3
Vienna = Wien, *Austria* 21 G6
Vienna, *U.S.A.* 109 G10
Vienne, *France* 27 C8
Vienne □, *France* 26 B4
Vienne →, *France* 24 E7
Vientiane, *Laos* 58 D4
Vientos, Paso de los, *Caribbean* 117 C5
Vierlingsbeek, *Neths.* 17 E8
Viersen, *Germany* 18 D2
Vierwaldstättersee, *Switz.* 23 C7
Vierzon, *France* 25 E9
Vieste, *Italy* 35 A9
Vietnam ■, *Asia* 58 C5
Vieux-Boucau-les-Bains, *France* 26 E2
Vif, *France* 27 C9
Vigan, *Phil.* 55 C4
Vigévano, *Italy* 32 C5
Vigia, *Brazil* 122 B2
Vigía Chico, *Mexico* 115 D7
Víglas, Ákra, *Greece* 37 D9
Vignemale, Pic du, *France* 26 F3
Vigneulles-lès-Hattonchâtel, *France* 25 D12
Vignola, *Italy* 32 D8
Vigo, *Spain* 30 C2
Vigo, Ría de, *Spain* 30 C2
Vihiers, *France* 24 E6
Vijayawada, *India* 61 L12
Vijfhuizen, *Neths.* 16 D5
Vík, *Iceland* 8 E4
Vikeke, *Indonesia* 57 F7
Viken, *Sweden* 11 F8
Viking, *Canada* 100 C6
Vikna, *Norway* 8 D14
Viksjö, *Sweden* 10 B11
Vikulovo, *Russia* 44 D8
Vila da Maganja, *Mozam.* 83 F4
Vila de João Belo = Xai-Xai, *Mozam.* 85 D5
Vila de Rei, *Portugal* 31 F2
Vila do Bispo, *Portugal* 31 H2
Vila do Chibuto, *Mozam.* 85 C5
Vila do Conde, *Portugal* 30 D2
Vila Franca de Xira, *Portugal* 31 G2
Vila Gamito, *Mozam.* 83 E3
Vila Gomes da Costa, *Mozam.* 85 C5
Vila Machado, *Mozam.* 83 F3
Vila Mouzinho, *Mozam.* 83 E3
Vila Nova de Foscôa, *Portugal* 30 D3
Vila Nova de Ourém, *Portugal* 31 F2
Vila Novo de Gaia, *Portugal* 30 D2
Vila Pouca de Aguiar, *Portugal* 30 D3
Vila Real, *Portugal* 30 D3
Vila Real de Santo António, *Portugal* 31 H3
Vila Vasco da Gama, *Mozam.* 83 E3
Vila Velha, *Amapá, Brazil* 121 C7
Vila Velha, *Espírito Santo, Brazil* 123 F3
Vila Viçosa, *Portugal* 31 G3
Vilaboa, *Spain* 30 C2
Vilaine →, *France* 24 E4
Vilanandro, Tanjona, *Madag.* 85 B7
Vilanculos, *Mozam.* 85 C6
Vilar Formosa, *Portugal* 30 E4
Vilareal □, *Portugal* 30 D3
Vilaseca-Salou, *Spain* 28 D6
Vilcabamba, Cordillera, *Peru* 124 C3
Vilcanchos, *Peru* 124 C3
Vileyka, *Belarus* 40 E4
Vilhelmina, *Sweden* 8 D17
Vilhena, *Brazil* 125 C5
Viliga, *Russia* 45 C16
Viliya →, *Lithuania* 9 J21
Viljandi, *Estonia* 9 G21
Vilkitskogo, Proliv, *Russia* 45 B11
Vilkovo = Vylkove, *Ukraine* 41 K5
Villa Abecia, *Bolivia* 126 A2
Villa Ahumada, *Mexico* 114 A3
Villa Ana, *Argentina* 126 B4
Villa Ángela, *Argentina* 126 B3
Villa Bella, *Bolivia* 125 C4
Villa Bens = Tarfaya, *Morocco* 74 C2
Villa Cañás, *Argentina* 126 C3
Villa Carlos, *Spain* 36 B11
Villa Cisneros = Dakhla, *W. Sahara* 74 D1
Villa Colón, *Argentina* 126 C2
Villa Constitución, *Argentina* 126 C3
Villa de Cura, *Venezuela* 120 A4
Villa de María, *Argentina* 126 B3
Villa del Rosario, *Venezuela* 120 A3
Villa Dolores, *Argentina* 126 C2
Villa Frontera, *Mexico* 114 B4
Villa Guillermina, *Argentina* 126 B4
Villa Hayes, *Paraguay* 126 B4
Villa Iris, *Argentina* 126 D3
Villa Juárez, *Mexico* 114 B4
Villa María, *Argentina* 126 C3
Villa Mazán, *Argentina* 126 B2
Villa Minozzo, *Italy* 32 D7
Villa Montes, *Bolivia* 126 A3
Villa Ocampo, *Argentina* 126 B4
Villa Ocampo, *Mexico* 114 B3
Villa Ojo de Agua, *Argentina* 126 B3
Villa San Giovanni, *Italy* 35 D8
Villa San José, *Argentina* 126 C4
Villa San Martín, *Argentina* 126 B3
Villa Santina, *Italy* 33 B9
Villa Unión, *Mexico* 114 C3
Villablino, *Spain* 30 C4
Villacañas, *Spain* 28 F1
Villacarriedo, *Spain* 28 B1
Villacarrillo, *Spain* 29 G1
Villacastín, *Spain* 30 E6
Villach, *Austria* 21 J3
Villacidro, *Italy* 34 C1
Villada, *Spain* 30 C6
Villadiego, *Spain* 30 C6
Villadóssola, *Italy* 32 B5
Villafeliche, *Spain* 28 D3
Villafranca, *Spain* 28 C3
Villafranca de los Barros, *Spain* 31 G4
Villafranca de los Caballeros, *Baleares, Spain* 36 B10
Villafranca de los Caballeros, *Toledo, Spain* 29 F1

Villafranca del Bierzo, *Spain* 30 C4
Villafranca del Cid, *Spain* 28 E4
Villafranca del Panadés, *Spain* 28 D6
Villafranca di Verona, *Italy* 32 C7
Villagarcía de Arosa, *Spain* 30 C2
Villagrán, *Mexico* 115 C5
Villaguay, *Argentina* 126 C4
Villaharta, *Spain* 31 G6
Villahermosa, *Mexico* 115 D6
Villahermosa, *Spain* 29 G2
Villaines-la-Juhel, *France* 24 D6
Villajoyosa, *Spain* 29 G4
Villalba, *Spain* 30 B3
Villalba de Guardo, *Spain* 30 C6
Villalcampo, Pantano de, *Spain* 30 D4
Villalón de Campos, *Spain* 30 C5
Villalpando, *Spain* 30 D5
Villaluenga, *Spain* 30 E7
Villamanán, *Spain* 30 C5
Villamartín, *Spain* 31 J5
Villamayor, *Spain* 28 F2
Villamblard, *France* 26 C4
Villanova Monteleone, *Italy* 34 B1
Villanueva, *Colombia* 120 A3
Villanueva, *U.S.A.* 111 J11
Villanueva de Castellón, *Spain* 29 F4
Villanueva de Córdoba, *Spain* 31 G6
Villanueva de la Fuente, *Spain* 29 G2
Villanueva de la Serena, *Spain* 31 G5
Villanueva de la Sierra, *Spain* 30 E4
Villanueva de los Castillejos, *Spain* 31 H3
Villanueva del Arzobispo, *Spain* 29 G1
Villanueva del Duque, *Spain* 31 G5
Villanueva del Fresno, *Spain* 31 G3
Villanueva y Geltrú, *Spain* 28 D6
Villaodrid, *Spain* 30 B3
Villaputzu, *Italy* 34 C2
Villar del Arzobispo, *Spain* 28 F4
Villar del Rey, *Spain* 31 F4
Villarcayo, *Spain* 28 C1
Villard-Bonnot, *France* 27 C9
Villard-de-Lans, *France* 27 C9
Villarino de los Aires, *Spain* 30 D4
Villarosa, *Italy* 35 E7
Villarramiel, *Spain* 30 C6
Villarreal, *Spain* 28 F4
Villarrica, *Chile* 128 A2
Villarrica, *Paraguay* 126 B4
Villarrobledo, *Spain* 29 F2
Villarroya de la Sierra, *Spain* 28 D3
Villarrubia de los Ojos, *Spain* 29 F1
Villars-les-Dombes, *France* 27 B9
Villarta de San Juan, *Spain* 29 F1
Villasayas, *Spain* 28 D2
Villaseca de los Gamitos, *Spain* 30 D4
Villastar, *Spain* 28 E3
Villatobas, *Spain* 28 F1
Villavicencio, *Argentina* 126 C2
Villavicencio, *Colombia* 120 C3
Villaviciosa, *Spain* 30 B5
Villazón, *Bolivia* 126 A2
Ville-Marie, *Canada* 98 C4
Ville Platte, *U.S.A.* 109 K8
Villedieu-les-Poêlles, *France* 24 D5
Villefort, *France* 26 D7
Villefranche-de-Lauragais, *France* 26 E5
Villefranche-de-Rouergue, *France* 26 D6
Villefranche-du-Périgord, *France* 26 D5
Villefranche-sur-Cher, *France* 25 E8
Villefranche-sur-Saône, *France* 27 C8
Villegrande, *Bolivia* 125 D5
Villel, *Spain* 28 E3
Villemaur-sur-Vanne, *France* 25 D10
Villemur-sur-Tarn, *France* 26 E5
Villena, *Spain* 29 G4
Villenauxe-la-Grande, *France* 25 D10
Villenave-d'Ornon, *France* 26 D3
Villeneuve, *Italy* 32 C4
Villeneuve, *Switz.* 22 D3
Villeneuve-l'Archevêque, *France* 25 D10
Villeneuve-lès-Avignon, *France* 27 E8
Villeneuve-St.-Georges, *France* 25 D9
Villeneuve-sur-Allier, *France* 26 B7
Villeneuve-sur-Lot, *France* 26 D4
Villeréal, *France* 26 D4
Villers-Bocage, *France* 24 C6
Villers-Bretonneux, *France* 25 C9
Villers-Cotterêts, *France* 25 C10
Villers-le-Bouillet, *Belgium* 17 G6
Villers-le-Gambon, *Belgium* 17 H5
Villers-sur-Mer, *France* 24 C6
Villersexel, *France* 25 E13
Villerupt, *France* 25 C12
Villerville, *France* 24 C7
Villiers, *S. Africa* 85 D4
Villingen-Schwenningen, *Germany* 19 G4
Villisca, *U.S.A.* 108 E7
Vilna, *Canada* 100 C6
Vilnius, *Lithuania* 9 J21
Vils →, *Germany* 19 G9
Vilsbiburg, *Germany* 19 G8
Vilshofen, *Germany* 19 G9
Vilusi, *Montenegro, Yug.* 21 N8
Vilvoorde, *Belgium* 17 G4
Vilyuy →, *Russia* 45 C13
Vilyuysk, *Russia* 45 C13
Vimercate, *Italy* 32 C6
Vimiosa, *Portugal* 30 D4
Vimoutiers, *France* 24 D7
Vimperk, *Czech.* 20 F3
Viña del Mar, *Chile* 126 C1
Vinaroz, *Spain* 28 E5
Vincennes, *U.S.A.* 104 F2
Vincent, *U.S.A.* 113 L8
Vinces, *Ecuador* 120 D2
Vinchina, *Argentina* 126 B2
Vindelälven →, *Sweden* 8 E18
Vindeln, *Sweden* 8 D18
Vinderup, *Denmark* 11 H2
Vindhya Ra., *India* 62 H7
Vineland, *U.S.A.* 104 F8
Vinga, *Romania* 38 D4
Vingnes, *Norway* 10 C4
Vinh, *Vietnam* 58 C5
Vinh Linh, *Vietnam* 58 D6
Vinh Long, *Vietnam* 59 G5
Vinh Yen, *Vietnam* 58 B5
Vinhais, *Portugal* 30 D3
Vinica, *Croatia* 33 B13
Vinica, *Slovenia* 33 C12
Vinita, *U.S.A.* 109 G7
Vinkeveen, *Neths.* 16 D5
Vinkovci, *Croatia* 21 K8
Vinnitsa = Vinnytsya, *Ukraine* 41 H5
Vinnytsya, *Ukraine* 41 H5
Vinstra, *Norway* 10 C3
Vinton, *Calif., U.S.A.* 112 F6
Vinton, *Iowa, U.S.A.* 108 D8
Vinton, *La., U.S.A.* 109 K8
Vințu de Jos, *Romania* 38 D6
Viöl, *Germany* 18 A5
Vipava, *Slovenia* 33 C10
Vipiteno, *Italy* 33 B8
Vir, *Croatia* 33 D12
Virac, *Phil.* 55 E6
Virachei, *Cambodia* 58 F6
Virago Sd., *Canada* 100 C2
Viramgam, *India* 62 H5
Virananşehir, *Turkey* 67 D8
Virden, *Canada* 101 D8
Vire, *France* 24 D6
Vire →, *France* 24 C5
Virgem da Lapa, *Brazil* 123 E3
Vírgenes, C., *Argentina* 128 D3
Virgin →, *Canada* 101 B7
Virgin →, *U.S.A.* 111 H6
Virgin Gorda, *Virgin Is.* 117 C7
Virgin Is. (British) ■, *W. Indies* 117 C7
Virgin Is. (U.S.) ■, *W. Indies* 117 C7
Virginia, *S. Africa* 84 D4
Virginia, *U.S.A.* 108 B8
Virginia □, *U.S.A.* 104 G7
Virginia Beach, *U.S.A.* 104 G8
Virginia City, *Mont., U.S.A.* 110 D8
Virginia City, *Nev., U.S.A.* 112 F7
Virginia Falls, *Canada* 100 A3
Virginiatown, *Canada* 98 C4
Virieu-le-Grand, *France* 27 C9
Viroqua, *U.S.A.* 108 D9
Virovitica, *Croatia* 21 K7
Virton, *Belgium* 17 J7
Virú, *Peru* 124 B2
Virudunagar, *India* 60 Q10
Vis, *Croatia* 33 E13
Vis Kanal, *Croatia* 33 E13
Visalia, *U.S.A.* 111 H4
Visayan Sea, *Phil.* 55 F5
Visby, *Sweden* 9 H18
Viscount Melville Sd., *Canada* 4 B2
Visé, *Belgium* 17 G7
Višegrad, *Bos.-H.* 21 M9
Viseu, *Brazil* 122 B2
Viseu, *Portugal* 30 E3
Viseu □, *Portugal* 30 E3
Vişeu de Sus, *Romania* 38 B7
Vishakhapatnam, *India* 61 L13
Viskafors, *Sweden* 11 G6
Visnagar, *India* 62 H5
Višnja Gora, *Slovenia* 33 C11
Viso, Mte., *Italy* 32 D4
Viso del Marqués, *Spain* 29 G1
Visoko, *Bos.-H.* 21 M8
Visokoi I., *Antarctica* 5 B1
Visp, *Switz.* 22 D5
Vispa →, *Switz.* 22 D5
Visselhövede, *Germany* 18 C5
Vissoie, *Switz.* 22 D5
Vista, *U.S.A.* 113 M9
Vistula = Wisła →, *Poland* 20 A8
Vit →, *Bulgaria* 38 F7
Vitanje, *Slovenia* 33 B12
Vitebsk = Vitsyebsk, *Belarus* 40 E6
Viterbo, *Italy* 33 F9
Viti Levu, *Fiji* 87 C7
Vitigudino, *Spain* 30 D4
Vitim, *Russia* 45 D12
Vitim →, *Russia* 45 D12
Vitória, *Brazil* 123 F3
Vitoria, *Spain* 28 C2
Vitória da Conquista, *Brazil* 123 D3
Vitória de São Antão, *Brazil* 122 C4
Vitorino Friere, *Brazil* 122 B2
Vitré, *France* 24 D5
Vitry-le-François, *France* 25 D11
Vitsi, Óros, *Greece* 39 J4
Vitsyebsk, *Belarus* 40 E6
Vitteaux, *France* 25 E11
Vittel, *France* 25 D12
Vittória, *Italy* 35 F7
Vittório Véneto, *Italy* 33 C9
Vivario, *France* 27 F13
Vivegnis, *Belgium* 17 G7
Viver, *Spain* 28 F4
Vivero, *Spain* 30 B3
Viviers, *France* 27 D8
Vivonne, *France* 26 B4
Vizcaíno, Desierto de, *Mexico* 114 B2
Vizcaíno, Sierra, *Mexico* 114 B2
Vizcaya □, *Spain* 28 B2
Vize, *Turkey* 66 B2
Vizianagaram, *India* 61 K13
Vizille, *France* 27 C9
Viziñada, *Croatia* 33 C10
Viziru, *Romania* 38 E10
Vizovice, *Czech.* 20 F7
Vizzini, *Italy* 35 E7
Vlaardingen, *Neths.* 16 E4
Vlădeasa, *Romania* 38 C5
Vladikavkaz, *Russia* 43 J7
Vladimir, *Russia* 42 B5
Vladimir Volynskiy = Volodymyr-Volynskyy, *Ukraine* 41 G3
Vladimirovac, *Serbia, Yug.* 21 K10
Vladimirovka, *Russia* 43 F8
Vladimorvka, *Kazakstan* 42 E10
Vladislavovka, *Ukraine* 41 K8
Vladivostok, *Russia* 45 E14
Vlamertinge, *Belgium* 17 G1
Vlasenica, *Bos.-H.* 21 L8
Vlasinsko Jezero, *Serbia, Yug.* 21 N12
Vleuten, *Neths.* 16 D6
Vlieland, *Neths.* 16 B5
Vliestroom, *Neths.* 16 B6
Vlijmen, *Neths.* 17 E6
Vlissingen, *Neths.* 17 F3
Vlóra, *Albania* 39 J2
Vlorës, Gjiri i, *Albania* 39 J2
Vltava →, *Czech.* 20 E4
Vo Dat, *Vietnam* 59 G6
Vobarno, *Italy* 32 C7
Voćin, *Croatia* 21 K7
Vodice, *Croatia* 33 E12
Vodnjan, *Croatia* 33 D10
Vogelkop = Doberai, Jazirah, *Indonesia* 57 E8
Vogelsberg, *Germany* 18 E5
Voghera, *Italy* 32 D6
Vohibinany, *Madag.* 85 B8
Vohimarina, *Madag.* 85 A9
Vohimena, Tanjon' i, *Madag.* 85 D8
Vohipeno, *Madag.* 85 C8
Voi, *Kenya* 82 C4
Void, *France* 25 D12
Voiron, *France* 27 C9
Voisey B., *Canada* 99 A7
Voitsberg, *Austria* 21 H5
Voiviïs Límni, *Greece* 39 K5
Vojens, *Denmark* 11 J3
Vojmsjön, *Sweden* 8 D17
Vojnić, *Croatia* 33 C12
Vojnik, *Italy* 33 B12
Vokhtoga, *Russia* 40 C11
Volborg, *U.S.A.* 108 C2
Volcano Is. = Kazan-Rettō, *Pac. Oc.* 92 E6
Volchansk = Vovchansk, *Ukraine* 41 G9
Volchayevka, *Russia* 45 E14
Volchya →, *Ukraine* 41 H8
Volda, *Norway* 9 E12
Volendam, *Neths.* 16 D6
Volga, *Russia* 42 A4
Volga →, *Russia* 43 G9
Volga Hts. = Privolzhskaya Vozvyshennost, *Russia* 42 E7
Volgo-Baltiyskiy Kanal, *Russia* 40 B9
Volgo-Donskoy Kanal, *Russia* 43 F7
Volgodonsk, *Russia* 43 G6
Volgograd, *Russia* 43 F7
Volgogradskoye Vdkhr., *Russia* 42 E8
Volgorechensk, *Russia* 42 B5
Volkach, *Germany* 19 F6
Volkerak, *Neths.* 17 E4
Volkhov, *Russia* 40 C7
Volkhov →, *Russia* 40 B7
Völklingen, *Germany* 19 F2
Volkovysk = Vawkavysk, *Belarus* 41 F3
Volksrust, *S. Africa* 85 D4
Vollenhove, *Neths.* 16 C7
Volnansk, *Ukraine* 41 H8
Volnovakha, *Ukraine* 41 J9
Volochanka, *Russia* 45 B10
Volodarsk, *Russia* 42 B6
Volodymyr-Volynskyy, *Ukraine* 41 G3
Vologda, *Russia* 40 C10
Volokolamsk, *Russia* 42 B2
Volokonovka, *Russia* 42 E3
Vólos, *Greece* 39 K5
Volosovo, *Russia* 40 C5
Volovets, *Ukraine* 41 H2
Volovo, *Russia* 42 D4
Volozhin = Valozhyn, *Belarus* 40 E4
Volsk, *Russia* 42 D8
Volta →, *Ghana* 79 D5
Volta, L., *Ghana* 79 D5
Volta Blanche = White Volta →, *Ghana* 79 D4
Volta Redonda, *Brazil* 123 F3
Voltaire, C., *Australia* 88 B4
Volterra, *Italy* 32 E7
Voltri, *Italy* 32 D5
Volturara Appula, *Italy* 35 A8
Volturno →, *Italy* 34 A6
Volubilis, *Morocco* 74 B3
Volvo, *Australia* 91 E3
Volzhsk, *Russia* 42 C9
Volzhskiy, *Russia* 43 F7
Vondrozo, *Madag.* 85 C8
Voorburg, *Neths.* 16 D4
Voorne Putten, *Neths.* 16 E4
Voorst, *Neths.* 16 D8
Voorthuizen, *Neths.* 16 D7
Vopnafjörður, *Iceland* 8 D6
Vóras Óros, *Greece* 39 J4
Vorbasse, *Denmark* 11 J3
Vorden, *Neths.* 16 D8
Vorderrhein →, *Switz.* 23 C8
Vordingborg, *Denmark* 11 K5
Voreppe, *France* 27 C9
Voríai Sporádhes, *Greece* 39 K6
Vórios Evvoïkos Kólpos, *Greece* 39 L6
Vorkuta, *Russia* 44 C7
Vorma →, *Norway* 10 D5
Vormsi, *Estonia* 9 G20
Vorona →, *Russia* 42 E6
Voronezh, *Russia* 42 E4
Voronezh, *Ukraine* 41 G7
Voronezh →, *Russia* 42 E4
Vorontsovo-Aleksandrovskoye = Zelenokumsk, *Russia* 43 H6
Voroshilovgrad = Luhansk, *Ukraine* 41 H10
Voroshilovsk = Alchevsk, *Ukraine* 41 H10
Vorovskoye, *Russia* 45 D16
Vorselaar, *Belgium* 17 F5
Vorskla →, *Ukraine* 41 H8
Võrts Järv, *Estonia* 9 G22
Võru, *Estonia* 9 H22
Vosges, *France* 25 D14
Vosges □, *France* 25 D13
Voskopoja, *Albania* 39 J3
Voskresensk, *Russia* 42 C4
Voskresenskoye, *Russia* 42 B7
Voss, *Norway* 9 F12
Vosselaar, *Belgium* 17 F5
Vostok I., *Kiribati* 93 J12
Vouga →, *Portugal* 30 E2
Vouillé, *France* 24 F7
Vouvray, *France* 24 E7
Vouvry, *Switz.* 22 D3
Voúxa, Ákra, *Greece* 37 D5
Vouzela, *Portugal* 30 E2
Vouziers, *France* 25 C11
Vovchansk, *Ukraine* 41 G9
Voves, *France* 25 D8
Voxna, *Sweden* 10 C9
Vozhe Ozero, *Russia* 40 B10
Vozhega, *Russia* 40 B11
Voznesenka, *Russia* 45 D10
Voznesensk, *Ukraine* 41 J6
Voznesenye, *Russia* 40 B8
Vrådal, *Norway* 10 E2
Vrakhnéïka, *Greece* 39 L4
Vrancei, Munții, *Romania* 38 D9
Vrangelya, Ostrov, *Russia* 45 B19
Vranica, *Bos.-H.* 21 M7
Vranje, *Serbia, Yug.* 21 N11
Vransko, *Slovenia* 33 B11
Vratsa, *Bulgaria* 38 F6
Vrbas, *Serbia, Yug.* 21 K9
Vrbas →, *Bos.-H.* 21 K7
Vrbnik, *Croatia* 33 C11
Vrbovec, *Croatia* 33 C13
Vrbovsko, *Croatia* 33 C12
Vrchlabí, *Czech.* 20 E5
Vrede, *S. Africa* 85 D4
Vredefort, *S. Africa* 84 D4
Vredenburg, *S. Africa* 84 E2
Vredendal, *S. Africa* 84 E2
Vreeswijk, *Neths.* 16 D6
Vrena, *Sweden* 11 F10
Vrgorac, *Croatia* 21 M7
Vrhnika, *Slovenia* 33 C11
Vrîdi, *Ivory C.* 78 D4
Vries, *Neths.* 16 B9
Vriezenveen, *Neths.* 16 D9
Vrindavan, *India* 62 F7
Vríses, *Greece* 37 D6
Vrnograč, *Bos.-H.* 33 C12
Vroomshoop, *Neths.* 16 D9
Vršac, *Serbia, Yug.* 21 K11
Vrsacki Kanal, *Serbia, Yug.* 21 K11
Vryburg, *S. Africa* 84 D3
Vryheid, *S. Africa* 85 D5
Vsetín, *Czech.* 20 F8
Vu Liet, *Vietnam* 58 C5
Vucha →, *Bulgaria* 39 G7
Vught, *Neths.* 17 E6
Vukovar, *Croatia* 21 K8
Vulcan, *Canada* 100 C6
Vulcan, *U.S.A.* 104 C2
Vulcanești, *Moldova* 41 K5
Vulcano, *Italy* 35 D7
Vŭlchedruma, *Bulgaria* 38 F6
Vulci, *Italy* 33 F8
Vulkaneshty = Vulcanești, *Moldova* 41 K5
Vunduzi →, *Mozam.* 83 F3
Vung Tau, *Vietnam* 59 G6
Vŭrbitsa, *Bulgaria* 38 G9
Vyartsilya, *Russia* 40 A6
Vyatka = Kirov, *Russia* 44 D5
Vyatka →, *Russia* 42 C10
Vyatskiye Polyany, *Russia* 42 B10
Vyazemskiy, *Russia* 45 E14
Vyazma, *Russia* 42 C2
Vyazniki, *Russia* 42 B6
Vyborg, *Russia* 40 B5
Vychegda →, *Russia* 44 C5
Vychodné Beskydy, *Europe* 41 H2
Vyerkhnyadzvinsk, *Belarus* 40 E4
Vyksa, *Russia* 42 C6
Vylkove, *Ukraine* 41 K5
Vynohradiv, *Ukraine* 41 H2
Vyrnwy, L., *U.K.* 12 E4
Vyshniy Volochek, *Russia* 42 B2
Vyškov, *Czech.* 20 F6
Vysoké Mýto, *Czech.* 20 F6
Vysokovsk, *Russia* 42 B3
Vytegra, *Russia* 40 B9

W

W.A.C. Bennett Dam, *Canada* 100 B4
Wa, *Ghana* 78 C4
Waal →, *Neths.* 16 E6
Waalwijk, *Neths.* 17 E6
Waarschoot, *Belgium* 17 F3
Waasmunster, *Belgium* 17 F4
Wabakimi L., *Canada* 98 B2
Wabana, *Canada* 99 C9
Wabasca, *Canada* 100 B6
Wabash, *U.S.A.* 104 E3
Wabash →, *U.S.A.* 104 G1
Wabeno, *U.S.A.* 104 C1
Wabi →, *Ethiopia* 77 F5
Wabigoon L., *Canada* 101 D10
Wabowden, *Canada* 101 C9
Wąbrzeźno, *Poland* 20 B8
Wabu Hu, *China* 53 A11
Wabuk Pt., *Canada* 98 A2
Wabush, *Canada* 99 B6
Wabuska, *U.S.A.* 110 G4
Wachtebeke, *Belgium* 17 F3
Wächtersbach, *Germany* 19 E5
Waco, *U.S.A.* 109 K6
Waconichi, L., *Canada* 98 B5
Wad Ban Naqa, *Sudan* 77 D3
Wad Banda, *Sudan* 77 E2
Wad el Haddad, *Sudan* 77 E3
Wad en Nau, *Sudan* 77 E3
Wad Hamid, *Sudan* 77 D3
Wâd Medanî, *Sudan* 77 E3
Wad Thana, *Pakistan* 62 F2
Wadai, *Africa* 70 E5
Wadayama, *Japan* 49 G7
Waddeneilanden, *Neths.* 16 B6
Waddenzee, *Neths.* 16 B6
Wadderin Hill, *Australia* 89 F2
Waddington, *U.S.A.* 107 B9
Waddington, Mt., *Canada* 100 C3
Waddinxveen, *Neths.* 16 D5
Waddy Pt., *Australia* 91 C5
Wadena, *Canada* 101 C8
Wadena, *U.S.A.* 108 B7
Wädenswil, *Switz.* 23 B7
Wadesboro, *U.S.A.* 105 H5
Wadhams, *Canada* 100 C3
Wādī as Sīr, *Jordan* 69 D4
Wadi Gemâl, *Egypt* 76 C4
Wadi Halfa, *Sudan* 76 C3
Wadian, *China* 53 A9
Wadowice, *Poland* 20 F9
Wadsworth, *U.S.A.* 110 G4
Waegwan, *S. Korea* 51 G15
Wafrah, *Si. Arabia* 64 D5
Wagenberg, *Neths.* 17 E5
Wageningen, *Neths.* 16 E7
Wageningen, *Surinam* 121 B6
Wager B., *Canada* 97 B11
Wager Bay, *Canada* 97 B10
Wagga Wagga, *Australia* 91 F4
Waghete, *Indonesia* 57 E9
Wagin, *Australia* 89 F2
Wagon Mound, *U.S.A.* 109 G2
Wagoner, *U.S.A.* 109 G7
Wagrowiec, *Poland* 20 C7
Wah, *Pakistan* 62 C5
Wahai, *Indonesia* 57 E7
Wahiawa, *U.S.A.* 102 H15

Wâḫid, Egypt 69 E1
Wahnai, Afghan. 62 C1
Wahoo, U.S.A. 108 E6
Wahpeton, U.S.A. 108 B6
Wai, Koh, Cambodia 59 H4
Waiau →, N.Z. 87 K4
Waibeem, Indonesia 57 E8
Waiblingen, Germany 19 G5
Waidhofen, Niederösterreich, Austria 20 G5
Waidhofen, Niederösterreich, Austria 21 H4
Waigeo, Indonesia 57 E8
Waihi, N.Z. 87 G5
Waihou →, N.Z. 87 G5
Waika, Zaïre 82 C2
Waikabubak, Indonesia 57 F5
Waikari, N.Z. 87 K4
Waikato →, N.Z. 87 G5
Waikerie, Australia 91 E2
Waikokopu, N.Z. 87 H6
Waikouaiti, N.Z. 87 L3
Waimakariri →, N.Z. 87 K4
Waimate, N.Z. 87 L3
Waimes, Belgium 17 H8
Wainganga →, India 60 K11
Waingapu, Indonesia 57 F6
Waini →, Guyana 121 B6
Wainwright, Canada 101 C6
Wainwright, U.S.A. 96 A3
Waiouru, N.Z. 87 H5
Waipara, N.Z. 87 K4
Waipawa, N.Z. 87 H6
Waipiro, N.Z. 87 H7
Waipu, N.Z. 87 F5
Waipukurau, N.Z. 87 J6
Wairakei, N.Z. 87 H6
Wairarapa, L., N.Z. 87 J5
Wairoa, N.Z. 87 H6
Waitaki →, N.Z. 87 L3
Waitara, N.Z. 87 H5
Waitsburg, U.S.A. 110 C5
Waiuku, N.Z. 87 G5
Wajima, Japan 49 F8
Wajir, Kenya 82 B5
Wajir □, Kenya 82 B5
Wakasa, Japan 49 G7
Wakasa-Wan, Japan 49 G7
Wakatipu, L., N.Z. 87 L2
Wakaw, Canada 101 C7
Wakayama, Japan 49 G7
Wakayama-ken □, Japan 49 H7
Wake Forest, U.S.A. 105 H6
Wake I., Pac. Oc. 92 F8
Wakefield, N.Z. 87 J4
Wakefield, U.K. 12 D6
Wakefield, Mass., U.S.A. 107 D13
Wakefield, Mich., U.S.A. 108 B10
Wakeham Bay = Maricourt, Canada 97 C12
Wakema, Burma 61 L19
Wakkanai, Japan 48 B10
Wakkerstroom, S. Africa 85 D5
Wakool, Australia 91 F3
Wakool →, Australia 91 F3
Wakre, Indonesia 57 E8
Wakuach L., Canada 99 A6
Walamba, Zambia 83 E2
Wałbrzych, Poland 20 E6
Walbury Hill, U.K. 13 F6
Walcha, Australia 91 E5
Walcheren, Neths. 17 E3
Walcott, U.S.A. 110 F10
Wałcz, Poland 20 B6
Wald, Switz. 23 B7
Waldbröl, Germany 18 E3
Waldburg Ra., Australia 88 D2
Waldeck, Germany 18 D5
Walden, Colo., U.S.A. 110 F10
Walden, N.Y., U.S.A. 107 E10
Waldenburg, Switz. 22 B5
Waldport, U.S.A. 110 D1
Waldron, U.S.A. 109 H7
Waldshut, Germany 19 H4
Walembele, Ghana 78 C4
Walensee, Switz. 23 B8
Walenstadt, Switz. 23 B8
Wales □, U.K. 13 E4
Walewale, Ghana 79 C4
Walgett, Australia 91 E4
Walgreen Coast, Antarctica 5 D15
Walhalla, Australia 91 F4
Walhalla, U.S.A. 101 D9
Walker, U.S.A. 108 B7
Walker L., Man., Canada 101 C9
Walker L., Qué., Canada 99 B6
Walker L., U.S.A. 110 G4
Walkerston, Australia 90 C4
Walkerton, Canada 106 B3
Wall, U.S.A. 108 C3
Walla Walla, U.S.A. 110 C4
Wallabadah, Australia 90 B3
Wallace, Idaho, U.S.A. 110 C6
Wallace, N.C., U.S.A. 105 H7
Wallace, Nebr., U.S.A. 108 E4
Wallaceburg, Canada 98 D3
Wallachia = Valahia, Romania 38 E8
Wallal, Australia 91 D4
Wallal Downs, Australia 88 C3
Wallambin, L., Australia 89 F2
Wallaroo, Australia 91 E2
Wallasey, U.K. 12 D4
Walldürn, Germany 19 F5
Wallerawang, Australia 91 E5
Wallhallow, Australia 90 B2
Wallingford, U.S.A. 107 E12
Wallis & Futuna, Is., Pac. Oc. 92 J10
Wallisellen, Switz. 23 B7
Wallowa, U.S.A. 110 D5
Wallowa Mts., U.S.A. 110 D5
Wallsend, Australia 91 E5
Wallsend, U.K. 12 C6
Wallula, U.S.A. 110 C4
Wallumbilla, Australia 91 D4
Walmsley, L., Canada 101 A7
Walney, I. of, U.K. 12 C4
Walnut Creek, U.S.A. 112 H4
Walnut Ridge, U.S.A. 109 G9
Walsall, U.K. 13 E6
Walsenburg, U.S.A. 109 G2
Walsh, U.S.A. 109 G3
Walsh →, Australia 90 B3
Walsh P.O., Australia 90 B3
Walshoutem, Belgium 17 G6
Walsrode, Germany 18 C5
Walterboro, U.S.A. 105 J5
Walters, U.S.A. 109 H5
Waltershausen, Germany 18 E6
Waltham, U.S.A. 107 D13
Waltham Station, Canada 98 C4
Waltman, U.S.A. 110 E10
Walton, U.S.A. 107 D9
Walvisbaai, Namibia 84 C1
Wamba, Kenya 82 B4
Wamba, Zaïre 82 B2
Wamego, U.S.A. 108 F6
Wamena, Indonesia 57 E9
Wamulan, Indonesia 57 E7
Wan Xian, China 50 E8
Wana, Pakistan 62 C3
Wanaaring, Australia 91 D3
Wanaka, N.Z. 87 L2
Wanaka L., N.Z. 87 L2
Wan'an, China 53 D10
Wanapiri, Indonesia 57 E9
Wanapitei L., Canada 98 C3
Wanbi, Australia 91 E3
Wandaik, Guyana 121 C6
Wandarrie, Australia 89 E2
Wandel Sea = McKinley Sea, Arctic 4 A7
Wanderer, Zimbabwe 83 F3
Wandoan, Australia 91 D4
Wandre, Belgium 17 G7
Wanfercée-Baulet, Belgium 17 H5
Wanfu, China 51 D12
Wang →, Thailand 58 D2
Wang Kai, Sudan 77 F2
Wang Noi, Thailand 58 E3
Wang Saphung, Thailand 58 D3
Wang Thong, Thailand 58 D3
Wanga, Zaïre 82 B2
Wangal, Indonesia 57 F8
Wanganella, Australia 91 F3
Wanganui, N.Z. 87 H5
Wangaratta, Australia 91 F4
Wangary, Australia 91 E2
Wangcang, China 52 A6
Wangdu, China 50 E8
Wangerooge, Germany 18 B3
Wangi, Kenya 82 C5
Wangiwangi, Indonesia 57 F6
Wangjiang, China 53 B11
Wangmo, China 52 E6
Wangqing, China 51 C15
Wankaner, India 62 H4
Wanless, Canada 101 C8
Wannian, China 53 C11
Wanon Niwat, Thailand 58 D4
Wanquan, China 50 D8
Wanrong, China 50 G6
Wanshan, China 52 D7
Wanshengchang, China 52 C6
Wanssum, Neths. 17 E8
Wanxian, China 52 B7
Wanyuan, China 52 A7
Wanzai, China 53 C10
Wanze, Belgium 17 G6
Wapakoneta, U.S.A. 104 E3
Wapato, U.S.A. 110 C3
Wapawekka L., Canada 101 C8
Wapikopa L., Canada 98 B2
Wappingers Falls, U.S.A. 107 E11
Wapsipinicon →, U.S.A. 108 E9
Warangal, India 60 L11
Waratah, Australia 90 G4
Waratah B., Australia 91 F4
Warburg, Germany 18 D5
Warburton, Vic., Australia 91 F4
Warburton, W. Austral., Australia 89 E4
Warburton Ra., Australia 89 E4
Ward, N.Z. 87 J5
Ward →, Australia 91 D4
Ward Cove, U.S.A. 100 B2
Ward Mt., U.S.A. 112 H8
Warden, S. Africa 85 D4
Wardha, India 60 J11
Wardha →, India 60 K11
Wardlow, Canada 100 C6
Ware, Canada 100 B3
Ware, U.S.A. 107 D12
Waregem, Belgium 17 G2
Wareham, U.S.A. 107 E14
Waremme, Belgium 17 G6
Waren, Germany 18 B8
Warendorf, Germany 18 D3
Warialda, Australia 91 D5
Wariap, Indonesia 57 E8
Warin Chamrap, Thailand 58 E5
Warkopi, Indonesia 57 E8
Warley, U.K. 13 E6
Warm Springs, U.S.A. 111 G5
Warman, Canada 101 C7
Warmbad, Namibia 84 D2
Warmbad, S. Africa 85 C4
Warmenhuizen, Neths. 16 C5
Warmeriville, France 25 C11
Warmond, Neths. 16 D5
Warnambool Downs, Australia 90 C3
Warnemünde, Germany 18 A8
Warner, Canada 100 D6
Warner Mts., U.S.A. 110 F3
Warner Robins, U.S.A. 105 J4
Warnes, Bolivia 125 D5
Warneton, Belgium 17 G1
Warnow →, Germany 18 A8
Warnsveld, Neths. 16 D8
Waroona, Australia 89 F2
Warracknabeal, Australia 91 F3
Warragul, Australia 91 F4
Warrawagine, Australia 88 D3
Warrego →, Australia 91 E4
Warrego Ra., Australia 90 C4
Warren, Australia 91 E4
Warren, Ark., U.S.A. 109 J8
Warren, Mich., U.S.A. 104 D4
Warren, Minn., U.S.A. 108 A6
Warren, Ohio, U.S.A. 106 E4
Warren, Pa., U.S.A. 106 E5
Warrenpoint, U.K. 15 B5
Warrensburg, U.S.A. 108 F8
Warrenton, S. Africa 84 D3
Warrenton, U.S.A. 112 D3
Warrenville, Australia 91 D4
Warri, Nigeria 79 D6
Warrina, Australia 91 D2
Warrington, U.K. 12 D5
Warrington, U.S.A. 105 K2
Warrnambool, Australia 91 F3
Warroad, U.S.A. 108 A7
Warsa, Indonesia 57 E9
Warsaw = Warszawa, Poland 20 C11
Warsaw, Ind., U.S.A. 104 E3
Warsaw, N.Y., U.S.A. 106 D6
Warsaw, Ohio, U.S.A. 106 F2
Warstein, Germany 18 D4
Warszawa, Poland 20 C11
Warta →, Poland 20 C4
Warthe = Warta →, Poland 20 C4
Waru, Indonesia 57 E8
Warwick, Australia 91 D5
Warwick, U.K. 13 E6
Warwick, U.S.A. 107 E13
Warwickshire □, U.K. 13 E6
Wasaga Beach, Canada 106 B4
Wasatch Ra., U.S.A. 110 F8
Wasbank, S. Africa 85 D5
Wasco, Calif., U.S.A. 113 K7
Wasco, Oreg., U.S.A. 110 D3
Waseca, U.S.A. 108 C8
Wasekamio L., Canada 101 B7
Wash, The, U.K. 12 E8
Washago, Canada 106 B5
Washburn, N. Dak., U.S.A. 108 B4
Washburn, Wis., U.S.A. 108 B9
Washim, India 60 J10
Washington, D.C., U.S.A. 104 F7
Washington, Ga., U.S.A. 105 J4
Washington, Ind., U.S.A. 104 F2
Washington, Iowa, U.S.A. 108 E9
Washington, Mo., U.S.A. 108 F9
Washington, N.C., U.S.A. 105 H7
Washington, N.J., U.S.A. 107 F10
Washington, Pa., U.S.A. 106 F4
Washington, Utah, U.S.A. 111 H7
Washington □, U.S.A. 110 C3
Washington, Mt., U.S.A. 107 B13
Washington I., U.S.A. 104 C2
Washougal, U.S.A. 112 E4
Wasian, Indonesia 57 E8
Wasior, Indonesia 57 E8
Waskaganish, Canada 98 B4
Waskaiowaka, L., Canada 101 B9
Waskesiu Lake, Canada 101 C7
Wasmes, Belgium 17 H3
Waspik, Neths. 17 E5
Wassen, Switz. 23 C7
Wassenaar, Neths. 16 D4
Wasserburg, Germany 19 G8
Wasserkuppe, Germany 18 E5
Wassy, France 25 D11
Waswanipi, Canada 98 C4
Waswanipi, L., Canada 98 C4
Watangpone, Indonesia 57 E6
Water Park Pt., Australia 90 C5
Water Valley, U.S.A. 109 H10
Waterberge, S. Africa 85 C4
Waterbury, Conn., U.S.A. 107 E11
Waterbury, Vt., U.S.A. 107 B12
Waterbury L., Canada 101 B8
Waterdown, Canada 106 C5
Waterford, Canada 106 D4
Waterford, Ireland 15 D4
Waterford, U.S.A. 112 H6
Waterford □, Ireland 15 D4
Waterford Harbour, Ireland 15 D5
Waterhen L., Man., Canada 101 C9
Waterhen L., Sask., Canada 101 C7
Wateringen, Neths. 16 D4
Waterloo, Belgium 17 G4
Waterloo, Ont., Canada 98 D3
Waterloo, Qué., Canada 107 A12
Waterloo, S. Leone 78 D2
Waterloo, Ill., U.S.A. 108 F9
Waterloo, Iowa, U.S.A. 108 D8
Waterloo, N.Y., U.S.A. 106 D8
Watermeal-Boitsford, Belgium 17 G4
Watersmeet, U.S.A. 108 B10
Waterton-Glacier International Peace Park, U.S.A. 110 B7
Watertown, Conn., U.S.A. 107 E11
Watertown, N.Y., U.S.A. 107 C9
Watertown, S. Dak., U.S.A. 108 C6
Watertown, Wis., U.S.A. 108 D10
Waterval-Boven, S. Africa 85 D5
Waterville, Canada 107 A13
Waterville, Maine, U.S.A. 99 D6
Waterville, N.Y., U.S.A. 107 D9
Waterville, Pa., U.S.A. 106 E7
Waterville, Wash., U.S.A. 110 C3
Watervliet, Belgium 17 F3
Watervliet, U.S.A. 107 D11
Wates, Indonesia 57 G14
Watford, Canada 106 D3
Watford, U.K. 13 F7
Watford City, U.S.A. 108 B3
Wathaman →, Canada 101 B8
Watheroo, Australia 89 F2
Wating, China 50 G4
Watkins Glen, U.S.A. 106 D8
Watling I. = San Salvador, Bahamas 117 B5
Watonga, U.S.A. 109 H5
Watou, Belgium 17 G1
Watrous, Canada 101 C7
Watrous, U.S.A. 109 H2
Watsa, Zaïre 82 B2
Watseka, U.S.A. 104 E2
Watson, Australia 89 F5
Watson, Canada 101 C8
Watson Lake, Canada 100 A3
Watsonville, U.S.A. 111 H3
Wattenwil, Switz. 22 C5
Wattiwarriganna Cr. →, Australia 91 D2
Wattwil, Switz. 23 B8
Watuata = Batuata, Indonesia 57 F6
Watubela, Kepulauan, Indonesia 57 E8
Watubela Is. = Watubela, Kepulauan, Indonesia 57 E8
Wau, Sudan 71 F6
Waubach, Neths. 17 G8
Waubamik, Canada 106 A4
Waubay, U.S.A. 108 C6
Waubra, Australia 91 F3
Wauchope, Australia 91 E5
Wauchula, U.S.A. 105 M5
Waugh, Canada 101 D9
Waukarlycarly, L., Australia 88 D3
Waukegan, U.S.A. 104 D2
Waukesha, U.S.A. 104 D1
Waukon, U.S.A. 108 D9
Wauneta, U.S.A. 108 E4
Waupaca, U.S.A. 108 C10
Waupun, U.S.A. 108 D10
Waurika, U.S.A. 109 H6
Wausau, U.S.A. 108 C10
Wautoma, U.S.A. 108 C10
Wauwatosa, U.S.A. 104 D2
Wave Hill, Australia 88 C5
Waveney →, U.K. 13 E9
Waverley, N.Z. 87 H5
Waverly, Iowa, U.S.A. 108 D8
Waverly, N.Y., U.S.A. 107 D8
Wavre, Belgium 17 G5
Wavreille, Belgium 17 H6
Wâw, Sudan 77 F2
Wāw al Kabīr, Libya 73 C8
Wawa, Canada 98 C3
Wawa, Nigeria 79 D5
Wawa, Sudan 76 C3
Wawanesa, Canada 101 D9
Wawona, U.S.A. 112 H7
Waxahachie, U.S.A. 109 J6
Way, L., Australia 89 E3
Wayabula Rau, Indonesia 57 D7
Wayatinah, Australia 90 G4
Waycross, U.S.A. 105 K4
Wayi, Sudan 77 F3
Wayne, Nebr., U.S.A. 108 D6
Wayne, W. Va., U.S.A. 104 F4
Waynesboro, Ga., U.S.A. 105 J4
Waynesboro, Miss., U.S.A. 105 K1
Waynesboro, Pa., U.S.A. 104 F7
Waynesboro, Va., U.S.A. 104 F6
Waynesburg, U.S.A. 104 F5
Waynesville, U.S.A. 105 H4
Waynoka, U.S.A. 109 G5
Wāzin, Libya 75 B7
Wazirabad, Pakistan 62 C6
We, Indonesia 56 C1
Weald, The, U.K. 13 F8
Wear →, U.K. 12 C6
Weatherford, Okla., U.S.A. 109 H5
Weatherford, Tex., U.S.A. 109 J6
Weaverville, U.S.A. 110 F2
Webb City, U.S.A. 109 G7
Webo = Nyaake, Liberia 78 E3
Webster, Mass., U.S.A. 107 D13
Webster, N.Y., U.S.A. 106 C7
Webster, S. Dak., U.S.A. 108 C6
Webster, Wis., U.S.A. 108 C8
Webster City, U.S.A. 108 D8
Webster Green, U.S.A. 108 F9
Webster Springs, U.S.A. 104 F5
Weda, Indonesia 57 D7
Weda, Teluk, Indonesia 57 D7
Weddell I., Falk. Is. 128 D4
Weddell Sea, Antarctica 5 D1
Wedderburn, Australia 91 F3
Wedel, Germany 18 B5
Wedgeport, Canada 99 D6
Wedza, Zimbabwe 83 F3
Wee Waa, Australia 91 E4
Weed, U.S.A. 110 F2
Weed Heights, U.S.A. 112 G7
Weedsport, U.S.A. 107 C8
Weedville, U.S.A. 106 E6
Weemelah, Australia 91 D4
Weenen, S. Africa 85 D5
Weener, Germany 18 B3
Weert, Neths. 17 F7
Weesp, Neths. 16 D6
Weggis, Switz. 23 B6
Węgliniec, Poland 20 D5
Węgorzewo, Poland 20 A11
Węgrów, Poland 20 C12
Wehl, Neths. 16 E8
Wei He →, Hebei, China 50 F8
Wei He →, Shaanxi, China 50 G6
Weichang, China 51 D9
Weichuan, China 50 G7
Weida, Germany 18 E8
Weiden, Germany 19 F8
Weifang, China 51 F10
Weihai, China 51 F12
Weilburg, Germany 18 E4
Weilheim, Germany 19 H7
Weimar, Germany 18 E7
Weinan, China 50 G5
Weinfelden, Switz. 23 A8
Weingarten, Germany 19 H5
Weinheim, Germany 19 F4
Weining, China 52 D5
Weipa, Australia 90 A3
Weir →, Australia 91 D4
Weir →, Canada 101 B10
Weir River, Canada 101 B10
Weirton, U.S.A. 106 F4
Weisen, Switz. 23 C9
Weiser, U.S.A. 110 D5
Weishan, Shandong, China 51 G9
Weishan, Yunnan, China 52 E3
Weissenburg, Germany 19 F6
Weissenfels, Germany 18 D8
Weisshorn, Switz. 22 D5
Weissmies, Switz. 22 D6
Weisstannen, Switz. 23 C8
Weisswasser, Germany 18 D10
Weiswampach, Belgium 17 H8
Weixi, China 52 D2
Weixin, China 52 D5
Weiyuan, China 50 G3
Weiz, Austria 21 H5
Weizhou Dao, China 52 G7
Wejherowo, Poland 20 A8
Wekusko L., Canada 101 C9
Welbourn Hill, Australia 91 D1
Welch, U.S.A. 104 G5
Weldya, Ethiopia 77 E4
Welega □, Ethiopia 77 F3
Welkenraedt, Belgium 17 G7
Welkite, Ethiopia 77 F4
Welkom, S. Africa 84 D4
Welland, Canada 98 D4
Welland →, U.K. 12 E7
Wellen, Belgium 17 G6
Wellesley Is., Australia 90 B2
Wellin, Belgium 17 H6
Wellingborough, U.K. 13 E7
Wellington, Australia 91 E4
Wellington, Canada 98 D4
Wellington, N.Z. 87 J5
Wellington, S. Africa 84 E2
Wellington, Shrops., U.K. 12 E5
Wellington, Somst., U.K. 13 G4
Wellington, Colo., U.S.A. 108 E2
Wellington, Kans., U.S.A. 109 G6
Wellington, Nev., U.S.A. 112 G7
Wellington, Ohio, U.S.A. 106 E2
Wellington, Tex., U.S.A. 109 H4
Wellington, I., Chile 128 C2
Wellington, L., Australia 91 F4
Wells, U.K. 13 F5
Wells, Maine, U.S.A. 107 C14
Wells, Minn., U.S.A. 108 D8
Wells, Nev., U.S.A. 110 F6
Wells, L., Australia 89 E3
Wells Gray Prov. Park, Canada 100 C4
Wells-next-the-Sea, U.K. 12 E8
Wells River, U.S.A. 107 B12
Wellsboro, U.S.A. 106 E7
Wellsburg, U.S.A. 106 F4
Wellsville, Mo., U.S.A. 108 F9
Wellsville, N.Y., U.S.A. 106 D7
Wellsville, Ohio, U.S.A. 106 F4
Wellsville, Utah, U.S.A. 110 F8
Wellton, U.S.A. 111 K6
Welmel, Wabi →, Ethiopia 77 F5
Welo □, Ethiopia 77 E4
Wels, Austria 21 G4
Welshpool, U.K. 13 E4
Wem, U.K. 12 E5
Wembere →, Tanzania 82 C3
Wemindji, Canada 98 B4
Wemmel, Belgium 17 G4
Wen Xian, Gansu, China 50 H3
Wen Xian, Henan, China 50 G7

Wenatchee, *U.S.A.* 110 C3
Wenchang, *China* 58 C8
Wencheng, *China* 53 D13
Wenchi, *Ghana* 78 D4
Wenchow = Wenzhou, *China* 53 C13
Wenchuan, *China* 52 B4
Wendell, *U.S.A.* 110 E6
Wenden, *U.S.A.* 113 M13
Wendeng, *China* 51 F12
Wendesi, *Indonesia* 57 E8
Wendo, *Ethiopia* 77 F4
Wendover, *U.S.A.* 110 F6
Wenduine, *Belgium* 17 F2
Weng'an, *China* 52 D6
Wengcheng, *China* 53 E9
Wengen, *Switz.* 22 C5
Wengyuan, *China* 53 E10
Wenjiang, *China* 52 B4
Wenling, *China* 53 C13
Wenlock ➛, *Australia* 90 A3
Wenshan, *China* 52 F5
Wenshang, *China* 50 G9
Wenshui, *Guizhou, China* 52 C6
Wenshui, *Shanxi, China* 50 F7
Wensu, *China* 54 B3
Wentworth, *Australia* 91 E3
Wenut, *Indonesia* 57 E8
Wenxi, *China* 50 G6
Wenzhou, *China* 53 C13
Weott, *U.S.A.* 110 F2
Wepener, *S. Africa* 84 D4
Werbomont, *Belgium* 17 H7
Werda, *Botswana* 84 D3
Werdau, *Germany* 18 E8
Werder, *Ethiopia* 68 F4
Werder, *Germany* 18 C8
Werdohl, *Germany* 18 D3
Wereilu, *Ethiopia* 77 E4
Weri, *Indonesia* 57 E8
Werkendam, *Neths.* 16 E5
Werne, *Germany* 18 D3
Werneck, *Germany* 19 F6
Wernigerode, *Germany* 18 D6
Werra ➛, *Germany* 18 D5
Werribee, *Australia* 91 F3
Werrimull, *Australia* 91 E3
Werris Creek, *Australia* 91 E5
Wersar, *Indonesia* 57 E8
Wertach ➛, *Germany* 19 G6
Wertheim, *Germany* 19 F5
Wertingen, *Germany* 19 G6
Wervershoof, *Neths.* 16 C6
Wervik, *Belgium* 17 G2
Wesel, *Germany* 18 D2
Weser ➛, *Germany* 18 B4
Wesiri, *Indonesia* 57 F7
Wesley Vale, *U.S.A.* 111 J10
Wesleyville, *Canada* 99 C9
Wesleyville, *U.S.A.* 106 D4
Wessel, C., *Australia* 90 A2
Wessel Is., *Australia* 90 A2
Wesselburen, *Germany* 18 A4
Wessem, *Neths.* 17 F7
Wessington, *U.S.A.* 108 C5
Wessington Springs, *U.S.A.* 108 C5
West, *U.S.A.* 109 K6
West Allis, *U.S.A.* 104 D1
West B., *U.S.A.* 109 L10
West Baines ➛, *Australia* 88 C4
West Bank □, *Asia* 69 C4
West Bend, *U.S.A.* 104 D1
West Bengal □, *India* 63 H12
West Beskids = Západné Beskydy, *Europe* 20 F9
West Branch, *U.S.A.* 104 C3
West Bromwich, *U.K.* 13 E5
West Cape Howe, *Australia* 89 G2
West Chazy, *U.S.A.* 107 B11
West Chester, *U.S.A.* 104 F8
West Columbia, *U.S.A.* 109 L7
West Covina, *U.S.A.* 113 L9
West Des Moines, *U.S.A.* 108 E8
West Dunbartonshire □, *U.K.* 14 F4
West End, *Bahamas* 116 A4
West Falkland, *Falk. Is.* 128 D4
West Fjord = Vestfjorden, *Norway* 8 C15
West Frankfort, *U.S.A.* 108 G10
West Hartford, *U.S.A.* 107 E12
West Haven, *U.S.A.* 107 E12
West Helena, *U.S.A.* 109 H9
West Ice Shelf, *Antarctica* 5 C7
West Indies, *Cent. Amer.* 117 C7
West Lorne, *Canada* 106 D3
West Lothian □, *U.K.* 14 F5
West Lunga ➛, *Zambia* 83 E1
West Memphis, *U.S.A.* 109 H9
West Midlands □, *U.K.* 13 E6
West Mifflin, *U.S.A.* 106 F5
West Monroe, *U.S.A.* 109 J8
West Newton, *U.S.A.* 106 F5
West Nicholson, *Zimbabwe* 83 G2
West Palm Beach, *U.S.A.* 105 M5
West Plains, *U.S.A.* 109 G9
West Point, *Ga., U.S.A.* 105 J3
West Point, *Miss., U.S.A.* 105 J1
West Point, *Nebr., U.S.A.* 108 E6
West Point, *Va., U.S.A.* 104 G7
West Pokot □, *Kenya* 82 B4
West Pt. = Ouest, Pte., *Canada* 99 C7
West Pt., *Australia* 91 F2
West Road ➛, *Canada* 100 C4
West Rutland, *U.S.A.* 107 C11
West Schelde = Westerschelde ➛, *Neths.* 17 F2
West Seneca, *U.S.A.* 106 D6
West Siberian Plain, *Russia* 46 C11
West Sussex □, *U.K.* 13 G7
West-Terschelling, *Neths.* 16 B6
West Valley City, *U.S.A.* 110 F8
West Virginia □, *U.S.A.* 104 F5
West-Vlaanderen □, *Belgium* 17 G2
West Walker ➛, *U.S.A.* 112 G7
West Wyalong, *Australia* 91 E4
West Yellowstone, *U.S.A.* 110 D8
West Yorkshire □, *U.K.* 12 D6
Westall Pt., *Australia* 91 E1
Westbrook, *Maine, U.S.A.* 105 D10
Westbrook, *Tex., U.S.A.* 109 J4
Westbury, *Australia* 90 G4
Westby, *U.S.A.* 108 A2
Westend, *U.S.A.* 113 K9
Westerbork, *Neths.* 16 C9
Westerland, *Germany* 9 J13
Western □, *Kenya* 82 B3
Western □, *Uganda* 82 B3
Western □, *Zambia* 83 F1
Western Australia □, *Australia* 89 E2
Western Cape □, *S. Africa* 84 E3
Western Dvina = Daugava ➛, *Latvia* 9 H21
Western Ghats, *India* 60 N9
Western Isles □, *U.K.* 14 D1
Western Sahara ■, *Africa* 74 D2
Western Samoa ■, *Pac. Oc.* 87 A13
Westernport, *U.S.A.* 104 F6
Westerschelde ➛, *Neths.* 17 F2
Westerstede, *Germany* 18 B3
Westervoort, *Neths.* 16 E7
Westerwald, *Germany* 18 E4
Westfield, *Mass., U.S.A.* 107 D12
Westfield, *N.Y., U.S.A.* 106 D5
Westfield, *Pa., U.S.A.* 106 E7
Westgat, *Neths.* 17 E3
Westhope, *U.S.A.* 108 A4
Westkapelle, *Belgium* 17 F2
Westkapelle, *Neths.* 17 E2
Westland Bight, *N.Z.* 87 K3
Westlock, *Canada* 100 C6
Westmalle, *Belgium* 17 F5
Westmeath □, *Ireland* 15 C4
Westminster, *U.S.A.* 104 F7
Westmorland, *U.S.A.* 111 K6
Weston, *Malaysia* 56 C5
Weston, *Oreg., U.S.A.* 110 D4
Weston, *W. Va., U.S.A.* 104 F5
Weston I., *Canada* 98 B4
Weston-super-Mare, *U.K.* 13 F5
Westport, *Canada* 107 B8
Westport, *Ireland* 15 C2
Westport, *N.Z.* 87 J3
Westport, *Oreg., U.S.A.* 112 D3
Westport, *Wash., U.S.A.* 110 C1
Westray, *Canada* 101 C8
Westray, *U.K.* 14 B6
Westree, *Canada* 98 C3
Westville, *Calif., U.S.A.* 112 F6
Westville, *Ill., U.S.A.* 104 E2
Westville, *Okla., U.S.A.* 109 G7
Westwood, *U.S.A.* 110 F3
Wetar, *Indonesia* 57 F7
Wetaskiwin, *Canada* 100 C6
Wethersfield, *U.S.A.* 107 E12
Wetteren, *Belgium* 17 G3
Wettingen, *Switz.* 23 B6
Wetzikon, *Switz.* 23 B7
Wetzlar, *Germany* 18 E4
Wevelgem, *Belgium* 17 G2
Wewoka, *U.S.A.* 109 H6
Wexford, *Ireland* 15 D5
Wexford □, *Ireland* 15 D5
Wexford Harbour, *Ireland* 15 D5
Weyburn, *Canada* 101 D8
Weyburn L., *Canada* 100 A5
Weyer, *Austria* 21 H4
Weyib ➛, *Ethiopia* 77 F5
Weymouth, *Canada* 99 D6
Weymouth, *U.K.* 13 G5
Weymouth, *U.S.A.* 107 D14
Weymouth, C., *Australia* 90 A3
Wezemaal, *Belgium* 17 G5
Wezep, *Neths.* 16 D7
Wha Ti, *Canada* 96 B8
Whakatane, *N.Z.* 87 G6
Whale ➛, *Canada* 99 A6
Whale Cove, *Canada* 101 A10
Whales, B. of, *Antarctica* 5 D12
Whalsay, *U.K.* 14 A7
Whangamomona, *N.Z.* 87 H5
Whangarei, *N.Z.* 87 F5
Whangarei Harb., *N.Z.* 87 F5
Wharfe ➛, *U.K.* 12 D6
Wharfedale, *U.K.* 12 C5
Wharton, *N.J., U.S.A.* 107 F10
Wharton, *Pa., U.S.A.* 106 E6
Wharton, *Tex., U.S.A.* 109 L6
Wheatland, *Calif., U.S.A.* 112 F5
Wheatland, *Wyo., U.S.A.* 108 D2
Wheatley, *Canada* 106 D2
Wheaton, *U.S.A.* 108 C6
Wheelbarrow Pk., *U.S.A.* 112 H10
Wheeler, *Oreg., U.S.A.* 110 D2
Wheeler, *Tex., U.S.A.* 109 H4
Wheeler ➛, *Canada* 101 B7
Wheeler Pk., *N. Mex., U.S.A.* 111 H11
Wheeler Pk., *Nev., U.S.A.* 111 G6
Wheeler Ridge, *U.S.A.* 113 L8
Wheeling, *U.S.A.* 106 F4
Whernside, *U.K.* 12 C5
Whidbey I., *U.S.A.* 100 D4
Whiskey Gap, *Canada* 100 D6
Whiskey Jack L., *Canada* 101 B8
Whistleduck Cr. ➛, *Australia* 90 C2
Whitby, *Canada* 106 C6
Whitby, *U.K.* 12 C7
White ➛, *Ark., U.S.A.* 109 J9
White ➛, *Ind., U.S.A.* 104 F2
White ➛, *S. Dak., U.S.A.* 108 D5
White ➛, *Utah, U.S.A.* 110 F9
White ➛, *Wash., U.S.A.* 112 C4
White, L., *Australia* 88 D4
White B., *Canada* 99 B8
White Bear Res., *Canada* 99 C8
White Bird, *U.S.A.* 110 D5
White Butte, *U.S.A.* 108 B3
White City, *U.S.A.* 108 F6
White Cliffs, *Australia* 91 E3
White Deer, *U.S.A.* 109 H4
White Hall, *U.S.A.* 108 F9
White Haven, *U.S.A.* 107 E9
White Horse, Vale of, *U.K.* 13 F6
White I., *N.Z.* 87 G6
White L., *Canada* 107 A8
White L., *U.S.A.* 109 L8
White Mts., *Calif., U.S.A.* 111 H4
White Mts., *N.H., U.S.A.* 107 B13
White Nile = Nîl el Abyad ➛, *Sudan* 77 D3
White Nile Dam = Khazzân Jabal el Awliyâ, *Sudan* 77 D3
White Otter L., *Canada* 98 C1
White Pass, *Canada* 100 B1
White Pass, *U.S.A.* 112 D5
White Plains, *U.S.A.* 107 E11
White River, *Canada* 98 C2
White River, *S. Africa* 85 D5
White River, *U.S.A.* 108 D4
White Russia = Belarus ■, *Europe* 40 F4
White Sea = Beloye More, *Russia* 44 C4
White Sulphur Springs, *Mont., U.S.A.* 110 C8
White Sulphur Springs, *W. Va., U.S.A.* 104 G5
White Swan, *U.S.A.* 112 D6
White Volta ➛, *Ghana* 79 D4
Whitecliffs, *N.Z.* 87 K3
Whitecourt, *Canada* 100 C5
Whiteface, *U.S.A.* 109 J3
Whitefield, *U.S.A.* 107 B13
Whitefish, *U.S.A.* 110 B6
Whitefish L., *Canada* 101 A7
Whitefish Point, *U.S.A.* 104 B3
Whitegull, L., *Canada* 99 A7
Whitehall, *Mich., U.S.A.* 104 D2
Whitehall, *Mont., U.S.A.* 110 D7
Whitehall, *N.Y., U.S.A.* 107 C11
Whitehall, *Wis., U.S.A.* 108 C9
Whitehaven, *U.K.* 12 C4
Whitehorse, *Canada* 100 A1
Whitemark, *Australia* 90 G4
Whitemouth, *Canada* 101 D9
Whiteplains, *Liberia* 78 D2
Whitesboro, *N.Y., U.S.A.* 107 C9
Whitesboro, *Tex., U.S.A.* 109 J6
Whiteshell Prov. Park, *Canada* 101 C9
Whiteside, Canal, *Chile* 128 D2
Whitetail, *U.S.A.* 108 A2
Whiteville, *U.S.A.* 105 H6
Whitewater, *U.S.A.* 104 D1
Whitewater Baldy, *U.S.A.* 111 K9
Whitewater L., *Canada* 98 B2
Whitewood, *Australia* 90 C3
Whitewood, *Canada* 101 C8
Whitfield, *Australia* 91 F4
Whithorn, *U.K.* 14 G4
Whitianga, *N.Z.* 87 G5
Whitman, *U.S.A.* 107 D14
Whitmire, *U.S.A.* 105 H5
Whitney, *Canada* 98 C4
Whitney, Mt., *U.S.A.* 111 H4
Whitney Point, *U.S.A.* 107 D9
Whitstable, *U.K.* 13 F9
Whitsunday I., *Australia* 90 C4
Whittier, *U.S.A.* 113 M8
Whittlesea, *Australia* 91 F4
Whitwell, *U.S.A.* 105 H3
Wholdaia L., *Canada* 101 A8
Whyalla, *Australia* 91 E2
Whyjonta, *Australia* 91 D3
Wiarton, *Canada* 98 D3
Wiawso, *Ghana* 78 D4
Wibaux, *U.S.A.* 108 B2
Wichabai, *Guyana* 121 C6
Wichian Buri, *Thailand* 58 E3
Wichita, *U.S.A.* 109 G6
Wichita Falls, *U.S.A.* 109 J5
Wick, *U.K.* 14 C5
Wickenburg, *U.S.A.* 111 K7
Wickepin, *Australia* 89 F2
Wickham, C., *Australia* 90 F3
Wickliffe, *U.S.A.* 106 E3
Wicklow, *Ireland* 15 D5
Wicklow □, *Ireland* 15 D5
Wicklow Hd., *Ireland* 15 D5
Widgiemooltha, *Australia* 89 F3
Widnes, *U.K.* 12 D5
Wiedenbrück, *Germany* 18 D4
Wiehl, *Germany* 18 E3
Wiek, *Germany* 18 A9
Wielbark, *Poland* 20 B10
Wieliczka, *Poland* 20 F10
Wieluń, *Poland* 20 D8
Wien, *Austria* 21 G6
Wiener Neustadt, *Austria* 21 H6
Wieprz ➛, *Koszalin, Poland* 20 A6
Wieprz ➛, *Lublin, Poland* 20 D11
Wierden, *Neths.* 16 D9
Wiers, *Belgium* 17 H3
Wiesbaden, *Germany* 19 E4
Wiesental, *Germany* 19 F4
Wigan, *U.K.* 12 D5
Wiggins, *Colo., U.S.A.* 108 E2
Wiggins, *Miss., U.S.A.* 109 K10
Wight, I. of □, *U.K.* 13 G6
Wigtown, *U.K.* 14 G4
Wigtown B., *U.K.* 14 G4
Wijchen, *Neths.* 16 E7
Wijhe, *Neths.* 16 D8
Wijk bij Duurstede, *Neths.* 16 E6
Wil, *Switz.* 23 B8
Wilber, *U.S.A.* 108 E6
Wilberforce, *Canada* 106 A6
Wilberforce, C., *Australia* 90 A2
Wilburton, *U.S.A.* 109 H7
Wilcannia, *Australia* 91 E3
Wilcox, *U.S.A.* 106 E6
Wildbad, *Germany* 19 G4
Wildervank, *Neths.* 16 B9
Wildeshausen, *Germany* 18 C4
Wildhorn, *Switz.* 22 D4
Wildrose, *Calif., U.S.A.* 113 J9
Wildrose, *N. Dak., U.S.A.* 108 A3
Wildspitze, *Austria* 19 J6
Wildstrubel, *Switz.* 22 D5
Wildwood, *U.S.A.* 104 F8
Wilge ➛, *S. Africa* 85 D4
Wilhelm II Coast, *Antarctica* 5 C7
Wilhelm-Pieck-Stadt-Guben, *Germany* 18 D10
Wilhelmina, Geb., *Surinam* 121 C6
Wilhelmina Kanaal, *Neths.* 17 E6
Wilhelmsburg, *Austria* 21 G5
Wilhelmshaven, *Germany* 18 B4
Wilhelmstal, *Namibia* 84 C2
Wilkes-Barre, *U.S.A.* 107 E9
Wilkesboro, *U.S.A.* 105 G5
Wilkie, *Canada* 101 C7
Wilkinsburg, *U.S.A.* 106 F5
Wilkinson Lakes, *Australia* 89 E5
Willamina, *U.S.A.* 110 D2
Willandra Billabong Creek ➛, *Australia* 91 E4
Willapa B., *U.S.A.* 110 C2
Willapa Hills, *U.S.A.* 112 D3
Willard, *N. Mex., U.S.A.* 111 J10
Willard, *Utah, U.S.A.* 110 F7
Willcox, *U.S.A.* 111 K9
Willebroek, *Belgium* 17 F4
Willemstad, *Neth. Ant.* 117 D6
Willeroo, *Australia* 88 C5
William ➛, *Canada* 101 B7
William Creek, *Australia* 91 D2
Williambury, *Australia* 89 D2
Williams, *Australia* 89 F2
Williams, *Ariz., U.S.A.* 111 J7
Williams, *Calif., U.S.A.* 112 F4
Williams Lake, *Canada* 100 C4
Williamsburg, *Ky., U.S.A.* 105 G3
Williamsburg, *Pa., U.S.A.* 106 F6
Williamsburg, *Va., U.S.A.* 104 G7
Williamson, *N.Y., U.S.A.* 106 C7
Williamson, *W. Va., U.S.A.* 104 G4
Williamsport, *U.S.A.* 106 E7
Williamston, *U.S.A.* 105 H7
Williamstown, *Australia* 91 F3
Williamstown, *Mass., U.S.A.* 107 D11
Williamstown, *N.Y., U.S.A.* 107 C9
Williamsville, *U.S.A.* 109 G9
Willimantic, *U.S.A.* 107 E12
Willis Group, *Australia* 90 B5
Willisau, *Switz.* 22 B6
Williston, *S. Africa* 84 E3
Williston, *Fla., U.S.A.* 105 L4
Williston, *N. Dak., U.S.A.* 108 A3
Williston L., *Canada* 100 B4
Willits, *U.S.A.* 110 G2
Willmar, *U.S.A.* 108 C7
Willoughby, *U.S.A.* 106 E3
Willow Bunch, *Canada* 101 D7
Willow L., *Canada* 100 A5
Willow Lake, *U.S.A.* 108 C6
Willow Springs, *U.S.A.* 109 G8
Willow Wall, The, *China* 51 C12
Willowlake ➛, *Canada* 100 A4
Willowmore, *S. Africa* 84 E3
Willows, *Australia* 90 C4
Willows, *U.S.A.* 112 F4
Willowvale = Gatyana, *S. Africa* 85 E4
Wills, L., *Australia* 88 D4
Wills Cr. ➛, *Australia* 90 C3
Wills Point, *U.S.A.* 109 J7
Willunga, *Australia* 91 F2
Wilmette, *U.S.A.* 104 D2
Wilmington, *Australia* 91 E2
Wilmington, *Del., U.S.A.* 104 F8
Wilmington, *Ill., U.S.A.* 104 E1
Wilmington, *N.C., U.S.A.* 105 H7
Wilmington, *Ohio, U.S.A.* 104 F4
Wilpena Cr. ➛, *Australia* 91 E2
Wilrijk, *Belgium* 17 F4
Wilsall, *U.S.A.* 110 D8
Wilson, *U.S.A.* 105 H7
Wilson ➛, *Queens., Australia* 91 D3
Wilson ➛, *W. Austral., Australia* 88 C4
Wilson Bluff, *Australia* 89 F4
Wilsons Promontory, *Australia* 91 F4
Wilster, *Germany* 18 B5
Wilton, *U.K.* 13 F6
Wilton, *U.S.A.* 108 B4
Wilton ➛, *Australia* 90 A1
Wiltshire □, *U.K.* 13 F6
Wiltz, *Lux.* 17 J7
Wiluna, *Australia* 89 E3
Wimereux, *France* 25 B8
Wimmera ➛, *Australia* 91 F3
Winam G., *Kenya* 82 C3
Winburg, *S. Africa* 84 D4
Winchendon, *U.S.A.* 107 D12
Winchester, *U.K.* 13 F6
Winchester, *Conn., U.S.A.* 107 E11
Winchester, *Idaho, U.S.A.* 110 C5
Winchester, *Ind., U.S.A.* 104 E3
Winchester, *Ky., U.S.A.* 104 G3
Winchester, *N.H., U.S.A.* 107 D12
Winchester, *Nev., U.S.A.* 113 J11
Winchester, *Tenn., U.S.A.* 105 H2
Winchester, *Va., U.S.A.* 104 F6
Wind ➛, *U.S.A.* 110 E9
Wind River Range, *U.S.A.* 110 E9
Windau = Ventspils, *Latvia* 9 H19
Windber, *U.S.A.* 106 F6
Windermere, L., *U.K.* 12 C5
Windfall, *Canada* 100 C5
Windflower L., *Canada* 100 A5
Windhoek, *Namibia* 84 C2
Windom, *U.S.A.* 108 D7
Windorah, *Australia* 90 D3
Window Rock, *U.S.A.* 111 J9
Windrush ➛, *U.K.* 13 F6
Windsor, *Australia* 91 E5
Windsor, *N.S., Canada* 99 D7
Windsor, *Nfld., Canada* 99 C8
Windsor, *Ont., Canada* 98 D3
Windsor, *U.K.* 13 F7
Windsor, *Colo., U.S.A.* 108 E2
Windsor, *Conn., U.S.A.* 107 E12
Windsor, *Mo., U.S.A.* 108 F8
Windsor, *N.Y., U.S.A.* 107 D9
Windsor, *Vt., U.S.A.* 107 C12
Windsorton, *S. Africa* 84 D3
Windward Is., *W. Indies* 117 D7
Windward Passage = Vientos, Paso de los, *Caribbean* 117 C5
Windy L., *Canada* 101 A8
Winefred L., *Canada* 101 B6
Winejok, *Sudan* 77 F2
Winfield, *U.S.A.* 109 G6
Wingate Mts., *Australia* 88 B5
Wingen, *Australia* 91 E5
Wingene, *Belgium* 17 F2
Wingham, *Australia* 91 E5
Wingham, *Canada* 98 D3
Winifred, *U.S.A.* 110 C9
Winisk, *Canada* 98 A2
Winisk ➛, *Canada* 98 A2
Winisk L., *Canada* 98 B2
Wink, *U.S.A.* 109 K3
Winkler, *Canada* 101 D9
Winlock, *U.S.A.* 112 D4
Winneba, *Ghana* 79 D4
Winnebago, *U.S.A.* 108 D7
Winnebago, L., *U.S.A.* 104 D1
Winnecke Cr. ➛, *Australia* 88 C5
Winnemucca, *U.S.A.* 110 F5
Winnemucca L., *U.S.A.* 110 F4
Winner, *U.S.A.* 108 D5
Winnett, *U.S.A.* 110 C9
Winnfield, *U.S.A.* 109 K8
Winnibigoshish, L., *U.S.A.* 108 B7
Winning, *Australia* 88 D1
Winnipeg, *Canada* 101 D9
Winnipeg ➛, *Canada* 101 C9
Winnipeg, L., *Canada* 101 C9
Winnipeg Beach, *Canada* 101 C9
Winnipegosis, *Canada* 101 C9
Winnipegosis L., *Canada* 101 C9
Winnipesaukee, L., *U.S.A.* 107 C13
Winnsboro, *La., U.S.A.* 109 J9
Winnsboro, *S.C., U.S.A.* 105 H5
Winnsboro, *Tex., U.S.A.* 109 J7
Winokapau, L., *Canada* 99 B7
Winona, *Minn., U.S.A.* 108 C9
Winona, *Miss., U.S.A.* 109 J10
Winooski, *U.S.A.* 107 B11
Winschoten, *Neths.* 16 B10
Winsen, *Germany* 18 B6
Winslow, *Ariz., U.S.A.* 111 J8
Winslow, *Wash., U.S.A.* 112 C4
Winsted, *U.S.A.* 107 E11
Winston-Salem, *U.S.A.* 105 G5
Winsum, *Neths.* 16 B9
Winter Garden, *U.S.A.* 105 L5
Winter Haven, *U.S.A.* 105 M5
Winter Park, *U.S.A.* 105 L5
Winterberg, *Germany* 18 D4
Winterhaven, *U.S.A.* 113 N12
Winters, *Calif., U.S.A.* 112 G5
Winters, *Tex., U.S.A.* 109 K5
Winterset, *U.S.A.* 108 E7
Wintersville, *U.S.A.* 106 F4
Winterswijk, *Neths.* 16 E9
Winterthur, *Switz.* 23 B7

Winthrop, *Minn., U.S.A.* 108 C7
Winthrop, *Wash., U.S.A.* 110 B3
Winton, *Australia* 90 C3
Winton, *N.Z.* 87 M2
Winton, *U.S.A.* 105 G7
Wintzenheim, *France* 25 D14
Wipper →, *Germany* 18 D7
Wirral, *U.K.* 12 D4
Wirrulla, *Australia* 91 E1
Wisbech, *U.K.* 12 E8
Wisconsin □, *U.S.A.* 108 C10
Wisconsin →, *U.S.A.* 108 D9
Wisconsin Dells, *U.S.A.* 108 D10
Wisconsin Rapids, *U.S.A.* 108 C10
Wisdom, *U.S.A.* 110 D7
Wishaw, *U.K.* 14 F5
Wishek, *U.S.A.* 108 B5
Wisła, *Poland* 20 F8
Wisła →, *Poland* 20 A8
Wisłok →, *Poland* 20 E12
Wisłoka →, *Poland* 20 E11
Wismar, *Germany* 18 B7
Wismar, *Guyana* 121 B6
Wisner, *U.S.A.* 108 E6
Wissant, *France* 25 B8
Wissembourg, *France* 25 C14
Wissenkerke, *Neths.* 17 E3
Witbank, *S. Africa* 85 D4
Witdraai, *S. Africa* 84 D3
Witham →, *U.K.* 12 D7
Withernsea, *U.K.* 12 D8
Witmarsum, *Neths.* 16 B6
Witney, *U.K.* 13 F6
Witnossob →, *Namibia* 84 D3
Wittdün, *Germany* 18 A4
Witten, *Germany* 17 F10
Wittenberg, *Germany* 18 D8
Wittenberge, *Germany* 18 B7
Wittenburg, *Germany* 18 B7
Wittenoom, *Australia* 88 D2
Wittingen, *Germany* 18 C6
Wittlich, *Germany* 19 F2
Wittmund, *Germany* 18 B3
Wittow, *Germany* 18 A9
Wittstock, *Germany* 18 B8
Witzenhausen, *Germany* 18 D5
Wlingi, *Indonesia* 57 H15
Włocławek, *Poland* 20 C9
Włodawa, *Poland* 20 D13
Włoszczowa, *Poland* 20 E9
Woburn, *U.S.A.* 107 D13
Wodian, *China* 50 H7
Wodonga, *Australia* 91 F4
Woerden, *Neths.* 16 D5
Woerth, *France* 25 D14
Woëvre, *France* 25 C12
Wognum, *Neths.* 16 C6
Wohlen, *Switz.* 23 B6
Woinbogoin, *China* 52 A2
Wokam, *Indonesia* 57 F8
Wolbrom, *Poland* 20 E9
Woldegk, *Germany* 18 B9
Wolf →, *Canada* 100 A2
Wolf Creek, *U.S.A.* 110 C7
Wolf L., *Canada* 100 A2
Wolf Point, *U.S.A.* 108 A2
Wolfe I., *Canada* 98 D4
Wolfenbüttel, *Germany* 18 C6
Wolfheze, *Neths.* 16 D7
Wolfsberg, *Austria* 21 J4
Wolfsburg, *Germany* 18 C6
Wolgast, *Germany* 18 A9
Wolhusen, *Switz.* 22 B6
Wolin, *Poland* 20 B4
Wollaston, Is., *Chile* 128 E3
Wollaston L., *Canada* 101 B8
Wollaston Pen., *Canada* 96 B8
Wollogorang, *Australia* 90 B2
Wollongong, *Australia* 91 E5
Wolmaransstad, *S. Africa* 84 D4
Wolmirstedt, *Germany* 18 C7
Wolseley, *Australia* 91 F3
Wolseley, *Canada* 101 C8
Wolseley, *S. Africa* 84 E2
Wolstenholme, C., *Canada* 94 C12
Wolsztyn, *Poland* 20 C6
Wolvega, *Neths.* 16 C7
Wolverhampton, *U.K.* 13 E5
Wommels, *Neths.* 16 B7
Wonarah, *Australia* 90 B2
Wonck, *Belgium* 17 G7
Wondai, *Australia* 91 D5
Wondelgem, *Belgium* 17 F3
Wongalarroo L., *Australia* 91 E3
Wongan Hills, *Australia* 89 F2
Wongawol, *Australia* 89 E3
Wŏnju, *S. Korea* 51 F14
Wonosari, *Indonesia* 57 G14
Wŏnsan, *N. Korea* 51 E14
Wonthaggi, *Australia* 91 F4
Woocalla, *Australia* 91 E2
Wood Buffalo Nat. Park, *Canada* 100 B6
Wood Is., *Australia* 88 C3
Wood L., *Canada* 101 B8
Wood Lake, *U.S.A.* 108 D4
Woodah I., *Australia* 90 A2
Woodanilling, *Australia* 89 F2
Woodbridge, *Canada* 106 C5
Woodburn, *Australia* 91 D5
Woodenbong, *Australia* 91 D5
Woodend, *Australia* 91 F3
Woodfords, *U.S.A.* 112 G7
Woodgreen, *Australia* 90 C1
Woodlake, *U.S.A.* 112 J7
Woodland, *U.S.A.* 112 G5
Woodlands, *Australia* 88 D2
Woodpecker, *Canada* 100 C4
Woodridge, *Canada* 101 D9
Woodroffe, Mt., *Australia* 89 E5
Woodruff, *Ariz., U.S.A.* 111 J8
Woodruff, *Utah, U.S.A.* 110 F8
Woods, L., *Australia* 90 B1
Woods, L., *Canada* 99 B6
Woods, L. of the, *Canada* 101 D10
Woodstock, *Queens., Australia* 90 B4
Woodstock, *W. Austral., Australia* 88 D2
Woodstock, *N.B., Canada* 99 C6
Woodstock, *Ont., Canada* 98 D3
Woodstock, *U.K.* 13 F6
Woodstock, *Ill., U.S.A.* 108 D10
Woodstock, *Vt., U.S.A.* 107 C12
Woodsville, *U.S.A.* 107 B13
Woodville, *N.Z.* 87 J5
Woodville, *U.S.A.* 109 K7
Woodward, *U.S.A.* 109 G5
Woody, *U.S.A.* 113 K8
Woolamai, C., *Australia* 91 F4
Woolgoolga, *Australia* 91 E5
Woombye, *Australia* 91 D5
Woomera, *Australia* 91 E2
Woonsocket, *R.I., U.S.A.* 107 D13
Woonsocket, *S. Dak., U.S.A.* 108 C5
Wooramel, *Australia* 89 E1
Wooramel →, *Australia* 89 E1
Wooroloo, *Australia* 89 F2
Wooster, *U.S.A.* 106 F3
Worb, *Switz.* 22 C5
Worcester, *S. Africa* 84 E2
Worcester, *U.K.* 13 E5
Worcester, *Mass., U.S.A.* 107 D13
Worcester, *N.Y., U.S.A.* 107 D10
Wörgl, *Austria* 19 H8
Workington, *U.K.* 12 C4
Worksop, *U.K.* 12 D6
Workum, *Neths.* 16 C6
Worland, *U.S.A.* 110 D10
Wormerveer, *Neths.* 16 D5
Wormhoudt, *France* 25 B9
Worms, *Germany* 19 F4
Wörth, *Germany* 19 F8
Wortham, *U.S.A.* 109 K6
Wörther See, *Austria* 21 J4
Worthing, *U.K.* 13 G7
Worthington, *U.S.A.* 108 D7
Wosi, *Indonesia* 57 E7
Wou-han = Wuhan, *China* 53 B10
Woubrugge, *Neths.* 16 D5
Woudenberg, *Neths.* 16 D6
Woudsend, *Neths.* 16 C7
Wour, *Chad* 73 D8
Wousi = Wuxi, *China* 53 B13
Wouw, *Neths.* 17 E4
Wowoni, *Indonesia* 57 E6
Woy Woy, *Australia* 91 E5
Wrangel I. = Vrangelya, Ostrov, *Russia* 45 B19
Wrangell, *U.S.A.* 96 C6
Wrangell I., *U.S.A.* 100 B2
Wrangell Mts., *U.S.A.* 96 B5
Wrath, C., *U.K.* 14 C3
Wray, *U.S.A.* 108 E3
Wrekin, The, *U.K.* 12 E5
Wrens, *U.S.A.* 105 J4
Wrexham, *U.K.* 12 D4
Wrexham □, *U.K.* 12 D5
Wriezen, *Germany* 18 C10
Wright, *Canada* 100 C4
Wright, *Phil.* 55 F6
Wrightson Mt., *U.S.A.* 111 L8
Wrightwood, *U.S.A.* 113 L9
Wrigley, *Canada* 96 B7
Wrocław, *Poland* 20 D7
Września, *Poland* 20 C7
Wschowa, *Poland* 20 D6
Wu Jiang →, *China* 52 C6
Wu'an, *China* 50 F8
Wubin, *Australia* 89 F2
Wubu, *China* 50 F6
Wuchang, *China* 51 B14
Wucheng, *China* 50 F9
Wuchuan, *Guangdong, China* 53 G8
Wuchuan, *Guizhou, China* 52 C7
Wuchuan, *Nei Mongol Zizhiqu, China* 50 D6
Wudi, *China* 51 F9
Wuding, *China* 52 E4
Wuding He →, *China* 50 F6
Wudu, *China* 50 H3
Wufeng, *China* 53 B8
Wugang, *China* 53 D8
Wugong Shan, *China* 53 D9
Wuhan, *China* 53 B10
Wuhe, *China* 51 H9
Wuhsi = Wuxi, *China* 53 B13
Wuhu, *China* 53 B12
Wujiang, *China* 53 B13
Wukari, *Nigeria* 79 D6
Wulajie, *China* 51 B14
Wulanbulang, *China* 50 D6
Wulehe, *Ghana* 79 D5
Wulian, *China* 51 G10
Wuliang Shan, *China* 52 E3
Wuliaru, *Indonesia* 57 F8
Wulumuchi = Ürümqi, *China* 44 E9
Wum, *Cameroon* 79 D7
Wuming, *China* 52 F7
Wuning, *China* 53 C10
Wunnummin L., *Canada* 98 B2
Wunsiedel, *Germany* 19 E8
Wunstorf, *Germany* 18 C5
Wuntho, *Burma* 61 H19
Wuping, *China* 53 E11
Wuppertal, *Germany* 18 D3
Wuppertal, *S. Africa* 84 E2
Wuqing, *China* 51 E9
Würenlingen, *Switz.* 23 A6
Wurung, *Australia* 90 B3
Würzburg, *Germany* 19 F5
Wurzen, *Germany* 18 D8
Wushan, *Gansu, China* 50 G3
Wushan, *Sichuan, China* 52 B7
Wusuli Jiang = Ussuri →, *Asia* 48 A7
Wutach →, *Germany* 19 H4
Wutai, *China* 50 E7
Wuting = Huimin, *China* 51 F9
Wutong, *China* 53 E8
Wutonghaolai, *China* 51 C11
Wutongqiao, *China* 52 C4
Wuustwezel, *Belgium* 17 F5
Wuwei, *Anhui, China* 53 B11
Wuwei, *Gansu, China* 54 C5
Wuxi, *Jiangsu, China* 53 B13
Wuxi, *Sichuan, China* 52 B7
Wuxiang, *China* 50 F7
Wuxing, *China* 53 B13
Wuxuan, *China* 52 F7
Wuyang, *China* 50 H7
Wuyi, *Hebei, China* 50 F8
Wuyi, *Zhejiang, China* 53 C12
Wuyi Shan, *China* 53 D11
Wuyo, *Nigeria* 79 C7
Wuyuan, *Jiangxi, China* 53 C11
Wuyuan, *Nei Mongol Zizhiqu, China* 50 D5
Wuzhai, *China* 50 E6
Wuzhi Shan, *China* 54 E5
Wuzhong, *China* 50 E4
Wuzhou, *China* 53 F8
Wyaaba Cr. →, *Australia* 90 B3
Wyalkatchem, *Australia* 89 F2
Wyalusing, *U.S.A.* 107 E8
Wyandotte, *U.S.A.* 104 D4
Wyandra, *Australia* 91 D4
Wyangala Res., *Australia* 91 E4
Wyara, L., *Australia* 91 D3
Wycheproof, *Australia* 91 F3
Wye →, *U.K.* 13 F5
Wyemandoo, *Australia* 89 E2
Wyk, *Germany* 18 A4
Wymondham, *U.K.* 13 E7
Wymore, *U.S.A.* 108 E6
Wynbring, *Australia* 91 E1
Wyndham, *Australia* 88 C4
Wyndham, *N.Z.* 87 M2
Wyndmere, *U.S.A.* 108 B6
Wynne, *U.S.A.* 109 H9
Wynnum, *Australia* 91 D5
Wynyard, *Australia* 90 G4
Wynyard, *Canada* 101 C8
Wyola, L., *Australia* 89 E5
Wyoming □, *U.S.A.* 110 E10
Wyong, *Australia* 91 E5
Wyszków, *Poland* 20 C11
Wyszogród, *Poland* 20 C10
Wytheville, *U.S.A.* 104 G5

X

Xaçmaz, *Azerbaijan* 43 K9
Xai-Xai, *Mozam.* 85 D5
Xainza, *China* 54 C3
Xambioá, *Brazil* 122 C2
Xangongo, *Angola* 84 B2
Xankändi, *Azerbaijan* 67 C12
Xanlar, *Azerbaijan* 43 K8
Xanten, *Germany* 18 D2
Xánthi, *Greece* 39 H7
Xanthos, *Turkey* 66 D3
Xapuri, *Brazil* 124 C4
Xar Moron He →, *China* 51 C11
Xau, L., *Botswana* 84 C3
Xavantina, *Brazil* 127 A5
Xenia, *U.S.A.* 104 F4
Xeropotamos →, *Cyprus* 37 E11
Xhora, *S. Africa* 85 E4
Xhumo, *Botswana* 84 C3
Xi Jiang →, *China* 53 F9
Xi Xian, *Henan, China* 53 A10
Xi Xian, *Shanxi, China* 50 F6
Xia Xian, *China* 50 G6
Xiachengzi, *China* 51 B16
Xiachuan Dao, *China* 53 G9
Xiaguan, *China* 52 E3
Xiajiang, *China* 53 D10
Xiajin, *China* 50 F8
Xiamen, *China* 53 E12
Xi'an, *China* 50 G5
Xian Xian, *China* 50 E9
Xianfeng, *China* 52 C7
Xiang Jiang →, *China* 53 C9
Xiangcheng, *Henan, China* 50 H8
Xiangcheng, *Henan, China* 50 H7
Xiangcheng, *Sichuan, China* 52 C2
Xiangdu, *China* 52 F6
Xiangfan, *China* 53 A9
Xianghuang Qi, *China* 50 C7
Xiangning, *China* 50 G6
Xiangquan, *China* 50 F7
Xiangshan, *China* 53 C13
Xiangshui, *China* 51 G10
Xiangtan, *China* 53 D9
Xiangxiang, *China* 53 D9
Xiangyin, *China* 53 C9
Xiangyun, *China* 52 E3
Xiangzhou, *China* 52 F7
Xianju, *China* 53 C13
Xianning, *China* 53 C10
Xianshui He →, *China* 52 B3
Xianyang, *China* 50 G5
Xianyou, *China* 53 E12
Xiao Hinggan Ling, *China* 54 B7
Xiao Xian, *China* 50 G9
Xiaofeng, *China* 53 B12
Xiaogan, *China* 53 B9
Xiaojin, *China* 52 B4
Xiaolan, *China* 53 F9
Xiaoshan, *China* 53 B13
Xiaoyi, *China* 50 F6
Xiapu, *China* 53 D12
Xiawa, *China* 51 C11
Xiayi, *China* 50 G9
Xichang, *China* 52 D4
Xichong, *China* 52 B5
Xichuan, *China* 50 H6
Xiemahe, *China* 53 B8
Xieng Khouang, *Laos* 58 C4
Xifei He →, *China* 50 H9
Xifeng, *Guizhou, China* 52 D6
Xifeng, *Liaoning, China* 51 C13
Xifengzhen, *China* 50 G4
Xigazê, *China* 54 D3
Xihe, *China* 50 G3
Xihua, *China* 50 H8
Xiliao He →, *China* 51 C12
Xilin, *China* 52 E5
Xilókastron, *Greece* 39 L5
Xin Jiang →, *China* 53 C11
Xin Xian, *China* 50 E7
Xinavane, *Mozam.* 85 D5
Xinbin, *China* 51 D13
Xincai, *China* 53 A10
Xinchang, *China* 53 C13
Xincheng, *Guangxi Zhuangzu, China* 52 E7
Xincheng, *Jiangxi, China* 53 D10
Xinfeng, *Guangdong, China* 53 E10
Xinfeng, *Jiangxi, China* 53 D11
Xinfeng, *Jiangxi, China* 53 E10
Xing Xian, *China* 50 E6
Xing'an, *Guangxi Zhuangzu, China* 53 E8
Xingan, *Jiangxi, China* 53 D10
Xingcheng, *China* 51 D11
Xingguo, *China* 53 D10
Xinghe, *China* 50 D7
Xinghua, *China* 51 H10
Xinghua Wan, *China* 53 E12
Xinglong, *China* 51 D9
Xingning, *China* 53 E10
Xingping, *China* 50 G5
Xingren, *China* 52 E5
Xingshan, *China* 53 B8
Xingtai, *China* 50 F8
Xingu →, *Brazil* 121 D7
Xingyang, *China* 50 G7
Xinhe, *China* 50 F8
Xinhua, *China* 53 D8
Xinhuang, *China* 52 D7
Xinhui, *China* 53 F9
Xining, *China* 54 C5
Xinjiang, *China* 50 G6
Xinjiang Uygur Zizhiqu □, *China* 54 B3
Xinjie, *China* 52 D3
Xinjin, *Liaoning, China* 51 E11
Xinjin, *Sichuan, China* 52 B4
Xinkai He →, *China* 51 C12
Xinle, *China* 50 E8
Xinlitun, *China* 51 D12
Xinlong, *China* 52 B3
Xinmin, *China* 51 D12
Xinning, *China* 53 D8
Xinping, *China* 52 E3
Xinshao, *China* 53 D8
Xintai, *China* 51 G9
Xintian, *China* 53 E9
Xinxiang, *China* 50 G7
Xinxing, *China* 53 F9
Xinyang, *China* 53 A10
Xinye, *China* 53 A9
Xinyi, *China* 53 F8
Xinyu, *China* 53 D10
Xinzhan, *China* 51 C14
Xinzheng, *China* 50 G7
Xinzhou, *China* 53 B10
Xiong Xian, *China* 50 E9
Xiongyuecheng, *China* 51 D12
Xiping, *Henan, China* 50 H8
Xiping, *Henan, China* 50 H6
Xiping, *Zhejiang, China* 53 C12
Xique-Xique, *Brazil* 122 D3
Xiruá →, *Brazil* 124 B4
Xisha Qundao = Paracel Is., *S. China Sea* 56 A4
Xishui, *China* 53 B10
Xituozhen, *China* 52 B7
Xiuning, *China* 53 C12
Xiuren, *China* 53 E8
Xiushan, *China* 52 C7
Xiushui, *China* 53 C10
Xiuwen, *China* 52 D6
Xiuyan, *China* 51 D12
Xixabangma Feng, *China* 61 E14
Xixia, *China* 50 H6
Xixiang, *China* 50 H4
Xiyang, *China* 50 F7
Xizang □, *China* 54 C3
Xlendi, *Malta* 37 C1
Xu Jiang →, *China* 53 D11
Xuan Loc, *Vietnam* 59 G6
Xuancheng, *China* 53 B12
Xuan'en, *China* 52 C7
Xuanhan, *China* 52 B6
Xuanhua, *China* 50 D8
Xuchang, *China* 50 G7
Xudat, *Azerbaijan* 43 K9
Xuefeng Shan, *China* 53 D8
Xuejiaping, *China* 53 B8
Xun Jiang →, *China* 53 F8
Xun Xian, *China* 50 G8
Xundian, *China* 52 E4
Xunwu, *China* 53 E10
Xunyang, *China* 50 H5
Xunyi, *China* 50 G5
Xupu, *China* 53 D8
Xushui, *China* 50 E8
Xuwen, *China* 53 G8
Xuyen Moc, *Vietnam* 59 G6
Xuyong, *China* 52 C5
Xuzhou, *China* 51 G9
Xylophagou, *Cyprus* 37 E12

Y

Ya Xian, *China* 58 C7
Yaamba, *Australia* 90 C5
Ya'an, *China* 52 C4
Yaapeet, *Australia* 91 F3
Yabassi, *Cameroon* 79 E6
Yabelo, *Ethiopia* 77 G4
Yablonovy Ra. = Yablonovyy Khrebet, *Russia* 45 D12
Yablonovyy Khrebet, *Russia* 45 D12
Yabrai Shan, *China* 50 E2
Yabrūd, *Syria* 69 B5
Yacuiba, *Bolivia* 126 A3
Yacuma →, *Bolivia* 125 C4
Yadgir, *India* 60 L10
Yadkin →, *U.S.A.* 105 H5
Yadrin, *Russia* 42 C8
Yagaba, *Ghana* 79 C4
Yagodnoye, *Russia* 45 C15
Yagoua, *Cameroon* 80 B3
Yaguas →, *Peru* 120 D3
Yaha, *Thailand* 59 J3
Yahila, *Zaïre* 82 B1
Yahk, *Canada* 100 D5
Yahotyn, *Ukraine* 41 G6
Yahuma, *Zaïre* 80 D4
Yahyalı, *Turkey* 66 C6
Yaita, *Japan* 49 F9
Yaiza, *Canary Is.* 36 F6
Yajiang, *China* 52 B3
Yajua, *Nigeria* 79 C7
Yakima, *U.S.A.* 110 C3
Yakima →, *U.S.A.* 110 C3
Yako, *Burkina Faso* 78 C4
Yakoruda, *Bulgaria* 39 G6
Yakovlevka, *Russia* 48 B6
Yaku-Shima, *Japan* 49 J5
Yakutat, *U.S.A.* 96 C6
Yakutia = Sakha □, *Russia* 45 C13
Yakutsk, *Russia* 45 C13
Yala, *Thailand* 59 J3
Yalbalgo, *Australia* 89 E1
Yalboroo, *Australia* 90 C4
Yale, *U.S.A.* 106 C2
Yalgoo, *Australia* 89 E2
Yalinga, *C.A.R.* 73 G9
Yalkubul, Punta, *Mexico* 115 C7
Yalleroi, *Australia* 90 C4
Yalobusha →, *U.S.A.* 109 J9
Yalong Jiang →, *China* 52 D3
Yalova, *Turkey* 66 B3
Yalpuh, Ozero, *Ukraine* 38 D11
Yalta, *Ukraine* 41 K8
Yalu Jiang →, *China* 51 E13
Yalutorovsk, *Russia* 44 D7
Yalvaç, *Turkey* 66 C4
Yam Ha Melah = Dead Sea, *Asia* 69 D4
Yam Kinneret, *Israel* 69 C4
Yamada, *Japan* 49 H5
Yamagata, *Japan* 48 E10
Yamagata □, *Japan* 48 E10
Yamaguchi, *Japan* 49 G5
Yamaguchi □, *Japan* 49 G5
Yamal, Poluostrov, *Russia* 44 B8
Yamal Pen. = Yamal, Poluostrov, *Russia* 44 B8
Yamanashi □, *Japan* 49 G9
Yamantau, Gora, *Russia* 44 D6
Yamba, *N.S.W., Australia* 91 D5
Yamba, *S. Austral., Australia* 91 E3
Yambah, *Australia* 90 C1
Yambarran Ra., *Australia* 88 C5
Yâmbiô, *Sudan* 77 G2
Yambol, *Bulgaria* 38 G9
Yamdena, *Indonesia* 57 F8
Yame, *Japan* 49 H5
Yamethin, *Burma* 61 J20
Yamil, *Nigeria* 79 C6
Yamma-Yamma, L., *Australia* 91 D3
Yamoussoukro, *Ivory C.* 78 D3

Yampa →, *U.S.A.* 110 F9
Yampi Sd., *Australia* 88 C3
Yampil, *Moldova* 41 H5
Yampol = Yampil, *Moldova* 41 H5
Yamrat, *Nigeria* 79 C6
Yamrukchal, *Bulgaria* 38 G7
Yamuna →, *India* 63 G9
Yamzho Yumco, *China* 54 D4
Yan, *Nigeria* 79 C7
Yana →, *Russia* 45 B14
Yanac, *Australia* 91 F3
Yanagawa, *Japan* 49 H5
Yanai, *Japan* 49 H6
Yan'an, *China* 50 F5
Yanbian, *China* 52 D3
Yanbu 'al Baḥr, *Si. Arabia* 64 F3
Yancannia, *Australia* 91 E3
Yanchang, *China* 50 F6
Yancheng, *Henan, China* 50 H7
Yancheng, *Jiangsu, China* 51 H11
Yanchi, *China* 50 F4
Yanchuan, *China* 50 F6
Yanco Cr. →, *Australia* 91 F4
Yandal, *Australia* 89 E3
Yandanooka, *Australia* 89 E2
Yandaran, *Australia* 90 C5
Yandoon, *Burma* 61 L19
Yanfeng, *China* 52 E3
Yanfolila, *Mali* 78 C3
Yang Xian, *China* 50 H4
Yangambi, *Zaïre* 82 B1
Yangbi, *China* 52 E2
Yangcheng, *China* 50 G7
Yangch'ü = Taiyuan, *China* 50 F7
Yangchun, *China* 53 F8
Yanggao, *China* 50 D7
Yanggu, *China* 50 F8
Yangjiang, *China* 53 G8
Yangliuqing, *China* 51 E9
Yangon = Rangoon, *Burma* 61 L20
Yangping, *China* 53 B8
Yangpingguan, *China* 50 H4
Yangquan, *China* 50 F7
Yangshan, *China* 53 E9
Yangshuo, *China* 53 E8
Yangtze Kiang = Chang Jiang →, *China* 53 B13
Yangxin, *China* 53 C10
Yangyang, *S. Korea* 51 E15
Yangyuan, *China* 50 D8
Yangzhou, *China* 53 A12
Yanhe, *China* 52 C7
Yanji, *China* 51 C15
Yanjin, *China* 52 C5
Yanjing, *China* 52 C2
Yankton, *U.S.A.* 108 D6
Yanna, *Australia* 91 D4
Yanonge, *Zaïre* 82 B1
Yanqi, *China* 54 B3
Yanqing, *China* 50 D8
Yanshan, *Hebei, China* 51 E9
Yanshan, *Jiangxi, China* 53 C11
Yanshan, *Yunnan, China* 52 F5
Yanshou, *China* 51 B15
Yantabulla, *Australia* 91 D4
Yantai, *China* 51 F11
Yanting, *China* 52 B5
Yantra →, *Bulgaria* 38 F8
Yanwa, *China* 52 D2
Yanykurgan, *Kazakstan* 44 E7
Yanyuan, *China* 52 D3
Yanzhou, *China* 50 G9
Yao, *Chad* 73 F8
Yao Xian, *China* 50 G5
Yao Yai, Ko, *Thailand* 59 J2
Yao'an, *China* 52 E3
Yaodu, *China* 52 A5
Yaoundé, *Cameroon* 79 E7
Yaowan, *China* 51 G10
Yap I., *Pac. Oc.* 92 G5
Yapen, *Indonesia* 57 E9
Yapen, Selat, *Indonesia* 57 E9
Yappar →, *Australia* 90 B3
Yaqui →, *Mexico* 114 B2
Yar-Sale, *Russia* 44 C8
Yaracuy □, *Venezuela* 120 A4
Yaracuy →, *Venezuela* 120 A4
Yaraka, *Australia* 90 C3
Yaransk, *Russia* 42 B8
Yardea P.O., *Australia* 91 E2
Yare →, *U.K.* 13 E9
Yaremcha, *Ukraine* 41 H3
Yarensk, *Russia* 44 C5
Yarí →, *Colombia* 120 D3
Yaritagua, *Venezuela* 120 A4
Yarkand = Shache, *China* 54 C2
Yarker, *Canada* 107 B8
Yarkhun →, *Pakistan* 63 A5
Yarmouth, *Canada* 99 D6
Yarmūk →, *Syria* 69 C4
Yaroslavl, *Russia* 42 B4
Yarqa, W. →, *Egypt* 69 F2
Yarra Yarra Lakes, *Australia* 89 E2
Yarraden, *Australia* 90 A3
Yarraloola, *Australia* 88 D2
Yarram, *Australia* 91 F4
Yarraman, *Australia* 91 D5
Yarranvale, *Australia* 91 D4
Yarras, *Australia* 91 E5
Yarrowmere, *Australia* 90 C4
Yartsevo, *Russia* 40 E7
Yartsevo, *Russia* 45 C10
Yarumal, *Colombia* 120 B2
Yasawa Group, *Fiji* 87 C7
Yaselda, *Belarus* 41 F4
Yashi, *Nigeria* 79 C6
Yashkul, *Russia* 43 G7
Yasin, *Pakistan* 63 A5
Yasinovataya, *Ukraine* 41 H9
Yasinski, L., *Canada* 98 B4
Yasinya, *Ukraine* 41 H3
Yasothon, *Thailand* 58 E5
Yass, *Australia* 91 E4
Yata →, *Bolivia* 125 C4
Yatağan, *Turkey* 66 D3
Yates Center, *U.S.A.* 109 G7
Yathkyed L., *Canada* 101 A9
Yatsushiro, *Japan* 49 H5
Yatta Plateau, *Kenya* 82 C4
Yauca, *Peru* 124 D3
Yauya, *Peru* 124 B2
Yauyos, *Peru* 124 C2
Yavari →, *Peru* 124 A3
Yavatmal, *India* 60 J11
Yavne, *Israel* 69 D3
Yavoriv, *Ukraine* 41 H2
Yavorov = Yavoriv, *Ukraine* 41 H2
Yavuzeli, *Turkey* 66 D7
Yawatahama, *Japan* 49 H6
Yawri B., *S. Leone* 78 D2
Yaxi, *China* 52 D6
Yayama-Rettō, *Japan* 49 M1
Yazd, *Iran* 65 D7
Yazd □, *Iran* 65 D7
Yazoo →, *U.S.A.* 109 J9
Yazoo City, *U.S.A.* 109 J9
Yding Skovhøj, *Denmark* 9 J13
Ye Xian, *Henan, China* 50 H7
Ye Xian, *Shandong, China* 51 F10
Yealering, *Australia* 89 F2
Yebyu, *Burma* 61 M21
Yechŏn, *S. Korea* 51 F15
Yecla, *Spain* 29 G3
Yécora, *Mexico* 114 B3
Yedintsy = Edinița, *Moldova* 41 H4
Yeeda, *Australia* 88 C3
Yeelanna, *Australia* 91 E2
Yefremov, *Russia* 42 D4
Yeghegnadzor, *Armenia* 67 C11
Yegorlyk →, *Russia* 43 G5
Yegorlykskaya, *Russia* 43 G5
Yegoryevsk, *Russia* 42 C4
Yegros, *Paraguay* 126 B4
Yehuda, Midbar, *Israel* 69 D4
Yei, *Sudan* 77 G3
Yei, Nahr →, *Sudan* 77 F3
Yejmiadzin, *Armenia* 43 K7
Yekaterinburg, *Russia* 44 D7
Yekaterinodar = Krasnodar, *Russia* 43 H4
Yelabuga, *Russia* 42 C11
Yelan, *Russia* 42 E6
Yelanskoye, *Russia* 45 C13
Yelarbon, *Australia* 91 D5
Yelatma, *Russia* 42 C5
Yelcho, L., *Chile* 128 B2
Yelets, *Russia* 42 D4
Yélimané, *Mali* 78 B2
Yelizavetgrad = Kirovohrad, *Ukraine* 41 H7
Yell, *U.K.* 14 A7
Yell Sd., *U.K.* 14 A7
Yellow Sea, *China* 51 G12
Yellowhead Pass, *Canada* 100 C5
Yellowknife, *Canada* 100 A6
Yellowknife →, *Canada* 100 A6
Yellowstone →, *U.S.A.* 108 B3
Yellowstone L., *U.S.A.* 110 D8
Yellowstone National Park, *U.S.A.* 110 D8
Yellowtail Res., *U.S.A.* 110 D9
Yelnya, *Russia* 40 E7
Yelsk, *Belarus* 41 G5
Yelvertoft, *Australia* 90 C2
Yelwa, *Nigeria* 79 C5
Yemen ■, *Asia* 68 E3
Yen Bai, *Vietnam* 58 B5
Yenakiyeve, *Ukraine* 41 H10
Yenakiyevo = Yenakiyeve, *Ukraine* 41 H10
Yenangyaung, *Burma* 61 J19
Yenbo = Yanbu 'al Baḥr, *Si. Arabia* 64 F3
Yenda, *Australia* 91 E4
Yendéré, *Ivory C.* 78 C4
Yendi, *Ghana* 79 D4
Yenice, *Ankara, Turkey* 66 C5
Yenice, *Çanakkale, Turkey* 66 C2
Yenice →, *Turkey* 66 D6
Yenisaía, *Greece* 39 H7
Yenişehir, *Turkey* 66 B3
Yenisey →, *Russia* 44 B9
Yeniseysk, *Russia* 45 D10
Yeniseyskiy Zaliv, *Russia* 44 B9
Yennádhi, *Greece* 37 C9
Yenne, *France* 27 C9
Yenotayevka, *Russia* 43 G8
Yenyuka, *Russia* 45 D13
Yeo, L., *Australia* 89 E3
Yeola, *India* 60 J9
Yeoryioúpolis, *Greece* 37 D6
Yeovil, *U.K.* 13 G5
Yepes, *Spain* 28 F1
Yeppoon, *Australia* 90 C5
Yeráki, *Greece* 39 N4
Yerbent, *Turkmenistan* 44 F6
Yerbogachen, *Russia* 45 C11
Yerevan, *Armenia* 43 K7
Yerilla, *Australia* 89 E3
Yerköy, *Turkey* 66 C6
Yermak, *Kazakstan* 44 D8
Yermakovo, *Russia* 45 D13
Yermo, *U.S.A.* 113 L10
Yerofey Pavlovich, *Russia* 45 D13
Yerólakkos, *Cyprus* 37 D12
Yeropol, *Russia* 45 C17
Yeropótamos →, *Greece* 37 D6
Yeroskipos, *Cyprus* 37 E11
Yerseke, *Neths.* 17 F4
Yershov, *Russia* 42 E9
Yerunaja, Cerro, *Peru* 124 C2
Yerushalayim = Jerusalem, *Israel* 69 D4
Yerville, *France* 24 C7
Yes Tor, *U.K.* 13 G4
Yesan, *S. Korea* 51 F14
Yeşilhisar, *Turkey* 66 C6
Yeşilırmak →, *Turkey* 66 B7
Yeşilkent, *Turkey* 66 D7
Yesnogorsk, *Russia* 42 C3
Yeso, *U.S.A.* 109 H2
Yessentuki, *Russia* 43 H6
Yessey, *Russia* 45 C11
Yeste, *Spain* 29 G2
Yeu, I. d', *France* 24 F4
Yevlakh = Yevlax, *Azerbaijan* 43 K8
Yevlax, *Azerbaijan* 43 K8
Yevpatoriya, *Ukraine* 41 K7
Yeya →, *Russia* 43 G4
Yeysk, *Russia* 43 G4
Yezd = Yazd, *Iran* 65 D7
Yezerishche, *Belarus* 40 E5
Yhati, *Paraguay* 126 B4
Yhú, *Paraguay* 127 B4
Yi →, *Uruguay* 126 C4
Yi 'Allaq, G., *Egypt* 69 E2
Yi He →, *China* 51 G10
Yi Xian, *Anhui, China* 53 C11
Yi Xian, *Hebei, China* 50 E8
Yi Xian, *Liaoning, China* 51 D11
Yiali, *Greece* 39 N10
Yialiás →, *Cyprus* 37 D12
Yi'allaq, G., *Egypt* 76 H8
Yialousa, *Cyprus* 37 D13
Yiáltra, *Greece* 39 L5
Yianisádhes, *Greece* 37 D8
Yiannitsa, *Greece* 39 J5
Yibin, *China* 52 C5
Yichang, *China* 53 B8
Yicheng, *Henan, China* 53 B9
Yicheng, *Shanxi, China* 50 G6
Yichuan, *China* 50 F6
Yichun, *Heilongjiang, China* 54 B7
Yichun, *Jiangxi, China* 53 D10
Yidu, *Hubei, China* 53 B8
Yidu, *Shandong, China* 51 F10
Yidun, *China* 52 B2
Yihuang, *China* 53 D11
Yijun, *China* 50 G5
Yıldızeli, *Turkey* 66 C7
Yiliang, *Yunnan, China* 52 D5
Yiliang, *Yunnan, China* 52 E4
Yilong, *China* 52 B6
Yimen, *China* 52 E4
Yimianpo, *China* 51 B15
Yinchuan, *China* 50 E4
Yindarlgooda, L., *Australia* 89 F3
Ying He →, *China* 50 H9
Ying Xian, *China* 50 E7
Yingcheng, *China* 53 B9
Yingde, *China* 53 E9
Yingjiang, *China* 52 E1
Yingjing, *China* 52 C4
Yingkou, *China* 51 D12
Yingshan, *Henan, China* 53 B9
Yingshan, *Hubei, China* 53 B10
Yingshan, *Sichuan, China* 52 B6
Yingshang, *China* 53 A11
Yingtan, *China* 54 D6
Yining, *China* 44 E9
Yinjiang, *China* 52 C7
Yinmabin, *Burma* 61 H19
Yinnietharra, *Australia* 88 D2
Yiofiros →, *Greece* 37 D7
Yioúra, *Greece* 39 K7
Yipinglang, *China* 52 E3
Yirga Alem, *Ethiopia* 77 F4
Yishan, *China* 52 E7
Yishui, *China* 51 G10
Yíthion, *Greece* 39 N5
Yitiaoshan, *China* 50 F3
Yitong, *China* 51 C13
Yiwu, *China* 53 C13
Yixing, *China* 53 B12
Yiyang, *Henan, China* 50 G7
Yiyang, *Hunan, China* 53 C9
Yiyang, *Jiangxi, China* 53 C11
Yizhang, *China* 53 E9
Yizheng, *China* 53 A12
Yli-Kitka, *Finland* 8 C23
Ylitornio, *Finland* 8 C20
Ylivieska, *Finland* 8 D21
Yngaren, *Sweden* 11 F10
Ynykchanskiy, *Russia* 45 C14
Yoakum, *U.S.A.* 109 L6
Yobe □, *Nigeria* 79 C7
Yog Pt., *Phil.* 57 B6
Yogan, *Togo* 79 D5
Yogyakarta, *Indonesia* 57 G14
Yoho Nat. Park, *Canada* 100 C5
Yojoa, L. de, *Honduras* 116 D2
Yŏju, *S. Korea* 51 F14
Yokadouma, *Cameroon* 80 D2
Yokkaichi, *Japan* 49 G8
Yoko, *Cameroon* 79 D7
Yokohama, *Japan* 49 G9
Yokosuka, *Japan* 49 G9
Yokote, *Japan* 48 E10
Yola, *Nigeria* 79 D7
Yolaina, Cordillera de, *Nic.* 116 D3
Yonago, *Japan* 49 G6
Yonaguni-Jima, *Japan* 49 M1
Yŏnan, *N. Korea* 51 F14
Yonezawa, *Japan* 48 F10
Yong Peng, *Malaysia* 59 L4
Yong Sata, *Thailand* 59 J2
Yongampo, *N. Korea* 51 E13
Yong'an, *China* 53 E11
Yongcheng, *China* 50 H9
Yŏngchŏn, *S. Korea* 51 G15
Yongchuan, *China* 52 C5
Yongchun, *China* 53 E12
Yongdeng, *China* 50 F2
Yongding, *China* 53 E11
Yŏngdŏk, *S. Korea* 51 F15
Yŏngdŭngpo, *S. Korea* 51 F14
Yongfeng, *China* 53 D10
Yongfu, *China* 52 E7
Yonghe, *China* 50 F6
Yŏnghŭng, *N. Korea* 51 E14
Yongji, *China* 50 G6
Yŏngju, *S. Korea* 51 F15
Yongkang, *Yunnan, China* 52 E2
Yongkang, *Zhejiang, China* 53 C13
Yongnian, *China* 50 F8
Yongning, *Guangxi Zhuangzu, China* 52 F7
Yongning, *Ningxia Huizu, China* 50 E4
Yongping, *China* 52 E2
Yongqing, *China* 50 E9
Yongren, *China* 52 D3
Yongshan, *China* 52 C4
Yongsheng, *China* 52 D3
Yongshun, *China* 52 C7
Yongtai, *China* 53 E12
Yŏngwŏl, *S. Korea* 51 F15
Yongxin, *China* 53 D10
Yongxing, *China* 53 D9
Yongxiu, *China* 53 C10
Yonibana, *S. Leone* 78 D2
Yonkers, *U.S.A.* 107 F11
Yonne □, *France* 25 E10
Yonne →, *France* 25 D9
York, *Australia* 89 F2
York, *U.K.* 12 D6
York, *Ala., U.S.A.* 105 J1
York, *Nebr., U.S.A.* 108 E6
York, *Pa., U.S.A.* 104 F7
York □, *U.K.* 12 D6
York, C., *Australia* 90 A3
York, Kap, *Greenland* 4 B4
York Sd., *Australia* 88 B4
Yorke Pen., *Australia* 91 E2
Yorkshire Wolds, *U.K.* 12 D7
Yorkton, *Canada* 101 C8
Yorktown, *U.S.A.* 109 L6
Yorkville, *U.S.A.* 112 G3
Yornup, *Australia* 89 F2
Yoro, *Honduras* 116 C2
Yoron-Jima, *Japan* 49 L4
Yos Sudarso, Pulau, *Indonesia* 57 F9
Yosemite National Park, *U.S.A.* 111 H4
Yosemite Village, *U.S.A.* 112 H7
Yoshkar Ola, *Russia* 42 B8
Yŏsu, *S. Korea* 51 G14
Yotala, *Bolivia* 125 D4
Yotvata, *Israel* 69 F4
You Xian, *China* 53 D9
Youbou, *Canada* 100 D4
Youghal, *Ireland* 15 E4
Youghal B., *Ireland* 15 E4
Youkounkoun, *Guinea* 78 C2
Young, *Australia* 91 E4
Young, *Canada* 101 C7
Young, *Uruguay* 126 C4
Younghusband, L., *Australia* 91 E2
Younghusband Pen., *Australia* 91 F2
Youngstown, *Canada* 101 C6
Youngstown, *N.Y., U.S.A.* 106 C5
Youngstown, *Ohio, U.S.A.* 106 E4
Youngsville, *U.S.A.* 106 E5
Youssoufia, *Morocco* 74 B3
Youxi, *China* 53 D12
Youyang, *China* 52 C7
Youyu, *China* 50 D7
Yoweragabbie, *Australia* 89 E2
Yozgat, *Turkey* 66 C6
Ypané →, *Paraguay* 126 A4
Yport, *France* 24 C7
Ypres = Ieper, *Belgium* 17 G1
Ypsilanti, *U.S.A.* 104 D4
Yreka, *U.S.A.* 110 F2
Ysleta, *U.S.A.* 111 L10
Yssingeaux, *France* 27 C8
Ystad, *Sweden* 11 J7
Ysyk-Köl, *Kyrgyzstan* 46 E11
Ysyk-Köl, Ozero, *Kyrgyzstan* 44 E8
Ythan →, *U.K.* 14 D7
Ytterhogdal, *Sweden* 10 B8
Ytyk Kyuyel, *Russia* 45 C14
Yu Jiang →, *China* 54 D6
Yu Xian, *Hebei, China* 50 E8
Yu Xian, *Henan, China* 50 G7
Yu Xian, *Shanxi, China* 50 E7
Yuan Jiang →, *Hunan, China* 53 C8
Yuan Jiang →, *Yunnan, China* 52 F4
Yuan'an, *China* 53 B8
Yuanjiang, *Hunan, China* 53 C9
Yuanjiang, *Yunnan, China* 52 F4
Yüanli, *Taiwan* 53 E13
Yüanlin, *Taiwan* 53 F13
Yuanlin, *Taiwan* 53 F13
Yuanling, *China* 53 C8
Yuanmou, *China* 52 E3
Yuanqu, *China* 50 G6
Yuanyang, *Henan, China* 50 G7
Yuanyang, *Yunnan, China* 52 F4
Yuba →, *U.S.A.* 112 F5
Yuba City, *U.S.A.* 112 F5
Yūbari, *Japan* 48 C10
Yūbetsu, *Japan* 48 B11
Yucatán □, *Mexico* 115 C7
Yucatán, Canal de, *Caribbean* 116 B2
Yucatán, Península de, *Mexico* 94 H11
Yucatán Basin, *Cent. Amer.* 94 H11
Yucatan Str. = Yucatán, Canal de, *Caribbean* 116 B2
Yucca, *U.S.A.* 113 L12
Yucca Valley, *U.S.A.* 113 L10
Yucheng, *China* 50 F9
Yuci, *China* 50 F7
Yudino, *Russia* 44 D7
Yudu, *China* 53 E10
Yuendumu, *Australia* 88 D5
Yueqing, *China* 53 C13
Yueqing Wan, *China* 53 C13
Yuexi, *Anhui, China* 53 B11
Yuexi, *Sichuan, China* 52 C4
Yueyang, *China* 53 C9
Yugan, *China* 53 C11
Yugoslavia ■, *Europe* 21 M10
Yuhuan, *China* 53 C13
Yujiang, *China* 53 C11
Yukhnov, *Russia* 42 C2
Yukon →, *U.S.A.* 96 B3
Yukon Territory □, *Canada* 96 B6
Yüksekova, *Turkey* 67 D11
Yukti, *Russia* 45 C11
Yukuhashi, *Japan* 49 H5
Yule →, *Australia* 88 D2
Yuli, *Nigeria* 79 D7
Yulin, *Guangxi Zhuangzu, China* 53 F8
Yulin, *Shaanxi, China* 50 E5
Yuma, *Ariz., U.S.A.* 113 N12
Yuma, *Colo., U.S.A.* 108 E3
Yuma, B. de, *Dom. Rep.* 117 C6
Yumbe, *Uganda* 82 B3
Yumbi, *Zaïre* 82 C2
Yumbo, *Colombia* 120 C2
Yumen, *China* 54 C4
Yumurtalık, *Turkey* 66 D6
Yun Ho →, *China* 51 E9
Yun Xian, *Hubei, China* 53 A8
Yun Xian, *Yunnan, China* 52 E3
Yunak, *Turkey* 66 C4
Yunan, *China* 53 F8
Yuncheng, *Henan, China* 50 G8
Yuncheng, *Shanxi, China* 50 G6
Yundamindra, *Australia* 89 E3
Yunfu, *China* 53 F9
Yungas, *Bolivia* 125 D4
Yungay, *Chile* 126 D1
Yungay, *Peru* 124 B2
Yunhe, *China* 53 C12
Yunlin, *Taiwan* 53 F13
Yunling, *China* 52 D2
Yunlong, *China* 52 E2
Yunmeng, *China* 53 B9
Yunnan □, *China* 52 E4
Yunquera de Henares, *Spain* 28 E1
Yunta, *Australia* 91 E2
Yunxi, *China* 50 H6
Yunxiao, *China* 53 F11
Yunyang, *China* 52 B7
Yuping, *China* 52 D7
Yupukarri, *Guyana* 121 C6
Yupyongdong, *N. Korea* 51 D15
Yuqing, *China* 52 D6
Yur, *Russia* 45 D14
Yurgao, *Russia* 44 D9
Yuribei, *Russia* 44 B8
Yurimaguas, *Peru* 124 B2
Yuryev-Polskiy, *Russia* 42 B4
Yuryevets, *Russia* 42 B6
Yuryung Kaya, *Russia* 45 B12
Yuscarán, *Honduras* 116 D2
Yushanzhen, *China* 52 C7
Yushe, *China* 50 F7
Yushu, *Jilin, China* 51 B14
Yushu, *Qinghai, China* 54 C4
Yusufeli, *Turkey* 67 B9
Yutai, *China* 50 G9
Yutian, *China* 51 E9
Yuxarı Qarabağ = Nagorno-Karabakh, *Azerbaijan* 67 C12
Yuxi, *China* 52 E4
Yuyao, *China* 53 B13
Yuzawa, *Japan* 48 E10
Yuzha, *Russia* 42 B6
Yuzhno-Sakhalinsk, *Russia* 45 E15
Yvelines □, *France* 25 D8
Yverdon, *Switz.* 22 C3
Yvetot, *France* 24 C7
Yvonand, *Switz.* 22 C3

Z

Zaamslag, *Neths.* 17 F3
Zaan →, *Neths.* 16 D5
Zaandam, *Neths.* 16 D5
Zab, Monts du, *Algeria* 75 B6
Žabalj, *Serbia, Yug.* 21 K10
Žabari, *Serbia, Yug.* 21 L11
Zabarjad, *Egypt* 76 C4
Zabaykalsk, *Russia* 45 E12
Zabid, *Yemen* 68 E3
Ząbkowice Śląskie, *Poland* 20 E6
Zabłudów, *Poland* 20 B13
Zābol, *Iran* 65 D9
Zābolī, *Iran* 65 E9
Zabré, *Burkina Faso* 79 C4
Zabrze, *Poland* 20 E8
Zacapa, *Guatemala* 116 D2
Zacapu, *Mexico* 114 D4
Zacatecas, *Mexico* 114 C4
Zacatecas □, *Mexico* 114 C4
Zacatecoluca, *El Salv.* 116 D2
Zacoalco, *Mexico* 114 C4
Zacualtipán, *Mexico* 115 C5
Zadar, *Croatia* 33 D12
Zadawa, *Nigeria* 79 C7
Zadetkyi Kyun, *Burma* 59 H2
Zadonsk, *Russia* 42 D4
Zafarqand, *Iran* 65 C7
Zafra, *Spain* 31 G4
Żagań, *Poland* 20 D5
Zagazig, *Egypt* 76 H7
Zāgheh, *Iran* 65 C6
Zaghouan, *Tunisia* 75 A7
Zaglivérion, *Greece* 39 J6
Zaglou, *Algeria* 75 C4
Zagnanado, *Benin* 79 D5
Zagorá, *Greece* 39 K6
Zagora, *Morocco* 74 B3
Zagorsk = Sergiyev Posad, *Russia* 42 B4
Zagreb, *Croatia* 33 C12
Zāgros, Kūhhā-ye, *Iran* 65 C6
Zagros Mts. = Zāgros, Kūhhā-ye, *Iran* 65 C6
Zaguinaso, *Ivory C.* 78 C3
Zāhedān, *Fārs, Iran* 65 D7
Zāhedān, *Sīstān va Balūchestān, Iran* 65 D9
Zahlah, *Lebanon* 69 B4
Zahna, *Germany* 18 D8
Zahrez Chergui, *Algeria* 75 A5
Zahrez Rharbi, *Algeria* 75 B5
Zainsk, *Russia* 42 C11
Zaïre ■, *Africa* 80 E4
Zaïre →, *Africa* 80 F2
Zaječar, *Serbia, Yug.* 21 M12
Zakamensk, *Russia* 45 D11
Zakataly = Zaqatala, *Azerbaijan* 43 K8
Zakhodnaya Dzvina = Daugava →, *Latvia* 9 H21
Zākhū, *Iraq* 67 D10
Zákinthos, *Greece* 39 M3
Zakopane, *Poland* 20 F9
Zákros, *Greece* 37 D8
Zala →, *Hungary* 21 J7
Zalaegerszeg, *Hungary* 21 J6
Zalalövö, *Hungary* 21 J6
Zalamea de la Serena, *Spain* 31 G5
Zalamea la Real, *Spain* 31 H4
Žalec, *Slovenia* 33 B12
Zaleshchiki = Zalishchyky, *Ukraine* 41 H3
Zalingei, *Sudan* 73 F9
Zalishchyky, *Ukraine* 41 H3
Zaltbommel, *Neths.* 16 E6
Zambeke, *Zaïre* 82 B2
Zambeze →, *Africa* 83 F4
Zambezi = Zambeze →, *Africa* 83 F4
Zambezi, *Zambia* 81 G4
Zambezia □, *Mozam.* 83 F4
Zambia ■, *Africa* 83 E2
Zamboanga, *Phil.* 55 H5
Zamboanguita, *Phil.* 55 G5
Zambrano, *Colombia* 120 B3
Zambrów, *Poland* 20 C12
Zametchino, *Russia* 42 D6
Zamora, *Ecuador* 120 D2
Zamora, *Mexico* 114 C4
Zamora, *Spain* 30 D5
Zamora □, *Spain* 30 D5
Zamora-Chinchipe □, *Ecuador* 120 D2
Zamość, *Poland* 20 E13
Zamuro, Sierra del, *Venezuela* 121 C5
Zan, *Ghana* 79 D4
Zanaga, *Congo* 80 E2
Záncara →, *Spain* 29 F1
Zandijk, *Neths.* 16 D5
Zandvoort, *Neths.* 16 D5
Zanesville, *U.S.A.* 106 G2
Zangābād, *Iran* 64 B5
Zangue →, *Mozam.* 83 F4
Zanjān, *Iran* 67 D13
Zanjān □, *Iran* 65 B6
Zannone, *Italy* 34 B6
Zante = Zákinthos, *Greece* 39 M3
Zanthus, *Australia* 89 F3
Zanzibar, *Tanzania* 82 D4
Zanzūr, *Libya* 75 B7
Zaouiet El-Kala = Bordj Omar Driss, *Algeria* 75 C6
Zaouiet Reggane, *Algeria* 75 C5
Zaoyang, *China* 53 A9
Zaozhuang, *China* 51 G9
Zap Suyu = Kabīr, Zab al →, *Iraq* 67 D10
Zapadna Morava →, *Serbia, Yug.* 21 M11
Zapadnaya Dvina, *Russia* 40 D7
Zapadnaya Dvina → = Daugava →, *Latvia* 9 H21
Západné Beskydy, *Europe* 20 F9
Zapala, *Argentina* 128 A2
Zapaleri, Cerro, *Bolivia* 126 A2
Zapata, *U.S.A.* 109 M5
Zapatón →, *Spain* 31 G4
Zapiga, *Chile* 124 D4
Zaporizhzhya, *Ukraine* 41 J8
Zaporozhye = Zaporizhzhya, *Ukraine* 41 J8
Zapponeta, *Italy* 35 A8
Zaqatala, *Azerbaijan* 43 K8
Zara, *Turkey* 66 C7
Zaragoza, *Colombia* 120 B3
Zaragoza, *Coahuila, Mexico* 114 B4
Zaragoza, *Nuevo León, Mexico* 115 C5
Zaragoza, *Spain* 28 D4
Zaragoza □, *Spain* 28 D4
Zarand, *Kermān, Iran* 65 D8
Zarand, *Markazī, Iran* 65 C6
Zărandului, Munţii, *Romania* 38 C5
Zaranj, *Afghan.* 60 D2
Zarasai, *Lithuania* 9 J22
Zarate, *Argentina* 126 C4
Zaraysk, *Russia* 42 C4
Zaraza, *Venezuela* 121 B4
Zāreh, *Iran* 65 C6
Zarembo I., *U.S.A.* 100 B2
Zaria, *Nigeria* 79 C6
Zarneh, *Iran* 64 C5
Zarós, *Greece* 37 D6
Zarqā' →, *Jordan* 69 C4
Zarrīn, *Iran* 65 C7
Zaruma, *Ecuador* 120 D2
Żary, *Poland* 20 D5
Zarza de Alange, *Spain* 31 G4
Zarza de Granadilla, *Spain* 30 E4
Zarzaïtine, *Algeria* 75 C6
Zarzal, *Colombia* 120 C2
Zarzis, *Tunisia* 75 B7
Zas, *Spain* 30 B2
Zashiversk, *Russia* 45 C15
Zaskar →, *India* 63 B7
Zaskar Mts., *India* 63 C7
Zastron, *S. Africa* 84 E4
Zaterechnyy, *Russia* 43 H7
Zavāreh, *Iran* 65 C7
Zaventem, *Belgium* 17 G4
Zavetnoye, *Russia* 43 G6
Zavidovići, *Bos.-H.* 21 L8
Zavitinsk, *Russia* 45 D13
Zavodovski, I., *Antarctica* 5 B1
Zavolzhsk, *Russia* 42 B6
Zavolzhye, *Russia* 42 B6
Zawiercie, *Poland* 20 E9
Zawyet Shammâs, *Egypt* 76 A2
Zâwyet Um el Rakham, *Egypt* 76 A2
Zâwyet Ungeîla, *Egypt* 76 A2
Zāyā, *Iraq* 64 C5
Zayarsk, *Russia* 45 D11
Zaysan, *Kazakstan* 44 E9
Zaysan, Oz., *Kazakstan* 44 E9
Zayü, *China* 52 C1
Zazir, O. →, *Algeria* 75 D6
Zbarazh, *Ukraine* 41 H3
Zbąszyń, *Poland* 20 C5
Zblewo, *Poland* 20 B8
Zdolbuniv, *Ukraine* 41 G4
Ždrelo, *Serbia, Yug.* 21 L11
Zduńska Wola, *Poland* 20 D8
Zeballos, *Canada* 100 D3
Zebediela, *S. Africa* 85 C4
Zedelgem, *Belgium* 17 F2
Zeebrugge, *Belgium* 17 F2
Zeehan, *Australia* 90 G4
Zeeland, *Neths.* 17 E7
Zeeland □, *Neths.* 17 F3
Zeelst, *Neths.* 17 F6
Zeerust, *S. Africa* 84 D4
Zefat, *Israel* 69 C4
Zegdou, *Algeria* 74 C4
Zege, *Ethiopia* 77 E4
Zegelsem, *Belgium* 17 G3
Zégoua, *Mali* 78 C3
Zehdenick, *Germany* 18 C9
Zeil, Mt., *Australia* 88 D5
Zeila, *Somali Rep.* 68 E3
Zeist, *Neths.* 16 D6
Zeitz, *Germany* 18 D8
Zele, *Belgium* 17 F4
Zelenodolsk, *Russia* 42 C9
Zelenogorsk, *Russia* 40 B5
Zelenograd, *Russia* 42 B3
Zelenogradsk, *Russia* 9 J19
Zelenokumsk, *Russia* 43 H6
Zelhem, *Neths.* 16 D8
Zell, *Baden-W., Germany* 19 H3
Zell, *Rhld-Pfz., Germany* 19 E3
Zell am See, *Austria* 21 H2
Zella-Mehlis, *Germany* 18 E6
Zelzate, *Belgium* 17 F3
Zembra, I., *Tunisia* 75 A7
Zémio, *C.A.R.* 82 A2
Zemmora, *Algeria* 75 A5
Zemmur, *W. Sahara* 74 C2
Zemoul, O. →, *Algeria* 74 C3
Zemst, *Belgium* 17 G4
Zemun, *Serbia, Yug.* 21 L10
Zengbe, *Cameroon* 79 D7
Zengcheng, *China* 53 F9
Zenica, *Bos.-H.* 21 L7
Žepce, *Bos.-H.* 21 L8
Zeraf, Bahr ez →, *Sudan* 77 F3
Zerbst, *Germany* 18 D8
Zermatt, *Switz.* 22 D5
Zernez, *Switz.* 23 C10
Zernograd, *Russia* 43 G5
Zerqani, *Albania* 39 H3
Zestaponi, *Georgia* 43 J6
Zetel, *Germany* 18 B3
Zetten, *Neths.* 16 E7
Zeulenroda, *Germany* 18 E7
Zeven, *Germany* 18 B5
Zevenaar, *Neths.* 16 E8
Zevenbergen, *Neths.* 17 E5
Zévio, *Italy* 32 C8
Zeya, *Russia* 45 D13
Zeya →, *Russia* 45 D13
Zêzere →, *Portugal* 31 F2
Zghartā, *Lebanon* 69 A4
Zgierz, *Poland* 20 D9
Zgorzelec, *Poland* 20 D5
Zhabinka, *Belarus* 41 F3
Zhailma, *Kazakstan* 44 D7
Zhambyl, *Kazakstan* 44 E8
Zhangaly, *Kazakstan* 43 G10
Zhangaqazaly, *Kazakstan* 44 E7
Zhangbei, *China* 50 D8
Zhangguangcai Ling, *China* 51 B15
Zhangjiakou, *China* 50 D8
Zhangping, *China* 53 E11
Zhangpu, *China* 53 E11
Zhangwu, *China* 51 C12
Zhangye, *China* 54 C5
Zhangzhou, *China* 53 E11
Zhanhua, *China* 51 F10
Zhanjiang, *China* 53 G8
Zhanyi, *China* 52 E4
Zhanyu, *China* 51 B12
Zhao Xian, *China* 50 F8
Zhao'an, *China* 53 F11
Zhaocheng, *China* 50 F6
Zhaojue, *China* 52 C4
Zhaoping, *China* 53 E8
Zhaoqing, *China* 53 F9
Zhaotong, *China* 52 D4
Zhaoyuan, *Heilongjiang, China* 51 B13
Zhaoyuan, *Shandong, China* 51 F11
Zharkovskiy, *Russia* 40 E7
Zhashkiv, *Ukraine* 41 H6
Zhashui, *China* 50 H5
Zhayyq →, *Kazakstan* 44 E6
Zhdanov = Mariupol, *Ukraine* 41 J9
Zhecheng, *China* 50 G8
Zhegao, *China* 53 B11
Zhejiang □, *China* 53 C13
Zheleznogorsk, *Russia* 42 D2
Zheleznogorsk-Ilimskiy, *Russia* 45 D11
Zheltyye Vody = Zhovti Vody, *Ukraine* 41 H7
Zhen'an, *China* 50 H5
Zhenfeng, *China* 52 E5
Zheng'an, *China* 52 C6
Zhengding, *China* 50 E8
Zhenghe, *China* 53 D12
Zhengyang, *China* 53 A10
Zhengyangguan, *China* 53 A11
Zhengzhou, *China* 50 G7
Zhenhai, *China* 53 C13
Zhenjiang, *China* 53 A12
Zhenlai, *China* 51 B12
Zhenning, *China* 52 D5
Zhenping, *Henan, China* 50 H7
Zhenping, *Shaanxi, China* 52 B7
Zhenxiong, *China* 52 D5
Zhenyuan, *Gansu, China* 50 G4
Zhenyuan, *Guizhou, China* 52 D7
Zherdevka, *Russia* 42 E5
Zherong, *China* 53 D12
Zhetiqara, *Kazakstan* 44 D7
Zhezqazghan, *Kazakstan* 44 E7
Zhidan, *China* 50 F5
Zhigansk, *Russia* 45 C13
Zhigulevsk, *Russia* 42 D9
Zhijiang, *Hubei, China* 53 B8
Zhijiang, *Hunan, China* 52 D7
Zhijin, *China* 52 D5
Zhilinda, *Russia* 45 C12
Zhirnovsk, *Russia* 42 E7
Zhitomir = Zhytomyr, *Ukraine* 41 G5
Zhizdra, *Russia* 42 D2
Zhlobin, *Belarus* 41 F6
Zhmerinka = Zhmerynka, *Ukraine* 41 H5
Zhmerynka, *Ukraine* 41 H5
Zhodino = Zhodzina, *Belarus* 40 E5
Zhodzina, *Belarus* 40 E5
Zhokhova, Ostrov, *Russia* 45 B16
Zhong Xian, *China* 52 B7
Zhongdian, *China* 52 D2
Zhongdong, *China* 52 F6
Zhongdu, *China* 52 E7
Zhongning, *China* 50 F3
Zhongshan, *Guangdong, China* 53 F9
Zhongshan, *Guangxi Zhuangzu, China* 53 E8
Zhongtiao Shan, *China* 50 G6
Zhongwei, *China* 50 F3
Zhongxiang, *China* 53 B9
Zhongyang, *China* 50 F6
Zhoucun, *China* 51 F9
Zhouning, *China* 53 D12
Zhoushan Dao, *China* 53 C14
Zhouzhi, *China* 50 G5
Zhovti Vody, *Ukraine* 41 H7
Zhovtneve, *Ukraine* 41 J7
Zhovtnevoye = Zhovtneve, *Ukraine* 41 J7
Zhuanghe, *China* 51 E12
Zhucheng, *China* 51 G10
Zhugqu, *China* 50 H3
Zhuhai, *China* 53 F9
Zhuji, *China* 53 C13
Zhukovka, *Russia* 42 D1
Zhumadian, *China* 50 H8
Zhuo Xian, *China* 50 E8
Zhuolu, *China* 50 D8
Zhuozi, *China* 50 D7
Zhupanovo, *Russia* 45 D16
Zhushan, *China* 53 A8
Zhuxi, *China* 52 A7
Zhuzhou, *China* 53 D9
Zhytomyr, *Ukraine* 41 G5
Zi Shui →, *China* 53 C9
Zīārān, *Iran* 65 B6
Ziarat, *Pakistan* 62 D2
Zibo, *China* 51 F10
Zichang, *China* 50 F5
Zichem, *Belgium* 17 F5
Zielona Góra, *Poland* 20 D5
Zierikzee, *Neths.* 17 E3
Ziesar, *Germany* 18 C8
Zifta, *Egypt* 76 H7
Zigey, *Chad* 73 F8
Zigong, *China* 52 C5
Zigui, *China* 53 B8
Ziguinchor, *Senegal* 78 C1
Zihuatanejo, *Mexico* 114 D4
Zijin, *China* 53 F10
Zile, *Turkey* 66 B6
Žilina, *Slovak Rep.* 20 F8
Zillah, *Libya* 73 C8
Zillertaler Alpen, *Austria* 19 H7
Zima, *Russia* 45 D11
Zimane, Adrar in, *Algeria* 75 D5
Zimapán, *Mexico* 115 C5
Zimba, *Zambia* 83 F2
Zimbabwe, *Zimbabwe* 83 G3
Zimbabwe ■, *Africa* 83 F2
Zimovniki, *Russia* 43 G6
Zinal, *Switz.* 22 D5
Zinder, *Niger* 79 C6
Zinga, *Tanzania* 83 D4
Zingem, *Belgium* 17 G3
Zingst, *Germany* 18 A8
Ziniaré, *Burkina Faso* 79 C4
Zinkgruvan, *Sweden* 11 F9
Zinnowitz, *Germany* 18 A9
Zion National Park, *U.S.A.* 111 H7
Zipaquirá, *Colombia* 120 C3
Zirc, *Hungary* 21 H7
Žiri, *Slovenia* 33 B11
Žirje, *Croatia* 33 E12
Zirl, *Austria* 19 H7
Ziros, *Greece* 37 D8
Zitácuaro, *Mexico* 114 D4
Žitava →, *Slovak Rep.* 21 G8
Zittau, *Germany* 18 E10
Zitundo, *Mozam.* 85 D5
Živinice, *Bos.-H.* 21 L8
Ziway, L., *Ethiopia* 77 F4
Zixi, *China* 53 D11
Zixing, *China* 53 E9
Ziyang, *Shaanxi, China* 50 H5
Ziyang, *Sichuan, China* 52 B5
Ziyun, *China* 52 E6
Ziz, Oued →, *Morocco* 74 B4
Zizhixian, *China* 53 E8
Zizhong, *China* 52 C5
Zlarin, *Croatia* 33 E12
Zlatar, *Croatia* 33 B13
Zlataritsa, *Bulgaria* 38 F8
Zlatitsa, *Bulgaria* 38 G7
Zlatograd, *Bulgaria* 39 H8
Zlatoust, *Russia* 44 D6
Zletovo, *Macedonia* 39 H5
Zlin, *Czech.* 20 F7
Zlītan, *Libya* 73 B7
Złocieniec, *Poland* 20 B6
Złoczew, *Poland* 20 D8
Złotoryja, *Poland* 20 D5
Złotów, *Poland* 20 B7
Zmeinogorsk, *Kazakstan* 44 D9
Żmigród, *Poland* 20 D6
Zmiyev, *Ukraine* 41 H9
Znamenka = Znamyanka, *Ukraine* 41 H7
Znamyanka, *Ukraine* 41 H7
Żnin, *Poland* 20 C7
Znojmo, *Czech.* 20 G6
Zobeyrī, *Iran* 64 C5
Zobia, *Zaïre* 82 B2
Zoetermeer, *Neths.* 16 D5
Zofingen, *Switz.* 22 B5
Zogang, *China* 52 C1
Zogno, *Italy* 32 C6
Zogqên, *China* 52 A2
Zolder, *Belgium* 17 F6
Zollikofen, *Switz.* 22 C4
Zollikon, *Switz.* 23 B7
Zolochev = Zolochiv, *Ukraine* 41 H3
Zolochiv, *Ukraine* 41 H3
Zolotonosha, *Ukraine* 41 H7
Zomba, *Malawi* 83 F4
Zomergem, *Belgium* 17 F3
Zongo, *Zaïre* 80 D3
Zonguldak, *Turkey* 66 B4
Zonhoven, *Belgium* 17 G6
Zonqor Pt., *Malta* 37 D2
Zonza, *France* 27 G13
Zorgo, *Burkina Faso* 79 C4
Zorita, *Spain* 31 F5
Zorritos, *Peru* 124 A1
Zorzor, *Liberia* 78 D3
Zossen, *Germany* 18 C9
Zottegem, *Belgium* 17 G3
Zou Xiang, *China* 50 G9
Zouar, *Chad* 73 D8
Zouérate, *Mauritania* 74 D2
Zousfana, O. →, *Algeria* 75 B4
Zoushan Dao, *China* 53 B14
Zoutkamp, *Neths.* 16 B8
Zrenjanin, *Serbia, Yug.* 21 K10
Zuarungu, *Ghana* 79 C4
Zuba, *Nigeria* 79 D6
Zubayr, *Yemen* 77 D5
Zubia, *Spain* 31 H7
Zubtsov, *Russia* 42 B2
Zudáñez, *Bolivia* 125 D5
Zuénoula, *Ivory C.* 78 D3
Zuera, *Spain* 28 D4
Zuetina = Az Zuwaytīnah, *Libya* 73 B9
Zufar, *Oman* 68 D5
Zug, *Switz.* 23 B7
Zug □, *Switz.* 23 B7
Zugdidi, *Georgia* 43 J5
Zugersee, *Switz.* 23 B7
Zugspitze, *Germany* 19 H6
Zuid-Holland □, *Neths.* 16 E5
Zuidbeveland, *Neths.* 17 F3
Zuidbroek, *Neths.* 16 B9
Zuidelijk-Flevoland, *Neths.* 16 D6
Zuidhorn, *Neths.* 16 B8
Zuidlaarder meer, *Neths.* 16 B9
Zuidlaren, *Neths.* 16 B9
Zuidwolde, *Neths.* 16 C8
Zújar, *Spain* 29 H2
Zújar →, *Spain* 31 F5
Zújar, Pantano del, *Spain* 31 G5
Zula, *Eritrea* 77 D4
Zulia □, *Venezuela* 120 B3
Zülpich, *Germany* 18 E2
Zumaya, *Spain* 28 B2
Zumbo, *Mozam.* 83 F3
Zummo, *Nigeria* 79 D7
Zumpango, *Mexico* 115 D5
Zundert, *Neths.* 17 F5
Zungeru, *Nigeria* 79 D6
Zunhua, *China* 51 D9
Zuni, *U.S.A.* 111 J9
Zunyi, *China* 52 D6
Zuoquan, *China* 50 F7
Zuozhou, *China* 52 F6
Županja, *Croatia* 21 K8
Zurbātīyah, *Iraq* 67 F12
Zürich, *Switz.* 23 B7
Zürich □, *Switz.* 23 B7
Zürichsee, *Switz.* 23 B7
Zuromin, *Poland* 20 B9
Zuru, *Nigeria* 79 C6
Zurzach, *Switz.* 23 A6
Žut, *Croatia* 33 E12
Zutendaal, *Belgium* 17 G7
Zutphen, *Neths.* 16 D8
Zuwārah, *Libya* 75 B7
Zūzan, *Iran* 65 C8
Žužemberk, *Slovenia* 33 C11
Zvenigorodka = Zvenyhorodka, *Ukraine* 41 H6
Zvenyhorodka, *Ukraine* 41 H6
Zverinogolovskoye, *Russia* 44 D7
Zvezdets, *Bulgaria* 38 G10
Zvishavane, *Zimbabwe* 83 G3
Zvolen, *Slovak Rep.* 20 G9
Zvonce, *Serbia, Yug.* 21 N12
Zvornik, *Bos.-H.* 21 L9
Zwaag, *Neths.* 16 C6
Zwanenburg, *Neths.* 16 D5
Zwarte Meer, *Neths.* 16 C7
Zwarte Waler, *Neths.* 16 C8
Zwartemeer, *Neths.* 16 C10
Zwartsluis, *Neths.* 16 C8
Zwedru = Tchien, *Liberia* 78 D3
Zweibrücken, *Germany* 19 F3
Zwenkau, *Germany* 18 D8
Zwevegem, *Belgium* 17 G2
Zwickau, *Germany* 18 E8
Zwiesel, *Germany* 19 F9
Zwijnaarde, *Belgium* 17 F3
Zwijndrecht, *Belgium* 17 F4
Zwijndrecht, *Neths.* 16 E5
Zwischenahn, *Germany* 18 B4
Zwolle, *Neths.* 16 C8
Zwolle, *U.S.A.* 109 K8
Zymoetz →, *Canada* 100 C3
Żyrardów, *Poland* 20 C10
Zyryan, *Kazakstan* 44 E9
Zyryanka, *Russia* 45 C16
Zyryanovsk = Zyryan, *Kazakstan* 44 E9
Zyyi, *Cyprus* 37 E12